INTERNATIONAL CRIMINAL PRACTICE

INTERNATIONAL CRIMINAL PRACTICE

The International Criminal Tribunal for the Former Yugoslavia
The International Criminal Tribunal for Rwanda
The International Criminal Court
The Special Court for Sierra Leone
The East Timor Special Panel for Serious Crimes
War Crimes Prosecutions in Kosovo

John R. W. D. Jones
MA. (Oxon.), M.A. In Law, LL.M.
of Lincoln's Inn, Barrister

Steven Powles
LL.B. (London), LL.M (Cantab.)
of Middle Temple, Barrister

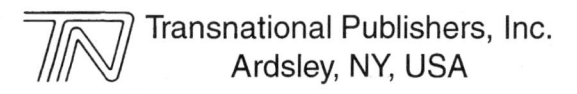

Transnational Publishers, Inc.
Ardsley, NY, USA

OXFORD
UNIVERSITY PRESS

Sold and distributed in North America by:
Transnational Publishers, Inc.
410 Saw Mill River Road
Ardsley, NY 10502 USA
Tel.: +1 (914) 693-5100
Fax: +1 (914) 693-4430
Email: info@transnationalpubs.com
www.transnationalpubs.com

Sold and distributed in the U.K. by:
Oxford University Press
Great Clarendon Street
Oxford, OX26DP UK
Tel: +44 (0) 1536 741 727

Email: book.orders@oup.co.uk
www.oup.com

Library of Congress Cataloging-in-Publication Data

Jones, John R. W. D., 1967–
    International criminal practice : the International Tribunal for the Former Yugoslavia, the International Criminal Tribunal for Rwanda, the International Criminal Court, The Special Court for Sierra Leone, the East Timor Special Panel for Serious Crimes, war crimes prosecution in Kosovo / John R.W.D. Jones, Steven Powles.
        p. cm.
    Includes bibliographical references and index.
    ISBN 1-57105-229-1 Transnational Publishers Edition
        1. International criminal courts-Rules and practice.   2. Criminal procedure.
    I. Powles, Steven.   II. Title.

KZ6310.J66 2003
341.7'7—dc21
2002045417

British Library Cataloging-in-Publication Data

Data available
ISBN 0-19-926436-8 Oxford University Press Edition

Copyright © 2003 Transnational Publishers, Inc.

Originally published as *The Practice of the International Criminal Tribunals for the Former Yugoslavia and Rwanda*: First Edition © 1998; Second Edition © 2000; published and distributed exclusively by Transnational Publishers, Inc.

This publication is protected by international copyright law.

All rights reserved. This book may not be reproduced, in whole or in part, in any form (beyond that copying permitted by U.S. Copyright Law in Section 107, "fair use" in teaching and research, Section 108, certain library copying, and except in published media by reviewers in limited excerpts), without written permission from the publisher.

Manufactured in the United States of America

"'The power of the precedent,' Mr. Justice Cardozo has said, 'is the power of the beaten path.' One of the chief obstacles to [the Nuremberg] trial was the lack of a beaten path. A judgement such has been rendered shifts the power of the precedent to the support of these rules of law. No one can hereafter deny or fail to know that the principles on which the Nazi leaders are adjudged to forfeit their lives constitute law and law with a sanction."

Mr. Justice Jackson, in his Report to the President of 7 October 1946 on the Judgement of the International Military Tribunal at Nuremberg

―――――――――――――

To our Parents

ACKNOWLEDGMENTS

The authors gratefully acknowledge the invaluable assistance of the scholars and students listed below in helping to revise, up-date, edit and add references for the following sections of this edition:

Ms. Lucia ALENI (*"Defences"*)
Mr. Luca D'AMBROSIO (*"Defences"*)
Mr. Amedeo BARLETTA (*"Offences against the Administration of Justice, Personal, Temporal and Territorial Jurisdiction"*)
Mr. David BOYLE (*"Genocide"*)
Mr. Andrea CALIGIURI (*"Elements of Crimes"*)
Dr. Andreana ESPOSITO (*"Elements of Crimes"*)
Dr. Emanuela FRONZA (*"Sentencing Procedure and Penalties"*)
Ms. Jessica LESC (*"Individual Criminal Responsibility"*)
Ms. May LUEKEN (*"Enforcement of Sentences"*)
Ms. Domenica LUPO (*"Elements of Crimes"*)
Professor Stefano MANACORDA (*"Defences"*)
Ms. Fabia de MELO E SILVA (*"Genocide"*)
Mr. Gabriele della MORTE (*"Primacy"*)
Mr. Nicola NAPOLETANO (*"Offences against the Administration of Justice, Personal, Temporal and Territorial Jurisdiction"*)
Ms. Raphaële PARIZOT (*"Legality"*)
Ms. Sarah PELLET (*"Relationship of the ICTs to the ICJ"*)
Judge Raffaele PICCIRILLO (*"Offences against the Administration of Justice, Personal, Temporal and Territorial Jurisdiction"*)
Dr. Carlo SOTIS (*"Sentencing Procedure and Penalties"*)
Mr. Pascal TURLAN (*"Kosovo, Special Court for Sierra Leone"*)
Dr. Judith VAILHE (*"The Prosecutor"*)

Thanks in particular to Dr. Emanuela Fronza for the wonderful job she did in coordinating and supervising these contributions and for up-dating the Bibliography. Professor Stefano Manacorda also deserves thanks for co-ordinating and supervising some of the contributions.

The authors also wish to thank Ms. Gillian Higgins, Barrister, 3 Gray's Inn Square, London, for her extremely helpful comments on a previous draft. Thanks are also due to Judge Sylver Ntumamzina and Michael Hartmann for their very helpful comments on the East Timor section and Kosovo section respectively.

The responsibility for any mistakes remains, of course, our own.

The index to this edition was adapted from *The Rome Statute of the International Criminal Court: A Commentary* (Cassese, Gaeta, Jones, eds., Oxford University Press, 2002). We thank the indexer, Kim Harris, and OUP, for permission to use their index. We are also grateful to Stella Harris (no relation), pupil of Chanber Chambers, for her work adapting the index materials.

The initial revision of this work from the format of previous editions, as well as a great deal of up-dating, was made possible by the Rockefeller Foundation, which granted John Jones a month's residence at the Foundation's Conference and Study Centre at the Villa Serbollini in Bellagio, in February, 2001. Profound gratitude is therefore due to the Rockefeller Foundation and to White and Case in Paris for granting John a month's paid leave to take up the residency.

Our thanks, finally, are due to Transnational Publishers and Oxford University Press, and in particular to Maria Angelini and Annabel Macris respectively, for their professionalism, help and above all, patience in the production of this book.

j.r.w.d.j., s.p.

CONTENTS

References are to pages.
See the first page of each part for detailed synopses and reference by paragraph.

Foreword .... *xix*
    Geoffrey Robertson, QC

Foreword to the Second Edition .... *xxiii*
    Thomas Buergenthal

Foreword to the First Edition .... *xxiv*
    Antonio Cassese

User's Guide .... *xxvii*

Introduction .... *xxix*

Glossary of Abbreviations Used in this Edition .... *xxxi*

Quick Index to ICTY Statute .... *xxxvii*

Quick Index to ICTR Statute .... *xxxix*

Quick Index to ICTY and ICTR Rules of Procedure and Evidence .... *xl*

Part 1: The Establishment of the International Tribunals

ICTY Preamble: Updated Statute of the International Tribunal 2
ICTR Preamble: Updated Statute of the International Tribunal
    for Rwanda 2

Part 2: Organisation of the International Tribunals

ICTY Article 11: Organization of the International Tribunal 41
ICTR Article 10: Organization of the International Tribunal for
    Rwanda 41
ICC Article 34: Organs of the Court 42

Section 1: Chambers 43

Composition of the Chambers 43
ICTY Article 12/ICTR Article 11: Composition of the Chambers 43
ICC Article 39: Chambers 45

Qualifications and Election of Judges 46
ICTY Article 13/ICTR Article 12: Qualifications of Judges 46
ICTY Article 13 *bis*/ ICTR Article 12 *bis:* Election of Permanent
  Judges 46
ICTY Article 13 *ter*/ ICTR Article 12 *ter:* Election and
  Appointment of *Ad Litem* Judges....................................... 48
ICTY Article 13 *quater*/ ICTR Article 12 *quater:* Status of *Ad Litem*
  Judges 49

Officers and Members of Chambers... 54
ICTY Article 14/ ICTR Article 13: Officers and Members of the
  Chambers... 54
ICTY Rule 14/ ICTR Rule 14: Solemn Declaration............................ 58
ICTR Rule 14 *bis*.. 59

Disqualification, Resignation, and Precedence of Judges 59
ICTY Rule 15/ICTR Rule 15: Disqualification of Judges 59
ICTY Rule 15 *bis*/ICTR Rule 15 *bis:* Absence of a Judge 64
ICTY Rule 16/ICTR Rule 16: Resignation 67
ICTY Rule 17/ICTR Rule 17: Precedence 67

President, Vice President, and the Bureau 68
ICTY Rule 18/ICTR Rule 18: Election of the President 68
ICTY Rule 19/ICTR Rule 19: Functions of the President 69
ICTY Rule 20/ICTR Rule 20: The Vice President 70
ICTY Rule 21/ICTR Rule 21: Functions of the Vice President 71
ICTY Rule 22/ICTR Rule 22: Replacements................................... 71
ICTY Rule 23/ICTR Rule 23: The Bureau..................................... 72
ICTY Rule 23 *bis:* The Coordination Council 73
ICTY Rule 23 *ter:* The Management Committee 73

Plenary Meetings 74
ICTY Rule 24/ICTR Rule 24: Plenary Meetings of the Tribunal............... 74
ICTY Rule 25/ICTR Rule 25: Dates of Plenary Sessions 74
ICTY Rule 26/ICTR Rule 26: Quorum and Vote 75

Rotation of Judges and Deliberations.................................... 75
ICTY Rule 27/ICTR Rule 27: Rotation 75
ICTY Rule 28: Reviewing and Duty Judges................................... 76
ICTR Rule 28: Duty Judges... 76
ICTY Rule 29/ICTR Rule 29: Deliberations 79

Section 2: The Registry 80

ICTY Article 17/ICTR Article 16: The Registry 80
ICTY Rule 30/ICTR Rule 30: Appointment of the Registrar 80
ICTY Rule 31/ICTR Rule 31: Appointment of the Deputy Registrar
  and Registry Staff 80
ICTY Rule 32/ICTR Rule 32: Solemn Declaration 81

ICTY Rule 33/ICTR Rule 33: Functions of the Registrar 81
ICTY Rule 33 *bis:* Functions of the Deputy Registrar 84

Section 3: Victims and Witnesses 85
ICTY Rule 34/ICTR Rule 34: Victims and Witnesses Section 85

Section 4: Minutes and Records 88
ICTY Rule 35/ICTR Rule 35: Minutes 88
ICTY Rule 36/ICTR Rule 36: Record Book 88

Section 5: The Prosecutor 90
ICTY Article 16/ICTR Article 15: The Prosecutor 90
ICTY Rule 37/ICTR Rule 37: Functions of the Prosecutor 97
ICC Article 15: Prosecutor 98
ICTY Rule 38/ICTR Rule 38: Deputy Prosecutor 100

Section 6: The Defence 101
ICTY Rule 44: Appointment, Qualifications, and Duties of Counsel 101
ICTR Rule 44: Appointment and Qualifications of Counsel 101
ICTR Rule 44 *bis*: Duty Counsel 103
ICTY Rule 45/ICTR Rule 45: Assignment of Counsel 104
ICTY Rule 45 *bis*/ICTR Rule 45 *bis:* Detained Persons 112
ICTR Rule 45 *ter:* Availability of Counsel 113
ICTR Rule 45 *quater* 113
ICTY Rule 46/ICTR Rule 46: Misconduct of Counsel 114

Part 3: The Status, Privileges and Immunities of the International Tribunals

ICTY Article 30: The Status, Privileges and Immunities of the
   International Tribunal 120
ICTY Article 29: The Status, Privileges and Immunities of the
International Tribunal for Rwanda 120
ICTY Article 31: Seat of the International Tribunal 120
ICTY Rule 4: Meetings Away from the Seat of Tribunal 121
ICTR Rule 4: Sittings Away from the Seat of the Tribunal 121
ICTY Article 32: Expenses of the International Tribunal 122
ICTR Article 30: Expenses of the International Tribunal for Rwanda 122
ICTY Article 33/ICTR Article 31: Working Languages 123
ICTY Article 34/ICTR Article 32: Annual Report 124

Part 4: Competence of the International Tribunals

ICTY Article 1: Competence of the International Tribunal 131
ICTR Article 1: Competence of the International Tribunal for Rwanda 131

Section 1: Sources of Law 136

Section 2: Subject-Matter Jurisdiction 143
Genocide 143
ICTY Article 4/ICTR Article 2: Genocide 143
ICC Article 6: Genocide 179
Crimes Against Humanity 180
ICTY Article 5/ICTR Article 3: Crimes Against Humanity 180
ICC Article 7: Crimes Against Humanity 218
War Crimes 219
ICTY Article 2: Grave Breaches of the Geneva Conventions of 1949 220
ICTY Article 3: Violations of the Laws or Customs of War 251
ICTR Article 4: Violations of Article 3 Common to the Geneva
  Conventions and of Additional Protocol II 266
ICC Article 8: War Crimes 274
Elements of the Offences 289
ICC Elements of Crimes 298
Offenses Against the Administration of Justice 322
ICTY Rule 77/ICTR Rule 77: Contempt of the Tribunal 322
ICTY Rule 77 *bis:* Payment of Fines 337
ICTY Rule 91/ICTR Rule 91: False Testimony Under Solemn
  Declaration 338
ICC Article 70: Offences Against the Administration of Justice ... 343
ICC Rule 162: Exercise of Jurisdiction 344
ICC Rule 163: Application of the Statute and the Rules 344
ICC Rule 164: Periods of Limitation 345
ICC Rule 165: Investigation, Prosecution and Trial 345
ICC Rule 166: Sanctions Under Article 70 345
ICC Rule 167: International Cooperation and Judicial Assistance ... 346
ICC Rule 168: *Ne Bis in Idem* 346
ICC Rule 169: Immediate Arrest 346
ICC Article 71: Sanctions for Misconduct Before the Court 347

Section 3: Personal Jurisdiction 348
ICTY Article 6/ICTR Article 5: Personal Jurisdiction 348
ICC Article 1: The Court 357
ICC Article 25: Individual Criminal Responsibility 357
ICC Article 26: Exclusion of Jurisdiction Over Persons
  Under Eighteen 358

Section 4: Temporal and Territorial Jurisdiction 354

ICTY Article 8/ICTR Article 7: Territorial and Temporal Jurisdiction......... 354
ICC Article 11: Jurisdiction *Ratione Temporis*........................... 357
ICC Article 4: Legal Status and Powers of the Court....................... 358
ICC Article 12: Preconditions to the Exercise of Jurisdiction 358
ICC Article 13: Exercise of Jurisdiction 358

Part 5: Primacy of the International Tribunals

ICTY Article 9/ ICTR Article 8: Concurrent Jurisdiction 367
ICTY Article 10/ICTR Article 9: *Non-Bis-in-Idem* 371
ICTY Rule 13/ICTR Rule 13: *Non-Bis-in-Idem*......................... 372
ICTY Rule 8/ICTR Rule 8: Request for Information...................... 376
ICTY Rule 9/ICTR Rule 9: Prosecutor's Request for Deferral.............. 377
ICTY Rule 10/ICTR Rule 10: Formal Request for Deferral................ 379
ICTY Rule 11 *bis*/ICTR Rule 11 *bis:* Referral of the Indictment to
    Another Court 385
ICTY Rule 12/ICTR Rule 12: Determinations of Courts of Any State........ 387
ICC Preamble.. 390
ICC Article 1: The Court 390
ICC Article 17: Issues of Admissibility 391
ICC Article 18: Preliminary Rulings Regarding Admissibility 392
ICC Article 19: Challenges to the Jurisdiction of the Court or the
    Admissibility of a Case 394
ICC Article 20: *Ne Bis in Idem* 396

Part 6: General Principles of Criminal Law

Section 1: Legality... 400

ICC Article 22: *Nullum Crimen Sine Lege*.............................. 400
ICC Article 23: *Nulla Poena Sine Lege* 401
ICC Article 24: Non-Retroactivity *Ratione Personae* 401

Section 2: Individual Criminal Responsibility........................... 408

ICTY Article 7/ICTR Article 6: Individual Criminal Responsibility 408
ICTY Article 7(3)/ICTR Article 6(3): Command Responsibility............ 424
ICC Article 28: Responsibility of Commanders and Other Superiors 442
ICC Article 33: Superior Orders and Prescription of Law 444

Section 3: Defences.. 445

ICC Article 31: Grounds for Excluding Criminal Responsibility............ 458
ICC Article 32: Mistake of Fact or Mistake of Law 459
ICC Article 33: Superior Orders and Prescription of Law 459

Part 7: Rules of Procedure and Evidence

ICTY Article 15/ICTR Article 14: Rules of Procedure and Evidence 462
ICC Article 51: Rules of Procedure and Evidence 467
ICC Article 52: Regulations of the Court............................... 467
ICTY Rule1/ICTR Rule1: Entry into Force 468
ICTY Rule 2/ICTR Rule 2: Definitions.................................. 468
ICTY Rule 3/ICTR Rule 3: Languages 470
ICTY Rule 5/ICTR Rule 5: Non-Compliance with Rules 473
ICTY Rule 6/ICTR Rule 6: Amendment of the Rules 474
ICTY Rule 7/ICTR Rule 7: Authentic Texts............................. 476

Part 8: International Criminal Proceedings

Section 1: Investigations 492

ICTY Rule 39/ICTR Rule 39: Conduct of Investigations.................. 492
ICTY Rule 40/ICTR Rule 40: Provisional Measures 494
ICTY Rule 40 *bis*/ICTR Rule 40 *bis*: Transfer and Provisional
  Detention of Suspects 495
ICTY Rule 41: Retention of Information................................ 500
ICTR Rule 41: Preservation of Information............................. 500
ICTY Rule 42/ICTR Rule 42: Rights of Suspects During
  Investigations... 501
ICTY Rule 43/ICTR Rule 43: Recording Questioning of Suspects 502

Section 2: Indictment 504

ICTY Article 18/ICTR Article 17: Investigation and Preparation of
  Indictment 504
ICTY Article 19/ICTR Article 18: Review of the Indictment.............. 508
ICTY Rule 47/ICTR Rule 47: Submission of Indictment by the
  Prosecutor 510
ICTY Rule 48/ICTR Rule 48: Joinder of Accused......................... 516
ICTR Rule 48 *bis*: Joinder of Trials..................................... 520
ICTY Rule 49/ICTR Rule 49: Joinder of Crimes.......................... 520
ICTY Rule 50/ICTR Rule 50: Amendment of Indictment 523
ICTY Rule 51/ICTR Rule 51: Withdrawal of Indictment................... 528
ICTY Rule 52/ICTR Rule 52: Public Character of Indictment.............. 531
ICTY Rule 53/ICTR Rule 53: Non-Disclosure of Indictment 531
ICTY Rule 53 *bis*/ICTR Rule 53 *bis*: Service of Indictment 533

Section 3: Cumulative Charging...................................... 534

Section 4: Orders and Warrants 538

ICTY Rule 54/ICTR Rule 54: General Rule 538
ICTY Rule 54 *bis*: Orders Directed to States for the Production of
  Documents... 552

ICTY Rule 55/ICTR Rule 55: Execution of Arrest Warrants 555
ICTR Rule 55 *bis*: Warrant of Arrest to All States 558
ICTY Rule 57/ICTR Rule 57: Procedure after Arrest 559
ICTY Rule 59 *bis*: Transmission of Arrest Warrants 560
ICTY Rule 60/ICTR Rule 60: Publication of Indictment................ 565
ICTY Rule 61/ICTR Rule 61: Procedure in Case of Failure to
   Execute a Warrant 566

Section 5: Commencement and Conduct of Trial Proceedings 574

ICTY Article 20/ICTR Article 19: Commencement and Conduct of
   Trial Proceedings.. 574
Rights of the Accused... 577
ICTY Article 21/ICTR Article 20: Rights of the Accused 577
ICTY Rule 63/ICTR Rule 63: Questioning of the Accused 596
ICTY Rule 64/ICTR Rule 64: Detention on Remand.................. 598
ICTY Rule 65/ICTR Rule 65: Provisional Release 599

Protection of Victims and Witnesses 612
ICTY Article 22/ICTR Article 21: Protection of Victims and Witnesses 612
ICTY Rule 69/ICTR Rule 69: Protection of Victims and Witnesses 612
ICTY Rule 75/ICTR Rule 75: Measure for the Protection of Victims
   and Witnesses.. 621

Time Limits 630
ICTY Rule 126: General Provision 630
ICTY Rule 126 *bis:* Time for Filing Responses to Motions 630
ICTY Rule 127: Variation of Time-Limits 631
ICTR Rule 7 *ter*: Time Limits 631

Preliminary Proceedings 632
ICTY Rule 62/ICTR Rule 62: Initial Appearance of Accused 632
ICTY Rule 62 *bis:* Guilty Pleas...................................... 639
ICTY Rule 62 *ter*: Plea Agreement Procedure........................ 642
ICTY Rule 65 *bis*/ICTR Rule 65 *bis:* Status Conferences 642
ICTY Rule 65 *ter:* Pre-Trial Judge................................... 644

Production of Evidence 647
ICTY Rule 66: Disclosure by the Prosecutor........................ 647
ICTR Rule 66: Disclosure of Materials by the Prosecutor 647
ICTY Rule 67: Reciprocal Disclosure 656
ICTR Rule 67: Reciprocal Disclosure of Evidence 656
ICTY Rule 68/ICTR Rule 68: Disclosure of Exculpatory Evidence 662
ICTY Rule 68 *bis:* Failure to Comply with Disclosure Obligations.......... 668
ICTY Rule 70/ICTR Rule 70: Matters Not Subject to Disclosure 668

Depositions 672
ICTY Rule 71/ICTR Rule 71: Depositions 672
ICTY Rule 71 *bis*: Testimony by Video-Conference Link 676

xvi • *International Criminal Practice*

Motions 676
ICTY Rule 72/ICTR Rule 72: Preliminary Motions. 676
ICTY Rule 73: Other Motions 686
ICTR Rule 73: Motions 686

Conferences 691
ICTY Rule 73 *bis*/ICTR Rule 73 *bis:* Pre-Trial Conference. 691
ICTY Rule 73 *ter*/ICTR Rule 73 *ter:* Pre-Defence Conference 694

Proceedings Before Trial Chambers 696
ICTY Rule 74/ICTR Rule 74: *Amicus Curiae* 696
ICTY Rule 74 *bis*/ICTR Rule 74 *bis:* Medical Examination of the Accused 702
ICTY Rule 76/ICTR Rule 76: Solemn Declaration by Interpreters
   and Translators. 702
ICTY Rule 78/ICTR Rule 78: Open Sessions 703
ICTY Rule 79/ICTR Rule 79: Closed Sessions 703
ICTY Rule 80/ICTR Rule 80: Control of Proceedings. 707
ICTY Rule 81/ICTR Rule 81: Records of Proceedings and Evidence 707
ICTY Rule 82/ICTR Rule 82: Joint and Separate Trials 708
ICTY Rule 83/ICTR Rule 83: Instruments of Restraint. 711
ICTY Rule 84/ICTR Rule 84: Opening Statements 712
ICTY Rule 84 *bis:* Statement of the Accused. 713
ICTY Rule 85/ICTR Rule 85: Presentation of Evidence 713
ICTY Rule 86/ICTR Rule 86: Closing Arguments. 719
ICTY Rule 87/ICTR Rule 87: Deliberations 721

Rules of Evidence. 725
ICTY Rule 89/ICTR Rule 89: General Provisions 725
ICTY Rule 90/ICTR Rule 90: Testimony of Witnesses 735
ICTY Rule 90 *bis*/ICTR Rule 90 *bis:* Transfer of a Detained Witness 741
ICTY Rule 92/ICTR Rule 92: Confessions 745
ICTY Rule 92 *bis*/ICTR Rule 92 *bis:* Proof of Facts Other Than by
   Oral Evidence 746
ICTY Rule 93/ICTR Rule 93: Evidence of Consistent Pattern of
   Conduct 749
ICTY Rule 94/ICTR Rule 94: Judicial Notice 749
ICTY Rule 94 *bis*/ICTR Rule 94 *bis:* Testimony of Expert
   Witnesses. 752
ICTY Rule 95: Exclusion of Certain Evidence 753
ICTR Rule 95: Exclusion of Evidence on the Grounds of the Means
   by Which It Was Obtained 753
ICTY Rule 96/ICTR Rule 96: Evidence in Cases of Sexual Assault 754
ICTY Rule 97/ICTR Rule 97: Lawyer-Client Privilege 757
ICTY Rule 98/ICTR Rule 98: Power of Chambers to Order
   Production of Additional Evidence 758

Section 6: Judgement 760

ICTY Article 23/ICTR Article 22: Judgement 760
ICTY Rule 98 *bis*/ICTR Rule 98 *bis*: Motion of Judgement of Acquittal. 761

ICTY Rule 98 *ter:* Judgement 763
ICTR Rule 88: Judgement 763
ICTY Rule 99/ICTR Rule 99: Status of the Acquitted Person 764

Part 9: Sentencing Procedure, Penalties and Enforcement of Sentences

ICTY Article 24/ICTR Article 23: Penalties 769
ICTY Rule 101/ICTR Rule 101: Penalties 769
ICTY Rule 100/ICTR Rule 100: Sentencing Procedure on a
   Guilty Plea 791
ICTY Rule 102/ICTR Rule 102: Status of the Convicted Person 796
ICTY Article 27/ICTR Article 26: Enforcement of Sentences 797
ICTY Rule 103/ICTR Rule 103: Place of Imprisonment 798
ICTY Rule 104/ICTR Rule 104: Supervision of Imprisonment 801
ICTY Rule 105/ICTR Rule 105: Restitution of Property 802
ICTY Rule 106/ICTR Rule 106: Compensation to Victims 803
ICTY Article 28/ICTR Article 27: Pardon or Commutation of
   Sentences 804
ICTY Rule 123/ICTR Rule 124: Notification by States 805
ICTY Rule 124/ICTR Rule 125: Determination by the President 805
ICTY Rule 125/ICTR Rule 126: General Standards for Granting
   Pardon or Commutation 806

Part 10: Appeal and Review Proceedings

Section 1: Appeal Proceedings 811

ICTY Article 25/Article 24: Appellate Proceedings 811
ICTY Rule 107/ICTR Rule 107: General Provision 814
ICTR Rule 107 *bis:* Practice Directions for the Appeals Chamber 815
ICTY Rule 108/ICTR Rule 108: Notice of Appeal 815
ICTR Rule 108 *bis:* Pre-Appeal Judge 816
ICTY Rule 108 *bis:* State Request for Review 816
ICTY Rule 109/ICTR Rule 109: Record on Appeal 818
ICTY Rule 110/ICTR Rule 110: Copies of Record 819
ICTY Rule 111/ICTR Rule 111: Appellant's Brief 819
ICTY Rule 112/ICTR Rule 112: Respondent's Brief 821
ICTY Rule 113/ICTR Rule 113: Brief in Reply 821
ICTY Rule 114/ICTR Rule 114: Date of Hearing 822
ICTY Rule 115/ICTR Rule 115: Additional Evidence 822
ICTR Rule 116: Extension of Time-Limits 826
ICTY Rule 116 *bis*/ICTR Rule 117: Expedited Appeals Procedure 827
ICTR Rule 117 *bis:* Parties' Books 828
ICTR Rule 117 *ter:* Filing of the Trial Records 829
ICTY Rule 117/ICTR Rule 118: Judgement on Appeal 829
ICTY Rule 118/ICTR Rule 119: Status of the Accused Following
   Appeal 830

Section 2: Review Proceedings 831

ICTY Article 26/ICTR Article 25: Review Proceedings 831
ICTY Rule 119/ICTR Rule 120: Request for Review 831
ICTY Rule 120/ICTR Rule 121: Preliminary Examination 832
ICTY Rule 121/ICTR Rule 122: Appeals 832
ICTY Rule 122/ICTR Rule 123: Return of Case to Trial Chamber 833

Part 11: State Cooperation

Section 1: General Obligation to Cooperate 836

ICTY Article 29/ICTR Article 28: Cooperation and Judicial Assistance 836
ICTY Rule 56/ICTR Rule 56: Cooperation of States 843
ICTR Rule 58/ICTR Rule 58: National Extradition Provisions 844

Section 2: Consequences of Non-Cooperation 846

ICTY Rule 7 *bis*/ICTR Rule 7 *bis:* Non-Compliance with Obligations 846
ICTY Rule 11/ICTR Rule 11: Non-Compliance with a Request for Deferral 846
ICTY Rule 59: Failure to Execute a Warrant or Transfer Order 847
ICTR Rule 59: Failure to Execute a Warrant of Arrest or Transfer Order 847

Annexes

Annex 1: Summary of Concluded Trials 851

Annex 2: Rome Statute for an International Criminal Court 859

Annex 3: International Criminal Court Rules of Procedure and Evidence 915

Annex 4: ICTY Directive on the Assignment of Defence Counsel 981

Annex 5: Statute of the Special Court for Sierra Leone 993

Annex 6: Special Court for Sierra Leone Rules of Procedure and Evidence 1001

Indices

Bibliography 1037
Biographical Note 1055
Index 1057

FOREWORD

This new edition of *International Criminal Practice* will take its place as an essential tool for all who work in the burgeoning business of delivering international criminal justice. It charts—comprehensibly as well as comprehensively—those procedural rules which, if fashioned with fairness, make "justice" attainable, in the difficult and different atmosphere of a court without a country. The authors, John Jones and Steven Powles, possess two inestimable advantages as guides to this new legal terrain: firstly they have been "insiders," John having worked for President Cassese at the ICTY and then as a legal officer at the ICTR during the tribunals' formative years, and recently as the acting Principal Defender of the Special Court for Sierra Leone, while Steven was both a judge's assistant at the ICTY and legal adviser on the Rules of Procedure and Evidence for the ICC. Secondly they are now both practicing barristers who prosecute and defend in domestic and international criminal trials. It is because any legal subject is in practice very different from its academic theory that they are so adept at identifying the issues which really matter and in predicting how some of the novel questions thrown up in this area will be resolved. Their analysis is street-wise as well as authoritative. Most importantly for the reader, they have been able to make some comparative sense of the rules adopted by the several tribunals, and to distill lengthy trial and appellate chamber judgments—often written about convoluted facts and in a turgid europrose—into short and meaningful propositions. For this relief, much thanks.

This exercise of synthesizing the procedural rules and jurisprudence of international criminal law has a special importance at a time when that body of doctrine, still at a rudimentary stage of development, is on the brink of exponential expansion. The International Criminal Court, its notional jurisdiction secure since 1st July, 2002, will take organizational shape in 2003–4; the Special Court established by the UN and Sierra Leone for trying the authors of crimes against humanity in that country commences its three-year mandate in 2003, and may serve as a model for other "hybrid" courts, probably in Cambodia and possibly in Afghanistan or even in post-regime-changed Iraq. It is relatively easy for politicians and diplomats to set up an international criminal court, but whether that court succeeds in its task of fair, effective and speedy justice-delivery will largely depend on the procedures and practices that develop interstitially, through gaps closed and rules interpreted by the judges or the registrar, and by codes of prosecution conduct and practices followed by the defence bar. It is at this unglamourous and somewhat technical level that problems have already begun to emerge which threaten to undermine the great cause of global justice.

The resolve to end impunity only dates from the turn into the twenty-first century. There was no precedent prior to Nuremberg: at Versailles, Woodrow Wilson insisted on immunity for the Kaiser and on leaving German war criminals to "losers' justice" in their own courts in Leipzig where almost all of them were wrongfully acquitted. The Nuremberg trials were vehemently opposed by Churchill and the British War Cabinet, who wanted simply to assassinate the Nazi leadership rather than let them use the dock as a soapbox:

Nuremberg only happened because of Truman's touching faith in due process and Stalin's liking for show trials (at least, for show trials in which all defendants were shot at the end). That Nuremberg and its satellite trials "succeeded," in terms of retributive justice and the production of an authoritative record of Nazi crimes, was partly attributable to the allied occupation of Germany, which put prosecutors in possession of all the devastating documentary evidence. We tend to forget the mishaps in Tokyo: the man who bore greatest responsibility for Japanese war mongering, Emperor Hirohito, was given immunity, while the luckless General Yamashita—in the course of whose case the US Supreme Court formulated the concept of "command responsibility"—was wrongfully convicted (and wrongfully executed).

For the next half-century, the Goddess Nemesis seemed to have flown to another planet: tyrants and torturers flourished on earth, and if forced to leave the bloody stage were allowed to make their exits with an amnesty in their back pocket and their Swiss bank account intact. The establishment of the ICTY in 1993 was at that time little more than a publicity stunt, a desperate attempt by the UN to provide a fig leaf for its abject failure to stop ethnic cleansing in Bosnia. It did not begin to be taken seriously until 1998–9, when NATO arrested some generals and concentration camp commanders. That was the time, at the far end of a century in which 160 million lives had been lost by war and genocide and other crimes against humanity, when impunity was first seriously called into question—by the Pinochet case, the Rome Treaty for the ICC, the Lockerbie proceedings and the use of force to stop atrocities in Kosovo and East Timor.

It should not be assumed that this millennium shift from expediency to justice means that the time for appeasing international criminals in political or military leadership positions is now past. Churchill's fear that political leaders would exploit international tribunals to propagate their doctrines was echoed in 2002 when Milosevic made his televised opening statement to rally Serb nationalists, whilst there is considerable political support—certainly in the US—for Henry Kissinger's view that decisions about the fate of ex-rulers should not be made by judges. Diplomats resent the intrusion of lawyers on what was hitherto their turf and still believe that amnesties are essential to produce peace settlements. These objections can be shown to be wrong in principle, but much more dangerous is the objection which is beginning to focus on the great expense of the ICTY and the ICTR. "Give the money to the victims, not the lawyers" is becoming a catchy and current refrain.

The performance of these tribunals is also coming under fire. The ICTR, hidden away in Arusha, has been the subject of critical review (see Report of the Expert Group to Conduct a Review of the Effective Operation and Functioning of the ICTY and ICTR: UNGA, 22 November 1999) and there have been many concerns expressed about the fact that it has managed only 8 completed trials in its first 8 years of operation. Innumerable interlocutory applications have caused delays in both *ad hoc* tribunals, and there have been some conflicting decisions on novel rules of procedure given by differently constituted trial chambers, whose rulings do not of course bind other chambers. One practical benefit of the 3rd edition of this book is to assist judges and practitioners in developing a consistent approach to the interpretation of procedural rules, especially those which relate to disclosure and protection of witnesses. In this early, 'shake down' period for international criminal justice, the authors have expertly cherry-picked the case law for the most helpful ratios on offer thus far, and their commentary is full of insights into the approaches most likely to commend themselves to future courts.

The first edition of this work was produced in 1998, when the rules were largely untouched by judicial hand. Five years on, they require rigorous re-evaluation, and amendments to those which have contributed to excessive delay and cost. Why, for example, do we find no provision for video-link appearance by lawyers, whose attachment to their home-town trials is one important cause of delays? In this day and age, interlocutory motions should be made and decided at video conferences or in routine cases by e-mail. The time limits, especially in the Arusha rules, are lax: 90 days is too permissive, even for the laziest lawyer, to put together an appeal on a point which will have already been argued in detail before a trial chamber. The rule which allows a defendant to prevent the continuation of a trial where one judge has to step down prematurely is also a recipe for delay. A conviction (or acquittal) by two judges is acceptable (since a 2-1 decision is permitted) and an appeal decision should be similarly satisfactory if it is rendered by three appellate justices in agreement, even if their 5 Judge chamber has been reduced to four or even three. ICTY rule 61 should certainly be repealed: it is a recipe for "trial in absentia," a futile exercise which is unnecessarily prejudicial to the defendant. (International arrest warrants should issue automatically once indictments are confirmed).

In some respects, the existing rules do not take full advantage of the fact that international criminal trials are, for good reason, held before a panel of judges rather than by jury. Such panels are capable of rationally evaluating *all* relevant material, as would any historian (and in analyzing the background to conflict situations, judges must *be* historians). The rules pertaining to what evidence is admissible on issues which do not concern the accused's conduct are much too narrow and are producing inexhaustible arguments by lawyers on all sides. Such background evidence should be received, when tendered, from any source—books, periodicals, television, video, etc— and its weight, rather than its admissibility, should be the crux of judicial assessment. There is still no satisfactory interpretation of ICTY Rule 95, the "fruit of the poisoned tree" provision, which inelegantly excludes evidence, "if its admission is antithetical to, and would seriously damage, the integrity of proceedings." This formula can be interpreted in many ways—a prosecution torture chamber is, one supposes, "antithetical to the integrity of proceedings" meant to secure justice, but evidence crucial to prove guilt of a crime as heinous as a crime against humanity hardly compromises the court if it has been obtained by breach of privacy or trickery or an offer of money or immunity. It is curious that so many of these evidential rules erect a barrier to admissibility, when the real issue for the court should be reliability.

The systemic defect in all international criminal courts at present concerns the co-ordination and competence of the disparate defending lawyers, ranged against an office of prosecutors in full time employment. At Nuremberg, the German defence counsel were ostracized and given inadequate facilities, and prosecution favouritism is built-in to the new tribunals where judges can be qualified by reference to their background as prosecutors, and Registries are harnessed to help the prosecution by running "victims and witnesses units." The defence bar, for its part, is often to blame for time and cost wastage: there is little "quality control," and some defenders from Britain and the US find that commitments in home courts take precedence over trials at the Hague or Arusha. The adversarial system only works effectively with "equality of arms" between the prosecution and the defence, and this principle requires in my opinion that responsibility for organizing defences should be removed from the Registrars and given to a new personage—a "Public Defender" who should occupy a full time post of equivalent rank and status to that of the Prosecutor. The occupant should be appointed from amongst the most distinguished and fearless defenders at the main private bars, and be provided with an adequate staff of attorneys and investigators. The "public defender" would then assume responsibility for all indigent defendants, except where a conflict of interest arises or if a defendant decides to make his own "counsel of choice" arrangements. This way, defendants would be represented by full-time and competent counsel from an office which builds up tribunal experience and has the duty of confronting the prosecutor within the adversarial arena. A salaried public defender's presence in every international tribunal would reduce the fees and traveling expenses of overseas members of the private bar and would substantially reduce delays, as well as guaranteeing an experienced and competent representation for indigent defendants without the danger of clandestine 'fee sharing' arrangements which have been exposed in respect of several ICTY and ICTR defendants.

The substantive jurisprudence emerging from international criminal tribunals is at this stage somewhat prolix and tentative—a reflection perhaps, of the influence of the somewhat abstruse doctrines of customary international law as a subject which until now have not had to embody the precision and predictability required of criminal law in domestic settings. At least the ICTY rulings in *Tadić* et seq are clearing away some of the conceptual confusion in the overlap between international humanitarian law and human rights law, and some of the bedevilments in the requirement to prove "international" armed conflict. There have been some ground breaking and creative decisions as well, such as *Randal* (testimony privilege for war correspondents), Appeals Chamber, 11 December 2002; *Foča* (rape and sexual slavery as crimes against humanity), Trial Chamber, 22 February 2001; *Krstić* (genocide in relation to events in Srebrenica), Trial Chamber, 2 August 2001; *Erdemović* (duress as a defence to crimes against humanity and war crimes), Appeals Chamber, 7 October 1997. But much more work of synthesis and simplification is needed. The fundamental proposition of international criminal law is, after all, that its offences should be instantly recognizable as such by all manner of combatants, from Heads of state to foot soldiers and policemen. It behoves the judges to fashion that law into a set of clear and incontestable principles, so that no indicted defendant can ever plead ignorance. This book will serve as a textbook for that challenge.

Geoffrey Robertson QC
President,
Special Court for Sierra Leone
Doughty Street Chambers
March 2003

FOREWORD TO THE SECOND EDITION*

For more than fifty years after the historic Nuremberg war crimes trials, the international community debated the need for the establishment of an international criminal court. And even though the Genocide Convention contemplated its creation as far back as 1948, most commentators concluded after a while that the idea of such a court would remain stillborn.

The situation changed dramatically when the United Nations Security Council, liberated of its Cold War paralysis and propelled to action by the horrendous crimes being committed in what used to be Yugoslavia and in Rwanda, established two interrelated ad hoc tribunals in 1993 and 1994, respectively, to try and punish those guilty of these crimes. The creation of the International Criminal Tribunal for the Former Yugoslavia and the International Criminal Tribunal for Rwanda revived the long-dormant debate on the need for a permanent international criminal tribunal. It led, finally, to the adoption in 1998 of the Statute of the permanent International Criminal Court. Although the Statute is not yet in force, there is little doubt that it will come into effect and that the Court will be established early in the new millennium. Recent events in Kosovo and East Timor demonstrate the urgent need for such a court and the sad realities that will continue to confront the international community as it seeks to prevent and punish genocide, crimes against humanity and war crimes.

This, the second edition of John R.W.D. Jones' work, is therefore a welcome addition to the growing literature on international criminal law. Source books, of which the present volume is a fine example, tend to be taken for granted by most of their users, and their authors seldom receive the recognition for the conceptualization and hard work required to assemble and organize the material they reproduce. Mr. Jones therefore deserves our appreciation for this expanded and much improved second edition of his book. The editorial comments, case summaries, helpful charts, and above all, a badly needed index make this second edition much more user-friendly than the first. The fact that he worked for some time as legal counsel to both the Tribunal for the Former Yugoslavia and the Rwanda Tribunal provided him with insights that enhance the value of his editorial contributions.

The jurisprudence of these two ad hoc tribunals, which is compiled in these pages, demonstrates that even in the few short years of their existence, their judges have been able to make impressive and intellectually creative contributions to contemporary international criminal law. Those wishing to understand how the permanent International Criminal Court is likely to approach its task will find much valuable information in

---

* Of the then-titled *"The Practice of the International Criminal Tribunals for the Former Yugoslavia and Rwanda"* by John R.W.D. Jones (Transnational Publishers, 2000).

the judgments reproduced in this volume as will those who are interested in the work of the Rwanda and Yugoslav tribunals. In short, this is a book practitioners and scholars alike can benefit from.

Thomas Buergenthal
Lobingier Professor of International and Comparative Law
The George Washington University Law School, Washington, D.C.
Former President, Inter-American Court of Human Rights.
October 1999

FOREWORD TO THE FIRST EDITION*

The International Criminal Tribunal for the former Yugoslavia ("ICTY") has now been in existence for four years; the International Criminal Tribunal for Rwanda ("ICTR") for three years. Speaking as the President of the ICTY, I should like to note that this Tribunal has, in the four years since it was established, evolved from a resolution of the Security Council, existing only on paper, to become a fully functioning court with one trial (*Tadić*) and one sentencing procedure (*Erdemović*) completed, two trials underway (*Čelebići* and *Blaškić*) and three more trials scheduled (*Aleksovski, Dokmanović* and *Kovačević*).

The ICTY has thus achieved a great deal so far—although much remains to be done—in its mission of bringing justice to the former Yugoslavia for the atrocities such as mass killings, rape and "ethnic cleansing" in all its manifestations, which were committed in the former Yugoslavia and which justified the ICTY's establishment. However, as everybody knows, Justice must not only be done but must also be seen to be done. Thus it is crucial to the pedagogical role of the ICTY and the ICTR that their Judgements and Decisions be as widely diffused as possible. This task John Jones' *Practice of the International Criminal Tribunals for the Former Yugoslavia and Rwanda* performs superbly. When John Jones, my assistant legal officer, circulated it internally at the ICTY it proved immediately popular, indeed indispensable, to Judges, prosecutors and defence counsel alike. I trust it will continue to be an extremely useful guide now that it is available to the world public in whose name the international tribunals were created.

Antonio Cassese
President, ICTY
The Hague, July 1997

---

* Of the then-titled *"The Practice of the International Criminal Tribunals for the Former Yugoslavia and Rwanda"* by John R.W.D. Jones (Transnational Publishers, 1998).

USER'S GUIDE

Unlike the first two editions of this work, published in 1998 and 2000, this edition is presented *thematically*, rather than as an article-by-article, rule-by-rule commentary. Given the emerging *corpus* of international criminal law generated by the Statutes, Rules of Procedure and Evidence and jurisprudence of the ICTY, ICTR, ICC and the courts in East Timor, Sierra Leone and Kosovo, among others, a subject-matter approach appears more logical and, indeed, user-friendly.

Where, however, the reader seeks exegesis of a specific article, he or she need only refer to the article-by-article, rule-by-rule index to find the appropriate page(s). This is in addition to the subject-matter index.

In order to shorten references to cases, a number of abbreviations are used (e.g., Tr. Ch. for Trial Chamber), which are set out in a list of abbreviations. There is also a glossary of frequently cited Judgements and Decisions, which provides the date of the Judgement or Decision to avoid the need to mention it each time reference is made to that Judgement or Decision (e.g., the *Blaškić Trial Judgement* stands for the Judgement of the Trial Chamber rendered in the case of *the Prosecutor v. Tihomir Blaškić* (IT-95-14-T) on 3 March, 2000).

Cases are referred to by their name, in italics (e.g., *Tadić*). Case numbers (e.g, IT-01-47-PT) are generally dispensed with, unless it is necessary so to refer to avoid ambiguity. The composition of each Chamber has also not been provided; in the last edition, a system was devised using footnote-type references to show which Judges constituted the Chamber, but the unwieldiness of the system did not seem justified in light of the limited information it provided. Where a Judge has attached a separate or dissenting opinion, that is indeed significant, and accordingly attention is paid in this edition to such opinions rather than to the composition of the Chamber rendering a unanimous opinion.

The authors welcome any comments and suggestions and, in particular, any corrections as to anything which may be inaccurate or out-of-date: please send any remarks to JohnRWDJones@hotmail.com. The law is stated as at 1 May 2003. This work is regularly up-dated at www.intcrimpractice.com.

j.r.w.d.j.
Freetown
Sierra Leone
May 2003

INTRODUCTION

The subject of this book is international criminal practice, that is the practice of international criminal courts and tribunals. There are, currently, four such bodies: the International Criminal Tribunal for the former Yugoslavia (the "**ICTY**"), the International Criminal Tribunal for Rwanda (the "**ICTR**"), the International Criminal Court (the "**ICC**") and the Special Court for Sierra Leone (albeit that it is a mixed international-domestic court) (the "**SCSL**"). Their predecessors, the International Military Tribunals at Nuremberg and Tokyo, for all the criticism that they were "victors' tribunals," were nonetheless international (the London Agreement on War Criminals, 1945, establishing the Nuremberg Tribunal, was signed by 5 states and acceded to by 19 others), and are therefore included in this study of international criminal courts and tribunals.

The courts in Kosovo and East Timor dealing with war crimes are also hybrid institutions applying international humanitarian law and so come within the scope of this study.

International criminal practice, as so defined, does not encompass the practice of purely national courts. Accordingly, this book does not deal with international criminal law as applied by national courts, except when those courts have referred in their decisions and judgements to international criminal practice.

The ICTY and ICTR have both held extensive trials, and appeals, while the ICC and SCSL are only commencing operation at the time of publication. Accordingly, the approach adopted here is to examine the law and practice of the ICTY and ICTR in parallel, with a comparison being made to the ICC and SCSL, where appropriate, at the end of each section.

GLOSSARY OF ABBREVIATIONS

I. Judgements and Decisions

The International Criminal Tribunal for the Former Yugoslavia

Aleksovski Trial Judgement — Prosecutor v. Zlatko Aleksovski, Case No. IT-95-14/1-T, Trial Chamber, Judgement, 25 June 1999

Aleksovski Appeals Judgement — Prosecutor v. Zlatko Aleksovski, Case No. IT-95-14/1-A, Appeals Chamber, Judgement, 24 March 2000

Blaškić Subpoenae Appeals Judgement — Prosecutor v. Tihomir Blaškić, Judgement on the Request of the Republic of Croatia for Review of the Decision of Trial Chamber II of 18 July 1997, Appeals Chamber, 29 October 1997

Blaškić Trial Judgement — Prosecutor v. Tihomir Blaškić, Case No. IT-95-14-T, Trial Chamber, Judgement, 3 March 2000

Delalić et al. Trial Judgement — Prosecutor v. Zejnil Delalić, Zdravko Mucić, Hazim Delić and Esad Landžo (also known as the "*Čelebići* case"), Case No. IT-96-21-T, Trial Chamber, Judgement, 16 November 1998

Delalić et al. Appeals Judgement — Prosecutor v. Zejnil Delalić, Zdravko Mucić, Hazim Delić and Esad Landžo (also known as the "*Čelebići* case"), Case No. IT-96-21-A, Appeals Chamber, Judgement, 20 February 2001

Erdemović Sentencing Judgement — Prosecutor v. Dražen Erdemović, Case No. IT-96-22-T, Trial Chamber, Sentencing Judgement, 29 November 1996

Erdemović Appeals Judgement — Prosecutor v. Dražen Erdemović, Case No. IT-96-22-A, Appeals Chamber, Judgement, 7 October 1997

Erdemović Sentencing Judgement II — Prosecutor v. Dražen Erdemović, Case No. IT-96-22-A, Trial Chamber, Judgement, 5 March 1998

Foča Trial Judgement — Prosecutor v. Dragoljub Kunarac, Radomir Kovac, Zoran Vuković, Case No. IT-96-23-T, Judgement of the Trial Chamber, 22 February 2001

Furundžija Trial Judgement	Prosecutor v. Anto Furundžija, Case No. IT-95-17/1-T, Trial Chamber, Judgement, 10 December 1998
Furundžija Appeals Judgement	Prosecutor v. Anto Furundžija, Case No. IT-95-17/1-A, Appeals Chamber, Judgement, 21 July 2000
Jelisić Trial Judgement	Prosecutor v. Goran Jelisić, Case No. IT-95-10-T, Trial Chamber, Judgement, 14 December 1999
Jelisić Appeals Judgement	Prosecutor v. Goran Jelisić, Case No. IT-95-10-A, Appeals Chamber, Judgement, 5 July 2001
Karadžić and Mladić Rule 61 Decision	Prosecutor v. Radovan Karadžić and Ratko Mladić, Case Nos IT-95-5-R61 and IT-95-18-R61, Review of the Indictments pursuant to Rule 61 of the Rules of Procedure and Evidence, Trial Chamber, 11 July 1996
Kordić and Čerkez Trial Judgement	Prosecutor v. Dario Kordić and Mario Čerkez, Case No. IT-95-14/2-T, Trial Chamber, Judgement, 26 February 2001
Krstić Trial Judgement	Prosecutor v. Radislav Krstić, Case No. IT-98-33-T, Trial Chamber, Judgement, 2 August 2001
Kupreškić Trial Judgement	Prosecutor v. Zoran Kupreškić, Mirjan Kupreškić, Vlatko Kupreškić, Drago Josipović, Dragan Papić and Vladimir Šantić, IT-95-16-T, Trial Chamber, Judgement, 14 January 2000
Kupreškić Appeals Judgement	Prosecutor v. Zoran Kupreškić, Mirjan Kupreškić, Vlatko Kupreškić, Drago Josipović, Dragan Papić and Vladimir Šantić, IT-95-16-T, Appeals Chamber, Judgement, 23 October 2001
Nikolić Rule 61 Decision	Prosecutor v. Dragan Nikolić, Case No. IT-94-2-R61, Review of the Indictment pursuant to Rule 61 of the Rules of Procedure and Evidence, Trial Chamber, 20 October 1995
Rajić Rule 61 Decision	Prosecutor v. Ivica Rajić, Case No. IT-95-12-R61, Trial Chamber, Review of the Indictment pursuant to Rule 61 of the Rules of Procedure and Evidence, 13 September 1996
Sikirica Judgement	Prosecutor v. Duško Sikirica, Case No. IT-95-8-T, Trial Chamber, Judgement on Defence Motions to Acquit, 3 September 2001
Tadić Jurisdiction Decision	Prosecutor v. Duško Tadić, Case No. IT-94-1, Trial Chamber, *Decision on the Defence Motion on the Jurisdiction of the Tribunal*, 10 August 1995
Tadić Jurisdiction Appeals Decision	Prosecutor v. Duško Tadić, Case No. IT-94-1/AR72, Appeals Chamber, Decision on Defence Motion for Interlocutory Appeal on Jurisdiction, 2 October 1995

Tadić Non-bis-in-idem Decision	*Prosecutor v. Duško Tadić*, Case No. IT-94-1/AR72, Trial Chamber, *Decision on Defence Motion on the Principle of non-bis-in-idem*, 14 November 1995
Tadić Opinion and Judgment	*Prosecutor v. Duško Tadić*, Case No. IT-94-1-T, Trial Chamber, Opinion and Judgement, 7 May 1997
Tadić Sentencing Judgment	*Prosecutor v. Duško Tadić*, Case No. IT-94-1-T, Trial Chamber, Judgement in Sentencing, 14 July 1997
Tadić Appeals Judgement	*Prosecutor v. Duško Tadić*, Case No. IT-94-1-A, Appeals Chamber, Judgement, 15 July 1999
Tadić Sentencing Judgment II	*Prosecutor v. Duško Tadić*, Case No. IT-94-1-A and IT-94-1-A*bis*-R117, Trial Chamber, Sentencing Judgement, 11 November 1999
Tadić Judgement in Sentencing Appeals	*Prosecutor v. Duško Tadić*, Case No. IT-94-1-A and IT-94-1-A*bis*, Appeals Chamber, Judgement in Sentencing Appeals, 26 January 2000
Todorović Sentencing Judgement	*Prosecutor v. Stevan Todorović*, Case No. IT-95-9-I, Trial Chamber, Judgement, 31 July 2001
Vukovar Rule 61 Decision	*Prosecutor v. Mile Mrkšić, Miroslav Radić and Veselin Šljivančanin*, Case No. IT-95-13-R61, Trial Chamber, Review of the Indictment pursuant to Rule 61 of the Rules of Procedure and Evidence, 3 April 1996

The International Criminal Tribunal for Rwanda

Akayesu Trial Judgement	*Prosecutor v. Jean-Paul Akayesu*, Case No. ICTR-96-4-T, Trial Chamber, Judgement, 2 September 1998
Akayesu Sentencing Judgement	*Prosecutor v. Jean-Paul Akayesu*, Case No. ICTR-96-4-S, Trial Chamber, Decision on Sentence, 2 October 1998
Akayesu Appeals Judgement	*Prosecutor v. Jean-Paul Akayesu*, Case No. ICTR-96-4-A, Appeals Chamber, Judgement, 1 June 2001
Bagilishema Trial Judgement	*Prosecutor v. Ignace Bagilishema*, Case No. ICTR-95-1A-T, Trial Chamber, Judgement, 7 June 2001
Kambanda Judgement and Sentence	*Prosecutor v. Jean Kambanda*, Case No. ICTR-95-23-S, Trial Chamber, Sentencing Judgement, 4 September 1998
Kambanda Appeals Judgement	*Prosecutor v. Jean Kambanda*, Judgement of the Appeals Chamber, Case No. ICTR-95-23-A, 19 October 2000

Kanyabashi Jurisdiction Decision	*Prosecutor v. Joseph Kanyabashi*, Case No. ICTR-96-15-T, Trial Chamber, *Decision on the Defence Motion on Jurisdiction*, 18 June 1997
Kayishema and Ruzindana Trial Judgement	*Prosecutor v. Clément Kayishema and Obed Ruzindana*, Case No. ICTR-95-1-T, Trial Chamber, Judgement and Sentence, 21 May 1999
Kayishema and Ruzindana Appeals Judgement	*Prosecutor v. Clément Kayishema and Obed Ruzindana*, Case No. ICTR-95-1-T, Trial Chamber, Judgement and Sentence, 1 July 2001
Musema Trial Judgement	*Prosecutor v. Alfred Musema*, Case No. ICTR-96-13-T, Trial Chamber, Judgement and Sentence, 27 January 2000
Ruggiu Judgement and Sentence	*Prosecutor v. Georges Ruggiu*, Case No. ICTR-97-32-T, Trial Chamber, Judgement and Sentence, 1 June 2000
Rutaganda Trial Judgement	*Prosecutor v. Georges Rutaganda*, Case No. ICTR-96-3-T, Trial Chamber, Judgement, 6 December 1999
Serushago Sentencing Judgement	*Prosecutor v. Omar Serushago*, Case No. ICTR-98-39-C, Sentencing Judgement, Trial Chamber, 5 February 1999

II. Other Abbreviations

App. Ch.	Appeals Chamber (of the ICTY or ICTR)
BH	Bosnia and Herzegovina
FRY	Federal Republic of Yugoslavia (Serbia and Montenegro)
GA or UNGA	General Assembly of the United Nations
ICJ	International Court of Justice
ICTs	The International Criminal Tribunal for the former Yugoslavia and the International Criminal Tribunal for Rwanda (also referred to collectively as the "*ad hoc* tribunals" or the "international tribunals)
ICTY	International Criminal Tribunal for the former Yugoslavia, established by UNSC Res. 827 of 27 May, 1993
ICTR	International Criminal Tribunal for Rwanda, established by UNSC Res. 955 of 8 November, 1994
ILC	International Law Commission
IMT	International Military Tribunal at Nuremberg
IMTFE	International Military Tribunal for the Far East (the Tokyo Tribunal)
PrepCom	Preparatory Committee on the Establishment of an International Criminal Court, established by UNGA Res. 50/46 of 11 December, 1995
Res	Resolution
RPE	Rules of Procedure and Evidence

SC or UNSC	Security Council of the United Nations
SG	Secretary-General of the United Nations
Tr. Ch.	Trial Chamber (of the ICTY or ICTR)
UN	United Nations

QUICK INDEX TO THE ICTY STATUTE

Article		Page
Preamble		2
Article 1	Competence of the International Tribunal	131
Article 2	Grave Breaches of the Geneva Conventions of 1949	220
Article 3	Violations of the Laws or Customs of War	251
Article 4	Genocide	143
Article 5	Crimes Against Humanity	180
Article 6	Personal Jurisdiction	348
Article 7	Individual Criminal Responsibility	408
Article 8	Territorial and Temporal Jurisdiction	354
Article 9	Concurrent Jurisdiction	367
Article 10	*Non-Bis-in-Idem*	371
Article 11	Organization of the International Tribunal	41
Article 12	Composition of the Chambers	43
Article 13	Qualifications of Judges	46
Article 13*bis*	Election of Permanent Judges	46
Article 13*ter*	Election and Appointment of *Ad Litem* Judges	48
Article 13*quater*	Status of *Ad Litem* Judges	49
Article 14	Officers and Members of the Chambers	54
Article 15	Rules of Procedure and Evidence	462
Article 16	The Prosecutor	90
Article 17	The Registry	80
Article 18	Investigation and Preparation of Indictment	504
Article 19	Review of the Indictment	508
Article 20	Commencement and Conduct of Trial Proceedings	574
Article 21	Rights of the Accused	577
Article 22	Protection of Victims and Witnesses	612
Article 23	Judgement	760
Article 24	Penalties	769
Article 25	Appellate Proceedings	811
Article 26	Review Proceedings	797
Article 27	Enforcement of Sentences	804
Article 28	Pardon or Commutation of Sentences	804
Article 29	Cooperation and Judicial Assistance	836
Article 30	The Status, Privileges and Immunities of the International Tribunal	120
Article 31	Seat of the International Tribunal	120
Article 32	Expenses of the International Tribunal	122
Article 33	Working Languages	123
Article 34	Annual Report	124

QUICK INDEX TO THE ICTR STATUTE

Article		Page
Preamble		2
Article 1	Competence of the International Tribunal for Rwanda	131
Article 2	Genocide	143
Article 3	Crimes Against Humanity	180
Article 4	Violations of Article 3 common to the Geneva Conventions and of Additional Protocol II	266
Article 5	Personal Jurisdiction	348
Article 6	Individual Criminal Responsibility	408
Article 7	Territorial and Temporal Jurisdiction	354
Article 8	Concurrent Jurisdiction	367
Article 9	*Non-Bis-in-Idem*	371
Article 10	Organization of the International Tribunal for Rwanda	41
Article 11	Composition of the Chambers	43
Article 12	Qualifications of Judges	46
Article 12 *bis*	Election of permanent Judges	46
Article 12 *ter*	Elections and Appointment of *Ad Litem* Judges	48
Article 12 *quater*	Status of *Ad litem* Judges	49
Article 13	Officers and Members of the Chambers	54
Article 14	Rules of Procedure and Evidence	462
Article 15	The Prosecutor	90
Article 16	The Registry	80
Article 17	Investigation and Preparation of Indictment	504
Article 18	Review of the Indictment	508
Article 19	Commencement and Conduct of Trial Proceedings	574
Article 20	Rights of the Accused	577
Article 21	Protection of Victims and Witnesses	612
Article 22	Judgement	760
Article 23	Penalties	769
Article 24	Appellate Proceedings	811
Article 25	Review Proceedings	831
Article 26	Enforcement of Sentences	797
Article 27	Pardon or Commutation of Sentences	804
Article 28	Cooperation and Judicial Assistance	836
Article 29	The Status, Privileges and Immunities of the International Tribunal for Rwanda	120
Article 30	Expenses of the International Tribunal for Rwanda	122
Article 31	Working Languages	123
Article 32	Annual Report	124

QUICK INDEX TO THE ICTY AND ICTR RULES OF PROCEDURE AND EVIDENCE

Rule	Page
Rule 1	468
Rule 2	468
Rule 3	470
Rule 4	121
Rule 5	473
Rule 6	474
Rule 7	476
Rule 7 *bis*	846
Rule 7 *ter*	631
Rule 8	376
Rule 9	377
Rule 10	379
Rule 11	846
Rule 11 *bis*	385
Rule 12	387
Rule 13	372
Rule 14	58
Rule 14 *bis*	59
Rule 15	59
Rule 15 *bis*	64
Rule 16	67
Rule 17	67
Rule 18	68
Rule 19	69
Rule 20	70
Rule 21	71
Rule 22	71
Rule 23	72
Rule 23 *bis*	73
Rule 23 *ter*	73
Rule 24	74
Rule 25	74
Rule 26	75
Rule 27	75
Rule 28	76
Rule 29	79

Rule 30	80
Rule 31	80
Rule 32	81
Rule 33	81
Rule 33 *bis*	84
Rule 34	85
Rule 35	88
Rule 36	88
Rule 37	97
Rule 38	100
Rule 39	492
Rule 40	494
Rule 40 *bis*	495
Rule 41	500
Rule 42	501
Rule 43	502
Rule 44	101
Rule 44 *bis*	103
Rule 45	104
Rule 45 *bis*	112
Rule 45 *ter*	113
Rule 45 *quater*	113
Rule 46	114
Rule 47	510
Rule 48	516
Rule 48 *bis*	520
Rule 49	520
Rule 50	523
Rule 51	528
Rule 52	531
Rule 53	531
Rule 53 *bis*	533
Rule 54	538
Rule 54 *bis*	552
Rule 55	555
Rule 55 *bis*	558
Rule 56	843
Rule 57	559
Rule 58	844
Rule 59	847
Rule 59 *bis*	560
Rule 60	565
Rule 61	566
Rule 62	632
Rule 62 *bis*	639
Rule 62 *ter*	642
Rule 63	596

Rule	Page
Rule 64	598
Rule 65	599
Rule 65 *bis*	642
Rule 65 *ter*	644
Rule 66	647
Rule 67	656
Rule 68	662
Rule 68 *bis*	668
Rule 69	612
Rule 70	668
Rule 71	672
Rule 71 *bis*	676
Rule 72	676
Rule 73	686
Rule 73 *bis*	691
Rule 73 *ter*	694
Rule 74	696
Rule 74 *bis*	702
Rule 75	621
Rule 76	702
Rule 77	322
Rule 77 *bis*	337
Rule 78	703
Rule 79	703
Rule 80	707
Rule 81	707
Rule 82	708
Rule 83	711
Rule 84	712
Rule 84 *bis*	713
Rule 85	713
Rule 86	719
Rule 87	721
Rule 88	763
Rule 89	725
Rule 90	735
Rule 90 *bis*	741
Rule 91	338
Rule 92	745
Rule 92 *bis*	746
Rule 93	749
Rule 94	749
Rule 94 *bis*	752
Rule 95	753
Rule 96	754
Rule 97	757
Rule 98	758

Rule 98 *bis*	761
Rule 98 *ter*	763
Rule 99	764
Rule 100	791
Rule 101	769
Rule 102	796
Rule 103	798
Rule 104	801
Rule 105	802
Rule 106	803
Rule 107	814
Rule 107 *bis*	815
Rule 108	815
Rule 108 *bis*	816
Rule 109	818
Rule 110	819
Rule 111	819
Rule 112	821
Rule 113	821
Rule 114	822
Rule 115	822
Rule 116	826
Rule 116 *bis*	827
Rule 117	827
Rule 117 *bis*	828
Rule 117 *ter*	829
Rule 118	829
Rule 119	830
Rule 120	831
Rule 121	832
Rule 122	833
Rule 123	805
Rule 124	805
Rule 125	806
Rule 126	630
Rule 126 *bis*	630
Rule 127	631

PART 1

THE ESTABLISHMENT OF THE INTERNATIONAL TRIBUNALS

ICTY Preamble: Updated Statute of the International Tribunal.	1.1
ICTR Preamble: Updated Statute of the International Tribunal for Rwanda	1.1
Historical Background.	1.2
The International Criminal Tribunal for the Former Yugoslavia (ICTY)	1.5
Amendment of the ICTY Statute	1.7
The International Criminal Tribunal for Rwanda (ICTR)	1.11
Amendment of the ICTR Statute	1.14
Lawfulness of Establishment of ICTY and ICTR	1.18
Violation of State Sovereignty	1.22
Lack of Competence on the Part of the Security Council	1.23
Humanitarian/Military Intervention.	1.34
Article 41 or 42 of the United Nations Charter.	1.35
The ICTY as a Military Tribunal	1.40
Relationship of the ICTs to the International Court of Justice (ICJ).	1.42
Relationship Between the ICTY and the European Court of Human Rights (ECHR)	1.57
The International Criminal Court (ICC)	1.62
The Special Court for Sierra Leone.	1.64
Historical Background	1.64
Competence and Functioning of the Special Court.	1.83
Competence of the Court	1.91
Composition of the Court.	1.101
Functioning of the Court	1.109
Prosecution of War and Ethnic Crimes and Other Serious Crimes Under the	
UN Interim Administration Mission in Kosovo.	1.116
International Judges and Prosecutors / International Staff in Local Courts.	1.121
The Kosovo War and Ethnic Crimes Court	1.134
Ombudsperson Institution.	1.137
Co-operation with the ICTY	1.141
The Serious Crimes Panel of the Dili District Court: East Timor	1.142
Background	1.142
Development of the Serious Crimes Panels	1.146
Applicable Law.	1.149
Operation.	1.150
The Proposed Extraordinary Chambers of the Courts of Cambodia	1.156
Background	1.156
Development of the Extraordinary Chambers.	1.160
Composition and Applicable Law	1.165

* * * * *

1.1

ICTY UPDATED STATUTE OF THE INTERNATIONAL TRIBUNAL	ICTR UPDATED STATUTE OF THE INTERNATIONAL TRIBUNAL FOR RWANDA
(ADOPTED 25 MAY 1993 BY RESOLUTION 827) (AS AMENDED 13 MAY 1998 BY RESOLUTION 1166) (AS AMENDED 30 NOVEMBER 2000 BY RESOLUTION 1329) (AS AMENDED 17 MAY 2002 BY RESOLUTION 1411)	(ADOPTED 8 NOVEMBER 1994 BY RESOLUTION 955) (AS AMENDED 30 APRIL 1998 BY RESOLUTION 1165) (AS AMENDED 30 NOVEMBER 2000 BY RESOLUTION 1329) (AS AMENDED 17 MAY 2002 BY RESOLUTION 1411)
Having been established by the Security Council acting under Chapter VII of the Charter of the United Nations, the International Tribunal for the Prosecution of Persons Responsible for Serious Violations of International Humanitarian Law Committed in the Territory of the Former Yugoslavia since 1991 (hereinafter referred to as "the International Tribunal") shall function in accordance with the provisions of the present Statute.	As amended by the Security Council acting under Chapter VII of the Charter of the United Nations, the International Criminal Tribunal for the Prosecution of Persons Responsible for Genocide and Other Serious Violations of International Humanitarian Law Committed in the Territory of Rwanda and Rwandan Citizens Responsible for Genocide and other such violations committed in the territory of neighbouring States, between 1 January 1994 and 31 December 1994 (hereinafter referred to as "the International Tribunal for Rwanda") shall function in accordance with the provisions of the present Statute.

Historical Background

1.2 The Charter of the United Nations was signed in San Francisco on 26 June 1945. Under Article 24 of the United Nations Charter, the Members of the United Nations "confer on the Security Council primary responsibility for the maintenance of international peace and security, and agree that in carrying out its responsibilities the Security Council acts on their behalf." In 1993, the Security Council, acting under Chapter VII of the United Nations Charter ("Action with respect to Threats to the Peace, Breaches of the Peace, and Acts of Aggression") determined that the situation in the former Yugoslavia posed a threat to international peace and security. It responded to this threat, *inter alia*, by establishing a tribunal to try persons suspected of being responsible for serious violations of international humanitarian law, i.e., genocide, crimes against humanity and war crimes. This was the first time that the United Nations had established a criminal tribunal to try individuals and such an effort had not been undertaken at the international level since the Nuremberg and Tokyo Tribunals were established after the Second World War. The next year, in 1994, the Security Council again reacted to a threat to international peace and security, this time in Rwanda, by establishing an international criminal tribunal.

1.3 The creation of these two, *ad hoc* tribunals had the effect of re-activating the project to establish a standing International Criminal Court ("ICC"), which had been stalled during the Cold War. This project came back to life and a treaty establishing the ICC was concluded at the Rome Conference in July, 1998. Subsequently, other international courts, or mixed international-domestic or national courts with major international involvement, have been established to try individuals in relation to situations of massive and widespread violence in places such as East Timor, Kosovo and Sierra Leone.

1.4 There are thus two main categories of international tribunals: those established by the United Nations Security Council and those established by treaty or other international arrangement. The ICTY and the ICTR were established by resolutions of the United Nations Security Council in 1993 and 1994, respectively. The ICC and SCSL, by contrast, are treaty-based courts. The ICC was established by the Rome Treaty of 17 July 1998. The SCSL was set up pursuant to an Agreement between the United Nations and the Government of Sierra Leone (see Security Council resolution 1315 of 14 August 2000). See 1.62 on the establishment of the ICC and 1.64 on the SCSL.

The International Criminal Tribunal for the Former Yugoslavia (ICTY)

1.5 Following a number of resolutions passed by the Security Council concerning the situation in the former Yugoslavia, the Security Council passed resolution 808 of 22 February 1993, in which it decided "that an international tribunal shall be established for the prosecution of persons responsible for serious violations of international humanitarian law committed in the territory of the former Yugoslavia since 1991." The resolution requested the Secretary-General "to submit for consideration by the Council at the earliest possible date . . . a report on all aspects of this matter." The Secretary-General's Report was submitted on 3 May 1993 (S/25704), and proposed a Statute for the ICTY.

1.6 The Security Council considered the Secretary-General's Report and subsequently adopted the proposed Statute unanimously and without amendment in its resolution 827 of 27 May, 1993. In that resolution, the Security Council determined that the situation in the former Yugoslavia, and in particular in Bosnia and Herzegovina—where there were "reports of mass killings, massive, organised and systematic detention and rape of women and [. . .] the practice of 'ethnic cleansing'"—constituted a threat to international peace and security under Chapter VII of the United Nations Charter. The Security Council considered that establishing an international tribunal would "contribute to ensuring that such violations are halted and effectively redressed." Accordingly, in operative paragraph 2 of resolution 827, the Council decided:

> hereby to establish an international tribunal for the sole purpose of prosecuting persons responsible for serious violations of international humanitarian law committed in the territory of the former Yugoslavia between 1 January 1991 and a date to be determined by the Security Council upon the restoration of peace and to this end to adopt the Statute of the International Tribunal annexed to the above-mentioned [Secretary-General's] report.

Article: For a useful general overview of the ICTY, see Patricia M. Wald, former ICTY Judge, "The International Criminal Tribunal for the Former Yugoslavia Comes of Age: Some Observations on Day to Day Dilemmas of an International Court," Vol 5 *Journal of Law and Policy* 87.

Amendment of the ICTY Statute

1.7 The ICTY Statute was adopted by the UN Security Council and may, therefore, only be amended by the Security Council. The Statute has so far been amended three times: by Security Council resolution 1166 (13 May 1998), resolution 1329 (30 November 2000) and resolution 1411 (17 May 2002).

1.8 The Security Council amended the ICTY Statute by resolution 1166 (1998) of 13 May 1998 to add a third Trial Chamber and three new Judges. Articles 11, 12 and 13 of the ICTY Statute were consequently amended to this effect.

1.9 The Security Council again amended the ICTY Statute by resolution 1329 (2000) of 30 November 2000, to establish a pool of *ad litem* judges at the ICTY and to increase the number of judges in the Appeals Chambers of the ICTY and ICTR "in order to enable the International Tribunals to expedite the conclusion of their work at the earliest possible date." Articles 12, 13 and 14 of the ICTY Statute were accordingly amended. This was done at the request of the ICTY and ICTR Presidents. See the letter from the Secretary-General to the President of the Security Council dated 7 September 2000 (S/2000/865), annexing letters from the ICTY and ICTR Presidents to the Secretary-General dated 12 May 2000 and 14 June 2000 respectively.

1.10 The amendments to the ICTY Statute made by SC resolution 1411 of 17 May 2002 dealt simply with the issue of the double nationality of Judges. Article 12 of the Statute was amended to add an additional para. (4).

The International Criminal Tribunal for Rwanda (ICTR)

1.11 The Security Council established the ICTR in its Resolution 955 of 8 November 1994, after having commissioned a number of reports on the situation in Rwanda that indicated that "genocide and other systematic, widespread and flagrant violations of international humanitarian law have been committed in Rwanda," and having determined that "this situation continues to constitute a threat to international peace and security."

1.12 It has been estimated that from 500,000 to one million people—the vast majority of them Tutsi civilians—were killed in the course of three months during the 1994 genocide in Rwanda (*Report on the Situation of Human Rights in Rwanda Submitted by René Degni-Ségui, Special Rapporteur of the Commission on Human Rights, under Paragraph 20 of Commission Resolution S-3/1 of 25 May 1994*, U.N. Doc. E/CN. 4/1995/7 (1994)).

1.13 On 14 April 2000, the United Nations Security Council publicly acknowledged the responsibility of the United Nations for not having succeeded in halting the 1994 genocide, while making recommendations on how to deal with future atrocities. The members of the Security Council agreed with the conclusions of a Report prepared by the "*Independent Inquiry into the actions of the United Nations during the 1994 Genocide in Rwanda*," commissioned by the United Nations, which accused the Organisation of having lacked the determination before the genocide to prevent it and for not having intervened once the massacres had begun. The Security Council members also recognised, as the Report had done, that the United Nations had lacked the resources to deal with the situation and that the members of the United Nations had lacked the political will to stop the killings (see UN doc. S/1999/1257 dated 16 December 1999).

Amendment of the ICTR Statute

1.14 The ICTR Statute has, like the ICTY Statute, been amended three times: by Security Council resolution 1165 (30 April 1998), resolution 1329 (30 November 2000) and resolution 1411 (17 May 2002).

1.15 The Statute of the ICTR was amended by the Security Council in its resolution 1165 (1998) of 30 April 1998 to provide for a third Trial Chamber. Articles 10, 11 and 12 of the ICTR Statute were amended to this end.

1.16 The Security Council again amended the ICTR Statute by resolution 1329 (2000) of 30 November 2000, to increase the number of judges in the Appeals Chambers of the ICTY and ICTR "in order to enable the International Tribunals to expedite the conclusion of their work at the earliest possible date." Articles 11, 12 and 13 of the ICTR Statute were amended accordingly.

1.17 The amendments to the ICTR Statute made by SC resolution 1411 of 17 May 2002 dealt simply with the issue of the double nationality of Judges. Article 11 of the Statute was amended to add an additional para. (2).

Lawfulness of Establishment of ICTY and ICTR

1.18 As noted above, the Security Council had never before established a court in order to counter a threat to international peace and security. Not unsurprisingly, therefore, there were those who, from the outset, questioned whether the Security Council had the power under Chapter VII of the United Nations Charter to establish the ICTY (and subsequently the ICTR).

1.19 When the legality of the Security Council's establishment of the ICTY was first raised in ICTY proceedings, in a motion filed in *Tadić* on 23 June 1995, the Trial Chamber ruled that it was not competent to review the lawfulness of the Tribunal's creation. (*Tadić Jurisdiction Decision*, 10 August 1995):

> 5. [. . .] this International Tribunal is not a constitutional court set up to scrutinise the actions of organs of the United Nations. It is [. . .] a criminal tribunal with clearly defined powers, involving a quite specific and limited criminal jurisdiction. If it is to confine itself to those specific limits, it will have no authority to investigate the legality of its creation by the Security Council.
>
> [. . .]

9. [Rule 73(A)(i)] relates to challenges to jurisdiction and is no authority for engaging in investigation, not into jurisdiction, but into the legality of the action of the Security Council in establishing the International Tribunal.

1.20 On appeal, the Appeals Chamber took a different approach, holding by a majority of four to one, Judge Li dissenting, that the ICTY *was* competent to review the legality of its own establishment. The Appeals Chamber then held that the ICTY *had* been lawfully established (*Tadić Jurisdiction Appeals Decision*, 2 October 1995). The *Tadić* Appeal Decision was reaffirmed by the Appeals Chamber in the *Krajisnik Decision on Interlocutory Motion Challenging Jurisdiction*, 25 May 2001.

1.21 The lawfulness of the ICTR's establishment was raised for the first time at the ICTR on a preliminary motion in *Kanyabashi*. The Trial Chamber held that the ICTR had been lawfully established (Kanyabashi, Tr. Ch., *Decision on the Defence Motion on Jurisdiction*, 18 June 1997). The Decision is worth quoting at length, as an introduction to the basic issues.

Violation of State Sovereignty

1.22 The first objection dealt with in the *Kanyabashi Jurisdiction Decision* was that, "the Sovereignty of States, in particular that of the Republic of Rwanda, was violated by the fact that the Tribunal was not established by a treaty through the General Assembly." The Trial Chamber held that, considered against the background of the law of the UN Charter, the ICTR has been lawfully set up by the Security Council:

9. The Defence Counsel submitted [. . .] that the Tribunal should and in fact could only have been established by an international treaty upon recommendation of the General Assembly, which would have permitted the member States of the United Nations to express their approval or disapproval of the establishment of an ad-hoc Tribunal. The Defence Counsel argued that by leaving the establishment of the Tribunal to the Security Council through a Resolution under Chapter VII of the UN Charter, the United Nations not only encroached upon the sovereignty of the Republic of Rwanda, and other Member States, but also frustrated the endeavours of its General Assembly to establish a permanent criminal court. The Tribunal, in the Defence Counsel's view, was therefore not lawfully established.

10. The Prosecutor, in response to this first objection raised by Defence Counsel, rejected the notion that the Tribunal was unlawfully established and contended that, since there was a need for an effective and expeditious implementation of the decision to establish the Tribunal, the treaty approach would have been ineffective because of the considerable time required for the establishment of an instrument and for its entry into force.

11. The Trial Chamber finds that two issues need to be addressed. One is whether the accused as an individual has *locus standi* to raise a plea of infringement of the sovereignty of States, in particular that of the Republic of Rwanda, and the other is whether the sovereignty of the Republic of Rwanda and other Member States were in fact violated in the present case.

12. As regards the first of these questions [. . .] [t]he Trial Chamber [. . .] accepts that the accused in the present case can raise the plea of State sovereignty. In any

event, it is the individual and not the State who has been subjected to the jurisdiction of the Tribunal.

13. As regards the second question whether the sovereignty of the Republic of Rwanda has been violated by the Security Council's decision to establish the Tribunal, the Trial Chamber notes that membership of the United Nations entail[s] certain limitations upon the sovereignty of the member States. This is true in particular by virtue of the fact that all member States, pursuant to Article 25 of the UN Charter, have agreed to accept and carry out the decisions of the Security Council in accordance with the Charter. [. . .]

14. The Trial Chamber notes, furthermore, that the establishment of the ICTR was called for by the Government of Rwanda itself, which maintained that an international criminal tribunal could assist in prosecuting those responsible for acts of genocide and crimes against humanity and in this way promote the restoration of peace and reconciliation in Rwanda. The Ambassador of Rwanda, during the discussion and adoption of Resolution 955 in the Security Council on 8 November 1994 declared that:

> The tribunal will help national reconciliation and the construction of a new society based on social justice and respect for the fundamental rights of the human person, all of which will be possible only if those responsible for the Rwandese tragedy are brought to justice.

15. Against this background, the Trial Chamber is of the view that the Security Council's establishment of the Tribunal through a Resolution under Chapter VII of the UN Charter and with the participation of the Government of Rwanda, rather than by a treaty adopted by the Member States under the auspices of the General Assembly, did not entail any violation of the sovereignty of the Republic of Rwanda and that of the Member States of the United Nations.

16. The Defence Counsel further argued that the establishment of the Tribunal through a resolution of the Security Council effectively undermined the General Assembly's initiative to set up a permanent International Criminal Court. The Trial Chamber, however, mindful of the fact that such a tribunal may well be created by an international treaty, finds that this question has no bearing on the jurisdiction of this Tribunal and must therefore be rejected.

In the event, of course, a permanent ICC was established, in July 1998.

Lack of Competence on the Part of the Security Council

1.23 Second, the Trial Chamber considered the defence argument that the Security Council was not competent to establish an *ad-hoc* Tribunal under Chapter VII of the UN Charter. The defence argued that the establishment of the Tribunal by the Security Council was unlawful for five basic reasons:

(1) The conflict in Rwanda did not pose any threat to international peace and security.
(2) There was no international conflict to warrant any action by the Security Council.
(3) The Security Council thus could not act within Chapter VII of the UN Charter.
(4) The establishment of an ad-hoc tribunal was never a measure contemplated by Article 41 of the UN Charter.

8 • International Criminal Practice

(5) The Security Council has no authority to deal with the protection of Human Rights.

1.24 The Trial Chamber rejected each of these arguments.

(1) **The conflict in Rwanda did not pose any threat to international peace and security.**

1.25 On this subject, the Trial Chamber concluded, first, that decisions of the Security Council as to what constitutes a threat to international peace and security are not justiciable. It is to be noted that this corresponds to the approach taken by the Trial Chamber in the *Tadić Jurisdiction Decision*. This approach had, however, already been overturned by the Appeals Chamber in the *Tadić Jurisdiction Appeals Decision* on 2 October 1995, in which the Chamber ruled (Judge Li dissenting) that it could review the legality of UNSC resolutions. Thus the ICTR Trial Chamber ruling in *Kanyabashi* could have taken the position that it was entitled to review the lawfulness of its establishment by SC resolutions.

1.25 The Chamber did in any event proceed to look at the merits of the claim. It held that a conflict, while internal, can present a threat to international peace and security due to the effects it has on the wider community, e.g. caused by the spill-over of refugees to neighbouring countries, its destabilising effect on the whole region, etc.

> 19. On several occasions, e.g. in Congo, Somalia and Liberia, the Security Council has established that incidents such as sudden migration of refugees across the borders to neighbouring countries and extension or diffusion of an internal armed conflict into foreign territory may constitute a threat to international peace and security. This might happen in particular where the areas immediately affected have exhausted their resources. The reports submitted by the Special Rapporteur for Rwanda of the United Nations Commission on Human Rights (see Doc. S/1994/1157) and also by the Commission of Experts appointed by the Secretary General (see Doc. S/1994/1125) concluded that the conflict in Rwanda as well as the stream of refugees had created a highly volatile situation in some of the neighbouring regions. As a matter of fact, this conclusion was subsequently shared by the Security Council and formed the basis for the adoption of Security Council's resolution 955 (1994) of 8 November 1994.
>
> 20. Although bound by the provisions in Chapter VII of the UN Charter and in particular Article 39 of the Charter, the Security Council has a wide margin of discretion in deciding when and where there exists a threat to international peace and security. By their very nature, however, such discretionary assessments are not justiciable since they involve the consideration of a number of social, political and circumstantial factors which cannot be weighed and balanced objectively by this Trial Chamber.
>
> 21. While it is true that the conflict in Rwanda was internal in the sense that it emerged from inherent tensions between the two major groups forming the population within the territory of Rwanda and otherwise did not involve the direct participation of armed forces belonging to any other State, the Trial Chamber cannot accept the Defence Counsel's notion that the conflict did not pose any threat to international peace and security. The question of whether or not the conflict posed a threat to international peace and security is a matter to be decided exclusively by the Security Council. The Trial Chamber nevertheless takes judi-

cial notice of the fact that the conflict in Rwanda created a massive wave of refugees, many of whom were armed, into the neighbouring countries which by itself entailed a considerable risk of serious destabilisation of the local areas in the host countries where the refugees had settled. The demographical composition of the population in certain neighbouring regions outside the territory of Rwanda, furthermore, showed features which suggest that the conflict in Rwanda might eventually spread to some or all of these neighbouring regions.

22. The Trial Chamber concludes that there is no merit in the Defence Counsel's argument that the conflict in Rwanda did not pose any threat to international peace and security and holds that this was a matter to be decided exclusively by the Security Council.

1.27 In effect, this approach amounts to a low standard of review; the Chamber was in fact noting that there was a rational basis for the SC's decision that the situation posed a threat to international peace and security, while granting to the SC a wide margin of appreciation or discretion in reaching this decision. Thus the Chamber did not, despite its protestations, treat the SC's decision as truly unjusticiable. To this extent, the approach *de facto* approximates to that taken in the *Tadić Jurisdiction Appeals Decision*.

(2)   There was no international conflict to warrant any action by the Security Council.

1.28 The Chamber responded to this objection by, in effect, declaring it irrelevant, since the basis for UNSC action is that there is a threat to international peace and security, not that there is an international armed conflict. The Chamber had already noted, paradoxical though it may sound, that a non-international conflict may nonetheless pose a threat to international peace and security:

23. The Defence Counsel further contends that there was no international conflict to warrant any action by the Security Council. This argument has been partly addressed in the preceding paragraphs in the sense that *if* the Security Council had decided that the conflict in Rwanda did in fact pose a threat to international peace and security, this conflict would thereby fall within the ambit of the Security Council's powers to restore and maintain international peace and security pursuant to the provisions in Chapter VII of the UN Charter.

24. The Security Council's authority to take such action, furthermore, exists independently of whether or not the conflict was deemed to be international in character. The decisive prerequisite for the Security Council's prerogative under Article 39 and 41 of the UN Charter is not whether there *exists* an *international* conflict, but whether the conflict at hand entails a threat to international peace and security. Internal conflicts, too, may well have international implications which can justify Security Council action. The Trial Chamber holds that there is no basis for the Defence Counsel's submission that the Security Council's competence to act rested on a pre-existing international conflict.

1.29 It is worth noting, nonetheless, that the UNSC did evidently consider the conflict in Rwanda to be an internal one, since the ICTR's jurisdiction over war crimes encompasses only violations of common Article 3 and of Additional Protocol II, both of which are applicable to internal conflicts. By contrast, the ICTY clearly has a Statute to cover an international, or at least partly international, armed conflict, since its jurisdiction encompasses the body of law applicable to international armed conflicts, namely the Geneva Conventions of 1949 and the laws or customs of war, as originally set out in the Hague Conventions of 1899 and 1907 (see below, on the internationality of the conflict in the former Yugoslavia, see 4.3.319).

(3)   The Security Council could not act within Chapter VII of the UN Charter.

1.30   This argument was, of course, based on the notion that there was no international armed conflict in Rwanda and that the situation did not pose a threat to international peace and security, or at least that peace and security had been re-established by the time the ICTR was established. The Chamber had already rejected these arguments.

> 26. The Trial Chamber observes, once again, that this argument entails a finding of fact based on evidence and that, in any case, the question of whether or not the Security Council was justified in taking actions under Chapter VII when it did, is a matter to be determined by the Security Council itself. The Trial Chamber notes, in particular, that cessation of the atrocities of the conflict does not necessarily imply that international peace and security had been restored, because peace and security cannot be said to be re-established adequately without justice being done. In the Trial Chamber's view, the achievement of international peace and security required that swift international action be taken by the Security Council to bring to justice those responsible for the atrocities in the conflict.

(4)   The establishment of an ad-hoc tribunal was never a measure contemplated by Article 41 of the UN Charter.

1.31   The Trial Chamber in *Kanyabashi* rejected this argument on the grounds that the establishment of the ICTR fell within the ambit of Article 41 of the UN Charter as a possible measure to be taken in response to a threat to the peace:

> 27. The thrust of this argument lies in the contention that establishment of an ad-hoc Tribunal to prosecute perpetrators of genocide and violations of international humanitarian law is not a measure contemplated by the provisions of Chapter VII of the UN Charter. While it is true that establishment of judicial bodies is not directly mentioned in Article 41 of the UN Charter as a measure to be considered in the restoration and maintenance of peace, it clearly falls within the ambit of measures to satisfy this goal. The list of actions contained in Article 41 is clearly not exhaustive but indicates some examples of the measures which the Security Council might eventually decide to impose on States in order to remedy a conflict or an imminent threat to international peace and security. This is also the view of the Appeals Chamber in the Tadić-case.

(5)   The Security Council has no authority to deal with the protection of Human Rights.

1.32   The Chamber gave this submission short shrift:

> Finally, the Defence Counsel holds that the international protection of Human Rights is embedded in particular international instruments such as the global International Covenants on Civil and Political Rights & Social, Economic and Cultural Rights and in the regional conventions on Human Rights for Europe and Africa, all of which have established particular international institutions entrusted with the task of protecting the body of international Human Rights. The Defence

Counsel claims, therefore, that the protection of Human Rights is not a matter for the Security Council.

29. The Trial Chamber cannot accept the Defence Counsel's argument that the existence of specialized institutions for the protection of Human Rights should effectively prevent the Security Council from taking part in the protection of this body of law. Rather to the contrary, the protection of international Human Rights is the responsibility of all United Nations organs, the Security Council included, without any limitation, in conformity with the UN Charter.

1.33 Many of the above arguments have also been introduced before the ICTY and have been dealt with by the Judges in much the same manner. (See the most recent ruling on this issue in *Milošević, Decision on Preliminary Motions*, 8 November 2001).

Article: Virginia Morris, "International Decisions: The Prosecutor v. Kanyabashi, Decision on Jurisdiction," 92 *American Journal of International Law* 66–70, (1998).

Humanitarian/Military Intervention

1.34 The creation of the ICTY and ICTR may be seen as a modern form of collective humanitarian intervention by the Security Council to deal with the massive human rights violations being committed in the former Yugoslavia and Rwanda. See Professor Theodor Meron, "War Crimes in Yugoslavia and the Development of International Law," 88 *American Journal of International Law* 78 (1994).

1.35 Indeed, some considered that the Nuremberg Tribunal was established pursuant to this principle. Sir Hartley Shawcross, the British Chief Prosecutor at the Nuremberg trials said:

The right of humanitarian intervention on behalf of the rights of man trampled upon by a State in a manner shocking the sense of mankind has long been considered to form part of the law of nations. Here too, the Charter [the London Charter establishing the International Military Tribunal] merely develops a pre-existing principle. (*Transcript of the Nuremberg trials*, p. 813)

Website: The website of the Avalon Project of the Yale Law School (http://www.yale.edu/lawweb/avalon/imt/imt.htm#key) has a vast collection of documents related to the Nuremberg Tribunal.

Article 41 or Article 42 of the United Nations Charter

1.35 It has often been assumed that the Security Council, when it established the ICTY and ICTR, acted under Article 41 of the United Nations Charter (see, in particular, *Tadić Jurisdiction Appeals Decision*, paras. 33–36). The relevant Security Council resolutions do not, however, state under which article of the Charter the Security Council acted when it established the tribunals, only that it acted pursuant to Chapter VII.

1.36 The establishment of the ICTY and ICTR may, however, be seen as military measures taken under Article 42 of the United Nations Charter to maintain or restore international peace and security. Article 42 of the United Nations Charter reads:

Should the Security Council consider the measures provided for in Article 41 would be inadequate or have proved to be inadequate, it may take such action by air, sea, or land forces as may be necessary to maintain or restore international peace and security. Such action may include demonstrations, blockade, and other operations by air, sea, or land forces of Members of the United Nations.

1.38 Thus Professor Conforti argues in *The Law and Practice of the United Nations* (1996), pages 206–207:

> As far as the Tribunal for the former Yugoslavia is concerned, the Tribunal itself has held the view that its creation can be fitted into Article 41 as an atypical measure not involving the use of force. . . . In our opinion, as the action in the former Yugoslavia as a whole—i.e. the action directly taken by the United Nations forces plus the action only authorised by the Security Council—may be defined as an action involving the use of force, the creation of the Tribunal, being an aspect of this action, must more appropriately be brought within the framework of Article 42. In fact, the right to punish the war criminals of the enemy's forces has always been considered as an international right of a belligerent State, and, according to the most convincing legal doctrine, also the Nuremberg trial in 1945 found its ultimate justification in this old rule. *Mutatis mutandis*, the creation of the Tribunal can thus be considered as a "belligerent" measure of the United Nations. The same can be said of the Tribunal for the crimes in Rwanda.

1.39 This argument is supported by the fact that a large number of the persons in the ICTY's custody were brought before the tribunal by use of military force, having been arrested by the NATO-led, international military force, SFOR (Stabilisation Force). Moreover, the international community reacted to "ethnic cleansing" by Serb forces in Kosovo in early 1999 by a bombing campaign conducted by NATO ('Operation Allied Force') from 24 March to 20 June 1999.

The ICTY as a Military Tribunal

1.40 The ICTY has on occasion compared itself to a military tribunal and distinguished itself from courts of ordinary criminal jurisdiction on this ground:

> the International Tribunal is adjudicating crimes which are considered so horrific as to warrant universal jurisdiction. The International Tribunal is in certain respects comparable to a military tribunal which often has limited rights of due process and more lenient rules of evidence. (*Tadić*, Tr. Ch. majority (Judges McDonald and Vohrah), *Protective Measures Decision*, 10 August 1995, paragraph 28)

1.41 A more persuasive argument, however, is that trials of horrific crimes require *heightened* "rights of due process," given the penalties and social opprobrium resulting from a conviction for war crimes or genocide. Given the seriousness of the crimes with which they are dealing, ICTY Judges should, one may argue, err on the side of being scrupulous rather than lenient with respect to the admission of evidence at trial. Indeed, on other occasions, the Tribunal has recognised this and emphasised that accused facing trial before the Tribunal are granted the highest of human rights protections. This would seem to be the more appropriate aim.

ICTY Publication: For information concerning the establishment of the ICTY, see the ICTY's publication, *The Path to The Hague (Selected Documents on the Origins of the ICTY)* (The Hague, 1996).

Relationship of the ICTs to the International Court of Justice (ICJ)

1.42 The ICTY and ICTR are autonomous international judicial bodies. While the ICJ is the "principal judicial organ" (Article 92 of the United Nations Charter) within the United Nations system to which the tribunals belong, "there is no hierarchical relationship between the two courts. Although the common ICTY/ICTR Appeals Chamber will necessarily take into consideration other decisions of international courts, it may, after careful consideration, come to a different conclusion" (*Delalić et al. Appeals Judgement*, 20 February 2001, para. 24).

1.43 The jurisprudence of the international criminal tribunals and of the ICJ have in fact diverged on two major issues: applicable law and substantive law.

1.44 With regard to applicable law, decisions regarding control over acts of the Security Council have crystallised the differences between the ICJ and the tribunals. As discussed above, both the ICTY and the ICTR have held that they are competent to review the legality of acts of the Security Council because of "the incidental or inherent jurisdiction of any judicial or arbitral tribunal" (*Tadić Jurisdiction Appeals Decision*, paras. 14 and 18). See also *Kanyabashi Jurisdiction Decision*, para. 20.

1.45 By contrast, the ICJ has stated that "it does not possess powers of judicial review or appeal in relation to [the Security Council]" (ICJ, *Legal Consequences for States of the Continued Presence of South Africa in Namibia (South West Africa) notwithstanding Security Council Resolution 276 (1970)*, Advisory Opinion, 21 June 1971, para. 89). At the same time, the ICJ has been tentatively moving towards claiming a power to review SC resolutions. See *Questions of Interpretation and Application of the 1971 Montreal Convention arising from the Aerial Incident at Lockerbie* (Libyan Arab Jamahiriya v. United Kingdom and Libyan Arab Jamahiriya v. Unites States of America), Provisional Measures, Orders of 14 April 1992, and *Application of the Convention on the Prevention and Punishment of the Crime of Genocide* (Bosnia and Herzegovina v. Yugoslavia), Further request for the indication of provisional measures, Order of 13 September 1993).

1.46 The ICJ's jurisprudence denying its competence to review SC resolutions is difficult to reconcile with its own statute: "[i]n the event of a dispute as to whether the Court has jurisdiction, the matter shall be settled by the decision of the Court." (Article 36(6) of the Statute of the International Court of Justice).

1.47 This jurisprudence made it difficult for the ICTY to itself claim a power of review. As the ICTY Trial Chamber concluded, after reviewing the ICJ case-law: "[t]hese opinions of the Court clearly provide no basis for the international tribunal to review the actions of the Security Council, indeed, they are authorities to the contrary." (*Tadić Jurisdiction Decision*). This makes it all the more important that the ICTY Appeals Chamber, in its *Tadić Jurisdiction Appeals Decision*, overturning the Trial Chamber, went against the jurisprudence of the ICJ in this matter, and thereby laid the foundations for an approach which, it is submitted, is more in conformity with international law.

1.48 Nonetheless, the ICTY does not ignore ICJ jurisprudence. On the contrary: "[s]o far as international law is concerned, the operation of the desiderata of consistency, stability, and predictability does not stop at the frontiers of the tribunal. [. . .] The Appeals Chamber cannot behave as if the general state of the law in the international community whose interests it serves is none of its concern" (Separate Opinion of Judge Shahabuddeen, appended to App. Ch. Decision in *Semanza* of 31 May 2000, paragraph 25, cited by the Appeals Chamber in its *Delalić et al. Appeals Judgement*, paragraph 24). See also *Kvočka and others, Decision on Interlocutory Appeal by the Accused Zoran Zigić against the Decision of Trial Chamber I dated 5 December 2000*, in which Zigić sought to argue that the proceedings of the Trial Chamber should be suspended pending the determination of the Genocide Case by the ICJ. He asserted that as the same issues would be determined by both the ICTY and ICJ, the Trial Chamber's proceedings should be suspended pending the outcome of the ICJ case. In the alternative, Zigić, urged the suspension of his case pending a determination of the issue by the ICJ rather than the ICTY. The Appeals Chamber rejected his arguments, relying on the lack of any hierarchical relationship between the ICTY and ICJ as explained by the Appeals Chamber in *Delalić*.

1.49 Shabtaï Rosenne has argued that the ICTY should not have found that it had the power to review SC resolutions. Rather, the tribunal should have asked the SC to request an advisory opinion from the ICJ. See also Georges Abi-Saab, "Fragmentation or Unification: Some Concluding Remarks," 31 *New York University Journal of International Law and Politics* 928, (1999). This position, while perhaps technically appropriate, is troublesome because in reality there was little chance that the Council would accept such a proposition. Other scholars have argued that a system enabling tribunals to request the ICJ for a preliminary ruling should have been included in their statutes in order to suspend decisions pending the observations of the ICJ on a legal issue, following the example of the system stated in Article 234 (former Article 177) of the European Treaty. (See Gilbert Guillaume, "Quelques propositions concrètes à l'occasion du cinquantenaire," 2 *Revue Générale de Droit International Public* 332–333, (1996)). This would help to reduce the risk of discrepancies created by the proliferation of international courts and tribunals.

1.50 This system has been proposed by the Working Group on the crime of aggression established by the Preparatory Commission on the International Criminal Court. On 27 August, 2001, Bosnia-Herzegovina, New Zealand and Romania presented a common proposition stating that: "Where the Security Council does not make a determination under Article 39 or invoke Article 16 of the Statute within 6 months from the date of notification, the Court may request the General Assembly to seek an advisory opinion from The International Court of Justice, in accordance with Article 96 of the Charter and Article 65 of the Statute of the International Court of Justice, on the legal question of whether or not an aggression has been committed by the State concerned." See Doc. PCNICC/2001/WGCA/DP.2/Add.1. Even if no decision has been taken on this proposal, it seems to have been generally well received by State Delegations, with the exception of the United States and Israel, and thus may be a feasible mechanism.

1.51 As regards applicable law, the ICTY and ICJ have diverged in their interpretations of the law of State responsibility. It should, first, be borne in mind that the ICJ is concerned with the law of State responsibility while the international tribunals are concerned with individual responsibility. As will be seen below (6.2.1), both the ICTY Statute and the ICTR Statute contain provisions that state "that a plea of head of State immunity or that an act was committed in the official capacity of the accused will not constitute a defence, nor will it mitigate punishment" (See Report of the Secretary-General Pursuant to Paragraph 2 of Security Council Resolution 808 (1993), 3 May 1993, Doc. S/25704; article 7 (2) of the ICTY Statute and 6 (2) of the ICTR Statute). In the *Furundžija Trial Judgement*, the ICTY recognized that "Individuals are personally responsible, whatever their official position, even if they are heads of State or government ministers: [these rules] are indisputably declaratory of customary international law" (para. 140). The Rome Statute also includes this principle. Pursuant to Article 27:

> 1. This Statute shall apply equally to all persons without any distinction based on official capacity. In particular, official capacity as a Head of State or Government, a member of a Government or parliament, an elected representative or a government official shall in no case exempt a person from criminal responsibility under this Statute, nor shall it, in and of itself, constitute a ground for reduction of sentence.
>
> 2. Immunities or special procedural rules which may attach to the official capacity of a person, whether under national or international law, shall not bar the Court from exercising its jurisdiction over such a person.

1.52 The fact that State officials may be implicated by the international criminalisation of certain crimes committed by individuals does not exempt States from responsibility (See *Case Concerning Application of the Convention on the Prevention and Punishment of the Crime of Genocide* (Bosnia-Herzegovina v. Yugoslavia), Preliminary Objections, Judgement, 11 July 1996, para. 50). Therefore, both the ICJ and the ICTY may end up judging the same acts; *i.e.* serious violations of international humanitarian law committed in the territory of the former Yugoslavia since 1991. Though the genocide case before the ICJ is still pending, the ICTY found Krstić guilty of genocide in relation to massacres in Srebrenica in July 1995, which are specifically mentioned in the Bosnian application. Therefore, conflicting jurisprudence could arise if the ICJ were to refuse to find that Serb forces had committed genocide in Bosnia-Herzegovina. Similar considerations apply with respect to the *Milosević* case, pending before the ICTY.

1.53 Second, the ICTY, in the *Tadić Appeals Judgement*, has taken a different approach from the ICJ in the *Nicaragua* case to the test of "effective control" in determining whether the acts of organs in one state can be attributed to another State. See 4.2.319 *et seq* on the discussion of the internationality of the conflict in the former Yugoslavia.

1.54 Finally, the recent judgement of the ICJ in the *Case concerning the Arrest Warrant of 11 April 2000* deserves mention. Indeed, this judgement concerning the lawfulness of an international arrest warrant issued in 2000 by a Belgian Judge against the incumbent Minister for Foreign Affairs of the Congo provides a profoundly different approach with respect to the nature and scope of the immunities enjoyed by Officials than the one adopted by international criminal courts for the past 50 years.

1.55 By making it clear that a careful distinction must be drawn between the jurisdiction of courts and the immunity of those appearing before them, the Court concluded that jurisdiction does not imply absence of immunity, while absence of immunity does not imply jurisdiction. It further emphasized that immunity from jurisdiction and individual criminal responsibility are two separate concepts.

1.56 It is a clearly established principle that "the fact that a person who committed an act which constitutes a crime under international law acted as a Head of State or responsible Government official does not relieve him from responsibility under international law" (see Principle 3 of the Nuremberg Principles confirmed by its subsequent codification, namely the statutes of the international Tribunals and the Statute of the International Criminal Court). The ICJ does not put into question this basic principle. The ICJ has, however, adopted a position that may create problems with respect to the interpretations developed by the Tribunals and the ICC, notwithstanding the fact that the ICJ was careful to affirm the powers which may be conferred in this area on international criminal courts (see *Case concerning the Arrest Warrant of 11 April 2000, para. 61*). See also below, 5.31 ("Concurrent jurisdiction between the ICTs and the ICJ").

Relationship Between the ICTY and the European Court of Human Rights (ECHR)

1.57 The ICTY and the European Court of Human Rights (ECHR) also overlap in several ways. First, the ICTY has often referred to the jurisprudence of the ECHR in developing its own case-law, in the same way that domestic courts do (e.g., in the UK since the *Human Rights Act 1998* incorporated the European Convention into domestic law). The ECHR may also invoke ICTY jurisprudence in its decisions. Second, since the ICTY has its seat in the Netherlands, which is a party to the European Convention on Human Rights, there may be problems of overlapping jurisdiction.

1.58 As pointed out by Adjovi and Della Morte (*"La notion de procès équitable devant les Tribunaux Pénaux Internationaux"*), in Hélène RUIZ FABRI (ed.) *Procès équitable et enchevêtrement des espaces normatifs*, Paris, Societé de Legislation Comparée de Paris (2002, forthcoming): *"in principle, it is possible for accused persons to have standing before the European Court of Human Rights on the basis of the same remedies as they would have before Dutch courts. This was the method taken by Milošević* [Editor's note: on Milošević's case before the ECHR, see next paragraph]: *however, the Court's decision that the application was inadmissible for non-exhaustion of domestic remedies raises a doubt about the possibility of such overlap, even if it remains an academic hypothesis. In any event, the primacy bestowed on the ICTs may also be valid for the ECHR. The latter may only respond to violations by State Parties to the Convention, in this case the Netherlands or other countries of the Council of Europe involved in the procedure, for example in the transfer. In these circumstances, any complaint before the ECHR must be based on the responsibility, albeit indirect, of a State Member of the Council of Europe."* (unofficial translation).

1.59 In this respect, reference should be made to the ECHR, Second Section's *Decision as to Admissibility of Application n° 77631/01 by Slobodan Milošević against the Netherlands*, 19 March 2001. According to the ECHR, Milošević had not exhausted all his domestic remedies for appealing the judgement of the Dutch court in The Hague of 31 August 2001.

1.60 Note also that the ECHR has, on at least one occasion, pronounced on the ICTY's respect for human rights. See the decision in *Naletelić v. Croatia* (4 May 2000, *Decision on the Admissibility of the Request N° 00051891/99*) stating that the ICTY was *"an international tribunal displaying all the necessary guarantees, including those of impartiality and independence, as is shown by the tenor of its Statute and Rules of Procedure and Evidence."*

1.61 As Adjovi and Della Morte point out in a footnote to the above-mentioned article, *"As regards the ICTR, there is for the moment no similar recourse* [to a regional Human Rights mechanism], *since there is no equivalent to the ECHR in Africa: it is necessary to await the entry into force of the Protocol to the African Charter on Human and Peoples' Rights, creating a Court. Nonetheless, the fact that the ICTY has a part of its organisation in The Hague might also permit Dutch judges to be seised."* (unofficial translation).

The International Criminal Court (ICC)

1.62 On 17 July 1998, in Rome, a permanent International Criminal Court was established by treaty at the United Nations Diplomatic Conference of Plenipotentiaries on the Establishment of an International Criminal Court. The ICC has jurisdiction over the "core crimes" under international law: genocide, crimes against humanity and war crimes, and will exercise jurisdiction over the crime of aggression "once a provision is adopted in accordance with articles 121 and 123 defining the crime and setting out the conditions under which the Court shall exercise jurisdiction with respect to this crime. Such a provision shall be consistent with the relevant provisions of the Charter of the United Nations." (Article 5(2) of the Rome Statute of the International Criminal Court (hereinafter the *"Rome Statute"*)).

1.63 The Rome Statute received the requisite 60 ratifications on 11 April 2002. Accordingly, pursuant to Article 126 of the Rome Statute, it entered into force on 1 July 2002. The ICC will therefore only have jurisdiction over crimes committed after 1 July 2002.

Website: Website of the Rome Statute of the International Criminal Court (http://www.un.org/law/icc/); Website of the Coalition for an International Criminal Court (http://www.igc.org/icc/).

Books:

Cassese, Antonio, Gaeta, Paola, and Jones, John R.W.D., (eds.), *The Rome Statute of the International Criminal Court: A Commentary* (3 vols., Oxford University Press: 2002).

Triffterer, Otto, (ed.), *Commentary on the Rome Statute of the International Criminal Court* (Baden-Baden: Nomos, 1999)

Lee, Roy S., (ed.), *The International Criminal Court: The Making of the Rome Statute* (Kluwer: 1999).

The Special Court for Sierra Leone

Historical Background

1.64 Since March 1991, Sierra Leone has suffered from a civil war characterised by massive and widespread violence. The Peace Agreement (*Lomé Peace Agreement*, S/1999/777) signed in Lomé, Togo, on 7 July, 1999, between the democratically elected Government of President Ahmed Tejan Kabbah and the Revolutionary United Front (RUF) put an end to an 8 year long civil war while granting amnesty to the RUF leader Foday Sankoh and his followers and setting up a Truth and Reconciliation Commission to document violations of international law.

1.65 On 17 May 2000 the RUF leader, Foday Sankoh, and other rebels were arrested near Freetown for having conducted attacks on both governmental forces and civilian population. This occurred shortly after the President of the United Nations (UN) Security Council charged him with responsibility for serious breaches of obligations under the Lomé Agreement (United Nations, Security Council, *Presidential Statement*, 4 May 2000, S/PRST/2000/14).

1.66 Following a declaration of the Government of Sierra Leone on 23 May 2000 announcing its intention to ratify the Rome Statute for the ICC (Sierra Leone ratified the Rome Statute on 15 September 2000), President Ahmad Tejan Kabbah together with his government declared on 20 June 2000 his plan to ask the UN Security Council to set up a tribunal for Sierra Leone, either by creating a special court or by extending the mandate of the ICTR to its territory. The latter proposal was rejected by Richard Holbrooke, the then US permanent representative to the UN.

1.67 On 14 August 2000, the Security Council, being *"deeply concerned at the very serious crimes committed within the territory of Sierra Leone . . . and at the prevailing situation of impunity,"* adopted by a majority vote resolution 1315 requesting the Secretary-General, Kofi Annan, *"to negotiate an agreement with the Government of Sierra Leone to create an independent special court consistent with this resolution, . . ."* and expressing *"its readiness to take further steps expeditiously . . ."* (S/RES/1315 (2000), §1.).

1.68 This new court would thus not be created by a resolution of the Security Council (like the ICTY and ICTR) but would depend upon an Agreement between the UN and the Sierra Leonean Government. Its subject matter jurisdiction *"should include notably crimes against humanity, war crimes and other serious violations of international humanitarian law"* and its personal jurisdiction should be *"over persons who bear the greatest responsibility . . . including those leaders who, in committing such crimes, have threatened the establishment of and implementation of the peace process in Sierra Leone."*

1.69 Within this text, the Security Council noted *"the steps taken by the Government of Sierra Leone in creating a national truth and reconciliation process, as required by Article XXVI of the Lomé Peace Agreement (. . .) to contribute to the promotion of the rule of law"* and recalled that the Special Representative of the Secretary-General appended to his signature of the said agreement a statement that the UN *"holds the understanding that the amnesty provisions of the Agreement shall not apply to international crimes of genocide, crimes against humanity, war crimes and other serious violations of international humanitarian law, ..."*

1.70 In the same Resolution, the Security Council requested the Secretary-General to discuss an agreement with the Sierra Leonean Government within 30 days and to submit a report on his consultations and on the implementation of the resolution, addressing in particular *"the questions of the temporal jurisdiction of the special court, an appeals process including the advisability, feasibility, and appropriateness of an Appeals Chamber in the special court or of sharing the Appeals Chamber of the* [ICTY and ICTR] *or other effective options. . . ."*

1.71 The Security Council also requested the Secretary-General to produce recommendations on *"any additional agreements that might be required (. . .); The level of participation, support and technical assistance of qualified persons required from Member States (. . .); The amount of voluntary contributions of funds (. . .);* [and] *whether the Special Court receive, as necessary and feasible, expertise and advice from the* [ICTY and ICTR]."

1.72 From 12 to 14 September 2000, the Minister of Justice and the Attorney General of Sierra Leone were in New York to negotiate. This first stage of the negotiations at the UN Headquarters focused on the legal framework and constitutive instruments establishing the Special Court, namely the Statute for the Court and the Agreement between the UN and the Government (*Report of the Secretary-General on the establishment of a Special Court for Sierra Leone*, 4 October 2000, S/2000/915). On 4 October 2000, the Secretary-General presented to the Security Council his Report on the establishment of a Special Court for Sierra Leone (the "Report") *"to prosecute persons who bear the greatest responsibility for the commission of crimes against humanity, war crimes and other serious violations of international humanitarian law, as well as crimes under relevant Sierra Leonean law committed within the territory of Sierra Leone"* (*ibid.*). The mission reached an agreement over the legal and practical arrangements necessary to establish a special court in the country to prosecute certain individuals which was set out in detail in the Report along with various options for financing.

1.73 The Report stressed the role of the Court in *"dealing with impunity and developing respect for the rule of law in Sierra Leone"* and *"its educative message"* conveyed through a *"broad public information and education campaign"* by the government together with UNAMSIL and non-governmental organizations (*ibid*, para. 7). It also recommended that the temporal jurisdiction of the Court extend from November 1996 to the date of the signing of the Abidjan Agreement (the first attempt at a peace settlement to the conflict). The relationship between the Special Court, on the one hand, and the national courts and the National Truth and Reconciliation Commission, on the other hand, had not yet been addressed in detail. Mr. Zacklin did, however, underline that *"there is no amnesty for international crimes.* [The Sierra Leone Government] *could only grant amnesty for their own domestic legislation"* in the Lomé Agreement.

1.74 Following the Report, and the draft Agreement and Statute for the Court annexed, the Special Court was to be *"established by an Agreement between the UN and the Government of Sierra Leone pursuant to Security Council resolution 1315 (2000) of 14 August 2000 (. . .) and is therefore a treaty-based sui generis court of mixed jurisdiction and composition."*

1.75 In the meantime and in the context of the peace process, the Secretary-General sent a mission to Sierra Leone from 7 to 14 October 2000 to visit the region and to meet with as many of the persons concerned with the regional crisis as possible.

1.76 In its own Report (UNSC, *Report of the Security Council mission to Sierra Leone*, S/2000/992, §47), this mission noted that the *"government of Sierra Leone referred to the need for an effective information campaign to explain to the public the limits of the powers of the Special Court and the delay in the commencement of its operations."* It added that the government *"considered that the Court should have powers under Chapter VII of the Charter of the UN so as to ensure that it had sufficient authority to try any individual under international and domestic law, including the requirement upon third countries to surrender persons subject to the jurisdiction of the Court* [and that it] *preferred to appoint a co-prosecutor rather than a deputy prosecutor."* The mission also stressed the government's wish that the Security Council expedite its decision on the Special Court *"so that trials could start in a reasonable time (i.e. six months) since the Government could not hold suspects indefinitely."*

1.77 The President of the Security Council addressed a letter to the Secretary-General on 22 December 2000 (S/2000/1234), conveying the *"deep appreciation"* of the Council members for the observations and recommendations set forth in his report and suggesting a number of amendments to incorporate the views of the Council on the draft Agreement and the proposed Statute, in particular regarding personal jurisdiction of the Special Court, funding and size of the Court.

1.78 The Secretary-General answered these points on 12 January 2001 (S/2001/40) and cautioned the Security Council of the risks involved in establishing a Court without sufficient funds to support its first three years of operation. Discussions and negotiations have since continued between the Security Council and the Secretary-General (see *Letter dated 31 January 2001 from the President of the Security Council addressed to the Secretary-General*, S/2001/95; *Letter dated 12 July 2001 from the Secretary-General addressed to the President of the Security Council*, S/2001/693; *Letter dated 23 July 2001 from the President of the Security Council to the Secretary-General*, S/2001/722).

1.79 The main problems being budgetary and practical, the Secretary-General appealed to all states to make contributions in funds, personnel and services. On 13 July 2001, the Secretary-General announced that he had received sufficient funds to launch the process of the establishing the Special Court. The Security Council agreed and declared its support for the process on 24 July 2001. On 13 December 2001, the Secretary-General recommended proceeding with the Special Court despite a remaining shortfall in funds. In a letter to the Security Council dated 28 December 2001, he expressed his wish to achieve an Agreement by January 2002.

1.80 On 16 January 2002, the Agreement between the United Nations and the Government of Sierra Leone on the establishment of a Special Court for Sierra Leone was signed in Freetown by Hans Corell, UN Legal Adviser, and Mr. Berewa, Sierra Leonean Minister of Justice.

1.81 The implementing legislation for the Special Court was passed on 19 March 2002 and assented to by the President of Sierra Leone on 29 March 2002. This ratification act, as required by the Sierra Leone's constitution, provides the *"framework by which Sierra Leone authorities may work with the Special Court within Sierra Leone"*

(No Peace Without Justice, *Implementing Legislation for the Special Court*, www.specialcourt. org/documents).

1.82 On 16 April 2002, the Deputy Permanent Representative of Sierra Leone, Ambassador Allieu Ibrahim Kanu and the UN legal Counsel, Hans Corell exchanged the instruments that brought the Agreement into force, and on 19 April 2002, the Secretary-General named David Crane as Chief Prosecutor and Robin Vincent as Registrar of the Court.

Competence and Functioning of the Special Court

1.83 The treaty-based Special Court, set up pursuant to a bilateral agreement between the UN and the affected state, is mandated to try those who allegedly bear the greatest responsibility for war crimes committed during Sierra Leone's 10-year civil war. It is one of the new models of supranational prosecutions of serious international crimes (genocide, crimes against humanity and war crimes) in post-conflict situations, combining international and domestic mechanisms and laws. Its mandate is to end impunity through an effective and fair legal procedure and thereby to contribute to peace and reconciliation.

1.84 The Special Court will be the third *ad hoc* international criminal court after the ICTY and ICTR but the first among them to sit in the country where the crimes were committed and the first where international—United Nations—and local judges sit side by side (the courts in Kosovo are working on a different legal basis and directly under a UN mission). It will permit individuals to be tried for offences under international and national law, for instance for crimes against humanity and diamond smuggling, in the same proceedings. This constitutes the main difference between the planned jurisdiction in Cambodia that would only be able to judge crimes under domestic law.

1.85 The Court differs from the two existing *ad hoc* tribunals in that it has a unique hybrid nature and by virtue of its Management Committee which oversees budgetary and administrative matters. The Court is also fully backed by the government of Sierra Leone.

1.86 Furthermore, following an Act establishing a Truth and Reconciliation Commission ("TRC") in line with Article XXVI of the Lomé Peace Agreement, which had been enacted by the President and Members of Parliament on 22 February 2000, it may also be possible for the Special Court to request information from the TRC. Moreover, the TRC and the Special Court will share common administrative services.

1.87 In principle, the TRC will not pass information on to the Special Court and both institutions will operate separately. In exceptional cases, however, information-sharing may be possible provided that two cumulative conditions are met: first, the information in question should only be obtainable from the TRC and second, that information should be crucial to a specific trial.

1.88 As the Security Council decided that the Court will be funded entirely from voluntary contributions, the fact that UN member states did not sufficiently contribute meant that the budget for the Court had to be revised and substantially reduced, which also entailed changes to the structure and jurisdiction originally envisioned for the Court.

1.89 The *Agreement between the UN and the Government of Sierra Leone on the establishment of a Special Court for Sierra Leone* (the "Agreement") and the *Statute of* the Special Court for Sierra Leone (the "Statute") constitute the framework for the prosecution of individuals allegedly responsible for war crimes during the civil war in Sierra Leone. The first text deals with the establishment of the Court itself, the second with its competencies and functions.

1.90 The Special Court shall have concurrent jurisdiction with the national courts of Sierra Leone, but at any stage it may formally request a national court to defer to its competence and thus it shall have primacy over national courts (Article 8, Statute). The *Non bis in idem* principle (Article 9, Statute) is to be respected by the Court.

Competence of the Court

1.91 The Special Court is competent to *"prosecute persons who bear the greatest responsibility for serious violations of international humanitarian law and Sierra Leonean law committed in the territory of Sierra Leone since 30 November 1996"* (Article 1 of the Agreement and Article 1(1) of the Statute).

1.92 Thus, as concerns its *rationae personae* jurisdiction, only those people who bear the greatest responsibility for the crimes committed during the conflict will be prosecuted. Individual criminal responsibility for those persons is dealt with in Article 6 of the Statute. This provision corresponds almost verbatim with ICTY Article 7 and ICTR Article 6. Article 6 removes any immunity related to the official position of the accused person and establishes both the responsibility of the superior and of any person acting under an order of a Government. This includes *"those leaders who, in committing such crimes, have threatened the establishment of and implementation of the peace process in Sierra Leone"* (Article 1(1), Statute), but does not include *"transgressions by peacekeepers and related personnel present in Sierra Leone"* with the consent of the Government (whether their presence is pursuant to the Status of Mission Agreement or to the specific consent of the Government). In that case, the primary competence belongs to the jurisdiction of the sending state (Article 1(2), Statute). The Special Court only again becomes competent if the State is unwilling or unable to prosecute, and then only subject to the authorisation of the Security Council (Article 1(3), Statute). A useful comparison may be made with Articles 17(1) and 98 of the Rome Statute for the ICC.

1.93 After a lengthy debate about whether to charge the many children who fought during the civil war and those juvenile offenders who committed crimes and acts of extreme barbarity, a compromise was reached: No child under the age of 15 may be prosecuted (Article 7, Statute), and defendants aged between 15 and 18 at the time of the alleged commission of the crime may be prosecuted by the Special Court but cannot be sentenced to imprisonment and will receive separate anonymous hearings and special counselling: *". . . he or she shall be treated with dignity and a sense of worth, taking into account his or her young age and the desirability of promoting his or her rehabilitation. . . ."* (Article 7, Statute). Specific sentences shall be ordered by the Court in this regard.

1.94 In addition, the fact that the Special Court will only prosecute *"those who bear the greatest responsibility for violations makes it unlikely that children will be prosecuted."* (No Peace without Justice, *The Special Court for Sierra Leone*, at www.specialcourt.org; Also see Ana Peyro Llopis, *Sierra Leone: La Sierra Leone, entre trafic* *de diamants, opération de paix et justice pénale internationale*, Actualité et droit international, 31 January 2002).

1.95 On the subject of children in armed conflict, see 4.3.17 *et seq.*

1.96 The Court's temporal jurisdiction runs from 30 November 1996 to a date to be decided by a subsequent agreement between the parties. The starting date was chosen by reference to the Abidjan Peace Agreement between the government and the RUF, as this *"would have the benefit of putting the Sierra Leone conflict in perspective without unnecessarily extending the temporal jurisdiction of the Special Court."* (Report of the Secretary-General on the Establishment of a Special Court for Sierra Leone, 4 October 2000, U.N. Doc. S/2000/915, para. 27)

1.97 Crimes committed between March 1991 and 1996 do not fall within the Court's jurisdiction. Moreover, only evidence collected after the Lomé Agreement in 1999 will be easily accessible since the Headquarters of the Police Investigation Office was destroyed in 1999.

1.98 The Court's *ratione loci* competence (i.e., territorial jurisdiction) only applies to Sierra Leonean territory.

1.99 Another difference between the Special Court and the ICTY and ICTR lies in its subject matter jurisdiction. In addition to war crimes and crimes against humanity, the Court's subject matter jurisdiction extends to a range of crimes under the law of Sierra Leone. Conversely, it does not have jurisdiction over the crime of genocide.

- Crimes against humanity (Article 2, Statute). This corresponds largely to ICTY Article 5 and ICTR Article 3.
  The definition of this crime perpetuated *"as part of a widespread or systematic attack against any civilian population,"* is the same as in the Rome Statute of the ICC, apart from the fact that it does not require *"knowledge of the attack."* A list of acts follows. The Statute confirms a definition of crimes against humanity which does not require any link with a war crime.
- Violations of Art. 3 common to the Geneva Conventions and of Additional Protocol II (Article 3, Statute) and other serious violations of international humanitarian law (Article 4, Statute). This corresponds to ICTR Article 4.
- Crimes under Sierra Leonean Law (Article 5, Statute).
  Article 5 of the Statute represents the main difference from the two existing *ad hoc* tribunals. It does not deal with violations of international humanitarian law, *"which are beyond doubt part of customary international law"* (Prof. Michael P. Scharf, *The Special Court for Sierra Leone*, ASIL Insights, October 2000). Instead it deals with specific crimes under Sierra Leonean law such as *Offences relating to the abuse of girls under the Prevention of Cruelty to Children Act, 1926* (abusing a girl under 13 years of age, or between 13 and 14 years of age; abduction of a girl for immoral purposes) and *Offences relating to the wanton destruction of property under the Malicious Damage Act, 1861* (Setting fire to dwelling-houses, any person being therein, or to public or other buildings).

1.100 The maximum penalty that may be imposed by the Court is life imprisonment. In addition to imprisonment, other penalties can be *"the forfeiture of the property, proceeds and any assets acquired unlawfully or by criminal conduct and their return to their rightful owner or to the State of Sierra Leone"* (Article 19(3), Statute).

Composition of the Court

1.101 According to the Secretary-General's Report, the Court *"has been conceived as a self-contained entity, consisting of three organs: the Chambers (. . .), the Prosecutor's Office and the Registry."*

1.102 Article 2 of the Agreement deals with the composition of the Court. The Court comprises one Trial Chamber and one Appeals Chamber. There will be from eight to eleven independent judges (Article 12(1), Statute), deemed to possess special qualifications and *"high moral character, impartiality and integrity"* (Article 13, Statute). They are appointed for a three-year period and are eligible for reappointment. The total number of judges will depend on whether a second Trial Chamber is created.

1.103 In the Trial Chamber, one judge is appointed by the Sierra Leone government and two judges are appointed by the UN Secretary-General (Article 12(1)(a), Statute). In the Appeals Chamber, two judges are appointed by the government and three by the Secretary-General (Articel 12(1)(b), Statute).

1.104 The following judges have been appointed to the Special Court:

1.105 Trial Chamber: Pierre Boutet (Canada) and Benjamin Mutanga Itoe (Cameroon) appointed by the Secretary General, and Bankole Thompson (Sierra Leone) appointed by the Government of Sierra Leone.

1.106 Appeals Chamber: Emmanuel Ayoola (Nigeria), Alhaji Hassan Jallow (The Gambia) and Renate Winter (Austria) appointed by the Secretary General, and Gelaga King (Sierra Leone) and Geoffrey Robertson (United Kingdom) appointed by the Government of Sierra Leone.

1.107 The President of the Special Court is the presiding judge of the Appeals Chamber (Article 12(3), Statute). Geoffrey Robertson, QC, has been elected President of the Special Court.

1.108 Article 11 of the Statute states that the Court also consists of a Prosecutor and a Registry.

Functioning of the Court

1.109 The Rules of Procedure and Evidence of the ICTR are applicable *mutatis mutandis* to the conduct of the legal proceedings before the Court (Article 14, Statute).

1.110 The Prosecutor is appointed by the U.N. Secretary-General for a three-year term and is eligible for re-appointment. He is responsible for investigation and prosecution. He acts independently as a separate organ of the Court, with the power to question suspects, victims and witnesses, to collect evidence and to conduct on-site investigations. The Prosecutor is assisted by a Deputy Prosecutor, Sierra Leonean and international staff, and the Sierra Leonean authorities, if necessary (Article 15, Statute). The Prosecutor is David Crane; the Deputy Prosecutor is Desmond de Silva, QC.

1.111 The Registry is responsible for the administration and servicing of the Court. It consists of a Registrar, appointed by the U.N. Secretary-General after consultation with the President of the Court amongst the staff members of the United Nations, and his staff. The Registrar is responsible for the setting up of a Victims and Witnesses Unit within the Registry (Article 16, Statute).

1.112 A majority of the Judges of any Chamber renders a judgement, delivered in public and accompanied by a reasoned opinion in writing (Article 18, Statute). Separate and dissenting opinions are allowed.

1.113 Appeals may be made on the grounds of procedural error, error on a question of law invalidating the decision and error of fact which have occasioned a miscarriage of Justice (Article 20, Statute). Appeals are to be heard before the Appeals Chamber from persons convicted by the Trial Chamber or from the Prosecutor. In their decision, the judges of the Appeals Chamber shall be guided by the decisions of the Appeals Chamber of the ICTY and ICTR, and by the decisions of the Supreme Court of Sierra Leone as concerns the interpretation and application of the laws of Sierra Leone.

1.114 Article 21 of the Statute sets out the procedure for review, i.e., when new facts have been discovered which could have been a decisive factor in reaching the decision. Article 22 deals with enforcement of sentences. It provides that convicted persons shall serve their terms of imprisonment in Sierra Leone or in *"any of the States which have concluded with the ICTY or ICTR an agreement on for the enforcement of sentences."* Article 23 provides for pardon or commutation of sentences following a decision of the President of the Court.

1.115 In general, the Statute of the Special Court closely tracks the ICTY and ICTR Statutes, and it is thus to be expected that its practice and procedure will closely resemble those of the ICTs.

Articles: Scharf, Michael P., "The Special Court for Sierra Leone," *ASIL Insight* (American Society of International Law: October 2000).

Frulli, Micaela, "The Special Court for Sierra Leone: Some Preliminary Comments,"11 *European Journal of International Law* 857–870 (2000).

Linton, Suzanna, "Cambodia, East Timor and Sierra Leone: Experiments in International Justice," 12 *Criminal Law Forum* 185 (2001).

Prosecution of War and Ethnic Crimes and Other Serious Crimes Under the UN Interim Administration Mission in Kosovo

1.116 Kosovo presents a special problem for international and national courts. While the ICTY's territorial jurisdiction covers genocide, crimes against humanity and war crimes committed in Kosovo (see 4.4.5), the extent of the unrest in Kosovo has meant that it has also been necessary for local courts to play a role in dealing with these crimes. Given, however, the ethnic tensions between Kosovo Albanians and Serbs, it has proved necessary to provide for international intervention in the local proceedings. This has been carried out under the auspices of the UN interim administration.

1.117 Thus the legal and judicial system in Kosovo under the UN interim administration represents a further approach to international criminal justice developed in addition to the direct establishment of the ICTY. It provides for the prosecution of serious international crimes by both local organs and the international community within the framework of a UN mission scheme and on the basis of a Security Council decision under Chapter VII.

1.118 An initial proposal for the establishment of a Kosovo War and Ethnic Crimes Court (see 1.134) was not realised, largely due to a lack of resources. Following this, UNMIK (United Nations Mission in Kosovo) introduced international judges and prosecutors into local courts, but without giving them adequate procedural guidance. Thereafter this deficiency was rectified by UNMIK providing procedural guidelines which ensured majority international control of court decisions. In addition, final discretion on the abandonment of cases was left to the international prosecutor

1.119 UNMIK's approach was to attempt to build and establish an independent, impartial and multi-ethnic judiciary through UN intervention. Indeed, a competent international criminal tribunal with jurisdiction over certain crimes committed in Kosovo already existed in the form of the ICTY. The task of the UN interim administration was thus to re-build local judicial institutions, to set out a new body of law based on the existing one, to appoint new judges under a new mandate and to act within the framework of international human rights standards and principles of non-discrimination in the local prosecution of war and ethnic crimes and other serious violations of international law.

1.120 The newly re-established local criminal courts soon became overwhelmed due to the increasing number of crimes. Moreover, there were local criticisms of bias and discrimination. Thus the international administration in Kosovo felt compelled to launch a process of internationalisation. The first step was the appointment of international judges to work with local judges. Subsequently a formal structure was created within which the local judges could examine and try cases appropriate to their jurisdiction and refer more serious cases on to the ICTY.

International Judges and Prosecutors/International Staff in Local Courts

1.121 Accusations of ethnic bias and discrimination, local judges' misunderstanding regarding the status of international human rights law in local law, and evidence of bias on the part of the local judiciary against minorities led to the establishment of a Joint Working Group to ensure the independence and impartiality of the judiciary.

1.122 To answer those concerns the first international Judge was sworn in to the District Court of Mitrovica on 15 February 2000 and the first international Prosecutor was appointed in Mitrovica on 17 February 2000 under UNMIK Regulation N° 2000/6 signed on 15 February 2000 (UNMIK, *Regulation N° 2000/6 on the Appointment and Removal from Office of International Judges and International Prosecutors*, 15 February 2000, UNMIK/REG/2000/6.), to work in tandem with the local judges and prosecutor in order to restore security in Mitrovica and to counter-act the *"pressure upon the fledgling local judiciary"* (UNMIK, Press Release, *First International Prosecutor Appointed in Mitrovica*, 17 February 2000, UNMIK/PR/162.). Both the international judge and international prosecutor began work shortly after their appointment. For security reasons they were first assigned offices in the French KFOR Camp, only moving to the Mitrovica Courthouse in April 2000. On 6 June 2000 the second international judge was appointed to the Pristina District Court. The appointment was made pursuant to UNMIK Regulation 34/2000 which had the effect of expanding Regulation 6 to all districts rather than just Mitrovica.

1.123 The Regulation provides:

> *International judges shall have the authority and responsibility to perform the functions of their office, including the authority to select and take responsibility for new and pending criminal cases within the jurisdiction of the court to which he or she is appointed*; and

> *International prosecutors shall have the authority and responsibility to perform the functions of their office, including the authority and responsibility to conduct criminal investigations and to select and take responsibility for new and pending criminal investigations or proceedings within the jurisdiction of the office of the prosecutor to which he or she is appointed.*

1.124 International judges must have a university degree in law, five years' service as a judge or prosecutor in their own country and high moral integrity. They must not have a criminal record.

1.125 They are selected through the UNMIK staff recruiting process without KJPC involvement. The SRSG appoints staff for six-month renewable terms and may remove them from office. The mechanism used for international officials is different from that used for local judicial officers since they are directly recruited and contracted by UNMIK within the regular UN framework

1.126 International judges were further appointed to each of the 5 district courts throughout Kosovo and to the Supreme Court. They work exclusively on criminal cases, dealing primarily with sensitive cases involving alleged war crimes or other serious crimes and inter-ethnic violence.

1.127 In order to clear the back-log of cases and to address the problems of Kosovo's crowded detention centres—some accused had been held in pre-trial detention for more than one year, arguably thereby violating Article 5 of the ECHR—the OSCE and UNMIK established new war crimes courts throughout the region with three-judge benches, comprising one Serb, one ethnic Albanian and an independent international chairman.

1.128 By 15 December 2000 there were already ten international judges and three international prosecutors serving throughout Kosovo, including one appointed to the Supreme Court and they already had completed a total of 35 trials and investigations (Security Council, *Report of the Secretary-General on the UNMIK*, 15 December 2000, S/2000/1196). There were twelve judges and five prosecutors by 13 March 2001 taking part in judicial proceedings at all levels on war/ethnic/organised crimes as well as other cases that may severely affect the peace process. The remaining problem of access to the judiciary being compounded by the difficulties in recruiting non-Albanian Kosovo judges and prosecutors means that the international presence in this area must be maintained.

1.129 With the growing involvement of international judges in cases of minorities accused of war crimes and other serious crimes, earlier concerns about fair trials and ethnic bias in the criminal justice system seem to have been partly addressed, not only by the conducting of current trials but also by the reviewing of past cases where there had been allegations of bias (see UNHCR-OSCE, *Ninth Assessment of the Situation of Ethnic Minorities in Kosovo (Period covering September 2001 to April 2002)*, Part 2, Access to Justice, p. 20.)

1.130 However, the simple placement of "international judges and prosecutors" into the Kosovo justice system did not entirely guarantee justice to minority (usually Serb) accused and victims. Frequently international judges and prosecutors would be "out-voted" or over-ruled by Kosovar Albanian members of the court.

1.131 To address concerns of a lack of judicial independence and impartiality, the SRSG issued on 15 December 2000 a regulation on Assignment of International Judges and Prosecutors and Change of Venue (UNMIK, *Regulation N° 2000/64 on Assignment of International judges/prosecutors and/or Change of venue*, 15 December 2000, UNMIK/REG/2000/64) allowing *"at any stage in the criminal proceedings, the competent prosecutor, the accused or the defence counsel* [to] *submit to the Department of Judicial Affairs a petition for an assignment of international judges/prosecutors and/or a change of venue where this is considered necessary to ensure the independence and impartiality of the judiciary or the proper administration of justice."* Then, on the basis of the said petition, the Department of Judicial Affairs may submit a recommendation to the SRSG for the assignment or change of venue requested. Upon approval of the SRSG, an international prosecutor or investigating judge or a panel composed of 3 judges including at least 2 international judges shall be designated to perform the functions of their office throughout Kosovo, as well as a new venue upon request (for a critical approach to the issue of independence and impartiality under Regulation 2000/64, see OSCE, *Kosovo review of the Criminal Justice System*, September 2001–February 2002, Section 3, p. 25).

1.132 Pursuant to the 15 December 2001 amendment (UNMIK, *Regulation N° 2001/34 amending UNMIK Regulation N° 2000/64*, 15 December 2001, UNMIK/REG/2001/34.), this Regulation will remain in force until 15 December 2002. Regulation 2000/64, although addressing part of the problem, still provides for a situation where potentially "biased" judges can sit on war crimes cases, albeit that they can be outvoted by the majority international judges. The perception of bias on the part of even one member of the court could be said to amount to a violation of basic and fundamental human rights in that an accused is not being tried by a truly "independent and impartial" tribunal.

1.133 On 17 July 2002 (Security Council, *Report of the Secretary-General on the UNMIK*, 17 July 2002, S/2002/779) there were 337 local judges and prosecutors, among whom were 314 Kosovo Albanians, but only 27 international judges and prosecutors out of a target of 34.

The Kosovo War and Ethnic Crimes Court

1.134 To deal with the case overload and accusations of ethnic bias particularly in serious crimes cases, the UNMIK also attempted to create a Kosovo War and Ethnic Crimes Court. The Court was never established. The Technical Advisory Commission on Judiciary and Prosecution Service recommended the creation of such a court by the end of 1999. In its report dated 3 March 2000, the Secretary-General underlined UNMIK concerted efforts to establish this Court as soon as possible. He declared that *"the particular nature of war and ethnically related crimes requires that these cases be tried by panels with both local and international representatives"* asking for Member States financial support and for their help in identifying and fielding experts.

1.135 It was proposed that the Court would be composed of two local judges—an ethnic Albanian and a Serb—and one international judge, and that it would be competent to hear cases of *"war crimes, crimes against humanity, genocide and other serious crimes committed on grounds of race, ethnicity, religion, nationality, association with an ethnic minority or political opinion"* (UNMIK, *UNMIK 1st Anniversary Backgrounder-Reviving Kosovo's Judicial Systems*, 5 June 2000, at www.unmikonline.org.)

1.136 After a few press articles published by June 2000 and allusions to the Court made by the SRSG in some of its reports, the project seems to have been abandoned since there is not a single word about this Court in any report made by the Secretary-General to the Security Council during the year 2002 (Security Council, 3 *Reports of the Secretary-general on the UNMIK*, 15 January 2002, S/2002/62; 22 April 2002, S/2002/436; 17 July 2002, S/2002/779.).

Ombudsperson Institution

1.137 To strengthen the rule of law, UNMIK developed mechanisms to ensure that any administration or security official is acting in accordance with international human rights standards.

1.138 To deal with potential complaints regarding any UNMIK or local authority abuse of power and any allegation of human rights violation by any person or authority in Kosovo, UNMIK Regulation 2000/38 of 30 June 2000 established Kosovo's first Ombudsperson institution, inaugurated on 21 November 2000. The OSCE drafted its rules of procedure and evidence and assisted in the development and establishment of the institution itself.

1.139 Having become an independent institution in May 2001, the Ombudsperson is in charge with the investigation and mediation of complaints made by *"any person or entity in Kosovo, concerning human rights violations and action constituting an abuse of authority by the interim civil administration as well as an emerging central or local institution"* (See OSCE Mission in Kosovo, Field activities, Independent bodies, Ombudsperson's institution, at www.osce.org/kosovo/bodies/ombudsperson/). Its office is composed of Kosovars assisted by national and international supporting staff.

1.140 Marek Antoni Nowicki (Poland) was appointed on 12 July 2000 as Ombudsperson by SRSG for a two-year term under UNMIK Regulation 2000/38 (UNMIK, Press Release, *Polish Human Rights Lawyer Appointed as Ombudsperson*, 12 July 2000, UNMIK/PR/289).

Co-operation with the ICTY

1.141 Upon deployment, UNMIK immediately established working relations with the ICTY and provided support for its activities of collecting evidence, processing crime scene sites throughout Kosovo, and supporting existing and new indictments.

The Serious Crimes Panel of the Dili District Court: East Timor

Background

1.142 On 7 December 1975, East Timor was invaded by the Indonesian military. At the time East Timor was a non-self-governing territory under the control of Portugal. It had begun a process of decolonisation and self-determination. Indonesia declared East Timor as its 27th Province on 17 July 1976. Indonesia's occupation lasted 25 years and was characterised by continuous repression and violence carried out predominantly by 'militia' forces, armed groups of mostly East Timorese irregulars, recruited, trained, paid and directed by members of the Indonesian military.

1.143 President Suharto of Indonesia stepped down from power on 21 May 1998, handing power over to his vice-president, B.J. Habibie. On 9 June 1998, President Habibie announced that he would consider offering special status to East Timor. After several months of diplomacy, President Habibie announced on 27 January 1999 that East Timor would be allowed to decide whether to accept autonomy within Indonesia. Rejection of this option was widely seen to be a vote for independence.

1.144 Militia activity increased in the months leading up to the popular consultation which was held on 30 August 1999. It was announced on 4 September 1999 that 78.5% of the East Timorese population had voted for independence. Within hours the militias launched a scorched earth campaign involving murder, rape, disappearances, torture, displacement and the systematic destruction of property.

1.145 The Indonesian government consented to international intervention and allowed the Australian led INTERFET to land on 20 September 1999. INTERFET acted under the authority of UN Security Council Resolution 1264 of 15 September 1999. On 25 October 1999 the Indonesian parliament ratified the result of the popular consultation and ceded control of the territory to the UN. The same day the UN Security Council established the United Nations Transitional Administration in East Timor (UNTAET). UNTAET's mission was, *inter alia*, to uphold the rule of law and develop institutions sufficient for its maintenance.

Development of the Serious Crimes Panels

1.146 In the aftermath of August and September 1999, East Timor's infrastructure was in ruins, including its legal system. There were no courthouses, law books or legal records. Moreover, there was a lack of experienced personnel. Regulation 1999/3 *On the Establishment of a Transitional Judicial Service Commission* established a Commission to recommend to the Special Representative of the Secretary-General candidates for judicial or prosecutorial office. The Commission was composed of three East Timorese individuals and two international experts.

1.147 Regulation 2000/11 established the court system of East Timor. It provided for the establishment of various District Courts and a Court of Appeal in Dili. Section 10 of Regulation 2000/11 reserved jurisdiction over "serious crimes" to the Dili District Court. "Serious crimes" were described as: War Crimes, Crimes Against Humanity, murder, sexual offences, and torture. Jurisdiction over murder, sexual offences and torture was limited to offences committed between 1 January and 25 October 1999. The regulation gave the Transitional Administrator the authority to establish special panels with exclusive jurisdiction over such crimes. Such panels are composed of both East Timorese and international judges.

1.148 Regulation 2000/15 created the first Serious Crimes Panel of the District Court of Dili. The Panels consist of two international judges and one East Timorese judge. Regulation 2000/16 established the office of the Deputy Prosecutor for Serious Crimes under the General Prosecutor. The Deputy Prosecutor's office includes an investigative unit.

Applicable Law

1.149 Pursuant to Regulation 2000/15, the Panels apply the law of East Timor as promulgated by UNTAET Regulation 1999/1, any subsequent UNTAET Regulations, and where appropriate, "applicable treaties and recognised principles and norms of international law, including the established principles of the international law of armed conflict." The Regulation also sets out the elements and definitions of the Serious Criminal Offences which in part defer to the Penal Code applicable in East Timor. The definitions of genocide, war crimes and crimes against humanity are all similar to the definitions contained in the Rome Statute of the International Criminal Court. The Regulation also contains general principles of international criminal law which, in the main, correspond to those set out in the ICC Statute.

Operation

1.150 *Pre-Trial Detention:* Pursuant to Section 20.11 of UNTAET Regulation N° 2000/30 on the Transitional Rules of criminal procedure, the detention of a person who has been held in pre-trial detention for six months may be extended by the Special Panel at Dili District Court for an additional three months if it is in the case of a crime carrying a penalty of more than 5 years and if the interests of justice so require, based on compelling grounds.

1.151 Under Section 20.12 of UNTAET Regulation N° 2000/30, on exceptional grounds, and taking into consideration the prevailing circumstances in East Timor, the Special Panel for Serious Crimes at Dili District Court may order the continued detention of a suspect, if the interests of justice so require, and as long as the length of pre-trial detention is reasonable in the circumstances, and having due regard to international standards of fair trial. Section 20 authorizes detention under certain circumstances, including the reasons provided in its point 7, (a) when there are reasons to believe that a crime has been committed, (b) there is sufficient evidence to support a reasonable belief that the individual is responsible for the crime, and (c) there are reasonable grounds to believe that such detention is necessary.

1.152 Furthermore, section 20.8 provides that reasonable grounds for detention exist when: (a) there are reasons to believe that the suspect will flee to avoid criminal proceedings; (b) there is a risk that the evidence may be tainted, lost or destroyed; (c) there are reasons to believe that witnesses or victims may be pressured, manipulated or their safety endangered; or (d) there are reasons to believe that the suspect will continue to commit offences or poses a danger to public safety or security.

1.153 *Preliminary Hearing:* Preliminary hearings are held for the purpose of the Court satisfying itself that the accused have read or have had the indictment read to them and understand the nature of the charges against them; to ensure that the right of the accused to counsel has been respected; to rule on any motions or requests for evidence or additional investigation or, if the accused has failed to file any motions or requests, to ensure that the accused understood his or her rights in that regard; to afford the accused the opportunity to make a statement concerning the charges, which may include a plea of not guilty or an admission of guilt as to all or any portion of the charges; and determine what evidence and witnesses the defence would intend to present to the Court.

1.154 The Serious Crimes Panels work has been hampered to some extent by the fact that the majority of those who planned and ordered the destruction of East Timor are in Indonesia. Moreover, co-operation from Indonesia has not been forthcoming. An internal Human Rights Commission identified a number of senior military officials as potential war crimes suspects. The Indonesian Government, however, resolutely refuses to surrender any indicted officials to stand trial in East Timor.

1.155 The Dili District Court has, however, already issued one extremely well-researched judgement, in the case of Joao Franca da Silva, alias, Jhoni Franca, dated 5 December 2002. The case is available at www.intcrimpractice.com.

Articles:

Strohmeyer, Hansjorg, "Collapse and Reconstruction of a Judicial System: The United Nations Missions in Kosovo and East Timor," 95 *American Journal of International Law* (2001).

Linton, Suzannah, "Cambodia, East Timor and Sierra Leone: Experiments in International Justice," 12 *Criminal Law Forum* 185 (2001).

Drew, Catriona, "The East Timor Story: International Law on Trial," 12(4) *European Journal of International Law* 651–684 (September 2001) (on the self-determination aspects of East Timor's struggle for independence).

Dunn, James, "*Crimes Against Humanity in East Timor, January to October 1999: Their Nature and Causes*," available at www.etan.org/news/2001a/dunn1.htm.

Linton, Suzannah, "Rising from the Ashes: The Creation of a Viable Criminal Justice System in East Timor," 25 *Melbourne University Law Review* 122 (2001).

The La'o Hamutuk Bulletin Vol. 2, Nos. 6 and 7: October 2001. Available at www.etan.org/lh/bulletins/bulletinv2n6.html.

Official Documents:

See *Internationalised Criminal Courts and Tribunals: Practice and Procedure: Collection of Documents and Materials*, materials from conference organised by *No Peace Without Justice*, Amsterdam Centre for International Law, and Project on International Courts and Tribunals in Amsterdam, The Netherlands between 25–26 January 2002.

Cases can be found at: www.jsmp.minihub.org. See also the "Case Summary" at Annex 1.

The Proposed Extraordinary Chambers of the Courts of Cambodia

Background

1.156 Discussions are ongoing between the United Nations and the government of Cambodia on the possibility of having Extraordinary Chambers of the Courts of Cambodia with jurisdiction over crimes committed under the Khmer Rouge.

1.157 After nearly 90 years of colonial rule, Cambodia achieved independence in 1953. Its first ruler was Prince Sihanouk. Cambodia attempted to protect itself from foreign incursions and insulate itself from regional conflict by issuing a declaration to the effect that it would not make military alliances and would remain neutral unless attacked. As the Vietnam war intensified, Cambodia's neutrality became harder to maintain and Sihanouk was overthrown by Lon Nol in a US backed coup in March 1970. Nol, a career soldier who had previously been commander in chief, defence minister, and premier under Sihanouk, reversed the policy of neutrality and allowed South Vietnamese and US forces to operate in Cambodian territory. Simultaneously, a rebel Communist group grew in the countryside. Its popularity grew from alienated and angered victims of a massive US bombing campaign, and gained support from supporters of Sihanouk. The Communists, or Khmer Rouge, made progress towards the capital and ousted Nol from Phnom Penh.

1.158 Upon taking power the Khmer Rouge, under the direction of Pol Pot, renamed the country Democratic Kampuchea and began a two-pronged plan to implement its vision. Firstly the Khmer Rouge systematically executed all of the middle and professional classes, as well as other perceived enemies of the revolution. Secondly, they forced the transfer of urban populations to rural areas where they were forced into hard labour. It is estimated that 1 to 1.5 million people out of Cambodia's 7 million died between 1975 and 1979.

1.159 Democratic Kampuchea was invaded by Vietnam in December 1978. Vietnamese forces took Phnom Penh in January 1979. The Khmer Rouge were forced from power and retreated to the rural areas of the country where they continued to control the area near the border with Thailand from where they continued a guerrilla resistance. In the early years of the People's Republic of Kampuchea, a puppet government under the Vietnamese and headed by Hun Sen, Pol Pot and a senior associate, Ieng Sary, were convicted *in absentia* for genocide. Amnesties were later granted to members of the Khmer Rouge to encourage them to refrain from violence against the state. The People's Republic of Kampuchea lasted until a 1991 peace accord. Hun Sen has since become Prime Minister of Cambodia and is the chief negotiator between the UN and Cambodia on the establishment of a Khmer Rouge Tribunal.

Development of the Extraordinary Chambers

1.160 In 1997, Thomas Hammarberg, Special Representative of the Secretary-General for Human Rights in Cambodia, exerted pressure on the Cambodian government to formally request the UN to assist it in bringing members of the Khmer Rouge to justice. In response the Secretary General established a three-member Group of Experts to investigate the situation in Cambodia and make recommendations for achieving accountability for past crimes. The Group had three basic tasks: (i) to examine the question of which crimes should be considered for prosecution in relation to any available evidence; (ii) to assess the feasibility of trying Khmer Rouge leaders, and (iii) to investigate the possible domestic and international mechanisms for such trials.

1.161 The Group reported on 15 March 1999 and released its *Report of the Group of Experts*. It recommended that the tribunal's mandate cover genocide, crimes against humanity, torture, forced labour, crimes against internationally protected persons, and several crimes under Cambodian criminal law in force during 1975–79. It was agreed that the temporal jurisdiction be limited to the period when the government of the Democratic Kampuchea was in power, i.e. 17 April 1975 to 8 January 1979. It was recommended that the tribunals exercise jurisdiction only over those "most responsible" for the crimes of the Khmer Rouge in order to preserve the stability of the country. The Group of Experts strongly favoured the establishment of a purely "international tribunal." It felt that the Cambodian judiciary lacked the sufficient experience and independence necessary effectively to carry out trials of such a complex and politically sensitive nature. This proved an extremely controversial recommendation. The Cambodian government immediately rejected the exclusion of its judiciary from the process.

1.162 As a result of Cambodian unease with solely international tribunals, the proposal was dropped. However, the main area of contention between the UN and the Cambodian government has continued to be the precise character and relationship between the Cambodian and international judges. Prime Minister Hun Sen was adamant that the trials take place within the Cambodian judicial system, under local control with international participation. The UN is equally adamant that there should be a degree of international involvement and control over the proceedings. A proposal was made in April 2000 that there be five person chambers in which three judges would be Cambodian and two international. The concept of "super-majority" was considered as a compromise with four votes required to reach a decision.

1.163 In January 2001 Cambodia's National Assembly passed the *Law of Extraordinary Chambers*. This differed in key respects from the Memorandum of Understanding with the UN and resulted in immediate criticism from the UN on issues such as the status of amnesties and pardons already granted to potential defendants. The Memorandum of Understanding provided that amnesties would not be a bar to prosecution for genocide, war crimes and crimes against humanity. The Law of Extraordinary Chambers replaced this with language to the effect that the government will not request amnesties or pardons, without prejudice to their being granted without such a request. Another area of contention has been the insistence by the Cambodians on the application of Cambodian criminal procedure which is in many respects inconsistent with international standards.

1.164 The *Law on the Establishment of Extra Ordinary Chambers in the Courts of Cambodia for the Prosecution of Crimes Committed During the Period of Democratic Kampuchea* became law on 10 August 2001 after it was signed by King Sihanouk. Consultations and dialogue between the UN and Cambodia has been ongoing on the possibility of collaboration. No compromise has been reached but efforts to reach an agreement continue. Cambodia has, however, indicated that it is prepared to continue with prosecutions under the new law with or without UN involvement.

Composition and Applicable Law

1.165 The Extraordinary Chambers will have three levels: (i) a Trial Court composed of five judges, (ii) an Appeals Court with seven judges, and (iii) a Supreme Court with nine judges. In each case Cambodian judges will make up the majority and internationals judges the remainder (see Article 9). All judicial appointments will be made by Cambodia's Supreme Council of the Magistracy; local judges on its own advice and international judges based on the recommendation of the Secretary-General of the United Nations. Decisions of the various Chambers must be reached by supermajority requiring a consenting vote of at least on international judge.

1.166 Investigations will be carried out by Co-Investigating Judges, one Cambodian and one international. They will apply existing procedural law, but if there are any lacuna in existing procedures, the Co-Investigating Judges may seek guidance in procedural rules established at the international level (see article 24). In the event that the Co-Investigating judges disagree on whether to proceed, a special Pre-Trial Chamber will be established to determine the issue. In the event that the five member Pre-Trial Chamber fail to arrive at a decision by at least four votes, the investigation will continue.

1.167 Indictments will be prepared and trials conducted by Co-Prosecutors, one Cambodian and one international. The prosecution shall be conducted in accordance with existing procedural law, but again, if there are lacunae, the Co-Prosecutors may seek guidance in procedural rules established under international law. (see article 20). Disputes between Co-Prosecutors will be settled in the same way as those between Co-Investigating Judges.

1.165 The Extraordinary Chamber will be competent to try senior members of the Khmer Rouge and as envisaged by the Group of Experts "those more responsible" for violations of Cambodian law, international humanitarian law and custom, and international conventions recognised by Cambodia. The temporal jurisdiction will be restricted to the period between 17 April 1975 and 6 January 1979. The subject matter jurisdiction will consist of genocide, crimes against humanity and grave breaches of the Geneva Conventions, violations of the Hague Convention for the Protection of Cultural Property in the Event of Armed Conflict, and crimes perpetrated against internationally protected persons according to the Vienna Convention on Diplomatic Relations. Additionally, the Chamber will have jurisdiction over murder, torture, and religious persecution under the 1956 Penal Code of Cambodia.

Conference Materials:

Internationalised Criminal Courts and Tribunals: Practice and Prospects Collection of Documents and Materials. Conference organised by *No Peace Without Justice*, Amsterdam Centre for International Law, and Project on International Courts and Tribunals in Amsterdam, The Netherlands between 25–26 January 2002.

Linton, Suzannah, "Cambodia, East Timor and Sierra Leone: Experiments in International Justice," 12 *Criminal Law Forum* 185 (2001).

Herder, Stephen and Tittemore, Brian D. , *"Seven Candidates for the Prosecution: Accountability for the Crimes of the Khmer Rouge,"* available at www.wcl.american.edu/pub/humright/ wcrimes/khmerrouge.pdf.

Official Documents:

Tribunal Memorandum of Understanding Between the United Nations and the Royal Government of Cambodia, published in Phnom Penh, Issue 9/22, October 27–November 9, 2000. Available at: www.yale.edu/cgp/tribunal/mou_v3.htm.

Law on the Establishment of Extraordinary Chambers in the Courts of Cambodia for the Prosecution of Crimes Committed During the Period of Democratic Kampuchea, adopted by the National Assembly on 2 January 2001. Available at: www.derechos.org/human-rights/seasia/doc/krlaw.html.

PART 2

ORGANISATION OF THE INTERNATIONAL TRIBUNALS

ICTY Article 11: Organization of the International Tribunal	2.1
ICTR Article 10: Organization of the International Tribunal for Rwanda	2.1
Structure of the ICTs	2.2
History of ICTY Article 11	2.3
History of ICTR Article 10	2.5
ICC Article 34: Organs of the Court	2.8
Organisation of the ICC	2.9

SECTION 1: CHAMBERS

COMPOSITION OF THE CHAMBERS	2.1.1
ICTY Article 12/ICTR Article 11: Composition of the Chambers	2.1.1
History of ICTY Article 12	2.1.3
History of ICTR Article 11	2.1.4
The Nature of the Common ICTY/ICTR Appeals Chamber	2.1.5
The Trial Chamber Can Only Act as Three Judges	2.1.7
ICC Article 39: Chambers	2.1.8
Trial and Appellate Levels at the ICC	2.1.9
QUALIFICATIONS AND ELECTION OF JUDGES	2.1.10
ICTY Article 13/ICTR Article 12: Qualifications of Judges	2.1.10
ICTY Article 13 bis/ICTR Article 12 bis: Election of Permanent Judges	2.1.11
ICTY Article 13 ter/ICTR Article 12 ter: Election and Appointment of Ad Litem Judges	2.1.12
ICTY Article 13 quater/ICTR Article 12 quater: Status of Ad Litem Judges	2.1.13
The Changing Structures of the ICTY and ICTR	2.1.14
Impartiality of Judges	2.1.20
Election of ICTY Judges	2.1.21
ICTY Article 13(3): Chambers Vacancies	2.1.27
Election of ICTR Judges	2.1.28
ICTY Article 13 bis (3)	2.1.32
Election of ICC Judges	2.1.36
OFFICERS AND MEMBERS OF CHAMBERS	2.1.38
ICTY Article 14/ICTR Article 13: Officers and Members of the Chambers	2.1.38
History of ICTY Article 14	2.1.39
History of ICTR Article 13	2.1.40
Composition of Chambers	2.1.42
OTP Plays No Role in Assignment of Case	2.1.43
Judicial Impartiality and Independence	2.1.45
Common ICTY/ICTR Appeals Chamber	2.1.46
ICTR President	2.1.48
ICTY Rule 14/ICTR Rule 14: Solemn Declaration	2.1.49
History of ICTY Rule 14	2.1.50

38 • *International Criminal Practice*

History of ICTR Rule 14 .... 2.1.50
Rule 14 Is the Guarantor of Tribunal's Impartiality and Independence 2.1.52
ICTR Rule 14 *bis* 2.1.53
History of ICTR Rule 14 *bis* 2.1.54
DISQUALIFICATION, RESIGNATION, AND PRECEDENCE OF JUDGES 2.1.56
ICTY Rule 15/ICTR Rule 15: Disqualification of Judges 2.1.56
History of ICTY Rule 15 .... 2.1.57
History of ICTR Rule 15 .... 2.1.59
Voluntary Withdrawal 2.1.62
Determination by Bureau of Judge's Disqualification 2.1.63
    Judge Not Disqualified from Hearing Trial(s) Arising From the
        Same Set of Events 2.1.64
    Judge Not Disqualified Based on Position Taken in Another Case on an
        Issue in Dispute in the Present Case 2.1.69
    Judge Not Disqualified Due to Holding Executive Office 2.1.70
Application to Disqualify Judge Must Be Made Before Trial Is Concluded 2.1.73
ICTY Rule 15 *bis*/ICTR Rule 15 *bis*: Absence of a Judge 2.1.74
History of ICTY Rule 15 *bis* 2.1.75
History of ICTR Rule 15 *bis* 2.1.76
Trial Chamber Sitting in Absence of Member 2.1.77
    Delivery of Decisions 2.1.78
    Hearing of Witnesses 2.1.79
ICTY Rule 16/ICTR Rule 16: Resignation 2.1.80
Resignations 2.1.81
ICTY Rule 17/ICTR Rule 17: Precedence 2.1.82
History of ICTY Rule 17 .... 2.1.83
PRESIDENT, VICE PRESIDENT, AND THE BUREAU 2.1.84
ICTY Rule 18/ICTR Rule 18: Election of the President 2.1.84
ICTY Rule 19/ICTR Rule 19: Functions of the President 2.1.85
History of ICTY Rule 19 .... 2.1.86
    Rule 19(A): Coordinating the Work of the Chambers 2.1.87
Practice Directions 2.1.88
Practice Directions Cannot Be Used as Form of Appeal 2.1.90
ICTY Rule 20/ICTR Rule 20: The Vice President 2.1.91
ICTY Rule 21/ICTR Rule 21: Functions of the Vice President 2.1.92
ICTY Rule 22/ICTR Rule 22: Replacements 2.1.94
History of ICTY Rule 22 .... 2.1.95
ICTY Rule 23/ICTR Rule 23: The Bureau 2.1.98
History of ICTY Rule 23 .... 2.1.99
    Decisions of the Bureau 2.1.100
    Other Tasks of the Bureau 2.1.101
ICTY Rule 23 *bis*: The Coordination Council 2.1.102
History of ICTY Rule 23 *bis* 2.1.103
ICTY Rule 23 *ter*: The Management Committee 2.1.104
History of ICTY Rule 23 *ter* 2.1.105
PLENARY MEETINGS 2.1.106
ICTY Rule 24/ICTR Rule 24: Plenary Meetings of the Tribunal 2.1.106
ICTY Rule 25/ICTR Rule 25: Dates of Plenary Sessions 2.1.107
History of ICTY Rule 25 .... 2.1.108
ICTY Rule 26/ICTR Rule 26: Quorum and Vote 2.1.109
History of ICTY Rule 26 .... 2.1.110

Organization of the Tribunals • 39

ROTATION OF JUDGES AND DELIBERATIONS 2.1.111
ICTY Rule 27/ICTR Rule 27: Rotation 2.1.111
ICTY Rule 27 and ICTR Rule 27.. 2.1.112
ICTY Rule 28: Reviewing and Duty Judges..................................... 2.1.115
ICTR Rule 28: Duty Judges 2.1.115
History of ICTY Rule 28 .... 2.1.116
History of ICTR Rule 28 .... 2.1.121
Powers and Duties of "Duty Judge" 2.1.122
ICTY Rule 29/ICTR Rule 29: Deliberations 2.1.126

SECTION 2: THE REGISTRY
ICTY Article 17/ICTR Article 16: The Registry 2.2.1
ICTY Rule 30/ICTR Rule 30: Appointment of the Registrar 2.2.2
ICTY Rule 31/ICTR Rule 31: Appointment of the Deputy Registrar and Registry Staff 2.2.3
ICTY Rule 32/ICTR Rule 32: Solemn Declaration 2.2.4
ICTY Rule 33/ICTR Rule 33: Functions of the Registrar 2.2.5
History of ICTY Rule 33 .... 2.2.6
ICTY Registrars 2.2.7
Directive and Instructions for the ICTY Registry................................ 2.2.10
ICTR Registrars 2.2.11
Purpose of the Registry 2.2.12
Orders Addressed to the Registry 2.2.14
The President's Authority over the Registrar 2.2.15
ICTY Rule 33 *bis:* Functions of the Deputy Registrar 2.2.18
History of ICTY Rule 33 *bis*.. 2.2.19

SECTION 3: VICTIMS AND WITNESSES
ICTY Rule 34/ICTR Rule 34: Victims and Witnesses Section.............. 2.3.1
History of ICTY Rule 34 .... 2.3.2
History of ICTR Rule 34 .... 2.3.3
Functions of the Victims and Witness Section 2.3.6
Impartial Role of VWS 2.3.8
Witness Relocation 2.3.10

SECTION 4: MINUTES AND RECORDS
ICTY Rule 35/ICTR Rule 35: Minutes... 2.4.1
History of ICTR Rule 35 .... 2.4.2
ICTY Rule 36/ICTR Rule 36: Record Book.................................... 2.4.5
History of ICTY Rule 36 .... 2.4.6

SECTION 5: THE PROSECUTOR
ICTY Article 16/ICTR Article 15: The Prosecutor 2.5.1
ICTY/ICTR Prosecutor... 2.5.2
ICTY Deputy Prosecutor 2.5.10
Structure of the ICTY OTP 2.5.12
ICTR Deputy Prosecutor 2.5.15
Structure of the ICTR OTP 2.5.17
Functions of the Prosecutor 2.5.19
Role of the Prosecutor 2.5.28
Prosecutorial Discretion.. 2.5.30
Trial Chamber Can Make Orders on Prosecution Conduct of a Case 2.5.34
ICTY Rule 37/ICTR Rule 37: Functions of the Prosecutor 2.5.35
ICC Article 15: Prosecutor.. 2.5.36

History of ICTY Rule 37 .... 2.5.37
The ICC Prosecutor 2.5.38
ICTY Rule 38/ICTR Rule 38: Deputy Prosecutor 2.5.45
History of ICTY Rule 38 .... 2.5.46

SECTION 6: THE DEFENCE

ICTY Rule 44: Appointment, Qualifications, and Duties of Counsel 2.6.1
ICTR Rule 44: Appointment and Qualifications of Counsel 2.6.1
History of ICTY Rule 44 .... 2.6.2
History of ICTR Rule 44 .... 2.6.5
Assignment of Counsel 2.6.6
Annotated Directive on the Assignment of Defence Counsel 2.6.11
ICTR Rule 44 *bis*: Duty Counsel 2.6.12
History of ICTR Rule 44 *bis* 2.6.13
ICTY Rule 45/ICTR Rule 45: Assignment of Counsel 2.6.15
History of ICTY Rule 45 .... 2.6.16
History of ICTR Rule 45 .... 2.6.19
Language Requirements 2.6.21
Counsel's Experience: ICTY vs. ICTR 2.6.23
Withdrawal of Counsel 2.6.26
    Appointment of Co-Counsel, Investigators, Etc., Is a Matter for
        Lead Counsel 2.6.35
    Registrar Has Primary Responsibility in Determining Issues Relating to
        Assignment of Counsel 2.6.37
    Review of Registrar's Decision on Appointment of Counsel by
        Trial Chamber 2.6.38
Code of Conduct 2.6.39
    Ignorance of the Tribunal's Rules and Procedures Could Amount to
        Failure to Perform Counsel's Obligations 2.6.44
    Counsel Found Guilty of Contempt Loses Rights of Audience 2.6.46
    Decisions Arising Under Code of Conduct 2.6.47
Further Decisions Under Rule 45 .... 2.6.49
ICTY Rule 45 *bis*/ICTR Rule 45 *bis*: Detained Persons 2.6.50
History of ICTY Rule 45 *bis* 2.6.51
History of ICTR Rule 45 *bis* 2.6.52
ICTR Rule 45 *ter*: Availability of Counsel 2.6.53
History of ICTR Rule 45 *ter* 2.6.54
ICTR Rule 45 *quater* 2.6.55
History of ICTR Rule 45 *quater* 2.6.56
ICTY Rule 46/ICTR Rule 46: Misconduct of Counsel 2.6.57
History of ICTY Rule 46 .... 2.6.58
History of ICTR Rule 46 .... 2.6.60
Warnings to Counsel and Prosecutors 2.6.62
    Failure to Attend Hearings 2.6.64
    Disputes with the Registry Not a Ground for Refusing to
        Attend Hearings 2.6.68
    Prosecution Warned Pursuant to Rule 46(A) 2.6.70
Fee Splitting 2.6.71
ICTR Directive on Assignment of Counsel Article 5 *bis*: Fee Splitting . 2.6.72

* * * * *

2.1

ICTY ARTICLE 11 ORGANIZATION OF THE INTERNATIONAL TRIBUNAL	ICTR ARTICLE 10 ORGANIZATION OF THE INTERNATIONAL TRIBUNAL FOR RWANDA
The International Tribunal shall consist of the following organs: (a) The Chambers, comprising three Trial Chambers and an Appeals Chamber; (b) The Prosecutor, and (c) A Registry, servicing both the Chambers and the Prosecutor.	The International Tribunal for Rwanda shall consist of the following organs: (a) The Chambers, comprising three Trial Chambers and an Appeals Chamber; (b) The Prosecutor, and (c) A Registry.

Structure of the ICTs

2.2 Articles 11 and 10 of the ICTY Statute and ICTR Statute, respectively, set out the basic structure of the International Tribunals, namely three organs: the Chambers (i.e., the Judges), the Prosecutor and the Registry. Defence Counsel are not an organ of the tribunals and are thus "outside" the tribunals' structure.

History of ICTY Article 11

2.3 Article 11 of the ICTY Statute was amended by Security Council resolution 1166 of 13 May 1998 as a consequential amendment upon the addition of a third Trial Chamber.

2.4 The Chambers, Office of the Prosecutor and Registry of the ICTY are located at: Churchillplein 1, 2517 JW, The Hague, the Netherlands (tel: +31 70 416 5000; fax: +31 70 512 8668). The ICTY's relations with the Host Country, the Netherlands, are governed by the Headquarters Agreement, initialled on 27 May 1994, and taking effect on a provisional basis as from the date of signature and formally entering into force the day after all legal requirements for entry into force have been met. The Headquarters Agreement contains some 29 articles, most of which relate to the normal incidents of a diplomatic or international relationship.

History of ICTR Article 10

2.5 Article 10 of the Statute of the ICTR is identical to Article 11 of the Statute of the ICTY. The reference to *three* Trial Chambers was the result of the amendment to Article 10 made by the Security Council in its Resolution 1165 of 30 April 1998, which added a third Trial Chamber.

2.6 The Chambers and Registry of the ICTR are located at Arusha International Conference Centre, P.O. Box 6016, Arusha, Tanzania (tel: +1 212 963 2850; fax: +1 212 963 2848), while the Office of the Prosecutor is located in Kigali, Rwanda and in the ICTY offices in The Hague, the Netherlands.

2.7 The Headquarters Agreement signed on 21 August 1995 between the ICTR and the United Republic of Tanzania (A/51/399; S/1996/778—appendix) governs the ICTR's relations with the Host Country, Tanzania.

2.8

ICC
ARTICLE 34
ORGANS OF THE COURT

The Court shall be composed of the following organs:
(a) The Presidency;
(b) An Appeals Division, a Trial Division and a Pre-Trial Division;
(c) The Office of the Prosecutor;
(d) The Registry.

Organisation of the ICC

2.9 The ICC has a similar organisation to that of the ICTY and the ICTR, with the Presidency as an additional organ which nonetheless corresponds to the *bureaux* introduced by Rule 23 of the ICTY and ICTR RPE.

Article:

For further comparisons between the structure of the ICTY/ICTR and the ICC, see John R.W.D. Jones, "Composition of the Court," Ch. 4.4., *in* Cassese, Antonio, Gaeta, Paola and Jones, John R.W.D., *The Rome Statute of the International Criminal Court: A Commentary* (Oxford University Press, 2002).

SECTION 1: CHAMBERS

COMPOSITION OF THE CHAMBERS

2.1.1

ICTY ARTICLE 12 COMPOSITION OF THE CHAMBERS	ICTR ARTICLE 11 COMPOSITION OF THE CHAMBERS
1. The Chambers shall be composed of sixteen permanent independent judges, no two of whom may be nationals of the same State, and a maximum at any one time of nine ad litem independent judges appointed in accordance with article 13 ter, paragraph 2, of the Statute, no two of whom may be nationals of the same State. 2. Three permanent judges and a maximum at any one time of six ad litem judges shall be members of each Trial Chamber. Each Trial Chamber to which ad litem judges are assigned may be divided into sections of three judges each, composed of both permanent and ad litem judges. A section of a Trial Chamber shall have the same powers and responsibilities as a Trial Chamber under the Statute and shall render judgement in accordance with the same rules. 3. Seven of the permanent judges shall be members of the Appeals Chamber. The Appeals Chamber shall, for each appeal, be composed of five of its members. 4. A person who for the purposes of membership of the Chambers of the International Tribunal could be regarded as a national of more than one State shall be deemed to be a national of the State in which that person ordinarily exercises civil and political rights.	1. The Chambers shall be composed of sixteen permanent independent judges, no two of whom may be nationals of the same State, and a maximum at any one time of four *ad litem* independent judges appointed in accordance with article 12 *ter*, paragraph 2, of the present Statute, no two of whom may be nationals of the same State. 2. Three permanent judges and a maximum at any one time of four *ad litem* judges shall be members of each Trial Chamber. Each Trial Chamber to which *ad litem* judges are assigned may be divided into sections of three judges each, composed of both permanent and *ad litem* judges. A section of a Trial Chamber shall have the same powers and responsibilities as a Trial Chamber under the present Statute and shall render judgement in accordance with the same rules. 3. Seven of the permanent judges shall be members of the Appeals Chamber. The Appeals Chamber shall, for each appeal, be composed of five of its members. 4. A person who for the purposes of membership of the Chambers of the International Tribunal for Rwanda could be regarded as a national of more than one State shall be deemed to be a national of the State in which that person ordinarily exercises civil and political rights.

2.1.2 "The Chambers" is the collective term for the Judges, organised into Trial and Appeals Chambers. The Appeals Chamber is common to the ICTY and the ICTR.

History of ICTY Article 12

2.1.3 Article 12 of the ICTY Statute was amended by SC resolution 1166 of 13 May 1998 as a consequential amendment upon the addition of a third Trial Chamber. It was further substantially amended by SC resolution 1329 of 30 November 2000 to provide for *ad litem* judges and was again amended by SC resolution 1411 of 17 May 2002, to add para. (4).

History of ICTR Article 11

2.1.4   The Security Council, in its Resolution 1165 of 30 April 1998, amended Article 11 of the ICTR Statute to provide for three Trial Chambers, and hence fourteen Judges. Previously Article 11 had read, "The Chambers shall be composed of *eleven* independent judges. . . ." It was further substantially amended by Security Council resolution 1329 of 30 November 2000 to increase the number of ICTR judges to sixteen and was again amended by SC resolution 1411 of 17 May 2002, to add para. (2).

The Nature of the Common ICTY/ICTR Appeals Chamber

2.1.5   The Appeals Chamber is not comprised of more senior Judges than those serving in the Trial Chambers. Therefore appeal judgements and decisions are authoritative only on a numerical basis, there being five appellate Judges as opposed to three trial Judges.

2.1.6   Pursuant to Rule 27(A), permanent Trial Chamber judges "rotate" into the Appeals Chamber. This practice was criticised by an experts' group on the functioning of the ICTY and ICTR appointed by the United Nations Secretary-General, which noted the "unsatisfactory consequences" of rotation and stated that "it would be preferable if judges were assigned exclusively to the Trial Chambers or Appeals Chamber for their entire terms" (Fondation Hirondelle, *News*, 31 January 2000).

The Trial Chamber Can Only Act as Three Judges

2.1.7   For this ruling, see the Appeals Chamber's *Decision on Appeal by Dragan Papić against ruling to proceed by deposition* of 15 July 1999. See also the *Separate Opinion* of Judge Hunt:

> 21.   . . . The oral decision as announced by the Presiding Judge was silent as to any participation by Judge May in it. The only conclusion which can be drawn is that it was at that time the decision of the other two judges only.
>
> 22.   As such, the decision was no mere procedural error. It was not made by a properly constituted Trial Chamber, and it was therefore invalid. . . .

2.1.8

> **ICC**
> **ARTICLE 39**
> **CHAMBERS**
>
> 1. As soon as possible after the election of the judges, the Court shall organize itself into the divisions specified in article 34, paragraph (b). The Appeals Division shall be composed of the President and four other judges, the Trial Division of not less than six judges and the Pre-Trial Division of not less than six judges. The assignment of judges to divisions shall be based on the nature of the functions to be performed by each division and the qualifications and experience of the judges elected to the Court, in such a way that each division shall contain an appropriate combination of expertise in criminal law and procedure and in international law. The Trial and Pre-Trial Divisions shall be composed predominantly of judges with criminal trial experience.
> 2. (a) The judicial functions of the Court shall be carried out in each division by Chambers.
>   (b) (i) The Appeals Chamber shall be composed of all the judges of the Appeals Division;
>   (ii) The functions of the Trial Chamber shall be carried out by three judges of the Trial Division;
>   (iii) The functions of the Pre-Trial Chamber shall be carried out either by three judges of the Pre-Trial Division or by a single judge of that division in accordance with this Statute and the Rules of Procedure and Evidence;
>   (c) Nothing in this paragraph shall preclude the simultaneous constitution of more than one Trial Chamber or Pre-Trial Chamber when the efficient management of the Court's workload so requires.
> 3. (a) Judges assigned to the Trial and Pre-Trial Divisions shall serve in those divisions for a period of three years, and thereafter until the completion of any case the hearing of which has already commenced in the division concerned.
>   (b) Judges assigned to the Appeals Division shall serve in that division for their entire term of office.
> 4. Judges assigned to the Appeals Division shall serve only in that division. Nothing in this article shall, however, preclude the temporary attachment of judges from the Trial Division to the Pre-Trial Division or vice versa, if the Presidency considers that the efficient management of the Court's workload so requires, provided that under no circumstances shall a judge who has participated in the pre-trial phase of a case be eligible to sit on the Trial Chamber hearing that case.

Trial and Appellate Levels at the ICC

2.1.9   The ICC is more hierarchical in its separation of the trial and appellate levels than the ICTY and ICTR, and imposes different requirements for the qualifications and expertise for trial and appellate judges. See Article 39 of the Rome Statute.

QUALIFICATIONS AND ELECTION OF JUDGES

2.1.10

ICTY ARTICLE 13 QUALIFICATIONS OF JUDGES	ICTR ARTICLE 12 QUALIFICATIONS OF JUDGES
The permanent and *ad litem* judges shall be persons of high moral character, impartiality and integrity who possess the qualifications required in their respective countries for appointment to the highest judicial offices. In the overall composition of the Chambers and sections of the Trial Chambers, due account shall be taken of the experience of the judges in criminal law, international law, including international humanitarian law and human rights law.	The permanent and *ad litem* judges shall be persons of high moral character, impartiality and integrity who possess the qualifications required in their respective countries for appointment to the highest judicial offices. In the overall composition of the Chambers and sections of the Trial Chambers, due account shall be taken of the experience of the judges in criminal law, international law, including international humanitarian law and human rights law.

2.1.11

ICTY ARTICLE 13 *bis* ELECTION OF PERMANENT JUDGES	ICTR ARTICLE 12 *bis* ELECTION OF PERMANENT JUDGES
1. Fourteen of the permanent judges of the International Tribunal shall be elected by the General Assembly from a list submitted by the Security Council, in the following manner: (a) The Secretary-General shall invite nominations for judges of the International Tribunal from States Members of the United Nations and non-member States maintaining permanent observer missions at United Nations Headquarters; (b) Within sixty days of the date of the invitation of the Secretary-General, each State may nominate up to two candidates meeting the qualifications set out in article 13 of the Statute, no two of whom shall be of the same nationality and neither of whom shall be of the same nationality as any judge who is a member of the Appeals Chamber and who was elected or appointed a judge of the International Criminal Tribunal for the Prosecution of Persons Responsible	1. Eleven of the permanent judges of the International Tribunal for Rwanda shall be elected by the General Assembly from a list submitted by the Security Council, in the following manner: (a) The Secretary-General shall invite nominations for permanent judges of the International Tribunal for Rwanda from States Members of the United Nations and non-member States maintaining permanent observer missions at United Nations Headquarters; (b) Within sixty days of the date of the invitation of the Secretary-General, each State may nominate up to two candidates meeting the qualifications set out in article 12 of the present Statute, no two of whom shall be of the same nationality and neither of whom shall be of the same nationality as any judge who is a member of the Appeals Chamber and who was elected or appointed a permanent judge of the International Tribunal for the Prosecution

for Genocide and Other Serious Violations of International Humanitarian Law Committed in the Territory of Rwanda and Rwandan Citizens Responsible for Genocide and Other Such Violations Committed in the Territory of Neighbouring States, between 1 January 1994 and 31 December 1994 (hereinafter referred to as "The International Tribunal for Rwanda") in accordance with article 12 of the Statute of that Tribunal;	of Persons Responsible for Serious Violations of International Humanitarian Law Committed in the Territory of the Former Yugoslavia since 1991 (hereinafter referred to as 'the International Tribunal for the Former Yugoslavia') in accordance with article 13 *bis* of the Statute of that Tribunal;
(c) The Secretary-General shall forward the nominations received to the Security Council. From the nominations received the Security Council shall establish a list of not less than twenty-eight and not more than forty-two candidates, taking due account of the adequate representation of the principal legal systems of the world;	(c) The Secretary-General shall forward the nominations received to the Security Council. From the nominations received the Security Council shall establish a list of not less than twenty-two and not more than thirty-three candidates, taking due account of the adequate representation on the International Tribunal for Rwanda of the principal legal systems of the world;
(d) The President of the Security Council shall transmit the list of candidates to the President of the General Assembly. From that list the General Assembly shall elect fourteen permanent judges of the International Tribunal. The candidates who receive an absolute majority of the votes of the States Members of the United Nations and of the non-member States maintaining permanent observer missions at United Nations Headquarters, shall be declared elected. Should two candidates of the same nationality obtain the required majority vote, the one who received the higher number of votes shall be considered elected.	(d) The President of the Security Council shall transmit the list of candidates to the President of the General Assembly. From that list the General Assembly shall elect eleven permanent judges of the International Tribunal for Rwanda. The candidates who receive an absolute majority of the votes of the States Members of the United Nations and of the non-member States maintaining permanent observer missions at United Nations Headquarters, shall be declared elected. Should two candidates of the same nationality obtain the required majority vote, the one who received the higher number of votes shall be considered elected.
2. In the event of a vacancy in the Chambers amongst the permanent judges elected or appointed in accordance with this article, after consultation with the Presidents of the Security Council and of the General Assembly, the Secretary-General shall appoint a person meeting the qualifications of article 13 of the Statute, for the remainder of the term of office concerned.	2. In the event of a vacancy in the Chambers amongst the permanent judges elected or appointed in accordance with this article, after consultation with the Presidents of the Security Council and of the General Assembly, the Secretary-General shall appoint a person meeting the qualifications of article 12 of the present Statute, for the remainder of the term of office concerned.
3. The permanent judges elected in accordance with this article shall be elected for a term of four years. The terms and conditions of service shall be those of the judges of the International Court of Justice. They shall be eligible for re-election.	3. The permanent judges elected in accordance with this article shall be elected for a term of four years. The terms and conditions of service shall be those of the permanent judges of the International Tribunal for the Former Yugoslavia. They shall be eligible for re-election.

2.1.12

ICTY ARTICLE 13 *ter* ELECTION AND APPOINTMENT OF *AD LITEM* JUDGES	ICTR ARTICLE 12 *ter* ELECTION AND APPOINTMENT OF *AD LITEM* JUDGES
1. The ad litem judges of the International Tribunal shall be elected by the General Assembly from a list submitted by the Security Council, in the following manner: (a) The Secretary-General shall invite nominations for ad litem judges of the International Tribunal from States Members of the United Nations and non-member States maintaining permanent observer missions at United Nations Headquarters; (b) Within sixty days of the date of the invitation of the Secretary-General, each State may nominate up to four candidates meeting the qualifications set out in article 13 of the Statute, taking into account the importance of a fair representation of female and male candidates; (c) The Secretary-General shall forward the nominations received to the Security Council. From the nominations received the Security Council shall establish a list of not less than fifty-four candidates, taking due account of the adequate representation of the principal legal systems of the world and bearing in mind the importance of equitable geographical distribution; (d) The President of the Security Council shall transmit the list of candidates to the President of the General Assembly. From that list the General Assembly shall elect the twenty-seven ad litem judges of the International Tribunal. The candidates who receive an absolute majority of the votes of the States Members of the United Nations and of the non-member States maintaining permanent observer missions at United Nations Headquarters shall be declared elected; (e) The ad litem judges shall be elected for a term of four years. They shall not be eligible for re-election. 2. During their term, ad litem judges will be appointed by the Secretary-General, upon	1. The *ad litem* judges of the International Tribunal for Rwanda shall be elected by the General Assembly from a list submitted by the Security Council, in the following manner: (a) The Secretary-General shall invite nominations for *ad litem* judges of the International Tribunal for Rwanda from States Members of the United Nations and non-member States maintaining permanent observer missions at United Nations Headquarters; (b) Within sixty days of the date of the invitation of the Secretary-General, each State may nominate up to four candidates meeting the qualifications set out in article 12 of the present Statute, taking into account the importance of a fair representation of female and male candidates; (c) The Secretary-General shall forward the nominations received to the Security Council. From the nominations received the Security Council shall establish a list of not less than thirty-six candidates, taking due account of the adequate representation of the principal legal systems of the world and bearing in mind the importance of equitable geographical distribution; (d) The President of the Security Council shall transmit the list of candidates to the President of the General Assembly. From that list the General Assembly shall elect the eighteen *ad litem* judges of the International Tribunal for Rwanda. The candidates who receive an absolute majority of the votes of the States Members of the United Nations and of the non-member States maintaining permanent observer missions at United Nations Headquarters shall be declared elected; (e) The *ad litem* judges shall be elected for a term of four years. They shall not be eligible for re-election. 2. During their term, *ad litem* judges will be appointed by the Secretary-General, upon

request of the President of the International Tribunal, to serve in the Trial Chambers for one or more trials, for a cumulative period of up to, but not including, three years. When requesting the appointment of any particular ad litem judge, the President of the International Tribunal shall bear in mind the criteria set out in article 13 of the Statute regarding the composition of the Chambers and sections of the Trial Chambers, the considerations set out in paragraphs 1 (b) and (c) above and the number of votes the ad litem judge received in the General Assembly.	request of the President of the International Tribunal for Rwanda, to serve in the Trial Chambers for one or more trials, for a cumulative period of up to, but not including, three years. When requesting the appointment of any particular *ad litem* judge, the President of the International Tribunal for Rwanda shall bear in mind the criteria set out in article 12 of the present Statute regarding the composition of the Chambers and sections of the Trial Chambers, the considerations set out in paragraphs 1 (b) and (c) above and the number of votes the *ad litem* judge received in the General Assembly.

2.1.13

ICTY ARTICLE 13 *quater* STATUS OF *AD LITEM* JUDGES	ICTR ARTICLE 12 *quater* STATUS OF *AD LITEM* JUDGES

1. During the period in which they are appointed to serve in the International Tribunal, ad litem judges shall:
(a) Benefit from the same terms and conditions of service mutatis mutandis as the permanent judges of the International Tribunal;
(b) Enjoy, subject to paragraph 2 below, the same powers as the permanent judges of the International Tribunal;
(c) Enjoy the privileges and immunities, exemptions and facilities of a judge of the International Tribunal.
2. During the period in which they are appointed to serve in the International Tribunal, ad litem judges shall not:
(a) Be eligible for election as, or to vote in the election of, the President of the Tribunal or the Presiding Judge of a Trial Chamber pursuant to article 14 of the Statute;
(b) Have power:
   (i) To adopt rules of procedure and evidence pursuant to article 15 of the Statute. They shall, however, be consulted before the adoption of those rules;
   (ii) To review an indictment pursuant to
	1. During the period in which they are appointed to serve in the International Tribunal for Rwanda, ad litem judges shall:
	(a) Benefit from the same terms and conditions of service mutatis mutandis as the permanent judges of the International Tribunal for Rwanda;
	(b) Enjoy, subject to paragraph 2 below, the same powers as the permanent judges of the International Tribunal for Rwanda;
	(c) Enjoy the privileges and immunities, exemptions and facilities of a judge of the International Tribunal for Rwanda.
	2. During the period in which they are appointed to serve in the International Tribunal for Rwanda, ad litem judges shall not:
	(a) Be eligible for election as, or to vote in the election of, the President of the International Tribunal for Rwanda or the Presiding Judge of a Trial Chamber pursuant to article 13 of the present Statute;
	(b) Have power:
	   (i) To adopt rules of procedure and evidence pursuant to article 14 of the Statute. They shall, however, be consulted before the adoption of those rules;

article 19 of the Statute; (iii) To consult with the President in relation to the assignment of judges pursuant to article 14 of the Statute or in relation to a pardon or commutation of sentence pursuant to article 28 of the Statute; (iv) To adjudicate in pre-trial proceedings.	(ii) To review an indictment pursuant to article 18 of the Statute; (iii) To consult with the President of the International Tribunal for Rwanda in relation to the assignment of judges pursuant to article 13 of the present Statute or in relation to a pardon or commutation of sentence pursuant to article 27 of the present Statute; (iv) To adjudicate in pre-trial proceedings.

The Changing Structures of the ICTY and ICTR

2.1.14 Article 13 of the ICTY Statute was amended by Security Council resolution 1166 of 13 May 1998 as a consequential amendment upon the addition of a third Trial Chamber. This article was then again substantially amended, adding Articles 13 *bis, ter* and *quater*, by Security Council resolution 1329 of 30 November 2000, as a result of adding *ad litem* judges. Furthermore, Security Council resolution 1431 (2002) of 14 August 2002 made a slight amendment to Article 13 *bis*.

2.1.15 The structure of the ICTY and ICTR Chambers has thus changed considerably since they were first established, when they comprised two Trial Chambers of three judges each and a common Appeals Chamber of five judges.

2.1.16 Under the present system, both the ICTY and ICTR are comprised of 16 permanent judges. At the ICTY, the judges are divided between three Trial Chambers and one Appeals Chamber. Each Trial Chamber consists of three permanent judges and, in the case of the ICTY, a maximum, at any one point, of six *ad litem* judges. An ICTY Trial Chamber may be divided into mixed sections of three judges (two permanent and one *ad litem* or one permanent and two *ad litem*). Each Trial Chamber can be comprised of up to three sections.

2.1.17 At the ICTR, the concept of *ad litem* judges was introduced by Security Council resolution 1431 (2002) of 14 August 2002, which provided for the creation of a pool of eighteen *ad litem* judges. Article 12 was amended and Articles 12 *bis, ter* and *quater* were added in order to deal with the election, appointment and status of both permanent and *ad litem* judges.

2.1.18 The common ICTY/ICTR Appeals Chamber consists of seven permanent judges: five from the permanent judges of the ICTY and two from the 11 permanent judges of the ICTR (see Article 14(4) of the ICTY Statute). These seven judges also constitute the ICTR Appeals Chamber. Each appeal is heard and decided by 5 judges.

2.1.19 As a result, only 11 judges are elected by the General Assembly to serve in the ICTR (two appeals judges and nine trial judges, three for each of the three Trial Chambers), while 14 judges are elected by the General Assembly to serve in the ICTY (five appeals judges and nine trial judges, three for each of the three Trial Chambers), as well as *ad litem* judges.

Impartiality of Judges

2.1.20 Impartiality is an obligation undertaken by judges upon assuming their duties (See Rules 14 and 15). In *Furundžija*, (paragraph 189) the ICTY Appeals Chamber defined the test of impartiality in the following way:

> a Judge should not only be subjectively free from bias, but also . . . there should be nothing in the surrounding circumstances which objectively gives rise to an appearance of bias. On this basis, the Appeals Chamber considers that the following principles should direct it in interpreting and applying the impartiality requirement of the Statute:
> A. A Judge is not impartial if shown that actual bias exists.
> B. There is an unacceptable appearance of bias if:
> (i) a Judge is a party to the case, or has a financial or propriety interests in the outcome of a case, or if the Judge's decision will lead to the promotion of a cause in which he or she is involved, together with one of the parties. Under these circumstances, a Judge's disqualification from the case is automatic; or
> (ii) the circumstances would lead a reasonable observer, properly informed, to reasonably apprehend bias.

See also 2.1.45, below ("Judicial Impartiality and Independence").

Election of ICTY Judges

2.1.21 The General Assembly elected the first Judges to serve at the ICTY in its Decision 47/328 of 17 September 1993. The following Judges were elected:

Georges ABI-SAAB (Egypt)
Antonio CASSESE (Italy)
Jules DESCHENES (Canada)
Adolphus KARIBI-WHYTE (Nigeria)
Germain LE FOYER DE COSTIL (France)
Haopei LI (China)
Gabrielle McDONALD (USA)
Elizabeth ODIO-BENITO (Costa Rica)
Rustam SIDHWA (Pakistan)
Ninian STEPHEN (Australia)
Lal Chand VOHRAH (Malaysia).

2.1.22 The second round of Judges were elected by the General Assembly on 20 May 1997. Five Judges were re-elected, namely Judge Antonio Cassese (Italy), Judge Gabrielle Kirk McDonald (United States), Judge Claude Jorda (France) (who had replaced Judge Le Foyer de Costil), Judge Lal Chand Vohrah (Malaysia), and Judge Fouad Riad (Egypt) (who had replaced Judge Abi-Saab). Judge Li (China) and Judge Stephen (Australia) did not seek re-election. The six newly elected Judges were:

Richard MAY (United Kingdom)
Florence MUMBA (Zambia)
Rafael NIETO-NAVIA (Columbia)
Almiro RODRIGUES (Portugal)
Mohamed SHAHABUDDEEN (Guyana)
Tieya WANG (China).

2.1.23 On 20 May 1998, three new judges were elected:

> David Anthony HUNT (Australia)
> Mohamed BENNOUNA (Morocco)
> Patrick Lipton ROBINSON (Jamaica)

2.1.24 The current, permanent Judges at the ICTY are:

> Carmel A. AGIUS (Malta)
> Liu DAQUN (China)
> Asoka de Zoysa GUNAWARDANA (Sri Lanka) (also serving at ICTR)
> Mehmet GÜNEY (Turkey) (also serving at ICTR)
> David Anthony HUNT (Australia)
> Claude JORDA (France), President
> O-gon KWON (South Korea)
> Amin EL MAHDI (Egypt)
> Richard George MAY (United Kingdom)
> Theodor MERON (United States of America)
> Florence Ndepele Mwachande MUMBA (Zambia)
> Alphonsus Martinus Maria ORIE (the Netherlands)
> Fausto POCAR (Italy)
> Patrick Lipton ROBINSON (Jamaica)
> Wolfgang SCHOMBURG (Germany)
> Mohamed SHAHABUDDEEN (Guyana), Vice President

2.1.25 The current, *ad litem* Judges at the ICTY are:

> Carmen Maria ARGIBAY (Argentina)
> Maureen Harding CLARK (Ireland)
> Fatoumata DIARRA (Mali)
> Ivana JANU (Czech Republic)
> Per-Johan Viktor LINDHOLM (Finland)
> Rafael NIETO-NAVIA (Colombia)
> Amarjeet SINGH (Singapore)
> Chikako TAYA (Japan)
> Volodymyr Vassylenko (Ukraine)
> Sharon A. WILLIAMS (Canada)

2.1.26 For details as to the Judges and Chambers dealing with each case, reference should be made to the following web address: http://www.un.org/icty/glance/index.htm.

ICTY Article 13(3): Chambers Vacancies

2.1.27 There have been a number of judicial replacements since the ICTY was established. Reference may be made to earlier editions of this work for details.

Election of ICTR Judges

2.1.28 At the first election, the General Assembly, in its Decision 324 in April, 1995, elected as ICTR Judges:

Trial Chamber Judges

Lennart ASPEGREN (Sweden)
Laïty KAMA (Senegal), President
Tafazzal H.KHAN (Bangladesh)
Yakov A. OSTROVSKY (Russia)
Navanethem PILLAY (South Africa)
William H. SEKULE (Tanzania)

Appeals Chamber Judges

Antonio CASSESE (Italy)
Georges Michel ABI-SAAB (Egypt)
Jules DESCHÊNES (Canada)
Haopei LI (China)
Sir Ninian STEPHEN (Australia)

2.1.29 The composition of the Appeals Chamber was subsequently modified in line with changes to the composition of the ICTY Trial Chamber.

2.1.30 At the second election by the General Assembly, in 1999, the following were elected as ICTR Judges:

Trial Chamber Judges

Pavel DOLENC (Slovenia)
Mehmet GÜNEY (Turkey)
Asoka de Zoysa GUNAWARDANA (Sri Lanka)
Erik MØSE (Norway)
Lloyd George WILLIAMS (Jamaica, St. Kitts and Nevis)
Laïy KAMA, (Senegal), President
Yakov A. OSTROVSKY (Russia)
Navanethem PILLAY (South Africa)
William H. SEKULE (Tanzania)

Appeals Chamber Judges

Gabrielle Kirk McDONALD (USA)
Mohamed SHAHABUDDEEN (Guyana)
Lal Chand VOHRAH (Malaysia)
Wang TIEYA (China)
Rafael Nieto NAVIA (Colombia)

2.1.31 The current ICTR judges, following the elections by the General Assembly on 31 January 2003, are:

Mansoor AHMED (Pakistan)
Sergei EGOROV (Russia)
Asoka de Zoysa GUNAWARDANA (Sri Lanka)
Mehmet GÜNEY (Turkey)
Erik MØSE (Norway)
Jai Ram REDDY (Fiji)
William H. SEKULE (Tanzania)
Andrésia VAZ (Senegal)
Inés WEINBERG DE ROCA (Argentina)

ICTY Article 13 *bis* (3)

2.1.32 This article provides that, "The terms and conditions of service shall be those of the judges of the International Court of Justice." This has proved relevant with respect to Article 13(3) of the ICJ Statute, which reads:

> The members of the Court shall continue to discharge their duties until their places have been filled. Though replaced, they shall finish any cases which they may have begun.

2.1.33 This same provision was enacted at the ICTR in Rule 14 *bis*, which reads, "The members of the Tribunal shall continue to discharge their duties until their places have been filled. Though replaced, they shall finish any cases which they may have begun." Rule 14 *bis* of the ICTR's Rules of Procedure and Evidence was added at the Fourth Plenary Session, held in Arusha 1–5 June 1997.

2.1.34 While Rule 14 *bis* has not been adopted at the ICTY, Judges Karibi-Whyte, Odio-Benito and Jan, although not re-elected, continued to sit in *Delalić et al.* until the trial was finished. Their terms of service were extended by Security Council resolution 1126 of 27 August 1997:

> endors[ing] the recommendation of the Secretary-General that Judges Karibi-Whyte, Odio-Benito and Jan, once replaced as members of the Tribunal, finish the *Čelebići* case which they have begun before expiry of their term of office; and [taking] note of the intention of the International Tribunal to finish the case before November 1998.

2.1.35 Even in the absence of Rule 14 *bis*, justification could be found for the Judges continuing to sit in *Delalić et al.* until it was finished by reading Article 13(4) of the ICTY's Statute ("The terms and conditions of service shall be those of the judges of the International Court of Justice"), together with Article 13(3) of the ICJ Statute (above).

Election of ICC Judges

2.1.36 After 33 ballots, the following eighteen judges were elected, on 7 February 2003, as judges of the International Criminal Court:

List A (Criminal Practitioners)

Maureen Harding CLARK (Ireland)	–	for 9 years
Fatoumata Dernbele DIARRA (Mali)	–	for 9 years
Adrian FULFORD (United Kingdom)	–	for 9 years
Karl T. HUDSON-PHILLIPS (Trinidad and Tobago)	–	for 9 years
Claude JORDA (France)	–	for 6 years
Elizabeth ODIO-BENITO (Costa Rica)	–	for 9 years
Gheorghios M. PIKIS (Cyprus)	–	for 6 years
Tuiloma Neroni SLADE (Samoa)	–	for 3 years
Sang-hyun SONG (Korea)	–	for 3 years
Sylvia H. de Figueiredo STEINER (Brazil)	–	for 9 years

List B (International Lawyers)

René BLATTMANN (Bolivia)	–	for 6 years
Hans Peter KAUL (Germany)	–	for 3 years
Philippe KIRSCH (Canada)	–	for 6 years
Erkki KOURULA (Finland)	–	for 3 years
Akua KUENYEHIA (Ghana)	–	for 3 years
Navanethem PILLAY (South Africa)	–	for 6 years
Mauro POLITI (Italy)	–	for 6 years
Anita USACKA (Latvia)	–	for 3 years

2.1.37   Only those judges who were selected by lot to serve a three-year term shall be eligible for re-election (Article 36(9) of the Rome Statute for the ICC).

OFFICERS AND MEMBERS OF CHAMBERS

2.1.38

ICTY ARTICLE 14 OFFICERS AND MEMBERS OF THE CHAMBERS	ICTR ARTICLE 13 OFFICERS AND MEMBERS OF THE CHAMBERS
1. The permanent judges of the International Tribunal shall elect a President from amongst their number. 2. The President of the International Tribunal shall be a member of the Appeals Chamber and shall preside over its proceedings. 3. After consultation with the permanent judges of the International Tribunal, the President shall assign four of the permanent judges elected or appointed in accordance with Article 13 *bis* of the Statute to the Appeals Chamber and nine to the Trial Chambers. 4. Two of the judges elected or appointed in accordance with article 12 of the Statute of the International Tribunal for Rwanda shall be assigned by the President of that Tribunal, in consultation with the President of the International Tribunal, to be members of the Appeals Chamber and permanent judges of the International Tribunal.	1. The judges of the International Tribunal for Rwanda shall elect a President from amongst their number. 2. The President of the International Tribunal for Rwanda shall be a member of one of its Trial Chambers. 3. After consultation with the permanent judges of the International Tribunal for Rwanda, the President shall assign two of the permanent judges elected or appointed in accordance with Article 12 *bis* of the present Statute to be members of the Appeals Chamber of the International Tribunal for the former Yugoslavia and eight to the Trial Chambers of the International Tribunal for Rwanda. 4. The members of the Appeals Chamber of the International Tribunal for the former Yugoslavia shall also serve as the members of the Appeals Chamber of the International Tribunal for Rwanda.

5. After consultation with the permanent judges of the International Tribunal, the President shall assign such *ad litem* judges as may from time to time be appointed to serve in the International Tribunal to the Trial Chambers. 6. A judge shall serve only in the Chamber to which he or she was assigned. 7. The permanent judges of each Trial Chamber shall elect a Presiding Judge from amongst their number, who shall oversee the work of the Trial Chamber as a whole.	5. After consultation with the permanent judges of the International Tribunal for Rwanda, the President shall assign such *ad litem* judges as may from time to time be appointed to serve in the International Tribunal for Rwanda to the Trial Chambers. 6. A judge shall only serve in the Chamber to which he or she was assigned. 7. The permanent judges of each Trial Chamber shall elect a Presiding Judge from amongst their number, who shall oversee the work of that Trial Chamber as a whole.

History of ICTY Article 14

2.1.39 ICTY Article 14 was substantially amended by Security Council resolution 1329 of 30 November 2000, which provided for *ad litem* judges. The amendment provided that only the permanent judges elect the President of the ICTY, and are consulted by the President regarding assignment to the Trial and Appeals Chambers, and that two judges of the ICTR serve in the common ICTY/ICTR Appeals Chamber. Article 14 was amended further by Security Council resolution 1431 (2002) of 14 August 2002.

History of ICTR Article 13

2.1.40 The Security Council, in its Resolution 1165 of 30 April 1998, amended Article 12(3) (c) and (d) to provide for a third Trial Chamber, and hence nine Trial Chamber judges as opposed to six. Article 12(3)(c) had previously read, ". . . From the nominations received the Security Council shall establish a list of not less than *twelve* and not more than *eighteen* candidates. . .", and Article 12(3)(d) had read, ". . . From that list the General Assembly shall elect the *six* judges of the Trial Chambers."

2.1.41 Articles 11, 12 and 13 of the ICTR Statute were substantially amended by Security Council resolution 1329 of 30 November 2000. Further amendments were made to these articles by Security Council resolution 1431 (2002) of 14 August 2002.

Composition of Chambers

2.1.42 For detail as to the Judges—permanent and *ad litem*—presently hearing each case, and the Presiding Judges, reference should be made to the ICTY website (http://www.un.org/icty/glance/index.htm) and ICTR website (www.ictr.org).

OTP Plays No Role in Assignment of Case

2.1.43 See the *Order of the President on Applications to Assign a Case to a Trial Chamber* issued in *Meakić and others* and *Sikirica and others* on 21 April 1998, dismissing the application:

FURTHER CONSIDERING the Application to be a misuse of Article 14 of the Statute of the International Tribunal and Rule 62 of the Rules of Procedure and Evidence as neither of these provisions contemplate a role for the Prosecution in the assignment of cases to Trial Chambers and the request affects the rights of all of the aforementioned accused without affording them the opportunity to be heard.

2.1.44   Even if the other could be heard, there is a danger, if Parties are given a say in which Judges will try their case, in "Judge-shopping," which would clearly be undesirable.

Judicial Impartiality and Independence

2.1.45   The requirements that Judges must meet in order to be considered to qualify to sit on the ICTY bench are intended to ensure the Tribunal's impartiality and independence. The accused has a right, under international human rights law (see 8.5.29) to be tried by an impartial and independent tribunal established by law. See the *Kanyabashi Decision on the Defence Motion on Jurisdiction* of 18 June 1997 (paragraph 42):

> In this Trial Chamber's view, the personal independence of the judges of the Tribunal and the integrity of the Tribunal are underscored by Article 12 (1) of the Statute of the Tribunal which states that persons of high moral character, integrity, impartiality who possess adequate qualifications to become judges in their respective countries and having widespread experience in criminal law, international law including international humanitarian law and human rights law, shall be elected.

Common ICTY/ICTR Appeals Chamber

2.1.46   For the purposes of ensuring uniformity and coherence of jurisprudence, the Appeals Chamber is common to the ICTY and the ICTR. On this subject, see the *Kanyabashi Jurisdiction Decision* (para. 8):

> The Trial Chamber notes that, in terms of Article 12(2) of the Statute, the two Tribunals share the same Judges of their Appeals Chambers and have adopted largely similar Rules of Procedure and Evidence for the purpose of providing uniformity in the jurisprudence of the two Tribunals. The Trial Chamber respects the persuasive authority of the . . . Appeals Chamber of the International Criminal Tribunal for the Former Yugoslavia. . . .

2.1.47   The ICTY President, but not the ICTR President, serves in the Appeals Chamber, as its Presiding Judge, and assigns the Judges thereto, pursuant to paras. (2) and (3) of Article 14 of the ICTY Statute.

ICTR President

2.1.48   The first President of the ICTR was Judge Laïty Kama of Senegal, who was elected in 1995. Judge Navanethem Pillay of South Africa succeeded him in 1999.

2.1.49

ICTY RULE 14 SOLEMN DECLARATION	ICTR RULE 14 SOLEMN DECLARATION
(A) Before taking up duties each Judge shall make the following solemn declaration: "I solemnly declare that I will perform my duties and exercise my powers as a Judge of the International Tribunal for the Prosecution of Persons Responsible for Serious Violations of International Humanitarian Law Committed in the Territory of the Former Yugoslavia since 1991 honourably, faithfully, impartially and conscientiously." (B) The declaration shall be signed by the Judge and witnessed by, or by a representative of, the Secretary-General of the United Nations shall be kept in the records of the Tribunal. (C) A Judge whose service continues without interruption after expiry of a previous period of service shall not make a new declaration.	(A) Before taking up his duties each Judge shall make the following solemn declaration: "I solemnly declare that I will perform my duties and exercise my powers as a Judge of the International Criminal Tribunal for the Prosecution of Persons Responsible for Genocide and other Serious Violations of International Humanitarian Law Committed in the Territory of Rwanda and Rwandan Citizens responsible for Genocide and other such violations committed in the territory of neighbouring States, between 1 January 1994 and 31 December 1994, honourably, faithfully, impartially and conscientiously." (B) The text of the declaration, signed by the Judge and witnessed by the Secretary-General of the United Nations or his representative, shall be kept in the records of the Tribunal.

History of ICTY Rule 14

2.1.50 Rule 14(C) was added at the fourteenth plenary session on 12 November 1997; sub-paras. (A) and (B) were also amended at the same session in minor ways.

History of ICTR Rule 14

2.1.51 The words of "text of the" were added to para. (B) at the eighth plenary session on 26 June 2000.

Rule 14 Is the Guarantor of Tribunal's Impartiality and Independence

2.1.52 See *Kanyabashi Jurisdiction Decision*, para. 41: "Further, the judges of the Tribunal exercise their *judicial* duties independently and freely and are under oath to act honourably, faithfully, impartially and conscientiously as stipulated in rule 14 of the Rules. Judges do not account to the Security Council for their judicial functions."

2.1.53

| ICTR only
RULE 14 *bis* |
|---|
| The members of the Tribunal shall continue to discharge their duties until their places have been filled. Though replaced, they shall finish any cases which they may have begun. |

History of ICTR Rule 14 *bis*

2.1.54 Rule 14 *bis* of the ICTR's Rules of Procedure and Evidence was added at the ICTR's fourth Plenary Session, held in Arusha 1–5 June 1997. The wording is identical to Article 13(3) of the Statute of the International Court of Justice (save for the reference to "Court" rather than "Tribunal"):

> The members of the Court shall continue to discharge their duties until their places have been filled. Though replaced, they shall finish any cases which they may have begun.

2.1.55 Rule 14 *bis* has not been adopted at the ICTY. Nonetheless where ICTY Judges continue to sit in a case until it is finished (as has happened, for example, in the *Čelebići* case, with respect to Judges Karibi-Whyte, Odio-Benito and Jan, who were not re-elected but who continued to sit in the case pursuant to Security Council Resolution 1126 of 27 August 1997), this may be justified by Article 13(*bis*)(3) of the ICTY's Statute ("The terms and conditions of service shall be those of the judges of the International Court of Justice"), taken in conjunction with Article 13(3) of the ICJ Statute of the International Court of Justice (see 2.1.32).

DISQUALIFICATION, RESIGNATION, AND PRECEDENCE OF JUDGES

2.1.56

| ICTY
RULE 15
DISQUALIFICATION OF JUDGES | ICTR
RULE 15
DISQUALIFICATION OF JUDGES |
|---|---|
| (A) A Judge may not sit on a trial or appeal in any case in which he has a personal interest or concerning which the Judge has or has had any association which might affect his or her impartiality. The Judge shall in any such circumstance withdraw, and the President shall assign another Judge to the case. | (A) A Judge may not sit on a trial or appeal in any case in which he has a personal interest or concerning which he has or has had any association which might affect his impartiality. He shall in any such circumstance withdraw from that case. Where the Judge withdraws from the Trial Chamber, the President shall assign another Trial Chamber Judge to sit in his place. Where a Judge withdraws from the |

(B) Any party may apply to the Presiding Judge of a Chamber for the disqualification and withdrawal of a Judge of that Chamber from a trial or appeal upon the above grounds. The Presiding Judge shall confer with the Judge in question, and if necessary the Bureau shall determine the matter. If the Bureau upholds the application, the President shall assign another Judge to sit in place of the disqualified Judge. (C) The Judge of the Trial Chamber who reviews an indictment against an accused, pursuant to Article 19 of the Statute and Rules 47 or 61, shall not be disqualified for sitting as a member of the Trial Chamber for the trial of that accused. Such a Judge shall also not be disqualified for sitting as a member of the Appeals Chamber, or as a member of a bench of three Judges appointed pursuant to Rules 65 (D) or 72 (E) to hear any appeal in that case. (D) (i) No Judge shall sit on any appeal or as a member of a bench of three Judges appointed pursuant to Rules 65 (D) or 72 (E) in a case in which that Judge sat as a member of the Trial Chamber. (ii) No Judge shall sit on any State Request for Review pursuant to Rule 108 bis in a matter in which that Judge sat as a member of the Trial Chamber whose decision is to be reviewed.	Appeals Chamber, the Presiding Judge of that Chamber shall assign another Judge to sit in his place. (B) Any party may apply to the Presiding Judge of a Chamber for the disqualification of a Judge of that Chamber from a trial or appeal upon the above grounds. After the Presiding Judge has conferred with the Judge in question, the Bureau, if necessary, shall determine the matter. If the Bureau upholds the application, the President shall assign another Judge to sit in place of the disqualified Judge. (C) The Judge of the Trial Chamber who reviews an indictment against an accused, pursuant to Article 18 of the Statute and Rules 47 and 61, shall not sit as a member of the Trial Chamber for the trial of that accused. (D) No member of the Appeals Chamber shall sit on any appeal in a case in which another Judge of the same nationality sat as a member of the Trial Chamber.

History of ICTY Rule 15

2.1.57   Para. (B) was amended at the fifth plenary session in January 1995 to add the words "or appeal," so that the provisions for disqualification of Judges apply to Judges of both the Trial and the Appeals Chambers. Para. (F) was amended at the seventh plenary session held on 2–16 June 1995 to clarify the meaning of the expression, "part-heard." The Judges adopted an amendment to para. (E) unanimously on 5 July 1996, regarding the procedure to be adopted in the event of illness of a Judge or an unfilled vacancy in the Chambers. This para. was further amended at the thirteenth plenary session on 25 July 1997, adding the words, "or in any other exceptional circumstances." Para. (D) was amended at the eighteenth plenary session on 9–10 July 1998, adding the reference to "a member of a bench of three Judges appointed pursuant to Rules 65 (D), 72 (B)(ii), 73 (B) or 77 (D)" in (i) and the new sub-section, (ii).

2.1.58 Rule 15 as a whole was amended at the nineteenth plenary session, on 17 December 1998, to render the language gender-neutral and as a consequential amendment to the amendment to Rule 77. The second sentence of para. (C) ("Such a Judge shall not be disqualified from sitting as a member of the Appeals Chamber, or as a member of a bench of three Judges appointed pursuant to Rules 63(D), 72(B)(ii), 73(B) or 77(J), to hear any appeal in that case"), was added at the twentieth plenary session on 30 June to 2 July 1999. At the twenty-first plenary session, effective 30 November 1999, para. (C) was again amended, this time to provide that the Judges of the Trial Chamber who reviewed the indictment would also not be disqualified from sitting as a member of the Trial Chamber for the trial of that accused. Previously such a judge *was* specifically disqualified because the fact of his or her having confirmed the indictment was perceived as colouring the Judge's judgement in the trial of the accused, throwing doubt on his or her ability to apply the presumption of innocence to the trial of the accused. At the same plenary session, paras. (E) and (F) were deleted, in favour of a more elaborate Rule 15 *bis* dealing with the same issue of absence of a Judge for "illness of other urgent personal reasons" (see next rule). Paras. (C) and (D) were amended on 19 January 2001, after the twenty-third plenary session, to remove the references to Rule 77(J). Paras. (C) and (D) were amended at the twenty-seventh plenary session on 12 December 2002 to refer to Rule 72 (E).

History of ICTR Rule 15

2.1.59 Rule 15 of the ICTR Rules of Procedure and Evidence was amended at the ICTR's fourth Plenary Session, held in Arusha 1–5 June 1997, so as to allow a Judge who has issued an order pursuant to Rule 40 *bis* for transfer and provisional detention of an accused to sit in the Trial Chamber for the trial of that accused. Para. (A) was further amended to distinguish between the consequences of a *Trial Chamber* Judge withdrawing from a case from those of an *Appeals Chamber* Judge withdrawing from a case.

2.1.60 Para. (F) was added at the ICTR's fifth Plenary Session, held in Arusha on 1–8 June 1998. It corresponds to Rule 15(E) of the ICTY's Rules of Procedure and Evidence ("In case of illness or an unfilled vacancy or in any other exceptional circumstances, the President may authorise a Chamber to conduct routine matters, such as the holding of an initial appearance under Rule 62 or the delivery of decisions, in the absence of one or more of its members"), with the difference that the ICTR Rule does not refer to initial appearances, evidently because initial appearances are not considered as "routine matters." The Rule was also amended further in minor ways.

2.1.61 Paras. (E) and (F) were removed from this rule at the tenth plenary session on 30–31 May, 2001; the subject-matter dealt with in those paragraphs was instead dealt with in the new rule 15 *bis*, introduced at the same plenary (see below).

Voluntary Withdrawal

2.1.62 ICTY Rule 15(A) has been applied to allow a Judge *voluntarily* to withdraw from a case, in the absence of any alleged personal interest or association which might affect the Judge's impartiality. See *Order of the President for the Assignment of a Judge to a Trial Chamber* of 9 April 1998 in *Kovačević*.

Determination by Bureau of Judge's Disqualification

2.1.63 In the *subpoena* hearings which took place before the Trial Chamber in *Blaškić* (see Rule 54, "subpoenas," 8.4.1), the Republic of Croatia, on 15 April 1997, requested Judge McDonald, the Presiding Judge, to "recuse yourself from participating in this hearing and rendering any decisions on it, since you are the judge who issued the order that is here at issue." Croatia added, "Although we, of course, do not doubt your integrity, we believe that both the appearance and substance of fairness and due process require you not to take part in this hearing, or in determining the validity of the subpoena at issue." At the request of Judge McDonald, the matter was referred, on 16 April 1997, to the Bureau of the Tribunal, which, pursuant to Rule 15, considered the matter and decided unanimously, in a reasoned decision, to reject the request for recusation.

Judge Not Disqualified from Hearing Trial(s) Arising from the Same Set of Events

2.1.64 See *Decision on the Application of the Accused for Disqualification of Judges Jorda and Riad* in the *Kordić and Čerkez* trial, dated 21 May 1998, as well as the Bureau Decision of 4 May 1998, both of which held that a Judge is not disqualified from hearing two or more criminal trials arising out of the same series of events. In this case, Judges Jorda and Riad were both sitting in the *Blaškić* trial, which involved the same events—"ethnic cleansing" by Bosnian Croat forces in central Bosnia in 1992–1993—as the *Kordić and Čerkez* trial. This was rejected as a ground for disqualifying the two Judges in the Decisions of the Bureau and of the Trial Chamber.

2.1.65 In the 4 May 1998 Decision, the Bureau stated:

> as is shown by the jurisprudence on the subject, it does not follow that a judge is disqualified from hearing two or more criminal trials arising out of the same series of events, where he is exposed to evidence relating to these events in both cases. This applies also to the situation where an accused in the later case was previously named as a co-accused in the first indictment in the first indictment. A judge is presumed to be impartial. In this case there is nothing to rebut that presumption.

2.1.66 The Defence renewed its application for disqualification on 21 May 1998, which was again rejected in a Decision of the Trial Chamber of 8 October 1998. The Chamber also rejected the argument that the fact that the Judges were sitting in the *Blaškić* trial would cause undue delay to the *Kordić and Čerkez* trial. In the event, however, the case was transferred to another Chamber, comprising Judges May, Bennouna and Robinson, for trial.

2.1.67 On a related point, see *Order on Emergency Motion to Limit Prosecutor's Inquiry relating to the accused Anto Furundžija* issued in *Kupreškić et al.* on 26 August 1998, in which the Trial Chamber affirmed that the Judges were professionals, able to compartmentalise evidence heard in one case from evidence heard in another case:

> CONSIDERING THAT, composed as it is of professional judges, the Trial Chamber is capable of disregarding any such evidence relating to Anto Furundžija offered in *Prosecutor v. Kupreškić et al. (IT-95-16-T)* when the members of this Trial Chamber sit in the case of *Prosecutor v. Furundžija*,

NOTING ALSO the Trial Chamber's ruling at the hearing of 24 August 1998, to the effect that whatever evidence relating to Anto Furundžija is produced in these proceedings, will not be regarded as evidence in *Prosecutor v. Furundžija*, because he is not present and not represented.

2.1.68 The fact that this requires the Judges to perform the mental gymnastics of discounting evidence heard in one case while relying on it another case should not, however, be lightly dismissed. It is submitted that, where possible, the situation contemplated above should not be allowed to arise.

Judge Not Disqualified Based on Position Taken in Another Case on an Issue in Dispute in the Present Case

2.1.69 See *Decision on Application by Momir Talić for the Disqualification and Withdrawal of a Judge* rendered by the Presiding Judge of one of the Trial Chambers on 18 May 2000. The defence requested Judge Mumba's disqualification because she had been a member of the Appeals Chamber which had found in *Tadić* that there had been an international armed conflict in Bosnia and Herzegovina, an issue that would also arise in the *Talić* trial. Judge Hunt declined the request:

> 19. To state the issue once more, it is whether the reaction of the hypothetical fair-minded observer (with sufficient knowledge of the actual circumstances to make a reasonable judgement) would be that Judge Mumba, having participated in the *Tadic* Conviction Appeal Judgement, might not bring an impartial and unprejudiced mind to the issues in the present case identified in pars 4 and 15, *supra*. It is *not* whether she would merely decide these issues in the same way as they were decided in that case. The distinction is an important one.
>
> 20. Having given the Request made by Talic careful consideration, I have *not* been satisfied by him that the reaction of the fair-minded observer would be that Judge Mumba might not bring an impartial and unprejudiced mind to any of the issues in this case. I have conferred with Judge Mumba, as Rule 15(B) requires. She has agreed with me that her participation in the *Tadic* Conviction Appeal Judgement provides no basis for her disqualification in the present case. Neither of us see any need to refer the matter to the Bureau for its determination.

Judge Not Disqualified Due to Holding Executive Office

2.1.70 See *Decision of the Bureau on Motion on Judicial Independence* issued in *Delalić et al* on 4 September 1998. Judge Odio Benito, who was sitting in the *Delalić et al*, had become Vice-President of Costa Rica during the trial proceedings, and the Defence challenged her independence on that ground. The Bureau rejected this as a ground for disqualification on the basis that she was not exercising any political or administrative function since "Judge Odio Benito has been holding the position of Vice-President in name only from the date she took the oath of office. She has committed herself not to take up the duties of her post until she has completed her judicial duties."

2.1.71 This finding was upheld on appeal from the *Delalić et al Trial Judgement*. See the *Delalić et al Appeals Judgement*, paras. 651–693. A similar ground of appeal based on the defence contention that Judge Odio-Benito should have been disqualified from sitting because her membership of the Board of Trustees of the United Nations Voluntary Fund for Victims of Torture rendered her partial, was also dismissed by the Appeals Chamber (paras. 694–709).

2.1.72 See also the *Decision of the Bureau on Motion to Disqualify Judges Pursuant to Rule 15 or in the Alternative that Certain Judges Recuse Themselves, Delalić et al*, 25 October 1999. The defence had submitted a motion pursuant to Rule 15, requesting that all ICTY Judges who either participated in the plenary session which found that Judge Odio Benito's nomination as Vice-President of Costa Rica would not be incompatible with service as Judge of the Tribunal or who took part in the plenary session after her election which approved her taking the oath as Vice-President of Costa Rica while remaining a Judge of the Tribunal be disqualified from sitting on the Appeals Chamber in *Delalić et al* on the appeal against conviction or, in the alternative, that these Judges recuse themselves. The Bureau unanimously rejected the Motion.

Application to Disqualify Judge Must Be Made Before Trial Is Concluded

2.1.73 See *Decision on post-trial application by Anto Furundžija to the Bureau of the Tribunal for the Disqualification of Presiding Judge Mumba, Motion to Vacate Conviction and Sentence, and Motion for a New Trial* rendered by the Bureau (President McDonald, Judges Jorda, Rodrigues, Hunt and Bennouna) on 11 March 1999. The Bureau, reconstituted pursuant to Rule 23(D), held that it was not competent in the matter since, under Rule 15(B), an application for disqualification of a Judge had to be made during the trial before the Judgement was issued. After that, it may be presumed, the matter is one for appeal on the merits. Accordingly, the Bureau dismissed the Application and Motions without ruling on the merits.

History of ICTY Rule 15 *bis*

2.1.74

ICTY RULE 15 *bis* ABSENCE OF A JUDGE	ICTR RULE 15 *bis* ABSENCE OF A JUDGE
(A) If (i) a Judge is, for illness or other urgent personal reasons, or for reasons of authorised Tribunal business, unable to continue sitting in a part-heard case for a period which is likely to be of short duration, and (ii) the remaining Judges of the Chamber are satisfied that it is in the interests of justice to do so, those remaining Judges of the Chamber may order	(A) If (i) a Judge is, for illness or other urgent personal reasons, or for reasons of authorised Tribunal business, unable to continue sitting in a part-heard case for a period which is likely to be of short duration, and (ii) the remaining Judges of the Chamber are satisfied that it is in the interests of justice to do so, those remaining Judges of the Chamber may order

that the hearing of the case continue in the absence of that Judge for a period of not more than five working days.
(B) If
(i) a Judge is, for illness or urgent personal reasons, or for reasons of authorised Tribunal business, unable to continue sitting in a part-heard case for a period which is likely to be of short duration, and
(ii) the remaining Judges of the Chamber are not satisfied that it is in the interests of justice to order that the hearing of the case continue in the absence of that Judge, then
    (a) those remaining Judges of the Chamber may nevertheless conduct those matters which they are satisfied it is in the interests of justice that they be disposed of notwithstanding the absence of that Judge, and
    (b) the Presiding Judge may adjourn the proceedings.
(C) If, by reason of death, illness, resignation from the Tribunal, or non-reelection, a Judge is unable to continue sitting in a part-heard case for a period which is likely to be longer than of a short duration, the Presiding Judge shall report to the President who may assign another Judge to the case and order either a rehearing or continuation of the proceedings from that point. However, after the opening statements provided for in Rule 84, or the beginning of the presentation of evidence pursuant to Rule 85, the continuation of the proceedings can only be ordered with the consent of the accused, except as provided for in paragraph (D).
(D) If, in the circumstances mentioned in the last sentence of paragraph (C), the accused withholds his consent, the remaining Judges may nonetheless decide to continue the proceedings before a Trial Chamber with a substitute Judge if, taking all the circumstances into account, they determine unanimously that doing so would serve the interests of justice. This decision is subject to appeal directly to a full bench of the Appeals Chamber by either party. If no appeal is taken or the Appeals

that the hearing of the case continue in the absence of that Judge for a period of not more than five working days.
(B) If
(i) a Judge is, for illness or other urgent personal reasons, or for reasons of authorised Tribunal business, unable to continue sitting in a part-heard case for a period which is likely to be of short duration, and
(ii) the remaining Judges of the Chamber are not satisfied that it is in the interests of justice to order that the hearing of the case continue in the absence of that Judge, then
    (a) those remaining Judges of the Chamber may nevertheless conduct those matters which they are satisfied should be disposed of in the interests of justice, notwithstanding the absence of that Judge, and
    (b) the Presiding Judge may adjourn the proceedings.
(C) If a Judge is, for any reason, unable to continue sitting in a part-heard case for a period which is likely to be longer than of a short duration, the Presiding Judge shall report to the President who may assign another Judge to the case and order either a rehearing or continuation of the proceedings from that point. However, after the opening statements provided for in Rule 84, or the beginning of the presentation of evidence pursuant to Rule 85, the continuation of the proceedings can only be ordered with the consent of the accused.
(D) In case of illness or an unfilled vacancy or in any other similar circumstances, the President may, if satisfied that it is in the interests of justice to do so, authorise a Chamber to conduct routine matters, such as the delivery of decisions, in the absence of one or more of its members.

Chamber affirms the decision of the Trial Chamber, the President shall assign to the existing bench a Judge, who, however, can join the bench only after he or she has certified that he or she has familiarised himself or herself with the record of the proceedings. Only one substitution under this paragraph may be made.

(E) Appeals under paragraph (D) shall be filed within seven days of filing of the impugned decision. When such decision is rendered orally, this time-limit shall run from the date of the oral decision, unless

    (i) the party challenging the decision was not present or represented when the decision was pronounced, in which case the time-limit shall run from the date on which the challenging party is notified of the oral decision; or

    (ii) the Trial Chamber has indicated that a written decision will follow, in which case, the time-limit shall run from filing of the written decision.

2.1.75 ICTY Rule 15 *bis* was adopted on 30 November 1999, after the twenty-first plenary session. The words, "or for reasons of authorised Tribunal business," were added to paras. (A) and (B) on 19 January 2001, after the twenty-third plenary session. New paras. (D) and (E) were added after the twenty-seventh plenary session on 12 December 2002.

History of ICTR Rule 15 *bis*

2.1.76 This rule was adopted by the ICTR at the tenth plenary session on 30–31 May, 2001.

Trial Chamber Sitting in Absence of Member

2.1.77 The old Rule 15 *bis* (D), which authorised a Trial Chamber to sit without one of its members, was amended after the twenty-seventh plenary session. The rule now provides for a "substitute judge" and more elaborate procedures for replacement of a judge.

Delivery of Decisions

2.1.78 See *Order of the President authorising the Appeals Chamber to conduct a matter in the absence of one of its members* of 2 July 1999 in *Tadić*.

Hearing of Witnesses

2.1.79 The hearing of witnesses is not a routine matter for the purposes of Rule 15 *bis* (D). *See* the Appeals Chamber's *Decision on Appeal by Dragan Papić against ruling to proceed by deposition* of 15 July 1999.

2.1.80

ICTY RULE 16 RESIGNATION	ICTR RULE 16 RESIGNATION
A Judge who decides to resign shall communicate his resignation in writing to the President who shall transmit it to the Secretary-General of the United Nations.	A Judge who decides to resign shall communicate his resignation in writing to the President who shall transmit it to the Secretary-General of the United Nations.

Resignations

2.1.81 To date, there have been a number of resignations at the ICTY and ICTR. Reference may be made to earlier editions of this work for details and to the tribunals' websites and annual reports.

2.1.82

ICTY RULE 17 PRECEDENCE	ICTR RULE 17 PRECEDENCE
(A) All Judges are equal in the exercise of their judicial functions, regardless of dates of election, appointment, age or period of service. (B) The Presiding Judges of the Trial Chambers shall take precedence according to age after the President and the Vice-President. (C) Permanent Judges elected or appointed on different dates shall take precedence according to the dates of their election or appointment; Judges elected or appointed on the same date shall take precedence according to age.	(A) All Judges are equal in the exercise of their judicial functions, regardless of dates of election, appointment, age or period of service. (B) The Presiding Judges of the Chambers shall take precedence according to the dates of their election or appointment as judges, after the President and the Vice-President. Presiding judges elected or appointed on the same date shall take precedence according to age. (C) Judges elected or appointed on different dates shall take precedence according to the dates of their election or appointment; Judges elected or appointed on the same date shall take precedence according to age.

(D) In case of re-election, the total period of service as a Judge of the Tribunal shall be taken into account. (E) *Ad litem* Judges shall take precedence after the permanent Judges according to the dates of their appointment. *Ad litem* Judges appointed on the same date shall take precedence according to age.	(D) In case of re-election, the total period of service as a Judge of the Tribunal shall be taken into account.

History of ICTY Rule 17

2.1.83 This rule has been amended in light of the institution of *ad litem* judges (see above, 2.1.12). It differs from ICTR Rule 17 in having an additional para. (E).

PRESIDENT, VICE-PRESIDENT, AND THE BUREAU

2.1.84

ICTY RULE 18 ELECTION OF THE PRESIDENT	ICTR RULE 18 ELECTION OF THE PRESIDENT
(A) The President shall be elected for a term of two years, or such shorter term as shall coincide with the duration of his term of office as a Judge. He may be re-elected once. (B) If the President ceases to be a member of the Tribunal or resigns his office before the expiration of his term, the Judges shall elect from among their number a successor for the remainder of the term. (C) The President shall be elected by a majority of the votes of the Judges composing the Tribunal. If no Judge obtains such a majority, the second ballot shall be limited to the two Judges who obtained the greatest number of votes on the first ballot. In the case of equality of votes on the second ballot, the Judge who takes precedence in accordance with Rule 17 shall be declared elected.	(A) The President shall be elected for a term of two years, or such shorter term as shall coincide with the duration of his term of office as a Judge. He may be re-elected once. (B) If the President ceases to be a member of the Tribunal or resigns his office before the expiration of his term, the Judges shall elect from among their number a successor for the remainder of the term. (C) The President shall be elected by a majority of the votes of the Judges composing the Tribunal. If no Judge obtains such a majority, the second ballot shall be limited to the two Judges who obtained the greatest number of votes on the first ballot. In the case of equality of votes on the second ballot, the Judge who takes precedence in accordance with Rule 17 shall be declared elected.

2.1.85

ICTY RULE 19 FUNCTIONS OF THE PRESIDENT	ICTR RULE 19 FUNCTIONS OF THE PRESIDENT
(A) The President shall preside at all plenary meetings of the Tribunal. The President shall coordinate the work of the Chambers and supervise the activities of the Registry as well as exercise all the other functions conferred on him by the Statute and the Rules. (B) The President may from time to time, and in consultation with the Bureau, the Registrar and the Prosecutor, issue Practice Directions, consistent with the Statute and the Rules, addressing detailed aspects of the conduct of proceedings before the Tribunal.	(A) The President shall preside at all plenary meetings of the Tribunal, co-ordinate the work of the Chambers and supervise the activities of the Registry as well as exercise all the other functions conferred on him by the Statute and the Rules. (B) The President may, in consultation with the Bureau, the Registrar, and the Prosecutor, issue Practice Directions, consistent with the Statute and the Rules, addressing detailed aspects of the conduct of proceedings before the Tribunal.

History of ICTY Rule 19

2.1.86 Sub-Rule (B), introducing "Practice Directions," was added to Rule 19 at the thirteenth plenary session on 25 July 1997.

Rule 19(A): Coordinating the Work of the Chambers

2.1.87 As an example of an Order issued pursuant to this Rule, see *Order on Defence Motion to Vacate the Indictment Confirmation* issued by President McDonald in *Kovačević* on 2 July 1998.

Practice Directions

2.1.88 The following Practice Directions have been issued by the ICTY President pursuant to ICTY Rule 19(B):

- *Practice Direction on the Procedure for the International Tribunal's Designation of the State in which a Convicted Person is to serve his/her Sentence of Imprisonment.* 9 July 1998.
- *Practice Direction on the Procedure for the Determination of Applications for Pardon, Commutation of Sentence and early release of Persons convicted by the International Tribunal* (IT/146). 7 April 1999.
- *Practice Direction on Procedure for the Proposal, Consideration of and Publication of Amendments to the Rules of Procedure and Evidence of the International Tribunal.* Revision 2, 24 January 2002.
- *Practice Direction on Procedure for the Filing of written Submissions in Appeal Proceedings before the International Tribunal* (IT/155). 1 October 1999. Revision 1, 7 March 2002.

- *Practice Direction on Formal Requirements for Appeals from Judgement,* 7 March 2002
- *Practice Direction on the Procedure for Amending Regulations Issued by the Registrar,* 12 July 2002.
- *Practice Direction on Procedure for the Implementation of Rule 92bis(b) of The Rules of Procedure and Evidence,* 20 July 2001.
- *Practice Direction on the Length of Briefs and Motions* (IT/184). 19 January, 2001. *Revision 1,* 5 March 2002. This Practice Direction has been applied to refuse to consider a Motion as filed (*Hadžihasanović et al.,* Pre-Trial Judge Mumba, *Order on Motion Not in Compliance with Practice Direction,* 9 November, 2001).

2.1.89   The following Practice Directions have been issued at the ICTR:

- *Practice Direction on Formal Requirements for Appeals from Judgement,* 16 September 2002.
- *Practice Direction on Procedure for the filing of written submissions in appeal proceedings before the Tribunal,* 16 September 2002.
- *Practice Direction on the Length of Briefs and Motions on Appeal,* 16 September 2002.

Practice Directions Cannot Be Used as a Form of Appeal

2.1.90   In his *Decision on the Application of the Defence to the President of the Tribunal of 8 July 1998* of 14 July 1998, Vice-President Shahabudeen ruled that, "the competence thereby conferred [by rule 19(B)] on the President to issue Practice Directions addressing detailed aspects of the conduct of proceedings before the International Tribunal does not include competence to entertain an appeal from a ruling in a case...." Practice Directions should thus deal with general matters and not aim to resolve a specific issue arising in a particular case.

2.1.91

ICTY RULE 20 THE VICE-PRESIDENT	ICTR RULE 20 THE VICE-PRESIDENT
(A) The Vice-President shall be elected for a term of two years, or such shorter term as shall coincide with the duration of his term of office as a Judge. He may be re-elected once. (B) The Vice-President may sit as a member of a Trial Chamber or of the Appeals Chamber. (C) Sub-rules 18(B) and (C) shall apply mutatis mutandis to the Vice-President.	(A) The Vice-President shall be elected for a term of two years, or such shorter term as shall coincide with the duration of his term of office as a Judge. He may be re-elected once. (B) Rules 18(B) and (C) shall apply mutatis mutandis to the Vice-President.

2.1.92

ICTY RULE 21 FUNCTIONS OF THE VICE-PRESIDENT	ICTR RULE 21 FUNCTIONS OF THE VICE-PRESIDENT
Subject to Sub-rule 22(B), the Vice-President shall exercise the functions of the President in case of his absence or inability to act.	The Vice-President shall exercise the functions of the President in case of his absence or inability to act.

2.1.93 For an example of the Vice-President exercising the functions of the President where the latter was unable to act, see the *Order of the Vice-President for the Assignment of Judges to the Appeals Chamber* of 20 January 1999 in *Delalić et al.*

2.1.94

ICTY RULE 22 REPLACEMENTS	ICTR RULE 22 REPLACEMENTS
(A) If neither the President nor the Vice-President remains in office or is able to carry out the functions of the President, these shall be assumed by the senior Judge, determined in accordance with Rule 17 (C). (B) If the President is unable to exercise his functions as Presiding Judge of the Appeals Chamber, that Chamber shall elect a Presiding Judge from among its number. (C) The President and the Vice-President, if still permanent Judges, shall continue to discharge their functions after the expiration of their terms until the election of the President and the Vice-President has taken place.	If neither the President nor the Vice-President can carry out the functions of the President, these shall be assumed by the senior Judge of the Trial Chambers, determined in accordance with Rule 17.

History of ICTY Rule 22

2.1.95 This rule was amended, with the words, "remains in office or is able to" being substituted for the word, "can" in paragraph (A) and paragraph (C) being added, on 19 July, 2001, after the twenty-fourth plenary session.

2.1.96 See the commentary to ICTY Article 14 ("Officers and members of the Chambers").

2.1.97 For an Order made pursuant to this rule, see *Order on the Request to the President on the Composition of the Bench of the Appeals Chamber* of 12 February 1999 made by Judge May, replacing the President and Vice-President and holding that "it is improper for counsel to address the composition of any bench of the Chambers of the International Tribunal," after the accused had requested that a Judge of a "major Common Law jurisdiction, specifically England, Canada or the United States, preside over the panel at the hearing of this appeal."

2.1.98

ICTY RULE 23 THE BUREAU	ICTR RULE 23 THE BUREAU
(A) The Bureau shall be composed of the President, the Vice-President and the Presiding Judges of the Trial Chambers. (B) The President shall consult the other members of the Bureau on all major questions relating to the functioning of the Tribunal. (C) The President may consult with the *ad litem* Judges on matters to be discussed in the Bureau and may invite a representative of the *ad litem* Judges to attend Bureau meetings. (D) A Judge may draw the attention of any member of the Bureau to issues that the Judge considers ought to be discussed by the Bureau or submitted to a plenary meeting of the Tribunal. (D) If any member of the Bureau is unable to carry out any of the functions of the Bureau, these shall be assumed by the senior available Judge determined in accordance with Rule 17.	(A) The Bureau shall be composed of the President, the Vice-President and the Presiding Judges of the Trial Chambers. (B) The President shall consult the other members of the Bureau on all major questions relating to the functioning of the Tribunal. (C) A Judge may draw the attention of any member of the Bureau to issues that in his opinion ought to be discussed by the Bureau or submitted to a plenary meeting of the Tribunal.

History of ICTY Rule 23

2.1.99 Pursuant to ICTY Rule 6(B) and paragraph 7 of the Practice Direction of 18 December 1998, a new para. (D) was added to ICTY Rule 23 by unanimous written approval of all the Judges of the ICTY. The amendment entered into force on 25 February 1999.

Decisions of the Bureau

2.1.100 The Bureau has rendered a large number of decisions on a variety of issues, in particular concerning the disqualification of judges pursuant to Rule 15(B) (see 2.1.63). The Bureau has declined competence on motions concerning remuneration of counsel (Bureau, *Decision*, 8 June 2000).

Other Tasks of the Bureau

2.1.101 Under the Rules of Detention, the Bureau may, at any time, appoint a Judge or the Registrar of the Tribunal to inspect the detention unit and to report to the Tribunal on the general conditions or on any particular aspect of the implementation of the Rules of Detention.

2.1.102

> **ICTY**
> **RULE 23 *bis***
> **THE COORDINATION COUNCIL**
>
> (A) The Coordination Council shall be composed of the President, the Prosecutor and the Registrar.
> (B) In order to achieve the mission of the Tribunal, as defined in the Statute, the Coordination Council ensures, having due regard for the responsibilities and independence of any member, the coordination of the activities of the three organs of the Tribunal.
> (C) The Coordination Council shall meet once a month at the initiative of the President. A member may at any time request that additional meetings be held. The President shall chair the meetings.
> (D) The Vice-President, the Deputy Prosecutor and the Deputy Registrar may *ex officio* represent respectively, the President, the Prosecutor and the Registrar.

History of ICTY Rule 23 *bis*

2.1.103 This new rule was adopted on 19 January 2001, after the twenty-third plenary session.

2.1.104

> **ICTY**
> **RULE 23 *ter***
> **THE MANAGEMENT COMMITTEE**
>
> (A) The Management Committee shall be composed of the President, the Vice-President, a Judge elected by the Judges in plenary session for a one year renewable mandate, the Registrar, the Deputy Registrar and the Chief of Administration.
> (B) The Management Committee shall assist the President with respect to the functions set forth in Rules 19 and 33, concerning in particular, all Registry activities relating to the administrative and judicial support provided to the Chambers and to the Judges. To this end, the Management Committee shall coordinate the preparation and implementation of the budget of the Tribunal with the exception of budgetary lines specific to the activities of the Office of the Prosecutor.
> (C) The Management Committee shall meet twice a month at the initiative of the President. Two members may at any time request that additional meetings be held. The President shall chair the meetings.
> (D) In the performance of its functions, the Management Committee may call on the services of one or several advisers or experts.

History of ICTY Rule 23 *ter*

2.1.105 This new rule was adopted on 19 January 2001, after the twenty-third plenary session.

PLENARY MEETINGS

2.1.106

ICTY RULE 24 PLENARY MEETINGS OF THE TRIBUNAL	ICTR RULE 24 PLENARY MEETINGS OF THE TRIBUNAL
The Judges shall meet in plenary to: (i) elect the President and Vice-President; (ii) adopt and amend the Rules; (iii) adopt the Annual Report provided for in Article 34 of the Statute; (iv) decide upon matters relating to the internal functioning of the Chambers and the Tribunal; (v) determine or supervise the conditions of detention; (vi) exercise any other functions provided for in the Statute or in the Rules.	The Judges shall meet in plenary to: (i) elect the President and Vice-President; (ii) adopt and amend the Rules; (iii) adopt the Annual Report provided for in Article 32 of the Statute; (iv) decide upon matters relating to the internal functioning of the Chambers and the Tribunal; (v) determine or supervise the conditions of detention; (vi) exercise any other functions provided for in the Statute or in the Rules.

2.1.107

ICTY RULE 25 DATES OF PLENARY SESSIONS	ICTR RULE 25 DATES OF PLENARY SESSIONS
(A) The dates of the plenary sessions of the Tribunal shall normally be agreed upon in July of each year for the following calendar year. (B) Other plenary meetings shall be convened by the President if so requested by at least eight Judges, and may be convened whenever the exercise of his functions under the Statute or the Rules so requires.	(A) The dates of the plenary sessions of the Tribunal shall normally be agreed upon in July of each year for the following calendar year. (B) Other plenary meetings shall be convened by the President if so requested by at least six Judges, and may be convened whenever the exercise of his functions under the Statute or the Rules so requires.

History of ICTY Rule 25

2.1.108 Rule 25(B) was amended at the ICTY nineteenth plenary session, on 17 December 1998, from a reference to "six Judges" to the present reference to "eight Judges," to reflect the fact that a new Trial Chamber of three Judges had since been added to the Tribunal, bringing the number of Judges from eleven to fourteen.

2.1.109

ICTY RULE 26 QUORUM AND VOTE	ICTR RULE 26 QUORUM AND VOTE
(A) The quorum for each plenary meeting of the Tribunal shall be ten permanent Judges. (B) Subject to Rules 6(A), (B) and 18(C), the decisions of the plenary meetings of the Tribunal shall be taken by the majority of the Judges present. In the event of an equality of votes, the President or the Judge acting in the place of the President shall have a casting vote.	(A) The quorum for each plenary meeting of the Tribunal shall be ten Judges. (B) Subject to Rule 6(A) and (B) and Rule 18(C), the decisions of the plenary meetings of the Tribunal shall be taken by the majority of the Judges present. In the event of an equality of votes, the President or the Judge who acts in his place shall have a casting vote.

History of ICTY Rule 26

2.1.110 Rule 26(A) was amended at the ICTY's nineteenth plenary session, on 17 December 1998, from a reference to "seven Judges" to the present reference to "nine Judges," no doubt to reflect the fact that a new Trial Chamber of three Judges had since been added to the Tribunal, bringing the number of Judges from eleven to fourteen. Rule 26(B) was amended at the same plenary session to render the language gender-neutral.

ROTATION OF JUDGES AND DELIBERATIONS

2.1.111

ICTY RULE 27 ROTATION	ICTR RULE 27 ROTATION
(A) Permanent Judges shall rotate on a regular basis between the Trial Chambers and the Appeals Chamber. Rotation shall take into account the efficient disposal of cases. (B) The Judges shall take their places in their new Chamber as soon as the President thinks it convenient, having regard to the disposal of part-heard cases. (C) The President may at any time temporarily assign a member of a Trial Chamber or of the Appeals Chamber to another Chamber.	(A) Judges shall rotate on a regular basis between the Trial Chambers. Rotation shall take into account the efficient disposal of cases. (B) The Judges shall take their places in their new Chamber as soon as the President thinks it convenient, having regard to the disposal of part-heard cases. (C) The President may at any time temporarily assign a member of a Trial Chamber to the other Trial Chamber.

ICTY Rule 27 and ICTR Rule 27

2.1.112 ICTY Rule 27 and ICTR Rule 27 are the same except that the references in the latter to the Appeals Chamber have been omitted, since ICTR Trial Chamber Judges do not rotate into the Appeals Chamber. Also the word, "permanent" was added to ICTY Rule 27(A) after the introduction of *ad litem* judges.

2.1.113 The practice of rotation of judges, although dictated by necessity at the ICTY and ICTR, there being an insufficient number of judges at the outset, has been much-criticised, principally on the basis that the authority of the appellate instance is lost where its judiciary is indistinct from the first instance judiciary. In that case, whence does its authority to overrule the trial chamber derive, apart from its greater numbers (five appeals judges versus three trials judges)? Moreover, even this numerical advantage is to no avail where both the Chambers are split. For example, if the Trial Chamber ruled unanimously that a conflict was international, and on appeal, the Appeals Chamber ruled 3 to 2 that it was internal, then 5 judges would have considered the conflict international and 4 judges that it was internal. Yet the (overall minority) opinion of the Appeals Chamber majority that the conflict was internal would prevail, due neither to (overall) numerical majority nor to any greater seniority on the part of the Appeals Chamber.

2.1.114 Indeed this scenario materialised to some degree in the *Tadić Jurisdiction Decision* and the *Tadić Jurisdiction Appeals Decision*. Three (trial) judges considered that the question of internationality did not matter (Judges McDonald, Stephen and Vohrah), and they were in some sense joined by Judge Li in the Appeals Chamber who held that the conflict as a whole was international and therefore did not need to be proved case-by-case. Judge Abi-Saab occupied an intermediate position. Yet the majority view in the Appeals Chamber (Judges Cassese, Sidhwa and Deschenes) prevailed, namely that the question of internationality had to be proved, case-by-case, at trial. Again, this was a somewhat anomalous result (see 4.2.319, on the internationality of the conflict).

2.1.115

ICTY RULE 28 REVIEWING AND DUTY JUDGES	ICTR RULE 28 DUTY JUDGES
(A) On receipt of an indictment for review from the Prosecutor, the Registrar shall consult with the President who shall designate one of the permanent Trial Chamber Judges for the review. (B) The President, in consultation with the Judges, shall maintain a roster designating one Judge as duty Judge for the assigned period of seven days. The duty Judge shall be available at all times, including out of normal Registry hours, for dealing with applications pursuant to Sub-rules (C) and (D) but may	Every six months and after consultation with the Judges, the President shall, designate for each month of the next six months one Judge from each Trial Chamber to whom indictments, warrants, and other submissions not pertaining to a case already assigned to a Chamber, shall be transmitted for review. The duty roster shall be published by the Registrar. However, in exceptional circumstances, a Judge on duty may request another Judge of the same Chamber to replace him, after having informed the President and the Registrar.

refuse to deal with any application out of normal Registry hours if not satisfied as to its urgency. The roster of duty Judges shall be published by the Registrar.

(C) All applications in a case not otherwise assigned to a Chamber, other than the review of indictments, shall be transmitted to the duty Judge. Where accused are jointly indicted, a submission relating only to an accused who is not in the custody of the Tribunal, other than an application to amend or withdraw part of the indictment pursuant to Rule 50 or Rule 51, shall be transmitted to the duty Judge, notwithstanding that the case has already been assigned to a Chamber in respect of some or all of the co-accused of that accused. The duty Judge shall act pursuant to Rule 54 in dealing with applications under this Rule.

(D) Where a case has already been assigned to a Trial Chamber:
(i) where an application is made out of normal Registry hours, the application shall be dealt with by the duty Judge if satisfied as to its urgency;
(ii) where the application is made within the normal Registry hours and the Trial Chamber is unavailable, it shall be dealt with by the duty Judge if satisfied as to its urgency or that it is otherwise appropriate to do so in the absence of the Trial Chamber.

In such case, the Registry shall serve a copy of all orders or decisions issued by the duty Judge in connection therewith on the Chamber to which the matter is assigned.

(E) During periods of court recess, regardless of the Chamber to which he or she is assigned, in addition to applications made pursuant to paragraph (D) above, the duty Judge may:
(i) take decisions on provisional detention pursuant to Rule 40 *bis*;
(ii) conduct the initial appearance of an accused pursuant to Rule 62.

The provisions of this Rule shall apply *mutatis mutandis* to applications before the Appeals Chamber.

History of ICTY Rule 28

2.1.116 Rule 28 was amended at the ICTY fifth plenary session in January 1995 "to improve the working of the Tribunal" (ICTY second Annual Report, para. 24) by providing for the monthly assignment of *one* Judge from *each Trial Chamber*, thereby spreading the work-load evenly between the two Trial Chambers.

2.1.117 This Rule was again amended at the ICTY tenth plenary session on 22–23 April 1996, adding paras. (B) and (C) and modifying the first paragraph, which had previously read, "The President shall, in July of each year and after consultation with the Judges, assign for each month of the next calendar year one Judge from each Trial Chamber as the Judges to whom indictments shall be transmitted for review under Rule 47, and shall publish the list of assignments."

2.1.118 This Rule was substantially amended at the ICTY fourteenth plenary session on 12 November 1997 (see Revision 11 of the ICTY Rules of Procedure and Evidence, or ICTR Rule 28, for comparison).

2.1.119 Rule 28 was again amended at the ICTY twenty-first plenary session on 30 November 1999. Among other changes, the title was changed from "Duty Judge" to "Reviewing and Duty Judges." Para. (E) was added to Rule 28 at the twenty-second plenary session, effective 2 August 2000.

2.1.120 The Rule was amended at the twenty-fifth plenary session held on 12 and 13 December 2001. The words, "other than an application to amend or withdraw part of the indictment pursuant to Rule 50 or Rule 51," were added to Rule 28(C). Para. (D) was substantially amended. The words, "in addition to applications made pursuant to paragraph (D) above," and, "the provisions of this Rule shall apply *mutatis mutandis* to applications before the Appeals Chamber," were added to para. (E).

History of ICTR Rule 28

2.1.121 This rule was amended to change "fortnight" to "month" at the eighth plenary session on 26 June, 2000.

Powers and Duties of "Duty Judge"

2.1.122 The powers and duties of the Duty Judge were considered by the Appeals Chamber in *Krajisnik, Decision on Interlocutory Appeal by Momčilo Krajisnik*, 26 February 2002. The Appeals Chamber held that Rule 28(D) must be read consistently with what is clearly intended by Rule 28(B) which contemplates that the Duty Judge will have the power, during normal Registry hours, to deal with applications in cases that have already been assigned to a Trial Chamber.

2.1.123 The Appeals Chamber held that the Trial Chamber will normally be in a better position to deal with any issue arising which requires a detailed knowledge of the case. However, where it is appropriate for the Duty Judge to deal with the issue, he should do so unless it is non-urgent.

2.1.124 To assist with determining whether an issue is urgent, the Appeals Chamber established two cumulative conditions:

1. whether the relief sought can only be granted if the application is determined at a time before the Trial Chamber is available to determine it;
2. whether the applicant would suffer significant prejudice if the application is not determined within that time.

2.1.125 Where an application in a case already assigned to a Trial Chamber cannot be dealt with by the Trial Chamber and if the Duty Judge seized of the matter refuses to deal with it since it failed to satisfy him as to its urgency, the only ruling the Duty Judge should make is refusal to examine the issue. See also *Jokić and Ademi, Decision on the Defence Motions for Provisional Release*, 21 December 2001, in which Judge Orie examined the powers of the duty judge to consider and order provisional release.

2.1.126

ICTY RULE 29 DELIBERATIONS	ICTR RULE 29 DELIBERATIONS
The deliberations of the Chambers shall take place in private and remain secret.	The deliberations of the Chambers shall take place in private and remain secret.

SECTION 2: THE REGISTRY

2.2.1

ICTY ARTICLE 17 THE REGISTRY	ICTR ARTICLE 17 THE REGISTRY
1. The Registry shall be responsible for the administration and servicing of the International Tribunal. 2. The Registry shall consist of a Registrar and such other staff as may be required. 3. The Registrar shall be appointed by the Secretary-General after consultation with the President of the International Tribunal. He or she shall serve for a four-year term and be eligible for reappointment. The terms and conditions of service of the Registrar shall be those of an Assistant Secretary-General of the United Nations. 4. The staff of the Registry shall be appointed by the Secretary-General on the recommendation of the Registrar.	1. The Registry shall be responsible for the administration and servicing of the International Tribunal for Rwanda. 2. The Registry shall consist of a Registrar and such other staff as may be required. 3. The Registrar shall be appointed by the Secretary-General after consultation with the President of the International Tribunal for Rwanda. He or she shall serve for a four-year term and be eligible for reappointment. The terms and conditions of service of the Registrar shall be those of an Assistant Secretary-General of the United Nations. 4. The staff of the Registry shall be appointed by the Secretary-General on the recommendation of the Registrar.

2.2.2

ICTY RULE 30 APPOINTMENT OF THE REGISTRAR	ICTR RULE 30 APPOINTMENT OF THE REGISTRAR
The President shall seek the opinion of the Judges on the candidates for the post of Registrar, before consulting with the Secretary-General of the United Nations pursuant to Article 17(3) of the Statute.	The President shall seek the opinion of the Judges on the candidates for the post of Registrar, before consulting with the Secretary-General of the United Nations pursuant to Article 16(3) of the Statute.

2.2.3

ICTY RULE 31 APPOINTMENT OF THE DEPUTY REGISTRAR AND REGISTRY STAFF	ICTR RULE 31 APPOINTMENT OF THE DEPUTY REGISTRAR AND REGISTRY STAFF
The Registrar, after consultation with the Bureau, shall make his recommendations to the Secretary-General of the United Nations for the appointment of the Deputy Registrar and other Registry staff.	The Registrar, after consultation with the President, shall make his recommendations to the Secretary-General of the United Nations for the appointment of the Deputy Registrar and other Registry staff.

2.2.4

ICTY RULE 32 SOLEMN DECLARATION	ICTR RULE 32 SOLEMN DECLARATION
(A) Before taking up his duties, the Registrar shall make the following declaration before the President: "I solemnly declare that I will perform the duties incumbent upon me as Registrar of the International Tribunal for the Prosecution of Persons Responsible for Serious Violations of International Humanitarian Law Committed in the Territory of the Former Yugoslavia since 1991 in all loyalty, discretion and good conscience and that I will faithfully observe all the provisions of the Statute and the Rules of Procedure and Evidence of the Tribunal." (B) Before taking up his duties, the Deputy Registrar shall make a similar declaration before the President. (C) Every staff member of the Registry shall make a similar declaration before the Registrar.	(A) Before taking up his duties, the Registrar shall make the following declaration before the President: "I solemnly declare that I will perform the duties incumbent upon me as Registrar of the International Criminal Tribunal for the Prosecution of Persons Responsible for Genocide and other Serious Violations of International Humanitarian Law Committed in the Territory of Rwanda and Rwandan Citizens responsible for Genocide and other such violations committed in the territory of neighbouring States, between 1 January 1994 and 31 December 1994, in all loyalty, discretion and good conscience and that I will faithfully observe all the provisions of the Statute and the Rules of Procedure and Evidence of the Tribunal." (B) Before taking up his duties, the Deputy Registrar shall make a similar declaration before the President. (C) Every staff member of the Registry shall make a similar declaration before the Registrar.

2.2.5

ICTY RULE 33 FUNCTIONS OF THE REGISTRAR	ICTR RULE 33 FUNCTIONS OF THE REGISTRAR
(A) The Registrar shall assist the Chambers, the plenary meetings of the Tribunal, the Judges and the Prosecutor in the performance of their functions. Under the authority of the President, he shall be responsible for the administration and servicing of the Tribunal and shall serve as its channel of communication. (B) The Registrar, in the execution of his or her functions, may make oral and written representations to the President or Chambers on any issue arising in the context of a specific case which affects or may affect the discharge of such functions, including that of implementing judicial decisions, with notice to the parties where necessary.	(A) The Registrar shall assist the Chambers, the Plenary Meetings of the Tribunal, the Judges and the Prosecutor in the performance of their functions. Under the authority of the President, he shall be responsible for the administration and servicing of the Tribunal and shall serve as its channel of communication. (B) The Registrar, in the execution of his functions, may make oral or written representations to Chambers on any issue arising in the context of a specific case which affects or may affect the discharge of such functions, including that of implementing judicial decisions, with notice to the parties where necessary.

| (C) The Registrar shall report regularly on his or her activities to the Judges meeting in plenary and to the Prosecutor. | (C) The Registrar may, in consultation with the President of the Tribunal and the Presiding Judge of the Appeals Chamber, as the case may be, issue Practice Directions addressing particular aspects of the practice and procedure in the Registry of the Tribunal and in respect of other matters within the powers of the Registrar. |

History of ICTY Rule 33

2.2.6 Para. (B) was added at the ICTY twenty-first plenary session on 30 November 1999. The words, "the President or" were added to this para. on 19 January 2001, after the twenty-third plenary session. At the same time, para. (C) was added. The Registrar had already, from the earliest plenary sessions, been reporting on his or her activities to the Judges meeting in plenary, but the provision that the Registrar should report regularly to the Prosecutor is novel, and indeed curious.

ICTY Registrars

2.2.7 The Secretary-General appointed Professor Theodor Cornelis van Boven as Acting Registrar on 1 January 1994 and appointed him Registrar on 1 July 1994. Professor van Boven served until December 1994.

2.2.8 The Secretary-General appointed Mrs. Dorothee Margarete Elisabeth de Sampayo Garrido-Nijgh on 29 December 1994. Mrs. de Sampayo Garrido-Nijgh succeeded Professor van Boven on 1 January 1995.

2.2.9 On 11 December 2000, the United Nations Secretary-General, Mr. Kofi Annan, announced that Mr. Henry Hans Holthuis would succeed Mrs. de Sampayo Garrido-Nijgh as the ICTY Registrar.

Directive and Instructions for the ICTY Registry

2.2.10 The ICTY Judges approved a "Directive for the Registry" at the ICTY's eleventh plenary on 25 June 1996. The Directive, and the more detailed "Instructions for the Registry," provides guidance to Registry staff on the performance of their duties.

ICTR Registrars

2.2.11 On 8 September 1995, Mr. Andronico O. Adede (Kenya) was appointed Registrar of the ICTR. Mr. Agwu U. Okali (Nigeria) replaced Mr. Adede on 26 February 1997. Mr. Adama Dieng (Senegal) replaced Mr. Okali upon the completion of the latter's mandate at the end of February 2001.

Purpose of the Registry

2.2.12 The Registry, in addition to its court management functions, administers a legal aid system of assigning defence counsel to indigent accused, manages a unit for the protection of victims and witnesses, superintends the United Nations Detention Unit and maintains diplomatic contact with States and Embassies. It thus combines the diverse roles played in a national system by court registry, legal aid board, social workers, prisons service and diplomatic corps.

2.2.13 The *Paschke Report*, (A/51/789, annex) affirmed that "the Registry is not an independent body in itself and its objective is to service the two other organs of the Tribunal" (Second Annual Report, paragraph 58).

Orders Addressed to the Registry

2.2.14 A Judge or Chamber is competent to issue orders addressed to the Registry or Registrar. For example, in *Đukić*, the Trial Chamber orally ordered the Registrar to procure medical examinations of the accused (Transcripts of hearing, 25 March 1996), and in *Krsmanović*, the Trial Chamber, on 29 March 1996, issued an Order of Transfer to the Required State which included an instruction to the Registrar to ensure the transfer of Krsmanović to the authorities of Bosnia and Herzegovina. See also *Decision on Nzirorera's Motion for Withdrawal of Counsel*, 3 October 2001, in which the Trial Chamber stated that allegations of fee-splitting between defence counsel and their clients should be "exhaustively examined by the Tribunal's Registry" (para. 26).

The President's Authority Over the Registrar

2.2.15 Rule 33 provides that:

> Under the authority of the President, (the Registrar) shall be responsible for the administration and servicing of the Tribunal and shall serve as its channel of communication.

2.2.16 The President's authority over the Registrar pursuant to Rule 33 was considered, in the context of the Registrar's management of the Detention Unit, by the Trial Chamber, in its *Decision on the Prosecutor's Motion for the Production of Notes Exchanged Between Zejnil Delalić and Zdravko Mucić*, rendered on 31 October 1996 in *Delalić et al*. Two of the accused allegedly attempted to exchange notes at the United Nations Detention Unit. The Registrar confiscated the notes. On a Motion by the Prosecutor to the Trial Chamber for production of the notes, the Chamber remitted the matter to the President of the Tribunal for determination, for the following reason:

> 29. Decisions of the Registrar are, in certain circumstances, subject to review by the President of the Tribunal. Rule 33 provides for the Registrar to perform her tasks "under the authority of the President." Review by the President of the International Tribunal is also prescribed by the Rules of Detention and the Communications Regulations themselves. . . .

30. The two detainees . . . have not requested such intervention (by the President of the International Tribunal). However, it is clear that they would have the right to seek the intervention of the President if they wished.

31. In all the circumstances, it seems appropriate to the Trial Chamber that a similar right of review of the Registrar's decision should apply with respect to the Prosecution. It seems illogical that one party to a dispute of this nature may seek to have it resolved by one authority, i.e. the Trial Chamber, while the other may have recourse to a different authority, i.e. the President of the Tribunal.

32. The Trial Chamber therefore remits the matter to the President of the International Tribunal for determination.

2.2.17 The President of the Tribunal, Judge Cassese, subsequently adopted this reasoning in his *Decision of the President on the Prosecutor's Motion for the Production of Notes Exchanged Between Zejnil Delalić and Zdravko Mucić*, dated 11 November 1996: "I find that the Trial Chamber took the correct position with regard to this question" (para. 9). Regarding the production of the notes in question, pursuant to Rule 33 and 54 (see below, Rule 54), the President directed the Registrar to produce certified copies of the notes for the Prosecutor and the defence.

2.2.18

ICTY
RULE 33 *bis*
FUNCTIONS OF THE DEPUTY REGISTRAR

(A) The Deputy Registrar shall exercise the functions of the Registrar in the event of the latter's absence from duty or inability to act or upon the Registrar's delegation.
(B) The Deputy Registrar, in consultation with the President, shall in particular:
(i) direct and administer the Chambers Legal Support Section; in particular, in conjunction with the administrative services of the Registrar, the Deputy Registrar shall oversee the assignment of appropriate resources to the Chambers with a view to enabling them to accomplish their mission;
(ii) take all appropriate measures so that the decisions rendered by the Chambers and Judges are executed especially sentences and penalties;
(iii) make recommendations regarding the mission of the Registry which affect the judicial activity of the Tribunal.

History of ICTY Rule 33 *bis*

2.2.19 This new rule was adopted on 19 January 2001, after the twenty-third plenary session.

SECTION 3: VICTIMS AND WITNESSES

2.3.1

ICTY RULE 34 VICTIMS AND WITNESSES SECTION	ICTR RULE 34 VICTIMS AND WITNESSES UNIT
(A) There shall be set up under the authority of the Registrar a Victims and Witnesses Section consisting of qualified staff to: (i) recommend protective measures for victims and witnesses in accordance with Article 22 of the Statute; and (ii) provide counselling and support for them, in particular in cases of rape and sexual assault. (B) Due consideration shall be given, in the appointment of staff, to the employment of qualified women.	(A) There shall be set up under the authority of the Registrar a Victims and Witnesses Unit consisting of qualified staff to: (i) recommend the adoption of protective measures for victims and witnesses in accordance with Article 21 of the Statute; and (ii) ensure that they receive relevant support, including physical and psychological rehabilitation, especially counselling in cases of rape and sexual assault. (iii) develop short and long term plans for the protection of witnesses who have testified before the Tribunal and who fear a threat to their life, property or family. (B) A gender sensitive approach to victims and witnesses protective and support measures should be adopted and due consideration given, in the appointment of staff within this Unit, to the employment of qualified women.

History of ICTY Rule 34

2.3.2   The name of the ICTY Victims and Witnesses *Unit* was changed to the Victims and Witnesses *Section* at the ICTY twentieth plenary session on 30 June 1999–2 July 1999.

History of ICTR Rule 34

2.3.3   Para. (A)(iii) was added to Rule 34 at the Fourth Plenary Session, held in Arusha 1–5 June 1997. The amendment was intended to ensure planning for the protection of witnesses who have testified before the Tribunal. Paras. (A)(i) and (ii) and (B) were amended at the Fifth Plenary Session, held in Arusha 1–8 June 1998.

2.3.4   The *Paschke Report* on the ICTR, dated 6 February 1997, recommended, *inter alia*, that ". . . the Victims and Witnesses Unit, now in the Registry, should be located within the Office of the Prosecutor. . . . The needs of defence witnesses, which could not appropriately be dealt with by the Office of the Prosecutor, could be delegated to the official in the Registry who administers all defence-related matters and who could then call on the experience of the Witness Protection Unit of the Office of the Prosecutor as appropriate" (paragraph 99).

2.3.5 To implement this recommendation, the above Rule would have to be amended. The Statute would not, however, require amendment, as it does not specify that victims and witnesses shall be under the protection of the Registrar, as opposed to that of the Prosecutor. Article 21 merely provides that:

> The International Tribunal for Rwanda shall provide in its rules of procedure and evidence for the protection of victims and witnesses. Such protection measures shall include, but shall not be limited to, the conduct of *in camera* proceedings and the protection of the victim's identity.

Functions of the Victims and Witnesses Section

2.3.6 The Victims and Witnesses Section (VWS) is under the authority of the Registrar of the Tribunal. In formulating its policy for witness support and protection, the Victims and Witnesses Section applies the relevant United Nations standards. Thus the United Nations Declaration of Basic Principles of Justice for Victims of Crime and Abuse of Power formed the basis for the decision to offer witnesses appropriate reimbursement for necessary expenses, including child care, during the period they gave testimony.

2.3.7 The VWS, when so authorised, reviews and redacts transcripts for witness protection purposes. See, e.g., the *Decision on the Prosecutor's Motion requesting protective measures for victims and witnesses*, rendered by the majority of the Trial Chamber in *Tadić* on 10 August 1995.

Impartial Role of the VWS

2.3.8 The VWS should be impartial as between the Prosecutor and the Defence. Its impartiality was called into question in *Delalić et al*, when the Section transmitted a letter from a protected witness, which appeared to implicate one of the accused, to the Prosecution. In its Decision of 19 January 1998, the Trial Chamber did not consider that the Section had acted with any bias:

> 36. ... the Defence raises a public policy issue relating to the role of the Victims and Witnesses Unit, pursuant to which, in any event, it claims the letter should not be admitted in evidence. This argument, which was made with considerable passion by the Defence, appears to the Trial Chamber to be misconceived. The Unit is statutorily recognised, as the Registrar is vested with powers under Rule 34 to establish it. The Unit is common to the parties in the discharge of its functions of ameliorating the problems of all witnesses. It is a neutral unit in the administration of justice.
>
> 37. A witness who receives what he considers to be a threat (sic) letter and who passes such a letter to the Unit, does so in the ordinary course of association with the Unit and its duties towards such a witness. It is only natural and legitimate for the Unit, whose primary function is the protection of victims and witnesses, to inform the relevant Trial Chamber or the Prosecution. This is by no means a biased or partial discharge of its statutory functions in favour of the Prosecution. The Trial Chamber is satisfied that no right of the accused is

necessarily violated and no public policy issue is involved by the conduct such that the Trial Chamber will be required to reject the letter because it was received through the Unit.

2.3.9 While it does seem legitimate for the Victims and Witnesses Section to pass such a letter to the *Trial Chamber*, or to the Registrar, for appropriate action to protect the witness, it is not apparent why it should be legitimate to pass such a letter to the *Prosecution*, whose mandate does not include witness protection (although Rule 39(ii), as amended, does give the Prosecutor the power to take "special measures to provide for the safety of potential witnesses and informants"). Moreover, if the Prosecution then seeks to use the material *as evidence against the accused at trial*, then it is using the material for a different purpose than that for which it was intended, as it is then being used not for witness protection but to secure a conviction against the accused. This is surely improper.

Witness Relocation

2.3.10 On 7 November 1997, the United Kingdom became the first State to enter into an Agreement with the ICTY to relocate Tribunal witnesses who face danger as a result of testifying.

SECTION 4: MINUTES AND RECORDS

2.4.1

ICTY RULE 35 MINUTES	ICTR RULE 35 MINUTES
Except where a full record is made under Rule 81, the Registrar, or Registry staff designated by him, shall take minutes of the plenary meetings of the Tribunal and of the sittings of the Chambers, other than private deliberations.	Except where a full record is made under Rule 81, the Registrar, or Registry staff designated by him, shall take minutes of the plenary meetings of the Tribunal and of the sittings of the Chambers or a Judge, other than private deliberations.

History of ICTR Rule 35

2.4.2 The words, "or a Judge," were added to this Rule at the eighth plenary session on 26 June 2000.

2.4.3 The Court Deputy, who is part of the Registry staff, takes minutes of sittings of the Chambers, although this is not strictly necessary as a full audio-visual record of the proceedings, including *verbatim* transcripts, is made pursuant to Rule 81. See Article 39 of the "Directive for the Registry," adopted by the eleventh plenary on 25 June 1996, and the accompanying "Instructions for the Registry."

2.4.4 Legal officers or law clerks attached to the Chambers usually make minutes of plenary meetings of the Judges.

2.4.5

ICTY RULE 36 RECORD BOOK	ICTR RULE 36 RECORD BOOK
The Registrar shall keep a Record Book which shall list, subject to any Practice direction under Rule 19 or any order of a Judge or Chamber providing for the non-disclosure of any document or information, all the particulars of each case brought before the Tribunal. The Record Book shall be open to the public.	The Registrar shall keep a Record Book which shall list, subject to Rule 53, all the particulars of each case brought before the Tribunal. The Record Book shall be open to the public.

History of ICTY Rule 36

2.4.6 Rule 36 was amended at the ICTY's fifth plenary session in January 1995 to add the words "subject to Rule 53" to clarify that where an indictment or other documents are subject to an order for non-disclosure, the Record Book is also subject to that order.

2.4.7 The Rule was further amended at the ICTY's fourteenth plenary session on 12 November 1997.

SECTION 5: THE PROSECUTOR

2.5.1

ICTY ARTICLE 16 THE PROSECUTOR	ICTR ARTICLE 16 THE PROSECUTOR
1. The Prosecutor shall be responsible for the investigation and prosecution of persons responsible for serious violations of international humanitarian law committed in the territory of the former Yugoslavia since 1 January 1991. 2. The Prosecutor shall act independently as a separate organ of the International Tribunal. He or she shall not seek or receive instructions from any Government or from any other source. 3. The Office of the Prosecutor shall be composed of a Prosecutor and such other qualified staff as may be required. 4. The Prosecutor shall be appointed by the Security Council on nomination by the Secretary-General. He or she shall be of high moral character and possess the highest level of competence and experience in the conduct of investigations and prosecutions of criminal cases. The Prosecutor shall serve for a four-year term and be eligible for reappointment. The terms and conditions of service of the Prosecutor shall be those of an Under-Secretary-General of the United Nations. 5. The staff of the Office of the Prosecutor shall be appointed by the Secretary-General on the recommendation of the Prosecutor.	1. The Prosecutor shall be responsible for the investigation and prosecution of persons responsible for serious violations of international humanitarian law committed in the territory of Rwanda and Rwandan citizens responsible for such violations committed in the territory of neighbouring States, between 1 January 1994 and 31 December 1994. 2. The Prosecutor shall act independently as a separate organ of the International Tribunal for Rwanda. He or she shall not seek or receive instructions from any Government or from any other source. 3. The Prosecutor of the International Tribunal for the Former Yugoslavia shall also serve as the Prosecutor of the International Tribunal for Rwanda. He or she shall have additional staff, including an additional Deputy Prosecutor, to assist with prosecutions before the International Tribunal for Rwanda. Such staff shall be appointed by the Secretary-General on the recommendation of the Prosecutor.

ICTY/ICTR Prosecutor

2.5.2   The Prosecutor is common to the ICTY and ICTR. He or she is responsible for initiating investigations, bringing indictments and presenting the case for the prosecution in court.

2.5.3 Unlike the Judges, who are elected by the General Assembly, the Security Council has reserved for itself the right itself to appoint the Prosecutor, for a four-year, renewable term, on the nomination of the Security Council (Article 16(4) of the ICTY Statute).

2.5.4 By Resolution 877, dated 21 October 1993, the Security Council appointed Mr. Ramon Escovar-Salom (Venezuela) as the first Prosecutor. Mr. Escovar-Salom resigned, however, without having ever served as Prosecutor.

2.5.5 It was not until 8 July, 1994, that, by Resolution 936, the Security Council appointed the Honourable Justice Richard J. Goldstone (South Africa) as Prosecutor. At the time of his appointment, Justice Goldstone was a Judge of the Appellate Division of the Supreme Court of South Africa and had been Chairman of the Standing Commission of Inquiry regarding Public Violence and Intimidation, which had investigated violence during the apartheid era. Justice Goldstone served as Prosecutor from 15 August 1994 until 30 September 1996.

2.5.6 By Resolution 1047, dated 29 February 1996, the Security Council appointed the Honourable Ms. Louise Arbour (Canada), a member of the Court of Appeals of Ontario and a criminal law specialist, who succeeded Mr. Goldstone on 1 October 1996.

2.5.7 On 11 June 1999, Ms. Arbour announced her intention to resign, following her appointment to the Supreme Court of Canada. She resigned on 15 September 1999, after serving three years of her four-year mandate. Ms. Carla Del Ponte (Switzerland), a former Swiss Attorney-General, replaced her on 15 September 1999.

2.5.8 While the Prosecutor is common to the ICTY and ICTR, there is a separate Deputy Prosecutor for each tribunal.

2.5.9 The office established around the Prosecutor is commonly referred to as the Office of the Prosecutor or OTP.

ICTY Deputy Prosecutor

2.5.10 Under Rule 38 of the RPE, the Deputy Prosecutor is appointed by the Secretary-General on the Prosecutor's recommendation and exercises the functions of the Prosecutor in the absence or inability to act of the latter, or upon the latter's express instructions.

2.5.11 On 20 January, 1994, Mr. Escovar-Salom recommended to the UN Secretary-General that Mr. Graham Blewitt, then Director of the Australian War Crime Prosecution Unit (established to prosecute Nazi war criminals), be appointed to the post of ICTY Deputy Prosecutor. He has been serving in this post since 15 February 1994.

Structure of the ICTY OTP

2.5.12 When the OTP was established, it comprised four sections:

— An Investigations Section, comprised of investigators.
— A Prosecutions Section, charged with examining in an independent manner the cases prepared by the investigators, to put together the indictments and to present the cases in court.

- A Special Legal Advisory consisting of experts in international law, on military codes of justice and laws of war, on the laws of the former Yugoslavia, on military questions, including chain of command and battle formations, and on cultural, historical and political issues relating to the former Yugoslavia. This section furnished advice and training to all the other sections of the OTP.
- An Information and Records Section, charged with managing the data and archives of the OTP, as well as recording all documents, evidence, statements and exhibits received or generated by the OTP.

2.5.13 From the assumption of his functions in July 1994, Richard Goldstone decided to create liasion offices in Belgrade, Sarajevo and Zagreb for the purposes of providing support to the investigative teams and a number of other purposes.

2.5.14 Towards the end of 1994, the Special Advisory Section was reorganised (see ICTY Annual Reports for details). At this time, a Legal Adviser specialising in sexual crimes was appointed for the purposes of advising both the ICTY and ICTR Prosecutors.

ICTR Deputy Prosecutor

2.5.15 Article 15 of the ICTR Statute stipulates that, while the ICTY Prosecutor also serves as the ICTR Prosecutor, he or she has additional staff, including a Deputy Prosecutor, to assist with prosecutions before the ICTR. The Deputy Prosecutor is appointed by the Secretary-General on the Prosecutor's recommendation, pursuant to Article 15(3) of the ICTR Statute. According to Rule 38, the Deputy Prosecutor exercises the functions of the Prosecutor in the absence or inability to act of the latter, or upon the latter's express instructions.

2.5.16 The first ICTR Deputy Prosecutor was Mr. Honoré Rakotomanana (Madagascar). He was replaced by Mr. Bernard Muna (Cameroon) on 29 April 1997. Mr. Muna served until May 2001. On 29 January 2003, the Prosecutor announced that Mr. Bongani Christopher Majola (South Africa) would serve as ICTR Deputy Prosecutor.

Structure of the ICTR OTP

2.5.17 The ICTR OTP consists of two sections:

- the Investigations Section, which is composed of teams charged with gathering evidence;
- The Prosecution Section, which is composed of lawyers, generally responsible for the conduct of the cases before the Tribunal and legal advisers for investigations and prosecutions;

2.5.18 An Information and Evidence Unit has also been instituted and placed directly under the Deputy Prosecutor.

Functions of the Prosecutor

2.5.19 Article 16(1) of the ICTY Statute and Article 15(1) of the ICTR Statute, by referring to both "investigation" (*l'instruction* in French) and "prosecution," provide for a dual role for the Prosecutor. The separation of the investigative and prosecutorial functions known to civil law systems is, therefore, not applied at the ICTY/ICTR (nor indeed at the ICC—see Article 15 of the Rome Statute). This separation in the civil law system aims at best preserving the rights of the accused by conferring upon an investigating magistrate the task of investigating both incriminating and exculpatory material. This procedure has some advantages in terms of ensuring a fair trial (it often being hard, particularly in international trials, for the accused to conduct extensive investigations and to gain access to sensitive archives, e.g. those of States' intelligence agencies, on the same footing as the OTP). If the accused before the ICTY and ICTR are provided adequate resources and means—both material and normative—to conduct full investigation to match the formidable powers of the Prosecutors, then the need for this separation of investigative and prosecutorial functions—indeed the need for an inquisitorial-style system—is diminished, although perhaps not removed altogether (for an analysis of the powers of the Prosecutor compared to the defence, see NIANG (2001)).

2.5.20 The Prosecutor's powers are set out in Article 18(1) of the ICTY Statute and Article 17(1) of the ICTR Statute. These provisions give the Prosecutor the task of assessing the information received or obtained and to decide whether there is a sufficient basis or not for proceeding. Articles 18(2) and 17(2) of the ICTY Statute and ICTR Statute, respectively, authorise him to carry out questioning, to collect evidence and to conduct on-site investigations.

2.5.21 The Prosecutor may also solicit the assistance of the State authorities concerned. The general obligation of cooperation obliges States to assist the Prosecutor in gathering information. Nonetheless, State cooperation has always been a stumbling block in the progress of international criminal justice, since States have on occasion considered that their cooperation could harm their sovereign interests. It is for this reason that in certain cases, cooperation is only achieved as the result of the application of pressure. The former Prosecutor, Louise Arbour, has stated, *"Nous sommes passés du régne de la coopération à celui de la contrainte des Etats qui, s'ils refusent, entrent en conflit avec le Conseil de sécurité"* (quoted by Antoine J. BULLIER, "Les Etats face à la justice pénale internationale: coopération ou contrainte?", *Les Petites Affiches*, 16 septembre 1999, N° 185, pp. 6–7, p. 7).

2.5.22 It is also due to resistance on the part of certain States, in particular the Federal Republic of Yugoslavia (Serbia and Montenegro), to cooperate, that the Prosecutor, Louise Arbour, implemented the practice of "sealed indictments," whereby when the Prosecutor requests a Judge to confirm a new indictment, she also requests the non-disclosure to the public of the indictment. Thus the former Mayor of Vukovar, Slavko Dokmanović, and the commander of the Bosnian Serb army, Momir Talić, were arrested on the basis of indictments that remained secret until their arrest, as indeed were several other accused.

2.5.23 If the powers of the Prosecutor as defined in the Statute appear large, it is also true that as a result of the amendments to the Rules of Procedure and Evidence of 9 and 10 July 1998, the procedure in force before the ICTY has re-adjusted the powers between the Judges, on the one hand, and the Prosecutor and Defence Counsel on the other.

2.5.24 In fact, before these amendments, no controls on the Prosecutor's investigations existed, apart from with respect to detention. It was to address this lack of judicial supervision that the Rules of Procedure and Evidence were amended, on 9 and 10 July 1998, to institute the pre-trial Judge. The French term, *"juge de la mise en état,"* adopted the formula existing in France, signifying that investigations are not exclusively in the hands of the Prosecutor (on this point, see, "L'émergence d'une justice pénale internationale: les expériences en cours, Entretien avec Pierre Truche," L'Astrée, 1 September 1999, n° 8, pp. 3–6, p. 4). After the amendments of July 1998, Rule 65 *ter* provided that the Trial Chamber could at any moment designate from among its (permanent) members a Judge responsible for all the pre-trial proceedings. This provision modified what was initially an option for the Trial Chamber into a mandatory designation in each case of a Pre-Trial Judge.

2.5.25 Without referring explicitly to the powers of the Prosecutor during the pre-trial proceedings and the absence of control over investigations before 1998, Claude Jorda, in his speech of 20 June 2000 before the Security Council, explained as follows the amendments to the Rules of Procedure and Evidence: *"dans une procédure au départ de type accusatoire trés accentué, la pratique nous a révélé qu'il convient de laisser plus d'initiative et de marge manœuvre aux Juges, seuls gardiens en définitive de la protection des valeurs universelles qui sous tendent les missions qui leur ont été assignées. Ce mouvement déjà amorcé depuis 1998 concerne au premier chef la phase préparatoire du proces (celle avant le début des audiences proprement dites) dont le déroulement rapide et efficace a été placé sous le contrôle du juge de la mise en état."*

2.5.26 Moreover, it should be emphasised that, if the Prosecutor had previously enjoyed a wide discretion in terms of managing evidence, having in particular the power to call witnesses without restriction, since the amendments to the Rules of Procedure and Evidence of 9 and 10 July 1998, the Trial Chamber, at the Pre-Trial conference, may set the number of witnesses the Prosecutor may call and may also ask questions of the witnesses. The role granted to the Trial Chamber since 1998 has therefore been considerably enlarged.

2.5.27 Following the amendments to the Rules of Procedure and Evidence on 9–10 July 1998, Rule 73 *bis* provided that, "the Trial Chamber may call upon the Prosecutor to reduce the number of witnesses if it considers that an excessive number of witnesses are being called to prove the same facts." It was also provided that, "the Trial Chamber may call upon the Prosecutor to shorten the estimated length of the examination-in-chief for some witnesses." Following its amendment on 13 December 2001, the article now provides that "in the light of the file submitted to the Trial Chamber by the pre-trial Judge pursuant to Rule 65 *ter* (L)(i), the Trial Chamber, after having heard the Prosecutor, shall set the number of witnesses the Prosecutor may call." It is also stated that, "After having heard the Prosecutor, the Trial Chamber shall determine the time available to the Prosecutor for presenting evidence."

Role of the Prosecutor

2.5.28 The Decicion of the Trial Chamber in *Kupreškić* concerning communications between the parties and their witnesses, rendered on 21 September 1998, anticipated these changes and the shifting of powers with respect to the handling of evidence. The Decision stated that, ""the Prosecutor of the Tribunal is not, or not only, a Party to adversarial proceedings but is an organ of the Tribunal and an organ of international criminal justice whose object is not simply to secure a conviction but to present the case for the Prosecution, which includes not only inculpatory, but also exculpatory evidence, in order to assist the Chamber to discover the truth in a judicial setting."

2.5.29 The Chamber considered that a witness, be it a prosecution or defence witness, becomes a witness of truth before the Tribunal once he has made the solemn declaration under Rule 90 of the Rules and that, to the extent that he is called to contribute to establishing the truth, he is no longer strictly the witness of one or other of the parties. Moreover to allow one or other of the parties to communicate with the witness after he has begun to testify could lead to the witness discussing, albeit not necessarily deliberately, the content of the testimony that he has already given, which could lead to the witness's subsequent testimony being influenced or modified in a way which is incompatible with the spirit of the Statute and Rules of the Tribunal. The Tribunal considered further that the Victims and Witnesses Unit, established pursuant to Article 22 of the Statute and Rule 34 of the Rules, had a mandate to treat all witnesses on an equal footing, to aid them and to take care of them during their stay in The Hague, as well as to arrange for all of the practical aspects relating to their appearance before the Tribunal, and that the Prosecution or the Defence must therefore not enter into communication with the witness in the period while he is testifying.

Prosecutorial Discretion

2.5.30 The Prosecutor's discretion is not unlimited (*Delalić et al Appeals Judgement*, paras. 600–619). The accused, Landžo, had raised the matter on appeal:

> 596. Landzo alleges that he was the subject of a selective prosecution policy conducted by the Prosecution. He defines a selective prosecution as one "in which the criteria for selecting persons for prosecution are based, not on considerations of apparent criminal responsibility alone, but on extraneous policy reasons, such as ethnicity, gender, or administrative convenience." Specifically, he alleges that he, a young Muslim camp guard, was selected for prosecution, while indictments "against all other Defendants without military rank," who were all " non-Muslims of Serbian ethnicity," were withdrawn by the Prosecution on the ground of changed prosecutorial strategies.

2.5.31 The Chamber rejected this ground of appeal:

> 602. . . . It is beyond question that the Prosecutor has a broad discretion in relation to the initiation of investigations and in the preparation of indictments. This is acknowledged in Article 18(1) of the Statute. . . . It is also clear that a discretion of this nature is not unlimited. A number of limitations on the discretion entrusted to the Prosecutor are evident in the Tribunal's Statute and Rules of Procedure and Evidence.
>
> . . .
>
> 604. The discretion of the Prosecutor at all times is circumscribed in a more general way by the nature of her position as an official vested with specific duties imposed by the Statute of the Tribunal. The Prosecutor is committed to discharge those duties with full respect of the law. . . .

605. One such principle is explicitly referred to in Article 21(1) of the Statute, which provides:

All persons shall be equal before the International Tribunal.

... Thus Article 21 and the principle it embodies prohibits discrimination in the application of the law based on impermissible motives such as, *inter alia*, race, colour, religion, opinion, national or ethnic origin. The Prosecutor, in exercising her discretion under the Statute in the investigation and indictment of accused before the Tribunal, is subject to the principle of equality before the law and to this requirement of non-discrimination.

607. The burden of the proof rests on Landzo, as an appellant alleging that the Prosecutor has improperly exercised prosecutorial discretion, to demonstrate that the discretion was improperly exercised in relation to him. Landzo must therefore demonstrate that the decision to prosecute him or to continue his prosecution was based on impermissible motives, such as race or religion, and that the Prosecution failed to prosecute similarly situated defendants.

612. Landzo argues that he was the only Bosnian Muslim accused without military rank or command responsibility held by the Tribunal, and he contends that he was singled out for prosecution "simply because he was the only person the Prosecutor's office could find to 'represent' the Bosnian Muslims." He was, it is said, prosecuted to give an appearance of "evenhandedness" to the Prosecutor's policy.

614. The crimes of which Landzo was convicted are described both in the Trial Judgement and in the present judgement at paragraphs 565–570. The Appeals Chamber considers that, in light of the unquestionably violent and extreme nature of these crimes, it is quite clear that the decision to continue the trial against Landzo was consistent with the stated policy of the Prosecutor to "focus on persons holding higher levels of responsibility, or on those who have been *personally responsible for the exceptionally brutal or otherwise extremely serious offences.*" A decision, made in the context of a need to concentrate prosecutorial resources, to identify a person for prosecution on the basis that they are believed to have committed *exceptionally* brutal offences can in no way be described as a discriminatory or otherwise impermissible motive.

...

618. Finally, even if in the hypothetical case that those against whom the indictments were withdrawn were identically situated to Landzo, the Appeals Chamber cannot accept that the appropriate remedy would be to reverse the convictions of Landzo for the serious offences with which he had been found guilty. Such a remedy would be an entirely disproportionate response to such a procedural breach. As noted by the Trial Chamber, it cannot be accepted that "unless all potential indictees who are similarly situated are brought to justice, there should be no justice done in relation to a person who has been indicted and brought to trial."

2.5.32 While there is some merit in these remarks of the Chamber to the effect that authors of terrible crimes should not escape punishment, the principal point raised by Landžo appears to have been overlooked. That is, the Chamber failed to answer the following question: *if* it were true that Landžo had been selected for prosecution only because he was a Muslim, in the sense that if he had been a Serb or a Croat he would not have been prosecuted, does that not offend against both the notion of justice and that of non-discrimination? In these circumstances should not the Chamber intervene to prevent a prosecution from going ahead which is, in effect, ethnically motivated?

2.5.33 See also the *Krajisnik Decision on Interlocutory Motion Challenging Jurisdiction*, 25 May 2001, in which the Appeals Chamber rejected Krajisnik's assertion that the Prosecutor had not acted with impartiality and independence in the discharge of her duties and functions.

Trial Chamber Can Make Orders on Prosecution Conduct of a Case

2.5.34 In *Milošević, Reasons for refusal of leave to appeal from decision to impose time limit*, 16 May 2002, the Prosecutor appealed against the Trial Chamber's decision placing a time limit on the Prosecution for the presentation of its case. The Prosecutor asserted that this interfered with prosecutorial discretion guaranteed by ICTY Article 16(2). This argument was rejected by the Appeals Chamber, which interpreted the true intent of Article 16(2) and its extent as being that "no government or other institution or person, including the judges of the Tribunal, can direct the Prosecutor as to whom he or she is to investigate or charge." That is a different question from that of judicial management of case presentation by the parties in court. Note also that the Trial Chamber has a duty under Article 20 of the ICTY Statute to *"ensure that a trial is fair and expeditious and that proceedings are conducted in accordance with the rules of procedure and evidence, with full respect for the rights of the accused and due regard for the protection of victims and witnesses"* (emphasis added).

2.5.35

ICTY RULE 37 FUNCTIONS OF THE PROSECUTOR	ICTR RULE 37 FUNCTIONS OF THE PROSECUTOR
(A) The Prosecutor shall perform all the functions provided by the Statute in accordance with the Rules and such Regulations, consistent with the Statute and the Rules, as may be framed by the Prosecutor. Any alleged inconsistency in the Regulations shall be brought to the attention of the Bureau to whose opinion the Prosecutor shall defer. (B) The Prosecutor's powers and duties under the Rules may be exercised by staff members of the Office of the Prosecutor authorised by the Prosecutor, or by any person acting under the Prosecutor's direction.	(A) The Prosecutor shall perform all the functions provided by the Statute in accordance with the Rules and such Regulations, consistent with the Statute and the Rules, as may be framed by him. Any alleged inconsistency in the Regulations shall be brought to the attention of the Bureau to whose opinion the Prosecutor shall defer. (B) The Prosecutor's powers under Parts Four to Eight of the Rules may be exercised by staff members of the Office of the Prosecutor authorised by him, or by any person acting under his direction.

2.5.36

> **ICC**
> **ARTICLE 15**
> **PROSECUTOR**
>
> 1. The Prosecutor may initiate investigations proprio motu on the basis of information on crimes within the jurisdiction of the Court.
> 2. The Prosecutor shall analyse the seriousness of the information received. For this purpose, he or she may seek additional information from States, organs of the United Nations, intergovernmental or non-governmental organizations, or other reliable sources that he or she deems appropriate, and may receive written or oral testimony at the seat of the Court.
> 3. If the Prosecutor concludes that there is a reasonable basis to proceed with an investigation, he or she shall submit to the Pre-Trial Chamber a request for authorization of an investigation, together with any supporting material collected. Victims may make representations to the Pre-Trial Chamber, in accordance with the Rules of Procedure and Evidence.
> 4. If the Pre-Trial Chamber, upon examination of the request and the supporting material, considers that there is a reasonable basis to proceed with an investigation, and that the case appears to fall within the jurisdiction of the Court, it shall authorize the commencement of the investigation, without prejudice to subsequent determinations by the Court with regard to the jurisdiction and admissibility of a case.
> 5. The refusal of the Pre-Trial Chamber to authorize the investigation shall not preclude the presentation of a subsequent request by the Prosecutor based on new facts or evidence regarding the same situation.
> 6. If, after the preliminary examination referred to in paragraphs 1 and 2, the Prosecutor concludes that the information provided does not constitute a reasonable basis for an investigation, he or she shall inform those who provided the information. This shall not preclude the Prosecutor from considering further information submitted to him or her regarding the same situation in the light of new facts or evidence.

History of ICTY Rule 37

2.5.37 Para. (A) was amended at the ICTY's fifth plenary session "to improve the working of the Tribunal" (ICTY Second Annual Report, para. 24) by providing for regulations to be issued by the Prosecutor while preserving an element of judicial control over the Prosecutor's activities, since the Prosecutor must defer to the opinion of the Bureau regarding any alleged inconsistency between those regulations and the Tribunal's Statute or Rules. Para. (B) was amended at the ICTY's thirteenth plenary session on 25 July 1997 to add the words "and duties."

The ICC Prosecutor

2.5.38 For comparison with the functions and powers of the ICC Prosecutor, see Article 15 of the Rome Statute.

2.5.39 Article 42 of the Rome Statute provides that, unlike the ICTY/ICTR Prosecutor, the ICC Prosecutor will be elected by secret ballot by an absolute majority of the members of the Assembly of States Parties.

2.5.40 If the organisation and powers of the ICC Office of the Prosecutor do not differ greatly from those enjoyed by the ICTY/ICTR Prosecutor, an essential difference should nonetheless be noted: the creation of a "Pre-Trial Chamber" which is charged with overseeing certain activities of the Prosecutor, issuing arrest warrants and confirming or declining to confirm the charges on which the accused will be tried.

2.5.41 While the ICC Prosecutor may always start investigations at his own initiative he must however obtain the authorisation of the pre-trial Chamber. This creation, considered as a victory of French diplomacy over the pre-existing hegemony of the Anglo-Saxon procedure, also stems from a dispute between the ICTY and France in December 1997 (Pierre NUSS, "La France et la Cour pénale internationale," *La Gazette du Palais*, 25 February 2000, N° 56, pp. 21–37, pp. 34–35). The institution of the Pre-Trial Chamber, moreover, creates a preventative control over the Prosecutor's discretion through the Judges of this Chamber and implies more generally a responsibility on the Court as a whole. The Prosecutor is, however, not subject to any political authority and enjoys wide powers. Thus he can take any initiatives to being investigations without having to refer to anyone.

2.5.42 In giving a new status to victims, the ICC Prosecutor's powers are also more limited than those enjoyed by the ICTY/ICTR Prosecutor. Article 19(3) of the Rome Statute enables victims to submit observations relating to admissibility (see also Article 68(3) of the Statute for an enlarged consideration of the interests of victims).

2.5.43 The powers of the ICC Prosecutor are also delimited by Article 16 of the Rome Statute which permits the Security Council, in effect, to force the Prosecutor to defer investigations or prosecutions for a twelve-month, renewable period if a resolution is adopted by the Council to that effect. While one may consider this facility granted to the Security Council as a safeguard of traditional international law, that is the international law of sovereigns (on this point, see Serge SUR, "Le droit international pénal, entre l'Etat et la société internationale," *Actualité et droit international*, October 2001 (www.ridi.org/adi)), it may also indicate the need to subordinate war crimes investigations to assessments of political or diplomatic expediency (see, on this point, "La genèse de la Cour pénale internationale, Entretien avec Pierre-Marie Dupuy," L'Astrée, 1 September 1999, n° 8, pp. 7–12, p. 9.). It remains the case that the lack of precision in the Statute regarding the number of times upon which the Council's request may be renewed is a shortcoming that could have grave consequences. For a critical commentary on Article 16 of the Rome Statute, see Marie-Pierre BESSON DE VEZAC, "La Convention du 17 juillet 1998 instituant la Cour pénale internationale: coup d'épée dans l'eau ou avancée décisive?", *Les Petites Affiches*, 11 November 1999, N° 225.

2.5.44 Note should also be taken of the negotiations within NATO and the EU, and between these organisations and the candidate member states, particularly in eastern Europe, on the one hand, and the US, on the other, for the purposes of signing bilateral immunities granting US servicemen immunity from the Court. This process was initiated by the negotiation of a UNSC resolution, adopted in response to Article 16 of the ICC Statute, suspending any possible prosecutions against U.S. peacekeepers for a period of one year.

2.5.45

ICTY RULE 38 DEPUTY PROSECUTOR	ICTR RULE 38 DEPUTY PROSECUTOR
(A) The Prosecutor shall make his recommendations to the Secretary-General of the United Nations for the appointment of a Deputy Prosecutor. (B) The Deputy Prosecutor shall exercise the functions of the Prosecutor in the event of his absence from duty or inability to act or upon the Prosecutor's express instructions.	(A) The Prosecutor shall make his recommendations to the Secretary-General of the United Nations for the appointment of a Deputy Prosecutor. (B) The Deputy Prosecutor shall exercise the functions of the Prosecutor in the event of his absence or inability to act or upon the Prosecutor's express instructions.

History of ICTY Rule 38

2.5.46 The words "from duty" were added to para. (B) at the ICTY's thirteenth plenary session on 25 July 1997.

SECTION 6: THE DEFENCE

2.6.1

ICTY RULE 44 APPOINTMENT, QUALIFICATIONS, AND DUTIES OF COUNSEL	ICTR RULE 44 APPOINTMENT AND QUALIFICATIONS OF COUNSEL
(A) Counsel engaged by a suspect or an accused shall file his power of attorney with the Registrar at the earliest opportunity. Subject to any determination by a Chamber pursuant to Rule 46 or 77, a counsel shall be considered qualified to represent a suspect or accused if he satisfies the Registrar that he is admitted to the practice of law in a State, or is a University professor of law, and speaks one of the two working languages of the Tribunal and is a member of an association of counsel practising at the Tribunal recognised by the Registrar. (B) At the request of the suspect or accused and where the interests of justice so demand, the Registrar may admit a counsel who does not speak either of the two working languages of the Tribunal but who speaks the native language of the suspect or accused. The Registrar may impose such conditions as deemed appropriate. A suspect or accused may appeal a decision of the Registrar to the President. (C) In the performance of their duties, counsel shall be subject to the relevant provisions of the Statute, the Rules, the Rules of Detention and any other rules or regulations adopted by the Tribunal, the Host Country Agreement, the Code of Professional Conduct for Defence Counsel and the codes of practice and ethics governing their profession and, if applicable, the Directive on the Assignment of Defence Counsel set out by the Registrar and approved by the permanent Judges. (D) An Advisory Panel shall be established to assist the President and the Registrar in all matters relating to defence counsel. The Panel members shall be selected from representatives of professional associations and from counsel who have appeared before the Tribunal. They shall have recognised professional legal experience. The composition of the Advisory Panel shall be representative of the different legal systems. A Directive of the Registrar shall set out the structure and areas of responsibility of the Advisory Panel.	(A) Counsel engaged by a suspect or an accused shall file his power of attorney with the Registrar at the earliest opportunity. Subject to verification by the Registrar, a counsel shall be considered qualified to represent a suspect or accused, provided that he is admitted to the practice of law in a State, or is a University professor of law. (B) In the performance of their duties counsel shall be subject to the relevant provisions of the Statute, the Rules, the Rules of Detention and any other rules or regulations adopted by the Tribunal, the Host Country Agreement, the Code of Conduct and the codes of practice and ethics governing their profession and, if applicable, the Directive on the Assignment of Defence Counsel.

History of ICTY Rule 44

2.6.2 Para. (B) was added at the ICTY thirteenth plenary session on 25 July 1997. The title of the Rule was also changed to add the words "and Duties." New paras. (B) and (D) were added at the twenty-second plenary session, effective 2 August 2000, with the previous para. (B) becoming (C). Both new paragraphs codified existing practices. The subject-matter of para. (B) had in fact previously been dealt with under Rule 45(B). This rule was again amended in minor ways on 19 January 2001, after the twenty-third plenary session.

2.6.3 The words, "Subject to any determination by a Chamber pursuant to Rule 46 or 77," and, "set out by the Registrar and approved by the permanent Judges," were added to paras. (A) and (C) respectively at the twenty-fifth plenary session held on 12 and 13 December, 2001.

2.6.4 The words, "and is a member of an association of counsel practising at the Tribunal recognised by the Registrar," were added at the end of para. (A) at the twenty-sixth plenary session held on 11 and 12 July 2002." An inaugural general assembly held for the purposes of establishing such an association was held on 14 September 2002. At this meeting, the Association of Defence Counsel Practising Before the ICTY ("ADC-ICTY") was created. It is a professional association organised under the laws of the Netherlands. The objectives of the Association are set out at www.ADCICTY.com).

History of ICTR Rule 44

2.6.5 This Rule was amended at the ICTR fifth plenary session on 8 June 1998. Para. (B) was added, and the present para. (A) was amended in minor ways.

Assignment of Counsel

2.6.6 Lawyers wishing to represent a defendant must write to the Registrar, attaching their *curriculum vitae* and copies of relevant certificates, expressing their wish to be added to the list of Counsel willing to be assigned to indigent suspects and accused. The office handling these matters in the Registry is known as OLAD (Office for Legal Aid and Detention Matters, Registry, International Criminal Tribunal for the former Yugoslavia, Churchillplein 1, 2517 JW, The Hague, The Netherlands).

2.6.7 The procedure for assigning counsel is governed by the ICTY Directive on the Assignment of Defence Counsel (no.1/94), which was adopted on 11 February 1994. It is attached at Annex 4.

2.6.8 The Directive addresses, *inter alia*, the right to counsel, the procedure for assessing the indigency of the accused, the pre-requisites for the assignment of counsel, the remuneration to be afforded to counsel assigned and the procedure for settlement of disputes. The Directive has been amended several times. For example, at the ICTY's eleventh plenary session, on 25 June 1996, a number of amendments were adopted by the Judges, including a provision for the assignment of co-counsel in exceptional circumstances. Co-counsel have in fact been assigned by the Registrar in most, if not all, cases. See Directive on assignment of Defence Counsel, dated 12 July 2002.

This seems only fair; the accused are facing trials of the utmost seriousness, and are being prosecuted by whole teams of prosecution lawyers, investigators and legal assistants. Two defence counsel on the other side seems the minimum necessary to create the conditions for a fair trial.

2.6.9 The ICTR Code of Professional Conduct for Defence Counsel, largely modelled on the ICTY Code of Conduct, was adopted at the ICTR's fifth Plenary Session on 8 June 1998.

2.6.10 When assigning counsel to an accused or, on occasion, to a detained witness transferred to the Tribunal under the provisions of Rule 90 *bis* (counsel was assigned to detained witnesses in the *Đukić, Krsmanović, Erdemović* and *Kremenović* cases), the Registrar issues a written decision stating that the requirements of indigency are met and that a defence lawyer has satisfied the criteria laid down in the Directive. See, for example, the decisions of the Registrar of 25 April 1995, 15 February 1996 and 29 May 1996 assigning counsel to Duško Tadić, Aleksa Krsmanović and Dražen Erdemović respectively. The Registrar may also issue a decision determining that counsel cease to be assigned, for example in *Krsmanović* (IT-96-19-Misc.1), in which, on 3 April 1996, the Registrar decided that due to the transfer of Aleksa Krsmanović back to the authorities of Bosnia and Herzegovina, he no longer had a right to assigned counsel provided by the Tribunal.

Annotated Directive on the Assignment of Defence Counsel

2.6.11 The Registry has produced an Annotated Directive on the Assignment of Defence Counsel for its internal use. The Directive is annotated with Orders, Decisions, communications and practice. The Annotated Directive has been adapted, *mutatis mutandis*, by the ICTR as "Guidelines on the Directive on the Assignment of Defence Counsel."

2.6.12

ICTR only
RULE 44 *bis*
DUTY COUNSEL

(A) A list of duty counsel who speak one or both of the working languages of the Tribunal and have indicated their willingness to be assigned pursuant to this Rule shall be kept by the Registrar.
(B) Duty counsel shall fulfil the requirements of Rule 44, and shall be situated within reasonable proximity to the Detention Facility and the Seat of the Tribunal.
(C) The Registrar shall at all times ensure that duty counsel will be available to attend the Detention Facility in the event of being summoned.
(D) If an accused, or suspect transferred under Rule 40 bis, is unrepresented at any time after being transferred to the Tribunal, the Registrar shall as soon as practicable summon duty counsel to represent the accused or suspect until counsel is engaged by the accused or suspect, or assigned under Rule 45.
(E) In providing initial legal advice and assistance to a suspect transferred under Rule 40 bis, duty counsel shall advise the suspect of his or her rights including the rights referred to in Rule 55(A).

History of ICTR Rule 44 *bis*

2.6.13 This new Rule was added on 8 June 1998 at the ICTR's fifth Plenary Session.

2.6.14 In *Nyiramasuhuko and Ntahobali, Decision on Ntahobali's Motion for Withdrawal of Counsel,* 22 June 2001, in deciding to grant the accused's motion for withdrawal of counsel with the result that the accused would conduct his own defence, the Trial Chamber held that where this would result in the accused cross-examining victims, that it would be in the interests of justice that a Duty Counsel be immediately appointed so as to ensure that the accused is assisted in the conduct of his defence pursuant to Rule 44 *bis* (D).

2.6.15

ICTY RULE 45 ASSIGNMENT OF COUNSEL	ICTR RULE 45 ASSIGNMENT OF COUNSEL
(A) Whenever the interests of justice so demand, counsel shall be assigned to suspects or accused who lack the means to remunerate such counsel. Such assignments shall be treated in accordance with the procedure established in a Directive set out by the Registrar and approved by the Judges. (B) A list of counsel who, in addition to fulfilling the requirements of Rule 44, have shown that they possess reasonable experience in criminal and/or international law and have indicated their willingness to be assigned by the Tribunal to any person detained under the authority of the Tribunal lacking the means to remunerate counsel, shall be kept by the Registrar. (C) In particular circumstances, upon the request of a person lacking the means to remunerate counsel, the Registrar may assign counsel whose name does not appear on the list but who otherwise fulfils the requirements of Rule 44. (D) If a request is refused, a further request may be made by a suspect or an accused to the Registrar.	(A) A list of counsel who speak one or both of the working languages of the Tribunal, meet the requirements of Rule 44, have at least 10 years' relevant experience, and have indicated their willingness to be assigned by the Tribunal to indigent suspects or accused, shall be kept by the Registrar. (B) The criteria for determination of indigence shall be established by the Registrar and approved by the Judges. (C) In assigning counsel to an indigent suspect or accused, the following procedure shall be observed: (i) a request for assignment of counsel shall be made to the Registrar; (ii) the Registrar shall enquire into the means of the suspect or accused and determine whether the criteria of indigence are met; (iii) if he decides that the criteria are met, he shall assign counsel from the list; if he decides to the contrary, he shall inform the suspect or accused that the request is refused. (D) If a request is refused, a further reasoned request may be made by a suspect or an accused to the Registrar upon showing a change in circumstances.

(E) The Registrar shall, in consultation with the permanent Judges, establish the criteria for the payment of fees to assigned counsel. (F) Where a person is assigned counsel and is subsequently found not to be lacking the means to remunerate counsel, the Chamber may make an order of contribution to recover the cost of providing counsel. (G) A suspect or an accused electing to conduct his or her own defence shall so notify the Registrar in writing at the first opportunity.	(E) The Registrar shall, in consultation with the Judges, establish the criteria for the payment of fees to assigned counsel. (F) If a suspect or an accused elects to conduct his own defence, he shall so notify the Registrar in writing at the first opportunity. (G) Where an alleged indigent person is subsequently found not to be indigent, the Chamber may make an order of contribution to recover the cost of providing counsel. (H) Under exceptional circumstances, at the request of the suspect or accused or his counsel, the Chamber may instruct the Registrar to replace an assigned counsel, upon good cause being shown and after having been satisfied that the request is not designed to delay the proceedings. (I) It is understood that Counsel will represent the accused and conduct the case to finality. Failure to do so, absent just cause approved by the Chamber, may result in forfeiture of fees in whole or in part. In such circumstances the Chamber may make an order accordingly. Counsel shall only be permitted to withdraw from the case to which he has been assigned in the most exceptional circumstances.

History of ICTY Rule 45

2.6.16 Rule 45 was amended at the ICTY fifth plenary session in January 1995 for the purpose of "clarifying the Rules" by adding para. (G) to address the situation where an accused wishes to represent himself. Para. (H), which was also added at the fifth plenary session, provides that where an allegedly indigent person is subsequently found not to be indigent, an order may be made to recover the costs of providing counsel. This latter provision establishes a mechanism to recover costs where an accused has, for example, concealed his assets in order to be considered indigent and accordingly assigned counsel at the Tribunal's expense.

2.6.17 Rule 45 was amended at the ICTY fourteenth plenary session on 12 November 1997 to render it gender-neutral. The rule was further amended at the ICTY eleventh plenary session on 24–25 June 1996 to allow the Registrar, in certain circumstances, to assign counsel who did not fulfil the language requirement of Rule 45(A), i.e. ability to speak English or French. The Registrar had, however, to be "authorised, by a

Judge or a Trial Chamber seised of the case" to do so. At the ICTY eighteenth plenary session, para. (B) was further amended to allow the Registrar to assign such counsel *without* the authorisation of a Judge or Trial Chamber.

2.6.18 The rule was amended on 2 August 2000, following the twenty-second plenary session, in a number of ways including by the addition of para. (A). The words, "whenever the interests of justice so demand" derive from Article 14(3)(d) of the International Covenant on Civil and Political Rights, which sets out the right of an accused "(d) . . . to have legal assistance assigned to him, *in any case where the interests of justice so require*, and without payment by him in any such case if he does not have sufficient means to pay for it" (emphasis added). Prior to this amendment, it was generally assumed that counsel would automatically be assigned to any indigent suspect or accused. This amendment conditions such assignment on whether the interests of justice demand it, an approach apparently consistent with international human rights norms.

History of ICTR Rule 45

2.6.19 Rule 45 was amended at the ICTR fourth plenary session, held in Arusha on 1–5 June 1997, to authorise the Registrar under exceptional circumstances to replace an assigned counsel. The amendment involved adding new para. (H). The rule 45 was amended at the ICTR fifth Plenary Session on 8 June 1998, notably to add the requirement that assigned counsel have at least ten years' relevant experience.

2.6.20 ICTR Rule 45 differs from ICTY Rule 45 in that the former has a para. (I) which does not appear in the ICTY Rule.

Cross Reference: 8.5.62 *et seq.* on ICTY Article 21(4)(d) and ICTR Article 20(4)(d).

Language Requirements

2.6.21 In *Erdemović*, the Registrar decided not to assign the counsel requested by the accused, since he did not meet the language requirement of Rule 45(A) (now ICTY Rule 44(A)). Following an application by the accused dated 9 April 1996, which was supported by the Prosecutor in an application dated 22 May 1996, in which the accused requested the assignment of the counsel in question, Judge Jorda issued an order on 28 May 1996 determining that an exceptional situation existed and that counsel should be assigned who did not speak one of the two working languages of the Tribunal. Those circumstances, as narrated in the Prosecutor's application, were as follows:

> 5. In the Federal Republic of Yugoslavia Mr. BABIĆ has represented the accused before the District Court of Novi Sad in connection with the charges upon which he has been ordered by that court to be detained. He is familiar with all aspects of the case against the accused, has earned his confidence, has already acted for him informally in discussions with the Prosecutor and has established good working relations with the Prosecutor. Further, Mr. BABIĆ is willing to be assigned by the Tribunal to indigent suspects or accused.
>
> 6. It appears to the Prosecutor that the circumstances of this case are unusual, and may not have been contemplated when Rule 45 was adopted; that it is in the interests of justice that Mr. BABIĆ should be allowed to continue to represent

the accused; and that this is an appropriate case in which the strict requirements of Rule 45 should be allowed to do him so. The Prosecutor therefore considers that an order to this effect under Rule 54 by the Presiding Judge of the Trial Chamber is necessary for the preparation or conduct of the trial. (Prosecutor's Application, D111-D109, 22 May 1996)

2.6.22 The assignment of Mr. Babić to Dražen Erdemović led, however, to problems of communication and misunderstandings (for example, concerning the effect of a guilty plea and concerning the difference between crimes against humanity and war crimes), which the Appeals Chamber raised *proprio motu* and which led it to remit the case to a new Trial Chamber for a re-plea. See the *Erdemović Appeals Judgement:*

> 16. . . . it appears to us that defence counsel consistently advanced arguments contradicting the admission of guilt and criminal responsibility implicit in a guilty plea. If the defence had truly understood the nature of a guilty plea, it would not have persisted in its arguments which were obviously at odds with such a plea. . . .
>
> . . .
>
> 18. . . . There is no indication that the Appellant understood the nature of the charges. Indeed, there is every indication that the Appellant had no idea what a war crime or a crime against humanity was in terms of the legal requirements of either of these two offences. Our conclusion is supported by what seems to have been some misapprehension on the part of defence counsel himself as to the nature of the charges. . . .

Cross Reference: Rule 3(D).

Counsel's Experience: ICTY vs. ICTR

2.6.23 A counsel wishing to be assigned to represent an accused before the ICTR must have at least 10 years' relevant experience. Rule 45(A) of the ICTR's Rules of Procedure and Evidence, following its amendment at the Fifth Plenary Session in Arusha on 8 June 1998, reads, "(A) A list of counsel who speak one or both of the working languages of the Tribunal, meet the requirements of Rule 44, have at least 10 years' relevant experience, and have indicated their willingness to be assigned by the Tribunal to indigent suspects or accused, shall be kept by the Registrar."

2.6.24 See also *Ntakirutimana and Ntakirutimana, Decision on the Motion of the Defence for the Assignment of Co-counsel for Elizaphan Ntakirutimana*, 13 July 2001, in which the Trial Chamber stated that the requirement of 10 years experience was not limited to 10 years of legal practice as a lawyer but could also include experience as a "professor of law" pursuant to Rule 44(A). Accordingly, the Trial Chamber requested documentation to prove that the proposed counsel had act as a visiting professor at a university with sufficient regularity.

2.6.25 The ICTY does not require 10 years' relevant experience for the assignment of counsel. Conversely, ICTY Rule 45 (B) now requires that assigned counsel "have shown that they possess reasonable experience in criminal and/or international law." Moreover, ICTY Rule 44(A) has recently been amended to require that counsel be "a member of an association of counsel practising at the Tribunal recognised by the Registrar."

Withdrawal of Counsel

2.6.26 Accused may, and do, request removal of their counsel and/or co-counsel. Such a request is not, however, always granted. If it were, it would create potential for great mischief; an accused could, in effect, postpone his trial indefinitely by constantly changing his counsel. In *Delalić et al, Decision on Request by Accused Mucić for Assignment of New Counsel*, 24 June 1996, the Trial Chamber held:

> the Trial Chamber . . . has a responsibility to examine the reasons for the Accused's dissatisfaction with the Counsel assigned and determine whether those reasons constitute good cause. The Trial Chamber must be satisfied that the reasons are genuine and that the request is not made by frivolous reasons or in order to pervert the course of justice eg by causing added delay.

2.6.27 The status and duties of counsel vis-à-vis their clients was clarified in *Nyiramasuhuko and Ntahobali, Decision on Ntahobali's Motion on Withdrawal of Counsel*, 22 June 2001, in which the Trial Chamber noted:

> in the exercise of his professional judgement, Counsel is independent of the Accused, even if Counsel is expected to maintain a proper Counsel-Client relationship. The Trial Chamber has to be assured that a Counsel properly conducts an accused's defence and protects the latter's lawful interest during trial, but also has to verify that the accused does not abuse this right . . . as a matter of principle, the Chamber finds that an accused is mistaken when saying that counsel must consult with him, whereas there are matters of professional judgement for which Counsel alone is liable. While Counsel should take full instructions about facts surrounding the case, this does not imply that Counsel have to consult with the accused whenever any step in his defence is taken by the Counsel. Nevertheless, Counsel have to keep the Accused informed of the steps taken to protect his interests and provide the Accused with a reasoned explanation as to why they took such steps.

2.6.28 In *Delalić et al*, on 21 April 1997, the Trial Chamber refused an application by the accused Landžo for the withdrawal of lead counsel in the absence of a finding that there was either "a conflict of interest" or "any dereliction of duty as counsel on the part of" lead counsel. The Chamber further considered that there was no substance to the accused's assertion "that his choice of Mr. Brackovic as counsel was not made by his own free will" and stated that it would be "failing in its . . . duty if it grant(ed) the request for the reasons cited."

2.6.29 For an ICTY Decision where a request was granted, see, e.g. *Delalić et al.*, Tr. Ch., *Order on Request for Withdrawal of Counsel*, 2 May 1997.

2.6.30 See also the Decisions issued by the Registrar in *Kupreškić et al* and *Kordić et al* on 10 August 1999 to withdraw counsel when it was reported in the media that an organisation, "Croatian Prisoners in The Hague" had raised legal defence funds for several Croatian accused. Certain of these Decisions were reversed by Trial Chambers. See, e.g., *Decision on the Registrar's Withdrawal of the Assignment of Defence Counsel* rendered by the Trial Chamber in *Kordić* on 3 September 1999:

4. The Trial Chamber finds that there was insufficient evidence for the Registrar to take the drastic step of reversing the accused's status of indigency and removing the assignment of his defence counsel in the middle of the trial. . . . In the view of this Trial Chamber, if media reports gave rise to doubt about the income of the accused, the matter should have been investigated further before any possible finding could be made.

2.6.31 A lead counsel may also request that his co-counsel be removed. The decision is one for the Registrar, in the first instance. See Article 19 of the ICTY Directive on the Assignment of Defence Counsel.

2.6.32 In its *Decision concerning a Replacement of an Assigned Defence Counsel and Postponement of the Trial*, of 31 October 1996 in *Akayesu*, the Trial Chamber granted the request of the accused to be assigned a new Defence Counsel, given the circumstance that the counsel then assigned had failed to appear at a scheduled court hearing. The trial proceedings were also postponed to allow the newly assigned counsel adequate time to prepare the defence. At that time, the ICTR's Directive on the Assignment of Defence Counsel, provided only for the assignment of *one Counsel*, unlike the ICTY's Directive which was amended to allow the assignment, in exceptional circumstances, of a co-counsel to assist Lead Counsel (see Article 16(C) of the ICTY Directive (IT/73.REV.3)).

2.6.33 In a further *Decision on the Request of the Accused for the Replacement of Assigned Counsel*, rendered by the same *Akayesu* Chamber on 20 November 1996, the assignment of counsel in the previous Decision of 31 October 1996 was withdrawn, at the request of the accused.

2.6.34 See also *Decision on Nzirorera's Motion for Withdrawal of Counsel*, 3 October 2001, in which the Trial Chamber denied the accused's motion to withdraw the appointment of his lead counsel. The Trial Chamber held that allegations of financial dishonesty (i.e. fee-splitting) directed towards counsel was an administrative matter and should therefore be considered by the Registrar and not the Trial Chamber. While it may be correct that, in the first instance, it is for the Registry to determine whether or not there has been fee-splitting, where such an allegation is found to be substantiated, it is surely for the Chamber to take action. The fact that Counsel has engaged or is engaging in such a practice must reflect on his or her fitness to appear as Counsel before the Court.

Appointment of Co-Counsel, Investigators, Etc., Is a Matter for Lead Counsel

2.6.35 In *Ngeze, Decision on the Accused's Request for Withdrawal of his Counsel*, 29 March 2001, the Trial Chamber noted:

> the appointment of co-counsel, assistants and investigators are administrative matters falling within the powers and discretion of the Registrar. Lead counsel must initiate requests for such appointments, and he is held responsible for complying with the practice directions of the LDFMS. It is clear that the accused is not entitled as of right to have co-counsel, investigators and assistants appointed; nor can he assert the right of decision over the appointment or termination of their contracts. As stated above, these are matters for Lead Counsel.

2.6.36 This indeed follows from the Directive on the Assignment of Defence Counsel, which provides that the lead counsel *"is responsible for the defence"* (Article 16(D), Directive).

Registrar Has Primary Responsibility in Determining Issues Relating to Assignment of Counsel

2.6.37 The Registrar has primary responsibility for deciding matters relating to qualification, appointment and the assignment of counsel. See *Hadžihasanović, Decision on Prosecution's Motion for Review of the Decision of the Registrar to Assign Mr Rodney Dixon as Co-Counsel to the Accused Kubura*, 26 March 2002.

Review of Registrar's Decision on Appointment of Counsel by Trial Chamber

2.6.38 In *Knezević, Decision on Accused's Request for Review of Registrar's Decision as to Assignment of Counsel*, 6 September 2002, the Trial Chamber held that in "exceptional circumstances" a Trial Chamber, pursuant to Rule 54 could review the decisions of the Registrar to ensure the proper conduct of the trial. The Trial Chamber found that the Registrar's decision not to appoint counsel of the defendant's choosing was correct as proposed counsel worked for the same law firm as counsel for an accused in separate ICTY proceedings. Hence a conflict of interest might arise. See also *Hadžihasanović, Alagić and Kubura, Decision on the Prosecution's Motion for Review of the Decision of the Registrar to Assign Mr Rodney Dixon as Co-counsel to the Accused Kubura*, 26 March 2002, in which the Trial Chamber reviewed a potential conflict of interest of a former ICTY prosecutor undertaking the defence of an accused at the ICTY.

Code of Conduct

2.6.39 Both the ICTY and the ICTR have issued a Code of Conduct to which Counsel appearing before the ICTY are subject. This Code was promulgated by the Registrar on the basis of Rules 44 to 46 of the Rules of Procedure and Evidence. See the Registrar's Decision, dated 12 June 1997:

> CONSIDERING Rules 44 to 46 of the Rules . . . concerning Counsel, which confer on the Registrar the responsibility for ensuring that only Counsel who are qualified to do so appear before the Tribunal,
> CONSIDERING that being subject to a professional Code of Conduct is an essential attribute of being qualified as Counsel,
> CONSIDERING that Counsel appearing before the Tribunal come from jurisdictions all over the world, and that it is in the interests of the Tribunal that they all be subject to the same Code of Conduct
>
> . . .
>
> HEREBY PROMULGATE this Code of Conduct. . . .

2.6.40 The Code was drafted on the basis of a review of a large number of Codes of Conduct from different legal systems, with the fundamental principles being extracted therefrom. On its own terms, the ICTY's Code of Conduct is to prevail, in case of conflict, over any Code of Conduct to which counsel may be subject in his home jurisdiction. (See The Code of Professional Conduct for Defence Counsel Appearing before the International Tribunal 12 July 2002.)

2.6.41 The ICTR also has a Code of Conduct to which counsel appearing before the ICTR are subject. During the 12th Plenary Session on 5–6 July 2002, amendments to the Code were made to introduce a provision to deal with the illegal practice of "Fee Splitting," whereby Counsel provide to the client a portion of the fees they receive from the Tribunal as Counsel (Art 5 *bis*).

2.6.42 Defence counsel in *Kovačević* requested in a Motion dated 28 April 1998 that a Code of Conduct for prosecutors also be promulgated. This was denied in an *Order on Defendant's Motion for a Prosecutorial Code of Conduct* on 12 May 1998, the Chamber considering that "the relief sought by the Defense is neither warranted in this particular case nor within the power of this Trial Chamber to order in respect of all cases before the International Tribunal."

2.6.43 It may nevertheless be assumed that lawyers in the Office of the Prosecutor are bound at least by the spirit of the Code of Conduct, if not by its letter. This could be considered an aspect of the principle of "equality of arms," enshrined in Article 21 of the Statute (see above, Article 21(4)(d): ". . . under the same conditions . . ." and equality of arms). On this point, see ICTR Rule 46 ("Misconduct of Counsel"), para. (A): "This provision is applicable *mutatis mutandis* to Counsel for the prosecution."

Ignorance of the Tribunal's Rules and Procedures Could Amount to Failure to Perform Counsel's Obligations

2.6.44 See *Order on the Defence Motion for Discovery* rendered by the Trial Chamber in *Galić* on 11 May 2000:

> STATES that any further Defence motion that so blatantly ignores the general rules and procedures governing the proceedings before the International Tribunal shall be considered a major failure of counsel for the Defence to perform his obligations.

2.6.45 There is more than a suggestion in this that the Counsel could be sanctioned for misconduct in the event of a repetition of the episode.

Counsel Found Guilty of Contempt Loses Rights of Audience

2.6.46 Counsel convicted of contempt does not have rights of audience before the Tribunal, even where the contempt decision is under appeal. See *Decision on the Request of the accused Radomir Kovac to allow Mr. Milan Vujin to appear as co-counsel acting pro bono* rendered by a Trial Chamber on 14 March 2000 in *Kunarac and Kovac*. See also Separate Opinion of Judge Hunt appended to this *Decision*.

Decisions Arising Under Code of Conduct

2.6.47 See *Decision on the Prosecution Motion to resolve conflict of interest regarding attorney Borislav Pisarević* of 25 March 1999. In that case counsel had personal knowledge of the events that were the subject of the trial, namely the attack on Bosanski Samac. The Chamber dealt with the matter as one of conflict of interest under Article 9 of the Code of Conduct ("Conflict of Interest"), ruling that the counsel could continue to represent his client provided that he obtained "the full and informed consent of his client to continue the representation." The issue would perhaps have more appropriately been dealt with as one of "Counsel as witness" under Article 16 of the ICTY Code of Conduct, which provides that:

> Counsel must not act as advocate in a trial in which the Counsel is likely to be a necessary witness except where the testimony relates to an uncontested issue or where substantial hardship would be caused to the Client if that Counsel does not so act.

2.6.48 The Trial Chamber had held that counsel "had personal knowledge of, and was intimately involved in many of the events at issue in this trial." In those circumstances, he was clearly a potential witness to contested issues and should perhaps not have been permitted to continue to represent his client even with the client's full and informed consent of the client. The exception to this would be if it would have caused the client substantial hardship to withdraw the counsel, but the Chamber made no finding on that matter.

Further Decisions Under Rule 45

2.6.49 See *Decision on Defence Request for Assignment of Co-Counsel* rendered in *Kupreskić* on 15 May 1998; *Order on Appellant Zejnil Delalić's Motion for Appointment of Co-Counsel* of 8 February 1998 (refusing to assign co-counsel for failure to demonstrate exceptional circumstances as required by Article 16(C) of the ICTY Directive on the Assignment of Defence Counsel); *Order on the Motion to withdraw as Counsel due to Conflict of Interest* of 24 June 1999 (refusing to authorise withdrawal of counsel where counsel had requested to withdraw on the basis "that he will be unable to provide effective assistance" to his client "without risking his employment"), *Decision on the Request of 24 June 1999 by Counsel for the accused Šantić to allow Mr. Mirko Vrdoljak to examine the defence witnesses* of 28 June 1999 (legal assistants are not ordinarily permitted to examine witnesses).

2.6.50

ICTY RULE 45 *bis* DETAINED PERSONS	ICTR RULE 45 *bis* DETAINED PERSONS
Rules 44 and 45 shall apply to any person detained under the authority of the Tribunal.	Rules 44 and 45 shall apply to any person detained under the authority of the Tribunal.

History of ICTY Rule 45 *bis*

2.6.51 Rule 45 *bis* was introduced at the ICTY's eleventh plenary session of the Tribunal on 24–25 June 1996. It is designed to provide for the legal representation of detainees who are not accused, i.e. persons detained by the Tribunal pursuant to either Rule 40 *bis* or Rule 90 *bis* whom the Tribunal has not indicted.

History of ICTR Rule 45 *bis*

2.6.52 ICTR Rule 45 *bis* first appeared in the 8 June 1998 version of the ICTR Rules of Procedure and Evidence.

2.6.53

ICTR
RULE 45 *ter*
AVAILABILITY OF COUNSEL

(A) Counsel and Co-Counsel, whether assigned by the Registrar or appointed by the client for the purposes of proceedings before the Tribunal, shall furnish the Registrar, upon date of such assignment or appointment, a written undertaking that he will appear before the Tribunal within a reasonable time as specified by the Registrar.
(B) Failure by Counsel or Co-Counsel to appear before the Tribunal, as undertaken, shall be a ground for withdrawal by the Registrar of the assignment of such Counsel or Co-Counsel of the refusal of audience by the Tribunal or the imposition of any such other sanctions by the Chamber concerned.

History of ICTR Rule 45 *ter*

2.6.54 Rule 45 *ter* first appeared in the 1 July 99 version of the ICTR Rules.

2.6.55

ICTR
RULE 45 *quater*

The Trial Chamber may, if it decides that it is in the interests of justice, instruct the Registrar to assign a counsel to represent the interests of the accused.

History of ICTR Rule 45 *quater*

2.6.56 ICTR Rule 45 *quater* was introduced in the 12th Plenary session on 5–7 July 2002. The purpose appears to be to give the Judges the ultimate power to assign a counsel to an accused, rather than the Registy.

2.6.57

ICTY RULE 46 MISCONDUCT OF COUNSEL	ICTR RULE 46 MISCONDUCT OF COUNSEL
(A) (i) A Chamber may, after a warning, refuse audience to counsel if, in its opinion, his conduct is offensive, abusive or otherwise obstructs the proper conduct of the proceedings. (ii) The Chamber may also determine that counsel is no longer eligible to represent a suspect or accused before the Tribunal pursuant to Rule 44 and 45. (B) A Judge or a Chamber may also, with the approval of the President, communicate any misconduct of counsel to the professional body regulating the conduct of counsel in his State of admission or, if a professor and not otherwise admitted to the profession, to the governing body of his University. (C) In addition to the sanctions envisaged by Rule 46, a Chamber may impose sanctions against counsel if counsel brings a motion, including a preliminary motion, that, in the opinion of the Chamber is frivolous or is an abuse of process. Such sanctions may include non-payment, in whole or in part, of fees associated with the motion and/or costs thereof. (D) Under the supervision of the President, the Registrar shall publish and oversee the implementation of a Code of Professional Conduct for defence counsel.	(A) A Chamber may, after a warning, impose sanctions against a counsel if, in its opinion, his conduct remains offensive or abusive, obstructs the proceedings, or is otherwise contrary to the interests of justice. This provision is applicable *mutatis mutandis* to Counsel for the prosecution. (B) A Judge or a Chamber may also, with the approval of the President, communicate any misconduct of counsel to the professional body regulating the conduct of counsel in his State of admission or, if a professor and not otherwise admitted to the profession, to the governing body of his University. (C) If a counsel assigned pursuant to Rule 45 is sanctioned in accordance with Sub-Rule (A) by being refused audience, the Chamber shall instruct the Registrar to replace the counsel. (D) The Registrar may set up a Code of Professional Conduct enunciating the principles of professional ethics to be observed by counsel appearing before the Tribunal, subject to adoption by the Plenary Meeting. Amendments to the Code shall be made in consultation with representatives of the Prosecutor and Defence Counsel, and subject to adoption by the Plenary Meeting. If the Registrar has strong grounds for believing that Counsel has committed a serious violation of the Code of Professional Conduct so adopted, he may report the matter to the President or the Bureau for appropriate action under this rule.

History of ICTY Rule 46

2.6.58 Para. (C) (which became para. (D) after the amendments of the twenty-fifth plenary session—see below) was added on 2 August 2000, following the twenty-second plenary session. A Code of Professional Conduct had in fact been adopted on 12 June 1997.

2.6.59 Rule 46 was amended at the twenty-fifth plenary session held on 12–13 December, 2001, adding new paras. (A)(ii) and (C).

History of ICTR Rule 46

2.6.60 Rule 46 was amended at the ICTR fourth Plenary Session, held in Arusha 1–5 June 1997, to authorise the Registrar in cases of misconduct to replace an assigned counsel. The amendment involved a modification to para. (A) and the addition of the new para. (C).

2.6.61 Para. (D) was adopted at the Fifth Plenary Session on 8 June 1998. A Code of Professional Conduct was adopted at the same plenary.

Warnings to Counsel and Prosecutors

2.6.62 For a Decision under this Rule, see the *Decision On The Motion Filed By Defence Counsel Concerning The Interfering Conduct Of Another Party* rendered by the Trial Chamber in *Akayesu* on 31 January 1997. A Counsel had complained that another Counsel had interfered, or tried to interfere, with his client while at the Detention Unit. While the second Counsel denied such conduct, the Commanding Officer of the Detention Unit confirmed it, and the Chamber found the allegation sufficiently substantiated. It stated:

> WHEREAS, pursuant to Article 16 of the Directive on Assignment of Defence Counsel ("the Directive"), assigned defence counsels are obliged to respect, i.a., the codes of practice and ethics governing their profession in the performance of their duties;
>
> WHEREAS the Tribunal is of the opinion that any interference aimed at or capable of disturbing the relations between other accused and their assigned counsels or the proper conduct of the proceedings before the Tribunal, constitutes a violation of Article 16 of the Directive and a breach of the ethics governing the profession of defence lawyers;
>
> WHEREAS Rule 46 (A) of the Rules of Procedure and Evidence ("the Rules") authorises a Chamber to issue a warning to counsel whose conduct is offensive, abusive or otherwise obstructs the proper conduct of the proceedings;
>
> WHEREAS Rule 46 (B) entitles a Judge or a Chamber, with the approval of the President, to communicate any misconduct of counsel to the professional body regulating the conduct of counsel in his State of admission;
>
> *DECIDES:*
> (1) to hereby warn to Mr. Luc de Temmerman that any further attempt to interfere with the relations between detainees other that his client and their assigned counsels, or to influence matters not relating to the defence of his client, or

otherwise to act in any manner conducive to the obstruction of the proper conduct of the proceedings, may motivate the Chamber to refuse him further audience before this Tribunal;
(2) to communicate, with the approval of the President, this warning to the Belgian Bar Association/the professional body regulating the conduct of counsel in Belgium.

2.6.63 See also the *Order* issued in *Delalić et al* on 16 June 1998 by the Trial Chamber:

REMINDS counsel for Mr. Mucić that he has already been warned twice pursuant to Sub-rule 46(A) of the Rules and that, should the present Order not be complied with in full, to the satisfaction of the Trial Chamber, counsel will be refused audience, the necessary consequence thus being that he will be withdrawn from representing Mr. Mucić and the defence case will be continued by co-counsel, with the assistance of such other counsel as the Registrar shall assign.

Failure to Attend Hearings

2.6.64 Repeated failure to attend scheduled court hearings may amount to misconduct. See the Decision of the Trial Chamber in *Musema* on 18 November 1997, following the repeated failure of assigned counsel to be present at the scheduled initial appearances of the accused.

2.6.65 Pursuant to ICTR Rule 46(A), the Trial Chamber first warned the Defence Counsel. In its *Warning and Notice to Counsel in terms of Rule 46(A) of the Rules of Procedure and Evidence*, the Chamber noted that the initial appearance of the accused before the Tribunal was adjourned twice due to the assigned Defence Counsel's disregard of the fixed dates for the initial appearance of the accused, who had on both occasions declined to accept another counsel. The Trial Chamber also noted that it was not prepared to countenance any further delays in the matter, particularly since the Tribunal was obliged under Rule 62 to record the accused's plea to the charges "without delay" after his transfer to the Tribunal.

2.6.66 After due consideration of the various unsuccessful attempts made by the legal staff of the Registry of the Tribunal to ascertain the assigned Counsel's availability for the initial appearance of the accused, the Chamber concluded that the conduct and lack of cooperation of Counsel was obstructing the proceedings and was contrary to the interests of justice, within the meaning of Rule 46(A). Accordingly, the Tribunal required Defence Counsel to be present in person before the Tribunal for the initial appearance of the accused on 18 November 1997, and issued a warning to the Counsel, pursuant to Rule 46(A), that she might be sanctioned by the refusal of further audience before the Tribunal if she defaulted in complying with the Tribunal's request, in which case the Tribunal would instruct the Registrar to replace her as counsel for the accused under Rule 46(C). The Chamber further instructed the Registrar to communicate the warning to the Swiss Bar Association.

2.6.67 As a consequence of counsel's subsequent failure to appear for her client's initial appearance on 18 November 1997, the Chamber decided, in accordance with Rule 46(C), to sanction the Defence Counsel by refusing her future audience, and instructed the Registrar to replace the Counsel.

Disputes with the Registry Not a Ground for Refusing to Attend Hearings

2.6.68 A similar situation arose in *Akayesu* on the day scheduled for closing arguments by the Prosecutor. On 19 March 1998, the Prosecution began its closing arguments, pursuant to Rule 86, before the Trial Chamber. The hearing had to be postponed for one hour due to the non-appearance of defence counsel, Nicholas Tiangaye and Patrice Monthe. Before commencing the hearing, the Chamber issued a formal warning to Messrs Tiangaye and Monthe pursuant to Rule 46(A). The Chamber then allowed the hearing to continue, noting that the presence of defence counsel during closing arguments was not mandatory under Rule 86 of the Rules of Procedure and Evidence, and observing that defence counsel could prepare their closing arguments on the basis of the transcripts of the hearing.

2.6.69 When defence counsel appeared for the afternoon hearing, the Chamber described the defence counsel's absence from the morning hearing as a "serious contempt." Counsel cited "problems with the Registry" as the ground for their non-appearance. The Chamber rejected this as a ground for leaving their client unrepresented at the morning's hearing.

Prosecution Warned Pursuant to Rule 46(A)

2.6.70 In *Nyiramasuhuko et al.*, in its *Decision on the Prosecutor's Allegations of Contempt* of 10 July 2001, the Trial Chamber found that the Prosecution had conducted itself improperly and recklessly by disclosing the identity of defence personnel allegedly in contempt of the Tribunal. The Prosecution were accordingly warned to desist from such conduct which the Trial Chamber found to be contrary to the interests of justice.

Fee Splitting

2.6.71 See 4.2.590. See also Article 5 *bis* of the ICTR Directive on the Assignment of Defense Counsel:

2.6.72

ICTR DIRECTIVE ON ASSIGNMENT OF COUNSEL
ARTICLE 5 *bis*
FEE SPLITTING

1. Fee-splitting arrangements, including but not limited to financial arrangements, between Counsel and their clients, relatives and/or agent of their clients are not permitted by the Tribunal.
2. Where Counsel are being requested, induced or encouraged by their clients to enter into fee-splitting arrangements, they shall advice their clients on the unlawfulness of such practice and shall report the incident to the Registrar forthwith.
3. Counsel shall inform the Registrar of any alleged fee-splitting arrangement by any member of his Defence team.
4. Following receipt of information regarding possible fee-splitting arrangements between Counsel and their clients, the Registrar shall investigate such information in order to determine whether it is substantiated.

5. Where Counsel is found to have engaged in a practice of fee splitting or to have entered into a fee-splitting arrangement with his client, the Registrar shall take action in accordance with Article 19 (A) (iii) of the Directive on Assignment of Defence Counsel.

6. In exceptional circumstances, and only where the Registrar has granted leave, Counsel may provide their clients with equipment and materials necessary for the preparation of their defence.

PART 3

THE STATUS, PRIVILEGES, AND IMMUNITIES OF THE INTERNATIONAL TRIBUNALS

Principle of the Inviolability of the Archives of the United Nations 3.1
ICTY Article 30: The Status, Privileges and Immunities of the International Tribunal 3.2
ICTR Article 29: The Status, Privileges and Immunities of the International. 3.2
Tribunal for Rwanda 3.2
ICTY Article 31: Seat of the International Tribunal 3.3
Headquarters Agreements 3.4
ICTY Rule 4: Meetings Away from the Seat of Tribunal. 3.6
ICTR Rule 4: Sittings Away from the Seat of the Tribunal. 3.6
History of ICTR Rule 4 . . . . 3.7
On-Site Visit 3.8
Sittings Away from the Seat of the Tribunal Must Be Necessary 3.11
ICTY Article 32: Expenses of the International Tribunal. 3.12
ICTR Article 30: Expenses of the International Tribunal for Rwanda. 3.12
Expenses of the International Tribunals. 3.13
ICTY Article 33/ICTR Article 31: Working Languages 3.16
Working Languages 3.17
ICTY Article 34/ICTR Article 32: Annual Report 3.19
ICTY Annual Reports 3.20
ICTR Annual Reports 3.21

* * * * *

Principle of the Inviolability of the Archives of the United Nations

3.1 See *Order for Limited Access to Registry Files* rendered by the Trial Chamber in *Simić et al* on 1 November 1999 (the principle of the inviolability of the archives of the United Nations set out in the Convention on the Privileges and Immunities of the United Nations of 13 February 1946 is primarily directed at national authorities and bodies external to the United Nations and does not apply to the ICTY with regard to information and material in the possession of the Registrar relevant to the discharge by the ICTY of its functions).

3.2

ICTY ARTICLE 30 THE STATUS, PRIVILEGES AND IMMUNITIES OF THE INTERNATIONAL TRIBUNAL	ICTR ARTICLE 29 THE STATUS, PRIVILEGES AND IMMUNITIES OF THE INTERNATIONAL TRIBUNAL FOR RWANDA
1. The Convention on the Privileges and Immunities of the United Nations of 13 February 1946 shall apply to the International Tribunal, the judges, the Prosecutor and his staff, and the Registrar and his staff. 2. The judges, the Prosecutor and the Registrar shall enjoy the privileges and immunities, exemptions and facilities accorded to diplomatic envoys, in accordance with international law. 3. The staff of the Prosecutor and of the Registrar shall enjoy the privileges and immunities accorded to officials of the United Nations under articles V and VII of the Convention referred to in paragraph 1 of this article. 4. Other persons, including the accused, required at the seat of the International Tribunal shall be accorded such treatment as is necessary for the proper functioning of the International Tribunal.	1. The Convention on the Privileges and Immunities of the United Nations of 13 February 1946 shall apply to the International Tribunal for Rwanda, the judges, the Prosecutor and his staff, and the Registrar and his or her staff. 2. The judges, the Prosecutor and the Registrar shall enjoy the privileges and immunities, exemptions and facilities accorded to diplomatic envoys, in accordance with international law. 3. The staff of the Prosecutor and of the Registrar shall enjoy the privileges and immunities accorded to officials of the United Nations under articles V and VII of the Convention referred to in paragraph 1 of this article. 4. Other persons, including the accused, required at the seat or meeting place of the International Tribunal for Rwanda shall be accorded such treatment as is necessary for the proper functioning of the International Tribunal for Rwanda.

3.3

ICTY ARTICLE 31 SEAT OF THE INTERNATIONAL TRIBUNAL
The International Tribunal shall have its seat at The Hague.

Headquarters Agreements

3.4 The "Agreement between the United Nations and the Kingdom of the Netherlands Concerning the Headquarters of the International Tribunal for the Prosecution of Persons Responsible for Serious Violations of International Humanitarian Law Committed in the Territory of the Former Yugoslavia Since 1991," (the "*Headquarters Agreement*"), was signed on 19 July 1994 (S/1994/848). It is found in the ICTY's *Basic Documents 1995*, pp. 239–283.

3.5 The ICTR's relations with the Host Country, Tanzania, are governed by the Headquarters Agreement signed on 21 August 1995 between the ICTR and the United Republic of Tanzania (A/51/399; S/1996/778—appendix).

3.6

ICTY RULE 4 MEETINGS AWAY FROM THE SEAT OF THE TRIBUNAL	ICTR RULE 4 SITTINGS AWAY FROM THE SEAT OF THE TRIBUNAL
A Chamber may exercise its functions at a place other than the seat of the Tribunal, if so authorised by the President in the interests of justice.	A Chamber or a Judge may exercise their functions at a place other than the seat of the Tribunal, if so authorised by the President in the interests of justice.

History of ICTR Rule 4

3.7 The title of ICTR Rule 4 was amended from "*Meetings* away from the Seat of the Tribunal"; the title adopted by the ICTY. The words, "or a Judge" and "their functions" as opposed to "its functions," were also added by the ICTR.

On-Site Visit

3.8 See, in the *Kupreškić* case, the *Request to the President to Authorise an On-Site Visit Pursuant To Rule 4 Of The Rules Of Procedure And Evidence* issued by the Trial Chamber on 28 August 1998, requesting a meeting away from the seat of the Tribunal in Ahmici in central Bosnia, and the subsequent authorisation by President McDonald in her *Authorisation By The President Of An On-Site Visit Pursuant To Rule 4 Of The Rules Of Procedure And Evidence* of 29 September 1998.

3.9 The grounds for the Trial Chamber's request were as follows:

> NOTING that it would appear to be in the interests of justice in this case for the Chamber to undertake an on-site visit to the places described in the indictment, notably Ahmici and its environs, including Vitez, in order to obtain first-hand knowledge and estimation of the topography of the region including distances between houses, missile trajectories and travel routes, and to assess the extent of destruction visited upon the locality,
>
> CONSIDERING that the facts of the present case, notably the peculiarity that it involves events occurring principally in one small village which can be visited in one day, and the fate of the inhabitants of that village and multiple descriptions of attacks upon and flight from various houses which are in close proximity to each other,
>
> CONSIDERING that the prospect of such an on-site visit was raised by the Chamber *proprio motu* at the hearing of 27 August 1998, and was fully supported by both Prosecution and Defence. . . .

CONSIDERING, moreover, that the Tribunal has a mandate, *inter alia*, to contribute through its judicial proceedings to national reconciliation and that such an end may also be promoted by the Trial Chamber evincing its willingness to travel to the region in a truth-finding mission to see at first-hand the places which are the subject of the indictment. . . .

. . .

CONSIDERING that similar provisions exist in both national and international legal systems, including that of the International Court of Justice (see Articles 55 and 66 of the Rules of the Court). . . .

3.10 The President of the Tribunal endorsed these reasons in her authorisation of the on-site visit. In the event, the trip was cancelled on 19 October 1998 due to safety concerns raised by SFOR (see ICTY Press Release CC/PIU/354-E).

Sittings Away from the Seat of the Tribunal Must Be Necessary

3.11 A defence motion was presented in *Akayesu* which requested the Trial Chamber and parties to travel to Taba Commune in Rwanda—where the acts charged in the indictment took place—in order to establish the existence or otherwise of several mass graves. The defence also requested the appointment of a medico-legal expert to establish by exhumation the death or otherwise of three specific persons. In an oral decision rendered on 17 February 1998, the Trial Chamber rejected the motion on the grounds that the visit to the scene of the mass graves was not necessary, nor was the appointment of a medico-legal expert. On the second point, the Tribunal noted that since the deaths of the three persons would have taken place some four years before, during which time the corpses could have been dug up and re-buried, the appointment of a medico-legal expert would be neither opportune nor useful in establishing the truth.

3.12

ICTY ARTICLE 32 EXPENSES OF THE INTERNATIONAL TRIBUNAL	ICTR ARTICLE 30 EXPENSES OF THE INTERNATIONAL TRIBUNAL FOR RWANDA
The expenses of the International Tribunal shall be borne by the regular budget of the United Nations in accordance with Article 17 of the Charter of the United Nations.	The expenses of the International Tribunal for Rwanda shall be expenses of the Organisation in accordance with Article 17 of the Charter of the United Nations.

Expenses of the International Tribunals

3.13 Article 30 of the Statute of the ICTR differs from Article 32 of the Statute of the ICTY in that it omits mention of the "regular budget of the United Nations," instead referring to "expenses of the Organisation."

3.14 Article 17 of the United Nations Charter reads in part:

> 1. The General Assembly shall consider and approve the budget of the Organization.

3.15 The budgetary process entails the tabling by the Secretary-General of the proposed budget prepared by the Tribunal's Registrar, for consideration by the Committee on Administration and Budgetary Questions. This Committee then advises the Fifth Committee of the General Assembly, which then considers the budget proposal and passes on its recommendations to the General Assembly, which in turns votes for approval by resolution.

3.16

ICTY ARTICLE 33 WORKING LANGUAGES	ICTR ARTICLE 31 WORKING LANGUAGES
The working languages of the International Tribunal shall be English and French.	The working languages of the International Tribunal shall be English and French.

Working Languages

3.17 Given that all proceedings, and all of the documents which the Prosecution intends to use at trial, must also be translated into the language of the accused, the *de facto* working languages of the ICTY are English, French and Bosnian-Croatian-Serbian ("BCS") and of the ICTR are English, French and Kinyarwanda.

3.18 In a Separate Declaration to the *Tadić* Interlocutory Appeal on Jurisdiction Decision of 2 October 1995, Judge Deschênes protested against the fact that the Decision was rendered only in English:

> 2. ... This offends two principles which should direct the Tribunal's conduct:
> a) the simultaneous publication of the English and French texts of the Judgements of the Tribunal;
> b) the equally authoritative character of both texts.
>
> 3. Most regretfully both principles are breached to-day. The Appeals Chamber renders this Judgement in English only, it endows this sole version with the character of authenticity and foresees that a non-authentic French version of its Judgement will be published at a later date. The Tribunal's other language is thus relegated to the role of a tool of questionable usefulness, contrary to the spirit and the letter of the instruments which ought to guide the Tribunal's action.
>
> ...
>
> 18. In light of the Statutes, Rules, Regulations and best international usages, one cannot and should not tolerate, in this Tribunal, that the French speaking jurists must, either work in a language with which they are less fluent, or risk to be scientifically overrun while awaiting an official text to which they are entitled.

3.19

ICTY ARTICLE 34 ANNUAL REPORT	ICTR ARTICLE 32 ANNUAL REPORT
The President of the International Tribunal shall submit an annual report of the International Tribunal to the Security Council and to the General Assembly.	The President of the International Tribunal for Rwanda shall submit an annual report of the International Tribunal for Rwanda to the Security Council and to the General Assembly.

Cross Reference: Rule 3.

ICTY Annual Reports

3.20 To date, the ICTY President has submitted nine Annual Reports to the United Nations General Assembly and Security Council:

- First Annual Report, dated 29 August 1994 (A/49/342);
- Second Annual Report, dated 23 August 1995 (A/50/365);
- Third Annual Report, dated 16 August 1996 (A/51/292);
- Fourth Annual Report, dated 7 August 1997(A/52/375);
- Fifth Annual Report, dated 10 August 1998 (A/53/219);
- Sixth Annual Report, dated 25 August 1999 (A/54/187);
- Seventh Annual Report, dated 7 August 2000 (A/55/273);
- Eighth Annual Report, dated 17 September 2001 (A/56/352); and
- Ninth Annual Report, dated 4 August 2002 (A/57/150).

ICTR Annual Reports

3.21 To date, the ICTR President has submitted seven Annual Reports to the General Assembly and Security Council:

- First Annual Report, dated 24 September 1996 (A/51/399);
- Second Annual Report, dated 13 November 1997 (A/52/582);
- Third Annual Report, dated 23 September, 1998 (A/53/429);
- Fourth Annual Report, dated 7 September, 1999 (A/54/315);
- Fifth Annual Report, dated 2 October 2000 (A/55/435);
- Sixth Annual Report, dated 14 September 2001 (A/56/351); and
- Seventh Annual Report, dated 2 July 2002 (A/57/163).

3.22 The ICTY and ICTR Annual Reports are extremely useful resources for staying up-to-date with the ICT's case-law and activities.

PART 4

COMPETENCE OF THE INTERNATIONAL TRIBUNALS

ICTY Article 1: Competence of the International Tribunal	4.1
ICTR Article 1: Competence of the International Tribunal for Rwanda	4.1
General	4.2
Competence *Ratione Materiae*	4.4
ICTY Statute Does Not Legislate New Offences into Being	4.5
Prosecution of Only *Serious* Violations of International Humanitarian Law	4.11
Sexual Assault as a Serious Violation of International Humanitarian Law	4.17
Competence *Ratione Personae*	4.18
Competence *Ratione Loci* and *Ratione Temporis*	4.19

SECTION 1: SOURCES OF LAW

General	4.1.1
Principles of Interpretation of the ICTY and ICTR Statutes	4.1.2
Applicability of National Law	4.1.4
The Effect of National Law on the ICTs	4.1.7
ICTY/ICTR Law as a Fusion of Common and Civil Law	4.1.8
Precedent at the ICTY/ICTR	4.1.9
Sources of Law	4.1.21
Principles of Interpretation	4.1.22
Restrictive Interpretation	4.1.22

SECTION 2: SUBJECT-MATTER JURISDICTION

GENOCIDE	4.2.1
ICTY Article 4/ICTR Article 2: Genocide	4.2.1
General	4.2.2
Genocide in the Former Yugoslavia	4.2.16
"Ethnic Cleansing" and Genocide	4.2.18
Genocide Indictments and Verdicts at the ICTY	4.2.22
Genocide in Rwanda	4.2.25
The ICTR's Primary Focus on Genocide	4.2.25
The Rwandan Genocide Treated as a Preliminary Question of Fact	4.2.29
Genocide Indictments and Verdicts at the ICTR	4.2.33
Elements of Genocide	4.2.34
Relationship Between the *Actus Reus* and the *Mens Rea* of Genocide	4.2.35
Actus Reus of Genocide	4.2.39
Killing Members of the Group	4.2.41
Causing Serious Bodily or Mental Harm to Members of the Group	4.2.43
Deliberately Inflicting on the Group Conditions of Life Calculated to Bring About Its Physical Destruction in Whole or in Part	4.2.46
Imposing Measures Intended to Prevent Births Within the Group	4.2.48
Forcibly Transferring Children of the Group to Another Group	4.2.49

Rape as Genocide	4.2.51
Mens Rea of Genocide	4.2.52
The Special Intent to Commit Genocide	4.2.53
Intent to Destroy a Group "As Such"	4.2.57
Whose Intent?	4.2.62
The Need to Prove Individual Intent	4.2.64
Proof of Individual Intent May Be Facilitated by Evidence of the Existence of a Genocidal Plan	4.2.66
An Approach Which Helps Explain Variations in ICT Case Law	4.2.68
A Variable Standard of Proof of Genocidal Intent?	4.2.75
Participation in a Genocidal Plan	4.2.77
Toward a "Constructive" Approach to Intention Where the Acts Form Part of an Ongoing Genocidal Plan?	4.2.80
Proof of Specific Intent	4.2.83
The Existence of a Genocidal Plan	4.2.87
The Way in Which Other Acts Coming Within the Material Definition of Genocide Were Perpetrated Against the Same Group	4.2.89
The Relative Scale of the Crimes	4.2.95
The Perpetration, Against the Same Group, of Other Atrocities Not Coming Within the Strict Definition of Genocide	4.2.97
Intent to Destroy a Group "in Whole or in Part"	4.2.99
The Protected Groups	4.2.103
Objective and Subjective Approaches	4.2.105
The Objective Approach and "Stable" Groups	4.2.106
Toward a Subjective Approach	4.2.108
The Importance of the Perpetrators' Perception of the Group	4.2.112
Groups May Be Defined by Positive or Negative Criteria	4.2.114
"National Group"	4.2.115
"Ethnic Group"	4.2.119
The Tutsi as an "Ethnic Group"	4.2.120
"Racial Group"	4.2.122
"Religious Group"	4.2.124
Other Forms of Responsibility for Genocide	4.2.127
Complicity in Genocide	4.2.130
The *Actus Reus* of Complicity in Genocide	4.2.132
The *Mens Rea* Required for Complicity	4.2.135
Complicity in Genocide as an *Alternative* to Commission	4.2.138
Direct and Public Incitement to Commit Genocide	4.2.140
The *Actus Reus* of Incitement	4.2.140
The *Mens Rea* Requirement for Incitement	4.2.144
Incitement an Inchoate Offence	4.2.145
Conspiracy to Commit Genocide	4.2.147
The *Actus Reus* of Conspiracy to Commit Genocide	4.2.148
The *Mens Rea* of Conspiracy to Commit Genocide	4.2.149
Conspiracy an Inchoate Offence	4.2.152
Co-Conspirators Should Be Named in the Indictment	4.2.153
Conspiracy and Commission to Be Considered as Mutually Exclusive	4.2.154
ICC Article 6: Genocide	4.2.157
The ICC and Genocide	4.2.158
Conclusion: Genocide—From a Vague Notion to an Increasingly Consolidated Incrimination	4.2.159

CRIMES AGAINST HUMANITY ... 4.2.161
ICTY Article 5/ICTR Article 3: Crimes Against Humanity ... 4.2.161
Historical Background ... 4.2.162
Gravity of Crimes Against Humanity ... 4.2.169
Crimes Against Humanity in the ICT Statutes ... 4.2.173
Nexus with Armed Conflict ... 4.2.179
Conditions of Applicability for Crimes Against Humanity ... 4.2.183
    Existence of an Armed Conflict ... 4.2.184
    Nexus Between the Acts and the Armed Conflict ... 4.2.185
        Irrelevance of Motive ... 4.2.190
    The Acts Were Part of a Widespread or Systematic Occurrence of Crimes Directed Against a Civilian Population ... 4.2.193
        "Civilian" ... 4.2.193
        "Population" ... 4.2.200
        Widespread or Systematic ... 4.2.204
        Attack ... 4.2.211
    Discriminatory Intent ... 4.2.213
    No Need for Formal or State Policy ... 4.2.220
    Mens Rea Requirement ... 4.2.225
        Intent ... 4.2.225
        Knowledge ... 4.2.228
Crimes Against Humanity and "Ethnic Cleansing" ... 4.2.233
Constituent Offences of Crimes Against Humanity ... 4.2.236
    Murder ... 4.2.240
    Extermination ... 4.2.246
    Enslavement ... 4.2.252
    Deportation ... 4.2.253
    Imprisonment ... 4.2.257
    Torture ... 4.2.264
    Rape ... 4.2.266
        Rape as Torture ... 4.2.273
    Persecutions on Political, Racial and Religious Grounds ... 4.2.276
        Definition of Persecution ... 4.2.276
        Murder as Persecution ... 4.2.282
        Persecution Can Take Various Forms ... 4.2.283
        Actus Reus ... 4.2.284
        Mens Rea ... 4.2.287
        ICC and Persecution ... 4.2.291
        Listed Discriminatory Grounds Are Disjunctive ... 4.2.294
    Other Inhumane Acts ... 4.2.295
ICC Article 7: Crimes Against Humanity ... 4.2.300
Crimes Against Humanity—ICC Jurisdiction ... 4.2.301

WAR CRIMES ... 4.2.302
ICTY Article 2: Grave Breaches of the Geneva Conventions of 1949 ... 4.2.304
Introduction ... 4.2.305
Requirement of Armed Conflict ... 4.2.307
Nexus with Armed Conflict ... 4.2.314
International Armed Conflict ... 4.2.319
    General ... 4.2.319
    Procedural History of the International Armed Conflict Debate at the ICTY ... 4.2.323
        The *Tadić Jurisdiction Decision* of 10 August 1995 ... 4.2.323

128 • *International Criminal Practice*

The Appeals Chamber's *Tadić Jurisdiction Appeals Decision*	4.2.325
Separate Opinions by Judge Abi-Saab and Judge Li to the *Tadić Jurisdiction Appeals Decision*	4.2.331
Developments After the *Tadić Jurisdiction Appeals Decision*	4.2.335
Trial and Appeals Judgments	4.2.337
Internationality of Conflict to Be Proved at Trial	4.2.358
Protected Persons	4.2.361
Tadić Opinion and Judgment	4.2.365
Tadić Appeals Judgment	4.2.372
Delalić et al. Trial Judgment	4.2.375
Delalić et al. Appeals Judgment	4.2.379
Aleksovski Trial Judgment	4.2.380
Aleksovski Appeals Judgment	4.2.388
Blaškić Trial Judgment	4.2.392
Kordić and Čerkez Trial Judgment	4.2.394
Protected Property/Occupation	4.2.398
Constituent Offences	4.2.401
Actus Reus and *Mens Rea*	4.2.402
Wilful Killing	4.2.404
Inhuman Treatment	4.2.407
Torture	4.2.412
Biological Experiments	4.2.413
Wilfully Causing Great Suffering or Serious Injury to Body and Health	4.2.415
Extensive Destruction of Property	4.2.417
Compelling POWs or Civilians to Serve in the Forces of a Hostile Power	4.2.419
Wilfully Depriving POWs or Civilians of the Rights of Fair and Regular Trial	4.2.421
Unlawful Confinement of Civilians	4.2.423
Unlawful Transfer or Deportation of Civilians	4.2.426
Taking Civilians Hostage	4.2.428
ICTY Article 3: Violations of the Laws or Customs of War	4.2.330
Background	4.2.431
Security Council Interpretation of Article 3	4.2.436
General *Mens Rea* Requirement	4.2.439
Common Article 3 Falling within Article 3	4.2.442
Individual Criminal Responsibility for Violations of Common Article 3	4.2.445
Article 3 Not Confined to "Hague Law"	4.2.446
Residual Nature of Article 3	4.2.448
Conditions for the Application of Article 3	4.2.452
Applicability of Article 3 to Internal Conflict	4.2.454
Common Article 3	4.2.461
Customary Nature	4.2.462
No Violation of *Nullum Crimen Sine Lege* in Applying Common Article 3	4.2.463
Common Article 3 Applies to Both Internal and International Armed Conflicts	4.2.464
Persons Taking No Active Part in the Hostilities	4.2.469
Constituent Offences of Article 3	4.2.471
Employment of Poisonous Weapons or Other Weapons Calculated to Cause Unnecessary Suffering	4.2.472
Wanton Destruction of Towns, Cities or Villages	4.2.473
Devastation Not Justified by Military Necessity	4.2.476
Attack, or Bombardment, by Whatever Means, of Undefended Towns, Villages, Dwellings, or Buildings	4.2.480

Competence of the Tribunals • 129

Destruction or Wilful Damage to Institutions Dedicated to Religion or Education 4.2.481
Plunder of Public or Private Property 4.2.468
Common Article 3 Offences Prosecuted Under Article 3 .... 4.2.485
Murder (Common Article 3(1)(a) of the Geneva Conventions) 4.2.485
Violence to Life and Person (Common Article 3(1)(a) of the Geneva
Conventions) 4.2.486
Cruel Treatment (Common Article 3(1)(a) of the Geneva Conventions) 4.2.488
Taking Hostages (Common Article 3(1)(b) of the Geneva Conventions) 4.2.490
Outrages upon Personal Dignity, in Particular Humiliating and Degrading
Treatment (Common Article 3(1)(c) of the Geneva Conventions) 4.2.494
Violations of Additional Protocol I... 4.2.495
Unlawful Attack Against Civilians (Article 51(2) of Additional Protocol I);
Attack upon Civilian Property (Article 52(1) of Additional Protocol I) 4.2.495
**ICTR Article 4: Violations of Article 3 Common to the Geneva Conventions and of
Additional Protocol II** 4.2.497
Background 4.2.498
Applicability of Additional Protocol II and Common Article 3 to Events in Rwanda in 1994...... 4.2.502
Objective Test as to Sufficient Intensity of Internal Armed Conflict 4.2.503
Applicability of Additional Protocol II 4.2.505
Norms of Article 4 Customary 4.2.506
Individual Criminal Responsibility.. 4.2.507
Common Article 3 Threshold.. 4.2.508
Additional Protocol II Threshold... 4.2.509
Ratione Personae 4.2.510
Class of Victims 4.2.510
Class of Perpetrators 4.2.511
Ratione Loci 4.2.514
Nexus Requirements 4.2.517
Serious Violations of Common Article 3 and Additional Protocol II 4.2.521
Constituent Crimes under Article 4... 4.2.522
Violence to Life, Health and Physical or Mental Well-Being of Persons,
in Particular Murder as well as Cruel Treatment such as Torture,
Mutilation or Any Form of Corporal Punishment............................ 4.2.522
Collective Punishments... 4.2.523
Taking of Hostages 4.2.524
Acts of Terrorism 4.2.525
Outrages upon Personal Dignity, in Particular Humiliating and Degrading
Treatment, Rape, Enforced Prostitution and Any Form of Indecent Assault 4.2.528
Pillage.. 4.2.529
The Passing of Sentences and the Carrying Out of Executions Without Previous
Judgement Pronounced by a Regularly Constituted Court, Affording All the
Judicial Guarantees Which Are Recognized as Indispensable by Civilized
Peoples 4.2.530
Threats to Commit any of the Foregoing Acts............................ 4.2.531
ICC Article 8: War Crimes... 4.2.532
War Crimes Under the ICC 4.2.533
ELEMENTS OF THE OFFENCES 4.2.535
ICTY and ICTR Offences 4.2.535
Wilful Killing/Murder 4.2.538
Torture.. 4.2.542
Rape as Torture 4.2.552

    Rape 4.2.557
    Wilfully Causing Great Suffering or Serious Injury to Body or Health 4.2.568
    Inhuman Treatment/Cruel Treatment 4.2.570
    Detention under Inhumane Conditions 4.2.573
    Unlawful Confinement of Civilians 4.2.574
    Plunder/Pillage 4.2.576
    Outrages Upon Personal Dignity 4.2.581
ICC Elements of Crimes 4.2.584
Article 6: Genocide 4.2.586
Article 7: Crimes Against Humanity 4.2.587
Article 8: War Crimes 4.2.589
OFFENSES AGAINST THE ADMINISTRATION OF JUSTICE 4.2.590
ICTY Rule 77/ICTR Rule 77: Contempt of the Tribunal 4.2.590
History of ICTY Rule 77 . . . . 4.2.591
History of ICTR Rule 77 . . . . 4.2.597
Jurisdiction over Contempt 4.2.599
Need to Specify the Charge 4.2.601
Convictions for Contempt of Tribunal 4.2.607
Counsel Guilty of Contempt Struck Off List of Counsel Eligible to Be Assigned 4.2.619
Right to Appeal Conviction by the Appeals Chamber for Contempt 4.2.628
Acquittal for Contempt 4.2.630
Cautioning Counsel 4.2.631
Contempt the Prerogative of the Chambers 4.2.632
Chamber May Initiate Contempt Proceedings *Proprio Motu* 4.2.633
Severance of Joint Trials Based on Outcome of Contempt Proceedings 4.2.634
Contempt for Failure to Comply with a Subpoena 4.2.638
In Absentia Trial for Contempt 4.2.639
ICTY Rule 77(B): Investigating a Complaint of Interfering with or Intimidating a Witness 4.2.640
Disclosure of Protected Witness's Statement 4.2.642
Counsel's Absence from Hearing 4.2.643
Orders for Cessation of Contempt 4.2.644
ICTY Rule 77 *bis:* Payment of Fines 4.2.645
History of ICTY Rule 77 *bis* 4.2.646
ICTY Rule 91/ICTR Rule 91: False Testimony Under Solemn Declaration 4.2.648
History of ICTY Rule 91 . . . . 4.2.649
History of ICTR Rule 91 . . . . 4.2.651
Direction by Chamber to Prosecutor to Investigate False Testimony 4.2.652
Mere Contradiction Does Not Amount to False Testimony 4.2.653
Onus to Prove "Knowingly and Wilfully" 4.2.656
Elements of False Testimony 4.2.657
Contempt and False Testimony Before the ICC 4.2.661
ICC Article 70: Offences Against the Administration of Justice 4.2.665
ICC Rule 162: Exercise of Jurisdiction 4.2.666
ICC Rule 163: Application of the Statute and the Rules 4.2.667
ICC Rule 164: Periods of Limitation 4.2.668
ICC Rule 165: Investigation, Prosecution and Trial 4.2.669
ICC Rule 166: Sanctions Under Article 70 . . . . 4.2.670
ICC Rule 167: International Cooperation and Judicial Assistance 4.2.671
ICC Rule 168: *Ne Bis in Idem* 4.2.672
ICC Rule 169: Immediate Arrest 4.2.673
ICC Article 71: Sanctions for Misconduct Before the Court 4.2.674

SECTION 3: PERSONAL JURISDICTION

ICTY Article 6/ICTR Article 5: Personal Jurisdiction	4.3.1
Background	4.3.2
Individuals Under International Law	4.3.4
Irrelevance of the Group to Which the Accused "Belongs"	4.3.10
ICC Article 1: The Court	4.3.11
ICC Article 25: Individual Criminal Responsibility	4.3.12
ICC Article 26: Exclusion of Jurisdiction Over Persons Under Eighteen	4.3.13
ICC—Personal Jurisdiction	4.3.14

SECTION 4: TEMPORAL AND TERRITORIAL JURISDICTION

ICTY Article 8/ICTR Article 7: Territorial and Temporal Jurisdiction	4.4.1
Link Between Temporal and Territorial Jurisdiction and Existence of Armed Conflict	4.4.2
The Territory of the Former Yugoslavia	4.4.3
Kosovo	4.4.5
Macedonia	4.4.16
ICTR—Temporal Jurisdiction	4.4.17
ICC Article 11: Jurisdiction *Ratione Temporis*	4.4.19
ICC Article 4: Legal Status and Powers of the Court	4.4.20
ICC Article 12: Preconditions to the Exercise of Jurisdiction	4.4.21
ICC Article 13: Exercise of Jurisdiction	4.4.22
ICC—Territorial Jurisdiction	4.4.23

* * * * *

4.1

ICTY Article 1 Competence of the International Tribunal	ICTR Article 1 Competence of the International Tribunal for Rwanda
The International Tribunal shall have the power to prosecute persons responsible for serious violations of international humanitarian law committed in the territory of the former Yugoslavia since 1991 in accordance with the provisions of the present Statute.	The International Tribunal for Rwanda shall have the power to prosecute persons responsible for serious violations of international humanitarian law committed in the territory of Rwanda and Rwandan citizens responsible for such violations committed in the territory of neighbouring States, between 1 January 1994 and 31 December 1994, in accordance with the provisions of the present Statute.

General

4.2 Article 1 of the ICTY and ICTR Statutes is a general article conferring competence on the tribunals. As ICTY Trial Chamber II stated in the *Tadić Opinion and Judgement:*

> 558. The competence of this International Tribunal and hence of this Trial Chamber is determined by the terms of the Statute. Article 1 of the Statute confers power to prosecute persons responsible for serious violations of international humanitarian

law committed in the territory of the former Yugoslavia since 1991. The Statute then, in Articles 2,3,4 and 5, specifies the crimes under international law over which the International Tribunal has jurisdiction.

4.3 The tribunals' specific competence is spelt out elsewhere in their Statutes—see below.

Competence *Ratione Materiae*

4.4 The ICTs' competence *ratione materiae*, or subject-matter jurisdiction, refers to the crimes which the ICTs have the power to prosecute. These are set out in articles 2 to 5 of the ICTY Statute and in articles 2, 3 and 4 of the ICTR Statute.

ICTY Statute Does Not Legislate New Offences into Being

4.5 It is of fundamental significance that the Statutes of the ICTY and ICTR are not *legislation*. The United Nations Security Council had no power to create new offences, or new forms of criminal responsibility in respect of those offences. This is made clear in the Report of the Secretary-General (S/25704) on the ICTY's Statute, para. 29:

> *It should be pointed out that, in assigning to the International Tribunal the task of prosecuting persons responsible for serious violations of international humanitarian law*, the Security Council would not be creating or purporting to 'legislate' that law. *Rather, the International Tribunal would have the task of applying existing international humanitarian law.* (emphasis added)

4.6 This is an aspect of the principle of legality, or *nullum crimen sine lege* (see below, 6.1.1 *et seq.*).

4.7 See also the *Decision on Application for Leave to Appeal (Form of the Indictment)* rendered in *Delalić et al* on 15 October 1996, by the Bench of the Appeals Chamber. The Bench stated with regard to the sources of the Tribunal's competence *ratione materiae:*

> 26. ... the Tribunal's Statute does not create new offences but rather serves to give the Tribunal jurisdiction over offences which are already part of customary law. As the Secretary-General comments in his Report on the Tribunal's Statute (S/25704): "... the international tribunal should apply rules of international humanitarian law which are beyond any doubt part of customary law so that the problem of adherence of some but not all States to specific conventions does not arise" (para. 34).
>
> 27. ... the Report of the Secretary-General to the Security Council of 1993 on the Statute of this Tribunal in his exposition of Articles 2,3,4 and 5 of the Statute clearly referred the crimes enumerated in them to their sources of international humanitarian law, for example, the Geneva Conventions of 1949, the Hague Convention (IV) of 1907, the Nuremberg Charter of 1945 and the Genocide Convention of 1948. The Bench takes the view, therefore, that Articles 2,3,4 and 5 of the Statute are shorthand for the corresponding norms of international humanitarian law. ...

4.8 On this point, in relation to the requirments of an indictment, see the Trial Chamber's *Kvočka Decision on the form of the Indictment* of 12 April 1999: "the Prosecutor is not conducting a tutorial when she drafts an indictment . . . The indication in the . . . Indictment of the Article of the Statute that is contravened, or pursuant to which an accused is alleged to have incurred individual criminal responsibility, incorporates by reference all the elements set out therein." (Para. 36)

4.9 See also the *Delalić et al. Trial Judgement:*

> 402. The principles *nullum crimen sine lege* and *nulla poena sine lege* are well recognised in the world's major criminal justice systems as being fundamental principles of criminality. Another such fundamental principle is the prohibition against *ex post facto* criminal laws with its derivative rule of non-retroactive application of criminal laws and criminal sanctions. Associated with these principles are the requirement of specificity and the prohibition of ambiguity in criminal legislation. These considerations are the solid pillars on which the principle of legality stands. Without the satisfaction of these principles no criminalisation process can be accomplished and recognised.
>
> . . .
>
> 417. . . . The Statute does not create substantive law, but provides a forum and framework for the enforcement of existing international humanitarian law.

4.10 See also the Trial Chamber's discussion of this issue at paras. 414–417 of the *Delalić et al. Trial Judgement.*

Prosecution of Only *Serious* Violations of International Humanitarian Law

4.11 See the *Delalić et al. Trial Judgement,* in which the Defence argued:

> 175. . . . that the International Tribunal was established by the United Nations Security Council to prosecute and punish only the most serious violators of international humanitarian law, that is, those persons in positions of political or military authority, responsible for the most heinous atrocities. The Defence states that the International Tribunal should not "become bogged down in trying lesser violators for lesser violations" as such persons are more appropriately the subjects of prosecution by national courts. In addition, it is argued on behalf of Mr. Landžo that he is but one of thousands of individuals who might be prosecuted for similar offences committed in the former Yugoslavia and this places him in the unfair position of being made into a kind of representative of all these other persons, who are not the subject of proceedings before the International Tribunal.

4.12 The Trial Chamber rejected this argument:

> 176. The provisions of Articles 2, 3, 4 and 5 of the Statute set out in some detail the offences over which the International Tribunal has jurisdiction and clearly all of these crimes were regarded by the Security Council as "serious violations of international humanitarian law. Article 7 further establishes that individual criminal responsibility attaches to the perpetrators of such offences and those who plan, instigate, order, or aid and abet the planning, preparation or execution of

such offences, as well as, in certain situations, their superiors. It is clear from this latter article that the Tribunal was not intended to concern itself only with persons in positions of military or political authority. This was recognised previously by Trial Chamber I in its "Sentencing Judgement" in the case of *Prosecutor v. Dražen Erdemović*, when it stated that "[t]he Trial Chamber considers that individual responsibility is based on Articles 1 and 7(1) of the Statute which grant the International Tribunal full jurisdiction not only over "great criminals" like in Nürnberg—as counsel for the accused maintains—but also over executors."

4.13 The argument can certainly be made, however, that the ICTY and ICTR should concentrate on leadership figures, even if, under the terms of the Statute, they are *not barred* from trying less important figures. See Article 7(1) of ICTY Statute ("historical responsibility at the highest level. . . ."). (On the discrimination point, see 4.3.10).

4.14 The need to concentrate on leadership figures has ultimately come to be accepted by the ICTY. See Security Council resolution 1329 of 30 November, 2000:

> *Having considered* the letter from the Secretary-General to the President of the Security Council dated 7 September 2000 (S/2000/865) and the annexed letters from the President of the International Tribunal for the Former Yugoslavia addressed to the Secretary-General dated 12 May 2000 and from the President of the International Tribunal for Rwanda dated 14 June 2000,
>
> . . .
>
> *Taking note* of the position expressed by the International Tribunals that civilian, military and paramilitary leaders should be tried before them in preference to minor actors. . . .

4.15 This seems also to have been the intention with respect to the Special Court for Sierra Leone which was set up to try "persons *who bear the greatest responsibility* for the commission of crimes . . . *including those leaders who, in committing such crimes, have threatened the establishment of and implementation of the peace process in Sierra Leone*." (S/RES/1315 of 14 August, 2000, emphasis added). Unfortunately, the Secretary-General, in his Report on the establishment of a Special Court for Sierra Leone (S/2000/915 of 4 October, 2000), appears to have diluted this recommendation by the Security Council to the point where it has almost no content:

> 29. In its resolution 1315 (2000), the Security Council recommended that the personal jurisdiction of the Special Court should extend to those 'who bear the greatest responsibility for the commission of the crimes,' which is understood as an indication of a limitation on the number of accused by reference to their command authority and the gravity and scale of the crime. I propose, however, that the more general term 'persons most responsible' should be used.
>
> 30. While those 'most responsible' obviously include the political or military leadership, others in command authority down the chain of command may also be regarded 'most responsible' judging by the severity of the crime or its massive scale. 'Most responsible,' therefore, denotes both a leadership or authority position of the accused, and a sense of the gravity, seriousness or massive scale of the crime. It must be seen, however, not as a test criterion or a distinct juris-

dictional threshold, but as a guidance to the Prosecutor in the adoption of a prosecution strategy and in making decisions to prosecute in individual cases.

31. Within the meaning attributed to it in the present Statute, the term 'most responsible' would not necessarily exclude children between 15 and 18 years of age. . . .

4.16 The ICC is also intended to focus on "the most serious crimes of concern to the international community as a whole" (Preamble). Note that, with respect to war crimes, the ICC shall have jurisdiction "particularly when [those crimes are] committed as part of a plan or policy or as part of a large-scale commission of such crimes." It is to be expected that leadership figures, predominantly, will be prosecuted by the ICC, especially given the principle of complementarity, lower-ranking figures being more easily prosecuted in national courts than leaders.

Sexual Assault as a Serious Violation of International Humanitarian Law

4.17 It was argued by the defence in *Kvočka and others* that an isolated sexual assault could not be said to constitute a "serious violation of international humanitarian law" coming within the competence of the Tribunal. The Chamber in its *Decision* of 1 April 1999 rejected this argument on the grounds that the sexual assault formed part of a context of several kinds of offences which could clearly constitute serious violations of international humanitarian law. This would seem to imply that a context-less sexual assault could not constitute a serious violation of international humanitarian law. This would clearly be wrong. It may be that such a crime would not constitute a *crime against humanity*, due to the absence of a widespread and systematic context; that does not, however, prevent it from constituting a serious war crime.

Competence *Ratione Personae*

4.18 This term refers to the ICTs' jurisdiction over persons. See articles 6 and 7 of the ICTY Statute and articles 5 and 6 of the ICTR Statute.

Competence *Ratione Loci* and *Ratione Temporis*

4.19 This term refers to the ICTs' geographical and temporal jurisdiction. See article 8 of the ICTY Statute and article 7 of the ICTR Statute.

SECTION 1: SOURCES OF LAW

General

4.1.1 The immediate sources of law applied by the ICTY and ICTR are their Statutes, followed by their Rules of Procedure and Evidence. The tribunals must also have recourse, however, to international law and to general principles of criminal law.

Principles of Interpretation of the ICTY and ICTR Statutes

4.1.2 In the *Decision on the Prosecutor's Motion Requesting Protective Measures for Victims and Witnesses*, rendered in *Tadić* on 10 August 1995, the Trial Chamber majority enquired into whether it was "bound by interpretations of other international judicial bodies or whether it is at liberty to adapt those rulings to its own context" (para. 17). Regarding interpretation, the Chamber stated that although the Statute "is a *sui generis* legal instrument and not a treaty" (para. 18), the rules governing treaty interpretation contained in the Vienna Convention on the Law of Treaties (1969) should apply. According to Article 31(1) of the Vienna Convention, "A treaty shall be interpreted in good faith in accordance with the ordinary meaning to be given to the terms of the treaty in their context and in the light of its object and purpose." Applying these concepts, the Chamber majority held that:

> 18. . . . The object and purpose of the International Tribunal is evident in the Security Council resolutions establishing the International Tribunal and has been described as threefold: to do justice, to deter further crimes and to contribute to the restoration and maintenance of peace. (First Annual Report of the International Tribunal . . .) In the case of the International Tribunal, the context of the Statute is indicated by the Report of the Secretary-General of 3 May 1993 (U.N. DOC S/25704), which contained a draft statute adopted by the Security Council without amendment.

4.1.3 After having considered the applicability of the Vienna Convention, the Chamber majority noted that there was little to aid the ICTY in the interpretation of its Statute and Rules. It then proceeded to analyse the Tribunal's unique features and concluded that it "must interpret its provisions within its own legal context and not rely in its application on interpretations made by other judicial bodies" (para. 27).

Applicability of National Law

4.1.4 Concepts from national law are not to be automatically transposed to the ICTY. See the *Separate and Dissenting Opinion of Judge Cassese to* the *Erdemović* Appeals Chamber Decision, 7 October 1997:

> 2. . . . The point at issue is the extent to which an international criminal court may or should draw upon national law concepts and transpose those concepts into international criminal proceedings.

> To my mind, notions, legal constructs and terms of art upheld in national law should not be automatically applied at the international level. They cannot be mechanically imported into international criminal proceedings. The International Tribunal, being an international body based on the law of nations, must first of all look to the object and purpose of the relevant provisions of its Statute and Rules.
>
> ...
>
> 6. ... It follows that—unless expressly or implicitly commanded by the very provisions of international criminal law—it would be inappropriate mechanically to incorporate into international criminal proceedings ideas, legal constructs, concepts or terms of art which only belong, and are unique, to a specific group of national legal systems, say, common-law or civil-law systems. Reliance upon one particular system may be admissible only where indisputably imposed by the very terms of an international norm, or where no autonomous notion can be inferred from the whole context and spirit of international norms.

4.1.5 This appears to reflect the *Separate Opinion* of Sir Arnold McNair in the *South West Africa* case, International Court of Justice, I.C.J. Reports 1950, at p. 148:

> In my opinion, the true view of the duty of international tribunals in this matter is to regard any features or terminology which are reminiscent of the rules and institutions of private law as an indication of policy and principles rather than as directly importing these rules and institutions.

4.1.6 On the transposition of concepts from international human rights law to international humanitarian law, see also the *Foča Trial Judgement:*

> 470. In attempting to define an offence under international humanitarian law, the Trial Chamber must be mindful of the specificity of this body of law. In particular, when referring to definitions which have been given in the context of human rights law, the Trial Chamber will have to consider two crucial structural differences between these two bodies of law:
>
>> (i) Firstly, the role and position of the state as an actor is completely different in both regimes. Human rights law is essentially born out of the abuses of the state over its citizens and out of the need to protect the latter from state-organised or state-sponsored violence. Humanitarian law aims at placing restraints on the conduct of warfare so as to diminish its effects on the victims of the hostilities.
>>
>> In the human rights context, the state is the ultimate guarantor of the rights protected and has both duties and a responsibility for the observance of those rights. In the event that the state violates those rights or fails in its responsibility to protect the rights, it can be called to account and asked to take appropriate measures to put an end to the infringements.
>>
>> In the field of international humanitarian law, and in particular in the context of international prosecutions, the role of the state is, when it comes to accountability, peripheral. Individual criminal responsibility for violation of international humanitarian law does not depend on the participation of the state and, conversely, its participation in the commission of the offence is no defence to the perpetrator . Moreover, international

> humanitarian law purports to apply equally to and expressly bind all parties to the armed conflict whereas, in contrast, human rights law generally applies to only one party, namely the state involved, and its agents.
>
> . . .
>
> (ii) Secondly, that part of international criminal law applied by the Tribunal is a penal law regime. It sets one party, the prosecutor, against another, the defendant. In the field of international human rights, the respondent is the state. Structurally, this has been expressed by the fact that human rights law establishes lists of protected rights whereas international criminal law establishes lists of offences.

471. The Trial Chamber is therefore wary not to embrace too quickly and too easily concepts and notions developed in a different legal context. The Trial Chamber is of the view that notions developed in the field of human rights can be transposed in international humanitarian law only if they take into consideration the specificities of the latter body of law. . . .

The Effect of National Law on the ICTs

4.1.7 It is a settled principle of international law that the effect of domestic laws on the international plane is determined by international law (*Delalić et al Appeals Judgement*, paras. 76–77). Questions at issue before the international tribunals must thus be decided on the basis of international law; to do so is consistent with the nature of the question and with the nature of the tribunals' own functions.

ICTY/ICTR Law as a Fusion of Common and Civil Law

4.1.8 The law of the ICTY and ICTR is largely a fusion of common law and civil law (*Delalić et al Trial Judgement*, para. 159). Among the applicable principles of statutory interpretation (*ibid*, paras. 158–171), the cornerstone is discovering the legislature's intention (para. 160). The first principle is the *literal interpretation* of the provision in question. If that approach leads to absurdity or repugnance, however, then there are methods for determining the legislative intent, including the "golden rule" and the "mischief rule":

> 170. The International Tribunal is an *ad hoc* international court, established with a specific, limited jurisdiction. It is *sui generis*, with its own appellate structure. The interpretation of the provisions of the Statute and Rules must, therefore, take into consideration the objects of the Statute and the social and political considerations which gave rise to its creation. The kinds of grave violations of international humanitarian law which were the motivating factors for the establishment of the Tribunal continue to occur in many other parts of the world, and continue to exhibit new forms and permutations. The international community can only come to grips with the hydra-headed elusiveness of human conduct through a reasonable as well as a purposive interpretation of the existing provisions of international customary law. Thus, the utilisation of the literal, golden and mischief rules of interpretation repays effort.

Precedent at the ICTY/ICTR

4.1.9 The binding or non-binding effect of the jurisprudence of the two *ad hoc* international tribunals on each other, and indeed on themselves, is not spelt out in the Statute nor in the Rules of either Tribunal. There is no formal doctrine of precedence (*stare decisis*). In the ICTY *Decision on the Motion to Allow Witnesses K, L and M to Give Their Testimony by Means of Video-Link Conference*, IT-96-21-T, rendered on 28 May 1997, the Trial Chamber stated (para. 16):

> Prior decisions of a Trial Chamber in another case have no binding force *per se* in the case before us.

4.1.10 See also the *Decision on the Pre-Trial Motion by the Prosecution requesting the Trial Chamber to take judicial notice of the nature of the conflict in Bosnia and Herzegovina* of 25 March 1999, in which the Trial Chamber stated that the findings of other Trial Chambers on the nature of the conflict in Bosnia and Herzegovina:

> have no binding force except between the parties in respect of a particular case . . . that the circumstances of each case are different, and that as regards the controversial issue of the nature of the conflict, which involve an interpretation of facts, both parties should be able to present arguments and evidence on them.

4.1.11 However, since the *Aleksovski Appeals Judgement* of 24 March 2000, a doctrine analogous to precedent has been applied at the appellate level. After reviewing the practice of other international courts, the Appeals Chamber stated in its *Aleksovski Appeals Judgement*:

> 107. The Appeals Chamber . . . concludes that a proper construction of the Statute, taking due account of its text and purpose, yields the conclusion that in the interests of certainty and predictability, the Appeals Chamber should follow its previous decisions, but should be free to depart from them for cogent reasons in the interests of justice.
>
> 108. Instances of situations where cogent reasons in the interests of justice require a departure from a previous decision include cases where the previous decision has been decided on the basis of a wrong legal principle or cases where a previous decision has been given *per incuriam*, that is a judicial decision that has been "wrongly decided, usually because the judge or judges were ill-informed about the applicable law.
>
> 109. It is necessary to stress that the normal rule is that previous decisions are to be followed, and departure from them is the exception. The Appeals Chamber will only depart from a previous decision after the most careful consideration has been given to it, both as to the law, including the authorities cited, and the facts.
>
> 110. What is followed in previous decisions is the legal principle (*ratio decidendi*), and the obligation to follow that principle only applies in similar cases, or substantially similar cases. This means less that the facts are similar or substantially similar, than that the question raised by the facts in the subsequent case is the same as the question decided by the legal principle in the previous decision. There is no obligation to follow previous decisions which may be distinguished for one reason or another from the case before the court.

111. Where, in a case before it, the Appeals Chamber is faced with previous decisions that are conflicting, it is obliged to determine which decision it will follow, or whether to depart from both decisions for cogent reasons in the interests of justice.

4.1.12 Judge Hunt appended a Declaration to the Judgement in which he agreed with the majority's conclusion but for different reasons:

> 7. ... how then is the Appeals Chamber to respond to the tension between the special needs of certainty and flexibility? In my respectful view, the answer to that question is not to be found in the practices of other international courts (which are necessarily not criminal courts) or in the doctrine of judicial precedent in the domestic courts where the situation in which those courts operate is quite different to that in which this Tribunal operates.
>
> 8. The need for certainty in the criminal law means that the Appeals Chamber should never disregard a previous decision simply because the members of the Appeals Chamber at that particular time do not personally agree with it. The Appeals Chamber should depart from its previous decisions only with caution. It is unwise to attempt an exhaustive tabulation of specific instances when it would be appropriate to do so. The appropriate test, in my view, is that a departure from a previous decision is justified only when the interests of justice require it. ...
>
> 9. I therefore agree with the Judgement where it says that the normal rule is that the Appeals Chamber follows its previous decisions and that a departure from them is the exception. The reference to a previous decision means the *ratio decidendi* of that decision, the precise principle upon which the decision depended. The *ratio decidendi* cannot be distinguished merely because the facts to which it is to be applied are different.
>
> 10. Although it is not necessary for the purposes of this appeal (and thus is not part of the *ratio decidendi* of the Judgement), I agree with the Judgement, largely for the reasons given, that a Trial Chamber is bound by the decisions of the Appeals Chamber directly in point, although it should be permitted at the same time to express a reasoned disagreement with that decision for the later consideration of the Appeals Chamber itself.
>
> 11. I also agree with the Judgement that a Trial Chamber is not bound by the decision of another Trial Chamber, although I believe that it should have respect for that decision and consider carefully whether it is appropriate to depart from it.

4.1.13 It is, of course, "boot-strapping," i.e., tautological, to try to establish a doctrine of precedent *by precedent*. A subsequent Appeals Chamber would only be bound to follow the above ruling in *Aleksovski* if there had *already existed a doctrine of precedent*. A doctrine of precedent cannot, therefore, be established by a precedent; it is rather a matter of judicial practice, that is it is a question of whether judges do indeed over time form a practice of deferring to past judgements.

4.1.14 The Appeals Chamber's ruling in *Aleksovski* was in fact followed by the Appeals Chamber in the *Delalić et al Appeals Judgement* (para. 8).

4.1.15 Even before the *Aleksovki Appeals* Judgement, the practice of the two Tribunals was to refer to former decisions as persuasive authority, where appropriate. See the

Decision on the Preliminary Motion submitted by the Prosecutor for Protective Measures for Witnesses, rendered by the Trial Chamber on 26 September 1996 in *Rutaganda:*

> TAKING INTO CONSIDERATION the jurisprudence of the International Criminal Tribunal for the Former Yugoslavia, notably its decisions of 10 August 1995 and 14 November 1995. . . .

4.1.16 See also the *Decision on the Defence Motion on Jurisdiction* in *Kanyabashi* rendered by the Trial Chamber on 18 June 1997:

> TAKING INTO CONSIDERATION the decision of 10 August 1995 of the Trial Chamber of the International Criminal Tribunal for the Former Yugoslavia in Case No. IT-94-1-T, The Prosecutor versus Duško Tadić . . .

4.1.17 Given that the Security Council decided that there should be a common Appeals Chamber and common Prosecutor for both Tribunals, in part to ensure uniformity of approach, this practice makes sense. This much was recognised in the above-mentioned *Kanyabashi* Decision when the Chamber stated:

> in terms of Article 12(2) of the Statute, the two Tribunals share the same Judges of their Appeals Chambers and have adopted largely similar Rules of Procedure and Evidence for the purpose of providing uniformity in the jurisprudence of the two Tribunals. The Trial Chamber respects the persuasive authority of the decision of the Appeals Chamber of the International Criminal Tribunal for the Former Yugoslavia and has taken careful note of the decision rendered by the Appeals Chamber in the Tadić case.

4.1.18 Naturally, the decisions of the *Appeals Chamber* of the ICTY would have a certain amount of binding authority on a Trial Chamber of the ICTY, particularly where the Appeals Chamber has pronounced in the same case, as recognised in the *Delalić et al. Trial Judgement*, para. 167:

> it might thus seem that decisions from the Appeals Chamber of the Tribunal on the provisions of the Statute ought to be binding on Trial Chambers, this being the fundamental basis of the appellate process. However, decisions from the same or other jurisdictions which have not construed the same provisions in their decisions as the case being considered, are of merely "persuasive" value.

4.1.19 Even the binding force of Appeals Chamber pronouncements is not, however, spelt out in the Statute or Rules, except to the extent that Article 25(2) of the Statute empowers the ICTY Appeals Chamber to "affirm, reverse or revise the decisions taken by the Trial Chambers."

4.1.20 See also *Decision on the Joint Defence Motion to Dismiss the Amended Indictment for lack of jurisdiction based on the limited jurisdictional reach of Articles 2 and 3* rendered by the Trial Chamber in *Kordić and Čerkez* on 2 March 1999 in which the Chamber stated that it "may not disregard a previous ruling of the Appeals Chamber that has already discussed in depth most of the arguments presently put forward by the Defence."

Sources of Law

4.1.21 The ICTR has indicated that, as an international tribunal, it is bound by *universal* legal instruments, e.g., the Universal Declaration of Human Rights, rather than by *regional* legal instruments, e.g., the European Convention on Human Rights:

> WHEREAS, in this regard, the Tribunal recalls that, although nothing inhibits references to regional Human Rights agreements, such as the African Charter on Human and Peoples' Rights or the European Covenant (sic) for the Protection of Human Rights and Fundamental Freedoms, the fact remains nonetheless that both the Statute of the Tribunal and its Rules refer to universal instruments of Human Rights, ratified by a larger number of States, such as the Universal Declaration of Human Rights and particularly the International Covenant on Political and Civil Rights, and Article 14 of this Covenant which directly inspired the drafting of Article 20 of the Statute and of the provisions of the Rules concerning the rights of the accused. (*Decision on the Preliminary Motion filed by the Defence*, Trial Chamber 1, *Kayishema* (ICTR-95-1-T), 6 November 1996).

Principles of Interpretation

Restrictive Interpretation

4.1.22 In a *Decision on the Motion of the Prosecutor to sever, to join in a superseding indictment and to amend the superseding indictment*, rendered on 27 March 1997, the Trial Chamber stated that the Statute and Rules should be interpreted "restrictively," by which it evidently meant, "interpreted in the light most favourable to the accused":

> WHEREAS . . . the Tribunal deems it appropriate to reiterate, as did the Defence, that this is a criminal matter and that the pertinent laws must be interpreted in a restrictive manner, in the interest of the rights of the accused.

4.1.23 See also the *Kayishema and Ruzindana Judgement* of 21 May, 1999 (para. 103):

> if a doubt exists, [as] a matter of statutory interpretation, that doubt must be interpreted in favour of the accused.

Articles on the ICTY's Jurisdiction:

Meron, Theodor, "War Crimes in Yugoslavia and the Development of International Law," 88 *American Journal of International Law* 76 (1994).

Meron, Theodor, "International Criminalization of Internal Atrocities," 89 *American Journal of International Law* 554 (1995).

Aldrich, George H., "Jurisdiction of the International Criminal Tribunal for the Former Yugoslavia," 90 *American Journal of International Law* 64 (1996).

SECTION 2: SUBJECT-MATTER JURISDICTION

GENOCIDE

4.2.1

ICTY Article 4 Genocide	ICTR Article 2 Genocide
1. The International Tribunal shall have the power to prosecute persons committing genocide as defined in para. 2 of this article or of committing any of the other acts enumerated in para. 3 of this article. 2. Genocide means any of the following acts committed with intent to destroy, in whole or in part, a national, ethnical, racial or religious group, as such: (a) killing members of the group; (b) causing serious bodily or mental harm to members of the group; (c) deliberately inflicting on the group conditions of life calculated to bring about its physical destruction in whole or in part; (d) imposing measures intended to prevent births within the group; (e) forcibly transferring children of the group to another group. 3. The following acts shall be punishable: (a) genocide; (b) conspiracy to commit genocide; (c) direct and public incitement to commit genocide; (d) attempt to commit genocide; (e) complicity in genocide.	1. The International Tribunal for Rwanda shall have the power to prosecute persons committing genocide as defined in para. 2 of this article or of committing any of the other acts enumerated in para. 3 of this article. 2. Genocide means any of the following acts committed with intent to destroy, in whole or in part, a national, ethnical, racial or religious group, as such: (a) killing members of the group; (b) causing serious bodily or mental harm to members of the group; (c) deliberately inflicting on the group conditions of life calculated to bring about its physical destruction in whole or in part; (d) imposing measures intended to prevent births within the group; (e) forcibly transferring children of the group to another group. 3. The following acts shall be punishable: (a) genocide; (b) conspiracy to commit genocide; (c) direct and public incitement to commit genocide; (d) attempt to commit genocide; (e) complicity in genocide.

General

4.2.2　The term, "genocide," is based on a combination of the Greek word *genos* (which means race, tribe or nation) and the Latin suffix *cide* (which means killing). It was coined by the jurist Rafael Lemkin, in *Axis Rule in Occupied Europe*, to describe the deliberate plan of the Nazis and their satellites to exterminate entire groups, mainly the Jews and the Gypsies, but also other national and ethnic groups (see also Rafael Lemkin, "Genocide as a Crime under International Law").

4.2.3　Genocide is not, however, a phenomenon restricted to this century, but rather a sadly recurrent feature of human history. Groups have regularly been decimated through the violent action of other groups. Some authors affirm that the Bible is the first written register of such acts, although they have also been recorded in India and China.

4.2.4 On genocide from a historical perspective, see Andreopoulos, *Genocide. Conceptual and Historical Dimensions* (Philadelphia, 1997); Chalk-Johnasson, *The History and Sociology of Genocide: Analyses and Case Studies* (New Haven; 1992); Dobkoski-Walliman, *Genocide in Our Time. An Annotated Bibliography with Analytical Introductions* (Michigan: 1992); Cassese, Antonio, "La Communauté Internationale et le Genocide," *in Le Droit International au service de la paix, de la justice et du développement* 183–194 (Mèlanges Michel Virally, Paris, 1991).

4.2.5 While the Holocaust of Jews and Gypsies committed by the Nazis during the Second World War may be the most infamous and abominable example of genocide in this century, other instances abound in modern history: the extermination of Tasmanian and Australian Aboriginals in the nineteenth century, the forced removal and elimination of American Indians in the United States, the German *Vernichtungsbefehl*, or extermination order, and subsequent annihilation of the Herero in Namibia in 1904, the Turkish extermination of the Armenians in 1915 and contemporary massacres of Rwandan Tutsi in 1994 and Bosnian Muslims in 1992–1995.

4.2.6 On the origins of twentieth-century genocide, see *Exterminate All the Brutes* by Sven Lindquist (Granta Books, London: 1992); *The Origins of Totalitarianism* by Hannah Arendt (Harcourt Brace: 1968) and *L'Etat criminel, les génocides au XXe siècle*, by Yves Ternon, (Paris, Editions du Seuil, 1995).

4.2.7 By the end of the Second World War, this sort of mass criminality was considered intolerable. Indeed, although genocide was not incriminated as such in the Nuremberg Charter, the IMT described some Nazi crimes against humanity as acts of genocide (see the Judgement of 30 September and 1 October 1946). Moreover, when the international community adopted the Convention on the Prevention and Punishment of the Crime of Genocide in Paris on 9 December 1948 (the "Genocide Convention"), the prohibition was drafted with Nazi atrocities in mind.

4.2.8 On the Nuremberg judgements, see Cherif Bassiouni, "L'expérience des premières juridictions pènales internationales" (in ASCENSIO 2000, pp. 635–659); Dick de Mildt, *In the Name of the People: Perpetrators of Genocide in the Reflection of their Post-war Prosecution in West Germany* (Martinus Nijhoff Publishers, The Netherlands, 1996); Michel Massé, *Le droit de Nuremberg*, Confèrence pour le 50ème anniversaire du procès (Mémorial du martyre juif inconnu, Centre de documentation juive contemporaine, 28 November 1995, in *Le Monde Juif*, Revue d'Histoire de la Shoah No.156, pp. 7–16.)

4.2.9 The development of this first normative text relating to the crime of genocide is remarkable if one considers that, until its entry into force on 12 January 1951, the international norms relating to war crimes prohibited the massacre of civilians by enemy soldiers during inter-State armed conflict but did not extend to mass murder and extermination of a civilian population by its *own* government, whether committed in time of war or peace (breaches of the provisions of common Article 3 to the 1949 Geneva Conventions, which provides for the protection of civilian populations during internal conflicts, were not considered to be "war crimes" at the time).

4.2.10 On the Genocide Convention see: Jescheck, *Die Internationale Genocidium Konvention vom 9. Dezember 1948 und das Voelkerstrafrecht*, (Zeitschrift für die Strafrechtswissenschaft, vol. 66, 1954, p. 193); Lippman, *The drafting of the 1948 Convention on the Prevention and Punishment of the Crime Genocide* in (BULJ, 1985);

Antonio Lopes Monteiro, *Crimes Hediondos: texto, coment·rios e aspectos polímicos* (2nd Ed., Sao Paulo, 1992, pp. 66–74); *Ruhashyankiko* 1978; William Schabas, *The Genocide Convention at Fifty* (USIP, Special Report, January, 1999); *Schabas* 2000; *Sunga* 1997, pp. 105–119; *Whitaker* 1985; Robinson, *The Genocide Convention. A Commentary* (New York, 1960).

4.2.11 However, due to the historical and political context surrounding the adoption of the Genocide Convention, other instances of brutal mass crimes, including political purges in the USSR, China, Cambodia or Latin America, may not technically qualify as genocide, because political and economic groups are excluded from the ambit of the Convention, as is cultural genocide (See *Delmas-Marty* 2001).

4.2.12 The provisions of the ICTY and ICTR Statutes dealing with genocide are drawn *verbatim* from Articles 2 and 3 of the Genocide Convention. Indeed, the Report of the UN Secretary-General on the ICTY Statute affirms, referring to the ICJ's 1951 Advisory Opinion on Reservations to the Genocide Convention, that the 1948 Convention has become part of international customary law (S/25704, para. 45).

4.2.13 One result of this direct transposition is that the inchoate forms of genocide (attempt, direct and public incitement and conspiracy), as well as complicity, are included in the article defining genocide, creating possible conflict with the general provision dealing with individual responsibility for all crimes coming within the jurisdiction of the ICTs, which uses slightly different terms (ICTY Article 7 / ICTR Article 6). The Rome Statute of the ICC avoids this problem (see below).

4.2.14 The difference in the nature of the crimes committed in the former Yugoslavia and Rwanda have led the two ICTs to vary their approach to genocide indictments. They have elucidated difficult questions such as the constitutive elements of the crime, the criteria for identifying the protected groups as well as the means of proving the existence of the specific intent to commit the crime and the extent of personal responsibility of the participants in such organised crimes. Thus both ICTs have made an undeniable contribution to the law of genocide in the few years of their existence.

4.2.15 On the definition of genocide in the framework of the ICTs and the ICC, see Fronza E., "Genocide in the Rome Statute," in *Lattanzi/Schabas* 2000, pp. 105–137; VERDIRAME 2000).

Genocide in the Former Yugoslavia

4.2.16 In the context of the former Yugoslavia, the essential question has been the extent to which the crimes against humanity constituting "ethnic cleansing" carried out in furtherance of plans of territorial expansion may amount to genocide. When the Security Council established the ICTY, it referred explicitly to "the practice of 'ethnic cleansing,' including for the acquisition and the holding of territory" (Security Council resolution 827 of 25 May 1993). All ICTY Trial Chambers have also referred to "ethnic cleansing" in their decisions (see, in particular, the *Karadžić and Mladić Rule 61 Decision*, Trial Chamber, 11 July 1996, para. 64).

4.2.17 As for the relation between this practice and the "Greater Serbia" project, the Tribunal noted in the *Karadžić and Mladić Rule 61 Decision* that the large Muslim and Croat populations native to and living in Bosnia and Herzegovina were considered an obstacle to the creation of a "Greater Serbia" and the practice of ethnic cleansing was chosen as way of resolving the problem. The intention was to create a smaller Yugoslavia with a substantially Serbian population composed of Serbia, its two autonomous provinces, the Serb-dominated portions of Croatia and Bosnia and Herzegovina and Montenegro. On this subject, reference should be made to the *Milošević case*. A similar plan existed to creat a "Greater Croatia" comprising Croatia and Croat-dominated parts of Bosnia and Herzegovina (see the *Tadić Opinion and Judgement*, paras. 84–96 and 473–477).

"Ethnic Cleansing" and Genocide

4.2.18 The crimes involved in "ethnic cleansing" have generally been characterised as crimes against humanity or war crimes in ICTY indictments. However, the ICTY has considered that exceptionally grave forms of "ethnic cleansing" may constitute genocide, a crime which, "by definition," always arises out of persecution-type crimes against humanity (*Jelisić Trial Judgement*, para. 68; *Nikolić Rule 61 Decision*, para. 34). It should be noted, however, that there is no general agreement in the literature on the distinction between the discriminatory intent for crimes against humanity and genocide (see Part 8, section 3 "Cumulative Charging" below; and Law Clinic—Paris, "La distinction entre l'intention discriminatoire du crime contre l'humanité et l'intention génocidaire dans l'affaire *Jelisić*," *Rapport Final 2000–2001*, forthcoming).

4.2.19 Consequently, the Trial Chambers have several times invited the Prosecutor to consider amending the indictment when the "policy of ethnic cleansing" took the form of discriminatory acts of extreme seriousness which tended to show its genocidal character (see, e.g., the *Nikolić Rule 61 Decision*). See, on "ethnic cleansing and genocide," the second *Srebrenica* indictment of 16 November 1995 against Radovan Karadžić and Ratko Mladić. In confirming the indictment, Judge Riad considered that:

> The mass executions described in the indictment were evidently systematic, being organised by the military and political hierarchy of the Serbian administration of Pale, apparently with close support from elements of the army of the Federal Republic of Yugoslavia (Serbia-Montenegro). These executions were committed in the context of a broader policy of 'ethnic cleansing' which is directed against the Bosnian Muslim population and which also includes massive deportations. This policy aims at creating new borders by violently changing the national or religious composition of the population. As a result of this policy, the Muslim population of Srebrenica was totally banished from the area.
>
> . . .
>
> The policy of 'ethnic cleansing' referred to above presents, in its ultimate manifestation, genocidal characteristics. Furthermore, in this case, the intent to destroy, in whole or in part, a national, ethnical, racial or religious group, which is specific to genocide, may clearly be inferred from the gravity of the 'ethnic cleansing' practiced in Srebrenica and its surrounding areas, i.e. principally, the mass killings of Muslims which occurred after the fall of Srebrenica in July 1995, which were committed in circumstances manifesting an almost unparalleled cruelty. (p. 4)

4.2.20 This interpretation has been followed by the German Courts. In the 1999 *Jorgić* case, the German Federal Court of Justice classified 'ethnic cleansing' as genocide in relation to events in the former Yugoslavia (see text in Neue Zeitschrift für Strafrecht, 19 (1999), 396–404). See also the *Sokolović* case, decided by a Court in Düsseldorf, and then the Federal Court of Justice, in which the accused, who had been head of a Bosnian Serb paramilitary unit during the war in Bosnia, was sentenced to nine years' imprisonment for, *inter alia*, complicity in genocide in respect of crimes committed against Bosnian Muslims during the war (see *The Times*, 30 November 1999, p. 19). See also the *Kusljić* case decided by the same Court (*Kusljić* and *Sokolović* are reported at BGH 3 StR 244/00 and BGH 3 StR 372/003, respectively).

4.2.21 Furthermore, in its *Karadžić and Mladić Rule 61 Decision*, the Trial Chamber invited the Prosecutor to "consider broadening the scope of the characterisation of genocide" (para. 95) in the indictment to include other criminal acts besides those committed in the detention camps. It noted that:

> 84. . . . the evidence and testimony submitted suffice at this stage to demonstrate the active participation of the highest political and military leaders in the commission of the crimes by Bosnian Serb military and police forces in the detention facilities.
>
> . . .
>
> 95. At this stage, the Trial Chamber considers that certain acts submitted for review could have been planned or ordered with a genocidal intent. This intent derives from the combined effect of speeches or projects laying the groundwork for and justifying the acts, from the massive scale of their destructive effect and from their specific nature, which aims at undermining what is considered to be the foundation of the group. The national Bosnian, Bosnian Croat and, especially, Bosnian Muslim national groups, are the targets of those acts.

See also the *Jelisić Trial Judgement*, para. 68; and the *Nikolić Rule 61 Decision*, para. 34.

Genocide Indictments and Verdicts at the ICTY

4.2.22 As the extent to which "ethnic cleansing" may be considered genocidal depends on the facts of each case and the incidents in question, the relevant case law of the ICTY will be further examined below. To date, the Tribunal has charged 15 persons with genocide or complicity in genocide: Zeljko *Meakić* (IT-95-4-I), Radovan *Karadžić* and General Ratko *Mladić* (IT-95-5-I and IT-95-18-I), Dusko *Sikirica* (IT-95-8-I), Milan *Kovačević* (IT-97-24-I), Goran *Jelisić* (IT-95-10-I), General Radislav *Krstić* (IT-98-33), Radoslav *Brđanin* and Momir *Talić* (IT-99-36-I), Dragan *Obrenović* (IT-01-43), Milomir *Stakić* (IT-97-24-PT), Vinko *Pandurević* (IT-98-33), Slobodan *Milošević* (IT-01-51-I) (charged with genocide in the "Bosnia" indictment only) and Momcilo *Krajisnik* and Biljana *Plavsić* (IT-00-39 and 40-PT). All genocide indictments relate to the activities of Serb forces in Bosnia.

4.2.23 Only three of these trials have so far concluded: *Jelisić*, *Krstić* and *Plavsić*. At first instance, Goran Jelisić was acquitted of genocide at the close of the prosecution case (see the *Jelisić Trial Judgement*); a decision with which the Appeals Chamber disagreed, but without reversing the ruling or sending the matter back to the Trial Chamber (see the *Jelisić Appeals Judgement*).

4.2.24 The only conviction for genocide at the ICTY so far has been of Radislav Krstić (see the *Krstić Trial Judgement*) for his role in the taking of Srebrenica. Biljana Plavsić pleaded guilty to crimes against humanity on 2 October 2002. The Prosecution withdrew charges relating to genocide and war crimes. (See Plea Agreement, 30 September 2002).

Genocide in Rwanda

The ICTR's Primary Focus on Genocide

4.2.25 In the debates on Resolution 955, establishing the ICTR (8 November 1994, S/PV.3453), the representative of Rwanda, Ambassador Bakuramutsa, made clear his government's view that the ICTR should deal, primarily, if not exclusively, with the prosecution of genocide, "the crime of crimes" instead of dispersing its resources by prosecuting other (lesser) crimes. The Ambassador also bemoaned the fact that, according to him, "nothing in the draft resolution and statute indicates the order of priority for crimes considered by the Tribunal. In these conditions, nothing could prevent the Tribunal from devoting its resources on a priority basis to prosecuting crimes of plunder, corporal punishment or the intention to commit such crimes, while relegating to a secondary level the genocide that brought about its establishment."

4.2.26 Despite the scepticism of the Rwandan Permanent Representative, the pre-eminence of genocide prosecutions at the ICTR is evidenced by the fact that genocide is twice explicitly mentioned in the title of the ICTR: "the International Criminal Tribunal for the Prosecution of Persons Responsible for *Genocide* and Other Serious Violations of International Humanitarian Law Committed in the Territory of Rwanda and Rwandan Citizens Responsible for *Genocide* and other such violations committed in the territory of neighbouring States, between 1 January 1994 and 31 December 1994," setting it apart from the ICTY in this respect. Moreover, ICTR case law has established a hierarchy in the gravity of the crimes under its jurisdiction, considering genocide and crimes against humanity to be more serious than violations of Additional Protocol II, and that genocide is "the crime of crimes" (*Kambanda Judgement and Sentence*, para. 16).

4.2.27 In accordance with this focus, every individual indicted by the ICTR has been charged with genocide or one of the other, punishable genocidal acts, such as conspiracy to commit genocide (Article 2(3)(b) of the ICTR's Statute), direct and public incitement to commit genocide (Article 2(3)(c)) and complicity in genocide (Article 2(3)(e)). A number of those accused are in the ICTR's custody.

4.2.28 On the Rwandan genocide see: BEM ACHOUR/LAGHMANI 2000; MAISON 1999; Michel Massé, "L'affaire du prête Rwandais," (*RSC*, 1998, p. 836); *Ex-Yougoslavie et Rwanda, Une compétence 'virtuelle' des juridictions françaises* (*RSC*, 1997, p. 893); and R. Verdier *et al, RWANDA. Un génocide du XXe Siècle* (L'Harmattan, Paris, 1995).

The Rwandan Genocide Treated as a Preliminary Question of Fact

4.2.29 On 1 May 1998, Jean Kambanda, who was the former Prime Minister of the Interim Government of the Republic of Rwanda during the genocide and the highest-ranking person indicted by the ICTR, pleaded guilty to Genocide, Conspiracy to commit Genocide, Direct and Public Incitement to commit Genocide and Complicity in Genocide. This was the first guilty plea to crimes of genocide ever recorded. The guilty pleas were confirmed in the *Kambanda Judgement and Sentence* of 4 September 1998. Kambanda appealed against his conviction and sentence but the Appeals Chamber dismissed his appeal on all grounds on 19 October 2000. In so doing, the ICTR confirmed that genocide had been planned and implemented by the Rwandan government.

4.2.30 However, judicial notice has not been taken of this fact in subsequent cases. The closest a trial Chamber has come was in the *Bagilishema Trial Judgement*, where it relied on previous ICTR case law (*Kayishema and Ruzindana Trial Judgement* and *Musema Trial Judgement*) in determining that the prosecution was not required to produce new evidence that "a large number of Tutsi were attacked and killed at Bisesero in 1994" (see paras. 793–794 and 804).

4.2.31 In the *Akayesu Trial Judgement* of 2 September 1998, the first to deal with proof of genocide, the Chamber, accepting the Prosecution strategy of treating the existence of the genocide in Rwanda as a preliminary matter of fact to be determined, held that a "meticulously organised" genocide of the Tutsi "ethnic group" had taken place in Rwanda in 1994. (See section entitled, "Genocide in Rwanda in 1994?"). The key passage, in this respect, is set out below:

> 128. ... The Chamber's opinion is that the genocide was organized and planned not only by members of the FAR, but also by the political forces who were behind the 'Hutu-power,' that it was executed essentially by civilians including the armed militia and even ordinary citizens, and above all, that the majority of the Tutsi victims were non-combatants, including thousands of women and children, even foetuses.

See also paras. 118 and 126 of the *Akayesu Trial Judgement*.

4.2.32 As regards the responsibility of persons holding public office in a specific part of Rwanda at the time of the genocide, the ICTR has also treated the existence of genocide in that area as a preliminary question of fact. See, on this subject, the *Kayishema and Ruzindana Trial Judgement*, section 5.2 ("Did genocide occur in Rwanda and Kibuye in 1994?"—paras. 273–312, 405–406 and 528–530).

Genocide Indictments and Verdicts at the ICTR

4.2.33 As noted above, every individual indicted by the ICTR has been charged with genocide or one of the other punishable genocidal acts, such as conspiracy to commit genocide (Article 2(3)(b) of the ICTR Statute), direct and public incitement to commit genocide (Article 2(3)(c)) and complicity in genocide (Article 2(3)(e)). A number of those accused have been tried and found guilty of genocide: Jean *Kambanda*, the former Prime Minister; Jean-Paul *Akayesu*, a *bourgmestre*, Omar *Serushago*, a former militia leader of the *Interahamwe*; Georges *Rutaganda*, former 2nd Vice-President of the *Interahamwe*; Georges *Ruggiu*, a broadcaster with the Rwandan *Radio Television Libre des Milles Collines* (for direct and public incitement to commit genocide); Clément *Kayishema*, the former prefect of Kibuye; Obed *Ruzindana*, a businessman in that province; Alfred *Musema*, the Director of the Gisovu Tea Factory in Kibuye. However, Ignace *Bagilishema*, the former *bourgmestre* of Mabanza (Kibuye) was acquitted on all counts of genocide. Others are in the ICTR's custody, awaiting trial.

Elements of Genocide

4.2.34 According to the traditional criminal law approach followed by the ICTs, the crime of genocide is comprised of a physical and a mental element, the *actus reus* and the *mens rea* (see, for example, para. 58 of the *Jelisić Appeals Judgement*). The ICTs have dealt with the complex question of identifying these two elements in great detail.

Relationship Between the *Actus Reus* and the *Mens Rea* of Genocide

4.2.35 One problem with the traditional distinction between the physical and mental elements of crimes, when applied to genocide, is that the *acts* set out in the international definition (with the possible exception of "causing serious bodily or mental harm to members of the group") themselves make express or implicit reference to an intentional element (e.g., "killing members of the group," where "killing" implies intentionally depriving another of life). As set out below, this problem arises in most cases of crimes involving a *dolus specialis* or specific intent. It suffices here to note that the physical act must have been carried out intentionally, subject to the question of criminal negligence raised in the *Bagilishema Trial Judgement* (see the discussion under Article 7 and "Individual Criminal Responsibility" at 6.2.1 *et seq.*).

4.2.36 As for the ICC, the "Elements of Crimes," specify that:

> With respect to mental elements associated with elements involving value judgement, such as those using the terms "inhumane" or "severe," it is not necessary that the perpetrator personally completed a particular value judgement, unless otherwise indicated. (General introduction, paragraph 4).

4.2.37 Separate proof of *premeditation* of the act is not necessary, although this is clearly entailed by the notion of genocide (*Akayesu Trial Judgement*, para. 501). Thus, in the *Kayishema and Ruzindana Trial Judgement*, the Chamber held that although the *mens rea* consisting of the specific intent to destroy a group in whole or in part must be formed prior to the commission of the genocidal acts, "[t]he individual acts themselves, however, do not require premeditation: the only consideration is that the act should be done in furtherance of the genocidal intent" (para. 91). This allows the inclusion of acts committed on the spur of the moment by a person "inflamed" by discriminatory speeches, or in the context of a mass movement.

4.2.38 Furthermore, in the *Krstić Trial Judgement* (para. 95), the Trial Chamber stated that it "is conceivable that, although the intention at the outset of an operation was not the destruction of a group, it may become the goal at some later point during the implementation of the operation." This means that the genocidal intent can be conceived during a series of acts that originally began without the aim of destroying a group.

Actus Reus of Genocide

4.2.39 Before turning to the five categories of acts enumerated in the international definition of genocide, it should be noted that, during preparatory work for the Genocide Convention, the notion of *cultural genocide* was rejected. Claiming the concept was too "vague," the drafters emphasised the need for physical or biological destruction of a protected group. However, in the recent *Krstić Trial Judgement*, the Trial Chamber discussed whether UN Declarations and the case law of the ICTs and national courts such as the German Federal Constitutional Court were not evidence of a wider customary law concept of genocide (see paras. 575–579). Finally, the Chamber found that, for the purposes of its Statute, the acts capable of being characterised as genocide must be limited to the physical or biological destruction of a group:

> 580. The Trial Chamber is aware that it must interpret the Convention with due regard for the principle of *nullum crimen sine lege*. It therefore recognises that, despite recent developments, customary international law limits the definition of genocide to those acts seeking the physical or biological destruction of all or part of the group. Hence, an enterprise attacking *only* the cultural or sociological characteristics of a human group in order to annihilate these elements which give to that group its own identity distinct from the rest of the community would not fall under the definition of genocide. . . .

4.2.40 Acts of "cultural destruction" may, however, be taken into account in establishing the *mens rea* of the crime (see 4.2.52 *et seq.* below). As to whether individual criminal liability for genocide requires the commission of a quantitatively large number of material acts, see "*Intent to destroy a group in whole or in part*" at 4.2.99 below. On the interpretation of the specific acts included in the definition, see also the ICC "Elements of Crimes" (pp. 6–7).

Killing Members of the Group

4.2.41 Within the meaning of the Genocide Convention, the French and English translations of which are equally authentic (and thus the corresponding article in statutes of the ICTs: ICTY Article 4 and ICTR Article 2), "killing" must be interpreted as "homicide committed with the intent to cause death," being the most favourable interpretation for the accused, as was clearly set out in the *Bagilishema Trial Judgement:*

> 57. Article 2(2)(a) of the Statute, like the corresponding provisions of the Genocide Convention, uses '*meurtre*' in the French version and 'killing' in the English version. The concept of killing includes both intentional and unintentional homicide, whereas *meurtre* refers exclusively to homicide committed with the intent to cause death. In such a situation, pursuant to the general principles of criminal law, the version more favourable to the Accused must be adopted. The Chamber also notes the Criminal Code of Rwanda, which provides, under Article 311, that 'Homicide committed with intent to cause death shall be treated as murder.'

See also para. 501 of the *Akayesu Trial Judgement*, paras. 100 to 104 of the *Kayishema and Ruzindana Trial Judgement* and para. 50 of the *Rutaganda Trial Judgement*.

4.2.42 Premeditation is not expressly required with respect to killing. In any event, it is necessarily entailed by the notion of genocide (*Akayesu Trial Judgement*, para. 501).

Causing Serious Bodily or Mental Harm to Members of the Group

4.2.43 The District Court of Jerusalem, in its 12 December 1961 Judgement in the *Eichmann* case, stated that serious bodily and mental harm of members of a group could be caused "by the enslavement, starvation, deportation and persecution . . . and by their detention in ghettos, transit camps and concentration camps in conditions which were designed to cause their degradation, deprivation of their rights as human beings, and to suppress them and cause them inhuman suffering and torture."

4.2.44 According to the ICTR, "serious bodily or mental harm" includes, but is not limited to, torture, inhumane or degrading treatment and persecution (para. 504, *Akayesu Trial Judgement*). This was slightly broadened in para. 51 of the *Rutaganda Trial Judgement:*

> 51. For the purposes of interpreting Article 2(2)(b) of the Statute, the Chamber understands the words 'serious bodily or mental harm' to include acts of bodily or mental torture, inhumane or degrading treatment, rape, sexual violence, and persecution. The Chamber is of the opinion that 'serious harm' need not entail permanent or irremediable harm.

4.2.45 See also paras. 105 to 113 of the *Kayishema and Ruzindana Trial Judgement* (the phrase "serious mental harm" is to be determined on a case-by-case basis) and para. 59 of the *Bagilishema Trial Judgement:* "'serious harm' entails more than minor impairment of mental or physical faculties, but it need not amount to permanent or irremediable harm."

Deliberately Inflicting on the Group Conditions of Life Calculated to Bring About Its Physical Destruction in Whole or in Part

4.2.46 This refers to methods of destruction by which the perpetrator of genocide "does not immediately kill the members of the group" but which ultimately seek the physical destruction of the group, for example "subjecting a group of people to a subsistence diet, the systematic expulsion from homes and the reduction of essential medical services below minimum requirements" (paras. 505–506, *Akayesu Trial Judgement*). See also paras. 104 to 116 of the *Kayishema and Ruzindana Trial Judgement* and para. 52 of the *Rutaganda Trial Judgement*.

4.2.47 In the *Kayishema and Ruzindana Trial Judgement*, the Chamber said that the conditions of life contemplated would include "rape, the starving of a group of people, reducing required medical services below a minimum, and with holding sufficient living accommodation for a reasonable period, provided the above would lead to the destruction of the group in whole or in part" (para. 116).

Imposing Measures Intended to Prevent Births Within the Group

4.2.48 As noted in paras. 507 and 508 of the *Akayesu Trial Judgement*, this includes:

sexual mutilation, the practice of sterilization, forced birth control, separation of the sexes and prohibition of marriages. In patriarchal societies, where membership of a group is determined by the identity of the father, an example of a measure intended to prevent births within a group is the case where, during rape, a woman of the said group is deliberately impregnated by a man of another group, with the intent to have her give birth to a child who will consequently not belong to its mother's group.

Furthermore, the Chamber notes that measures intended to prevent births within the group may be physical, but can also be mental. For instance, rape can be a measure intended to prevent births when the person raped refuses subsequently to procreate, in the same way that members of a group can be led, through threats or trauma, not to procreate.

See also para. 117 of the *Kayishema and Ruzindana Trial Judgement* and para. 53 of the *Rutaganda Trial Judgement*.

Forcibly Transferring Children of the Group to Another Group

4.2.49 This act, originally seen as a form of "cultural genocide," was included in the Convention as a compromise when that concept was rejected, because it was argued that it would *eventually* lead to physical or biological destruction of the group. According to the ICTR, it would apply not only to the forcible transfer of children by the perpetrator of genocide but also to "threats or trauma which would lead to the forcible transfer of children from one group to another" (para. 509, *Akayesu Trial Judgement*; see also para. 118 of the *Kayishema and Ruzindana Trial Judgement* and para. 54 of the *Rutaganda Trial Judgement*).

4.2.50 It should be noted that, as a question of pure interpretation, it would not seem necessary that the transfer of children be carried out with the intention of destroying those children actually transferred. Such transfer would constitute an act of genocide as long as the intention was to destroy the *group* to which the children belong (at least in part), even if the intention was to *save* those children from destruction by transferring them. A practical example might be the transfer of children of mixed parentage to save them from the destruction of the group to which one of their "pure blood" parents belonged, as was arguably the case for the Australian Aboriginal population up until recently (see *Delmas-Marty* 2001, pp. 246–256). However, this concept sits uneasily with the notion that genocide only covers physical, not cultural, destruction.

Rape as Genocide

4.2.51 Rape and sexual violence may be used as an instrument of genocide, if committed with the genocidal intent to destroy the group. See paras. 731–734 of the *Akayesu Trial Judgement*. It can either be—as it was found to be in *Akayesu*—that the rapes of women were accompanied with the intent to kill the women or that the rapes were committed with the intent to impregnate the woman with a different "ethnic seed" or to so traumatise the woman that she would not want, or be physically able, to reproduce within her group afterwards.

Article:

Karagiannakis, M., "The Definition of Rape and Its Characterization as an Act of Genocide—A Review of the Jurisprudence of the International Criminal Tribunals for Rwanda and the Former Yugoslavia," 12 *Leiden Journal of International Law* 479–490 (1999).

Mens Rea of Genocide

4.2.52 The *mens rea,* or mental element, requirement is referred to as the "psychological" or "moral" element of criminal conduct in Civil Law systems. When considering the *mens rea* of genocide, it is useful to identify, on the one hand, the *dolus specialis*, or special/specific intent, being the intention to *destroy, in whole or in part*, certain human groups, *as such*, and on the other hand, the existence of a national, ethnical, racial or religious group the subject of the criminal intent. Indeed, whereas some national legislation, such as that of France, tends to treat the existence of a group as a question of fact (see *Delmas-Marty* 2001, pp. 263–265), ICT case law formally includes it as part of the *mens rea* of the crime.

The Special Intent to Commit Genocide

4.2.53 Underlying the concept of *dolus specialis*, or special intent, is the requirement that the author of an act commit that act not only with intention, but also with the intention to achieve a specific aim through that act. The specific aim of genocide is to "destroy, in whole or in part, a national, ethnical, racial or religious group, as such." This special intent must be formed before the commission of the genocidal acts, although premeditation of the acts is not required (see above). As the Trial Chamber noted in the *Akayesu Trial Judgement*:

> 518. Special intent is a well-known criminal law concept in the Roman-continental legal systems. It is required as a constituent element of certain offences and demands that the perpetrator have the clear intent to cause the offence charged. According to this meaning, special intent is the key element of an intentional offence, which offence is characterized by a psychological relationship between the physical result and the mental state of the perpetrator.
>
> . . .
>
> 521. In concrete terms, for any of the acts charged under Article 2 (2) of the Statute to be a constitutive element of genocide, the act must have been committed against one or several individuals, because such individual or individuals were members of a specific group, and specifically because they belonged to this group. Thus, the victim is chosen not because of his individual identity, but rather on account of his membership of a national, ethnical, racial or religious group. The victim of the act is therefore a member of a group, chosen as such, which, hence, means that the victim of the crime of genocide is the group itself and not only the individual.

4.2.54 United Nations General Assembly resolution 96 (I) defined genocide as "a denial of the right of existence of entire human groups," just as homicide is "a denial of the right to live of individual human beings." In 1996, the International Law Commission insisted that the victim of genocide is the group as a separate entity (see para. 552 of the *Krstić Trial Judgement*).

4.2.55 In the *Kayishema and Ruzindana Trial Judgement*, the Chamber observed that genocide "is a type of crime against humanity," differing from the latter in that "genocide requires the . . . specific intent to exterminate a group (in whole or in part) while crimes against humanity require the civilian population to be targeted as part of a widespread or systematic attack" (para. 89). During preparatory work on the Genocide Convention, the possibility of replacing the word "intent" by the expression "*having for effect*," was discussed as a way of providing an objective definition of genocide, but this was not accepted, as it is this special intent which creates the singularity of genocide as a crime (see *Ruhashyankiko* 1978, p. 25).

4.2.56 It should be noted, however, as pointed out in the *Jelisić Appeals Judgement*, that the content of the "specific intent" required for genocide is determined by the terms of the Statute of the ICT and not by the requirements for proof of *dolus specialis* in any particular legal system (paras. 42–52; see also "Participation in a genocidal plan" at 4.2.77 below). The ICTY in the *Sikirica Judgement*, noted that:

> an examination of theories of intent is unnecessary in construing the requirement of intent in Article 4 (2). What is needed is an empirical assessment of all the evidence to ascertain whether the very specific intent required by Article 4 (2) is established. . . (para. 59).

Intent to Destroy a Group "As Such"

4.2.57 The *travaux préparatoires* for the Genocide Convention show that the term, "as such," was added to the definition of genocide as a compromise, in the absence of agreement concerning the inclusion of the *motive* as a constitutive element of the crime. Indeed, while the phrase may be interpreted as introducing considerations of motive, most writers have seen it as simply reinforcing the fact that the individuals are chosen to be victimised due to their membership of a group (see *Ruhashyankiko* 1978, paras. 101–106; *Whitaker* 1985, para. 38; ILC 1996, Commentary 7 on proposed Article 17—Genocide).

4.2.58 The ICTR Trial Chamber seemed to lean towards the latter interpretation in the *Akayesu Trial Judgement*, holding that the victims were chosen because they belonged to the Tutsi ethnic group and not for their particular characteristics (paras. 124 and 521). However, the Trial Chamber took a more ambiguous approach in the *Kayishema and Ruzindana Trial Judgement*. Despite noting that "the 'destroying' has to be directed at the group *as such*, that is '*qua group*,*'* the Trial Chamber made a number of references to the need for the acts to be directed towards a specific group on 'discriminatory grounds,' and to massacres motivated by 'purely ethnic reasons' (Trial Judgement, 21 May 1999, paras. 98, 99 and 638), which seemingly suggest the relevance of motive. This ambiguity was expressly dealt with in the *Jelisić Appeals Judgement*:

49. The Appeals Chamber further recalls the necessity to distinguish specific intent from motive. The personal motive of the perpetrator of the crime of genocide may be, for example, to obtain personal economic benefits, or political advantage or some form of power. The existence of a personal motive does not preclude the perpetrator from also having the specific intent to commit genocide. In the *Tadić* appeal judgement the Appeals Chamber stressed the irrelevance and "inscrutability of motives in criminal law."

4.2.59 In that case, referring to Jelisić, the Appeals Chamber noted that "the fact that he took 'pleasure' from the killings does not detract in any way from his intent to perform such killings" (para. 71). The ICTs have not found it necessary to determine the exact motive of the accused in order to find him guilty of genocide. In the *Kambanda* case, for example, despite admitting his guilt, the former Prime Minister never stated the reasons for his acts. Moreover, in the *Kayishema and Ruzindana* case, evidence of radio announcements to the effect that all Tutsis had to be killed because they were the "accomplices" of the RPF Army, was rejected as proof of a non-prohibited intention by the Trial Chamber of the ICTR, which considered this to be a false pretext (*Kayishema and Ruzindana Judgement*, 21 May 1999, paras. 601–603). This pretext cannot, thus, be seen as the motivation for the attacks, and the underlying reason was not elucidated during the trial.

4.2.60 It follows that, although political groups were not included in the ambit of the Genocide Convention, if the acts in question were aimed at a protected group (national, racial, ethnical or religious) but for political motives, they may still be characterised as acts of genocide, as long as the perpetrator's intention was to destroy the protected group. *Why* he intended to do so is irrelevant to his guilt (see SUNGA 1997). Of course, this practical confirmation of the fact that the motives do not form part of the elements of the crime of genocide does not mean that declarations by the accused will not be taken into consideration by the tribunal as a factual element in determining whether he had the intention to destroy the group (see below), or in sentencing.

4.2.61 Finally, in the *Sikirica Judgement*, the Trial Chamber identified two cumulative elements, noting that "the Prosecution must not only establish an intention to destroy the Bosnian Muslim or Bosnian Croat populations in whole or in part, but it must also establish the intention to destroy those groups as such" (para. 61). However, the Chamber went on to state that:

> The evidence must establish that it is the group that has been targeted, and not merely specific individuals within that group. That is the significance of the phrase 'as such' in the chapeau (para. 89).

Whose Intent?

4.2.62 A recurring controversy with respect to the crime of genocide is whether the prosecution must prove that *the accused* possessed the requisite genocidal intent or whether the prosecution must rather prove that there existed a *plan or policy* which had a genocidal aim, and that the accused *participated* in that plan or policy by, for example, killing members of the group. The drafters of the Genocide Convention of 1948 were not necessarily thinking of *mens rea* in the technical sense in which it is applied in a criminal trial when they decided that genocide meant "any of the following acts committed with intent to destroy, in whole or in part, a national, ethnical, racial or religious group, as such . . ." (Article 2 of the Convention). Genocide was then conceived of as a mass crime, characterised by the fact that the aim of the particular crimes in question was to eliminate an entire human group. The emphasis being placed on those planning and implementing such mass crimes, it is unlikely that the reference to "intent" was meant to describe the state of mind of individual perpetrators of the plan for the purposes of criminal prosecutions.

On this point, see John R.W.D. Jones, "Whose Intent Is It Anyway? Genocide and the Intent to Destroy a Group," Ch. 22 *in Man's Inhumanity to Man: Essays in Honour of Antonio Cassese* (eds. Vohrah and Bohlander, Kluwer 2003).

4.2.63 Faced with the obligation of deciding questions of individual responsibility for genocide, both the ICTY and ICTR have struggled with the special intent requirement of genocide, especially whether it applies to the individual perpetrator of a genocidal plan or to the plan itself. The compromise that seems to be emerging in ICTY and ICTR Chambers and the Appeals Chamber is based on a two stage approach differentiating between the requirement for individual intent and the means of proving that intent in any particular case.

The Need to Prove Individual Intent

4.2.64 In the first place, it is accepted that the general principles of criminal law require the *ad hoc* tribunals to find an individualised intent. The Trial Chamber in the *Rutaganda Trial Judgement*, clearly set out the "individualised" approach:

> 59. . . . A person may be convicted of genocide only where it is established that he committed one of the acts referred to under Article 2(2) of the Statute with the specific intent to destroy, in whole or in part, a particular group.

See also para. 399 of the *Rutaganda Trial Judgement*.

4.2.65 The *Jelisić Appeals Judgement* stated that (emphasis added):

> 46. The specific intent requires that the *perpetrator*, by one of the prohibited acts enumerated in Article 4 of the Statute, seeks to achieve the destruction, in whole or in part, of a national, ethnical, racial or religious group, as such.

Proof of Individual Intent May Be Facilitated by Evidence of the Existence of a Genocidal Plan

4.2.66 At the second stage, however, when it comes to *proving* the existence of the author's individual intent, both direct evidence of intent and proof of participation in a genocidal plan appear to be considered as being equally probative alternatives. In other words, the *mens rea* requirement may be satisfied by proving either that the author committed the act with the *individual intention* to destroy a protected group, or alternatively, that he or she committed the act with the intention of *participating* in a genocidal plan. The *Jelisić Appeals Judgement* continued thus:

> 48. The Appeals Chamber is of the opinion that the existence of a plan or policy is not a legal ingredient of the crime. However, in the context of proving

specific intent, the existence of a plan or policy may become an important factor in most cases. The evidence may be consistent with the existence of a plan or policy, or may even show such existence, and the existence of a plan or policy may facilitate proof of the crime.

4.2.67 A concrete example was given in the *Kayishema and Ruzindana Trial Judgement*, where the Chamber stated that, "[t]he killers had the common intent to exterminate the ethnic group and Kayishema was instrumental in the realisation of that intent" (para. 533; see also the *Sikirica Judgement*, para. 62; and the *Krstić Trial Judgement*, para. 572).

An Approach Which Helps Explain Variations in ICT Case Law

4.2.68 The differing weight given to one or other approach in ICT case law may be attributed to various factors such as the place of the accused in the hierarchy of the organisation responsible for planning and implementing the genocide. Thus, in its *Karadžić and Mladić Rule 61 Decision*, relating to the Bosnian Serb leaders, the Chamber made the following observation:

> 94. In this case, the Trial Chamber considers that it must focus more specifically on the analysis of the intention 'to destroy in whole or in part a national, ethnical, racial or religious group.' Insofar as it is considering command responsibility, it must carry out its examination in order to discover whether the pattern of conduct of which it is seised, namely 'ethnic cleansing,' taken in its totality, reveals such a genocidal intent.

4.2.69 Conversely, in the *Jelisić* case, which involved a mid-level commander who personally committed the alleged acts, the Trial Chamber considered the two approaches as alternatives (see paras. 88–108—"The intention to commit 'all-inclusive' genocide" versus "Jelisić's intention to commit genocide"). The Trial Chamber concluded that it had not been proved "beyond a reasonable doubt" that there was a plan to destroy the Muslims in Brčko or beyond, nor that the acts of Goran Jelisić were the physical expression of an affirmed resolve to destroy in whole or in part a group as such.

4.2.70 Part of the explanation for this decision lies in the fact that the Chamber evidently considered that the Prosecution had failed (or perhaps not attempted, believing it unnecessary to do so) to prove that Jelisić's acts were committed in a broader context of genocide waged by Bosnian Serbs against Muslims in Brčko, and in Bosnia generally (see para. 98). The absence of this context, the Chamber hinted, would make it harder to prove genocide against an individual: "it will be very difficult in practice to provide proof of the genocidal intent of an individual if the crimes committed are not widespread and if the crime charged is not backed by an organisation or a system" (para. 101).

4.2.71 The Chamber might, however, have found the relevant broader context by reference to the fact that Jelisić's murder of large numbers of Muslims, and apparently genocidal boasts, were clearly condoned, if not encouraged by the Bosnian Serb entity that installed him as camp commander. Instead, the Chamber proceeded against Jelisić as if he were a "lone individual."

4.2.72 This conclusion was overturned on appeal, on the basis that Jelisić's acts may have been sufficient to show his individual intention to commit genocide regardless of the absence of proof that the wider context was genocidal (paras. 64–68). The Appeals Chamber thus agreed with the Prosecutor that it was open to the Tribunal to find that Jelisić was a "a one-man genocide mission, intent upon personally wiping out the protected group in whole or part" (para. 66). For this purpose, the Appeals Chamber relied on evidence of the clearly discriminatory words of the accused which the Trial Chamber had found to have been carried into action (see, in particular, paras. 73–77 and 102–103 of the Trial Judgement). It only disagreed with the Trial Chamber on the relative weight to be given to evidence that Jelisić had a "disturbed personality" and that he tended to kill "randomly." The Appeals Chamber found, on the contrary, that "[a] reasonable trier of fact could have discounted the few incidents where he showed mercy as aberrations in an otherwise relentless campaign against the protected group" (para. 71). Nevertheless, the Appeals Chamber did not consider it appropriate to convict Jelisić or to send the case back to a trial chamber for retrial.

Implicit in the *Jelisić Appeals Judgement* is the assumption that genocide may be committed in a strictly limited geographical area, in that case Brčko (see below). This was confirmed in the *Krstić Trial Judgement*, which related solely to Srebrenica and its surrounding area.

4.2.73 The *nature* of the crimes in question will equally influence the approach adopted. Due to the overwhelming number of victims killed in a systematic way, the ICTR has consistently found that a genocidal plan existed in Rwanda and in the specific regions in which the various accused held positions of responsibility (see the *Kayishema and Ruzindana Trial Judgement*, paras. 528–529). This undoubtedly explains the *obiter dicta* of the Trial Chamber in that case, to the effect that "although a specific plan to destroy does not constitute an element of genocide, it would appear that it is not easy to carry out a genocide without such a plan, or organisation" (para. 94). The ICTR's task has thus consisted in the much simpler one of determining whether the accused knowingly participated in the execution of that plan. In the *Rutaganda Trial Judgement*, the Chamber clearly established the relation between the individual intent and the broader context:

> 400. ... From the widespread nature of such atrocities, throughout the Rwandan territory, and the fact that the victims were systematically and deliberately selected owing to their being members of the Tutsi group, to the exclusion of individuals who were not members of the said group, the Chamber is able to infer a general context within which acts aimed at destroying the Tutsi group were perpetrated. Consequently, the Chamber notes that such acts as are charged against the Accused were part of an overall context within which other criminal acts systematically directed against members of the Tutsi group, targeted as such, were committed.

4.2.74 Conversely, in the absence of proof of a general plan to commit genocide in the former Yugoslavia, the ICTY has had to determine whether such a plan existed in a particular area or, if not, pass on to the much more difficult task of determining whether the accused himself had the requisite special intent.

A Variable Standard of Proof of Genocidal Intent?

4.2.75 The ICTY and ICTR Statutes do not refer to proof of guilt "beyond a reasonable doubt." The standard of proof is only referred to in ICTY and ICTR Rule 87 ("Deliberations"), para. (A) of which provides that, ". . . A finding of guilt may be reached only when a majority of the Trial Chamber is satisfied that *guilt* has been proved beyond reasonable doubt." (emphasis added). Clearly, then, when the Prosecutor seeks to show that the author of the act personally had the special intention, this must be proved beyond a reasonable doubt (See the *Jelisić Appeal Judgement*, paras. 30–40).

4.2.76 However, where the prosecution is relying on the author's *participation* in a genocidal plan, it is not clear whether the "beyond a reasonable doubt" standard is the appropriate norm to apply in determining whether a genocidal plan existed. Arguably, being a simple question of fact for the tribunal, this would not appear to be a question of *the accused's* guilt. It should not, therefore, require proof "beyond a reasonable doubt" according to Rule 87. A "balance of probabilities" or some other standard could be used. Accordingly, the only element needing to be proved beyond a reasonable doubt would be the accused's *intention to participate* in the execution of the plan. On this point, the Trial Chamber in *Jelisić* may have misdirected itself on the law (para. 48 of the *Jelisić Appeals Judgement*, quoted above, seems to support this argument).

Participation in a Genocidal Plan

4.2.77 The Judgement of the Appeals Chamber in the *Jelisić* case stated that "[t]he specific intent requires that the perpetrator, by one of the prohibited acts enumerated in Article 4 of the Statute, *seeks to achieve* the destruction, in whole or in part, of a national, ethnical, racial or religious group, as such" (para. 46, emphasis added). Although the Appeal Chamber did not positively distinguish between individualised intent and participation, it quoted elements of the prosecution case tending to establish such a distinction, without stating that the Prosecutor had erred on this point:

> 42. The Appeals Chamber understands the prosecution submission to be that an accused has the required *mens rea* for genocide if: i) he consciously desired the committed acts to result in the destruction, in whole or in part, of the group, as such; or ii) he knew that his acts were destroying, in whole or in part, the group, as such; or iii) he, acting as an aider or abettor, commits acts knowing that there is an ongoing genocide which his acts form part of, and that the likely consequence of his conduct would be to destroy, in whole or in part, the group as such.

4.2.78 The prosecution admitted, during oral argument, that simple participation with knowledge of a genocidal plan might only lead to a finding of aiding and abetting genocide (see para. 42, note 77). It is unclear whether in those circumstances, aiding and abetting genocide should be classified as complicity in genocide under ICTY Article 4(3)(e)/ ICTR Article 2(3)(e), or as genocide proper, taking ICTY Article 4(3)(a)/ ICTR Article 2(3)(a) in conjunction with the reference in ICTY Article 7(1)/ ICTR Article 6(1) to "*aided and abetted*." On alleged differences between complicity in genocide and aiding and abetting genocide, see below, 4.2.134.

4.2.79 The *Krstić Trial Judgement* dealt extensively with this question. The Trial Chamber held that "General Krstić participated in a joint criminal enterprise to kill the military-aged Bosnian Muslim men of Srebrenica with the awareness that such killings would lead to the annihilation of the entire Bosnian Muslim community at Srebrenica. His intent to kill the men thus amounts to a genocidal intent to destroy the group in part. . . . In sum, in view of both his *mens rea* and *actus reus*, General Krstić must be considered a principal perpetrator of these crimes" (para. 644). The following extracts from the Judgement provide an insight into the exact nature of what the Chamber found to be General Krstić's criminal participation in the genocidal plan:

> 633. . . . General Krstić may not have devised the killing plan, or participated in the initial decision to escalate the objective of the criminal enterprise from forcible transfer to destruction of Srebrenica's Bosnian Muslim military-aged male community, but there can be no doubt that, from the point he learned of the widespread and systematic killings and became clearly involved in their perpetration, he shared the genocidal intent to kill the men. This cannot be gainsaid given his informed participation in the executions through the use of Drina Corps assets.
>
> 634. . . . Having already played a key role in the forcible transfer of the Muslim women, children and elderly out of Serb-held territory, General Krstić undeniably was aware of the fatal impact that the killing of the men would have on the ability of the Bosnian Muslim community of Srebrenica to survive, as such. General Krstić thus participated in the genocidal acts of "killing members of the group" under Article 4(2)(a) with the intent to destroy a part of the groupî.
>
> 635. . . . While the agreed objective of the joint criminal enterprise in which General Krstić participated was the actual killing of the military aged Bosnian Muslim men of Srebrenica, the terrible bodily and mental suffering of the few survivors clearly was a natural and foreseeable consequence of the enterprise. General Krstić must have been aware of this possibility and he therefore incurs responsibility for these crimes as well.

Toward a "Constructive" Approach to Intention Where the Acts Form Part of an Ongoing Genocidal Plan?

4.2.80 Taken together with the fact that the existence of a genocidal plan may be considered a matter of fact, and that the motives for committing the act are legally irrelevant, the ICTs seem to be coming close to establishing that a person having committed a material act constitutive of genocide, in the context of an overall genocidal plan, may be presumed to have had the requisite intention to participate in that plan for the purposes of characterising those acts as aiding and abetting genocide, if not genocide itself. For example, in the *Jelisić Appeals Judgement*, although the Chamber re-iterated that the "intention necessary for the commission of a crime of genocide may not be presumed even in the case where the existence of a group is at least in part threatened," the Chamber reproduced, nevertheless, without criticism, the following extract from the Trial Judgement in that case:

> an individual knowingly acting against the backdrop of the widespread and systematic violence being committed against only one specific group could not

reasonably deny that he chose his victims discriminatorily. (Emphasis added; paras. 63 of the *Jelisić Trial Judgement*, and para. 60 of the *Jelisić Appeals Judgement*.)

4.2.81 Thus, while a presumption of intention is formally excluded, the Tribunal seems prepared to take a constructive or objective approach to the existence of intent in certain circumstances. Furthermore, it would appear that the onus of proof would then be on the accused to show that he or she did *not* have the requisite intent. As regards knowledge of the genocidal plan, quoting MORRIS and SCHARF (1995, p. 168), the Chamber in the *Kayishema and Ruzindana Trial Judgement* concurred with the view that "it is unnecessary for an individual to have knowledge of all details of the genocidal plan or policy" (para. 94).

4.2.82 This tendency towards a "constructive" approach to intent seems to be supported by the consistent ICT case law on the appropriate means of proving that intent.

Proof of Specific Intent

4.2.83 Assuming that the Tribunal is satisfied that the accused has committed the material *acts* charged in the indictment, one consequence of the two-step approach to proving the existence of special intent, set out above, is that the perpetrator's *dolus specialis*, or specific intention, may be *inferred from the surrounding circumstances*. In the *Karadžić and Mladić Rule 61 Decision*, the Trial Chamber, elaborating on *obiter* in the *Nikolić Rule 61 Decision*, made the following observations:

> 94. ... The intent which is peculiar to the crime of genocide need not be clearly expressed. ... the intent may be *inferred* from a certain number of facts such as the general political doctrine which gave rise to the acts possibly covered by the definition in Article 4, or the repetition of destructive and discriminatory acts. The intent may also be *inferred* from the perpetration of acts which violate, or which the perpetrators themselves consider to violate, the very foundation of the group—acts which are not in themselves covered by the list in Article 4(2) but which are committed as part of the same pattern of conduct. (Emphasis added.)

4.2.84 Given that this principle of *inferred* intent was laid down in some of the earliest ICT case law, it may be argued that the two step approach to genocidal intent has emerged as a theoretical justification of the tribunals' pragmatic need to make up for the lack of direct evidence of intention. Indeed, the Chamber ruling in the *Akayesu Trial Judgement* stated that, "... intent is a mental factor which is difficult, even impossible, to determine. This is the reason why, in the absence of a confession from the accused, his intent can be inferred from a certain number of presumptions of fact." (para. 523). Taking inspiration from this approach, the ICC "Elements of Crimes" acknowledge that the "existence of intent and knowledge can be inferred from relevant facts and circumstances." (General introduction, para. 3).

4.2.85 Nevertheless, the ICTR recently reiterated that the context surrounding the crimes is only a supplementary means of proving intent, which must be determined principally from the acts and declarations of the accused (*Bagilishema Trial Judgement*, para. 63).

4.2.86 The case law of the two *ad hoc* Tribunals concerning the surrounding circumstances which may be taken into account can thus be divided into a number of general categories. Taking as a starting point the abovementioned quotation from para. 94 of the *Karadžić and Mladić Rule 61 Decision* (approved in para. 523 of the *Akayesu Trial Judgement*, para. 93 of the *Kayishema and Ruzindana Trial Judgement*, para. 62 of the *Bagilishema Trial Judgement*, para. 47 of the *Jelisić Appeals Judgement*), these categories may be set out as follows:

The Existence of a Genocidal Plan

4.2.87 The *Karadžić and Mladić Rule 61 Decision* mentions "the general political doctrine which gave rise to the acts possibly covered by the definition in Article 4" (para. 94). The Trial Chamber went on to specify that "this intent derives from the combined effect of speeches or projects laying the groundwork for and justifying the acts" (*ibid.*). Having analysed the indictment presented to it, the Chamber went on to state that:

> 94. ... In this case, the plans of the SDS [Serbian Democratic Party] in Bosnia and Herzegovina contain elements which would lead to the destruction of the non-Serbian groups. The project of an ethnically homogeneous State formulated against a backdrop of mixed populations necessarily envisages the exclusion of any group not identified with the Serbian one. The concrete expressions of these plans by the SDS before the conflict would confirm the existence of an intent to exclude those groups by violence. The project does not exclude the use of force against civilian populations. Furthermore, it appears that a certain group which had been targeted could not, in accordance with the SDS plans, lay claim to any other specific territory. In this case, the massive deportations may be construed as the first step in a process of elimination. These elements, taken together, would confirm that the project which inspired the offences before the Trial Chamber, contemplates the destruction of the non-Serbian groups, and specifically the Bosnian Muslim group, as the ultimate step.

4.2.88 The existence of such a plan may not be required to be proved beyond a reasonable doubt (see above, 4.2.76). As shown in the *Akayesu Trial Judgement* (paras. 118 and 126), the elements indicating the existence of a plan for "centrally organized and supervised massacres" form part of the relevant context.

The Way in Which Other Acts Coming Within the Material Definition of Genocide Were Perpetrated Against the Same Group

4.2.89 As noted in the *Karadžić and Mladić Rule 61 Decision*, "the repetition of destructive and discriminatory acts" is also relevant. In particular, the Chamber mentioned "their specific nature, which aims at undermining what is considered to be the foundation of the group" (para. 95). This principle was enlarged upon in the *Akayesu Trial Judgement*, in which the Chamber inferred genocidal intent from other factors such as "the fact of deliberately and systematically targeting victims" from one group and excluding persons from other groups (para. 523).

4.2.90 In the *Kayishema and Ruzindana Trial Judgement*, the Chamber held that:

93. ... the intent can be inferred either from words or deeds and may be demonstrated by a pattern of purposeful action. In particular, the Chamber considers evidence such as the physical targeting of the group or their property; the use of derogatory language toward members of the targeted group; the weapons employed and the extent of bodily injury; the methodical way of planning, the systematic manner of killing. Furthermore, the number of victims from the group is also important.

4.2.91 In accordance with this principle (specifically confirmed in para. 47 of the *Jelisić Appeals Judgement*), the Trial Chamber in the *Kayishema and Ruzindana Trial Judgement* concluded that "this consistent and methodical pattern of killing is further evidence of the specific intent. Kayishema was instrumental in executing this pattern of *killing*." (paras. 534–535). For an analysis of the ICT case law concerning the inference of intention from the factual context, see *Jurovics*, pp. 316–322.

4.2.92 Interestingly, the ICC "Elements of Crimes" *require* that the conduct of the accused "took place in the context of a *manifest pattern of similar conduct* directed against that group," except to the extent that the perpetrator's conduct "could itself effect such destruction." While this does not formally require proof of a genocidal *plan*, it raises the existence of a contextual pattern of conduct from a pragmatic source of evidence of the accused's intention to the status of a constitutive element of the crime of genocide. Although clearly restrictive in other ways, this requirement can only reinforce the assumption that the accused's intention will still be open to *inference* from such surrounding circumstances under the ICC Statute. It should be noted, in this context, that the term "similar conduct" should be interpreted as referring to any conduct coming within the *actus reus* of genocide, and not as being limited to conduct identical to that charged against the accused (see also VON HEBEL & KELT, pp. 282–283). Moreover, the "Elements of Crimes" stipulate that "[t]he term "manifest" is an *objective* qualification," from which it follows that the need to prove the accused *knew* of the surrounding circumstances is for the Court to determine "on a case by case basis." (ICC Elements of Crimes, Article 6: Genocide.)

4.2.93 Finally, in this respect, it is submitted that the way in which vulnerable members of the group are treated (children, the elderly, women and even unborn children), will generally be an important factor in inferring genocidal intent. Indeed, it will be difficult to claim that these persons were political opponents or a military threat. The main support for this submission comes from the *Akayesu Trial Judgement*, which relied on the fact that "even newborn babies were not spared. Even pregnant women, including those of Hutu origin, were killed," in support of its rejection of defence argument that only "enemies" of the regime were attacked (see paras. 121, 125 and 128). It continued thus:

128. ... The Chamber's opinion is that the genocide was organized and planned not only by members of the FAR, but also by the political forces who were behind the 'Hutu-power,' that it was executed essentially by civilians including the armed militia and even ordinary citizens, and above all, that the majority of the Tutsi victims were non-combatants, including thousands of women and children, even foetuses.

4.2.94 See also the *Kayishema and Ruzindana Trial Judgement*, which found that, as a result of Ruzindana's conduct "thousands of Tutsis were killed or seriously wounded; men, women and children alike" (para. 544).

The Relative Scale of the Crimes

4.2.95 All of the relevant case law mentions this criterion. In particular, in the *Kayishema and Ruzindana Judgement*, the Trial Chamber stated:

> 93. . . . In the Report of the Sub-Commission on Genocide, the Special Rapporteur stated that 'the relative proportionate scale of the actual or attempted destruction of a group, by any act listed in Articles II and III of the Genocide Convention, is strong evidence to prove the necessary intent to destroy a group in whole or in part.'

4.2.96 Thus, in the *Kayishema and Ruzindana Trial Judgement*, the Chamber held that "[t]he number of the Tutsi victims is clear evidence of intent to destroy this ethnic group in whole or in part" (para. 533). For a similar ruling in the context of the Bosnian conflict, see the *Karadžić and Mladić Rule 61 Decision*, para. 94.

The Perpetration, Against the Same Group, of Other Atrocities Not Coming Within the Strict Definition of Genocide

4.2.97 The ICTs have raised the possibility of inferring genocidal intent from acts which are not enumerated in their Statutes, as long as they could contribute to the elimination of the group. See, for example, para. 94 of the *Karadžić and Mladić Rule 61 Decision* set out above. In that *Decision*, the Chamber went on to give the following concrete examples (although the approach to rape has since evolved):

> 94. . . . Furthermore, the specific nature of some of the means used to achieve the objective of 'ethnic cleansing' tends to underscore that the perpetration of the acts is designed to reach the very foundations of the group or what is considered as such. The systematic rape of women, to which material submitted to the Trial Chamber attests, is in some cases intended to transmit a new ethnic identity to the child. In other cases, humiliation and terror serve to dismember the group. The destruction of mosques or Catholic churches is designed to annihilate the centuries-long presence of the group or groups; the destruction of the libraries is intended to annihilate a culture which was enriched through the participation of the various national components of the population.

4.2.98 Despite excluding acts of "cultural destruction" from the *actus reus* of genocide (see above) the Trial Chamber in the *Krstić Trial Judgement* pointed out that:

> 580. . . . where there is physical or biological destruction there are often simultaneous attacks on the cultural and religious property and symbols of the targeted group as well, attacks which may legitimately be considered as evidence of an intent to physically destroy the group. In this case, the Trial Chamber will thus take into account as evidence of intent to destroy the group the deliberate destruction of mosques and houses belonging to members of the group.

Intent to Destroy a Group "in Whole or in Part"

4.2.99 The question of the total or partial destruction of a group was analysed in the *Jelisić Trial Judgement* (paras. 80–83). After analysing the relevant doctrine and case law, the Chamber acknowledged that "the intention to destroy must target at least a substantial part of the group," implicitly rejecting the stricter test suggested by the ICTR, requiring the intention to destroy a "considerable" number (*Akayesu Trial Judgement*, para. 97). However, the Chamber noted that partial destruction may be quantitative, where the acts affect "a major part" of the group, or qualitative, where they are perpetrated against "a representative fraction" of the group, such as its leaders (para. 81; see also the *Krstić Trial Judgement*, paras. 582 and 586).

4.2.100 In the *Krstić Trial Judgement*, the Trial Chamber noted that under the Genocide Convention, the term "in whole or in part" refers to the "intent" as opposed to the physical destruction. Regardless of the final result, any act committed with the *dolus specialis* of destroying a protected group in whole or in part, constitutes an act of genocide (para. 584).

4.2.101 While they are consistent with this approach to intent, the ICC "Elements of Crimes" may exclude the sort of "one-man genocide mission" envisaged by the ICTY Appeals Chamber in the *Jelisić* case (para. 66), as they require that "[t]he conduct took place in the context of a manifest pattern of similar conduct directed against that group." Thus, under the ICC Statute a single crime by the accused may only constitute an act of genocide if it "was conduct that could itself" effect the destruction of the group, or if it was committed in a genocidal context. The "Elements of Crimes" specify, in this respect, that the "the initial acts in an emerging pattern" may constitute acts of genocide (Elements of Crimes, Article 6: Genocide).

4.2.102 The Chamber in the *Krstić Trial Judgement* also confirmed that genocide may be *geographically limited*, not only to a particular country, but even to a zone or region within a country, i.e., in that case, Srebrenica, a town in eastern Bosnia. It referred to United Nations recognition of the massacres at the Sabra and Shatila camps as genocide and the object of the Genocide Convention (*Krstić Trial Judgement*, paras. 581–599; see also the *Sikirica Judgement*, para. 68).

The Protected Groups

4.2.103 Under the 1948 Genocide Convention, and thus Article 2 of the ICTR and Article 4 of the ICTY Statutes, the only groups which may be the subject of genocide are "national, ethnical, racial or religious" groups, and not, for example, political, social or economic groups. While various conceptual explanations were provided to justify this choice, including the desire to counter Nazi atrocities (see the introduction to this sub-section) and the reference to "stable" groups (see below), the principle reason for excluding political, but also social and economic groups, was to convince as wide a range of countries to ratify the Convention as possible. Indeed, given their previous recourse to political purges, various communist countries were strongly against the extension of the list to political groups. Similarly, numerous countries with indigenous minorities fought the inclusion of references to cultural genocide (see Ruhashyankiko 1978).

4.2.104 The most developed case law on the question of groups has come from the ICTR, confronted from the outset with the need to classify the Tutsi as either a national, ethnic, racial or religious group. Before commenting upon the four specific categories of groups, a difficulty needs to be analysed, which arises from the fact that the simple act of classifying individuals as belonging to a group for the purposes of protecting them seems to be playing into the hands of those who differentiate between human groups in order to discriminate against them. Not only is it widely considered to be no longer acceptable in international law to reason in such terms, but at least as regards "racial" groups, the *travaux préparatoires* show that it was not acceptable to do so at the time the Genocide Convention was drafted in 1948. Indeed, the fact that an international court held that such a group existed could be turned against the group in the future. Surprisingly, given the complexity of this question, the ICC "Elements of Crimes" make no attempt to clarify the meaning of these terms. Faced with this dilemma, the ICTR originally developed two approaches to determining the existence of a protected group within the meaning of the Genocide Convention (objective and subjective), although the subjective approach now appears dominant.

Objective and Subjective Approaches

4.2.105 In the *Akayesu* and *Kayishema and Ruzindana Trial Judgements*, the two ICTR Trial Chambers (the two Judgements were rendered before the addition of a third Trial Chamber at the ICTR) took different approaches to the problem of determining whether the Tutsi formed a protected group within the definition of genocide. The former attempted an objective examination of the existence of an ethnic group, whereas the latter took a more flexible approach, at least as concerns ethnic groups, taking account of subjective elements such as the perceptions of the members of the group itself, or of others, including the perpetrators of the crimes (see para. 98).

The Objective Approach and "Stable" Groups

4.2.106 Under the objective test of the existence of groups adopted by the ICTR in the *Akayesu Trial Judgement*, the Trial Chamber was obliged to conclude that, strictly speaking, the Tutsi did not fall within any of the groups protected by the definition of genocide. The Chamber was, thus, forced to adopt an extensive interpretation of the object of the Genocide Convention in order to find that a genocide had been committed in Rwanda. The Chamber accepted that *other relatively stable groups besides the four specified categories* could also fall within the scope of the crime of genocide without doing violence to the spirit of the Genocide Convention:

> 511 On reading through the *travaux préparatoires* of the Genocide Convention, it appears that the crime of genocide was allegedly perceived as targeting only 'stable' groups, constituted in a permanent fashion and membership of which is determined by birth, with the exclusion of the more 'mobile' groups which one joins through individual voluntary commitment, such as political and economic groups. Therefore, a common criterion in the four types of groups protected by the Genocide Convention is that membership in such groups would seem to be normally not challengeable by its members, who belong to it automatically, by birth, in a continuous and often irremediable manner.

> 516. ... the question that arises is whether it would be impossible to punish the physical destruction of a group as such under the Genocide Convention, if the said group, although stable and membership is by birth, does not meet the definition of any one of the four groups expressly protected by the Genocide Convention. In the opinion of the Chamber, it is particularly important to respect the intention of the drafters of the Genocide Convention, which according to the *travaux préparatoires*, was patently to ensure the protection of any stable and permanent group.

4.2.107 The Chamber held that the Tutsi came within the definition because they were classified as an "ethnic" group in a *stable way*. In reality, the Trial Chamber in the *Akayesu* case was forced to look at subjective questions, including self-conceptions of ethnicity, in finding the existence of a stable group (see para. 702). Thus, while the underlying premise of the objective existence of such groups seems scientifically flawed, and the Chamber's interpretation of the *travaux préparatoires* open to criticism, one may wonder whether there is any great difference between the "objective" and "subjective" approaches in practice.

Toward a Subjective Approach

4.2.108 Faced with the "stable groups" test and the more "subjective" approach used in the *Kayishema and Ruzindana Trial Judgement*, the Chamber equivocated, although a closer analysis shows its preference for the latter approach. Indeed, in the *Rutaganda Trial Judgement*, the Chamber considered that, "for the purposes of applying the Genocide Convention, membership of a group is, in essence, a subjective rather than an objective concept." Nevertheless, it accepted that a subjective test was not sufficient on its own, as "the Convention was presumably intended to cover relatively stable and permanent groups" (see paras. 55 and 56).

4.2.109 Yet, given that there was no generally accepted definition of these groups, each of them having to be assessed "in the light of a particular political, social and cultural context," the Chamber concluded, not surprisingly, that the question had to be examined on a case-by-case basis (paras. 55–57). In the *Krstić Trial Judgement*, the ICTY concurred with this approach, holding that "the group's cultural, religious, ethnical or national characteristics must be identified within the socio-historic context which it inhabits" (para. 80).

4.2.110 In the *Krstić Trial Judgement*, the Chamber also went back on previous interpretations of the object of the Genocide Convention, noting that, at the time, the conception of protected groups was synonymous with "national minorities":

> 556. The preparatory work of the Convention shows that setting out such a list was designed more to describe a single phenomenon, roughly corresponding to what was recognised, before the second world war, as 'national minorities,' rather than to refer to several distinct prototypes of human groups. To attempt to differentiate each of the named groups on the basis of scientifically objective criteria would thus be inconsistent with the object and purpose of the Convention. (See also para. 78.)

4.2.111 For an analysis of these *"seriatim"* and *"ensemble"* approaches to group classification, see Diane Amann, "Group Mentality, Expressivism, and Genocide," 1 *International Criminal Law* 2 (2002).

The Importance of the Perpetrators' Perception of the Group

4.2.112 This tendency to minimise the *Akayesu* approach has been confirmed by the recent case-law of both ICTs. In the *Jelisić Trial Judgement*, despite the surprising conclusions drawn by the Trial Chamber with regard to genocide on the facts, it is submitted that the Chamber rightly applied a *subjective* test to determine whether the victims of the accused's acts "belonged to a group" protected by the Genocide Convention:

> 69. Article 4 of the Statute protects victims belonging to a national, ethnical, racial or religious group and excludes members of political groups. The preparatory work of the Convention demonstrates that a wish was expressed to limit the field of application of the Convention to protecting "stable" groups objectively defined and to which individuals belong regardless of their own desires.
>
> 70. Although the objective determination of a religious group still remains possible, to attempt to define a national, ethnical or racial group today using objective and scientifically irreproachable criteria would be a perilous exercise whose result would not necessarily correspond to the perception of the persons concerned by such categorisation. Therefore, it is more appropriate to evaluate the status of a national, ethnical or racial group from the point of view of those persons who wish to single that group out from the rest of the community. The Trial Chamber consequently elects to evaluate membership in a national, ethnical or racial group using a subjective criterion. It is the stigmatisation of a group as a distinct national, ethnical or racial unit by the community which allows it to be determined whether a targeted population constitutes a national, ethnical or racial group in the eyes of the alleged perpetrators. This position corresponds to that adopted by the Trial Chamber in its Review of the Indictment Pursuant to Article 61 filed in the *Nikolić* case.

4.2.113 Similarly, while recognising the objective and subjective aspects of the question, the *Bagilishema Trial Judgement* considered that the perception of the perpetrator should be determinative:

> 65. ... Moreover, the perpetrators of genocide may characterize the targeted group in ways that do not fully correspond to conceptions of the group shared generally, or by other segments of society. In such a case, the Chamber is of the opinion that, on the evidence, if a victim was perceived by a perpetrator as belonging to a protected group, the victim could be considered by the Chamber as a member of the protected group, for the purposes of genocide.

Groups May Be Defined by Positive or Negative Criteria

4.2.114 Finally, applying the subjective criterion of the perpetrators' perception, the Trial Chamber in the *Jelisić* case made an interesting distinction between the stigmatisation of a group by virtue of "positive" or "negative" criteria (para. 71). A "positive" approach consists for the authors of the crime of distinguishing the group by virtue of what they consider to be the group's particular national, racial, religious or ethnical characteristics. A "negative" approach consists of identifying members of the group as not belonging to the group to which the authors of the crime believe they, the authors, belong. The group of individuals thus rejected constitute, by exclusion, a distinct group. Given the facts of the case, the Chamber considered that the attack on the Bosnian Muslims, as a group, involved a "positive" approach, *i.e.*, the group was identified by virtue of characteristics which it was believed to possess.

"National Group"

4.2.115 The term "national group" is capable of two contradictory interpretations within the context of the Genocide Convention: a national *minority*, or any group having the same nationality. The *travaux préparatoires* of the Convention seem to indicate that, given the precedent of the Second World War, its drafters had national minorities in mind (see para. 556 of the *Krstić Trial Judgement*, set out above): *i.e.*, persons who have the culture, language and traditional lifestyle of one nation, but who are living in another State (see RUHASHYANKIKO 1978, para. 61).

4.2.116 Yet, in the *Akayesu Trial Judgement*, the ICTR preferred an approach linked to citizenship:

> 512. ... Based on the *Nottebohm* decision rendered by the International Court of Justice, the Chamber holds that a national group is defined as a collection of people who are perceived to share a legal bond based on common citizenship, coupled with reciprocity of rights and duties.

4.2.117 While this approach is clearly of wider potential application than the former, it does not necessarily encompass those national minorities which are no longer seen as citizens of the mother, or host country. Furthermore, the *Nottebohm* case did not define this concept within the framework of the Genocide Convention. On the other hand, it is true that none of the other groups protected by the Convention are limited to a minority of the population. Nevertheless, such a definition of national groups creates the potential for widening Genocide Convention protection to cover cases of "auto-genocide" which would not otherwise be covered, especially when it is coupled with the fact that genocide may be "partial" and the concept of "negative" definitions of groups. As an example, the physical "purging" by a dominant political party of all "reactionary" fellow citizens would normally be seen as the destruction of a non-protected political group. However, under the wider "citizenship" definition, it might equally be characterised as flowing from an intention to destroy *part* of the "national group" in question, although this raises the question whether there was an intention to destroy the national group "as such." For the application of this approach to the atrocities perpetrated by the Khmer Rouge against their own population, see the Report of the UN Group of Experts on Cambodia (UN Doc. A/53/850, 16 March 1999, para. 63). Given that *everyone* belongs to a "national group" thus defined, the potential for extension of Genocide Convention protection to *all* discriminatory crimes is, thus, undeniable.

4.2.118 In the *Krstić Trial Judgement*, the ICTY relied on the *subjective* criterion of the "perpetrator's perception" developed in that case (see above), to find that the Bosnian Muslims were considered to be a specific *national* group by the accused, before preferring a classification corresponding to the victims' perception of themselves as members of the Bosnian Muslim group (see "*Participation in a Genocidal Plan*" above):

> 82. Originally viewed as a religious group, the Bosnian Muslims were recognised as a 'nation' by the Yugoslav Constitution of 1963. The evidence tendered at trial also shows very clearly that the highest Bosnian Serb political authorities and the Bosnian Serb forces operating in Srebrenica in July 1995 viewed the Bosnian Muslims as a specific national group. Conversely, no national, ethnical, racial or religious characteristic makes it possible to differentiate the Bosnian Muslims residing in Srebrenica, at the time of the 1995 offensive, from the other Bosnian Muslims. The only distinctive criterion would be their geographical location, not a criterion contemplated by the Convention. In addition, it is doubtful that the Bosnian Muslims residing in the enclave at the time of the offensive considered themselves a distinct national, ethnical, racial or religious group among the Bosnian Muslims. Indeed, most of the Bosnian Muslims residing in Srebrenica at the time of the attack were not originally from Srebrenica but from all around the central Podrinje region. Evidence shows that they rather viewed themselves as members of the Bosnian Muslim group.

"Ethnic Group"

4.2.119 As noted above, following its objective approach, the Trial Chamber in the *Akayesu* case found that "The term ethnic group is, in general, used to refer to a group whose members speak the same language and/or have the same culture" (para. 122, note 56). However, in the *Kayishema/Ruzindana Trial Judgement* (confirmed in para. 65 of the *Bagilishema Trial Judgement*—see above), the Trial Chamber applied a wider test, including subjective factors:

> 98. ... An ethnic group is one whose members share a common language and culture; or, a group which distinguishes itself, as such (self identification); or, a group identified as such by others, including perpetrators of the crimes (identification by others).

The Tutsi as an "Ethnic Group"

4.2.120 Using the subjective approach, the Chamber in the *Kayishema and Ruzindana Trial Judgement* had no trouble finding that the Tutsi formed an ethnic group, not only in their own perception but also in that of the perpetrators. However, following its objective test, the Chamber in the *Akayesu Trial Judgement* noted that:

> one can hardly talk of ethnic groups as regards Hutu and Tutsi, given that they share the same language and culture. (Para. 122, note 56; see also para. 513.)

4.2.121 Nevertheless, in reaching the conclusion that the Tutsi had been the victims of genocide, the *Akayesu* Chamber concluded that the Tutsi formed a "*stable* group" for the purposes of the definition of genocide because they were *perceived of* as an ethnic group. Thus, despite their theoretical reliance on the concept of permanent stable groups, an analysis of the Judgement shows that what was important was the perception of those involved at the time of the crime, regardless of whether that situation has evolved over time. Behind the rhetoric, thus, this seems perfectly compatible with the more flexible approach to ethnicity adopted in the *Kayishema and Ruzindana Trial Judgement*. Indeed, the *Akayesu* Chamber made the following observations:

> 171. ... The identification of persons as belonging to the group of Hutu or Tutsi (or Twa) had thus become embedded in Rwandan culture. The Rwandan witnesses who testified before the Chamber identified themselves by ethnic group, and generally knew the ethnic group to which their friends and neighbours belonged. Moreover, the Tutsi were conceived of as an ethnic group by those who targeted them for killing.
>
> 172. As the expert witness, Alison Desforges, summarised:
>
>> The primary criterion for [defining] an ethnic group is the sense of belonging to that ethnic group. It is a sense which can shift over time. In other words, the group, the definition of the group to which one feels allied may change over time. But, if you fix any given moment in time, and you say, how does this population divide itself, then you will see which ethnic groups are in existence in the minds of the participants at that time. The Rwandans currently, and for the last generation at least, have defined themselves in terms of these three ethnic groups. In addition reality is an interplay between the actual conditions and peoples' subjective perception of those conditions. In Rwanda, the reality was shaped by the colonial experience which imposed a categorisation which was probably more fixed, and not completely appropriate to the scene. But, the Belgians did impose this classification in the early 1930's when they required the population to be registered according to ethnic group. The categorisation imposed at that time is what people of the current generation have grown up with. They have always thought in terms of these categories, even if they did not, in their daily lives have to take cognizance of that. ... This practice was continued after independence by the First Republic and the Second Republic in Rwanda to such an extent that this division into three ethnic groups became an absolute reality.

On this point, see also para. 702 of the *Akayesu Trial Judgement*.

"Racial Group"

4.2.122 Not having been relied upon as the basis for any finding of genocide by either of the *ad hoc* Tribunals, the fraught notion of "racial groups" has been the subject of little attempt at detailed analysis. The conventional definition was considered to be based on hereditary physical traits identified with a geographical region in the *Kayishema and Ruzindana Trial Judgement* (para. 98), irrespective of linguistic, cultural, national or religious factors (*Akayesu Trial Judgement*, para. 514).

4.2.123 However, race is clearly included in those categories not being susceptible to an objective approach in the *Jelisić Trial Judgement* (para. 70, set out above).

"Religious Group"

4.2.124 See the *Akayesu Trial Judgement:*

> 514. ... The religious group is one whose members share the same religion, denomination or mode of worship.

4.2.125 The *Kayishema and Ruzindana Trial Judgement* expanded slightly on this definition:

> 98. ... A religious group includes denomination or mode of worship or a group sharing common beliefs.

4.2.126 The Trial Chamber in the *Jelisić* case considered that it was the Muslim population which was discriminated against *as a religious group* (paras. 73–77 of the Judgement). See also the *Krstić Trial Judgement*, para. 559.

Other Forms of Responsibility for Genocide

4.2.127 As a result of the transposition of Article 3 of the Genocide Convention directly into the definition of genocide in the ICTs' Statutes, both Statutes incriminate forms of responsibility for genocide other than the direct perpetration of genocidal acts already described. These other forms of responsibility are *conspiracy* to commit genocide, *direct and public incitement* to commit genocide, *attempted* genocide and *complicity* in genocide (Article 4(3), ICTY Statute and Article 2(3), ICTR Statute).

4.2.128 The ICTs have principally dealt with these forms of genocide as a question of individual criminal responsibility, which is dealt with by Article 7(1) of the ICTY Statute and Article 6(1) of the ICTR Statute. There are variations in language between the articles on individual criminal responsibility and the definitions of the other punishable genocide acts. The question is whether these other punishable acts are characterised as forms of participation in acts of genocide or as inchoate offences, i.e. punishable even where no act of genocide has actually been perpetrated (or where no proof need be adduced of any causal link between the acts, on the one hand, and the commission of genocide, on the other).

4.2.129 There is no doubt on this point, as regards *attempted genocide*. In such cases the genocidal act clearly must have been commenced, although for some reason the act could not be completed. The other forms of responsibility are analysed below.

Complicity in Genocide

4.2.130 Complicity as a form of criminal participation exists under both Common Law and Civil Law systems. It has been expressly included in international humanitarian law since Nuremberg. The accomplice to genocide may be defined as a person who does not directly commit the incriminated act, but who associates himself with the genocidal conduct of another (*Musema Trial Judgement*, paras. 169–170). Thus complicity may be seen as "borrowed criminality." The "physical act which constitutes the act of complicity does not have its own inherent criminality, but rather it borrows the criminality of the act committed by the principal perpetrator of the criminal enterprise." (*Akayesu Trial Judgement*, para. 528).

4.2.131 It follows that the principal offence must have been committed for liability to arise in complicity. Thus, before complicity in genocide can arise, the *existence* of genocide must have been proven beyond a reasonable doubt (*Akayesu Trial Judgement*, para. 530; *Musema Trial Judgement*, para. 173). This does not, however, imply that there must first be a *conviction* for genocide before the Tribunal can proceed against an individual for complicity in genocide. Both under Common Law and Civil Law Systems, there is no need to identify the principal perpetrator, nor find him guilty of genocide, in order to punish the accomplice:

> an accomplice may also be tried, even where the principal perpetrator of the crime has not been identified, or where, for any other reasons, guilt could not be proven. (*Akayesu Trial Judgement*, para. 531; see also the *Musema Trial Judgement*, para. 174.)

The *Actus Reus* of Complicity in Genocide

4.2.132 The forms that complicity may take are similar in both Common and Civil Law systems. However, faced with minor terminological differences, the Trial Chamber in the *Akayesu* case chose to interpret Article 2(3)(e) of the ICTR Statute in conformity with the three forms of complicity referred to in Article 91 of the Rwandan Penal Code (based on Civil Law terminology):

> 536. For the purposes of interpreting Article 2(3)e) of the Statute, which does not define the concept of complicity, the Chamber is of the opinion that it is necessary to define complicity as per the Rwandan Penal Code, and to consider the first three forms of criminal participation referred to in Article 91 of the Rwandan Penal Code as being the elements of complicity in genocide, thus:
> — complicity by *procuring means*, such as weapons, instruments or any other means, used to commit genocide, with the accomplice knowing that such means would be used for such a purpose;
> — complicity by knowingly *aiding or abetting* a perpetrator of a genocide in the planning or enabling acts thereof;
> — complicity by *instigation*, for which a person is liable who, though not directly participating in the crime of genocide crime (*sic*), gave instructions to commit genocide, through gifts, promises, threats, abuse of authority or power, machinations or culpable artifice, or who directly incited to commit genocide.

4.2.133 The *Akayesu Trial Judgement* approach has been followed in a number of other cases (see also the *Musema Trial Judgement*, para. 179; and the *Bagilishema Trial Judgement*, para. 69).

4.2.134 The Chamber also distinguished complicity in genocide under Article 2(3)(e) of the ICTR Statute from aiding and abetting genocide under Article 6(1) of the ICTR Statute, stating that the former implies a positive action while the latter may be committed by omission (*Akayesu Trial Judgement*, paras. 536 and 548).

The *Mens Rea* Required for Complicity

4.2.135 Conversely, the *mens rea* requirement for complicity in genocide is lower than that required for aiding and abetting genocide, as only the latter requires the specific intent to commit genocide. The accomplice does not need to have the "specific intent" of destroying a group, but he must know that the principal author has such an intention (*Akayesu Trial Judgement*, paras. 538–539). It follows that:

> anyone who knowing of another's criminal purpose, voluntarily aids him or her in it, can be convicted of complicity even though he regretted the outcome of the offence. (*Akayesu Trial Judgement*, paras. 540 and 547.)

4.2.136 In the *Akayesu Trial Judgement*, the Trial Chamber gave the following example of a sufficient *mens rea* to justify a conviction for complicity in genocide:

> 541. Thus, if for example, an accused knowingly aided or abetted another in the commission of a murder, while being unaware that the principal was committing such a murder, with the intent to destroy, in whole or in part, the group to which the murdered victim belonged, the accused could be prosecuted for complicity in murder, and certainly not for complicity in genocide. However, if the accused knowingly aided and abetted in the commission of such a murder while he knew or had reason to know that the principal was acting with genocidal intent, the accused would be an accomplice to genocide, even though he did not share the murderer's intent to destroy the group.

4.2.137 In sum, according to the Trial Chamber, complicity in genocide has a higher *actus reus* requirement, i.e. some positive action, but a lower *mens rea* requirement, i.e. knowingly assisting another to commit genocide, than aiding and abetting genocide. Aiding and abetting genocide does not require a positive action—omission may be sufficient—but does require the specific intent to destroy a national, ethnic, racial or religious group as such. What is the rationale for this distinction? If complicity in genocide under Article 2(3)(e) is regarded as secondary liability and Article 6(1) as principal liability, then the ICTR has, in effect, laid down a rule of law by which to distinguish these principal and secondary forms of liability.

Complicity in Genocide as an *Alternative* to Commission

4.2.138 It follows from the above that an accused cannot be convicted of both the principal offence and of complicity in relation to the same set of facts. Thus, as regards genocide, the offences of genocide and complicity in genocide, arising from the same set of facts, are mutually exclusive. This has been confirmed several times by the ICTR (*Akayesu Trial Judgement*, para. 532; *Musema Trial Judgement*, para. 175; *Bagilishema Trial Judgement*, para. 67).

4.2.139 In its *Decision on the Preliminary Motion filed by the Defence based on defects in the form of the indictment* handed down in the *Ntagerura* case on 28 November 1997, the Trial Chamber also confirmed the decision in the *Delalić et al.* case to the effect that, "there should be a clear identification of particular acts of participation by the accused" (para. 15). Nevertheless, it should be noted that, in the *Kambanda Judgement and Sentence*, the former Prime Minister pleaded guilty to both of these forms of criminal conduct, based essentially on the same facts, and was convicted of both.

Direct and Public Incitement to Commit Genocide

The *Actus Reus* of Incitement

4.2.140 Common Law Systems define "incitement" as *encouraging* or *persuading* someone to commit a crime, whereas Civil Law Systems define it as a form of *provocation*, which usually has to be direct and public. The definition of this form of criminal participation was discussed at length in the *Akayesu Trial Judgement* (see paras. 549–562). The principle consideration was as follows:

> 559. ... whatever the legal system, direct and public incitement must be defined for the purposes of interpreting Article 2(3)(c), as directly provoking the perpetrator(s) to commit genocide, whether through speeches, shouting or threats uttered in public places or at public gatherings, or through the sale or dissemination, offer for sale or display of written material or printed matter in public places or at public gatherings, or through the public display of placards or posters, or through any other means of audiovisual communication.

4.2.141 Under the Rwandan Penal Code, encouraging someone to perpetrate genocide is punishable as direct and public incitement to commit genocide. However, where this encouragement is accompanied by "gifts, promises, threats, abuse of authority or power, machinations or culpable artifice," it shall be punished as complicity in genocide (see the *Akayesu Trial Judgement*, para. 534).

4.2.142 A further issue is the interpretation of the words "direct" and "public" in cases of incitement. As for "public," two factors must be taken into account: the place where the provocation occurred and the relative number of people hearing it. Although the "direct" element must be analysed in light of the cultural and linguistic specificity of the country, initiation cannot be implicit.

4.2.143 The Appeals Chamber has held that incitement is only required to be "direct and public" in the case of genocide. This is not required by the general provision relating to individual criminal responsibility for *instigation* under ICTY Article 7(1)/ ICTR Article 6(1) (see the *Ruggiu Judgement*, paras. 480–483; and the *Akayesu Appeals Judgement*, paras. 474–483).

The *Mens Rea* Requirement for Incitement

4.2.144 The *mens rea* required for direct and public incitement to commit genocide is "the intent to directly prompt or provoke another to commit genocide" and comprises the *dolus specialis* of genocide, namely the specific intent to destroy, in whole or in part, a national, ethnical, racial or religious group, as such (*Akayesu Trial Judgement*, para. 560). The author of the incitement must thus personally have the intention to destroy the group, but rather than—or in addition to—perpetrating genocide himself, he chooses to provoke others to do so. The problem with this approach is that it creates a "double intention" requirement, i.e. the intent to prompt to provoke another to commit genocide and the intent to destroy the group in whole or in part. It is submitted that the former alone should suffice.

Incitement an Inchoate Offence

4.2.145 This form of criminal participation is considered to be an inchoate offence, *i.e.* the crime exists once the incitement is direct and public, without requiring any result. The ICTR Trial Chamber justified this exceptional treatment on the basis of the gravity of the crime of genocide, which is deemed to be so serious that "public and direct incitement to commit it must be punished as such, even when it produces no effects. The result is that there is no need to prove causation. Although such effects are not required, they may be an aggravating factor" (see paras. 562, and 674–675 of the *Akayesu Trial Judgement*). The Chamber also took the preventive aim of the Genocide Convention into account, even though the drafters of the Convention had not explicitly followed this approach (see para. 562 of the *Akayesu Trial Judgement*).

4.2.146 This interpretation simplifies the prosecutor's job, particularly in prosecution of Rwandan media personalities, as it is not necessary to prove any causal connection between the incitement and any particular act of genocide actually committed.

Conspiracy to Commit Genocide

4.2.147 Conspiracy is approached differently in Common and Civil Law Systems. In the former case, it is directly punishable as a form of criminal participation. In the latter, a person cannot generally be convicted for mere criminal intent or the commission of "preparatory acts." This is only possible for extremely serious crimes, such as undermining State security. Given the gravity of the crime of genocide, it was thus proposed to include conspiracy as a crime in itself during drafting of the Genocide Convention.

The *Actus Reus* of Conspiracy to Commit Genocide

4.2.148 The Trial Chamber in the *Musema Trial Judgement* discussed this crime in some detail. After considering related concepts under Civil and Common Law traditions, the Chamber noted the similarity between the elements of the crime in both systems, and thus defined conspiracy as "an agreement between two or more persons to commit the crime of genocide" (*Musema Trial Judgement*, paras. 189–191).

The *Mens Rea* of Conspiracy to Commit Genocide

4.2.149 The *mens rea* of conspiracy to commit genocide is the same as the *mens rea* for genocide itself, namely the intent to destroy a national, ethnical, racial or religious group in whole or in part (*Musema Trial Judgement*, para. 192).

4.2.150 The problem with this definition is that the usual *mens rea* requirement for a conspiracy (to commit *any* crime) is the intention to carry the conspiracy into effect. By defining the *mens rea* for conspiracy to commit genocide as the intent to destroy a group in whole or in part, the requirement that the accused intend to carry out the conspiracy has been inadvertently omitted.

4.2.151 It is submitted that this problem, and the analagous problem of the "double intention" requirement for direct and public incitement to commit genocide (4.2.144), both stem from the misapprehension that the genocidal intent to destroy a group must refer to an individualised *mens rea* requirement rather than to a feature of a genocidal plan. See 4.2.52 *et seq*.

Conspiracy an Inchoate Offence

4.2.152 It is the process of conspiring itself that is punishable and not the result. Conspiracy is, thus, also an inchoate offence (*Musema Trial Judgement*, para. 194).

Co-Conspirators Should Be Named in the Indictment

4.2.153 In the *Nahimana* case, the Trial Chamber held, in its *Decision on the Preliminary Motion filed by the Defence based on defects in the form of the indictment* of 24 November 1997, that an accused who is charged with conspiracy to commit genocide must (in order to have adequate notice of the charges against him) be informed of the names of his alleged co-conspirators (paras. 26–27; see also the *Decision on the Preliminary Motion filed by the Defence based on defects in the form of the indictment* rendered in the *Ntagerura* case on 28 November 1997, para. 19). That does not mean that all the co-conspriators have to be tried, or even convicted, in the same trial; only that the alleged co-conspirators must be *named*. This is only fair as a matter of notice to the accused of the charges against him.

Conspiracy and Commission to Be Considered as Mutually Exclusive

4.2.154 The *travaux préparatoires* of the Genocide Convention indicate that the crime of conspiracy was included to allow the punishment of acts that do not, in themselves, constitute genocide. This contrasts with the position in Common Law systems, where an accused can be convicted for both conspiracy to commit a crime (the mere agreement to commit the crime being itself a crime) and for the crime itself, if the conspiracy is carried out successfully. The ICTR has raised the question whether the two should be regarded as mutually exclusive (*Musema Trial Judgement*, para. 195). In that case, the Civil Law approach was applied, whereby a person can only be convicted of conspiracy if the principal crime has not been perpetrated, or if the accused has not participated directly in the acts perpetrated by his co-conspirators (*Musema Trial Judgement*, paras. 196–197). See para. 198 in particular:

> 198. In the instant case, the Chamber has adopted the definition of conspiracy most favourable to Musema, whereby an accused cannot be convicted of both genocide and conspiracy to commit genocide on the basis of the same acts. Such a definition is in keeping with the intention of the Genocide Convention. Indeed, the "*Travaux Préparatoires*" show that the crime of conspiracy was included to punish acts which, in and of themselves, did not constitute geno-

cide. The converse implication of this is that no purpose would be served in convicting an accused, who has already been found guilty of genocide, for conspiracy to commit genocide, on the basis of the same acts.

4.2.155 This "converse implication" does not, however, follow. The purpose served by recording a conviction for conspiracy to commit genocide alongside a conviction for genocide is to reflect the fact (if it has been established beyond a reasonable doubt) that the accused not only committed genocide but had also planned and agreed with another to commit genocide beforehand. A similar justification supported the Nuremberg Tribunal's decision to convict a number of accused of both the charge of "Common Plan or Conspiracy" to commit crimes against peace as well as the charge of crimes against peace. Establishing that there was an agreement or plan to commit a crime can be significant, not the least as a matter of historical fact.

4.2.156 In any event, the degree to which Musema, in the above *Judgement*, benefited from a *"favourable"* definition of conspiracy is open to question, since he was in any event sentenced to life impisonment. The decision not to record a conviction for conspiracy could not, therefore, have been motivated by any desire to avoid excessive punishment. On the contrary, it may well be that there was no conviction on this count simply because the evidence for it was lacking.

4.2.157

ICC
Article 6
Genocide

For the purpose of this Statute, "genocide" means any of the following acts committed with intent to destroy, in whole or in part, a national, ethnical, racial or religious group, as such:
(a) Killing members of the group;
(b) Causing serious bodily or mental harm to members of the group;
(c) Deliberately inflicting on the group conditions of life calculated to bring about its physical destruction in whole or in part;
(d) Imposing measures intended to prevent births within the group;
(e) Forcibly transferring children of the group to another group.

The ICC and Genocide

4.2.158 The problems caused for the ICTs by the direct transposition of the inchoate forms of genocide into the definitional articles themselves, do not arise in the ICC Statute because the inchoate forms of genocide (attempt, direct and public incitement and conspiracy) as well as complicity in genocide, do not appear in Article 6 which defines genocide. The other forms of genocide are covered by the general article on individual criminal responsibility, Article 25 of the Rome Statute. This Article does not include conspiracy to commit genocide; however, it does include liability for direct and public incitement in cases of genocide. Any new elements concerning the definition of genocide in the ICC "Elements of Crimes" are dealt with in the "Elements" section (4.2.586).

Conclusion: Genocide—From a Vague Notion to an Increasingly Consolidated Incrimination

4.2.159 The definition of genocide adopted in the Genocide Convention has been copied by the ICTs and the ICC, thus giving a sort of "consolidated definition." Despite this, there have been many doctrinal controversies concerning the exact nature and content of this crime.

4.2.160 In particular, it has been unclear whether genocide is an aggravated form of crime against humanity or a separate crime. In the *Kayishema and Ruzindana Trial Judgement*, the ICTR held that genocide is a crime against humanity in the form of persecution, following the lead given by the Israeli Courts in the *Eichmann* case. In the *Jelisić Trial Judgement*, the Chamber affirmed that genocide, by definition, *always* arises out of persecution-type crimes against humanity (para. 68). Thus, according to the ICTs, the principal difference between these crimes lies in the *"dolus specialis"* required for genocide, on the basis that, in the case of crimes against humanity, there is no intention to destroy the group as such (see the *Krstić Trial Judgement*, para. 553; and the *Sikirica Judgement*, para. 58). This seems to be the correct approach, although there will no doubt be further developments and refinements by the ICTs of the law of genocide in the years to come, paving the way, it is to be hoped, for the ICC to adopt a coherent approach to genocide from the outset of its activities.

* * * * *

CRIMES AGAINST HUMANITY

4.2.161

ICTY Article 5 Crimes Against Humanity	ICTR Article 3 Crimes Against Humanity
The International Tribunal shall have the power to prosecute persons responsible for the following crimes when committed in armed conflict, whether international or internal in character, and directed against any civilian population: (a) murder; (b) extermination; (c) enslavement; (d) deportation; (e) imprisonment; (f) torture; (g) rape; (h) persecutions on political, racial and religious grounds; (i) other inhumane acts.	The International Tribunal for Rwanda shall have the power to prosecute persons responsible for the following crimes when committed as part of a widespread or systematic attack against any civilian population on national, political, ethnic, racial or religious grounds: (a) murder; (b) extermination; (c) enslavement; (d) deportation; (e) imprisonment; (f) torture; (g) rape; (h) persecutions on political, racial and religious grounds; (i) other inhumane acts.

Historical Background

4.2.162 Phrases such as "crimes against mankind" and "crimes against the human family" have long appeared in human history (see 12 N.Y.L. Sch. J. Hum. Rts 545 (1995)). In 1874, George Curtis called slavery a "crime against humanity." The Martens clause of the Hague Convention (IV) of 1907 referred to "the usages established among civilised peoples, [. . .] the laws of humanity, and the dictates of the public conscience."

4.2.163 On 28 May 1915, the Governments of France, Great Britain and Russia made a declaration regarding the massacres of the Armenian population in Turkey, denouncing them as "crimes against humanity and civilisation for which all the members of the Turkish government will be held responsible together with its agents implicated in the massacres." See Vahakn Dadrian, *The History of the Armenian Genocide* (1995), *passim*. The 1919 Report of the Commission on the Responsibility of the Authors of the War and on Enforcement of Penalties formulated by representatives from several States and presented to the Paris Peace Conference also referred to "offences against . . . the laws of humanity."

4.2.164 See also Oppenheim, *International Law*, Vol. I (3rd ed.) (1920), p. 229: "The international concern over the commission of crimes against humanity has been greatly intensified in recent years. The fact of such concern is not a recent phenomenon, however. England, France and Russia intervened to end the atrocities in the Greco-Turkish warfare in 1827."

4.2.165 Thus, the concept of crimes against humanity was recognised long before Nuremberg, where it was first prosecuted. It is, therefore, inaccurate for the Secretary-General, in his Report on the ICTY Statute, to state, "Crimes against humanity were *first recognised* in the Charter and Judgement of the Nürnberg Tribunal, as well as in Law No. 10 of the Control Council for Germany." (para. 47, emphasis added). In the same paragraph, the Secretary-General went on to state, "Crimes against humanity are aimed at any civilian population and are prohibited regardless of whether they are committed in an armed conflict, international or internal in character."

4.2.166 Article 6(c) of the Charter of the Nuremberg Tribunal defined Crimes against Humanity thus:

> (c) CRIMES AGAINST HUMANITY: namely, murder, extermination, enslavement, deportation, and other inhumane acts committed against any civilian population, before or during the war; or persecutions on political, racial or religious grounds in execution of or in connection with any crime within the jurisdiction of the Tribunal, whether or not in violation of the domestic law of the country where perpetrated.

4.2.167 Article II(1)(c) of Control Council Law No. 10 defined Crimes against Humanity as:

> (a) Crimes against Humanity. Atrocities and offenses, including but not limited to murder, extermination, enslavement, deportation, imprisonment, torture, rape, or other inhumane acts committed against any civilian population, or persecutions on political, racial or religious grounds whether or not in violation of the domestic laws of the country where perpetrated.

4.2.168 As well as the genocides listed above in the Genocide section, which would also constitute crimes against humanity by virtue of the fact that the greater includes the lesser crime, other instances of crimes against humanity in recent history would, according to the findings of the *Russell* International War Tribunal, include the intentional bombing of civilian installations and other inhuman acts committed by the United States during the Vietnam war. The *Russell* Tribunal, which held sessions in Stockholm, Sweden (2–10 May 1967) and Roskilde, Denmark (20 November–1 December 1967), concluded that the United States had committed aggression, war crimes and crimes against humanity against North Vietnam. Crimes against humanity as distinct from genocide encompass such widespread attacks on a civilian population where there is, however, no intention to *destroy* an ethnic, racial, religious or national group as such.

Gravity of Crimes Against Humanity

4.2.169 It was at one time held by the ICTY that crimes against humanity were, other things being equal, *more serious* than ordinary war crimes. So held the Trial Chamber in the *Tadić Sentencing Judgement:*

> 73. A prohibited act committed as part of a crime against humanity, that is with an awareness that the act formed part of a widespread or systematic attack on a civilian population, is, all else being equal, a more serious offence than an ordinary war crime. This follows from the requirement that crimes against humanity be committed on a widespread or systematic scale, the quantity of the crimes having a qualitative impact on the nature of the offence which is seen as a crime against more than just the victims themselves but against humanity as a whole.

4.2.170 The same view was implicit in the *Erdemović Sentencing Judgement*, in which the Trial Chamber referred to the concept of "humanity as victim" characterising crimes against humanity, and observed that:

> 27. Generally speaking, crimes against humanity are recognised as very grave crimes which shock the collective conscience. The indictment supporting the charges against the accused at the Nuremberg Trial specified that the crimes against humanity constituted breaches of international conventions, domestic law, and the general principles of criminal law as derived from the criminal law of all civilised nations. The Secretary-General of the United Nations, in his report which proposed the Statute of International Tribunal, considered that "crimes against humanity refer to inhumane acts of *extreme gravity*, such as wilful killing, torture or rape, committed as part of a widespread or systematic attack against any civilian population on national, political, ethnic, racial or religious grounds" [. . .].
>
> 28. Crimes against humanity are serious acts of violence which harm human beings by striking what is most essential to them: their life, liberty, physical welfare, health, and or dignity. They are inhumane acts that by their extent and gravity go beyond the limits tolerable to the international community, which must perforce demand their punishment. But crimes against humanity also transcend the individual because when the individual is assaulted, humanity comes under attack and is negated. It is therefore the concept of humanity as victim which essentially characterises crimes against humanity.

4.2.171 This notion has now, however, been abandoned in favour of the view that there is "in law no distinction between the seriousness of a crime against humanity and that of a war crime," (*Foča Trial Judgement*, paras. 851 and 860; *Tadić Judgement in Sentencing Appeals*, para. 69 (although see dissent of Judge Cassese on this point); *Furundžija Appeals Judgement*, paras. 242–243).

4.2.172 See also Judge Li's Separate and Dissenting Opinion to the *Erdemović Appeals Judgement*. Judge Li's Separate and Dissenting Opinion was endorsed in Judge Robinson's Separate Opinion to the *Tadić Sentencing Judgement II*:

> . . . There is, in principle, no warrant either in past or contemporary practice for the conclusion that crimes against humanity are more serious than war crimes, and, in any event, for sentencing purposes, there is no justification for this approach when both crimes have precisely the same factual bases.
>
> . . .
>
> 8. the proper meaning of a crime against humanity is not that it is a crime against the whole of humanity, but rather that it is a crime which offends humaneness, i.e. a certain quality of behaviour.
>
> . . .
>
> It is well-established that the purpose of creating the new offense of crimes against humanity in 1945 was not to establish a crime of a graver nature than the existing war crimes, but simply to fill a gap in the law as to culpability for crimes committed by a combatant against its own nationals.
>
> . . .
>
> The mere fact that crimes against humanity are generally required to be committed on a widespread and systematic basis does not, by itself, make them more serious than war crimes, and, certainly, this cannot be the case where they are constituted by the very same acts as war crimes. . . . As a matter of fact, many of the war crimes charged in the Tribunal's indictments are committed as part of a plan or policy or on a large-scale.

For an in-depth treatment of this question, see Micaela Frulli, "Are crimes against humanity more serious than war crimes?" 12(2) *European Journal of International* 329–35 (April 2001).

Crimes Against Humanity in the ICT Statutes

4.2.173 There are three crucial differences between the definition of crimes against humanity in Article 3 of the ICTR Statute and the definition in Article 5:

- ICTY Article 5 refers to armed conflict, whereas ICTR Article 3 does not. Thus at the ICTY it is necessary to prove a nexus, or link, between the crime and an armed conflict, which is not required at the ICTR. (See para. 627 of the *Tadić Opinion and Judgement:* "In the Statute of the International Tribunal for Rwanda, the requirement of an armed conflict is omitted, requiring only that the acts be committed as part of an attack against a civilian population"). The ICC article on crimes against humanity (Article 7) does not have the requirement of a nexus with armed conflict.

- ICTY Article 5 does not refer to the attack on a civilian population as being "widespread or systematic," while ICTR Article 3 does. As a matter of case-law, however, the ICTY has come to recognise this criterion as a requirement for crimes against humanity, so the ICTY and ICTR share a common position on this point. The ICC has also taken up this wording (see ICC Article 7(1)).
- ICTR Article 3 requires the crimes against humanity coming within its jurisdiction to have been committed with a discriminatory intent (". . . on national, political, ethnic, racial or religious grounds"), while ICTY Article 5 only requires this in relation to persecution (ICTY Article 5(h)). The ICTY did introduce discriminatory intent as a requirement for all crimes against humanity in the *Tadić Opinion and Judgement*; this finding was, however, overturned on appeal, with the result that discriminatory intent is now required at the ICTY only in relation to persecution and not in relation to other crimes against humanity. ICC Article 7 does not require a discriminatory intent for all crimes against humanity, only for "persecution-type" crimes against humanity.
  See, however, the Appeals Chamber's subtle modification of the requirement of discriminatory intent set out in the *Akayesu Appeals Judgement* (see below, 4.2.214).
- Thus it can be seen that the ICC article on crimes against humanity agrees with ICTR Article 3 in two out of three respects. It appears that the earlier ICTY draft on crimes against humanity deviated in its literal wording from the common conception of crimes against humanity, a matter which has been arighted to a certain extent by its jurisprudence.

4.2.174 The article of the Special Court for Sierra Leone dealing with crimes against humanity (Article 2, SCSL Statute) most closely tracks ICTR Article 3, albeit without the reference in the latter to the attack being "on national, political, ethnic, racial or religious grounds." See Annex 5 for SCSL Statute.

4.2.175 The Secretary-General, in his report on the ICTY Statute, stated in relation to crimes against humanity:

> Crimes against humanity refer to inhumane acts of a very serious nature . . . committed as part of a *widespread or systematic attack against any civilian population on national, political, ethnic, racial or religious grounds. . . .*"
> (S/25704, para. 48, emphasis added.)

4.2.176 This was also the interpretation of Mrs. Madeleine Albright, the then Permanent Representative of the United States of America to the United Nations, speaking in the Security Council after the adoption of Resolution 827:

> it is understood that Article 5 applies to all acts listed in that article, when committed contrary to law during a period of armed conflict in the territory of the former Yugoslavia, as part of a widespread or systematic attack against any civilian population on national, political, ethnic, racial, gender or religious grounds. (UN Doc. S/PV.3217, at 15 (25 May,1993).)

4.2.177 The ICTY has, somewhat inconsistently, adopted in its case-law part of the above interpretation, incorporating the requirement of a "widespread or systematic attack," but not the part relating to discriminatory intent ("on national, political, ethnic, racial or religious grounds").

4.2.178 In light of the differences between Article 5 of the ICTY Statute and Article 3 of the ICTR Statute, the ICTR Appeals Chamber held in the *Akayesu Appeals Judgement*, para. 462, that the jurisprudence and interpretation of Article 5 of the ICTY Statute are, in certain cases, of limited relevance.

Nexus with Armed Conflict

4.2.179 Under customary international law, there is no requirement that crimes against humanity be committed in an armed conflict. Indeed, Article 6(c) of the Charter of the Nuremberg Tribunal refers to "murder-type" crimes against humanity committed "*before or during the war*" (emphasis added), thus expressly contemplating prosecution for crimes against humanity committed in peacetime.

4.2.180 Thus in the *Tadić Jurisdiction Appeals Decision*, the Appeals Chamber affirmed that under customary law crimes against humanity may be committed even in the absence of an armed conflict:

> 141. It is by now a settled rule of customary international law that crimes against humanity do not require a connection to international armed conflict. Indeed, as the Prosecutor points out, customary international law may not require a connection between crimes against humanity and any conflict at all. Thus, by requiring that crimes against humanity be committed in either internal or international armed conflict, the Security Council may have defined the crime in Article 5 more narrowly than necessary under customary international law. . . .

4.2.181 This raises the question whether the Tribunal would be bound by the more restrictive definition contained in the ICTY Statute or by customary law. The consesnsus which seems to be emerging on this point is that, in accordance with general principles of interpretation in criminal law, where the Statute is more favourable to the accused than customary law, then the former prevails, whereas where it is less favourable, customary law prevails. Thus in this case, since ICTY Article 5 imports an additional requirement to be proved by the Prosecution, making a conviction thereby more difficult to secure, the Statute would prevail over customary international law's less stringent definition.

4.2.182 *A fortiori*, the Appeals Chamber concluded that:

> 142. . . . Article 5 may be invoked as a basis of jurisdiction over crimes committed in either internal or international armed conflicts.

Conditions of Applicability for Crimes Against Humanity

4.2.183 The Trial Chamber ruling in the *Tadić Opinion and Judgement*, identified six conditions for crimes against humanity to apply:

(1) the existence of an armed conflict;
(2) a nexus between the acts in question and the armed conflict;
(3) the acts were part of a widespread or systematic occurrence of crimes directed against a civilian population;
(4) there was a discriminatory intent behind the crimes;
(5) there was a policy behind the discrimination (this may not strictly be necessary); and
(6) the accused acted with the requisite *intent*.

These conditions will be examined in turn.

Existence of an Armed Conflict

4.2.184   See para. 628 of the *Tadić Opinion and Judgement* and 4.2.179, above.

Nexus Between the Acts and the Armed Conflict

4.2.185   Subject to two caveats, the Trial Chamber held in the *Tadić Opinion and Judgement* that, "it is sufficient for purposes of crimes against humanity that the act occurred in the course or duration of an armed conflict":

> 633. . . . The first such caveat, a seemingly obvious one, is that the act be linked geographically as well as temporally with the armed conflict. In this regard it is important to note that the Appeals Chamber found that:
>
>> the temporal and geographic scope of both internal and international armed conflicts extends beyond the exact time and place of hostilities.
>
> . . .
>
> Secondly, the act and the conflict must be related or, to reverse this proposition, the act must not be *unrelated* to the armed conflict, must not be done for purely personal motives of the perpetrator.

4.2.186   The Prosecution in its cross-appeal appealed the finding that an act committed by the accused for "purely personal motives" cannot constitute a crime against humanity. See *Brief of Argument of the Prosecution (Cross-Appellant)* filed on 12 January 1998, pp. 59–67, and the cases cited therein.

4.2.187   The Prosecution objection was upheld on appeal. Following its discussion of the issue, in particular considering the irrelevance of motive in criminal law, the Appeals Chamber, in its *Tadić Appeals Judgement*, concluded:

> 271. The Trial Chamber correctly recognised that crimes which are unrelated to widespread or systematic attacks on a civilian population should not be prosecuted as crimes against humanity. Crimes against humanity are crimes of a special nature to which a greater degree of moral turpitude attaches than to an ordinary crime. Thus to convict an accused of crimes against humanity, it must be proved that the crimes were *related* to the attack on a civilian population (occurring during an armed conflict) and that the accused *knew* that his crimes were so related.

272. For the above reasons, however, the Appeals Chamber does not consider it necessary to further require, as a substantive element of *mens rea*, a nexus between the specific acts allegedly committed by the accused and the armed conflict, or to require proof of the accused's *motives*. Consequently, in the opinion of the Appeals Chamber, the requirement that an act must not have been carried out for the purely personal motives of the perpetrator does not form part of the prerequisites necessary for conduct to fall within the definition of a crime against humanity under Article 5 of the Tribunal's Statute.

4.2.188 This has been interpreted to mean that there is now *no nexus requirement* between the accused's acts and the armed conflict. See the *Foča Trial Judgement*, where the Trial Chamber stated:

413. The existence of an armed conflict with respect to crimes against humanity goes beyond the stipulations of customary international law. It has been interpreted by the Appeals Chamber as a general pre-requisite—peculiar to the Tribunal's Statute—which supposes the *existence* of an armed conflict at the time and place relevant to the Indictment. The requirement that there exists an armed conflict does not necessitate any substantive relationship between the acts of the accused and the armed conflict whereby the accused should have intended to participate in the armed conflict. The Appeals Chamber has held that a nexus between the acts of the accused and the armed conflict is not required. The armed conflict requirement is satisfied by proof that there was an armed conflict at the relevant time and place.

4.2.189 The Trial Chamber ruling in the *Foča Trial Judgement* did insist on the need for a nexus, but a nexus between the acts of the accused and the attack on a civilian population, not (as seemed to be the case previously) a nexus between the acts of the accused and the armed conflict:

418. There must exist a nexus between the acts of the accused and the attack, which consists of:

(i) the commission of an act which, by its nature or consequences, is objectively part of the attack; coupled with

(ii) knowledge on the part of the accused that there is an attack on the civilian population and that his act is part of the attack.

419. It is sufficient to show that the act took place in the context of an accumulation of acts of violence which, individually, may vary greatly in nature and gravity.

420. Finally, the Trial Chamber notes that, although the attack must be part of the armed conflict, it can also outlast it.

Irrelevance of Motive

4.2.190 The irrelevance of motive to crimes against humanity (apart from persecution) was affirmed by the Trial Chamber ruling in the *Kupreškić Trial Judgement*:

558. ... Subsequent to the Appeals Chamber's decision in *Prosecutor v. Tadić*, crimes against humanity need be committed with a discriminatory intent only

with regard to the category of "persecutions" under Article 5(h); ie. the sole category in which discrimination comprises an integral element of the prohibited conduct. Otherwise, a discriminatory animus is not an essential ingredient of the *mens rea* of crimes against humanity. Nor are the *motives* (as distinct from the *intent*) of the accused, as such, of special pertinence.

4.2.191 See also para. 433 of the *Foča Trial Judgement:* "The Appeals Chamber in the *Tadić* case made it clear that the motives of the accused for taking part in the attack are irrelevant and that a crime against humanity may be committed for purely personal reasons." This is, of course, provided that the accused knows of the attack against the civilian population and that his acts form part of that attack.

4.2.192 Some controversy remains on this issue, however, since ICTR jurisprudence continues to mention as part of the requirements of crimes against humanity that the crimes not be committed "for purely personal reasons." See the *Kayishema and Ruzindana Trial Judgement* (paras. 122–123).

The Acts Were Part of a Widespread or Systematic Occurrence of Crimes Directed Against a Civilian Population

"Civilian"

4.2.193 When considering the definition of "civilian" under this heading, the Trial Chamber ruling in the *Tadić Opinion and Judgement* held, on the basis of various sources, including the *Vukovar Rule 61 Decision*, that "a wide definition of civilian population . . . is justified":

> 643. . . . Thus the presence of those actively involved in the conflict should not prevent the characterization of a population as civilian and those actively involved in a resistance movement can qualify as victims of crimes against humanity.

4.2.194 In the *Vukovar* case, patients in a hospital who had been part of the resistance movement and laid down their arms were considered victims of crimes against humanity. In its *Vukovar Rule 61 Decision*, the Trial Chamber considered crimes against humanity applicable even where the victims at one time bore arms:

> 29. . . . Although according to the terms of Article 5 of the Statute of this Tribunal . . . combatants in the traditional sense of the term cannot be victims of a crime against humanity, this does not apply to individuals who, at one particular point in time, carried out acts of resistance. As the Commission of Experts, established pursuant to Security Council resolution 780, noted, "it seems obvious that Article 5 applies first and foremost to civilians, meaning people who are not combatants. This, however, should not lead to any quick conclusions concerning people who at one particular point in time did bear arms. . . . Information of the overall circumstances is relevant for the interpretation of the provision in a spirit consistent with its purpose." (Doc S/1994/674, para. 78). This conclusion is supported by case law. In the Barbie case, the French *Cour de Cassation* said that "inhumane acts and persecution which, in the name of a State practising a policy of ideological hegemony, were

committed systematically or collectively not only against individuals because of their membership in a racial or religious group but also against the adversaries of that policy whatever the form of the opposition" could be considered a crime against humanity. (Cass. Crim. 20 December 1985).

See also the *Kupreškić Trial Judgement*, paras. 547–549 and the *Blaškić Trial Judgement*, paras. 208–213.

4.2.195   See para. 582 of the *Akayesu Trial Judgement*:

> 582. ... Members of the civilian population are people who are not taking any active part in the hostilities, including members of the armed forces who laid down their arms and those persons placed *hors de combat* by sickness, wounds, detention or any other cause. Where there are certain individuals within the civilian population who do not come within the definition of civilians, this does not deprive the population of its civilian character.

4.2.196   This was also the approach taken in the *Kayishema and Ruzindana Trial Judgement*:

> 127. Traditionally, legal definitions of 'civilian' or 'civilian population' have been discussed within the context of armed conflict. However, under the Statute, crimes against humanity may be committed inside or outside the context of an armed conflict. Therefore, the term civilian must be understood within the context of war as well as relative peace. The Trial Chamber considers that a wide definition of civilian is applicable and, in the context of the situation of Kibuye *Prefecture* where there was no armed conflict, includes all persons *except* those who have the duty to maintain public order and have the legitimate means to exercise force. Non-civilians would include, for example, members of the FAR, the RPF, the police and the Gendarmerie Nationale.
>
> 128. With regard to the targeting of any civilian population, the Trial Chamber concurs with the finding in the *Tadic* decision that the targeted population must be predominantly civilian in nature but the presence of certain non-civilians in their midst does not change the character of that population.

4.2.197   See also the *Blaškić Trial Judgement* where it was held that individuals who at one time performed acts of resistance may in certain circumstances be victims of a crime against humanity:

> 214. Crimes against humanity therefore do not mean only acts committed against civilians in the strict sense of the term but include also crimes against two categories of people: those who were members of a resistance movement and former combatants—regardless of whether they wore uniforms or not—but who were no longer taking part in hostilities when the crimes were perpetrated because they had either left the army or were no longer bearing arms or, ultimately, had been placed *hors de combat*, in particular due to their wounds or their being detained. It also follows that the specific situation of the victim at the moment the crimes were committed, rather than his status, must be taken into account in determining his standing as a civilian. Finally, it can be concluded that the presence of soldiers within an intentionally targeted civilian population does not alter the civilian nature of that population.

This was quoted and adopted in the *Kordić Trial Judgement*, para. 180.

4.2.198 In essence, the approach seems to be that victims of crimes against humanity must be *non-combatants*, which would include, under Geneva law, prisoners-of-war and the wounded, sick and shipwrecked.

4.2.199 It would seem possible to broaden the class of victims still further. If one army had massive superiority over another, and attacked the enemy combatants in a systematically atrocious manner, e.g., by consistently committing war crimes against enemy combatants and employing illegal weapons designed to cause unnecessary suffering, then it could be said that crimes against humanity were being committed, even where the victims were all combatants. The elimination of barbarism, not legal formalism, should be the touchstone.

"Population"

4.2.200 As regards the term "population," the Trial Chamber in the *Tadić Opinion and Judgement* noted:

> 644. . . . the emphasis is not on the individual victim but rather on the collective, the individual being victimised not because of his individual attributes but rather because of his membership of a targeted civilian population. This has been interpreted to mean [. . .] that the acts must occur on a widespread or systematic basis, that there must be some form of a governmental, organisational or group policy to commit these acts and that the perpetrator must know of the context within which his actions are taken, as well as the requirement [. . .] that the actions be taken on discriminatory grounds.

4.2.201 On the meaning of the phrase, "directed against any civilian population," see also the *Foča Trial Judgement* (paras. 421–435).

4.2.202 The test of what constitutes the population against which the attacks are directed, in line with the test adopted for genocide (see 4.2.108 *et seq.*), appears to be a *subjective* one, i.e., the test adopted it is a part of the population identified as such *by the perpetrators*. See the *Nikolić Rule 61 Decision:*

> 26. The second circumstance, whereby crimes must be "directed against any civilian population" is specific to crimes against humanity. Set forth in broad terms in the Statute, it covers, according to prevailing opinion, three distinct components. First, the crimes must be directed at a civilian population, *specifically identified as a group by the perpetrators of those acts*. Secondly, the crimes must, to a certain extent, be organised and systematic. Although they need not be related to a policy established at State level, in the conventional sense of the term, they cannot be the work of isolated individuals alone. Lastly, the crimes, considered as a whole, must be of a certain scale and gravity. (Emphasis added.)

4.2.203 It may be also derived from the requirement that a "population" be targeted, as well as from the requirement that the crimes be part of a widespread and systematic context, that isolated acts cannot constitute crimes against humanity. See the *Decision on Defence Motion on the Form of the Indictment*, rendered on 14 November 1995 in *Tadić*, in which the Trial Chamber stated:

> 11. ... The very nature of the criminal acts in respect of which competence is conferred upon the International Tribunal by Article 5, that they be "directed against any civilian population," ensures that what is to be alleged will not be one particular act but, instead, a course of conduct.

Widespread or Systematic

4.2.204 The Trial Chamber ruling in the *Tadić Opinion and Judgement* stated, "it is now well established that the requirement that the acts be directed against a civilian "population" can be fulfilled if the acts occur on either a widespread basis or in a systematic manner. Either one of these is sufficient to exclude isolated or random acts" (para. 646). In other words, the requirement is disjunctive rather than conjunctive.

4.2.205 On the related issue of "whether a single act by a perpetrator can constitute a crime against humanity" (para. 649), the Trial Chamber emphasised the link between the act and a criminal political system:

> Clearly, a single act by a perpetrator taken within the context of a widespread or systematic attack against a civilian population entails individual criminal responsibility and an individual perpetrator need not commit numerous offences to be held liable. Although it is correct that isolated, random acts should not be included in the definition of crimes against humanity, that is the purpose of requiring that the acts be directed against a civilian *population* and thus "[e]ven an isolated act can constitute a crime against humanity if it is the product of a political system based on terror or persecution." (para. 649)

4.2.206 Thus a single act can be a crime against humanity if it occurs in the "appropriate" context. For example an act of denouncing a Jewish neighbour to the Nazi authorities—if committed against a background of widespread persecution—could amount to a crime against humanity. An *isolated* act, however—i.e. a context-less atrocity—could not. On this point, see the *Vukovar Rule 61 Decision:*

> 30. Crimes against humanity are to be distinguished from war crimes against individuals. In particular, they must be widespread or demonstrate a systematic character. However, as long as there is a link with the widespread or systematic attack against a civilian population, a single act could qualify as a crime against humanity. As such, an individual committing a crime against a single victim or a limited number of victims might be recognised as guilty of a crime against humanity if his acts were part of the specific context identified above.

4.2.207 In the *Akayesu Trial Judgement*, the requirements were explained thus:

> 580. The concept of 'widespread' may be defined as massive, frequent, large scale action, carried out collectively with considerable seriousness and directed against a multiplicity of victims. The concept of 'systematic' may be defined as thoroughly organised and following a regular pattern on the basis of a common policy involving substantial public or private resources. There is no requirement that this policy must be adopted formally as the policy of a state. There must however be some kind of preconceived plan or policy.

> 581. The concept of 'attack' may be defined as an unlawful act of the kind enumerated in Article 3(a) to (i) of the Statute, like murder, extermination, enslavement etc. An attack may also be non violent in nature, like imposing a system of apartheid, which is declared a crime against humanity in Article 1 of the Apartheid Convention of 1973, or exerting pressure on the population to act in a particular manner, may come under the purview of an attack, if orchestrated on a massive scale or in a systematic manner.

4.2.208 The terms "widespread" and "systematic" were defined by the Trial Chamber ruling in the *Kayishema and Ruzindana Trial Judgement* as follows:

> 123. A widespread attack is one that is directed against a multiplicity of victims. A systematic attack means an attack carried out pursuant to a preconceived policy or plan. Either of these conditions will serve to exclude isolated or random inhumane acts committed for purely personal reasons.

4.2.209 The meaning and requirements of the term "systematic" were clarified in the *Blaškić Trial Judgement*, para. 203. It held that the "systematic" requirement referred to the following four elements:

> (1) the existence of a political objective, a plan pursuant to which the attack is perpetrated or an ideology, in the broad sense of the word, that is, to destroy, persecute or weaken a community;
> (2) the perpetration of a criminal act on a very large scale against a group of civilians or the repeated and continuous commission of inhumane acts linked to one another;
> (3) the preparation and use of significant public or private resources, whether military or other;
> (4) the implication of high-level political and/or military authorities in the definition and establishment of the methodical plan.

4.2.210 It was held in the *Blaškić Trial Judgement*, para. 206, that a crime may be "widespread" or committed on a large scale by the "cumulative effect of a series of inhumane acts or the singular effect of an inhumane act of extraordinary magnitude." This was adopted in the *Kordić and Čerkez Trial Judgement*, para. 179.

Attack

4.2.211 The Trial Chamber ruling in the *Foča Trial Judgement* distinguished the use of the word "attack" in the context of crimes against humanity (i.e. "... widespread or systematic attack against any civilian population...") from its use in the context of war crimes:

> 416. The term "attack" in the context of a crime against humanity carries a slightly different meaning than in the laws of war. In the context of a crime against humanity, "attack" is not limited to the conduct of hostilities. It may also encompass situations of mistreatment of persons taking no active part in hostilities, such as someone in detention. However, both terms are based on a

similar assumption, namely that war should be a matter between armed forces or armed groups and that the civilian population cannot be a legitimate target.

4.2.212 The underlying offence does not need to constitute the attack but only to form part of the attack or to comprise part of a pattern of widespread and systematic crimes directed against any civilian population.

Discriminatory Intent

4.2.213 As noted above, a discriminatory intent *is* formally a requirement at the ICTR by virtue of the plain wording of Article 3 of the ICTR Statute: ". . . *when committed . . . on national, political, ethnic, racial or religious grounds.*" The matter has not posed much of a problem, since the genocide against the Tutsi was clearly an attack on a civilian population on discriminatory grounds.

4.2.214 Nonetheless the Appeals Chamber has modified this requirement in light of the *mens rea* requirement that the accused known of the context in which his acts are committed. It was held in the *Akayesu Appeals Judgement* that:

> 467. The meaning to be collected from Article 3 of the Statute is that even if the accused did not have a discriminatory intent when he committed the act charged against a particular victim, he nevertheless knew that his act could further a discriminatory attack against a civilian population; the attack could even be perpetrated by other persons and the accused could even object to it. As a result, where it is shown that the accused had knowledge of such objective nexus, the Prosecutor is under no obligation to go forward with a showing that the crime charged was committed against a particular victim with a discriminatory intent. In this connection, the only known exception in customary international law relates in cases of persecutions.
>
> 468. In light of this interpretation and the finding that persecution is the only crime which requires a discriminatory intent, the Appeals Chamber is of the view that any interpretation of the chapeau of Article 3 of the Statute such as would add a requirement for a showing of a discriminatory intent with respect to all crimes against humanity would likely render redundant the express if more succinct reference to discrimination—contained in Article 3 of the Statute (Persecutions), which reference is understood as a requirement of a discriminatory intent. As is known, one of the basic rules of interpretation requires that a provision or part thereof should not be interpreted in a manner to render it redundant or bereft of any object, unless such a conclusion is inevitable. One must proceed from the assumption that the lawmakers intended to give some effect to *each* of the words used.
>
> 469. For the foregoing reasons, the Appeals Chamber considers the present ground of appeal and finds that:
>
> > (1) Article 3 of the Statute does not require that all crimes against humanity enumerated therein be committed with a discriminatory intent.
> >
> > (2) Article 3 restricts the jurisdiction of the Tribunal to crimes against humanity committed in a specific situation, that is, "as part of a widespread or systematic attack against any civilian population" on discriminatory grounds.

4.2.215 In the former Yugoslavia, the crimes committed against the Muslim, Croat and Serb populations, whenever they were widespread and systematic evidently targeted a part of the population on discriminatory grounds, namely national or religious grounds. It is perhaps surprising, therefore, that there has been so much discussion at the ICTY as to whether or not a discriminatory intent was a requirement of crimes against humanity under Article 5 of the ICTY Statute.

4.2.216 The result of the jurisprudential debate has in any event now been resolved in favour of the opinion that a discriminatory intent is *not* required for all crimes against humanity under Article 5 of the ICTY Statute.

4.2.217 Initially, the Trial Chamber ruling in the *Tadić Opinion and Judgement* had concluded that a discriminatory intent was necessary for *all* acts constituting crimes against humanity:

> 652. . . . because the requirement of discriminatory intent on national, political, ethnic, racial or religious grounds for all crimes against humanity was included in the *Report of the Secretary-General*, and since several Security Council members stated that they interpreted Article 5 as referring to acts taken on a discriminatory basis, the Trial Chamber adopts the requirement of discriminatory intent for all crimes against humanity under Article 5. Factually, the inclusion of this additional requirement that the inhumane acts must be taken on discriminatory grounds is satisfied by the evidence discussed above that the attack on the civilian population was conducted against only the non-Serb portion of the population because they were non-Serbs.

4.2.218 This finding was cross-appealed by the Prosecution (see the Cross-Appellant's Brief, 12 January 1998). The Appeals Chamber, in the *Tadić Appeals Judgement*, upheld the Prosecution cross-appeal and reversed the Trial Chamber on this point:

> 285. . . . The aim of those drafting the Statute was to make all crimes against humanity punishable, including those which, while fulfilling all the conditions required by the notion of such crimes, may not have been perpetrated on political, racial or religious grounds as specified in para. (h) of Article 5. In light of the humanitarian goals of the framers of the Statute, one fails to see why they should have seriously restricted the class of offences coming within the purview of "crimes against humanity," thus leaving outside this class all the possible instances of serious and widespread or systematic crimes against civilians on account only of their lacking a discriminatory intent. For example, a discriminatory intent requirement would prevent the penalization of random and indiscriminate violence intended to spread terror among a civilian population as a crime against humanity. *A fortiori*, the object and purpose of Article 5 would be thwarted were it to be suggested that the discriminatory grounds required are limited to the five grounds put forth by the Secretary-General in his Report and taken up (with the addition, in one case, of the further ground of gender) in the statements made in the Security Council by three of its members. Such an interpretation of Article 5 would create significant *lacunae* by failing to protect victim groups not covered by the listed discriminatory grounds. The experience of Nazi Germany demonstrated that crimes against humanity may be committed on discriminatory grounds other than those enumerated in Article 5 (h), such as physical or mental disability, age or infirmity, or sexual preference. Similarly, the extermination of "class enemies" in the Soviet Union

during the 1930s (admittedly, as in the case of Nazi conduct before the Second World War, an occurrence that took place in times of peace, not in times of armed conflict) and the deportation of the urban educated of Cambodia under the Khmer Rouge between 1975–1979, provide other instances which would not fall under the ambit of crimes against humanity based on the strict enumeration of discriminatory grounds suggested by the Secretary-General in his Report.

...

2. Article 5 and Customary International Law

287. The same conclusion is reached if Article 5 is construed in light of the principle whereby, in case of doubt and whenever the contrary is not apparent from the text of a statutory or treaty provision, such a provision must be interpreted in light of, and in conformity with, customary international law. In the case of the Statute, it must be presumed that the Security Council, where it did not explicitly or implicitly depart from general rules of international law, intended to remain within the confines of such rules.

288. A careful perusal of the relevant practice shows that a discriminatory intent is not required by customary international law for all crimes against humanity.

...

3. The Report of the Secretary-General

293. The interpretation suggested so far is not in keeping with the Report of the Secretary-General and the statements made by three members of the Security Council before the Tribunal's Statute was adopted by the Council. The Appeals Chamber is nevertheless of the view that these two interpretative sources do not suffice to establish that all crimes against humanity need be committed with a discriminatory intent.

...

C. Conclusion

305. The Prosecution was correct in submitting that the Trial Chamber erred in finding that all crimes against humanity require a discriminatory intent. Such an intent is an indispensable legal ingredient of the offence only with regard to those crimes for which this is expressly required, that is, for Article 5 (h), concerning various types of persecution.

4.2.219 As stated, the question may be academic in the context of Rwanda and the former Yugoslavia; it is true, however, that this solution might prove preferable when other contexts are considered, e.g. the random killings practiced by the Khmer Rouge in Cambodia or the Euthanasia programme of the Nazis, where there is either no discernible discriminatory intent or the group discriminated against does not fall within one of the enumerated categories ("*national, political, ethnic, racial or religious*").

No Need for Formal or State Policy

4.2.220 The Trial Chamber in the *Tadić Opinion and Judgement* held that the concept of crimes against humanity necessarily *implies* a policy element (see paras. 653–655), but did not strictly stipulate this aspect as a *requirement* for crimes against humanity. The Chamber also held that such a policy need not be explicitly formulated, nor need it be the policy of a *State:*

653. ... the reason that crimes against humanity so shock the conscience of mankind and warrant intervention by the international community is because they are not isolated, random acts of individuals but rather result from a deliberate attempt to target a civilian population. Traditionally this requirement was understood to mean that there must be some form of policy to commit these acts. As explained by the Netherlands *Hoge Raad* in *Public Prosecutor v. Menten:*

> The concept of 'crimes against humanity' also requires—although this is not expressed in so many words in the above definition [Article 6(c) of the Nürnberg Charter]—that the crimes in question form a part of a system based on terror or constitute a link in a consciously pursued policy directed against particular groups of people.

Importantly, however, such a policy need not be formalized and can be deduced from the way in which the acts occur. Notably, if the acts occur on a widespread or systematic basis that demonstrates a policy to commit those acts, whether formalized or not. Although some doubt the necessity of such a policy the evidence in this case clearly establishes the existence of a policy.

654. An additional issue concerns the nature of the entity behind the policy. The traditional conception was, in fact, not only that a policy must be present but that the policy must be that of a State, as was the case in Nazi Germany. The prevailing opinion was, as explained by one commentator, that crimes against humanity, as crimes of a collective nature, require a State policy "because their commission requires the use of the state's institutions, personnel and resources in order to commit, or refrain from preventing the commission of, the specified crimes described in Article 6(c) [of the Nürnberg Charter]." While this may have been the case during the Second World War, and thus the jurisprudence followed by courts adjudicating charges of crimes against humanity based on events alleged to have occurred during this period, this is no longer the case.... Therefore, although a policy must exist to commit these acts, it need not be the policy of a State.

4.2.221 This was confirmed by the Trial Chamber ruling in the *Kayishema and Ruzindana Trial Judgement*, which held that a policy formulated by an organisation or group was sufficient:

> 124. For an act of mass victimisation to be a crime against humanity, it must include a policy element. Either of the requirements of widespread or systematic are enough to exclude acts not committed as part of a broader policy or plan. Additionally, the requirement that the attack must be committed against a "civilian population" inevitably demands some kind of plan and, the discriminatory element of the attack is, by its very nature, only possible as a consequence of a policy.

> 125. Who or what must instigate the policy? Arguably, customary international law requires a showing that crimes against humanity are committed pursuant to an action or policy of a State. However, it is clear that the ICTR Statute does not demand the involvement of a State....

> 126.... To have jurisdiction over either of the accused, the Chamber must be satisfied that their actions were instigated or directed by a Government *or by any organisation or group*. (Emphasis added.)

4.2.222 The *Kupreškić Trial Judgement*, para. 551, similarly stipulated that "a policy need not be explicitly formulated, nor need it be the policy of a *State*" (emphasis in the original). The *Blaškić Trial Judgement*, para. 204, after holding that the plan "need not necessarily be declared expressly or even stated clearly and precisely," went on to refer to events from which the existence of a plan may be inferred.

4.2.223 The *Kordić and Čerkez Trial Judgement*, para. 182, similarly stated that it is not appropriate to adopt a strict view in relation to the plan or policy requirement. It endorsed the *Kupreškić* finding that "although the concept of crimes against humanity necessarily implies a policy element, there is some doubt as to whether it is strictly a *requirement*, as such, for crimes against humanity." In the *Kordić Trial Judgement* it was held that "the existence of a plan or policy should better be regarded as indicative of the systematic character of offences charged as crimes against humanity" (*ibid.*).

4.2.224 The debate is, again, more important at the ICTY than at the ICTR, because in Rwanda, the genocide was almost certainly directed by the Rwandan State, that is by the Hutu-led government then in power. In the former Yugoslavia, on the other hand, the more immediate evidence of systematically criminal policies stems from the activities of non-State actors, i.e., the Bosnian Serb entity and the HVO, while evidence that these policies were also those of neighbouring States, i.e., the Federal Republic of Yugoslavia and Croatia, might be more difficult to demonstrate to the requisite standard of proof.

Mens Rea Requirement

Intent

4.2.225 The Trial Chamber ruling in the *Tadić Opinion and Judgement* held that the requisite *mens rea* for crimes against humanity was (1) *intent* to commit the underlying offence, combined with (2) *knowledge* of the broader context in which that offence occurs. The Trial Chamber added the negative requirement that "the act must not be taken for purely personal reasons unrelated to the armed conflict" (para. 656):

> 659. Thus if the perpetrator has knowledge, either actual or constructive, that these acts were occurring on a widespread or systematic basis and does not commit his act for purely personal motives completely unrelated to the attack on the civilian population, that is sufficient to hold him liable for crimes against humanity. Therefore the perpetrator must know that there is an attack on the civilian population, know that his act fits in with the attack and the act must not be taken for purely personal reasons unrelated to the armed conflict.

4.2.226 The issue of personal motives is dealt with in more detail above, under the section, "(2) nexus between the acts and the armed conflict" (4.2.185). It should be noted that the finding of the Chamber in the *Tadić Opinion and Judgement* on the question of "personal motives" was over-turned by the Appeals Chamber in the *Tadić Appeals Judgement*, para. 255, and that it is now settled jurisprudence of the ICTY that:

> crimes against humanity can be committed for purely personal reasons, provided it is understood that the two aforementioned conditions—that the crimes

must be committed in the context of widespread or systematic crimes against a civilian population and that the accused must have *known* that his acts, in the words of the Trial Chamber, 'fitted into such a pattern'—are met.

4.2.227 The *mens rea* requirement for crimes against humanity laid down in the *Tadić Opinion and Judgement* was confirmed in the *Kupreškić Trial Judgement* (para. 556).

Knowledge

4.2.228 As regards the knowledge requirement, the Trial Chamber ruling in the *Kayishema and Ruzindana Trial Judgement* stated:

> 133. The perpetrator must knowingly commit crimes against humanity in the sense that he must understand the overall context of his act. The Defence for Ruzindana submitted that to be guilty of crimes against humanity the perpetrator must know that there is an attack on a civilian population and that his act is part of the attack. This issue has been addressed by the ICTY where it was stated that the accused must have acted with knowledge of the broader context of the attack; a view which conforms to the wording of the Statute of the International Criminal Court (ICC) Article 7.
>
> 134. The Trial Chamber agrees with the Defence. Part of what transforms an individual's act(s) into a crime against humanity is the inclusion of the act within a greater dimension of criminal conduct; therefore an accused should be aware of this greater dimension in order to be culpable thereof. Accordingly, actual or constructive knowledge of the broader context of the attack, meaning that the accused must know that his act(s) is part of a widespread or systematic attack on a civilian population and pursuant to some kind of policy or plan, is necessary to satisfy the requisite *mens rea* element of the accused. This requirement further compliments the exclusion from crimes against humanity of isolated acts carried out for purely personal reasons.

4.2.229 The Trial Chamber ruling in the *Blaškić Trial Judgement* pointed out that "knowledge" of the broader context in which his act occurred does not imply, however, that the accused must have intended to support the regime carrying out the attack on a civilian population (paras. 254 to 257). This was affirmed by the French *Cour de Cassation* ruling in the *Papon* case with regard to Article 6 of the Nuremberg Charter, which "does not require that the accomplice to a crime against humanity support the policy of ideological hegemony of the principal perpetrators."

4.2.230 On this basis the Trial Chamber in the *Blaškić Trial Judgement* held that:

> 257. . . . the *mens rea* specific to a crime against humanity does not require that the agent be identified with the ideology, policy or plan in whose name mass crimes were perpetrated nor even that he supported it. It suffices that he knowingly took the risk of participating in the implementation of the ideology, policy or plan. This specifically means that it must [. . .] be proved that:
> — the accused willingly agreed to carry out the functions he was performing;
> — that these functions resulted in his collaboration with the political, military or civilian authorities defining the ideology, policy or plan at the root of the crimes;

- that he received orders relating to the ideology, policy or plan; and lastly
- that he contributed to its commission through intentional acts or by simply refusing of his own accord to take the measures necessary to prevent their perpetration.

4.2.231 This list of elements is, however, problematic. If the accused "simply refus[ed] of his own accord to take the measures necessary to prevent . . . perpetration" of criminal acts, then the first two conditions would not apply at all, since the accused, who has simply abstained from any action, has not "willingly agreed to carry out the functions he was performing [which] resulted in collaboration with the authorities." The third condition does not relate to the accused's guilt at all. Thus the only basis for liability is then the second half of the fourth condition—failure to prevent crimes—which is the form of liability provided for under Article 7(3) of the ICTY Statute but which has nothing, or nothing specific, to do with the *mens rea* requirement of crimes against humanity.

4.2.232 It is worth noting that the same knowledge-based *mens rea* requirement could be applied to genocide, i.e. an accused is guilty of genocide if he performed certain acts intentionally and with the knowledge that the acts were part of a genocidal plan or policy. The Chamber in the *Krstić Trial Judgement* ventured in this direction (see above, 4.2.79).

Crimes Against Humanity and "Ethnic Cleansing"

4.2.233 It follows from the above that "ethnic cleansing" is usually a crime against humanity. Indeed, as pointed out above (4.2.168), in its ultimate manifestations (e.g., the Final Solution for making Europe *Judenfrei*, i.e., empty of Jews), "ethnic cleansing" is genocidal.

4.2.234 In the *Nikolić Rule 61 Decision*, the Trial Chamber applied the definition of crimes against humanity to "ethnic cleansing" by Bosnian Serbs in the Vlasenica region. The Chamber concluded that Nikolić participated in a systematic and widespread policy directed against a civilian population identified as a group, "specifically, if not exclusively" the Muslim population (see para. 27):

> The implementation of that discriminatory policy, commonly referred to as "ethnic cleansing," over the region of Vlasenica alone seems to have been so wide-spread as to fall within the Tribunal's jurisdiction under Article 5.

4.2.235 The tentative language in the preceding paras. reflects the fact that this was a Rule 61 Decision—an *ex parte* proceeding—and not a final Judgement.

Constituent Offences of Crimes Against Humanity

4.2.236 As described by the Trial Chamber ruling in the *Kayishema and Ruzindana Judgement*, the crimes enumerated as crimes against humanity under Article 3 of the ICTR Statute (and Article 5 of the ICTR Statute) "must be committed as part of a widespread or systematic attack against any civilian population on national, political, ethnic, racial or religious grounds" (discriminatory grounds are not, however, required under Article 5 of the ICTY Statute). *"The crimes themselves need not contain the three elements of the attack* (i.e., widespread or systematic, against any civilian population, on discriminatory grounds), but must form *part of* such an attack." (emphasis added)

4.2.237 The Trial Chamber ruling in the *Akayesu Trial Judgement*, added that, "the act must be inhumane in nature and character, causing great suffering, or serious injury to body or to mental or physical health" (paras. 578 and 585). It is difficult to see the basis, however, for adding this element, especially as it appears to conflict with the Chamber's statement in the same Judgement that, "an attack may also be non violent in nature, like imposing a system of apartheid, which is declared a crime against humanity in Article 1 of the Apartheid Convention of 1973, or exerting pressure on the population to act in a particular manner, may come under the purview of an attack, if orchestrated on a massive scale or in a systematic manner" (para. 581). To take an example, an accused deliberately and on discriminatory grounds committing acts of imprisonment, in the context of a widespread or systematic attack on a targeted population, should come within the purview of crimes against humanity even if the acts themselves do not necessarily cause "great suffering, or serious injury to body or to mental or physical health." Nonetheless this ruling has been followed. See para. 66 of the *Rutaganda Trial Judgement* and para. 201 of the *Musema Trial Judgement*.

4.2.238 More controversially, the Chamber ruling in the *Kayishema and Ruzindana Trial Judgement* required that the perpetrator's belief that the group he is discriminating against be an objectively reasonable one:

> 132. The second relevant scenario is where the perpetrator attacks people on the grounds and in the *belief* that they are members of a group but, in fact, they are not, for example, where the perpetrator believes that a group of Tutsi are supporters of the RPF and therefore accomplices. In the scenario, the Trial Chamber opines that the Prosecution must show that the perpetrator's belief was objectively reasonable—based upon real facts—rather than being mere speculation or perverted deduction.

4.2.239 For a criticism of this holding, among others, in the *Kayishema and Ruzindana Trial Judgement*, see Hervé Ascensio and Rafaëlle Maison, "L'activité des tribunaux Pénaux Internationaux (1999)" *in Annuaire français de droit international* (1999):

> Cette affirmation, introduisant un critère objectif dans l'identification du groupe victime du crime contre l'humanité, est tout à fait contestable: la repression du crime contre l'humanité dans ses aspects discriminatoires n'a pas pour fondement unique la protection de groupes objectivement identifiables mais également la sanction de la démarche discriminatoire.

Murder

4.2.240 "Murder" for the purposes of crimes against humanity was defined by the Chamber in the *Akayesu Trial Judgement* "as the unlawful, intentional killing of a human being":

> 589. The Chamber defines murder as the unlawful, intentional killing of a human being. The requisite elements of murder are:
> 1. the victim is dead;
> 2. the death resulted from an unlawful act or omission of the accused or a subordinate;
> 3. at the time of the killing the accused or a subordinate had the intention to kill or inflict grievous bodily harm on the deceased having known that such bodily harm is likely to cause the victim's death, and is reckless whether death ensures or not.
>
> 590. Murder must be committed as part of a widespread or systematic attack against a civilian population. The victim must be a member of this civilian population. The victim must have been murdered because he was discriminated against on national, ethnic, racial, political or religious grounds.

4.2.241 See also the *Kayishema and Ruzindana Trial Judgement:*

> 140. The accused is guilty of murder if the accused, engaging in conduct which is unlawful:
> 1. causes the death of another;
> 2. by a premeditated act or omission;
> 3. intending to kill any person or,
> 4. intending to cause grievous bodily harm to any person.
>
> Thus, a premeditated murder that forms part of a widespread or systematic attack, against civilians, on discriminatory grounds will be a crime against humanity. Also included will be extrajudicial killings, that is "unlawful and deliberate killings carried out with the order of a Government or with its complicity or acquiescence."

4.2.242 The Chamber found that the standard of *mens rea* required for murder "is intentional and premeditated killing. The result is premeditated when the actor formulated his intent to kill after a cool moment of reflection. The result is intended when it is the actor's purpose, or the actor is aware that it will occur in the ordinary course of events" (para. 139).

4.2.243 The requirement of premeditation seems excessive if it is construed to mean that in each case the prosecution will have to prove that the accused killed only after "a cool moment of reflection." Moreover where large-scale crimes such as crimes against humanity are concerned, the attempt to analyse each killing and to discover each of the above-noted features in the surrounding circumstances seems inappropriate, if not impossible, particularly if the accused is a high-ranking official, charged with having ordered or aided and abetted murders, rather than of having actually committed murders himself. In that case, will it be necessary to prove that each of the underlying murders was committed by the subordinate or principal with premeditation? This would surely be a nonsense.

4.2.244 See also the Trial Chamber ruling in the *Kupreškić Trial Judgement:*

> 560. The constituent elements of murder under Article 5(a) of the Statute are well known. They comprise the death of the victim as a result of the acts or omissions of the accused, where the conduct of the accused was a substantial cause of the death of the victim. It can be said that the accused is guilty of

murder if he or she engaging in conduct which is unlawful, intended to kill another person or to cause this person grievous bodily harm, and has caused the death of that person.

561. The requisite *mens rea* of murder under Article 5(a) is the intent to kill or the intent to inflict serious injury in reckless disregard of human life. In *Kayishema* it was noted that the standard of *mens rea* required is intentional and premeditated killing. The result is premeditated when the actor formulated his intent to kill after a cool moment of reflection. The result is intended when it is the actor's purpose, or the actor is aware that it will occur in the ordinary course of events.

4.2.245 See also paras. 79–81 of the *Rutaganda Judgement* and *Blaškić Trial Judgement*, para. 217. It is, however, contradictory to state that the *mens rea* of murder is intentional killing while at the same time stating that the mere intent to inflict serious injury also suffices.

Extermination

4.2.246 Extermination as a crime against humanity requires an element of mass destruction, but it remains distinct from genocide in that it does not require the intent to eradicate a protected group. See paras. 591–592 of the *Akayesu Trial Judgement*:

591. . . . Extermination differs from murder in that it requires an element of mass destruction which is not required for murder.

592. The Chamber defines the essential elements of extermination as the following :
1. the accused or his subordinate participated in the killing of certain named or described persons;
2. the act or omission was unlawful and intentional.
3. the unlawful act or omission must be part of a widespread or systematic attack;
4. the attack must be against the civilian population;
5. the attack must be on discriminatory grounds, namely: national, political, ethnic, racial, or religious grounds.

The definition does not, however, fully encompass the idea of mass destruction, since—under the above definition—the killing of two persons would, if the other conditions were met, constitute extermination. Nor does it appear to require an intent to exterminate, which raises the question of what is the qualitative difference between several murders committed as crimes against humanity and extermination committed as a crime against humanity. The Chamber probably did not wish to attach a figure to the number of victims required in order for an act to constitute extermination, and therefore simply specified that there had to be more than one victim; hence the reference to "persons." Nevertheless the notion of extermination is, it is submitted, more akin to mass murder with intent to destroy the group. In other words, extermination is very close to the idea of genocide, except that it would encompass more diverse groups than genocide, for example it would embrace the physical destruction of political and economic groups, as well as the ethnical, racial, religious and national groups protected by the Genocide Convention.

4.2.247 This same criticism may be made of the concept of extermination provided in the *Kayishema and Ruzindana Trial Judgement:*

> 142. ... the difference between murder and extermination is the scale; extermination can be said to be murder on a massive scale.

4.2.248 The Trial Chamber ruling in the *Kayishema and Ruzindana Trial Judgement* went on to offer the following definition of extermination:

> 144. ... The actor participates in the mass killing of others or in the creation of conditions of life that lead to the mass killing of others, through his act(s) or omission(s); having intended the killing, or being reckless, or grossly negligent as to whether the killing would result and; being aware that his act(s) or omission(s) forms part of a mass killing event; where, his act(s) or omission(s) forms part of a widespread or systematic attack against any civilian population on national, political, ethnic, racial or religious grounds.

See also para. 82 of the *Rutaganda Judgement*.

4.2.249 Again these definitions fail to capture the idea that extermination is to do with *elimination* of a group. On the contrary, this notion *is* captured in the Rome Statute for an ICC:

> "Extermination" includes the intentional infliction of conditions of life, *inter alia* the deprivation of access to food and medicine, *calculated to bring about the destruction of part of a population.* (ICC Article 7(2)(b), emphasis added.)
>
> "*Elements*. 1. The perpetrator killed one or more persons, including by inflicting conditions of life *calculated to bring about the destruction of part of a population.*" (Elements, ICC Article 7(1)(b), emphasis added.)

4.2.250 The position at the ICTY is now that no discriminatory element is required for extermination. The "Tribunal argues that the act of extermination is distinguishable from genocide by the fact that it is not committed on account of a person's national, ethnical, racial or religious affiliation and that, moreover, the commission of the act does not require any special intention, that is, the intent to destroy the group in whole or in part" (*Krstić Trial Judgement*, para. 494).

4.2.251 The elements of the crime, according to the *Krstić* Trial Chamber, are:

1. the accused or his subordinate participated in the killing of certain named or described persons;
2. the act or omission was unlawful and intentional;
3. the unlawful act or omission must be part of a widespread or systematic attack;
4. the attack must be against the civilian population. (*Id*., para. 492.)

Enslavement

4.2.252 In the *Foča* case, the accused were charged with crimes against humanity for the systematic rape and enslavement of woman in the city of Foča after its takeover by Bosnian Serb forces in April 1992. The Chamber found the accused guilty, *inter alia*, of enslavement. The Chamber dealt with enslavement at length (the *Foča Trial Judgement*, paras. 515–543), defining it as follows:

> 539. ... at the time relevant to the indictment , enslavement as a crime against humanity in customary international law consisted of the exercise of any or all of the powers attaching to the right of ownership over a person.
>
> 540. Thus, the Trial Chamber finds that the *actus reus* of the violation is the exercise of any or all of the powers attaching to the right of ownership over a person. The *mens rea* of the violation consists in the intentional exercise of such powers.
>
> 541. This definition may be broader than the traditional and sometimes apparently distinct definitions of either slavery, the slave trade and servitude or forced or compulsory labour found in other areas of international law. This is evidenced in particular by the various cases from the Second World War [. . .], which have included forced or compulsory labour under enslavement as a crime against humanity. . . .
>
> 542. Under this definition, indications of enslavement include elements of control and ownership; the restriction or control of an individual's autonomy, freedom of choice or freedom of movement; and, often, the accruing of some gain to the perpetrator. The consent or free will of the victim is absent. It is often rendered impossible or irrelevant by, for example, the threat or use of force or other forms of coercion; the fear of violence, deception or false promises; the abuse of power; the victim's position of vulnerability; detention or captivity, psychological oppression or socio-economic conditions. Further indications of enslavement include exploitation; the exaction of forced or compulsory labour or service, often without remuneration and often, though not necessarily, involving physical hardship; sex; prostitution; and human trafficking. With respect to forced or compulsory labour or service, international law, including some of the provisions of Geneva Convention IV and the Additional Protocols, make clear that not all labour or service by protected persons, including civilians, in armed conflicts, is prohibited—strict conditions are, however, set for such labour or service. The "acquisition" or "disposal" of someone for monetary or other compensation, is not a requirement for enslavement. Doing so, however, is a prime example of the exercise of the right of ownership over someone. The duration of the suspected exercise of powers attaching to the right of ownership is another factor that may be considered when determining whether someone was enslaved; however, its importance in any given case will depend on the existence of other indications of enslavement. Detaining or keeping someone in captivity, without more, would, depending on the circumstances of a case, usually not constitute enslavement.
>
> 543. The Trial Chamber is therefore in general agreement with the factors put forward by the Prosecutor, to be taken into consideration in determining whether enslavement was committed. These are the control of someone's movement, control of physical environment, psychological control, measures taken to prevent or deter escape, force, threat of force or coercion, duration, assertion of exclusivity, subjection to cruel treatment and abuse, control of sexuality and forced labour. The Prosecutor also submitted that the mere ability to buy, sell, trade or inherit a person or his or her labours or services could be a relevant factor. The Trial Chamber considers that the *mere ability* to do so is insufficient, such actions actually occurring could be a relevant factor.

Article:

Bassiouni, M. Cherif, "Enslavement," in M. Cherif Bassiouni (ed.), *International Criminal Law–Crimes* 663–704 (Transnational Publishers, 1998).

Dixon, Rosalind, "Rape as a Crime in International Humanitarian Law: Where to from Here?," 13(3) *European Journal of International Law* 697–719 (June 2002).

Deportation

4.2.253 In the *Nikolić Rule 61 Decision* (para. 23), the Trial Chamber considered that deportation could be characterised as both a "grave breach" of the Geneva Conventions and as a crime against humanity.

4.2.254 As regards the obligation under international humanitarian law in certain circumstances to transfer populations, the Chamber in the *Krstić Trial Judgement* referred to the commentary to Article 49 of the 4th Geneva Convention, which suggests that deportations motivated by the fear of discrimination are not necessarily in violation of the law:

> The Diplomatic Conference preferred not to place an absolute prohibition on transfers of all kinds, as some might up to a certain point have the consent of those being transferred. The Conference had particularly in mind the case of protected persons belonging to ethnic or political minorities who might have suffered discrimination or persecution on that account and might therefore wish to leave the country. In order to make due allowances for that legitimate desire the Conference decided to authorise voluntary transfers by implication, and only to prohibit 'forcible' transfers (para. 528).

4.2.255 The Chamber in the *Krstić Trial Judgement* also referred, at para. 529, to the finalised draft text of the elements of the crimes adopted by the Preparatory Commission for the International Criminal Court that requires for the offence of deportation that:

> 1. The perpetrator deported or forcibly transferred, *without grounds permitted under international law*, one or more persons to another State or location, by expulsion or other coercive acts.
>
> 2. Such person or persons were lawfully present in the area from which they were so deported or transferred.
>
> 3. The perpetrator was aware of the factual circumstances that established the lawfulness of such presence.
>
> 4. The conduct was committed as part of a widespread or systematic attack directed against a civilian population.
>
> 5. The perpetrator knew that the conduct was part of or intended the conduct to be part of a widespread or systematic attack directed against a civilian population. (Emphasis added.)

4.2.256 Thus it is clear from the above that, at least under ICC law, it is a defence to a charge of deportation that the deportation was carried out on grounds permitted under international law, e.g. for the safety of the deported population. It will, of course, be a question of fact in each case to determine whether the grounds are sufficiently made out.

Imprisonment

4.2.257 Imprisonment as a crime against humanity was first considered by the ICTY in the *Kordić and Čerkez Trial Judgement*, paras. 292–303. The Trial Chamber concluded that the underlying elements of imprisonment as a crime against humanity are the same as those for unlawful confinement under Article 2 of the ICTY Statute. Accordingly, the discussion of unlawful confinement is relevant to imprisonment as a crime against humanity (see below, 4.2.423 *et seq.*, "War Crimes/Article 2 of the ICTY Statute/unlawful confinement"). Zdravko Mucić was convicted of this offence in the *Delalić et al. Trial Judgement* (see paras. 1125–1145).

4.2.258 The Trial Chamber in the *Kordić and Čerkez Trial Judgement* held that the term imprisonment in Article 5(e) of the ICTY Statute should be understood as arbitrary imprisonment, namely, the deprivation of liberty of an individual without due process of law, as part of a widespread or systematic attack directed against a civilian population.

4.2.259 Accordingly, a Chamber considering an allegation of "imprisonment" will have to determine the legality of the imprisonment as well as the procedural safeguards pertaining to the subsequent imprisonment of the person or group of persons, before determining whether or not they occurred as part of a widespread or systematic attack directed against a civilian population.

4.2.260 The Trial Chamber in the *Kordić and Čerkez Trial Judgement* concluded (paras. 302–303) that the imprisonment of civilians will be unlawful where:

— civilians have been detained in contravention of Article 42 of Geneva Convention IV, i.e., they are detained without reasonable grounds to believe that the security of the Detaining Power makes it absolutely necessary;

— the procedural safeguards required by Article 43 of Geneva Convention IV are not complied with in respect of detained civilians, even where initial detention may have been justified; and

— they occur as part of a widespread or systematic attack directed against a civilian population.

4.2.261 In its definition of crimes against humanity, the International Law Commission, in its 1996 ILC Report (p. 101), referred to the prohibited act of "arbitrary imprisonment" under sub-para. (h):

> The term imprisonment encompasses deprivation of liberty of the individual and the term "arbitrary" establishes the requirement that the deprivation be without due process of law.

4.2.262 The International Law Commission further indicated (*ibid.*) that arbitrary imprisonment is contrary to Article 9 of the Universal Declaration of Human Rights and to Article 9 of the International Covenant on Civil and Political Rights ("No one shall be deprived of his liberty except on such grounds and in accordance with such procedures as are established by law") and would cover the practice of concentration camps or detention camps or "other forms of long-term detention."

4.2.263 Article 7(1)(e) of the ICC Statute mentions "imprisonment or other severe deprivation of physical liberty in violation of fundamental rules of international law." Thus, this provision prohibits imprisonment only where it is contrary to international law and draws a distinction between lawful and unlawful imprisonments. According to Professor Bassiouni, by adding the language "other severe deprivation of physical liberty," Article 7(1)(e) of the ICC Statute has broadened the scope of the meaning of "imprisonment" to include other conduct which under the previous formulations may have been outside the scope of "imprisonment" (Bassiouni, *Crimes Against Humanity in International Criminal Law*, 362–363).

Torture

4.2.264 The essential elements of torture were defined in the *Akayesu Trial Judgement* (para. 594):

> (i) The perpetrator must intentionally inflict severe physical or mental pain or suffering upon the victim for one or more of the following purposes:
> (a) to obtain information or a confession from the victim or a third person;
> (b) to punish the victim or a third person for an act committed or suspected of having been committed by either of them;
> (c) for the purpose of intimidating or coercing the victim or the third person;
> (d) for any reason based on discrimination of any kind.
>
> (ii) The perpetrator was himself an official, or acted at the instigation of, or with the consent or acquiescence of, an official or person acting in an official capacity.

4.2.265 This definition was modified in the *Foča Trial Judgement*, removing, in effect (ii) from the *Akayesu* definition (above):

> 496. The Trial Chamber concludes that the definition of torture under international humanitarian law does not comprise the same elements as the definition of torture generally applied under human rights law. In particular, the Trial Chamber is of the view that the presence of a state official or of any other authority-wielding person in the torture process is not necessary for the offence to be regarded as torture under international humanitarian law.
>
> 497. On the basis of what has been said, the Trial Chamber holds that, in the field of international humanitarian law, the elements of the offence of torture, under customary international law are as follows:
> (i) The infliction, by act or omission, of severe pain or suffering, whether physical or mental.
> (ii) The act or omission must be intentional.
> (iii) The act or omission must aim at obtaining information or a confession, or at punishing , intimidating or coercing the victim or a third person, or at discriminating, on any ground, against the victim or a third person.

Rape

4.2.266 In the *Akayesu Trial Judgement* (para. 598), the Trial Chamber defined rape as:

> a physical invasion of a sexual nature, committed on a person under circumstances which are coercive.

In the same paragraph, the Chamber defined sexual violence as:

> any act of a sexual nature which is committed on a person under circumstances which are coercive.

4.2.267 See also the discussion in paras. 687–688 of the *Akayesu Trial Judgement:*

> 687. The Tribunal considers that rape is a form of aggression and that the central elements of the crime of rape cannot be captured in a mechanical description of objects and body parts. The Tribunal also notes the cultural sensitivities involved in public discussion of intimate matters and recalls the painful reluctance and inability of witnesses to disclose graphic anatomical details of sexual violence they endured. . . .
>
> 688. The Tribunal defines rape as a physical invasion of a sexual nature, committed on a person under circumstances which are coercive. The Tribunal considers sexual violence, which includes rape, as any act of a sexual nature which is committed on a person under circumstances which are coercive. Sexual violence is not limited to physical invasion of the human body and may include acts which do not involve penetration or even physical contact. The incident described by Witness KK in which the Accused ordered the Interahamwe to undress a student and force her to do gymnastics naked in the public courtyard of the bureau communal, in front of a crowd, constitutes sexual violence. . . .

4.2.268 Subsequently, the Trial Chamber ruling in the *Furundžija Trial Judgement* provided a more mechanical definition of rape (although not in the context of crimes against humanity):

> 185. . . . the Trial Chamber finds that the following may be accepted as the objective elements of rape:
>
> (i) the sexual penetration, however slight:
>
> (a) of the vagina or anus of the victim by the penis of the perpetrator or any other object used by the perpetrator; or
>
> (b) of the mouth of the victim by the penis of the perpetrator;
>
> (ii) by coercion or force or threat of force against the victim or a third person.

4.2.269 The Trial Chamber ruling in *Musema* preferred the *Akayesu* approach to the *Furundžija* approach (see paras. 226–229 of the *Musema Trial Judgement*).

4.2.270 The Trial Chamber ruling in the *Foča Trial Judgement* reexamined the definition of rape in considerable depth (paras. 436–460), starting from the *Furundžija* definition (above). The Chamber concluded—on the basis of a review of national case-law and legislation—that what was important in terms of the absence of consent was the serious violation of sexual autonomy which rape involved rather than the accomplishment of intercourse "by coercion or force or threat of force against the victim or a third person," the element emphasised by the *Furundžija* Trial Chamber. Thus the Chamber stated:

> 460. ... the *actus reus* of the crime of rape in international law is constituted by: the sexual penetration, however slight: (a) of the vagina or anus of the victim by the penis of the perpetrator or any other object used by the perpetrator; or (b) of the mouth of the victim by the penis of the perpetrator; where such sexual penetration occurs without the consent of the victim. Consent for this purpose must be consent given voluntarily, as a result of the victim's free will, assessed in the context of the surrounding circumstances. The *mens rea* is the intention to effect this sexual penetration, and the knowledge that it occurs without the consent of the victim.

4.2.271 Thus there is a split in the jurisprudence between the *Akayesu/Musema* approach, on the one hand, and the *Furundžija/Foča* approach, on the other. It is submitted that the latter is to be preferred in that it better respects the principle of legality by clearly defining the offence in advance. Indeed, the ICC seems to have elected, at least in part, for the *Furundžija/Foča* approach in the Elements:

> *Elements.* 1. The perpetrator invaded the body of a person by conduct resulting in penetration, however slight, of any part of the body of the victim or of the perpetrator with a sexual organ, or of the anal or genital opening of the victim with any object or any other part of the body. (Elements, Article 7(1)(g)-1, Crime against Humanity of Rape.)

4.2.272 This is, however, rather an odd definition, in particular with its reference to "... *penetration* ... *of any part of the body* ... *of the perpetrator with a sexual organ.*" This may be intended to cover a "rape" in which the perpetrator forces the victim to have sex by penetrating the perpetrator.

Rape as Torture

4.2.273 See also "Rape as Torture" in the "Elements of the Offences" section (4.2.552 *et seq.*).

4.2.274 In the *Nikolić Rule 61 Decision*, the Chamber considered the applicability of crimes against humanity to acts of sexual assault, particularly as defined as acts of torture (para. 33):

> the Chamber considers that rape and other forms of sexual assault inflicted on women in circumstances such as those described by the witnesses, may fall within the definition of torture submitted by the Prosecutor.

4.2.275 Trial Chamber I also treated this issue in the *Karadžić and Mladić Rule 61 Decision:*

64. Further, the Trial Chamber considers that, among the methods of "ethnic cleansing," sexual assaults warrant special attention owing to their systematic nature and the gravity of the suffering thereby inflicted on civilians. The Trial Chamber wished to hear an *amicus curiae* in relation to this issue as a whole.

In his indictment of 25 July 1995, the Prosecutor focused on the sexual assaults committed in the detention facilities of the Bosnian Serbs: camp guards or commanders, soldiers, members of the police or of paramilitary groups and even civilians had access to those camps and allegedly perpetrated sexual assaults on civilian Bosnian Muslim and Bosnian Croat detainees. It seems to the Trial Chamber however that sexual assaults in the camps constitute but one aspect of a broader practice. Sexual assaults were committed by individuals or groups before the conflict broke out, in a context of looting and intimidation of the population. During military attacks on civilian gatherings, there was sexual abuse, in particular public rapes. It seems that some women were particularly affected by the practice of sexual assault. Some camps were specially devoted to rape, with the aim of forcing the birth of Serbian offspring, the women often being interned until it was too late for them to undergo an abortion. It would seem that there were also hostels or private homes where women were raped for the soldiers' entertainment.

On the basis of the features of all these sexual assaults, it may be inferred that they were part of a widespread policy of "ethnic cleansing": the victims were mainly "non-Serbian" civilians, the vast majority being Muslims. Sexual assaults occurred in several regions of Bosnia and Herzegovina, in a systematic fashion and using recurring methods (e.g. gang rape, sexual assault in camps, use of brutal means, together with other violations of international humanitarian law). They were performed together with an effort to displace civilians and such as to increase the shame and humiliation of the victims and of the community they belonged to in order to force them to leave. It would seem that the aim of many rapes was enforced impregnation; several witnesses also said that the perpetrators of sexual assault—often soldiers—had been given orders to do so and that camp commanders and officers had been informed thereof and participated therein.

Article: Rees, Madeleine and Sarah Maguire, "Rape as a Crime Against Humanity," *Tribunal* (a Publication of the Institute for War & Peace Reporting), No. 6, Nov.–Dec. 1996.

Persecutions on Political, Racial and Religious Grounds

Definition of Persecution

4.2.276 The Chamber, in the *Kupreškić Trial Judgement*, discussed persecution at length (see paras. 567–636) and on the basis of the case-law drew the following conclusions:

(a) A narrow definition of persecution is not supported in customary international law. Persecution has been described by courts as a wide and particularly serious genus of crimes committed against the Jewish people and other groups by the Nazi regime.

(b) In their interpretation of persecution courts have included acts such as murder, extermination, torture, and other serious acts on the person such as those presently enumerated in Article 5.

(c) Persecution can also involve a variety of other discriminatory acts, involving attacks on political, social, and economic rights. . . .

(d) Persecution is commonly used to describe a series of acts rather than a single act. Acts of persecution will usually form part of a policy or at least of a patterned practice, and must be regarded in their context. In reality, persecutory acts are often committed pursuant to a discriminatory policy or a widespread discriminatory practice. . . .

(e) As a corollary to (d), discriminatory acts charged as persecution must not be considered in isolation. Some of the acts mentioned above may not, in and of themselves, be so serious as to constitute a crime against humanity. For example, restrictions placed on a particular group to curtail their rights to participate in particular aspects of social life (such as visits to public parks, theatres or libraries) constitute discrimination, which is in itself a reprehensible act; however, they may not in and of themselves amount to persecution. These acts must not be considered in isolation but examined in their context and weighed for their cumulative effect.

4.2.277 See also the *Kordić and Čerkez Trial Judgement* (paras. 193–194), in which the Trial Chamber held that:

> the wording of Article 5(h) does not contain any requirement of a connection between the crime of persecution and other crimes enumerated in the Statute. The jurisprudence of Trial Chambers of the International Tribunal thus far appears to have accepted that the crime of persecution can also encompass acts not explicitly listed in the Statute. The *Kupreškić* Trial Chamber placed particular emphasis upon the principle of legality when considering in some detail the issue now before this Chamber. It found that the *actus reus* for persecution requires no link to crimes enumerated elsewhere in the Statute.
>
> This Trial Chamber concurs with the *Kupreškić* decision . . . But of equal importance, and in order to comply with the principle of legality, this Trial Chamber also adopts the *Kupreškić* position that there must be "*clearly defined limits* on the expansion of the types of acts which qualify as persecution."

4.2.278 The *Kordić* Trial Chamber considered whether specific acts either enumerated or not enumerated in the Statute also give rise to the same level of gravity as other Article 5 crimes against humanity.

4.2.279 The Trial Chamber held, at paras. 203–207 of the *Kordić and Čerkez Trial Judgement*, that the following acts (enumerated elsewhere in the Statute), when performed with the requisite discriminatory intent, may amount to the crime of persecution:

— Attacking cities, towns and villages (akin to an "attack, or bombardment, by whatever means, of undefended towns, villages, dwellings, or buildings," a violation under Article 3(c) of the ICTY Statute).
— Trench-digging and use of hostages as human shields (recognised as grave breaches of the Geneva Conventions of 1949 and criminal under Article 2 of the ICTY Statute).
— Wanton destruction and plundering (similar to "wanton destruction of cities, towns or villages" and the "plunder of public or private property" violations under Articles 3 (b) and 3(e) of the ICTY Statute).

— Destruction and damage of religious or educational institutions (the same as "destruction or wilful damage done to institutions dedicated to religion" a violation of Article 3(d) of the ICTY Statute).

4.2.280 The Trial Chamber found, at paras. 208–210, that the following acts are not enumerated elsewhere in the Statute nor do they give rise to the same level of gravity as other acts enumerated in Article 5 of the Statute:

— Encouraging and promoting hatred on political, etc. grounds.
— Dismissing and removing Bosnian Muslims from government, etc..

4.2.281 Note that "persecution" is a key notion in refugee law. The 1951 Refugee Convention refers to a "well-founded fear of being persecuted." The English Court of Appeal has stated that there is no universally accepted definition of persecution so the word must be given its ordinary meaning; it is a matter of fact, no law (Kegema (1997) IMMAR 137).

Murder as Persecution

4.2.282 In the *Tadić Opinion and Judgement*, the accused was found guilty of one count of persecution, which included two murders (see para. 397). These murders could, however, have been charged equally, and perhaps more appropriately, under Article 5(a) (murder) of the ICTY Statute.

Persecution Can Take Various Forms

4.2.283 The Trial Chamber noted in the *Tadić Opinion and Judgement:*

> 707. ... persecution can take numerous forms, so long as the common element of discrimination in regard to the enjoyment of a basic or fundamental right is present, and persecution does not necessarily require a physical element.

Actus Reus

4.2.284 In the *Kupreškić Trial Judgement*, the Chamber defined the *actus reus* of persecution:

> 621. ... as the gross or blatant denial, on discriminatory grounds, of a fundamental right, laid down in international customary or treaty law, reaching the same level of gravity as the other acts prohibited in Article 5.

4.2.285 Thus a charge of persecution would have to contain the following elements (para. 627, *Kupreškić Trial Judgement*):

(a) those elements required for all crimes against humanity under the Statute;

(b) a gross or blatant denial of a fundamental right reaching the same level of gravity as the other acts prohibited under Article 5;

(c) discriminatory grounds.

4.2.286   See also the *Blaškić Trial Judgement* on the acts that constitute persecution:

> 220. There is no doubt that serious bodily and mental harm and infringements upon individual freedom may be characterised as persecution when . . . they target the members of a group because they belong to a specific community. The Trial Chamber considers that infringements of the elementary and inalienable rights of man, which are "the right to life, liberty and the security of person," the right not to be "held in slavery or servitude," the right not to "be subjected to torture or to cruel, inhuman or degrading treatment or punishment" and the right not to be "subjected to arbitrary arrest, detention or exile" as affirmed in Articles 3 , 4, 5 and 9 of the Universal Declaration of Human Rights, by their very essence may constitute persecution when committed on discriminatory grounds.
>
> . . .
>
> 222. In the part of the Judgement of the major war criminals specifically devoted to the persecution of the Jews, the Nuremberg Tribunal affirmed that the murder of the Jews, the brutal acts which they suffered, their confinement in ghettos and their being used to perform forced labour were all forms of persecution. The Nuremberg Tribunal thus noted *inter alia* that:
>
>> The Nazi *persecution of Jews* in Germany before the war, severe and repressive as it was, cannot compare, however, with the policy pursued during the war in the occupied territories. . . .
>>
>> In the summer of 1941, however, plans were made for the "final solution" of the Jewish question in Europe. This "final solution" meant the *extermination* of the Jews. . . .
>>
>> *Beating, starvation, torture and killing* were general. The inmates were subjected to cruel experiments. . . .
>
> In the paragraphs describing the role played by SS units in the persecution of the Jews, that Tribunal also brought out the fact that the units had participated in their deportation and extermination. Furthermore, in its analysis of the individual responsibility of the accused Frank , it pointed out that:
>
>> The persecution of the Jews was immediately begun in the General government. The area originally contained from 2½ million to 3½ million Jews. They were *forced into ghettos*, subjected to discriminatory laws, *deprived of the food necessary to avoid starvation*, and finally systematically and brutally *exterminated*.
>
> As regards the accused Bormann, the Judges also stated that:
>
>> Bormann was extremely active in the persecution of the Jews, not only in Germany but also in the absorbed and conquered countries. *He took part in the discussions which led to the removal* of 60,000 Jews from Vienna to Poland in co-operation with the SS and the Gestapo. *He signed the decree of 31 May 1941* extending the Nuremberg Laws to the annexed Eastern territories. In an order of 9 October 1942 *he declared that the permanent elimination of Jews in Greater German territory* could no longer be solved by emigration, but only by applying "ruthless force" in the special camps in the East. On 1 July 1943 *he signed an ordinance withdrawing Jews from the protection of the law courts* and placing them under the exclusive jurisdiction of Himmler's Gestapo.

...

227. However, persecution may take forms other than injury to the human person, in particular those acts rendered serious not by their apparent cruelty but by the discrimination they seek to instil within humankind. . . . persecution may thus take the form of confiscation or destruction of private dwellings or businesses, symbolic buildings or means of subsistence belonging to the Muslim population of Bosnia-Herzegovina.

228. The Nuremberg International Tribunal expressly recognised that, as of autumn 1938, the persecution of the Jews was designed to exclude them from German life and was particularly apparent in the "[p]ogroms [which] were organized, which included the burning and demolishing of synagogues, the looting of Jewish businesses, and the arrest of prominent Jewish business men" and the imposition of a billion mark fine. Furthermore, the Nuremberg Tribunal found Göring guilty of crimes against humanity, in particular, for being ". . . the active authority in the spoliation of conquered territory" and for having imposed the fine of a billion reichsmarks on the Jews. It added that:

> Göring persecuted the Jews . . . not only in Germany . . . but in the conquered countries. His own utterances then and his testimony now shows this interest was primarily economic—how to *get their property* and how to *force them out of the economic life* of Europe.

Rosenberg too was convicted of war crimes and crimes against humanity for "a system of organised plunder of both public and private property throughout the invaded countries of Europe." The Judgement also noted in this respect that:

> [a]cting under Hitler's orders of January 1940 to set up the "Hohe Schule," he organized and directed the "Einsatzstab Rosenberg," which plundered museums and libraries, confiscated art treasures and collections, and pillaged private houses.

In addition, the Nuremberg Tribunal found the accused Streicher guilty of crimes against humanity *inter alia* for the boycott on Jewish businesses and the fire at the Nuremberg synagogue.

...

233. The Trial Chamber finds from this analysis that the crime of "persecution" encompasses not only bodily and mental harm and infringements upon individual freedom but also acts which appear less serious, such as those targeting property, so long as the victimised persons were specially selected on grounds linked to their belonging to a particular community.

Mens Rea

4.2.287 The Trial Chamber ruling in the *Kupreškić Trial Judgement* held that discriminatory intent was key to the *mens rea* of persecution, which was a higher threshold than the *mens rea* required for other crimes against humanity:

> 636. . . . the *mens rea* requirement for persecution is higher than for ordinary crimes against humanity, although lower than for genocide. . . . persecution as a crime against humanity is an offence belonging to the same *genus* as genocide. Both persecution and genocide are crimes perpetrated against persons that belong to a particular group and who are targeted because of such belong-

ing. In both categories what matters is the intent to discriminate: to attack persons on account of their ethnic, racial, or religious characteristics (as well as, in the case of persecution, on account of their political affiliation). While in the case of persecution the discriminatory intent can take multifarious inhumane forms and manifest itself in a plurality of actions including murder, in the case of genocide that intent must be accompanied by the intention to destroy, in whole or in part, the group to which the victims of the genocide belong. Thus, it can be said that, from the viewpoint of *mens rea*, genocide is an extreme and most inhuman form of persecution. To put it differently, when persecution escalates to the extreme form of wilful and deliberate acts designed to destroy a group or part of a group, it can be held that such persecution amounts to genocide.

4.2.288 See also the *Blaškić Trial Judgement* on the necessary *mens rea* for persecution:

> 235. The underlying offence of persecution requires the existence of a *mens rea* from which it obtains its specificity. As set down in Article 5 of the Statute, it must be committed for specific reasons whether these be linked to political views, racial background or religious convictions. It is the specific intent to cause injury to a human being because he belongs to a particular community or group, rather than the means employed to achieve it, that bestows on it its individual nature and gravity and which justifies its being able to constitute criminal acts which might appear in themselves not to infringe directly upon the most elementary rights of a human being, for example, attacks on property. In other words, the perpetrator of the acts of persecution does not initially target the individual but rather membership in a specific racial, religious or political group.

4.2.289 See also the *Kordić and Čerkez Trial Judgement*, para. 220, citing with approval para. 634 of the *Kupreškić Trial Judgement*, concluding that:

> in order to possess the necessary heightened *mens rea* for the crime of persecution, the accused must have shared the aim of the discriminatory policy: "the removal of those persons from the society in which they live alongside the perpetrators, or eventually from humanity itself.

4.2.290 Thus persecution eventually shades into genocide.

ICC and Persecution

4.2.291 "Persecution" is enumerated as a crime against humanity under the Rome Statute for an ICC. See Article 7(1)(h) of the Rome Statute:

> Persecution against any identifiable group or collectivity on political, racial, national, ethnic, cultural, religious, gender as defined in para. 3, or other grounds that are universally recognized as impermissible under international law, in connection with any act referred to in this para. or any crime within the jurisdiction of the Court.

4.2.292 Persecution is defined under the Rome Statute (Article 7(2)(g)) as follows:

(g) "Persecution" means the intentional and severe deprivation of fundamental rights contrary to international law by reason of the identity of the group or collectivity.

4.2.293 The definition of "persecution" in the Rome Statute, which maintains the hitherto defunct requirement at Nuremberg that "persectuion-type" crimes against humanity must be committed in connection with another act or crime under the Statute, has been held to be "more restrictive than is necessary under customary international law." (*Kordić and Čerkez Trial Judgement*, para. 197).

Listed Discriminatory Grounds Are Disjunctive

4.2.294 In the *Tadić Opinion and Judgement*, the Trial Chamber held that the persecutory acts in question must be carried out on one of the discriminatory grounds listed in Article 5(h), i.e. "political, racial and religious grounds." It stated the obvious that these grounds should be read *disjunctively*, i.e. it suffices that the acts be carried out on *one of* the three listed grounds (i.e. political *or* racial *or* religious grounds), and it is not required, as the language might suggest, that the act be carried out on the basis of *all three* grounds. See paras. 711–713 of the *Tadić Opinion and Judgement* on this point.

Other Inhumane Acts

4.2.295 The following acts have been considered by Trial Chambers as falling within the category of "other inhumane acts": mutilation and other types of severe bodily harm, beatings and other acts of violence (*Tadić Opinion and Judgement*, para. 730), serious physical and mental injury (*Blaškić Trial Judgement*, para. 239), forcible transfer (*Kupreškić Trial Judgement*, para. 566, *Krstić Trial Judgement*, para. 523), inhumane and degrading treatment (*Kupreškić Trial Judgement*, para. 566), forced prostitution (*Kupreškić Trial Judgement*, para. 566) and forced disappearance (*Kupreškić Trial Judgement*, para. 566).

4.2.296 In *Akayesu*, the Trial Chamber considered charges of inhumane acts in the context of sexual violence, in particular forcing women to undress in public and publicly to parade and to perform exercises while naked (*Akayesu Trial Judgement*, para. 697).

4.2.297 The Chamber ruling in the *Kayishema and Ruzindana Trial Judgement* stated the following in relation to inhumane acts:

> 149. Since the Nuremberg Charter, the category "other inhumane acts" has been maintained as a useful category for acts not specifically stated but which are of comparable gravity. The importance in maintaining such a category was elucidated by the ICRC when commenting on inhumane treatment contained in Article 3 of the Geneva Conventions,
>
>> It is always dangerous to try to go into too much detail—especially in this domain. However much care were taken in establishing a list of all the various forms of infliction, one would never be able to catch up with the imagination of future torturers who wished to satisfy their bestial instincts; and the more specific and complete a list tries to be, the more

restrictive it becomes. The form of wording adopted is flexible and, at the same time, precise. . . .

154. In summary, for an accused to be found guilty of crimes against humanity for other inhumane acts, he must commit an act of similar gravity and seriousness to the other enumerated crimes, with the intention to cause the other inhumane act, and with knowledge that the act is perpetrated within the overall context of the attack.

4.2.298 Later on in the *Kayishema and Ruzindana Judgement*, the Trial Chamber stated that inhumane acts comprise a distinct category "with its own culpable conduct and *mens rea*" (para. 583) and is not, therefore, a "catch-all" (paras. 583 and 586).

4.2.299 The Chamber ruling in the *Kupreškić Trial Judgement* was more specific in describing what might be covered by the term "inhumane acts":

562. The expression "other inhumane acts" was drawn from Article 6(c) of the London Agreement and Article II(1)(c) of Control Council Law No. 10.

563. There is a concern that this category lacks precision and is too general to provide a safe yardstick for the work of the Tribunal and hence, that it is contrary to the principle of the "specificity" of criminal law. It is thus imperative to establish what is included within this category. The phrase "other inhumane acts" was deliberately designed as a residual category, as it was felt to be undesirable for this category to be exhaustively enumerated. An exhaustive categorization would merely create opportunities for evasion of the letter of the prohibition. . . .

564. In interpreting the expression at issue, resort to the *ejusdem generis* rule of interpretation does not prove to be of great assistance. Under this rule, that expression would cover *actions similar* to those specifically provided for.

566. Less broad parameters for the interpretation of "other inhumane acts" can instead be identified in international standards on human rights such as those laid down in the Universal Declaration on Human Rights of 1948 and the two United Nations Covenants on Human Rights of 1966. Drawing upon the various provisions of these texts, it is possible to identify a set of basic rights appertaining to human beings, the infringement of which may amount, depending on the accompanying circumstances, to a crime against humanity. Thus, for example, serious forms of cruel or degrading treatment of persons belonging to a particular ethnic, religious, political or racial group, or serious widespread or systematic manifestations of cruel or humiliating or degrading treatment with a discriminatory or persecutory intent no doubt amount to crimes against humanity: inhuman or degrading treatment is prohibited by the United Nations Covenant on Civil and Political Rights (Article 7), the European Convention on Human Rights, of 1950 (Article 3), the Inter-American Convention on Human Rights of 9 June 1994 (Article 5) and the 1984 Convention against Torture (Article 1). Similarly, the expression at issue undoubtedly embraces the forcible transfer of groups of civilians (which is to some extent covered by Article 49 of the IV Convention of 1949 and Article 17(1) of the Additional Protocol II of 1977), enforced prostitution (indisputably a serious attack on human dignity pursuant to most international instruments on human rights), as well as the enforced disappearance of persons (prohibited by General Assembly Resolution 47/133 of 18 December 1992 and the

Inter-American Convention of 9 June 1994). Plainly, all these, and other similar acts, must be carried out in a systematic manner and on a large scale. In other words, they must be as serious as the other classes of crimes provided for in the other provisions of Article 5. Once the legal parameters for determining the content of the category of "inhumane acts" are identified, resort to the *ejusdem generis* rule for the purpose of comparing and assessing the gravity of the prohibited act may be warranted. See also the *Kordić and Čerkez Trial Judgement*, paras. 269–272.

4.2.300

ICC
Article 7
Crimes Against Humanity

1. For the purpose of this Statute, "crime against humanity" means any of the following acts when committed as part of a widespread or systematic attack directed against any civilian population, with knowledge of the attack:
(a) Murder;
(b) Extermination;
(c) Enslavement;
(d) Deportation or forcible transfer of population;
(e) Imprisonment or other severe deprivation of physical liberty in violation of fundamental rules of international law;
(f) Torture;
(g) Rape, sexual slavery, enforced prostitution, forced pregnancy, enforced sterilization, or any other form of sexual violence of comparable gravity;
(h) Persecution against any identifiable group or collectivity on political, racial, national, ethnic, cultural, religious, gender as defined in paragraph 3, or other grounds that are universally recognized as impermissible under international law, in connection with any act referred to in this para. or any crime within the jurisdiction of the Court;
(i) Enforced disappearance of persons;
(j) The crime of apartheid;
(k) Other inhumane acts of a similar character intentionally causing great suffering, or serious injury to body or to mental or physical health.
2. For the purpose of paragraph 1:
(a) "Attack directed against any civilian population" means a course of conduct involving the multiple commission of acts referred to in para. 1 against any civilian population, pursuant to or in furtherance of a State or organizational policy to commit such attack;
(b) "Extermination" includes the intentional infliction of conditions of life, *inter alia* the deprivation of access to food and medicine, calculated to bring about the destruction of part of a population;
(c) "Enslavement" means the exercise of any or all of the powers attaching to the right of ownership over a person and includes the exercise of such power in the course of trafficking in persons, in particular women and children;
(d) "Deportation or forcible transfer of population" means forced displacement of the persons concerned by expulsion or other coercive acts from the area in which they are lawfully present, without grounds permitted under international law;
(e) "Torture" means the intentional infliction of severe pain or suffering, whether physical or mental, upon a person in the custody or under the control of the accused; except that torture shall not include pain or suffering arising only from, inherent in or incidental to, lawful sanctions;

(f) "Forced pregnancy" means the unlawful confinement of a woman forcibly made pregnant, with the intent of affecting the ethnic composition of any population or carrying out other grave violations of international law. This definition shall not in any way be interpreted as affecting national laws relating to pregnancy;
(g) "Persecution" means the intentional and severe deprivation of fundamental rights contrary to international law by reason of the identity of the group or collectivity;
(h) "The crime of apartheid" means inhumane acts of a character similar to those referred to in paragraph 1, committed in the context of an institutionalized regime of systematic oppression and domination by one racial group over any other racial group or groups and committed with the intention of maintaining that regime;
(i) "Enforced disappearance of persons" means the arrest, detention or abduction of persons by, or with the authorization, support or acquiescence of, a State or a political organization, followed by a refusal to acknowledge that deprivation of freedom or to give information on the fate or whereabouts of those persons, with the intention of removing them from the protection of the law for a prolonged period of time.
3. For the purpose of this Statute, it is understood that the term "gender" refers to the two sexes, male and female, within the context of society. The term "gender" does not indicate any meaning different from the above.

Crimes Against Humanity—ICC Jurisdiction

4.2.301 For an in-depth discussion of crimes against humanity in the Rome Statute of the ICC, see Cassese, Antonio, "Crimes against Humanity," ch. 11.2 in Cassese, Gaeta and Jones (eds.), *The Rome Statute of the International Criminal Court: A Commentary* (OUP, 2002); Boot, Dixon and Hall, "Article 7: Crimes against Humanity," in Triffterer (ed.), *Commentary on the Rome Statute of the International Criminal Court: Observers' Notes, Article-by-Article* (Nomos, 1999).

* * * * *

WAR CRIMES

4.2.302 The law of war crimes has traditionally been divided into two main branches: "Hague Law" (the law relating to the means and methods of waging war) and "Geneva Law" (the law relating to the protection of non-combatants). "Hague Law" is so named after the Hague Conventions, in particular the 1907 Hague Convention Respecting the Laws and Customs of War on Land and the Regulations annexed thereto. "Geneva Law" is named after the Geneva Conventions, in particular the four Geneva Conventions of 1949 and the two Additional Protocols of 1977.

4.2.303 War crimes are prosecuted at the ICTY and ICTR pursuant to three articles: Article 2 ("Grave breaches of the Geneva Conventions of 1949") and Article 3 ("Violations of the laws or customs of war") of the ICTY Statute and Article 4 of the ICTR Statute ("Violations of Article 3 common to the Geneva Conventions and of Additional Protocol II").

4.2.304

> **ICTY**
> **Article 2**
> **Grave Breaches of the Geneva Conventions of 1949**
>
> The International Tribunal shall have the power to prosecute persons committing or ordering to be committed grave breaches of the Geneva Conventions of 12 August 1949, namely the following acts against persons or property protected under the provisions of the relevant Geneva Convention:
> (a) wilful killing;
> (b) torture or inhuman treatment, including biological experiments;
> (c) wilfully causing great suffering or serious injury to body or health;
> (d) extensive destruction and appropriation of property, not justified by military necessity and carried out unlawfully and wantonly;
> (e) compelling a prisoner of war or a civilian to serve in the forces of a hostile power;
> (f) wilfully depriving a prisoner of war or a civilian of the rights of fair and regular trial;
> (g) unlawful deportation or transfer or unlawful confinement of a civilian;
> (h) taking civilians as hostages.

Introduction

4.2.305 The Secretary-General, in his Report on the ICTY Statute submitted pursuant to Security Council Resolution 808 (1993) (S/25704), noted the customary law status of Article 2 of the ICTY Statute:

> 34. In the view of the Secretary-General, the application of the principle *nullum crimen sine lege* requires that the international tribunal should apply rules of international humanitarian law which are beyond any doubt part of customary law so that the problem of adherence of some but not all States to specific conventions does not arise. This would appear to be particularly important in the context of an international tribunal prosecuting persons responsible for serious violations of international humanitarian law.
>
> 35. The part of conventional international humanitarian law which has beyond doubt become part of international customary law is the law applicable in armed conflict as embodied in: the Geneva Conventions of 12 August 1949 for the Protection of War Victims. . . .

4.2.306 The customary status of ICTY Article 2 was also considered in the *Tadić Opinion and Judgement* (para. 577).

Requirement of Armed Conflict

4.2.307 There must be an armed conflict for the ICTY to have jurisdiction to prosecute "grave breaches" of the Geneva Conventions, pursuant to Article 2 of the Statute.

4.2.308 The Appeals Chamber, in its *Tadić Jurisdiction Appeals Decision*, expounded the following test for determining whether there was an armed conflict:

> 70. ... we find that an armed conflict exists whenever there is a resort to armed force between States or protracted armed violence between governmental authorities and organized armed groups or between such groups within a State. International humanitarian law applies from the initiation of such armed conflicts and extends beyond the cessation of hostilities until a general conclusion of peace is reached; or, in the case of internal conflicts, a peaceful settlement is achieved. Until that moment, international humanitarian law continues to apply in the whole territory of the warring States or, in the case of internal conflicts, the whole territory under the control of a party, whether or not actual combat takes place there.

4.2.309 This test has subsequently been frequently cited by Chambers to determine whether an armed conflict existed at the relevant time and place. In the *Tadić Jurisdiction Appeals Decision*, the Chamber applied this test to the former Yugoslavia and rejected the defence argument that there were no hostilities at the relevant time and place. The Chamber thus held that the alleged crimes *were* committed in the context of an armed conflict:

> Fighting among the various entities within the former Yugoslavia began in 1991, continued through the summer of 1992 when the alleged crimes are said to have been committed, and persists to this day. Notwithstanding various temporary cease-fire agreements, no general conclusion of peace has brought military operations in the region to a close. These hostilities exceed the intensity requirements applicable to both international and internal armed conflicts. There has been protracted, large-scale violence between the armed forces of different States and between governmental forces and organized insurgent groups (para. 70).

4.2.310 This Decision was rendered while the conflict was still on-going, that is before the Dayton Peace Agreement was signed in December 1995, bringing an end to the hostilities in Bosnia and Herzegovina.

4.2.311 Turning to the specific question of the existence of hostilities in Opština Prijedor in April/May 1992, where the accused's acts took place, the Appeals Chamber in the *Tadić Jurisdiction Appeals Decision* held that:

> Even if substantial clashes were not occurring in the Prijedor region at the time and place the crimes allegedly were committed . . . international humanitarian law applies. It is sufficient that the alleged crimes were closely related to the hostilities occurring in other parts of the territories controlled by the parties to the conflict (para. 70).

4.2.312 Applying this test, the Trial Chamber in the *Tadić Opinion and Judgement* found an armed conflict existed:

> 566. In considering the conflict relating to the events in Opština Prijedor, the Trial Chamber is not . . . bound to confine its attention to the immediate area of that opština or to the time of the alleged offences but may consider the ongoing conflict between the Government of the Republic of Bosnia and Herzegovina and the Bosnian Serb forces in its entirety. . . .

568. Having regard then to the nature and scope of the conflict in the Republic of Bosnia and Herzegovina and the parties involved in that conflict . . . the Trial Chamber finds that, at all relevant times, an armed conflict was taking place between the parties to the conflict in the Republic of Bosnia and Herzegovina of sufficient scope and intensity for the purposes of the application of the laws or customs of war embodied in Article 3 common to the four Geneva Conventions of 12 August 1949, applicable as it is to armed conflicts in general, including armed conflicts not of an international character.

4.2.313 On the point made in para. 566, of the *Tadić Opinion and Judgement*, see also the *Blaškić Trial Judgement:* "It is not necessary to establish the existence of an armed conflict within each municipality concerned. It suffices to establish the existence of the conflict within the whole region of which the municipalities are a part."

Nexus with Armed Conflict

4.2.314 The *Tadić Opinion and Judgement* further stated that, "(t)he existence of an armed conflict or occupation and the applicability of international humanitarian law to the territory is not sufficient to create international jurisdiction over each and every serious crime committed in the territory of the former Yugoslavia. For a crime to fall within the jurisdiction of the International Tribunal, a sufficient nexus must be established between the alleged offence and the armed conflict which gives rise to the applicability of international humanitarian law" (para. 572). This criterion, which is meant to exclude, for example, domestic crimes, is discussed in the *Tadić Opinion and Judgement* at paras. 572–576.

4.2.315 These tests were again applied in the *Delalić et al. Trial Judgement*. The Trial Chamber found "that there was an 'armed conflict' in Bosnia and Herzegovina in the period relevant to the Indictment and . . . that, regardless of whether or not this conflict is considered internal or international, it incorporated the municipality of Konjic" (para. 192). It further found that there was a sufficient *nexus* between the armed conflict and the actions of the accused (paras. 193–198).

4.2.316 On the existence of an armed conflict, the Chamber said, *inter alia:*

> 186. . . . in Bosnia and Herzegovina as a whole there was continuing armed violence at least from the date of its declaration of independence—6 March 1992—until the signing of the Dayton Peace Agreement in November 1995. Certainly involved in this armed violence, and relevant to the present case, were the JNA, the Bosnian Army (consisting of the TO and MUP), the HVO and the VRS.

4.2.317 On the *nexus* requirement, the Chamber stated:

> 193. It is axiomatic that not every serious crime committed during the armed conflict in Bosnia and Herzegovina can be regarded as a violation of international humanitarian law. There must be an obvious link between the criminal act and the armed conflict. Clearly, if a relevant crime was committed in the course of fighting or the take-over of a town during an armed conflict, for example, this would be sufficient to render the offence a violation of international humanitarian law. Such a direct connection to actual hostilities is not, however, required in every situation.

4.2.318 The *Delalić* Trial Chamber endorsed the view of the Appeals Chamber in the *Tadić Appeals Judgement* that "[i]t is sufficient that the alleged crimes were closely related to the hostilities occurring in other parts of the territories controlled by the parties to the conflict." The *Delalić* Trial Chamber also agreed with the *Tadić* Trial Chamber that "it is not necessary that a crime 'be part of a policy or of a practice officially endorsed or tolerated by one of the parties to the conflict, or that the act be in actual furtherance of a policy associated with the conduct of war or in the actual interest of a party to the conflict'" for the nexus requirement of Article 2 to be met. See also the *Nikolić Rule 61 Decision* rendered by the Trial Chamber on 20 October 1995 (para. 29).

International Armed Conflict

General

4.2.319 There has been an enormous amount of discussion and disagreement at the ICTY both with respect to the test of internationality of the conflicts in the former Yugoslavia and as to whether the test, whatever it is, is satisfied in any particular instance.

4.2.320 The governing law, as laid down by the Appeals Chamber in the *Tadić Jurisdiction Appeals Decision*, and endorsed in the *Tadić Appeals Judgement*, is that an international armed conflict *is* required for Article 2 of the Statute (grave breaches of the Geneva Conventions of 1948) to apply, i.e., a conflict involving two or more States, and not a civil war. This "internationality" requirement is assessed on a *case-by-case* basis.

4.2.321 This has now been confirmed in several decisions. See, for example, *Decision on the Joint Defence Motion to Dismiss the Amended Indictment for lack of jurisdiction based on the limited jurisdictional reach of Articles 2 and 3* rendered by the Trial Chamber in *Kordić and Čerkez* on 2 March 1999, in which the Chamber confirmed that ICTY Article 2 is only applicable to international armed conflicts (while noting ICTY Decisions that suggested that customary law may be evolving to a position where the grave breaches regime was also applicable to internal conflicts) and that whether or not there was an international armed conflict, and the test to be applied in making the determination, was a matter for trial. For a summary of the other positions expressed by Judges and Chambers on this issue, see the second edition of this work, pages 55–56.

Articles:

See Stewart, Michael, "Atone and Move Forward" *in* 19(24) *London Review of Books*, (11 December 1997), reviewing Michael Scharf's book, *Balkan Justice:*

> Yet the progress of the [*Blaškić*] trial is being hampered, as Tadic's was, by two procedural difficulties that derive from the terms on which the Tribunal was established within the UN. The first concerns the classification of the war: was it an internal or an international conflict? During the drafting of the Tribunal's Statute, Scharf says it was proposed that, for the purpose of the Tribunal, the war "on or after 25 June 1991 shall be deemed of an international character." This was done to ensure that all the Geneva Conventions and additional protocols should be applicable, not just the weaker ones concerning

"internal conflicts." But the Secretary General removed this clause. Since on numerous occasions military leaders on all sides had claimed to be abiding by the Geneva Conventions, and since Yugoslavia had signed a treaty extending these to all military conflicts, Boutros Boutros Ghali's intervention has cost the Tribunal pointless legal grief and precious resources. In each trial where the prosecution brings charges of war crimes under the Geneva Conventions, the Judges have to determine whether the relevant acts were committed in a context tantamount to that of an international conflict. . .

4.2.322 In practice, what has happened is that the Prosecutor has often amended indictments to *drop* charges under the Geneva Conventions, for example in the *Kupreškić, Jelisić,* and *Hadžihasanović et al.* cases, in order to avoid having to prove the existence of an international armed conflict.

Procedural History of the International Armed Conflict Debate at the ICTY

The Tadić Jurisdiction Decision of 10 August 1995

4.2.323 The issue of international armed conflict was first considered by a Trial Chamber in *Tadić*. The accused submitted a preliminary motion, pursuant to Rule 73, objecting to the Tribunal's jurisdiction on the grounds that no international armed conflict existed at the relevant time and place.

4.2.324 The Chamber, ruling on the motion in its *Tadić Jurisdiction Decision,* held that "the element of internationality forms no jurisdictional criterion of the offences created by Article 2 of the Statute of the International Tribunal" (para. 53):

> 50. What is contended is that for Article 2 to have any application there must exist a state of international conflict and that none in fact existed at any relevant time or place. However, the requirement of international conflict does not appear on the face of Article 2. Certainly, nothing in the words of the Article expressly require its existence; once one of the specified acts is allegedly committed upon a protected person the power of the International Tribunal to prosecute arises if the spatial and temporal requirements of Article 1 are met.
>
> 51. The Report of the Secretary-General, (U.N. Doc. S/25704 (3 May 1993)) (the "Report") makes it clear, in para. 34, that it was intended that the rules of international law that were to be applied should be "beyond any doubt part of customary law," so that problems of non-adherence of particular States to any international Convention should not arise. Hence, no doubt, the specific reference to the law of the Geneva Conventions in Article 2 since, as the Report states in para. 35, that law applicable in armed conflict has beyond doubt become part of customary law. But there is no ground for treating Article 2 as in effect importing into the Statute the whole of the terms of the Conventions, including the reference in common Article 2 of the Geneva Convention to international conflicts. As stated, Article 2 of the Statute is on its face, self-contained, save in relation to the definition of protected persons and things. It simply confers subject matter jurisdiction to prosecute what, if one were concerned with the Conventions, would indeed be grave breaches of those Conventions, but which are, in the present context, simple enactments of the Statute.
>
> 52. When what is in issue is what the Geneva Conventions contemplate in the case of grave breaches, namely their prosecution before a national court and

not before an international tribunal, it is natural enough that there should be a requirement of internationality; a nation might well view with concern, as an unacceptable infringement of sovereignty, the action of a foreign court in trying an accused for grave breaches committed in a conflict internal to that nation. Such considerations do not apply to the International Tribunal, any more than do the references in the Conventions to High Contracting Parties and much else in the Conventions; all these are simply inapplicable to the International Tribunal. They do not apply because the International Tribunal is not in fact, applying conventional international law but, rather, customary international law, as the Secretary-General makes clear in his Report, and is doing so by virtue of the mandate conferred upon it by the Security Council. In the case of what are commonly referred to as "grave breaches," this conventional law has become customary law, though some of it may well have been conventional law before being written into the predecessors of the present Geneva Conventions.

53. It follows that the element of internationality forms no jurisdictional criterion of the offences created by Article 2 of the Statute of the International Tribunal. . . .

The Appeals Chamber's Tadić Jurisdiction Appeals Decision

4.2.325 The Appeals Chamber, in its *Tadić Jurisdiction Appeals Decision* of 2 October 1995, reversed the Trial Chamber's *Tadić Jurisdiction Decision*. The Appeals Chamber agreed with the Trial Chamber that, "the international armed conflict element generally attributed to the grave breaches provisions of the Geneva Conventions is merely a function of the system of universal mandatory jurisdiction that those provisions create" (para. 80). In other words, the States Parties to the Geneva Conventions, anxious to preserve their sovereignty, adopted the "grave breaches" system of universal mandatory jurisdiction only for crimes committed in international conflicts, and not in relation to crimes committed in internal armed conflicts.

4.2.326 It is submitted that the Trial Chamber's reasoning on this point is indeed persuasive. Considerations of state sovereignty are not strictly relevant to the ICTY's jurisdiction. The Security Council created the ICTY as an enforcement measure under Chapter VII of the United Nations Charter. Pursuant to Article 2(7) of the United Nations Charter, "Nothing contained in the present Charter shall authorize the United Nations to intervene in matters which are essentially within the domestic jurisdiction of any state or shall require the Members to submit such matters to settlement under the present Charter; *but this principle shall not prejudice the application of enforcement measures under Chapter VII*" (emphasis added). The ICTY, on behalf of the United Nations is, therefore, authorised "to intervene in matters which are essentially within the domestic jurisdiction of any state," including by prosecuting war crimes irrespective of whether they were committed in internal or international armed conflicts.

4.2.327 The Appeals Chamber also agreed with the Trial Chamber that the "grave breaches" themselves did not on their face require any element of internationality:

> 80. . . . The grave breaches system of the Geneva Conventions establishes a twofold system: there is on the one hand an enumeration of offences that are regarded so serious as to constitute "grave breaches"; closely bound up with

this enumeration a mandatory enforcement mechanism is set up, based on the concept of a duty and a right of all Contracting States to search for and try or extradite persons allegedly responsible for "grave breaches." The international armed conflict element generally attributed to the grave breaches provisions of the Geneva Conventions is merely a function of the system of universal mandatory jurisdiction that those provisions create. The international armed conflict requirement was a necessary limitation on the grave breaches system in light of the intrusion on State sovereignty that such mandatory universal jurisdiction represents. State parties to the 1949 Geneva Conventions did not want to give other States jurisdiction over serious violations of international humanitarian law committed in their internal armed conflicts—at least not the mandatory universal jurisdiction involved in the grave breaches system.

81. The Trial Chamber is right in implying that the enforcement mechanism has of course not been imported into the Statute of the International Tribunal, for the obvious reason that the International Tribunal itself constitutes a mechanism for the prosecution and punishment of the perpetrators of "grave breaches."

4.2.328 Where the Appeals Chamber disagreed with the Trial Chamber was in holding that the concept of "protected persons" imposed a requirement of internationality.

4.2.329 The Appeals Chamber held that, "persons or objects [are] protected only to the extent that they are caught up in an international armed conflict." It is not entirely clear how the Appeals Chamber reached this conclusion. Nevertheless, having done so, it followed that "Article 2 of the Statute only applies to offences committed within the context of international armed conflicts":

81. the Trial Chamber has misinterpreted the reference to the Geneva Conventions contained in the sentence of Article 2: "persons or property protected under the provisions of the relevant Geneva Conventions".... this reference is clearly intended to indicate that the offences listed under Article 2 can only be prosecuted when perpetrated against persons or property regarded as "protected" by the Geneva Conventions under the strict conditions set out by the Conventions themselves. This reference in Article 2 to the notion of "protected persons or property" must perforce cover the persons mentioned in Articles 13, 24, 25 and 26 (protected persons) and 19 and 33 to 35 (protected objects) of Geneva Convention I; in Articles 13, 36, 37 (protected persons) and 22, 24, 25 and 27 (protected objects) of Convention II; in Article 4 of Convention III on prisoners of war; and in Articles 4 and 20 (protected persons) and Articles 18, 19, 21, 22, 33, 53, 57 etc. (protected property) of Convention IV on civilians. Clearly, these provisions of the Geneva Conventions apply to persons or objects protected only to the extent that they are caught up in an international armed conflict. By contrast, those provisions do not include persons or property coming within the purview of common Article 3 of the four Geneva Conventions.

...

83. We find that our interpretation of Article 2 is the only one warranted by the text of the Statute and the relevant provisions of the Geneva Conventions, as well as by a logical construction of their interplay as dictated by Article 2....

4.2.330 It should be noted that the Trial Chamber did *not*, as the Appeals Chamber appeared to suggest ("... by contrast, those provisions do not include persons or property coming within the purview of common Article 3 of the four Geneva Conventions"), rely on Common Article 3 to conclude that internationality was not a jurisdictional prerequisite for Article 2. Rather the Chamber had based itself on the plain wording of Article 2 and on customary law.

Separate Opinions by Judge Abi-Saab and Judge Li to the Tadić Jurisdiction Appeals Decision

4.2.331 Judges Abi-Saab and Li appended separate opinions to the *Tadić Jurisdiction Appeals Decision*, in which they differed from the majority on the applicability of Article 2 of the Statute and "grave breaches" of the Geneva Conventions.

4.2.332 *Judge Abi-Saab* held that Article 2 of the Statute might apply even in internal armed conflicts:

> Instead of reaching, as the Decision does, for the acts expressly mentioned in Article 2 via Article 3 when they are committed in the course of an internal armed conflict, I consider, on the basis of the material presented in the Decision itself, that a strong case can be made for the application of Article 2, even when the incriminated act takes place in an internal conflict." (page 5)

4.2.333 Judge Abi-Saab's phrase, "reaching, as the Decision does, for the acts expressly mentioned in Article 2 via Article 3 when they are committed in the course of an internal armed conflict," requires some explanation. The Appeals Chamber's Decision concerning Article 2 of the Statute meant that the wilful killing or torture of a civilian in a civil war could not be prosecuted as a "grave breach" under Article 2. In order to ensure that such an act would not go unpunished, however, the Appeals Chamber turned to Article 3 of the Statute ("Violations of the laws or customs of war"), and held that Article 3 would cover such violations. Judge Abi-Saab felt that this manoeuvre was unnecessary, however, since in his view there was already sufficient justification in state practice for prosecuting such a violation under Article 2 of the ICTY Statute as a "grave breach" of the Geneva Conventions.

4.2.334 On the interpretation of Article 2 of the Statute, *Judge Li* considered that the Tribunal should view the armed conflict in the former Yugoslavia, *as a whole*, as international. Hence Article 2 would be generally applicable:

> 17. I am of the opinion that the submission of the Prosecution to view the conflict in the former Yugoslavia in its entirety and to consider it international in character is correct.
>
> The armed conflict in the former Yugoslavia started shortly after the date on which Slovenia and Croatia declared their independence on 25 June 1991 between the military forces of the SFRY and Slovenia and Croatia. Such armed conflict should of course be characterized as internal because the declarations of independence were suspended in consequence of the proposal of the EC for three months. After the expiration of the three months' period, on 7 October 1991, Slovenia proclaimed its independence with effect from that date, and Croatia with effect from 8 October 1991. So the armed conflict in the former

Yugoslavia should be considered international as from 8 October 1991 because the independence of these two States was definite on that date.

But there were some internal armed conflicts in the whole course of the conflict, for instance, Bosnians against Bosnians, and the question is how to treat such internal conflicts. This question is correctly answered by O'Brien as follows:

> the conflict is clearly international: three nations have fought, primarily in the territory of two of them (thus far), with a number of fronts and partisans or proxy groups participating on behalf of each. Once this determination is made, it should not matter that some combatants are citizens of the same nation-State. It is virtually unthinkable that, for example, a Ukrainian fighting for the German Army in World War II would have succeeded in arguing that his fight was internal (against the Soviet State), regardless of the character of the broader conflict." (O'Brien, *The International Tribunal for Violations of International Humanitarian Law in the Former Yugoslavia*, 87 AJIL 639, 647–648 (1993).)

18. Of the three nations mentioned by O'Brien in the passage quoted above, one is surely SFRY, afterwards FRY, and the other two are of course Croatia and Bosnia-Herzegovina. Indeed, there is sufficient evidence of probative value for proving that SFRY, afterwards FRY, participated, and FRY is still participating in the armed conflict against Croatia and Bosnia-Herzegovina. In the following I briefly list some:

1. The Final Report of the Commission of Experts established pursuant to Security Council resolution 780 (1992) states that both the "Bosnian Serb Army" operating in Bosnia and the "Krajina Serb Army" operating in Croatia are "armed and supported by the JNA" (Annexes to the Final Report, UN Doc. S/1994/674, Annex Summaries and Conclusions, para. 29). Furthermore, it says that the Bosnian Serb Army is carrying out the FRY objective of creating a new Yugoslav State from parts of Croatia and Bosnia and Herzegovina, and that the 110,000 troops nominally subordinated to the "Serbian Republic of Bosnia" and the "Serbian Republic of Croatia" receive instructions, arms and ammunition and other support from the JNA and the FRY (Annex III to the Final Report, paras. 17 and 124).

2. The Reports of Mr Mazowiecki give a clear account of the policy of the so-called "ethnic cleansing" consistently employed by the FRY for the purpose of creating a Greater Serbia by the forceful incorporation of the parts of territory of Croatia and Bosnia-Herzegovina into a Greater Serbia. For instance, his third Report of November 1992 further describes the methods used for "ethnic cleansing" and states: "This lends credence to the fear that the ultimate goal may be to incorporate Serbian-occupied areas of Croatia and Bosnia and Herzegovina into a 'Greater Serbia'." (UN Doc. A/47/666, para. 13.)

3. The statement submitted by Mr Andrew J.W. Gow, dated 30 January 1995, corroborates in detail the above-mentioned statements of the Reports of the United Nations Commission of Experts and Mr Mazowiecki. (Documents presented to the Trial Chamber by the Prosecution, Vol. III, Document 101.)

4. Many resolutions of the Security Council reflect that there was a continuing international armed conflict in the former Yugoslavia. For instance,

resolution 757 of 30 May 1992 imposed a series of economic sanctions against the FRY, which were to apply until the Security Council decided that the authorities of the FRY, including the JNA, had taken effective measures to fulfil the requirement of resolution 752 for the withdrawal of their forces from Bosnia and the cessation of their interference in Bosnia. The Council has never found that these requirements have been met and has not lifted all sanctions imposed. In effect, the Council's actions amount to a recognition of the continuing international character of the conflict. (*The* Amicus Curiae *Brief of the U.S.*, 25 July 1995, p. 32.)

5. The Bosnia-Herzegovina Government declared formally on 20 June 1992 the state of war in the country. It announced that Bosnia-Herzegovina was "the victim of aggression carried out by the Republic of Serbia, the Republic of Montenegro, the Yugoslav Army and terrorists of the Serbian Democratic Party. . . ." (UN Doc. S/24214, Annex.) According to common Article 2(1) of the Geneva Conventions of 1949, the Conventions shall apply to all cases of declared war. So because of the declaration of war by the Government of Bosnia-Herzegovina, the armed conflict in that country must also be considered as international.

19. Moreover, it is to be noted that the Commission of Experts mentioned in para. 8 has consistently held the view that the conflicts in the former Yugoslavia should be envisaged in their entirety, to which the law applicable in international armed conflict should be applied. In its Final Report, the Commission declares its definite position clearly as follows:

> [A]s indicated in para. 45 of its first interim report, the Commission is of the opinion that the character and complexity of the armed conflicts concerned, combined with the web of agreements on humanitarian law that the parties have concluded among themselves, justifies the Commission's approach in applying the law applicable in international armed conflicts to the entirety of the armed conflicts in the territory of the former Yugoslavia." (S/1994/674, p. 13, para. 44.)

Article: Greenwood, Christopher, "International Humanitarian Law and the *Tadić* Case," 7 *European Journal of International Law* 265–283 (1996).

Developments After the Tadić Jurisdiction Appeals Decision

4.2.335 The Appeals Chamber's ruling in the *Tadić Jurisdiction Appeals Decision* that an *international* armed conflict was required to invoke Article 2 has been applied in a number of cases: in confirmations of indictments (e.g. *Vukovar*), four Rule 61 proceedings (*Nikolić, Vukovar, Karadžić and Mladić* and *Rajić*), five final judgements (*Tadić, Delalić et al, Aleksovski, Blaškić* and *Kordić and Čerkez*) and two final appeals (*Tadić* and *Delalić et al*).

4.2.336 Note should be taken of the *Delalić Trial Judgement* (para. 232), where the Chamber stated that where the conflict had been found to be international up to a certain date, namely 19 May 1992, there should be a "presumption" that the conflict remained international unless the contrary be proven.

Trial and Appeals Judgements

Tadić Opinion and Judgement of 7 May 1997

4.2.337 In the *Tadić Opinion and Judgement* rendered on 7 May 1997, the Trial Chamber found that the armed conflict in Bosnia was international prior to 19 May 1992:

> 569. ... it is clear from the evidence before the Trial Chamber that, from the beginning of 1992 until 19 May 1992, a state of international armed conflict existed in at least part of the territory of Bosnia and Herzegovina. This was an armed conflict between the forces of the Republic of Bosnia and Herzegovina on the one hand and those of the Federal Republic of Yugoslavia (Serbia and Montenegro), being the JNA (later the VJ), working with sundry paramilitary and Bosnian Serb forces, on the other. ...
>
> 570. For evidence of this it is enough to refer generally to the evidence presented as to the bombardment of Sarajevo, the seat of government of the Republic of Bosnia and Herzegovina, in April 1992 by Serb forces, their attack on towns along Bosnia and Herzegovina's border with Serbia on the Drina River and their invasion of south-eastern Herzegovina from Serbia and Montenegro."

4.2.338 The Chamber went on to add, however:

> 571. ... the extent of the application of international humanitarian law from one place to another in the Republic of Bosnia and Herzegovina depends upon the particular character of the conflict with which the Indictment is concerned. This depends in turn on the degree of involvement of the VJ and the Government of the Federal Republic of Yugoslavia (Serbia and Montenegro) after the withdrawal of the JNA on 19 May 1992. ...

On this issue, see the "protected persons" section below.

4.2.339 Judge McDonald, presiding, dissented from the Judgement, holding that the conflict was international and the victims in question "protected persons" at all relevant times.

Tadić Appeals Judgement of 15 July 1999

4.2.340 On the Prosecutor's cross-appeal, the Appeals Chamber held that there was an international armed conflict at all relevant times, and thus the grave breaches regime of the 1949 Geneva Conventions applied, and that the victims were "protected persons" under the 4th Geneva Convention.

4.2.341 The Appeals Chamber examined the test that the International Court of Justice laid down in the *Nicaragua* case (ICJ Reports, 1986) for determining whether a group of individuals or a paramilitary structure operated as a *de facto* organ of a State, for the purposes of attributing responsibility to that State under international law. After an examination of the case-law, the Chamber concluded that the *Nicaragua* case was not persuasive since international law imposed different tests for *de facto* agency depending on whether the putative agents were individuals or organised into a paramilitary structure:

> 137. ... the Appeals Chamber holds the view that international rules do not always require the same degree of control over armed groups or private individuals for the purpose of determining whether an individual not having the status of a State official under internal legislation can be regarded as a *de facto* organ of the State. The extent of the requisite State control varies. Where the question at issue is whether a *single* private individual or a *group that is not militarily organised* has acted as a *de facto* State organ when performing a specific act, it is necessary to ascertain whether specific instructions concerning the commission of that particular act had been issued by that State to the individual or group in question; alternatively, it must be established whether the unlawful act had been publicly endorsed or approved *ex post facto* by the State at issue. By contrast, control by a State over subordinate *armed forces or militias or paramilitary units* may be of an overall character (and must comprise more than the mere provision of financial assistance or military equipment or training). This requirement, however, does not go so far as to include the issuing of specific orders by the State, or its direction of each individual operation. Under international law it is by no means necessary that the controlling authorities should plan all the operations of the units dependent on them, choose their targets, or give specific instructions concerning the conduct of military operations and any alleged violations of international humanitarian law. The control required by international law may be deemed to exist when a State (or, in the context of an armed conflict, the Party to the conflict) *has a role in organising, coordinating or planning the military actions* of the military group, in addition to financing, training and equipping or providing operational support to that group. Acts performed by the group or members thereof may be regarded as acts of *de facto* State organs regardless of any specific instruction by the controlling State concerning the commission of each of those acts.

4.2.342 Applying that finding to the case at hand, the Appeals Chamber stated:

> 145. ... given that the Bosnian Serb armed forces constituted a "military organization," the control of the FRY authorities over these armed forces required by international law for considering the armed conflict to be international was *overall control* going beyond the mere financing and equipping of such forces and involving also participation in the planning and supervision of military operations. By contrast, international rules do not require that such control should extend to the issuance of specific orders or instructions relating to single military actions, whether or not such actions were contrary to international humanitarian law.

4.2.343 The Appeals Chamber found *overall control* in the case of the FRY and the Bosnian Serb forces, particularly in light of the fact that officers of the Bosnian Serb army were paid by the JNA. Indeed the two armies were not separate at all:

> 150. The Trial Chamber clearly found that even after 19 May 1992, the command structure of the JNA did not change after it was renamed and redesignated as the VJ. Furthermore, and more importantly, it is apparent from the decision of the Trial Chamber and more particularly from the evidence as evaluated by Judge McDonald in her Separate and Dissenting Opinion, that even after that date the VJ continued to control the Bosnian Serb Army in Bosnia

and Herzegovina, that is the VRS. The VJ controlled the political and military objectives, as well as the military operations, of the VRS. Two "factors" emphasised in the Judgement need to be recalled: first, "the transfer to the 1st Krajina Corps, as with other units of the VRS, of former JNA Officers who were not of Bosnian Serb extraction from their equivalent postings in the relevant VRS unit's JNA predecessor" and second, with respect to the VRS, "the continuing payment of salaries, to Bosnian Serb and non-Bosnian Serb officers alike, by the Government of the Federal Republic of Yugoslavia (Serbia and Montenegro)." According to the Trial Chamber, these two factors did not amount to, or were not indicative of, effective control by Belgrade over the Bosnian Serb forces. The Appeals Chamber shares instead the views set out by Judge McDonald in her Separate and Dissenting Opinion, whereby these two factors, in addition to others shown by the Prosecution, did indicate control.

. . .

152. . . . even after 19 May 1992 the Bosnian Serb army continued to act in pursuance of the military goals formulated in Belgrade. . . .

4.2.344 The Appeals Chamber also pointed out the dangers of adopting the rigid approach taken by the Trial Chamber majority in the *Tadić Opinion and Judgement:*

154. . . . the finding of the Trial Chamber that the relationship between the FRY/VJ and VRS amounted to cooperation and coordination rather than overall control suffered from having taken largely at face value those features which had been put in place intentionally by Belgrade to make it seem as if their links with Pale were as partners acting only in cooperation with each other. Such an approach is not only flawed in the specific circumstances of this case, but also potentially harmful in the generality of cases. Undue emphasis upon the ostensible structures and overt declarations of the belligerents, as opposed to a nuanced analysis of the reality of their relationship, may tacitly suggest to groups who are in *de facto* control of military forces that responsibility for the acts of such forces can be evaded merely by resort to a superficial restructuring of such forces or by a facile declaration that the reconstituted forces are henceforth independent of their erstwhile sponsors.

4.2.345 The Appeals Chamber concluded, therefore, that, "for the period material to this case (1992), the armed forces of the *Republika Srpska* were to be regarded as acting under the overall control of and on behalf of the FRY. Hence, even after 19 May 1992 the armed conflict in Bosnia and Herzegovina between the Bosnian Serbs and the central authorities of Bosnia and Herzegovina must be classified as an *international* armed conflict" (para. 162).

4.2.346 In a Separate Opinion to the *Tadić Appeals Judgement* of 15 July 1999, Judge Shahabuddeen considered that the question raised was distinguishable from that raised in *Nicaragua:*

17. . . . The question . . . is whether the FRY was using force through the VRS against BH, not whether the FRY was responsible for any breaches of international humanitarian law committed by the VRS.

4.2.347 Judge Shahabuddeen felt that the "command and control" test applied by the Trial Chamber in *Tadić* was "too high a threshold . . . for the purpose of determining whether a state was using force through a foreign military entity, as distinguished from whether the state was committing breaches of international humanitarian law through that entity" (para. 16).

Delalić et al. Trial Judgement

4.2.348 The Trial Chamber ruling in the *Delalić et al. Trial Judgement* also found that the conflict between Bosnia and Herzegovina and the Federal Republic of Yugoslavia (Serbia and Montenegro) was international in character. The Chamber differed from the *Tadić* Trial Chamber in finding that the conflict remained international *throughout 1992*:

> 234. . . . the Trial Chamber is in no doubt that the international armed conflict occurring in Bosnia and Herzegovina, at least from April 1992, continued throughout that year and did not alter fundamentally in its nature. The withdrawal of JNA troops who were not of Bosnian citizenship, and the creation of the VRS and VJ, constituted a deliberate attempt to mask the continued involvement of the FRY in the conflict while its Government remained in fact the controlling force behind the Bosnian Serbs. From the level of strategy to that of personnel and logistics the operations of the JNA persisted in all but name. It would be wholly artificial to sever the period before 19 May 1992 from the period thereafter in considering the nature of the conflict and applying international humanitarian law.

4.2.349 The Trial Chamber examined (paras. 199–277) whether the two conditions for the application of Article 2 had been met, namely, (i) the existence of an international armed conflict, and (ii) whether the victims of the crimes in question were "protected persons" under the Geneva Conventions (para. 201).

4.2.350 On the first point, the Trial Chamber held that "an international armed conflict existed in Bosnia and Herzegovina at the date of its recognition as an independent State on 6 April 1992" (para. 214). The purported withdrawal of the JNA from Bosnia and Herzegovina in May 1992 was a ruse which did not change the nature of the conflict—"the plan to divide the JNA into the VRS and the VJ, so as to disguise its presence in Bosnia and Herzegovina once that Republic became an independent State, was conceived several months earlier in Belgrade" (para. 218). The Chamber went on to say, "the Government of Bosnia and Herzegovina, for its part, undoubtedly considered itself to be involved in an armed conflict as a result of aggression against that State by Serbia and Montenegro, the Yugoslav Army and the SDS. On 20 June 1992, it proclaimed a state of war, identifying these parties as the aggressors, despite the insistence of the FRY that it was no longer involved in the conflict. In addition, it clearly considered the Bosnian Serb forces organised by the SDS to be a party to that same armed conflict." (para. 225). Thus, "it is clear that the 'new' army belonging to the Bosnian Serbs constituted no more than a re-designation of the JNA units in Bosnia and Herzegovina" (para. 226).

4.2.351 Regarding the test applied by the *Tadić* majority using the *Nicaragua* case in the ICJ, the Trial Chamber instead held that *Nicaragua* was of little use to the ICTY. While the case:

230. ... constitutes an important source of jurisprudence on various issues of international law, it is always important to note the dangers of relying upon the reasoning and findings of a very different judicial body concerned with rather different circumstances from the case in hand. The International Tribunal is a criminal judicial body, established to prosecute and punish individuals for violations of international humanitarian law, and not to determine State responsibility for acts of aggression or unlawful intervention. It is, therefore, inappropriate to transpose wholesale into the present context the test enunciated by the ICJ to determine the responsibility of the United States for the actions of the contras in Nicaragua.

4.2.352 The Chamber distinguished *Nicaragua* from the case before it:

231. ... In that case, the ICJ was charged with determining whether there had been a use of force in violation of customary international law and article 2(4) of the United Nations Charter by the United States against Nicaragua, as well as an unlawful intervention in the internal affairs of Nicaragua on the part of the United States. ... More specifically, what was in question was the incursion of the forces of one such distinct, bounded entity into another and the operation of agents of that entity within the boundaries of the other. In contrast, the situation with which we are here concerned, is characterised by the breakdown of previous State boundaries and the creation of new ones. ...

232. ... the forces constituting the VRS had a prior identity as an actual organ of the SFRY, as the JNA. When the FRY took control of this organ and subsequently severed the formal link between them, by creating the VJ and VRS, the presumption remains that these forces retained their link with it, unless demonstrated otherwise.

233. The Trial Chamber's position accords fully with that taken by Judge McDonald in her Dissent to the majority Judgement in the *Tadić* case. Judge McDonald found that:

> [t]he evidence proves that the creation of the VRS was a legal fiction. The only changes made after the 15 May 1992 Security Council resolution were the transfer of troops, the establishment of a Main Staff of the VRS, a change in the name of the military organisation and individual units, and a change in the insignia. There remained the same weapons, the same equipment, the same officers, the same commanders, largely the same troops, the same logistics centres, the same suppliers, the same infrastructure, the same source of payments, the same goals and mission, the same tactics, and the same operations.
>
> ...
>
> [i]t would perhaps be naïve not to recognize that the creation of the VRS, which coincided with the announced withdrawal by the JNA, was in fact nothing more than a ruse.

234. In light of the above discussion, the Trial Chamber is in no doubt that the international armed conflict occurring in Bosnia and Herzegovina, at least from April 1992, continued throughout that year and did not alter fundamentally in its nature. The withdrawal of JNA troops who were not of Bosnian citizenship, and the creation of the VRS and VJ, constituted a deliberate attempt to mask the continued involvement of the FRY in the conflict while its Government remained in fact the controlling force behind the Bosnian Serbs.

From the level of strategy to that of personnel and logistics the operations of the JNA persisted in all but name. It would be wholly artificial to sever the period before 19 May 1992 from the period thereafter in considering the nature of the conflict and applying international humanitarian law.

235. Having reached this conclusion, the Trial Chamber makes no finding on the question of whether Article 2 of the Statute can only be applied in a situation of international armed conflict, or whether this provision is also applicable in internal armed conflicts. The issue which remains to be decided is simply whether the victims of the acts alleged in the Indictment were "persons protected" by the Geneva Conventions of 1949.

4.2.353 On this issue—whether the victims of the crimes in question were "protected persons" under the Geneva Conventions—see 4.2.361 *et seq.* below. On the issue of "effective control," and the relevance of funding, training, and equipping to the question of control, see 6.2.119 *et seq.* ICTY Article 7 (3).

The *Delalić et al. Appeals Judgement*

4.2.354 In this judgement, the Chamber affirmed the holding in the *Tadić Appeals Judgement* and the *Aleksovski Appeal Judgement* regarding international conflict that, where it is a matter of the acts of armed forces or militias or paramilitary units, the prosecution must establish that the foreign intervening party was in "overall control" of those forces or forces (paras. 10–51 of the *Judgement*). In this case, the Appeals Chamber affirmed the Trial Chamber's finding that the conflict was international.

The *Blaškić Trial Judgement*

4.2.355 The *Blaškić* case involved the conflict between the Bosnian Muslims and Croats in central Bosnia in 1992–1993. The accused was charged, *inter alia*, with violations of Article 2 of the ICTY Statute. In the *Blaškić Trial Judgement*, the Chamber considered two aspects by which the conflict might be deemed to be international: (i) by direct intervention of Croatian troops in the conflict, (ii) by Bosnian Croat troops acting as agents of Croatia. For direct intervention, the Trial Chamber found "ample proof to characterise the conflict as international" "based on Croatia's direct intervention in [Bosnia-Herzegovina]" (para. 94).

4.2.356 For indirect intervention, the Trial Chamber followed the ruling of the Appeals Chamber in *Tadić* and examined whether Croatia exercised "overall control" over Bosnian Croat troops in Bosnia and Herzegovina such that the conflict was international. It found that it did:

122. In the light of all the foregoing and, in particular, the Croatian territorial ambitions in respect of Bosnia-Herzegovina detailed above, the Trial Chamber finds that Croatia, and more specifically former President Tudjman, was hoping to partition Bosnia and exercised such a degree of control over the Bosnian Croats and especially the HVO that it is justified to speak of overall control. Contrary to what the Defence asserted, the Trial Chamber concluded that the close ties between Croatia and the Bosnian Croats did not cease with the establishment of the HVO.

123. Croatia's indirect intervention would therefore permit the conclusion that the conflict was international.

The *Kordić and Čerkez Trial Judgement*

4.2.357 The conflict was also found to be international in the *Kordić Trial Judgement* (see para. 146).

Internationality of Conflict to Be Proved at Trial

4.2.358 The Trial Chamber, in its *Decision Rejecting a Motion of the Defence to dismiss counts 4,7,10,14,16 and 18 based on the failure to adequately plead the existence of an international armed conflict* rendered in *Blaškić* on 4 April 1997, followed the Appeals Chamber interlocutory decision on jurisdiction in *Tadić*, and held that proof of the internationality of the armed conflict in question was a matter for trial:

> it [the Appeals Chamber in the *Tadić* Decision] did not settle the issue of whether in that case, given the circumstances of time and place covered by the indictment, the said conflict was international. It thus considered that the Trial Chamber should settle this issue involving factual and legal questions only on the merits.
>
> For the same reason, the Trial Chamber is of the opinion that it is premature to rule on this point since it can be considered properly only on its merits.

4.2.359 This has been confirmed in several cases. See, for example, *Decision on the Joint Defence Motion to Dismiss the Amended Indictment for lack of jurisdiction based on the limited jurisdictional reach of Articles 2 and 3* rendered by the Trial Chamber in *Kordić and Čerkez* on 2 March 1999.

4.2.360 In *Hadžihasanović and Others, Decision on Form of Indictment* (para. 29), 7 December, 2001, the Trial Chamber ordered the Prosecution clearly to plead in the indictment the states between which it was alleged that an international conflict existed.

Protected Persons

4.2.361 Article 2 of the ICTY Statute requires that the crimes be committed against "*persons or property protected under the provisions of the relevant Geneva Convention.*" That is, the victims must be "protected persons," which are defined categories within each of the four Geneva Conventions of 1949. ICTY Trial and Appeals Chambers have consistently applied the ruling set out in para. 80 of the *Tadić Jurisdiction Appeals Decision* that "protected persons" are those individuals mentioned in "Articles 13, 24, 25 and 26 . . . of Geneva Convention I; in Articles 13, 36, 37 . . . of Convention II; in Article 4 of Convention III on prisoners of war; and in Articles 4 and 20 . . . of Convention IV on civilians" (para. 81; see 4.2.329, above).

4.2.362 The Trial Chamber noted in its *Nikolić Rule 61 Decision*:

30. For Article 2 of the Statute, relating to the grave breaches provisions of the Geneva Conventions of 1949, to apply, the victims of the alleged crimes must be "persons . . . protected under the provisions of the relevant Geneva Convention."

The Muslim population of Vlasenica was systematically disarmed and it does not appear that there was any resistance movement in the region. The Chamber considers that all the detainees at Sušica camp were civilians and therefore "protected persons" within the meaning of Article 4 of Geneva Convention IV of 1949.

4.2.363 The Trial Chamber in its *Vukovar Rule 61 Decision* found that:

25. The general conditions for application of Article 2 of the Statute are the existence of an international armed conflict and the classification of victims as protected persons as defined by the relevant Geneva Convention. . . . The 260 men taken from the Vukovar hospital were . . . either civilians or medical personnel, wounded persons and other persons falling within the categories of protected persons as defined in the four Geneva Conventions of 1949.

4.2.364 In the *Rajić Rule 61 Decision*, the Trial Chamber found that the 4th Geneva Convention Relative to Protection of Civilian Persons in the Time of War applied and that the victims in question fell within that Convention's definition of "Protected Persons":

37. . . . although the residents of Stupni Do were not directly or physically "in the hands of" Croatia, they can be treated as being constructively "in the hands of" Croatia, a country of which they were not nationals. The Trial Chamber therefore finds that the civilian residents of the village of Stupni Do were—for the purposes of the grave breaches provisions of Geneva Convention IV—protected persons *vis-à-vis* the Bosnian Croats because the latter were controlled by Croatia. The Trial Chamber notes this holding is solely for the purpose of establishing subject-matter jurisdiction over the offences allegedly committed by the accused.

Tadić Opinion and Judgement

4.2.365 The first occasion on which the issue of "Protected Persons" under the Geneva Conventions—in particular Article 4 of the Fourth (Civilians) Geneva Convention—has been dealt with in a final Judgement is in the *Tadić Opinion and Judgement* rendered by the Trial Chamber on 7 May 1997.

4.2.366 The Trial Chamber majority (Judges Stephen and Vohrah) held that, while the conflict in question was at least initially international in character, the victims of Tadić's acts were not, at the relevant time, "protected persons" under the 4th Geneva Convention, i.e. they were not in the hands of a party to the conflict or occupying power of which they were not nationals (Article 4 of the 4th Geneva Convention). This was because on 19 May 1992—as a result of pressure from the international community, in particular resolutions of the Security Council threatening sanctions—the JNA (the Yugoslav army, later the rump Yugoslav army (Serbia and Montenegro)) nominally withdrew from the Republic of Bosnia and Herzegovina. According to the Trial Chamber majority, this rendered the conflict non-international after that date and the 4th Geneva Convention inapplicable.

4.2.367 Since an act is only a "grave breach" of the Geneva Conventions if the victim of the act is a "protected person" as defined by the relevant Convention, the finding that Tadić's victims were not "protected persons" meant that the "grave breaches" provisions of the Geneva Conventions would not apply. The Chamber therefore declared inapplicable all the counts of the indictment which charged "grave breaches" under Article 2 of the Statute. Tadić was nonetheless convicted of the crime under Article 3 of the Statute.

4.2.368 The Presiding Judge, Judge McDonald, disagreed, holding that the victims in question *were* protected persons under Article 4 of the 4th Geneva Convention of 1949 and that Article 2 of the Statute therefore applied.

4.2.369 Judge McDonald opined that the majority, which had relied on *Nicaragua* for their conclusion that the Bosnian Serbs did not act as agents for FRY after 19 May 1992, had in fact misapplied the case. In her view, *Nicagarua* posited two tests for the attribution of responsibility to a State for acts of a third party, namely (i) an *agency* relationship of *dependency and control*; or (ii) in the absence of an agency relationship, direct attributability on the basis of *effective control*. She held that both tests were satisfied in the relationship between the Bosnian Serb army and the Federal Republic of Yugoslavia (Serbia and Montenegro). Hence the acts of Bosnian Serbs committed against the citizens of Bosnia and Herzegovina ("Bosnians") were attributable to the Federal Republic of Yugoslavia (Serbia and Montenegro); thus the conflict was international. Bosnians in the hands of Bosnian Serbs were, therefore, constructively, if not actually, in the hands of the Federal Republic of Yugoslavia (Serbia and Montenegro)—a Party to the conflict or Occupying Power of which they were not nationals. Such Bosnians were, therefore, "protected persons" under the Fourth (Civilian) Geneva Convention. Article 2 of the ICTY's Statute therefore applied to them and to acts of violence committed against them by the accused, Duško Tadić, a Bosnian Serb, in pursuance of the policy of "ethnic cleansing" to create a "Greater Serbia."

4.2.370 Judge McDonald also considered that the *Nicaragua* case was easily distinguishable on the facts and the law from *Tadić's case* since the former involved the attribution of State responsibility while the latter concerned the determination of individual criminal liability for violations of international humanitarian law.

4.2.371 For extensive discussion of the Judgement of 7 May 1997, see the second edition of this work (Jones, John R.W.D., *The Practice of the International Criminal Tribunals for the former Yugoslavia and Rwanda,* pp. 70–81 (Transnational Publishers, 2d ed. 2000).

Tadić Appeals Judgement

4.2.372 The verdict of the Trial Chamber majority was overturned on appeal, on the grounds that the conflict was international (see the discussion of international armed conflict above). The Appeals Chamber, in the *Tadić Appeals Judgement* of 15 July 1999, construed the "nationality" requirement (to be a "protected person," the person must be "in the hands of a Party to the conflict or Occupying Power of which they are not nationals") of Article 4 of the 4th Geneva Convention *broadly* so that the crucial question was that of *allegiance* to a party to the conflict (paras. 163–169). The Appeals Chamber found:

> 164. Article 4(1) of Geneva Convention IV (protection of civilians), applicable to the case at issue, defines "protected persons"—hence possible victims of grave breaches—as those "in the hands of a Party to the conflict or Occupying Power of which they are not nationals." In other words, subject to the provisions of Article 4(2), the Convention intends to protect civilians (in enemy territory, occupied territory or the combat zone) who do not have the nationality of the belligerent in whose hands they find themselves, or who are stateless persons. In addition, as is apparent from the preparatory work, the Convention also intends to protect those civilians in occupied territory who, while having the nationality of the Party to the conflict in whose hands they find themselves, are refugees and thus no longer owe allegiance to this Party and no longer enjoy its diplomatic protection (consider, for instance, a situation similar to that of German Jews who had fled to France before 1940, and thereafter found themselves in the hands of German forces occupying French territory).
>
> 165. Thus already in 1949 the legal bond of nationality was not regarded as crucial and allowance was made for special cases. In the aforementioned case of refugees, the lack of both allegiance to a State and diplomatic protection by this State was regarded as more important than the formal link of nationality. In the cases provided for in Article 4(2), in addition to nationality, account was taken of the existence or non-existence of diplomatic protection: nationals of a neutral State or a co-belligerent State are not treated as "protected persons" unless they are deprived of or do not enjoy diplomatic protection. In other words, those nationals are not "protected persons" as long as they benefit from the normal diplomatic protection of their State; when they lose it or in any event do not enjoy it, the Convention automatically grants them the status of "protected persons."
>
> 166. This legal approach, hinging on substantial relations more than on formal bonds, becomes all the more important in present-day international armed conflicts. While previously wars were primarily between well-established States, in modern inter-ethnic armed conflicts such as that in the former Yugoslavia, new States are often created during the conflict and ethnicity rather than nationality may become the grounds for allegiance. Or, put another way, ethnicity may become determinative of national allegiance. Under these conditions, the requirement of nationality is even less adequate to define protected persons. In such conflicts, not only the text and the drafting history of the Convention but also, and more importantly, the Convention's object and purpose suggest that allegiance to a Party to the conflict and, correspondingly, control by this Party over persons in a given territory, may be regarded as the crucial test.

...

4.2.373 The Appeals Chamber held (at para. 167) that, while the Bosnian Serbs arguably had the same nationality as the victims (i.e. being both nationals of Bosnia and Herzegovina), Bosnian Serb forces acted as *de facto* organs of another State, namely, the FRY. Thus the requirements set out in Article 4 of Geneva Convention IV were met: the victims were "protected persons" as they found themselves in the hands of armed forces of a State of which they were not nationals. Observing that, "in granting its protection, Article 4 intends to look to the substance of relations, not to their legal characterisation as such" (para. 168), the Chamber went on to state (at para. 169) that:

> even if in the circumstances of the case the perpetrators and the victims were to be regarded as possessing the same nationality, Article 4 would still be applicable. Indeed, the victims did not owe allegiance to (and did not receive the diplomatic protection of) the State (the FRY) on whose behalf the Bosnian Serb armed forces had been fighting.

4.2.374 The Appeals Chamber therefore reinstated all of the Article 2 counts ("Grave Breaches") of which the accused had been acquitted (paras. 170–171).

Delalić et al. Trial Judgement

4.2.375 Unlike the majority in the *Tadić Opinion and Judgement*, the *Delalić* Chamber, in its *Delalić et al. Trial Judgement*, unanimously found an on-going international armed conflict and that the victims in question were at all relevant times "protected persons."

4.2.376 The Trial Chamber first held that the victims of the acts alleged in the indictment were "protected persons" under the Fourth (Civilian) Geneva Convention, and not as Prisoners of War under the 3rd Geneva Convention. In order to qualify as a "protected person" under the Fourth (Civilian) Geneva Convention, the persons had to be "in the hands of a Party to the conflict of which they are not nationals." The Chamber discussed the issue of nationality in this context (paras. 245–266), and concluded:

> 265. Without yet entering the discussion of whether or not their detention was unlawful, it is clear that the victims of the acts alleged in the Indictment were arrested and detained mainly on the basis of their Serb identity. As such, and insofar as they were not protected by any of the other Geneva Conventions, they must be considered to have been "protected persons" within the meaning of the Fourth Geneva Convention, as they were clearly regarded by the Bosnian authorities as belonging to the opposing party in an armed conflict and as posing a threat to the Bosnian State.
>
> 266. This interpretation of the Convention is fully in accordance with the development of the human rights doctrine which has been increasing in force since the middle of this century. It would be incongruous with the whole concept of human rights, which protect individuals from the excesses of their own governments, to rigidly apply the nationality requirement of article 4, that was apparently inserted to prevent interference in a State's relations with its own nationals. Furthermore, the nature of the international armed conflict in Bosnia and Herzegovina reflects the complexity of many modern conflicts and not, perhaps, the paradigm envisaged in 1949. In order to retain the relevance and effectiveness of the norms of the Geneva Conventions, it is necessary to adopt the approach here taken. As was recently stated by Meron,
>
>> "[i]n interpreting the law, our goal should be to avoid paralyzing the legal process as much as possible and, in the case of humanitarian conventions, to enable them to serve their protective goals.

4.2.377 The Chamber rejected the Prosecutor's contention that the victims in question were prisoners-of-war by virtue of being a levée-en-masse (see paras. 268 and 270). Instead the Chamber chose to treat all the victims as civilians (para. 270), while noting that the 4th (Civilian) Convention could be used in this way as a residual catch-all, as it contained a negative definition of civilians, i.e. civilians are those who are neither the wounded and sick, the shipwrecked nor prisoners-of-war (the categories of non-combatants protected by the other three Geneva Conventions):

> 271. It is important, however, to note that this finding is predicated on the view that there is no gap between the Third and the Fourth Geneva Conventions. If an individual is not entitled to the protections of the Third Convention as a prisoner of war (or of the First or Second Conventions) he or she necessarily falls within the ambit of Convention IV, provided that its article 4 requirements are satisfied.

4.2.378 Thus, the Chamber found that all of the victims of the acts alleged in the indictment were "persons protected" by the 4th Geneva Convention of 1949:

> 274. . . . For the purposes of the application of Article 2 of the Statute, these victims must be regarded as having been in the hands of a party to the conflict of which they were not nationals, being Bosnian Serbs detained during an international armed conflict by a party to that conflict, the State of Bosnia and Herzegovina.
>
> 275. This finding is strengthened by the Trial Chamber's fundamental conviction that the Security Council, in persistently condemning the widespread violations of international humanitarian law committed throughout the conflict in Bosnia and Herzegovina and, indeed, in establishing the International Tribunal to prosecute and punish such violations, did not consider that the protection of the whole corpus of international humanitarian law could be denied to particular groups of individuals on the basis of the provisions of domestic citizenship legislation. The International Tribunal must, therefore, take a broad and principled approach to the application of the basic norms of international humanitarian law, norms which are enunciated in the four Geneva Conventions. In particular, all of those individuals who took no active part in hostilities and yet found themselves engulfed in the horror and violence of war should not be denied the protection of the Fourth Geneva Convention, which constitutes the very basis of the law concerned with such persons.
>
> 276. The Trial Chamber does not consider it necessary to discuss at length in the present context the development of the law of the Third Geneva Convention relating to prisoners of war, for even if none of the victims can be viewed as prisoners of war, there is no gap between the Geneva Conventions and they must, therefore, be considered protected civilians, along with the other detainees. This finding does not prejudice the later discussion of whether the authorities of Bosnia and Herzegovina were legitimately entitled to detain all of these civilians.

Delalić et al. Appeals Judgement

4.2.379 The Trial Chamber's findings in *Delalić et al.* were upheld on appeal. The Appeals Chamber affirmed that a person "may be accorded protected person status, notwithstanding the fact that he is of the same nationality as his captors" (paras. 52–84, *Delalić et al. Appeals Judgement*). The nationality of the victims for the purposes of the application of the 4th Geneva Convention should not be determined on the basis of formal national characteristics or domestic laws but rather nationality should take into account the differing ethnicities of the victims and the perpetrators and their bonds with a foreign intervening state.

Article: Brown, Bartram S., "Nationality and Internationality in International Humanitarian Law," 34 *Stanford Journal of International Law*. 347 (1998).

Aleksovski Trial Judgement

4.2.380 In this case, the majority of the Trial Chamber (Judges Vohrah and Nieto-Navia) found Zlatko Aleksovski not guilty of the two counts of grave breaches of the 1949 Geneva Conventions, charged under Article 2 of the Statute of the Tribunal, on the grounds that it had not been proved that the conflict in question was international and that the victims in question were "protected persons" within the meaning of the 1949 Geneva Conventions. Judge Rodrigues, the Presiding Judge, dissented on this point.

4.2.381 The majority posed the question "whether the acts of the HVO can be imputed to the Government of Croatia" to render the conflict an international armed conflict between Bosnia and Herzegovina and Croatia. The majority followed the *Tadić* Trial Chamber majority (*Tadić Opinion and Judgement*) in relying on the test of "effective control" formulated by the ICJ in the *Nicaragua* case for the imputability of acts of a group of individuals to a State:

> In the view of the majority of the Trial Chamber, there must be some evidence of the control, direction or command of the State that is sufficiently strong to impute the rebel force's acts to it. The requisite degree of control depends on the circumstances of each case.

4.2.382 Applying the test to Croatia as State and the HVO as "rebel force," the majority found that the test was not satisfied (see para. 27)

4.2.383 It should be noted that this finding contradicts the *Rajić Rule 61 Decision* in which the Trial Chamber found that the HVO was *de facto* an agent of Croatia.

4.2.384 The majority also found that the victims in the indictment were not "protected persons" within the meaning of the Geneva Conventions and Article 2 of the Statute (paras. 28–35).

4.2.385 Judge Rodrigues, on the other hand, held that Article 2 *did* apply. He argued, first, that the element of internationality that derives from Article 2 common to the Geneva Conventions did not need to be incorporated into Article 2 of the ICTY Statute. Article 2 of the Statute is in this sense *autonomous* (see paras. 28–49) and can be applied without determining the nature of the conflict. This approximates to the approach taken in the *Tadić Jurisdiction Decision* (see above, 4.2.323 *et seq.*).

4.2.386 Second, Judge Rodrigues argued that, even if internationality were required for Article 2 to apply, the evidence adduced in the trial sufficed to prove the internationality of the conflict beyond a reasonable doubt (para. 15). To reach this conclusion, Judge Rodrigues held that many Bosnian Croats, in particular the accused, could be considered Croatian nationals; thus Bosnian victims in their hands would be in the hands of a party to the conflict or occupying power of which they were not nationals (Article 4 of the 4th Geneva Convention). Second, Croatia funded the HVO and involved itself in its military activities. This meant that Croatia was effectively at war with Bosnia and Herzegovina and thus the conflict in question was international.

4.2.387 Third, Judge Rodrigues considered that the conflict in the former Yugoslavia should in any event be seen *in its entirety* as one large-scale international armed conflict between FRY, Croatia and Bosnia and Herzegovina. This was the approach taken by Judge Li in his separate opinion to the *Tadić Jurisdiction Appeals Decision*, by the Commission of Experts, by the United States as *amicus curiae* and by several learned authors. Moreover it was supported by the consideration that the rules of international humanitarian law should apply to all victims equally "across the board" (see paras. 24–27 of Judge Rodrigues' dissenting opinion).

Aleksovski Appeals Judgement

4.2.388 In this Judgement, the Appeals Chamber took two approaches to the issue of "protected persons." First, it agreed with the Prosecutor that, "if it is established that the conflict was international by reason of Croatia's participation [in the war in Bosnia and Herzegovina], it follows that the Bosnian Muslim victims were in the hands of a party to the conflict, Croatia, of which they were not nationals and that, therefore, Article 4 of Geneva Convention IV is applicable" (para. 150).

4.2.389 This does not, however, necessarily follow. A conflict in State X (Bosnia and Herzegovina) can be international due to the intervention of another State, State Y (Croatia), but unless the victims are in the hands of State Y, or agents of State Y (Bosnian Croats), they would not be "protected." Thus if it were proved that Crotia intervened in the conflict in Bosnia, but it were *not* proved that Bosnian Croats acted as agents of Croatia, then Bosnians in the hands of Bosnian Croats would not be "protected persons" for the purposes of the 4th Geneva Convention and Article 2 of the ICTY Statute.

4.2.390 Second, the Appeals Chamber also confirmed the finding in the *Tadić Appeals Judgement*, "that, in certain circumstances, Article 4 [of Geneva Convention IV] may be given a wider construction so that a person may be accorded protected status notwithstanding the fact that he is of the same nationality as his captors" (para. 151).

4.2.391 The Chamber did not, however, reverse the Trial Chamber's findings on this point, since the crimes were already covered by the conviction under Article 3 of the Statute.

Blaškić Trial Judgement

4.2.392 Ruling on this issue for the purposes of determining whether ICTY Article 2 could apply or not, the Trial Chamber in the *Blaškić Trial Judgement* applied the principle set out by the Appeals Chamber in the *Tadić Appeals Judgement*, namely that ethnicity "may be regarded as a decisive factor in determining to which nation he owes his allegiance and may thus serve to establish the status of the victims as protected persons":

127. ... In an inter-ethnic armed conflict, a person's ethnic background may be regarded as a decisive factor in determining to which nation he owes his allegiance and may thus serve to establish the status of the victims as protected persons. The Trial Chamber considers that this is so in this instance.

128. ... The disintegration of Yugoslavia occurred along "ethnic" lines. Ethnicity became more important than nationality in determining loyalties or commitments. One historian, a Defence witness, stated that Yugoslavia was a multi-ethnic State in which each of the nations that had formed had followed differing "ideologies": Orthodox, Catholic or Muslim. The witness made reference to the ethnic principle and the historic principle whereby even 150 years ago Serbia and Croatia considered that they had a right to Bosnia. For their part, the Bosnians regarded themselves as a distinct people.

129. These trends became manifest in 1990 during the first multi-party elections held in Yugoslavia. The parties with nationalist leanings won in each constitutive republic. In Bosnia-Herzegovina, the dominant parties were the SDS, the SDA and the HDZ.

130. Croatia's policy towards the Bosnian Croats placed more emphasis on their ethnic background than on their nationality. A provision adopted by the Republic of Croatia gave to all members of the Croatian nation the right to citizenship.... Another law authorised all Croats to vote in the elections in Croatia, thus allowing the Bosnian Croats with Bosnian nationality to vote in the parliamentary elections in the Republic of Croatia. The "Agreement on Friendship and Co-operation between the Republic of Bosnia-Herzegovina and the Republic of Croatia" stipulated that the two republics would reciprocally authorise their citizens to obtain dual nationality. The Trial Chamber deems that all these texts were used by Croatia to steer the Croats of Bosnia-Herzegovina towards Croatia and contributed to the fact that the people identified more with ethnicity than formal nationality when expressing their loyalty. Approximately 10% of the representatives in the Sabor came from the diaspora. Two Bosnian Croat members of the HVO were elected to the Croatian parliament ...

...

133. ... Keeping in mind the sense in which the notion of nationality was used in the former Yugoslavia and more specifically in central Bosnia, the Trial Chamber is of the opinion that the Bosnian Muslim victims in the hands of the HVO must be considered as protected persons within the meaning of the Geneva Conventions.

4.2.393 The Trial Chamber also found that certain victims referred to in the indictment were "protected persons" under the 3rd Geneva Convention (Prisoners-of-War) (see para. 147 of the Judgement).

Kordić and Čerkez Trial Judgement

4.2.394 Applying the decisions of the Appeals Chamber in *Tadić, Aleksovski and Čelebići*, the Trial Chamber found that Bosnian Muslim victims were in the hands of a party to the conflict, namely Bosnian Croats, to whom they owed no allegiance (para. 154).

4.2.395 The Trial Chamber rejected two specific arguments raised by the Defence for both accused. Firstly, the Defence argued that by reason of Article 4(2) of the 4th Geneva Convention, the Bosnian Muslims were not protected persons, since Croatia and Bosnia and Herzegovina were co-belligerents in a conflict with the Serbs. The Chamber held that as the Indictment was concerned not with a conflict between Bosnia and Herzegovina and Croatia on the one hand, and the Serbs on the other, but with a conflict between Bosnian Croats and Bosnian Muslims in Bosnia and Herzegovina, in respect of that conflict, Bosnia and Herzegovina and Croatia were clearly not co-belligerents (paras. 156–157).

4.2.396 Secondly, the Defence argued that the finding that Bosnian Muslims were protected persons in that they were in the hands of a party to the conflict, Croatia, of which they were not nationals, gave rise to unequal treatment, in that Bosnian Croat victims would not, on the basis of that finding, qualify as protected persons, since there would be no corresponding foreign State as captor.

4.2.397 The Trial Chamber held that under the "allegiance test" no unequal treatment would arise since, in the same way that Bosnian Muslims owed no allegiance to Bosnian Croats, Bosnian Croats owed no allegiance to Bosnian Muslims.

Protected Property/Occupation

4.2.398 The "grave breaches" regime of the Geneva Conventions, and hence Article 2 of the ICTY Statute, protects property as well as persons, but the former only in the event of an occupation. Due to the nature of the crimes being dealt with by the Tribunal, i.e. involving for the most part extremely serious crimes against the person, the question of protected property has not frequently arisen. Where certain types of property have been unlawfully targeted or confiscated, the Prosecutor has usually chosen to prosecute these crimes under Article 3 of the Statute, e.g. Article 3(b) ("*Wanton destruction of cities, towns, etc.*"), (d) ("*seizure or, destruction or wilful damage done to institutions dedicated to religion, charity and education . . . .*"), or (e) ("*plunder of public or private property*").

4.2.399 In its *Rajić Rule 61 Decision*, the Trial Chamber concluded that the property of individuals living in the village of Stupni Do, in Bosnia-Herzegovina, was "protected" by the Geneva Conventions, given the control exercised over the area by Croatia, a foreign State (paras. 38–42):

> 42. The Trial Chamber has held that the Bosnian Croats controlled the territory surrounding the village of Stupni Do and that Croatia may be regarded as being in control of this area. Thus, when Stupni Do was overrun by HVO forces, the property of the Bosnian village came under the control of Croatia, in an international conflict. The Trial Chamber therefore finds that the property of Stupni Do became protected property for the purposes of the grave breaches provisions of Geneva Convention IV. . . .

4.2.400 The Trial Chamber ruling in the *Blaškić Trial Judgement* followed this reasoning in finding that there was "protected property" for the purposes of the commission of grave breaches of the Geneva Conventions (see paras. 148–150).

Articles:

Scharf, Michael P., "International Decisions: *Prosecutor v. Tadi_*," 91(4) *American Journal of International Law* (October 1997).

Meron, Theordor, "Classification of Armed Conflict in the Former Yugoslavia: Nicaragua's Fallout," 92(2) *American Journal of International Law* 236 (April 1998).

Brown, Bartram S., "Nationality and Internationality in International Humanitarian Law," 34(2) *Stanford Journal of International Law* 347–406 (1998).

Constituent Offences

4.2.401 Having determined whether the jurisdictional requirements are met for ICTY Article 2 to apply, namely international armed conflict and the status of the persons or property affected as "protected," a Trial Chamber applying Article 2 must then proceed to determine whether the constituent offences have been committed. The definitions of these crimes are dealt with here and in the "Elements" section.

Actus Reus and Mens Rea

4.2.402 In the *Blaškić Trial Judgement*, the Chamber stated that "the *mens rea* constituting all the violations of Article 2 of the Statute *includes both guilty intent and recklessness which may be likened to serious criminal negligence*" (para. 152, emphasis added).

4.2.403 This reference to negligence is, however, somewhat surprising. One would not ordinarily expect an accused who had been merely negligent, or even seriously negligent, to be convicted by the ICTY of a "serious violation of international humanitarian law." The Chamber may have been thinking here of liability under Article 7(3) of the ICTY Statute, which may be seen as creating liability on the part of a commander for negligence under certain circumstances. But this is a separate issue from the requisite *mens rea* for liability under Article 2 of the Statute, and it is submitted that negligence of any sort would not suffice. Only intention or, under certain circumstances, recklessness should be sufficient to ground a change for a "grave breach" of the Geneva Conventions. In this regard, it is worth nothing that Article 30(1) ("Mental Element") of the Rome Statute for the ICC provides that, "Unless otherwise provided, a person shall be criminally responsible and liable for punishment for a crime within the jurisdiction of the Court *only if the material elements are committed with intent and knowledge*" (emphasis added). Of course, the wording, "unless otherwise provided" would cover the exception for command responsibility which is in ICTY Article 7(3)/ICTR Article 6(3) and ICC Article 28.

Wilful Killing

4.2.404 For a conviction for wilful killing, it must be proved that the death of the victim was the result of the actions of the accused and that the accused intended to cause death or serious bodily injury to the victim in reckless disregard of human life (see *Delalić et al. Trial Judgement*, para. 439 and *Blaškić Trial Judgement*, para. 153).

4.2.405 See also the *Kordić and Čerkez Trial Judgement*, para. 229, in which the Chamber, applying the definitions set out in the *Delalić et al., Blaskić* and *Tadić* cases, set out the *actus reus* of wilful killing as follows:

— The physical act necessary for the offence is the death of a victim as a result of the actions or omissions of the accused.
— That the conduct of the accused must be a *substantial cause* of the death of the victim; and
— The victim was a "protected person."

4.2.406 The Chamber held that the *mens rea* requirement was as follows:

— That the accused had the intent to kill, or to inflict serious bodily injury in reckless disregard of human life.

Inhuman Treatment

4.2.407 Inhuman treatment has been defined (para. 543 of the *Delalić et al. Trial Judgement*, affirmed in paras. 154–155 of the *Blaškić Trial Judgement*, and para. 256 of the *Kordić and Čerkez Trial Judgement*, where the Chamber held that "injuries, inhuman treatment of detainees, and the use of persons as human shields" may be characterised as "inhuman treatment"):

an intentional act or omission, that is an act which, judged objectively, is deliberate and not accidental, which causes serious mental harm or physical suffering or injury or constitutes a serious attack on human dignity [. . .]. Thus, inhuman treatment is intentional treatment which does not conform with the fundamental principle of humanity, and forms the umbrella under which the remainder of the listed "grave breaches" in the Conventions fall. Hence, acts characterised in the Conventions and Commentaries as inhuman, or which are inconsistent with the principle of humanity, constitute examples of actions that can be characterised as inhuman treatment.

4.2.408 The Trial Chamber, in the *Delalić et al. Trial Judgement*, also suggested a negative definition of inhuman treatment, namely that inhuman treatment is treatment which causes severe mental or physical suffering *but which falls short of*, or lacks one of the elements of, torture (e.g., being done for prohibited purpose or with official sanction) (para. 542). The Chamber added that whether given conduct constitutes inhuman treatment is ultimately a question of fact.

4.2.409 The victim of the war crime of an "inhuman act" need not be living since certain acts against a dead body offend philosophical and religious notions of respect for the human being upon death. Thus, in *Trial of Max Schmid* (cited in the *Tadić Opinion and Judgement*, para. 748), the accused was convicted of having wilfully, deliberately, and wrongfully participated in the maltreatment of a dead prisoner of war by mutilating his corpse and denying him an honourable burial.

4.2.410 The Trial Chamber has entered a number of convictions for inhuman treatment in cases in which the defendant has also been convicted for cruel treatment (see *Delalić et al. Trial Judgement*, paras. 1052–1059), as well as in cases in they were convicted for the wilful infliction of great suffering or causing serious physical or mental injury (see *Delalić et al. Trial Judgement*, paras. 1015–1018, 1035–1040), all offences arising out of the same facts.

4.2.411 ICTY case-law establishes that inhuman treatment is synonymous with "cruel treatment" (a prohibition contained in common article 3 and prosecuted under Article 3 of the ICTY Statute). See "Elements of the Offences" section, 4.2.570 *et seq*.

Torture

4.2.412 See the definition of torture in the "Elements of the Offences" section, 4.2.542 *et seq*.

Biological Experiments

4.2.413 This offence is a form of inhuman treatment and it appears in Article 50 of the 1st Geneva Convention, Article 52 of the 2nd Geneva Convention, Article 140 of the 3rd Geneva Convention and Article 147 of the 4th Geneva Convention under the common formulation "torture or inhuman treatment, including biological experiments."

4.2.414 The ICTY has not yet defined the elements of this crime.

Wilfully Causing Great Suffering or Serious Injury to Body or Health

4.2.415 This offence is "an intentional act or omission consisting of causing great suffering or serious injury to body or health, including mental health. This category of offences includes those acts which do not fulfil the conditions set for the characterisation of torture, even though acts of torture may also fit the definition given" (*Blaškić Trial Judgement*, para. 156, citing in support the *Delalić et al. Trial Judgement*, para. 511).

4.2.416 See also *Kordić and Čerkez Trial Judgement*, para. 245, in which the Chamber distinguished "wilfully causing great suffering . . ." from inhuman treatment, in that "wilfully causing great suffering . . ." requires a showing of serious mental or physical injury. Accordingly, acts where the resultant harm relates solely to an individual's human dignity are not included in within the offence.

Extensive Destruction of Property

4.2.417 An occupying Power is prohibited from destroying movable and non-movable property except where such destruction is made absolutely necessary by military operations. To constitute a grave breach, the destruction must be extensive, unlawful and wanton, as well as being unjustified by military necessity. The notion of "extensive" is evaluated according to the facts of the case—a single act, such as the destruction of a hospital, may suffice to characterise an offence under this count. See para. 157 of the *Blaškić Trial Judgement*.

4.2.418 See also the *Kordić and Čerkez Trial Judgement*, paras. 335–341. The Chamber concluded that the crime of extensive destruction of property as a grave breach consisted of the following elements:

(i) Where the property destroyed is of a type accorded general protection under the Geneva Conventions of 1949, regardless of whether or not it is situated in occupied territory; and the perpetrator acted with the intent to destroy the property in question or in reckless disregard of the likelihood of its destruction; or

(ii) Where the property destroyed is accorded protection under the Genva Conventions, on account of its location in occupied territory; and the destruction occurs on a large scale; and

(iii) The destruction is not justified by military necessity; and the perpetrator acted with the intent to destroy the property in question in reckless disregard of the likelihood of its destruction.

Compelling POWs or a Civilian to Serve in the Forces of a Hostile Power

4.2.419 The US Military Tribunal operating under Control Council Law No. 10 held in the *Ministries* Case (see *In re von Weizsaecker et al.*, US Military Tribunal at Nuremberg, 14 April 1949, Annual Digest and Reports of Public International Law Cases, vol.16, 1955) that while it is not illegal to recruit prisoners of war who volunteer to fight against their own country, "pressure or coercion to compel such persons to enter into the armed services obviously violates international law."

4.2.420 The ICTY has not yet defined the elements of this crime.

Wilfully Depriving POWs or Civilians of the Rights of Fair and Regular Trial

4.2.421 This provision covers grave breaches that are common to the 3rd Geneva Convention (Article 130) and the 4th Geneva Convention (Article 147).

4.2.422 Neither the ICTY nor the ICTR have yet defined the elements of this crime (this crime is covered in part by Article 4(g) of the ICTR Statute).

Unlawful Confinement of Civilians

4.2.423 See also the discussion of this offence in the "Elements of the Offences" section, 4.2.574.

4.2.424 Zdravko Mucić, as commander of Čelebići camp, was convicted of this offence in the *Delalić et al. Trial Judgement* (see paras. 1125–1145). In finding him guilty, the Trial Chamber held that:

- Certain civilians confined in Čelebići camp could arguably be considered lawfully detained because they had arms and had participated in defending their villages (para. 1131);
- Other civilians, however, clearly could not be lawfully detained, for example a mother of two who was detained in the camp as a hostage (para. 1132);
- Some civilians were simply detained because they were Serbs, and "the mere fact that a person is a national of, or aligned with, an enemy party cannot be considered as threatening the security of

the opposing party where he is living, and is not, therefore, a valid reason for interning him" (para. 1134);
- The confinement of civilians was unlawful, moreover, because there was non-compliance with the requirements of the 4th Geneva Convention (para. 1142), although the further requirements relating to occupation did not need to be met as there was no occupation in this case (para. 578).

See also the *Kordić and Čerkez Trial Judgement*, paras. 280–291, and *Delalić et al. Appeals Judgement*, para. 322.

4.2.425 The Appeals Chamber in the *Delalić et al. Appeals Judgement* (para. 378) concluded that the confinement of civilians is unlawful in the following circumstances:

(i) when a civilian or civilians have been detained in contravention of Article 42 of the 4th Geneva Convention, *ie*, they are detained without reasonable grounds for believing that the security of the Detaining power makes it absolutely necessary; and
(ii) where the procedural safeguards required by Article 43 of 4th Geneva Convention are not complied with in respect of detained civilians, even where their initial detention may have been justified.

Unlawful Transfer or Deportation of Civilians

4.2.426 This offence is derived directly from Article 147 of the Geneva Convention IV (1949).

4.2.427 The ICTY has not yet defined the elements of the crime, although it has been considered, in particular in the *Krstić Trial Judgement* (see above, 4.2.255).

Taking Civilians Hostage

4.2.428 Civilian hostages "are persons unlawfully deprived of their freedom, often arbitrarily and sometimes under threat of death" (para. 158, *Blaškić Trial Judgement*). Since detention may be lawful under certain circumstances—for example, when carried out for the detainee's own safety—to secure a conviction the prosecution must also prove that, at the time of the detention, the person was detained "in order to obtain a concession or gain an advantage" (*ibid*). See also the *Kordić and Čerkez Trial Judgement*, where the Trial Chamber, following the *Blaškić Trial Judgement*, held that "an individual commits the offence of taking civilians as hostage when he threatens to subject civilians, who are unlawfully detained, to inhuman treatment or death as a means of achieving the fulfilment of a condition" (para. 314).

4.2.429 As Trial Chamber I noted in its *Decision on the Defence Motion to dismiss the Indictment based upon Defects thereof (vagueness/Lack of adequate Notice of Charges)* rendered in *Blaškić* on 4 April 1997, hostage-taking may fall under both ICTY Article 2(h), as a grave breach of the Geneva Conventions, and under Article 3(1)(b) common to the Geneva Conventions and thus, according to the *Tadić Jurisdiction Appeals Decision*, under ICTY Article 3. Since the former only applies to hostage-taking of *civilians*, whereas common Article 3's prohibition is broader, the Chamber considered that the Prosecutor should specify in the indictment to which form of hostage-taking reference was being made.

4.2.430

**ICTY
Article 3
Violations of the Laws or Customs of War**

The International Tribunal shall have the power to prosecute persons violating the laws or customs of war. Such violations shall include, but not be limited to:
(a) employment of poisonous weapons or other weapons calculated to cause unnecessary suffering;
(b) wanton destruction of cities, towns or villages, or devastation not justified by military necessity;
(c) attack, or bombardment, by whatever means, of undefended towns, villages, dwellings, or buildings;
(d) seizure of, destruction or wilful damage done to institutions dedicated to religion, charity and education, the arts and sciences, historic monuments and works of art and science;
(e) plunder of public or private property.

Background

4.2.431 The Secretary-General noted in his Report on the ICTY Statute (S/25704, 3 May 1993) that Article 3 is based on the 1907 Hague Conventions (IV) Respecting the Laws and Customs of War on Land and the Regulations annexed thereto (para. 41). As noted above, "Hague Law" concerns "the means and methods of warfare," in contrast to "Geneva Law" (Article 2 above), which concerns the treatment of non-combatants. There may, however, be some overlap between the two (para. 43, *Ibid*). Indeed, the distinction between Hague Law and Geneva Law has become more fluid since Additional Protocol I of 1977 to the Geneva Conventions of 1949 codified a number of aspects of Hague Law.

4.2.432 The Secretary-General stated in his Report that:

> many of the provisions contained in the Hague Regulations, although innovative at the time of their adoption were, by 1939, recognised by all civilised nations and were regarded as being declaratory of the laws or customs of war. The Nuremberg Tribunal also recognised that war crimes defined in article 6(b) of the Nuremberg Charter were already recognised as war crimes under international law, and covered in the Hague Regulations, for which guilty individuals were punishable (para. 42).

4.2.433 Article 6(b) of the Nuremberg Charter defined war crimes as:

> (b) *WAR CRIMES:* namely, violations of the laws or customs of war. Such violations shall include, but not be limited to, murder, ill-treatment or deportation to slave labor or for any other purpose of civilian population of or in occupied territory, murder or ill-treatment of prisoners of war or persons on

the seas, killing of hostages, plunder of public or private property, wanton destruction of cities, towns or villages, or devastation not justified by military necessity.

4.2.434 Thus the Hague rules of customary law, as interpreted and applied at Nuremberg, form the basis for Article 3 of the Statute.

4.2.435 Like ICTY Article 2, ICTY Article 3 can only apply where there is an armed conflict (although not necessarily an *international* armed conflict—see below, 4.2.454). See ICTY Article 2 for the criteria for determining the existence of an armed conflict (4.2.307 *et seq.*).

Security Council Interpretation of Article 3

4.2.436 The Security Council, when adopting the ICTY Statute, indicated that Article 3 would encompass common article 3 and Additional Protocol II, both of which apply to internal armed conflicts. Mrs. Madeleine Albright, the then Permanent Representative of the United States to the United Nations, stated in the Security Council following the adoption of resolution 827 establishing the ICTY, that common article 3 and Additional Protocol II of 1977 came within ICTY Article 3, since they formed part of the law in force in the former Yugoslavia:

> While the Council has adopted the Statute for the Tribunal as proposed in that report, the members of the Council have recognised that the Statute raises several technical issues that can be addressed through interpretative Statements.
>
> In particular, we understand that other members of the Council share our view regarding the following clarifications related to the Statute.
>
> Firstly, it is understood that the "laws or customs of war" referred to in Article 3 include all obligations under humanitarian law agreements in force in the territory of the former Yugoslavia at the time the acts were committed, including common article 3 of the 1949 Geneva Conventions, and the 1977 Additional Protocols to these Conventions. (UN Doc. S/PV.3217, at 15 (25 May 1993.))

4.2.437 The English and French Permanent Representatives shared this position.

4.2.438 Note that Article 4 of the ICTR Statute specifically covers *violations of Article 3 common to the Geneva Conventions and of Additional Protocol II* (see 4.2.497 *et seq.*, below).

General *Mens Rea* Requirement

4.2.439 In the *Blaškić Trial Judgement*, the Chamber said that the general *mens rea* requirement under Article 3 of the ICTY Statute was the same as for Article 2, namely "intentionality of the acts or omissions, a concept containing both guilty intent and recklessness [that may be likened to] to serious criminal negligence" (para. 179). As stated above (4.2.402), it is suspect to consider that "serious criminal negligence" would suffice to convict an accused of serious violations of international humanitarian law.

4.2.440 The Tribunal has also made clear that Article 3 does not contain a general requirement of discriminatory intent, nor is it required that the accused be "motivated by a contempt towards other persons' dignity in [a] racial, religious, social, sexual or other discriminatory sense" (*Aleksovski Appeals Judgement*, paras. 17–28).

4.2.441 For the specific *actus reus* and *mens rea* requirements of each crime, see below.

Common Article 3 Falling Within ICTY Article 3

4.2.442 The defence in *Kvočka et al.* argued that common article 3 could not be included within Article 3 of the ICTY Statute on the grounds, *inter alia*, that ICTY Article 2 deals with "Geneva-type law," which is concerned with victims, whereas ICTY Article 3 deals with "Hague law" which is concerned with behaviour in war. Common article 3, being a victim-orientated type of offence, and being part of the Geneva Conventions, would therefore appropriately belong in Article 2 of the Statute, and not Article 3.

4.2.443 The Trial Chamber rejected this submission in its *Decision on Preliminary Motions filed by Mlađo Radić and Miroslav Kvočka* of 1 April 1999, following its own ruling in the *Kordić Jurisdiction Decision* of 2 March 1999 (in which the same arguments had been raised), and based on the approach taken by the Appeals Chamber to common article 3 and article 3 of the Statute in the *Tadić Jurisdiction Appeals Decision* (see below).

4.2.444 The finding that common article 3 falls within Article 3 of the ICTY Statute was also confirmed in the *Delalić et al. Appeals Judgement* (para. 136) and in the *Foča Trial Judgement* (para. 406).

Individual Criminal Responsibility for Violations of Common Article 3

4.2.445 In several decisions, the Chambers have confirmed that the perpetrator of violations of common article 3 incurs individual criminal responsibility for those violations; a finding that is in any event implied in the finding that violations of common Article 3 may be prosecuted under Article 3 of the ICTY Statute. See paras. 153–174 of the *Delalić et al. Appeals Judgement*.

Article 3 Not Confined to "Hague Law"

4.2.446 In the *Delalić et al. Trial Judgement*, the Trial Chamber stated that Article 3 is not limited to offences under "Hague Law" (para. 278). The defence had argued "that the listed offences in Article 3 of the Statute are illustrative of offences under 'Hague law'—that is the laws enunciated in the 1907 Hague Convention (IV) and annexed Regulations—which relates to the conduct of hostilities, not to the protection of victims taking no active part in the fighting. The defence submitted that if the Security Council had intended to include certain provisions of "Geneva law"—such as common article 3—within Article 3 of the Statute, it would have done so explicitly" (para. 289). The Chamber rejected this argument (see paras. 295–306).

4.2.447 This was confirmed in the *Decision on the Joint Defence Motion to Dismiss the Amended Indictment for lack of jurisdiction based on the limited jurisdictional reach of Articles 2 and 3* rendered by the Trial Chamber in *Kordić and Čerkez* on 2 March 1999.

Residual Nature of Article 3

4.2.448 In the *Tadić Jurisdiction Appeals Decision*, the Appeals Chamber (Judge Li dissenting, see 4.2.459, below) held that Article 3 was of a residual nature:

> 87. ... Article 3 may be taken to cover *all violations* of international humanitarian law other than the "grave breaches" of the four Geneva Conventions falling under Article 2 ...
>
> 91. Article 3 thus confers on the International Tribunal jurisdiction over *any* serious offence against international humanitarian law not covered by Article 2, 4 or 5. Article 3 is a fundamental provision laying down that any "serious violation of international humanitarian law" must be prosecuted by the International Tribunal. In other words, Article 3 functions as a residual clause designed to ensure that no serious violation of international humanitarian law is taken away from the jurisdiction of the International Tribunal. Article 3 aims to make such jurisdiction watertight and inescapable.
>
> 92. ... Thus, if correctly interpreted, Article 3 fully realises the primary purpose of the establishment of the International Tribunal, that is, not to leave unpunished any person guilty of any such serious violation, whatever the context within which it may have been committed.

4.2.449 This was confirmed in the *Foča Trial Judgement* (para. 401).

4.2.450 In his Separate Opinion to the *Tadić Jurisdiction Appeals Decision*, Judge Sidhwa stated in respect of Article 3:

> 113.... What are the laws of war? ... They would include (a) treaties, conventions, agreements, declarations and protocols (b) constitutions and statutes of international war crimes tribunals and (c) decisions of international judicial tribunals. The 1907 Hague Convention (IV) respecting the Laws and Customs of War on Land and the Regulations annexed to it, the four Geneva Conventions of 1949 and the two Additional Protocols I and II, the decision of the Nürnberg and Tokyo Tribunals and a host of international declarations, treaties, conventions and rules entered into by States ... all constitute laws of war. I would exclude national manuals of military law, because they do not have an international character, although they may have a function in providing evidence of the law.
>
> 114. The customs of war are those which arise out of State practices extending over a period of time, coupled with *opinio juris*. Where a certain practice followed by a number of States in the international community over long use or a period of time has established a status as to be regarded by them as legally obligatory or binding, an international custom develops. Though this is the normal interpretation, State practices may consist of treaties, decisions of international and national courts, national legislation, diplomatic correspondence, practice of international organisations ... , policy statements, official manuals on legal questions (e.g. manuals of military law), executive decisions and practices, orders to the armed forces, etc., and comments by governments on drafts of the International Law Commission. ...
>
> 115. Abrupt development of customary law is not unusual. In the field of international human rights law, convention and custom have sometimes sprung up

almost instantaneously, leading to almost overlapping developments in conventional and customary law.

116..... A good part of the conventional laws of war contain customary law, but not all of customary law is embodied in conventional law. Likewise, a good part of the conventional laws of war is treated as customary international law, but not all. Here, I think, the dichotomy arises. If States are parties to certain conventions dealing with laws of war, they are bound both favourably and unfavourably to the same, and should they be in armed conflict, it should matter little whether the conventions have reached the customary threshold, for they are bound by the conventions and, having knowledge of them, the rule of *nullum crimen sine lege* should not prevail. Thus, since both laws of war and customs of war are covered, not jointly but severally, the question that the laws of war must be reinforced by custom, or that customs of war must be embodied in conventions, does not arise. Both, however, must cover violations of international humanitarian law, that being the grund norm under Article 1 of the Statute.

4.2.451 The implication that the ICTY could apply laws of war applicable on the territory of the former Yugoslavia that had not attained customary status would conflict with the often-cited statement of the Secretary-General in his Report on the ICTY Statute that, "the application of the principle *nullum crimen sine lege* requires that the international tribunal should apply rules of international humanitarian law *which are beyond any doubt part of customary law* so that the problem of adherence of some but not all States to specific conventions does not arise. This would appear to be particularly important in the context of an international tribunal prosecuting persons responsible for serious violations of international humanitarian law" (para. 34, emphasis added). The general view seems to be that the ICTY, and ICTR, should only apply their Statutes to the extent that the provisions reflect customary law.

Conditions for the Application of Article 3

4.2.452 The Appeals Chamber, Judge Li dissenting, in the *Tadić Jurisdiction Appeals Decision*, laid down four conditions for Article 3 to apply (para. 94):

> (i) the violation must constitute an infringement of a rule of international humanitarian law;
>
> (ii) the rule must be customary in nature or, if it belongs to treaty law, the required conditions must be met . . .;
>
> (iii) the violation must be "serious," that is to say, it must constitute a breach of a rule protecting important values, and the breach must involve grave consequences for the victim. . . .
>
> (iv) the violation of the rule must entail, under customary or conventional law, the individual criminal responsibility of the person breaching the rule.
>
> It follows that it does not matter whether the "serious violation" has occurred within the context of an international or an internal armed conflict, as long as the requirements set out above are met.

4.2.453 Judge Li dissented from the Chamber's ruling that, subject to these conditions, Article 3 could be deemed to cover *all* serious violations of international humanitarian law not captured by the other articles of the Statute (see 4.2.459 below).

Applicability of Article 3 to Internal Conflict

4.2.454 It follows from the *Tadić Jurisdiction Appeals Decision* that Article 3 could apply to *internal* armed conflicts. Thus the majority view in the *Tadić Jurisdiction Appeals Decision* was that:

> 127. . . . it cannot be denied that customary rules have developed to govern internal strife. These rules . . . cover such areas as protection of civilians from hostilities, in particular from indiscriminate attacks, protection of civilian objects, in particular cultural property, protection of all those who do not (or no longer) take active part in hostilities, as well as prohibition of means of warfare proscribed in international armed conflicts and ban of certain methods of conducting hostilities.
>
> . . .
>
> 130. Furthermore, many elements of international practice show that States intend to criminalize serious breaches of customary rules and principles on internal conflicts. . . . [D]uring the Nigerian Civil War, both members of the Federal Army and rebels were brought before Nigerian courts and tried for violations of principles of international humanitarian law. . . ."

4.2.455 The Appeals Chamber then referred to other elements of international practice to demonstrate that serious breaches of customary rules and principles on internal conflicts entailed individual criminal responsibility. These elements included punitive sanctions in various military manuals and national legislation designed to implement the Geneva Conventions. The Chamber also found the requisite *opinio juris* accompanying this practice:

> 134. All of these factors confirm that customary international law imposes criminal liability for serious violations of common Article 3, as supplemented by other general principles and rules on the protection of victims of internal armed conflict, and for breaching certain fundamental principles and rules regarding means and methods of combat in civil strife.
>
> . . .
>
> 137. In the light of the intent of the Security Council and the logical and systematic interpretation of Article 3 as well as customary international law, the Appeals Chamber concludes that, under Article 3, the International Tribunal has jurisdiction over the acts alleged in the indictment, regardless of whether they occurred within an internal or an international armed conflict. Thus, to the extent that Appellant's challenge to jurisdiction under Article 3 is based on the nature of the underlying conflict, the motion must be denied.

4.2.456 Judge Li dissented from this view in a Separate Opinion to the *Tadić Jurisdiction Appeals Decision*, holding that Article 3 only applied in an international armed conflict.

4.2.457 The majority had reasoned that Article 3 applied irrespective of the nature of the armed conflict, because there were undoubtedly "laws or customs of war" which were applicable to both internal and international armed conflicts. Since Article 3 was open-ended and not exhaustive, such laws or customs of war could come within Article 3, even when not enumerated in (a) to (e) of Article 3. In Judge Li's opinion, however, Article 3 was limited to "Hague Law," which applied solely to international armed conflicts:

> 10. Now, I may turn to the difference of my opinion from that of the Decision. The Decision asserts that there has been development of customary international law to such an extent that all the various violations of the laws or customs of war as enumerated in lit. (a)–(e) of Article 3 of the Statute of this Tribunal are liable to be prosecuted and punished even if they are committed in internal armed conflict. I cannot agree with this assertion.
>
> 11. According to Article 38 I (b) of the Statute of the International Court of Justice, for the establishment of a customary rule of international law, two requirements must be met:
>
>   1. the existence of a general practice of States; and
>   2. the acceptance of the general practice as law by States.
>
> There is no proof of the fulfilment of these two requirements. On the contrary, the Decision itself admits that not all, but only "a number of rules and principles governing international armed conflicts have gradually been extended to apply to internal conflicts". . . .

4.2.458 The *Tadić Appeals* majority, however, never in fact addressed the question whether the *enumerated* provisions in Article 3 were violations whether committed in internal or international armed conflict. The majority had held, rather, that, ". . . under Article 3, the International Tribunal has jurisdiction *over the acts alleged in the indictment*, regardless of whether they occurred within an internal or international armed conflict" (para. 137, emphasis added). Crucially, the acts alleged in the indictment were all charged as *violations of common article 3*—an offence not specifically enumerated under Article 3 of the ICTY Statute. Indeed common article 3 to the Geneva Conventions is "Geneva Law," not "Hague Law" at all. The majority thus never stated that "Hague Law"—of which the enumerated provisions (a) to (e) are classic examples—applied irrespective of the nature of the conflict. Their notion depended on another consideration, namely that common article 3 fell within the ambit of Article 3 of the ICTY Statute.

4.2.459 Judge Li, however, also dissented from this position. He disagreed that ICTY Article 3 was a "residual" provision covering *all* serious violations of international humanitarian law not covered by Article 2, 4 and 5:

> 13. And I cannot agree with the Decision that Article 3 "confers on the International Tribunal jurisdiction over *any* serious offence[s] against international humanitarian law not covered by Article 2, 4 or 5" (Decision at p. 51, para. 91) and that "the conditions to be fulfilled for Article 3 to become applicable" (Decision at p. 52, para. 94) may be laid down by the Decision. The Decision on this question is in fact an unwarranted assumption of legislative power which has never been given to this Tribunal by any authority.

4.2.460 The fourfold requirements laid down in the *Tadić Jurisdiction Appeals Decision* (see above) were first applied in the *Tadić Opinion and Judgement* (see paras. 609–617), namely:

> (i) the violation must constitute an infringement of a rule of international humanitarian law;
>
> (ii) the rule must be customary in nature or, if it belongs to treaty law, the required conditions must be met;
>
> (iii) the violation must be "serious," that is to say, it must constitute a breach of a rule protecting important values, and the breach must involve grave consequences for the victim . . . ; and
>
> (iv) the violation of the rule must entail, under customary or conventional law, the individual criminal responsibility of the person breaching the rule.
>
> Those requirements apply to any and all laws or customs of war which Article 3 covers. (Para. 610, *Tadić Opinion and Judgement*.)

Common Article 3

4.2.461 Article 3 common to the Geneva Conventions of 1949 provides as follows:

> In the case of armed conflict not of an international character occurring in the territory of one of the High Contracting Parties, each Party to the conflict shall be bound to apply, as a minimum, the following provisions:
>
> 1. Persons taking no active part in the hostilities, including members of armed forces who have laid down their arms and those placed hors de combat by sickness, wounds, detention, or any other cause, shall in all circumstances be treated humanely, without any adverse distinction founded on race, colour, religion or faith, sex, birth or wealth, or any other similar criteria.
>
> To this end, the following acts are and shall remain prohibited at any time and in any place whatsoever with respect to the above-mentioned persons:
>
> > (a) Violence to life and person, in particular murder of all kinds, mutilation, cruel treatment and torture;
> >
> > (b) Taking of hostages;
> >
> > (c) Outrages upon personal dignity, in particular humiliating and degrading treatment;
> >
> > (d) The passing of sentences and the carrying out of executions without previous judgement pronounced by a regularly constituted court, affording all the judicial guarantees which are recognized as indispensable by civilized peoples.
>
> 2. The wounded and sick shall be collected and cared for.
>
> An impartial humanitarian body, such as the International Committee of the Red Cross, may offer its services to the Parties to the conflict.
>
> The Parties to the conflict should further endeavour to bring into force, by means of special agreements, all or part of the other provisions of the present Convention.
>
> The application of the preceding provisions shall not affect the legal status of the Parties to the conflict.

Customary Nature

4.2.462 Common article 3, which is generally accepted (with the exception of Judge Li's dissent in the *Tadić Jurisdiction Appeals Decision* (above)) as falling within ICTY Article 3, is considered to form a part of international customary law. See para. 609 of the *Tadić Opinion and Judgement*, and paras. 89, 98, 102, 116 and 134 of the *Tadić Jurisdiction Appeals Decision*, as well as para. 218 of the *Nicaragua* case in the I.C.J. (1986 I.C.J. Reports, 14). See also para. 316 of the *Delalić et al Trial Judgement*, paras. 164–174 of the *Blaškić Trial Judgement* and para. 608 of the ICTR's *Akayesu Trial Judgement*.

No Violation of *Nullum Crimen Sine Lege* in Applying Common Article 3

4.2.463 It follows from the customary nature of common Article 3 that its application does not violate *nullum crimen sine lege*. On this point, see paras. 311–318 of the *Delalić et al. Trial Judgement*. The Chamber held that there was no violation of *nullum crimen sine lege* in applying common article 3 since the relevant acts were already criminalized under the criminal code of the SFRY and Bosnia and Herzegovina ("each of the accused in the present case could have been held individually criminally responsible under their own national law for the crimes alleged in the Indictment," para. 312). Moreover the acts were in any event "criminal according to the general principles of law recognised by the community of nations," and hence, according to Article 15(2) of the International Covenant of Civil and Political Rights (*"Nothing in this article shall prejudice the trial and punishment of any person for any act or omission which, at the time when it was committed, was criminal according to the general principles of law recognized by the community of nations."*), an accused could be tried and punished for those acts without violating the principle of *nullum crimen sine lege:*

> 316. ... both the substantive prohibitions in common article 3 of the Geneva Conventions, and the provisions of the Hague Regulations, constitute rules of customary international law which may be applied by the International Tribunal to impose individual criminal responsibility for the offences alleged in the Indictment. As a consequence of the division of labour between Articles 2 and 3 of the Statute thus far articulated by the Appeals Chamber, such violations have been considered as falling within the scope of Article 3."

Common Article 3 Applies to Both Internal and International Armed Conflicts

4.2.464 Violations of common article 3 may be charged both in respect of internal armed conflict and international armed conflict, according to the *Decision on the Defendant's Motion to dismiss counts 13 and 14 of the indictment (lack of subject matter jurisdiction)* rendered by the Trial Chamber in *Furundžija* on 29 May 1998:

> 14. ... Common Article 3 is expressed in the Geneva Conventions as being applicable in the case of "armed conflict not of an international character," that is, internal armed conflicts. However, the Appeals Chamber found that in customary international law, the norms reflected in Common Article 3 applied in all situations of armed conflict. It cited the dicta in the *Case of Paramilitary*

Activities In and Around Nicaragua, whereby the International Court of Justice opined that the rules contained in Common Article 3 reflected "elementary considerations of humanity" applicable under customary international law to any armed conflict, whether it is of internal or international character. The Prosecution, which continues to insist the conflict was international, can rely on the rules of customary international law emerging from Common Article 3 and is therefore entitled to charge Anto Furundžija with violating Article 3 of the Statute."

4.2.465 This was also confirmed in the *Delalić et al. Appeals Judgement* (paras. 140–150).

4.2.466 A step in the reasoning to this conclusion seems, however, to have been left unspoken, namely: there has traditionally been *less* protection given to victims of internal armed conflicts than to victims of international armed conflicts. Therefore any measure of protection which is afforded to victims of an internal armed conflict is *a fortiori* afforded to victims of international armed conflict. This is the case of common Article 3.

4.2.467 The finding that common Article 3, which according to the Appeals Chamber falls within ICTY Article 3, also applies to international armed conflicts is, however, rendered superfluous in light of the Chamber's ruling on cumulative charging and the overlap of ICTY Articles 2 and 3. The result of that ruling is that convictions cannot be entered for violations of common Article 3 (and thus ICTY Article 3) when convictions for the same violations have, pursuant to a finding of international armed conflict, been entered under ICTY Article 2. Thus whenever there is an international armed conflict, convictions will be recorded under ICTY Article 2, and not ICTY Article 3, so it will never be necessary to apply common Article 3 to the situation of an international armed conflict.

4.2.468 Moreover, the position taken by the Chamber has no bearing on the question whether, in an internal armed conflict, common article 3 may be used in conjunction with Article 7(3) of the Statute to impose criminal responsibility. On this point, see the challenge by counsel in *Hadžihasanović, Alagić and Kubura* to the Tribunal's jurisdiction where only an internal conflict was alleged and where the sole basis of responsibility alleged was Article 7(3). See the briefs filed simultaneously by the Parties on 9 May 2002, 24 May 2002 and 31 May 2002. The Trial Chamber rejected the defence challenge in its Decision dated 12 November 2002, which the defence has appealed. See 6.2.106 *et seq.*, below.

Persons Taking No Active Part in the Hostilities

4.2.469 Those protected by Common Article 3 are *"persons taking no active part in the hostilities"* (Common Article 3, para. (1)). The Trial Chamber in the *Tadić Opinion and Judgement* considered the conditions for Common Article 3 to apply:

> 614. The rules contained in para. 1 of Common Article 3 proscribe a number of acts which: (i) are committed within the context of an armed conflict; (ii) have a close connection to the armed conflict; and (iii) are committed against persons taking no active part in hostilities. The first and second of these require-

ments have already been dealt with above. Consequently, the Trial Chamber turns to the third requirement.

615. The customary international humanitarian law regime governing conflicts not of an international character extends protection, from acts of murder, torture and other acts proscribed by Common Article 3, to:

> Persons taking no active part in the hostilities, including members of armed forces who have laid down their arms and those placed *hors de combat* by sickness, wounds, detention, or any other cause . . . without any adverse distinction founded on race, colour, religion or faith, sex, birth or wealth, or any other similar criteria. . . .

This protection embraces, at the least, all of those protected persons covered by the grave breaches regime applicable to conflicts of an international character: civilians, prisoners of war, wounded and sick members of the armed forces in the field and wounded, sick and shipwrecked members of the armed forces at sea. Whereas the concept of "protected person" under the Geneva Conventions is defined positively, the class of persons protected by the operation of Common Article 3 is defined negatively. For that reason, the test the Trial Chamber has applied is to ask whether, at the time of the alleged offence, the alleged victim of the proscribed acts was directly taking part in hostilities, being those hostilities in the context of which the alleged offences are said to have been committed. If the answer to that question is negative, the victim will enjoy the protection of the proscriptions contained in Common Article 3.

616. It is unnecessary to define exactly the line dividing those taking an active part in hostilities and those who are not so involved. It is sufficient to examine the relevant facts of each victim and to ascertain whether, in each individual's circumstances, that person was actively involved in hostilities at the relevant time. . . .

4.2.470 Applying that test to the victims in question in *Tadić*, the Chamber found that the victims were not taking an active part in the hostilities and were therefore protected by common article 3, and hence by Article 3 of the Statute (as well as by Article 2 of the Statute as "protected persons). See paras. 616–617 of the *Tadić Opinion and Judgement*.

Constituent Offences of Article 3

4.2.471 Like Articles 2, 4 and 5 of the ICTY Statute, once the Chamber is satisfied that the jurisdictional requirements for each of the crimes are met (armed conflict, "protected persons," widespread and systematic attack, etc., as the case may be), the Chamber must examine whether the individual crimes charged in the indictment have been met. The violations set out in Article 3 are now examined in turn.

Employment of Poisonous Weapons or Other Weapons Calculated to Cause Unnecessary Suffering (Article 3 (a))

4.2.472 This provision is derived directly from Article 23(a) of the Hague Regulations (1907). The ICTY has not yet defined the elements of this crime.

Wanton Destruction of Towns, Cities or Villages (Article 3 (b))

4.2.473 Of this offence, the Chamber in the *Blaškić Trial Judgement* said that it is "similar to the grave breach constituting part of Article 2(d) of the Statute. . . . So as to be punishable, the devastation must have been perpetrated intentionally or have been the foreseeable consequence of the acts of the accused." (para. 183) The Trial Chamber did not specify whether the requirement of foreseeability means that the accused must have actually foreseen the consequences of his acts or whether it is merely that *a reasonable person* would have foreseen such consequences (although the accused himself might not have done so due to gross negligence). One suspects, given the Trial Chamber's references elsewhere to criminal negligence being sufficient to ground a conviction, that it would be the latter.

4.2.474 In the *Rajić Rule 61 Decision*, the Trial Chamber found that it had jurisdiction in respect of violations of Article 3(b) committed in an international armed conflict, but it did not rule on the question of whether Article 3(b) would apply in an internal armed conflict:

> 46. One of the enumerated violations over which the International Tribunal has jurisdiction under Article 3(b) is the "wanton destruction of cities, towns or villages, or devastation not justified by military necessity." The prohibitions listed in Article 3 clearly are applicable in cases of international armed conflict and may also apply in internal armed conflicts. . . . The Trial Chamber has held that there is sufficient evidence to conclude that the conflict at issue here was international in character. Accordingly, the Trial Chamber does not have to consider whether the prohibition on wanton destruction reflected in Article 3(b) of the Statute extends—as a matter of customary international law—to internal armed conflicts.

4.2.475 In the *Kordić and Čerkez Trial Judgement* (para. 346), the Trial Chamber considered that the elements for the crime of wanton destruction not justified by military necessity charged under Article 3 (b) of the ICTY Statute were satisfied where:

> (i) the destruction of property occurs on a large scale;
> (ii) the destruction is not justified by military necessity; and
> (iii) the perpetrator acted with the intent to destroy the property in question or in reckless disregard of the likelihood of its destruction.

Devastation Not Justified by Military Necessity (Article 3 (b))

4.2.476 Devastation is essentially large-scale destruction. This offence is "similar to the grave breach constituting part of Article 2(d) of the Statute . . . . to be punishable, the devastation must have been perpetrated intentionally or have been the foreseeable consequence of the acts of the accused" (para. 183, *Blaškić Trial Judgement*). The same considerations apply here as above (4.2.473) with respect to the Trial Chamber's failure to specify whether the requirement of foreseeability means that the accused must have actually foreseen the consequences of his acts or merely that a reasonable person would have foreseen them.

4.2.477 For the definition of this offence, see 4.2.417, above. As to whether this offence applies in internal armed conflict, the same considerations outlined in the *Rajić Rule 61 Decision* (para. 46), set out above (4.2.474), apply.

4.2.478 As regards military necessity, this is, strictly speaking, a defence rather than an element of the offence (see "Defences," 6.3.1 *et seq.*).

4.2.479 The Trial Chamber in the *Kordić Trial Judgement* observed that while property situated on enemy territory is not protected under the Geneva Conventions, and is therefore not included in the crime of extensive destruction of property listed as a grave breach of the Geneva Conventions, the destruction is criminalised under Article 3 of the Statute (para. 347).

Attack, or Bombardment, by Whatever Means, of Undefended Towns, Villages, Dwellings, or Buildings (Artticle 3 (c))

4.2.480 This provision is derived directly from Article 25 of the Hague Regulations (1907). The ICTY has not yet defined the elements of this crime.

Destruction or Wilful Damage to Institutions Dedicated to Religion or Education (Artticle 3 (d))

4.2.481 For this offence to be committed, "The damage or destruction must have been committed intentionally to institutions which may clearly be identified as dedicated to religion or education and which were not being used for military purposes at the time of the acts. In addition, the institutions must not have been in the immediate vicinity of military objectives" (*Blaškić Trial Judgement*, para. 185)

4.2.482 What seems to be missing from the above definition is this: if the accused deliberately destroys a church, for example by dynamiting it, it should not matter at all whether the church is in the immediate vicinity of a military objective or not. The point is, rather, that if the church were destroyed *as collateral damage during an attack on an adjacent military objective*, then such destruction may not amount to a war crime under ICTY Article 3(d).

4.2.483 In the *Kordić Trial Judgement* (paras. 360 and 361), the Chamber noted that:

> educational institutions are undoubtedly immovable property of great importance to the cultural heritage of peoples in that they are without exception centres of learning, arts, and sciences, with their valuable collections of books and works of arts and science. The Trial Chamber also notes one international treaty (Protection of Artistic and Scientific Institutions and Historic Monuments, known as "Roerich Pact," 15 April 1935, Art.1. . . . which requires respect and protection to be accorded to educational institutions in time of peace as well as in war.

> This offence overlaps to a certain extent with the offence of unlawful attacks on civilian objects except that the object of this offence is more specific: the cultural heritage of a certain population. Educational institutions are certainly civilian objects. The offence this section is concerned with is the *lex specialis* as far as acts against cultural heritage are concerned. The destruction or damage is committed wilfully and the accused intends by his acts to cause the

destruction or damage of institutions dedicated to religion or education and not used for a military purpose. The Trial Chamber intends to apply this more specialised offence to the facts of this case.

Plunder of Public or Private Property (Article 3 (e))

4.2.484 See the discussion of "Plunder/Pillage" in the "Elements of the Offences" section, below (4.2.576 *et seq.*).

Common Article 3 Offences Prosecuted Under ICTY Article 3

Murder (Common Article 3(1)(a) of the Geneva Conventions)

4.2.485 "The content of the offence of murder under Article 3 is the same as for wilful killing under Article 2" (para. 181, *Blaškic Trial Judgement*), i.e. the death of the victim was the result of the actions or omissions of the accused and the accused intended to cause death or serious bodily injury to the victim in reckless disregard of human life (see *Delalić et al Trial Judgement*, para. 439; *Blaškić Trial Judgement*, para. 153; *Kordić Trial Judgement*, para. 233). See also "murder" in the "Elements of the Offences" section, below (4.2.538 *et seq.*). Note that for killing as genocide, the ICTR has held that the intent must be to kill, not only to cause serious bodily injury (4.2.41). This is due to the French version of ICTR Article 2 (2) (a) which refers to "meurtre."

Violence to Life and Person (Common Article 3(1)(a) of the Geneva Conventions)

4.2.486 Violence to life and person is "a broad offence which, at first glance, encompasses murder, mutilation, cruel treatment and torture and which is accordingly defined by the cumulation of the elements of these specific offences" (*Blaškić Trial Judgement*, para. 182). The *Blaškić* Trial Chamber defined the *mens rea* requirement as the intent "to commit violence to the life or person of the victims deliberately or through recklessness. See also the *Kordić Trial Judgement*, para. 260.

4.2.487 This definition is, however, puzzling. First, it is unclear how an accused can "intend[.] to commit violence to the life or person of the victims . . . through recklessness." Intention and recklessness are mutually exclusive. Second, to the extent that violence to life and person encompasses murder, it is difficult to see how it can be charged at the same time as murder without creating double jeopardy.

Cruel Treatment (Common Article 3(1)(a) of the Geneva Conventions)

4.2.488 Cruel treatment is "an intentional act or omission . . . which causes serious mental or physical suffering or injury or constitutes a serious attack on human dignity. As such, it carries an equivalent meaning and therefore the same residual function for the purposes of Common article 3 of the Statute, as inhuman treatment does in relation to grave breaches of the Geneva Convention" (*Delalić et al. Trial Judgement*, para. 552). This definition was followed in the *Blaškić Trial Judgement* (para. 186). In the same paragraph, the *Blaškić* Chamber held, moreover, that "treatment may be cruel whatever the status of the person concerned," and thus it was not a requirement that the victims be "foreigners in enemy territory, inhabitants of an occupied territory or detainees."

4.2.489 See also the discussion of "cruel treatment" in the "Elements of the Offences" section, below (4.2.570 *et seq.*).

Taking Hostages (Common Article 3(1)(b) of the Geneva Conventions)

4.2.490 Civilian hostages "are persons unlawfully deprived of their freedom, often arbitrarily and sometimes under threat of death" (para. 158, *Blaškić Trial Judgement*). Since detention may be lawful under certain circumstances—for example, when carried out for the detainee's own safety—to secure a conviction the prosecution must also prove that, at the time of the detention, the person was detained "in order to obtain a concession or gain an advantage" (*ibid*).

4.2.491 As the Trial Chamber noted in its *Decision on the Defence Motion to dismiss the Indictment based upon Defects thereof (vagueness/Lack of adequate Notice of Charges)* rendered in *Blaškić* on 4 April 1997, hostage-taking may fall under both ICTY Article 2(h), as a grave breach of the Geneva Conventions, and under Article 3(1)(b) common to the Geneva Conventions and thus, according to the Appeals Chamber's *Tadić Jurisdiction Appeals Decision*, under ICTY Article 3. Since the former only applies to hostage-taking of *civilians*, whereas common Article 3's prohibition is broader, the Chamber considered that the Prosecutor should specify in the indictment to which form of hostage-taking reference was being made.

4.2.492 See *Blaškić Trial Judgement*, para. 187:

> The definition of hostages must be understood as being similar to that of civilians taken as hostages within the meaning of grave breaches under Article 2 of the Statute, that is—persons unlawfully deprived of their freedom, often wantonly and sometimes under threat of death. The parties did not contest that to be characterised as hostages the detainees must have been used to obtain some advantage or to ensure that a belligerent, other person or other group of persons enter into some undertaking.

4.2.493 See also the definition of hostages in the Commentary to the Geneva Conventions:

> hostages are nationals of a belligerent State who of their own free will or through compulsion are in the hands of the enemy and are answerable with their freedom or their life for the execution of his orders and the security of his armed forces.

Outrages upon Personal Dignity, in Particular Humiliating and Degrading Treatment (Common Article 3(1)(c) of the Geneva Conventions)

4.2.494 See the definition of this offence set out in the "Elements of the Offences" section, below (4.2.581 *et seq.*).

Violations of Additional Protocol I

Unlawful Attack Against Civilians (Article 51(2) of Additional Protocol I); Attack upon Civilian Property (Article 52(1) of Additional Protocol I)

4.2.495   Unlawful attacks "are those launched deliberately against civilians or civilian objects in the course of an armed conflict and are not justified by military necessity. They must have caused deaths and/or serious bodily injuries within the civilian population or extensive damage to civilian objects" (*Kordić and Čerkez Trial Judgement*, para. 328).

4.2.496   See also the *Blaškić Trial Judgement:*

> 180. . . . the attack must have caused deaths and/or serious bodily injury within the civilian population or damage to civilian property. The parties to the conflict are obliged to attempt to distinguish between military targets and civilian persons or property. Targeting civilians or civilian property is an offence when not justified by military necessity. Civilians within the meaning of Article 3 are persons who are not, or no longer, members of the armed forces. Civilian property covers any property that could not be legitimately considered a military objective. Such an attack must have been conducted intentionally in the knowledge, or when it was impossible not to know, that civilians or civilian property were being targeted not through military necessity.

4.2.497

ICTR
Article 4
Violations of Article 3 Common to the Geneva Conventions and of Additional Protocol II

The International Tribunal for Rwanda shall have the power to prosecute persons committing or ordering to be committed serious violations of Article 3 common to the Geneva Conventions of 12 August 1949 for the Protection of War Victims, and of Additional Protocol II thereto of 8 June 1977. These violations shall include, but shall not be limited to:

(a) Violence to life, health and physical or mental well-being of persons, in particular murder as well as cruel treatment such as torture, mutilation or any form of corporal punishment;
(b) Collective punishments;
(c) Taking of hostages;
(d) Acts of terrorism;
(e) Outrages upon personal dignity, in particular humiliating and degrading treatment, rape, enforced prostitution and any form of indecent assault;
(f) Pillage;
(g) The passing of sentences and the carrying out of executions without previous judgement pronounced by a regularly constituted court, affording all the judicial guarantees which are recognized as indispensable by civilized peoples;
(h) Threats to commit any of the foregoing acts.

Background

4.2.498 One of the principal differences between the conflict and genocide in Rwanda and the wars in the former Yugoslavia, is that the former was pre-eminently an internal conflict, albeit with international consequences, while the conflict in the former Yugoslavia was, at least in some respects, and if considered as a whole, international.

4.2.499 Accordingly, the law applicable to international armed conflicts (Geneva law and Hague law) applies, at least in part, to the conflict in the former Yugoslavia, while the law applicable to internal conflict (Common Article 3 and Additional Protocol II) applies in Rwanda. This is why the war crimes provisions of the two tribunals (Articles 2 and 3 of the ICTY Statute; Article 4 of the ICTR Statute) differ. Conversely, both tribunals have jurisdiction over genocide and crimes against humanity, as these crimes can be committed in either an internal or international conflict (or indeed in the absence of any conflict at all).

4.2.500 Thus the ICTR Statute does not contain an article that is analogous to Articles 2 and 3 of the ICTY Statute, covering "Geneva Law" and "Hague Law" applicable in international armed conflicts. Article 4 provides the ICTR with competence over violations of common Article 3 to the Geneva Conventions and of Additional Protocol II to the Geneva Conventions, the core of law applicable to *internal* armed conflicts.

4.2.501 The ICTY has stated that ICTY Article 3 may also cover violations of common Article 3 to the Geneva Conventions and possibly Additional Protocol II (see para. 89 of the *Tadić Jurisdiction Appeals Decision*), i.e. the subject-matter of Article 4 of the ICTR Statute (see 4.2.442 *et seq.* above).

Applicability of Additional Protocol II and Common Article 3 to Events in Rwanda in 1994

4.2.502 The question of the applicability of Additional Protocol II and common Article 3 to events in Rwanda in 1994 was first considered in the first trial before the ICTR, the *Akayesu* case. The following points emerge from the *Akayesu Trial Judgement* in relation to Article 4 of the Statute:

Objective Test as to Sufficient Intensity of Internal Armed Conflict

4.2.503 It should first be noted that both common Article 3 and Additional Protocol II have threshold conditions for their application. Article 3 applies to an "*armed conflict.*" Additional Protocol II only applies to conflicts "*which take place in the territory of a High Contracting Party between its armed forces and dissident armed forces or other organized groups which, under responsible command, exercise such control over a part of its territory as to enable them to carry out sustained and concerted military operations and to implement this Protocol*" (Article 1(1)) which breaks down into a number of conditions. Additional Protocol II (APII) is expressly stated *not* to apply to "*situations of internal disturbances and tensions, such as riots, isolated and sporadic acts of violence and other acts of violence and other acts of a similar nature*, as not being armed conflicts"" (Article 1(2), emphasis added). It can be inferred from this, that since common Article 3 applies only to "*armed conflicts,*" it too does *not* apply to "*internal disturbances and tensions, such as riots, isolated and sporadic acts of violence*," etc. So conflicts must be of a certain threshold intensity for common Article 3 and APII to be triggered. Because of the conditions set out in Article 1(1) of APII, it is commonly thought that APII requires a higher threshold intensity than common Article 3.

4.2.504 The question of whether the threshold intensity is reached is one to be assessed by reference to objective features. As noted in the *Akayesu Trial Judgement* (para. 603), "It should be stressed that the ascertainment of the intensity of a non-international conflict does not depend on the subjective judgement of the parties to the conflict." See also paras. 169–172 of the *Kayishema and Ruzindana Trial Judgement*.

Applicability of Additional Protocol II

4.2.505 The Chamber has to determine whether Additional Protocol II applies and not simply "take its Statute as it finds it." See para. 607 of the *Akayesu Trial Judgement*, "the Chamber finds it necessary and reasonable to establish the applicability of both Common Article 3 and Additional Protocol II individually."

Norms in Article 4 Customary

4.2.506 The norms in Article 4 of the Statute are *customary*. See para. 610 of the *Akayesu Trial Judgement*, "All of the guarantees, as enumerated in Article 4 reaffirm and supplement Common Article 3 and, as discussed above, Common Article 3 being customary in nature, the Chamber is of the opinion that these guarantees did also at the time of the events alleged in the Indictment form part of existing international customary law." See also paras. 156–158 of the *Kayishema and Ruzindana Trial Judgement*.

Individual Criminal Responsibility

4.2.507 Violations of common article 3 and Additional Protocol II give rise to individual criminal responsibility. See paras. 611–617 of the *Akayesu Trial Judgement:*

> 611. For the purposes of an international criminal Tribunal which is trying individuals, it is not sufficient merely to affirm that Common Article 3 and parts of Article 4 of Additional Protocol II—which comprise the subject-matter jurisdiction of Article 4 of the Statute—form part of international customary law.... it must also be shown that an individual committing serious violations of these customary norms incurs, as a matter of custom, individual criminal responsibility thereby. Otherwise, it might be argued that these instruments only state norms applicable to States and Parties to a conflict, and that they do not create crimes for which individuals may be tried.
>
> 612. As regards individual criminal responsibility for serious violations of Common Article 3, the ICTY has already affirmed this principle in the Tadić case. In the ICTY Appeals Chamber, the problem was posed thus:
>
>> Even if customary international law includes certain basic principles applicable to both internal and international armed conflicts, Appellant

argues that such provisions do not entail individual criminal responsibility when breaches are committed in internal armed conflicts; these provisions cannot, therefore, fall within the scope of the International Tribunal's jurisdiction.

Basing itself on rulings of the Nüremberg Tribunal, on "elements of international practice which show that States intend to criminalise serious breaches of customary rules and principles on internal conflicts," as well as on national legislation designed to implement the Geneva Conventions, the ICTY Appeals Chamber reached the conclusion:

> All of these factors confirm that customary international law imposes criminal liability for serious violations of common Article 3, as supplemented by other general principles and rules on protection of victims of internal armed conflict, and for breaching certain fundamental principles and rules regarding means and methods of combat in civil strife.

614. This was affirmed by the ICTY Trial Chamber when it rendered the Tadić judgement.

615. The Chamber considers this finding of the ICTY Appeals Chamber convincing and dispositive of the issue, both with respect to serious violations of Common Article 3 and of Additional Protocol II.

616. It should be noted, moreover, that Article 4 of the ICTR Statute states that, "The International Tribunal for Rwanda shall have the power to prosecute persons committing or ordering to be committed *serious violations* of Article 3 common to the Geneva Conventions of 12 August 1949 for the Protection of War Victims, and of Additional Protocol II thereto of 8 June 1977" (emphasis added). The Chamber understands the phrase "serious violation" to mean "a breach of a rule protecting important values [which] must involve grave consequences for the victim," in line with the above-mentioned Appeals Chamber Decision in Tadić, para. 94. The list of serious violations which is provided in Article 4 of the Statute is taken from Common Article 3—which contains fundamental prohibitions as a humanitarian minimum of protection for war victims—and Article 4 of Additional Protocol II, which equally outlines "Fundamental Guarantees." The list in Article 4 of the Statute thus comprises *serious* violations of the fundamental humanitarian guarantees which, as has been stated above, are recognized as part of international customary law. In the opinion of the Chamber, it is clear that the authors of such egregious violations must incur individual criminal responsibility for their deeds.

617. The Chamber, therefore, concludes the violation of these norms entails, as a matter of customary international law, individual responsibility for the perpetrator. In addition to this argument from custom, there is the fact that the Geneva Conventions of 1949 (and thus Common Article 3) were ratified by Rwanda on 5 May 1964 and Additional Protocol II on 19 November 1984, and were therefore in force on the territory of Rwanda at the time of the alleged offences. Moreover, all the offences enumerated under Article 4 of the Statute constituted crimes under Rwandan law in 1994. Rwandan nationals were therefore aware, or should have been aware, in 1994 that they were amenable to the jurisdiction of Rwandan courts in case of commission of those offences falling under Article 4 of the Statute.

Common Article 3 Threshold

4.2.508 Common Article 3 clearly applied to the situation in Rwanda in 1994, as the war between the government forces (FAR) and the Rwandan Patriotic Front (RPF) was clearly of sufficient intensity to amount to an *"armed conflict"* (see 4.2.503 *et seq.*, above). See para. 621 of the *Akayesu Trial Judgement:*

> 621. ... the testimony of Major-General Dallaire has shown there to have been a civil war between two groups, being on the one side, the governmental forces, the FAR, and on the other side, the RPF. Both groups were well-organized and considered to be armies in their own right. Further, as pertains to the intensity of conflict, all observers to the events, including UNAMIR and UN Special rapporteurs, were unanimous in characterizing the confrontation between the two forces as a war, an internal armed conflict. Based on the foregoing, the Chamber finds there existed at the time of the events alleged in the Indictment an armed conflict not of an international character as covered by Common Article 3 of the 1949 Geneva Conventions.

Additional Protocol II Threshold

4.2.509 Equally, the (higher) threshold of APII-type conflict (see 4.2.503 *et seq.*, above) was found to have been reached with respect to the conflict in Rwanda. See para. 627 of the *Akayesu Trial Judgement:*

> 627. ... evidence has been presented to the Chamber which showed there was at the least a conflict not of a international character in Rwanda at the time of the events alleged in the Indictment. The Chamber, also taking judicial notice of a number of UN official documents dealing with the conflict in Rwanda in 1994, finds, in addition to the requirements of Common Article 3 being met, that the material conditions listed above relevant to Additional Protocol II have been fulfilled. It has been shown that there was a conflict between, on the one hand, the RPF, under the command of General Kagame, and, on the other, the governmental forces, the FAR. The RPF increased its control over the Rwandan territory from that agreed in the Arusha Accords to over half of the country by mid-May 1994, and carried out continuous and sustained military operations until the cease fire on 18 July 1994 which brought the war to an end. The RPF troops were disciplined and possessed a structured leadership which was answerable to authority. The RPF had also stated to the International Committee of the Red Cross that it was bound by the rules of International Humanitarian law. The Chamber finds the said conflict to have been an internal armed conflict within the meaning of Additional Protocol II. Further, the Chamber finds that conflict took place at the time of the events alleged in the Indictment.

Ratione Personae

Class of Victims

4.2.510 The class of victims under Article 4 of the Statute comprises "persons not taking an active part in the hostilities (para. 629 of the *Akayesu Trial Judgement*). See also paras. 169–183 of the *Kayishema and Ruzindana Trial Judgement*. In the *Kayishema* *and Ruzindana Trial Judgement*, the Trial Chamber favoured a negative definition of civilian as someone who is *not* a member of the armed forces (para. 180). The presence of a few non-civilians among a civilian population would not, however, deprive the population of its civilian character.

Class of Perpetrators

4.2.511 The class of perpetrators under Article 4 of the Statute comprises civilians as well as combatants: "the laws of war must apply equally to civilians as to combatants in the conventional sense" (para. 634 of the *Akayesu Trial Judgement*). In the event, however, the Chamber found that Article 4 did not apply to the accused since it had not been proved that the accused's acts formed part of the war efforts of the Rwandan government:

> 641. ... The duties and responsibilities of the Geneva Coventions and the Additional, hence, will normally appy only to individuals of all ranks belonging to the armed forces under military command of either of the belligerent parties, or to individuals who were legitimately mandated and expected, as public officials or agents or persons otherwise holding public authority or *de facto* representing the Government, to support or fulfil the war efforts .

> 643. ... the Chamber finds that it has not been proved beyond reasonable doubt that the acts perpetrated by Akayesu in the commune of Taba at the time of the events alleged in the Indictment were committed in conjunction with the armed conflict. The Chamber further finds that it has not been proved beyond reasonable doubt that Akayesu was a member of the armed forces, or that he was legitimately mandated and expected, as a public official or agent or person otherwise holding public authority or *de facto* representing the Government, to support or fulfil the war efforts.

> 644. The Tribunal therefore finds that Jean-Paul Akayesu did not incur individual criminal responsibility under counts 6, 8, 10, 12 & 15 of the Indictment.

4.2.512 The Prosecution appealed this conclusion on the basis that there was no basis either in the Statute to support the 'public agency test' and that the Chamberl's holding was contrary to the object and purpose of the Geneva Conventions and Additional Protocols, international jurisprudence and doctrine.

4.2.513 In the *Akayesu Appeals Judgement*, the Appeals Chamber agreed with the Prosecution and held that:

> 443. ... the minimum protection provided for victims under common Article 3 implies necessarily effective punishment on persons who violate it. Now, such punishment must be applicable to everyone without discrimination, as required by the principles governing individual criminal responsibility as laid down by the Nuremburg Tribunal in particular. The Appeals Chamber is therefore of the opinion that international humanitarian law would be lessened and called into question if it were to be admitted that certain persons be exonerated from individual criminal responsibility for a violation of common Article 3 under the pretext that they did not belong to a specific category.

> 444. In paragraph 630 of the [Trial] Judgement, the Trial Chamber found that the four Geneva Conventions "were adopted primarily to protect the victims

as well as potential victims of armed conflicts." It went on to hold that "the catergory of persons to be held accountable in this respect then, would in most cases be limited to commanders, combatants and other members of the armed forces." Such a finding is *prima facie* not without reason. In actuality authors of violations of common Article 3 will likely fall into one of these categories. This stems from the fact that common Article 3 requires a close nexus between violations and the armed conflict. This nexus between violations and the armed conflict implies that, in most cases, the perpetrator of the crime will probably have a special relationship with one party to the conflict. However, such a special relationship is not a condition precedent to the application of common Article 3 and, hence of Article 4 of the Statute. In the opinion of the Appeals Chamber, the Trial Chamber erred in requiring that a special relationship should be a separate condition for triggering criminal responsibility for a violation of Article 4 of the Statute.

On this point, see also para. 176 of the *Kayishema/Ruzindana Judgement* of 21 May 1999.

Ratione Loci

4.2.514 Once the law of war starts to apply, it applies across *the whole territory* of the State in question. See the *Akayesu Trial Judgement*:

> 636. Thus the mere fact that Rwanda was engaged in an armed conflict meeting the threshold requirements of Common Article 3 and Additional Protocol II means that these instruments would apply over the whole territory hence encompassing massacres which occurred away from the 'war front.' From this follows that it is not possible to apply rules in one part of the country (i.e. Common Article 3) and other rules in other parts of the country (i.e. Common Article 3 and Additional Protocol II). The aforesaid, however, is subject to the *caveat* that the crimes must not be committed by the perpetrator for purely personal motives.

4.2.515 It should be noted, however, that in para. 643 of the *Akayesu Trial Judgement*, the Chamber found that the accused's acts in Taba were not committed in conjunction with the armed conflict occurring in Rwanda at the time.

4.2.516 In the *Kayishema and Ruzindana Trial Judgement*, the Trial Chamber held that the *ratione loci* requirement should not be too narrowly construed. It would be satisfied by there being a nexus between the conflict and the crime (para. 183).

Nexus Requirements

4.2.517 Two links need to be established for ICTR Article 4 to apply: a link between the accused and the armed forces, and a link between the crime and the armed conflict (*Kayishema and Ruzindana Trial Judgement*, paras. 169, 173–176, 185–189). The presence or absence of these links are matters are to be decided on a case-by-case basis (para. 188).

4.2.518 In that case, no link was found between the armed conflict and the civilian massacres, thus ICTR Article 4 did not apply (paras. 615–623, *Kayishema and Ruzindana Trial Judgement*):

> 602. ... Tutsis were being sought out *on the pretext* that they were accomplices [of the RPF].
>
> 603. ... These allegations show only that the armed conflict had been used as [a] pretext to unleash an official policy of genocide. Therefore, such allegations cannot be considered as evidence of a direct link between the alleged crimes and the armed conflict.

4.2.519 The link or nexus is not something vague or indefinite: "a direct connection between the alleged crimes referred to in the indictment, and the armed conflict should be established factually" (para. 604, *Kayishema and Ruzindana Trial Judgement*). The Chamber concluded:

> 619. [Tutsi] men, women and children were killed not as a result of the military operations between the FAR and the RPF but because of the policy of extermination of the Tutsi, pursued by the official authorities of Rwanda.

4.2.520 The massacres of Tutsi "were committed as part of a distinct policy of genocide; they were committed parallel to, and not as a result of, the armed conflict" (para. 621, *Kayishema and Ruzindana Trial Judgement*).

Serious Violations of Common Article 3 and Additional Protocol II

4.2.521 In the *Kayishema and Ruzindana Trial Judgement*, the Chamber drew attention to the words, "*serious violations*," and interpreted them to mean "breaches involving grave consequences" (para. 184). One problem with this consequentialist definition is that encompassed in ICTR Article 4 is "(h) Threats to commit any of the foregoing acts." A threat, like an attempt, may not result in any consequences, but may nonetheless constitute a serious violation (for example, threatening, or attempting, to detonate a nuclear weapon).

Constituent Crimes under Article 4

Violence to Life, Health and Physical or Mental Well-Being of Persons, in Particular Murder as Well as Cruel Treatment such as Torture, Mutilation or Any Form of Corporal Punishment

4.2.522 See the discussion of "murder," "cruel treatment" and "torture" in the "Elements of the Offences" section, below (4.2.535 *et seq.*).

Collective Punishments

4.2.523 Collective punishments are a war crime under Article 4, para. 2 (b), of the Protocol II Additional to the Geneva Conventions. The ICTR has not yet defined the elements of this crime.

Taking of Hostages

4.2.524 See the discussion of "hostage-taking" under Article 3 of the ICTY Statute, above (4.2.490).

Acts of Terrorism

4.2.525 Acts of terrorism are a war crime under Article 4, para. 2 (d), of Protocol II Additional to the Geneva Conventions. The ICTR has not yet defined the elements of this crime.

4.2.526 The only general definition of this crime given in an international instrument was made in 1937 through the League of Nations by the adoption of a Convention for the Prevention and Punishment of Terrorism. Article 1, para. 2, of that Convention, which required merely three ratifications to come into force, but received only one and was subsequently abandoned, defined:

> acts of terrorism [as] criminal acts directed against a State and intended or calculated to create a state of terror in the minds of particular persons, or groups of persons or the general public.

General Assembly Resolution 53 on "Measures to Eliminate Terrorism" of 11 December 1995 (UN Doc. A/RES/5/53) implicitly adopted and improved upon the definition of terrorism under the now defunct 1937 Convention. It "reiterates" that "criminal acts intended or calculated to provoke a state of terror in the general public, a group of persons or particular persons for political purposes are in any circumstances unjustifiable, whatever the considerations of a political, philosophical, ideological, racial, ethnic, religious or any other nature that may be invoked to justify them." The same definition is enbodied in Article 5 of the "UN Convention for the Suppression of Terrorist Bombing" of 1998 (not yet in force).

4.2.527 In the ICC Rome Statute, there is no reference to acts of terrorism as a war crime.

Articles:

Guillaume, G., "Terrorisme et droit international," 215 *Recueil des cours de l'Académie de droit international de La Haye* (1998–III).

Higgins, R. (ed.), *Terrorism and International Law* (London:Routledge, 1997).

Outrages upon Personal Dignity, in Particular Humiliating and Degrading Treatment, Rape, Enforced Prostitution and Any Form of Indecent Assault

4.2.528 See the discussion of this offence as set out in the "Elements of the Offences" section, below (4.2.581).

Pillage

4.2.529 See the discussion of this offence ("Plunder/Pillage") as set out in the "Elements of the Offences" section, below (4.2.576).

The Passing of Sentences and the Carrying Out of Executions Without Previous Judgement Pronounced by a Regularly Constituted Court, Affording All the Judicial Guarantees Which Are Recognized as Indispensable by Civilized Peoples

4.2.530 The ICTR has not yet applied this paragraph.

Threats to Commit any of the Foregoing Acts

4.2.531 The ICTR has not yet applied this paragraph.

4.2.532

ICC
Article 8
War Crimes

1. The Court shall have jurisdiction in respect of war crimes in particular when committed as part of a plan or policy or as part of a large-scale commission of such crimes.
2. For the purpose of this Statute, "war crimes" means:
(a) Grave breaches of the Geneva Conventions of 12 August 1949, namely, any of the following acts against persons or property protected under the provisions of the relevant Geneva Convention:
   (i) Wilful killing;
   (ii) Torture or inhuman treatment, including biological experiments;
   (iii) Wilfully causing great suffering, or serious injury to body or health;
   (iv) Extensive destruction and appropriation of property, not justified by military necessity and carried out unlawfully and wantonly;
   (v) Compelling a prisoner of war or other protected person to serve in the forces of a hostile Power;
   (vi) Wilfully depriving a prisoner of war or other protected person of the rights of fair and regular trial;
   (vii) Unlawful deportation or transfer or unlawful confinement;
   (viii) Taking of hostages.
(b) Other serious violations of the laws and customs applicable in international armed conflict, within the established framework of international law, namely, any of the following acts:
   (i) Intentionally directing attacks against the civilian population as such or against individual civilians not taking direct part in hostilities;
   (ii) Intentionally directing attacks against civilian objects, that is, objects which are not military objectives;
   (iii) Intentionally directing attacks against personnel, installations, material, units or vehicles involved in a humanitarian assistance or peacekeeping mission in accordance with the Charter of the United Nations, as long as they are entitled to the protection given to civilians or civilian objects under the international law of armed conflict;
   (iv) Intentionally launching an attack in the knowledge that such attack will cause incidental loss of life or injury to civilians or damage to civilian objects or widespread, long-term and severe damage to the natural environment which would be clearly excessive in relation to the concrete and direct overall military advantage anticipated;

(v) Attacking or bombarding, by whatever means, towns, villages, dwellings or buildings which are undefended and which are not military objectives;
(vi) Killing or wounding a combatant who, having laid down his arms or having no longer means of defence, has surrendered at discretion;
(vii) Making improper use of a flag of truce, of the flag or of the military insignia and uniform of the enemy or of the United Nations, as well as of the distinctive emblems of the Geneva Conventions, resulting in death or serious personal injury;
(viii) The transfer, directly or indirectly, by the Occupying Power of parts of its own civilian population into the territory it occupies, or the deportation or transfer of all or parts of the population of the occupied territory within or outside this territory;
(ix) Intentionally directing attacks against buildings dedicated to religion, education, art, science or charitable purposes, historic monuments, hospitals and places where the sick and wounded are collected, provided they are not military objectives;
(x) Subjecting persons who are in the power of an adverse party to physical mutilation or to medical or scientific experiments of any kind which are neither justified by the medical, dental or hospital treatment of the person concerned nor carried out in his or her interest, and which cause death to or seriously endanger the health of such person or persons;
(xi) Killing or wounding treacherously individuals belonging to the hostile nation or army;
(xii) Declaring that no quarter will be given;
(xiii) Destroying or seizing the enemy's property unless such destruction or seizure be imperatively demanded by the necessities of war;
(xiv) Declaring abolished, suspended or inadmissible in a court of law the rights and actions of the nationals of the hostile party;
(xv) Compelling the nationals of the hostile party to take part in the operations of war directed against their own country, even if they were in the belligerent's service before the commencement of the war;
(xvi) Pillaging a town or place, even when taken by assault;
(xvii) Employing poison or poisoned weapons;
(xviii) Employing asphyxiating, poisonous or other gases, and all analogous liquids, materials or devices;
(xix) Employing bullets which expand or flatten easily in the human body, such as bullets with a hard envelope which does not entirely cover the core or is pierced with incisions;
(xx) Employing weapons, projectiles and material and methods of warfare which are of a nature to cause superfluous injury or unnecessary suffering or which are inherently indiscriminate in violation of the international law of armed conflict, provided that such weapons, projectiles and material and methods of warfare are the subject of a comprehensive prohibition and are included in an annex to this Statute, by an amendment in accordance with the relevant provisions set forth in articles 121 and 123;
(xxi) Committing outrages upon personal dignity, in particular humiliating and degrading treatment;
(xxii) Committing rape, sexual slavery, enforced prostitution, forced pregnancy, as defined in article 7, para. 2 (f), enforced sterilization, or any other form of sexual violence also constituting a grave breach of the Geneva Conventions;
(xxiii) Utilizing the presence of a civilian or other protected person to render certain points, areas or military forces immune from military operations;
(xxiv) Intentionally directing attacks against buildings, material, medical units and transport, and personnel using the distinctive emblems of the Geneva Conventions in conformity with international law;

(xxv) Intentionally using starvation of civilians as a method of warfare by depriving them of objects indispensable to their survival, including wilfully impeding relief supplies as provided for under the Geneva Conventions;
(xxvi) Conscripting or enlisting children under the age of fifteen years into the national armed forces or using them to participate actively in hostilities.

(c) In the case of an armed conflict not of an international character, serious violations of article 3 common to the four Geneva Conventions of 12 August 1949, namely, any of the following acts committed against persons taking no active part in the hostilities, including members of armed forces who have laid down their arms and those placed *hors de combat* by sickness, wounds, detention or any other cause:
  (i) Violence to life and person, in particular murder of all kinds, mutilation, cruel treatment and torture;
  (ii) Committing outrages upon personal dignity, in particular humiliating and degrading treatment;
  (iii) Taking of hostages;
  (iv) The passing of sentences and the carrying out of executions without previous judgement pronounced by a regularly constituted court, affording all judicial guarantees which are generally recognized as indispensable.

(d) Para. 2 (c) applies to armed conflicts not of an international character and thus does not apply to situations of internal disturbances and tensions, such as riots, isolated and sporadic acts of violence or other acts of a similar nature.

(e) Other serious violations of the laws and customs applicable in armed conflicts not of an international character, within the established framework of international law, namely, any of the following acts:
  (i) Intentionally directing attacks against the civilian population as such or against individual civilians not taking direct part in hostilities;
  (ii) Intentionally directing attacks against buildings, material, medical units and transport, and personnel using the distinctive emblems of the Geneva Conventions in conformity with international law;
  (iii) Intentionally directing attacks against personnel, installations, material, units or vehicles involved in a humanitarian assistance or peacekeeping mission in accordance with the Charter of the United Nations, as long as they are entitled to the protection given to civilians or civilian objects under the international law of armed conflict;
  (iv) Intentionally directing attacks against buildings dedicated to religion, education, art, science or charitable purposes, historic monuments, hospitals and places where the sick and wounded are collected, provided they are not military objectives;
  (v) Pillaging a town or place, even when taken by assault;
  (vi) Committing rape, sexual slavery, enforced prostitution, forced pregnancy, as defined in article 7, para. 2 (f), enforced sterilization, and any other form of sexual violence also constituting a serious violation of article 3 common to the four Geneva Conventions;
  (vii) Conscripting or enlisting children under the age of fifteen years into armed forces or groups or using them to participate actively in hostilities;
  (viii) Ordering the displacement of the civilian population for reasons related to the conflict, unless the security of the civilians involved or imperative military reasons so demand;
  (ix) Killing or wounding treacherously a combatant adversary;
  (x) Declaring that no quarter will be given;
  (xi) Subjecting persons who are in the power of another party to the conflict to physical mutilation or to medical or scientific experiments of any kind which are neither justified by the medical, dental or hospital treatment of the person concerned nor carried out in

> his or her interest, and which cause death to or seriously endanger the health of such person or persons;
> (xii) Destroying or seizing the property of an adversary unless such destruction or seizure be imperatively demanded by the necessities of the conflict;
> (f) Para. 2 (e) applies to armed conflicts not of an international character and thus does not apply to situations of internal disturbances and tensions, such as riots, isolated and sporadic acts of violence or other acts of a similar nature. It applies to armed conflicts that take place in the territory of a State when there is protracted armed conflict between governmental authorities and organized armed groups or between such groups.
> 3. Nothing in para. 2 (c) and (e) shall affect the responsibility of a Government to maintain or re-establish law and order in the State or to defend the unity and territorial integrity of the State, by all legitimate means.

War Crimes under the ICC

4.2.533 War crimes that may be prosecuted by the ICC are set out in Article 8 of the Rome Statute. It incorporates crimes in both internal and international conflict.

4.2.534 For an in-depth discussion of war crimes in the Rome Statute of the ICC, see Bothe, Michael, "War Crimes," ch. 11.3 *in* Cassese, Gaeta and Jones (eds.), *The Rome Statute of the International Criminal Court: A Commentary* (OUP, 2002); Cottier, Fenrick, Viseur Sellers and Zimmermann, "Article 8: War Crimes," *in* Triffterer (ed.), *Commentary on the Rome Statute of the International Criminal Court: Observers' Notes, Article-by-Article* (Nomos, 1999).

* * * * *

ELEMENTS OF THE OFFENCES

ICTY and ICTR Offences

4.2.535 Unlike the Rome Statute for an International Criminal Court (Article 9), neither the ICTY Statute nor the ICTR Statute contains an article on the elements of the offences that may be prosecuted by the *ad hoc* tribunals. Generally, it is necessary in criminal law to spell out precisely what a crime such as murder or rape consists of, so that the public is on notice as to what sort of behaviour is criminal and what is not and, among behaviour which is criminal, to specify which acts constitute which crimes and to indicate how severely those crimes may be punished. At the ICTY and ICTR—as at Nuremberg and Tokyo, and in international criminal law—the crimes usually involved are composite, large-scale crimes committed by State actors; hence it is necessary to describe the crimes broadly (the crimes committed by the Nazis, for example, could not be neatly encapsulated in a precise definition of requisite acts and mental states). Since prosecutions before the ICTY, and ICTR, have not, however, only focused on leaders and organisers of State or quasi-State crimes, but also on individual killers and rapists, it has become necessary to adopt the approach taken in national systems and to provide clear definitions of some of these crimes such as rape, murder, plunder, etc..

4.2.536   Reference should be made to the subject-matter articles of the ICTY and ICTR Statutes (Articles 2, 3, 4 and 5 of the ICTY Statute and Articles 2, 3 and 4 of the ICTR Statute) for the elements of the crimes specifically falling under those articles.

4.2.537   The elements of certain crimes prosecuted under the ICTY and ICTR Statutes are common to several articles and accordingly the elements of those crimes are, for convenience, set out here.

Wilful Killing/Murder

4.2.538   Note that, whereas the English versions of the ICTY and ICTR Statutes refer variously to "wilful killing" (ICTY Article 2(a)), "killing" (ICTY Article 4(2)(a) and ICTR Article 2(2)(e)) and "murder" (ICTY Article 5(a) and ICTR Article 3(a)), the French versions refer, respectively, to "l'homicide intentionnel," "meurtre" and "assassinat." The meanings do not always neatly coincide.

4.2.539   In English law, the term "killing" refers to any act causing death without specifying the perpetrator's degree of intention. The *Akayesu Trial Judgement* observed that the notion of "meurtre" or "murder" should be preferred to that of "killings" in accordance with the general principles of criminal law which provide that where there are two possible interpretations the one which is more favourable to the accused must be used (*Akayesu Trial Judgement*, para. 501). The Chamber also noted (at para. 588) that the term "murder" is translated in French by "assassinat" (which supposes premeditation and may involve, if proven, a higher sentence) and stated that the term "meurtre" in French should be preferred, in keeping with customary international law.

4.2.540   In the *Delalić et al. Trial Judgement* (para. 422), the Chamber stated that there was no difference between "wilful killing," prosecuted as a grave breach under Article 2 of the Statute, and "murder" prosecuted under Article 3 of the Statute as a violation of common article 3 of the Geneva Conventions and "murder" prosecuted as a crime against humanity under Article 5(a) of the Statute. Each may be defined as follows:

> *Actus reus:* The death of the victim as a result of the acts or omissions of the accused (para. 424). Moreover, the conduct of the accused must be a substantial cause of the death of the victim (para. 424).
>
> *Mens rea:* The intent to kill or the intent to inflict serious injury in reckless disregard of human life (para. 439).

4.2.541   See also the *Akayesu Trial Judgement*, para. 589; *Blaškić Trial Judgement*, paras. 153, 181, and 217; *Krstić Trial Judgement*, para. 485; *Kayishema and Ruzindana Trial Judgement*, para. 140; *Kupreškić Trial Judgement*, paras. 560–561, *Rutaganda Judgement*, paras. 79–81.

Article:

Hogan-Doran, J., "Murder as a Crime Under International Law and the Statute of the International Criminal Tribunal for the Former Yugoslavia: Of Law, Legal Language, and a Comparative Approach to Legal Meaning," *Leiden Journal of International Law*, 165–181 (1998).

Torture

4.2.542 Torture is a norm of customary law and, further, a norm of *jus cogens*, i.e. a peremptory, absolute and non-derogable prohibition (*Delalić et al. Trial Judgement*, para. 454).

4.2.543 Torture appears in several places in the ICTs' Statutes: ICTY Article 2(b), ICTY Article 5(f) and, indirectly through common Article 3(1)(a), under ICTY Article 3, and in ICTR Article 3(f) and ICTR Article 4(a).

4.2.544 Both the ICTY and ICTR have so far based their interpretations of the definition of the offences of torture in their respective Statutes on the definition contained in the UN Torture Convention 1984 as embodying the concept of torture under customary international law.

4.2.545 For example, in the *Akayesu Trial Judgement*, the Trial Chamber explicitly invoked the definition contained in Article 1 of the UN Torture Convention as a means of defining the offence of torture in Article 3 (f) of its own Statute (see para. 593). The Trial Chamber defined the "essential elements of torture" such that (see paras. 594–595).

> (i) The perpetrator must intentionally inflict severe physical or mental pain or suffering upon the victim for one or more of the following purposes:
>> (a) to obtain information or a confession from the victim or a third person;
>> (b) to punish the victim or a third person for an act committed or suspected of having been committed by either of them;
>> (c) for the purpose of intimidating or coercing the victim or the third person;
>> (d) for any reason based on discrimination of any kind.
>
> (ii) The perpetrator was himself an official, or acted at the instigation of, or with the consent or acquiescence of, an official or person acting in an official capacity.

4.2.546 See also the *Delalić et al. Trial Judgement* which contains extensive discussion of torture (paras. 446–496). The Judgement defines torture (para. 494) as follows:

> (i) There must be an act or omission that causes severe pain or suffering, whether mental or physical,
>
> (ii) which is inflicted intentionally,
>
> (iii) and for such purposes as obtaining information or a confession from the victim, or a third person, punishing the victim for an act he or she or a third person has committed or is suspected of having committed, intimidating or coercing the victim or a third person, or for any reason based on discrimination of any kind,
>
> (iv) and such act or omission being committed by, or at the instigation of, or with the consent or acquiescence of, an official or other person acting in an official capacity.

4.2.547 This definition was followed in the *Furundžija Trial Judgement* which also discussed torture at length. It defined torture, when committed in armed conflict, as follows:

> (i) it consists of the infliction, by act or omission, of severe pain or suffering, whether physical or mental;

(ii) the act or omission must be intentional;

(iii) it must aim at obtaining information or a confession, or at punishing, intimidating, humiliating or coercing the victim or a third person, or at discriminating, on any ground, against the victim or a third person;

(iv) it must be linked to an armed conflict;

(v) at least one of the persons involved in the torture process must be a public official or must at any rate act in a non-private capacity, e.g. as a de facto organ of a State or any other authority-wielding entity.

4.2.548 The inclusion of "humiliating" in (iii) was new in that it did not appear in the UN Torture Convention nor in the *Akayesu Trial Judgement* nor the *Delalić et al. Trial Judgement*.

4.2.549 The definition was, however, modified in the *Foča Trial Judgement*, removing the need for the conduct to have an official aspect before it could constitute torture. The *Foča Trial Judgement* suggested that the term "torture" may be appropriately applied to the case of private acts which do not have the nexus to the state required by the UN Torture Convention:

> 496. The Trial Chamber concludes that the definition of torture under international humanitarian law does not comprise the same elements as the definition of torture generally applied under human rights law. In particular, the Trial Chamber is of the view that the presence of a state official or of any other authority-wielding person in the torture process is not necessary for the offence to be regarded as torture under international humanitarian law.
>
> 497. On the basis of what has been said, the Trial Chamber holds that, in the field of international humanitarian law, the elements of the offence of torture, under customary international law are as follows:
>
> (i) The infliction, by act or omission, of severe pain or suffering, whether physical or mental.
>
> (ii) The act or omission must be intentional.
>
> (iii) The act or omission must aim at obtaining information or a confession, or at punishing, intimidating or coercing the victim or a third person, or at discriminating, on any ground, against the victim or a third person.

4.2.550 A possible reason for considering the nexus with state action unnecessary in international criminal law is that the nexus in human rights instruments is required in order to engage the State's responsibility. Private acts of torture do not engage States' responsibility so there would be little point in including them in a human rights instrument. Conversely, in international criminal law, where individual criminal responsibility is concerned, it is possible to prosecute and punish individual acts of sadism. Ther question remains, however, whether such acts are appropriately prosecuted by an international tribunal, which would usually concern itself with crimes of a massive or systematic nature, sponsored by States or quasi-State entities. See also para. 141 of the *Kvočka et al. Judgement* of 2 November 2001 in this regard.

4.2.551 On the definition of torture, see also the Judgement of the East Timor (Dili District Tribunal) serious crimes panel in the case of Joao Franca da Silva, alias Jhoni

Franca, dated 5 December 2002, where a definition of torture as a crime against humanity is provided (at para. 140). The Judgement is available at www.intcrimpractice.com.

Articles:

Derby, D., "Torture" *in* M. Cherif Bassiouni (ed.), *International Criminal Law - Crimes* 705–749 (Transnational Publishers, 1998).

Wauters, J.M., "Torture and Related Crimes—A Discussion of the Crimes Before the International Criminal Tribunal for the Former Yugoslavia," *Leiden Journal of International Law* 155–164 (1998).

Byrnes, A., "Torture and Other Offences Involving the Violation of the Physical or Mental Integrity of the Human Person," *in* G.K. McDonald and O. Swaak-Goldman (eds.), *Substantive and Procedural Aspect of International Law* 197–245 (Kluwer Law International, 2000).

Rape as Torture

4.2.552 Rape, as sexually violent conduct, could fall within the concept of torture if the other conditions for torture are met.

In the *Akayesu Trial Judgement*, the ICTR classified rape as torture when:

> 598. [i]nflicted by or at the instigation of or with the consent or acquiescence of a public official or other person acting in an official capacity.

4.2.553 In other words, rape is torture when it falls within the definition of torture (for the definition of torture, see 4.2.542 *et seq.*).

4.2.554 In the *Nikolić Rule 61 Decision* (see para. 33), the Trial Chamber considered that rape and sexual assault could come within the definition of torture. See also the *Karadžić and Mladić Rule 61 Decision*, especially para. 64, in which the Chamber found that sexual assaults committed by Serb forces:

> were part of a widespread policy of "ethnic cleansing": the victims were mainly "non-Serbian" civilians, the vast majority being Muslims. Sexual assaults occurred in several regions of Bosnia and Herzegovina, in a systematic fashion and using recurring methods (e.g. gang rape, sexual assault in camps, use of brutal means, together with other violations of international humanitarian law). They were performed together with an effort to displace civilians and such as to increase the shame and humiliation of the victims and of the community they belonged to in order to force them to leave. It would seem that the aim of many rapes was enforced impregnation; several witnesses also said that the perpetrators of sexual assault—often soldiers—had been given orders to do so and that camp commanders and officers had been informed thereof and participated therein.

4.2.555 In the *Delalić et al. Trial Judgement*, the Trial Chamber also concluded that rape could constitute torture:

495. The Trial Chamber considers the rape of any person to be a despicable act which strikes at the very core of human dignity and physical integrity. The condemnation and punishment of rape becomes all the more urgent where it is committed by, or at the instigation of, a public official, or with the consent or acquiescence of such an official. Rape causes severe pain and suffering, both physical and psychological. The psychological suffering of persons upon whom rape is inflicted may be exacerbated by social and cultural conditions and can be particularly acute and long lasting. Furthermore, it is difficult to envisage circumstances in which rape, by, or at the instigation of a public official, or with the consent or acquiescence of an official, could be considered as occurring for a purpose that does not, in some way, involve punishment, coercion, discrimination or intimidation. In the view of this Trial Chamber this is inherent in situations of armed conflict.

496. Accordingly, whenever rape and other forms of sexual violence meet the aforementioned criteria, then they shall constitute torture, in the same manner as any other acts that meet this criteria.

4.2.556 The *Furundžija Trial Judgement* also held that rape may qualify as torture, provided the above conditions were met (para. 163), as indeed they were in that case. In the event Furundžija was convicted of torture, with rape as the act which caused great suffering, and of rape as an aider and abettor.

Cross Reference: See also Rape as Genocide at 4.2.51.

Articles:

Niarchos, C.N., "Women, War and Rape: Challenges Facing the International Tribunal for the Former Yugoslavia," *Human Rights Quarterly* 649–690 (1995).

Healy, A., "Prosecuting Rape under the Statute of the War Crimes Tribunal for the Former Yugoslavia," *Brooklyn Journal of International Law* 327–384 (1995).

Rees, M. & S. Maguire, "Rape as a Crime Against Humanity," *Tribunal* (a Publication of the *Institute for War & Peace Reporting*), No. 6, (Nov.–Dec. 1996).

Fitzgerald, K., "Problems of Prosecution and Adjudication of Rape and Other Sexual Assaults under International Law," *European Journal of International Law* 638–663 (1997).

Askin, Kelly D., "Sexual Violence in Decisions and Indictments of the Yugoslav and Rwandan Tribunals: Current Status," 93 *American Journal of International Law* 97 - 123 (1999).

Askin, Kelly D., "The International War Crimes Trial of Anto Furundžija: Major Progress Toward Ending the Cycle of Impunity for Rape Crimes," *Leiden Journal fo International Law* 935–955 (1999).

Davis, P.H., "The Politics of Prosecuting Rape as War Crime," *The International Lawyer* 1223–1248 (2000).

Pipe, S. C. Kennedy, "Rape in War: Lessons of the Balkan Conflicts in the 1990s," *International Journal of Human Rights* 67–84 (2000).

Sellers, P. V., "The Context of Sexual Violence: Sexual Violence as Violations of International Humanitarian Law," *in* G.K. McDonald and O. Swaak-Goldman (eds.), *Substantive and Procedural Aspects of International Law* 263–322 (Kluwer Law International, 2000).

Rape

4.2.557 Oddly, rape is mentioned nowhere in the Geneva Conventions of 1949. It is first referred to, in Geneva law, in the 1977 Protocols (Art. 76(1) API, Art.4(2)(e) APII).

4.2.558 The ICTY and ICTR Statutes do not contain a definition of rape. The ICTR and ICTY have sought to define rape in international law using different approaches and as a consequence a different definition: on the one hand a conceptual definition, on the other hand a more mechanical definition.

4.2.559 For a "conceptual" definition of rape, see the *Akayesu Trial Judgement* (paras. 596–598 and 687–688), which was followed by the *Delalić et al. Trial Judgement*. In the former, the Trial Chamber said that "the central elements of the crime of rape cannot be captured in a mechanical description of objects and body parts" (*Akayesu Trial Judgement*, p. 241,). The *Akayesu Trial Judgement* went on to define rape as "a physical invasion of a sexual nature, committed on a person under circumstances that are coercive" (*ibid.*). The Trial Chamber in the *Delalić et al. Trial Judgement* applied this definition:

> Rape: A physical invasion of a sexual nature, committed on a person under circumstances that are coercive. (para. 479)

4.2.560 The *Akayesu Trial Judgement* defined *sexual violence* as "any act of a sexual nature which is committed under circumstances that are coercive" (p. 241), but it is not clear whether, and to what extent, the Trial Chamber in *Delalić et al.* adopted this definition.

4.2.561 The *Furundžija Trial Judgement* offered a more mechanical definition of rape. The Chamber in *Furundžija* started by noting that no definition of rape existed in international law (para. 175). The Trial Chamber then adopted the following definition (para. 185):

> (i) the sexual penetration, however slight:
>   (a) of the vagina or anus of the victim by the penis of the perpetrator or any other object used by the perpetrator; or
>   (b) of the mouth of the victim by the penis of the perpetrator;
> (ii) by coercion or force or threat of force against the victim or a third person.

4.2.562 As regards any defence that the victim consented to the intercourse, the Chamber said that consent could not be found in circumstances where the victim was in custody: "any form of captivity vitiates consent" (*Furundžija Trial Judgement*, para. 271).

4.2.563 As between the *Akayesu/ Delalić et al.* and *Furundžija*, approaches, it is submitted that the latter has the advantage of being precise and hence better puts potential defendants on notice as to the nature of the crime; an important consideration in terms of respect for the principle of legality. It also would seem better to reflect common perceptions of rape; inserting an object other than the penis in the mouth of the victim would rarely be considered rape, although depending on the context, it may be an act of sexual violence. Moreover the *Furundžija* definition is already considerably broader than the definition in many national jurisdictions; forcible oral sex, for example, is not considered "rape" under English criminal law.

4.2.564 The ICTR Trial Chamber ruling in *Musema* preferred the *Akayesu* approach to the *Furundžija* approach (see paras. 226–229 of the *Musema Trial Judgement*).

4.2.565 The Trial Chamber ruling in the *Foča Trial Judgement* reexamined the definition of rape in considerable depth (paras. 436–460), starting from the *Furundžija* definition (above). The Chamber concluded, on the basis of a review of national case-law and legislation, that what was important in terms of the absence of consent was the serious violation of sexual autonomy which rape involved rather than the accomplishment of intercourse "by coercion or force or threat of force against the victim or a third person," the element emphasised by the *Furundžija* Trial Chamber. Thus the Chamber stated in the *Foča Trial Judgement*:

> 460. ... the *actus reus* of the crime of rape in international law is constituted by: the sexual penetration, however slight: (a) of the vagina or anus of the victim by the penis of the perpetrator or any other object used by the perpetrator; or (b) of the mouth of the victim by the penis of the perpetrator; where such sexual penetration occurs without the consent of the victim. Consent for this purpose must be consent given voluntarily, as a result of the victim's free will, assessed in the context of the surrounding circumstances. The *mens rea* is the intention to effect this sexual penetration, and the knowledge that it occurs without the consent of the victim.

4.2.566 Thus, in terms of the *actus reus*, the *Foča* Trial Chamber largely followed the *Furundžija* definition, with a modification as regards the element of coercion. See also 4.2.266 *et seq.* on the definitions of rape. In terms of *mens rea*, the above suggests that knowledge, and not mere recklessness, as to consent is required. This is a high threshold; in many jurisdictions recklessness suffices.

4.2.567 Note that the ICC, in the Elements of Crimes, has adopted the more "mechanical" definition of rape (see, e.g., the elements for Article 7 (1) (g)-1, crime against humanity of rape, below at 4.2.588).

Wilfully Causing Great Suffering or Serious Injury to Body or Health

4.2.568 This offence has been defined so as to encompass actions which would not qualify as torture because they were not inflicted for one of the purposes required under the traditional definitions of torture. The offence was defined in the *Delalić et al. Trial Judgement* at para. 511:

> An act or omission that is intentional, being an act which, judged objectively, is deliberate and not accidental, which causes serious mental or physical suffering or injury. It covers those acts that do not meet the purposive requirements for the offence of torture, although clearly all acts constituting torture could also fall within the ambit of this offence.

4.2.569 According to this definition, wilfully causing great suffering or serious injury is a lesser included offence to torture (i.e. the definition of the greater offence necessarily includes the definition of the lesser offence). Thus whenever an accused is found guilty of torture, he has necessarily also committed the offence of wilfully causing great suffering or serious injury. Equally, where all the elements of torture are present except the intention, for example, to obtain information, the accused would not be guilty of torture (the greater offence) but would be guilty of wilfully causing great suffering or serious injury. This can be important as a matter of alternative verdicts that are available to the trier of fact. See also the *Blaškić Trial Judgement*, para. 156. See, on "cumulative charging," 8.3.1 *et seq.*

Inhuman Treatment/Cruel Treatment

4.2.570 Cruel treatment under common Article 3, prosecuted under Article 3 of the Statute, is the same as inhuman treatment under Article 2 of the Statute (*Delalić et al. Trial Judgement*, para. 552).

4.2.571 The Chamber in the *Delalić et al. Trial Judgement* noted that inhuman treatment, unlike torture, has not been defined in international human rights instruments. It therefore fell to the Trial Chamber to provide such a definition (para. 517). The definition of inhuman treatment is provided at para. 543 of the *Delalić et al. Trial Judgement:*

> An intentional act or omission which causes serious mental or physical suffering or injury or constitutes a serious attack on human dignity.

4.2.572 The Trial Chamber also suggested a negative definition, namely that inhuman treatment is treatment which causes severe mental or physical suffering but which falls short of torture, or lacks one of the elements of torture (e.g. prohibited purpose or official sanction) (*ibid.*, para. 542). The Chamber added that whether a given conduct constitutes inhuman treatment is ultimately a question of fact. See also para. 186 of the *Blaškić Trial Judgement:*

> The Defence asserted *inter alia* that using human shields and trench digging constituted cruel treatment only if the victims were foreigners in enemy territory, inhabitants of an occupied territory or detainees. The Trial Chamber is of the view that treatment may be cruel whatever the status of the person concerned. The Trial Chamber entirely concurs with the *Celebici* Trial Chamber which arrived at the conclusion that cruel treatment constitutes an intentional act or omission "which causes serious mental or physical suffering or injury or constitutes a serious attack on human dignity. As such, it carries an equivalent meaning and therefore the same residual function for the purposes of Common article 3 of the Statute, as inhuman treatment does in relation to grave breaches of the Geneva Convention."

Detention Under Inhumane Conditions

4.2.573 Being detained under inhumane conditions could constitute wilfully causing great suffering or serious injury to body or health and cruel treatment (*Delalić et* al. *Trial Judgement*, para. 554). The standard that determined whether conditions were inhumane or not was an absolute and not a relative standard (*ibid*, para. 557), i.e., the question was not to be determined by assessing prevailing conditions nor what was possible under the circumstances. If humane conditions of detention were not possible, then the detaining Power must not detain people. This corresponds to the principle of European human rights law that lack of means and resources is not an excuse for failure to fulfill a human rights obligation.

Unlawful Confinement of Civilians

4.2.574 The confinement or internment of civilians during armed conflict is permissible in the limited cases where it is "absolutely necessary" (*Delalić et al. Trial Judgement*, paras. 559–583). Internment is permissible if a Party to the conflict had "serious and legitimate reasons" for thinking that the internees would otherwise "seriously prejudice its security" by engaging in sabotage or espionage. But the Party to the conflict could not automatically intern all enemy nationals or allies on the grounds that they all posed a threat, or because the internee was male and of military age. In short, the decision to intern could not be taken "on a collective basis" (*ibid*, para. 583). Any confinement or internment has to respect the internees' basic procedural rights under Articles 42 and 43 of the 4th Geneva Convention, in particular the right to review by a court or administrative board of the grounds for their detention.

4.2.575 The Trial Chamber's findings were upheld on appeal (see *Delalić et al. Appeals Judgement*, paras. 315–387).

Plunder/Pillage

4.2.576 This offence has long been known to international law, and it is prohibited as a matter of both conventional and customary law: see Hague Regulations, Article 46; the Charter of the International Military Tribunal 1945, Art. 6(b); The Trial of German Major War Criminals (Proceedings of the International Military Tribunal sitting at Nuremberg, Germany), Part 22, the IMT Judgement, p. 457; *U.S. v. Carl Krauch*, Law Reports of Trials of War Criminals, vol. x, pp. 42–47, which considered the term "spoliation" to be synonymous with that of "plunder."

4.2.577 Plunder and pillage both "embrace all forms of unlawful appropriation of property in armed conflict for which individual criminal responsibility attaches under international law, including those acts traditionally described as "pillage"." (*Delalić et al. Trial Judgement*, para. 591). Whether a given act of misappropriation is serious enough to constitute plunder is a factual question to be decided in each case (*ibid*, para. 592).

4.2.578 Basing itself on the *Delalić et al. Trial Judgement* (paras. 590–591), the Trial Chamber ruling in the *Blaškić Trial Judgement* held that:

> 184. The prohibition on the wanton appropriation of enemy public or private property extends to both isolated acts of plunder for private interest and to the "organized seizure of property undertaken within the framework of a systematic economic exploitation of occupied territory." Plunder "should be understood to embrace all forms of unlawful appropriation of property in armed

conflict for which individual criminal responsibility attaches under international law, including those acts traditionally described as 'pillage.'

4.2.579 Charges under this head were rejected in the *Delalić et al. Trial Judgement* (paras. 1151–1154), since the property in question, even if had been taken, was of little or no value and therefore its misappropriation could not constitute a *serious* violation of international humanitarian law. This conclusion was reached on the basis of the third condition laid down by the Appeals Chamber, in the *Tadić* interlocutory appeal, for Article 3 to apply, namely that the "breach must involve grave consequences for the victim":

> 1154. . . . even when considered in the light most favourable to the Prosecution, the evidence before the Trial Chamber fails to demonstrate that any property taken from the detainees in the Celebici prison-camp was of sufficient monetary value for its unlawful appropriation to involve grave consequences for the victims.

4.2.580 This seems, however, to take insufficient account of the relative poverty of many of the victims, for whom an object of small monetary value may have a high relative value. Moreover, inexpensive objects may nonetheless have sentimental value, so that being summarily deprived of them can cause mental suffering. Finally, stripping persons of their belongings dehumanises them, and is thus often the first step in a series of increasingly serious inhumane acts. At the same time, the Chamber's attempt to establish *some* threshold for "seriousness" of crimes is to be welcomed. See also the *Kordić Trial Judgement*, paras. 358–362.

Outrages Upon Personal Dignity

4.2.581 The *actus reus* and *mens rea* of this offence were defined by the Trial Chamber in the *Aleksovski Trial Judgement* (para. 56) as:

> *Actus reus:* The accused submits the victim to humiliation of sufficient intensity that any reasonable person would be outraged by it.
>
> *Mens rea:* The accused is aware of the logical and foreseeable consequences of his acts.

4.2.582 Whether a particular act or set of acts could qualify as an outrage upon personal dignity, however, was very much a question of fact (*ibid*, para. 57).

4.2.583 The Chamber ruling in the *Foča Trial Judgement* examined this offence in considerable depth (paras. 498–514). The Chamber disagreed with the definition put forward in the *Aleksovski Trial Judgement* (above) to the extent that it required the humiliation or degradation to cause "lasting" suffering to the victim. For the Chamber, it was sufficient that the humiliation was "real and serious" (para. 501). The Chamber saw outrages upon personal dignity as a category of inhuman treatment dealt with in common Article 3 (prosecuted under Article 3 of the ICTY Statute) (para. 502). The Chamber defined the offence as requiring (para. 514):

(i) that the accused intentionally committed or participated in an act or omission which would be generally considered to cause serious humiliation, degradation or otherwise be a serious attack on human dignity, and

(ii) that he knew that the act or omission could have that effect.

ICC Elements of Crimes

4.2.584 As noted above, the ICC—unlike the ICTY and ICTR—Judges will be "assisted" in their "interpretation and application" of the subject-matter articles of the Rome Statute, by the "Elements of the Crimes." See Article 9 of the Rome Statute (Annex 2). The "Finalised Draft Text of the Elements of the Crimes" was adopted by the Preparatory Commission for the International Criminal Court at its 23rd meeting on 30 June 2000. The text is here reproduced for convenience.

4.2.585

**ICC
Elements of Crimes**

General Introduction
1. Pursuant to article 9, the following Elements of Crimes shall assist the Court in the interpretation and application of articles 6, 7 and 8, consistent with the Statute. The provisions of the Statute, including article 21 and the general principles set out in Part 3, are applicable to the Elements of Crimes.
2. As stated in article 30, unless otherwise provided, a person shall be criminally responsible and liable for punishment for a crime within the jurisdiction of the Court only if the material elements are committed with intent and knowledge. Where no reference is made in the Elements of Crimes to a mental element for any particular conduct, consequence or circumstance listed, it is understood that the relevant mental element, i.e., intent, knowledge or both, set out in article 30 applies. Exceptions to the article 30 standard, based on the Statute, including applicable law under its relevant provisions, are indicated below.
3. Existence of intent and knowledge can be inferred from relevant facts and circumstances.
4. With respect to mental elements associated with elements involving value judgement, such as those using the terms "inhumane" or "severe," it is not necessary that the perpetrator personally completed a particular value judgement, unless otherwise indicated.
5. Grounds for excluding criminal responsibility or the absence thereof are generally not specified in the elements of crimes listed under each crime.
6. The requirement of "unlawfulness" found in the Statute or in other parts of international law, in particular international humanitarian law, is generally not specified in the elements of crimes.
7. The elements of crimes are generally structured in accordance with the following principles:
— As the elements of crimes focus on the conduct, consequences and circumstances associated with each crime, they are generally listed in that order;
— When required, a particular mental element is listed after the affected conduct, consequence or circumstance;
— Contextual circumstances are listed last.
8. As used in the Elements of Crimes, the term "perpetrator" is neutral as to guilt or innocence. The elements, including the appropriate mental elements, apply, *mutatis mutandis*, to all those whose criminal responsibility may fall under articles 25 and 28 of the Statute.
9. A particular conduct may constitute one or more crimes.
10. The use of short titles for the crimes has no legal effect.

4.2.586

Article 6
Genocide

Introduction

With respect to the last element listed for each crime:
— The term "in the context of" would include the initial acts in an emerging pattern;
— The term "manifest" is an objective qualification;
— Notwithstanding the normal requirement for a mental element provided for in article 30, and recognizing that knowledge of the circumstances will usually be addressed in proving genocidal intent, the appropriate requirement, if any, for a mental element regarding this circumstance will need to be decided by the Court on a case-by-case basis.

Article 6 (a)
Genocide by killing

Elements
1. The perpetrator killed one or more persons.
2. Such person or persons belonged to a particular national, ethnical, racial or religious group.
3. The perpetrator intended to destroy, in whole or in part, that national, ethnical, racial or religious group, as such.
4. The conduct took place in the context of a manifest pattern of similar conduct directed against that group or was conduct that could itself effect such destruction.

Article 6 (b)
Genocide by causing serious bodily or mental harm

Elements
1. The perpetrator caused serious bodily or mental harm to one or more persons.
2. Such person or persons belonged to a particular national, ethnical, racial or religious group.
3. The perpetrator intended to destroy, in whole or in part, that national, ethnical, racial or religious group, as such.
4. The conduct took place in the context of a manifest pattern of similar conduct directed against that group or was conduct that could itself effect such destruction.

Article 6 (c)
Genocide by deliberately inflicting conditions of life calculated to bring about physical destruction

Elements
1. The perpetrator inflicted certain conditions of life upon one or more persons.
2. Such person or persons belonged to a particular national, ethnical, racial or religious group.
3. The perpetrator intended to destroy, in whole or in part, that national, ethnical, racial or religious group, as such.
4. The conditions of life were calculated to bring about the physical destruction of that group, in whole or in part.

5. The conduct took place in the context of a manifest pattern of similar conduct directed against that group or was conduct that could itself effect such destruction.

Article 6 (d)
Genocide by imposing measures intended to prevent births

Elements
1. The perpetrator imposed certain measures upon one or more persons.
2. Such person or persons belonged to a particular national, ethnical, racial or religious group.
3. The perpetrator intended to destroy, in whole or in part, that national, ethnical, racial or religious group, as such.
4. The measures imposed were intended to prevent births within that group.
5. The conduct took place in the context of a manifest pattern of similar conduct directed against that group or was conduct that could itself effect such destruction.

Article 6 (e)
Genocide by forcibly transferring children

Elements
1. The perpetrator forcibly transferred one or more persons.
2. Such person or persons belonged to a particular national, ethnical, racial or religious group.
3. The perpetrator intended to destroy, in whole or in part, that national, ethnical, racial or religious group, as such.
4. The transfer was from that group to another group.
5. The person or persons were under the age of 18 years.
6. The perpetrator knew, or should have known, that the person or persons were under the age of 18 years.
7. The conduct took place in the context of a manifest pattern of similar conduct directed against that group or was conduct that could itself effect such destruction.

Comment:

In defining the Elements of Genocide, the drafters have opted for an objective notion of "group," somewhat in contradiction to the approach increasingly being taken by the ICTY and ICTR. According to the Elements, in each case the victim must *actually* have "belonged to a particular national, ethnical, racial or religious group," and not merely be believed by the perpetrator(s) to belong to such a group. Many would consider this a retrograde definition. See the discussion above, under "Genocide," of the subjective and objective approaches to "groups" (4.2.103 *et seq.*).

4.2.587

Article 7
Crimes against humanity

Introduction
1. Since article 7 pertains to international criminal law, its provisions, consistent with article 22, must be strictly construed, taking into account that crimes against humanity as defined in article 7 are among the most serious crimes of concern to the international community as a whole, warrant and entail individual criminal responsibility, and require conduct which is impermissible under generally applicable international law, as recognized by the principal legal systems of the world.
2. The last two elements for each crime against humanity describe the context in which the conduct must take place. These elements clarify the requisite participation in and knowledge of a widespread or systematic attack against a civilian population. However, the last element should not be interpreted as requiring proof that the perpetrator had knowledge of all characteristics of the attack or the precise details of the plan or policy of the State or organization. In the case of an emerging widespread or systematic attack against a civilian population, the intent clause of the last element indicates that this mental element is satisfied if the perpetrator intended to further such an attack.
3. "Attack directed against a civilian population" in these context elements is understood to mean a course of conduct involving the multiple commission of acts referred to in article 7, para. 1, of the Statute against any civilian population, pursuant to or in furtherance of a State or organizational policy to commit such attack. The acts need not constitute a military attack. It is understood that "policy to commit such attack" requires that the State or organization actively promote or encourage such an attack against a civilian population.

Article 7 (1) (a)
Crime against humanity of murder

Elements
1. The perpetrator killed one or more persons.
2. The conduct was committed as part of a widespread or systematic attack directed against a civilian population.
3. The perpetrator knew that the conduct was part of or intended the conduct to be part of a widespread or systematic attack against a civilian population.

Article 7 (1) (b)
Crime against humanity of extermination

Elements
1. The perpetrator killed one or more persons, including by inflicting conditions of life calculated to bring about the destruction of part of a population.
2. The conduct constituted, or took place as part of, a mass killing of members of a civilian population.
3. The conduct was committed as part of a widespread or systematic attack directed against a civilian population.
4. The perpetrator knew that the conduct was part of or intended the conduct to be part of a widespread or systematic attack directed against a civilian population.

Article 7 (1) (c)
Crime against humanity of enslavement

Elements
1. The perpetrator exercised any or all of the powers attaching to the right of ownership over one or more persons, such as by purchasing, selling, lending or bartering such a person or persons, or by imposing on them a similar deprivation of liberty.
2. The conduct was committed as part of a widespread or systematic attack directed against a civilian population.
3. The perpetrator knew that the conduct was part of or intended the conduct to be part of a widespread or systematic attack directed against a civilian population.

Article 7 (1) (d)
Crime against humanity of deportation or forcible transfer of population

Elements
1. The perpetrator deported or forcibly transferred, without grounds permitted under international law, one or more persons to another State or location, by expulsion or other coercive acts.
2. Such person or persons were lawfully present in the area from which they were so deported or transferred.
3. The perpetrator was aware of the factual circumstances that established the lawfulness of such presence.
4. The conduct was committed as part of a widespread or systematic attack directed against a civilian population.
5. The perpetrator knew that the conduct was part of or intended the conduct to be part of a widespread or systematic attack directed against a civilian population.

Article 7 (1) (e)
Crime against humanity of imprisonment or other severe deprivation of physical liberty

Elements
1. The perpetrator imprisoned one or more persons or otherwise severely deprived one or more persons of physical liberty.
2. The gravity of the conduct was such that it was in violation of fundamental rules of international law.
3. The perpetrator was aware of the factual circumstances that established the gravity of the conduct.
4. The conduct was committed as part of a widespread or systematic attack directed against a civilian population.
5. The perpetrator knew that the conduct was part of or intended the conduct to be part of a widespread or systematic attack directed against a civilian population.

Article 7 (1) (f)
Crime against humanity of torture

Elements
1. The perpetrator inflicted severe physical or mental pain or suffering upon one or more persons.
2. Such person or persons were in the custody or under the control of the perpetrator.
3. Such pain or suffering did not arise only from, and was not inherent in or incidental to, lawful sanctions.
4. The conduct was committed as part of a widespread or systematic attack directed against a civilian population.
5. The perpetrator knew that the conduct was part of or intended the conduct to be part of a widespread or systematic attack directed against a civilian population.

Comment:

Two ingredients are absent from this definition of torture which are found in ICTY and ICTR jurisprudence: (1) the need for a State actor to be implicated in the torutre, and (2) the need to prove a specific purpose for this crime.

4.2.588

Article 7 (1) (g)-1
Crime against humanity of rape

Elements
1. The perpetrator invaded the body of a person by conduct resulting in penetration, however slight, of any part of the body of the victim or of the perpetrator with a sexual organ, or of the anal or genital opening of the victim with any object or any other part of the body.
2. The invasion was committed by force, or by threat of force or coercion, such as that caused by fear of violence, duress, detention, psychological oppression or abuse of power, against such person or another person, or by taking advantage of a coercive environment, or the invasion was committed against a person incapable of giving genuine consent.
3. The conduct was committed as part of a widespread or systematic attack directed against a civilian population.
4. The perpetrator knew that the conduct was part of or intended the conduct to be part of a widespread or systematic attack directed against a civilian population.

Article 7 (1) (g)-2
Crime against humanity of sexual slavery

Elements
1. The perpetrator exercised any or all of the powers attaching to the right of ownership over one or more persons, such as by purchasing, selling, lending or bartering such a person or persons, or by imposing on them a similar deprivation of liberty.

2. The perpetrator caused such person or persons to engage in one or more acts of a sexual nature.
3. The conduct was committed as part of a widespread or systematic attack directed against a civilian population.
4. The perpetrator knew that the conduct was part of or intended the conduct to be part of a widespread or systematic attack directed against a civilian population.

Comment:

The definition of rape corresponds to the ICTY/ICTR's "mechanical" definition (see 4.2.557 above). It is stated, in a footnote to these Elements, that "It is understood that such deprivation of liberty may, in some circumstances, include exacting forced labour or otherwise reducing a person to a servile status as defined in the Supplementary Convention on the Abolition of Slavery, the Slave Trade, and Institutions and Practices Similar to Slavery of 1956. It is also understood that the conduct described in this element includes trafficking in persons, in particular women and children."

Article 7 (1) (g)-3
Crime against humanity of enforced prostitution

Elements
1. The perpetrator caused one or more persons to engage in one or more acts of a sexual nature by force, or by threat of force or coercion, such as that caused by fear of violence, duress, detention, psychological oppression or abuse of power, against such person or persons or another person, or by taking advantage of a coercive environment or such person's or persons' incapacity to give genuine consent.
2. The perpetrator or another person obtained or expected to obtain pecuniary or other advantage in exchange for or in connection with the acts of a sexual nature.
3. The conduct was committed as part of a widespread or systematic attack directed against a civilian population.
4. The perpetrator knew that the conduct was part of or intended the conduct to be part of a widespread or systematic attack directed against a civilian population.

Article 7 (1) (g)-4
Crime against humanity of forced pregnancy

Elements
1. The perpetrator confined one or more women forcibly made pregnant, with the intent of affecting the ethnic composition of any population or carrying out other grave violations of international law.
2. The conduct was committed as part of a widespread or systematic attack directed against a civilian population.
3. The perpetrator knew that the conduct was part of or intended the conduct to be part of a widespread or systematic attack directed against a civilian population.

Comment:

It seems odd that "*ethnic* composition" alone should be a prohibited intent, and not the intent to affect a racial, religious or national composition, which might well also be aims of perpetrators of this offence.

Article 7 (1) (g)-5
Crime against humanity of enforced sterilization

Elements
1. The perpetrator deprived one or more persons of biological reproductive capacity.
2. The conduct was neither justified by the medical or hospital treatment of the person or persons concerned nor carried out with their genuine consent.
3. The conduct was committed as part of a widespread or systematic attack directed against a civilian population.
4. The perpetrator knew that the conduct was part of or intended the conduct to be part of a widespread or systematic attack directed against a civilian population.

Article 7 (1) (g)-6
Crime against humanity of sexual violence

Elements
1. The perpetrator committed an act of a sexual nature against one or more persons or caused such person or persons to engage in an act of a sexual nature by force, or by threat of force or coercion, such as that caused by fear of violence, duress, detention, psychological oppression or abuse of power, against such person or persons or another person, or by taking advantage of a coercive environment or such person's or persons' incapacity to give genuine consent.
2. Such conduct was of a gravity comparable to the other offences in article 7, para. 1 (g), of the Statute.
3. The perpetrator was aware of the factual circumstances that established the gravity of the conduct.
4. The conduct was committed as part of a widespread or systematic attack directed against a civilian population.
5. The perpetrator knew that the conduct was part of or intended the conduct to be part of a widespread or systematic attack directed against a civilian population.

Article 7 (1) (h)
Crime against humanity of persecution

Elements
1. The perpetrator severely deprived, contrary to international law, one or more persons of fundamental rights.
2. The perpetrator targeted such person or persons by reason of the identity of a group or collectivity or targeted the group or collectivity as such.
3. Such targeting was based on political, racial, national, ethnic, cultural, religious, gender as defined in article 7, para. 3, of the Statute, or other grounds that are universally recognized as impermissible under international law.

> 4. The conduct was committed in connection with any act referred to in article 7, para. 1, of the Statute or any crime within the jurisdiction of the Court.
> 5. The conduct was committed as part of a widespread or systematic attack directed against a civilian population.
> 6. The perpetrator knew that the conduct was part of or intended the conduct to be part of a widespread or systematic attack directed against a civilian population.

> **Article 7 (1) (i)**
> **Crime against humanity of enforced disappearance of persons**
>
> Elements
> 1. The perpetrator:
> (a) Arrested, detained or abducted one or more persons; or
> (b) Refused to acknowledge the arrest, detention or abduction, or to give information on the fate or whereabouts of such person or persons.
> 2. (a) Such arrest, detention or abduction was followed or accompanied by a refusal to acknowledge that deprivation of freedom or to give information on the fate or whereabouts of such person or persons; or
> (b) Such refusal was preceded or accompanied by that deprivation of freedom.
> 3. The perpetrator was aware that:
> (a) Such arrest, detention or abduction would be followed in the ordinary course of events by a refusal to acknowledge that deprivation of freedom or to give information on the fate or whereabouts of such person or persons; or
> (b) Such refusal was preceded or accompanied by that deprivation of freedom.
> 4. Such arrest, detention or abduction was carried out by, or with the authorization, support or acquiescence of, a State or a political organization.
> 5. Such refusal to acknowledge that deprivation of freedom or to give information on the fate or whereabouts of such person or persons was carried out by, or with the authorization or support of, such State or political organization.
> 6. The perpetrator intended to remove such person or persons from the protection of the law for a prolonged period of time.
> 7. The conduct was committed as part of a widespread or systematic attack directed against a civilian population.
> 8. The perpetrator knew that the conduct was part of or intended the conduct to be part of a widespread or systematic attack directed against a civilian population.

Comment:

Two footnotes to the above article are worth noting. One footnote states, "Given the complex nature of this crime, it is recognized that its commission will normally involve more than one perpetrator as a part of a common criminal purpose." Another states, "This crime falls under the jurisdiction of the Court only if the attack referred to in elements 7 and 8 occurs after the entry into force of the Statute.'''' This latter footnote seems designed to keep "disappearances" of the past, notably those of South America which occurred in the 1970s, from the ICC's jurisdiction. This would seem to run counter to the idea of "continuing disappearances" developed in the *Velasquez-Rodriguez case* before the Inter-American Court of Human Rights, whereby a State can incur responsibility for a "disappearance" long in the past if it fails to take appropriate action to locate the person or to punish the perpetrators in the present.

Article 7 (1) (j)
Crime against humanity of apartheid

Elements
1. The perpetrator committed an inhumane act against one or more persons.
2. Such act was an act referred to in article 7, para. 1, of the Statute, or was an act of a character similar to any of those acts.
3. The perpetrator was aware of the factual circumstances that established the character of the act.
4. The conduct was committed in the context of an institutionalized regime of systematic oppression and domination by one racial group over any other racial group or groups.
5. The perpetrator intended to maintain such regime by that conduct.
6. The conduct was committed as part of a widespread or systematic attack directed against a civilian population.
7. The perpetrator knew that the conduct was part of or intended the conduct to be part of a widespread or systematic attack directed against a civilian population.

Article 7 (1) (k)
Crime against humanity of other inhumane acts

Elements
1. The perpetrator inflicted great suffering, or serious injury to body or to mental or physical health, by means of an inhumane act.
2. Such act was of a character similar to any other act referred to in article 7, para. 1, of the Statute.
3. The perpetrator was aware of the factual circumstances that established the character of the act.
4. The conduct was committed as part of a widespread or systematic attack directed against a civilian population.
5. The perpetrator knew that the conduct was part of or intended the conduct to be part of a widespread or systematic attack directed against a civilian population.

4.2.589

Article 8
War crimes

Introduction
The elements for war crimes under article 8, para. 2 (c) and (e), are subject to the limitations addressed in article 8, para. 2 (d) and (f), which are not elements of crimes.
The elements for war crimes under article 8, para. 2, of the Statute shall be interpreted within the established framework of the international law of armed conflict including, as appropriate, the

international law of armed conflict applicable to armed conflict at sea.
With respect to the last two elements listed for each crime:
- There is no requirement for a legal evaluation by the perpetrator as to the existence of an armed conflict or its character as international or non-international;
- In that context there is no requirement for awareness by the perpetrator of the facts that established the character of the conflict as international or non-international;
- There is only a requirement for the awareness of the factual circumstances that established the existence of an armed conflict that is implicit in the terms "took place in the context of and was associated with."

Article 8 (2) (a)
Article 8 (2) (a) (i)
War crime of wilful killing

Elements
1. The perpetrator killed one or more persons.
2. Such person or persons were protected under one or more of the Geneva Conventions of 1949.
3. The perpetrator was aware of the factual circumstances that established that protected status.
4. The conduct took place in the context of and was associated with an international armed conflict.
5. The perpetrator was aware of factual circumstances that established the existence of an armed conflict.

Article 8 (2) (a) (ii)-1
War crime of torture

Elements
1. The perpetrator inflicted severe physical or mental pain or suffering upon one or more persons.
2. The perpetrator inflicted the pain or suffering for such purposes as: obtaining information or a confession, punishment, intimidation or coercion or for any reason based on discrimination of any kind.
3. Such person or persons were protected under one or more of the Geneva Conventions of 1949.
4. The perpetrator was aware of the factual circumstances that established that protected status.
5. The conduct took place in the context of and was associated with an international armed conflict.
6. The perpetrator was aware of factual circumstances that established the existence of an armed conflict.

Comment:
Unlike torture as a crime against humanity, torture as a war crime *does* require that the perpetrator inflicted the torture for a specific purpose. The reason why this distinction was introduced is not entirely clear.

Article 8 (2) (a) (ii)-2
War crime of inhuman treatment

Elements
1. The perpetrator inflicted severe physical or mental pain or suffering upon one or more persons.
2. Such person or persons were protected under one or more of the Geneva Conventions of 1949.
3. The perpetrator was aware of the factual circumstances that established that protected status.
4. The conduct took place in the context of and was associated with an international armed conflict.
5. The perpetrator was aware of factual circumstances that established the existence of an armed conflict.

Article 8 (2) (a) (ii)-3
War crime of biological experiments

Elements
1. The perpetrator subjected one or more persons to a particular biological experiment.
2. The experiment seriously endangered the physical or mental health or integrity of such person or persons.
3. The intent of the experiment was non-therapeutic and it was neither justified by medical reasons nor carried out in such person's or persons' interest.
4. Such person or persons were protected under one or more of the Geneva Conventions of 1949.
5. The perpetrator was aware of the factual circumstances that established that protected status.
6. The conduct took place in the context of and was associated with an international armed conflict.
7. The perpetrator was aware of factual circumstances that established the existence of an armed conflict.

Article 8 (2) (a) (iii)
War crime of wilfully causing great suffering

Elements
1. The perpetrator caused great physical or mental pain or suffering to, or serious injury to body or health of, one or more persons.
2. Such person or persons were protected under one or more of the Geneva Conventions of 1949.
3. The perpetrator was aware of the factual circumstances that established that protected status.
4. The conduct took place in the context of and was associated with an international armed conflict.
5. The perpetrator was aware of factual circumstances that established the existence of an armed conflict.

Article 8 (2) (a) (iv)
War crime of destruction and appropriation of property

Elements
1. The perpetrator destroyed or appropriated certain property.
2. The destruction or appropriation was not justified by military necessity.
3. The destruction or appropriation was extensive and carried out wantonly.
4. Such property was protected under one or more of the Geneva Conventions of 1949.
5. The perpetrator was aware of the factual circumstances that established that protected status.
6. The conduct took place in the context of and was associated with an international armed conflict.
7. The perpetrator was aware of factual circumstances that established the existence of an armed conflict.

Article 8 (2) (a) (v)
War crime of compelling service in hostile forces

Elements
1. The perpetrator coerced one or more persons, by act or threat, to take part in military operations against that person's own country or forces or otherwise serve in the forces of a hostile power.
2. Such person or persons were protected under one or more of the Geneva Conventions of 1949.
3. The perpetrator was aware of the factual circumstances that established that protected status.
4. The conduct took place in the context of and was associated with an international armed conflict.
5. The perpetrator was aware of factual circumstances that established the existence of an armed conflict.

Article 8 (2) (a) (vi)
War crime of denying a fair trial

Elements
1. The perpetrator deprived one or more persons of a fair and regular trial by denying judicial guarantees as defined, in particular, in the third and the fourth Geneva Conventions of 1949.
2. Such person or persons were protected under one or more of the Geneva Conventions of 1949.
3. The perpetrator was aware of the factual circumstances that established that protected status.
4. The conduct took place in the context of and was associated with an international armed conflict.
5. The perpetrator was aware of factual circumstances that established the existence of an armed conflict.

Article 8 (2) (a) (vii)-1
War crime of unlawful deportation and transfer

Elements
1. The perpetrator deported or transferred one or more persons to another State or to another location.
2. Such person or persons were protected under one or more of the Geneva Conventions of 1949.
3. The perpetrator was aware of the factual circumstances that established that protected status.
4. The conduct took place in the context of and was associated with an international armed conflict.
5. The perpetrator was aware of factual circumstances that established the existence of an armed conflict.

Article 8 (2) (a) (vii)-2
War crime of unlawful confinement

Elements
1. The perpetrator confined or continued to confine one or more persons to a certain location.
2. Such person or persons were protected under one or more of the Geneva Conventions of 1949.
3. The perpetrator was aware of the factual circumstances that established that protected status.
4. The conduct took place in the context of and was associated with an international armed conflict.
5. The perpetrator was aware of factual circumstances that established the existence of an armed conflict.

Article 8 (2) (a) (viii)
War crime of taking hostages

Elements
1. The perpetrator seized, detained or otherwise held hostage one or more persons.
2. The perpetrator threatened to kill, injure or continue to detain such person or persons.
3. The perpetrator intended to compel a State, an international organization, a natural or legal person or a group of persons to act or refrain from acting as an explicit or implicit condition for the safety or the release of such person or persons.
4. Such person or persons were protected under one or more of the Geneva Conventions of 1949.
5. The perpetrator was aware of the factual circumstances that established that protected status.
6. The conduct took place in the context of and was associated with an international armed conflict.
7. The perpetrator was aware of factual circumstances that established the existence of an armed conflict.

Article 8 (2) (b)
Article 8 (2) (b) (i)
War crime of attacking civilians

Elements
1. The perpetrator directed an attack.
2. The object of the attack was a civilian population as such or individual civilians not taking direct part in hostilities.
3. The perpetrator intended the civilian population as such or individual civilians not taking direct part in hostilities to be the object of the attack.
4. The conduct took place in the context of and was associated with an international armed conflict.
5. The perpetrator was aware of factual circumstances that established the existence of an armed conflict.

Article 8 (2) (b) (ii)
War crime of attacking civilian objects

Elements
1. The perpetrator directed an attack.
2. The object of the attack was civilian objects, that is, objects which are not military objectives.
3. The perpetrator intended such civilian objects to be the object of the attack.
4. The conduct took place in the context of and was associated with an international armed conflict.
5. The perpetrator was aware of factual circumstances that established the existence of an armed conflict.

Article 8 (2) (b) (iii)
War crime of attacking personnel or objects involved in a humanitarian assistance or peacekeeping mission

Elements
1. The perpetrator directed an attack.
2. The object of the attack was personnel, installations, material, units or vehicles involved in a humanitarian assistance or peacekeeping mission in accordance with the Charter of the United Nations.
3. The perpetrator intended such personnel, installations, material, units or vehicles so involved to be the object of the attack.
4. Such personnel, installations, material, units or vehicles were entitled to that protection given to civilians or civilian objects under the international law of armed conflict.
5. The perpetrator was aware of the factual circumstances that established that protection.
6. The conduct took place in the context of and was associated with an international armed conflict.
7. The perpetrator was aware of factual circumstances that established the existence of an armed conflict.

Article 8 (2) (b) (iv)
War crime of excessive incidental death, injury, or damage

Elements
1. The perpetrator launched an attack.
2. The attack was such that it would cause incidental death or injury to civilians or damage to civilian objects or widespread, long-term and severe damage to the natural environment and that such death, injury or damage would be of such an extent as to be clearly excessive in relation to the concrete and direct overall military advantage anticipated.
3. The perpetrator knew that the attack would cause incidental death or injury to civilians or damage to civilian objects or widespread, long-term and severe damage to the natural environment and that such death, injury or damage would be of suchan extent as to be clearly excessive in relation to the concrete and direct overall military advantage anticipated.
4. The conduct took place in the context of and was associated with an international armed conflict.
5. The perpetrator was aware of factual circumstances that established the existence of an armed conflict.

Comment:

There are two footnotes to this provision. The footnote to para. 2 states, "The expression 'concrete and direct overall military advantage' refers to a military advantage that is foreseeable by the perpetrator at the relevant time. Such advantage may or may not be temporally or geographically related to the object of the attack. The fact that this crime admits the possibility of lawful incidental injury and collateral damage does not in any way justify any violation of the law applicable in armed conflict. It does not address justifications for war or other rules related to *jus ad bellum*. It reflects the proportionality requirement inherent in determining the legality of any military activity undertaken in the context of an armed conflict."

The footnote to para. 3 states, "As opposed to the general rule set forth in para. 4 of the General Introduction, this knowledge element requires that the perpetrator make the value judgement as described therein. An evaluation of that value judgement must be based on the requisite information available to the perpetrator at the time."

Article 8 (2) (b) (v)
War crime of attacking undefended places

Elements
1. The perpetrator attacked one or more towns, villages, dwellings or buildings.
2. Such towns, villages, dwellings or buildings were open for unresisted occupation.
3. Such towns, villages, dwellings or buildings did not constitute military objectives.
4. The conduct took place in the context of and was associated with an international armed conflict.
5. The perpetrator was aware of factual circumstances that established the existence of an armed conflict.

Comment:
The footnote to the title of this article states: "The presence in the locality of persons specially protected under the Geneva Conventions of 1949 or of police forces retained for the sole purpose of maintaining law and order does not by itself render the locality a military objective."

Article 8 (2) (b) (vi)
War crime of killing or wounding a person *hors de combat*

Elements
1. The perpetrator killed or injured one or more persons.
2. Such person or persons were *hors de combat*.
3. The perpetrator was aware of the factual circumstances that established this status.
4. The conduct took place in the context of and was associated with an international armed conflict.
5. The perpetrator was aware of factual circumstances that established the existence of an armed conflict.

Article 8 (2) (b) (vii)-1
War crime of improper use of a flag of truce

Elements
1. The perpetrator used a flag of truce.
2. The perpetrator made such use in order to feign an intention to negotiate when there was no such intention on the part of the perpetrator.
3. The perpetrator knew or should have known of the prohibited nature of such use.
4. The conduct resulted in death or serious personal injury.
5. The perpetrator knew that the conduct could result in death or serious personal injury.
6. The conduct took place in the context of and was associated with an international armed conflict.
7. The perpetrator was aware of factual circumstances that established the existence of an armed conflict.

Article 8 (2) (b) (vii)-2
War crime of improper use of a flag, insignia or uniform of the hostile party

Elements
1. The perpetrator used a flag, insignia or uniform of the hostile party.
2. The perpetrator made such use in a manner prohibited under the international law of armed conflict while engaged in an attack.
3. The perpetrator knew or should have known of the prohibited nature of such use.
4. The conduct resulted in death or serious personal injury.
5. The perpetrator knew that the conduct could result in death or serious personal injury.
6. The conduct took place in the context of and was associated with an international armed conflict.
7. The perpetrator was aware of factual circumstances that established the existence of an armed conflict.

Article 8 (2) (b) (vii)-3
War crime of improper use of a flag, insignia or uniform of the United Nations

Elements
1. The perpetrator used a flag, insignia or uniform of the United Nations.
2. The perpetrator made such use in a manner prohibited under the international law of armed conflict.
3. The perpetrator knew of the prohibited nature of such use.
4. The conduct resulted in death or serious personal injury.
5. The perpetrator knew that the conduct could result in death or serious personal injury.
6. The conduct took place in the context of and was associated with an international armed conflict.
7. The perpetrator was aware of factual circumstances that established the existence of an armed conflict.

Article 8 (2) (b) (vii)-4
War crime of improper use of the distinctive emblems of the Geneva Conventions

Elements
1. The perpetrator used the distinctive emblems of the Geneva Conventions.
2. The perpetrator made such use for combatant purposes in a manner prohibited under the international law of armed conflict.
3. The perpetrator knew or should have known of the prohibited nature of such use.
4. The conduct resulted in death or serious personal injury.
5. The perpetrator knew that the conduct could result in death or serious personal injury.
6. The conduct took place in the context of and was associated with an international armed conflict.
7. The perpetrator was aware of factual circumstances that established the existence of an armed conflict.

Article 8 (2) (b) (viii)
The transfer, directly or indirectly, by the Occupying Power of parts of its own civilian population into the territory it occupies, or the deportation or transfer of all or parts of the population of the occupied territory within or outside this territory

Elements
1. The perpetrator:
(a) Transferred, directly or indirectly, parts of its own population into the territory it occupies; or
(b) Deported or transferred all or parts of the population of the occupied territory within or outside this territory.
2. The conduct took place in the context of and was associated with an international armed conflict.
3. The perpetrator was aware of factual circumstances that established the existence of an armed conflict.

Article 8 (2) (b) (ix)
War crime of attacking protected objects

Elements
1. The perpetrator directed an attack.
2. The object of the attack was one or more buildings dedicated to religion, education, art, science or charitable purposes, historic monuments, hospitals or places where the sick and wounded are collected, which were not military objectives.
3. The perpetrator intended such building or buildings dedicated to religion, education, art, science or charitable purposes, historic monuments, hospitals or places where the sick and wounded are collected, which were not military objectives, to be the object of the attack.
4. The conduct took place in the context of and was associated with an international armed conflict.
5. The perpetrator was aware of factual circumstances that established the existence of an armed conflict.

Article 8 (2) (b) (x)-1
War crime of mutilation

Elements
1. The perpetrator subjected one or more persons to mutilation, in particular by permanently disfiguring the person or persons, or by permanently disabling or removing an organ or appendage.
2. The conduct caused death or seriously endangered the physical or mental health of such person or persons.
3. The conduct was neither justified by the medical, dental or hospital treatment of the person or persons concerned nor carried out in such person's or persons' interest.
4. Such person or persons were in the power of an adverse party.
5. The conduct took place in the context of and was associated with an international armed conflict.
6. The perpetrator was aware of factual circumstances that established the existence of an armed conflict.

Comment:

The footnote to para. (3) states: "Consent is not a defence to this crime. The crime prohibits any medical procedure which is not indicated by the state of health of the person concerned and which is not consistent with generally accepted medical standards which would be applied under similar medical circumstances to persons who are nationals of the party conducting the procedure and who are in no way deprived of liberty. This footnote also applies to the same element for article 8(2)(b)(x)–2.".

Article 8 (2) (b) (x)-2
War crime of medical or scientific experiments

Elements
1. The perpetrator subjected one or more persons to a medical or scientific experiment.
2. The experiment caused death or seriously endangered the physical or mental health or integrity of such person or persons.

3. The conduct was neither justified by the medical, dental or hospital treatment of such person or persons concerned nor carried out in such person's or persons' interest.
4. Such person or persons were in the power of an adverse party.
5. The conduct took place in the context of and was associated with an international armed conflict.
6. The perpetrator was aware of factual circumstances that established the existence of an armed conflict.

Article 8 (2) (b) (xi)
War crime of treacherously killing or wounding

Elements
1. The perpetrator invited the confidence or belief of one or more persons that they were entitled to, or were obliged to accord, protection under rules of international law applicable in armed conflict.
2. The perpetrator intended to betray that confidence or belief.
3. The perpetrator killed or injured such person or persons.
4. The perpetrator made use of that confidence or belief in killing or injuring such person or persons.
5. Such person or persons belonged to an adverse party.
6. The conduct took place in the context of and was associated with an international armed conflict.
7. The perpetrator was aware of factual circumstances that established the existence of an armed conflict.

Article 8 (2) (b) (xii)
War crime of denying quarter

Elements
1. The perpetrator declared or ordered that there shall be no survivors.
2. Such declaration or order was given in order to threaten an adversary or to conduct hostilities on the basis that there shall be no survivors.
3. The perpetrator was in a position of effective command or control over the subordinate forces to which the declaration or order was directed.
4. The conduct took place in the context of and was associated with an international armed conflict.
5. The perpetrator was aware of factual circumstances that established the existence of an armed conflict.

Article 8 (2) (b) (xiii)
War crime of destroying or seizing the enemy's property

Elements
1. The perpetrator destroyed or seized certain property.
2. Such property was property of a hostile party.
3. Such property was protected from that destruction or seizure under the international law of armed conflict.
4. The perpetrator was aware of the factual circumstances that established the status of the property.
5. The destruction or seizure was not justified by military necessity.
6. The conduct took place in the context of and was associated with an international armed conflict.
7. The perpetrator was aware of factual circumstances that established the existence of an armed conflict.

Article 8 (2) (b) (xiv)
War crime of depriving the nationals of the hostile power of rights or actions

Elements
1. The perpetrator effected the abolition, suspension or termination of admissibility in a court of law of certain rights or actions.
2. The abolition, suspension or termination was directed at the nationals of a hostile party.
3. The perpetrator intended the abolition, suspension or termination to be directed at the nationals of a hostile party.
4. The conduct took place in the context of and was associated with an international armed conflict.
5. The perpetrator was aware of factual circumstances that established the existence of an armed conflict.

Article 8 (2) (b) (xv)
War crime of compelling participation in military operations

Elements
1. The perpetrator coerced one or more persons by act or threat to take part in military operations against that person's own country or forces.
2. Such person or persons were nationals of a hostile party.
3. The conduct took place in the context of and was associated with an international armed conflict.
4. The perpetrator was aware of factual circumstances that established the existence of an armed conflict.

Article 8 (2) (b) (xvi)
War crime of pillaging

Elements
1. The perpetrator appropriated certain property.
2. The perpetrator intended to deprive the owner of the property and to appropriate it for private or personal use.
3. The appropriation was without the consent of the owner.
4. The conduct took place in the context of and was associated with an international armed conflict.
5. The perpetrator was aware of factual circumstances that established the existence of an armed conflict.

Article 8 (2) (b) (xvii)
War crime of employing poison or poisoned weapons

Elements
1. The perpetrator employed a substance or a weapon that releases a substance as a result of its employment.
2. The substance was such that it causes death or serious damage to health in the ordinary course of events, through its toxic properties.

3. The conduct took place in the context of and was associated with an international armed conflict.
4. The perpetrator was aware of factual circumstances that established the existence of an armed conflict.

Article 8 (2) (b) (xviii)
War crime of employing prohibited gases, liquids, materials or devices

Elements
1. The perpetrator employed a gas or other analogous substance or device.
2. The gas, substance or device was such that it causes death or serious damage to health in the ordinary course of events, through its asphyxiating or toxic properties.
3. The conduct took place in the context of and was associated with an international armed conflict.
4. The perpetrator was aware of factual circumstances that established the existence of an armed conflict.

Comment:

The footnote to para. (2) states: "Nothing in this element shall be interpreted as limiting or prejudicing in any way existing or developing rules of international law with respect to the development, production, stockpiling and use of chemical weapons." This represents a compromise, which many would term unfortunate, on the issue of chemical, biological and nuclear weapons.

Article 8 (2) (b) (xix)
War crime of employing prohibited bullets

Elements
1. The perpetrator employed certain bullets.
2. The bullets were such that their use violates the international law of armed conflict because they expand or flatten easily in the human body.
3. The perpetrator was aware that the nature of the bullets was such that their employment would uselessly aggravate suffering or the wounding effect.
4. The conduct took place in the context of and was associated with an international armed conflict.
5. The perpetrator was aware of factual circumstances that established the existence of an armed conflict.

Article 8 (2) (b) (xx)
War crime of employing weapons, projectiles or materials or methods of warfare listed in the Annex to the Statute

Elements
[Elements will have to be drafted once weapons, projectiles or material or methods of warfare have been included in an annex to the Statute.]

Article 8 (2) (b) (xxi)
War crime of outrages upon personal dignity

Elements
1. The perpetrator humiliated, degraded or otherwise violated the dignity of one or more persons.
2. The severity of the humiliation, degradation or other violation was of such degree as to be generally recognized as an outrage upon personal dignity.
3. The conduct took place in the context of and was associated with an international armed conflict.
4. The perpetrator was aware of factual circumstances that established the existence of an armed conflict.

Article 8 (2) (b) (xxii)-1
War crime of rape

Elements
1. The perpetrator invaded the body of a person by conduct resulting in penetration, however slight, of any part of the body of the victim or of the perpetrator with a sexual organ, or of the anal or genital opening of the victim with any object or any other part of the body.
2. The invasion was committed by force, or by threat of force or coercion, such as that caused by fear of violence, duress, detention, psychological oppression or abuse of power, against such person or another person, or by taking advantage of a coercive environment, or the invasion was committed against a person incapable of giving genuine consent.
3. The conduct took place in the context of and was associated with an international armed conflict.
4. The perpetrator was aware of factual circumstances that established the existence of an armed conflict.

Article 8 (2) (b) (xxii)-2
War crime of sexual slavery

Elements
1. The perpetrator exercised any or all of the powers attaching to the right of ownership over one or more persons, such as by purchasing, selling, lending or bartering such a person or persons, or by imposing on them a similar deprivation of liberty.
2. The perpetrator caused such person or persons to engage in one or more acts of a sexual nature.
3. The conduct took place in the context of and was associated with an international armed conflict.
4. The perpetrator was aware of factual circumstances that established the existence of an armed conflict.

Article 8 (2) (b) (xxii)-3
War crime of enforced prostitution

Elements
1. The perpetrator caused one or more persons to engage in one or more acts of a sexual nature by force, or by threat of force or coercion, such as that caused by fear of violence, duress, detention, psychological oppression or abuse of power, against such person or persons or another person, or by taking advantage of a coercive environment or such person's or persons' incapacity to give genuine consent.
2. The perpetrator or another person obtained or expected to obtain pecuniary or other advantage in exchange for or in connection with the acts of a sexual nature.
3. The conduct took place in the context of and was associated with an international armed conflict.
4. The perpetrator was aware of factual circumstances that established the existence of an armed conflict.

Article 8 (2) (b) (xxii)-4
War crime of forced pregnancy

Elements
1. The perpetrator confined one or more women forcibly made pregnant, with the intent of affecting the ethnic composition of any population or carrying out other grave violations of international law.
2. The conduct took place in the context of and was associated with an international armed conflict.
3. The perpetrator was aware of factual circumstances that established the existence of an armed conflict.

Article 8 (2) (b) (xxii)-5
War crime of enforced sterilization

Elements
1. The perpetrator deprived one or more persons of biological reproductive capacity.
2. The conduct was neither justified by the medical or hospital treatment of the person or persons concerned nor carried out with their genuine consent.
3. The conduct took place in the context of and was associated with an international armed conflict.
4. The perpetrator was aware of factual circumstances that established the existence of an armed conflict.

Article 8 (2) (b) (xxii)-6
War crime of sexual violence

Elements
1. The perpetrator committed an act of a sexual nature against one or more persons or caused such person or persons to engage in an act of a sexual nature by force, or by threat of force or coercion, such as that caused by fear of violence, duress, detention, psychological oppression or abuse of power, against such person or persons or another person, or by taking advantage of a coercive environment or such person's or persons' incapacity to give genuine consent.

2. The conduct was of a gravity comparable to that of a grave breach of the Geneva Conventions.
3. The perpetrator was aware of the factual circumstances that established the gravity of the conduct.
4. The conduct took place in the context of and was associated with an international armed conflict.
5. The perpetrator was aware of factual circumstances that established the existence of an armed conflict.

Article 8 (2) (b) (xxiii)
War crime of using protected persons as shields

Elements
1. The perpetrator moved or otherwise took advantage of the location of one or more civilians or other persons protected under the international law of armed conflict.
2. The perpetrator intended to shield a military objective from attack or shield, favour or impede military operations.
3. The conduct took place in the context of and was associated with an international armed conflict.
4. The perpetrator was aware of factual circumstances that established the existence of an armed conflict.

Article 8 (2) (b) (xxiv)
War crime of attacking objects or persons using the distinctive emblems of the Geneva Conventions

Elements
1. The perpetrator attacked one or more persons, buildings, medical units or transports or other objects using, in conformity with international law, a distinctive emblem or other method of identification indicating protection under the Geneva Conventions.
2. The perpetrator intended such persons, buildings, units or transports or other objects so using such identification to be the object of the attack.
3. The conduct took place in the context of and was associated with an international armed conflict.
4. The perpetrator was aware of factual circumstances that established the existence of an armed conflict.

Article 8 (2) (b) (xxv)
War crime of starvation as a method of warfare

Elements
1. The perpetrator deprived civilians of objects indispensable to their survival.
2. The perpetrator intended to starve civilians as a method of warfare.
3. The conduct took place in the context of and was associated with an international armed conflict.
4. The perpetrator was aware of factual circumstances that established the existence of an armed conflict.

Article 8 (2) (b) (xxvi)
War crime of using, conscripting or enlisting children

Elements
1. The perpetrator conscripted or enlisted one or more persons into the national armed forces or used one or more persons to participate actively in hostilities.
2. Such person or persons were under the age of 15 years.
3. The perpetrator knew or should have known that such person or persons were under the age of 15 years.
4. The conduct took place in the context of and was associated with an international armed conflict.
5. The perpetrator was aware of factual circumstances that established the existence of an armed conflict.

Article 8 (2) (c)
Article 8 (2) (c) (i)-1
War crime of murder

Elements
1. The perpetrator killed one or more persons.
2. Such person or persons were either *hors de combat*, or were civilians, medical personnel, or religious personnel taking no active part in the hostilities.
3. The perpetrator was aware of the factual circumstances that established this status.
4. The conduct took place in the context of and was associated with an armed conflict not of an international character.
5. The perpetrator was aware of factual circumstances that established the existence of an armed conflict.

Article 8 (2) (c) (i)-2
War crime of mutilation

Elements
1. The perpetrator subjected one or more persons to mutilation, in particular by permanently disfiguring the person or persons, or by permanently disabling or removing an organ or appendage.
2. The conduct was neither justified by the medical, dental or hospital treatment of the person or persons concerned nor carried out in such person's or persons' interests.
3. Such person or persons were either *hors de combat*, or were civilians, medical personnel or religious personnel taking no active part in the hostilities.
4. The perpetrator was aware of the factual circumstances that established this status.
5. The conduct took place in the context of and was associated with an armed conflict not of an international character.
6. The perpetrator was aware of factual circumstances that established the existence of an armed conflict.

Article 8 (2) (c) (i)-3
War crime of cruel treatment

Elements
1. The perpetrator inflicted severe physical or mental pain or suffering upon one or more persons.
2. Such person or persons were either *hors de combat*, or were civilians, medical personnel, or religious personnel taking no active part in the hostilities.
3. The perpetrator was aware of the factual circumstances that established this status.
4. The conduct took place in the context of and was associated with an armed conflict not of an international character.
5. The perpetrator was aware of factual circumstances that established the existence of an armed conflict.

Article 8 (2) (c) (i)-4
War crime of torture

Elements
1. The perpetrator inflicted severe physical or mental pain or suffering upon one or more persons.
2. The perpetrator inflicted the pain or suffering for such purposes as: obtaining information or a confession, punishment, intimidation or coercion or for any reason based on discrimination of any kind.
3. Such person or persons were either *hors de combat*, or were civilians, medical personnel or religious personnel taking no active part in the hostilities.
4. The perpetrator was aware of the factual circumstances that established this status.
5. The conduct took place in the context of and was associated with an armed conflict not of an international character.
6. The perpetrator was aware of factual circumstances that established the existence of an armed conflict.

Article 8 (2) (c) (ii)
War crime of outrages upon personal dignity

Elements
1. The perpetrator humiliated, degraded or otherwise violated the dignity of one or more persons.
2. The severity of the humiliation, degradation or other violation was of such degree as to be generally recognized as an outrage upon personal dignity.
3. Such person or persons were either *hors de combat*, or were civilians, medical personnel or religious personnel taking no active part in the hostilities.
4. The perpetrator was aware of the factual circumstances that established this status.
5. The conduct took place in the context of and was associated with an armed conflict not of an international character.
6. The perpetrator was aware of factual circumstances that established the existence of an armed conflict.

Article 8 (2) (c) (iii)
War crime of taking hostages

Elements
1. The perpetrator seized, detained or otherwise held hostage one or more persons.
2. The perpetrator threatened to kill, injure or continue to detain such person or persons.
3. The perpetrator intended to compel a State, an international organization, a natural or legal person or a group of persons to act or refrain from acting as an explicit or implicit condition for the safety or the release of such person or persons.
4. Such person or persons were either *hors de combat*, or were civilians, medical personnel or religious personnel taking no active part in the hostilities.
5. The perpetrator was aware of the factual circumstances that established this status.
6. The conduct took place in the context of and was associated with an armed conflict not of an international character.
7. The perpetrator was aware of factual circumstances that established the existence of an armed conflict.

Article 8 (2) (c) (iv)
War crime of sentencing or execution without due process

Elements
1. The perpetrator passed sentence or executed one or more persons.
2. Such person or persons were either *hors de combat*, or were civilians, medical personnel or religious personnel taking no active part in the hostilities.
3. The perpetrator was aware of the factual circumstances that established this status.
4. There was no previous judgement pronounced by a court, or the court that rendered judgement was not "regularly constituted," that is, it did not afford the essential guarantees of independence and impartiality, or the court that rendered judgement did not afford all other judicial guarantees generally recognized as indispensable under international law.
5. The perpetrator was aware of the absence of a previous judgement or of the denial of relevant guarantees and the fact that they are essential or indispensable to a fair trial.
6. The conduct took place in the context of and was associated with an armed conflict not of an international character.
7. The perpetrator was aware of factual circumstances that established the existence of an armed conflict.

Article 8 (2) (e)
Article 8 (2) (e) (i)
War crime of attacking civilians

Elements
1. The perpetrator directed an attack.
2. The object of the attack was a civilian population as such or individual civilians not taking direct part in hostilities.
3. The perpetrator intended the civilian population as such or individual civilians not taking direct part in hostilities to be the object of the attack.

4. The conduct took place in the context of and was associated with an armed conflict not of an international character.
5. The perpetrator was aware of factual circumstances that established the existence of an armed conflict.

Article 8 (2) (e) (ii)
War crime of attacking objects or persons using the distinctive emblems of the Geneva Conventions

Elements
1. The perpetrator attacked one or more persons, buildings, medical units or transports or other objects using, in conformity with international law, a distinctive emblem or other method of identification indicating protection under the Geneva Conventions.
2. The perpetrator intended such persons, buildings, units or transports or other objects so using such identification to be the object of the attack.
3. The conduct took place in the context of and was associated with an armed conflict not of an international character.
4. The perpetrator was aware of factual circumstances that established the existence of an armed conflict.

Article 8 (2) (e) (iii)
War crime of attacking personnel or objects involved in a humanitarian assistance or peacekeeping mission

Elements
1. The perpetrator directed an attack.
2. The object of the attack was personnel, installations, material, units or vehicles involved in a humanitarian assistance or peacekeeping mission in accordance with the Charter of the United Nations.
3. The perpetrator intended such personnel, installations, material, units or vehicles so involved to be the object of the attack.
4. Such personnel, installations, material, units or vehicles were entitled to that protection given to civilians or civilian objects under the international law of armed conflict.
5. The perpetrator was aware of the factual circumstances that established that protection.
6. The conduct took place in the context of and was associated with an armed conflict not of an international character.
7. The perpetrator was aware of factual circumstances that established the existence of an armed conflict.

Article 8 (2) (e) (iv)
War crime of attacking protected objects

Elements
1. The perpetrator directed an attack.
2. The object of the attack was one or more buildings dedicated to religion, education, art, science or charitable purposes, historic monuments, hospitals or places where the sick and wounded are collected, which were not military objectives.

3. The perpetrator intended such building or buildings dedicated to religion, education, art, science or charitable purposes, historic monuments, hospitals or places where the sick and wounded are collected, which were not military objectives, to be the object of the attack.
4. The conduct took place in the context of and was associated with an armed conflict not of an international character.
5. The perpetrator was aware of factual circumstances that established the existence of an armed conflict.

Article 8 (2) (e) (v)
War crime of pillaging

Elements
1. The perpetrator appropriated certain property.
2. The perpetrator intended to deprive the owner of the property and to appropriate it for private or personal use.
3. The appropriation was without the consent of the owner.
4. The conduct took place in the context of and was associated with an armed conflict not of an international character.
5. The perpetrator was aware of factual circumstances that established the existence of an armed conflict.

Article 8 (2) (e) (vi)-1
War crime of rape

Elements
1. The perpetrator invaded the body of a person by conduct resulting in penetration, however slight, of any part of the body of the victim or of the perpetrator with a sexual organ, or of the anal or genital opening of the victim with any object or any other part of the body.
2. The invasion was committed by force, or by threat of force or coercion, such as that caused by fear of violence, duress, detention, psychological oppression or abuse of power, against such person or another person, or by taking advantage of a coercive environment, or the invasion was committed against a person incapable of giving genuine consent.
3. The conduct took place in the context of and was associated with an armed conflict not of an international character.
4. The perpetrator was aware of factual circumstances that established the existence of an armed conflict.

Article 8 (2) (e) (vi)-2
War crime of sexual slavery

Elements
1. The perpetrator exercised any or all of the powers attaching to the right of ownership over one or more persons, such as by purchasing, selling, lending or bartering such a person or persons, or by imposing on them a similar deprivation of liberty.
2. The perpetrator caused such person or persons to engage in one or more acts of a sexual nature.

3. The conduct took place in the context of and was associated with an armed conflict not of an international character.
4. The perpetrator was aware of factual circumstances that established the existence of an armed conflict.

Article 8 (2) (e) (vi)-3
War crime of enforced prostitution

Elements
1. The perpetrator caused one or more persons to engage in one or more acts of a sexual nature by force, or by threat of force or coercion, such as that caused by fear of violence, duress, detention, psychological oppression or abuse of power, against such person or persons or another person, or by taking advantage of a coercive environment or such person's or persons' incapacity to give genuine consent.
2. The perpetrator or another person obtained or expected to obtain pecuniary or other advantage in exchange for or in connection with the acts of a sexual nature.
3. The conduct took place in the context of and was associated with an armed conflict not of an international character.
4. The perpetrator was aware of factual circumstances that established the existence of an armed conflict.

Article 8 (2) (e) (vi)-4
War crime of forced pregnancy

Elements
1. The perpetrator confined one or more women forcibly made pregnant, with the intent of affecting the ethnic composition of any population or carrying out other grave violations of international law.
2. The conduct took place in the context of and was associated with an armed conflict not of an international character.
3. The perpetrator was aware of factual circumstances that established the existence of an armed conflict.

Article 8 (2) (e) (vi)-5
War crime of enforced sterilization

Elements
1. The perpetrator deprived one or more persons of biological reproductive capacity.
2. The conduct was neither justified by the medical or hospital treatment of the person or persons concerned nor carried out with their genuine consent.
3. The conduct took place in the context of and was associated with an armed conflict not of an international character.
4. The perpetrator was aware of factual circumstances that established the existence of an armed conflict.

Article 8 (2) (e) (vi)-6
War crime of sexual violence

Elements
1. The perpetrator committed an act of a sexual nature against one or more persons or caused such person or persons to engage in an act of a sexual nature by force, or by threat of force or coercion, such as that caused by fear of violence, duress, detention, psychological oppression or abuse of power, against such person or persons or another person, or by taking advantage of a coercive environment or such person's or persons' incapacity to give genuine consent.
2. The conduct was of a gravity comparable to that of a serious violation of article 3 common to the four Geneva Conventions.
3. The perpetrator was aware of the factual circumstances that established the gravity of the conduct.
4. The conduct took place in the context of and was associated with an armed conflict not of an international character.
5. The perpetrator was aware of factual circumstances that established the existence of an armed conflict.

Article 8 (2) (e) (vii)
War crime of using, conscripting and enlisting children

Elements
1. The perpetrator conscripted or enlisted one or more persons into an armed force or group or used one or more persons to participate actively in hostilities.
2. Such person or persons were under the age of 15 years.
3. The perpetrator knew or should have known that such person or persons were under the age of 15 years.
4. The conduct took place in the context of and was associated with an armed conflict not of an international character.
5. The perpetrator was aware of factual circumstances that established the existence of an armed conflict.

Article 8 (2) (e) (viii)
War crime of displacing civilians

Elements
1. The perpetrator ordered a displacement of a civilian population.
2. Such order was not justified by the security of the civilians involved or by military necessity.
3. The perpetrator was in a position to effect such displacement by giving such order.
4. The conduct took place in the context of and was associated with an armed conflict not of an international character.
5. The perpetrator was aware of factual circumstances that established the existence of an armed conflict.

Article 8 (2) (e) (ix)
War crime of treacherously killing or wounding

Elements
1. The perpetrator invited the confidence or belief of one or more combatant adversaries that they were entitled to, or were obliged to accord, protection under rules of international law applicable in armed conflict.
2. The perpetrator intended to betray that confidence or belief.
3. The perpetrator killed or injured such person or persons.
4. The perpetrator made use of that confidence or belief in killing or injuring such person or persons.
5. Such person or persons belonged to an adverse party.
6. The conduct took place in the context of and was associated with an armed conflict not of an international character.
7. The perpetrator was aware of factual circumstances that established the existence of an armed conflict.

Article 8 (2) (e) (x)
War crime of denying quarter

Elements
1. The perpetrator declared or ordered that there shall be no survivors.
2. Such declaration or order was given in order to threaten an adversary or to conduct hostilities on the basis that there shall be no survivors.
3. The perpetrator was in a position of effective command or control over the subordinate forces to which the declaration or order was directed.
4. The conduct took place in the context of and was associated with an armed conflict not of an international character.
5. The perpetrator was aware of factual circumstances that established the existence of an armed conflict.

Article 8 (2) (e) (xi)-1
War crime of mutilation

Elements
1. The perpetrator subjected one or more persons to mutilation, in particular by permanently disfiguring the person or persons, or by permanently disabling or removing an organ or appendage.
2. The conduct caused death or seriously endangered the physical or mental health of such person or persons.
3. The conduct was neither justified by the medical, dental or hospital treatment of the person or persons concerned nor carried out in such person's or persons' interest.
4. Such person or persons were in the power of another party to the conflict.
5. The conduct took place in the context of and was associated with an armed conflict not of an international character.
6. The perpetrator was aware of factual circumstances that established the existence of an armed conflict.

Article 8 (2) (e) (xi)-2
War crime of medical or scientific experiments

Elements
1. The perpetrator subjected one or more persons to a medical or scientific experiment.
2. The experiment caused the death or seriously endangered the physical or mental health or integrity of such person or persons.
3. The conduct was neither justified by the medical, dental or hospital treatment of such person or persons concerned nor carried out in such person's or persons' interest.
4. Such person or persons were in the power of another party to the conflict.
5. The conduct took place in the context of and was associated with an armed conflict not of an international character.
6. The perpetrator was aware of factual circumstances that established the existence of an armed conflict.

Article 8 (2) (e) (xii)
War crime of destroying or seizing the enemy's property

Elements
1. The perpetrator destroyed or seized certain property.
2. Such property was property of an adversary.
3. Such property was protected from that destruction or seizure under the international law of armed conflict.
4. The perpetrator was aware of the factual circumstances that established the status of the property.
5. The destruction or seizure was not required by military necessity.
6. The conduct took place in the context of and was associated with an armed conflict not of an international character.
7. The perpetrator was aware of factual circumstances that established the existence of an armed conflict.

* * * * *

OFFENCES AGAINST THE ADMINISTRATION OF JUSTICE

4.2.590

ICTY Rule 77 Contempt of the Tribunal	ICTR Rule 77 Contempt of the Tribunal
(A) The Tribunal in the exercise of its inherent power may hold in contempt those who knowingly and wilfully interfere with its administration of justice, including any person who	(A) Subject to the provisions of Rule 90(E), a witness who refuses or fails contumaciously to answer a question relevant to the issue before a Chamber may be found in contempt of the Tribunal.

(i) being a witness before a Chamber, contumaciously refuses or fails to answer a question;
(ii) discloses information relating to those proceedings in knowing violation of an order of a Chamber;
(iii) without just excuse fails to comply with an order to attend before or produce documents before a Chamber;
(iv) threatens, intimidates, causes any injury or offers a bribe to, or otherwise interferes with, a witness who is giving, has given, or is about to give evidence in proceedings before a Chamber, or a potential witness; or
(v) threatens, intimidates, offers a bribe to, or otherwise seeks to coerce any other person, with the intention of preventing that other person from complying with an obligation under an order of a Judge or Chamber.
(B) Any incitement or attempts to commit any of the acts punishable under para. (A) is punishable as contempts of the Tribunal with the same penalties.
(C) When a Chamber has reason to believe that a person may be in contempt of the Tribunal, it may:
(i) direct the Prosecutor to investigate the matter with a view to the preparation and submission of an indictment for contempt;
(ii) where the Prosecutor, in the view of the Chamber, has a conflict of interest with respect to the relevant conduct, direct the Registrar to appoint an *amicus curiae* to investigate the matter and report back to the Chamber as to whether there are sufficient grounds for instigating contempt proceedings; or
(iii) initiate proceedings itself.
(D) If the Chamber considers that there are sufficient grounds to proceed against a person for contempt, the Chamber may:
(i) in circumstances described in para. (C)(i), direct the Prosecutor to prosecute the matter; or
(ii) in circumstances described in para. (C)(ii) or (iii), issue an order in lieu of an indictment and either direct *amicus curiae* to prosecute the matter or prosecute the matter itself.

The Chamber may impose a fine not exceeding US$10,000 or a term of imprisonment not exceeding six months.
(B) The Chamber may, however, relieve the witness of the duty to answer, for reasons which it deems appropriate.
(C) Any person who attempts to interfere with or intimidate a witness may be found guilty of contempt and sentenced in accordance with Sub-rule (A).
(D) Any decision rendered under this Rule shall be subject to appeal within 15 days of the impugned decision.
(E) Payment of a fine shall be made to the Registrar to be held in a separate account.

(E) The rules of procedure and evidence in Parts Four to Eight shall apply *mutatis mutandis* to proceedings under this Rule.

(F) Any person indicted for or charged with contempt shall, if that person satisfies the criteria for determination of indigency established by the Registrar, be assigned counsel in accordance with Rule 45.

(G) The maximum penalty that may be imposed on a person found to be in contempt of the Tribunal shall be a term of imprisonment not exceeding seven years, or a fine not exceeding Eur 100,000, or both.

(H) Payment of a fine shall be made to the Registrar to be held in a separate account.

(I) If a Counsel is found guilty of contempt of the Tribunal pursuant to this Rule, the Chamber making such finding may also determine that counsel is no longer eligible to represent a suspect or accused before the Tribunal or that such conduct amounts to misconduct of counsel pursuant to Rule 46, or both.

(J) Any decision rendered by a Trial Chamber under this Rule shall be subject to appeal. Notice of appeal shall be filed within fifteen days of filing of the impugned decision. Where such decision is rendered orally, the application shall be filed within fifteen days of the oral decision, unless

(i) the party challenging the decision was not present or represented when the decision was pronounced, in which case the time-limit shall run from the date on which the challenging party is notified of the oral decision; or

(ii) the Trial Chamber has indicated that a written decision will follow, in which case, the time-limit shall run from filing of the written decision.

(K) In the case of decisions under this Rule by the Appeals Chamber sitting as a Chamber of first instance, an appeal may be submitted in writing to the President within fifteen days of the filing of the impugned decision. Such appeal shall be decided by five different Judges as assigned by the President. Where the impugned decision is rendered orally, the appeal shall be filed within fifteen days of the oral decision, unless

(i) the party challenging the decision was not present or represented when the decision was pronounced, in which case the time-limit shall run from the date on which the challenging party is notified of the oral decision; or
(ii) the Appeals Chamber has indicated that a written decision will follow, in which case the time-limit shall run from filing of the written decision.

History of ICTY Rule 77

4.2.591 Rule 77 was amended at the fifth plenary session in January 1995, to add paras. (C) and (D). Rule 77 was again substantially amended at the fourteenth plenary session on 12 November 1997 (see Revision 11 or ICTR Rule 77 for comparison). The last sentence of Rule 77(J) and paras. (i) and (ii) were added at the eighteenth plenary session. Identical amendments were added to Rules 65, 72 and 73. These amendments are designed to deal with the situation where a party seeks leave to appeal from an *oral* decision.

4.2.592 Rule 77 was amended at the nineteenth plenary session, on 17 December 1998, to amend references to "Trial Chamber" to "Chamber," thus incorporating the Appeals Chamber directly into the rule. A former sub-para. (A)(ii), which made "interfer[ing] with or intimidat[ing] a witness who is giving, has given, or is about to give evidence before a Trial Chamber" contempt of the Tribunal, was moved to para. (B) and elaborated at the same plenary session. New paras. (C) and (D) were also added, with the subsequent paras—which were also substantially amended and reorganised—being renumbered accordingly. Old para. (F) was also moved to para. (E), and para. (E) became para. (I).

4.2.593 Para. (J) was amended on 19 January 2001, after the twenty-third plenary session, to render appeal from a conviction for contempt *a matter of right*, rather than of leave from a Bench of the Appeals Chamber, as had previously been provided for.

4.2.594 As a conviction for contempt is a criminal conviction, carrying a maximum term of imprisonment of seven years, this amendment was no doubt considered necessary in order to comply with Article 14(5) of the International Covenant on Civil and Political Rights, which provides that, "Everyone convicted of a crime shall have the right to his conviction and sentence being reviewed by a higher tribunal according to law." A Bench of the Appeals Chamber is not a "higher tribunal" established by law; only the full Appeals Chamber would fit that description.

4.2.595 The rule was substantially amended at the ICTY's twenty-fifth plenary session, held on 12–13 December, 2001, in particular in relation to paras. (A), (C), (D), (E), (G) and (I).

4.2.596   Para. (K) was added at the twenty-sixth plenary session held on 11 and 12 July 2002, to deal with the problem posed by the absence of an avenue of appeal where an individual is convicted of contempt by the *Appeals Chamber* (as occurred in the *Vujin case*; see 4.2.628 *et seq.* below).

History of ICTR Rule 77

4.2.597   Rule 77(D) was amended at the twelfth plenary session on 5–6 July 2002 to provide a fifteen-day time period within which a decision rendered under this Rule may be appealed.

4.2.598   It is worth noting the considerable difference between the ICTY and ICTR rule on contempt. At the ICTR, contempt is limited to where a witness "*refuses or fails contumaciously to answer a [relevant] question*" and to where a person "*attempts to interfere with or intimidate a witness*," whereas ICTY Rule 77(A) covers a broader range of conduct.

Jurisdiction over Contempt

4.2.599   The ICTY's jurisdiction to deal with contempt was considered in detail by the Appeals Chamber in *Tadić* (App. Ch., *Judgement on Allegations of Contempt against Prior Counsel, Milan Vujin*, 31 January 2000) and again in the Trial Chamber's *Judgement in the Matter of Contempt Allegations against an Accused and his Counsel* of 30 June 2000:

> 91. . . . the power to deal with contempt [i]s within the inherent jurisdiction of the Tribunal, deriving from its judicial function, in order to ensure that its exercise of the jurisdiction which is expressly given to it by its Statute is not frustrated and that its basic judicial functions are safeguarded. The inherent power is to hold in contempt those who knowingly and wilfully interfere with the Tribunal's administration of justice. It includes intimidation of, interference with, or an offer of a bribe to, a potential witness before the Tribunal, or any attempt to intimidate or to interfere with such a witness. That inherent power exists independently of the terms of Rule 77, and the amendments made to that Rule from time to time do not limit that inherent power.

4.2.600   Following his conviction for contempt, Milan Vujin appealed the decision of the Appeals Chamber to a differently composed Appeals Chamber. (See 4.2.615 below) Vujin argued *inter alia* that the Tribunal does not have the power to set up a procedure for contempt and to punish such contempt. In the *Appeal Judgement on Allegations of Contempt Against Prior Counsel, Milan Vujin*, 27 February 2001, the Appeals Chamber rejected this argument. The Appeals Chamber referred to paras. 12 to 29 of their Judgement of 31 January 2000 "in which the basis of the International Tribunal's power to prosecute and punish matters of contempt is clearly set out" and held that the "adoption of rules to prosecute contempt falls within the within the purview of "other appropriate matters" required by Article 15 of the Statute."

Need to Specify the Charge

4.2.601 Not every example of misconduct in the investigation or conduct of a case amounts to contempt. Accordingly, where the Prosecutor alleges contempt, it is not sufficient merely to relate instances of misconduct, or inappropriate behaviour. The Prosecutor must also detail why the alleged conduct would amount to contempt within the terms of the ICT's rules.

4.2.602 In the *Kanyabashi* case the Prosecutor requested that there be contempt investigations of allegations that members of the Kanyabashi Defence team had approached four prosecution witnesses and attempted to make them change their mind not to testify for the Prosecution, and that they *"knowingly and falsely presented themselves to third parties* [authorities of the Ngoma Commune Office in the Butare Prefecture] *as 'ICTR investigators'"* with the intention of *"tamper[ing] with evidence."* According to the Prosecution, these acts amounted to Misconduct of Counsel pursuant to Rule 46 and Contempt of the Tribunal pursuant to Rule 77(C).

4.2.603 The Chamber dismissed the Prosecution's request in a Decision dated 10 July 2001 *(Decision on the Prosecutor's Allegations of Contempt, the Harmonization of the Witness Protection Measures and Warning to the Prosecutor's Counsel. Rules 46, 54, 73 and 77 of the Rules and Article 9(3)(c)(ii) of the Code of Professional Conduct for Defence Counsel)*. The Chamber explained the reasons for the dismissal noting that:

> bearing in mind the principle of the presumption of innocence, any allegations of contempt are to be handled with due care. Consequently, the Prosecution is to justify its request for investigations by *prima facie* satisfying the Trial Chamber that there are reasonable grounds to believe that contemptuous conduct may have taken place.

However,

> the Prosecutor does not "formulat[e] at [this] early stage the nature of the charge with the precision expected of an indictment," as expected for allegations of contempt.

and:

> neither have sworn statements emanating from the witnesses who were allegedly approached been produced, nor any official statement emanating from . . . [third parties] referring to the allegations of tampering with evidence held in their archives.

4.2.604 In this regard, the Chamber made reference to the ICTY's jurisprudence, namely in *Simić et al.* (Tr. Ch., *Scheduling Order in the Matter of Allegations against Accused Milan Simić and his Counsel*, 7 July 1999) and in *Aleksovski* (App. Ch., *Judgement on Appeal by Anto Nobilo Against Finding of Contempt*, 30 May 2001).

4.2.605 Therefore, the Trial Chamber was:

> not satisfied that the contemptuous conduct alleged may have taken place, and/or may be attributed to the Defence teams concerned, so as to justify an order for investigations.

4.2.606 See Bohlander, Michael, "International Criminal Tribunals and their Power to Punish Contempt and False Testimony," 12 *Criminal Law Forum* 91–118, in which he questions the basis of the Tribunal's power to prosecute and punish contempt. It is true that the absence of an explicit basis in the ICTs' statutes to prosecute—and potentially to fine and/or imprison—persons for contempt gives concern for the legality of such an action.

Convictions for Contempt of Tribunal

4.2.607 The ICTY has convicted a number of persons, both defence counsel, for contempt. The Appeals Chamber overturned the conviction of Anto Nobilo.

Anto Nobilo

4.2.608 Mr. Anto Nobilo, counsel for Tihomir Blaškić was found guilty of contempt of Tribunal in a *Finding of Contempt of the Tribunal* of 11 December 1998 in *Aleksovski*. Nobilo, while acting as counsel for Blaškić, divulged in public session in the *Blaškić* hearings the identity of a protected witness in violation of an Order of the Chamber issued in *Aleksovksi*. He was thus arguably in violation of what is now Rule 77(A)(ii). As regards the *mens rea* requirement that the person in contempt must "disclose information relating to those proceedings *in knowing violation* of an order of a Chamber," the Chamber held that this was satisfied where the person did not know of a witness's protected status but deliberately abstained from trying to discover what the witness's status was. Nobilo was fined Dfl. 10,000 guilders (approximately US $4,000) although Dfl. 6,000 was suspended for one year, provided no further contempt was committed. The remaining Dfl. 4,000 had to be paid within seven days of the Decision.

4.2.609 Nobilo was granted leave to appeal this Decision by a Bench of the Appeals Chambers in its *Decision on Application of Mr. Nobilo for leave to appeal the Trial Chamber finding of contempt* of 22 December 1998. The Bench considered "that good cause or good grounds have been shown for leave to appeal to be granted in that the proper interpretation of the expression 'in knowing violation' of an Order of a Chamber and the obligations imposed on counsel appearing before the International Tribunal are matters of general importance to proceedings before the International Tribunal or in international law generally."

4.2.610 On 30 May 2001 the Appeals Chamber reversed Nobilo's conviction for contempt. There were three principal issues in the Appeal:

> (i) Is it necessary for the prosecution to establish *actual* knowledge of the order of the Chamber which was violated?
> (ii) Is it necessary for the prosecution to *also* establish an *intention* to violate or disregard that order?
> (iii) Was the offence (so far as it imposed any standard other than actual knowledge) known to international law at the time the offence was alleged to have been committed?

4.2.611 On these points, the Appeals Chamber answered as follows:

4.2.612 On issue (i), the Chamber held that *actual knowledge* was a necessary requirement for the offence to be committed. They also found that it had not been established that Nobilo had such actual knowledge. They also held that wilful blindness to an order could also amount to contempt but similarly found that such wilful blindness had not been proven. (*Decision*, 30 May 2001, paras. 39–52).

4.2.613 On issue (ii), in light of their conclusions on actual knowledge, it was not strictly necessary for the Appeals Chamber to determine whether it was also necessary for the prosecution to establish intention. However, for the sake of future prosecutions the Appeals Chamber considered the point. They stated that in most cases where it is established that a contemnor had knowledge of the existence of an order (either actual knowledge or wilful blindness), a finding that he intended to violate the order would necessary follow. They stated:

> There may, however, be cases where such an alleged contemnor acted with reckless indifference as to whether his act was in violation of the order. In the opinion of the Appeals Chamber, such conduct is sufficiently capable to warrant punishment as contempt, even though it does not establish a specific intention to violate the order. (Para. 54.)

4.2.614 On issue (iii), the Appeals Chamber held that:

> The Tribunal's inherent power to deal with contempt has necessarily existed ever since its creation, and the extent of that power has not altered by reason of the amendments made to the Tribunal's Rules, or by reason of its decisions interpreting or clarifying that power. (Para. 38.)

Milan Vujin

4.2.615 Milan Vujin, former counsel for Duško Tadić, was found guilty of contempt in the *Judgement on Allegations of Contempt against Prior Counsel, Milan Vujin* rendered by the Appeals Chamber on 31 January 2000. The Chamber regarded Vujin's contempt as serious:

> 166. ... Courts and tribunals necessarily rely very substantially upon the honesty and propriety of counsel in the conduct of litigation. Counsel are permitted important privileges by the law which are justified only upon the basis that they can be trusted not to abuse them.
>
> 167. It unfortunately happens that counsel occasionally do abuse those privileges or act dishonestly or improperly. Such cases usually involve conduct on the part of counsel which is intended, for whatever reason, to assist in winning the case for the client whom counsel represents. That is bad enough. In the present case, the Respondent's conduct has been *against* the interests of his client. That is even worse, particularly where the client is in custody and relies so heavily upon his counsel for assistance. The conduct of the Respondent in this case strikes at the very heart of the criminal justice system. The Appeals Chamber has not considered the extent to which the interests of Tadić may in fact have been disadvantaged by the conduct in question. That is a matter which would require substantial investigation, and no such investigation was either suggested or undertaken in these proceedings. The contempt in this case remains a serious one, no matter what disadvantage was or was not in fact caused to Tadić.

> 168. The contempt requires punishment which serves not only as retribution for what has been done but also as deterrence of others who may be tempted to act in the same way...

4.2.616 In the event, Vujin was ordered to pay a fine of Dfl. (guilders) 15,000 (approximately US $6,000), but not imprisoned. In the same judgement, the Appeals Chamber directed the Registrar to consider striking the Appellant off the list of assigned counsel maintained pursuant to Rule 45. It was also ordered that Vujin's conduct as found by the Appeals Chamber be reported to the professional body to which he belonged.

4.2.617 Vujin was granted leave to appeal against the Judgement on 25 October 2000, it having been concluded that "the arguments advanced in support of the Application for leave to appeal justify a more thorough review by the Appeals Chamber." Vujin argued that (i) the Tribunal does not have the power to set up a procedure for contempt and to punish such contempt (see 4.2.599 above); that Rule 77 of the Rules does not provide for the striking off the list of eligible counsel by the Registrar (see 4.2.619 *et seq.* below), and (iii) that the Appeals Chamber had made various errors of fact in finding him guilty of contempt.

4.2.618 The Appeals Chamber rejected all of Vujin's arguments and upheld the judgement of the Appeals Chamber ruling in the first instance, *Appeal Judgement on Allegations of Contempt Against Prior Counsel, Milan Vujin*, 27 February 2001.

Counsel Guilty of Contempt Struck Off List of Counsel Eligible to Be Assigned

4.2.619 In *Vujin's* case, the Appeals Chamber ruling in the first instance fined Vujin and directed the Registrar to consider striking him off the list of assigned counsel kept pursuant to Rule 45 of the Rules. On appeal Vujin argued that as Rule 77 does not provide for the striking off the list of eligible counsel as a punishment upon conviction of contempt, the Appeals Chamber had acted *ultra vires*.

4.2.620 The Appeals Chamber ruling of 27 February 2001 rejected this argument. The Appeals Chamber held:

> that when convicted of contempt pursuant to Rule 77 of the Rules, counsel can expect to be either suspended or struck off the list of assigned counsel kept by the Registrar pursuant to Rule 45 of the Rules;

4.2.621 The Appeals Chamber further noted that Vujin was not struck off by the Appeals Chamber ruling in the first instance, but that the Appeals Chamber had "merely directed the Registrar to "consider" striking the Appellant off the list." The Chamber reiterated that:

> the Registrar may consider, bearing in mind the factual findings against the Appellant by the Appeals Chamber ruling in the first instance and in accordance with his powers, to strike off or suspend the Appellant for a set period from the list of assigned counsel kept pursuant to Rule 45...

4.2.622 Accordingly, the question of whether and for how long counsel is to be removed from the list of assigned counsel kept pursuant to Rule 45 for a conviction of contempt is a matter for the Registrar. It is of course open to the Chamber that convicts counsel of contempt to recommend an appropriate period of suspension to the Registrar, but it is ultimately a matter for the Registrar whether to follow such a recommendation. Furthermore it is submitted that counsel convicted of contempt should be given an opportunity to address the Registrar as to the appropriate length of any suspension or removal from the list of assigned counsel.

4.2.623 On 12 June 2001, the Registrar ordered that Vujin be withdrawn from the list of assigned defence counsel "in order to safeguard the administration of justice before the Tribunal." On 12 September 2001, the President of the Tribunal, Judge Jorda, dismissed a request for review of the Registrar's decision filed by Vujin on 25 June 2001.

4.2.624 In light of the above contempt of court decision, on 18 June 2001, Tadić, who had been represented by Vujin, filed a request for review of his complete case as well as the Trial Chamber and Appeals Chamber proceedings before the ICTY.

4.2.625 It is an open question, when the Registrar strikes a counsel off the list of assigned counsel or suspends him for a given period and reports his conduct to the professional body to which he belongs, whether the Registrar's decision may be appealed by a suspect or accused to the President of the Tribunal pursuant to Rule 44(B).

4.2.626 It should be noted that counsel who do not appear at the Tribunal as "assigned counsel," but as private counsel clearly cannot be struck off the list of assigned counsel if convicted of contempt. Consideration needs to be given to the possibility of denying rights of audience to privately paid counsel convicted of contempt, since there is no justification for maintaining a distinction between privately- and publicly-funded counsel in this regard.

4.2.627 The express power to strike off a Counsel who has been found guilty of contempt was added to Rule 77, as para. (I) at the ICTY's twenty-fifth plenary session, held on 12–13 December, 2001.

Right to Appeal Conviction by the Appeals Chamber for Contempt

4.2.628 The Appeals Chamber, in its ruling in *Tadić* on 27 February 2001, considered whether Vujin had a right to appeal the Appeals Chamber's Judgement of 31 January 2000. The Chamber noted that Rule 77, as it then stood, did not expressly provide for the right to appeal a conviction of contempt *by the Appeals Chamber*. (Rule 77 was amended at the twenty-sixth plenary session held on 11 and 12 July 2002 to provide for such an appeal by adding para. (K)). The Chamber majority found that, despite the lack of provision for a right to appeal in the Rules, it would nonetheless consider the Appeal in order to adhere to accepted human rights standards:

> NOTING that Rule 77 of the Rules does not expressly provide for the right to appeal a contempt conviction of the Appeals Chamber;
>
> CONSIDERING, however, that the Rules must be interpreted in conformity with the International Tribunal's Statute which, as the United Nations Secretary-General states in his report of 3 May 1993 (S/25704) must respect the "internationally recognized standards regarding the rights of the accused" including Article 14 of the International Covenant on Civil and Political Rights (hereinafter "the International Covenant");

CONSIDERING moreover that Article 14 of the International Covenant reflects an imperative norm of international law to which the Tribunal must adhere;

CONSIDERING that the procedure established under Rule 77 of the Rules is of a penal nature, and that a person convicted pursuant to Rule 77 of the Rules faces a potential custodial sentence of up to 7 years imprisonment;

CONSIDERING that the preferred course in this case would have been for the contempt trial to have been initially referred to a Trial Chamber, thereby providing for the possibility of appeal, rather than being heard by the Appeals Chamber, ruling in the first instance;

CONSIDERING however that it is the duty of the International Tribunal to guarantee and protect the rights of those who appear as accused before it;

DECIDES therefore that due to the special circumstances of this case, it is appropriate for the Appeals Chamber to consider the merits of the Appellant's complaints;

4.2.629 Judge Wald appended a strong and persuasive dissenting opinion to the majority's finding that the Chamber had jurisdiction:

> I am . . . unable to agree that the Appeals Chamber has jurisdiction under the ICTY Statute or the Rules of Procedure and Evidence adopted thereunder to entertain an appeal from one of its own decisions.
>
> . . . I do not agree that human rights considerations require the creation of a two-tiered system of appeal in cases such as the one before us, where a finding of contempt has been initially made by the Appeals Chamber. Such an interpretation goes against the plain language of the Statute and Rules, and I do not believe that we can reasonably construe our governing documents to permit such an appeal.
>
> . . .
>
> First, the Statute lays down the organization and jurisdiction of the Tribunal. . . . It nowhere states that an appeal may be taken from one duly constituted Appeals Chamber to another duly constituted Appeals Chamber, and I do not think we have the power to create such a two-level process in that Chamber on our own.
>
> . . .
>
> Second, the Tribunal has never attempted in its Rules to create the two-tiered appeal system accepted by the majority in this case. . . . Rule 77(J) states that "(a)ny decision rendered by a Trial Chamber under this Rule shall be subject to appeal . . ." At the 1998 Plenary Session in conjunction with the amendment of Rule 77 specifically to include contempt actions by the Appeals Chamber, no action was taken as to any right to appeal therefrom. The Appeals Chamber judgement now before us acknowledges that at the December 1998 Plenary Session "the right to appeal was limited to decisions made by a Trial Chamber."
>
> Thus I can find no basis in our Rules any more than in our Statute for an appeal from one Appeals Chamber bench to another. Nor do I believe this fatal omission can be rectified by declaring that the Judgement of the Appeals Chamber was a ruling "in the first instance." The Judgement is clearly labeled as one "In the Appeals Chamber."
>
> . . .

Lastly my colleagues justify their ruling because to deny someone convicted of contempt by the Appeals Chamber any further appeal would violate human rights norms such as those contained in Article 14(5) of the International Covenant on Civil and Political Rights which declares that "(e)veryone convicted of a crime shall have the right to have his conviction and sentenced reviewed by a higher tribunal according to law."

In my view, the failure to provide a right of appeal for convictions that originate in the highest tribunal is not a fundamental violation of this right. Indeed, a number of western European States have submitted reservations to Article 14(5) to make it clear that an appellate court may impose an aggravated sentence, without giving rise to a further right of appeal, although there was no consensus that such a reservation was strictly necessary.

...

Moreover, the right in Article 14(5) of the ICCPR relates to persons who have been convicted of "crimes." Although contempt is a crime in the sense that it is potentially punishable by imprisonment, it is a *sui generis* offence. This is reflected in the fact that various procedural safeguards that apply in relation other criminal offences do not apply in the case of contempt. . . . Various national judicial systems, including the United Kingdom and the United States, recognise convictions for contempt before the highest tribunal without any appeal therefrom. Thus, I cannot conclude that the creation of a new right to appeal an Appeals Chamber judgement is necessary so as to avoid a flagrant violation of accepted human rights norms.

Nonetheless the goal of providing an appeal from all conviction for criminal contempt is an eminently worthy one. However, it must be accomplished without wrenching all meaning form the constraints on the jurisdiction of the Appeals Chamber as set out in the Statute and Rules.

...

the rule of law .. . requires that courts acknowledge the statutes and rules that bind them in the exercise of their powers, even when those restraints interfere with understandable aspirations to maximize human rights norms. Courts must lead the way in following the law if there is to be a rule of law.

Acquittal for Contempt

4.2.630 In its *Judgement in the Matter of Contempt Allegations against an Accused and his Counsel* of 30 June 2000, the Trial Chamber found that the allegations of contempt against the accused Milan Simić and against his counsel, Branislav Avramović, had not been proved beyond a reasonable doubt.

Cautioning Counsel

4.2.631 Counsel may of course be cautioned before being found in contempt, and it would seem only fair to do so, where possible. On this point, see *Order for Non-disclosure* issued in *Kupreškić* on 24 August 1998, cautioning Ranko Radović, who had disclosed a protected witness's identity in open session, "that the Orders of the Tribunal must be complied with categorically and unquestioningly, and that any further disclosure of a protected witness's identity could lead to contempt proceedings under . . . Rule 77."

Contempt the Prerogative of the Chambers

4.2.632 In his *Decision of the President on the Prosecutor's Motion for the Production of Notes Exchanged between Zejnil Delalić and Zdravko Mucić*, dated 11 November 1996, President Cassese stated, *obiter dicta*, that Contempt of Tribunal was the prerogative of the Chambers, since it derived from the inherent power of the court to control its own proceedings:

> the Prosecutor seems erroneously to conceive that he has not only the authority, but perhaps even the *exclusive* authority, to investigate and prosecute Contempt of Tribunal. This is far from being the case. Rule 77 does not state that the Prosecutor shall bring charges of contempt; on the contrary, in Rule 77(A), contempt is primarily conceived as occurring in the presence of the Chamber and the Chamber, therefore, in the exercise of its inherent power to control its own proceedings, has the power to react to such contempt. The Judges acting in plenary had the authority to adopt a rule on contempt only by virtue of this inherent power; clearly the Statute does not contain any article conferring on the Prosecutor the ultimate responsibility for bringing a contempt action.

> It is apparent from Sub-rule 77(C), read in conjunction with Sub-rule 77(A), that the power to sentence someone for contempt lies within the province of the Chamber. The Prosecutor may investigate and bring to the Chamber's attention such interference with or intimidation of a witness as may come within the terms of Sub-rule 77(A), but, equally, so may the Defence or the Chamber, *proprio motu*, and it remains the prerogative of the Chambers whether or not to convict someone of contempt. (footnote 1—It bears pointing out that both prosecution witnesses and persons in the Office of the Prosecutor are also subject to the rule on contempt; the former if he "refuses or fails contumaciously to answer a question relevant to the issue before a Chamber," the latter if he "attempts to interfere with or intimidate a witness"). It is simply not true, therefore, that, as the Prosecutor claims in his pleadings, the Prosecutor "is ultimately responsible for bringing a contempt action in court" (point IV, Prosecutor's Motion, RP1123). Even when the Prosecutor brings a contempt action before the Chamber, his authority to do so derives from the inherent powers of the Chambers, not from any independent, prosecutorial authority. (footnote 2—This may be contrasted with national systems where a prosecutor may indeed enjoy a statute-based power to prosecute contempt of court. But at the International Tribunal, the Prosecutor's powers derive from the Statute, and the Statute only confers on the Prosecutor the authority to prosecute "serious violations of international humanitarian law committed in the territory of the former Yugoslavia since 1 January 1991" (Article 16(1))).

Chamber May Initiate Contempt Proceedings *Proprio Motu*

4.2.633 Rule 77 makes clear that the power to initiate contempt proceedings lies with the Chamber acting *proprio motu*. The Appeals Chamber stated in *Aleksovski*, 30 May 2001, *Judgement On Appeal By Anto Nobilo Against Finding of Contempt* that where a Chamber initiates proceedings for contempt itself, it is essential that it formulates at an early stage the nature of the charge with the precision expected of an indictment so as to give the parties the opportunity to debate what is required to be proved. "It is only in this way that the alleged contemnor can be afforded a fair trial." (para. 56) The Appeals Chamber also noted the suggestion that it should be for the Prosecutor to initiate proceedings for contempt by way of indictment or, where the alleged contemnor is associated with the prosecution, for an *amicus curiae* to be appointed by the Chamber to do so. (para. 55). See also, *Nyiramasuhuko et al., Decision on the Prosecutor's Allegation of Contempt*, 10 July 2001, paras. 6 and 7. The Trial Chamber held that the Prosecution had not established *prima facie* grounds for contempt. The Trial Chamber further warned the Prosecution pursuant to Rule 46(A) for having 'improperly and recklessly' disclosed the identity of defence personnel in making the allegations of contempt.

Severance of Joint Trials Based on Outcome of Contempt Proceedings

4.2.634 The question whether persons accused jointly should be tried separately "in order to avoid a conflict of interests that might cause serious prejudice to an accused, or to protect the interests of justice" (Rule 82) in the case of contempt proceedings pursuant to Rule 77 was considered by the Trial Chamber in *Simić* (Tr. Ch., *Decision denying de novo motion to sever the trial of Stevan Todorović from that of the accused Milan Simić*, 31 May 2000).

4.2.635 On 19 March 1999, the Trial Chamber, in its *Decision on Defence Motion to Sever Defendants and Counts* had denied Stevan Todorović's application for separate trial on the ground that the *"interests of justice are best served by a joint trial in this case."* In the *Decision denying De Novo Motion to Sever the Trial on the Indictment of Stevan Todorović from that of the Accused Milan Simic,* 31 May 2000, the Trial Chamber noted that:

> the reason stated by counsel for the accused [for bringing the Motion] was to "renew all of the arguments heretofore advanced in support of the earlier motion" together with the "additional ground of the on-going Rule 77 Contempt Proceedings," arguing that any ruling "adverse to the Accused Milan Simic and his counsel Branislav Avramovic will 'poison' this Trial Chamber's impartiality" and that a separate trial should be ordered "in that justice so requires."

4.2.636 However, the Trial Chamber considered that:

> the acquittal by the Trial Chamber of both the accused, Milan Simic, and his counsel, Branislav Avramovic, removes the only new ground relied upon by the accused, Stevan Todorović in the Todorovic Motion for Separate Trial, that of possible prejudice to the accused.

4.2.637 The Chamber left open the question whether or not a conviction for contempt of Tribunal pursuant to Rule 77 was a necessary or sufficient reason for granting a Motion to sever joint trials.

Contempt for Failure to Comply with a Subpoena

4.2.638 In an order issued by Judge McDonald on 28 February 1997 in *Blaškić*, the Defence Minister of the Federation of Bosnia and Herzegovina was requested, in the event of a failure to comply with the order, to appear in person before the Judge "to show cause why he should not be held in contempt for failure to comply with this order." In the event, contempt proceedings were not initiated.

In Absentia Trial for Contempt

4.2.639 In its *Subpoena* Judgement (IT-95-14-AR108*bis*) of 29 October 1997, the Appeals Chamber held that "*in absentia* proceedings may be exceptionally warranted in cases involving contempt of the International Tribunal, where the person charged fails to appear in court, thus obstructing the administration of justice" (para. 59).

Cross Reference:

See Rule 74, *Amicus Curiae*, and the *amicus* briefs there referred to, which should be consulted for discussions of the subpoena/contempt issue (8.5.507).

ICTY Rule 77(B): Investigating a Complaint of Interfering With or Intimidating a Witness

4.2.640 In *Delalić et al*, the Prosecutor brought a complaint before the Chamber that the names of some of its witnesses had been published in a newspaper. The witness names constituted confidential information by virtue of two orders of the Chamber. The Chamber decided to order a judicial investigation, and referred the matter to the President of the Tribunal (see *Referral of Complaint* dated 16 May 1997). The President subsequently reported back to the Chamber (see *Report of the President in the Matter of the Referral of Complaint*, dated 27 May 1997). The Chamber accepted the conclusion in the President's Report that "there is no evidence of misconduct on the part of . . . counsel for Zejnil Delalić," but rejected the conclusion that Zejnil Delalić himself might have acted in contempt "on the grounds that the findings in the Report disclose no evidence on which the President could have relied for casting any element of doubt on the uncontradicted and unequivocal denial of the accused Zejnil Delalić that he did not (sic) grant any interview or disclose any information" to the newspaper in question. The Chamber also accepted the conclusion that the investigation with regard to the writer and editor of the newspaper in question was "inconclusive." On this basis, the Chamber found "that there is no rational basis for proceeding with any investigation with a view to charging the accused Zejnil Delalić or any of the other participants in the current proceedings with contempt" and declared the matter closed.

4.2.641 In *Blaškić*, a similar situation arose with respect to a witness, albeit not a protected one. The Prosecution requested an investigation into the matter, which the Trial Chamber refused, in a Decision dated 6 June 1997, on the grounds that, "the said witness was not covered by any protective measures insofar as no request was made that he be covered and no decision granting such request was ever issued" (para. 7). Moreover, it noted that, "it would be extremely difficult to determine who is responsible for such disclosure" (*ibid*).

Disclosure of Protected Witness's Statement

4.2.642 In *Ntakirutimana, Decision on Prosecution Motion for Contempt*, 16 July 2001, the Trial Chamber decided that the disclosure of a protected witness's statement by one accused to another in the Detention Unit was not a serious enough breach of the witness protection order to amount to contempt as the statement was exculpatory and should have been disclosed in any event pursuant to Rule 68. See also *Rwamakuba, Decision on Prosecution Motion for Contempt of Court and on two Defence Motions for Disclosure etc*, 16 July 2001.

Counsel's Absence from Hearing

4.2.643 Counsel's absence from a scheduled hearing may constitute contempt under ICTY Rule 77(A)(iii). See *Order for Appearance of Counsel*, Trial Chamber, 10 March 1998, *Gagović et al.*: "Orders Mr. Slaviša Prodanović to appear before the Trial Chamber . . . and to explain to the Trial Chamber the circumstances of his absence from today's hearing, failing which the Tribunal will consider instituting proceedings for contempt."

Orders for Cessation of Contempt

4.2.644 See, e.g., the Trial Chamber's *Order for the Immediate Cessation of Violations of Protective Measures for Witnesses, Blaškić*, 1 December 2000; and the Trial Chamber's *Order for the Immediate Cessation of Violations of Protective Measures for Witnesses, Milošević*, 18 June 2002.

4.2.645

ICTY
Rule 77 *bis*
Payment of Fines

(A) In imposing a fine under Rule 77 or Rule 91, a Chamber shall specify the time for its payment.
(B) When a fine imposed under Rule 77 or Rule 91 is not paid within the time specified, the Chamber imposing the fine may issue an order requiring the person on whom the fine is imposed to appear before, or to respond in writing to, the Tribunal to explain why the fine has not been paid.
(C) After affording the person on whom the fine is imposed an opportunity to be heard, the Chamber may make a decision that appropriate measures be taken, including:
(i) extending the time for payment of the fine;
(ii) requiring the payment of the fine to be made in instalments;
(iii) in consultation with the Registrar, requiring that the moneys owed be deducted from any outstanding fees owing to the person by the Tribunal where the person is a counsel retained by the Tribunal pursuant to the Directive on the Assignment of Defence Counsel;
(iv) converting the whole or part of the fine to a term of imprisonment not exceeding twelve months.
(D) In addition to a decision under Sub-rule (C), the Chamber may find the person in contempt of the Tribunal and impose a new penalty applying Rule 77(H)(i), if that person was able to pay the fine within the specified time and has wilfully failed to do so. This penalty for contempt of the Tribunal shall be additional to the original fine imposed.
(E) The Chamber may, if necessary, issue an arrest warrant to secure the person's presence where he or she fails to appear before or respond in writing pursuant to an order under Sub-Rule (B). A State or authority to whom such a warrant is addressed, in accordance with Article 29 of the

> Statute, shall act promptly and with all due diligence to ensure proper and effective execution thereof. Where an arrest warrant is issued under this Sub-rule, the provisions of Rules 45, 57, 58, 59, 59 *bis* and 60 shall apply *mutatis mutandis*. Following the transfer of the person concerned to the Tribunal, the provisions of Rules 64, 65 and 99 shall apply *mutatis mutandis*.
>
> (F) Where under this Rule a penalty of imprisonment is imposed, or a fine is converted to a term of imprisonment, the provisions of Rules 102, 103 and 104 and Part Nine shall apply *mutatis mutandis*.
>
> (G) Any finding of contempt or penalty imposed under this Rule shall be subject to appeal as allowed for in Rule 77 (J).

History of ICTY Rule 77 *bis*

4.2.646 This new rule was introduced at the twentieth plenary session on 30 June–2 July 1999. It was amended in minor ways at the twenty-first session on 30 November 1999.

4.2.647 The rule was amended at the twenty-fifth plenary session on 12–13 December, 2001 to remove references to a "Judge" exercising powers under this Rule so that, as amended, only a Chamber may do so.

4.2.648

ICTY Rule 91 False Testimony Under Solemn Declaration	ICTR Rule 91 False Testimony Under Solemn Declaration
(A) A Chamber, *proprio motu* or at the request of a party, may warn a witness of the duty to tell the truth and the consequences that may result from a failure to do so. (B) If a Chamber has strong grounds for believing that a witness has knowingly and wilfully given false testimony, it may (i) direct the Prosecutor to investigate the matter with a view to the preparation and submission of an indictment for false testimony; or (ii) where the Prosecutor, in the view of the Chamber, has a conflict of interest with respect to the relevant conduct, direct the Registrar to appoint an *amicus curiae* to investigate the matter and report back to the Chamber as to whether there are sufficient grounds for instigating proceedings for false testimony. (C) If the Chamber considers that there are sufficient grounds to proceed against a person for giving famse testimony, the Chamber may:	(A) A Chamber, on its own initiative or at the request of a party, may warn a witness of the duty to tell the truth and the consequences that may result from a failure to do so. (B) If a Chamber has strong grounds for believing that a witness may have knowingly and wilfully given false testimony, the Chamber may direct the Prosecutor to investigate the matter with a view to the preparation and submission of an indictment for false testimony. (C) The rules of procedure and evidence in Parts Four to Eight shall apply *mutatis mutandis* to proceedings under this Rule. (D) The maximum penalty for false testimony under solemn declaration shall be a fine of US$10,000 or a term of imprisonment of twelve months, or both. The payment of any fine imposed shall be made to the Registrar to

(i) in circumstances described in para. (B)(i), direct the Prosecutor to prosecute the matter; or
(ii) in circumstances described in para. (B)(ii), issue an order in lieu of an indictment and direct *amicus curiae* to prosecute the matter.

(D) The rules of procedure and evidence in Parts Four to Eight shall apply *mutatis mutandis* to proceedings under this Rule.

(E) Any person indicted for or charged with false testimony shall, if that person satisfies the criteria for determination of indigency established by the Registrar, be assigned counsel in accordance with Rule 45.

(F) No Judge who sat as a member of the Trial Chamber before which the witness appeared shall sit for the trial of the witness for false testimony.

(G) The maximum penalty for false testimony under solemn declaration shall be a fine of Eur 100,000 or a term of imprisonment of seven years, or both. The payment of any fine imposed shall be paid to the Registrar to be held in the account referred to in Rule 77(H).

(H) Paragraphs (B) to (E) apply *mutatis mutandis* to a person who knowingly and willingly makes a false statement in a written statement taken in accordance with Rule 92 *bis* which the person knows or has reason to know may be used as evidence in proceedings before the Tribunal.

(I) Any decision rendered by a Trial Chamber under this Rule shall be subject to appeal. Notice of appeal shall be filed within fifteen days of filing of the impugned decision. Where such decision is rendered orally, the application shall be filed within fifteen days of the oral decision, unless
(i) the party challenging the decision was not present or represented when the decision was pronounced, in which case the time-limit shall run from the date on which the challenging party is notified of the oral decision; or
(ii) the Trial Chamber has indicated that a written decision will follow, in which case, the time-limit shall run from filing of the written decision.

be held in the separate account referred to in Rule 77(E).

(E) Paragraphs (B) to (D) shall apply *mutatis mutandis* to a person who knowingly and willingly makes a false statement in a written statement taken in accordance with Rule 92 *bis* which the person knows or has reason to know may be used as evidence in proceedings before the Tribunal.

(F) In case of decisions under this Rule, an application to appeal may be submitted in writing to the Appeals Chamber within 15 days of the impugned decision.

History of ICTY Rule 91

4.2.649 Para. (E) was amended at the nineteenth plenary, on 17 December 1998, to increase the maximum penalty for false testimony from twelve months' to seven years' imprisonment, and the maximum fine from US $10,000 to Dfl. 200,000 (approximately US $130,000). Para. (F) was added at the twenty-first plenary session on 30 November 1999. Para. (G) was added, and minor changes made to other sub-Rules, on 19 January 2001, after the twenty-third plenary session.

4.2.650 This rule was substantially amended at the twenty-fifth plenary session held on 12–13 December, 2001. The changes largely track those made to Rule 77, which is in many ways a corresponding rule, namely one which creates a substantive offence based on the ICTY's inherent jurisdiction, a procedure for trying the offence, and for imposing penalties, and avenues of appeal and representation by Counsel.

History of ICTR Rule 91

4.2.651 ICTR Rule 91 was amended at the ICTR fourth plenary session, held in Arusha on 1–5 June 1997, to clarify the procedure for prosecution and trial of witnesses who have given false testimony. It was further amended in minor ways at the fifth plenary session on 8 June 1998. During the twelfth plenary session on 5–6 July 2002, the rule was amended further so that paras. (B) to (D) of the Rule apply *mutatis mutandis* to statements given under the 92 *bis* procedure. Para. (F) provides that any appeal must be made within 15 days of the impugned decision.

Direction by Chamber to Prosecutor to Investigate False Testimony

4.2.652 On 10 December 1996, in its *Order for the Prosecution to investigate the false testimony of Dragan Opacić*, rendered in *Tadić*, the Trial Chamber "direct[ed] the Prosecution to investigate the matter of the presentation of false testimony by Dragan Opacić and evaluate the possibility of the preparation and submission of an indictment against him." (p. 2) See also *Decision Withdrawing Protective Measures for Witness "L,"* rendered by the the Trial Chamber in the same case on 5 December 1996. In the event, no such indictment was submitted.

Mere Contradiction Does Not Amount to False Testimony

4.2.653 Mere contradiction in witness testimony is not sufficient to ground a charge of false testimony. In *Akayesu*, the defence submitted a motion requesting that an indictment be brought against a witness for false testimony, pointing out inconsistencies in the witness's testimony. The Trial Chamber rejected the Motion on the grounds that mere contradictions and inconsistencies in a witness's testimony, without more, did not establish that the witness had "knowingly and wilfully given false testimony," as required under Rule 91(B), and thus could not sustain a charge of false testimony. See the oral *Decision* rendered by the Chamber on 9 March 1998. The Chamber stated that the question of inexactitudes and other contradictions in witness statements was more appropriately dealt with as a question of the witness's *credibility*, which would be assessed at the end of the trial. The oral decision was followed by a written *Decision* also rendered on 9 March 1998.

4.2.654 In essence, the Chamber was saying that the defence had made no showing of the requisite *mens rea* on the part of the witness whose testimony was allegedly inconsistent.

4.2.655 The Chamber affirmed its position in the *Akayesu Trial Judgement:*

> 139. ... the Chamber held in the decision, that the onus is on the party pleading a case of false testimony to prove the falsehoods of the witness statements, that they were made with harmful intent, or at least that they were made by a witness who was fully aware that they were false, and their possible bearing upon the judge's decisions. The Chamber found that for the Defence to raise only doubts as to the credibility of the statements made by the witness was not sufficient to establish strong grounds for believing that the witness may have knowingly and wilfully given false testimony, and that the assessment of credibility pertains to the rendering of the final judgement.
>
> 140. The majority of the witnesses who appeared before the Chamber were eye-witnesses, whose testimonies were based on events they had seen or heard in relation to the acts alleged in the Indictment. The Chamber noted that during the trial, for a number of these witnesses, there appeared to be contradictions or inaccuracies between, on the one hand, the content of their testimonies under solemn declaration to the Chamber, and on the other, their earlier statements to the Prosecutor and the Defence. This alone is not a ground for believing that the witnesses gave false testimony. Indeed, an often levied criticism of testimony is its fallibility. Since testimony is based mainly on memory and sight, two human characteristics which often deceive the individual, this criticism is to be expected. Hence, testimony is rarely exact at to the events experienced. To deduce from any resultant contradictions and inaccuracies that there was false testimony, would be akin to criminalising frailties in human perceptions. Moreover, inaccuracies and contradictions between the said statements and the testimony given before the Court are also the result of the time lapse between the two. Memory over time naturally degenerates, hence it would be wrong and unjust for the Chamber to treat forgetfulness as being synonymous with giving false testimony. Moreover, false testimony requires the necessary *mens rea* and not a mere wrongful statement.

Onus to Prove "Knowingly and Wilfully"

4.2.656 Where a party seeks to plead a case of false testimony, the onus is on that party to prove that the testimony was given "knowingly and wilfully" (Trial Chamber, *Nahimana, Decision on the Defence Motion to Direct the Prosecutor to Investigate the Matter of False Testimony by Witness "AEN" in Terms of Rule 91(B)*, 27 February 2001). In that case, the Trial Chamber considered that no strong grounds had been made out to conclude that the witness had given false testimony. See also *Decision on the Defence motion to Direct the Prosecutor to Investigate the Matter of False Testimony by Witness "CC," Rutaganda*, 10 March 1998.

Elements of False Testimony

4.2.657 The constituent elements of false testimony were dealt with by the Trial Chamber in *Bagilishema* (*Decision on the Request of the Defence for the Chamber to Direct the Prosecutor to Investigate a Matter with a View to the Preparation and Submission of an Indictment for False Testimony*, 11 July 2000). The Chamber, making reference to *Akayesu* (Tr. Ch., *Decision on the Defence Motions to Direct the Prosecutor to Investigate the False Testimony of Witness "R,"* 9 March 1998), stated that:

> the constituent elements of false testimony are:
>
> the witness must make a solemn declaration;
>
> the false statement must be contrary to the solemn declaration;
>
> the witness must believe at the time the statement was made that it was false; and
>
> there must be a relevant relationship between the statement and a material matter within the case.

4.2.658 Moreover the burden of proving each of these elements is on the party alleging false testimony.

> the onus is on the party pleading a case of false testimony to prove:
>
> the falsehood of the witness statements;
>
> that these statements were made with harmful intent, or at least that they were made by a witness who was fully aware that they were false [in other words, the false testimony was given knowingly and wilfully]; and
>
> the possible bearing of the said statements upon the judge's decision.

4.2.659 In *Nahimana* (Tr. Ch., *Decision on the Defence Motion to Direct the Prosecutor to Investigate the Matter of False Testimony by Witness "AEN" in Terms of Rule 91 (b)*, 27 February 2001), the Chamber specified that:

> the weight to be attached to the witness's responses is a matter for evaluation by the Trial Chamber when assessing the merits of the case, . . . follow[ing] the reasoning laid down in the case of *The Prosecutor v. Georges Rutaganda* [Trial Chamber I, *Decision on the Defence motion to Direct the Prosecutor to Investigate the Matter of False Testimony by Witness "CC,"* 10 March 1998], in which the Tribunal stated:
>
>> In the context of the ongoing trials before the Tribunal, inaccuracies and other contradictions could eventually be raised during the overall evaluation of credibility upon the final determination of the probative value of the evidence presented at trial.

4.2.660 The ICC Elements of Crimes do not provide elements for the offence of false testimony, which is regrettable since false testimony is a crime under Article 70 of the Rome Statute, which therefore needs to have its constituent features defined as much as any other crime under the Statute.

Contempt and False Testimony Before the ICC

4.2.661 Article 70 of the Rome Statute gives the ICC jurisdiction over offences against the administration of justice. Article 70 covers *inter alia:* giving false testimony, presenting evidence that the party knows is false, interfering with witnesses, and interfering with officials of the Court. Upon conviction the Court may impose a term of imprisonment of up to five years, a fine, or both. Article 71 gives the Court the power to sanction persons before it who commit misconduct, including disruption of its proceedings or deliberate refusal to comply with its directions. The penalties provided for by Article 71 are to fine the individual or have them removed from the courtroom; unlike Article 70, imprisonment is not an option.

4.2.662 It is clear from the ICC Rules of Procedure and Evidence that it is intended that the offences set out in Article 71 will be dealt with summarily by the Chamber before whom the individual is appearing (Rules 170 and 171). Appeals will be permissible from penalties ordered by a Trial Chamber under Article 71. Rule 172 provides that if the conduct covered by Article 71 also constitutes one of the offences defined in Article 70, the Court shall proceed in accordance with Article 70 and Rules 162–169.

4.2.663 Rule 165 sets out the procedure for *"Investigation, prosecution and trial"* of offences against the administration of justice under Article 70. Proceedings are to be initiated by the Prosecutor and commenced at the ICC before the Pre-Trial Chamber, proceeding to trial before a Trial Chamber, with a right of appeal to the Appeals Chamber under Article 81 of the Rome Statute.

4.2.664 This consolidated approach to matters of contempt and false testimony is, it is submitted, a preferable basis upon which to proceed in such matters than the existing procedures before the *ad hoc* Tribunals.

4.2.665

ICC
Article 70
Offences Against the Administration of Justice

1. The Court shall have jurisdiction over the following offences against its administration of justice when committed intentionally:
   (a) Giving false testimony when under an obligation pursuant to article 69, para. 1, to tell the truth;
   (b) Presenting evidence that the party knows is false or forged;
   (c) Corruptly influencing a witness, obstructing or interfering with the attendance or testimony of a witness, retaliating against a witness for giving testimony or destroying, tampering with or interfering with the collection of evidence;
   (d) Impeding, intimidating or corruptly influencing an official of the Court for the purpose of forcing or persuading the official not to perform, or to perform improperly, his or her duties;
   (e) Retaliating against an official of the Court on account of duties performed by that or another official;
   (f) Soliciting or accepting a bribe as an official of the Court in connection with his or her official duties.
2. The principles and procedures governing the Court's exercise of jurisdiction over offences under this article shall be those provided for in the Rules of Procedure and Evidence. The conditions for providing international cooperation to the Court with respect to its proceedings under this article shall be governed by the domestic laws of the requested State.

3. In the event of conviction, the Court may impose a term of imprisonment not exceeding five years, or a fine in accordance with the Rules of Procedure and Evidence, or both.
4. (a) Each State Party shall extend its criminal laws penalizing offences against the integrity of its own investigative or judicial process to offences against the administration of justice referred to in this article, committed on its territory, or by one of its nationals;
(b) Upon request by the Court, whenever it deems it proper, the State Party shall submit the case to its competent authorities for the purpose of prosecution. Those authorities shall treat such cases with diligence and devote sufficient resources to enable them to be conducted effectively.

4.2.666

ICC
Rule 162
Exercise of Jurisdiction

1. Before deciding whether to exercise jurisdiction, the Court may consult with States Parties that may have jurisdiction over the offence.
2. In making a decision whether or not to exercise jurisdiction, the Court may consider, in particular:
(a) The availability and effectiveness of prosecution in a State Party;
(b) The seriousness of an offence;
(c) The possible joinder of charges under article 70 with charges under articles 5 to 8;
(d) The need to expedite proceedings;
(e) Links with an ongoing investigation or a trial before the Court; and
(f) Evidentiary considerations.
3. The Court shall give favourable consideration to a request from the host State for a waiver of the power of the Court to exercise jurisdiction in cases where the host State considers such a waiver to be of particular importance.
4. If the Court decides not to exercise its jurisdiction, it may request a State Party to exercise jurisdiction pursuant to article 70, para. 4.

4.2.667

ICC
Rule 163
Application of the Statute and the Rules

1. Unless otherwise provided in sub-rules 2 and 3, rule 162 and rules 164 to 169, the Statute and the Rules shall apply mutatis mutandis to the Court's investigation, prosecution and punishment of offences defined in article 70.
2. The provisions of Part 2, and any rules thereunder, shall not apply, with the exception of article 21.
3. The provisions of Part 10, and any rules thereunder, shall not apply, with the exception of articles 103, 107, 109 and 111.

4.2.668

> **ICC**
> **Rule 164**
> **Periods of Limitation**

1. If the Court exercises jurisdiction in accordance with rule 162, it shall apply the periods of limitation set forth in this rule.
2. Offences defined in article 70 shall be subject to a period of limitation of five years from the date on which the offence was committed, provided that during this period no investigation or prosecution has been initiated. The period of limitation shall be interrupted if an investigation or prosecution has been initiated during this period, either before the Court or by a State Party with jurisdiction over the case pursuant to article 70, para. 4 (a).
3. Enforcement of sanctions imposed with respect to offences defined in article 70 shall be subject to a period of limitation of 10 years from the date on which the sanction has become final. The period of limitation shall be interrupted with the detention of the convicted person or while the person concerned is outside the territory of the States Parties.

4.2.669

> **ICC**
> **Rule 165**
> **Investigation, Prosecution and Trial**

1. The Prosecutor may initiate and conduct investigations with respect to the offences defined in article 70 on his or her own initiative, on the basis of information communicated by a Chamber or any reliable source.
2. Articles 53 and 59, and any rules thereunder, shall not apply.
3. For purposes of article 61, the Pre-Trial Chamber may make any of the determinations set forth in that article on the basis of written submissions, without a hearing, unless the interests of justice otherwise require.
4. A Trial Chamber may, as appropriate and taking into account the rights of the defence, direct that there be joinder of charges under article 70 with charges under articles 5 to 8.

4.2.670

> **ICC**
> **Rule 166**
> **Sanctions Under Article 70**

1. If the Court imposes sanctions with respect to article 70, this rule shall apply.
2. Article 77, and any rules thereunder, shall not apply, with the exception of an order of forfeiture under article 77, para. 2 (b), which may be ordered in addition to imprisonment or a fine or both.
3. Each offence may be separately fined and those fines may be cumulative. Under no circumstances may the total amount exceed 50 per cent of the value of the convicted person's identifiable assets, liquid or realizable, and property, after deduction of an appropriate amount that would satisfy the financial needs of the convicted person and his or her dependants.

4. In imposing a fine the Court shall allow the convicted person a reasonable period in which to pay the fine. The Court may provide for payment of a lump sum or by way of instalments during that period.

5. If the convicted person does not pay a fine imposed in accordance with the conditions set forth in sub-rule 4, appropriate measures may be taken by the Court pursuant to rules 217 to 222 and in accordance with article 109. Where, in cases of continued wilful non-payment, the Court, on its own motion or at the request of the Prosecutor, is satisfied that all available enforcement measures have been exhausted, it may as a last resort impose a term of imprisonment in accordance with article 70, para. 3. In the determination of such term of imprisonment, the Court shall take into account the amount of fine paid.

4.2.671

ICC
Rule 167
International Cooperation and Judicial Assistance

1. With regard to offences under article 70, the Court may request a State to provide any form of international cooperation or judicial assistance corresponding to those forms set forth in Part 9. In any such request, the Court shall indicate that the basis for the request is an investigation or prosecution of offences under article 70.

2. The conditions for providing international cooperation or judicial assistance to the Court with respect to offences under article 70 shall be those set forth in article 70, para. 2.

4.2.672

ICC
Rule 168
Ne bis in idem

In respect of offences under article 70, no person shall be tried before the Court with respect to conduct which formed the basis of an offence for which the person has already been convicted or acquitted by the Court or another court.

4.2.673

ICC
Rule 169
Immediate Arrest

In the case of an alleged offence under article 70 committed in the presence of a Chamber, the Prosecutor may orally request that Chamber to order the immediate arrest of the person concerned.

4.2.674

ICC
Article 71
Sanctions for Misconduct Before the Court

1. The Court may sanction persons present before it who commit misconduct, including disruption of its proceedings or deliberate refusal to comply with its directions, by administrative measures other than imprisonment, such as temporary or permanent removal from the courtroom, a fine or other similar measures provided for in the Rules of Procedure and Evidence.
2. The procedures governing the imposition of the measures set forth in para. 1 shall be those provided for in the Rules of Procedure and Evidence.

SECTION 3: PERSONAL JURISDICTION

4.3.1

ICTY Article 6 Personal Jurisdiction	ICTR Article 5 Personal Jurisdiction
The International Tribunal shall have jurisdiction over natural persons pursuant to the provisions of the present Statute.	The International Tribunal for Rwanda shall have jurisdiction over natural persons pursuant to the provisions of the present Statute.

Background

4.3.2 The ICTs have jurisdiction only over natural persons. They do not have jurisdiction to judge States or organisations, although they may order States and organisations to provide various forms of cooperation and they may declare to the United Nations that a State or organisation is failing to cooperate (see 11.1.1 *et seq.* on State Cooperation). The ICTs also do not have the power to declare criminal certain organisations, e.g., "Arkan's Tigers" or the Rwandan Interahamwe. This is in contrast to the International Military Tribunal at Nuremberg (see Articles 9 and 10 of the IMT Charter):

> Art. 9. At the trial of any individual member of any group or organisation the Tribunal may declare (in connection with any act of which the individual may be convicted) that the group or organisation of which the individual was a member was a criminal organisation. . . .
>
> Art. 10. In cases where a group or organisation is declared criminal by the Tribunal, the competent national authority of any Signatory shall have the right to bring individuals to trial for membership therein before national, military or occupation courts. In any such case the criminal nature of the group or organisation is considered proved and shall not be questioned.

4.3.3 The French Government's proposal for the ICTY Statute did include a provision dealing with criminal organisations. See the letter dated 10 February 1993 from the Permanent Representative of France to the United Nations (S/25266), paras. 92–94, in particular para. 92: "In addition, membership in a *de jure* or *de facto* group whose primary or subordinate goal is to commit crimes coming within the jurisdiction of the Tribunal would constitute a specific offence." The proposal was not accepted.

Individuals Under International Law

4.3.4 The notion that the ICTs should have jurisdiction, under international law, over individuals is, however, in some ways perplexing. Traditionally international law was only concerned with inter-state conflicts. In terms of criminal jurisdiction, individuals were subject only to their national and local courts or if they were subject to international organs, e.g. before the Nuremberg Tribunal, it was only as *agents of a State*. See Article 6 of the Charter of the Nuremberg Tribunal: "The Tribunal . . . shall have the power to try and punish persons who, *acting in the interests of the European Axis countries . . . committed any of the following crimes. . . ,*" i.e. individuals were only to be prosecuted by the IMT insofar as they had acted as agents of the Axis countries.

4.3.5 It may thus be argued that international law should only be concerned with individuals insofar as they act as agents of a State. For a comprehensive development of this concept, see the doctoral thesis of Professor R. Maison, *"La responsabilité individuelle pour crime d'Etat en droit international public" (Université Panthéon-Assas (Paris II)—17 January 2000).*

4.3.6 It is logical that if States are not responsible for the criminality in question, then they may be trusted to prosecute the perpetrators of international crimes in their domestic courts. Accordingly international organs need not intervene. Conversely, if the individuals in question enjoy impunity, it can only be because the State in question acquiesces in and/or tolerates the crime, in which case the State itself partakes of the criminality. Thus, it can be argued, individuals acting in a purely personal capacity and not as agents of a State (or of a quasi-State entity) should not be brought before international courts or tribunals, but should be left to their national courts.

4.3.7 A similar argument was raised in *Kanyabashi*. See the *Kanyabashi Jurisdiction Decision*, 18 June 1997, where the Trial Chamber dealt with the "the Defence Counsel's Objections Against the Tribunal's Jurisdiction over Individuals Directly under International Law":

> 33. The Defence Counsel further contends that bestowing the Tribunal with jurisdiction over individuals is inconsistent with the UN Charter, for the reason that the Security Council has no authority over individuals, and that only States can pose threats to international peace and security.
>
> 34. The Prosecution responded to this contention by citing the Nüremberg Trials which, in the Prosecution's view, established that individuals who have committed crimes against international law can be held criminally responsible directly under international law. The Prosecutor further contended that attribution of individual criminal responsibility is a fundamental expression of the need for enforcement action by the Security Council. It is indeed difficult to separate the individual from the State, as the duties and rights of States are only duties and rights of the individuals who compose them, and as international criminal law, like other branches of law, deals with the regulation of human conduct. It is to individuals, not the abstract, that international law applies, and it is against individuals that it should provide sanctions. In the words of the Deputy Prosecutor in the trial against *Frank Hans* in 1946:
>
>> It seems intolerable to every sensitized human being that the men who put their good will at disposition of the State entity in order to make use of the power and material resources of this entity to slaughter, as they have done, millions of human beings in the execution of a policy long since determined, should be assured of immunity. The principle of State sovereignty which might protect these men is only a mask; this mask removed, the man's responsibility reappears.
>
> 35. The Trial Chamber recalls that the question of direct individual criminal responsibility under international law is and has been a controversial issue within and between various legal systems for several decades and that the Nüremberg trials in particular have been interpreted differently in respect of the position of

the individual as a subject under international law. By establishing the two International Criminal Tribunals for the Former Yugoslavia and Rwanda, however, the Security Council explicitly extended international legal obligations and criminal responsibilities directly to individuals for violations of international humanitarian law. In doing so, the Security Council provided an important innovation of international law, but there is nothing in the Defence Counsel's motion to suggest that this extension of the applicability of international law against individuals was not justified or called for by the circumstances, notably the seriousness, the magnitude and the gravity of the crimes committed during the conflict.

36. In his submissions, furthermore, the Defence Counsel referred to a number of other areas of conflicts and incidents in which the Security Council took no action to establish an international criminal tribunal, e.g. Congo, Somalia and Liberia, and the Defence Counsel seems to infer from the lack of such action in these cases that individual criminal responsibility should not be taken in the case of the conflict in Rwanda. The Trial Chamber, however, disagrees entirely with this perception. The fact that the Security Council, for previously prevailing geo-strategic and international political reasons, was unable in the past to take adequate measures to bring to justice the perpetrators of crimes against international humanitarian law is not an acceptable argument against introducing measures to punish serious violations of international humanitarian law when this becomes an option under international law. The Trial Chamber, thus, cannot accept the Defence Counsel's objections against the Tribunal's jurisdiction over individuals.

4.3.8 While this reasoning is, on the whole, convincing, the following needs to be borne in mind. As pointed out above, the Nuremberg Tribunal precedent establishes that individuals may be prosecuted under international law *insofar as they have acted as agents of a State*, not that they may be so prosecuted when they acted in a purely personal capacity. If the defendants before the ICTR had not acted as agents of the Rwandan State, implementing a nation-wide criminal plan, it would be questionable whether they could be put on trial by an international court. Moreover, once the Rwandan Patriotic Front won the war in Rwanda and took over the government, the Rwandan State ceased to be a criminal one and in those circumstances it would have been proper, perhaps even mandatory, to leave the prosecutions to the national courts in Rwanda.

4.3.9 Second, the argument raised by some defendants at Nuremberg that they enjoyed impunity because they acted as agents of a State, i.e. that they enjoyed functional or State immunity, was rejected at Nuremberg. But that does not mean that the question of whether or not an individual acted as an agent of the State loses all relevance. It is only that the fact of acting as an agent of a State no longer creates an immunity. Yet it may remain highly relevant to the question of whether or not the person should be judged *under international law*. To derive from Nuremberg the proposition that State criminality is no longer important, and that only individual criminality may now be considered, is to throw the baby out with the bath water.

Irrelevance of the Group to Which the Accused "Belongs"

4.3.10 See the second Annual Report of the Tribunal: "The Tribunal does not prosecute members of 'ethnic groups,' but individuals who are accused of grave crimes' (para. 196). This was in response to demands that Tribunal operate a sort of "quota policy" of indicting similar numbers of members of each "ethnic group" involved in the conflict in the former Yugoslavia. It is submitted that this approach, rightly rejected by the Prosecutor at the time, is the antithesis of justice, as it means that individuals are selected for prosecution because of their "ethnic identity" and not, or not solely, because of the seriousness of the crimes that they are alleged to have committed. On this point, see 4.11. Moreover, a "quota" policy suggests complete moral equivalence between the parties involved in the war in the former Yugoslavia, as if there were no difference between the siegers and the besieged. This is clearly a nonsense.

4.3.11

ICC
Article 1
The Court

An International Criminal Court ("the Court") is hereby established. It shall be a permanent institution and shall have the power to exercise its jurisdiction over persons for the most serious crimes of international concern, as referred to in this Statute, and shall be complementary to national criminal jurisdictions. The jurisdiction and functioning of the Court shall be governed by the provisions of this Statute.

4.3.12

ICC
Article 25
Individual Criminal Responsibility

---

1. The Court shall have jurisdiction over natural persons pursuant to this Statute.
2. A person who commits a crime within the jurisdiction of the Court shall be individually responsible and liable for punishment in accordance with this Statute.
3. In accordance with this Statute, a person shall be criminally responsible and liable for punishment for a crime within the jurisdiction of the Court if that person:
(a) Commits such a crime, whether as an individual, jointly with another or through another person, regardless of whether that other person is criminally responsible;
(b) Orders, solicits or induces the commission of such a crime which in fact occurs or is attempted;
(c) For the purpose of facilitating the commission of such a crime, aids, abets or otherwise assists in its commission or its attempted commission, including providing the means for its commission;
(d) In any other way contributes to the commission or attempted commission of such a crime by a group of persons acting with a common purpose. Such contribution shall be intentional and shall either:
  (i) Be made with the aim of furthering the criminal activity or criminal purpose of the group, where such activity or purpose involves the commission of a crime within the jurisdiction of the Court; or
  (ii) Be made in the knowledge of the intention of the group to commit the crime;

> (e) In respect of the crime of genocide, directly and publicly incites others to commit genocide;
> (f) Attempts to commit such a crime by taking action that commences its execution by means of a substantial step, but the crime does not occur because of circumstances independent of the person's intentions. However, a person who abandons the effort to commit the crime or otherwise prevents the completion of the crime shall not be liable for punishment under this Statute for the attempt to commit that crime if that person completely and voluntarily gave up the criminal purpose.
>
> 4. No provision in this Statute relating to individual criminal responsibility shall affect the responsibility of States under international law.

4.3.13

> **ICC**
> **Article 26**
> **Exclusion of Jurisdiction Over Persons Under Eighteen**
>
> The Court shall have no jurisdiction over any person who was under the age of 18 at the time of the alleged commission of a crime.

ICC—Personal Jurisdiction

4.3.14 Compare the provisions on personal jurisdiction of the ICC.

4.3.15 The ICC, as provided for by Article 1 of the Statute:

> shall have the power to exercise its jurisdiction over persons for the most serious crimes of international concern . . .

4.3.16 Article 25 specifies that *"persons"* refers only to *"natural persons."* Moreover, Article 26 limits the Court's jurisdiction:

> The Court shall have no jurisdiction over any person who was under the age of 18 at the time of the alleged commission of a crime.

4.3.17 This provision excludes under-18-year olds from the ICC's ambit *as a matter of jurisdiction*. The ICC Statute does not, however, state that under-18 year olds are incapable of forming the requisite criminal intent (*doli incapax*); in which case, the provision would have been part of Article 25 ("Individual Criminal Responsibility"), Article 30 ("Mental Element") or Article 31 ("Grounds for excluding criminal responsibility").

4.3.18 It is therefore to be presumed that under-18 year olds could be tried in national courts, where, however, they might enjoy lower standards of protection than before the ICC. On this paradox, see Frulli, Micaela, "Jurisdiction *Ratione Personae*," in The *Rome Statute of the International Criminal Court: A Commentary* (eds. Antonio Cassese, Paola Gaeta, John R.W.D. Jones, OUP, 2002).

4.3.19 The following should also be noted in this regard: (1) Article 8(2)(b)(xxvi) ("*War Crimes*") provides that the following is a war crime, "*Conscripting or enlisting* *children under the age of fifteen years into the national armed forces or using them to participate actively in hostilities."* Article 8(2)(e)(vii) (*"War Crimes"*) is to the same effect in non-international armed conflicts. This reflects an international consensus that under-15 year olds should not participate in any way in armed conflict (see the 1989 *Convention on the Rights of the Child*, Article 38(2); *Additional Protocol I to the 1977 Geneva Conventions*, Article 77; *Additional Protocol II to the 1977 Geneva Conventions*, Article 4(3)(c)). (2) There is an emerging consensus that the age for this prohibition should be raised to 18 years old. See the *2000 Optional Protocol to the Convention on the Rights of the Child on the involvement of children in armed conflict*, which entered into force on 12 February 2002 and the 1999 *African Charter on the Rights and Welfare of the Child.* (3) The Statute of the Special Court for Sierra Leone fixes at 15 the age at which individuals may be prosecuted. At same time, it establishes a special regime for juvenile offenders granting them a whole set of protective measures and guarantees, including that they may not be sentenced to imprisonment. Instead the focus is on their treatment and rehabilitation (see 1.93 *et seq.* on the Special Court for Sierra Leone).

* * * * *

SECTION 4: TEMPORAL AND TERRITORIAL JURISDICTION

4.4.1

ICTY Article 8 Territorial and Temporal Jurisdiction	ICTR Article 7 Territorial and Temporal Jurisdiction
The territorial jurisdiction of the International Tribunal shall extend to the territory of the former Socialist Federal Republic of Yugoslavia, including its land surface, airspace and territorial waters. The temporal jurisdiction of the International Tribunal shall extend to a period beginning on 1 January 1991.	The territorial jurisdiction of the International Tribunal for Rwanda shall extend to the territory of Rwanda including its land surface and airspace as well as to the territory of neighbouring States in respect of serious violations of international humanitarian law committed by Rwandan citizens. The temporal jurisdiction of the International Tribunal for Rwanda shall extend to a period beginning on 1 January 1994 and ending on 31 December 1994.

Link Between Temporal and Territorial Jurisdiction and Existence of Armed Conflict

4.4.2   At the ICTY, Articles 2 and 3 only apply if there is a nexus between the acts charged against the accused and an armed conflict. This imposes temporal and territorial requirements which are, in a sense, more restrictive than the ICTY's general territorial and temporal jurisdiction. See the *Tadić Jurisdiction Appeals Decision* (see also 4.2.325 *et seq.*):

> 70. . . . we find that an armed conflict exists whenever there is a resort to armed force between States or protracted armed violence between governmental authorities and organized armed groups or between such groups within a State. International humanitarian law applies from the initiation of . . . armed conflicts and extends beyond the cessation of hostilities until a general conclusion of peace is reached; or, in the case of internal conflicts, a peaceful settlement is achieved. Until that moment, international humanitarian law continues to apply in the whole territory of the warring States or, in the case of internal conflicts, the whole territory under the control of a party, whether or not actual combat takes place there.

The Territory of the Former Yugoslavia

4.4.3   The dissolution of the Socialist Federal Republic of Yugoslavia (SFRY) resulted in the creation of five new States: Slovenia, Croatia, Bosnia and Herzegovina, the Federal Republic of Yugoslavia (Serbia and Montenegro) (FRY) and Macedonia. Within the FRY, Kosovo is increasingly autonomous.

4.4.4   The wording of ICTY Article 8 makes clear that all of the above States fall within the ICTY's territorial competence. Indeed, cases have been brought involving all of the new States (except Slovenia).

Kosovo

4.4.5 Although it might not appear open to challenge, the ICTY Prosecutor asserted on 10 March 1998 that the ICTY's jurisdiction covered events taking place in Kosovo in 1998—when Serb forces were reportedly committing serious violations of international humanitarian law—Kosovo being on the territory of the former Socialist Federal Republic of Yugoslavia. Security Council resolutions 1160 (1998) and 1207 (1998) confirmed this, urging the Office of the Prosecutor to investigate violations of humanitarian law being committed in Kosovo.

4.4.6 See also the letter of 1 September 1998 from the Prosecutor to the ICTY President:

> the international community is gravely concerned about the hostilities in Kosovo, and the possibility that war crimes and crimes against humanity are being committed there. As you know, my Office has launched an investigation into the events in Kosovo. I believe that the strongest deterrent message that could possibly be sent to those who may be involved in criminal activities falling within the jurisdiction of the Tribunal would be to demonstrate unambiguously that indicted persons will indeed be brought to justice in The Hague. The present tolerance of the default by the FRY to arrest indictees on its territory is inconsistent with the expressed desired to see the Tribunal play its full role as an instrument of international peace and security, in particular in Kosovo.

4.4.7 See also the letter dated 16 September 1998 from the ICTY President to the Security Council, reporting the FRY's refusal to arrest indictees and noting that, "closely related to this is the situation in the province of Kosovo."

4.4.8 In March–June 1999, when Serb forces attacked ethnic Albanians in Kosovo, the United Nations, governments and the ICTY reaffirmed the same principle—that the events fell within the jurisdiction of the ICTY—on countless occasions.

4.4.9 The Commission on Human Rights adopted a resolution on the situation in the countries of the former Yugoslavia (E/CN.4/1999/L.34/Rev.1) on 21 April 1999:

> *Shocked and horrified* by ongoing massacres and other brutal repressive measures committed by Serbian security and paramilitary forces in Kosovo with the intent of ethnic cleansing, in clear violation of international human rights standards and international humanitarian law and resulting in the loss of lives and a massive humanitarian tragedy affecting the entire region,
>
> . . .
>
> . . . demands that the authorities in the Federal Republic of Yugoslavia (Serbia and Montenegro) comply with their obligation to cooperate with the Tribunal, including with regard to events in Kosovo, on the basis of resolution 1160 (1998) of the Security Council and all its subsequent resolutions on the subject, including 1207 (1998), and commends the Office of the Prosecutor of the Tribunal for its efforts to gather information relating to the violence in Kosovo.

4.4.10 On 27 May 1999, an Indictment confirmed on 24 May 1999 was made public which charged Slobodan Milošević, Milan Milutinović, Nikola Šainović, Dragoljub Ojdanić and Vlajko Stojiljković with crimes against humanity and war crimes in relation to the events in Kosovo. The Prosecutor has stated that her investigations are continuing and that she might seek to amend the indictment at a later stage to add new charges.

4.4.11 See also the *Presentation of an Indictment for Review and Application for Warrants of Arrest and for Related Orders* dated 23 May 1999 and the *Decision on Review of Indictment and Application for Consequential Orders* rendered by Judge Hunt on 24 May 1999. The *Presentation* requested, *inter alia*, that:

> an order be made under Rule 54, that each State make enquiries to discover whether any of the accused have assets located in their territory, and that any State finding such assets adopt provisional measures to freeze such assets, without prejudice to the rights of third parties, until the accused are taken into custody.

4.4.12 Judge Hunt granted this request in his *Decision* of 24 May 1999 (Disposition, point 2(5)). Judge Hunt also directed warrants for the arrest of the accused to be sent to all States Members of the United Nations, Switzerland, the FRY and the Prosecutor.

4.4.13 Regarding the scale of the massacres in Kosovo, see *The Independent*, 18 June 1999, page 1 ("The student hostel that became a torturers' den") and page 3 ("100 massacres, 10,000 dead—a catalogue of horror reveals depth of Serb depravity") and *The Times*, 18 June 1999, page 13 ("Balkans War: atrocities").

4.4.14 The ICTY Prosecutor has decided not to launch an investigation against NATO leaders for the 1999 bombing campaign which was launched against Serbia in response to these atrocities. See *Guardian Weekly*, June 8–14, 2000, page 32, "U.N. Tribunal rejects call to put NATO in dock. File closed on Western nations being charged with committing war crimes against the Serbs":

> Carla Del Ponte, chief prosecutor of the International Criminal Tribunal for the Former Yugoslavia, told the Security Council last weekend that, after an 11-month assessment of charges that NATO forces committed crimes against Serbian civilians, her office had decided not to open a formal investigation. 'Although some mistakes were made by NATO, I am very satisfied that there was no deliberate targeting of civilians or unlawful military targets by NATO during the bombing campaign,' she said.
>
> . . .
>
> Del Ponte said that judging the legitimacy of the NATO campaign 'is not our task and is not part of our brief, just as we cannot decide on general responsibilities of countries or international organisations. It is our task to pinpoint possible individual responsibilities.'

4.4.15 See "The Kosovo Report" of the Independent International Commission on Kosovo (Oxford University Press, 2000).

Articles:

"Symposium: The International Legal Fallout from Kosovo," 12 (3) *European Journal of International Law* (June 2001), especially W.J. Fenrick, "Targeting and Proportionality during the NATO Bombing Campaign against the Federal Republic of Yugoslavia," *ibid.*, pp. 489–502.

Macedonia

4.4.16 See the ICTY's Macedonia deferral case (Decision on the Prosecutor's Request for Deferral and Motion for Order to the Former Yugoslav Republic of Macedonia, IT-02-55-MISC.6, 4 October 2002). National war crimes prosecutions are increasingly taking place in Macedonia, although legitimate doubts may be raised as to whether some of the crimes charged partake of the necessary nexus with armed conflict to qualify as war crimes. See 4.2.314.

ICTR—Temporal Jurisdiction

4.4.17 It is now settled case-law that ICTR indictments may *refer* to events or crimes which occurred prior to 1994, i.e. outside the ICTR's temporal jurisdiction, for which evidence may be admissible at trial, and on which the Trial Chamber may rely in its Judgement "for historical purposes or as information." The Trial Chamber may not, however, "hold any accused accountable for crimes committed prior to 1994," as this would clearly be *ultra vires*. The Tribunal's temporal jurisdiction is not exceeded provided that the "Trial Chamber will not rely upon [any] event occurring prior to 1994 as the independent basis of a count." See *Ngeze and Nahimana, Decision on Interlocutory Appeals*, 5 September 2000.

4.4.18 The admissibility of evidence regarding specific events pre-dating 1994 may be raised at trial. See *Nsengiyumva, Decision on the Defence Motions Objecting to the Jurisdiction of the Trial Chamber on the Amended Indictment*, 3 April 2000; *Nahimana, Decision of the Defence Preliminary Motion, Pursuant to Rule 72*, 12 July 2000; *Kabiligi and Ntabakuze, Decision on the Defence Motions Objecting to a Lack of Jurisdiction and Seeking to Declare the Indictment Void* Ab Initio, 13 April 2000; *Niyitegeka, Decisions and Preliminary Motion based on Defects in the Form of the Indictment and lack of jurisdiction*, 20 November 2000; and *Kajelijeli, Decision on the Defence Motion Objecting to the Jurisdiction of the Tribunal*, 13 March 2001.

4.4.19

ICC
Article 11
Jurisdiction *Ratione Temporis*

1. The Court has jurisdiction only with respect to crimes committed after the entry into force of this Statute.
2. If a State becomes a Party to this Statute after its entry into force, the Court may exercise its jurisdiction only with respect to crimes committed after the entry into force of this Statute for that State, unless that State has made a declaration under article 12, para. 3.

4.4.20

ICC
Article 4
Legal Status and Powers of the Court

---

1. The Court shall have international legal personality. It shall also have such legal capacity as may be necessary for the exercise of its functions and the fulfilment of its purposes.
2. The Court may exercise its functions and powers, as provided in this Statute, on the territory of any State Party and, by special agreement, on the territory of any other State.

4.4.21

ICC
Article 12
Preconditions to the Exercise of Jurisdiction

---

1. A State which becomes a Party to this Statute thereby accepts the jurisdiction of the Court with respect to the crimes referred to in article 5.
2. In the case of article 13, para. (a) or (c), the Court may exercise its jurisdiction if one or more of the following States are Parties to this Statute or have accepted the jurisdiction of the Court in accordance with para. 3:
(a) The State on the territory of which the conduct in question occurred or, if the crime was committed on board a vessel or aircraft, the State of registration of that vessel or aircraft;
(b) The State of which the person accused of the crime is a national.
3. If the acceptance of a State which is not a Party to this Statute is required under para. 2, that State may, by declaration lodged with the Registrar, accept the exercise of jurisdiction by the Court with respect to the crime in question. The accepting State shall cooperate with the Court without any delay or exception in accordance with Part 9.

4.4.22

ICC
Article 13
Exercise of Jurisdiction

The Court may exercise its jurisdiction with respect to a crime referred to in article 5 in accordance with the provisions of this Statute if:
(a) A situation in which one or more of such crimes appears to have been committed is referred to the Prosecutor by a State Party in accordance with article 14;
(b) A situation in which one or more of such crimes appears to have been committed is referred to the Prosecutor by the Security Council acting under Chapter VII of the Charter of the United Nations; or
(c) The Prosecutor has initiated an investigation in respect of such a crime in accordance with article 15.

ICC—Territorial Jurisdiction

4.4.23 As provided in Article 4 of the Rome Statute, the Court may exercise its functions and powers on the territory of any State Party and, by special agreement, on the territory of any other State. A State which becomes a Party to the Statute thereby accepts the jurisdiction of the Court with respect to the crimes referred to in Article 5 (Article 12).

4.4.24 Limits to the jurisdiction of the Court are given by the preconditions to the exercise of jurisdiction: these are set out in Article 12 (2), if a situation is referred to the Prosecutor by a State Party, pursuant to Article 14, or if the Prosecutor has initiated an investigation in respect of a crime, pursuant to Article 15. Article 12 (2) provides that:

> ... the Court may exercise its jurisdiction if one or more of the following States are Parties to this Statute or have accepted the jurisdiction of the Court in accordance with para. 3:
>
> (a) The State on the territory of which the conduct in question occurred or, if the crime was committed on board a vessel or aircraft, the State of registration of that vessel or aircraft;
>
> (b) The State of which the person accused of the crime is a national."

4.4.25 In the case of a State which is not a Party to the Statute:

> .... that State may, by declaration lodged with the Registrar, accept the exercise of jurisdiction by the Court with respect to the crime in question... (Article 12 (3)).

4.4.26 These limits do not, however, apply when:

> a situation [...] is referred to the Prosecutor by the Security Council acting under Chapter VII of the Charter of the United Nations (*Article 13 (b)*).

4.4.27 In other words, the Security Council may refer a situation to the ICC concerning *any* state, not only where the crimes were committed on the territory, or by a national, of a State Party to the Rome Statute.

4.4.28 Pursuant to Article 18 (Preliminary rulings regarding admissibility), when a situation is referred to the Prosecutor by the Security Council acting under Chapter VII of the Charter of the United Nations, the Prosecutor need not "notify all States Parties and those States which, taking into account the information available, would normally exercise jurisdiction over the crimes concerned [...]," of the commencement of an investigation.

4.4.29 Therefore, in the case of referral pursuant to Article 13 (b), there are no limits *ratione loci* to the exercise of the jurisdiction of the Court.

PART 5

PRIMACY OF THE INTERNATIONAL TRIBUNALS

Introduction	5.1
Historical Background	5.2
The ICTs—General	5.4
National War Crimes Cases	5.8
National Cases in Rwanda and Former Yugoslavia	5.9
National Cases in Other Countries	5.11
ICTY Article 9/ICTR Article 8: Concurrent Jurisdiction	5.21
General	5.22
History of ICTY Article 9	5.23
History of ICTR Article 8	5.27
Justification for Trying International Crimes Before ICTs	5.28
Challenge to the Grant of Primacy to the ICTR	5.30
Concurrent Jurisdiction Between the ICTs and the ICJ	5.31
ICTY Article 10/ICTR Article 9: *Non-Bis-in-Idem*	5.35
ICTY Rule 13/ICTR Rule 13: *Non Bis in Idem*	5.36
General	5.37
History of ICTY Rule 13	5.40
Applicable Only When Accused Already Tried	5.41
Right to Be Tried by National Courts Does Not Exclude Trial by ICTs	5.44
Exceptions to *Non-Bis-in-Idem*	5.46
Exceptions Not *Necessary Conditions* for the Exercise of Primacy	5.47
Justification for Deferral to the ICTs	5.49
ICTY Rule 8/ICTR Rule 8: Request for Information	5.51
History of ICTY Rule 8	5.52
ICTY Rule 9/ICTR Rule 9: Prosecutor's Request for Deferral	5.53
History of ICTY Rule 9	5.54
History of ICTR Rule 9	5.55
ICTY Rule 10/ICTR Rule 10: Formal Request for Deferral	5.61
History of ICTY Rule 10	5.62
History of ICTR Rule 10	5.62
ICTY Requests for Deferral	5.65
Chamber Must Be Seised of a Proposal for Deferral	5.68
Timing of the Application	5.71
Grounds for Prosecutor's Proposal	5.72
Subject of the Deferral	5.73
Consent of the Government	5.74
The Macedonia Deferrals	5.75
ICTR Requests for Deferral	5.79
Government as *Amicus Curiae* at Deferral Hearings	5.82
History of ICTR Rule 11 *bis*	5.83

362 • International Criminal Practice

ICTY Rule 11 *bis*/ICTR Rule 11 *bis:* Referral of the Indictment to Another Court............5.84
History of ICTR Rule 11 *bis*...5.89
ICTY Rule 12/ICTR Rule 12: Determinations of Courts of Any State....................5.92
History of ICTY Rule 12..5.93
The ICC and Complementarity with National Courts—General.........................5.94
ICC Preamble...5.98
ICC Article 1: The Court..5.99
ICC Article 17: Issues of Admissibility..5.103
ICC Article 18: Preliminary Rulings Regarding Admissibility.............................5.109
ICC Article 19: Challenges to the Jurisdiction of the Court or the
Admissibility of a Case..5.114
ICC Article 20: *Ne Bis in Idem*...5.120

* * * * *

Introduction

5.1 International criminal courts and tribunals are not intended to replace national courts in prosecuting international crimes. Where national courts are willing and able to try individuals for crimes falling within the jurisdiction of the ICTY and ICTR, it is perfectly permissible—indeed desirable—that they do so in preference to ICTs, which do not have the resources to deal with every alleged perpetrator and crime. The only requirement is that the trials in the national courts be fair and impartial, and not designed to shield the accused from criminal justice. Nevertheless, the mechanisms established for dealing with the division of labour between the ICTs and national courts, which is based on concurrent jurisdiction, and the complementarity regime of the ICC, in fact establish primacy of the ICTs and the ICC over national courts, at least under certain circumstances.

Historical Background

5.2 The need to regulate the interplay between international and domestic criminal proceedings did not arise in relation to the International Military Tribunal at Nuremberg (IMT). According to the *Agreement for the Prosecution and Punishment of the Major War Criminals of the European Axis*, signed in London in 1945, the IMT was founded "for the trial of war criminals whose offences have no particular geographical location" (Article 1). This solved the problem of the relationship between the IMT and national courts. All offences having no geographical location came within the jurisdiction of the IMT, the rest would be dealt with by domestic courts. Article 6 of the IMT Charter left open the possibility of war crimes trials in domestic courts by explicitly providing that, "Nothing in this Agreement shall prejudice the jurisdiction or the powers of any national or occupation court established or to be established in any Allied territory or in Germany for the trial of war criminals."

5.3 This also indirectly solved the problem of double jeopardy. The Charter laid down certain consequences for national courts following from the imposition of a sentence by the IMT. Article 11 of the IMT Charter provided that, "any person convicted by the Tribunal may be charged before a national, military or occupation court [. . .] with a crime other than of membership in a criminal group or organization and such court may, after convicting him, impose upon him punishment independent of and additional to the punishment imposed by the Tribunal for participation in the criminal activities of such group or organization". The Charter was silent about the effect of national courts' judgements and sentences on the IMT. The question did not, in fact, arise since none of the Nuremberg defendants had already been tried for the same crimes by national courts or courts-martial.

Articles:

Donnedieu de Vabres, Henri, "Le procès de Nuremberg devant les principes modernes du droit pénal international," *in* I *Recueil des Cours de l'Académie de Droit International* (1947).

Kelsen, "Will the Judgement in the Nuremberg Trial Constitute a Precedent in International Law?," *in* 1 *International Law Quarterly* 153 (1947).

Vassalli, "Prolusione letta il 31 gennaio 1946 dalla cattedra di diritto penale dell'Università di Genova," *in La giustizia penale internazionale, studi,* (Milano: Giuffrè, 1995).

Web Site:

The Avalon Project at the Yale Law School on the Nuremberg Trial: http://www.yale.edu/lawweb/avalon

Cross References:
ICTY, Articles 9 and 10; Rules 8, 9, 10, 11, 11 *bis*, 12 and 13.
ICTR, Articles 8 and 9; Rules 8, 9, 10, 11, 12 and 13.
ICC, Preamble and Articles 1, 15, 17, 18, 19 and 20.

The ICTs—General

5.4   As noted above, the ICTs do not have exclusive jurisdiction over the crimes in their Statutes. Rather they operate in a concurrent regime with national courts. The latter continue, therefore, to have jurisdiction over these crimes, at least to the extent that their national law allows. Thus, for example, persons have been tried in Germany and Belgium for war crimes committed, respectively, in the former Yugoslavia and in Rwanda, the domestic courts in each case applying their own domestic law, albeit exercising extra-territorial jurisdiction on the basis of the principle of universal jurisdiction.

5.5   As the Secretary-General highlighted in his *Report* on the ICTY Statute (UN Doc. S/25704 (1993)):

> 64. In establishing an international tribunal for the prosecution of persons responsible for serious violations committed in the territory of the former Yugoslavia, it was not the intention of the Security Council to preclude or prevent the exercise of jurisdiction by national courts with respect to such acts. Indeed national courts should be encouraged to exercise their jurisdiction in accordance with their national laws and procedures.

5.6   In practical terms, the solution adopted in the ICTs' statutes allows the ICTs to exercise primacy over national courts in two different ways: directly, in terms of the power of *deferral*, given that "At any stage of the procedure, the International Tribunal may formally request national courts to defer to the competence of the International Tribunal" (ICTY Article 9(2); ICTR Article 8(2)); and indirectly, in terms of the *ne bis in idem* principle, i.e. "No person shall be tried before a national court for acts constituting serious violations of international humanitarian law under the present Statute, for which he or she has already been tried by the International Tribunal" and "a person who has been tried by a national court for acts constituting serious violations of international humanitarian law may be subsequently tried by the International Tribunal" under certain circumstances (ICTY Article 10; ICTR Article 9).

5.7 There is also the power of *referral*, which does not appear in the ICTs' statutes but which was introduced in the ICTY's Rules of Procedure and Evidence, allowing referral of case from the ICTY back to national courts (see ICTY Rule 11 *bis* (Referral of the Indictment to Another Court), 5.84)

National War Crimes Cases

5.8 Since the establishment of the ICTs, several trials have been conducted by national courts against persons accused of serious violations of international humanitarian law falling within the jurisdiction of the tribunals. Reference should be made to the following:

National Cases in Rwanda and Former Yugoslavia

5.9 **Former Yugoslavia**, as reported in the ICTY's Eighth Annual Report (para. 36):

> On 12 May 2001, a conference entitled "An idea whose time has come: a Truth and Reconciliation Commission in Bosnia and Herzegovina" was organized in Sarajevo to allow all the parties concerned by the draft law, namely, the representatives of the international community and those from the civil society of Bosnia and Herzegovina, to air their views on the appropriateness of the commission, its legitimacy and its compatibility with the International Tribunal. The President gave a speech in which he proposed the establishment of a system of reconciliation complementary to the work of the Tribunal, which would allow for a more effective contribution to the reconstruction of national unity. Nonetheless, he underscored that the mandate of the commission should in no case impinge on that of the International Tribunal.

There have been war crimes prosecutions in Bosnia, Kosovo (see 1.116 *et seq.*) and Macedonia (5.75).

5.10 **Rwanda**, on August 30, 1996, the "*Loi organique sur l'organisation des poursuites des infractions constitutives du crime de génocide ou de crimes contre l'humanité, commises à partir du 1° octobre 1990*" was issued. Moreover, "participative" traditional courts ("gacaca") have been established and declared constitutional by Rwanda's Constitutional Court on 18 January 2001. These courts are intended to shed light on what happened during the 1994 genocide and to accelerate the trials of 120,000 people detained in Rwanda's jails charged with genocide and crimes against humanity.

Articles:

Kritz and Finci, "A Truth Reconciliation Commission in Bosnia and Herzegovina: An Idea Whose Time Has Come," *in* 3(1) *International Law FORUM du droit international* (2001).

Reydams, L., "Justice dans l'après-Apartheid. La Commission de vérité et de réconciliation sud-africaine," *in* 9 *Yearbook of African Law* (1995).

Schabas, W., "Justice, Democracy and Impunity in Post-Genocide Rwanda: Searching for Solutions to Impossible Problems," *in* 7(3) *Criminal Law Forum.*

National Cases in Other Countries

5.11 Belgium, with the adoption on 1993 of the *"Loi relative à la répression des infractions graves aux conventions internationales de Genève du 12 août 1949 et aux protocoles I et II du 8 juin 1977, additionnels à ce convention,"* as amended, on 10 February 1999, by the *"Loi relative à la répression des violations graves du droit international humanitaire,"* Belgium has assumed universal jurisdiction over serious violations of international humanitarian law. It should be noted that the scope for applying this law has, however, been restricted following the ruling of the ICJ in the *Case concerning the Arrest Warrant of 11 April 2000* between Congo and Belgium, which incidentally brought a stop, among other things, to the Belgian investigations against Prime Minister Sharon of Israel.

5.12 The *Butare four case* opened on 17 April 2001 before the Brussels Court of Assizes against Vincent Ntezimana, Alphonse Higaniro, Consolata Mukangango and Julienne Mukabutera (respectively a former academic, a former director of the Butare match factory and two Nuns from Sovu), was also brought under the 1993 law.

Articles:

A series of reports by S. MAUPAS on this trial are published in *Diplomatie judiciaire (Internet magazine on the international criminal law)*—http://www.diplomatiejudiciaire.com/.

5.13 Denmark, *Sarik Case*, in which an eight year term of imprisonment was imposed for several violations of the 3rd Geneva Convention in the POW camp of Dretelj in Bosnia (see "High Court of Denmark, III Chamber, 25 November 1994, S-3396-94").

Articles:

The case is briefly mentioned in: Graditzky, "Individual Criminal Responsibility for Violations of International Humanitarian Law Committed in Non-International Armed Conflicts," *in International Review of the Red Cross* 29–56, No. 322 (1 March 1998).

5.14 France, *Javor Case*, concerning a decision of inadmissibility to prosecute a person accused of several acts of ethnic cleaning in the Kozarac area. The accused was not detained in France. The *Parquet* of first instance dealt with the issue as one of admissibility. The *Cour de Cassation* confirmed the decision of first instance—see, respectively, "Ordonnance d'incompétence partielle, May 6 1994, N. Parquet 94 0522002/7, Chambre d'accusation de la Cour d'appel de Paris, Quatrième Chambre, n. A 94/02071," and "Cour de Cassation, Chambre criminelle, May 26, 1996, N.° D95-

81.527.PF").

Article:
Case note by B. Stern *in* 93 *AJIL* 525 (1999).

5.15 See also the *Munyeshyaka Case*, concerning a priest working in France accused of involvement in genocide near Kigali. Here, too, problems arose as to admissibility (see "Juge d'istructions de Privas, Ordonnance d'incompétence partielle, January 9 1996, N° d'instruction 95/081"; "Chambre d'accusation de la Cour d'appel de Nîmes, March 1996, N° 96-0160," and "Cour de Cassation, Chambre criminelle, 6 January 1998, N° X 96-82.491 PF").

Article: On this topic, see B. Stern, "La compétence universelle en France: le cas de crimes commis en ex-Yougoslavie et au Rwanda," *in* 40 *German Yearbook of International Law* 280–299.

5.16 Germany, *Jorgić Case*, in which the accused was convicted and sentenced to life imprisonment for several acts (including murders) committed by the accused as leader of a paramilitary group involved, *inter alia*, in the ethnic cleansing of the Doboj municipality in the spring and summer of 1992 (see "Oberlandesgericht Düsseldorf, 5 January 1998, 3 ST 20/96").

5.17 See also *Djajić Case*, in which the accused was convicted and sentenced to five years' imprisonment for, among other things, murder in Bosnia and Herzegovina ("Bayerisches Oberstes Landesgericht, 25 May 1996, 3 ST 20/96").

Article:
Case note with commentary by Safferling *in* 92 *AJIL* 528–532 (1998).

5.18 *Netherlands*, *Knesevi Case*, This is a series of decisions mainly on jurisdictional issues ("Rechter-commissaris of the Arrondissementsrechtbank Arnhem—militaire kamer, raadkamer—decision of 1 December 1995"; "Arrondissementsrechtbank Arnhem (militaire kamer, raadkamer), Decision of 21 February 1996"; "Hoge Raad (Netherlands Supreme Court)," Judgement of 22 October 1996"; "Arrondissementsrechtbank Arnhem (militaire kamer, raadkamer), Judgement of 19 March 1997"; "Hoge Raad, two separate judgements of 11 November 1997 Strafkamer, Nr. 3717 AB and Nr, 3718").

5.19 Switzerland, the *Niyonteze Case*, in which a former Rwandan Mayor was convicted by a Swiss Military Tribunal in 1999 for violations of the Geneva Conventions. Niyonteze was sentenced to life imprisonment, but this was subsequently reduced to 14 years.

5.20 See also *In re G. Case*, where the Military Tribunal acquitted the accused on the grounds that the evidence was insufficient to establish that he was in the camps at the time of the crimes (G. was accused of having beaten and injured civilian prisoners in the Omarska and Keraterm camps in Bosnia-Herzegovina in 1992).

Articles:

Case note with Commentary by Ziegler, *in* 92 *AJIL* 78–82 (1998).

Brown, Bartram S., "Primacy or Complementarity: Reconciling the Jurisdiction of National Courts and International Criminal Tribunals," in 23 *Yale Journal of International Law* 383 (1998).

Lattanzi, F., "La primazia del tribunale internazionale per l'ex Jugoslavia sulle giurisdizioni interne," *in Rivista di Diritto Internazionale,"*597ss. (1996). See also "La competenza delle giurisdizioni degli Stati terzi a ricercare e processare i responsabili dei crimini nella ex Jugoslavia e nel Ruanda," *in Rivista di Diritto Internazionale*707ss. (1995).

5.21

ICTY Article 9 Concurrent Jurisdiction	ICTR Article 8 Concurrent Jurisdiction
1. The International Tribunal and national courts shall have concurrent jurisdiction to prosecute persons for serious violations of international humanitarian law committed in the territory of the former Yugoslavia since 1 January 1991.	1. The International Tribunal for Rwanda and national courts shall have concurrent jurisdiction to prosecute persons for serious violations of international humanitarian law committed in the territory of Rwanda and Rwandan citizens for such violations committed in the territory of neighbouring States, between 1 January 1994 and 31 December 1994.
2. The International Tribunal shall have primacy over national courts. At any stage of the procedure, the International Tribunal may formally request national courts to defer to the competence of the International Tribunal in accordance with the present Statute and the Rules of Procedure and Evidence of the International Tribunal.	2. The International Tribunal for Rwanda shall have primacy over the national courts of all States. At any stage of the procedure, the International Tribunal for Rwanda may formally request national courts to defer to its competence in accordance with the present Statute and the Rules of Procedure and Evidence of the International Tribunal for Rwanda.

General

5.22   The ICTs' provisions on concurrent jurisdiction, on the one hand, recognize the concurrent nature of the judicial work performed by the Tribunal and national courts, while on the other hand, they raise the question of which court(s) should prevail in the event of conflict and solve the problem by conferring upon the ICTs primacy over the national courts of all States.

Cross References:

IMT, Article 1.

ICC, Preamble, Articles 1, 15, 17, 18 and 19.

History of ICTY Article 9

5.23 During the debates on Security Council Resolution 827, four of the five permanent members of the Security Council (France, United States, United Kingdom and Russia) asserted the need to circumscribe the primacy of the *ad hoc* Tribunals over national courts. They expressed the view that the ICTY's primacy should be limited to those cases where the *ne bis in idem* exceptions applied, i.e., where "(a) the act for which [the accused] was tried was characterized as an ordinary crime; (b) the national court proceedings were not impartial or independent, were designed to shield the accused from international criminal responsibility, or the case was not diligently prosecuted."

5.24 As reported in U.N. Doc. S/PV.3217, at 11, France proposed that (for the positions of the United States, United Kingdom and Russia, *See*, respectively, at 16, 18 and 46)

> the Tribunal may intervene at any stage of the procedure and assert its primacy, including from the stage of investigations where appropriate, in the situations covered under Article 10, para. 2.

5.25 The suggestion was not, however, adopted. If it had been, it would have precluded the first trial before the ICTY of Duško Tadić, given that the proceedings against him in Germany appeared to be impartial and independent, were not designed to shield him from international criminal responsibility and were being diligently prosecuted. Moreover, not only were the crimes with which Tadić was charged in Germany not characterised as ordinary crimes, but he was also charged in Germany with Genocide which was not prosecuted before the ICTY. In light of this, and in the spirit of the positions of four of the five Permanent Members of the Security Council on this point, it is submitted that it was inappropriate and unwise to order the deferral of the proceedings in Germany to the ICTY. The decision was evidently taken in order to have *an accused* before the Tribunal at a time when no-one was in custody; however this was, it is submitted, an unduly pragmatic and short-sighted view, given that the ICTY has been trying ever since to move away from prosecutions of "minor players" towards the prosecution of leadership figures (see 4.13 and 6.2.9 *et seq.*).

5.26 The ICTY Judges subsequently decided, however, at the suggestion of the Prosecutor, to amend the Rules of Procedure and Evidence to include in ICTY Rule 9 other situations in which the Prosecutor may propose to the Trial Chamber that a formal request for deferral be made to a State. Among these are where the national proceedings involve "significant factual or legal questions which may have implications for investigations or prosecutions before the Tribunal"—ICTY Rule 9(iii). While there may be good practical reasons for the adoption of such a rule, it is arguably *ultra vires* given the provisions of the Statute and the comments made by the permanent members of the Security Council when the ICTY Statute was adopted. On this point, see ICTY Rule 9, below.

History of ICTR Article 8

5.27 ICTR Article 8 is directly inspired by ICTY Article 9. However, differences exist between the two *ad hoc* Tribunals in relation to the reasons for asserting primacy (see, below, 5.53 *et seq.*, the similarities and the differences between ICTY/ICTR Rule 9).

Justification for Trying International Crimes Before ICTs

5.28 For a justification of the grant of primacy to the Tribunal, see Judge Sidhwa's separate opinion to the *Tadić Jurisdiction Appeals Decision:*

> 83. At the root of primacy is a demand for justice at the international level by all States and constitutes the first step towards implementation of international judicial competence. The rule enhances the role of the Prosecutor in giving him a right to move for transfer of competence and to the International Tribunal the option whether to exercise its discretion to secure competence for itself. The rule obliges States to accede to and accept requests for deferral on the ground of suspension of their sovereign rights to try the accused themselves and compels States to accept the fact that certain domestic crimes are really international in character and endanger international peace and that such international crimes should be tried by an international tribunal, that being an appropriate and competent legal body duly established for this purpose by law. The rule cuts [across] national borders to bring to justice persons guilty of serious international crimes, as they concern all States and require to be dealt with for the benefit of all civilized nations. Last but not least, the rule recognizes the right of all nations to ensure the prevention of such violations by establishing international criminal tribunals appropriately empowered to deal with these matters, or else international crimes would be dealt with as ordinary crimes and the guilty would not be adequately punished.

5.29 This last reason is, however, flawed: national courts are able to try international crimes as such, if their legislation allows, and are not obliged to treat them as "ordinary crimes."

Challenge to the Grant of Primacy to the ICTR

5.30 The defence in *Kanyabashi* challenged the grant of primacy to the ICTR. The Trial Chamber rejected this challenge in its *Kanyabashi Jurisdiction Decision:*

> 30. Although the Defence Counsel did not explicitly challenge the primacy of the Tribunal's jurisdiction over national courts, this objection is implied in the Defence Counsel's contention that establishment of the Tribunal violated the principle of *jus de non evocando*.
>
> 31. This principle, originally derived from constitutional law in civil law jurisdictions, establishes that persons accused of certain crimes should retain their right to be tried before the regular domestic criminal Courts rather than by politically founded ad-hoc criminal tribunals which, in times of emergency, may fail to provide impartial justice. As stated by the Appeals Chamber in the *Tadić* case: "As a matter of fact and of law the principle advocated by the Appellant aims at one very specific goal: to avoid the creation of special or extraordinary courts designed to try political offences in times of social unrest without guarantees of a fair trial." In the Trial Chamber's opinion, however, the Tribunal is far from being an institution designed for the purpose of removing, for political reasons, certain criminal offenders from fair and impartial justice and have them prosecuted for political crimes before prejudiced arbitrators.
>
> 32. It is true that the Tribunal has primacy over domestic criminal Courts and may at any stage request national Courts to defer to the competence of the Tribunal

pursuant to Article 8 of the Statute of the Tribunal, according to which the Tribunal may request that national Courts defer to the competence of the Tribunal at any stage of their proceedings. The Tribunal's primacy over national Courts is also reflected in the principle of *non bis in idem* as laid down in Article 9 of the Statute and in Article 28 of the Statute which establishes that States shall comply without undue delay with any request for assistance or an order issued by a Trial Chamber. The primacy thereby entrenched for the Tribunal, however, is exclusively derived from the fact that the Tribunal is established under Chapter VII of the UN Charter, which in turn enables the Tribunal to issue directly binding international legal orders and requests to States, irrespective of their consent. Failure of States to comply with such legally binding orders and requests may, under certain conditions, be reported by the President of the Tribunal to the Security Counsel for further action. The Trial Chamber concludes, therefore, that the principle of *jus de non evocando* has not been violated.

Concurrent Jurisdiction Between the ICTs and the ICJ

5.31 The issue whether the ICTs should follow a decision rendered by the International Court of Justice on a question of law was considered in the *Delalić et al. Appeals Judgement*. The Appeals Chamber held that, while it would take into account the decisions of other international courts as much as possible so as to ensure consistency and predictability as much as possible in international law, the Tribunal was an autonomous legal body and therefore not bound by ICJ rulings:

> 24. The Appeals Chamber agrees that "so far as international law is concerned, the operation of the desiderata of consistency, stability, and predictability does not stop at the frontiers of the Tribunal. . . . The Appeals Chamber cannot behave as if the general state of the law in the international community whose interests it serves is none of its concern." However, this Tribunal is an autonomous international judicial body, and although the ICJ is the "principal judicial organ" within the United Nations system to which the Tribunal belongs, there is no hierarchical relationship between the two courts. Although the Appeals Chamber will necessarily take into consideration other decisions of international courts, it may, after careful consideration, come to a different conclusion.

5.32 The same issue arises, of course, for the ICTR. See the Separate Opinion of Judge Shahabuddeen, a former judge of the ICJ, to the Appeals Chamber's Decision in *Semanza* dated 31 May 2000, in which he noted that:

> 32. . . . whereas the Tribunal was established by a principal organ of the United Nations, the ICJ is itself a principal organ of that Organisation and, indeed, its 'principal judicial organ' as provided by the supreme law of both judicial bodies. . . . The lawgiver might reasonably be supposed to have envisaged that the Tribunal would in consequence show deference to, if not take the law from, decisions of the ICJ as to what was customary international law and depart from them only in the clearest and most compelling cases. Subject to such narrow exceptions, when there is a conflict in holdings the Appeals Chamber should accordingly be prepared to bring its previous decisions into conformity with those of the ICJ. If not, the consequences may be noted.

5.33 In *Kvočka et al.*, Zoran Zigić filed a motion in which he requested the Trial Chamber to suspend its decision on questions pending before the ICJ or to rule that such questions should not be decided and, furthermore to request an advisory opinion from the ICJ. The accused submitted that questions as to the nature of the armed conflict in Bosnia and Herzegovina, the identity of the parties to the conflict, and whether crimes were committed in the course of that conflict, were subject to determination by both the ICTY in his case and by the ICJ in an application filed by Bosnia and Herzegovina on 20 March 1993, alleging violations of the 1948 Convention on the Prevention and Punishment of the Crime of Genocide and of several other international obligations by the FRY. In the *Decision on the Defence Motion regarding concurrent procedures before International Criminal Tribunal for the former Yugoslavia and International Court of Justice on the same questions* rendered on 5 December 2000, the Chamber dismissed the motion on a procedural ground, being in reality a challenge to jurisdiction which was brought out of time. The Chamber also noted the respective competences of the ICJ and the ICTY:

> Considering that the ICJ, the principal judicial organ of the United Nations, deals with State responsibility, while the Tribunal, established by the Security Council on the basis of Chapter VII of the United Nations Charter, deals with individual criminal responsibility.

5.34 The Appeal Chamber confirmed this in the *Decision on Interlocutory Appeal by the accused Zoran Zigić against the decision of Trial Chamber I dated 5 December 2000*, (*Prosecutor v. Kvočka et al.*, 25 May 2001). The Chamber, dismissing the interlocutory appeal, considered that

> 17. ... no legal basis exists for suggesting that the International Tribunal must defer to the International Court of Justice such that the former would be legally bound by decisions of the latter.

See also 1.42 above ("Relationship between the ICTY and the ICJ").

5.35

ICTY Article 10 *Non-Bis-in-Idem*	ICTR Article 9 *Non-Bis-in-Idem*
1. No person shall be tried before a national court for acts constituting serious violations of international humanitarian law under the present Statute, for which he or she has already been tried by the International Tribunal. 2. A person who has been tried by a national court for acts constituting serious violations of international humanitarian law may be subsequently tried by the International Tribunal only if:	1. No person shall be tried before a national court for acts constituting serious violations of international humanitarian law under the present Statute, for which he or she has already been tried by the International Tribunal for Rwanda. 2. A person who has been tried by a national court for acts constituting serious violations of international humanitarian law may be subsequently tried by the International Tribunal for Rwanda only if:

(a) the act for which he or she was tried was characterized as an ordinary crime; or (b) the national court proceedings were not impartial or independent, were designed to shield the accused from international criminal responsibility, or the case was not diligently prosecuted. 3. In considering the penalty to be imposed on a person convicted of a crime under the present Statute, the International Tribunal shall take into account the extent to which any penalty imposed by a national court on the same person for the same act has already been served.	(a) the act for which he or she was tried was characterized as an ordinary crime; or (b) the national court proceedings were not impartial or independent, were designed to shield the accused from international criminal responsibility, or the case was not diligently prosecuted. 3. In considering the penalty to be imposed on a person convicted of a crime under the present Statute, the International Tribunal for Rwanda shall take into account the extent to which any penalty imposed by a national court on the same person for the same act has already been served.

5.36

ICTY Rule 13 *Non Bis in Idem*	ICTR Rule 13 *Non Bis in Idem*
When the President receives reliable information to show that criminal proceedings have been instituted against a person before a court of any State for a crime for which that person has already been tried by the Tribunal, a Trial Chamber shall, following *mutatis mutandis* the procedure provided in Rule 10, issue a reasoned order requesting that court permanently to discontinue its proceedings. If that court fails to do so, the President may report the matter to the Security Council.	When the President receives reliable information to show that criminal proceedings have been instituted against a person before a court of any State for a crime for which that person has already been tried by the Tribunal, a Trial Chamber shall, following *mutatis mutandis* the procedure provided in Rule 10, issue a reasoned order requesting that court permanently to discontinue its proceedings. If that court fails to do so, the President may report the matter to the Security Council.

General

5.37 The *non bis in idem* principle (or double jeopardy) is designed to ensure that a person is never judged twice in respect of the same events.

5.38 The articles in the ICTs dealing with *non bis in idem* regulate this matter with a general rule and an exception. The general provision is embodied in the prohibition on national courts from trying a person in respect of acts for which he has already been tried before the ICTs. The exception consists in the provision whereby a person who has been tried by national courts may be subsequently tried before the ICTs for the same acts under certain specific circumstances.

5.39 *Non bis in idem* is a fundamental principle of criminal law recognized in universal (e.g. ICCPR, Article 14(7)) and regional (e.g. ECHR, Protocol 7, Article 4) international human rights instruments, as well as in criminal co-operation conventions and in most national criminal systems. As has been pointed out in the Secretary General's Report (UN Doc. S/25704)

> 66. ... In the present context, given the primacy of the International Tribunal, the principle of non bis in idem would preclude subsequent trial before a national court. However, the principle of non bis in idem would not preclude a subsequent trial before the International Tribunal in the following two circumstances:
>
>> (a) The characterization of the act by the national court did not correspond to its characterization under the statute; or
>>
>> (b) Conditions of impartiality, independence or effective means of adjudication were not guaranteed in the proceedings before the national courts.

Cross References:

IMT, Article 11 of the Charter.

ICC, Article 20.

History of ICTY Rule 13

5.40 Like ICTY Rules 8, 9, 10 and 12, Rule 13 was amended at the ICTY fifth plenary session in January 1995 to remove the previous reference to "national" courts, the word "national" being "a term which has a particular or restrictive meaning in some jurisdictions."

Applicable Only When Accused Already Tried

5.41 *Non-bis-in-idem* applies only when a person has already been *tried*, i.e. convicted or acquitted after a trial. See the *Tadić Non-bis-in-idem Decision*:

> 9. The principle of *non-bis-in-idem*, appears in some form as part of the international legal code of many nations. Whether characterized as *non-bis-in-idem*, double jeopardy or autrefois acquit, autrefois convict, this principle normally protects a person from being tried twice or punished twice for the same acts. This principle has gained a certain international status since it is articulated in Article 14(7) of the International Covenant on Civil and Political Rights as a standard of a fair trial, but it is generally applied so as to cover only double prosecution within the same State. The principle is binding upon this International Tribunal to the extent that it appears in Statute, and in the form that it appears there.
>
> 10. The deferral which occurred in this case does not raise a genuine issue of *non-bis-in-idem* according to the terms of the Statute, for this principle clearly applies only in cases where a person has already been tried.

5.42 The Defence had argued that *non-bis-in-idem* arose because proceedings against the accused were still pending in Germany. The Trial Chamber agreed that the principle of *non-bis-in-idem would* be violated if the accused were to be retried in Germany after having been tried by the Tribunal, but it stated that that possibility was excluded by the deferral proceedings which had been held in relation to Germany:

13. The Defence has raised an issue of *non-bis-in-idem* by suggesting that the stage of the proceedings in Germany in such that there is a possibility that the accused might be retried in Germany after being tried by this International Tribunal. If true this would indeed raise an issue of *non-bis-in-idem* under Article 10 of the Statute. But, having deferred the case of the accused to the International Tribunal, Germany could not proceed to retry him for the same acts after the disposition of his case here. Article 10(1) of the Statute makes this unequivocally clear.

5.43 Moreover, at the deferral hearings at the ICTY, the accused had agreed, through his legal representative, for his case to be transferred from Germany to the ICTY.

Right to Be Tried by National Courts Does Not Exclude Trial by ICTs

5.44 The right of an accused to be tried by his national courts under his national laws does not exclude trial by an international tribunal. See the *Tadić Jurisdiction Appeals Decision*:

> 61. ... No one has questioned the right of Appellant [to be tried by his national courts under his national laws]. The problem is elsewhere: is that right exclusive? Does it prevent Appellant from being tried ...—and having an equally fair trial—before an international tribunal? ...
>
> 62. ... This principle is not breached by the transfer of jurisdiction to an international tribunal created by the Security Council acting on behalf of the community of nations. No rights of accused are thereby infringed or threatened; quite to the contrary, they are all specifically spelt out and protected under the Statute of the International Tribunal. No accused can complain. True, he will be removed from his "natural" national forum; but he will be brought before a tribunal at least equally fair, more distanced from the facts of the case and taking a broader view of the matter.
>
> Furthermore, one cannot but rejoice at the thought that, universal jurisdiction being nowadays acknowledged in the case of international crimes, a person suspected of such offences may finally be brought before an international judicial body for a dispassionate consideration of his indictment by impartial, independent and disinterested judges coming, as it happens here, from all continents of the world.

5.45 This reasoning is not, however, entirely convincing. First, if it is acknowledged that an accused has a "right" to be tried by his national forum, it means little to say that the right may be displaced by other considerations. In that case, it is not truly speaking a "right" at all, or at least a right of which the accused can avail himself. A right which cannot be enjoyed is not of much use. Second, the argument appears to be that the accused's right to be tried by his national courts may be overcome because "*he will be brought before a tribunal at least equally fair, more distanced from the facts of the case and taking a broader view of the matter.*" But does that mean that whether the right to demand trial by the national court may be exercised depends on whether the tribunal is equally fair, etc.? If it could be empirically shown that the national court would have tried the matter as fairly, impartially and independently as the international tribunal, would the accused then have a right to insist on his acknowledged right to be tried by his own courts? Would the Tribunal even agree to examine such an argument based on the equally fair treatment he would receive in the national court? Probably not. Finally, if this really is the consideration, then trial by an international court is meant to be an option more favourable to the accused—but if the advantage is meant to accrue to the accused, why can the accused not "waive" the option of having such an advantage conferred on him, electing instead for trial by the allegedly "less fair" national courts? The answers to these questions remain unclear.

Exceptions to *Non-Bis-in-Idem*

5.46 ICTY Article 10(2) reflects special circumstances, which act "as a limited exception to [the] principle of *non-bis-in-idem*" (*Tadić Non-bis-in-idem Decision*, para. 33). In other words, as a general principle, a person cannot be tried twice. The exception to this is when, in the first set of proceedings, the act for which the accused was tried was characterised as an ordinary crime, or the proceedings were not impartial or independent, or the proceedings were designed to shield the accused from international criminal responsibility, or the case was not diligently prosecuted.

Exceptions Not *Necessary Conditions* for the Exercise of Primacy

5.47 In *Tadić*, the accused argued that the Tribunal was only justified in exercising its primacy if the exceptions to the principle of *non-bis-in-idem* listed in Article 10(2) of the ICTY Statute applied. Therefore if the national proceedings in respect of which the Tribunal was requesting deferral were impartial and independent proceedings, diligently pursued and not designed to shield the accused from international criminal responsibility (as they apparently were in Germany), then the Tribunal was not justified in exercising its primacy. The Appeals Chamber rejected this argument in its Decision of 2 October 1995:

> 52. ... One recognizes at once that this vocabulary [referring to "impartial and independent proceedings diligently pursued and not designed to shield the accused from international criminal responsibility"] is borrowed from Article 10, para. 2, of the Statute. This provision has nothing to do with the present case. This is not an instance of an accused being tried anew by this International Tribunal, under the exceptional circumstances described in Article 10 of the Statute. Actually, the proceedings against Appellant were deferred to the International Tribunal on the strength of Article 9 of the Statute, which provides that a request for deferral may be made "at any stage of the procedure." ... The Prosecutor has never sought to bring Appellant before the International Tribunal for a new trial for the reason that one or the other of the conditions enumerated in Article 10 would have vitiated his trial in Germany. Deferral of the proceedings against Appellant was requested in accordance with the procedure set down in Rule 9(iii). ... After the Trial Chamber had found that that condition was satisfied, the request for deferral followed automatically. The conditions alleged by Appellant in his Brief were irrelevant.

5.48 The Appellant's argument was not, however, altogether unreasonable; in fact, it corresponds to the view taken by the four of the permanent members of the Security Council upon the adoption of the ICTY Statute (see above, 5.23).

Justification for Deferral to the ICTs

5.49 Where national courts lack competence to prosecute genocide and crimes against humanity, and therefore can only prosecute crimes committed in Rwanda and the former Yugoslavia, or elsewhere, as ordinary crimes, that is a good reason for deferring the prosecutions to the ICTY or ICTR, who can prosecute the crimes upon a truer characterisation of their criminality. See the *Decision on the Application by the Prosecutor for a Formal Request for Deferral*, rendered by the Trial Chamber on 17 May 1996 in *Bagosora*, in which the Chamber approved the Prosecutor's reasons, with respect to *non bis in idem*, for making the request:

> 13. Moreover, the Prosecutor rightly observes that Article 9.2 of the Tribunal's Statute, concerning the principle of *non bis in idem*, sets limits to the subsequent prosecution by the Tribunal of persons who have been tried by a national court for acts constituting serious violations of international humanitarian law. And, in the case of Théoneste Bagosora, as Belgian law does not contain any provision concerning genocide or crimes against humanity, it was only for murder and serious violations of the Geneva Conventions of 12 August 1949 and Additional Protocols I and II of 8 June 1977 that the Belgian authorities were able to prosecute him, given the facts that he is charged with. Therefore, should the Prosecutor subsequently wish to prosecute Théoneste Bagosora for the same facts, characterizing them as genocide and crimes against humanity, he would not be able to do so, if Théoneste Bagosora had already been tried by Belgian jurisdictions.

5.50 This same reasoning had been applied in the earlier *Decisions on the Formal Request for Deferral presented by the Prosecutor*, rendered by the Trial Chamber on 12 March 1996 in *Musema* with respect to Switzerland and its investigations and prosecution of the suspect, i.e. under Swiss law, the accused could not be prosecuted for genocide nor for crimes against humanity (see para. 12 of the Decision), and in the *Radio Télévision Libre des Mille Collines* case, with respect to the investigations of the Belgian authorities (see para. 11 of the Decision).

Articles:

Christine Van den Wyngaert and Tom Ongena, *"Ne bis in idem Principle,* Including the Issue of Amnesty," Ch. 18.4., *in* Antonio Cassese, Paola Gaeta and John R.W.D. Jones (eds.), *The Rome Statute of the International Criminal Court: A Commentary* (Oxford University Press: 2002).

5.51

ICTY Rule 8 Request for Information	ICTR Rule 8 Request for Information
Where it appears to the Prosecutor that a crime within the jurisdiction of the Tribunal is or has been the subject of investigations or criminal proceedings instituted in the courts of any State, he may request the State to forward to him all relevant information in that respect, and the State shall transmit to him such information forthwith in accordance with Article 29 of the Statute.	Where it appears to the Prosecutor that a crime within the jurisdiction of the Tribunal is or has been the subject of investigations or criminal proceedings instituted in the courts of any State, he may request the State to forward to him all relevant information in that respect, and the State shall transmit to him such information forthwith in accordance with Article 28 of the Statute.

History of ICTY Rule 8

5.52   ICTY Rule 8, as well as Rules 9, 10, 12 and 13, was amended at the fifth plenary session in January 1995 to remove the previous reference to "national" courts, the word "national" being "a term which has a particular or restrictive meaning in some jurisdictions." In international law, the term "municipal" is used in contrast to "international," and "municipal courts" in contrast to "international courts." However, for many ICTY Judges, the term "municipal" in their national systems suggested *local*, i.e. the law or courts of a municipality, town or village. Equally, the term "national courts" could suggest a distinction, in a federal State like Germany or the United States, between the federal courts and the courts of the Länder or States. Hence the above terminology was used to cover all the courts of any State.

5.53

ICTY Rule 9 Prosecutor's Request for Deferral	ICTR Rule 9 Prosecutor's Request for Deferral

Where it appears to the Prosecutor that in any such investigations or criminal proceedings instituted in the courts of any State:
(i)   the act being investigated or which is the subject of those proceedings is characterized as an ordinary crime;
(ii) there is a lack of impartiality or independence, or the investigations or proceedings are designed to shield the accused from international criminal responsibility, or the case is not diligently prosecuted; or
 	
(iii) what is in issue is closely related to, or otherwise involves, significant factual or legal questions which may have implications for investigations or prosecutions before the Tribunal,
the Prosecutor may propose to the Trial Chamber designated by the President that a formal request be made that such court defer to the competence of the Tribunal.
	Where it appears to the Prosecutor that crimes which are the subject of investigations or criminal proceedings instituted in the courts of any State:
	(i) are the subject of an investigation by the Prosecutor;
	(ii) should be the subject of an investigation by the Prosecutor considering, *inter alia*:
	  (a) the seriousness of the offences;
	  (b) the status of the accused at the time of the alleged offences;
	  (c) the general importance of the legal questions involved in the case;
	(iii) are the subject of an indictment in the Tribunal,
	the Prosecutor may propose to the Trial Chamber designated by the President that a formal request be made that such court defer to the competence of the Tribunal.

History of ICTY Rule 9

5.54   Like ICTY Rule 8, Rule 9 was amended at the ICTY fifth plenary session in January 1995 to remove the previous reference to "national" courts, the word "national" being a term which has a particular or restrictive meaning in some jurisdictions. Paras. (i) and (ii) of Rule 9 are based, respectively, on Article 10(2)(a) and (b) of the Statute which enshrine the principle of *non-bis-in-idem*. Para. (iii) does not, however, derive from Article 10(2) of the Statute but was introduced as an amendment to Rule 9. While there are sound practical reasons for such a sub-Rule—to avoid witnesses being confused by being called to testify before two prosecuting/investigating authorities and, generally, to avoid duplication of work—it is not justified by reference to the *non-bis-in-idem* exceptions, but can only be justified by invoking the ICTY's primacy under Article 9(2) of the Statute.

History of ICTR Rule 9

5.55 ICTR Rule 9 was amended at the ICTR fourth plenary session, held in Arusha from 1–5 June 1997. The amendment was made in order to clarify the procedure for requests for deferral of national investigations and criminal proceedings instituted in the courts of any State to the competence of the Tribunal.

5.56 As at the ICTY, prior to this Rule being amended in June 1996, the Prosecutor relied in his deferral requests exclusively on Rule 9(iii), viz. "what is in issue is closely related to, or otherwise involves, significant factual or legal questions which may have implications for investigations or prosecutions before the Tribunal." This was unfortunate inasmuch as Rule 9(iii), unlike Rule 9 (i) and (ii), was introduced into the Rules without any basis in the Statute. Article 9 of the ICTR Statute, which admittedly deals with *non bis in idem* rather than deferral proceedings (although the two may be considered two sides of the same coin) only contemplates intervention by the ICTR in national proceedings where:

(a) the act for which the accused was tried was characterized as an ordinary crime; or
(b) the national court proceedings were not impartial or independent, were designed to shield the accused from international criminal responsibility, or the case was not diligently prosecuted.

5.57 It seems logical for these grounds to be relied on equally in deferral proceedings, and where neither condition is met, to allow the national prosecutions to go ahead. This may be the reason for the Judges' decision to amend ICTR Rule 9 at the Fourth Plenary Session so that the old Rule (iii) can no longer be exclusively relied upon, and requiring that an indictment be confirmed before a proposal for deferral is tendered.

5.59 The amended ICTR Rule 9, which now specifies that the Prosecutor must have regard to whether his investigation "*should be* the subject of an investigation by the Prosecutor considering, *inter alia:* . . . the status of the accused at the time of the alleged offences," is a rare instance of textual support for the notion that the two *ad hoc* international tribunals should only occupy themselves with prosecuting individuals of high status. The *Paschke Report* (A/51/789, 6 February 1997) also referred to the need to give priority to the indictment of high-ranking individuals. See para. 56, criticising the fact that the former ICTR Deputy Prosecutor "did not redirect the limited resources of the Office of the Prosecutor to pursue *key figures in the genocide*" (emphasis added).

5.60 Rule 11 *bis* of the ICTY's Rules would also presumably operate as a device for referring prosecutions of low-ranking figures *back* to national courts, in order to retain a focus on the prosecution of leadership figures at the ICTY (see below, 4.13 and 6.2.9 *et seq.*).

5.61

ICTY Rule 10 Formal Request for Deferral	ICTR Rule 10 Formal Request for Deferral
(A) If it appears to the Trial Chamber seised of a proposal for deferral that, on any of the grounds specified in Rule 9, deferral is appropriate, the Trial Chamber may issue a formal request to the State concerned that its court defer to the competence of the Tribunal. (B) A request for deferral shall include a request that the results of the investigation and a copy of the court's records and the judgement, if already delivered, be forwarded to the Tribunal. (C) Where deferral to the Tribunal has been requested by a Trial Chamber, any subsequent trial shall be held before another Trial Chamber.	(A) If it appears to the Trial Chamber seized of a request by the Prosecutor under Rule 9 that para. (i), (ii) or (iii) of Rule 9 is satisfied, the Trial Chamber shall issue a formal request to the State concerned that its court defer to the competence of the Tribunal. (B) A request for deferral shall include a request that the results of the investigation and a copy of the court's records and the judgement, if already delivered, be forwarded to the Tribunal. (C) The State to which the formal request for deferral is addressed shall comply without undue delay in accordance with Article 28 of the Statute.

History of ICTY Rule 10

5.62 Like ICTY Rules 8 and 9, Rule 10 was amended at the ICTY fifth plenary session in January 1995 to remove the previous reference to "national" courts, the word "national" being a term which has a particular or restrictive meaning in some jurisdictions.

5.63 Para. (C) was also amended at the ICTY sixth plenary session in May 1995 to help clarify how the work of the Tribunal would be divided between the two Trial Chambers. It was amended to provide that where deferral to the Tribunal has been requested by a Trial Chamber, "any subsequent trial" would be held before the other Trial Chamber. The previous version of the Rule had called for "any subsequent proceedings" to be held before the other Trial Chamber, creating a possible impression that Judges of a Trial Chamber which had heard a deferral would not be permitted to participate in either a Rule 47 or a Rule 61 proceeding. Following the amendment, Rule 10 deferral proceedings, Rule 47 indictment review and Rule 61 proceedings in any given case will be dealt with by the same Trial Chamber or Judge thereof, with the other Trial Chamber standing in reserve for the actual trial, should it take place. The fact that the Trial Chamber hearing the trial proper will be wholly unacquainted with the facts and history of the case at first hand is intended to ensure fairness and impartiality at trial.

5.64 At the twenty-first plenary session, the last words of para. (C) were changed from "before the other Trial Chamber" to "before another Trial Chamber," to reflect the fact that there were now more than two Trial Chambers.

History of ICTR Rule 10

5.65 This rule was amended at the ICTR fourth plenary session, held in Arusha from 1–5 June 1997. The amendment was made in order to clarify the procedure for requests for deferral of national investigations and criminal proceedings instituted in the courts of any State to the competence of the Tribunal.

ICTY Requests for Deferral

5.66 To date, the ICTY has held six deferral hearings on proposals by the Prosecutor for requests for deferral, all of which have been granted by the Chambers: *Tadić, Bosnian Serb leadership* (Karadžić, Mladić and Stanišić), *Lašva River Valley, Erdemović, Vukovar,* and the Macedonian deferrals (See 5.75, below).

5.67 The *Vukovar case* was also the subject of Security Council resolution 1207 adopted on 17 November 1998:

> 2. *Calls again upon* the Federal Republic of Yugoslavia, and all other States which have not already done so, to take any measures necessary under their domestic law to implement the provisions of resolution 827 (1993) and the Statute of the Tribunal, and *affirms* that a State may not invoke provisions of its domestic law as justification for its failure to perform binding obligations under international law;
>
> 3. *Condemns* the failure to date of the Federal Republic of Yugoslavia to execute the arrest warrants issued by the Tribunal against the three individuals referred to in the letter of 8 September 1998 [the letter of the President of the International Tribunal for the Former Yugoslavia to the President of the Security Council] and *demands* the immediate and unconditional execution of those arrest warrants, including the transfer to the custody of the Tribunal of those individuals.

Chamber Must Be Seised of a Proposal for Deferral

5.68 Under Rule 10(A), a Chamber has to be seised by the Prosecutor before it may entertain a request for deferral (Tr. Ch., *Delalić et al., Decision regarding preliminary motion to the Prosecutor by the accused Zdravko Mucić requesting deferral,* 30 September 1996, page 2):

> The Trial Chamber
>
> FINDS that the Rules contemplate that, before issuing a request for deferral, the Trial Chamber must be "seised of a proposal" to do so by the Prosecutor;
>
> FINDS further that an order requiring the Prosecution to submit to the Trial Chamber a proposal of deferral is inappropriate and not within the authority of the Trial Chamber.

5.69 The second finding is in line with the *Decision on Preliminary Motions of the Accused* (*Đukić*, 26 April 1996), in which the Trial Chamber held that, under Rule 9, the Prosecutor "has the power to assess the suitability and timing for submitting to the Trial Chamber a proposal for deferral," but cautioned that "the Prosecutor must, however, take care not to place the Defence in a position which, in the future, might prejudice the rights of the [Accused], as recognized in Article 21 of the Statute ["Rights of the Accused"] (paras 7 and 8). The Chamber had held earlier in its Decision (para. 6) that:

> the mere fact of two trials being held simultaneously for the same crimes against the same accused is likely to prejudice the rights of the accused as stated in Article 14 of the International Covenant on Civil and Political Rights and reiterated in Article 21 of the Statute of the Tribunal, particularly in para. 4(b) of that Article according to which the accused has the right "to have adequate time and facilities for the preparation of his defence."

5.70 More importantly, the holding of two trials for the same crimes would sooner or later fall foul of the non-bis-in-idem principle, which is precisely intended to guard against this type of situation.

Timing of the Application

5.71 Deferral applications have taken place at the ICTY both *before* and *after* the indictment of the subject of the deferral application, as well as *before* and *after* the accused's delivery to the Tribunal. In *Tadić* (IT-94-1-D), the deferral application took place before the accused was indicted and then delivered to the Tribunal. In *Erdemović* (IT-96-22-D), the accused had been transferred to the Tribunal for questioning pursuant to an Order of a Judge of the Tribunal under Rule 90 *bis*, before an indictment was confirmed and before the subsequent deferral decision. In the *Bosnian Serb Leadership* case (IT-95-5-D), the deferral took place before any of the suspects had been indicted; since then two of the suspects, Karadžić and Mladić, have been indicted, twice (IT-95-5-I and IT-95-18-I), but not delivered to the Tribunal. The other suspect, Stanišić, has not yet been publicly indicted. It appears only logical that an individual who has been the subject of a deferral proceeding should eventually be indicted by the Tribunal. If he is not indicted, the Tribunal should refer the matter back to the national courts (see Rule 11 *bis* on this issue, which, however, presupposes that the individual has been arrested and delivered to the Tribunal by the national authorities, and, further, that the Tribunal has indicted him) or otherwise discharge the case, in order to enable the national authorities to continue with their investigations or prosecutions. Otherwise, the individual is effectively shielded from justice by the Tribunal.

Grounds for Prosecutor's Proposal

5.72 To date, all but one of the applications by the Prosecutor have been based on Rule 9(iii) (i.e. what is in issue may have implications for investigations or prosecutions before the Tribunal). In the *Vukovar* deferral, of 10 December 1998, however, the Prosecution based its argument for deferral on the ground that "the continuing refusal of the Federal Republic of Yugoslavia (Serbia and Montenegro) to surrender the said accused indicates that the proceedings initiated in its territory would be neither impartial nor independent and would be designed to shield the accused from [their] international criminal responsibility" (page 3), i.e., Rule 9(ii) (i.e. lack of impartiality or independence, etc., in the courts of the requested State)—which, unlike Rule 9(iii), is statutorily based, being reproduced from Article 10(2)(a) and (b) of the Statute of the Tribunal on analogy with the principle of *non-bis-in-idem*. The Trial Chamber, in its Decision of 10 December 1998 granting the Prosecutor's proposal, fell back, however, on the less contentious ground—i.e., what is in issue may have implications for investigations or prosecutions before the Tribunal—thus refraining from criticising the Serbian courts for lack of impartiality and independence:

> CONSIDERING that, in the case in point . . . the proceedings instituted in the Federal Republic of Yugoslavia (Serbia and Montenegro) relate to facts or points of law which have implications for investigations or proceedings currently before the Tribunal;
>
> CONSIDERING that this circumstance alone fully justifies that the national court defer to the Tribunal.

Subject of the Deferral

5.73 Deferral requests have not always named individual suspects but have on occasion referred to general investigations of unnamed persons. In the *Lašva River Valley* deferral (IT-95-6-D), the request did not state the name of any perpetrator but addressed itself solely to events at a certain time and place. See also the ICTR's *Decision on the Formal Request for Deferral presented by the Prosecutor*, rendered by Trial Chamber 1 on 12 March 1996 in the *Radio Télévision Libre des Mille Collines* case (ICTR-96-6-D), where, again, no individual suspects were named in the deferral proposal and request, the reference being solely to the activities of the radio station in question and to persons implicated in those activities. This was also true of the Macedonia deferrals in respect of the "Ljuboten" and "Neprošteno" investigations (see 5.75 *et seq.* below).

Consent of the Government

5.74 As might be expected of a tribunal acting as a Chapter VII enforcement measure, the consent of the government is not essential to the granting of a request. Although in the *Tadić* deferral (IT-94-1-D), and the *Bosnian Serb Leadership* (IT-95-5-D) and *Lašva River Valley* (IT-95-6-D) deferrals, the governments in question, the Federal Republic of Germany and the Republic of Bosnia and Herzegovina, respectively, acceded to the requests at the time of the hearing, in the *Erdemović* deferral (IT-96-22-D), the representative of the Federal Republic of Yugoslavia (Serbia and Montenegro) said that any request concerning Erdemović had to be addressed to the Ministry of Justice of the Federal Republic of Yugoslavia (Serbia and Montenegro) and that he had no instructions to oppose or accede to the proposal for a request for deferral. The Chamber nonetheless granted the request on 29 May 1996.

The Macedonia Deferrals

5.75 The Former Yugoslav Republic of Macedonia ("Macedonia") did not altogether escape the violence occasioned by the dissolution of the former Yugoslavia. The conflict in Macedonia between Macedonian security forces and ethnic Albanians, in particular those fighting in the National Liberation Army—the Macedonian equivalent of the KLA—took place between January and September 2001, but remained of low intensity. Subsequently, the Macedonian authorities initiated investigations and prosecutions in a number of "war crimes" cases.

5.76 On 5 September 2002, the ICTY Prosecutor requested the deferral, on the basis of ICTY Rule 9 (iii), by Macedonia to the ICTY of five specific cases and investigations. The ICTY Prosecutor also requested deferral by Macedonia of "all current and future investigations and prosecutions of alleged crimes committed by members of the NLA during 2001 as well as all current and future investigations and prosecutions of allegations concerning the activities of the Macedonian forces against Macedonian Albanian civilians in Macedonia in 2001." See the Prosecutor's Request for Deferral and Motion for Order to the Former Yugoslav Republic of Macedonia, dated 5 September 2002.

5.77 The Trial Chamber seised of the proposal for deferral issued its *Decision on the Prosecutor's Request for Deferral and Motion for Order to the Former Yugoslav Republic of Macedonia* (the "Macedonia Deferral Decision") on 4 October 2002. The Chamber granted the five specific proposals for deferral but declined to make the "open-ended" deferral sought by the OTP:

- *"NLA Leadership" case*. The OTP and Macedonia agreed on deferral and it was granted by the Chamber pursuant to ICTY Rule 9 (iii);
- *"Lipkovo Water Reserve" case*. The OTP and Macedonia agreed on deferral and it was granted by the Chamber pursuant to ICTY Rule 9 (iii);
- *"Mavrova Road Workers" case*. This presented the Chamber with a "unique situation" as the OTP had reviewed the case and announced that it considered there was no *prima facie* against the two individuals charged in Macedonia (Macedonia Deferral Decision, para. 36). While recognising the legitimate interests of both the OTP and Macedonia in deferring the case, the Chamber was concerned about the possible "blocking effect" of granting a request for deferral where there was no intention by the OTP to prosecute the subjects of the deferral (para. 38, *ibid*.), i.e., granting the request would essentially confer impunity—national and international—on them. Thus the Chamber came up with its own procedural solution. It granted deferral, while allowing the parties to apply back to the Chamber within 9 months for a hearing "to reconsider whether the blocking effect of the deferral on the exercise of the national jurisdiction is still fully justified" (paras. 40–41, *ibid*.)
- *"Ljuboten" and "Neprošteno" investigations*. In these cases, the perpetrators of the crimes were not yet known. Deferral was not opposed by Macedonia. The Chamber granted the proposal for deferral under ICTY Rule 9 (iii). (Paras. 42–44, ibid.)
- The Chamber declined to grant the Prosecutor's proposal for deferral of all current and future cases, since the Prosecutor had not submitted "substantial reasoning for her far-reaching application" (para. 46, *ibid*.). Moreover, the request was opposed by Macedonia . The Chamber con-

sidered that granting the proposal "would have an intense frustrating effect on the national jurisdiction with regard to crimes committed during the year 2001" (para. 48, *ibid.*).

5.78 It should be noted that Macedonia adopted as amnesty law, on 8 March 2002, which presents certain difficulties for its prosecuting authorities to pursue war crimes investigations and prosecutions.

ICTR Requests for Deferral

5.79 The ICTR has held several deferral proceedings. On 10 January 1996, the Trial Chamber heard a Prosecution proposal for deferral, made under Rule 9(iii) of the Rules of Procedure and Evidence, in respect of three persons who had been detained by the Belgian authorities—Elie Ndayambaje, Joseph Kanyabashi and Alphonse Higaniro. The Chamber approved the Prosecutor's proposal in a Decision dated 11 January 1997, and requested the Belgian authorities to defer their investigations and proceedings in favour of the Tribunal. The Belgian government had been fully cooperative and agreeable to the request.

5.80 On 12 March 1996, the Trial Chamber reviewed and granted two proposals for deferral submitted by the Prosecutor. The first request (ICTR-96-6-D) concerned investigations by the Belgian authorities of persons in charge of the station, *Radio Télévision Libre des Mille collines SARL*. The second request (ICTR-96-5-D) was addressed to the Swiss authorities in respect of their investigations and prosecution of Alfred Musema, a Rwandan citizen detained by the Swiss authorities. The Swiss government was willing to cooperate with the Tribunal on the request (see para. 14 of the Decision).

5.81 On 17 May 1996, the Trial Chamber granted the Prosecutor's proposal to address a formal request to the Belgian authorities to defer their investigations and prosecution of Théoneste Bagosora in favour of the ICTR.

Government as *Amicus Curiae* at Deferral Hearings

5.82 It has been common practice for the government to whom it is proposed that a request for deferral be addressed to appear at the deferral hearing as *amicus curiae*, pursuant to ICTY Rule 74. Thus, the Federal Republic of Germany appeared as *amicus* in the *Tadić* deferral (IT-94-1-D), the Republic of Bosnia and Herzegovina in the *Bosnian Serb leadership* deferral (*Karadžić, Mladić and Stanišić*) (IT-95-5-D) and the *Lašva River Valley* deferral (IT-95-6-D), and the Federal Republic of Yugoslavia (Serbia and Montenegro) in the *Erdemović* deferral (IT-96-22-D). In the *Erdemović* deferral, counsel for the accused was also present as *amicus curiae*.

History of ICTY Rule 11 *bis*

5.83 As the French Commission of Experts already noted in its proposal for the Statute of International Tribunal (UN Doc. S/25266 (1993)):

> 136. The possibility of relinquishing jurisdiction is recommendable both for practical reasons (decongesting the international court) and for political reasons. It would seem desirable, in fact, to restore as quickly as possible the exercise of

5.84

ICTY Rule 11 *bis* Referral of the Indictment to Another Court	ICTR Rule 11 *bis* Suspension of Indictment in Case of Proceedings before National Courts
(A) If an indictment has been confirmed, irrespective of whether or not the accused is in the custody of the Tribunal, the President may appoint a Trial Chamber for the purpose of referring a case to the authorities of a State: (i) in whose territory the crime was committed; or (ii) in which the accused was arrested, so that those authorities should forthwith refer the case to the appropriate court for trial within that State. (B) The Trial Chamber may order such referral *proprio motu* or at the request of the Prosecutor, after having given to the Prosecutor and, where applicable, the accused, the opportunity to be heard. (C) In determining whether to refer the case in accordance with paragraph (A), the Trial Chamber shall, in accordance with Security Council Presidential Statement S/PRST/2002/21, consider the gravity of the crimes charged and the level of responsibility of the accused. (D) Where an order is issued pursuant to this rule: i. the accused, if in the custody of the Tribunal, shall be handed over to the authorities of the State concerned; ii. the Chamber may order that protective measures for certain witnesses or victims remain in force; iii. the Prosecutor shall provide to the authorities of the State concerned all of the information relating to the case which the Prosecutor considers appropriate and, in particular, the material supporting the indictment; iv. the Prosecutor may send observers to monitor the proceedings in the national courts on her behalf. (E) The Trial Chamber may issue a warrant for the arrest of the accused, which shall specify the State to which he is to be transferred for trial.	(A) Where, on application by the Prosecutor or *proprio motu*, it appears to the Trial Chamber that: (i) the authorities of the State in which the accused was arrested (the arresting State) are prepared to prosecute the accused in their own courts; or (ii) the authorities of another State (the receiving State) are prepared to do so, and the authorities of the arresting State do not object; and (iii) it is appropriate in the circumstances for the courts of the arresting or receiving State, as the case may be, to exercise jurisdiction over the accused; the Trial Chamber, after affording the opportunity to an accused already in the custody of the Tribunal to be heard, may order that the indictment against the accused be suspended, pending the proceedings before the national courts. (B) If an order is made under this Rule: (i) the accused, if in the custody of the Tribunal, shall be transferred to the authorities of the State concerned; (ii) the Prosecutor may transmit to the authorities of the State concerned such information relating to the case, as the Prosecutor considers appropriate; (iii) the Prosecutor may direct trial observers to monitor proceedings before the national courts on the Prosecutor's behalf. (C) At any time after the making of an order under this Rule and before the accused is convicted or acquitted by a national court, the Trial Chamber may, upon the Prosecutor's application and after affording an opportunity to the authorities of the State concerned to be heard, rescind the order and issue a formal request for deferral under Rule 10.

(F) At any time after the making of an order under this Rule and before the accused is convicted or acquitted by a national court, the Trial Chamber may, upon the Prosecutor's application and after affording an opportunity to the authorities of the State concerned to be heard, rescind the order and issue a formal request for deferral under Rule 10. (G) If an order under this Rule is rescinded by the Trial Chamber, the Trial Chamber may formally request the State concerned to transfer the accused to the seat of the Tribunal, and the State shall comply without undue delay in accordance with Article 29 of the Statute. The Trial Chamber or a Judge may also issue a warrant for the arrest of the accused.	(D) If an order under this Rule is rescinded by the Trial Chamber, the Trial Chamber may formally request the State concerned to transfer the accused to the seat of the Tribunal, and the State shall comply without undue delay in accordance with Article 28 of the Statute. The Trial Chamber or a Judge may also issue a warrant for the arrest of the accused.

normal jurisdiction to the courts of the States resulting from the breakup of the Socialist Federal Republic of Yugoslavia, and thus help to re-establish the normal operation of judicial authority in the countries in question.

5.85 This Rule was introduced at the ICTY fourteenth plenary session on 12 November 1997, in recognition of the fact that, given the increasing number of indictees in custody at the ICTY, some awaiting trial for a long time, a 'division of labour' between the ICTY and national courts willing to prosecute indictees might be beneficial.

5.86 Rule 11 *bis* was amended at the eighteenth plenary session on 9–10 July 1998 to allow a Trial Chamber to invoke the Rule *proprio motu*, where previously the prerogative was solely that of the Prosecutor. Paras. (A) to (E), and the title of the rule, were further substantially amended by decision of the Judges at the extraordinary plenary session of the Tribunal held on 30 September 2002.

5.87 The rule was further amended by decision of the Judges at the extraordinary plenary session of the Tribunal held on 30 September 2002, the amendment entering into force on 17 October 2002.

5.88 The rule has not yet been applied by the ICTY.

History of ICTR Rule 11 *bis*

5.89 Rule 11 *bis* was recently added to the ICTR Rules of Procedure and Evidence. Before its adoption, the Prosecutor had simply to withdraw ICTR indictments when he/she wished to defer to national courts. This situation arose in *Ntuyahaga*. Major Bernard Ntuyahaga is a former Rwandan army officer who was charged by the ICTR with the murder of Rwandan Prime Minister Agathe Uwilingiyimana and ten Belgian United Nations peacekeepers in Kigali on 7 April 1994. Ntuyahaga was released by the ICTR on 29 May 1999 after the Prosecutor's application to withdraw the indictment against him was granted on 18 May 1999. The Prosecutor had made the application so that Ntuyahaga might be tried in Belgium. The Chamber hearing the application held, however, that it did not have jurisdiction to order his transfer to national authorities. See the *Decision on the Prosecutor's Motion to Withdraw the Indictment* in *Ntuyahaga*, Tr. Ch., 18 March 1999, pp. 4–5:

> the Tribunal wishes to emphasize, in line with the General Assembly and the Security Council of the United Nations, that it encourages all States, in application of the principles of universal jurisdiction, to prosecute and judge those responsible for serious crimes such as genocide, crimes against humanity and other grave violations of international humanitarian law.

5.90 Consequently, Ntuyahaga was released and arrested the same day by the Tanzanian authorities. Extradition proceedings are underway to transfer him for trial from Tanzania to Rwanda. Belgium also submitted an extradition request to the Tanzanian authorities. This was rejected, however, on the grounds that the extradition treaty between Tanzania and Belgium did not allow extradition to a country other than where the alleged crimes were committed.

5.91 In a Press Release dated 1 October 1999, several ICTR defence lawyers opposed the extradition of Ntuyahaga to Rwanda, where he would face the death penalty if convicted, as his potential testimony as a defence witness would then be lost.

5.92

ICTY Rule 12 Determinations of Courts of Any State	ICTR Rule 12 Determinations of Courts of Any State
Subject to Article 10(2) of the Statute, determinations of courts of any State are not binding on the Tribunal.	Subject to Article 9(2) of the Statute, determinations of courts of any State are not binding on the Tribunal.

History of ICTY Rule 12

5.93 Like ICTY Rules 8, 9, 10 and 13, Rule 12 was amended at the fifth plenary session in January 1995 to remove, both in the text and in the title, the previous reference to "national" courts, the word "national" being a term which has a particular or restrictive meaning in some jurisdictions.

ICC and Complementarity with National Courts—General

5.94 In general terms during the ICC negotiation process, the specific issue of the relationship between the ICC and proceedings before national courts did not raise any particularly critical questions. The original idea of establishing an International Criminal Court which would be *complementary* to national courts was never seriously challenged (see, on this point, the ILC report, UN Doc. A/49/10, 1994, p. 29). Nevertheless, it seems important to underline that the complementary character of the Court was one of the issues included in Part II of the draft elaborated during the *PrepCom* and presented for negotiations at the Rome Conference (U.N. Doc. A/CONF.183/2/Add.1).

Part II of the draft, dedicated to "Jurisdiction, Admissibility and Applicable Law" (articles 5–21), had a crucial role in the context of the Rome negotiations, in terms of the problems raised and the resolutions adopted. Moreover, during the plenipotentiary conference, the other parts of the draft statute were discussed and approved point by point, while articles 5–21 were negotiated as a block and were the object of a series of unitary proposals presented by the *Committee of the Whole* of the Rome Conference to be accepted or refused, as a whole (the "*package deal*").

5.95 This negotiation policy produced double results. On the one hand, it allowed the Rome Statute to be adopted within a concentrated schedule (five weeks) of the plenipotentiary conference. On the other hand, the Statute that has emerged as a product of competing and sometimes opposed interests is one in which the resistance of individual States has triumphed over the construction of a homogeneous *corpus iuris* which would arguably be more consistent with the aim of the project.

Articles:

Arbour and Bergsmo, "Conspicuous Absence of Jurisdictional Overreach," *in* H. von Hebel, J. Lammers and J. Schukking (eds.), *Reflections on the International Criminal Court—Essays in Honour of Adriaan Bos* 129–140 (The Hague: T.M.C. Asser Press, 1999).

Arsanjani, M., "Reflections on the Jurisdiction and Trigger-Mechanism of the International Criminal Court," in *Reflections on the International Criminal Court . . . , op. cit.*, at. 57–77;

Benvenuti, P., "Complementarity of the International Criminal Court to National Criminal Jurisdictions," *in* F. Lattanzi and W.A. Schabas (eds.), 1 *Essays on the Rome Statute of the International Criminal Court* 21–51 (Il Sirente, Ripa Fagnano Alto (AQ), 1999).

Broomhall, B., "La Cour Pénale Internationale: Présentation générale et Coopération des Etats," *in* 13–4 *Nouvelles études pénales* 48–81 (1999).

Cassese, A., "The Statute of the International Criminal Court: Some Preliminary Reflections," 10 *European Journal of International Law* 144–172 (1999).

Della Morte, G., "La potestà giurisdizione della Corte Penale Internazionale: complementarità, condizione di procedibilità, soggetti legittimati a richiedere l'esercizio dell'azione penale e ne bis in idem," *in* G. Della Morte, A. Marchesi and S. Laurenti (eds.), *La Corte Penale Internazionale: problemi e prospettive* (*The International Criminal Court: Issues and Perspectives*) (Napoli: Vivarium, 2002) (forthcoming).

Hall, K., "The Principle of Complementarity," *in The International Criminal Court, The Making of the Rome Statute, Issues, Negotiations, Results* 41–79 (The Hague/London/Boston: 1999).

Holmes, J., "Complementarity: National Courts versus the ICC," *in* A. Cassese, P. Gaeta, J.R.W.D. Jones (eds.), *The Rome Statute of the International Criminal Court. A Commentary*, three vols. (OUP 2002).

Kirsch, P., and Holmes, J. "The Rome Conference on an International Criminal Court: The Negotiating Process," 93 *AJIL* 2–12 (1999).

Lattanzi, F., "The Rome Statute and State Sovereignty, ICC Competence, Jurisdiction Links, Trigger Mechanism," *in Essays on the Rome Statute of the International Criminal Court, op. cit.*, at 51–67.

———, "Compétence de la Cour pénale internationale et consentement des Etats," *in* 2 *RGDIP*, 426–444 (1999).

———, "Rapporti fra giurisdizioni penali internazionali e giurisdizioni penali interne," *in Crimini di guerra e competenza delle giurisdizioni nazionali* 47–75 (Milano).

Schabas, W., *An Introduction to the International Criminal Court* 54–70 (Cambridge, 2001).

Zappalà, S., "Il Procuratore della Corte Penale Internazionale: luci e ombre," *in* 1 *RDI* 39–85 (1999).

Cross References:

IMT, Article 1 of the Agreement and Article 11 of the Charter.
ICTY, Articles 9 and 10; Rules 8, 9, 10, 11, 11-*bis*, 12 and 13.
ICTR, Articles 8 and 9; Rules 8, 9, 10, 11, 12 and 13.

Web Sites:

United Nations Web Site on the Rome Statute of the ICC—http://www.un.org/law/icc/index.html
Coalition for an International Criminal Court—http://www.igc.org/icc/

5.96 The complementary character of the ICC is stated in the Preamble, and is confirmed in Article 1 of the ICC Statute. Nevertheless, the explanation of how complementarity works in practice is principally set out in the "Issues of admissibility" (Article 17) and "ne bis in idem" (Article 20) provisions.

5.97 In the Preamble, the principle of complementarity is set out implicitly and expressly. Implicitly, because points 4 and 6 respectively state that the effective prosecution of crimes of international concern "must be ensured by taking measures at the national level and by enhancing international cooperation" and that "it is the duty of every State to exercise its criminal jurisdiction over those responsible for international crimes." Expressly, at point 10, when is announced that the ICC "shall be complementary to national criminal jurisdictions."

5.98

ICC Preamble
The States Parties to this Statute, *Conscious* that all peoples are united by common bonds, their cultures pieced together in a shared heritage, and concerned that this delicate mosaic may be shattered at any time, *Mindful* that during this century millions of children, women and men have been victims of unimaginable atrocities that deeply shock the conscience of humanity,

Recognizing that such grave crimes threaten the peace, security and well-being of the world,
Affirming that the most serious crimes of concern to the international community as a whole must not go unpunished and that their effective prosecution must be ensured by taking measures at the national level and by enhancing international cooperation,
Determined to put an end to impunity for the perpetrators of these crimes and thus to contribute to the prevention of such crimes,
Recalling that it is the duty of every State to exercise its criminal jurisdiction over those responsible for international crimes,
Reaffirming the Purposes and Principles of the Charter of the United Nations, and in particular that all States shall refrain from the threat or use of force against the territorial integrity or political independence of any State, or in any other manner inconsistent with the Purposes of the United Nations,
Emphasizing in this connection that nothing in this Statute shall be taken as authorizing any State Party to intervene in an armed conflict or in the internal affairs of any State,
Determined to these ends and for the sake of present and future generations, to establish an independent permanent International Criminal Court in relationship with the United Nations system, with jurisdiction over the most serious crimes of concern to the international community as a whole,
Emphasizing that the International Criminal Court established under this Statute shall be complementary to national criminal jurisdictions,
Resolved to guarantee lasting respect for and the enforcement of international justice,
Have agreed as follows

5.99

ICC
Article 1
The Court

An International Criminal Court ("the Court") is hereby established. It shall be a permanent institution and shall have the power to exercise its jurisdiction over persons for the most serious crimes of international concern, as referred to in this Statute, and shall be complementary to national criminal jurisdictions. The jurisdiction and functioning of the Court shall be governed by the provisions of this Statute.

5.100 Immediately after the Preamble, Article 1 of the Statute reaffirms the complementarity of the ICC in respect of national criminal jurisdictions as regards "the most serious crimes of international concern."

5.101 It is clear from the outset, however, that the relationship of complementarity between national and international jurisdictions is not symmetrical. In ordinary circumstances, national criminal tribunals preserve their jurisdiction, the ICC exercising its role just in those cases in which the domestic criminal system is experiencing some political or practical difficulty in working effectively, or, in other words, if "the State is unwilling or unable genuinely to carry out the investigation or prosecution" (Article 17 (1) (a).

5.102 Considering the lack of reciprocity in the relationship between international and national criminal jurisdictions, some scholars hold that the ICC has a subsidiary character rather than a complementary one in the strict sense (see F. Lattanzi, "The Rome Statute and State Sovereignty", *op cit*.at 53 and Sur, "Vers une Cour Pénale Internationale: La convention de Rome entre les ONG et le Conseil de Sécurité", *in RGDIP*, 40 (1999)).

5.103

ICC
Article 17
Issues of Admissibility

1. Having regard to paragraph 10 of the Preamble and Article 1, the Court shall determine that a case is inadmissible where:
(a) The case is being investigated or prosecuted by a State which has jurisdiction over it, unless the State is unwilling or unable genuinely to carry out the investigation or prosecution;
(b) The case has been investigated by a State which has jurisdiction over it and the State has decided not to prosecute the person concerned, unless the decision resulted from the unwillingness or inability of the State genuinely to prosecute;
(c) The person concerned has already been tried for conduct which is the subject of the complaint, and a trial by the Court is not permitted under Article 20, paragraph 3;
(d) The case is not of sufficient gravity to justify further action by the Court.
2. In order to determine unwillingness in a particular case, the Court shall consider, having regard to the principles of due process recognized by international law, whether one or more of the following exist, as applicable:
(a) The proceedings were or are being undertaken or the national decision was made for the purpose of shielding the person concerned from criminal responsibility for crimes within the jurisdiction of the Court referred to in Article 5;
(b) There has been an unjustified delay in the proceedings which in the circumstances is inconsistent with an intent to bring the person concerned to justice;
(c) The proceedings were not or are not being conducted independently or impartially, and they were or are being conducted in a manner which, in the circumstances, is inconsistent with an intent to bring the person concerned to justice.
3. In order to determine inability in a particular case, the Court shall consider whether, due to a total or substantial collapse or unavailability of its national judicial system, the State is unable to obtain the accused or the necessary evidence and testimony or otherwise unable to carry out its proceedings.

5.104 Pursuant to Article 17 of the Rome Statute, the Court (here having the narrow meaning of the Judges only, despite the fact that Article 1 refers to the Court as the institution as a whole) can declare a case inadmissible in three situations.

5.105 First, when the same case "*is being* investigated or prosecuted by a State which has jurisdiction over it, unless the State is unwilling or unable genuinely to carry out the investigation or prosecution"; or "*has been* investigated by a State which has jurisdiction over it, and the State has decided not to prosecute the person concerned," unless—for both situations—the investigation or the decision resulted from the unwillingness or inability of the State genuinely to prosecute (Article 17 (1) (a) and (b), emphasis added).

5.106 Second, when the Court is subject to the *ne bis in idem* principle, here also, "unless the proceedings in the other court: (a) Were for the purpose of shielding the person concerned from criminal responsibility for crimes within the jurisdiction of the Court; or (b) Otherwise not conducted independently or impartially . . ." Article 17 (2) (c) and, see after, Article 20 (3)).

5.107 Third, when "the case is not of sufficient gravity to justify further action by the Court" (Article 17 (1) (d)).

5.108 In fact, these three situations may be reduced to two in substance: if the ICC is the only jurisdiction seised of the case, the only condition imposed is that the case has to be of sufficient gravity; if not, e.g., if there is another court or jurisdiction that has started, disclaimed or terminated a prosecution, the State which has jurisdiction over it will have a kind of primacy over the ICC, unless an element of unwillingness or inability is manifested.

Articles:

Williams, "Article 17—Issues of Admissibility," *in Commentary on the Rome Statute of the International Criminal Court—Observers' Notes, Article by Article* 383–394 (Baden-Baden: Nomos Verlagsgesellschaft, 1999).

Adjovi and Della Morte, "La notion de procès équitable devant les Tribunaux Pénaux Internationaux," *in* Ruiz Fabri (ed.), *La notion de procès équitable en droit international* (Paris, forthcoming 2002).

Cross Reference: ICC Rule 51.

5.109

ICC
Article 18
Preliminary Rulings Regarding Admissibility

1. When a situation has been referred to the Court pursuant to Article 13 (a) and the Prosecutor has determined that there would be a reasonable basis to commence an investigation, or the Prosecutor initiates an investigation pursuant to articles 13 (c) and 15, the Prosecutor shall notify all States Parties and those States which, taking into account the information available, would normally exercise jurisdiction over the crimes concerned. The Prosecutor may notify such States on a confidential basis and, where the Prosecutor believes it necessary to protect persons, prevent destruction of evidence or prevent the absconding of persons, may limit the scope of the information provided to States.
2. Within one month of receipt of that notification, a State may inform the Court that it is investigating or has investigated its nationals or others within its jurisdiction with respect to criminal acts which may constitute crimes referred to in Article 5 and which relate to the information provided in the notification to States. At the request of that State, the Prosecutor shall defer to the State's investigation of those persons unless the Pre-Trial Chamber, on the application of the Prosecutor, decides to authorize the investigation.
3. The Prosecutor's deferral to a State's investigation shall be open to review by the Prosecutor six months after the date of deferral or at any time when there has been a significant change of circumstances based on the State's unwillingness or inability genuinely to carry out the investigation.
4. The State concerned or the Prosecutor may appeal to the Appeals Chamber against a ruling of the Pre-Trial Chamber, in accordance with Article 82. The appeal may be heard on an expedited basis.

> 5. When the Prosecutor has deferred an investigation in accordance with paragraph 2, the Prosecutor may request that the State concerned periodically inform the Prosecutor of the progress of its investigations and any subsequent prosecutions. States Parties shall respond to such requests without undue delay.
>
> 6. Pending a ruling by the Pre-Trial Chamber, or at any time when the Prosecutor has deferred an investigation under this article, the Prosecutor may, on an exceptional basis, seek authority from the Pre-Trial Chamber to pursue necessary investigative steps for the purpose of preserving evidence where there is a unique opportunity to obtain important evidence or there is a significant risk that such evidence may not be subsequently available.
>
> 7. A State, which has challenged a ruling of the Pre-Trial Chamber under this Article, may challenge the admissibility of a case under Article 19 on the grounds of additional significant facts or significant change of circumstances.

5.110 Article 18 of the Rome Statute sets out the preliminary rules that have to be followed before the beginning of a trial. The general scope of this provision is to allow the entry into force of the complementarity regime, principally instituting a system of communication between the ICC Prosecutor and the State party and between the former and "those States which, taking into account the information available, would normally exercise jurisdiction over the crimes concerned" (Article 18.1). The specific aim is to put on the Prosecutor the burden of proving the inability or unwillingness of the State to carry out the prosecution (the contrary provision, i.e., putting the burden on the States to prove their ability to prosecute, was strongly opposed principally by the United States during the Rome conference—see UN Doc. A/AC.249/1998/W.G.3/DP.2—1998).

5.111 Concerning the ICC trigger mechanism (see Articles 13 and 15 of the Rome Statute), the notification is requested only in those cases in which a situation is referred to the Prosecutor by a State Party, or by the Prosecutor acting *proprio motu*. If a situation is referred to the Prosecutor by the Security Council acting under Chapter VII of the Charter of the United Nations, the duty to notify does not apply. This seems reasonable because in this case it is equally unnecessary to inform the States that the Prosecutor has started an investigation.

5.112 A special problem related to Article 18 concerns the identification of the States that are subject to the duty of the Prosecutor to notify. The above mentioned provision refers expressly to the States which "would normally exercise jurisdiction over the crimes concerned." This must be taken to refer to a State's territorial or personal jurisdiction, since if a State were permitted to declare an interest based on universal jurisdiction as set out in its domestic law (as Belgium, for example, could do), then that State would be able continuously to challenge the jurisdiction of the ICC, thereby complicating and unhelpfully delaying the ICC's work.

5.113 As explained in Article 18, once the notification has been given, the State concerned has one month to inform the Court that it is investigating or has investigated its nationals or others within its jurisdiction. The Prosecutor, at that stage, shall defer to the State's investigation of those persons unless the Pre-Trial Chamber decides otherwise on the Prosecutor's application. The Prosecutor's deferral is not definitive, nor is the decision of the Pre-Trial Chamber. The latter decision could be the object of an appeal by both the Prosecutor and the State concerned.

Articles: Nsereko, Ntanda, "Article 18—Preliminary Rulings Regarding Admissibility", in *Commentary on the Rome Statute of the International Criminal Court—Observers' Notes, Article by Article*, 395–405 (Baden-Baden, Nomos Verlagsgesellschaft, 1999).

Cross Reference: ICC Rules 52–57.

5.114

**ICC
Article 19
Challenges to the Jurisdiction of the Court or the Admissibility of a Case**

1. The Court shall satisfy itself that it has jurisdiction in any case brought before it. The Court may, on its own motion, determine the admissibility of a case in accordance with Article 17.
2. Challenges to the admissibility of a case on the grounds referred to in Article 17 or challenges to the jurisdiction of the Court may be made by:
(a) An accused or a person for whom a warrant of arrest or a summons to appear has been issued under Article 58;
(b) A State which has jurisdiction over a case, on the ground that it is investigating or prosecuting the case or has investigated or prosecuted; or
(c) A State from which acceptance of jurisdiction is required under Article 12.
3. The Prosecutor may seek a ruling from the Court regarding a question of jurisdiction or admissibility. In proceedings with respect to jurisdiction or admissibility, those who have referred the situation under Article 13, as well as victims, may also submit observations to the Court.
4. The admissibility of a case or the jurisdiction of the Court may be challenged only once by any person or State referred to in paragraph 2. The challenge shall take place prior to or at the commencement of the trial. In exceptional circumstances, the Court may grant leave for a challenge to be brought more than once or at a time later than the commencement of the trial. Challenges to the admissibility of a case, at the commencement of a trial, or subsequently with the leave of the Court, may be based only on Article 17, paragraph 1 (c).
5. A State referred to in paragraph 2 (b) and (c) shall make a challenge at the earliest opportunity.
6. Prior to the confirmation of the charges, challenges to the admissibility of a case or challenges to the jurisdiction of the Court shall be referred to the Pre-Trial Chamber. After confirmation of the charges, they shall be referred to the Trial Chamber. Decisions with respect to jurisdiction or admissibility may be appealed to the Appeals Chamber in accordance with Article 82.
7. If a challenge is made by a State referred to in paragraph 2 (b) or (c), the Prosecutor shall suspend the investigation until such time as the Court makes a determination in accordance with Article 17.
8. Pending a ruling by the Court, the Prosecutor may seek authority from the Court:
(a) To pursue necessary investigative steps of the kind referred to in Article 18, paragraph 6;
(b) To take a statement or testimony from a witness or complete the collection and examination of evidence which had begun prior to the making of the challenge; and
(c) In cooperation with the relevant States, to prevent the absconding of persons in respect of whom the Prosecutor has already requested a warrant of arrest under Article 58.
9. The making of a challenge shall not affect the validity of any act performed by the Prosecutor or any order or warrant issued by the Court prior to the making of the challenge.
10. If the Court has decided that a case is inadmissible under Article 17, the Prosecutor may submit a request for a review of the decision when he or she is fully satisfied that new facts have arisen which negate the basis on which the case had previously been found inadmissible under Article 17.

> 11. If the Prosecutor, having regard to the matters referred to in Article 17, defers an investigation, the Prosecutor may request that the relevant State make available to the Prosecutor information on the proceedings. That information shall, at the request of the State concerned, be confidential. If the Prosecutor thereafter decides to proceed with an investigation, he or she shall notify the State to which deferral of the proceedings has taken place.

5.115 Article 19 sets out the rules for resolving a conflict of jurisdiction when it appears.

5.116 First, the ICC is the only judge of its own jurisdiction. This is a general principle concerning the jurisdiction function (*"Kompetenz-Kompetenz"* or *"la compétence de la compétence"*) in international law. It has also been affirmed in the practice of the ICTs (for the ICTY, see the *Tadić Jurisdiction Appeals Decision*, para. 18; for the ICTR, see the *Kanyabashi Jurisdiction Decision*).

5.117 In addition to the Court being responsible for determining its jurisdiction (e.g., that the crime was committed on the territory of a State Party, according to Article 12 (2) (a)) "on its own motion," the subjects which the ICC Statute recognises as having standing to challenge admissibility (e.g., that the case is sufficiently serious, under Article 17 (d)), are three-fold. First, the accused or person sought; second, the investigating or prosecuting States; third, the States from which acceptance of jurisdiction is required under the provision on preconditions (i.e., the State on the territory on which the conduct occurred or the national State of the accused). All these three have the right to challenge admissibility once, unless exceptional circumstances subsequently arise.

5.118 If a challenge is brought by either of the categories of State referred to, "the Prosecutor shall suspend the investigation until the Court makes a determination in accordance with Article 17" (Article 19 (7)).

5.119 A similar right to challenge jurisdiction as well as the admissibility of a case is given to the Prosecutor, who has the power to seek a ruling from the Court regarding a similar question at any stage. Moreover, when a ruling by the Court is pending, the Prosecutor may seek authority from the Court to take measures to preserve evidence or to prevent persons from absconding.

Articles: K. HALL, "Article 19—Challenges to the Jurisdiction of the Court or the Admissibility of a Case", *in Commentary on the Rome Statute of the International Criminal Court—Observers' Notes, Article by Article*, 405–419 (Nomos Verlagsgesellschaft, Baden-Baden, 1999).

Cross References: ICC Rules 58–62 and 133.

5.120

ICC
Article 20
Ne Bis in Idem

> 1. Except as provided in this Statute, no person shall be tried before the Court with respect to conduct that formed the basis of crimes for which the person has been convicted or acquitted by the Court.

> 2. No person shall be tried by another court for a crime referred to in Article 5 for which that person has already been convicted or acquitted by the Court.
> 3. No person who has been tried by another court for conduct also proscribed under Article 6, 7 or 8 shall be tried by the Court with respect to the same conduct unless the proceedings in the other court:
> (a) Were for the purpose of shielding the person concerned from criminal responsibility for crimes within the jurisdiction of the Court; or
> (b) Otherwise were not conducted independently or impartially in accordance with the norms of due process recognized by international law and were conducted in a manner which, in the circumstances, was inconsistent with an intent to bring the person concerned to justice.

5.121 The *ne bis idem* principle is, in the context of the Rome Statute, another of the fundamentals on which the complementary architecture of the Court stands. In particular, it has a strong connection with Article 17 (1) (c) on issues of admissibility, which does not allow the ICC to prosecute in a case in which "the person concerned has already been tried for conduct which is the subject of the complaint." In general terms, this principle protects several interests: those of the accused (not to be prosecuted twice for the same conduct) as well as those related to the administration of justice, i.e. the ICC's limited resources should not be squandered where justice has already been done.

5.122 Article 20 of the ICC Statute contains three different provisions, one concerning the effect of a decision of the ICC on its own jurisdiction, and the other two regarding the effects of ICC decisions in relation to other courts and the effects of the other courts' decisions on the ICC.

5.123 The first provision, Article 20 (1), establishes respect for the double jeopardy principle for the Court itself, as well as for a person who has been convicted or acquitted by the Court. This provision is always valid except as otherwise provided in the Statute, for example in Article 84 of the ICC Statute (permitting revision of a conviction or sentence) and Article 81 which grants the prosecutor a right to appeal against an acquittal.

5.124 Concerning the articulation of the *ne bis in idem* principle in relation to other courts, as underlined above, the effects *from* and *on* the ICC decision should be distinguished. The first issue that embodies the consequences of the ICC decisions on the other courts is set out in Article 20 (2). Here it is provided that if the ICC has convicted or acquitted a person, other courts (i.e. national courts) are not allowed to re-try that person. The major problem, therefore, is the definition of the *idem* aspects, which are generally interpreted in a narrow sense (the focus is generally on the crime and not on the conduct, e.g. a person acquitted for genocide under the ICC for lack of *dolus specialis* could be tried under a national court for an ordinary crime).

5.125 Regarding the opposite situation, the effects of other decisions *on* the ICC, Article 20(3) establishes that a person who has been tried by another court cannot be tried by the ICC unless either (a) or (b) of that paragraph apply.

Articles:

Bohlander, M., "Possible Conflicts of Jurisdiction with Ad-hoc International Tribunal," *in* A. Cassese, P. Gaeta, J.R.W.D. Jones (eds.), *The Rome Statute of the International Criminal Court. A Commentary*, three vols. (OUP, 2002).

Dugard, J., "Possible Conflicts of Jurisdiction with Truth Commission," in *The Rome Statute of the International Criminal Court. A Commentary*, in A. Cassese, P. Gaeta, J.R.W.D. Jones (eds.), *The Rome Statute of the International Criminal Court. A Commentary*, three vols. (OUP, 2002).

Tallgren, "Article 20—Ne bis in idem," *in Commentary on the Rome Statute of the International Criminal Court—Observers' Notes, Article by Article*319–443 (Baden-Baden: Nomos Verlagsgesellschaft, 1999).

Van Den Wyngaert, C. and Ongena, "Ne bis in idem Principle, Including the Issue of Amnesty," *in* A. Cassese, P. Gaeta, J.R.W.D. Jones (eds.), *The Rome Statute of the International Criminal Court. A Commentary*, three vols. (OUP, 2002).

Cross References:

IMT, Article 11.

ICTY, Article 10.

ICTR, Article 9.

PART 6

GENERAL PRINCIPLES OF CRIMINAL LAW

SECTION 1: LEGALITY
ICC Article 22: *Nullum Crimen Sine Lege* 6.1.1
ICC Article 23: *Nulla Poena Sine Lege* 6.1.2
ICC Article 24: Non-Retroactivity *Ratione Personae* 6.1.3
The Principle of Legality—General 6.1.4
Who Makes the Law? 6.1.10
Extent of Judges' Power of Interpretation 6.1.12
Strict Interpretation 6.1.14
Legality of Punishment (*Nulla Poena Sine Lege*) 6.1.18
Non-Retroactivity of Criminal Law 6.1.21

SECTION 2: INDIVIDUAL CRIMINAL RESPONSIBILITY
ICTY Article 7/ICTR Article 6: Individual Criminal Responsibility 6.2.1
General 6.2.2
Levels of Individual Criminal Responsibility 6.2.9
Lower-Ranking Accused and Complementarity with National Courts 6.2.21
Individual Criminal Responsibility in Internal Armed Conflict 6.2.26
Need to Determine Form of Liability 6.2.28
Intent and Participation 6.2.30
Forms of Participation 6.2.32
Common Criminal Purpose and Joint Criminal Enterprise 6.2.38
    Burden of Proof Where Voluntariness of Participation in Joint Criminal
        Enterprise Is in Issue 6.2.45
Instigating 6.2.46
Aiding and Abetting 6.2.49
    The Accused's Presence at the Crime 6.2.57
    Torture: Co-Perpetrator or Aider and Abettor 6.2.62
No State Immunity 6.2.64
ICTY Article 7(3)/ICTR Article 6(3): Command Responsibility 6.2.69
The Origins of Command Responsibility 6.2.70
Pre-World War II Cases 6.2.71
World War II Cases 6.2.75
Post-World War II Cases 6.2.81
Additional Protocol I of 1977 .... 6.2.87
Command Responsibility at the ICTs 6.2.95
Charging Command Responsibility 6.2.100
Customary Nature of Command Responsibility 6.2.103
Command Responsibility in Internal Conflict 6.2.106
Elements of Command Responsibility 6.2.112
    Element I: Superior/Subordinate Relationship 6.2.113
    Element II: *Mens Rea*—Knew or Had Reason to Know 6.2.124

Knowledge... 6.2.125
    Had Reason to Know 6.2.126
    Element III: Failure to Take Necessary and Reasonable Measures................... 6.2.136
Causation Not Required... 6.2.143
Relationship Between Paragraphs (1) and (3) of ICTY Article 7/ ICTR Article 6................ 6.2.144
    Position of Command as Aiding and Abetting 6.2.145
    Simultaneous Liability Pursuant to 6(1)/7(1) and 6(3)/7(3) for the Same Conduct......... 6.2.148
ICC Article 28: Responsibility of Commanders and Other Superiors 6.2.149
Superior Orders 6.2.152
ICC Article 33: Superior Orders and Prescription of Law.......................... 6.2.156
Superior Orders as a Factor to Be Considered in Mitigation of Punishment 6.2.158

SECTION 3: DEFENCES

Introduction.. 6.3.1
Burden of Proof on Defences 6.3.4
Alibi... 6.3.9
Diminished Responsibility and Lack of Mental Capacity 6.3.17
Duress.. 6.3.38
No Defence of *Tu Quoque*... 6.3.54
Reprisals 6.3.58
Self Defence 6.3.62
ICC Article 31: Grounds for Excluding Criminal Responsibility 6.3.64
ICC Article 32: Mistake of Fact or Mistake of Law 6.3.65
ICC Article 33: Superior Orders and Prescription of Law 6.3.66
Defences under the Rome Statute for an ICC.............................. 6.3.67

* * * * *

SECTION 1: LEGALITY

6.1.1

ICC
Article 22
Nullum Crimen Sine Lege

1. A person shall not be criminally responsible under this Statute unless the conduct in question constitutes, at the time it takes place, a crime within the jurisdiction of the Court.
2. The definition of a crime shall be strictly construed and shall not be extended by analogy. In case of ambiguity, the definition shall be interpreted in favour of the person being investigated, prosecuted or convicted.
3. This article shall not affect the characterization of any conduct as criminal under international law independently of this Statute.

6.1.2

> **ICC**
> **Article 23**
> ***Nulla Poena Sine Lege***
>
> A person convicted by the Court may be punished only in accordance with this Statute.

6.1.3

> **ICC**
> **Article 24**
> **Non-Retroactivity *Ratione Personae***
>
> 1. No person shall be criminally responsible under this Statute for conduct prior to the entry into force of the Statute.
> 2. In the event of a change in the law applicable to a given case prior to a final judgement, the law more favourable to the person being investigated, prosecuted or convicted shall apply.

The Principle of Legality—General

6.1.4 The principle of legality of crime and punishment, the guiding light of criminal law, means that a person can only be judged or punished in accordance with a law which precedes the act in question, defining the crime and setting out the corresponding punishment.

6.1.5 This principle, which is not expressly set out in the Statutes of the ICTY and ICTR, is enshrined in Part 3—"General Principles of Criminal Law"—of the Rome Statute for an ICC. The absence of an explicit reference to the principle of legality in the ICTs' applicable texts does not mean, however, that the principle is not recognised in practice. It is referred to in the Secretary-General's report on the ICTY Statute (S/25704):

> 34. In the view of the Secretary-General, the application of the principle *nullum crimen sine lege* requires that the international tribunal should apply rules of international humanitarian law which are beyond any doubt part of customary law so that the problem of adherence of some but not all States to specific conventions does not arise. This would appear to be particularly important in the context of an international tribunal prosecuting persons responsible for serious violations of international humanitarian law.

6.1.6 The reason given by the Secretary-General for acknowledging the principle—"so that the problem of adherence of some but not all States to specific conventions does not arise"—seems, however, to miss the point. The principle of legality is founded upon the rights of the accused rather than state adherence to treaties, particularly considering that the States of the former Yugoslavia are all parties to the relevant conventions, namely the four Geneva Conventions, the Hague Conventions and the Genocide Convention.

6.1.7 In the *Delalić et al. Trial Judgement*, the judges recognised the fundamental importance of this principle:

> 402. The principles *nullum crimen sine lege* and *nulla poena sine lege* are well recognised in the world's major criminal justice systems as being fundamental principles of criminality. Another such fundamental principle is the prohibition against *ex post facto* criminal laws and criminal sanctions. Associated with these principles are the requirement of specificity and the prohibition of ambiguity in criminal legislation. These considerations are the solid pillars on which the principle of legality stands. Without the satisfaction of these principles no criminalisation process can be accomplished and recognised.

6.1.8 However the principle of legality, which is relatively uniform between different national legal systems, does not necessarily exhibit the same characteristics in international law. Indeed, the Judges ruling in the *Delalić et al. Trial Judgement* went on to state:

> 403. The above principles of legality exist and are recognised in all the world's major criminal justice systems. It is not certain to what extent they have been admitted as part of international legal practice, separate and apart from the existence of the national legal systems. This is essentially because of the different methods of criminalisation of conduct in national and international criminal justice systems.
>
> 404. Whereas the criminalisation process in a national criminal justice system depends upon legislation which dictates the time when conduct is prohibited and the content of such prohibition, the international criminal justice system attains the same objective through treaties or conventions, or after a customary practice of the unilateral enforcement of a prohibition by States.
>
> 405. It could be postulated, therefore, that the principles of legality in international criminal law are different from their related national legal systems with respect to their application and standards. They appear to be disjunctive, in the obvious objective of maintaining a balance between the preservation of justice and fairness towards the accused and taking into account the following factors, *inter alia:* the nature of international law; the absence of international legislative policies and standards; the *ad hoc* processes of technical drafting; and the basic assumption that international criminal law norms will be embodied into the national criminal law of the various States.

6.1.9 The problem in international law is thus to know what the law is and who makes the law.

Who Makes the Law?

6.1.10 The equivalent of law on the international level consists of conventions, international custom and general principles of law. See the *Delalić et al. Trial Judgement:*

> 414. It is obvious that the subject matter jurisdiction of the Tribunal is constituted by provisions of international law. It follows, therefore, that recourse would be had to the various sources of international law as listed in Article 38 of the Statute of the ICJ, namely international conventions, custom, and general principles of law, as well as other subsidiary sources such as judicial decisions and

the writings of jurists. Conversely, it is clear that the Tribunal is not mandated to apply the provisions of the national law of any particular legal system.

415. With respect to the content of the international humanitarian law to be applied by the Tribunal, the Secretary-General, in his Report, stated the position with unequivocal clarity, in paragraph 29 as follows:

> It should be pointed out that, in assigning to the International Tribunal the task of prosecuting persons responsible for serious violations of international humanitarian law, the Security Council would not be creating or purporting to "legislate" that law. Rather, the International Tribunal would have the task of applying existing international humanitarian law.

6.1.11 The Chamber then went on to refer to para. 34 of the Secretary-General's report on the ICTY Statute (S/25704), discussed above, concluding that:

> 417. The implication of these explanations is that the Security Council, not being a legislative body, cannot create offences. It therefore vests in the Tribunal the exercise of jurisdiction in respect of offences already recognised in international humanitarian law. The Statute does not create substantive law, but provides a forum and framework for the enforcement of existing international humanitarian law.

Extent of Judges' Powers of Incrimination

6.1.12 The powers of incrimination granted to the ICTs are exercised in the context of international humanitarian law; they are, therefore, limited. Clarification regarding the extent of the Judges' powers was given in the *Decision* of 31 January 2000 rendered by the Appeals Chamber in *Tadić* concerning allegations of contempt against Mr. Vujin under Rule 77 of the Rules of Procedure and Evidence. In that Decision (see especially para. 24), the Appeals Chamber affirmed that the power to punish contempt of Tribunal derived not from Article 15 of the ICTY Statute, as that provision only allowed the judges to adopt new rules of procedure and evidence, and not to create new offences, but from the ordinary sources of international law.

6.1.13 The creative power of the Judges is therefore limited to matters of procedure and evidence. But even this creative power has engendered numerous discussions, including the question whether the Appeals Chamber has the power to create an avenue of appeal to itself. See the Separate and Dissenting Opinion of Judge Wald dated 27 February 2001 (discussed above, "Contempt of Tribunal," 4.2.629), in which she answered this question in the negative, concluding that:

> the rule of law ... requires that courts acknowledge the statutes and rules that bind them in the exercise of their powers, even when those restraints interfere with understandable aspirations to maximize human rights norms. Courts must lead the way in following the law if there is to be a rule of law.

Strict Interpretation

6.1.14 The main corollary of the principle of legality is the strict interpretation of criminal law (Article 22(2) of the Rome Statute for an ICC). This rule of interpretation, like that of legality, is meant to be respected by the ICTs, even in the absence of a specific text setting it out. Thus the Chamber stated in the *Delalić et al. Trial Judgement*:

> 410. The rule of strict construction requires that the language of a particular provision shall be construed such that no cases shall be held to fall within it which do not fall both within the reasonable meaning of its terms and within the spirit and scope of the enactment. In the construction of a criminal statute no violence must be done to its language to include people within it who do not ordinarily fall within its express language. The accepted view is that if the legislature has not used words sufficiently comprehensive to include within its prohibition all the cases which should naturally fall within the mischief intended to be prevented, the interpreter is not competent to extend them. The interpreter of a provision can only determine whether the case is within the intention of a criminal statute by construction of the express language of the provision.
>
> 411. A strict construction requires that no case shall fall within a penal statute which does not comprise all the elements which, whether morally material or not, are in fact made to constitute the offence as defined by the statute. In other words, a strict construction requires that an offence is made out in accordance with the statute creating it only when all the essential ingredients, as prescribed by the statute, have been established.

6.1.15 If the text is not explicit, the Judges cannot create law:

> 412. It has always been the practice of courts not to fill omissions in legislation when this can be said to have been deliberate. It would seem, however, that where the omission was accidental, it is usual to supply the missing words to give the legislation the meaning intended. The paramount object in the construction of a criminal provision, or any other statute, is to ascertain the legislative intent. The rule of strict construction is not violated by giving the expression its full meaning or the alternative meaning which is more consonant with the legislative intent and best effectuates such intent.

6.1.16 If the text is ambiguous, it has to be interpreted in favour of the accused:

> 413. The effect of strict construction of the provisions of a criminal statute is that where an equivocal word or ambiguous sentence leaves a reasonable doubt of its meaning which the canons of construction fail to solve, the benefit of the doubt should be given to the subject and against the legislature which has failed to explain itself. This is why ambiguous criminal statutes are to be construed *contra proferentem*.

6.1.17 The ICTR Chamber in the *Kayishema and Ruzindana Trial Judgement* was of the same view:

> 103. The Trial Chamber agrees that if a doubt exists, for a matter of statutory interpretation, that doubt must be interpreted in favour of the accused.

Legality of Punishment (*Nulla Poena Sine Lege*)

6.1.18 As regards legality of punishment, there has been an evolution in the ICC Statute vis-à-vis the ICT Statutes. Thus, Article 24 of the ICTY Statute (to which Article 23 of the ICTR Statute corresponds) provides that:

> 1. The penalty imposed by the Trial Chamber shall be limited to imprisonment. In determining the terms of imprisonment, the Trial Chambers shall have recourse to the general practice regarding prison sentences in the courts of the former Yugoslavia.
>
> 2. In imposing the sentences, the Trial Chambers should take into account such factors as the gravity of the offence and the individual circumstances of the convicted person.

6.1.19 It is difficult to consider that the principle of legality is respected with regard to punishment when the ICTY judges, e.g., in the *Kuprešić Trial Judgement*, have pointed out the non-mandatory nature of ICTY Article 24(1):

> 839. Pursuant to Article 24(1) of the Statute, the Trial Chamber "shall have recourse to the general practice regarding prison sentences in the courts of the former Yugoslavia" in determining the terms of imprisonment. Rule 101(B) also requires the Trial Chamber to "take into account" such general practice.
>
> 840. It is clear from these provisions—in particular the phrase "have recourse to" and "take into account"—that the Trial Chamber is not bound to follow the sentencing practice of the courts of the former Yugoslavia. Reference should be made to the said sentencing practice as an aid in determining the sentences to be imposed by the Trial Chamber.

6.1.20 Article 23 of the Rome Statute sets out the principle of legality of punishment and refers it to the Statute's provisions on penalties. See Part 7 of the Rome Statute, in particular Article 77 on the applicable penalties.

Non-Retroactivity of Criminal Law

6.1.21 This is a second corollary of the principle of legality. It means that a person cannot be judged or punished by virtue of a law which entered into force after the occurrence of the act in question.

6.1.22 The ICTs may be accused of having undermined, through their Statutes, the principle of non-retroactivity of criminal law. The ICTY Statute dates from 25 May 1993 and aims at prosecuting crimes committed since 1991 (therefore giving rise to the possibility of a violation of the non-retroactivity principle between 1991 and 1993). In the same way, the ICTR Statute dates from 8 November 1994 and aims at prosecuting crimes committed between 1 January 1994 and 31 December 1994 (there might therefore be retroactivity between 1 January 1994 and 8 November 1994).

6.1.23 This criticism is, however, met by the observation that creating a new court to try existing offences does not amount to creating new offences. This is only procedural, not substantive, retroactivity. To avoid substantive retroactivity, however, the new court must ensure that it only punishes offences *as they were defined and penalised at the time of their commission*.

6.1.24 This problem—procedural and substantive—does not arise for the ICC since Article 24 of the Rome Statute enshrines the principle of non-retroactivity *ratione personae* and non-retroactivity *in mitius* (i.e. the application of law retroactively when it is to the accused's benefit):

1. No person shall be criminally responsible under this Statute for conduct prior to the entry into force of the Statute.

2. In the event of a change in the law applicable to a given case prior to a final judgement, the law more favourable to the person being investigated, prosecuted or convicted shall apply.

6.1.25 As regards non-respect for the legality principle in the ICTs Statutes, some have argued that the Statutes only enshrine that which has existed for a long time on the international level. They only codify general principles of law and international customs, which considerably ante-dated the acts in question. This may or may not be true. The question may not be answered *in abstracto* but only by examining each provision defining crimes and forms of criminal responsibility case-by-case. For example, in *Hadžihasanović, Alagić and Kubura*, the Defense have argued that applying Article 7(3) to a non-international armed conflict offends the prohibition on non-retroactivity. The Trial Chamber rejected the argument in it's Decision of 12 November 2002, but that Decision is under appeal.

6.1.26 The ICT judges have affirmed the importance of the non-retroactivity principle. In the *Delalić et al. Trial Judgement*, the Chamber stated:

> 408. To put the meaning of the principle of legality beyond doubt, two important corollaries must be accepted. The first of these is that penal statutes must be strictly construed, this being a general rule which has stood the test of time. Secondly, they must not be given retroactive effect. This is in addition to the well-recognised paramount duty of the judicial interpreter, or judge, to read into the language of the legislature, honestly and faithfully, its plain and rational meaning and to promote its object. This rule would appear to have been founded on the firm principle that it is for the legislature and not the court or judge to define a crime and prescribe its punishment.

6.1.27 The affirmation of this principle is reinforced in the practice of the ICTs with respect to the rule of precedent. According to the doctrine of precedent, not only do the judges respect the existing law, but they also respect prior judicial decisions (see the section, "The Role of Precedent at the ICTR/ICTY," 4.1.9 *et seq.*).

Articles:

Donnedieu de Vabres, Henri, "Le jugement de Nuremberg et le principe de légalité des délits et des peines," *RDPC* 813 (1946–47).

Glaser, Stefan, "Le principe de légalité et le procès criminel de guerre," RDPC 230 (1947–48).

Delmas Saint-Hilaire, Jean-Pierre, "Les principes de la légalité des délits et des peines, *in* mélanges *Bouzat, Pédone* 149 (1980).

Delmas-Marty, Mireille, "Légalité pénale et prééminence du droit selon la Convention européenne de sauvegarde des droits de l'homme et des libertés fondamentales," *in* mélanges *Vitu* 151.

Koering-Joulin, Renée, "Pour un retour à une interprétation stricte...du principe de la légalité criminelle (à propos de l'article 7 1° de la Convention européenne des droits de l'homme)," in mélanges *Vitu* 247.

Kress, Claus, "Zur Methode der Rechtsfindung im Allgemeinen Teil des Völkerstrafrechts," *In Zeitschrift für die Gesamte Strafrechtswissenschaft*, 111. Band, 1999, Heft 3, S.597ff.

Lamb, Susan "*Nullum Crimen, Nulla Poena Sine Lege* in International Criminal Law," *in* Cassese, Gaeta, Jones (eds.), *The Rome Statute of the International Criminal Court: A Commentary* (OUP, 2002).

Padovani, Tullio, *Il crepuscolo della legalità nel processo penale. Riflessioni antistoriche sui momenti processuali della legalità penale* (IP, 1999).

Books:

Beccaria, Cesare, *Dei delitti e delle pene* (1764).

Lombois, Claude, *Droit pénal international* (Paris, 1971).

Bassiouni, M. Cherif, *International Criminal Law*, Vol. 1 (Transnational Publishers, 1999).

Triffterer, Otto, *Commentary on the Rome Statute of the International Criminal Court Article by Article* (Baden-Baden, 1999).

Illuminati, Stortoni, Virgilio (a cura di), *Crimini internazionali tra diritto e giustizia: dai Tribunali internazionali alle Commissioni Verità e riconciliazione* 40–67 (Giappichelli, Torino, 2000).

Ascensio, Decaux, Pellet, *Droit International Pénal* (Paris: Pédone, 2000).

Lattanzi and Schabas, *Essays on the Rome Statute of the International Criminal Court* (Il Sirente, Teramo, 2000).

* * * * *

SECTION 2: INDIVIDUAL CRIMINAL RESPONSIBILITY

6.2.1

ICTY Article 7 Individual Criminal Responsibility	ICTR Article 6 Individual Criminal Responsibility
1. A person who planned, instigated, ordered, committed or otherwise aided and abetted in the planning, preparation or execution of a crime referred to in articles 2 to 5 of the present Statute, shall be individually responsible for the crime. 2. The official position of any accused person, whether as Head of State or Government or as a responsible Government official, shall not relieve such person of criminal responsibility nor mitigate punishment. 3. The fact that any of the acts referred to in articles 2 to 5 of the present Statute was committed by a subordinate does not relieve his superior of criminal responsibility if he knew or had reason to know that the subordinate was about to commit such acts or had done so and the superior failed to take the necessary and reasonable measures to prevent such acts or to punish the perpetrators thereof. 4. The fact that an accused person acted pursuant to an order of a Government or of a superior shall not relieve him of criminal responsibility, but may be considered in mitigation of punishment if the International Tribunal determines that justice so requires.	1. A person who planned, instigated, ordered, committed or otherwise aided and abetted in the planning, preparation or execution of a crime referred to in articles 2 to 4 of the present Statute, shall be individually responsible for the crime. 2. The official position of any accused person, whether as Head of State or Government or as a responsible Government official, shall not relieve such person of criminal responsibility nor mitigate punishment. 3. The fact that any of the acts referred to in articles 2 to 4 of the present Statute was committed by a subordinate does not relieve his superior of criminal responsibility if he knew or had reason to know that the subordinate was about to commit such acts or had done so and the superior failed to take the necessary and reasonable measures to prevent such acts or to punish the perpetrators thereof. 4. The fact that an accused person acted pursuant to an order of a Government or of a superior shall not relieve him of criminal responsibility, but may be considered in mitigation of punishment if the International Tribunal determines that justice so requires.

General

6.2.2 At the end of World War I, there were declarations that war crimes would be punished, and lists of criminals were prepared by a fact-finding committee, but aside from a few unsatisfactory trials by the Leipzig Supreme Court—with the exception of the *Llandovery Castle* case, which produced a useful judgement—little of practical significance was effected.

6.2.3 Both the Treaty of Sèvres, which was signed on 10 August 1920 but never ratified—and which dealt, *inter alia*, with the responsibility of the "Young Turks" for the Armenian genocide of 1915 in which some 1 million Armenians were killed—and the Treaty of Versailles contained provisions relating to individual criminal responsibility for war crimes and crimes against civilisation or humanity. So, too, did the Treaties of Neuilly-sur-Seine (Treaty with Bulgaria) (Articles 118–120), St. Germain-en-Laye

(Treaty with Austria) (Articles 173–176) and Trianon (Treaty with Hungary)(Articles 157–160). While the Treaty of Sèvres did lead to unsuccessful Allied attempts at retributive justice, and trials at Istanbul conducted by the Turkish authorities did take place (see Vahakn Dadrian, *The History of the Armenian Genocide (1995))*, it is not known by the authors whether the penal provisions of the Treaties of Neuilly, St. Germain or Trianon were ever implemented.

6.2.4 Under Article 227 of the Treaty of Versailles of 28 June 1919, the Allied and Associate Powers, "publicly arraign[ed] William II of Hohenzollern, formerly Germany Emperor, for a supreme offence against international morality and sanctity of treaties." Article 227 further stipulated that, "A special tribunal will be constituted to try the accused, thereby assuring him the guarantees essential to the right of defence. It will be composed of five judges, one appointed by each of the following powers; namely, the United States of America, Great Britain, France, Italy and Japan." However, the trial of the Kaiser never took place, as the Netherlands, who had given William II refuge, refused to surrender him for trial. Article 227 remained a dead letter.

6.2.5 Trials of "the major war criminals" of the Axis countries were held at Nuremberg and Tokyo after the Second World War, in which the principle of individual responsibility for crimes against peace, war crimes and crimes against humanity was further affirmed.

6.2.6 After Nuremberg and Tokyo, the principles of individual criminal responsibility were formulated into the "Nuremberg Principles," prepared by the International Law Commission, submitted to and affirmed by the General Assembly of the United Nations in 1950:

PRINCIPLE I

Any person who commits an act which constitutes a crime under international law is responsible therefor and liable to punishment.

PRINCIPLE II

The fact that internal law does not impose a penalty for an act which constitutes a crime under international law does not relieve the person who committed the act from responsibility under international law.

PRINCIPLE III

The fact that a person who committed an act which constitutes a crime under international law acted as Head of State or responsible Government official does not relieve him from responsibility under international law.

PRINCIPLE IV

The fact that a person acted pursuant to order of his Government or of a superior does not relieve him from responsibility under international law, provided a moral choice was in fact possible to him.

PRINCIPLE V

Any person charged with a crime under international law has the right to a fair trial on the facts and law.

PRINCIPLE VI

The crimes hereinafter set out are punishable as crimes under international law:
(a) Crimes against peace. . . .
(b) War crimes. . . .
(c) Crimes against humanity. . . .

PRINCIPLE VII

Complicity in the commission of a crime against peace, a war crime, or a crime against humanity as set forth in Principle VI is a crime under international law.

6.2.7 ICTY Article 7 (and subsequently ICTR Article 6) were partly inspired by these principles (see para. 55 of the Report of the Secretary-General (S/25704): "Virtually all of the written comments received by the Secretary-General have suggested that the Statute of the International Tribunal should contain provisions with regard to the individual criminal responsibility of heads of State, government officials and persons acting in an official capacity. These suggestions draw upon the precedents following the Second World War").

6.2.8 As noted above (4.3.2), however, the concept of "criminal organisations" employed at Nuremberg (see Articles 9 and 10 of the Charter of the International Military Tribunal) was not formulated as a "Nuremberg principle," nor was it retained in the ICTY and ICTR Statutes (see para. 51 of the Report of the Secretary-General on the ICTY Statute (S/25704, 3 May 1993)).

Levels of Individual Criminal Responsibility

6.2.9 In an armed conflict such as took place in the former Yugoslavia, criminal responsibility may arise on a number of levels—on the part of political leaders for planning and conspiring to commit criminal acts, on high-ranking military leaders for putting those plans into effect by ordering the commission of criminal acts by their subordinates and on lower-ranking soldiers for carrying out those illegal orders.

6.2.10 At both the ICTY and ICTR, there is a subtle and often complex interplay between these diffferent levels of responsibility, and policy choices to be made as to whom it is most appropriate to prosecute given the ICTs' limited resources.

6.2.11 In the *Martić Rule 61 Decision*, the Trial Chamber I stated that those who have the ability criminally to influence events through their positions of superior authority should be brought to justice as they have the ability to "undermine international public order" more than those who merely followed orders.

> 21. The Tribunal has particularly valid grounds for exercising its jurisdiction over persons who, through their position of political or military authority, are able to order the commission of crimes falling within its competence *ratione materiae* or who knowingly refrain from preventing or punishing the perpetrators of such crimes. In a Decision of 16 May 1995, this Trial Chamber considered that such persons "more so than those just carrying out orders (. . .) would thus undermine international public order" (*Karadžić, Mladić and Stanišić*, IT-95-5-D, official request for deferral, para. 25). Since the criminal intent is formulated at a high level of the administrative hierarchy, the violation of the norm

of international humanitarian law is part of a system of criminality specifically justifying the intervention of the Tribunal.

6.2.12 Under ICTY Article 7(1)/ ICTR Article 6(1), the ICTs clearly have jurisdiction over both leaders and individual executants. See the *Erdemović Sentencing Judgement*, para. 83:

> The Trial Chamber considers that individual responsibility is based on Articles 1 and 7.1 of the Statute which grant to the International Tribunal full jurisdiction not only over *"great criminals"* like Nuremberg—as counsel for the accused maintains—but also over executors.

6.2.13 Nevertheless it is equally clear that the ICTY—and the ICTR—should first and foremost prosecute leadership figures, i.e., those who have planned, conspired and orchestrated crimes of such magnitude as to attract international concern, rather than the individual executants—the "small fry"—who are better prosecuted by national courts than by international tribunals.

6.2.14 This was particularly recognised in Security Council resolution 1329 of 30 November 2000:

> *Having considered* the letter from the Secretary-General to the President of the Security Council dated 7 September 2000 (S/2000/865) and the annexed letters from the President of the International Tribunal for the Former Yugoslavia addressed to the Secretary-General dated 12 May 2000 and from the President of the International Tribunal for Rwanda dated 14 June 2000,
>
> . . .
>
> *Noting* the significant progress being made in improving the procedures of the International Tribunals, and convinced of the need for their organs to continue their efforts to further such progress,
>
> *Taking note* of the position expressed by the International Tribunals that civilian, military and paramilitary leaders should be tried before them in preference to minor actors. . . .

6.2.15 This was earlier recognised by the Trial Chamber in the *Delalić et al Trial Judgement*, when it recognised that the prosecution of "brutal" offenders was an exception to the "new policy" that only persons of some military or political authority should be prosecuted before the ICTY:

> 1283. The Defence for Mr. Landžo also raises once again the argument that he was merely an ordinary soldier and, as such, should not be subject to the jurisdiction of the International Tribunal, which is limited to persons in positions of superior authority. This argument has been considered and dismissed above and the Trial Chamber finds no reason to revisit it in detail. It does, however, note that the statement issued in May of this year (1998) by the Tribunal Prosecutor concerning the withdrawal of charges against several indicted persons, quoted by the Defence, indicates that an exception to the new policy of maintaining the investigation and indictment only of persons in positions of some military or political authority, is made for those responsible for exceptionally brutal or

otherwise extremely serious offences. From the facts established and the findings of guilt made in the present case, the conduct of Esad Landžo would appear to fall within this exception.

6.2.16 The ICTR's Rules of Procedure and Evidence refer to "the status of the accused at the time of the alleged offences" as a relevant factor to be considered by the Prosecutor, under Rule 9, and the Trial Chamber under Rule 10, in deciding whether the accused "should be the subject of an investigation by the Prosecutor" and hence whether a State should be asked to defer its proceedings to the Tribunal. Presumably the implication is that an accused should be of an elevated status to be properly the subject of investigation by the ICTR Prosecutor.

6.2.17 The *Paschke Report* (A/51/789, 6 February 1997) also referred to the need to give priority to the indictment of high-ranking individuals. See para. 56 of this report, criticising the fact that the former ICTR Deputy Prosecutor "did not redirect the limited resources of the Office of the Prosecutor to pursue *key figures in the genocide*" (emphasis added).

6.2.18 ICTY Rule 11 *bis* appears to be a device for referring prosecutions of low-ranking figures *back* to national courts, in order to retain a focus on the prosecution of leadership figures at the ICTY.

6.2.19 The *Karadžić and Mladić Rule 61 Decision* raised the question of the "appropriate hierarchical level" at which to analyse the system criminality evidenced in the planned take-over by Bosnian Serbs of parts of Bosnia and Herzegovina and the practice of "ethnic cleansing" carried out for the acquisition of territory (para. 41). The Chamber concluded that it was necessary for the ICTY to focus on suspects at the "top of the pyramid" (see paras. 41–79).

6.2.20 See also the Macedonia Deferral Decision, 4 October 2002, para. 51, where the Trial Chamber referred to the statement of the President of the Security Council (S/PRST/2002/21, 23 July) "that the prosecution of perpetrators, for the remaining time of the Tribunal's mission, should concentrate on high-level perpetrators only." The exact words of the President of the Security Council were that:

> [T]he ICTY should concentrate its work on the prosecution and trial of the civilian, military, and paramilitary leaders suspected of being responsible for serious violations of international humanitarian law committed in the territory of the former Yugoslavia since 1991, rather than on minor actors.

On the Macedonia Deferral Decision, see 5.75 *et seq.*

Lower-Ranking Accused and Complementarity with National Courts

6.2.21 In light of the above, there have consistently been moves at the ICTY to transfer lower-ranking accused persons to be tried by national courts. See the *Order granting leave for withdrawal of charges against Janjić, Kondić, Lajić, Šaponja and Timarac* dated 5 May 1998, in which the Prosecutor acknowledged that non-leadership figures could "appropriately be tried in another forum, such as a State forum." This notion of the appropriate forum—national court or international tribunal—calls to mind the concept of "complementarity" between national courts and international criminal courts, a principle enshrined in the Rome Statute for an International Criminal Court.

6.2.22 See on this point, particularly, the Security Council Presidential Statement (S/PRST/2002/21) and the latest version of ICTY Rule 11 *bis* (IT/210, 10 October 2002), which requires the ICTY Trial Chamber considering referral of the indictment to another court to take into account *"the gravity of the crimes charged and the level of responsibility of the accused."* See 5.84 *et seq.*

6.2.23 The principle of complementarity is indeed one of the centrepieces of the ICC. The Preamble of the Rome Statute emphasises that the ICC "shall be a permanent institution and shall have the power to exercise its jurisdiction over persons for the most serious crimes of international concern" and that it "shall be complementary to national criminal jurisdiction." The definition of complementarity can be found in Article 17 of the Statute and is *a contrario*. This article in effect stipulates that a matter is for the national courts (a) if it is being investigated or prosecuted by a State which has jurisdiction over it, unless the State is unwilling or unable genuinely to carry out investigation or prosecution, or (b) if the case has been investigated by a State which has jurisdiction over it and the State has decided not to prosecute the person concerned, unless the decision resulted from the unwillingness or inability of the State genuinely to prosecute, or (c) if the person concerned has already been tried for conduct which is the subject of the complaint, and a trial by the Court is not permitted under article 20, para. 3, or (d) if the case is not of sufficient gravity to justify action by the Court.

6.2.24 Consequently, the ICC will only exceptionally have jurisdiction. As a rule, national courts should prosecute even crimes of international concern. Paras. 2 and 3 of Article 17 set out the criteria for determining whether the ICC has jurisdiction. In other words, these paragraphs explain how to determine whether the State is unwilling or unable genuinely to carry out the investigation or prosecution. To determine whether the State is unwilling, the Court shall consider, having regard to the principles of due process recognised by international law, whether the proceedings were or are being undertaken or the national decision was made for the purpose of shielding the person concerned from criminal responsibility for crimes within the jurisdiction of the Court. The Court will have to consider also whether there has been an unjustified delay in the proceedings which in the circumstances is inconsistent with an intent to bring the person concerned to justice. Finally, the Court will have to consider whether the proceedings were not or are not being conducted independently or impartially, or are being conducted in a manner which is inconsistent with an intent to bring the person concerned to justice. In order to determine inability (to investigate or prosecute) in a particular case, the Court shall consider whether, due to a total or substantial collapse or unavailability of its national judicial system, the State is unable to obtain the accused or the necessary evidence and testimony or otherwise to carry out its proceedings.

6.2.25 Article 19 of the Rome Statute sets out the procedure for dealing with a challenge to the jurisdiction of the Court or the admissiblity of case. This procedure can be used by the accused or a person for whom a warrant of arrest or a summons to appear has been issued, a State which has jurisdiction over a case, on the ground that it is investigating or prosecuting the case or has investigated or prosecuted it; a State on the territory of which the conduct in question occurred or, if the crime was committed on board a vessel or aircraft, the State of registration of that vessel or that craft. The Prosecutor may submit a request for a review of the decision when he or she is fully satisfied that new facts have arisen which negate the basis on which the case had previously been found inadmissible under article 17.

Individual Criminal Responsibility in Internal Armed Conflict

6.2.26 In the *Tadić Jurisdiction Appeals Decision*, the Chamber affirmed that the principle of individual criminal responsibility applies even in internal armed conflicts:

> 128. Even if customary international law includes certain basic principles applicable to both internal and international armed conflicts, Appellant argues that such prohibitions do not entail individual criminal responsibility when breaches are committed in internal armed conflicts. . . . The Nuremberg Tribunal considered a number of factors relevant to its conclusion that the authors of particular prohibitions incur individual responsibility: the clear and unequivocal recognition of the rules of warfare in international law and State practice indicating an intention to criminalize the prohibition, including statements by government officials and international organizations, as well as punishment of violations by national courts and military tribunals (*Id.*, at 445–47, 467). Where these conditions are met, individuals must be held criminally responsible, because, as the Nuremberg Tribunal concluded:
>
>> "[c]rimes against international law are *committed by men, not by abstract entities*, and only by punishing individuals who commit such crimes can the provisions of international law be enforced." (*Id.*, at 447.) (emphasis added)
>
> 129. Applying the foregoing criteria to the violations at issue here, we have no doubt that they entail individual criminal responsibility, regardless of whether they are committed in internal or international armed conflicts. Principles and rules of international humanitarian law reflect "elementary considerations of humanity" widely recognized as the mandatory minimum for conduct in armed conflicts of any kind. No one can doubt the gravity of the acts at issue, nor the interest of the international community in their prohibition.

6.2.27 The Chamber went on to affirm that the other "conditions" referred to above were met in the case of violations of common Article 3; hence the accused, charged with such violations, incurred individual criminal responsibility.

Need to Determine Form of Liability

6.2.28 Given that ICTY Article 7(1)/ ICTR Article 6(1) refer to several heads of liability, the Trial Chamber in its Judgement—if not the Prosecutor in its indictment—has to specify which head of liability applies to the accused. See the *Furundžija Trial Judgement*:

> 189. The Trial Chamber finds that as the Prosecution has relied on Article 7(1) without specification and left the Trial Chamber the discretion to allocate criminal responsibility, it is empowered and obliged, if satisfied beyond reasonable doubt that the accused has committed the crimes alleged against him, to convict the accused under the appropriate head of criminal responsibility within the limits of the Amended Indictment.

6.2.29 Indeed this is essential both because of the accused's basic human right to know of what he has been convicted and so that the Chamber has a factual basis for sentencing the accused. There may be an enormous difference in terms of sentencing between an instigator, an aider and abettor and a direct perpetrator of a completed offence. Ideally, the form of participation alleged should be spelt out in the indictment.

Intent and Participation

6.2.30 In the *Tadić Opinion and Judgement,* Trial Chamber II identified, on the basis of post-World War II case-law, *intent* and *participation* as the key ingredients of individual responsibility under Article 7(1) of the ICTY Statute (Article 6(1) of the ICTR Statute):

> 674. ... First, there is a requirement of intent, which involves awareness of the act of participation coupled with a conscious decision to participate by planning, instigating, ordering, committing, or otherwise aiding and abetting in the commission of a crime. Second, the prosecution must prove that there was participation in that the conduct of the accused contributed to the commission of the illegal act.

6.2.31 This was followed, *inter alia*, in the *Aleksovski Trial Judgement* (paras 60–65).

Forms of Participation

6.2.32 On one view of ICTY Article 7(1)/ ICTR Article 6(1), and following general principles of criminal law, a person who "committed" a crime would be the author or perpetrator, while a person who "planned" or "insitigated" or "ordered" a crime would be a co-author or co-perpetrator of the crime, while a person who "otherwise aided and abetted in the planning, preparation or execution of a crime," with knowledge that his acts would assist the perpetrator or author, would be an aider and abettor or accomplice.

6.2.33 A person who participates in a crime with intent may, according to the ICTY's jurisprudence, also be a co-perpetrator under the "common criminal purpose" doctrine. This classification has been adhered to, *inter alia*, in the *Furundžija Trial Judgement*. The *Delalić et al. Trial Judgement* also followed this scheme to a certain extent, in particular applying the "common criminal purpose" doctrine.

6.2.34 These categories have been further recognised in the jurisprudence of both ICTs. It was held in the *Foča Trial Judgement* that, "there can be several perpetrators in relation to the same crime where the conduct of each one of them fulfills the requisite elements of the definition of the substantive offence" (para. 390). The *Krstić Trial Judgement* stated that committing "covers physically perpetrating a crime or engendering a culpable omission in violation of criminal law" (para. 601). The *Kayishema Appeals Judgement* also dealt with common criminal purpose (see para. 187). The Appeals Chamber in that case observed that it is not necessary to prove the common criminal purpose to determine that a plan was organised (para. 192).

6.2.35 Concerning the person who planned, instigated or ordered a crime, the *Akayesu Trial Judgement* held that "planning implies that one or several persons contemplate designing the commission of a crime at both the preparatory and executive phases" (para. 480). This decision was followed by the *Blaškić Trial Judgement* and the *Krstić Trial Judgement*. The *Kordić Trial Judgement* further held that a person found to have committed a crime should not also be found responsible for planning the same crime. In that case, the Trial Chamber insisted that an accused will only be held responsible for planning, instigating or ordering a crime if he directly or indirectly intended that the crime be committed. The Trial Chamber held moreover that a causal relationship between the instigation and the physical perpetration of the crime needed to be demonstrated. The contribution of the accused must have had a substantial effect on the commission of the crime. To determine that the accused ordered a crime, it is sufficient to show that he had enough authority to give orders, but it is not necessary to show that a superior-subordinate relationship existed (see *Kordić Trial Judgement*, para. 388).

6.2.36 As regards liability for participation in an offence other than by direct commission, the *Delalić Trial Judgement* stated:

> 326. . . . in order for there to be individual criminal responsibility for degrees of involvement in a crime under the Tribunal's jurisdiction which do not constitute a direct performance of the acts which make up the offence, a showing must be made of both a physical and a mental element. The requisite *actus reus* for such responsibility is constituted by an act of participation which in fact contributes to, or has an effect on, the commission of the crime. Hence, this participation must have "a direct and substantial effect on the commission of the illegal act." The corresponding intent, or *mens rea*, is indicated by the requirement that the act of participation be performed with knowledge that it will assist the principal in the commission of the criminal act. Thus, there must be "awareness of the act of participation coupled with a conscious decision to participate by planning, instigating, ordering, committing, or otherwise aiding and abetting in the commission of a crime."

6.2.37 This approach does not, however, distinguish between perpetration (by committing), co-perpetration (by planning, instigating, or ordering), and aiding and abetting.

Common Criminal Purpose and Joint Criminal Enterprise

6.2.38 The Chamber found, in the *Delalić Trial Judgement*, that to prove co-perpetration, it is not necessary for the Prosecutor to prove that that there was a pre-existing plan to engage in the criminal conduct in question. Outlining the common criminal purpose doctrine, the Chamber went on to say that "where such a plan exists, or where there otherwise is evidence that members of a group are acting with a common criminal purpose, all those who knowingly participate in, and directly and substantially contribute to, the realisation of this purpose may be held criminally responsible under Article 7(1) for the resulting criminal conduct. Depending upon the facts of any given situation, the culpable individual may, under such circumstances, be held criminally responsible either as a direct perpetrator of, or as an aider and abetter to, the crime in question" (para. 328).

6.2.39 This doctrine of common purpose was explicitly endorsed, and applied, in the *Tadić Appeals Judgement*. Applying this doctrine, the accused was convicted of killings of which he had been acquitted at trial (on the Prosecutor's Cross-Appeal). The doctrine is developed at paras. 185–192 of the Judgement. The Chamber concluded, "international criminal responsibility embraces actions perpetrated by a collectivity of persons in furtherance of a common criminal design" (para. 193). The Chamber noted, however, that "the Tribunal's Statute does not specify (either expressly or by implication) the objective and subjective elements (*actus reus* and *mens rea*) of this category of collective criminality. To identify these elements one must turn to customary international law. Customary rules on this matter are discernible on the basis of various elements: chiefly case law and a few instances of international legislation" (para. 194). After an analysis of the case law and international legislation (paras 195–226), the Appeals Chamber concluded that "the notion of common design as a form of accomplice liability is firmly established in customary international law and in addition is upheld, albeit implicitly, in the Statute of the International Tribunal" (para. 220). It then identified three categories of such cases:

> 220. . . . First, in cases of co-perpetration, where all participants in the common design possess the same criminal intent to commit a crime (and one or more of them actually perpetrate the crime, with intent). Secondly, in the so-called "concentration camp" cases, where the requisite *mens rea* comprises knowledge of the system of ill-treatment and intent to further the common design of ill-treatment. . . .

6.2.40 The third category of case is set out more fully earlier in the Judgement:

> 204. The third category concerns cases involving a common design to pursue one course of conduct where one of the perpetrators commits an act which, while outside the common design, was nevertheless a natural and foreseeable consequence of the effecting of that common purpose. An example of this would be a common, shared intention on the part of a group to forcibly remove members of one ethnicity from their town, village or region (to effect "ethnic cleansing") with the consequence that, in the course of doing so, one or more of the victims is shot and killed. While murder may not have been explicitly acknowledged to be part of the common design, it was nevertheless foreseeable that the forcible removal of civilians at gunpoint might well result in the deaths of one or more of those civilians. Criminal responsibility may be imputed to all participants within the common enterprise where the risk of death occurring was both a predictable consequence of the execution of the common design and the accused was either reckless or indifferent to that risk. Another example of a common plan to forcibly evict civilians belonging to a particular ethnic group by burning their houses; if some of the participants in the plan, in carrying out this plan, kill civilians by setting their houses on fire, all the other participants in the plan are criminally responsible for the killing if these deaths were predictable.

6.2.41 The Trial Chamber identified, in its *Decision on Form of Further Amended Indictment and Proseution Application to Amend*, 26 June 2001 in *Brdjanin and Talić*, further details for determining foreseeability. The Trial Chamber held that the state of mind of the accused which must be proved by the prosecution varies depending on whether the crime charged was "within the object of the criminal enterprise, or went beyond the object of that enterprise, but was nevertheless a natural and foreseeable consequence of that enterprise. If the crime charged fell within the object of the enterprise, the prosecution must establish that the accused shared with the person who personally perpetrated the crime the state of mind required for that crime. If the crime charged went beyond the object of the joint criminal enterprise, the prosecution need only establish that the accused was aware that the further crime was a possible consequence in the execution of that enterprise and that, with that awareness, he participated in that enterprise." The *Krstić Trial Judgement* followed this reasoning (see para. 613).

6.2.42 The Appeals Chamber in the *Tadić Appeals Judgement* formulated the *actus reus* and *mens rea* as regards the three categories of common design (set out above), as follows:

> 227. In sum, the objective elements (*actus reus*) of this mode of participation in one of the crimes provided for in the Statute (with regard to each of the three categories of cases) are as follows:
>
>> i. *A plurality of persons.* They need not be organised in a military, political or administrative structure . . .
>>
>> ii. *The existence of a common plan, design or purpose which amounts to or involves the commission of a crime provided for in the Statute.* There is no necessity for this plan, design or purpose to have been previously arranged or formulated. The common plan or purpose may materialise extemporaneously and be inferred from the fact that a plurality of persons act in unison to put into effect a joint criminal enterprise.
>>
>> iii. *Participation of the accused in the common design* involving the perpetration of one of the crimes provided for in the Statute. This participation need not involve commission of a specific crime under one of those provisions (for example, murder, extermination, torture, rape, etc.), but may take the form of assistance in, or contribution to, the execution of the common plan or purpose.
>
> 228. By contrast, the *mens rea* element differs according to the category of common design under consideration. With regard to the first category, what is required is the intent to perpetrate a certain crime (this being the shared intent on the part of all co-perpetrators). With regard to the second category . . . personal knowledge of the system of ill-treatment is required (whether proved by express testimony or a matter of reasonable inference from the accused's position of authority), as well as the intent to further this common concerted system of ill-treatment. With regard to the third category, what is required is the *intention* to participate in and further the criminal activity or the criminal purpose of a group and to contribute to the joint criminal enterprise or in any event to the commission of a crime by the group. In addition, responsibility for a crime other than the one agreed upon in the common plan arises only if, under the circumstances of the case, (i) it was *foreseeable* that such a crime might be perpetrated by one or other members of the group and (ii) the accused *willingly took that risk.*

6.2.43 The Prosecutor has now started explicitly charging this form of liability in indictments. See *Decision on form of second amended indictment* rendered by a Trial Chamber on 11 May 2000 in *Krnojelac* (para. 9: "This complaint raises an issue as to the nature of the 'common purpose' case now pleaded for the first time in the second amended indictment. . . ."). Common purpose is also charged in the indictments against Milošević.

6.2.44 It is understandable that this form of liability, commonly found in national criminal law, should have been incorporated in the Tribunal's practice as a matter of jurisprudence. Nonetheless, basing convictions on a form of liability which is nowhere set out in the Statute may be criticised on legality grounds (see above, 6.1.4 *et seq.*). If this form of liability *is* applied, it is submitted that it should be done in an extremely restrictive manner. Otherwise mere presence on the scene of a crime may become a basis for convicting persons of extremely serious crimes, which can work a great injustice.

Burden of Proof Where Voluntariness of Participation in Joint Criminal Enterprise Is in Issue

6.2.45 If the accused wishes to raise an issue as to the voluntary nature of his participation in the joint criminal enterprise pleaded and if it is a relevant issue in the case, he must point to or elicit evidence at the trial from which it could be inferred that there is at least a reasonable possibility that his participation was not voluntary. Only then does the prosecution bear the onus of establishing that his action was voluntary. The legal onus in relation to the issue, however, remains at all times with the prosecution. See *Brdjanin and Talić, Decision on Form of Further Amended Indictment and Prosecution application to Amend*, 26 June 2001. This is an instance of shifting burdens of proof.

Instigating

6.2.46 ICTY Article 7(1) and ICTR Article 6(1) both refer to *"instigat[ing]"* crimes within the jurisdiction of the ICTs. The ICTs have held that such instigation need not be public nor direct, in contrast to direct and public incitement under ICTY Article 4 (3)(c) / ICTR Article 2(3)(c). In the *Akayesu Appeals Judgement*, para. 478, the Appeals Chamber stated that:

> There is a glaring disparity between the English and French text; indeed, the English word "instigated" is translated into French as *"incite."* That said, the Appeals Chamber is of the opinion that linguistically the two terms are synonymous. The Appeals Chamber points out in particular that neither text contains any suggestion or recommendation that incitement must be direct and public. Consequently, by interpreting this provision "in accordance with its ordinary meaning," the Appeals Chamber holds that, although instigation may, in certain circumstances, be direct and public, this does not however, constitute a requirement. Nothing in Article 6(1) suggests that there is such a requirement. The Appeals Chamber concurs with the Prosecution's argument that "if the drafters of the Statute had wished to similarly confine 'instigation' to situations where it is 'public and direct,' it would be reasonable to expect that they would have specifically required it."

6.2.47 The Appeals Chamber also reached this conclusion by referring to Article 31 of the 1969 Vienna Convention on the Law of Treaties (*Akayesu Appeals Judgement*, paras. 478–479). This provides that *"a treaty shall be interpreted in good faith in accordance with the ordinary meaning to be given to the terms of the treaty in their context and in the light of its object and purpose."* Since neither ICTY Article 7(1) nor ICTR Article 6(1) explicitly state any requirement that instigation be direct and public, the correct interpretation of the plain words of these articles is that it is *not* required. As regards direct and public incitement to commit genocide, there are special reasons why that inchoate offence has those elements (see 4.2.140 *et seq.* on "direct and public incitement to commit genocide").

6.2.48 In the jurisprudence of the Tribunals, "instigating" has been defined to mean "prompting another to commit an offence." (see *Kvočka, Kos, Radić, Žigić, Prcać Trial Judgement*, para. 243; *Krstić Trial Judgement*, para. 601; *Akayesu Trial Judgement*, para. 482; *Blaškić Trial Judgement*, para. 280; and *Kordić and Čerkez Trial Judgement*, para. 387).

Aiding and Abetting

6.2.49 According to the *Furundžija Trial Judgement*, the *actus reus* of aiding and abetting in international law "consists of practical assistance, encouragement, or moral support which has a substantial effect on the perpetration of the crime" (para. 249).

6.2.50 The importance of a "substantial effect" has been followed in the *Aleksovski Trial Judgement*, the *Foča Trial Judgement*, the *Kordić and Čerkez Trial Judgement* and the *Krstić Trial Judgement*. In this last case, the Trial Chamber added that aiding and abetting means: "rendering a substantial contribution to the commission of a crime" (para. 601). The *Akayesu Trial Judgement* emphasized that aiding and abetting "which may appear as synonymous, are indeed different. Aiding means giving assistance to someone. Abetting, on the other hand, would involve facilitating the commission of an act by being sympathetic thereto" (see para. 484).

6.2.51 The *actus reus* of this form of liability may be very broad. Moreover, the acts required to hold an accused responsible may consist of encouragement and moral support that has a substantial effect on the perpetration of a crime. The Chamber held in the *Blaškić Trial Judgement* that the *actus reus* can consist of an omission, provided that the failure to act had a decisive effect on the commission of the crime and that was coupled with the requisite *mens rea* (para. 284). For the *mens rea* requirement, see below, 6.2.55.

6.2.52 Note that liability for omissions usually only arises, as a general principle of criminal law, where there was a pre-existing *duty to act*.

6.2.53 The Trial Chamber in the *Bagilishema Trial Judgement* held that the assistance rendered by the aider and abettor need not be provided at the same time that the offence is committed, i.e., it could come afterwards, e.g., by hiding the perpetrator.

6.2.54 The *mens rea* required to prove aiding and abetting is the *knowledge* that these acts assist the commission of the offence" (*Furundžija Trial Judgement*, para. 249). The Trial Chamber added that aiding and abetting had to be distinguished from the notion of common design "where the *actus reus* consists of participation in a joint criminal enterprise and the *mens rea* required is intent to participate" (*ibid.*)—a distinction which it also found in the Rome Statute for an ICC. In reaching this definition of aiding and abetting, the Trial Chamber relied on a number of post-World War II cases—*Schonfeld, Rohde*, the *Synagogue* case, the *Pig-cart parade* case, the *Dachau Concentration Camp* case, the *Auschwitz Concentration Camp* case, the *Einsatzgruppen* case, the *Zyklon B* case, the *Hechingen deportation* case, as well as the *Tadić* and *Akayesu* cases.

6.2.55 As regards the *mens rea* of aiding and abetting, namely *knowledge* that the aider or abettor's acts will assist the principal, the *Furundžija* Trial Chamber added that, "it is not necessary that the aider and abettor should know the precise crime that was intended and which in the event was committed. If he is aware that one of a number of crimes will probably be committed, and one of those crimes is in fact committed, he has intended to facilitate the commission of that crime, and is guilty as an aider and abettor" (para. 246). This definition of aiding and abetting was followed in the *Foča Trial Judgement* (paras 391–392) and the *Bagilishema Trial Judgement* (para. 32).

6.2.56 Aiding and abetting "includes all acts of assistance by words or acts that lend encouragement or support, as long as the requisite intent is present" (*Tadić Opinion and Judgement*, para. 689).

The Accused's Presence at the Crime

6.2.57 In this context, the accused's mere presence at the scene of a crime's commission could constitute aiding and abetting, provided it was a "knowing" and contributory presence. See the *Tadić Opinion and Judgement*:

> 689. ... Under this theory, presence alone is not sufficient if it is an ignorant or unwilling presence. However, if the presence can be shown or inferred, by circumstantial or other evidence, to be knowing and to have a direct and substantial effect on the commission of the illegal act, then it is sufficient on which to base a finding of participation and assign the criminal culpability that accompanies it.
>
> 690. Moreover, when an accused is present and participates in the beating of one person and remains with the group when it moves on to beat another person, his presence would have an encouraging effect, even if he does not physically take part in this second beating, and he should be viewed as participating in this second beating as well. This is assuming that the accused has not actively withdrawn from the group or spoken out against the conduct of the group.
>
> 691. However, actual physical presence when the crime is committed is not necessary; just as with the defendants who only drove victims to the woods to be killed, an accused can be considered to have participated in the commission of a crime based on the precedent of the Nürnberg war crimes trials if he is found to be "concerned with the killing." However, the acts of the accused must be direct and substantial.
>
> 692. In sum, the accused will be found criminally culpable for any conduct where it is determined that he knowingly participated in the commission of an offence that violates international humanitarian law and his participation directly and substantially affected the commission of that offence through supporting the actual commission before, during, or after the incident. He will also be responsible for all that naturally results from the commission of the act in question.

6.2.58 This reasoning—and comparable reasoning in the *Akayesu Trial Judgement*—was followed in the *Delalić et al. Trial Judgement* where the Chamber stated that physical presence at the scene of the offence may be adequate encouragement or support. In the *Furundžija Trial Judgement*, the Chamber stated that "presence, when combined with authority, can constitute assistance in the form of moral support, that is, the *actus reus* of the offence. The supporter must be of a certain status for this to be sufficient for criminal responsibility." (para. 209).

6.2.59 The *Aleksovski Trial Judgement* confirmed this decision and insisted that to determine the impact of the accused's presence on the commission of the crime, it was necessary to consider the relevant facts to ascertain whether his presence had a significant effect on the perpetration of the crime (paras 63–65). The Chamber concluded that mere presence, *particularly when coupled with a position of authority occupied by the accused*, could be sufficient for criminal liability to arise under Article 7(1) of the Statute (para. 65).

6.2.60 The Chamber in the *Foča Trial Judgement* stated that, "presence alone at the scene of the crime is not conclusive of aiding and abetting unless it is shown to have a significant legitimising effect on the principal" (para. 393). In the same vein, the *Akayesu Trial Judgement* held that the defendant had previously provided verbal encouragement for the commission of crimes, and that his status as "bourgemeister" conferred upon him a position of authority. His subsequent silence was a signal in the face of crimes of violence committed nearby of official tolerance for the crimes (para. 693). See also the *Kayishema and Ruzindana Appeals Judgement*, para. 201.

6.2.61 The Trial Chamber in the *Bagilishema Trial Judgement* observed that the accused's "presence is to have the required effect on the perpetrators, such as encouragement, moral support or tacit approval. As long as the accomplice has the requisite *mens rea*, all acts of assistance that lend encouragement or support will constitute aiding and abetting, even where the "act" is mere presence" (para. 36).

Torture: Co-Perpetrator or Aider and Abettor

6.2.62 In light of the above principles, the Chamber in the *Furundžija Trial Judgement* distinguished liability for torture as a co-perpetrator from liability as an aider and abettor. For a co-perpetrator, the *actus reus* consists of participating in an integral part of the torture (para. 257), while the *mens rea* consists of acting with the intent to obtain information or a confession, to punish or intimidate, humiliate, coerce or discriminate against the victim or a third person (paras 252 and 257).

6.2.63 For an aider or abettor, the *actus reus* consists of assisting the torture in some way which has a substantial effect on the perpetration of the crime. The *mens rea* of aiding and abetting torture consists of knowledge that torture is taking place and that the accused's acts are assisting the perpetrator to commit torture. The Trial Chamber stated that all co-perpetrators are equally liable, in accordance with the principle enunciated by the English House of Lords in the now annulled *Pinochet* (No. 1) decision of 25 November 1998, that "there is no distinction between the man who strikes and a man who orders another to strike."

No State Immunity

6.2.64 ICTY Article 7(2)/ ICTR Article 6(2) provide that, "*The official position of any accused person, whether as Head of State or Government or as a responsible Government official, shall not relieve such person of criminal responsibility nor mitigate punishment.*" This provision clearly rules out claims of state or functional immunity, but it is not clear whether it would remove the *personal* immunity of a serving Head of State. In other words, in terms of subject-matter, the fact that the accused performed a certain act as a high State official does not mean that the acts are screened from scrutiny as being, in essence, acts of State. Thus an ex-President cannot raise this claim. But it is a separate issue whether an accused *who is currently serving as a Head of State with the attendant personal immunities* may be lawfully arrested.

6.2.65 In *Milošević*, the Trial Chamber dealt with the issue of whether or not the Tribunal had jurisdiction over Milošević notwithstanding his status as a former President (of Serbia). In its *Decision on Preliminary Motion*, 8 November 2001, the Trial Chamber stated with respect to ICTY Article 7(2) that:

The history of this rule can be traced to the development of the doctrine of individual criminal responsibility after the Second World War, when it was incorporated in Article 7 of the Nuremberg Charter and Article 6 of the Tokyo Tribunal Charter. The customary character of the rule is further supported by its incorporation in a wide number of other instruments, as well as case law.

As for instruments, the following may be mentioned: Article IV of the Convention for the Prevention and the Punishment of the Crime of Genocide; Principle III of the Nuremberg Principles; Article 6 of the Statute of the International Criminal Tribunal for Rwanda; Article 6, paragraph 2, of the Statute of the Special Court for Sierra Leone; Article 27 of the Rome Statute of the International Criminal Court ("ICC"), and Article 7 of the Draft Code of Crimes against the Peace and Security of Mankind.

Particular mention must be made of the Rome Statute of the ICC which, although not yet in force, has been signed by 139 States and now has 43 of the 60 ratifications required for its entry into force [*editor's note:* the Rome Statute entered into force on 1 July 2002]. This is a multilateral instrument of the greatest importance, which, even at this stage, has attracted fairly widespread support. The Chamber also attaches particular significance to the International Law Commission's Draft Code of Crimes against the Peace and Security of Mankind, prepared in 1996. The Chamber cites two modern instruments as evidence of the customary character of the rule that a Head of State cannot plead his official position as a bar to criminal liability in respect of crimes over which the International Tribunal has jurisdiction.

Moreover, case law also confirms the rule: in the Nuremberg judgement, it was said:

> The Principle of international law, which, under certain circumstances, protects the representative of a State, cannot be applied to acts which are condemned as criminal by international law. The authors of these acts cannot shelter themselves behind their official position in order to be freed from punishment in appropriate proceedings . . . the very essence of the Charter is that individuals have international duties which transcend the national obligations of obedience imposed by the individual State. He who violates the laws of war cannot obtain immunity while acting in pursuance of the authority of the State if the State in authorizing action moves outside its competence under international law.

More recently in the *Pinochet* case, the House of Lords held that Senator Pinochet was not entitled to immunity in respect of acts of torture and conspiracy to commit torture, alleged to have been committed in his capacity as a Head of State. In particular, Lord Millett stated:

> In future those who commit atrocities against civilian populations must expect to be called to account if fundamental human rights are to be properly protected. In this context, the exalted rank of the accused can afford no defence.

Accordingly, this ground is dismissed.

6.2.66 Of course, the position with respect to claimed immunities depends on whether the trying court is an international or a national one, as the rationale for the international rules on state immunities is that sovereign states should not and may not stand in judgement on other states (*par in parem non habet imperium*). This consideration does not apply to international courts. Hence prosecutions of heads of state and former heads of state *in national courts* have encountered obstacles. See in particular the judgement of the ICJ in the *Case concerning the Arrest Warrant of 11 April 2000* between Congo and Belgium. As a result of this case, Belgium's proceedings against Prime Minister Sharon of Israel were also declared inadmissible by the Belgian courts.

6.2.67 Moreover, in the *Pinochet* case, the House of Lords implicitly held that personal immunities of heads of state would be a bar to prosecution, and that state immunity was only lost, or waived, with respect to torture, where the States in question were parties to the UN Convention against Torture 1984. State immunity was not necessarily lost with respect to all international crimes. On the *Pinochet* case, and also the distinction between state immunity and personal immunity, see John R.W.D. Jones, "Immunity and Double Criminality: General Augusto Pinochet before the House of Lords" in *International Law in the Post-Cold War World: Essays in Honour of Judge Li*, eds. Sienho Yee and Wang Tieya (Routledge, 2001).

6.2.68 See also Salvatore Zappalà, "Do Heads of State in Office enjoy Immunity from Jurisdiction for International Crimes? The Ghaddafi case before the French Cour de Cassation," *European Journal of International Law*, Vol. 12, No. 3, June 2001, pp. 595–612; and articles by Professors Cassese, Wirth and Spinedi in "Symposium: The Democratic Republic of the Congo v. Belgium case before the ICJ," *European Journal of International Law*, Vol. 13, No. 4, September 2002, pp. 853–899.

6.2.69

ICTY Article 7(3)/ICTR Article 6(3): Command Responsibility
The fact that any of the acts referred to in articles 2 to 5 [articles 2 to 4 at the ICTR] of the present Statute was committed by a subordinate does not relieve his superior of criminal responsibility if he knew or had reason to know that the subordinate was about to commit such acts or had done so and the superior failed to take the necessary and reasonable measures to prevent such acts or to punish the perpetrators thereof.

The Origins of Command Responsibility

6.2.70 The doctrine of command responsibility, namely the responsibility of a commander for the actions of his subordinates, was first clearly enunciated in its modern form in war crimes cases decided after World War II. It has been suggested that a new term of art should be formulated, such as "superior criminal responsibility" so as to make clear that in its modern form the doctrine also applies to civilian and well as military commanders. See W.J. Fenrick, "Some International Law Problems Related to Prosecution Before the International Criminal Tribunal for the former Yugoslavia," 6 (1) *Duke Journal of Comparative and International Law* 103 n. 21 (1995).

Pre-World War II Cases

6.2.71 The origins of the doctrine can be traced back to feudal times when it was established that a commander might be liable for offences committed by those under his command. In 1439, Charles VII of Orleans promulgated an Ordinance providing as follows:

> The King orders that each captain or lieutenant be held responsible for the abuses, ills and offences committed by members of his company, and that as soon as he receives any complaint concerning any such misdeed or abuse, he bring the offender to justice.... If he fails to do so or covers up the misdeed or delays taking action, or if, because of his negligence of otherwise, the offender escapes and thus evades punishment, the captain shall be deemed responsible for the offence as if he had committed it himself and be punished in the same way as the offender would have been.
>
> (Charles VII's "Ordinance des Rois de France de la Troisieme Race" *cited in* Theodor Meron, *Henry's Laws and Shakepeare's Wars* (Cambridge University Press, 1993.)

6.2.72 Command responsibility became a matter of international concern at the end of World War I as a result of the work of the Commission on the Responsibility of the Authors of War and on Enforcement of Penalties. The Commission considered that:

> all persons belonging to enemy countries, however high their position may have been, without distinction of rank, including Chiefs of Staff, who may have been guilty of offences against the laws and customs of war or the laws of humanity, are liable to criminal prosecution.

6.2.73 They further recommended that a tribunal be established for the prosecution of those who:

> ordered, or with knowledge thereof and with the power to intervene, abstained from preventing or taking measures to prevent, putting an end to or repressing violations of the laws or customs of war.
>
> (Commission Report, 19 March 1919, 14 *American Journal of International Law* 25 (1920)).

6.2.74 The provision was not put into effect as ultimately no international military tribunal was established following World War I. However, twelve people eventually stood trial in German courts, one of whom was convicted on the basis of ordering war crimes.

World War II Cases

6.2.75 It was not until the post-World War II trials of alleged war criminals that the doctrine of command responsibility for failure to act received judicial recognition for the first time. Neither the Nuremberg nor the Tokyo Charter provided for the prosecution of commanders who failed to prevent or punish the offences of their subordinates. The Statutes only placed liability on commanders for their participation as conspirators, principals or as accomplices when they shared in the design or purpose of their subordinates. No liability was expressly stated for failure effectively to command. It was therefore during the war crimes trials themselves that the doctrine of command responsibility was developed, leading some defendants who were prosecuted pursuant to the doctrine to complain that it amounted to retrospective law. See Major Michael Smidt "Yamahita, Medina, and Beyond: Command Responsibility in Contemporary Military Operations," 164 *Mil.L.Rev*. 155 at 176. The most cited World

War II case on command responsibility is the case of General Tomoyuki Yamashita. It was the first World War II case to consider the liability of a commander for the actions of his troops and was ultimately considered by the US Supreme Court, which was divided on the matter. See *Re* Yamashita, 327 US 1 (1946) The US Supreme Court stated that commanders have a duty to control their troops and prevent war crimes. Commanders in charge of occupying forces are additionally required to take affirmative steps to protect civilians and prisoners of war. For the majority, Chief Justice Harlan Fiske Stone stated:

> The question is whether the law of war imposes on an army commander a duty to take such appropriate measures as are within his power to control the troops under his command for the prevention of the specified acts which are violations of the law of war and which are likely to attend the occupation of hostile territory by an uncontrolled soldiery, and whether he may be charged with personal responsibility for his failure to take such measures when violations result. . . . It is evident that the conduct of military operations by troops whose excesses are unrestrained by the orders or efforts of their commander would almost certainly result in violations which it is the purpose of the law of war to prevent. Its purpose to protect civilian populations and prisoners of war from brutality would largely be defeated if the commander of an invading army could with impunity neglect to take reasonable measures for their protection. Here the law of war presupposes that its violation is to be avoided through the control of the operations by commanders who are to some extent responsible for their subordinates. *Re Yamashita* p 43

6.2.76 In his strong dissent to the majority decision, Justice Murphy stated:

> Nothing in all history or in international law . . . justifies such a charge against a fallen commander of a defeated force. To use the very inefficiency and disorganization created by the victorious forces as the primary basis for condemning officers of the defeated armies bears no resemblance to justice or to military reality.

6.2.77 In the *High Command Case*, 11 *Trials of War Criminals* 462 (1948), thirteen high ranking German officials were charged with crimes against peace, war crimes, crimes against humanity and conspiracy to commit those crimes. The tribunal held:

> A high commander cannot keep completely informed of the details of military operation of his subordinates. . . . He has the right to assume that the details entrusted to responsible subordinates will be largely executed. . . . There must be a personal dereliction. That can only occur where the act is directly traceable to him or where his failure to properly supervise his subordinates constitutes criminal negligence on his part. In the latter case, it must be personal neglect amounting to a wanton, immoral disregard of the action of his subordinates amounting to acquiescence. Any other interpretation of international law would go far beyond the basic principles of criminal law as known to civilized nations.

6.2.78 Accordingly, the tribunal held that the commander must have some knowledge of the crimes committed by subordinates. The tribunal further stated that for the commander to incur liability he:

> must have knowledge of these offences and acquiesce or participate or criminally neglect to interfere in their commission and . . . the offences must be patently criminal.

General Principles of Criminal Law • 427

6.2.79 From this it appears that the tribunal determined that guilt rested with a commander who wilfully disregarded information of his subordinates' criminal acts. The tribunal also considered the liability of a commander for crimes committed within his command as a result of orders from his superiors independent of him. It was held that:

> Under basic principles of command authority and responsibility, an officer who merely stands by while his subordinates execute a criminal order of his superiors which he knows is criminal violates a moral obligation under international law. By doing nothing he cannot wash his hands of international responsibility.

6.2.80 Other World War II cases in which command responsibility was considered are: *The Hostage Case*, 11 *Trials of War Criminals* 1230 (1948); *The Abbaye Ardenne Case*, 4 *Law Reports of Trials of War Criminals* 97 (1945); *Trial of Hideki Tojo*, 20 *Tokyo Trials* 49845–49846.

Post-World War II Cases

6.2.81 Since World War II, the doctrine of command responsibility has been considered in various domestic tribunals. In 1959, the Israeli Military Court of Appeal considered the liability of an Israeli lieutenant for the killing by Israeli reserves of 43 villagers out in violation of a curfew. The Court stated:

> D[ahan]'s responsibility for the acts of [these] men derives from his orders to fire at the victims which he issued to his unit. . . . This makes D liable for procuring an offence under . . . the Criminal Code. . . . Although D was not present [when the] squad committed the murders . . . he was patrolling in the village, driving his car, and from time to time appeared near the [area from which the firing took place]; he was aware of what was taking place . . . and did not take any measures to stop the killings. Under these circumstances, bearing in mind his authority over [the group], his omission to act to stop the killings is the same as being accessory to the offence. . . . This is a sufficient ground to convict D as an accomplice . . . besides his responsibility for procuring the offences.
>
> *Melenki v. Chief Military Prosecutor*, reprinted and translated in "Kafr Qassem: A Civilian Massacre," 2 *Palestine Yearbook of International Law* (1985).

6.2.82 Given, however, that the Court considered that the accused had given the orders to fire at the victims, this case is perhaps not best regarded as one of liability for omissions by virtue of the command responsibility principle but rather one of liability for giving illegal orders under classic principles of criminal responsibility for ordering.

6.2.83 Following the killing of 200 Vietnamese civilians in Mai Lai by US troops in Vietnam, the company commander, Captain Ernest Medina was put on trial. The jury were directed as follows

> a commander is also responsible if he has actual knowledge that troops or other persons subject to his control are in the process of committing or are about to commit a war crime and he wrongfully fails to take the necessary and reasonable steps to insure compliance with the law of war. . . . These legal requirements placed upon a commander require actual knowledge plus a wrongful failure to act. Thus mere presence at the scene will not suffice. That is, the commander-

subordinate relationship alone will not allow an inference of knowledge. While it is not necessary that a commander actually see an atrocity being committed, it is essential that he know that his subordinates are in the process of committing atrocities or are about to commit atrocities.

US v. Medina (1971) Court Martial 427162, Appeal Court Martial Reports, 1971.

6.2.84 The different *mens rea* requirement between *Yamashita* and *Medina* is difficult to reconcile considering that both decisions were propounded by US courts. Could it be that the differing treatment of Yamashita and Medina was due to the fact that Yamashita was Japanese and an enemy of the US, while Medina a US soldier fighting on his country's behalf? One would hope not. However the treatment meted out to Lieutenant Calley for the My Lai massacre—two years' house arrest followed by an executive pardon—supports the inference that US courts do not always treat their soldiers and enemy civilians equally under the law.

6.2.85 In September 1982, during the Israeli invasion of Lebanon, Israeli forces permitted Phalangists to enter two Palestinian refugee camps at Sabra and Shatila. It was feared in some Israeli quarters that a bloodbath might ensue at the hands of the Phalangists. They were nevertheless allowed to enter the camps and duly massacred most of the refugee inhabitants. The Israelis established a Commission of Inquiry presided over by the Chief Justice of the Supreme Court resulting in the Kahan Report. The Kahan Commission held that the incursion into Lebanon by Israel amounted to war and that accordingly the basic principles of humanitarian law were applicable. Although the atrocities were committed by Phalangists, they had been supplied by Israel. Furthermore, Israeli authorities knew of the potential dangers of allowing the Phalangists into the camps. The Commission held that Israel was not "directly" responsible for the massacre as it had not been committed by its own forces nor at its request. However, there was scope for various political and military leaders to be held "indirectly" responsible. Indirect responsibility was defined in the following terms:

> If it indeed becomes clear that those who decided on the entry of the Phalangists into the camps should have foreseen—from the information at their disposal and from things which were common knowledge—that there was danger of a massacre, and no steps were taken which might have prevented this danger or at least greatly reduced the possibility that deeds of this type might be done, then those who made the decision and those who implemented them are indirectly responsible for what ultimately occurred, even if they did not intend this to happen and merely disregarded the anticipated danger. A similar indirect responsibility also falls on those who knew of the decision; it was their duty, by virtue of their position and their office, to warn of the danger, and they did not fulfil this duty. It is also not possible to absolve of such indirect responsibility those persons who, when they received the first reports of what was happening in the camps, did not rush to prevent the continuation of the Phalangist's actions and did not do anything within their power to stop them. (Commission Report, 22 ILM 472 at 476.)

6.2.86 With regard to the then Minister for Defence, Ariel Sharon, the Commission held:

> responsibility is to be imputed to the Minister of Defence for having disregarded the danger of acts of vengeance and bloodshed by the Phalangists against the population of the refugee camps, and having failed to take this danger into account

when he decided to have the Phalangist enter the camps. In addition responsibility is to be imputed to the minister for not ordering appropriate measures for preventing or reducing the danger of massacre as a condition of the Phalangists' entry into the camps. These blunders constitute the non-fulfilment of a duty with which the Defence Minister was charged. (Commission Report, 22 ILM 472 at p. 503)

Additional Protocol I of 1977

6.2.87 The responsibility of superiors for failure to prevent crimes of subordinates was set out for the first time in a binding instrument in Additional Protocol I of 1977 to the Geneva Conventions of 1949 (API). Articles 86 and 87 gave the doctrine of command responsibility a clear conventional basis. At the time it was adopted, the protocol reflected the customary international law position with regard to command responsibility. Article 87(3) established a duty of commanders to prevent violations of the Geneva Conventions and Article 86(2) a liability for failure to prevent violations.

6.2.88 Article 86 (Failure to act) of API provides:

> 1. The High Contracting Parties and the Parties to the conflict shall repress grave breaches, and take measures necessary to suppress all other breaches, of the Conventions or of this Protocol which result from a failure to act when under a duty to do so.
>
> 2. The fact that a breach of the Conventions or of this Protocol was committed by a subordinate does not absolve his superiors from penal or disciplinary responsibility, as the case may be, if they knew, or had information which should have enabled them to conclude in the circumstances at the time, that he was committing or was going to commit such a breach and if they did not take all feasible measures within their power to prevent or repress the breach.

6.2.89 Article 87 (Duty of Commanders) of API provides:

> 1. The High Contracting Parties and the Parties to the conflict shall require military commanders, with respect to members of the armed forces under their command and other persons under their control, to prevent and, where necessary, to suppress and report to competent authorities breaches of the Conventions and of this Protocol.
>
> 2. In order to prevent and suppress breaches, High Contracting Parties and Parties to the conflict shall require that, commensurate with their level of responsibility, commanders ensure that members of the armed forces under their command are aware of their obligations under the Conventions and this Protocol.
>
> 3. The High Contracting Parties and Parties to the conflict shall require any commander who is aware that subordinates or other persons under his control are going to commit or have committed a breach of the Conventions or of this Protocol, to initiate such steps as are necessary to prevent such violations of the Conventions or this Protocol, and where appropriate, to initiate disciplinary action against violators thereof.

6.2.90 The ICRC Commentary on Protocol I (para. 3543) sets out three conditions which must be met for a superior to incur responsibility for an omission relating to an offence committed or about to be committed by a subordinate.

6.2.91 First, the person to be held responsible must be the superior of the person or persons committing the breach of the convention. Article 87(3) refers to "commanders" while Article 86(2) refers to "superiors." The ICRC Commentary states that the term superiors encompasses military commanders and extends to a further category of persons with similar powers of control over subordinates. The Commentary on Article 87 provides that the duty to prevent crimes extends to all persons in the armed forces who exercise command "from the highest to the lowest level of the hierarchy." The duty extends to all persons under the commander's control, not just members of the armed forces. The Commentary to Article 86 stipulates that the provision is concerned with the "superior who has personal responsibility with regard to the perpetrator of the acts concerned because the latter, being his subordinate, is under his control."

6.2.92 Secondly, the superior must have known or had information which should have enabled him to conclude that a breach was being committed or was going to be committed. The Commentary states that a superior cannot be absolved from responsibility by pleading ignorance of reports addressed to him or by citing temporary absence as an excuse. In certain cases, knowledge of breaches committed by subordinates can be assumed. The Commentary makes clear that responsibility pursuant to Article 86 may be incurred by negligence, however, that negligence must be so serious as to amount to malicious intent.

6.2.93 Thirdly, it must be demonstrated that the superior did not take all feasible measures within his power to prevent the breach. The Commentary stipulates that as a matter of common sense a superior is only under an obligation to take measures that are "within his power."

6.2.94 The fact that the command responsibility principle did not appear in Additional Protocol II, which deals with non-international conflicts, was invoked by the Defense in *Hadzihasanović et al.* to argue that, at least prior to 1993, States did not recognise the principle as being applicable in internal conflicts. Accordingly the principle was not part of international—customary or conventional—law where internal conflicts were concerned. Thus the ICTY could not prosecute accused solely on the basis of Article 7(3) in internal conflicts (as was the case for all three accused in *Hadzihasanović et al.*). See the *Joint Challenge to Jurisdiction Arising from the Amended Indictment* dated 21 February 2002. The Trial Chamber's Decision, dated 12 November 2002, rejecting the defence motion, is currently under appeal.

Command Responsibility at the ICTs

6.2.95 The Secretary-General's Report on the ICTY Statute states the following on Article 7(3):

> A person in a position of superior authority should, therefore, be held individually responsible for giving the unlawful order to commit a crime under the present statute. But he should also be held responsible for failure to prevent a crime or deter the unlawful behaviour of his subordinates. This imputed responsibility or criminal negligence is engaged if the person in superior authority knew or had reason to know that his subordinates were about to commit or had committed crimes and yet failed to take the necessary and reasonable steps to prevent or repress the commission of such crimes or to punish those who had committed them.

6.2.96 At the Security Council meeting where the Secretary-General's report was considered and the resolution establishing the ICTY adopted, the US was the only delegation to mention the Statute's provision on command responsibility. The U.S. stated their understanding that the principle of individual liability for failure to take reasonable measures to prevent or punish crimes extended to both military and civilian leaders. (UN Doc S/PV 3217, 25 May 1993.)

6.2.97 The Commission of Experts, established to examine and analyse information with a view to providing conclusions on the evidence of violations of international humanitarian law committed in the territory of the former Yugoslavia to the Secretary-General considered Article 7(3) in their Final Report. The Commission found that the doctrine of command responsibility is directed primarily at military commanders as they have an obligation to ensure the discipline of troops under their command. The Commission stated that the mental element could take one of the following forms:

> (a) actual knowledge; (b) such serious personal dereliction on the part of the commander as to constitute wilful and wanton disregard of the possible consequences; or (c) an imputation of constructive knowledge, that is, despite pleas to the contrary, the commander, under the facts and circumstances of the particular case, must have known of the offences charged and acquiesced therein.

6.2.98 For (c), it is not clear whether the concept is (i) given the facts and circumstances of the case, the accused *should have known* of the offences (but perhaps did not *in fact* know of the offences) and he is being punished for his negligence in not finding out about the offences and doing something about it, or (ii) that the accused knew of the crime and this can be proved inferentially on the basis of the facts and circumstances of the case (i.e., it can be proved that he *must* have known, i.e., that he knew). There is a considerable difference between the two concepts, as an example illustrates: A commander receives a sealed envelope marked "urgent for the attention of the commander" from one of his subordinates. Inside the envelope is a report of war crimes committed by the superior's subordinates. It can be proved that the commander received the envelope. It can also be assumed that a reasonable, i.e., non-negligent, commander would have opened the envelope, i.e., that he *should have* opened the envelope, which would have informed him of the crimes. Thus he *should have known* about the crimes. But what if it can be affirmatively proved by other evidence that the commander *never opened the envelope*, and thus never knew of the crimes? According to concept (i), it makes no difference—he can be convicted and punished, because he *should have known* of the crimes. According to concept (ii), however, he will be acquitted because—whatever he *should* have done and *should* have known—the fact is that he *did not know* of the offences. The inference of knowledge—constructive knowledge—can be rebutted by evidence of actual lack of knowledge. The ICTY has yet to tackle this problem.

6.2.99 In answering this question, it should be remembered that the ICTs' jurisdiction is limited to crimes and bases of liability existing under customary international law. In his Report to the Security Council, the Secretary-General stated that (para. 29):

> It should be pointed out that, in assigning to the International Tribunal the task of prosecuting persons responsible for serious violations of international humanitarian law, the Security Council would not be creating or purporting to "legislate" that law. Rather, the International Tribunal would have the task of applying existing international humanitarian law.

Charging Command Responsibility

6.2.100 Command responsibility under Article 7(3) of the ICTY Statute should be clearly and specifically pleaded in the indictment with reference to the elements comprised in this form of liability (See *Decision on Preliminary Motion on Form of Amended Indictment, Krnojelac*, 11 February 2000).

6.2.101 When the "command responsibility" principle is not specifically alleged in the Indictment in relation to a specific charge, it is inapplicable.

6.2.102 See the *Akayesu Trial Judgement:*

> 691. The Tribunal has found that the Accused had reason to know and in fact knew that acts of sexual violence were occurring on or near the premises of the bureau communal and that he took no measures to prevent these acts or punish the perpetrators of them. The Tribunal notes that it is only in consideration of Counts 13, 14 and 15 that the Accused is charged with individual criminal responsibility under Section 6(3) of its Statute. As set forth in the Indictment, under Article 6(3) "an individual is criminally responsible as a superior for the acts of a subordinate if he or she knew or had reason to know that the subordinate was about to commit such acts or had done so and the superior failed to take the necessary and reasonable measures to prevent such acts or punish the perpetrators thereof." Although the evidence supports a finding that a superior/subordinate relationship existed between the Accused and the Interahamwe who were at the bureau communal, the Tribunal notes that there is no allegation in the Indictment that the Interahamwe, who are referred to as "armed local militia," were subordinates of the Accused. This relationship is a fundamental element of the criminal offence set forth in Article 6(3). The amendment of the Indictment with additional charges pursuant to Article 6(3) could arguably be interpreted as implying an allegation of the command responsibility required by Article 6(3). In fairness to the Accused, the Tribunal will not make this inference. Therefore, the Tribunal finds that it cannot consider the criminal responsibility of the Accused under Article 6(3).

Customary Nature of Command Responsibility

6.2.103 The first and most comprehensive trial judgement considering the doctrine of command responsibility at the ICTY was the *Delalić Trial Judgement* (see paras. 330–400). The Trial Chamber held (para. 333):

> That military commanders and other persons occupying positions of superior authority may be held criminally responsible for the unlawful conduct of their subordinates is a well-established norm of customary and conventional law.

6.2.104 See also *Decision on the Defence Motion to Strike Portions of the Amended Indictment Alleging "Failure to Punish Liability,"* Tr. Ch., *Blaškić* 4 April 1997 and *Decision On The Joint Defence Motion To Dismiss For Lack Of Jurisdiction Portions Of The Amended Indictment Alleging "Failure To Punish" Liability*, Tr. Ch., *Kordić and Čerkez*, 2 March 1999, para. 12.

6.2.105 The Trial Chamber in *Delalić et al.* held that "Command responsibility" in the sense of Article 7(3) of the ICTY Statute is a species of liability for omissions and, therefore, in accordance with criminal law as it relates to omissions, liability is only incurred "where there exists a legal obligation to act" (para. 334).

Command Responsibility in Internal Conflict

6.2.106 In *Hadžihasanović, Alagić and Kubura*, the Defence argued that, at the times relevant to the indictment (1993–1994), there was no clear incrimination of command responsibility in internal armed conflict. Therefore to charge the accused on the sole basis of command responsibility in internal conflict—as all three accused were—violated the principle of legality or *nullum crimen sine lege*.

The argument, in summary, was set out in the *Submissions of Alagić* filed on 10 May 2002:

> (1) The Statute does not create new law, the Tribunal has to apply existing international humanitarian law;
> (2) The principle of legality requires a written text (a conventional source) and a customary source;
> (3) the only sources for Article 7(3) Command Responsibility are Additional Protocol I and post-World War II cases; these apply only to *international* armed conflicts;
> (4) there are *no* conventional or customary sources for Command Responsibility in *internal* armed conflicts;
> (5) there is a difference, recognised by the ICTY Appeals Chamber, between the law applicable to international, and the law applicable to internal, armed conflicts;
> (6) the principle of legality prohibits reasoning by analogy from the position in international conflicts to the position in internal conflicts.
> (7) if there is any doubt or ambiguity, it must be resolved in favour of the Accused.

6.2.107 The Defence also pointed out the strange hybrid nature of Article 7(3), as a form of liability for omissions yet under which the superior was held responsible, on the basis of imputed liability, for the crimes of his subordinates as if he had committed the crimes himself. The Defence also pointed out the injustice of holding a superior, who had not acted intentionally, responsible for the intentional crimes, e.g., murders, of his subordinates.

6.2.108 Pursuant to an Order by the Trial Chamber, briefs were filed on this issue simultaneously by the Parties on 9 May 2002, 24 May 2002 and 31 May 2002. After several months' deliberation, the Trial Chamber rendered its *Decision on Joint Challenge to Jurisdiction* on 12 November 2002, rejecting the Defence's challenge (as well as two other jurisdictional challenges). On the challenge to Article 7(3)-type liability in internal conflict, the Trial Chamber Trial Chamber found that:

> a. No codification in an international agreement or treaty exists for the doctrine of command responsibility applying to internal conflict (para. 93);
> b. No international judicial organ has ruled that the doctrine of command responsibility applies to internal conflicts, and since the

1950s no international judicial organ had applied the doctrine of command responsibility in internal or international conflict until the ICTY was established (paras. 77, 93, and 155);
c. As the conflicts in relation to which the various international judicial bodies after the Second World War had been established were of an international character, obviously the principle of command responsibility was only used against persons who had acted in such international conflicts (para. 151);
d. Additional Protocol II did not include a provision on command responsibility similar to Additional Protocol I (paras. 157 and 164);
e. There is practically no national legislation or military manual touching upon command responsibility in the context of internal conflicts (para. 165); and
f. The issue of command responsibility in an internal conflict has not been extensively discussed in any of the works of highly qualified publicists on this subject (fn. 278).

6.2.109 Despite these findings, the Trial Chamber ruled that "the doctrine of command responsibility already in—and since—1991 was applicable in the context of an internal conflict under customary international law."

6.2.110 In its *Interlocutory Appeal on Decision on Joint Challenge to Jurisdiction* filed on 26 November 2002, the Defence argued that the Trial Chamber had erred in two respects:

A. Failed to respect the principle of legality in reaching its conclusion that it had jurisdiction in the present case; and
B. Wrongly found that there was a basis in customary international law for the applicability of the doctrine of command responsibility in internal conflict at the material time of the indictment.

6.2.111 The matter remains under appeal.

Elements of Command Responsibility

6.2.112 In the *Delalić et al. Trial Judgement*, the Chamber identified three elements for liability pursuant to Article 7(3): (i) the existence of a superior-subordinate relationship; (ii) that the superior knew or had reason to know that the criminal act was about to be or had been committed; and (iii) that the superior failed to take the necessary and reasonable measures to prevent the criminal act or the perpetrator thereof. (para. 346). Various aspects of the Trial Chamber's Judgement in relation to command responsibility were appealed to the Appeals Chamber. The Appeals Chamber rendered its Judgement on 20 February 2001. The Trial Chamber's conclusions as to elements (i) and (ii) were upheld, element (iii) was not in issue in the appeal.

Element I: Superior/Subordinate Relationship

6.2.113 In the *Delalić et al. Trial Judgement*, the Chamber held that superiors, both military and civilian, may be held responsible for the actions of their subordinates. The crucial factor is the possession of power over subordinates by the superior (see paras. 330–400).

6.2.114 The Trial Chamber held that Command responsibility applies to *de facto* as well as to *de jure* authority (para. 354: "individuals in positions of authority, whether civilian or within military structures, may incur criminal responsibility under the doctrine of command responsibility on the basis of their *de facto* as well as *de jure* positions as superiors"). On the sufficiency of *de facto* authority for command responsibility to arise, see also the *Aleksovski Trial Judgement* (para. 76), the *Foča Trial Judgement* (paras 394–399), the *Delalić et al Appeals Judgement*, 20 February 2001, (paras 182–198), and the *Kayishema and Ruzindana Trial Judgement* (paras 218–222).

6.2.115 Command responsibility applies to political and civilian leaders, and not only to military leaders (para. 356: "its applicability extends beyond the responsibility of military commanders to also encompass political leaders and other civilian superiors in positions of authority"; para. 363: "Thus, it must be concluded that the applicability of the principle of superior responsibility in Article 7(3) extends not only to military commanders but also to individuals in non-military positions of superior authority"). The Appeals Chamber, in confirming that civilian superiors also bear the responsibility of subordinates for their offences, raised the question as to how clear the responsibility is on the basis of customary international law and whether the responsibility contains identical elements to that of military commanders (*Delalić et al Appeals Judgement*, para. 240).

6.2.116 Command responsibility is only incurred when the accused is in a position of *command* (para. 370: "a position of command is indeed a necessary precondition for the imposition of command responsibility. However, this statement must be qualified by the recognition that the existence of such a position cannot be determined by reference to formal status alone. Instead, the factor that determines liability for this type of criminal responsibility is the actual possession, or non-possession, of powers of control over the actions of subordinates.")

6.2.117 This seems to suggest that the test is indeed solely one of *de facto* authority, and that *de jure* authority alone, without *de facto* authority, would not suffice for liability to arise under the command responsibility doctrine. Thus the test would seem to be whether the accused *in fact* had the power effectively to control his subordinates.

6.2.118 In reviewing post World War II cases, the Trial Chamber ruling in the *Delalić et al Trial Judgement* found that command responsibility had been applied to (i) armed forces commanders in respect of acts of persons they could control but not formally under their authority in the chain of command; (ii) a commander in charge of occupied territory for acts committed in that territory by persons not formally under their command; (iii) an officer with operational, but not administrative authority; (iv) the business manager of an industry employing concentration camp labour; (v) a chief of staff to a military governor; and (vi) the foreign minister of a country (paras 370–376).

6.2.119 Ultimately, the question was whether the accused had *power* over his subordinates:

> 377. ... The doctrine of command responsibility is ultimately predicated upon the power of the superior to control the acts of his subordinates. A duty is placed upon the superior to exercise this power so as to prevent and repress

the crimes committed by his subordinates, and a failure by him to do so in a diligent manner is sanctioned by the imposition of individual criminal responsibility in accordance with the doctrine. It follows that there is a threshold at which persons cease to possess the necessary powers of control over the actual perpetrators of offences and, accordingly, cannot properly be considered their "superiors" within the meaning of Article 7(3) of the Statute. While the Trial Chamber must at all times be alive to the realities of any given situation and be prepared to pierce such veils of formalism that may shield those individuals carrying the greatest responsibility for heinous acts, great care must be taken lest an injustice be committed in holding individuals responsible for the acts of others in situations where the link of control is absent or too remote.

378. Accordingly, it is the Trial Chamber's view that, in order for the principle of superior responsibility to be applicable, it is necessary that the superior have effective control over the persons committing the underlying violations of international humanitarian law, in the sense of having the material ability to prevent and punish the commission of these offences. With the caveat that such authority can have a *de facto* as well as a *de jure* character, the Trial Chamber accordingly shares the view expressed by the International Law Commission that the doctrine of superior responsibility extends to civilian superiors only to the extent that they exercise a degree of control over their subordinates which is similar to that of military commanders.

6.2.120 Regarding the factors to be taken into account in determining whether or not the accused occupied a command position, see also the *Rajić Rule 61 Decision* (paras 60–61). Effective control is often largely a question of funding (see the *Tadić Appeals Judgement*, 4.2.343, above); "he who pays the piper calls the tune."

6.2.121 In the *Delalić et al. Trial Judgement*, Zejnil Delalić was acquitted of responsibility under ICTY Article 7(3), since the Trial Chamber found that Delalić at no time had command and actual control over the Čelebići prison camp, which were indispensable elements of command responsibility (see paras. 605–721). Zdravko Mucić, on the other hand, was the *de facto* commander of Čelebići prison camp and was therefore liable through the principle of command responsibility (para. 775). Mucić appealed the finding of his being a *de facto* commander. The Appeals Chamber upheld the Trial Chamber findings on law and fact (*Appeals Judgement*, 20 February 2001) As regards Hazim Delić, the Prosecution failed to prove beyond a reasonable doubt that he was a superior, so he did not incur liability as a commander (para. 810). The fourth defendant, Landžo, was not charged with command responsibility.

6.2.122 In the *Aleksovski Trial Judgement*, the Trial Chamber convicted Aleksovski under Article 7(3) for the acts of the prison guards as he was commander of the prison. However, he was not convicted for the actions of the HVO soldiers who committed atrocities in the camp as he was not their superior and did not exercise control over them.

6.2.123 The test now accepted at the ICTs for a superior-subordinate relationship is one of "*effective control*"; a concept which has been developed in international law in a number of contexts (see, e.g., the Nicaragua case at the ICJ).

Element II: *Mens Rea*—Knew or Had Reason to Know

6.2.124 The Chamber in the *Delalić et al. Trial Judgement* made clear that command responsibility does not impose a standard of strict liability upon superiors (para. 383).

Article 7(3) requires that a superior either knew or had reason to know that subordinates were about to or had committed crimes. The Chamber stipulated that (para. 383):

> A superior may possess the *mens rea* required to incur criminal liability where: (1) he had actual knowledge, established through direct or circumstantial evidence, that his subordinates were committing or about to commit crimes referred to under Article 2 to 5 of the ICTY Statute, or (2) where he had in his possession information of a nature, which at the least, would put him on notice of the risk of such offences by indicating the need for additional investigation in order to ascertain whether such crimes were committed or were about to be committed by his subordinates.

Knowledge

6.2.125 The Chamber in the *Delalić et al. Trial Judgement* held that knowledge cannot be *presumed*, but it can be established by *circumstantial evidence*. See para. 386:

> It is, accordingly, the Trial Chamber's view that, in the absence of direct evidence of the superior's knowledge of the offences committed by his subordinates, such knowledge cannot be presumed, but must be established by way of circumstantial evidence. In determining whether a superior, despite pleas to the contrary, in fact must have possessed the requisite knowledge, the Trial Chamber may consider, *inter alia*, the following indicia, listed by the Commission of Experts in its Final Report:

(a) The number of illegal acts;
(b) The type of illegal acts;
(c) The scope of illegal acts;
(d) The time during which the illegal acts occurred;
(e) The number and type of troops involved;
(f) The logistics involved, if any;
(g) The geographical location of the acts;
(h) The widespread occurrence of the acts;
(i) The tactical tempo of operations;
(j) The modus operandi of similar illegal acts;
(k) The officers and staff involved;
(l) The location of the commander at the time.

Had Reason to Know

6.2.126 The requirement of having reason to know was spelt out by the Chamber in the *Delalić et al. Trial Judgement* to mean that the superior had available to him "some specific information . . . which would provide notice of offences committed by his subordinates" (para. 393). In the *Blaškić Trial Judgement*, another Trial Chamber held that no such specific information was required in order to find that a superior "had reason to know." The Appeals Chamber in the *Delalić et al. Appeals Judgement* confirmed, however, that some specific information was in fact required (para. 241).

6.2.127 The information need not, however, be such as to indicate the existence of such crimes, all that is required is that (*Delalić et al. Trial Judgement,* para. 393):

> the superior was put on further inquiry by the information, or, in other words, that it indicated the need for additional investigation in order to ascertain whether offences were being committed or about to be committed by his subordinates.

6.2.128 The accused is not permitted to remain "wilfully blind to the acts of his subordinates" (*Delalić et al. Trial Judgement,* para. 387).

6.2.129 Where the accused is ignorant that his subordinates are committing crimes because of his own failure to supervise them, this will not avail him of a defence or excuse.

6.2.130 Post-World War II jurisprudence has established a principle whereby absence of such knowledge is no defence where the superior was at fault for having failed to acquire such knowledge (*Delalić et al. Trial Judgement,* para. 388).

6.2.131 A higher *mens rea* requirement was laid down by the ICTR held in the *Akayesu Trial Judgement*. In that Judgement, the Chamber held that the *mens rea* required for the command responsibility principle is malicious intent or negligence amounting to acquiescence:

> 488. There are varying views regarding the *Mens rea* required for command responsibility. According to one view it derives from a legal rule of strict liability, that is, the superior is criminally responsible for acts committed by his subordinate, without it being necessary to prove the criminal intent of the superior. Another view holds that negligence which is so serious as to be tantamount to consent or criminal intent, is a lesser requirement. Thus, the "Commentary on the Additional Protocols of 8 June 1977 to the Geneva Conventions of 12 August 1949" stated, in reference to Article 86 of the Additional Protocol I, and the *mens rea* requirement for command responsibility that:
>
>> ... the negligence must be so serious that it is tantamount to malicious intent, apart from any link between the conduct in question and the damage that took place. This element in criminal law is far from being clarified, but it is essential, since it is precisely on the question of intent that the system of penal sanctions in the Conventions is based.
>
> 489. The Chamber holds that it is necessary to recall that criminal intent is the moral element required for any crime and that, where the objective is to ascertain the individual criminal responsibility of a person Accused of crimes falling within the jurisdiction of the Chamber, such as genocide, crimes against humanity and violations of Article 3 Common to the Geneva Conventions and of Additional Protocol II thereto, it is certainly proper to ensure that there has been malicious intent, or, at least, ensure that negligence was so serious as to be tantamount to acquiescence or even malicious intent.

6.2.132 See 6.2.149, below on the differing *mens rea* requirements for military and civilian superiors pursuant to Article 28 of the Rome Statute of the International Criminal Court. See also the *Kayishema and Ruzindana Trial Judgement*, in which the Trial Chamber, following the Rome Statute, distinguished the *mens rea* requirement for military and civilian superiors. For military superiors, the *mens rea* requirement is "knew or should have known" while non-military superiors' *mens rea* is "knew or consciously disregarded information which clearly indicated or put him on notice" that subordinates had committed or were about to commit offences (paras 227–228). However, see also *Kronjelac Trial Judgement*, in which the Trial Chamber held that the knowledge requirement of commanders has been applied uniformly to both civilian and military commanders. The Trial Chamber was accordingly of the view that the same state of knowledge is required for both civilian and military commanders. (para 94).

6.2.133 In *Blaškić*, the defence requested the Trial Chamber to specify the *mens rea* requirement for command responsibility under Article 7(3) of the Statute prior to the commencement of the trial, so that the defence could make adequate preparations for his defence. In its Decision, the Trial Chamber replied:

> In the present case, the Defence has requested that Trial Chamber I rule on points of substantive law which are essential for determining the criminal liability of the accused.
>
> It is obvious that any question related to the guilt of the accused must be considered in hearings on the merits of the case and cannot be regarded as a pretrial matter. At this stage, the Trial Chamber, which has heard no evidence, is therefore not in a position to make a ruling.

6.2.134 This is not convincing. Since the accused was requesting clarification as to a legal definition which had nothing to do with evidentiary matters or with the specifics of his case, but with the law generally, it should not have been necessary for him to await the presentation of evidence in his trial before clarifying the matter. The presentation of evidence raises factual issues specific to that case, but it does not, or at least it should not, change the applicable legal rules and definitions, which remain the same for all cases.

6.2.135 The applicable law and definitions should in any event be made clear to the accused before the start of his trial—indeed before the crimes themselves are committed—in order to avoid offending the principle *nullum crimen sine lege* (the principle of legality). The Secretary-General said in his Report on the Tribunal's Statute that this principle, "requires that the international tribunal should apply rules of international humanitarian law which are beyond any doubt part of customary law" (para. 34) The *mens rea* for command responsibility is clearly one of those rules of international humanitarian law. If the rule is beyond any doubt part of customary law, it should be possible for the Chamber to enunciate it prior to the start of the trial, and thereby enable the accused to tailor his evidence to that rule. Moreover this helps to ensure that the parties do not waste time by presenting irrelevant evidence at trial, in ignorance of the applicable legal rules.

Element III: Failure to Take Necessary and Reasonable Measures

6.2.136 In the *Delalić et al. Trial Judgement*, the Chamber held that a legal duty exists upon superiors to take all necessary and reasonable measures to prevent the commission of offences, or, if crimes have been committed, to punish the perpetrators. What constitutes "necessary and reasonable measures" depends on the situation and cannot be formulated *in abstracto* (para. 394). A superior can only be required to take such measures as are within his powers; international law cannot oblige a superior to perform the impossible (para. 395).

6.2.137 In the *Aleksovski Trial Judgement*, the Chamber confirmed that the accused does not need to have the power to impose sanctions on the authors of the crime in order to incur responsibility pursuant to Article 7(3). It is sufficient that the superior has the power to transmit a report which could result in sanctions being imposed (para. 78). This seems rather unfair in the sense that practically anyone in any organisation has the "power" to submit a report or to send a memo to someone else in the hierarchy. Moreover, it completely side-steps the requirement that the superior exercise effective control over the subordinates committing crimes.

6.2.138 In *Blaškić, Decision on the Defence Motion to Strike Portions of the Amended Indictment Alleging "Failure to Punish" Liability,* 4 April 1997, the Defence applied to strike out parts of the indictment which alleged "failure to punish" liability under Article 7(3), on the grounds that the failure to punish subordinates who had committed crimes:

> a) would be an offence not found in customary international humanitarian law and conventional humanitarian law;
>
> b) does not in itself involve the criminal responsibility of a commanding officer;
>
> c) violates the rule *nullum crimen sine lege*; and accordingly
>
> d) is not an offence falling within the Tribunal's jurisdiction.

6.2.139 The Trial Chamber rejected these arguments, finding a sufficient basis for "failure to punish" liability in both conventional and customary international law.

6.2.140 The Chamber's Decision appeared to assume that the Security Council had the power to declare the state of customary law. In support of its holding that command responsibility was part of international customary law, the Chamber stated that "it would . . . be wholly unfounded for the Tribunal to now declare unconstitutional and invalid part of its jurisdiction which the Security Council, with the Secretary-General's assent, has asserted to be part of "existing international humanitarian law"" (para. 8). Since, however, neither the Security Council nor the Secretary-General are judicial organs equipped with law-making powers, it is eminently for the Tribunal, which *is* a judicial organ, to ascertain the law and to determine what is validly within its jurisdiction and what is not. As was established by the Appeals Chamber in the *Tadić Interlocutory Appeal on Jurisdiction Decision*, the Tribunal has competence to decide upon its own competence (known in English as *competence/competence*, in German as *Kompetenz/Kompetenz*, and in French as *compétence de la compétence*). Moreover, as the Chamber stated in the *Delalić et al. Trial Judgement:*

> 417. . . . the Security Council, not being a legislative body, cannot create offences. It therefore vests in the Tribunal the exercise of jurisdiction in respect of offences already recognised in international humanitarian law. The Statute does not create substantive law, but provides a forum and framework for the enforcement of existing international humanitarian law.

6.2.141 Thus the Trial Chamber has the power, and the duty, to determine whether what is asserted to be part of existing international humanitarian law—in this case the principle of command responsibility—really is so.

6.2.142 The same arguments raised by *Blaškić* defence counsel were subsequently raised by the defense of *Kordić* and *Čerkez*, but were rejected by the Trial Chamber in its *Decision On The Joint Defence Motion To Dismiss For Lack Of Jurisdiction Portions Of The Amended Indictment Alleging "Failure To Punish" Liability,* 2 March 1999.

Causation Not Required

6.2.143 In the *Delalić et al. Trial Judgement*, the Chamber rejected the notion that an element of command responsibility was *causation*, i.e., that the superior's omissions *caused* the subordinates' criminal acts in some way. This, the Chamber said, was not required as regards failure to prevent crimes (para. 398) and indeed could not be a requirement as regards failure to punish, as, in that case, the crimes had already been committed and so there could be no question of causation.

Relationship Between Paragraphs (1) and (3) of ICTY Article 7/ ICTR Article 6

6.2.144 The close relationship between Articles 6(1)/7(1) and Article 6(3)/7(3) means that in some cases there may be an overlap between an accused's responsibility pursuant to each limb.

Position of Command as Aiding and Abetting

6.2.145 In the *Furundžija Trial Judgement*, the Chamber held that "presence, when combined with authority, can constitute assistance in the form of moral support, that is, the *actus reu* of the offence." The person in a position of authority must be of a certain status for his mere presence at the commission of a crime to give rise to criminal responsibility (para. 209).

6.2.146 In the *Akayesu Trial Judgement*, the Chamber held (para. 692):

> the Accused, having had reason to know that sexual violence was occurring, aided and abetted the following acts of sexual violence, by allowing them to take place on or near the premises of the bureau communal and by facilitating the commission of such sexual violence through his words of encouragement in other acts of sexual violence which, by virtue of his authority, sent a clear signal of official tolerance for sexual violence, without which these acts would not have taken place. . . .

6.2.147 In the *Kordić and Čerkez Trial Judgement*, the Chamber stated (para. 371):

> Where the omissions of an accused in a position of superior authority contribute (for instance by encouraging the perpetrator) to the commission of a crime by a subordinate, the conduct of the superior may constitute a basis of liability under Article 7(1).

On this subject, see 6.2.58 *et seq.*, above.

Simultaneous Liability Pursuant to 6(1)/7(1) and 6(3)/7(3) for the Same Conduct

6.2.148 In the *Blaškić Trial Judgement*, the Trial Chamber stated that it would be "illogical to hold a commander criminally responsible for planning, instigating or ordering the commission of crimes and, at the same time, reproach him for not preventing or punishing them" (para. 337). In the *Kayishema and Ruzindana Trial Judgement*, it was held that responsibility pursuant to 6(1) and 6(3) are not mutually exclusive and that a finding under both limbs would be possible. However, the Trial Chamber stated that it would be unnecessary to consider whether an accused had tried to prevent crimes and irrelevant whether he tried to punish if he had ordered the crimes in question (para.

223). By contrast, in *Kordić and Čerkez*, it had been argued by the prosecution that an accused could be convicted cumulatively for responsibility under Articles 7(1) and 7(3) on the grounds that "any additional responsibility under Article 7(3) increases the responsibility of the accused attracting enhanced punishment" (para. 370). The accused Čerkez was found guilty for the same crimes pursuant to both Article 7(1) and 7(3). The question of cumulative conviction pursuant to 6(1)/7(1) and 6(3)/7(3) is yet to be considered by the Appeals Chamber. On "cumulative charging," see 8.3.1 *et seq.*

6.2.149

ICC
Article 28
Responsibility of Commanders and Other Superiors

In addition to other grounds of criminal responsibility under this Statute for crimes within the jurisdiction of the Court:

1. A military commander or person effectively acting as a military commander shall be criminally responsible for crimes within the jurisdiction of the Court committed by forces under his or her effective command and control, or effective authority and control as the case may be, as a result of his or her failure to exercise control properly over such forces, where:
   (a) That military commander or person either knew or, owing to the circumstances at the time, should have known that the forces were committing or about to commit such crimes; and
   (b) That military commander or person failed to take all necessary and reasonable measures within his or her power to prevent or repress their commission or to submit the matter to the competent authorities for investigation and prosecution.
2. With respect to superior and subordinate relationships not described in para. 1, a superior shall be criminally responsible for crimes within the jurisdiction of the Court committed by subordinates under his or her effective authority and control, as a result of his or her failure to exercise control properly over such subordinates, where:
   (a) The superior either knew, or consciously disregarded information which clearly indicated, that the subordinates were committing or about to commit such crimes;
   (b) The crimes concerned activities that were within the effective responsibility and control of the superior; and
   (c) The superior failed to take all necessary and reasonable measures within his or her power to prevent or repress their commission or to submit the matter to the competent authorities for investigation and prosecution.

6.2.150 Article 28 of the Rome Statute imposes similar liability upon commanders as ICTY Article 7 (3) and ICTR Article 6 (3). Article 28 deals with the responsibility of both military and civilian superiors respectively. During negotiations, some delegations, among them China, took the view that liability should not extend to civilian superiors, however, the majority view was that it should. However, the US delegation questioned whether civilian superiors would normally have the same degree of control as military commanders and whether they should therefore incur the same degree of liability. For example it was questioned whether civilian superiors would be in the same position to prevent or repress the commission of crimes by subordinates or to punish the perpetrators. In particular attention was given to whether superiors, and especially civilian superiors, would always be in a position to prosecute offences. Accordingly it was decided that submission of the crimes to the competent authorities for investigation and prosecution would suffice. Article 28 also imposes a different mental requirement on military and civilian superiors so as to reflect their different positions. A military superior is responsible for crimes that he "should have know" about, whereas a civilian superior is responsible if he "consciously disregarded information which clearly indicated" that subordinates were committing or about to commit a crime. A matter raised but not reflected in ICC Article 28 is the degree of responsibility, if any, of a superior with regard to crimes committed by subordinates before the superior took up their post.

6.2.151 The *Kayishema and Ruzindana Trial Judgement* also distinguished—as the Rome Statute does—between military and non-military superiors. For military superiors, the *mens rea* requirement is "knew or should have known." For non-military superiors, the *mens rea* requirement is "knew or consciously disregarded information which clearly indicated or put him on notice" that his subordinates had committed or were about to commit crimes (paras 227–228).

Articles:

Burnette, W., "Command Responsibility of Israeli Military Commanders for the Pogrom at Shatila and Sabra," 107 *Mil. L. Rev.* 71 (1985).

Crowe, C., "Command Responsibility in the Former Yugoslavia: The Chances of Successful Prosecution," 29 *U. Rich. L. Rev.* 191 (1994).

Eckhardt, W.G., "Command Responsibility: A Plea for a Workable Standard," 97 *Mil. L. Rev.* 1 (1982).

Green, Leslie, "Command Responsibility in International Humanitarian Law," 5 *Transnational Law and Contemporary Problems* 320 (1995).

Howard, K., "Command Responsibility for War Crimes," 21 *J. Pub. L.* 7 (1972).

Parks, W., "Command Responsibility for War Crimes," 62 *Mil. L. Rev.* 1 (1973).

Fenrick, W.J., "Some International Law Problems Related to Prosecution Before the International Criminal Tribunal for the Former Yugoslavia," 6 (1) *Duke Journal of Comparative and International Law*, (1995).

Sarooshi, D., "Command Responsibility and the Blaskic Case," 50 *ICLQ* 452.

Smidt, M., "Yamashita, Medina and Beyond: Command Responsibility in Contemporary Military Operations," 164 *Mil. L. Rev.* 155.

Solf, W., "A Response to Telford Taylor's Nuremburg and Vietnam: An American Tragedy," 5 *Akron L. Rev.* 43 (1972).

Superior Orders

6.2.152 ICTY Article 7(4) and ICTR Article 6(4) state categorically that "The fact that an accused person acted pursuant to an order of a Government or of a superior shall not relieve him of criminal responsibility. . . ." In other words, superior orders is not a defence to a charge of war crimes, crimes against humanity or genocide. This is commonly considered one of the legacies of the Nuermberg trials.

6.2.153 The position was, not, however, so clear when the proposed Statute was debated at the United Nations Security Council. Regarding the defence of superior orders, Mrs. Albright, then Permanent Representative of the United States to the United Nations, commented in the Security Council after the adoption of resolution 827, establishing the ICTY:

> It is, of course, a defence that the accused was acting pursuant to orders where he or she did not know the orders were unlawful and a person of ordinary sense and understanding would not have known the orders to be unlawful (UN Doc. S/PV.3217, at 15 (25 May,1993))

6.2.154 This assertion stands in stark contrast to the widespread assertion that "superior orders are no defence." Nevertheless it appears to be a correct statement of the position under international law and under most national laws (see, e.g., prosecutions by the United States of its military personnel in Vietnam applying this standard, e.g. *U.S. v. Keenan*, 39 CMR 108 (1969) and *U.S. v. Walter Griffen 39 CMR 293*. See also Gary Solis, *Marines and Military Law in Vietnam* (1989) and *Son Thang: An American War Crime* (1997)). It is only in respect of orders that are "manifestly illegal," not illegal *simpliciter*, that the defence of superior orders is unavailable.

6.2.155 Indeed, this qualified approach is the one adopted in the Rome Statute for an International Criminal Court:

6.2.156

ICC
Article 33
Superior Orders and Prescription of Law

1. The fact that a crime within the jurisdiction of the Court has been committed by a person pursuant to an order of a Government or of a superior, whether military or civilian, shall not relieve that person of criminal responsibility unless:

    (a) The person was under a legal obligation to obey orders of the Government or the superior in question;

    (b) The person did not know that the order was unlawful; and

    (c) The order was not manifestly unlawful.

2. For the purposes of this article, orders to commit genocide or crimes against humanity are manifestly unlawful.

6.2.157 This formulation, somewhat awkwardly, lays down a rule of law whereby the defence of superior orders can *never* be a defence to charges of genocide and crimes against humanity. It may, however, be a defence to charges of war crimes provided the above-enumerated conditions are met.

Superior Orders as a Factor to Be Considered in Mitigation of Punishment

6.2.158 In the *Erdemović Sentencing Judgement*, the Chamber took superior orders (in a context in which the defence of superior orders was very closely, if not, inextricably, linked with the defence of *duress*) into account in mitigation of the accused's punishment. See Commentary to ICTY Article 24, 9.1 *et seq.*, below.

SECTION 3: DEFENCES

Introduction

6.3.1 Unlike the Rome Statute for the ICC (see, in particular, Article 31 ("Grounds for excluding criminal responsibility"), and Articles 32 and 33, 6.3.64 below), the ICTY and ICTR Statutes do not explicitly set out what constitute defences to violations of international humanitarian law, although Rule 67(A)(ii) of the Rules of Procedure and Evidence does mention alibi and diminished responsibility in the context of disclosure obligations on the defence.

6.3.2 The Report of the Secretary General, submitted pursuant to paragraph 2 of Security Council Resolution 808, in relation to superior orders, states that ". . . the International Tribunal may consider the factor of superior orders in connection with *other defences such as coercion or lack of moral choice*" (para. 57, emphasis added), suggesting that "coercion" and "lack of moral choice" may be complete defences which, if proved, would entitle the accused to an acquittal.

6.3.3 The Secretary General's Report goes on to state that: "The International Tribunal itself will have to decide on various personal defences which may relieve a person of individual criminal responsibility, such as minimum age or mental incapacity, drawing upon general principles of law recognised by all nations" (para. 58).

Burden of Proof on Defences

6.3.4 Generally, it is for the Accused to raise the issue of a defence rather than being for the Prosecution to prove, much less beyond a reasonable doubt, that no possible defence applies (except where in proving the elements of the crimes beyond a reasonable doubt, the Prosecution has necessarily proved the absence of the defence in question). However, having raised a defence, the accused is usually not obliged to prove beyond a reasonable doubt that the defence applies; rather, once the accused has discharged the evidentiary burden—that is, the burden of proving that the defence *might* apply—the burden shifts back to the prosecution to prove beyond a reasonable doubt that the defence does *not* apply. On another view, having raised the defence, the accused has the persuasive burden of proving, usually on a balance of probabilities, that the defence applies.

6.3.5 This latter view seems to be the one adopted at the ICTY. See *Order on Esad Landžo's Submission regarding diminished or lack of mental capacity* issued in *Delalić et al.* on 18 June 1998:

> CONSIDERING that the burden of proving guilt beyond reasonable doubt lies on the Office of the Prosecutor;
>
> NOTING that, pursuant to Sub-rule 67(A)(ii)(a), the special defence of diminished or lack of mental responsibility is a plea offered by the Defence;
>
> FOR THE FOREGOING REASONS, PURSUANT TO RULES 54 and 67;
>
> HEREBY DECIDES that the Defence offering a special defence of diminished or lack of mental responsibility carries the burden of proving this defence on the balance of probabilities.

6.3.6 The Chamber did not define the special defence of diminished or lack of mental capacity, but reserved the matter to final judgement (see the *Delalić et al. Trial Judgement*). See also *Order on Landžo's Request for Definition of diminished or lack of mental capacity* issued on 15 July 1998 to the same effect (definition reserved to final judgement).

6.3.7 Concerning the moment to submit defences, the Appeals Chamber in the *Aleksovski Appeals Judgement* held:

> 51. In general, accused before this Tribunal have to raise all possible defences, where necessary in the alternative, during the trial, and where so required under the Rules of Procedure and Evidence of the International Tribunal ("Rules"), before trial. It follows that accused, generally, cannot raise a defence for the first time on appeal.

6.3.8 It is important to note, however, that at the ICC, there are no "shifting burdens of proof." See Article 67(1)(i) of the Rome Statute, which stipulates that the accused has the right, *inter alia*, "not to have imposed on him or her any reversal of the burden of proof or any onus of rebuttal." This provision—which is a novel supplement to the usual fair trial rights listed, e.g. in Article 14 of the ICCPR, Article 6 of the ECHR, ICTY Article 21 and ICTR Article 20, although the notion arguably arises from the presumption of innocence guaranteed in these articles—has the potential to be of great importance to the defence at the ICC.

Alibi

6.3.9 Alibi is not strictly a defence, but rather a special form of denial by the accused that he is the perpetrator of the crimes in question, as the Appeals Chamber recognised in the *Delalic et al. Appeals Judgement:*

> 581. It is a common misuse of the word to describe an alibi as a "defence." If a defendant raises an alibi, he is merely denying that he was in a position to commit the crime with which he is charged. That is not a *defence* in its true sense at all. By raising that issue, the defendant does no more than require the Prosecution to eliminate the reasonable possibility that the alibi is true.

6.3.10 This was re-affirmed in the *Kayishema and Ruzindana Appeals Judgement* (para. 103).

6.3.11 Thus the implication which arises for most defences, namely that the burden of proof shifts onto the accused, does not apply to alibi. Once the accused raises an alibi, the burden of proof on all elements remains on the Prosecutor and the accused is only required to fulfil the specific requirements set out in Rule 67(A)(ii) of the Rules of Procedure and Evidence.

6.3.12 On this point, see the *Kayishema and Ruzindana Trial Judgement:*

> 234. In the instant case, the Trial Chamber holds that the burden of proof rests upon the Prosecution to prove its case beyond a reasonable doubt in all aspects notwithstanding that the Defence raised alibi. After all, the accused is presumed innocent until the Prosecution has proved his guilt under Article 20(3) of the Statute.

6.3.13 The Appeals Chamber upheld this decision in the *Kayishema and Ruzindana Appeals Judgement* (para. 110). The Chamber held that Rule 67(A)(ii) does not place any burden of proof on the defence since it merely requires the defence to notify the prosecution of certain information, not to prove the relevant facts.

6.3.14 The Appeals Chamber itself underlined that these findings were confirmed in the *Foča Trial Judgement*. See para. 625 of the *Foča Trial Judgement*:

> The Prosecution bore the onus of establishing the facts alleged in the Indictment. Having raised the issue of alibi, the accused bore no onus of establishing that alibi. It was for the Prosecution to establish that, despite the evidence of the alibi, the facts alleged in the Indictment were nevertheless true.

6.3.15 Accordingly, even if the procedural requirements of Rule 67(A)(ii)(a)—notification by the accused of his intention to raise alibi—are not met, this cannot prevent the accused from raising the defence, for by doing so the accused is effectively merely asserting his innocence, which the Chamber will have to examine in any event. Thus Rule 67(B) states that "the failure of the defence to provide notice shall not limit the right of the accused to testify on the above defences." This was confirmed in the *Rutaganda Trial Judgement* (para. 139).

6.3.16 However, the failure to provide notification may be taken into account as regards the credibility of the defence. See the *Musema Trial Judgement*, para. 107.

Diminished Responsibility and Lack of Mental Capacity

6.3.17 Rule 67(A)(ii) of the Rules of Procedure and Evidence refers to diminished responsibility, setting out a requirement that the defence give notice of its intent to raise the defence.

> (ii) The defence shall notify the Prosecutor of its intent to offer: . . . (b) any special defence, including that of diminished or lack of mental responsibility; in which case the notification shall specify the names and addresses of witnesses and any other evidence upon which the accused intends to rely to establish the special defence.

6.3.18 In the *Delalić et al. Trial Judgement*, the Trial Chamber distinguished between the plea of diminished mental responsibility and the plea of insanity (lack of mental responsibility).

> 1156. . . . A plea of diminished responsibility is to be distinguished from a plea of insanity which, in this case, was expressly disavowed by the Defence for Mr. Landžo. It should be noted, however, that both pleas are founded on an abnormality of mind. In the case of the plea of insanity, the accused is, at the time of commission of the criminal act, unaware of what he is doing or incapable of forming a rational judgement as to whether such an act is right or wrong. By contrast, the plea of diminished responsibility is based on the premise that, despite recognising the wrongful nature of his actions, the accused, on account of his abnormality of mind, is unable to control his actions.

6.3.19 Landžo argued that Rule 67(a)(ii) made diminished mental responsibility a complete defence to any charge. This argument was accepted by the Trial Chamber, which considered that Rule 67 should not be interpreted restrictively.

> 1157. ... The special defences referred to in sub-Rule 67(A)(ii)(b) may be construed *ejusdem generis* to be limited to special defences of the category relating to lack of mental capacity. If thus construed, mental incapacity resulting from insanity and partial delusion will be included. However, since the Rule is expressed as requiring a special defence without qualification or limitation, the expression cannot be so limited. It should be construed to include any special defence relied upon by the accused. The expression "includes" used in an enactment is one of enlargement and cannot be construed restrictively to deprive the accused of any special defence properly available.
>
> 1158. In this instance, the most favourable meaning for the accused that can be read into sub-Rule 67(A)(ii)(b) is that a special defence is one apart from the general defence open to accused persons and is peculiar to the accused in the circumstances of a given case.

6.3.20 The Trial Chamber concluded that:

> 1164. Sub-Rule 67(A)(ii)(b) would indeed appear to suggest a complete defence since the words are without qualification or limitation.

6.3.21 A "complete defence" would be one which, if made out, would entitle the accused to a complete acquittal rather than a reduction of sentence or re-classification of the offence charged (for example, in English law, diminished responsibility only reduces a charge of murder to manslaughter).

6.3.22 To reach the definition of diminished responsibility eventually employed by the Trial Chamber, it had resort to national laws, notably Section 2 of the English Homicide Act 1957, which allows the defence when:

> 1162. [the accused] was suffering from such abnormality of mind (whether arising from a condition of arrested or related development of mind or any inherent causes or induced by disease or injury) as substantially impaired his mental responsibility for his acts and omissions in doing or being a party to the killing.

6.3.23 Although the Trial Chamber did not explicitly so state, therefore, it seems that the essential element of diminished responsibility is *loss of self-control* by the accused, presumably for reasons for which the accused is not himself to blame, i.e. organic disease or inherent causes, rather than self-induced frenzy or loss of temper.

> 1166. Thus, the accused must be suffering from an abnormality of mind which has substantially impaired his mental responsibility for his acts or omissions. The abnormality of mind must have arisen from a condition of arrested or retarded development of the mind, or inherent causes induced by disease or injury.

6.3.24 In Landžo's case, however, the Trial Chamber rejected the plea of diminished responsibility on the grounds that the accused suffered from a personality disorder but that he "*was quite capable of controlling his actions*" at the relevant time (para. 1186).

General Principles of Criminal Law • 449

6.3.25 Until the contrary was proven, there was a presumption of sanity (para. 1157). The burden of proof was, therefore, on the defendant "to rebut the presumption of sanity" (para. 1158), including where he wished to adduce the partial defence of diminished responsibility (para. 1172). Landžo had failed to rebut this presumption.

6.3.26 The Trial Chamber noted that the accused had requested that the definition of diminished responsibility be settled *before* trial, so that he could present his case accordingly (para. 1159). The Chamber considered, however, that since the accused raised the defence, it was for him to present it within the parameters he deemed appropriate:

> 1160. . . . The Trial Chamber is convinced that the evidence to support a special defence involves matters peculiarly within the knowledge of the accused and is thus a matter which the Trial Chamber cannot know until the evidence is adduced. The Trial Chamber has provided the accused with the necessary guidance for the defence it relies upon, namely, the nature of the burden and the required standard of proof.

6.3.27 This raises the question whether the principle of legality applies equally to *defences* as it does to *offences*. If it does, then defences need to be clearly defined in law prior to an accused being charged so that he is on notice as to what sort of behaviour would acquit him. At the same time, it has to be admitted that the potential injustice is mitigated when it is the defence rather than the offence which is poorly, or not at all, defined at the time of the commission of the offence. Moreover, if an accused is permitted to raise novel arguments which, he says, entitles him to an acquittal, then it is impossible to require the law, or the judges, to anticipate and define the elements of all these myriad, possible defences in advance. This latter was in effect the reasoning of the *Delalić* Trial Chamber.

6.3.28 The plea of limited physical capacity raised by Landžo was also rejected in the *Delalić Trial Judgement* on the grounds that, while the accused *did* have some physical problems, he admitted to having killed and beaten detainees, and was thus clearly physically capable of doing so (para. 1187).

6.3.29 The Appeals Chamber upheld these findings in the *Delalić et al. Appeals Judgement*. It found no error by the Trial Chamber for not having defined the elements of "diminished responsibility" before the trial began.

6.3.30 Nevertheless, the Appeals Chamber denied that diminished responsibility constituted a defence in international law by reason of Rule 67(A)(ii), as the Trial Chamber had held.

6.3.31 First, there was no reference to the defence in the ICTY Statute and the Judges could not create new defences.

> 583. . . . there is no reference to any defence of diminished mental responsibility in the Tribunal's Statute. The description of diminished mental responsibility as a "special defence" in Rule 67(A)(ii) is insufficient to constitute it as such. The rule-making powers of the judges are defined by Article 15 of the Tribunal's Statute, which gives power to the judges to adopt only—. . . *rules of procedure and evidence* for the conduct of the pre-trial phase of the proceedings, trials and appeals, the admission of evidence, the protection of victims and witnesses and other appropriate matters. The Appeals Chamber has held that this

power does not permit rules to be adopted which constitute new *offences*, but only *rules of procedure and evidence* for the conduct of matters falling within the jurisdiction of the Tribunal. It follows that there is, therefore, no power to adopt rules which constitute new *defences*.

6.3.32 It does not in fact follow, however, that the absence of a power to *incriminate* necessarily implies the absence of a power to *exonerate*. The former has its basis in *nullum crimen* concerns and the rights of the accused. No such factors militate against the recognition of defences which were not incorporated in the Statute, not least since the Statute does not refer to *any* defences and since the Secretary-General in his Report, and the Security Council, expressly conferred this power on the (Judges of the) Tribunal (see paras. 57 and 58 of the Secretary-General's Report, referred to above at 6.3.2 and 6.3.3). Finally, the Tribunal may—indeed must—apply those defences which exist as a matter of international customary law. Recognising a defence that is not explicitly referred to in the Statute does not necessarily amount to recognising a "new" defence; it may be merely a question of recognising, or codifying, an existing defence under international humanitarian law.

6.3.33 The Appeals Chamber did, however, go on to address this point. As a second ground, the Appeals Chamber held that a special defence of diminished responsibility cannot be found in the usual sources of international law (customary or conventional law), nor in the general principles of law recognised by all nations. Concerning the English *Homicide Act* 1957, an abnormality of mind is a partial defence, not a complete defence, to a charge of murder.

> 588. in many other countries where the defendant's total mental incapacity to control his actions or to understand that they are wrong constitutes a complete defence, his diminished mental responsibility does not constitute either a partial or a complete defence, but it is relevant in mitigation of sentence.

6.3.34 The Appeals Chamber's conclusion was that the issue of diminished responsibility was relevant to the sentence imposed on an accused as a mitigating circumstance, but not to the question of his guilt or innocence.

> 590. The Appeals Chamber accepts that the relevant general principle of law upon which, in effect, both the common law and the civil law systems have acted is that the defendant's diminished mental responsibility is relevant to the sentence to be imposed and is not a defence leading to an acquittal in the true sense. This is the appropriate general legal principle representing the international law to be applied in the Tribunal. Rule 67(A)(ii)(b) must therefore be interpreted as referring to diminished mental responsibility where it is to be raised by the defendant as a matter in mitigation of sentence. As a defendant bears the onus of establishing matters in mitigation of sentence, where he relies upon diminished mental responsibility in mitigation, he must establish that condition on the balance of probabilities—that more probably than not such a condition existed at the relevant time.

6.3.35 See also the *Todorović Trial Judgement*, where the defence gave notice of its intent to raise diminished responsibility *"in mitigation of sentence only"* (para. 93).

6.3.36 If the accused proves *lack* of mental capacity, he may be acquitted, as the Appeals Chamber stated, referring to *M'Naghten's Case* (1843) 10 Cl & Fin 200, in the *Delalić et al. Appeals Judgement*:

> 582. On the other hand, if the defendant raises the issue of *lack* of mental capacity, he is challenging the presumption of sanity by a plea of insanity. That is a defence in the true sense, in that the defendant bears the onus of establishing it—that, more probably than not, at the time of the offence he was labouring under such a defect of reason, from disease of the mind, as not to know the nature and quality of his act or, if he did know it, that he did not know that what he was doing was wrong. Such a plea, if successful, is a complete defence to a charge and it leads to an acquittal.

6.3.37 The Appeals Chamber considered this issue was confirmed in the Rome Statute of the ICC.

> 587. The ICC Statute provides that a defendant shall not be criminally responsible if, at the relevant time, he or she—
>
>> suffers from a mental disease or defect that destroys that person's capacity to appreciate the unlawfulness or nature of his or her conduct, or capacity to control his or her conduct to conform to the requirements of law.
>
> This is not the same as any partial defence of diminished mental responsibility, as it requires the *destruction* of (and not merely the *impairment* to) the defendant's capacity, and it leads to an acquittal. It is akin to the defence of insanity. There is no express provision in the ICC Statute which is concerned with the consequences of an impairment to such a capacity.

Duress

6.3.38 The question of duress arose in *Erdemović*, in tandem with that of superior orders. The two points must be clearly distinguished. See the *Erdemović Sentencing Judgement*:

> 5. The defence of obedience to superior orders has been addressed expressly in Article 7(4) of the Statute. This defence does not relieve the accused of criminal responsibility....
>
> 16. In respect of the physical and moral duress accompanied by the order from a military superior (sometimes referred to as "extreme necessity"), which has been argued in this case, the Statute provides no guidance.

6.3.39 The Trial Chamber concluded that duress may afford a complete defence, although it found that the defence did not apply in the present case.

> 14. ... Depending on the probative value and force which may be given to them [i.e. orders of military superior and duress], they may also be regarded as a defence for the criminal conduct which might go so far as to eliminate the mens rea of the offence and therefore the offence itself.
>
> ...
>
> 20. On the basis of the case-by-case approach and in light of all the elements before it, the Trial Chamber is of the view that proof of the specific circumstances which would fully exonerate the accused of his responsibility has not been provided. Thus, the defence of duress accompanying the superior order

will, as the Secretary-General seems to suggest in his report, be taken into account at the same time as other factors in the consideration of mitigating circumstances.

...

91. [. . .] as regards the acts in which the accused is personally implicated and which, if sufficiently proved, would constitute grounds for granting mitigating circumstances, the Defence has produced no testimony, evaluation or any other elements to corroborate what the accused has said. For this reason, the Judges deem that they are unable to accept the plea of extreme necessity.

6.3.40 For a criticism of this ruling, see 8.5.261 *et seq.* The question of duress was in any event reconsidered before the Appeals Chamber. After the filing of the parties' briefs, the Appeals Chamber, *proprio motu*, in a *Scheduling Order* issued on 5 May 1997, set a hearing on "three preliminary questions" which was held on 26 May 1997. In the Order, the parties were instructed to submit written briefs on, *inter alia*, whether:

(1) In law, may duress afford a complete defence to a charge of crimes against humanity and/or war crimes such that, if the defence is proved at trial, the accused is entitled to an acquittal?

6.3.41 The Appeals Chamber pronounced on the matter in its *Erdemović Appeals Judgement*. The majority (Judges Li, McDonald and Vohrah) held that duress could *not* afford a complete defence to a charge of crimes against humanity or war crimes *where the underlying offence involved the killing of an innocent human being.* Judge Li too attached a separate opinion. The majority judges all agreed that no international rule (either conventional or customary) nor general principle of law (based on national law and practice), could be found in order to excuse an unlawful killing on the grounds that the killing was committed under duress. As a consequence, the Appellant's plea of guilty—in which he invoked duress while pleading guilty—was therefore not equivocal (i.e., the accused did not at one and the same time raise a *bona fide* defence to the charge while pleading guilty to it).

6.3.42 Judge Cassese and Judge Stephen dissented on these points in two separate opinions. Judge Cassese contended, on the basis of a copious survey of international case-law, that no *special* rule excluding duress as a defence in case of *murder* had evolved in international criminal law. In the absence of such a special rule, it was necessary to apply the general rule, which recognised duress as a defence *without specification as to the crimes to which it applied and those to which it did not apply.* Consequently, and subject to strict requirements enumerated in his dissent, Judge Cassese held that duress could be admitted as a complete defence even to the crime of killing innocent persons, it being of course a question of fact in each case whether the defence applied in the circumstances.

6.3.43 The four requirements, set out in para. 16 of Judge Cassese's dissent, were:

(i) The act charged was done under an immediate threat of severe and irreparable harm to life or limb;

(ii) There was no adequate means of averting such evil;

(iii) The crime committed was not disproportionate to the evil threatened (it would, for example, be disproportionate to kill an innocent in order to avoid being beaten by a third party);

(iv) The situation creating the duress must not have been voluntarily brought about by the person coerced (e.g. by joining a criminal organization where it was foreseeable that one might at some stage be forced to commit criminal deeds).

6.3.44 Dissenting on this point from the majority, Judge Cassese held that:

> 12. ... For offences involving killing, it is true, however, that one of the requirements (discussed at paragraph 42 below)—proportionality—would usually not be fulfilled. Nevertheless, in exceptional circumstances this requirement might be met, for example, when the killing would be in any case perpetrated by persons other than the one acting under duress (since then it is not a question of saving your own life by killing another person, but of simply saving your own life when the other person will inevitably die, which may not be 'disproportionate' as a remedy).

6.3.45 Judge Stephen agreed with Judge Cassese that duress might in principle be urged as a defence even to unlawful killing. He held that no rule of customary international law either expressly allowed or expressly forbade duress as a defence to unlawful killing. In the absence of guidance from international custom, it was necessary to turn to the general principles of law recognised by civilised nations. Most legal systems recognised duress as a general defence, with no exception for homicide. Anglo-American common law, however, did expressly exclude duress as a defence to homicide, while allowing it for other crimes. However, Judge Stephen found that this exception was not based on any satisfying or reasoned principle. At its heart was the notion to be found in the old English authorities (principally Hale and Blackstone) that one should not balance one life against another or, alternatively, that is "better to die oneself, than to kill an innocent." The situation in which the Appellant allegedly found himself, however, where the victims would die irrespective of whether he lived or died, was not answered by this rationale nor otherwise addressed by the Anglo-American authorities. The proportionality of duress, which is the most controversial and inscrutable requirement when the crime at issue is homicide, is satisfied in "the case of an accused, forced to take lives which he cannot save and who can only add to the toll by the sacrifice of his own life" (para. 67, Judge Stephen's dissent).

6.3.46 In these circumstances, Judge Stephen argued, general principles of law favoured the recognition of duress as a general defence. Thus even where an innocent were killed, the accused should in principle be allowed to raise the defence. Having raised the defence, it would, of course, be up to the trier of fact to decide whether the defence succeeded on the particular facts of the case:

> 65. ... I am ... alive to the concerns expressed by other members of this Appeals Chamber of the need to protect innocent life in conflicts such as that in the former Yugoslavia which involve so great a threat to innocent life. However, to my mind, that aim is not achieved by the denial of a just defence to one who is in no position to effect by his own will the protection of innocent life.
>
> 67. The stringent conditions always surrounding that defence will have to be met, including the requirement that the harm done is not disproportionate to the harm threatened. The case of an accused, forced to take lives which he cannot save and who can only add to the toll by the sacrifice of his own life, is entirely consistent with that requirement.

6.3.47 Despite its finding that Erdemović's plea was not equivocal, the Appeals Chamber majority nonetheless held that the Appellant's plea had not been "informed," since he had not received adequate explanation as to the difference between crimes against humanity and war crimes, nor of the implications of pleading guilty to crimes against humanity. Hence the matter was remanded to a new Trial Chamber for entry of an informed plea.

6.3.48 The new Trial Chamber, in the *Erdemović Sentencing Judgement II*, applied the ruling of the Appeals Chamber majority that:

> duress does not afford a complete defence to a soldier charged with a crime against humanity and/or a war crime involving the killing of innocent human beings . . . and may be taken into account only by way of mitigation.

6.3.49 Duress was accordingly taken into account in mitigation, with other factors. Moreover *Erdemović* was permitted to change his guilty plea from crimes against humanity to war crimes. His sentence was reduced from 10 years' imprisonment to 5 years.

6.3.50 The main conclusion raised by the majority on the Appeals Chamber in *Erdemović* was confirmed in the *Krstić Trial Judgement*:

> 714. The jurisprudence of the Tribunal established that, while duress cannot afford a "complete defence to a soldier charged with crimes against humanity or war crimes in international law involving the taking of innocent lives," it may be taken into account as a mitigating circumstance.

6.3.51 See also the *Jelisić Appeals Judgement* and the *Todorović Trial Judgement*.

6.3.52 In *Aleksovski*, the appellant argued before the Appeals Chamber that duress must be distinguished from extreme necessity. It was submitted that the criminal law concept of extreme necessity had to be applied to the facts and that it excuses the perpetrator's unlawful actions since such actions are motivated by the intent to avoid a worse violation (see paras. 40–44). The Appellant further submitted that the concept of extreme necessity (*exceptio casu necessitatis*) is familiar to civil law and that in civil law procedure the court is authorised to apply the concept of its own motion in accordance with the principle *iura novit curia*. A provision similar to extreme necessity is found in Article 31(1)(d) of the ICC Statute (see 6.6.64 below). The appellant argued that this concept, although absent from the ICTY Statute, should be applied as a general principle of law derived from national legal systems, as provided for in Article 21(1)(c) of the ICC Statute.

6.3.53 The Appeals Chamber, in the *Aleksovski Appeals Judgement*, refused to decide this point, on the technical ground that the argument had not been raised before the Trial Chamber (para. 51). In any event, the Appeals Chamber held that the ground of appeal was entirely misplaced (see paras. 53–54) and accordingly it was "unnecessary to dwell on whether necessity constitutes a defence under international law."

Articles:

Swaak-Goldman, Olivia, "International Decisions: Prosecutor v. Erdemović," 92 (2) *American Journal of International Law*. (April 1998).

Oellers-Frahm, Karin and Specht,Britta, *Die Erdemovic-Rechsprechung des Jugoslawien-tribunals: Probleme bei der Entwicklung eines internationalen Strafrechts, dargestellt am Beispiel des Notstands* (*The Erdemovic Case before the International Criminal Tribunal for the former Yugoslavia: Problems concerning the Development of International Criminal Law, with particular emphasis on Duress*).

Cavicchioli, Lucia, "Il Costringimento Psichico come causa di esclusione dell colpevolezza nei crimini contro l'umanità: il caso *Erdemović*," LXXX *Rivista di Diritto Internazionale* 2 (1997).

Yee, Sienho, "The *Erdemović* Sentencing Judgement: A Questionable Milestone for the International Criminal Tribunal for the former Yugoslavia," 2 (2) *Georgia Journal of International and Comparative Law* (1997).

Cross-References: ICTY Articles 7(4) and 24(2), ICTR Articles 6(3) and 23(2), Rule 62 and Rule 62 *bis* of the ICTY/ICTR Rules of Procedure and Evidence; Article 31(1)(d) of the Rome Statute for an ICC.

No Defence of *Tu Quoque*

6.3.54 The defence of *tu quoque*, i.e., that the other Party has committed similar atrocities, was rejected as a defence at Nuremberg. It is also not a defence at the ICTY, where it has been implicitly raised. See the Trial Chamber's *Decision On Defence Motion to Summon Witness, Kupreškić et al.*, 3 February 1999:

> Defence counsel has so far not persuasively proved the relevance to the issue of innocence or guilt of the accused of the alleged commission by Bosniaks (Bosnian Muslims), or forces of the Bosnian army, of large-scale crimes against Croats in Bosnia and Herzegovina. In this connection the Chamber reiterates what it indicated to all defence counsel at the hearing of 11 January 1999, namely that the *tu quoque* principle does not apply to international humanitarian law. This body of law does not lay down synallagmatic obligations, i.e obligations based on reciprocity, but obligations *erga omnes* (or, in the case of treaty obligations, obligations *erga omnes contractantes*) which are designed to safeguard fundamental human values and therefore must be complied with regardless of the conduct of the other party or parties.

6.3.55 The Chamber reiterated this point in its *Decision on Evidence of the Good Character of the Accused and the Defence of Tu Quoque* of 17 February 1999 and in the *Kupreškić et al. Trial Judgement* (paras 515–520 and 765). In the latter, the Chamber pointed out that, "although *tu quoque* was raised as a defence in war crimes trials following the Second World War, it was universally rejected . . . there is in fact no support either in State practice or in the opinions of publicists for the validity of such a defence" (para. 516). The Chamber held that the *tu quoque* argument was "flawed in principle" because "it envisages humanitarian law as based upon a narrow bilateral exchange of rights and obligations," whereas in fact humanitarian law "lays down absolute obligations, namely obligations that are unconditional or in other words not based on reciprocity" (para. 517). Moreover, "most norms of international humanitarian law, in particular those prohibiting war crimes, crimes against humanity and genocide, are also peremptory norms of international law or *jus cogens*, i.e. of a non-derogable and overriding character" (para. 520); therefore these norms cannot be breached on the grounds that the other party is breaching them.

6.3.56 In the *Kordić and Čerkez Trial Judgement* (para 520), the Trial Chamber found that persecution of Muslims took place in several central Bosnian municipalities taken over by the HVO and clearly stated that "the fact that there may have been persecution of Croats by Muslims in other municipalities does not detract from this finding and in no way justifies the HVO persecution."

6.3.57 Notwithstanding the invalidity of the principle of *tu quoque* as a defence, Trial Chambers have recognised that under certain conditions, evidence related to crimes allegedly committed by other parties to the conflict may be admissible. The Trial Chamber in *Kupreškić* held that "evidence of events occurring in villages other than Ahmići may be admissibile in so far as it tends to disprove allegations made by the Prosecution that Bosnian Muslims were subjected to persecution by the Bosnian Croats, or to disprove any other material averments by the Prosecution." (See *Kupreškić, Decision on Evidence of the Good Character of the Accused and the Defence of Tu Quoque*, 17 February 1999). It may also be relevant to the notion of reprisals (see next heading).

Reprisals

6.3.58 The issue of reprisals was considered in the *Martić Rule 61 Decision*. The question was raised: "does the fact that the attack was carried out as a reprisal reverse the illegality of the attack?" The Chamber excluded such a possibility as regards attacks on civilians. The "great majority of legal authorities" supported the conclusion "that no circumstances would legitimise an attack against civilians even if it were a response proportionate to a similar violation perpetrated by the other party" (para. 15).

6.3.59 The Chamber ruling in the *Kupreškić Trial Judgement* noted that reprisals against civilians are designed to ensure compliance with international humanitarian law. It held, however, that developments in international human rights law have rendered the practice obsolete, particularly since compliance could now be ensured by prosecuting violations of international humanitarian law:

> 528. ... reprisals against civilians are inherently a barbarous means of seeking compliance with international law ... they may not only be arbitrary but are also not directed specifically at the individual authors of the initial violation. Reprisals typically are taken in situations where the individuals personally responsible for the breach are either unknown or out of reach. These retaliatory measures are aimed instead at other more vulnerable individuals or groups. ...
>
> 529. In addition, the reprisal killing of innocent persons ... can safely be characterized as a blatant infringement of the most fundamental principles of human rights ... a slow but profound transformation of humanitarian law under the pervasive influence of human rights has occurred. As a result belligerent reprisals against civilians and fundamental rights of human beings are absolutely inconsistent legal concepts. ...
>
> 530. ... while reprisals could have had a modicum of justification in the past, when they constituted practically the only effective means of compelling the enemy to abandon unlawful acts of warfare and to comply in future with inter-

national law, at present they can no longer be justified in this manner. A means of inducing compliance with international law is at present more widely available and, more importantly, is beginning to prove fairly efficacious: the prosecution and punishment of war crimes and crimes against humanity by national or international courts. This means serves the purpose of bringing to justice those who are responsible for any such crime, as well as, albeit to a limited extent, the purpose of deterring at least the most blatant violations of international humanitarian law.

6.3.60 The Chamber did not, however, conclude that reprisals were ruled out altogether under international customary law:

> 535. ... at any rate, even when considered lawful, reprisals are restricted by: (a) the principle whereby they must be a last resort in attempts to impose compliance by the adversary with legal standards (which entails, amongst other things, that they may be exercised only after a prior warning has been given which has failed to bring about the discontinuance of the adversary's crimes); (b) the obligation to take special precautions before implementing them (they may be taken only after a decision to this effect has been made at the highest political or military level; in other words they may not be decided by local commanders); (c) the principle of proportionality (which entails not only that the reprisals must not be excessive compared to the precedent unlawful act of warfare, but also that they must stop as soon as that unlawful act has been discontinued) and; (d) 'elementary considerations of humanity' (as mentioned above).

6.3.61 The issue was, in any event, moot since the applicable law on the territory of the former Yugoslavia outlawed reprisals. As the Chamber went on to say in the *Kupreškić Trial Judgement:*

> 536. Finally, it must be noted, with specific regard to the case at issue, that whatever the content of the customary rules on reprisals, the treaty provisions prohibiting them were in any event applicable in the case in dispute. In 1993, both Croatia and Bosnia and Herzegovina had ratified Additional Protocol I and II, in addition to the four Geneva Conventions of 1949. Hence, whether or not the armed conflict of which the attack on Ahmici formed part is regarded as internal, indisputably the parties to the conflict were bound by the relevant treaty provisions prohibiting reprisals.

Self-Defence

6.3.62 In *Kordić and Čerkez*, the Defence presented to the Trial Chamber evidence of ABiH attacks and offensives in Central Bosnia and sought to demonstrate that the Bosnian Croats were victims of a policy of Muslim aggression and were acting in self-defence.

6.3.63 The Trial Chamber, ruling on this issue in the *Kordić and Čerkez Trial Judgement*, paras. 448–452, noted that the ICTY Statute did not provide for self-defence as a ground for excluding criminal responsibility. "Defences" do, however, form part of the general principles of criminal law which the Tribunal must take into account in deciding the cases before it. The Trial Chamber held:

449. The notion of 'self-defence' may be broadly defined as providing a defence to a person who acts to defend or protect himself or his property (or another person or person's property) against attack, provided that the acts constitute a reasonable necessary and proportionate reaction to the attack . . .

. . .

451. The principle of self-defence enshrined in [Article 31(1)(c) of the Statute of the ICC (see below)] reflects provisions found in most national criminal codes and may be regarded as constituting a rule of customary international law. Article 31(1)(c) of the ICC Statute sets forth two conditions which must be met in order for self-defence to be accepted as a ground for excluding criminal liability: (a) the act must be in response to "an imminent and unlawful use of force" against an attack on a "protected" person or property; (b) the act of defence must be "proportionate to the degree of danger." In relation to the specific circumstances of war crimes, the provision takes into account the principle of military necessity.

452. Of particular relevance to this case is the last sentence of [Article 31(1)(c) of the ICC Statute] to the effect that the involvement of a person in a "defensive operation" does not "in itself" constitute a ground for excluding criminal responsibility. It is therefore clear that any argument raising self-defence must be assessed on its own facts and in the specific circumstances relating to each charge. The Trial Chamber will have regard to this condition when deciding whether the defence of self-defence applies to any of the charges. The Trial Chamber, however, would emphasise that military operations in self-defence do not provide a justification for serious violations of humanitarian law."

6.3.64

ICC
Article 31
Grounds for Excluding Criminal Responsibility

1. In addition to other grounds for excluding criminal responsibility provided for in this Statute, a person shall not be criminally responsible if, at the time of that person's conduct:
(a) The person suffers from a mental disease or defect that destroys that person's capacity to appreciate the unlawfulness or nature of his or her conduct, or capacity to control his or her conduct to conform to the requirements of law;
(b) The person is in a state of intoxication that destroys that person's capacity to appreciate the unlawfulness or nature of his or her conduct, or capacity to control his or her conduct to conform to the requirements of law, unless the person has become voluntarily intoxicated under such circumstances that the person knew, or disregarded the risk, that, as a result of the intoxication, he or she was likely to engage in conduct constituting a crime within the jurisdiction of the Court;
(c) The person acts reasonably to defend himself or herself or another person or, in the case of war crimes, property which is essential for the survival of the person or another person or property which is essential for accomplishing a military mission, against an imminent and unlawful use of force in a manner proportionate to the degree of danger to the person or the other person or property protected. The fact that the person was involved in a defensive operation conducted by forces shall not in itself constitute a ground for excluding criminal responsibility under this subparagraph;

(d) The conduct which is alleged to constitute a crime within the jurisdiction of the Court has been caused by duress resulting from a threat of imminent death or of continuing or imminent serious bodily harm against that person or another person, and the person acts necessarily and reasonably to avoid this threat, provided that the person does not intend to cause a greater harm than the one sought to be avoided. Such a threat may either be:
  (i) Made by other persons; or
  (ii) Constituted by other circumstances beyond that person's control.
2. The Court shall determine the applicability of the grounds for excluding criminal responsibility provided for in this Statute to the case before it.
3. At trial, the Court may consider a ground for excluding criminal responsibility other than those referred to in paragraph 1 where such a ground is derived from applicable law as set forth in article 21. The procedures relating to the consideration of such a ground shall be provided for in the Rules of Procedure and Evidence.

6.3.65

ICC
Article 32
Mistake of Fact or Mistake of Law

1. A mistake of fact shall be a ground for excluding criminal responsibility only if it negates the mental element required by the crime.
2. A mistake of law as to whether a particular type of conduct is a crime within the jurisdiction of the Court shall not be a ground for excluding criminal responsibility. A mistake of law may, however, be a ground for excluding criminal responsibility if it negates the mental element required by such a crime, or as provided for in article 33.

6.3.66

ICC
Article 33
Superior Orders and Prescription of Law

1. The fact that a crime within the jurisdiction of the Court has been committed by a person pursuant to an order of a Government or of a superior, whether military or civilian, shall not relieve that person of criminal responsibility unless:
(a) The person was under a legal obligation to obey orders of the Government or the superior in question;
(b) The person did not know that the order was unlawful; and
(c) The order was not manifestly unlawful.
2. For the purposes of this article, orders to commit genocide or crimes against humanity are manifestly unlawful.

Defences under the Rome Statute for an ICC

6.3.67 Unlike the ICTY and ICTR Statutes, the Rome Statute for an ICC spells out the applicable defences, in Articles 31, 32 and 33 (set out above). For an in-depth discussion of defences under the Rome Statute, see ch. 24 ("*Defences*") in Antonio Cassese, Paola Gaeta and John R.W.D. Jones, *The Rome Statute of the International Criminal Court: A Commentary*. (Oxford University Press, 2002).

PART 7

RULES OF PROCEDURE AND EVIDENCE

ICTY Article 15/ICTR Article 14: Rules of Procedure and Evidence	7.1
The ICTY Rules of Procedure and Evidence	7.2
History of ICTY Plenary Sessions	7.5
The ICTR Rules of Procedure and Evidence	7.30
History of ICTR Plenary Sessions	7.31
Adversarial Versus Inquisitorial System	7.41
Rule-Making	7.43
ICC—Judges Are Not Rule-Makers	7.44
ICC Article 51: Rules of Procedure and Evidence	7.46
ICC Article 52: Regulations of the Court	7.48
ICTY Rule1/ICTR Rule1: Entry into Force	7.49
ICTY Rule 2/ICTR Rule 2: Definitions	7.50
History of ICTY Rule 2	7.51
History of ICTR Rule 2	7.56
ICTY Rule 3/ICTR Rule 3: Languages	7.57
History of ICTY Rule 3	7.58
History of ICTR Rule 3	7.60
Working Languages	7.61
Defence Not Entitled to Documents in Language of the Accused	7.63
ICTY Rule 5/ICTR Rule 5: Non-Compliance with Rules	7.68
History of ICTY Rule 5	7.69
Rule 5 Does Not Permit the Annulment of the Prosecution Against an Accused	7.71
ICTY Rule 6/ICTR Rule 6: Amendment of the Rules	7.72
History of ICTY Rule 6	7.73
History of ICTR Rule 6	7.74
ICTY Rule 6(A)	7.75
ICTY Rule 6(B)	7.76
ICTY Rule 6(D)	7.77
ICTR Quorum	7.81
ICTY Rule 7/ICTR Rule 7: Authentic Texts	7.82
In Case of Discrepancy, the Version More Favourable to the Accused Should Be Upheld	7.85

* * * * *

7.1

ICTY Article 15 Rules of Procedure and Evidence	ICTR Article 14 Rules of Procedure and Evidence
The judges of the International Tribunal shall adopt rules of procedure and evidence for the conduct of the pre-trial phase of the proceedings, trials and appeals, the admission of evidence, the protection of victims and witnesses and other appropriate matters.	The judges of the International Tribunal for Rwanda shall adopt, for the purpose of proceedings before the International Tribunal for Rwanda, the rules of procedure and evidence for the conduct of the pre-trial phase of the proceedings, trials and appeals, the admission of evidence, the protection of victims and witnesses and other appropriate matters of the International Tribunal for the Former Yugoslavia with such changes as they deem necessary.

The ICTY Rules of Procedure and Evidence

7.2 The ICTY Rules of Procedure and Evidence were first adopted in plenary on 11 February 1994. With four exceptions (see ICTY Rule 6(B)), the Rules have been amended in plenary. Rule 6(A) reads, "Proposals for amendment of the Rules may be made by a Judge, the Prosecutor or the Registrar and shall be adopted if agreed to by not less than ten permanent Judges at a plenary meeting of the Tribunal convened with notice of the proposal addressed to all Judges," while Rule 6(B) provides that "An amendment to the Rules may be otherwise adopted, provided it is unanimously approved by the Judges."

7.3 The Rules were amended on 5 May 1994, 4 October 1994, 30 January 1995, 3 May 1995, 15 June 1995, 6 October 1995, 18 January 1996, 23 April 1996, 25 June 1996, 5 July 1996, 3 December 1996, 25 July 1997, 20 October and 12 November 1997, 9–10 July 1998, 4 December 1998, 25 February 1999, 2 July 1999, 17 November 1999, 14 July 2000, 1 and 13 December 2000, 19 January 2001, 12 April 2001, 12 July 2001, 13 December 2001, 23 April 2002, 11 and 12 July 2002 and 10 October 2002.

7.4 The latest version of the ICTY Rules used in this book is Revision 26 (see IT/32/Rev. 26, which entered into force on 30 December 2002. Updates are found at www.intcrimpractice.com.

History of ICTY Plenary Sessions

7.5 The inaugural plenary session took place in November and December 1993, when the judges were sworn in and a general debate took place, particularly regarding the rules of procedure and evidence. The second plenary session took place in January–February 1994 and was devoted mainly to discussion and adoption of the Rules of Procedure and Evidence.

7.6 At the third session in April–May 1994, rules of detention were adopted to regulate the conditions under which detainees would be held, together with guidelines concerning the assignment of counsel for indigent detainees. Rule 96 was amended.

Rules of Procedure and Evidence • 463

7.7 The fourth plenary session was held in July 1994.

7.8 At the fifth plenary session, in January 1995, Rules 2, 3, 5, 8, 9, 10, 12, 13, 15, 28, 36, 37, 39, 40, 42, 43, 45, 47, 49 (French text only), 53, 54, 55, 57, 61, 62, 65, 66, 68, 70, 72, 75, 77, 88, 90, 93, 95, 96, 101, 105, 108, 116 *bis* and 117 were amended or introduced.

7.9 At the sixth plenary session, on 1–3 May 1995, Rules 10, 61 and 99 (French text only) were amended.

7.10 At the seventh plenary session, on 2–16 June 1995, Rules 15, 62, 69 and 75 were amended.

7.11 At the eighth plenary session, in October 1995, Rules 70 and 90 *bis* were amended or introduced.

7.12 At the ninth plenary session, in January 1996, Rules 50, 55, 59 *bis* and 61 were amended or introduced.

7.13 At the tenth plenary session, on 22–23 April 1996, Rules 28, 40 *bis* and 61 were amended or introduced.

7.14 At the eleventh plenary session, on 24–25 June 1996, Rules 45, 45 *bis*, 53, 72, 100 were amended or introduced.

7.15 At the twelfth plenary session, on 2–3 December 1996, Rules 50, 51, 63, 66 were amended.

7.16 At the thirteenth plenary session, on 25 July 1997, Rules 2,3,7 *bis*, 11, 15, 19, 37, 38, 40 *bis*, 44, 47, 55, 60, 61, 64, 65, 65 *bis*, 70, 72, 77, 81, 90, 108, 108 *bis* and 116 *bis* were amended or introduced. Gender-neutral language was also adopted and the rules were "harmonised" as between the English and French versions.

7.17 At the fourteenth plenary session, on 12 November 1997, Rules 2, 5, 13, 14, 28, 36, 40, 40 *bis*, 44, 45, 47, 50, 51, 55, 59 *bis*, 60, 61, 62, 65, 66, 72, 73, 77, 81, 88, 89, 90 *bis*, 95, 99, 108, 108 *bis*, 111 and 116 were amended. The following new Rules were adopted: 11 *bis*, 53 *bis*, 62 *bis*, 126 and 127. Old Rule 116 was deleted, being replaced by old Rule 116 *bis*. In addition, the text was further revised to be gender-neutral.

7.18 No amendments were formally adopted at the fifteenth plenary session in March 1998.

7.19 At the eighteenth plenary session on 9–10 July 1998, the following Rules were amended: Rules 11 *bis*, 15, 45, 47(F), 50, 62 *bis*, 65, 66, 72, 73, 77, 85, 86, 87, 88 (also moved), 88 *bis* (also moved), 90, 94, 99, 100, 101, 102, 103, 108 *bis* and 111. New Rules adopted were: 65 *ter*, 73 *bis*, 73 *ter*, 74 *bis*, 94 *bis* and 98 *ter*.

7.20 At the nineteenth plenary session on 4–5 December 1998, the following Rules were amended: Rules 6, 15, 25, 26, 40, 53, 62, 62 *bis*, 65 *bis*, 77, 83, 91, 103, 115 (French text only), 119 (French text only) and 122 (French text only). One new rule was adopted, namely Rule 94 *ter*.

7.21 At the twentieth plenary session on 30 June–2 July 1999, two new Rules were adopted, Rules 77 *bis* and 84 *bis*, and the following rules were amended: Rules 15(C), 34, 69(B), 72(A), 75(A), 108 and 108 *bis* (A). These amendments entered into force on 22 July 1999.

7.22 At the twenty-first plenary session, Rules 15 *bis*, 54 *bis* and 71 *bis* were adopted and Rules 2, 10, 15, 28, 33, 50, 62, 65, 65 *bis*, 65 *ter*, 66, 71, 72, 73 *bis*, 73 *ter*, 75, 77 *bis*, 85 (French only), 90, 91, 94 *ter*, 98 *bis*, 105, 108, 108 *bis*, 111, 112 and 116 *bis* were amended, effective 30 November 1999.

7.23 On 2 August 2000, after the twenty-second plenary session, Rules 28, 44, 45, 46, 50, 65, 73, 85, 94 *bis* and 116 *bis* were amended.

7.24 On 19 January 2001, after the twenty-third plenary session, new rules 23 *bis*, 23 *ter*, 33 *bis* and 92 *bis* were adopted, while the following rules were amended: Rules 6, 15, 15 *bis*, 28, 33, 41, 44, 47, 65, 65 *ter*, 66, 71, 72, 75, 77, 81, 86, 87, 89, 90, 91, 94 *bis*, 101, 109, 116 *bis* and 127. Rule 94 *ter* was deleted.

7.25 On 19 July, 2001, after the twenty-fourth plenary session, the following rules were amended: rules 22, 65 *ter*, 68, 119 and 120.

7.26 At the twenty-fifth plenary session, held on 12–13 December, 2001, rules 62 *ter*, 68 *bis* and 126 *bis* were adopted, while the following rules were amended: rules 28, 44, 46, 54 *bis*, 65, 65 *ter*, 67, 69, 73, 75, 77, 77 *bis*, 91, 94 *bis*, 108, 111, 112, 116 *bis*, 119 and 126.

7.27 At the extraordinary plenary session held on 30 September 2002, Rule 11 *bis* was amended.

7.28 At the twenty-seventh plenary session on 12 December 2002, the following rules were amended: Rules 2, 15, 15 *bis*, 28, 43, 51, 54 *bis*, 65 *bis*, 68, 72, 75, 94 *bis*, and 116 *bis*.

7.29 The basic rationale for amendment of the Rules is given in the ICTY Third Annual Report (A/51/292), para. 66:

> The Rules constituted the first international criminal procedural and evidentiary code ever adopted; given that the Statute was not sufficiently detailed to be a guide to the conduct of proceedings, it was necessary to adopt these Rules to govern all the various aspects of criminal trials. It was, of course, not possible at the outset to anticipate every eventuality which would arise; accordingly the Rules have been amended from time to time, by a plenary of the Judges, to take account of various eventualities.

The ICTR Rules of Procedure and Evidence

7.30 Article 14 of the ICTR Statute differs slightly from Article 15 of the ICTY Statute. The ICTY Rules of Procedure and Evidence were adopted, *mutatis mutandis*, as the ICTR Rules of Procedure and Evidence at the ICTR first plenary session held in The Hague on 26–30 June 1995. The Rules were then subsequently amended on 12 January 1996, 15 May 1996, 4 July 1996, 5 June 1997, 8 June 1998, 1 July 1999, 21 February 2000, 26 June 2000, 3 November 2000 and 30–31 May, 2001.

History of ICTR Plenary Sessions

7.31 The ICTR Rules were adopted on 29 June 1995 at the first plenary session, held in The Hague, adapting the ICTY Rules *mutatis mutandis*. The Rules have since been amended on the following occasions: 12 January 1996, 15 May 1996, 4 July 1996, 5 June 1997, 8 June 1998, 1 July 1999, 21 February 2000, 26 June 2000, 3 November

2000, 31 May 2001 and 6 July 2002. The latest version of the ICTR Rules used in this book is the revision as amended on 6 July 2002. Updates are found at www.intcrimpractice.com.

7.32 Rule 40 *bis* was amended on 15 May 1996, at the Third Plenary Session. The following rules were amended or introduced on 5 June 1997, following the Fourth Plenary Session, held in Arusha on 1–5 June 1997: Rules 7 *bis*, 9, 10, 14 *bis*, 15, 34, 45, 46, 66, 70, 72, 73, and 91.

7.33 The following rules were amended or introduced on 8 June 1998, at the Fifth Plenary Session, held in Arusha on 1–8 June 1998: Rules 2, 15, 34, 40 *bis*, 44, 45, 46, 47, 50, 51, 55, 60, 61, 62, 63, 65, 65 *bis*, 66, 67, 69, 72, 73 *bis*, 73 *ter*, 74 *bis*, 75, 85, 86, 87, 90, 91, 94 *bis*, 98. 98 *bis*, 99, 100, 101, 102, 111 and 112.

7.34 The following rules were amended at the Eighth plenary session, on 26 June, 2000: rules 2, 6, 11, 14, 16, 18, 28, 35, 39, 40, 40 *bis*, 61, 62, 63, 65, 73, 73 *bis*, 73 *ter*, 75, 85, 109, 117 *ter* and 118.

7.35 The following rules were amended at the ninth plenary session, on 3 November, 2000: rules 48 *bis*, 94, 108, 109, 117, 117 *bis* and 117 *ter*.

7.36 The following rules were amended at the tenth plenary session, on 30–31 May, 2001: rules 3, 7 *ter*, 15, 15 *bis*, 40 *bis*, 41, 55 *bis*, 73 *bis* and 73 *ter*.

7.37 The following rules were amended at the twelfth plenary session on 5–6 July 2002: rules 11 *bis*, 17, 45, 65, 65 *bis*, 69, 72, 77, 91, 92 *bis*, 98 *bis*, 108, 108 *bis*, 111, 112, 114, 116 and 117. The Code of Professional Conduct for defence counsel was also amended at this plenary session to include a provision on fee splitting. (See Article 5 *bis* of the Code).

7.38 For the nature of the amendments made to each Rule, reference should be made to the pertinent Rule.

7.39 In *Kanyabashi, Decision on the Defence Motion for the Provisional Release of the Accused*, 21 February 2001, it was argued by the defence that amendments to ICTY Rule 65(B) should apply to ICTR Rule 65(B) despite no express change being made to the ICTR Rules by the Judges. This argument was rejected by the Trial Chamber on the basis that pursuant to Article 14, the judges of the ICTR shall adopt ICTY Rules with "such changes as they deem necessary." Accordingly, the amendments to ICTY Rule 65(B) could only be incorporated into the ICTR Rules if the ICTR Judges decided to do so and to the extent they deemed necessary (para. 5).

7.40 Note that the ICTR RPE are adopted, *mutatis mutandis*, to govern proceedings at the Special Court for Sierra Leone.

Adversarial Versus Inquisitorial System

7.41 It has been said on a number of occasions, both by the tribunals themselves and by commentators, that their Rules of Procedure and Evidence enshrine a basically adversarial approach, in which the procedure is "advocate-led," rather than inquisitorial, in which the procedure is "judge-led." As to the difference between these two procedures, Lord Justice Staughton has put it thus:

> To my mind the essence of adversarial procedure is that the judge listens to the evidence and arguments of the parties, and decides between them; he does not

make his own enquiries as to the facts, or adopt conclusions of fact not proposed by either party; nor does he propose or adopt arguments or conclusions of law differing from those which the parties put forward. By contrast, where the procedure is inquisitorial the judge can and does exercise all of these functions. ("Common Law and Civil Law Procedures: Which is the more Inquisitorial? A Common Lawyer's Response," *Arbitration International*, (1989), Vol. 5, No. 4, p. 352)

7.42 While it is true that at the outset, the Rules of the ICTY and ICTR were closely modelled on a common law, adversarial system—due in large part to the fact that the first proposal for the Rules was by the U.S., whose proposal was based on the U.S. *Federal Rules of Evidence*—both tribunals have since amended the Rules in a number of ways to move away from the adversarial paradigm towards a more inquisitorial approach, seemingly striving to achieve a "golden mean between them if it can be found" (Staughton, *Op. Cit.*).

Further Reading:

Orie, Alphonse, "Accusatorial v. Inquisitiorial Approach in International Criminal Proceedings," Ch. 34, *in* Antonio Cassese, Paola Gaeta and John R.W.D. Jones (eds.), *The Rome Statute of the International Criminal Court: A Commentary* (Oxford University Press, 2002).

Rule-Making

7.43 The terms used in the Rules of Procedure and Evidence are to be interpreted in the ICTY's context. They do not necessarily bear the same meaning as in a national context. As the Trial Chamber stated in the *Blaškić Subpoena Trial Decision*:

> 60. ... the Judges of the International Tribunal were responsible for the drafting of its Rules. Every Rule adopted was the result of extensive discussion and debate among the Judges and, therefore, the terms used therein carry their own specific meaning, suited for an international judicial institution with criminal jurisdiction.
>
> 61. ... Terminology utilized which originates in one or another domestic legal system does not convey its full meaning in the International Tribunal's context. Likewise, the Judges did not reject a term simply because it was peculiar to one legal system.

ICC—Judges Are Not Rule-Makers

7.44 A notable difference between the ICTY and ICTR, on the one hand, and the ICC, on the other, is that at the latter, the Judges are not responsible for drafting and adopting the Rules of Procedure and Evidence. This task is entrusted to the Assembly of States Parties established under the Rome Statute. The ICC Rules are adopted and amended by the Assembly of States Parties voting with a two-thirds majority. See ICC Article 51 (*"Rules of Procedure and Evidence"*). The ICC Rules are set out at Annex 3 herein.

7.45 ICC Article 51(2)(b) does, however, endow the Judges with the limited power of acting by an absolute majority to propose amendments to the Rules of Procedure and Evidence. Amendments may also be proposed by any State party or the Prosecutor. See also Article 51(3) on the adoption by the Judges of provisional Rules.

7.46

**ICC
Article 51
Rules of Procedure and Evidence**

1. The Rules of Procedure and Evidence shall enter into force upon adoption by a two-thirds majority of the members of the Assembly of States Parties.
2. Amendments to the Rules of Procedure and Evidence may be proposed by:
(a) Any State Party;
(b) The judges acting by an absolute majority; or
(c) The Prosecutor.
Such amendments shall enter into force upon adoption by a two-thirds majority of the members of the Assembly of States Parties.
3. After the adoption of the Rules of Procedure and Evidence, in urgent cases where the Rules do not provide for a specific situation before the Court, the judges may, by a two-thirds majority, draw up provisional Rules to be applied until adopted, amended or rejected at the next ordinary or special session of the Assembly of States Parties.
4. The Rules of Procedure and Evidence, amendments thereto and any provisional Rule shall be consistent with this Statute. Amendments to the Rules of Procedure and Evidence as well as provisional Rules shall not be applied retroactively to the detriment of the person who is being investigated or prosecuted or who has been convicted.
5. In the event of conflict between the Statute and the Rules of Procedure and Evidence, the Statute shall prevail.

7.47 The ICC Rules of Procedure and Evidence were adopted by general agreement by the Preparatory Commission for the International Criminal Court at its 23rd meeting on 30 June 2000.

7.48

**ICC
Article 52
Regulations of the Court**

1. The judges shall, in accordance with this Statute and the Rules of Procedure and Evidence, adopt, by an absolute majority, the Regulations of the Court necessary for its routine functioning.
2. The Prosecutor and the Registrar shall be consulted in the elaboration of the Regulations and any amendments thereto.
3. The Regulations and any amendments thereto shall take effect upon adoption unless otherwise decided by the judges. Immediately upon adoption, they shall be circulated to States Parties for comments. If within six months there are no objections from a majority of States Parties, they shall remain in force.

7.49

ICTY Rule 1 Entry into Force	ICTR Rule 1 Entry into Force
These Rules of Procedure and Evidence, adopted pursuant to Article 15 of the Statute of the Tribunal, shall come into force on 14 March 1994.	These Rules of Procedure and Evidence, adopted pursuant to Article 14 of the Statute of the Tribunal, shall come into force on 29 June 1995.

7.50

ICTY Rule 2 Definitions	ICTR Rule 2 Definitions
(A) In the Rules, unless the context otherwise requires, the following terms shall mean: Rules: The Rules of Procedure and Evidence in force; Statute: The Statute of the Tribunal adopted by Security Council resolution 827 of 25 May 1993; Tribunal: The International Tribunal for the Prosecution of Persons Responsible for Serious Violations of International Humanitarian Law Committed in the Territory of the Former Yugoslavia since 1991, established by Security Council resolution 827 of 25 May 1993. Accused: A person against whom one or more counts in an indictment have been confirmed in accordance with Rule 47; Ad litem Judge: A Judge appointed pursuant to Article 13 ter of the Statute; Arrest: The act of taking a suspect or an accused into custody pursuant to a warrant of arrest or under Rule 40 by a national authority; Bureau: A body composed of the President, the Vice-President and the Presiding Judges of the Trial Chambers; Defence: The accused, and/or the accused's counsel	(A) In the Rules, unless the context otherwise requires, the following terms shall mean: Rules: The Rules referred to in Rule 1; Statute: The Statute of the Tribunal adopted by Security Council resolution 955 of 8 November 1994; Tribunal: The International Criminal Tribunal for the Prosecution of Persons Responsible for Genocide and other Serious Violations of International Humanitarian Law Committed in the Territory of Rwanda and Rwandan Citizens responsible for Genocide and other such violations committed in the territory of neighbouring States, between 1 January 1994 and 31 December 1994, established by Security Council resolution 955 of 8 November 1994. Accused: A person against whom one or more counts in an indictment have been confirmed in accordance with Rule 47; Arrest: The act of apprehending and taking a suspect or an accused into custody pursuant to a warrant of arrest or under Rule 40; Bureau: A body composed of the President, the Vice-President and the more senior Presiding Judge of the Trial Chambers;

Investigation: All activities undertaken by the Prosecutor under the Statute and the Rules for the collection of information and evidence, whether before or after an indictment is confirmed; Parties: The Prosecutor and the Defence; Permanent Judge: A Judge elected or appointed puruant to Article 13 *bis* of the Statute; President: The President of the Tribunal; Prosecutor: The Prosecutor appointed pursuant to Article 16 of the Statute; Regulations: The provisions framed by the Prosecutor pursuant to Sub-rule 37(A) for the purpose of directing the functions of his Office; State: (i) A State Member or non-Member of the United Nations; (ii) an entity recognised by the constitution of Bosnia and Herzegovina, namely, the Federation of Bosnia and Herzegovina and the Republika Srpska; or (iii) a self-proclaimed entity de facto exercising governmental functions, whether recognised as a State or not; Suspect: A person concerning whom the Prosecutor possesses reliable information which tends to show that he may have committed a crime over which the Tribunal has jurisdiction; Transaction: A number of acts or omissions whether occurring as one event or a number of events, at the same or different locations and being part of a common scheme, strategy or plan; Victim: A person against whom a crime over which the Tribunal has jurisdiction has allegedly been committed. (B) In the Rules, the singular shall include the plural, and vice-versa.	Investigation: All activities undertaken by the Prosecutor under the Statute and the Rules for the collection of information and evidence, whether before or after confirmation of an indictment; Party: The Prosecutor or the accused; President: The President of the Tribunal; Prosecutor: The Prosecutor designated pursuant to Article 15 of the Statute; Regulations: The provisions framed by the Prosecutor pursuant to Rule 37(A) for the purpose of directing the functions of the Office of the Prosecutor; Suspect: A person concerning whom the Prosecutor possesses reliable information which tends to show that he may have committed a crime over which the Tribunal has jurisdiction; Transaction: A number of acts or omissions whether occurring as one event or a number of events, at the same or different locations and being part of a common scheme, strategy or plan; Victim: A person against whom a crime over which the Tribunal has jurisdiction has allegedly been committed. (B) In the Rules, the masculine shall include the feminine and the singular the plural, and vice-versa.

History of ICTY Rule 2

7.51 The definition of "State" in Rule 2(A) was amended at the fifth plenary session in January 1995, "to take account of the political entities now found in the territory of the former Yugoslavia" (ICTY second Annual Report, para. 23), i.e. to allow judicial documents to be transmitted to entities which are not States, and, in particular, to allow arrest warrants issued under Rules 55 and 61 to be transmitted to the

Bosnian Serb administration in Pale, the former "Croatian Community of Herceg-Bosna," the former Krajina Serb Republic and the Federation of Bosnia and Herzegovina (see the *Nikolić Rule 61 Decision*, para. 35). This Rule has also meant that *de facto* States may be reported to the Security Council for failure to co-operate with the Tribunal. See the *Karadžić and Mladić Rule 61 Decision:* "On the basis of all the Tribunal's rules and regulations, and in particular Article 29 of the Statute and Rule 2(A) ("State") of the Rules of Procedure and Evidence, the Bosnian Serb administration . . . is bound to co-operate with the Tribunal." (Para. 98)

7.52 This Rule was also amended at the fifth plenary session for the purposes of "completeness" (second Annual Report, para. 21, fn.6) to define the term "Regulations," following provision for such Regulations under amended sub-Rule 37(A), and the term, "Transaction," to define the phrase as used in Rules 48 and 49.

7.53 The word "reliable" was added before the word "information" in the definition of "Suspect" at the fifth plenary session, at the suggestion of the Prosecutor, to allow him* to make a qualitative analysis of the information available to him and thus determine whether a person to whom he wishes to speak is likely to be viewed as a suspect and therefore entitled to the benefit of the provisions of Rules 42 and 43.

7.54 The definitions of "Rules," "Accused," "Arrest" and "Investigation" were amended in minor ways at the thirteenth plenary session on 25 July 1997. Rule 2(B) was amended in a minor way at the fourteenth plenary session on 12 November 1997.

7.55 The definition of "Defence" was added at the twenty-first plenary session, effective 30 November 1999, and the definition of "Party" as "the Prosecutor or the accused" was changed to a definition of "Parties" as "the Prosecutor and the Defence." The definition of "State" was amended to include the BH entities on 12 December 2002.

History of ICTR Rule 2

7.56 Para. (A) and the definition of "arrest" were amended at the eighth plenary session on 26 June 2000.

7.57

ICTY Rule 3 Languages	ICTR Rule 3 Languages
(A) The working languages of the Tribunal shall be English and French. (B) An accused shall have the right to use his own language. (C) Other persons appearing before the Tribunal, other than as counsel, who does not have sufficient knowledge of either of the two working languages, may use his own language.	(A) The working languages of the Tribunal shall be English and French. (B) The accused or suspect shall have the right to use his own language. (C) Counsel for the accused may apply to a Judge or a Chamber for leave to use language other than the two working ones or the language of the accused. If such leave is

---

* The Prosecutor is either referred to as "he" or "she," "him" or "her," depending on who of Richard Goldstone, Louise Arbour or Carla del Ponte was serving at the time.

(D) Counsel for an accused may apply to the Presiding Judge of a Chamber for leave to use a language other than the two working ones or the language of the accused. If such leave is granted, the expenses of interpretation and translation shall be borne by the Tribunal to the extent, if any, determined by the President, taking into account the rights of the defence and the interests of justice. (E) The Registrar shall make any necessary arrangements for interpretation and translation into and from the working languages. (F) If: (i) a party is required to take action within a specified time after the filing or service of a document by another party; and (ii) pursuant to the Rules, that document is filed in a language other than one of the working languages of the Tribunal, time shall not run until the party required to take action has received from the Registrar a translation of the document into one of the working languages of the Tribunal.	granted, the expenses of interpretation and translation shall be borne by the Tribunal to the extent, if any, determined by the President, taking into account the rights of the Defence and the interests of justice. (D) Any other person appearing before the Tribunal, who does not have sufficient knowledge of either of the two working languages, may use his own language. (E) The Registrar shall make any necessary arrangements for interpretation and translation into and from the working languages.

History of ICTY Rule 3

7.58 ICTY Rule 3 was amended at the ICTY fifth plenary session in January 1995 by adding the words, "other than as counsel" to clarify the relationship between paras. (C) and (D) (second Annual Report, para. 21, fn. 6).

7.59 Para. (F) was added at the thirteenth plenary session on 25 July 1997.

History of ICTR Rule 3

7.60 The words, "or suspect" were added to para. (B) at the ICTR's tenth plenary session on 30–31 May, 2001.

Working Languages

7.61 While the working languages of the ICTs are English and French, all proceedings are also interpreted into Bosnian/Croatian/Serbian ("BCS") at the ICTY, and Kinyarwanda at the ICTR. It is possible under the ICTY Statute for there to be an accused whose language is not BCS. Neither the ICTY nor the ICTR Statute is restricted in its personal jurisdiction by reference to nationality. The ICTR has indeed indicted a non-Rwandan, namely Georges Ruggio, a Belgian.

7.62 Official documents of the ICTs are also typically translated into all three of the above-mentioned languages. Certain documents are also available in Albanian, as a result of the *Milošević* trial for events in Kosovo in which many Albanian-speaking witnesses appeared.

Defence Not Entitled to Documents in Language of the Accused

7.63 In *Delalić et al.*, on 15 May 1996, defence counsel for Delalić applied for copies of transcripts and other documents to be forwarded to her in Bosnian, citing Rule 3(B) and (D) in support of her application. On 31 May 1996, after a response by the Prosecutor, the Trial Chamber noted that translation was a matter for the Registrar pursuant to Article 17 of the Statute and Rule 33, and it directed the Registrar to respond to the Application. The Registrar accordingly sent a letter on 14 June 1996, stating that, under the Tribunal's Rules, the transcripts did not have to be submitted in the language of the accused. The defence then filed an additional application on 23 July 1996, to which the Prosecutor responded on 31 July 1996. The defence argued that the right of the accused to a fair trial necessarily included the right of his counsel to all relevant documents in the language of the accused and the right to file motions and responses in the language of the accused. The defence also argued that the requirement that counsel address the Tribunal in one of its working languages was a restriction on the right of the accused to choose his own counsel.

7.64 In its *Decision on Defence Application for Forwarding the Documents in the Language of the Accused* of 25 September 1996, the Trial Chamber held that the Defence was not entitled as of right to be served with all documents in the language of the accused. The Chamber found that:

> 8. ... neither Rule 3 nor Article 21 entitles the Defence to receive all discovery from the Prosecution in the language of the accused. The guarantees of Article 21(4) do not extend to all material, but only to evidence which forms the basis of the determination by the Trial Chamber of the charges against the accused.
>
> ...
>
> 10. Implicit in the concept of "working languages" in Article 33 of the Statute and Rule 3(A) is that all papers which are filed with the International Tribunal be in either English or French.
>
> ...
>
> 12. Sub-rule 3(C) clearly provides that, unlike others appearing before the International Tribunal, counsel do not have an *automatic* right to use their own language, even if that is the same as the language of the accused. However, counsel are permitted to address the Trial Chamber in the language of the accused, pursuant to Sub-rule 3(D). The right under Sub-rule 3(D) for counsel to use the language of the accused without requiring leave of the Trial Chamber is based on the premise that it is desirable for counsel to be able to communicate easily with the accused.
>
> ...
>
> 14. The transcripts of the proceedings are provided in one or both of the working languages on request simply as an aide memoire for courtroom participants. As with motions and other similar documents, the Defence is not entitled to have the transcripts translated into the language of the accused.

7.65 This last paragraph was endorsed by the Trial Chamber in its *Order on the Motion for Application of Redress of the Accused's Right of Information pursuant to Articles 20 and 21 of the Statute of the International Tribunal* rendered in the same case on 16 January 1998.

7.66 Nevertheless, the Trial Chamber recognised that the defence would often have to arrange for translation of the documents disclosed to it by the Prosecutor, a fact which would have to be taken into account in scheduling the trial date. This was not because the defence did not speak either of the two working languages, but rather because the accused had to be able to consult the documents in his own language. This meant that disclosure had to occur in sufficient time before the trial date to allow the defence time to translate the documents into the language of the accused. See the *Decision on the Applications for Adjournment of the Trial Date*, rendered in *Delalić* by the Trial Chamber on 3 February 1997:

> 22. The Trial Chamber is cognisant of the fact that unless there is prompt and proper disclosure to the Defence, the Defence cannot make a decision on what evidence it will use at trial, and cannot therefore be adequately prepared for trial. This is especially so in this case where the disclosure was in English, making translation into the language of the accused necessary.

7.67 See also *Kajelijeli, Decision on Defence Motion Seeking to Interview Prosecutor's Witnesses or Alternatively to be Provided with a Bill of Particulars*, 12 March 2001, para. 13, in which the Trial Chamber stipulated that material recorded in

7.68

ICTY Rule 5 Non-Compliance with Rules	ICTR Rule 5 Non-Compliance with Rules
(A) Where an objection on the ground of non-compliance with the Rules or Regulations is raised by a party at the earliest opportunity, the Trial Chamber shall grant relief if it finds that the alleged non-compliance is proved and that it has caused material prejudice to that party. (B) Where such an objection is raised otherwise than at the earliest opportunity, the Trial Chamber may in its discretion grant relief if it finds that the alleged non-compliance is proved and that it has caused material prejudice to the objecting party. (C) The relief granted by a Trial Chamber under this Rule shall be such remedy as the Trial Chamber considers appropriate to ensure consistency with the fundamental principles of fairness.	(A) Where an objection on the ground of non-compliance with the Rules or Regulations is raised by a party at the earliest opportunity, the Trial Chamber shall grant relief, if it finds that the alleged non-compliance is proved and that it has caused material prejudice to that party. (B) Where such an objection is raised otherwise than at the earliest opportunity, the Trial Chamber may in its discretion grant relief, if it finds that the alleged non-compliance is proved and that it has caused material prejudice to the objecting party. (C) The relief granted by a Trial Chamber under this Rule shall be such remedy as the Trial Chamber considers appropriate to ensure consistency with fundamental principles of fairness.

the language of the accused could be disclosed to the Defence in that form in addition to either of the official languages of the Tribunal.

Cross Reference: ICTY Article 21(4)(f), and ICTY Rule 45(A) on the language requirements for Counsel.

History of ICTY Rule 5

7.69 Rule 5 was amended at the ICTY fifth plenary session in January 1995 to add the words, "or regulations," to be consistent with the provision for such regulations under amended sub-Rule 37(A).

7.70 Rule 5 was substantially amended at the ICTY fourteenth plenary session on 12 November 1997.

Rule 5 Does Not Permit the Annulment of the Prosecution Against an Accused

7.71 This Rule was considered by the Trial Chamber in its *Decision on the Preliminary Motion filed by the Defence*, rendered in *Kayishema* on 6 November 1996. The Chamber, rejecting a defence motion, stated:

> it is the opinion of the Tribunal that even if the Prosecutor had not complied with the said provisions [Rule 66], the annulment of the disclosed materials or that of the proceedings, as moved by the Defence, could not have been ordered, as this sanction is not provided for by the Rules.

See also *Kanyabashi, Decision on the Defense Extremely Urgent Motion on Habeas Corpus and Stoppage of Proceedings*, 23 May 2000, (para. 81) and *Niyitegeka, Decision on Two Defence Motions . . .* , 27 February 2001 (para. 55).

7.72

ICTY Rule 6 Amendment of the Rules	ICTR Rule 6 Amendment of the Rules
(A) Proposals for amendment of the Rules may be made by a Judge, the Prosecutor or the Registrar and shall be adopted if agreed to by not less than ten permanent Judges at a plenary meeting of the Tribunal convened with notice of the proposal addressed to all Judges. (B) An amendment to the Rules may be otherwise adopted, provided it is unanimously approved by the Judges. (C) Proposals for amendment of the Rules may otherwise be made in accordance with the Practice Direction issued by the President.	(A) Proposals for amendment of the Rules may be made by a Judge, the Prosecutor or the Registrar and shall be adopted if agreed to by not less than ten Judges at a plenary meeting of the Tribunal convened with notice of the proposal addressed to all Judges. (B) An amendment of the Rules may be adopted otherwise than as stipulated in Sub-Rule (A) above, provided it is approved unanimously by any appropriate means either done in writing or confirmed in writing.

(D) An amendment shall enter into force seven days after the date of issue of an official Tribunal document containing the amendment, but shall not operate to prejudice the rights of the accused or of a convicted or acquitted person in any pending case.	(C) An amendment shall enter into force immediately, but shall not operate to prejudice the rights of the accused in any pending case.

History of ICTY Rule 6

7.73 This rule was amended at the ICTY nineteenth plenary session, on 17 December 1998. The reference in para. (A) to "seven Judges" was changed to the present reference to "nine Judges," in consequence of the fact that a new Trial Chamber of three Judges had since been added to the Tribunal, bringing the number of Judges from eleven to fourteen. At the same plenary session, a new para. (C) was added, with the previous para. (C) becoming para. (D) and also being amended to provide that "an amendment shall enter into force seven days after the date of issue of an official Tribunal document containing the amendment," where before the Rule provided "An amendment shall enter into force immediately." The words, "or of a convicted or acquitted person," were added to para. (D) on 19 January 2001, after the twenty-third plenary session.

History of ICTR Rule 6

7.74 Para. (B) was amended at the eighth plenary session on 26 June 2000.

ICTY Rule 6(A)

7.75 To date, twenty-seven plenary sessions have been held by the ICTY and a great many amendments have been adopted. Reference should be made in this regard to the Tribunal's Annual Reports, in particular to "Regulatory Activity" in the "Chambers" sections of the Reports.

ICTY Rule 6(B)

7.76 Four rules have, to date, been amended by unanimous vote outside plenary session under Rule 6(B), rather than in plenary session under Rule 6(A). Rule 70(B) was so amended in October 1994, to meet an urgent problem encountered by the Prosecutor in obtaining information from non-governmental organisations and other bodies. Rule 15 was amended in July 1996, to address the situation posed by the sudden resignation of a judge. Rule 23 was amended to add para. (D) on 25 February 1999. Rule 115 was amended pursuant to Rule 6(B) on 17 October 2002.

ICTY Rule 6(D)

7.77 This para., when it was para. (C) and before it was amended to provide that "an amendment shall enter into force seven days after the date of issue of an official Tribunal document containing the amendment," was considered in relation to the introduction of a new Rule, Rule 108 *bis*, in two Decisions of the Appeals Chamber rendered in *Blaškić* (IT-95-14-AR108*bis*), on 29 July 1997 (see paras. 10–11) and 12 August 1997 (see paras. 11–13).

7.78 It was also considered by the Trial Chamber in *Blaškić* in relation to an amendment to Rule 66(A). The Chamber held that the amendment in question did not change the sense of Rule 66(A), but merely clarified its spirit and meaning and that there was therefore no violation of Rule 6 in applying the new Rule immediately. See *Decision on the Defence Motion to Compel the Disclosure of Rule 66 and 68 material relating to Statements made by a Person known as "X"* rendered on 15 July 1998.

7.79 It has also been held that amendments which do not prejudice the rights of the accused in a pending case come into effect immediately. See *Decision on the Prosecution's Alternative Request to Reopen the Prosecution's Case, Delalić et al.*, 19 August 1998.

7.80 See also ICTR Rule 6(C) and its application in *Ntakirutimana, Decision on the Prosecutor's Motion to Join the Indictments*, 22 February 2001, in which the Trial Chamber held that the accused would not suffer any prejudice by the retrospective application of Rule 48 *bis* and accordingly applied it to the case before them.

ICTR Quorum

7.81 A quorum is constituted at the ICTR by ten Judges—the same number as required by the ICTY. To understand this, it must be remembered that in addition to the nine Trial Chamber Judges of the ICTR, the ICTR consists of the five Appeals Judges based at the ICTY in The Hague. Thus all fourteen Judges must meet together—either in Arusha or The Hague—for plenary sessions, and a minimum of ten votes is required in order to amend a Rule.

7.82

ICTY Rule 7 Authentic Texts	ICTR Rule 7 Authentic Texts
The English and French texts of the Rules shall be equally authentic. In case of discrepancy, the version which is more consonant with the spirit of the Statute and the Rules shall prevail.	The English and French texts of the Rules shall be equally authentic. In case of discrepancy, the version which is more consonant with the spirit of the Statute and the Rules shall prevail.

7.83 Judge Deschênes, in his Declaration in the *Tadić Jurisdiction Appeals Decision*, said that this Rule, when read with the Statute, made it "manifestly apparent that the English and French languages benefit of a status of equality in the Tribunal." He concluded that Decisions of the Tribunal should be simultaneously published in both languages, and that both texts should be equally authoritative.

7.84 In some cases, Judge Deschênes' injunction has been followed and both texts have been declared to be equally "authoritative." However the term "authoritative" is generally understood to mean that the decision has been *drafted* in that language. Rarely, if ever, is a decision drafted in both working languages. In any case, however, both English and French versions are always equally *official* and authentic, even where the decision in question has been "done" only in one of the languages. For example, for a decision that is proclaimed to be "DONE in English and French, the English version being authoritative," the English version is authoritative, but both English and French versions are equally official and authentic. The authoritative version would create a presumption that it should prevail in case of discrepancy, although if the non-authoritative version were "more consonant with the spirit of the Statute and the Rules," Rule 7 would dictate that the non-authoritative version prevail.

In Case of Discrepancy the Version More Favourable to the Accused Should Be Upheld

7.85 In the *Akayesu Trial Judgement*, the Trial Chamber held that in case of discrepancy between the French and English versions of a text, with regard either to a provision of the Statute, or to specific paragraphs of the Indictment, the version most favourable to the Accused should be upheld. In *Karemera, Decision on the Defence Motion pursuant to Rule 72*, 25 April 2001, the Trial Chamber concurred with this reasoning and decided to apply Rule 72(F) in its French version, as it appeared more favourable to the Accused and therefore more consonant with the spirit of the Statute and Rules.

PART 8

INTERNATIONAL CRIMINAL PROCEEDINGS

SECTION 1: INVESTIGATIONS
ICTY Rule 39/ICTR Rule 39: Conduct of Investigations 8.1.1
History of ICTY Rule 39 .... 8.1.2
Request Must Be Made to Trial Chamber or Judge 8.1.3
Requests for Assistance 8.1.6
ICTY Rule 40/ICTR Rule 40: Provisional Measures 8.1.8
History of ICTY Rule 40 .... 8.1.9
History of ICTR Rule 40 .... 8.1.11
ICTY Rule 40 bis/ICTR Rule 40 bis: Transfer and Provisional Detention of Suspects 8.1.12
History of ICTY Rule 40 bis 8.1.13
History of ICTR Rule 40 bis 8.1.16
ICTR Rule 40 bis (F) Applied Only in Exceptional Circumstances 8.1.19
Rule 40 bis and Submission of Indictment 8.1.20
Release Due to Violations of Rule 40 bis 8.1.21
Rule 40 bis Decisions 8.1.27
ICTY Rule 41: Retention of Information 8.1.28
ICTR Rule 41: Preservation of Information 8.1.28
History of ICTY Rule 41 .... 8.1.29
History of ICTR Rule 41 .... 8.1.30
Rule 41(B): Prosecutor Must Return Material Seized from the Accused 8.1.31
ICTY Rule 42/ICTR Rule 42: Rights of Suspects During Investigations 8.1.32
History of ICTY Rule 42 .... 8.1.33
ICTY Rule 43/ICTR Rule 43: Recording Questioning of Suspects 8.1.36
History of Rule 43 .... 8.1.37
SECTION 2: INDICTMENT
ICTY Article 18/ICTR Article 17: Investigation and Preparation of Indictment 8.2.1
General 8.2.2
Status of Indictments and Proceedings 8.2.3
Requirements of an Indictment 8.2.4
Indictment Bad for Duplicity 8.2.5
Indictment Must Contain a Concise Statement of Facts and Crimes Charged 8.2.8
ICTY Article 19/ICTR Article 18: Review of the Indictment 8.2.11
General 8.2.12
Standard of Proof for Review of Indictment 8.2.13
The Meaning of "*Prima Facie* Case" 8.2.14
ICTY Rule 47/ICTR Rule 47: Submission of Indictment by the Prosecutor 8.1.17
History of ICTY Rule 47 .... 8.2.18
History of ICTR Rule 47 .... 8.2.19
Requirements of an Indictment 8.2.20

Defence Motions on Form of Indictment Brought After Requesting Further Particulars from Prosecutor	8.2.22
Rule 47 (C): Indictment Must Contain Concise Statement of Facts	8.2.23
Excessive Vagueness	8.2.26
Decision of Confirming Judge Unreviewable Except Where Flagrantly in Violation of the Statute/Rules	8.2.30
Dismissal of Counts of Indictment	8.2.34
Superseding Indictments	8.2.35
Substitution of New Indictment Must Be Pursuant to Rules 50 and 51	8.2.36
ICTY Rule 48/ICTR Rule 48: Joinder of Accused	8.2.39
General	8.2.40
Application Must Be *Inter Partes*	8.2.41
Joinder for Better Administration of Justice	8.2.42
Joinder of Accused and Joint Trials	8.2.43
Meaning of "Same Transaction"	8.2.44
Joinder to Protect Victims and Witnesses	8.2.51
ICTR Rule 48 *bis*: Joinder of Trials	8.2.55
History of ICTR Rule 48 *bis*	8.2.56
ICTY Rule 49/ICTR Rule 49: Joinder of Crimes	8.2.58
History of ICTY Rule 49	8.2.59
Decisions Under Rule 49	8.2.60
ICTY Rule 50/ICTR Rule 50: Amendment of Indictment	8.2.69
History of ICTY Rule 50	8.2.70
History of ICTR Rule 50	8.2.72
Prerogative of Prosecutor to Amend	8.2.73
Withdrawal of Counts "With Prejudice"	8.2.75
Addition of New Counts Without Leave	8.2.76
No Need for Additional Time Where Charges Are Simply Withdrawn	8.2.77
Substantial Amendment of Indictment	8.2.78
Prosecution Must Disclose Supporting Material Proffered for Additional Counts to Defence and Judges	8.2.82
Schedule of Changes to Indictment	8.2.83
Procedure Upon Showing Defects in Form of Indictment	8.2.84
No Need to Notify Defence of Motion to Amend Indictment	8.2.85
Rule 50 Must Be Applied in Accordance with ICTY Articles 19 and 20 and ICCPR Article 9(2)	8.2.86
Amendment Allowed Based on Investigations Carried Out After Trial Has Commenced	8.2.87
ICTY Rule 51/ICTR Rule 51: Withdrawal of Indictment	8.2.88
History of ICTY Rule 51	8.2.89
History of ICTR Rule 51	8.2.90
Ill-Health Not Ground for Withdrawal	8.2.91
Death Ground for Withdrawal	8.2.92
Withdrawal for Lack of Evidence	8.2.93
Withdrawal for Trial in Domestic Courts	8.2.95
ICTY Rule 52/ICTR Rule 52: Public Character of Indictment	8.2.100
Rule 52 Subject to Rule 53	8.2.101
ICTY Rule 53/ICTR Rule 53: Non-Disclosure of Indictment	8.2.102
History of ICTY Rule 53	8.2.103
Sealed Indictments	8.2.105
ICTY Rule 53 *bis*/ICTR Rule 53 *bis*: Service of Indictment	8.2.110
History of ICTY Rule 53 *bis*	8.2.111
History of ICTR Rule 53 *bis*	8.2.112

SECTION 3: CUMULATIVE CHARGING

Charges Must Protect Different Values or Contain Different Elements	8.3.1
Cumulative Convictions Permitted if *Blockburger* Test Met	8.3.4
Cumulative or Alternative Counts	8.3.11
ICTY Rule 87(C)	8.3.20

SECTION 4: ORDERS AND WARRANTS

ICTY Rule 54/ICTR Rule 54: General Rule	8.4.1
History of ICTY Rule 54	8.4.2
Necessary for Purpose of Investigation, Preparation, or Conduct of Trial	8.4.3
Examples of Orders, Summonses, Subpoenas and Warrants Issued	8.4.5
Summonses	8.4.6
Subpoenae Duces Tecum	8.4.8
Subpoenas to States	8.4.12
Developments on Subpoenas/Binding Orders to States	8.4.15
Subpoenas and Protection of National Security	8.4.21
Subpoenas to Private Individuals	8.4.28
Subpoenas Cannot Be Issued to International Organizations	8.4.31
Subpoena to ICRC	8.4.32
Subpoena to Tribunal Officials	8.4.35
Subpoena to Journalists: War Correspondents	8.4.40
Subpoena or Order Not Issued in Vain	8.4.45
Vacating a Subpoena	8.4.46
Safe Conducts	8.4.47
Safe Conducts May Only Be Granted by a Judge or Chamber	8.4.52
Safe Conducts: Other Decisions	8.4.54
ICTR Subpoena	8.4.55
Arrest Warrants	8.4.58
Orders	8.4.59
Orders for Detention of Suspects	8.4.60
Order to Remedy and Error *in Personam*	8.4.61
Order to Confirm that Status of an Indictment Remains Unchanged	8.4.63
Order for Return of Materials	8.4.64
Order Regarding Fitness to Stand Trial	8.4.65
Other Examples of Orders	8.4.66
Stipulations/Formal Admissions	8.4.67
ICTY Rule 54 *bis*: Orders Directed to States for the Production of Documents	8.4.71
History of ICTY Rule 54 *bis*	8.4.72
Rule 54 *bis* Also Applies to Orders to International Organisations	8.4.74
ICTY Rule 55/ICTR Rule 55: Execution of Arrest Warrants	8.4.75
History of ICTY Rule 55	8.4.76
History of ICTR Rule 55	8.4.79
General	8.4.80
Meaning of "Arrest"	8.4.82
Rule 55 Not Exclusive Method of Procuring Arrest	8.4.83
Registrar Must Serve Documents on National States	8.4.84
ICTR Rule 55 *bis*: Warrant of Arrest to All States	8.4.87
History of ICTR Rule 55 *bis*	8.4.88
Relationship to Rule 61	8.4.89
ICTY Rule 57/ICTR Rule 57: Procedure after Arrest	8.4.90
History of ICTY Rule 57	8.4.92

482 • International Criminal Practice

ICTY Rule 59 *bis*: Transmission of Arrest Warrants 8.4.93
History of ICTY Rule 59 *bis* 8.4.94
Arrest by UNTAES 8.4.96
Luring of Accused Not Unlawful 8.4.98
Accused Has Standing to Raise Violation of State Sovereignty 8.4.106
Authority of UNTAES 8.4.108
Transmission of Arrest Warrants to Prosecutor 8.4.109
Dismissal of Indictment as a Result of Illegal Conduct During Course of Arrest .. 8.4.110
Mala Captus—Bene Detentus 8.4.112
Remedy for Violation of Human Rights During Arrest 8.4.113
ICTY Rule 60/ICTR Rule 60: Publication of Indictment 8.4.114
History of ICTY Rule 60 .... 8.4.115
History of ICTR Rule 60 .... 8.4.116
General 8.4.117
Proof of Publication Not Necessary 8.4.118
ICTY Rule 61/ICTR Rule 61: Procedure in Case of Failure to Execute a Warrant ... 8.4.119
History of ICTY Rule 61 .... 8.4.120
History of ICTR Rule 61 .... 8.4.126
Differences Between ICTY and ICTR on Rule 61 Hearings 8.4.127
Type of Proceedings 8.4.128
Rule 61 Hearing Not a Trial 8.4.130
Rule 61 Akin to Committal Proceedings 8.4.132
Representation of Accused 8.4.133
Amicus Curiae 8.4.135
Protection of Victims and Witnesses 8.4.138
"Reasonable Time" Dependent on Circumstances 8.4.139
Additional Evidence Tendered by Prosecutor 8.4.140
International Arrest Warrants to All States and to IFOR 8.4.142
Provisional Measures to Freeze Assets 8.4.144
Notification to Security Council 8.4.145

SECTION 5: COMMENCEMENT AND CONDUCT OF TRIAL PROCEEDINGS

ICTY Article 20/ICTR Article 19: Commencement and Conduct of Trial Proceedings 8.5.1
General 8.5.2
Fair Trial, Truth Finding and Effective Cross-Examination 8.5.3
Fair Trial and Appointment of *Amicus Curiae* 8.5.6
Custody 8.5.7
    Death in Custody: Inquest 8.5.8
    Persons in ICTY Custody 8.5.9
    Persons in ICTR Custody 8.5.10
The Plea 8.5.11
Public Hearings 8.5.12
RIGHTS OF THE ACCUSED
ICTY Article 21/ICTR Article 20: Rights of the Accused 8.5.13
ICTY Article 21/ ICTR Article 20 Based on ICCPR Article 14 .... 8.5.15
Equality Before the Tribunals 8.5.20
Public Hearing 8.5.22
Presumption of Innocence 8.5.25
Burdens of Proof 8.5.27
Independent and Impartial Tribunal 8.5.29

Prompt, Detailed Information as to Nature and Cause of Charge	8.5.32
Languages	8.5.39
Adequate Time and Facilities	8.5.46
Expeditious Trial	8.5.47
Right To Be Tried Without Undue Delay	8.5.47
Expeditious Trial Not To Be Compromised by Motions to Amend Indictment	8.5.49
Use of Pre-Trial Briefs and Stipulations	8.5.50
Use of Pre-Trial Judge	8.5.54
No Oral Argument Unless Requested by Counsel	8.5.57
Length of Trials	8.5.60
Accused May Not Waive Right to Expeditious Trial	8.5.61
Assignment of Defence Counsel	8.5.62
Equality of Arms Does Not Mean Equality of Means and Resources	8.5.70
Proceeding in Absence of Counsel	8.5.72
"Under the Same Conditions"—Equality of Arms	8.5.73
Right of Confrontation and Exceptions	8.5.83
Trial Chamber Can Order Party To Close Its Case	8.5.86
To Examine, or Have Examined, Witnesses Against Him	8.5.88
Requests for Interpretation	8.5.91
Privilege Against Self Incrimination	8.5.92
Non-Enumerated Rights	8.5.97
Legitimate Expectation	8.5.97
ICTY Rule 63/ICTR Rule 63: Questioning of the Accused	8.2.98
History of ICTY Rule 63	8.5.99
History of ICTR Rule 63	8.5.100
Right to Silence	8.5.101
Questioning by the Prosecution in the Absence of Counsel	8.5.102
Timing at Which to Challenge Compliance with Rule 63	8.5.106
History of ICTY Rule 64	8.5.107
ICTY Rule 64/ICTR Rule 64: Detention on Remand	8.5.108
Modification of Conditions of Detention	8.5.109
Test To Be Applied	8.5.113
ICTY Rule 65/ICTR Rule 65: Provisional Release	8.5.114
History of ICTY Rule 65	8.5.115
History of ICTR Rule 65	8.5.119
Granting of Provisional Release	8.5.120
Timing of Application for Provisional Release	8.5.122
State of Health a Factor To Be Considered in Granting Provisional Release	8.5.123
Jurisdiction of Appeals Chamber to Order Provisional Release	8.5.127
Four Conditions for Provisional Release	8.5.128
Exceptional Circumstances	8.5.130
Presumption of Detention	8.5.132
Factors in Deciding Exceptional Circumstances	8.5.139
Length of Detention	8.5.144
Ill-Health of the Accused	8.5.147
Accused Will Appear for Trial	8.5.151
Accused Will Not Pose a Danger To Victims, Witnesses, or Others	8.5.154
Host Country Must Be Heard	8.5.156
Position of the Host Country with Regard to Provisional Release	8.5.156
Appeal of Refusal To Grant Provisional Release	8.5.159
Other Decisions on Rule 65	8.5.161

Emergency Application for Provisional Release Can Be Considered by Duty Judge 8.5.169
PROTECTION OF VICTIMS AND WITNESSES................................... 8.5.170
ICTY Article 22/ICTR Article 21: Protection of Victims and Witnesses 8.5.170
General.. 8.5.171
ICTY Rule 69/ICTR Rule 69: Protection of Victims and Witnesses..................... 8.5.174
History of ICTY Rule 69... 8.5.175
History of ICTR Rule 69 .... 8.5.177
General.. 8.5.178
Witness with a Criminal Record... 8.5.179
Meaning of the "Identity" of the Victim or Witness 8.5.181
Relationship of Rule 69 to Rule 75 .... 8.5.182
Witness Anonymity 8.5.186
    Five Conditions for Witness Anonymity................................. 8.5.187
    Three Further Criteria.. 8.5.189
    Guidelines for Witness Anonymity 8.5.191
    Withdrawal of Anonymity 8.5.192
    Measures Stopping Short of Anonymity 8.5.195
Protective Measures Must Be Objectively Grounded............................ 8.5.196
Redaction of Witness Statements 8.5.199
Decisions on the Protection of Victims and Witnesses 8.5.202
ICTY Rule 75/ICTR Rule 75: Measures for the Protection of Victims and Witnesses 8.5.205
History of ICTY Rule 75... 8.5.206
History of ICTR Rule 75 .... 8.5.208
Measures Taken 8.5.209
Precarious Security Situation in Rwanda..................................... 8.5.210
Testifying Away from the Seat of the ICTR as a Safety Measure 8.5.214
Preventing Disclosure of Witness Statements to the Public and Media 8.5.215
Meaning of "Public" for the Purposes of "Non-Disclosure to the Public"........... 8.5.216
Exception to Ban on Disclosure to Third Parties 8.5.217
Protective Orders for Victims of Sexual Offences 8.5.218
Ex Parte Hearings.. 8.5.219
Tadić Victims and Witnesses Decision of 10 August 1995 .... 8.5.220
Protective Measures Must Be Exceptional 8.5.223
Witness Protection and State Cooperation Pursuant to Article 28................ 8.5.224
Refusal of Measures to Protect Against Self-Incrimination by a Witness.......... 8.5.225
Refusal to Limit Accused's Possession of Protected Material 8.5.226
Measures to Prevent Intimidation and Harassment of Witnesses 8.5.227
Prohibition on Making Independent Determination of the Identity of Any
    Protected Witness 8.5.228
Protective Measures for Family Members 8.5.230
Review of Protective Measures... 8.5.231
Other Decisions and Orders Under Rule 75 .... 8.5.233
TIME LIMITS.. 8.5.235
ICTY Rule 126: General Provision 8.5.235
History of ICTY Rule 126.. 8.5.236
ICTY Rule 126 *bis*: Time for Filing Responses to Motions 8.5.237
History of ICTY Rule 126 *bis*.. 8.5.238
ICTY Rule 127: Variation of Time-Limits.................................... 8.5.239
History of ICTY Rule 127.. 8.5.240
Orders Made Under Rule 127 .... 8.5.241

ICTR Rule 7 *ter:* Time Limits	8.5.242
History of ICTR Rule 7 *ter*	8.5.243
PRELIMINARY PROCEEDINGS	
ICTY Rule 62/ICTR Rule 62: Initial Appearance of Accused	8.5.244
History of ICTY Rule 62	8.5.245
History of ICTR Rule 62	8.5.247
ICTY Initial Appearances	8.5.248
Prosecutor Has No Role in Assignment of a Case to a Trial Chamber	8.5.250
Conditions for Accepting a Guilty Plea	8.5.251
Equivocal Plea	8.5.258
The *Erdemović* Case on Appeal	8.5.263
Failure to Enter a Plea	8.5.267
Guilty Pleas	8.5.271
ICTY	8.5.271
Erdemović	8.5.272
Kunarac	8.5.273
Jelisić	8.5.274
ICTR	8.5.277
Kambanda	8.5.278
Serushago	8.5.280
Other Rule 62 Decisions	8.5.281
ICTY Rule 62 *bis:* Guilty Pleas	8.5.282
History of ICTY Rule 62 *bis*	8.5.283
Plea Bargains	8.5.286
ICTY Rule 62 *ter:* Plea Agreement Procedure	8.5.292
History of ICTY Rule 62 *ter*	8.5.293
ICTY Rule 65 *bis*/ICTR Rule 65 *bis:* Status Conferences	8.5.295
History of ICTY Rule 65 *bis*	8.5.296
History of ICTR Rule 65 *bis*	8.5.297
ICTY Rule 65 *ter:* Pre-Trial Judge	8.5.298
History of ICTY Rule 65 *ter*	8.5.299
Juge d'Instruction	8.5.301
Defence Pre-Trial Brief	8.5.302
PRODUCTION OF EVIDENCE	8.5.305
ICTY Rule 66: Disclosure by the Prosecutor	8.5.305
ICTR Rule 66: Disclosure of Materials by the Prosecutor	8.5.305
History of ICTY Rule 66	8.5.306
History of ICTR Rule 66	8.5.312
Orders Issued by the Accused Are Not "Prior Statements Obtained by the Prosecutor from the Accused" Within the Meaning of Rule 66(A)(i)	8.5.313
Accused's Access to His Prior Statements and Those of Prosecution Witnesses Applies Irrespective of How They Were Obtained by the Prosecution	8.5.314
Hearsay Declarant Is Not a Witness Whose Prior Statements Must Be Disclosed to the Defence, Although Prior Statements Must Be Disclosed If Exculpatory Pursuant to Rule 68	8.5.318
Accused Entitled to Witness Statements in Language He Understands	8.5.319
Relationship Between Rule 66(A)(ii) and Rule 73 *bis* (E) on Variation of Witnesses to Be Called by Prosecution at Trial	8.5.320
Disclosure Must Be "Timely"	8.5.323
Prosecution Under Obligation to Obtain Previous Statements of Prosecution Witnesses Taken by Other Authorities	8.5.325

Defence Not Entitled to Interview Prosecution Witnesses Prior to Trial or to Request a
  "Bill of Particulars" 8.5.327
Requirement that Defence Show Materiality of Evidence Requested 8.5.328
Obligation to Disclose Arises Only After the Initial Appearance of the Accused 8.5.333
Sanctioning the Prosecution for Failure to Comply with Its Disclosure Obligations 8.5.334
Other Decisions on Rule 66. .... 8.5.337
Redaction of Witness Statements Can Only Be Done Pursuant to an Order by the
  Chamber 8.5.338
Disclosure Pursuant to Rule 66(A) Not To Be Withheld Due to Pendency of a Motion for
  Protective Measures 8.5.340
Dilatory Disclosure by the Prosecutor 8.5.343
ICTY Rule 67: Reciprocal Disclosure 8.5.344
ICTR Rule 67: Reciprocal Disclosure of Evidence 8.5.344
History of ICTY Rule 67. .... 8.5.345
History of ICTR Rule 67 .... 8.5.346
Names of Prosecution Witnesses Must Be Given in a Comprehensive Document. 8.5.347
Unlike Prosecution, Defence Is Not Obliged to Disclose Its Witnesses' Names Prior to
  Trial 8.5.348
Alibi Notice 8.5.353
    Consequences of Failure to Serve Alibi Notice at the Proper Time. 8.5.356
Notice of Special Defence 8.5.358
Diminished Responsibility Versus Unfitness to Stand Trial 8.5.359
Disclosure of Addresses of Witnesses to Special Defence 8.5.360
Decisions 8.5.362
Para. (C) Only Requires Defence to Make Reciprocal Disclosure of Evidence That It
  "Intends" to Use at Trial 8.5.363
Circumvention by Reliance Not on Rule 66(B) but on Rule 68 ("Disclosure of
  Exculpatory Evidence") 8.5.364
Defence Must Present a *Prima Facie* Case that Would Make Probable the Exculpatory
  Nature of the Materials Sought 8.5.368
ICTY Rule 68/ICTR Rule 68: Disclosure of Exculpatory Evidence 8.5.370
History of ICTY Rule 68. .... 8.5.371
Definition of 'Exculpatory Material" 8.5.372
Lack of Evidence Is Not "Exculpatory Evidence" 8.5.373
Exculpatory Evidence in Case-Files of Other Accused 8.5.376
Duty on the Prosecutor 8.5.377
Exculpatory Evidence Must Be in Possession of Prosecutor 8.5.380
Test To Be Applied for Discovery Under Rule 68 .... 8.5.384
Exculpatory Evidence Not Limited to Admissible Evidence 8.5.388
Obligation Pursuant to Rule 68 Continues after Trial 8.5.389
Subjective Element To What Is Exculpatory; Presumption of Good Faith on the
  Part of the Prosecutor 8.5.390
Sanctions for Prosecutor's Failure to Comply with Rule 68 .... 8.5.391
Re-Opening of Trial Due to Failure to Comply with Rule 68. .... 8.5.392
ICTY Rule 68 *bis:* Failure to Comply with Disclosure Obligations 8.5.397
History of Rule 68 *bis* 8.5.398
ICTY Rule 70/ICTR Rule 70: Matters Not Subject to Disclosure 8.5.399
History of ICTY Rule 70. .... 8.5.400
History of ICTR Rule 70 .... 8.5.404
Applicability of Rule 70 to the Accused 8.5.405
Applicability to Witness Statements. 8.5.406
Examples 8.5.407

DEPOSITIONS
ICTY Rule 71/ICTR Rule 71: Depositions 8.5.411
History of ICTY Rule 71. . . . . 8.5.412
Use of Rule 71 in the Event of the Temporary Unavailability of a Judge 8.5.413
Video Conference 8.5.418
Video Conference and the Right of Confrontation 8.5.424
ICTY Rule 71 *bis*: Testimony by Video-Conference Link 8.5.428
History of ICTY Rule 71 *bis* 8.5.429
MOTIONS
ICTY Rule 72/ICTR Rule 72: Preliminary Motions 8.5.430
History of ICTY Rule 72. . . . . 8.5.431
History of ICTR Rule 72 . . . . 8.5.438
Motions Should Be Respectful 8.5.440
Decisions on Motions Challenging Jurisdiction 8.5.441
    ICTY Challenges to Jurisdiction 8.5.442
    ICTR Challenges to Jurisdiction 8.5.447
Decisions on Objections Based on Defects in the Form of the Indictment 8.5.449
Distinguishing Between Forms of Individual Criminal Responsibility 8.5.451
Averring the Names of the Accused's Alleged Co-Conspirators. 8.5.452
Decisions on Applications for Severance of Crimes Joined in One Indictment under
    Rule 49, or for Separate Trials under Sub-Rule 82(B) 8.5.454
Objections Based on Denial of Request for Assignment of Counsel 8.5.455
Interlocutory Appeal 8.5.456
    Interlocutory Appeal on Jurisdiction in *Tadić*. 8.5.457
    Interlocutory Appeal Only Available to Parties 8.5.462
    No Hearing Necessary 8.5.464
Interpretation of ICTY Rule 72(B)(ii) 8.5.465
ICTY Rule 73: Other Motions 8.5.468
ICTR Rule 73: Motions 8.5.468
History of ICTY Rule 73. . . . . 8.5.469
History of ICTR Rule 73 . . . . 8.5.472
ICTY Motions Practice. 8.5.473
    Written Motions 8.5.474
    Oral Motions at Trial 8.5.475
ICTR Motions Practice 8.5.477
Types of Motion. 8.5.479
    Motions to Reconsider 8.5.480
Interlocutory Appeal under Rule 73. . . . . 8.5.482
Denial of Payment. 8.5.484
CONFERENCES
ICTY Rule 73 *bis*/ICTR Rule 73 *bis*: Pre-Trial Conference 8.5.486
History of ICTY Rule 73 *bis* 8.5.487
History of ICTR Rule 73 *bis* 8.5.488
Pre-Trial Brief 8.5.489
Reinstatement of Witness 8.5.490
Varying the Witness List at Trial 8.5.491
ICTY Rule 73 *ter*/ICTR Rule 73 *ter*: Pre-Defence Conference 8.5.492
History of ICTY Rule 73 *ter* 8.5.493
History of ICTR Rule 73 *ter* 8.5.494

Defence Can Be Ordered to Provide Information Identifying Their Witnesses and
    Summaries of Their Witnesses' Testimony 8.5.495
Order to Submit Detailed Witness Statements.................................. 8.5.496
PROCEEDINGS BEFORE TRIAL CHAMBERS.. 8.5.499
ICTY Rule 74/ICTR Rule 74: *Amicus Curiae*.. 8.5.499
Guidelines for Submission of *Amicus* Briefs 8.5.500
History of *Amicus* Submissions 8.5.501
    The UN Secretary-General as *Amicus* 8.5.502
    Governments as *Amicus*... 8.5.504
    Blaškić Supoena Hearings 8.5.507
    Concerned Organisations... 8.5.510
    Milošević and the Appointment of *Amicus*................................. 8.5.512
Relationship Between *Amicus* and *Partie Civile* 8.5.513
    Belgium 8.5.514
        Bagosora and *Nahimana*... 8.5.514
        Semanza... 8.5.520
ICTY Rule 74 *bis*/ICTR Rule 74 *bis*: Medical Examination of the Accused 8.5.522
History of ICTY Rule 74 *bis*... 8.5.523
History of ICTR Rule 74 *bis*... 8.5.524
ICTY Rule 76/ICTR Rule 76: Solemn Declaration by Interpreters and Translators 8.5.525
ICTY Rule 78/ICTR Rule 78: Open Sessions 8.5.527
ICTY Rule 79/ICTR Rule 79: Closed Sessions 8.5.529
General Principle.. 8.5.530
National Security.. 8.5.531
Protection of Victims and Witnesses 8.5.532
Transcripts of Closed Sessions 8.5.533
Lašva River Valley Cases: Access to Non-Public Materials 8.5.534
ICTY Rule 80/ICTR Rule 80: Control of Proceedings............................... 8.5.535
ICTY Rule 81/ICTR Rule 81: Records of Proceedings and Evidence 8.5.537
History of ICTY Rule 81.. 8.5.538
Orders and Decisions under Rule 81... 8.5.539
Authorisation of Photography 8.5.541
ICTY Rule 82/ICTR Rule 82: Joint and Separate Trials 8.5.542
Conflict of Interest Necessitating Separate Trials 8.5.543
Relevance to Joint Trials of the Absence of a Jury............................... 8.5.544
Conflicting Defences... 8.5.545
Concurrent Presentation of Evidence 8.5.546
Intention to Call Co-Accused to Testify 8.5.547
Command Responsibility... 8.5.549
Drawbacks to Separate Trials 8.5.550
Co-Accused Not in Custody 8.5.551
Deadline for Application for Severance 8.5.553
ICTY Rule 83/ICTR Rule 83: Instruments of Restraint............................. 8.5.556
History of ICTY Rule 83.. 8.5.557
ICTY Rule 84/ICTR Rule 84: Opening Statements 8.5.559
ICTY Rule 84 *bis*: Statement of the Accused................................... 8.5.563
History of ICTY Rule 84 *bis*.. 8.5.564
ICTY Rule 85/ICTR Rule 85: Presentation of Evidence 8.5.567
History of ICTY Rule 85.. 8.5.568
History of ICTR Rule 85 .... 8.5.569
Order of Presentation of Evidence 8.5.570

International Criminal Proceedings • 489

Evidence Called at the Proper Time	8.5.571
Defence Motion to Dismiss Charges	8.5.573
Distinction Between Motion to Dismiss and Judgement of Acquittal	8.5.576
Order of Presentation of Rebuttqal Evidence	8.5.579
Re-Cross-Examination	8.5.581
Accused Sworn before Giving Testimony	8.5.584
Accused Cannot Be Ordered to Appear as First Defence Witness	8.5.589
Rules of Examination of Witnesses	8.5.593
Rule Against Comment	8.5.593
Scope of Cross-Examination	8.5.595
Accused Has No Right to Polygraph Test	8.5.599
ICTY Rule 86/ICTR Rule 86: Closing Arguments	8.5.601
History of ICTY Rule 86	8.5.602
History of ICTR Rule 86	8.5.604
Unfairness to the Accused of Having to Address Sentencing Matters at the Sentencing Stage	8.5.605
Examples	8.5.607
ICTY Rule 87/ICTR Rule 87: Deliberations	8.5.608
History of ICTY Rule 87	8.5.609
History of ICTR Rule 87	8.5.611
Proof of Guilt Beyond a Reasonable Doubt	8.5.612
Elements to Be Proved at Trial	8.5.616
Corroboration	8.5.617
Reliability of Witnesses	8.5.618
Pre-Trial Media Coverage and the Infection of Testimonial Evidence	8.5.619
"Dock Identification"	8.5.620
Hearsay	8.5.622
Meaning of Separate Findings	8.5.623
ICTY Rule 87	8.5.625
RULES OF EVIDENCE	8.5.626
ICTY Rule 89/ICTR Rule 89: General Provisions	8.5.626
History of Rule 89	8.5.627
Comparison Between ICTY Rule 89 and ICTR Rule 89	8.5.628
"Chambers Shall Not Be Bound by National Rules of Evidence"	8.5.631
Guidance as to What Constitute "General Principles of Law"	8.5.633
Proof of Death	8.5.634
Corroboration	8.5.636
Rules of Evidence/Comment	8.5.639
Weight To Be Given to Witness Testimony	8.5.641
Hearsay	8.5.642
Definition of Hearsay	8.5.642
Hearsay Not *Per Se* Excluded; Test Is Reliability of the Evidence	8.5.643
Non-Admission of Hearsay Evidence	8.5.653
Admission of Hearsay Does Not Indicate Finding as to Its Probative Value	8.5.654
Hearsay and the Statement of a Deceased Witness	8.5.655
Relevant Evidence	8.5.656
Character Evidence	8.5.662
Direct Versus Indirect Evidence	8.5.664
"Conciousness of Guilt" Not of Probative Value	8.5.665
Evidence of Acts Not Charged in the Indictment	8.5.666
Probative Value Outweighed by Prejudicial Effect	8.5.668
Authentication	8.5.669

490 • *International Criminal Practice*

No Corroboration Requirement	8.5.670
Submission of Documents to Chamber	8.5.671
Other ICTY and ICTR Decisions on Rule 89	8.5.672
ICTY Rule 90/ICTR Rule 90: Testimony of Witnesses	8.5.673
History of ICTY Rule 90	8.5.674
History of ICTR Rule 90	8.5.676
The "Best Evidence Rule" at the ICTs	8.5.677
Video-Link Testimony	8.5.679
Improper for Witness to Send *Ex Parte* Communications to Judge about Merits of Issues before the Tribunal	8.5.680
Communication with a Witness after He Has Been Sworn	8.5.681
Prevention of Contamination of Witness Testimony	8.5.686
Investigations Are Not "Expert Witnesses"	8.5.689
Publications of Expert Witnesses Are Public Property and Do Not Have To Be Disclosed	8.5.692
Expert Witnesses	8.5.693
Expert Witness Must Be Impartial and an Acknowledged Expert	8.5.695
Sequestration of Witnesses	8.5.696
Immunised Testimony	8.5.697
Credibility of Witnesses	8.5.698
Cross-Examination: Leading Questions	8.5.699
ICTY Rule 90 *bis*/ICTR Rule 90 *bis*: Transfer of a Detained Witness	8.5.700
History of ICTR Rule 90 *bis*	8.5.701
General	8.5.702
Precursor to Rule 90 *bis*: The *Opačić* Case	8.5.704
Detention by National Authorities Not Justiciable	8.5.706
Extension of Time for Detention	8.5.707
Expiry of Time Limits	8.5.709
Necessity for Request Must Be Demonstrated	8.5.711
Detained Witness Not Required for Criminal Proceedings in Progress in the State	8.5.712
Communication between Detained Witnesses	8.5.713
ICTY Rule 92/ICTR Rule 92: Confessions	8.5.714
Appropriate Stage to Challenge Admissibility of Confessions	8.5.715
ICTY Rule 92 *bis*/ICTR Rule 92 *bis*: Proof of Facts Other Than by Oral Evidence	8.5.716
History of ICTY Rule 92 *bis*	8.5.717
ICTY Rule 93/ICTR Rule 93: Evidence of Consistent Pattern of Conduct	8.5.720
History of ICTY Rule 93	8.5.721
ICTY Rule 94/ICTR Rule 94: Judicial Notice	8.5.723
History of ICTY Rule 94	8.5.724
History of ICTR Rule 94	8.5.725
General	8.5.726
Judicial Notice and *Res Judicata*	8.5.727
Judicial Notice and Stipulations/Formal Admissions	8.5.728
Judicial Notice of Adjudicated Facts	8.5.729
Citing Authorities and Judicial Notice	8.5.734
ICTY Rule 94 *bis*/ICTR Rule 94 *bis*: Testimony of Expert Witnesses	8.5.735
History of ICTY Rule 94 *bis*	8.5.736
History of ICTR Rule 94 *bis*	8.5.739
ICTY Rule 95: Exclusion of Certain Evidence	8.5.741

**ICTR Rule 95: Exclusion of Evidence on the Grounds of the Means by Which
It Was Obtained** 8.5.741
History of ICTY Rule 95. .... 8.5.742
Decisions, Orders, and Opinions under Rule 95 .... 8.5.743
ICTY Rule 96/ICTR Rule 96: Evidence in Cases of Sexual Assault 8.5.745
History of ICTY Rule 96. .... 8.5.746
Protection of Alleged Victims of Sexual Assault. 8.5.748
"Consent Shall Not Be Allowed as a Defence". 8.5.749
No Waiver of Victim's Right Not To Have His/Her Prior Sexual Conduct Admitted In
    Evidence 8.5.750
Expert Medical Evidence Not Required in Relation to Sexual Offences. 8.5.751
ICTY Rule 97/ICTR Rule 97: Lawyer-Client Privilege. 8.5.752
General 8.5.753
Transmission of Privileged Correspondence between Counsel and Accused by
    Investigators 8.5.754
**ICTY Rule 98/ICTR Rule 98: Power of Chambers to Order Production of
Additional Evidence** 8.5.758
Hisory of ICTR Rule 98 .... 8.5.759
Witness Summoned by the Chamber 8.5.760

SECTION 6: JUDGEMENT

ICTY Article 23/ICTR Article 22: Judgement 8.6.1
Judgements Drafted by Legal Assistants. 8.6.2
ICTY Trial Judgements 8.6.4
ICTR Final Judgements. 8.6.5
ICTY Rule 98 *bis*/ICTR Rule 98 *bis*: Motion of Judgement of Acquittal 8.6.6
History of ICTY Rule 98 *bis*. 8.6.7
Standard To Be Applied under Rule 98 *bis* 8.6.9
Rule 98 *bis* Can Be Applied to Individual Incidents 8.6.10
Decisions under Rule 98 *bis* 8.6.11
ICTY Rule 98 *ter*: Judgement 8.6.16
ICTR Rule 88: Judgement 8.6.16
History of ICTY Rule 98 *ter*. 8.6.17
Sentencing Matters May Be Dealt with Before Judgment Handed Down 8.6.19
ICTY Rule 99/ICTR Rule 99: Status of the Acquitted Person 8.6.20
History of ICTY Rule 99. .... 8.6.21
History of ICTR Rule 99 .... 8.6.22
Application of Rule 8.6.23

* * * * *

SECTION 1: INVESTIGATIONS

8.1.1

ICTY Rule 39 Conduct of Investigations	ICTR Rule 39 Conduct of Investigations
In the conduct of an investigation, the Prosecutor may: (i) summon and question suspects, victims and witnesses and record their statements, collect evidence and conduct on-site investigations; (ii) undertake such other matters as may appear necessary for completing the investigation and the preparation and conduct of the prosecution at the trial, including the taking of special measures to provide for the safety of potential witnesses and informants; (iii) seek, to that end, the assistance of any State authority concerned, as well as of any relevant international body including the International Criminal Police Organization (INTERPOL); and (iv) request such orders as may be necessary from a Trial Chamber or a Judge.	In the conduct of an investigation, the Prosecutor may: (i) summon and question suspects, victims and witnesses and record their statements, collect evidence and conduct on-site investigations; (ii) take all measures deemed necessary for the purpose of the investigation and to support the prosecution at trial, including the taking of special measures to provide for the safety of potential witnesses and informants; (iii) seek, to that end, the assistance of any State authority concerned, as well as of any relevant international body including the International Criminal Police Organization (INTERPOL); and (iv) request such orders as may be necessary from a Trial Chamber or a Judge.

History of ICTY Rule 39

8.1.2 Rule 39(ii) was amended at the fifth plenary session in January 1995 to allow the Prosecutor to take special measures for the protection of victims and witnesses. The amendment, proposed by the Prosecution, would permit it to offer assistance to potential witnesses and informants without removing overall responsibility for the protection of victims and witnesses from the Registrar and the Victims and Witnesses Unit (ICTY second Annual Report, para. 27).

Request Must Be Made to Trial Chamber or Judge

8.1.3 Rule 39(iv) is, on its terms, similar to Rule 54, and the Prosecutor has on occasion sought orders pursuant to both Rules simultaneously.

8.1.4 This test of whether it is "necessary" to grant the order sought was considered by the ICTY President in the *Decision of the President on the Prosecutor's Motion for the Production of Notes Exchanged Between Zejnil Delalić and Zdravko Mucić*, rendered in *Delalić et al.* on 11 November 1996, on a Motion made pursuant to Rules 39, 54 and 72 by the Prosecutor to a Trial Chamber, which had been remitted to the ICTY President for determination:

38. The Prosecutor's Motion before the Trial Chamber is founded on three Rules: Rules 39(iv), 54 and 72. Rule 72 is no help in this regard—it simply gives the Prosecutor the *right* to file preliminary motions, but says nothing about when those motions will be granted. Rule 39(iv) refers to "such orders *as may be necessary* ...," and Rule 54 refers to "such ... orders *as may be necessary for the purposes of an investigation or for the preparation or conduct of the trial.*" In the light of these two Rules, I find that the appropriate test is: *is it necessary (not simply useful or helpful) for the purposes of the investigation or for the preparation or conduct of the trial that the Registrar be ordered to produce the notes in question?*

39. The test entails two parts: (a) an order of the International Tribunal must be necessary for the Prosecutor to obtain such material; and (b) the material being sought must be relevant to an investigation or prosecution being conducted by the Prosecutor. As with any search or seizure warrant, the Prosecutor cannot simply conduct a "fishing expedition" through the Registrar's records.

8.1.5 In this last regard, the ICTY President considered the criteria applicable to disclosure under Rule 66 of the Rules as laid down in the Trial Chamber's *Decision on the Motion by the Accused Zejnil Delalić for the Disclosure of Evidence*, dated 26 September 1996 (see Rules 54 and 66). In the event, the President found that it *was* necessary for the Registrar to be ordered to produce the notes in question.

Requests for Assistance

8.1.6 On 2 August 1995, the Trial Chamber, on a motion from the Prosecutor submitted under Article 29 of the Statute and Rules 39 and 40, issued an Order requesting States to assist in the arrests of Radovan Karadžić, Ratko Mladić and Milan Martić by providing information as to their movements and location. This Order, and accompanying documents, were sent to all Permanent Missions to the United Nations in New York, including the Observer Missions of Switzerland, the Holy See and Palestine, on 3 August 1995.

8.1.7 In his Motion, the Prosecutor stated, "In view of the terms of Article 29 of the Statute, the Prosecutor considers it appropriate that a formal request for assistance ... should (be) addressed to states by a Trial Chamber rather than by the Prosecutor." (para. 10)

Cross Reference: Rule 54.

8.1.8

ICTY Rule 40 Provisional Measures	ICTR Rule 40 Provisional Measures
In case of urgency, the Prosecutor may request any State: (i) to arrest a suspect or an accused provisionally; (ii) to seize physical evidence; (iii) to take all necessary measures to prevent the escape of a suspect or an accused, injury to or intimidation of a victim or witness, or the destruction of evidence. The State concerned shall comply forthwith, in accordance with Article 29 of the Statute.	(A) In case of urgency, the Prosecutor may request any State: (i) to arrest a suspect provisionally; (ii) to seize physical evidence; (iii) to take all necessary measures to prevent the escape of a suspect or an accused, injury to or intimidation of a victim or witness, or the destruction of evidence. The State concerned shall comply forthwith, in accordance with Article 28 of the Statute. (B) Upon showing that a major impediment does not allow the State to keep the suspect under provisional detention or to take all necessary measures to prevent his escape, the Prosecutor may apply to a Judge designated by the President for an order to transfer the suspect to the seat of the Tribunal or to such other place as the Bureau may decide, and to detain him provisionally. After consultation with the Prosecutor and the Registrar, the Registrar shall be arranged between the State authorities concerned, the authorities of the host Country and the Registrar. (C) In the cases referred to in para. (B), the suspect shall, from the moment of his transfer, enjoy all the rights provided for in Rule 42 and may apply for review to a Trial Chamber of the Tribunal. The Chamber, after hearing the Prosecutor, shall rule upon the application. (D) The suspect shall be released if (i) the Chamber so rules, or (ii) the Prosecutor fails to issue an indictment within twenty days of the transfer.

History of ICTY Rule 40

8.1.9 Rule 40 was amended at the ICTY fifth plenary session in January 1995, adding the phrase, "the State concerned shall comply forthwith, in accordance with Article 29 of the Statute," which is based on a similar phrase in Rule 8 (See second Annual Report, para. 24).

8.1.10 Rule 40 was amended at the ICTY nineteenth plenary session, on 17 December 1998, adding the words "or an accused" to para. (i).

History of ICTR Rule 40

8.1.11 Paras (B), (C) and (D) were added to Rule 40 by the ICTR in a plenary session. The ICTY has not adopted these paras. which, to a certain extent, anticipate Rule 40 *bis* (see next Rule).

8.1.12

ICTY Rule 40 *bis* Transfer and Provisional Detention of Suspects	ICTR Rule 40 *bis* Transfer and Provisional Detention of Suspects
(A) In the conduct of an investigation, the Prosecutor may transmit to the Registrar, for an order by a Judge assigned pursuant to Rule 28, a request for the transfer to and provisional detention of a suspect in the premises of the detention unit of the Tribunal. This request shall indicate the grounds upon which the request is made and, unless the Prosecutor wishes only to question the suspect, shall include a provisional charge and a summary of the material upon which the Prosecutor relies. (B) The Judge shall order the transfer and provisional detention of the suspect if the following conditions are met: (i) the Prosecutor has requested a State to arrest the suspect provisionally, in accordance with Rule 40, or the suspect is otherwise detained by State authorities; (ii) after hearing the Prosecutor, the Judge considers that there is a reliable and consistent body of material which tends to show that the suspect may have committed a crime over which the Tribunal has jurisdiction; and (iii) the Judge considers provisional detention to be a necessary measure to prevent the escape of the suspect, injury to or intimidation of a victim or witness or the destruction of evidence, or to be otherwise necessary for the conduct of the investigation. (C) The order for the transfer and provisional detention of the suspect shall be signed by the Judge and bear the seal of the Tribunal. The order shall set forth the basis of the application made by the Prosecutor under Sub-rule	(A) In the conduct of an investigation, the Prosecutor may transmit to the Registrar, for an order by a Judge assigned pursuant to Rule 28, a request for the transfer to and provisional detention of a suspect in the premises of the detention unit of the Tribunal. This request shall indicate the grounds upon which the request is made and, unless the Prosecutor wishes only to question the suspect, shall include a provisional charge and a summary of the material upon which the Prosecutor relies. (B) The Judge shall order the transfer and provisional detention of the suspect if the following conditions are met: (i) the Prosecutor has requested a State to arrest the suspect provisionally, in accordance with Rule 40, or the suspect is otherwise detained by State authorities; (ii) after hearing the Prosecutor, the Judge considers that there is a reliable and consistent body of material which tends to show that the suspect may have committed a crime over which the Tribunal has jurisdiction; and (iii) the Judge considers provisional detention to be a necessary measure to prevent the escape of the suspect, physical or mental injury to or intimidation of a victim or witness or the destruction of evidence, or to be otherwise necessary for the conduct of the investigation. (C) The provisional detention of a suspect may be ordered for a period not exceeding 30 days from the day after the transfer of the suspect to the detention unit of the Tribunal.

(A), including the provisional charge, and shall state the Judge's grounds for making the order, having regard to Sub-rule (B). The order shall also specify the initial time-limit for the provisional detention of the suspect, and be accompanied by a statement of the rights of a suspect, as specified in this Rule and in Rules 42 and 43.

(D) The provisional detention of a suspect shall be ordered for a period not exceeding thirty days from the date of the transfer of the suspect to the seat of the Tribunal. At the end of that period, at the Prosecutor's request, the Judge who made the order, or another Judge of the same Trial Chamber, may decide, subsequent to an *inter partes* hearing of the Prosecutor and the suspect assisted by his counsel, to extend the detention for a period not exceeding thirty days, if warranted by the needs of the investigation. At the end of that extension, at the Prosecutor's request, the Judge who made the order, or another Judge of the same Trial Chamber, may decide, subsequent to an *inter partes* hearing of the Prosecutor and the suspect assisted by his counsel, to extend the detention for a further period not exceeding thirty days, if warranted by special circumstances. The total period of detention shall in no case exceed ninety days, at the end of which, in the event the indictment has not been confirmed and an arrest warrant signed, the suspect shall be released or, if appropriate, be delivered to the authorities of the requested State.

(E) The provisions in Rules 55(B) to 59 *bis* shall apply *mutatis mutandis* to the execution of the transfer order and the provisional detention order relative to a suspect.

(F) After being transferred to the seat of the Tribunal, the suspect, assisted by counsel, shall be brought, without delay, before the Judge who made the order, or another Judge of the same Trial Chamber, who shall ensure that the rights of the suspect are respected.

(G) During detention, the Prosecutor and the suspect or the suspect's counsel may submit to the Trial Chamber of which the Judge who

(D) The order for the transfer and provisional detention of the suspect shall be signed by the Judge and bear the seal of the Tribunal. The order shall set forth the basis of the application made by the Prosecutor under Sub-rule (A), including the provisional charge, and shall state the Judge's grounds for making the order, having regard to Sub-rule (B). The order shall also specify the initial time limit for the provisional detention of the suspect, and be accompanied by a statement of the rights of a suspect, as specified in this Rule and in Rules 42 and 43.

(E) As soon as possible, copies of the order and of the request by the Prosecutor are served upon the suspect and his counsel by the Registrar.

(F) At the Prosecutor's request indicating the grounds upon which it is made and if warranted by the needs of the investigation, the Judge who made the order, or another Judge of the same Trial Chamber, may decide, subsequent to an *inter partes* hearing and before the end of the period of detention, to extend the detention for a further period not exceeding 30 days.

(G) At the Prosecutor's request indicating the grounds upon which it is made and if warranted by special circumstances, the Judge made the order is a member, all applications relative to the propriety of provisional detention or to the suspect's release.

(H) Without prejudice to Sub-rule (D), the Rules relating to the detention on remand of accused persons shall apply *mutatis mutandis* to the provisional detention of persons under this Rule.

who made the order, or another Judge of the same Trial Chamber, may decide, subsequent to an *inter partes* hearing and before the end of the period of detention, to extend the detention for a further period not exceeding 30 days.

(H) The total period of detention shall in no case exceed 90 days after the day of transfer of the suspect to the Tribunal, at the end of which, in the event the indictment has not been confirmed and an arrest warrant signed, the suspect shall be released or, if appropriate, be delivered to the authorities of the State to which the request was initially made.

(I) The provisions in Rules 55(B) to 59 shall apply *mutatis mutandis* to the execution of the order for the transfer and provisional detention order of the suspect.

(J) After his transfer to the seat of the Tribunal, the suspect, assisted by his counsel, shall be brought, without delay, before the Judge who made the initial order, or another Judge of the same Trial Chamber, who shall ensure that his rights are respected.

(K) During detention, the Prosecutor and the suspect or his counsel may submit to the Trial Chamber of which the Judge who made the initial order is a member, all applications relative to the propriety of provisional detention or to the suspect's release.

(L) Without prejudice to Sub-rules (C) to (H), the Rules relating to the detention on remand of accused persons shall apply *mutatis mutandis* to the provisional detention of persons under this Rule.

History of ICTY Rule 40 *bis*

8.1.13 This new Rule was adopted at the ICTY tenth plenary session on 22–23 April 1996. It gives the Prosecutor the authority to request an order from a Judge for the transfer and provisional detention of a *suspect* to the Detention Unit in The Hague. A regime governing the period of such detention, taking into account applicable international standards, was prepared by the Judicial Department of the Registry and approved by the Judges.

8.1.14 Rule 40 *bis* (D) was amended at the ICTY thirteenth plenary session on 25 July 1997, substituting the words, "date of the transfer of the suspect to the seat of the Tribunal" for "signing of the provisional detention order." The significance of this amendment may be understood in light of the use of this Rule at the ICTR, where the previous wording of the Rule required the detention order to be renewed even when the accused was not yet in custody (see History of ICTR Rule 40 *bis* below).

8.1.15 Gender-neutral language was adopted for this Rule at the fourteenth plenary session on 12 November 1997.

Cross References: This Rule should be contrasted with Rule 90 *bis*, which concerns transfer and detention of a *witness*. See Rule 90 *bis* and commentary at 8.5.700 *et seq.* below.

History of ICTR Rule 40 *bis*

8.1.16 This rule was adopted by the ICTR on 15 May 1996, following the adoption of the same rule by the ICTY (see above, ICTY Rule 40 *bis*). It was applied in the *Ntagerura* (ICTR-96-10-DP), *Bagosora* (ICTR-96-7-D), *Nsengiyumva* (ICTR-96-9-DP) and *Nahimana* (ICTR-96-8-DP) cases on 17 May 1996, in Decisions rendered by Judge Aspegren ordering provisional detention and transfer of the suspects. In light of the 30 day period imposed by Rule 40 *bis* (D), Decisions were rendered by Judge Aspegren in the last three cases on 18 June 1996 ordering the *continued* detention on remand of the suspects for a further 30 day period. In the *Bagosora* case (ICTR-96-7-D), a further Decision ordering the suspect's continued detention for another 30 days was ordered by Judge Kama on 15 July 1996. It is worth noting that the suspect was still not in the custody of the ICTR by the time the third order was made; it was necessary for the Prosecutor to seek the further Orders because the time-limits under Rule 40 *bis* (D) ran from the date at which the provisional detention order was *signed*, not from the date at which the suspect was transferred to the custody of the Tribunal. It was to avoid this problem that the amendment to Rule 40 *bis* (C) was adopted.

8.1.17 This Rule was further amended in minor ways at the Fifth Plenary Session on 8 June 1998. Paras. (F) and (G) were amended at the eighth plenary session on 26 June 2000. The words, "after the day of transfer of the suspect to the Tribunal" were added to para. (H) at the tenth plenary session on 30–31 May, 2001.

8.1.18 ICTR's Rule 40 *bis* is structurally somewhat different from ICTY Rule 40 *bis*, but in substance it is the same.

ICTR Rule 40 *bis* (F) Applied Only in Exceptional Circumstances

8.1.19 This provision "can only be applied where exceptional circumstances prevail, such as, in particular, serious problems which may arise during the investigations" (*Decision on the Extension of the Provisional Detention for a Maximum Period of Thirty Days in accordance with Rule 40 bis (F) of the Rules of Procedure and Evidence*, Judge Kama (nevertheless granting the Prosecutor's request), *Kabiligi* (ICTR-97-34-DP), 14 August 1997, p. 2).

Rule 40 *bis* and the Submission of Indictment

8.1.20 Judge Ostrovsky in his *Decision to Confirm the Indictment* in *Kambanda* of 16 October 1997, while confirming the indictment against the accused, nevertheless deplored the submission by the Prosecutor of an indictment one day before the suspect's detention under Rule 40 *bis* was due to expire:

> FINDS IT unacceptable that this indictment was filed on 15 October 1997, a day before the expiry of the suspect's detention under Rule 40 BIS (G) on 16 October 1997 as ordered by Judge Navanethem Pillay on 16 September 1997;
>
> DECLARES that such late submission of indictment is incompatible with the due process and the interests of justice and is an irresponsible conduct of the Office of the Prosecutor.

Release Due to Violations of Rule 40 *bis*

8.1.21 The Appeals Chamber (Judges McDonald, Shahabuddeen, Vohrah, Wald and Nieto-Navia) ordered the release of Jean-Bosco Barayagwiza in a *Decision* dated 3 November 1999 on the following grounds:

- the accused's right to be promptly charged pursuant to international standards as reflected in Rule 40 *bis* was violated (para. 100 of the *Decision*);
- the accused's right to an initial appearance, without delay upon his transfer to the Tribunal's detention unit, under Rule 62 was violated (para. 100);
- the delay amounted to an "abuse of process" (para. 101);
- the "failure to resolve the appellant's 'writ of habeas corpus' in a timely manner violated his right to challenge the legality of his continued detention (para. 101);
- the Prosecutor failed to prosecute the case with due diligence (para. 101)

8.1.22 The Appeals Chamber rejected the Prosecutor's suggestions that the appropriate remedy for these violations would be either to order an expedited trial or to give the accused credit for time served and instead ordered the dismissal of the indictment "with prejudice," so that the accused could no longer be tried by the ICTR. By four votes to one, the Appeals Chamber ordered the release of Barayagwiza to Cameroon. Judge Shahabudeen thought that the accused should be completely released, and not released to Cameroon:

> I should have thought that the proper order was to set the appellant at liberty and to direct the Registrar to provide him with reasonable facilities to leave Tanzania, if he so wishes (page 7).

8.1.23 Judge Nieto-Navia opined that Rule 40 *bis* provides for release of the detainee to the national authorities "if appropriate." Under the circumstances, therefore, the tribunal should first have verified with the Cameroonian authorities that such release *was* appropriate.

8.1.24 This decision caused an outcry in Rwanda, which suspended relations with the ICTR as a result.

8.1.25 As a result, in an *Order* dated 25 November 1999, the Appeals Chamber, under the new ICTY President Jorda, who had replaced President McDonald, suspended execution of its Decision of 3 November 1999 pending resolution of the Prosecutor's application for review of that Decision pursuant to ICTR Rule 120.

8.1.26 In the Appeals Chamber's *Decision (Prosecutor's Request for Review or Reconsideration)* of 31 March 2000, the earlier decision was reversed and Barayagwiza kept in ICTR custody for trial. The Appeals Chamber decided that, as remedy for the violations of his rights, he would receive financial compensation if found not guilty and if found guilty, would have his sentence reduced to take account of the violation of his rights.

Rule 40 *bis* Decisions

8.1.27 *Order of Provisional Detention and of Transfer* rendered in *Nsengiyumva* (ICTR-96-9-DP) by Judge Aspegren on 17 May 1996; *Continued Detention on Remand of Anatole Nsengiyumva* rendered in *Nsengiyumva* (ICTR-96-9-DP) by Judge Aspegren on 18 June 1996; *Order of Provisional Detention and of Transfer* rendered in *Ntagerura* (ICTR-96-10-DP) by Judge Aspegren on 17 May 1996; *Continued Detention on Remand of André Ntagerura* rendered in *Ntagerura* (ICTR-96-10-DP) by Judge Aspegren on 18 June 1996; *Decision on the Extension of the Provisional Detention for a Maximum Period of Thirty Days* rendered in *Nsabimana* (ICTR-97-29-DP) by Judge Kama on 14 August 1996; *Decision on the Extension of the Provisional Detention for a Maximum Period of Thirty Days* rendered in *Ngeze* (ICTR-97-27-DP) by Judge Kama on 18 August 1997.

8.1.28

ICTY Rule 41 Retention of Information	ICTR Rule 41 Preservation of Information
Subject to Rule 81, the Prosecutor shall be responsible for the retention, storage and security of information and physical evidence obtained in the course of his investigations until formally tendered into evidence.	(A) The Prosecutor shall be responsible for the preservation, storage and security of information and physical evidence obtained in the course of his investigations. (B) The Prosecutor shall draw up an inventory of all materials seized from the accused, including documents, books, papers, and other objects, and shall serve a copy thereof on the accused. Materials that are of no evidentiary value shall be returned without delay to the accused.

History of ICTY Rule 41

8.1.29 The words, "subject to Rule 81" and "until formally tendered into evidence" were added to this Rule on 19 January 2001, after the twenty-third plenary session, to reflect the fact that, once the Prosecutor had tendered an original exhibit into evidence, the responsibility for retention and preservation of that physical evidence would pass to the Registrar pursuant to Rule 81(C).

History of ICTR Rule 41

8.1.30 Para. (B) was added at the tenth plenary session on 30–31 May 2001.

Rule 41(B): Prosecutor Must Return Material Seized from the Accused

8.1.31 In *Ndindiliyimana, Decision on Defence Urgent Motion for the Disclosure of Evidence and for the Return of Seized Items*, 24 September 2001, the Trial Chamber held that Rule 41(B) applies only to those materials 'seized from the accused' and not material belonging to the accused seized by the Prosecutor from third parties (para. 6).

8.1.32

ICTY Rule 42 Rights of Suspects During Investigation	ICTR Rule 42 Rights of Suspects During Investigation
(A) A suspect who is to be questioned by the Prosecutor shall have the following rights, of which he shall be informed by the Prosecutor prior to questioning, in a language he speaks and understands: (i) the right to be assisted by counsel of his choice or to have legal assistance assigned to him without payment if he does not have sufficient means to pay for it; (ii) the right to have the free assistance of an interpreter if he cannot understand or speak the language to be used for questioning; and (iii) the right to remain silent, and to be cautioned that any statement he makes shall be recorded and may be used in evidence. (B) Questioning of a suspect shall not proceed without the presence of counsel unless the suspect has voluntarily waived his right to counsel. In case of waiver, if the suspect subsequently expresses a desire to have counsel, questioning shall thereupon cease, and shall only resume when the suspect has obtained or has been assigned counsel.	(A) A suspect who is to be questioned by the Prosecutor shall have the following rights, of which he shall be informed by the Prosecutor prior to questioning, in a language he speaks and understands: (i) the right to be assisted by counsel of his choice or to have legal assistance assigned to him without payment if he does not have sufficient means to pay for it; (ii) the right to have the free assistance of an interpreter if he cannot understand or speak the language to be used for questioning; and (iii) the right to remain silent, and to be cautioned that any statement he makes shall be recorded and may be used in evidence. (B) Questioning of a suspect shall not proceed without the presence of counsel unless the suspect has voluntarily waived his right to counsel. In case of waiver, if the suspect subsequently expresses a desire to have counsel, questioning shall thereupon cease, and shall only resume when the suspect has obtained or has been assigned counsel.

History of ICTY Rule 42

8.1.33 Rule 42(A) was amended at the ICTY fifth plenary session in January 1995 "to broaden the rights of suspects and accused persons" (second Annual Report, para. 26, fn. 9). The new para. (iii) was added, on the basis that the right was of such fundamental importance that it should be explicitly mentioned in the Rules.

8.1.34 This Rule was considered by the Trial Chamber in *Delalić* on a motion by the accused that his rights as a suspect had been violated. The Chamber denied the Motion in its *Decision on the Motion on the Exclusion and Restitution of Evidence and Other Material seized from the Accused Zejnil Delalić*, rendered on 9 October 1996.

8.1.35 The Rules do not explicitly state what the remedy should be when a suspect's rights are violated. An "exclusionary rule," applying Rules 89(D) and 95, to exclude from evidence, for example, a confession which has been obtained in violation of any of those rights, as well as any "fruits" of that violation—is one possibility, although other remedies could be envisaged, e.g. holding the person committing the violation in contempt under Rule 77.

8.1.36

ICTY Rule 43 Recording Questioning of Suspects	ICTR Rule 43 Recording Questioning of Suspects
Whenever the Prosecutor questions a suspect, the questioning shall be audio-recorded or video-recorded, in accordance with the following procedure: (i) the suspect shall be informed in a language he speaks and understands that the questioning is being audio-recorded or video-recorded; (ii) in the event of a break in the course of the questioning, the fact and the time of the break shall be recorded before audio-recording or video-recording ends and the time of resumption of the questioning shall also be recorded; (iii) at the conclusion of the questioning the suspect shall be offered the opportunity to clarify anything he has said, and to add anything he may wish, and the time of conclusion shall be recorded; (iv) A copy of the recorded tape will be supplied to the suspect or, if multiple recording apparatus was used, one of the original recorded tapes; and (v) after a copy has been made, if necessary, of the recorded tape, the original recorded tape	Whenever the Prosecutor questions a suspect, the questioning shall be audio-recorded or video-recorded, in accordance with the following procedure: (i) the suspect shall be informed in a language he speaks and understands that the questioning is being audio-recorded or video-recorded; (ii) in the event of a break in the course of the questioning, the fact and the time of the break shall be recorded before audio-recording or video-recording ends and the time of resumption of the questioning shall also be recorded; (iii) at the conclusion of the questioning the suspect shall be offered the opportunity to clarify anything he has said, and to add anything he may wish, and the time of conclusion shall be recorded; (iv) the tape shall then be transcribed as soon as practicable after the conclusion of questioning and a copy of the transcript supplied to the suspect, together with a copy of the recorded tape or, if multiple recording apparatus was used, one of the original recorded tapes; and

or one of the original tapes shall be sealed in the presence of the suspect under the signature of the Prosecutor and the suspect. (vi) the tape shall be transcribed if the suspect becomes an accused.	(v) after a copy has been made, if necessary, of the recorded tape for purposes of transcription, the original recorded tape or one of the original tapes shall be sealed in the presence of the suspect under the signature of the Prosecutor and the suspect.

History of ICTY Rule 43

8.1.37 Rule 43(iv) was amended at the ICTY fifth plenary session in January 1995 to add "new language . . . to indicate that the Prosecutor's obligation to have an audio or video tape recording of a suspect's testimony transcribed must be met 'as soon as practicable after the conclusion of the questioning.' This amendment removes any suggestion that the transcript is to be provided immediately following the questioning—something which could be impossible, especially in the field" (ICTY Second Annual Report, para. 22, fn. 7). Para. (vi) was added, and paras. (iv) and (v) amended accordingly, on 12 December 2002.

8.1.38 This Rule was considered by the Trial Chamber on a motion by the accused in *Delalić* alleging an irregularity in the recording procedure prescribed by Rule 43. The Chamber denied the Motion in its *Decision on the Motion on the Exclusion and Restitution of Evidence and Other Material seized from the Accused Zejnil Delalić*, rendered on 9 October 1996.

SECTION 2: INDICTMENT

8.2.1

ICTY Article 18 Investigation and Preparation of Indictment	ICTR Article 17 Investigation and Preparation of Indictment
1. The Prosecutor shall initiate investigations ex-officio or on the basis of information obtained from any source, particularly from Governments, United Nations organs, inter-governmental and non-governmental organizations. The Prosecutor shall assess the information received or obtained and decide whether there is sufficient basis to proceed. 2. The Prosecutor shall have the power to question suspects, victims and witnesses, to collect evidence and to conduct on-site investigations. In carrying out these tasks, the Prosecutor may, as appropriate, seek the assistance of the State authorities concerned. 3. If questioned, the suspect shall be entitled to be assisted by counsel of his own choice, including the right to have legal assistance assigned to him without payment by him in any such case if he does not have sufficient means to pay for it, as well as to necessary translation into and from a language he speaks and understands. 4. Upon a determination that a prima facie case exists, the Prosecutor shall prepare an indictment containing a concise statement of the facts and the crime or crimes with which the accused is charged under the Statute. The indictment shall be transmitted to a judge of the Trial Chamber.	1. The Prosecutor shall initiate investigations ex-officio or on the basis of information obtained from any source, particularly from Governments, United Nations organs, inter-governmental and non-governmental organizations. The Prosecutor shall assess the information received or obtained and decide whether there is sufficient basis to proceed. 2. The Prosecutor shall have the power to question suspects, victims and witnesses, to collect evidence and to conduct on-site investigations. In carrying out these tasks, the Prosecutor may, as appropriate, seek the assistance of the State authorities concerned. 3. If questioned, the suspect shall be entitled to be assisted by counsel of his own choice, including the right to have legal assistance assigned to him without payment by him in any such case if he does not have sufficient means to pay for it, as well as to necessary translation into and from a language he speaks and understands. 4. Upon a determination that a prima facie case exists, the Prosecutor shall prepare an indictment containing a concise statement of the facts and the crime or crimes with which the accused is charged under the Statute. The indictment shall be transmitted to a judge of the Trial Chamber.

General

8.2.2 The Prosecution has the task of drawing up indictments based on investigations conducted by OTP investigators. Once a *prima facie* case has, in the Prosecutor's view, been made out, the indictment is submitted to a judge for review. In the course of conducting his investigations, the Prosecutor has certain powers, which are set out in the above articles.

Status of Indictments and Proceedings

8.2.3 See Annex 1 for the status of completed cases. For the ICTY, see also the "Fact Sheet on ICTY Proceedings" on the ICTY website (*http://www.un.org/icty/glance/procfact-e.htm*) which provides information regarding the numbers of indictments issued and accused charged and in custody.

Requirements of an Indictment

8.2.4 ICTY Article 18/ICTR Article 17—taken in conjunction with ICTY Article 21(4)(a)/ICTR Article 20(4)(a)—means that "there is a minimum level of information that must be provided by the indictment; there is a floor below which the level of information must not fall if the indictment is to be valid as to form" (*Kvočka*, Tr. Ch., *Decision on Defence Preliminary Motions on the Form of the Indictment*, 12 April 1999, para. 14). See further the Commentary to ICTY/ICTR Rule 47. See also the *Kupreškić Appeal Judgement* and various Trial Chamber decisions in *Brdjanin* and *Tradić* on the form of the indictment.

Indictments Bad for Duplicity

8.2.5 Under many national laws, the indictment must not be "duplicitous":

> The indictment must not be double; that is to say, no one count of the indictment should charge the defendant with having committed two or more separate offences. (ARCHBOLD CRIMINAL PLEADING, EVIDENCE AND PRACTICE, 2002, §1–135.)

8.2.6 The notion of duplicity in an indictment has been raised at the ICTR. In the *Gerard Ntakirutimana* case, Counsel for the accused submitted, on 17 April 1997, a *Preliminary Motion for an Order to Quash Counts 1,2,3 and 6 of the Indictment*, in which it requested the Trial Chamber to quash certain counts of the indictment on the grounds of duplicity and vagueness. As regards the former objection, Counsel for the accused argued that a single specific act should be the subject of one and only one count of the indictment and that this principle was violated in the indictment against Ntakirutimana.

8.2.7 The Prosecution replied on 6 October 1997 in a *Factum of the Prosecutor in Response to Preliminary Motions of the Defence in Relation to two indictments*. The Prosecution opposed the defence motion on the grounds that (1) none of the counts in the indictment were duplicitous, as the rule against duplicity did not prohibit using the description of several means of committing a single offence in one count; (2) using cumulative or alternative counts in the indictment was valid where different offences were concerned; (3) the counts alleged to be vague were sufficiently informative to enable the accused to prepare his defence; and (4) defective counts should be the subject of an order for amendment, not of quashing. On Cumulative Charging, see 8.3.1 *et seq.* below.

Indictment Must Contain a Concise Statement of Facts and Crimes Charged

8.2.8 The indictment must contain "a concise statement of the facts and the crime or crimes with which the accused is charged under the Statute" (ICTY Article 18(4)/ICTR Article 17(4)). A number of defence motions have been brought under Rules 72 and 73 alleging that the indictments in question failed to meet the requirements laid down in the Statute. Reference should therefore be made to those two Rules, as well as to Rule 47 ("Submission of Indictment by the Prosecutor").

8.2.9 At the ICTY, where the Trial Chamber has rejected such motions, there have, on occasion, been applications to the Bench of the Appeals Chamber under Rule 72(B)(ii) for leave to appeal the decision of the Trial Chamber. In one such case (IT-96-21-AR72.5, *Decision on Application for Leave to Appeal by Hazim Delić (Defects in the Form of the Indictment,* 6 December 1996), the Bench of the Appeals Chamber gave guidance for the interpretation of Article 18(4):

> (b) *That the Indictment is incomplete and/or violates the principle nullum crimen sine lege;*
>
> 25. To the Accused's objection that the Indictment is incomplete and violates the principle of *nullum crimen sine lege,* the Trial Chamber replied:
>
>> The Trial Chamber finds that the allegation that this Indictment violates the principle of *nullum crimen sine lege* does not hold. The Indictment cites the applicable provisions of the Statute which support the alleged criminal responsibility for the acts mentioned in the Indictment. In so doing, the Indictment puts the Defence on notice of the legal classification of the crime and sufficiently enables the accused to prepare his defence. (para. 21)
>
> 26. The Accused is no doubt correct when he states that the Tribunal's Statute does not create new offences but rather serves to give the Tribunal jurisdiction over offences which are already part of customary law. As the Secretary-General comments in his Report on the Tribunal's Statute (S/25704): ". . . the international tribunal should apply rules of international humanitarian law which are beyond any doubt part of customary law so that the problem of adherence of some but not all States to specific conventions does not arise" (para. 34).
>
> 27. This does not, however, have any bearing on whether *the Indictment* should refer for each offence to both the pertinent Article of the Statute and the pertinent norm of international humanitarian law. Provided that it is clear in each count of the Indictment which serious violation of international humanitarian law is being charged, it matters little whether the Indictment refers to, for example, Article 2 of the Statute or to the relevant Articles of the Geneva Conventions of 1949. Indeed the Statute appears to favour the former approach; Article 18(4) mentions "a concise statement of facts and of the crime or crimes with which the accused is charged *under the Statute."* Moreover, the Report of the Secretary-General to the Security Council of 1993 on the Statute of this Tribunal in his exposition of Articles 2,3,4 and 5 of the Statute clearly referred the crimes enumerated in them to their sources of international humanitarian law, for example, the Geneva Conventions of 1949, the Hague Convention (IV) of 1907, the Nuremberg Charter of 1945 and the Genocide Convention of 1948. The Bench takes the view, therefore, that Articles 2,3,4 and 5 of the Statute are shorthand for the corresponding norms of international humanitarian laws, and if there is any dispute as to those norms, that is a matter for trial, not for pre-trial objections to the form of the Indictment.
>
> 28. The Accused argues that it is difficult for him to defend against the Indictment when it does not mention the norms relied on. In particular, he says that in these circumstances the principle *nullum crimen sine lege* is violated and his right to a fair trial is jeopardised. In light of the above comments, the Bench does not consider this concern to be justified.

(c) *That the Indictment is vague*;

29. The defence further avers that the Indictment is not "a concise statement of facts and of the crime or crimes with which the accused is charged under the Statute" as required by Article 18(4) of the Statute.

30. In particular, the accused complains that many charges contain mutually exclusive alternative formulations of guilt, e.g. "knew" versus "had reason to know," "were about to commit" versus "committed," "failed to prevent" versus "failed to punish."

31. The Trial Chamber, in its *Decision*, did not fully address this issue, which the Accused raised in its Motion before the Trial Chamber in para. 5. The Bench considers, however, that this is not a grave error on the Trial Chamber's part. These sets of alternatives, recognised in military manuals and under international humanitarian law, do not render the Indictment fatally vague, although wherever possible the Prosecutor should make clear the precise line of conduct and mental element alleged.

(d) *That the Indictment fails to separate distinct charges and therefore subjects the accused to the danger of "double jeopardy" and/or falls foul of the principle non bis in idem*;

32. The Accused submits that a charge for crimes individually committed must be separated from a charge as a superior, whereas he is charged for certain offences, both as a direct participant and as a superior, for example Paras. 35 (Counts 46 and 47), 36 (count 48) and 37 (count 49).

33. The Trial Chamber, in response to this objection, stated:

> The Trial Chamber finds that the Indictment sufficiently informs the accused of the acts for which he is being charged both as a direct participant and as a superior. Moreover, the Indictment does separate the acts for which the accused is being held responsible as a direct participant and as a superior. The Indictment therefore fulfils its purpose in an adequate manner. . . . (*para. 18, Decision*).

The Trial Chamber therefore rejected the objection; in the view of this Bench, with reason.

34. It is worth noting, however, that there is one respect in which the Accused's concern is justified with respect to the distinction between being charged as a direct participant and being charged as a superior; namely the failure, in those counts of the indictment which charge command responsibility for the acts of subordinates, to refer to the statutory source for liability for the acts of subordinates, i.e. Article 7(3) of the Tribunal's Statute. While the Bench is of the view that the said sub-Article should be explicitly mentioned whenever it is relied on, nevertheless there is no possibility in this Indictment of the Accused being mistaken as to which Article is being referred to when the "knew or had reason to know" formula is employed.

35. The accused also complains of being charged on multiple occasions throughout the Indictment with two different crimes arising from one act or omission, namely being charged in each case with both a grave breach "and" a violation of the laws or customs of war for the same acts. On this matter, the Trial Chamber endorsed its reasoning on an identical issue in the *Tadić* case:

> In any event, since this is a matter that will only be relevant insofar as it might affect penalty, it can best be dealt with if and when matters of penalty fall

for consideration. What can, however, be said with certainty is that penalty cannot be made to depend upon whether offences arising from the same conduct are alleged cumulatively or in the alternative. What is to be punished by penalty is proven criminal conduct and that will not depend upon technicalities of pleading. (*Prosecutor v. Tadić*, Decision on Defence Motion on Form of the Indictment at p. 10 (No. IT-94-1-T, T.Ch.II, 14 Nov, 1995)

36. The Bench does not consider that the reasoning reveals an error, much less a grave one, justifying the granting of leave to appeal.

(e) *That the Indictment alleges facts which are false.*

37. The accused complains under this heading that the Indictment offers no facts concerning Delić's position as Deputy Commander, nor does it demonstrate how a Deputy Commander can be responsible as a commander. Also as a factual issue, the Accused avers that the Prosecutor has wrongfully characterised the conflict in Bosnia and Herzegovina.

38. The Bench considers that the Trial Chamber was correct to state that these are factual issues to be determined at trial. . . .

39. The accused raises two miscellaneous issues which, however, do not allege an error on the part of the Trial Chamber, much less a "serious cause" justifying leave to appeal, namely:

(a) That the *ex parte* review of the Indictment under Rule 47 offends the principle *audi alteram partes*.

(b) that there must be a "reasonable suspicion" that the accused has committed the offences alleged.

40. The Bench does not consider that either of these arguments raise a "serious cause" justifying the granting of leave to appeal under Rule 72(B)(ii)."

8.2.10 Thus the Appeals Chamber rejected the application for leave to appeal, finding no error in the Trial Chamber's judgement. Nonetheless, its lengthy exposition on what an indictment should contain, and what it need not contain, is a useful touchstone for analysing a given indictment.

8.2.11

ICTY Article 19 Review of the Indictment	ICTR Article 18 Review of the Indictment
1. The judge of the Trial Chamber to whom the indictment has been transmitted shall review it. If satisfied that a *prima facie* case has been established by the Prosecutor, he shall confirm the indictment. If not so satisfied, the indictment shall be dismissed. 2. Upon confirmation of an indictment, the judge may, at the request of the Prosecutor, issue such orders and warrants for the arrest, detention, surrender or transfer of persons, and any other orders as may be required for the conduct of the trial.	1. The judge of the Trial Chamber to whom the indictment has been transmitted shall review it. If satisfied that a *prima facie* case has been established by the Prosecutor, he shall confirm the indictment. If not so satisfied, the indictment shall be dismissed. 2. Upon confirmation of an indictment, the judge may, at the request of the Prosecutor, issue such orders and warrants for the arrest, detention, surrender or transfer of persons, and any other orders as may be required for the conduct of the trial.

General

8.2.12 Once the Prosecutor has drawn up an indictment, he has to submit it to a Judge of the Tribunal for confirmation. Until it is confirmed, the indictment has no binding force. The test to be applied by the Judge who is reviewing the indictment is whether or not the indictment and supporting material establish a *prima facie* case against the accused. Obviously, since the decision to confirm an indictment or not has such dramatic effects for an accused—it usually leads to their incarceration for a number of years pending trial and widespread notoriety, and usually the collapse of any business that the accused might have had (see, e.g., the case of *Delalić*)—the decision of the reviewing judge must be taken very solemnly and carefully, having regard to all the supporting material submitted by the Prosecutor as evidence of the charges. There have been instances where accused have spent many years in custody, only to be acquitted subsequently, and where the lack of evidence at trial raises suspicions as to whether there was a *prima facie* case to begin with. It is, therefore, clear that the reviewing judge's decision to confirm or not confirm an indictment must not be a mere "rubber stamp," since the consequences of an erroneous decision are dramatic indeed for the innocent person.

Standard of Proof for Review of Indictment

8.2.13 ICTY Article 19 has to be read in conjunction with ICTY Rule 47, which, prior to its amendment on 25 July 1997, referred to the standard of proof of "sufficient evidence to provide reasonable grounds for believing that a suspect has committed a crime within the jurisdiction of the Tribunal," and not to the "*prima facie* case" standard of proof. Note, however, that ICTY Rule 47 has now been amended to refer directly to "the standard set forth in ICTY Article 19, paragraph 1 of the Statute," therefore bringing the Rule into line with the Statute. (See Rule 47). ICTR Rule 47 has been likewise amended to refer to "the standard set forth in Article 18 of the [ICTR] Statute."

The Meaning of "*Prima Facie* Case"

8.2.14 Several Judges have, upon confirmation of an indictment, pronounced upon the meaning of the terms, "*prima facie*" and "*reasonable grounds for believing.*" Judge Sidhwa, in his review of the indictment against *Rajić* on 29 August 1995, noted that Articles 18(4) and 19(1) of the Statute both refer to a "*prima facie* case" as the appropriate standard of proof when confirming an indictment. Noting that "[t]he Statute of the Tribunal does not define or outline the principles to be taken into consideration when assessing the expression "*prima facie case*" (page 212), Judge Sidhwa went on to consider the possible meaning of the expression:

> In Latin the expression "*prima facie*" means at first sight, or on the face of it, or on first impression. However, the extended expression "*prima facie case*" means the assessment of the case by way of first impression. But the matter does not end here. In the legal context, the amplitude of its meaning varies (page 217).

8.2.15 Judge McDonald, in the *Kordić et al.* confirmation of the indictment of 10 November 1995, adhered to the definition of "*prima facie* case" contained in the Draft

Statute for an International Criminal Court adopted by the International Law Commission:

> a *prima facie* case for this purpose is understood to be a credible case which would (if not contradicted by the Defence) be a sufficient basis to convict the accused on the charge. (p. 1675)

8.2.16 This dictum has been followed in a number of indictment confirmations (for example, by Judge Hunt in his *Decision on review of indictment and application for consequential orders* in *Milošević et al* of 24 May 1999).

Cross Reference: See Part Five ("Pre-Trial Proceedings") of the ICTY Rules of Procedure and Evidence.

8.2.17

ICTY Rule 47 Submission of Indictment by the Prosecutor	ICTR Rule 47 Submission of Indictment by the Prosecutor
(A) An indictment, submitted in accordance with the following procedure, shall be reviewed by a Judge designated in accordance with Rule 28 for this purpose. (B) The Prosecutor, if satisfied in the course of an investigation that there is sufficient evidence to provide reasonable grounds for believing that a suspect has committed a crime within the jurisdiction of the Tribunal, shall prepare and forward to the Registrar an indictment for confirmation by a Judge, together with supporting material. (C) The indictment shall set forth the name and particulars of the suspect, and a concise statement of the facts of the case and of the crime with which the suspect is charged. (D) The Registrar shall forward the indictment and accompanying material to the designated Judge, who will inform the Prosecutor of the date fixed for review of the indictment. (E) The reviewing Judge shall examine each of the counts in the indictment, and any supporting materials the Prosecutor may provide, to determine, applying the standard set forth in Article 19, paragraph 1, of the Statute, whether a case exists against the suspect. (F) The reviewing Judge may: (i) request the Prosecutor to present additional material in support of any or all	(A) An indictment, submitted in accordance with the following procedure, shall be reviewed by a Judge designated in accordance with Rule 28 for this purpose. (B) The Prosecutor, if satisfied in the course of an investigation that there is sufficient evidence to provide reasonable grounds for believing that a suspect has committed a crime within the jurisdiction of the Tribunal, shall prepare and forward to the Registrar an indictment for confirmation by a Judge, together with supporting material. (C) The indictment shall set forth the name and particulars of the suspect, and a concise statement of the facts of the case and of the crime with which the suspect is charged. (D) The Registrar shall forward the indictment and accompanying material to the designated Judge, who will inform the Prosecutor of the date fixed for review of the indictment. (E) The reviewing Judge shall examine each of the counts in the indictment, and any supporting materials the Prosecutor may provide, to determine, applying the standard set forth in Article 18 of the Statute, whether a case exists against the suspect. (F) The reviewing Judge may: (i) request the Prosecutor to present additional material in support of any or all

counts, or to take any further measures which appear appropriate; (ii) confirm each count; (iii) dismiss each count; or (iv) adjourn the review so as to give the Prosecutor the opportunity to modify the indictment. (G) The indictment as confirmed by the Judge shall be retained by the Registrar, who shall prepare certified copies bearing the seal of the Tribunal. If the accused does not understand either of the official languages of the Tribunal and if the language understood is known to the Registrar, a translation of the indictment in that language shall also be prepared, and shall be included as part of each certified copy of the indictment. (H) Upon confirmation of any or all counts in the indictment, (i) the Judge may issue an arrest warrant, in accordance with Sub-rule 55 (A), and any orders as provided in Article 19 of the Statute, and (ii) the suspect shall have the status of an accused. (I) The dismissal of a count in an indictment shall not preclude the Prosecutor from subsequently bringing an amended indictment based on the acts underlying that count if supported by additional evidence.	counts, or to take any further measures which appear appropriate; (ii) confirm each count; (iii) dismiss each count; or (iv) adjourn the review so as to give the Prosecutor the opportunity to modify the indictment. (G) The indictment as confirmed by the Judge shall be retained by the Registrar, who shall prepare certified copies bearing the seal of the Tribunal. If the accused does not understand either of the official languages of the Tribunal and if the language understood is known to the Registrar, a translation of the indictment in that language shall also be prepared, and a copy of the translation attached to each certified copy of the indictment. (H) Upon confirmation of any or all counts in the indictment, (i) the Judge may issue an arrest warrant, in accordance with Sub-rule 55 (A), and any orders as provided in Article 18 of the Statute, and (ii) the suspect shall have the status of an accused. (I) The dismissal of a count in an indictment shall not preclude the Prosecutor from subsequently bringing an amended indictment based on the acts underlying that count if supported by additional evidence.

History of ICTY Rule 47

8.2.18 Rule 47(C), as it then was, was amended at the ICTY fifth plenary session in January 1995, as a consequence of the amendment to Rule 28 that was adopted at the same session. Rule 47 was substantially amended at the thirteenth plenary session on 25 July 1997 (see Revision 10 of the Rules for comparison). In particular, the Rule was amended in order explicitly to state that the standard of proof to be exercised by a Judge reviewing the indictment is "the standard set forth in Article 19, paragraph 1 of the Statute," where before it was silent on this point. The Rule was further amended, in particular by adding para. (G), at the fourteenth plenary session on 12 November 1997. The words, "or to take any further measures which appear appropriate," were added to para. (F)(i) at the eighteenth plenary session on 9–10 July 1998.

History of ICTR Rule 47

8.2.19 ICTR Rule 47 was substantially amended at the ICTR fifth plenary session on 8 June 1998 to bring it in line with ICTY Rule 47, which was amended at the ICTY thirteenth plenary session on 25 July 1997. In particular, the Rule was amended in order explicitly to state that the standard of proof to be exercised by a Judge reviewing the indictment is "the standard set forth in Article 18 of the Statute," where before it was silent on this point.

Requirements of an Indictment

8.2.20 An indictment must make clear the capacity in which it is alleged the accused committed the offences and the material facts by which this will be established (*Kunarac and Kovac*, Tr. Ch., *Decision on the Form of the Indictment,* 4 November 1999):

> 6. . . . the capacity in which the accused allegedly committed the charged offence must be clearly defined. The indictment must also leave no doubt as to what the accused is alleged to have done at a particular venue on a particular date during a particular time period, with whom, to whom, or to what purpose. It must describe the full conduct complained of which amounts to the crime(s) charged. It must identify with reasonable clarity other persons involved, or affected, where necessary.
>
> 7. It further follows that neither the supporting material nor the witness statements made available to an accused under Rule 66 of the Rules of Procedure and Evidence ("Rules") can be used to fill in any gaps in the indictment. An accused could be prejudiced were the Prosecutor to be allowed, for example, to introduce material facts through the calling of additional witnesses at trial instead of applying for leave to amend the indictment.

8.2.21 See also *Decision on Preliminary Motions in Došen and Kolundžija*, 10 February 2000, where the Trial Chamber held that, where possible, the Prosecutor must provide information as to the place and time of the alleged offences, the identity of victims and co-perpetrators and the means by which the crimes were perpetrated.

Defence Motions on Form of Indictment Brought After Requesting Further Particulars from Prosecutor

8.2.22 A defence motion for an order by the Chamber for the amendment of an indictment to provide greater specificity should only be brought "after a refusal by the Prosecution of a request for further particulars which specifies the counts in question, the respect in which it is said that the material already in the possession of the Defence is inadequate and the particulars necessary to remedy that inadequacy" (*Tadić* Tr. Ch., *Form of the Indictment Decision,* 14 November 1995). In fact, this practice is more honored in the breach than in the observance.

Cross References: See also ICTY Article 18(4) and Rules 72 and 73 and the Commentary thereto.

Rule 47(C): Indictment Must Contain Concise Statement of Facts

8.2.23 The requirement that the indictment provide a "concise statement of the facts of the case and of the crime with which the suspect is charged" was considered by the Trial Chamber in its *Tadić Form of the Indictment Decision* of 14 November 1995. In respect of one count of the indictment, the Chamber decided that there was not sufficient detail to meet the requirements of Rule 47 since, *inter alia*, it did not "provide the accused with any specific, albeit concise, statement of the facts of the case and of the crimes with which he is charged. It says nothing specific about the accused's conduct, about what was the nature and extent of his participation in the several courses of conduct which are alleged over the months in question" (para. 12).

The same Decision stated that a single count of the indictment should not allege distinct types of conduct (see para. 12).

8.2.24 In its *Delić Form of the Indictment Decision* of 15 November 1996, the Trial Chamber, affirming its earlier Decision on the same Motion filed by Zejnil Delalić, stated:

> The Indictment should articulate each charge specifically and separately, and identify the particular acts in a satisfactory manner in order sufficiently to inform the accused of the charges against which he has to defend himself.

8.2.25 In considering whether an indictment is defective or not, the Chamber should consider its "summary nature" and that its purpose is "very succinctly [to] demonstrate . . . that the accused allegedly committed a crime." (*Delalić Indictment Decision*, 2 October 1996, p. 11, quoting the *Đukić Preliminary Motions Decision*, 26 April 1996, para. 14).

Excessive Vagueness

8.2.26 The formulations "including, but not limited to . . . ," "among others," and "about," which appeared in the *Blaškić* indictment, were considered excessively vague and were stricken by the Trial Chamber in its *Decision on the Defence Motion to dismiss the Indictment based upon Defects thereof (vagueness/Lack of adequate Notice of Charges)* rendered on 4 April 1997. The Chamber agreed with the Defence that such phrases were "vague and subject to interpretation and that they do not belong in the indictment when it is issued against the accused." (para. 22)

8.2.27 In the same Decision, the Chamber intimated that Article 7(1) and Article 7(3) should be separately charged:

> In conclusion, the Trial Chamber is of the opinion that the indictment should be amended as to the nature and the legal basis of the criminal responsibility for which the accused is liable. Nothing prevents the Prosecutor from pleading an alternative responsibility (Article 7(1) or 7(3) of the Statute), but the factual allegations supporting either alternative must be sufficiently precise so as to permit the accused to prepare his defence on either or both alternatives. . . . (para. 32)

8.2.28 See also the Chamber's *Decision on the Defence Request for Enforcement of an Order of the Trial Chamber*, dated 23 May 1997, in *Blaškić*. In that Decision, the Trial Chamber noted that its Order of 4 April 1997 had been complied with to the extent of removing the offending phrases such as "including, but not limited to. . . ." However, the indictment remained defective with respect to the allegations concerning the type of responsibility charged, i.e. Article 7(1) or Article 7(3) responsibility. The Prosecutor was not, however, given more time to amend the indictment, the matter being left for trial:

the Trial Chamber will not fail to draw all the legal consequences at trial of the possible total or partial failure to satisfy the obligations incumbent on the Prosecutor insofar as that failure *inter alia* might not have permitted the accused to prepare his defence pursuant to Article 21 of the Statute and the principles identified in its Decision. (p. 5)

8.2.29 In the event, Blaškić was convicted at trial; it is thus unclear how this dictum of the Chamber was given practical effect.

Decision of Confirming Judge Unreviewable Except Where Flagrantly in Violation of the Statute/Rules

8.2.30 The Decision of a confirming Judge to confirm an indictment pursuant to Rule 47 is a matter of discretion and not reviewable by a Trial Chamber except in exceptional circumstances. As the Trial Chamber stated in its *Decision on the Preliminary Motion filed by the Defence based on Defects in the form of the Indictment*, rendered in *Nahimana* on 24 November 1997:

> 8. The purpose of the confirmation . . . is merely to ensure that the investigations carried out by the Prosecutor have reached an acceptable level of probability to justify a belief that the suspect may have committed certain crimes, without going into any specific evaluation of the culpability of the suspect. The autonomous power of discretion exercised by the confirming Judge in this endeavour is by its very nature subjective and could therefore be reviewable in circumstances where the confirming decision was in flagrant violation of the Statute and/or the Rules or was inconsistent with the fundamental principles of fairness, and had entailed a miscarriage of justice. Under such circumstances only could there be room for consideration of annulment pursuant to the principle included in Rule 5 of the Rules. However, none of these circumstances apply in the present case.

8.2.31 Rule 5, however, does not on its face allow the annulment of a *judicial decision*, but only of an "act of another party." Rule 5 reads, "Any objection by a party to an act of another party on the ground of non-compliance with the Rules or Regulations shall be raised at the earliest opportunity; it shall be upheld, and the act declared null, only if the act was inconsistent with the fundamental principles of fairness and has occasioned a miscarriage of justice." A "party" is defined in the Rules as "The Prosecutor or the accused."

8.2.32 The above decision in *Nahimana* was followed by the Trial Chamber in a Decision in *Ntagerura* on 28 November 1997:

> 32. . . . Only if the confirming decision would appear to be manifestly inconsistent with fundamental principles of fairness and had entailed a miscarriage of justice could there have been room for consideration by the Trial Chamber of annulment pursuant to the principle included in Rule 5 of the Rules, but this is not at all the case in the present case.

8.2.33 See also *Decision on the Defence Motion to strike confirmed amended indictment* rendered in *Kovačević* on 3 July 1998; *Decision on Motion to Dismiss Indictment* rendered in *Brdjanin* of 5 October 1999 (Trial Chamber has no power to review the decision of the confirming Judge by way of appeal or otherwise); *Decision on Motion for Release* rendered in *Talić* on 10 December 1999 (when considering the lawfulness of a detainee's detention, the Trial Chamber or a Pre-Trial Judge cannot review the adequacy of the supporting material produced before the confirming Judge); *Decision on Motion to dismiss indictment* rendered in *Brdjanin* on 5 October 1999 (the requirement is for the indictment to disclose a *prima facie* case against the accused, not for the evidence submitted in support to do so. This Decision may be criticised in that it would allow an accused, in respect of whom there is *no evidence at all*, to be indicted and brought before the Tribunal. Moreover it is hard to understand how *an indictment* can *disclose* a case against a person. An indictment simply states a case against a person. Furthermore, this ruling would mean that there would be no need to submit supporting material to the confirming judge).

Dismissal of Counts of Indictment

8.2.34 Judge Aspegren dismissed one count of the indictment against Hasan Ngeze in the indictment review of 3 October 1997. Judge Aspegren held:

> WHEREAS the Tribunal notes that although Article 6 of the Statute sets out the conditions for individual criminal responsibility for the crimes referred to in Articles 2 to 4 of the Statute, it does not by itself establish an independent crime;
>
> WHEREAS, in light thereof, the Tribunal is of the opinion that the supporting material does not provide reasonable grounds for believing that the accused himself executed the crime which he is alleged to have committed in Count 1 in violation of Article 2(2)(a) and/or (b) and Article 2(3)(a) of the Statute;
>
> ...
>
> DISMISSES Count 1 of the indictment.

Superseding Indictments

8.2.35 A superseding indictment which unaccountably adds new charges to the existing indictment is likely to be rejected by the Chamber, particularly if the superseding indictment is submitted close to the trial date and therefore prejudices the accused's right to have adequate time for the preparation of his defence and to be tried without undue delay (see Article 20(4)(b) and (c) of the Statute). See the *Decision on the Motion filed by the Prosecutor for Confirmation of the Trial Date and Submission of a Superseding Indictment* rendered by the Trial Chamber in *Kayishema and Ruzindana* (ICTR-95-1-T) on 10 April 1997.

Substitution of New Indictment Must Be Pursuant to Rules 50 and 51

8.2.36 See *Decision on the Prosecution Motion for Adjournment* by the Trial Chamber in *Bagosora* of 17 March 1998:

> The Trial Chamber is aware that the Tribunal has been seized of a joint indictment pursuant to rule 47 of the Rules in which the accused and several others have been indicted. However, the Chamber also observes that there is still an existing indictment which is yet to be withdrawn.

8.2.37 In the same case and on the same date, see the *Separate Opinion of Judge Yakov Ostrovsky on the Prosecutor's Motion for Adjournment:*

> 8. ... I cannot agree with my colleagues who recognize, in the Trial Chamber's decision, that the Tribunal has been seized of a joint indictment pursuant to rule 47 of the Rules. This joint indictment should not be seen to be based on rule 47. The Prosecutor informed us that new charges have been added against Bagosora. In accordance with rule 50 of the Rules this cannot be done without leave of the Trial Chamber. The Prosecutor also recognized that the previous Bagosora indictment should be withdrawn because a joint indictment has been prepared. But in accordance with rule 51 of the Rules, the existing Bagosora indictment cannot be withdrawn without preliminary permission from the Trial Chamber. I question why the Prosecutor disregards the Rules and finds it possible to present the Judges with a *fait accompli*?

8.2.38 Judge Khan confirmed this view in his *Dismissal of Indictment* decision of 31 March 1998 in the case of *Bagosora and 28 others*. Dismissing a new indictment that the Prosecutor sought to have confirmed, Judge Khan commented:

> If the Prosecutor in her continuing investigations has, in fact, collected information which may jointly implicate new suspects and the existing accused for a specific offense, in my opinion she must follow the provision of Rules 50 (amendment of indictments) or 51 (withdrawal of indictments) of the Rules [...] Rule 47 cannot be used as a panacea for all the difficulties that the learned Prosecutor may confront during this process. Although such an approach may seem time consuming, under no circumstances can rule 47 supersede the mandatory provision of the other rules.

Cross References: See also ICTR Article 17(4) and Rules 72 and 73.

8.2.39

ICTY Rule 48 Joinder of Accused	ICTR Rule 48 Joinder of Accused
Persons accused of the same or different crimes committed in the course of the same transaction may be jointly charged and tried.	Persons accused of the same or different crimes committed in the course of the same transaction may be jointly charged and tried.

Cross Reference: Rule 82 ("Joint and Separate Trials.")

General

8.2.40 Joint trials avoid duplication of evidence, minimise hardship to witnesses and are generally in the interests of judicial economy (Tr. Ch., *Decision on Motions for Separate Trial for Simo Zarić*, 3 February 2000, page 4).

Application Must Be *Inter Partes*

8.2.41 Judge Vohrah held, in his *Decision rejecting Prosecutor's Request for leave to amend the indictment* of 6 July 1999 in *Kolundžija*, that he did not have jurisdiction to entertain, in an *ex parte* hearing, an application to amend an indictment in order to join two accused when both the accused were in the tribunal's custody and had had their initial appearances before the tribunal.

Joinder for Better Administration of Justice

8.2.42 Joinder of accused under Rule 48 was ordered for the accused Clément Kayishema and Obed Ruzindana in the interests of "a better administration of justice, by ensuring at the same time a more consistent and detailed perception of the evidence presented by the Prosecutor, better protection of the victims' and witnesses' physical and mental safety, and by eliminating the need for them to make several journeys and to repeat their testimony" and to "obviate risks of contradiction in the decision rendered when related and indivisible facts are examined" (*Kayishema*, Tr. Ch., *Decision on the Joinder of the Accused and Setting the Date for Trial*, 6 November 1996).

Joinder of Accused and Joint Trials

8.2.43 The joinder of accused does not presuppose a joint trial. The Trial Chamber pointed out in a *Decision on Preliminary Motions filed by the Defence* on 21 March 1997 that "the joinder of accused does not in itself presuppose that all accused must be tried together at the same time." The accused, Obed Ruzindana, had argued that he had to be tried simultaneously with his co-accused (of which there were several besides Clément Kayishema), because if he were tried individually, exculpatory evidence might subsequently come to light in the trials of his co-accused, and he would thereby have been denied the right to a fair trial. The Trial Chamber rejected this argument. It pointed out that if exculpatory evidence were to emerge after the accused's conviction, then he could always seek review of the judgement under Rule 120 of the Rules of Procedure and Evidence. Nonetheless, it would seem odd to join accused in one indictment if a joint trial were not envisaged.

Meaning of "Same Transaction"

8.2.44 A defence motion for a separate trial was filed by Delalić on 29 May 1996, in which he argued that it would run counter to the principle of individual criminal responsibility for Delalić to be tried jointly with his co-accused. In its *Decision on Motions for Separate Trial filed by the Accused Zejnil Delalić and the Accused Zdravko Mucić* of 25 September 1996, the Trial Chamber stated that the relevant Rule was Rule 48 "read in light of the definition of 'transaction' in Rule 2, and Rule 82, in particular, Sub-rule (B)." In the opinion of the Chamber, the acts alleged were part of the same transaction and severance could only occur if necessary under Rule 82(B): "There is no provision in the Rules for separate trial of distinct issues arising in the one indictment" (para. 2).

8.2.45 The Trial Chamber dealt with the meaning of "the same transaction" in its *Kayishema Decision* rendered on 27 March 1997, delivered orally on 1 April 1997 and filed on 29 May 1997. The Prosecutor had applied to join three accused—Clément Kayishema, Gérard Ntakirutimana and Obed Ruzindana—and thus try them together. The Prosecutor argued that the three accused had committed their crimes as part of the same transaction, as they had all participated in the elimination of Tutsis from Kibuye prefecture in 1994.

8.2.46 The Trial Chamber rejected this argument, finding this contention for "the same transaction" too vague and imprecise, since it failed to specify the ingredients of this transaction:

> the Tribunal considers that involvement in a same transaction must be connected to specific material elements which demonstrate on the one hand the existence of an offence, of a criminal act which is objectively punishable and specifically determined in time and space, and on the other hand prove the existence of a common scheme, strategy or plan, and that the accused therefore acted together and in concert;
>
> WHEREAS thereby the definition of a same transaction submitted by the Prosecutor, as mentioned above, [the elimination of Tutsis from Kibuye prefecture in 1994], appears to be too vague and imprecise, as it makes no reference either to the material elements, or to the mental elements which must surround the said concept;
>
> WHEREAS the Tribunal is therefore of the opinion that the Defence has grounds to think that it would be a gross generalisation to deduce solely from the "elimination of Tutsis in Kibuye Prefecture" the existence of a same transaction.

8.2.47 The requirement of proving "the existence of a common scheme, strategy or plan, and that the accused therefore acted together and in concert" may, however, be too strict inasmuch as it may seem to require proof of *conspiracy* between two accused in order to join them in one indictment and try them together. This would be too stringent; clearly two accused do not have to be co-conspirators in order to be tried together.

8.2.48 The Chamber considered a reference to the elements comprising the same transaction particularly necessary with respect to *genocide* which required proof of an intention to destroy a national, ethnic or religious group in whole or in part, and *crimes against humanity*, which required proof of a widespread or systematic attack against a civilian population:

> WHEREAS, moreover, the Prosecutor did not offer any evidence which would demonstrate the nature of the common scheme, strategy or plan, particularly with regards to the count of Genocide, defined by Article 2 of the Statute of the Tribunal, which provides that the offences must have been committed with the intent to destroy, in whole or in part, a national, ethnical, or religious group, and the count of Crimes against Humanity, defined by Article 3 of the Statute, which provides that the offences must have been committed as part of a widespread or systematic attack against any civilian population.

8.2.49 In *Ntabakuze* and *Kabiligi, Decision on the Defence Motion Requesting an Order for Separate Trials*, 30 September 1998, the Trial Chamber held that the interpretation of Rule 48 in the *Kayishema Decision* (8.2.45, above) had created some argument as to whether the acts or omissions which allegedly constituted the same transaction had to be criminal or illegal in themselves or not. The Trial Chamber was of the opinion that the acts of the accused need not be criminal or illegal in themselves. They held that the acts of the accused should satisfy the following criteria:

1. Be *connected to* material elements of a criminal act. For example the acts of the accused may be non-criminal/legal acts in furtherance of future criminal acts;
2. The criminal acts which the acts of the accused are to be connected to must be capable of specific determination in time and space, and;
3. The criminal acts which the acts of the accused are connected to must illustrate the existence of a *common scheme, strategy or plan.*

8.2.50 The Trial Chamber stated that "these guidelines are not intended to be a rigid insurmountable three prong test." See also *Ntakirutimana et al, Decision on the Prosecutor's Motion to Join the Indictments*, 22 February 2001, in which it was held that the 'same transaction' test was satisfied.

Joinder to Protect Victims and Witnesses

8.2.51 In the same application by the Prosecutor (8.2.45), the Prosecutor also argued that joinder of the three accused—Clément Kayishema, Gérard Ntakirutimana and Obed Ruzindana—would better protect the witnesses that were coming to testify, for if they had to come to the Tribunal thrice, to testify against each of the three accused individually, they would be at greater risk than if they had to testify only once, in a joint trial against all three accused.

8.2.52 The Trial Chamber held that it was a question of balancing the protection of witnesses, on the one hand, against the need for full protection of the rights of the accused. It averred that witnesses might, in fact, be more traumatised by being subjected to cross-examination by three counsel—for each of the accused—all at one time. Thus it rejected the Prosecutor's argument, mentioning that, in any event, nothing prevented the Prosecutor from applying, at the appropriate moment, for protective measures for the said witnesses.

8.2.53 The third argument in favour of joinder advanced by the Prosecutor—that it would be a better administration of justice to hear the three cases together—was also rejected by the Chamber, which believed that joining the cases might slow down rather than expedite the trials:

> WHEREAS the Prosecutor submits that the joinder of the cases should allow for a better administration of justice;
>
> WHEREAS the Tribunal does not share this opinion, and deems that, on the contrary, there would be a risk of retarding all the proceedings.

8.2.54 Also on Rule 48 and joinder of accused, see *Decision on the Prosecution Motion for Adjournment* and para. 6 of *Separate Opinion of Judge Yakov Ostrovsky on the Prosecution's Motion for Adjournment* rendered in *Bagosora* on 17 March 1998.

8.2.55

| ICTR
Rule 48 *bis*
Joinder of Trials |
|---|
| Persons who are separately indicted, accused of the same or different crimes committed in the course of the same transaction, may be tried together, with leave granted by a Trial Chamber pursuant to Rule 73. |

History of ICTR Rule 48 *bis*

8.2.56 This Rule was adopted in 1999. It was amended in minor ways at the ICTR ninth plenary session on 3 November 2000.

8.2.57 In *Ntagerura* and *Bagambiki, Imanishimwe and Munyakazi, Decision on Prosecutor's Motion for Joinder*, 11 October 1999, the Trial Chamber stated that "at the 1999 Plenary Session, the Tribunal added Rule 48 *bis* to the Rules. This was merely a clarification of Rule 48." In *Ntakirutimana, Decision on the Prosecutor's Motion to Join the Indictments*, 22 February 2001, the Chamber held that Rule 48 *bis* did not create a new means by which to seek joinder.

8.2.58

| ICTY
Rule 49
Joinder of Crimes | ICTR
Rule 49
Joinder of Crimes |
|---|---|
| Two or more crimes may be joined in one indictment if the series of acts committed together form the same transaction, and the said crimes were committed by the same accused. | Two or more crimes may be joined in one indictment if the series of acts committed together form the same transaction, and the said crimes were committed by the same accused. |

History of ICTY Rule 49

8.2.59 The French version of this Rule was amended at the fifth plenary session, replacing "mêmes faits" with the words "la même opération," to correct a defective translation in the original Rule and to adapt the French version to the definition of "transaction" adopted at the fifth plenary session.

Decisions Under Rule 49

8.2.60 See *Decision on Motions by Momir Talić for a Separate Trial and for Leave to file a reply* rendered by the Trial Chamber on 9 March 2000 in *Brdjanin and Talić*. On the notion of a "transaction":

21. The case pleaded against these two accused clearly asserts the existence of the one campaign (for the execution of which both accused are charged with criminal responsibility), carried out by the same people, against the same people, during the one period of time and in the same area. The Trial Chamber is satisfied that, in accordance with Rule 48, it was proper to have charged the two accused jointly.

8.2.61 The issue nevertheless remained as to whether, in the circumstances of the case, it was appropriate for the two accused to be tried jointly. This is a matter dealt with under ICTY Rule 82(B), i.e. separate trials are required in order to avoid any conflict of interest that may cause serious prejudice or to protect the interests of justice. The Trial Chamber did not find that separate trials were required in that case.

8.2.62 In *Milošević*, the Prosecution sought joinder of three indictments (Croatia, Bosnia and Kosovo) in a single trial pursuant to Rule 49. The Prosecution submitted that all three indictments concerned "the same transaction in the sense of a common scheme, strategy or plan, namely the accused Milošević's overall conduct in attempting to create a "Greater Serbia"—a centralised Serbian state encompassing the Serb-populated areas of Croatia and Bosnia and Hercegovina, and all of Kosovo."

8.2.63 In its *Decision on Prosection's Motion for Joinder*, 13 December 2001, the Trial Chamber referred to the Separate Opinion to an Appeals Chamber Decision on the amendment of indictment in *Kovačević*, where Judge Shahabuddeen stated that: "Joinder of offences is of course possible, within limits. Additional charges must bear a reasonable relationship to the matrix of facts involved in the original charge." The test of the relationship is laid down by Rule 49 the language of which "recognises both the convenience to each side of trying several charges together and the injustice which might enure to the accused if he was required to answer unrelated charges at the same time." The Trial Chamber noted Judge Shahabuddeen's assessment of Rule 49, namely that it appears to have taken its inspiration from the "same transaction" test used in the federal system of the United States of America, according to which it has been said that "it is proper . . . to join offenses which are closely related in that they were interrelated parts of a particular criminal episode." (*Criminal Procedure* 762 (3d ed.), by Wayne R. Lafave and Jerold H. Israel)

8.2.64 Judge Shahabuddeen had concluded that "the question is whether all the counts, old and new, represent interrelated parts of a particular criminal episode. It is not necessary for all of the facts to be identical. It is enough if the new charges cannot be alleged but for the facts which give rise to the old." (See *Decision Stating Reasons for Appeals Chamber's Order of 29 May 1998, 2 July 1998, Separate Opinion of Judge Mohamed Shahabuddeen, p. 2.*).

8.2.65 Pursuant to the filing of written briefs by the Prosecution and the Amici Curiae, and an oral hearing on 11 December 2001, the Trial Chamber in *Milošević* allowed the Prosecution's Motion on Joinder, to the extent that it ordered that the Croatia and Bosnia Indictments be joined. The Trial Chamber decided that the Kosovo indictment would be tried separately, beginning on 12 February 2002. (See Discussion Section of the *Decision on Prosecution's Motion for Joinder* for further detail.)

8.2.66 On 20 December 2001, the Prosection sought leave to file an interlocutory appeal against the Trial Chamber's Decision on Joinder, pursuant to Rule 73(D). One of the grounds upon which the Prosecution submitted that the Trial Chamber had abused its discretion was by "misinterpreting Rule 49 and finding that the Prosecution failed to meet the "same transaction" test." (Rule 73 was amended at the ICTY's twenty-fifth Plenary session on 12–13 December 2001, although the new amendments were not in force when the Prosecution sought leave).

8.2.67 The Appeals Chamber granted leave to appeal on 9 January 2002, pursuant to which the Prosecution filed further written submissions on the interpretation of Rule 49, some of which had not been raised at the joinder hearing, before the Trial Chamber. As part of its submissions, the Prosecution conducted a review of national law approaches to the "same transaction test," submitting that the "law in other national jurisdictions reflects a non-restrictive attitiude toward joinder of counts against the same accused, permitting a variety of possible connections, any of which would be sufficient for joinder." (For more detail, see *Milošević, Interlocutory Appeal of the Prosecution against "Decision on Prosecution's Motion for Joinder*)

8.2.68 The Appeals Chamber held for the Prosecution in its *Decision on Prosecution's Interlocutory Appeal From Refusal to Order Joinder* on 1 February 2002. In this Decision, the Appeals Chamber held that "upon the correct interpretation of Rule 49, the acts alleged in the Croatia, Bosnia and Kosovo Indictments form the same transaction."

> CONSIDERING that the interpretation of the expression "the same transaction" in Rule 49 of the Rules of Procedure and Evidence ("Rules") is a question of law;
>
> AND CONSIDERING that the decision of a Trial Chamber under Rule 49 as to whether there should be a joinder is a discretionary one;
>
> BEING SATISFIED that, based upon arguments as to the correct interpretation of Rule 49 which had not been put by the Prosecution to the Trial Chamber for its consideration, the Trial Chamber misdirected itself as to the correct interpretation of the Rule, and that this error of law invalidated that decision and vitiated the exercise by the Trial Chamber of its discretion;
>
> CONSIDERING that, in accordance with usual appellate practice, the Appeals Chamber should therefore exercise its own discretion in substitution for that of the Trial Chamber;
>
> BEING SATISFIED that, upon the correct interpretation of Rule 49, the acts alleged in the Croatia, Bosnia and Kosovo Indictments ("Three Indictments") form the same transaction;
>
> BEING ALSO SATISFIED in accordance with Rule 49 that the crimes charged in the Three Indictments are alleged to have been committed by the Accused; . . . .
>
> HEREBY ALLOWS the Prosecution's appeal and ORDERS as follows:
> 1. The Three Indictments shall be tried together in the one trial.
> 2. For the purposes of the one trial, the Three Indictments shall be deemed to constitute one Indicment. . . .

See also App. Ch., *Milošević, Reasons for Decision on Prosecution Interlocutory Appeal from Refusal to Order Joinder*, 18 April 2002.

8.2.69

ICTY Rule 50 Amendment of Indictment	ICTR Rule 50 Amendment of Indictment
(A) (i) The Prosecutor may amend an indictment: (a) at any time before its confirmation, without leave; (b) between its confirmation and the assignment of the case to a Trial Chamber, with the leave of the Judge who confirmed the indictment, or a Judge assigned by the President; and (c) after the assignment of the case to a Trial Chamber, with the leave of that Trial Chamber or a Judge of that Chamber, after having heard the parties. (ii) After the assignment of the case to a Trial Chamber, it shall not be necessary for the amended indictment to be confirmed. (iii) Rule 47(G) and Rule 53 *bis* apply *mutatis mutandis* to the amended indictment. (B) If the amended indictment includes new charges and the accused has already appeared before a Trial Chamber in accordance with Rule 62, a further appearance shall be held as soon as practicable to enable the accused to enter a plea on the new charges. (C) The accused shall have a further period of thirty days in which to file preliminary motions pursuant to Rule 72 in respect of the new charges and, where necessary, the date for trial may be postponed to ensure adequate time for the preparation of the defence.	(A) The Prosecutor may amend an indictment, without prior leave, at any time before its confirmation, but thereafter, until the initial appearance of the accused before a Trial Chamber pursuant to Rule 62, only with leave of the Judge who confirmed it or, in exceptional circumstances, by leave of a Judge assigned by the President. At or after such initial appearance, an amendment of an indictment may only be made by leave granted by that Trial Chamber pursuant to Rule 73. If leave to amend is granted, Rule 47 (G) and Rule 53 *bis* apply *mutatis mutandis* to the amended indictment. (B) If the amended indictment includes new charges and the accused has already appeared before a Trial Chamber in accordance with Rule 62, a further appearance shall be held as soon as practicable to enable the accused to enter a plea on the new charges. (C) The accused shall have a further period of sixty days in which to file preliminary motions pursuant to Rule 72 in respect of the new charges.

History of ICTY Rule 50

8.2.70 Paras (B) and (C) were added at the ICTY ninth plenary session in January 1996. Para. (A) has been amended three times. Initially it stipulated that, "if at trial," then leave of the Trial Chamber was required in order to amend an indictment. At the twelfth plenary session, held 2–3 December 1996, the words, "if at trial" were deleted, and the words, "after the presentation of evidence in terms of Rule 85 has commenced," were substituted. Those words were subsequently deleted at the fourteenth plenary session on 12 November 1997 in favour of wording which referred to "the initial appearance of the accused before a Trial Chamber pursuant to Rule 62" as the threshold when the leave of the whole Trial Chamber was required, as opposed to that of a single Judge. Finally, at the eighteenth plenary session, on 9–10 July 1998, the wording reverted to the "commencement of the presentation of evidence in terms of Rule 85" threshold. The requirement that, "If leave to amend is granted, the amended indictment shall be reviewed by the Judge or Trial Chamber granting leave. Rule 47 (G) and Rule 53 *bis* apply *mutatis mutandis* to the amended indictment," was also added at the same plenary. Para. (C) was also amended to reduce the period permitted for the accused to file preliminary motions in respect of the new charges from sixty days to thirty days.

8.2.71 Rule 50 was further amended at the ICTY twenty-first plenary session on 30 November 1999 to distinguish between amended indictments that needed to be confirmed and those that did not need to be confirmed, the distinction to be made in accordance with the criteria set out in para. (A)(iii). This distinction was abolished in favour of the present regime when para. (A) was again amended on 2 August 2000 after the twenty-second plenary session.

History of ICTR Rule 50

8.2.72 ICTR Rule was amended at the ICTR fifth Plenary Session on 8 June 1998 to bring it in line with ICTY Rule 50.

Prerogative of Prosecutor to Amend

8.2.73 In the *Nikolić Rule 61 Decision*, the Trial Chamber observed that "it is the prerogative of the Prosecutor, not the Chamber, to amend the indictment (Rule 50)." The Chamber can, it said, "only express its belief and invite the Prosecutor to amend the indictment accordingly, should he share such belief" (para. 32).

8.2.74 It is, however, clearly in the power of the Chambers to dismiss counts of an indictment or to strike out an indictment altogether.

Withdrawal of Counts "With Prejudice"

8.2.75 In *Delalić et al.*, the Trial Chamber issued an *Order on Prosecution's Motion to withdraw Counts 9 and 10 of the Indictment* in which it "grant(ed) the Prosecution leave to withdraw counts 9 and 10 of the Indictment with prejudice such that the charges set forth in the said counts shall not be raised against any of the four accused persons at a later date." The Prosecutor in her Motion requested the "with prejudice" designation.

Addition of New Counts Without Leave

8.2.76 The Trial Chamber, in a Decision rendered in *Blaškić* on 23 May 1997, considered that the Prosecutor, who had amended the indictment pursuant to an Order of the Chamber, had added a new count—"devastation not justified by military necessity"—and it therefore referred the Prosecutor to the confirming Judge for leave to add the count:

> In the absence of any factual indications in support (of) Count 2, the Trial Chamber notes that the count is new. The Trial Chamber, pursuant to Rule 50 of the Rules, can therefore merely refer the Prosecutor to the confirming judge unless she considers that the count might be covered by the wording and contents of Counts 3 and 4. (pages 5–6)

It is unclear whether "she" here refers to the Prosecutor or to the Confirming Judge.

No Need for Additional Time Where Charges Are Simply Withdrawn

8.2.77 See *Decision on the Prosecutor's Motion for Leave to Amend the Indictment* rendered in *Jelisić* on 12 May 1998, where the charges under Article 2 of the Statute were withdrawn by amendment of the indictment, the Prosecutor deciding, in order to expedite the trial, not to tender evidence of an international armed conflict as required under Article 2, as interpreted by the Tribunal. The Trial Chamber stated that, "since the amendment involves only the withdrawal of some of the counts, the proceedings initiated thus far must follow their normal course with no need to grant additional time for the preparation of the defence of the accused."

Substantial Amendment of Indictment

8.2.78 See *Decision on Prosecutor's Request to file an amended indictment* rendered by the Trial Chamber in *Kovačević* on 5 March 1998, denying the Prosecutor's request to amend the indictment:

> 12. The Trial Chamber's reasons for refusing this Request for Leave to Amend are as follows:
>
> (a) The proposed amendment (consisting of 14 added counts, and factual allegations which would increase the size of the Indictment from 8 to 18 pages) is so substantial as to amount to a substitution of a new indictment; an amendment of this proportion should have been made much more promptly (and not nearly a year after confirmation; and seven months after the arrest of the accused).

8.2.79 This Decision was, however, successfully appealed. Upholding the appeal in part, the Appeals Chamber on 29 May 1998 ordered the Trial Chamber to grant leave to amend the indictment. This seems contradictory inasmuch as leave is a *discretionary* remedy and while it would appear that the Appeals Chamber could itself grant leave, it is not obvious that it could order a Trial Chamber to grant leave. In any event, however, the Trial Chamber did grant leave to amend the indictment in its *Order granting leave to amend the Indictment* of 2 June 1998.

8.2.80 The Appeals Chamber gave the reasons for its Order in its *Decision stating reasons for Appeals Chamber's Order of 29 May 1998*, dated 2 July 1998, in which it held that (1) the *size* of the new indictment was not a valid reason for the Trial Chamber to reject it (para. 25); (2) that undue delay on the part of the Prosecutor was also not a valid reason for the Trial Chamber to reject the new indictment (para. 31). The matter had to be looked at in the context of the case, especially in relation to the concept of *fairness* to an accused; (3) as to whether there had been a failure to disclose the new charges to the accused *promptly* upon his arrest, it was acceptable if the accused were told of at least certain of the crimes charged against him upon his arrest, even if further charges were added subsequently (Judge Shahabuddeen added a Separate Opinion on this issue); and (4) as to whether there existed a "specialty" principle under customary international law which would prohibit the prosecution of the accused on charges other than those on which he was arrested in Bosnia and Herzegovina and brought to the Netherlands, the Appeals Chamber rejected this argument (para. 37). Thus the Appeals Chamber considered that "in the circumstances of this case, the prosecution was entitled to leave to amend the indictment by the addition of the new charges."

8.2.81 In his Separate Opinion, Judge Shahabuddeen affirmed a principle "which recognises that the prosecution has a right not to institute charges as soon as it has enough material to do so; it may competently defer doing so until it has inquired into the possibility of obtaining better or alternative forms of evidence." Judge Shahabuddeen also turned to the test laid down in Rule 49 for justification for the addition of new charges, namely whether the additional crimes formed "the same transaction" and were committed by the same accused. Judge Shahabuddeen also considered Article 9(2) of the International Covenant on Civil and Political Rights ("ICCPR"), which reads: "Anyone who is arrested shall be informed, at the time of arrest, of the reasons for his arrest and shall promptly be informed of any charges against him." Judge Shahabuddeen agreed with defence counsel that "any charges" meant "all charges," not "some charges": "The purpose of the provision being to put the arrested person in a position to challenge the lawfulness of his arrest, all of the grounds on which the arrest was made are important." This did not mean, however, that the accused could not subsequently be informed of *additional* charges against him; this was permissible provided that such additional charges did not form the basis of his arrest and that he was therefore not informed of those charges at the time of his arrest, which is what Article 9(2) of the ICCPR, and Article 21(4)(a) of the ICTY Statute, expressly require.

Prosecution Must Disclose Supporting Material Proffered for Additional Counts to Defence and Judges

8.2.82 See *Scheduling Order*, Trial Chamber, *Kupreškić et al.*, 13 February 1998.

Schedule of Changes to Indictment

8.2.83 When an indictment is amended, the Prosecution should ordinarily file a schedule showing what is new and what is old in the amended indictment. See *Order on the Disclosure of Additional Information in respect of the Prosecutor's Motion for Leave to Amend the Indictment* issued by the Trial Chamber in *Kordić and Čerkez* on 21 May 1998:

> NOTING therefore that, in respect of the above, it appears indispensable that the Prosecutor provide to the Trial Chamber a detailed exhaustive comparative table of the proposed amendments: that, in the case in point, the Prosecutor specify for each act indicated in the initial indictment whether it also appears in the draft and, if so, in respect of which count(s); that, furthermore, the Prosecutor specify what in the draft, in her opinion, constitutes a new count and, if necessary, that she clearly indicate the facts on which each of the new crimes is based,
> FOR THE FOREGOING REASONS,
> ORDERS the Prosecutor to submit to the Trial Chamber by 15 June 1998, a brief containing the above-mentioned information.

Procedure Upon Showing Defects in Form of Indictment

8.2.84 For the procedure to be followed upon a successful motion alleging defects in the form of the indictment, see the *Decision on Prosecutor's Response to Decision of 24 February 1999* rendered in *Krnojelac* on 20 May 1999, in particular paras. 4–14. Noting that, "the practice within the Tribunal has not been consistent as to the precise nature of the relief granted when upholding a complaint by an accused in relation to the form of the indictment pursuant to what is now Rule 72," the Trial Chamber stated that:

> 8. There is no difference in substance between granting leave to amend the indictment and ordering or directing the Prosecution to amend it. In either such case, any application made to the confirming judge pursuant to Rule 50(A) for leave to make the particular amendments which have already been permitted or directed by a Trial Chamber would serve no useful purpose, and the Trial Chamber is satisfied that such a procedure is not contemplated by the wording of the rule....
>
> 9. What happens next depends on whether the amendments do or do not go beyond what was permitted or directed by the Trial Chamber.
>
> 10. If the amendments made by the prosecution *do* go beyond what was permitted or directed by the Trial Chamber and add new charges, Rule 50(A) does apply, and leave to make those amendments is required. Such leave must be sought from the confirming judge or another judge assigned by the President. The reason why the Trial Chamber which heard the Motion by the accused ... cannot also grant leave to add new charges at this stage lies in the structure of the Rules of Procedure and Evidence. The Rules adopt a division of functions ...
>
> 11. ... The intention of this division of functions is to avoid any contamination spreading from the *ex parte* nature of the confirming procedure to the Trial Chamber.
>
> 12. Once evidence has been presented before the Trial Chamber, it is not practicable for the confirming judge to continue to be the authority from whom leave to amend in order to add new charges must be sought.... That is why para. (iii) has been added to Rule 50(A). The need to confirm the indictment remains where an application for leave to amend is granted, although the review which must be undertaken by the Trial Chamber for that purpose is performed *inter partes*.... The possibility of contamination spreading from the *ex parte* nature of the confirming procedure is therefore effectively eliminated.
>
> 13. If the amendments made by the Prosecution do *not* go beyond what was permitted or directed by the Trial Chamber in relation to defects found in the form of the indictment, and so do not add new charges, leave to amend the indictment need not be sought from the confirming judge or other judge assigned by the President pursuant to Rule 50(A)....

No Need to Notify Defence of Motion to Amend Indictment

8.2.85 See the *Motion for Leave to Amend the Indictment* submitted by the Prosecutor in *Akayesu* on 17 June 1997, which was granted in a Decision by the Trial Chamber on 3 October 1997. The Chamber noted, in reply to a defence objection that it had had insufficient time to respond to the Prosecutor's Motion, that the Prosecutor had no obligation to transmit to the defence the request to amend the indictment which was before the Chamber. This suggests that the amendment of an indictment is essentially an *ex parte* matter between the Prosecutor and Judges. This is arguable given that the amendment of an indictment affects the rights of the accused in a number of ways. It is submitted that the accused should be fully heard on its view of the proposed amendment.

Rule 50 Must Be Applied in Accordance with ICTY Articles 19 and 20 and ICCPR Article 9(2)

8.2.86 In *Kovačević, Decision Stating Reasons for Appeals Chamber's Order of 29 May 1998*, 2 July 1998, the Appeals Chamber held that Rule 50 must be applied in accordance with Articles 19 and 20 of the ICTY Statute and Article 9(2) of the ICCPR (*"Anyone who is arrested shall be informed, at the time of arrest, of the reasons for his arrest and shall be promptly informed of any charges against him."*)

Amendment Allowed Based on Investigations Carried Out After Trial Has Commenced

8.2.87 In the *Akayesu Appeals Judgement* (para. 121), the Appeals Chamber, citing a Decision in *Barayagwiza*, held that an amendment to the Indictment may be sought by the Prosecution, even during trial, based on the results of ongoing investigations. The Appeals Chamber dismissed Akayesu's complaint that the Trial Chamber had wrongly allowed the Prosecution to amend the indictment during trial. The Prosecution had conducted further investigations after the testimony of a Prosecution witness. Based upon the results of those investigations, the Prosecution sought to amend the indictment. The amendment added crimes to the indictment that had been covered at trial by witnesses who had testified before the amendment. As a result the Defence had not cross-examined these witnesses about these offences. The Appeals Chamber held that in such circumstances, if the Defence had wished to challenge the evidence of the witnesses who had testified prior to amendment they should have requested that the witnesses be recalled for cross-examination.

8.2.88

ICTY Rule 51 Withdrawal of Indictment	ICTR Rule 51 Withdrawal of Indictment
(A) The Prosecutor may withdraw an indictment: (i) at any time before its confirmation, without leave; (ii) between its confirmation and the assignment of the case to a Trial Chamber, with the leave of the Judge who confirmed the indictment, or a Judge assigned by the President; and (iii) after the assignment of the case to a Trial Chamber, by motion before that Trial Chamber pursuant to Rule 73. (B) The withdrawal of the indictment shall be promptly notified to the suspect or the accused and to the counsel of the suspect or accused.	(A) The Prosecutor may withdraw an indictment, without prior leave, at any time before its confirmation, but thereafter, until the initial appearance of the accused before a Trial Chamber pursuant to Rule 62, only with leave of the Judge who confirmed it or, in exceptional circumstances, by leave of a Judge assigned by the President. At or after such initial appearance an indictment may only be withdrawn by leave granted by that Trial Chamber pursuant to Rule 73. (B) The withdrawal of the indictment shall be promptly notified to the suspect or the accused and to the counsel of the suspect or accused.

History of ICTY Rule 51

8.2.89 Para. (A) has been amended three times. Initially it stipulated that leave of the Trial Chamber was required for the withdrawal of an indictment "if at trial." At the twelfth plenary session, held 2–3 December 1996, the words, "if at trial" were deleted, and the words, "after the presentation of evidence in terms of Rule 85 has commenced," were substituted. Those words were subsequently deleted at the fourteenth plenary session on 12 November 1997 in favour of the wording which referred to "the initial appearance of the accused before a Trial Chamber pursuant to Rule 62" as the threshold of when the leave of the whole Trial Chamber is required as opposed to that of a single Judge. The current wording of para. (A) was adopted on 12 December 2002.

History of ICTR Rule 51

8.2.90 This Rule was amended at the ICTR fifth plenary session on 8 June 1998.

Ill-Health Not Ground for Withdrawal

8.2.91 The Trial Chamber in *Đukić* rejected a motion to withdraw the indictment against the accused for reasons of ill-health (*Decision rejecting the application to withdraw the indictment and order for provisional release*, 24 April 1996). The Chamber recognised that Đorđe Đukić was suffering from an incurable illness but stated that, "... no matter how critical the medical reasons cited may be, nothing in the Statute or Rules authorises the withdrawal for those reasons of an indictment for major crimes which the International Criminal Tribunal must judge. . ." (p. 3). The Chamber noted that "during the Nuremberg and Tokyo trials, identical situations arose (accused Krupp von Bohlen und Halbach and Osawa) and that the International Military Tribunals did not consider it necessary to withdraw the indictments" (p. 3). The Chamber instead issued an order pursuant to Rule 65 for the provisional release of Đukić on purely humanitarian grounds.

Death Ground for Withdrawal

8.2.92 The indictment against Stipo Alilović was withdrawn, upon the Prosecutor's application, after confirmation that the accused was dead. See *Decision on Motion by the Prosecutor for Withdrawal of Indictment against Stipo Alilović*, Trial Chamber, 23 December 1997.

Withdrawal for Lack of Evidence

8.2.93 Clearly, an indictment may be withdrawn if there is insufficient evidence to justify proceeding to trial against the accused. See *Prosecutor's Motion under Rule 51 for leave to withdraw the indictment against the accused Marinko Katava* dated 18 December 1997, *Prosecutor's Motion under Rule 51 for leave to withdraw the indictment against the accused Ivan Šantić* dated 18 December 1997, and *Prosecutor's Motion under Rule 51 for leave to withdraw the indictment against the accused Pero Skopljak* dated 18 December 1997. These Motions were granted in Orders issued by the Trial Chamber on 19 December 1997 (Katava), and by Judge Riad (pursuant to an *Order of the President authorising a Trial Chamber to conduct a matter in the absence of two* *of its members* of the same day) on 19 December 1997 (Šantić and Skopljak). In all three cases, the immediate release of the accused was ordered at the same time as withdrawal of the indictment.

8.2.94 In a *Decision on The Prosecutor's Ex Parte Application for Leave to Withdraw the Indictment* in *Rusatira (ICTR-2002-80-I)*, Judge Pillay granted leave to the Prosecutor, pursuant to Rule 51, to withdraw the Indictment against Leonidas Rusatira without prejudice to the Prosecutor seeking the confirmation of another indictment against him, based on new or additional evidence. The arrest warrant against Rusatira was immediately withdrawn, although clearly a new arrest warrant could be issued once a new indictment was confirmed.

Withdrawal for Trial in Domestic Courts

8.2.95 An indictment may be withdrawn because the accused would be more appropriately tried in another forum. This notion is analogous to that of complementarity with national courts which will be applied before the ICC. See *Order granting leave for withdrawal of charges against Govedarica, Gruban, Janjić, Kostić, Paspalj, Popović, Predojević, Savić, Babić and Šaponja* issued by Judge Riad on 8 May 1998, in which he granted leave for the withdrawal of charges against the above-mentioned accused on the following grounds, *inter alia:*

> CONSIDERING the submission of the Prosecutor that the increase in the number of arrests . . . has compelled her to re-evaluate all outstanding indictments vis-à-vis the overall investigative and prosecutorial strategies of the Office of the Prosecutor;
>
> . . .
>
> CONSIDERING that the named accused could appropriately be tried in another forum, such as a State forum . . .

8.2.96 Note the principle of concurrent jurisdiction, expressed in Article 9 of the Statute: "The International Tribunal and national courts shall have concurrent jurisdiction to prosecute persons for serious violations of international humanitarian law committed in the territory of the former Yugoslavia since 1 January 1991." While the ICTY has primacy over national courts (Article 9(2) of the Statute), the International Criminal Court established by the Rome Statute operates on the principle of *complementarity*. See Preamble, "Emphasizing that the International Criminal Court established under this Statute shall be complementary to national criminal jurisdictions" and Article 17 of the Rome Statute. It can be seen from the above that the ICTY, too, applies the principle of complementarity in deciding whether it is appropriate for a case to be tried before it, although in this case it does not appear that any State or national court was proceeding against any of the accused, only that the accused "*could* appropriately be tried" by such courts.

8.2.97 See also the *Order granting leave for withdrawal of charges against Janjić, Kondić, Lajić, Šaponja and Timarac* dated 5 May 1998, in which the Prosecutor also acknowledged that these non-leadership figures could "appropriately be tried in another forum, such as a State forum."

8.2.98 In *Ntuyahaga*, the accused was released after the indictment was withdrawn. This was despite the fact that the Belgian authorities had requested that the accused be surrendered to them. Belgium wished to prosecute Ntuyahaga for the murder of ten Belgian United Nations peacekeepers on 7 April 1994. The Chamber held, however, that "it does not have jurisdiction to order the release of a person who is no longer under indictment into the custody of any given state, including the Host State, the United Republic of Tanzania" (*Decision on the Prosecutor's Motion to Withdraw the Indictment*, Trial Chamber 1, 18 March 1999). The Tribunal noted that neither Rule 40 *bis* (H)("Transfer and Provisional Detention of Suspects") nor Rule 65 ("Provisional Release") could be called in aid, and bemoaned the fact that:

> the primacy recognised by the Statute is clear inasmuch as the Tribunal may request any national jurisdiction to defer investigations or ongoing proceedings, whereas the reverse, namely the deferral of investigations and proceedings by the Tribunal to any national jurisdiction, is not provided for.

8.2.99 In this connection, it is interesting to refer to Rule 11 *bis* of the ICTY's Rules of Procedure and Evidence ("Suspension of Indictment in Case of Proceedings before National Courts"), although the conditions for the application of that rule would not be met *in casu* since Belgium had not arrested the accused.

8.2.100

ICTY Rule 52 Public Character of Indictment	ICTR Rule 52 Public Character of Indictment
Subject to Rule 53, upon confirmation by a Judge of a Trial Chamber, the indictment shall be made public.	Subject to Rule 53, upon confirmation by a Judge of a Trial Chamber, the indictment shall be made public.

Rule 52 Subject to Rule 53

8.2.101 Rule 52 confirms the public character of indictments. The general rule is that upon confirmation of an indictment it is to be made public. However, Rule 52 is subject to Rule 53 (below).

8.2.102

ICTY Rule 53 Non-Disclosure of Indictment	ICTR Rule 53 Non-Disclosure
(A) In exceptional circumstances, a Judge or a Trial Chamber may, in the interests of justice, order the non-disclosure to the public of any documents or information until further order.	(A) In exceptional circumstances, a Judge or a Trial Chamber may, in the interests of justice, order the non-disclosure to the public of any documents or information until further order.

(B) When confirming an indictment the Judge may, in consultation with the Prosecutor, order that there be no public disclosure of the indictment until it is served on the accused, or, in the case of joint accused, on all the accused. (C) A Judge or Trial Chamber may, in consultation with the Prosecutor, also order that there be no disclosure of an indictment, or part thereof, or of all or any part of any particular document or information, if satisfied that the making of such an order is required to give effect to a provision of the Rules, to protect confidential information obtained by the Prosecutor, or is otherwise in the interests of justice. (D) Notwithstanding paragraphs (A), (B) and (C), the Prosecutor may disclose an indictment or part thereof to the authorities of a State or an appropriate authority or international body where the Prosecutor deems it necessary to prevent an opportunity for securing the possible arrest of an accused from being lost.	(B) When confirming an indictment the Judge may, in consultation with the Prosecutor, order that there be no public disclosure of the indictment until it is served on the accused, or, in the case of joint accused, on all the accused. (C) A Judge or Trial Chamber may, in consultation with the Prosecutor, also order that there be no disclosure of an indictment, or part thereof, or of all or any part of any particular document or information, if satisfied that the making of such an order is required to give effect to a provision of the Rules, to protect confidential information obtained by the Prosecutor, or is otherwise in the interests of justice.

History of ICTY Rule 53

8.2.103 Para. (B) (now para. (C)) was amended at the ICTY fifth plenary session in January 1995 for the purpose of "clarifying the Rules" (second Annual Report, para. 21). The words "of all or any part" were inserted, as well as the words, "required to give effect to a provision of the Rules, to protect confidential information obtained by the Prosecutor, or is otherwise . . . ," to make clear that non-disclosure orders may be available to protect such information.

8.2.104 Para. (A) was amended at the eleventh plenary session, on 24–25 June 1996, at the suggestion of the Judicial Department of the Registry, to provide a general rule for non-disclosure, not limited, as was the case beforehand, to an indictment or part thereof. Para. (D) was added at the nineteenth plenary session, on 17 December 1998.

Cross References: See also, on non-disclosure, Rules 36, 66(C), 69(A), 70, 75 and 79.

Sealed Indictments

8.2.105 Rule 53 empowers the Tribunals to order the non-disclosure of an indictment where this would be in the interests of justice. When it is no longer in the interests of justice to keep it under seal, a non-disclosure order can be lifted. This is usually at the time of arrest but an indictment can sometimes be disclosed prior to an arrest.

8.2.106 Pursuant to Rule 53(C), indictments have been confirmed which have remained undisclosed—or "sealed"—pursuant to an Order of the confirming Judge, until the accused has been arrested. For example, Slavko Dokmanović, Milan Kovačević and Radislav Krstić were taken into custody pursuant to "sealed" indictments.

8.2.107 The ICTY/ICTR Prosecutor, Louise Arbour, who succeeded Richard Goldstone in this capacity, stated that her policy was to issue only sealed indictments, in order to facilitate the arrest of accused persons. This proved to be a very successful strategy.

8.2.108 Exceptionally, however, the Prosecutor has made the existence of sealed indictments known, notably the indictments of "Tuta" (on 21/12/98) and "Arkan." Concerning the indictment of "Arkan," see ICTY Press Release of 31 March 1999 (CC/PIU/391-E):

8.2.109 The Prosecutor was able to disclose the existence of the arrest warrant due to the *Decision to vacate in part an order for non-disclosure* rendered by an ICTY Judge on 31 March 1999. In fact "Arkan" was killed in Belgrade and was, therefore, never transferred to the ICTY.

8.2.110

ICTY Rule 53 *bis* Service of Indictment	ICTR Rule 53 *bis* Service of Indictment
(A) Service of the indictment shall be effected personally on the accused at the time the accused is taken into custody or as soon as reasonably practicable thereafter. (B) Personal service of an indictment on the accused is effected by giving the accused a copy of the indictment certified in accordance with Rule 47(G).	(A) Service of the indictment shall be effected personally on the accused at the time the accused is taken into the custody of the Tribunal or as soon as possible thereafter. (B) Personal service of an indictment on the accused is effected by giving the accused a copy of the indictment certified in accordance with Rule 47 (G).

History of ICTY Rule 53 *bis*

8.2.111 This Rule was adopted at the fourteenth plenary on 12 November 1997.

History of ICTR Rule 53 *bis*

8.2.112 This Rule was introduced on 1 July 1999.

SECTION 3: CUMULATIVE CHARGING

Charges Must Protect Different Values or Contain Different Elements

8.3.1 The practice of cumulative charging refers to the charging, in an indictment, of more than one crime in relation to the same set of events. ICTY jurisprudence allows cumulative charging under certain circumstances. See the *Decision on Defence Challenges to Form of the Indictment* rendered in *Kupreškić et al* on 15 May 1998:

> the Prosecutor may be justified in bringing cumulative charges when the Articles of the Statute referred to are designed to protect different values and when each Article requires proof of a legal element not required by the others.

8.3.2 In the *Decision on the Defence Preliminary Motion on the Form of the Indictment* rendered in *Krnojelac* on 24 February 1999, the Trial Chamber upheld the practice of allowing cumulative charging (paras 5–10). The Chamber based itself on both ICTY jurisprudence and the *Akayesu Trial Judgement:*

> 10. The prosecution must be allowed to frame charges within the one indictment on the basis that the tribunal of fact may not accept a particular element of one charge which does not have to be established for the other charges, and in any event in order to reflect the totality of the accused's criminal conduct, so that the punishment will do the same. Of course, great care must be taken in sentencing that an offender convicted of different charges arising out of the same or substantially the same facts is not punished more than once for his commission of the individual acts (or omissions) which are common to two or more of those charges. But there is no breach of the double jeopardy principle by the inclusion in the one indictment of different charges arising out of the same or substantially the same facts.

8.3.3 The test set out in *Kupreškić*, above, differs from that enunciated by the ICTR in the *Akayesu Trial Judgement* in two respects: (1) the *Akayesu* Judgement added a third condition ("where it is necessary to record a conviction for both offences in order fully to describe what the accused did") and (2) presented the three conditions as *disjunctive* ("or") as opposed to the conjunctive ("and") applied in *Kupreškić*. See para. 468 of the *Akayesu Trial Judgement:*

> On the basis of national and international law and jurisprudence, the Chamber concludes that it is acceptable to convict the accused of two offences in relation to the same set of facts in the following circumstances: (1) where the offences have different elements; or (2) where the provisions creating the offences protect different interests; or (3) where it is necessary to record a conviction for both offences in order fully to describe what the accused did. However, the Chamber finds that it is not justifiable to convict an accused of two offences in relation to the same set of facts where (a) one offence is a lesser included offence of the other, for example, murder and grievous bodily harm, robbery and theft, or rape and indecent assault; or (b) where one offence charges accomplice liability and the other offence charges liability as a principal, e.g. genocide and complicity in genocide.

Cumulative Convictions Permitted if *Blockburger* Test Met

8.3.4 In the *Delalić et al. Appeals Judgement* (paras 316–359), the Chamber allowed cumulative convictions (as opposed to cumulative charging, which the Chamber allowed generally (para. 327)), only in one situation, namely when each statutory provision involved has a materially distinct element not contained in the other (para. 339). This has been referred to as the *Blockburger* test, after the U.S. case of the same name.

8.3.5 Where this test is not met, a decision must be made in relation to which offence the Chamber will enter a conviction, on the basis that the conviction must be for the offence containing the more specific provision (para. 340). Where the evidence establishes the guilt of an accused based upon the same conduct under both Article 2 and Article 3 of the Statute, the conviction must be entered for the offence under Article 2 (para. 354), because Article 2 has the more specific requirement that the crimes were committed in the context of an international armed conflict.

8.3.6 This approach was followed in the *Foča Trial Judgement* (paras. 548–549):

> 550. Accordingly, once all the evidence has been assessed, before deciding which convictions, if any, to enter against an accused, a Trial Chamber first has to determine whether an accused is charged with more than one statutory offence based upon the same conduct. Secondly, if there is evidence to establish both offences, but the underlying conduct is the same, the Trial Chamber has to determine whether each relevant statutory provision has a materially distinct element not contained in the other. This involves a comparison of the elements of the relevant statutory provisions—the facts of a specific case play no role in this determination. Thirdly, if the relevant provisions do not each have a materially distinct element, the Trial Chamber should select the more specific provision.

8.3.7 When it comes to sentencing, the sentence must "reflect the totality of the criminal conduct and overall culpability of the offender" (para. 551).

8.3.8 See also the *Kordić and Čerkez Trial Judgement*, paras. 814–826. The Trial Chamber, applied the test enunciated by the Appeals Chamber in the *Delalić et al. Appeals Judgement* and set out the appropriate charges to convict upon in situations of overlapping counts.

8.3.9 This approach was also taken in the *Kayishema and Ruzindana Trial Judgement* in relation to the charges of genocide and crimes against humanity:

> 577. . . . in this particular case the crimes against humanity in question are completely absorbed by the crime of genocide. All counts for these crimes are based on the same facts and the same criminal conduct. These crimes were committed at the same massacre sites, against the same people, belonging to the Tutsi ethnic group with the same intent to destroy this group in whole or in part.
> 578. Considering the above . . . it . . . [would] be improper to convict the accused persons for genocide as well as for crimes against humanity based on murder and extermination because the later [sic] two offences are subsumed fully by the counts of genocide. . . .

8.3.10 Judge Khan, in a separate and dissenting opinion, dissented from this approach, believing it was proper in that case to record convictions for both genocide and crimes against humanity.

Cumulative or Alternative Counts

8.3.11 There seem to be two approaches at the ICTY to the question whether crimes in an indictment may be charged cumulatively or in the alternative. The *Tadić* Trial Chamber, when confronted with this issue, postponed it *to the sentencing stage* (*Tadić Form of the Indictment Decision*, 14 November 1995):

> since this is a matter that will only be relevant insofar as it might affect penalty, it can best be dealt with if and when matters of penalty fall for consideration. What can, however, be said with certainty is that penalty cannot be made to depend upon whether offences arising from the same conduct are alleged cumulatively or in the alternative. What is to be punished by penalty is proven criminal conduct and that will not depend upon technicalities of pleading. (para. 17).

8.3.12 The *Delalić* Trial Chamber followed its own reasoning in its *Delalić Form of the Indictment Decision* of 2 October 1996 (p. 14); its *Landžo Form of the Indictment Decision* of 15 November 1996 (para. 7), and its *Delić Form of the Indictment Decision* of 15 November 1996 (para. 22).

8.3.13 When the *Tadić* trial concluded, the Trial Chamber imposed concurrent sentences, both as between Article 3 and Article 5 charges relating to the same conduct, and as between different instances of misconduct (e.g. different beatings).

8.3.14 This approach does not, however, entirely address the issue. First, the matter of whether crimes are being charged cumulatively or in the alternative is not a "technicality of pleading"; it goes to the very question of whether an accused has committed one crime or several and it is thus a question of *substance*.

8.3.15 Second, since *concurrent* sentences were imposed in *Tadić*—a practice which could be adopted for both alternative verdicts and cumulative charges—the Trial Chamber was able to side-step the issue. The Chamber would only have had to clarify the matter if it had wished to impose *consecutive* sentences under Rule 101(C), since that would only appear to be permissible where the charges are cumulative (since separate crimes are then being punished) and not where they are alternative (since the accused would then be punished twice for the same crime).

8.3.16 Indeed, an accused should not even be *convicted* of two crimes if they really are alternatives, but if concurrent sentences are imposed, the injustice of the double conviction is mitigated by the fact that it makes no difference in terms of penalty, as noted above (although it can make a difference to an accused to be convicted of fifteen crimes rather than five crimes, even if the overall sentence is the same).

8.3.17 Thus the question of cumulative/alternative verdicts was not answered in *Tadić*.

8.3.18 A different approach was taken in *Kupreškić*, where it was held that cumulative charges are permitted where the crimes charged protect different values or contain different elements (see 8.3.1, above).

8.3.19 See also *Prosecutor's Response to the Trial Chamber's Request for a Brief on the Use of Cumulative Criminal Charges in relation to a proposed "substantive"* non bis in idem *principle in international criminal law* submitted in *Dokmanović* on 10 February 1998, for a discussion of the cumulative charges/*non bis in idem*/double jeopardy issue.

ICTY Rule 87(C)

8.3.20   Reference should be made to ICTY Rule 87(C) in this regard:

> If the Trial Chamber finds the accused guilty on one or more of the charges contained in the indictment, it shall impose a sentence in respect of each finding of guilt and indicate whether such sentences shall be served consecutively or concurrently, unless it decides to exercise its power to impose a single sentence reflecting the totality of the criminal conduct of the accused.

Walther, Suzanne, "Cumulation of Offences," Ch. 11.6, *in* Antonio Cassese, Paola Gaeta and John R.W.D. Jones, *The Rome Statute of the International Criminal Court: A Commentary* (Oxford University Press, 2002).

SECTION 4: ORDERS AND WARRANTS

8.4.1

| ICTY
Rule 54
General Rule | ICTR
Rule 54
General Rule |
| --- | --- |
| At the request of either party or *proprio motu*, a Judge or a Trial Chamber may issue such orders, summonses, subpoenas, warrants and transfer orders as may be necessary for the purposes of an investigation or for the preparation or conduct of the trial. | At the request of either party or *proprio motu*, a Judge or a Trial Chamber may issue such orders, summonses, subpoenas, warrants and transfer orders as may be necessary for the purposes of an investigation or for the preparation or conduct of the trial. |

History of ICTY Rule 54

8.4.2 Rule 54 was amended at the fifth plenary session in January 1995, by adding the word "subpoenas," for the purpose of "clarifying the rules" (ICTY second Annual Report, para. 21).

Necessary for Purpose of Investigation, Preparation or Conduct of Trial

8.4.3 The test for whether a Judge or Chamber will issue an order, etc. under Rule 54 is whether to do so is "necessary for the purposes of an investigation or for the preparation or conduct of the trial." This test was considered by the President of the Tribunal, Judge Cassese, in the *Decision on the Prosecutor's Motion for the Production of Notes Exchanged Between Zejnil Delalić and Zdravko Mucić*, rendered in *Delalić et al.* on 11 November 1996. The Prosecutor had submitted a Motion pursuant to Rules 39, 54 and 72 to a Trial Chamber. The Trial Chamber then remitted the Motion to the President for determination, deeming it to be a matter within his competence (see Rule 33, "under the authority of the President"). The President, in his Decision, stated with respect to Rule 54:

> 38. The Prosecutor's Motion before the Trial Chamber is founded on three Rules: Rules 39(iv), 54 and 72. Rule 72 is no help in this regard—it simply gives the Prosecutor the *right* to file preliminary motions, but says nothing about when those motions will be granted. Rule 39(iv) refers to "such orders *as may be necessary*...," and Rule 54 refers to "such ... orders *as may be necessary for the purposes of an investigation or for the preparation or conduct of the trial*." In the light of these two Rules, I find that the appropriate test is: *is it necessary (not simply useful or helpful) for the purposes of the investigation or for the preparation or conduct of the trial that the Registrar be ordered to produce the notes in question?*
>
> 39. The test entails two parts: (a) an order of the International Tribunal must be necessary for the Prosecutor to obtain such material; and (b) the material being sought must be relevant to an investigation or prosecution being conducted by the Prosecutor. As with any search or seizure warrant, the Prosecutor cannot simply conduct a "fishing expedition" through the Registrar's records.

8.4.4 In this last regard, the President considered the criteria applicable to disclosure under Rule 66 of the Rules as laid down in the *Decision on the Motion by the Accused Zejnil Delalić for the Disclosure of Evidence*, rendered by the Trial Chamber in *Delalić et al* on 26 September 1996 (see Rule 39 above and Rule 66 below).

Examples of Orders, Summonses, Subpoenas and Warrants Issued

8.4.5 Rule 54 is, on its terms, a general rule, for the issuance of orders, summonses, subpoenas, etc..

Summonses

8.4.6 Summonses were issued by the Trial Chamber in *Tadić* in its *Decision on the Defence Motion to Summon and Protect Defence Witnesses, and on the Giving of Evidence by Video-Link* rendered on 25 June 1996. The Chamber ordered that the summons in question, "shall provide instructions relating to identification, insofar as possible, (shall) specify the time and place for the appearance, and shall set out the penalty for non-compliance. It shall also indicate the approximate allowances payable and the travelling and subsistence expenses which are reimbursable or pre-paid" (para. 7).

8.4.7 Summonses were also issued by the Trial Chamber in *Kupreškić* to summons a witness to appear as a witness for the Tribunal rather than as a *defence* witness (*Decision On Defence Motion to Summon Witnesses* dated 6 October 1998). Witnesses sometimes prefer to be called to testify by the Tribunal rather than by one party, particularly the defence, as there may be a perception of partisanship in so doing. The *Kupreškić Decision* also specified the order of examination of the witness. See also the *Witness Summons by the Chamber pursuant to Rule 98 of the Rules of Procedure and Evidence* issued in *Kupreškić* on 30 September 1998.

Subpoenae Duces Tecum

8.4.8 A *Subpoena duces tecum* and *Order of a Judge to ensure compliance with a Subpoena duces tecum* were issued by Judge McDonald in *Blaškić* on 15 January 1997 and 14 February 1997, respectively. The Order was addressed to the Minister of Defence of the Republic of Croatia and to the Minister of Defence of the Federation of Bosnia and Herzegovina, and directed the authorities of those Republics to produce certain documents described in the subpoena. It further provided that in the event of a failure to produce the said documents, representatives of the authorities would have to appear before the Judge to explain their non-compliance.

8.4.9 The order to Croatia was suspended on 19 February 1997 to allow the matter to be resolved informally. Croatia had challenged the legality of the order and subpoena, maintaining that neither international law nor the Tribunal's Statute nor its Rules empowered the Tribunal to subpoena state officials:

> The assistance request can be directed to a State, but not to a specifically named high government official to appear on behalf of the State. A State is to decide freely on who is to appear before the Tribunal on its behalf. (para. 6, Reply of the Republic of Croatia)

8.4.10 The order to Bosnia and Herzegovina was supplemented by an order issued by Judge McDonald on 24 February 1997 requesting the Minister of Defence of the Federation of Bosnia and Herzegovina to appear before the Tribunal to explain non-compliance with the subpoena. In a further order dated 28 February 1997, the Defence Minister was directed to produce the subpoenaed documents or face contempt proceedings. In the event, the latter course did not prove necessary.

8.4.11 In light of non-compliance with the subpoena, and objections raised to its having been issued, notably by the Republic of Croatia, Judge McDonald subsequently convened a full Trial Chamber to consider the issue. In an *Order Submitting the Matter to Trial Chamber II and inviting Amicus Curiae*, issued on 14 March 1997, Judge McDonald directed that a hearing on the issuance of a *subpoena duces tecum*, scheduled for 16 April 1997, be held before the Trial Chamber, composed of Judges McDonald, Odio-Benito and Jan, and not a single Judge, "considering the significance of the issues to be addressed." In the order, Judge McDonald invited *amicus curiae* briefs on the following questions to be submitted by 7 April 1997:

> the power of a Judge or Trial Chamber of the International Criminal Tribunal for the former Yugoslavia to issue a subpoena duces tecum to a sovereign State;
>
> the power of a Judge or Trial Chamber of the International Criminal Tribunal for the former Yugoslavia to make a request or issue a subpoena duces tecum to a high government official of a State;
>
> the appropriate remedies to be taken if there is non-compliance of a subpoena duces tecum or request issued by a Judge or a Trial Chamber of the International Criminal Tribunal for the former Yugoslavia;
>
> any other issue concerning this matter.

See also *Scheduling Order* issued by the same Chamber on 27 May 1997, and the *Order to Give Evidence* issued by the Chamber on 29 May 1997.

Subpoenas to States

8.4.12 The *Decision on the Objection of the Republic of Croatia to the Issuance of subpoenae duces tecum* was rendered on 18 July 1997 by a Trial Chamber comprised of Judges McDonald, Odio-Benito and Jan. The Trial Chamber held, in a lengthy decision, that (1) the Tribunal has inherent and express powers to issue a *subpoena duces tecum*; (2) States and their officials are under an obligation to comply with such subpoenae; (3) the subpoena must be relevant and specific; and (4) national security is a valid challenge to a subpoena, but the validity of such a challenge is for the Trial Chamber to settle.

8.4.13 The Republic of Croatia appealed this decision on 25 July 1997. The Appeals Chamber rendered its *Blaškić Subpoenae Appeals Judgement* on 29 October 1997. The Chamber quashed the subpoena addressed to Croatia and its Defence Minister, Mr. Sušak.

8.4.14 In the *Blaškić Subpoenae Appeals Judgement*, the Appeals Chamber held that:

> (1) a subpoena—in the sense of a compulsory order backed by threat of penalty for non-compliance—may only be issued by the ICTY to individuals acting in

a private capacity, and not to States nor State officials. The penalty for non-compliance with such an order is to be held in contempt of Tribunal;

(2) binding orders or requests—as distinct from subpoenae, i.e. without threat of penalty—may be issued by the ICTY to States. The Appeals Chamber laid down four substantive criteria for binding orders addressed to States for the production of documents (para. 32). They must:

(i) identify specific documents and not broad categories;

(ii) set out succinctly the reasons why such documents are deemed relevant to the trial;

(iii) not be unduly onerous;

(iv) give the requested State sufficient time for compliance.

(3) the remedy for non-compliance with a binding order addressed to a State is a judicial finding by the Tribunal that a State has failed to comply, coupled with the power to report this finding to the Security Council, the Tribunal's parent body;

(4) binding orders cannot be issued by the Tribunal to specifically named State officials (para. 43), but only to the State in question;

(5) States may not withhold documents because of national security concerns. However, *in camera, ex parte* proceedings might be held before a Chamber or, (Judge Karibi-Whyte dissenting), a single Judge, to scrutinise the validity of such concerns (para. 67).

Developments on Subpoenae/Binding Orders to States

8.4.15 Following the *Blaškić Subpoenae Appeals Judgement* (see previous para.), the Trial Chambers have issued *binding orders* to States, as opposed to subpoenae; and have continued to issue subpoenae to private individuals.

8.4.16 In accordance with the Appeals Chamber decision, binding orders to States must (i) identify specific documents and not broad categories; (ii) set out succinctly the reasons why such documents are deemed relevant to the trial; (iii) not be unduly onerous; and (iv) give the requested State sufficient time for compliance.

8.4.17 It is not necessary, however, for the State in question to be notified and heard prior to the issuance of a Binding Order. Nor does a State does have standing to challenge the relevance of documents, this being a matter for the Trial Chamber to determine in its discretion. (App. Ch., *Decision on the Request of the Republic of Croatia for Review of a Binding Order, Kordić and Čerkez*, 9 September 1999).

8.4.18 Binding orders have also on occasion been challenged by the States under Rule 108 *bis* ("State Request for Review"). See the following decisions in the *Blaškić* case:

- *Decision on the Prosecutor's Request for the Issuance of a Binding Order to Bosnia and Herzegovina for the Production of Documents*, Trial Chamber, 17 December 1997, issued at the request of the Prosecutor and ordering Bosnia and Herzegovina to produce certain documents.
- *Confidential and* ex parte *Order*, Trial Chamber, 30 January 1998, issued at the request of the Prosecutor and ordering the Republic of Croatia to produce certain documents.

- *Judgement* delivered by the Appeals Chamber on 26 February 1998, at the request of the Republic of Croatia by virtue of Rule 108 *bis*.
- *Decision on the Prosecutor's Request for the Issuance of a Binding, Order to Bosnia and Herzegovina for the Production of Documents*, Trial Chamber, 27 February 1998.
- *Order for a Hearing following the Appeals Chamber Judgement concerning the Chamber's Order of 30 January 1998 to the Republic of Croatia*, Trial Chamber, 6 April 1998.
- *Order to Bosnia and Herzegovina for the production of documents* Trial Chamber, 29 April 1998.
- *Order to the Republic of Croatia for the production of documents,* Trial Chamber, 21 July 1998.

8.4.19 In the *Separate Opinion of Judge Mohamed Shahabuddeen*, attached to an *Order* rendered in *Blaškić* on 21 July 1998, Judge Shahabuddeen held that: (1) for a *subpoena duces tecum, specific* documents must be requested, but this can include *categories* of documents. The test is whether the order is sufficiently specific that the witness can conveniently find it and bring it to court; (2) that the notion of "broad," in the sense that requests for "broad categories" of documents was proscribed by the Appeals Chamber in its Decision of 29 October 1997, was a relative concept, and did not mechanically exclude a demand for "hundreds of documents"; (3) that "oppressiveness" is the test, rather than broadness of the demand; (4) that the Chamber can order the production of documents even if it does not know whether or not they exist; and (5) that the Chamber can order a State to cooperate and if it does not do so, report the State in question to the Security Council (see page 10 of the Separate Opinion).

8.4.20 Judge Shahabuddeen concluded:

> In the result, I hold that, provided that a category is defined with sufficient clarity to permit of ready identification of its members and that it is not so broad as to be oppressive, a State may be ordered to say whether it has any documents within the category even if particulars of each document are not given, and, if it has, to produce them either to a party or the Chamber, barring valid considerations of State security.

Subpoenas and Protection of National Security

8.4.21 It is natural that States may often not wish to comply with *subpoena* due to national security concerns. If this situation arises, the State must communicate these concerns, rather than refusing to comply with the *subpoena* outright and without explanation (see the *Blaškić Subpoenae Appeals Judgement,* para. 68).

8.4.22 In exceptional cases of national security concerns, the State concerned my submit to the Trial Judges a signed affidavit by the responsible minister:

(1) stating that he has personally examined the document in question;
(2) summarily describing the document's contents;
(3) setting out precisely the grounds on which the State considers that the document is not of great relevance to the trial proceedings; and
(4) concisely indicating the principal reasons for the desire of the State to withhold those documents.

8.4.23 It will then be for the Judge to appraise the grounds offered. He may request a more detailed affidavit or *ex parte, in camera* proceedings. If the Judge is ultimately not satisfied that the reasons adduced are valid or persuasive, the Trial Chamber may make a finding of non-compliance by the State with its obligations under Article 29 of the ICTY Statute and ask the President to transmit such finding to the Security Council (para. 68, *ibid.*).

8.4.24 The potential for lack of judicial scrutiny in this process, certainly if it occurred in domestic proceedings, would be likely to fall foul of the right to a fair trial, enshrined in ICCPR Article 14 and ECHR Article 6.

8.4.25 An important decision on this matter is the *Decision of Trial Chamber I on Protective Measures for General Philippe Morillon, witness of the Trial Chamber*, rendered in *Blaškić* on 12 May 1999. Morillon, when subpoenaed by the Trial Chamber to testify, raised the following objections based on the French law of "national defence secrecy" and the duty of "discretion of public servants":

> his testimony might endanger not only his own safety but also that of the French civilian and military personnel assigned to the territory of the Former Yugoslavia,
>
> ... that if no protective measures were to be granted, his testimony might disclose information whose disclosure would run contrary to the essential security interests of France ...

8.4.26 Morillon's immunity as a former UNPROFOR officer had, however, already been lifted by the Secretary-General of the United Nations and the Chamber considered that, subject to the conditions mentioned below, he could therefore safely testify without transgressing the necessary bounds of confidentiality:

> ORDERS that the scope of the questions asked by the Prosecutor and the Defence be limited to the scope of the Witness' initial statement with the Trial Chamber reserving for itself the right to settle any dispute in that respect;
>
> AUTHORISES the Witness to state to the Judges that the requested information is, wholly or in part, confidential;
>
> AUTHORISES the representatives of the United Nations Secretary-General and the French government to be present in the courtroom while the Witness testifies with a maximum of two persons per delegation and to address the Trial Chamber, if necessary outside the presence of the Witness and/or parties, and to present any reasoned request which they believe necessary for the protection of the higher interests they have been assigned to protect. ...

8.4.27 In other cases on the *subpoena* issue besides *Blaškić*, see:

- *Order to Republika Srpska*, issued by the Appeals Chamber, *Tadić* (IT-94-1-A), 2 February 1998.
- *Decision on Defence Motion to issue Subpoena to United Nations Secretariat*, rendered by the Trial Chamber in *Kovačević* on 1 July 1998 (refusing to issue the *subpoena* on grounds of irrelevance and suggesting that the defence should first "approach the United Nations Secretariat and request the material from it, providing sufficient information to the

- *Order on the Motion of the Defence for Hazim Delić for the issuance of subpoenas, Delalić et al*, 25 June 1998

Cross Reference: See Rule 74 (*Amicus Curiae*) and the *amicus curiae* briefs there referred to for discussions of the subpoena issue (8.5.507 *et seq.*).

Subpoenas to Private Individuals

8.4.28 A *subpoena ad testificandum* is an order to appear to testify, as opposed to a *subpoena duces tecum* which is an order to appear to produce documents. On 15 October 1997, the Trial Chamber, sitting in *Delalić et al.* granted from the bench an application by the Prosecutor for the issuance of *subpoenae ad testificandum* to six witnesses, who were residing on the territory of Bosnia and Herzegovina and/or were employed by the government of Bosnia and Herzegovina. The Chamber affirmed that, "the Trial Chamber can grant the issue of subpoenae against private individuals," as opposed to public officials, against whom a Chamber cannot issue subpoenae, according to the Appeals Chamber decision mentioned above (8.4.14). This was affirmed in a *Request* issued in the same case by the same Chamber on 1 July 1998: "the Trial Chamber may issue subpoenas to individuals acting in their private capacity," and in a subpoena dated 25 July 1998.

8.4.29 It follows from the above that a Chamber must first ascertain whether an individual or organisation is a State organ before ordering it to appear or to produce documents; if it is a State organ, it cannot be *subpoenaed* and any order should only be issued, as a matter of policy, after the cooperation of the State concerned has first been solicited. See *Scheduling Order* rendered in *Delalić et al.* on 26 June 1998, which raised the issue whether Konjić Hospital was an organ of the State of Bosnia and Herzegovina. Once the Trial Chamber was satisfied that Konjić Hospital was *not* a State organ, the Chamber issued a *subpoena* on 6 July 1998.

8.4.30 See also *Subpoena ad testificandum* to a private individual issued in *Delalić et al.* on 25 June 1998.

Subpoenas Cannot Be Issued to International Organisations

8.4.31 *Subpoenae* cannot be issued to international organisations such as the Organisation for Security and Cooperation in Europe ("OSCE"). See the *Decision refusing Defence Motion for Subpoena* issued in *Kovačević* on 23 June 1998:

> NOTING FURTHER THAT information essentially the same as, or similar to, that sought to be obtained by the issue of such subpoena is already in the public domain and has been submitted to the International Tribunal in other matters.
>
> CONSIDERING THAT the International Tribunal has no authority to issue such subpoena to the OSCE, it being an international organisation and not a State. . . .

Subpoena to ICRC

8.4.32 Binding Orders cannot be addressed to the International Committee of the Red Cross (ICRC) or to former ICRC employees. The ICRC enjoys a right to non-disclosure under international customary law and therefore cannot be ordered to disclose such information in its possession (Tr. Ch., *Decision on the Prosecution Motion under Rule 73 for a Ruling Concerning the Testimony of a Witness, Simić et al*, 27 July 1999). In a Separate Opinion, Judge Hunt dissented from this finding, holding that it was not established that an absolute right of non-disclosure on the part of the ICRC existed under international law.

8.4.33 See also *Decision on (1) Application by Stevan Todorović to re-open the Decision of 27 July 1999, (2) Motion by ICRC to re-open Scheduling Order of 18 November 1999, and (3) Conditions for access to material*, Trial Chamber, 28 February 2000.

8.4.34 See also *Decision denying request for assistance in securing documents and witnesses from the International Committee of the Red Cross*, Trial Chamber, *Simić et al.*, 7 June 2000.

Subpoena to Tribunal Officials

8.4.35 In *Delalić et al.*, the defece sought to subpoenae tribunal officials. The Appeals Chamber, in its *Delalić et al. Decision on Motion to Preserve and Provide Evidence* of 22 April 1999, stated:

> The Appellant is seeking to rely on the alleged admissions of the former President and Legal Officer in order to establish that there was no waiver of the right to complain [that the Presiding Judge was asleep during portions of the trial] and to show the need for access to the video recording [of the trial]. They cannot be subpoenaed to testify as witnesses on matters relating to their official duties or functions because their work is integral to the operation of the Tribunal which must be protected by confidentiality.

8.4.36 This immunity from subpoena was not, however, supported by reference to any provision in the Statute, Rules, Headquarters Agreement or other regulations. It would seem, in line with other Tribunal decisions relating to *subpoenae* and confidential information (for example, the *Decision of Trial Chamber I on Protective Measures for General Philippe Morillon, witness of the Trial Chamber*, rendered in *Blaškić* on 12 May 1999) that if appropriate safeguards were put in place to protect the confidential information, for example closed sessions, there is no reason why tribunal officials could not be subpoenaed to testify, particularly where it concerns so important a matter as whether the accused waived his right to complain of a major irregularity in the trial.

8.4.37 See also the *Separate Opinion of Judge David Hunt on Motion by Esad Landžo to preserve and provide evidence* of 22 April 1999 (also discussing the prohibition on a party conducting a "fishing expedition" and on the meaning of this phrase).

8.4.38 The matter came up again, and was again dismissed, by the Appeals Chamber in its *Order on Motion of the Appellant, Esad Landžo, for permission to obtain and adduce further evidence on appeal* of 7 December 1999 (judicial deliberations and observations in relation to matters upon which the Judges are adjudicating may not be the subject of compelled evidence before the tribunal; tribunal officials assisting the Judges may not be compelled to testify in relation to their knowledge of the Judges' performance of their functions).

8.4.39 In the *Delalić et al. Appeals Judgement*, the Chamber, while disagreeing with the defence contention that the evidence established that the Presiding Judge "was asleep during substantial portions of the trial," nonetheless did find that it established "a recurring pattern of behaviour where Judge Karibi-Whyte appears not to have been fully conscious of the proceedings for short periods at a time" (para. 628). The Chamber rebuked Judge Karibi-Whyte for such behaviour, but did not find that any prejudice had been caused to the appellants thereby (paras 630–639).

Subpoena to Journalists: War Correspondents

8.4.40 In *Brdjanin and Talić, Decision on Motion to Set Aside Confidential Subpoena to Give Evidence*, 7 June 2002, the Trial Chamber considered an application by a journalist, Jonathan Randal, to set aside a subpoena compelling him to give evidence. Randal sought a qualified privilege that would exempt journalists from giving testimony unless the evidence sought is crucial to the case of either the prosecution or defence. The basis for this argument was essentially that journalists in conflict zones perform a vital public watchdog role in bringing to the international community's attention the horrors of the conflict. It is this media coverage that in part led to the establishment of the ICTY. If journalists are routinely compellable by International Tribunals there is a serious risk that they will lose their independence and impartiality and moreover be in a position of added danger in present and future conflicts. As the former ICTY Chief Prosecutor, Richard Goldstone, has stated:

> Not infrequently, journalists come across evidence of war crimes—as eye witnesses, in discovering a mass grave, or through being privy to statements made by commanders in the heat of the actions. Like aid workers and Red Cross or red Crescent delegates, if reporters become identified as would-be witnesses, their safety and future ability to be present at a field of battle will be compromised. In my opinion the law takes too little account of that reality.
>
> I would therefore support a rule of law to protect journalists from becoming unwilling witnesses in situations that would place them or their colleagues in future jeopardy. . . . They should not be compelled to testify lest they give up their ability to work in the field, but they may, of course, testify voluntarily.

[From Foreword to Roy Gutman's *The Crimes of War.*]

8.4.41 The Trial Chamber seemed to accept and follow the European Court of Human Rights decision of *Goodwin v UK* (1996) 22 EHRR 123, in that, where a journalist's confidential sources are at risk, a journalist should be granted a qualified privilege (see Trial Chamber Decision para. 31). However, the Trial Chamber held that as no question of confidential sources arose in Randal's case, the subpoena would not be set aside. On 3 October 2002, the Appeals Chamber heard oral argument on behalf of Randal and *amici curiae* on behalf of at least 30 international media organisations. The Appeals

Chamber delivered its decision on 11 December 2002. It stressed that its Decision was of application only to war zone correspondents, not all journalists. The Chamber held that a subpoena should not be issued against a war zone correspondent unless a two-part test had been satisfied:

> *First*, the petitioning party must demonstrate that the evidence sought is of direct and important value in determining a core issue in the case. *Second*, it must demonstrate that the evidence cannot reasonably be obtained elsewhere (para. 50).

8.4.42 The Appeals Chamber recognized the "particularly clear and weighty" public interest in protecting the free flow of information to war correspondents.

> Wars necessarily involve death, destruction and suffering on a large scale, and, too frequently, atrocities of many kinds, as the conflict in the former Yugoslavia illustrates. In war zones, accurate information is often difficult to obtain and may be difficult to distribute or disseminate as well. The transmission of information is essential to keeping the international public informed about matters of life and death. It may also be vital to assisting those who would prevent or punish the crimes under international humanitarian law that fall within the jurisdiction of this Tribunal. In this ground, it may be recalled that the images of the terrible suffering of the detainees at the Omarska Camp that played such an important role in awakening the international community to the seriousness of the human rights situation during the conflict in Bosnia-Herzegovina were broadcast by war correspondents (para. 36).

8.4.43 The Appeals Chamber held that compelling war correspondents to testify on a routine basis "may have a significant impact upon their ability to obtain information and thus their ability to inform the public on issues of greatest concern." The Appeals Chamber stated:

> If war correspondents were to be perceived as potential witnesses for the prosecution, two consequences may follow: First, they may have difficulties in gathering significant information because the interviewed persons, particularly those committing human right violations, may talk less freely with them and may deny access to conflict zones. Second, war correspondents may shift from being observers of those committing human rights violations to being their targets, thereby putting their own lives at risk (para. 43).

8.4.44 The problem with this reasoning is that it applies even if war correspondents are competent, but not compellable, to testify. In other words, if war correspondents may still testify voluntarily—albeit they may not be forced to testify—then they remain "potential witnesses for the prosecution," and thus potential targets for perpetrators of atrocities who wish to ensure that there are no witnesses to their deeds.

Subpoena or Order Not Issued in Vain

8.4.45 In a *Decision* rendered in *Delalić et al* on 22 June 1998, the Trial Chamber, refusing an application to subpoena witnesses, stated, "the Trial Chamber does not, and should not, do anything in vain. . . . This application is made too late to be meaningful." It also refused to issue an Order to Bosnia and Herzegovina when the latter was known to cooperate with the Tribunal:

> 52. The Government of Bosnia and Herzegovina has officially indicated its willingness and readiness to co-operate with the International Tribunal in the service of process and has in some cases practically demonstrated its willingness to do so. The Motion has not shown any previous efforts made by Counsel to seek assistance from the Government of Bosnia and Herzegovina that has been refused, or that there has been inordinate delay in answering a request already made. The Trial Chamber does not consider it ripe in this circumstance to issue an order to a sovereign Government which is known to be willing to co-operate without such an order.

Vacating a Subpoena

8.4.46 See the *Order on the Prosecution's Oral Request for the Release from the Subpoena ad testificandum issued by the Trial Chamber*, Trial Chamber, *Delalić et al.* 23 October 1997.

Safe Conducts

8.4.47 Orders for safe conduct protect a person from prosecution and restriction of liberty in the requesting country in relation to acts which preceded his departure from the requested country for purposes of appearing and testifying in response to a request (*Tadić*, Tr. Ch., *Decision on the Defence Motion to Summon and Protect Defence Witnesses, and on the Giving of Evidence by Video-Link*, 25 June 1996, para. 9). In this *Decision*, the Chamber observed that, while safe conducts are not specifically provided for in the Statute or the Rules, "an order in terms can . . . be made under the general power of Rule 54" (para. 8, *ibid.*).

8.4.48 In the same *Decision*, the Chamber set out guidelines for the procedure to be followed when witnesses appear before the Tribunal pursuant to a Safe Conduct:

> 13. . . . First, the summons served on the witnesses should contain the clause that safe conduct does not bar prosecution for offences which the witness might commit after his departure from his home country. . . .

> 14. Additionally, the safe conduct must be limited in time. The safe conduct will commence a reasonable time before the witness is to appear before the International Tribunal. . . .

8.4.49 Accordingly, the Chamber made the following order:

> 15. . . . that, while in the Netherlands for the purpose of appearing before the International Tribunal to testify, [the witnesses in question] . . . shall not be prosecuted, detained or subjected to any other restriction of their personal liberty in respect of acts or convictions prior to their departure from their home country. The immunity provided for shall cease when the witness, having had for a period of fifteen (15) consecutive days from the date when his presence is no longer required by the International Tribunal an opportunity of leaving, has nevertheless remained in the Netherlands, or having left it, has returned. . . .

8.4.50 Subsequently, safe conducts have been issued in similar terms. In that case, the Chamber declined to make an order requested by the Defence for "protection in the countries through which the witnesses travel to reach the International Tribunal," without explanation beyond stating that it "declines the request of the Defence to issue such a general order for immunity of persons in transit for the purpose of appearing before the International Tribunal."

8.4.51 A safe conduct was also granted in *Dokmanović* by the Trial Chamber in a Decision of 27 August 1997. See also *Order on Defence Motion for Safe Conduct* issued in *Dokmanović* on 12 June 1998, limiting the scope of the safe conduct, however, to immunity from prosecution, detention, etc. "by or on behalf of the Prosecution, in respect of acts committed within the jurisdiction of the International Tribunal . . . ," so that the witness could, for example, be arrested by the Dutch or other national authorities, for "ordinary crimes" or for serious violations of international humanitarian law, committed before or after the witness's departure from his or her home country, so long as the arrest was not carried out "by or on behalf of the Prosecution."

Safe Conducts May only Be Granted by a Judge or Chamber

8.4.52 See also the application of the above criteria to assurances allegedly made to the accused that he would not be arrested in the *Decision on the Motion for Release by the Accused Slavko Dokmanović*, 22 October 1997, paras. 79–85. The alleged assurances did not meet the above criteria, in that Dokmanović was not sought as a witness, the alleged assurances were not limited in time and place and they did not specify the purpose for which they were allegedly issued. More importantly, they were not issued by a Judge or Chamber. The Trial Chamber affirmed that:

> 84. . . . Only a Judge or Trial Chamber has the authority to provide a guarantee of safe conduct—this cannot be issued by the OTP or UNTAES.

8.4.53 On the issue of the legality of Dokmanović's arrest, see 8.4.96 *et seq*.

Safe Conducts: Other Decisions

8.4.54 *Decision on Defence Motions for Safe Conduct* rendered in *Dokmanović* on 22 April 1998; *Order granting Safe Conduct to Defence Witnesses* issued in *Delalić et al.* on 25 June 1998.

ICTR Subpoena

8.4.55 See the *Decision on the Motion to Subpoena a Witness* in *Akayesu* rendered by the Trial Chamber on 19 November 1997. This followed a defence motion of 11 November 1997, which was not opposed by the Prosecutor, in which the defence requested the Tribunal to issue a summons to Major-General Romeo Dallaire, a Canadian national and former Force Commander of the United Nations Assistance Mission in Rwanda (UNAMIR) peacekeeping force, for the purpose of securing his testimony.

8.4.56 In the *Decision on the Motion to Subpoena a Witness*, rendered after a hearing held on 19 November 1997, the Trial Chamber considered, *inter alia*, the explanation of the Defence in its motion that the United Nations peacekeeping troops were in Rwanda when the massacres began following the attack that cost the lives of President Juvénal Habyarimana and his Burundian counterpart, Cyprien Ntaryamira; and that hearing General Dallaire would throw light on events. Accordingly, it declared the motion by the Defence to be admissible and well-founded, summoned Major-General Romeo Dallaire to appear as a witness for the defence in the ongoing legal proceedings against Jean-Paul Akayesu, and requested the Secretary-General of the United Nations, consequently, to waive the immunity he enjoyed by virtue of his position as former Force Commander of UNAMIR.

8.4.57 In a letter of 13 January 1998 from Mr. Hans Corell, Under-Secretary-General for Legal Affairs and the Legal Counsel of the United Nations, addressed to the President of the Tribunal, Judge Kama, Mr. Corell stated that the Secretary-General's agreement to waive General Dallaire's immunity "is limited to General Dallaire's appearance as a witness before the Tribunal [in the *Akayesu* case] and to matters of direct relevance to the charges made against the accused. This waiver does not relate to the release of confidential documents of the United Nations which is subject to the authorization of the Secretary-General."

Cross Reference: Rule 74 ("Amicus curiae"). A representative of the UN Secretary-General appeared at the *Akayesu* hearings in which Dallaire testified as *amicus curiae*.

Arrest Warrants

8.4.58 On 24 December 1995, Judge Jorda issued an order pursuant to Rule 54 requiring that copies of all indictments and arrest warrants issued by the Tribunal up to that date be transmitted to IFOR.

Cross References: See Rule 61(D) with respect to international arrest warrants, which have also been transmitted to IFOR. See also Rules 55 and 59 *bis*.

Orders

8.4.59 See, for example, *Order Pursuant to Rule 54*, dated 13 May 1997, issued by Judge Vohrah in *Gagović et al*, which ordered the Prosecutor to report on the status of negotiations to obtain custody of one of the accused in the indictment.

Orders for Detention of Suspects

8.4.60 In *Đukić and Krsmanović* (IT-96-19-Misc.1), Judge Stephen was asked to make an order under Rule 54 for the detention of two suspects who had not been indicted by the Tribunal. Judge Stephen issued an order for their detention, but under Rule 90 *bis* in addition to Rule 54, thus treating them as witnesses. See *Transfer Order for General Đorđe Đukić and Colonel Aleksa Krsmanović* and *Order for Detention of General - Đorđe Đukić and Colonel Aleksa Krsmanović*, both dated 12 February 1996, and the *Amended Orders for Transfer and Detention of General Đorđe Đukić and Colonel Aleksa Krsmanović*, dated 24 February 1996, all signed by Judge Stephen. In the first of these Orders, Judge Stephen noted the request of the Prosecutor, in accordance with Rule 54, for the appearance of Đorđe Đukić and Aleksa Krsmanović, and ordered their transfer pursuant to Article 29 of the Statute and Rules 54, 56 and 90 *bis*, considering that the conditions of Rule 90 *bis* (B)(i) and (ii) were satisfied. In the second, Judge Stephen ordered the detention of Đukić and Krsmanović pursuant to Rules 54 and 90 *bis* of the Rules. In the third order, an amendment was made to the expiry date of the prior two orders.

Order to Remedy an Error *in Personam*

8.4.61 Rule 54 was applied in *Keraterm Camp* (IT-95-8-T), where a person named Goran Lajić, who bore the same name as one of the accused in the indictment, had been arrested and detained at the United Nations Detention Unit. In that case, on 17 June 1996, Trial Chamber issued an *Order for the Withdrawal of the Charges Against the Person Named Goran Lajić and for His Release*, under Rules 54 and 72.

8.4.62 See also *Scheduling Order* of 18 June 1999, again in *Keraterm Camp* (scheduling an evidentiary hearing to resolve the identity of the accused) and *Scheduling Order* of 25 June 1999 in the same case, noting that it was determined at the evidentiary hearing "that the accused is the person identified in the indictment."

Order to Confirm that Status of an Indictment Remains Unchanged

8.4.63 On 22 November 1996, at the request of the Prosecutor, Judge McDonald issued an *Order on Status of Indictment*, pursuant to Rule 54, in light of the amendments to the indictment against the accused Tihomir Blaškić, which confirmed that the status of the original indictment, *Kordić and Others*, remained "unchanged and valid" (p. 2).

Order for Return of Materials

8.4.64 See *Order for Return of Video-Tapes* of 9 April 1999 in *Kovačević*.

Order Regarding Fitness to Stand Trial

8.4.65 See *Order on the Prosecution's Request for a Formal Finding of the Trial Chamber that the Accused Landžo is fit to stand trial*, issued on 23 June 1997 by the Trial Chamber in which, in response to a Motion by the Prosecutor, the Chamber found, on the basis of reports of mental health experts, the submissions of defence counsel and the behaviour of the accused—who had filed notice of his intent to offer the defence of diminished responsibility at trial—that the accused was fit to stand trial.

Cross Reference: Rule 67(A)(ii)(b) on the defence of diminished responsibility.

Other Examples of Orders

8.4.66 To dismiss counts of an indictment (see Tr. Ch., *Order, Delalić et al.*, 16 January 1998); to order the publication of a newspaper advertisement (Tr. Ch., *Decision on*

Prosecution Motion for an Order for Publication of Newspaper Advertisement and an Order for Service of Documents, Mrkšić et al., 19 December 1997); to order a State to serve documents on accused persons on their territory (Tr. Ch., *Order to the Federal Republic of Yugoslavia for Service of Documents, Mrkšić et al.*, 19 December 1997); to order the Defence to disclose its witness list (Tr. Ch., *Decision on the Prosecutor's Motion for an Order requiring Advance Disclosure of Witnesses by the Defence, Delalić et al.*, 4 February 1998); to order a State to allow an individual access to that State's territory (Tr. Ch., *Urgent Request for Assistance to the Republic of Croatia, Dokmanović*, 15 June 1998); to terminate proceedings when an accused has died (Tr. Ch., *Order terminating the proceedings against Milan Kovačević*, 24 August 1998. See also *Order denying request for return of materials* issued the same day. See also *Order terminating proceedings against Slavko Dokmanović* issued on 15 July 1998 by Trial Chamber II.)

Stipulations/Formal Admissions

8.4.67 In a *Scheduling Order* issued in *Dokmanović* on 20 November 1997, the Trial Chamber contemplated ordering the Defence, pursuant to Rules 54 and 65 *bis* ("Status Conferences"), to make any formal admissions, or stipulations, within a certain time-limit, for the purposes of expediting the trial and defining the issues therein:

> HEREBY ORDERS that a status conference shall be held . . . for the following purposes:
>
> . . .
>
> (4) to consider ordering that the Defence, within a time limit to be set by the Trial Chamber, set out in writing:
>
>   (a) those points (if any) in the Indictment which are admitted;
>
>   (b) those points in the Indictment which are denied and the grounds for so doing; and
>
>   (c) set out in general terms their defence to the Indictment.

8.4.68 The same device of seeking formal admissions was employed by the Trial Chamber in the *Decision on Pre-Trial Motions* in the same case on 21 January 1998; the *Scheduling Order* issued by the Trial Chamber in *Kovačević* on 5 March 1998; and the *Scheduling Order* issued by the Trial Chamber in *Aleksovski* on 3 December 1997.

8.4.69 This practice of seeking stipulations or admissions to expedite trial proceedings was codified in Rules 73 *bis* and 73 *ter* at the eighteenth plenary session on 9–10 July 1998. See Rule 73 *bis* (B) (i)(ii) and (iii) and (F), and Rule 73 *ter* (B) (i) and (ii).

8.4.70 For an example of stipulations, see the *Stipulations* signed for the Prosecutor and for the defence in *Krstić* on 7 March 2000.

Cross References:

Article 19(2) of the ICTY Statute, Rule 39(iv) and Rule 98 which, *per* Judge McDonald, "supplements" Rule 54 (see p. 15367, IT-94-1-T, Opinion of 27 November 1996 in *Tadić*).

8.4.71

ICTY
Rule 54 *bis*
Orders Directed to States for the Production of Documents

(A) A party requesting an order under Rule 54 that a State produce documents or information shall apply in writing to the relevant Judge or Trial Chamber and shall:
(i) identify as far as possible the documents or information to which the application relates;
(ii) indicate how they are relevant to any matter in issue before the Judge or Trial Chamber and necessary for a fair determination of that matter; and
(iii) explain the steps that have been taken by the applicant to secure the State's assistance.
(B) The Judge or Trial Chamber may reject an application under para. (A) *in limine* if satisfied that:
(i) the documents or information are not relevant to any matter in issue in the proceedings before them or are not necessary for a fair determination of any such matter; or
(ii) no reasonable steps have been taken by the applicant to obtain the documents or information from the State.
(C)
(i) A decision by a Judge or a Trial Chamber under paragraph (B) or (E) shall be subject to:
  (a) review under Rule 108 *bis*; or
  (b) appeal with the leave of a bench of three Judges of the Appeals Chamber which may grant such leave
   (1) if the impugned decision would cause such prejudice to the party seeking leave to appeal as could not be cured by the final disposal of the trial including post-judgement appeal; or
   (2) if the issue in the proposed appeal is of general importance to proceedings before the Tribunal or in international law generally.
(ii) Applications for leave to appeal under paragraph (i) shall be filed within seven days of filing of the impugned decision. Where such decision is rendered orally, this time-limit shall run from the date of the oral decision, unless
  (a) the party challenging the decision was not present or represented when the decision was pronounced, in which case the time-limit shall run from the date on which the challenging party is notified of the oral decision; or
  (b) the Trial Chamber has indicated that a written decision will follow, in which case, the time-limit shall run from filing of the written decision.
(D)
(i) Except in cases where a decision has been taken pursuant to paragraph (B) or paragraph (E), the State concerned shall be given notice of the application, and not less than fifteen days' notice of the hearing of the application, at which the State shall have an opportunity to be heard.
(ii) Except in cases where the Judge or Trial Chamber determines otherwise, only the party making the application and the State concerned shall have the right to be heard.
(E) If, having regard to all circumstances, the Judge or Trial Chamber has good reasons for so doing, the Judge or Trial Chamber may make an order to which this Rule applies without giving the State concerned notice or the opportunity to be heard under para. (D), and the following provisions shall apply to such an order:
(i) the order shall be served on the State concerned;
(ii) subject to para. (iv), the order shall not have effect until fifteen days after such service;

(iii) a State may, within fifteen days of service of the order, apply by notice to the Judge or Trial Chamber to have the order set aside, on the grounds that disclosure would prejudice national security interests. Para. (F) shall apply to such a notice as it does to a notice of objection;

(iv) where notice is given under para. (iii), the order shall thereupon be stayed until the decision on the application;

(v) paras. (F) and (G) shall apply to the determination of an application made pursuant to para. (iii) as they do to the determination of an application of which notice is given pursuant to para. (D);

(vi) the State and the party who applied for the order shall, subject to any special measures made pursuant to a request under paras. (F) or (G), have an opportunity to be heard at the hearing of an application made pursuant to paragraph (E)(iii) of this Rule.

(F) The State, if it raises an objection pursuant to para. (D), on the grounds that disclosure would prejudice its national security interests, shall file a notice of objection not less than five days before the date fixed for the hearing, specifying the grounds of objection. In its notice of objection the State:

(i) shall identify, as far as possible, the basis upon which it claims that its national security interests will be prejudiced; and

(ii) may request the Judge or Trial Chamber to direct that appropriate protective measures be made for the hearing of the objection, including in particular:

(a) hearing the objection in camera and *ex parte*;

(b) allowing documents to be submitted in redacted form, accompanied by an affidavit signed by a senior State official explaining the reasons for the redaction;

(c) ordering that no transcripts be made of the hearing and that documents not further required by the Tribunal be returned directly to the State without being filed with the Registry or otherwise retained.

(G) With regard to the procedure under para. (F) above, the Judge or Trial Chamber may order the following protective measures for the hearing of the objection:

(i) the designation of a single Judge from a Chamber to examine the documents or hear submissions; and/or

(ii) that the State be allowed to provide its own interpreters for the hearing and its own translations of sensitive documents.

(H) Rejection of an application made under this Rule shall not preclude a subsequent application by the requesting party in respect of the same documents or information if new circumstances arise.

(I) An order under this Rule may provide for the documents or information in question to be produced by the State under appropriate arrangements to protect its interests, which may include those arrangements specified in paras. (F)(ii) or (G).

History of ICTY Rule 54 *bis*

8.4.72 This rule was introduced at the ICTY twenty-first plenary session on 30 November 1999. The rule sets out the procedure for requesting documents from States which had hitherto been dealt with by reference to the *Blaškić subpoenae* jurisprudence (see Rule 54, "subpoenae," above).

8.4.73 The rule was amended at the twenty-fifth plenary session held on 12–13 December, 2001. The appeals procedure set out in para. (C) was modified and a new para. (D)(ii) was added. Para. (C) was again extensively amended on 12 December 2002.

Rule 54 *bis* Also Applies to Orders to International Organisations

8.4.74 Applying this rule to international organizations affords them the right to be heard. See *Scheduling Order for Hearing on Defence Motion for Judicial Assistance* rendered by a Trial Chamber in *Simić* on 1 June 2000:

> CONSIDERING that Rule 54 *bis* (D) requires that, where a request for an Order for the production of documents or information by a State is sought, the State concerned shall be given notice of the application and shall have the opportunity to be heard,
>
> . . .
>
> CONSIDERING that the Trial Chamber is of the view that a similar procedure should be applied to requests seeking orders for production of documents and materials from an international organization and that the international organization should be afforded the opportunity to address the Trial Chamber. . . .

8.4.75

ICTY Rule 55 Execution of Arrest Warrants	ICTR Rule 55 Execution of Arrest Warrants
(A) A warrant of arrest shall be signed by a Judge. It shall include an order for the prompt transfer of the accused to the Tribunal upon the arrest of the accused. (B) The original warrant shall be retained by the Registrar, who shall prepare certified copies bearing the seal of the Tribunal. (C) Each certified copy shall be accompanied by a copy of the indictment certified in accordance with Rule 47(G) and a statement of the rights of the accused set forth in Article 21 of the Statute, and in Rules 42 and 43 *mutatis mutandis*. If the accused does not understand either of the official languages of the Tribunal and if the language understood by the accused is known to the Registrar, each certified copy of the warrant of arrest shall also be accompanied by a translation of the statement of the rights of the accused in that language. (D) Subject to any order of a Judge or Chamber, the Registrar may transmit a certified copy of a warrant of arrest to the person or authorities to which it is addressed, including the national authorities of a State in whose territory or under whose jurisdiction the accused resides, or was last known to be, or is believed by the Registrar to be likely to be found.	(A) A warrant of arrest shall be signed by a Judge and shall bear the seal of the Tribunal. It shall be accompanied by a copy of the indictment, and a statement of the rights of the accused. These rights include those set forth in Article 20 of the Statute, and in Rules 42 and 43 *mutatis mutandis*, together with the right of the accused to remain silent, and to be cauioned that any statement he makes shall be recorded and may be used in evidence. (B) The Registrar shall transmit to the national authorities of the State in whose territory or under whose jurisdiction or control the accused resides, or was last known to be, three sets of certified copies of: (i) the warrant for arrest of the accused and an order for his surrender to the Tribunal; (ii) the confirmed indictment; (iii) a statement of the rights of the accused; and ifnecessary a translation thereof in a language understood by the accused. (C) The Registrar shall instruct the said authorities to: (i) cause the arrest of the accused and his transfer to the Tribunal; (ii) serve a set of the aforementioned documents upon the accused;

(E) The Registrar shall instruct the person or authorities to which a warrant is transmitted that at the time of arrest the indictment and the statement of the rights of the accused be read to the accused in a language that he or she understands and that the accused be cautioned in that language that the accused has the right to remain silent, and that any statement he or she makes shall be recorded and may be used in evidence.
(F) Notwithstanding Sub-rule (E), if at the time of arrest the accused is served with, or with a translation of, the indictment and the statement of rights of the accused in a language that the accused understands and is able to read, these need not be read to the accused at the time of arrest.
(G) When an arrest warrant issued by the Tribunal is executed by the authorities of a State, or an appropriate authority or international body, a member of the Office of the Prosecutor may be present as from the time of the arrest.

(iii) cause the documents to be read to the accused in a language understood by him and to caution him as to his rights in that language, and
(iv) return one set of the documents together with proof of service to the Tribunal.
(D) When an arrest warrant issued by the Tribunal is executed, a member of the Prosecutor's Office may be present as from the time of arrest.

History of ICTY Rule 55

8.4.76 The old para. (B) was amended at the fifth plenary session in January 1995 for the purpose of "clarifying the rules" (second Annual Report, para. 21), by adding the words "an order for," since, strictly speaking, a warrant for arrest is not the same as an order for surrender, although they are commonly contained in one document. Para. (A), following its amendment at the fourteenth plenary session, now clarifies this further by stipulating that a warrant of arrest "shall *include* an order for the prompt transfer of the accused . . ." (emphasis added).

8.4.77 The old para. (B)—which is now para. (D)—was again amended, at the ninth plenary session, on 17–18 January 1996 by adding the words, "or is believed by the Registrar to be likely to be found." The same para. was further amended at the thirteenth plenary session on 25 July 1997, adding the words, "subject to any Order of a Judge or Chamber," and, "to the person or authorities to which it is addressed," and adding gender-neutral language.

8.4.78 This Rule was substantially amended at the fourteenth plenary session on 12 November 1997 (see earlier Revisions and ICTR Rule 55 for comparison).

History of ICTR Rule 55

8.4.79 ICTR Rule 55 was substantially amended at the Fifth Plenary Session on 8 June 1998.

General

8.4.80 Arrest warrants have been sent to the authorities in appropriate States with respect to every indictment confirmed by a Judge of the Tribunal. In addition, after the signing of the Dayton Accord, all the arrest warrants previously issued by the Tribunal were transmitted, pursuant to an order by Judge Jorda under Rule 54 on 24 December 1995, to the International Implementation Force ("IFOR") deployed on the territory of Bosnia and Herzegovina pursuant to the Dayton Accord.

8.4.81 On 29 December 1995, the Registrar wrote a letter to the Legal Advisor at Supreme Headquarters of the Allied Powers in Europe, including copies of all prior indictments and warrants of arrest for transmission to IFOR personnel.

Meaning of "Arrest"

8.4.82 "Arrest" has been said to occur when "by physical restraint or conduct, or by words, an individual is made aware that he is not free to leave" (*Decision on the Motion for Release by the Accused Slavko Dokmanović*, 22 October 1997, para. 51). This test is reminiscent of that applied under U.S. Federal Criminal Law to determine whether a person has been "stopped" within the meaning of *Terry v. Ohio, S.Ct, 1968* (see *U.S. v. Mendenhall* (1980); see also Saltzburg and Capra, *American Criminal Procedure* (1996, 5th ed.), pp. 175–176) and it is also the test applied in the context of Article 5 of the European Convention on Human Rights as to whether there has been an arrest or detention (see para. 28 of the above-mentioned *Decision*; see also *Guzzardi v. Italy* (1981) 3 EHRR 333 at para. 92).

Rule 55 Not Exclusive Method of Procuring Arrest

8.4.83 Rule 55 provides the *primary* means of securing the arrest of an indictee, but it is not the *only* means. In particular, Rule 59 *bis* furnishes an alternative means, namely by use of international forces and/or the Prosecutor, rather than arrest *by States*. See *Decision on the Motion for Release by the Accused Slavko Dokmanović*, 22 October 1997, para. 40:

> The Judges . . . adopted Rule 59 *bis* within the parameters of Articles 19 and 20 of the Statute to provide for a mechanism additional to that of Rule 55, which, however, remains the primary method for the arrest and transfer of persons to the Tribunal.

Cross References: See also Rules 54, 59 *bis* and, with respect to international arrest warrants, Rule 61(D).

Registrar Must Serve Documents on National States

8.4.84 Rule 55 requires the Registrar to serve documents on national authorities, but does not require him or her to prove that the national authorities served the documents on the accused. Once the Registrar has transmitted the arrest warrant and order for surrender to the relevant national authorities, with the appropriate instructions, there has been compliance with Rule 55, and this is not vitiated by possible non-compliance with those instructions by the national authorities. It was so held in the *Decision on the Preliminary Motion filed by the Defence based on defects in the form of the indictment* rendered by the Trial Chamber in *Nahimana* on 24 November 1997:

> 12. . . . the Registrar's obligation under Rule 55(B) of the Rules is to transmit the warrant of arrest and order for surrender to the national authorities together with a copy of the indictment and a statement of the rights of the accused, and to instruct the national authorities to read out these documents to the accused upon his arrest in a language he understands. Having done so, which in this case is verified by production in Court of a copy of the Registrar's aforementioned letter to the Cameroonian Minister of Justice, the Registrar had complied fully with the requirements contained in Rule 55. The Chamber is not in possession of any verified information of whether or not the warrant of arrest and the accompanying documents were actually served by the Cameroonian authorities on the accused. Even if this did not take place, however, the Chamber cannot but regret this fact, but failure of the Cameroonian authorities to serve the documents on the accused does not constitute any intentional breach of the Statute or the Rules by the Registrar and thus cannot entail the nullification of the indictment as requested by the Defence.

8.4.85 This para. was cited *verbatim* by the Trial Chamber in *Ntagerura* in a Decision of 28 November 1997 (para. 35).

8.4.86 ICTR Rule 55(C)(iv), which was introduced after this Decision, now provides for the authorities to return proof of service of the documents on the accused.

Cross References: See also Rules 54, 59 *bis* and, with respect to international arrest warrants, Rule 61(D).

8.4.87

ICTR Rule 55 *bis* Warrant of Arrest to All States
(A) Upon the request of the Prosecutor, and if satisfied that to do so would facilitate the arrest of an accused who may move from State to State, or whose whereabouts are unknown, a Judge may without having recourse to the procedures set out in Rule 61, and subject to sub-rule (B), address a warrant of arrest to all States. (B) The Registrar shall transmit such a warrant to the national authorities of such States as may be indicated by the Prosecutor.

History of ICTR Rule 55 *bis*

8.4.88 This rule was added at the tenth plenary session on 30–31 May, 2001.

Relationship to Rule 61

8.4.89 Prior to the introduction of this rule, it was widely believed, at least at the ICTY, that to be permitted to send an arrest warrant to all States—an international arrest warrant—the Tribunal had to hold Rule 61 proceedings. There is no particular rationale for this, however—Rule 54 would in any event permit a Judge or Chamber to address an arrest warrant to all States without holding a Rule 61 hearing. Moreover, the point of an arrest warrant being to secure the detention of the accused, once a Judge is satisfied that there is enough evidence against the accused to justify his arrest in the country where he normally resides, there seems no good reason why additional hurdles should be erected before the accused's arrest may be sought worldwide.

8.4.90

ICTY Rule 57 Procedure after Arrest	ICTR Rule 57 Procedure after Arrest
Upon the arrest of the accused, the State concerned shall detain him, and shall promptly notify the Registrar. The transfer of the accused to the seat of the Tribunal shall be arranged between the State authorities concerned, the authorities of the host country and the Registrar.	Upon the arrest of the accused, the State concerned shall detain him, and shall promptly notify the Registrar. The transfer of the accused to the seat of the Tribunal, or to such other place as the Bureau may decide, after consultation with the Prosecutor and the Registrar, shall be arranged by the State authorities concerned, in liaison with the authorities of the host country and the Registrar.

8.4.91 ICTR Rule 57 differs from ICTY Rule 57 with the addition of the words, "or to such other place as the Bureau may decide, after consultation with the Prosecutor and the Registrar," which do not appear in the latter. . Thus, the ICTR rule contemplates that the accused may be detained somewhere other than at the seat of the Tribunal.

History of ICTY Rule 57

8.4.92 Rule 57 was amended at the ICTY fifth plenary session in January 1995 "to take account of practical problems that have arisen or may arise in the implementation of the Statute or the Rules." See the ICTY second Annual Report, para. 22, fn. 7: "Rule 57 deals with the transfer of the accused to the seat of the Tribunal. The Rule had formerly contemplated only that "the State authorities concerned" and the Registrar would arrange the transfer; at the request of the Dutch government, however, the Rule was amended to include a reference to the "authorities of the host country" in arranging the transfer."

8.4.93

> **ICTY**
> **Rule 59 *bis***
> **Transmission of Arrest Warrants**
>
> (A) Notwithstanding Rules 55 to 59, on the order of a Judge, the Registrar shall transmit to an appropriate authority or international body or the Prosecutor a copy of a warrant for the arrest of an accused, on such terms as the Judge may determine, together with an order for the prompt transfer of the accused to the Tribunal in the event that the accused be taken into custody by that authority or international body or the Prosecutor.
> (B) At the time of being taken into custody an accused shall be informed immediately, in a language the accused understands, of the charges against him or her and of the fact that he or she is being transferred to the Tribunal. Upon such transfer, the indictment and a statement of the rights of the accused shall be read to the accused and the accused shall be cautioned in such a language.
> (C) Notwithstanding Sub-rule (B), the indictment and statement of rights of the accused need not be read to the accused if the accused is served with these, or with a translation of these, in a language the accused understands and is able to read.

History of ICTY Rule 59 *bis*

8.4.94 Rule 59 *bis* was adopted at the ninth plenary session on 17–18 January 1996 to provide for the transmission of arrest warrants to, *inter alia*, the NATO-led International Implementation Force (IFOR), deployed in Bosnia and Herzegovina under the Dayton Accord.

8.4.95 The Rule was further amended at the fourteenth plenary session on 12 November 1997, adding gender-neutral language and a new para. (C).

Arrest by UNTAES

8.4.96 Rule 59 *bis* was the basis for the Order, issued by Judge Riad, for the arrest by the United Nations Transitional Administration for Eastern Slavonia ("UNTAES") and investigators of the Office of the Prosecutor, of Slavko Dokmanović, which took place on 27 June 1997. The indictment of Dokmanović, who was charged in an amendment to the *Vukovar* indictment (IT-95-13-I), was kept confidential prior to his arrest in order to facilitate apprehension.

8.4.97 In a Preliminary Motion filed on 7 July 1997, the accused argued that his arrest had been illegal (see Rule 73 and Commentary thereto). The Motion was rejected by the Trial Chamber in its *Decision on the Motion for Release by the Accused Slavko Dokmanović*, rendered on 22 October 1997. The Chamber held that the arrest was lawful under Rule 59 *bis* and that UNTAES and OTP investigators had "neither violated principles of international law nor the sovereignty of the Federal Republic of Yugoslavia (Serbia and Montenegro)." The Chamber concluded that "UNTAES, in discharging its obligation to cooperate with the International Tribunal and enforcing its Chapter VII mandate is ensuring the effectiveness of the Tribunal and thus contributing to the maintenance of international peace and security as it is intended to do." Leave to appeal this Decision was refused by a Bench of the Appeals Chamber on 11 November 1997.

Luring of Accused Not Unlawful

8.4.98 Luring the accused into territory, i.e. the territory of another State, for the purposes of arrest is not unlawful. In the *Decision on the Motion for Release by the Accused Slavko Dokmanović*, rendered on 22 October 1997, the Chamber held that "luring" the accused, from the Federal Republic of Yugoslavia (Serbia and Montenegro) into Eastern Slavonia, is "consistent with principles of international law and the sovereignty of the FRY" (para. 57). This use of trickery or ruse did not amount to forcible abduction or kidnapping, which the Tribunal suggested might be illicit. It was important in this regard to note that national case-law either sanctioned "luring" or, where such practice was disapproved of, it was either on the grounds of circumvention of an existing extradition treaty or because of unjustified violence used against the suspect (para. 74). Neither of these elements were present in the case at hand. In particular, since the ICTY was not a party to any extradition treaty (and indeed could not be, as an organ of the United Nations established by the Security Council), "there was no extradition treaty which was circumvented in securing the arrest of the accused" (para. 75).

8.4.99 This holding follows the Kerr-Frisbie doctrine, or *mala captus bene detentus* rule (see below, 8.4.112), upheld in the *Eichmann* case in Israel and in the U.S. Supreme Court Decision in *Alvarez-Machain*. This doctrine or rule is that a Court will not enquire into how an accused came to be brought before it. The Trial Chamber did, however, retrench on this principle to the extent of indicating that it would not sanction kidnapping or abduction, which is how the accused were brought before the courts in the *Eichmann* and *Alvarez-Machain* cases.

8.4.100 See also on this point, in *Todorović*, the Trial Chamber's *Decision* of 25 March 1999 and the Appeals Chamber's *Decision and Scheduling Order* of 18 May 1999. The Trial Chamber rejected the issue for evidentiary deficiency, as the only evidence put forward by the accused was an e-mail posting. This is odd inasmuch as one would expect the accused himself to be able to provide evidence on this matter in the form of an affidavit.

8.4.101 On appeal, the Appeals Chamber held that the *mala captus* issue was not a *jurisdictional* issue that would give rise to an automatic right of interlocutory appeal pursuant to Rule 72(B)(i). Hence, *in casu*, the Appeals Chamber was "not properly seised of the matter," as the accused would have to apply to a bench of the Appeals Chamber for *leave* to appeal under Rule 73(B) (*Decision and Scheduling Order*, 18 May 1999).

8.4.102 The Appeals Chamber's holding indirectly supports the Kerr-Frisbie approach since it says, in effect, that wrongful detention—even if made out on the facts—would not deprive the court of jurisdiction. But in that case, one wonders what effect a wrongful detention would have, and at what stage of the proceedings. If the matter is not one of jurisdiction, it is not really one for trial either. The purpose of the trial is to determine the accused's guilt or innocence, not to enquire into the circumstances of the accused's subsequent arrest. Thus on the Appeals Chamber's approach, the issue of unlawful arrest—even a blatant, egregious case of violent abduction or kidnapping—

could never be raised. This may be the approach that the Chamber desired, but in that case it would have been clearer to state that the Tribunal strictly follows the Kerr-Frisbie doctrine/*mala captus bene detentus* rule and would in no circumstances entertain a motion based on a wrongful arrest. This approach would, however, hardly be consistent with respect for international human rights standards and would also be inconsistent with current trends in this area of the law (e.g., see the English case, *Bennett v. Horseferry Road Magistrates Court* [1993] 3 All ER 138).

8.4.103 It is submitted that the correct approach is to treat an allegation of unlawful arrest as a matter which does affect the Tribunal's jurisdiction. A decision rendered by the Trial Chamber on the matter would then be appealable as of right, as a decision on a motion "challenging jurisdiction" under Rule 72(B)(i). That is not to say that the allegation, if found to be true, would necessarily bar jurisdiction in every case. That would depend on the nature, and severity, of the unlawful arrest. An arrest that was unlawful, albeit in a minor way, might not be sufficient to taint the entire proceedings.

8.4.104 In *Todorović*, the accused did apply for leave to appeal to a Bench of the Appeals Chamber and the Bench granted leave to appeal in its *Decision* of 1 July 1999 on the grounds that ". . . the Trial Chamber's decision not to grant the Defence requests could cause such prejudice to the accused Stevan Todorović as could not be cured by the final disposal of the trial including post-judgement appeal." The matter then went before the full Appeals Chamber. See the Appeals Chamber's *Scheduling Order* of 8 July 1999 in *Todorović*.

8.4.105 On the *mala captus bene detentus* rule, see further below, 8.4.112.

Accused Has Standing to Raise Violation of State Sovereignty

8.4.106 The Trial Chamber held in the *Decision on the Motion for Release by the Accused Slavko Dokmanović* dated 22 October 1997 that the accused *could* raise an alleged violation of State sovereignty as an objection to his arrest, although the objection failed on the merits:

> 76. Finally, the Defence argument that the sovereignty of the FRY was violated by the fraudulent luring of the accused into Croatia is without merit. However, contrary to the Prosecution's assertions, the accused is at liberty to raise this claim.

8.4.107 This is consistent with the holding in the *Tadić Jurisdiction Appeals Decision* that the accused had *locus standi* to raise the issue of "unjustified primacy of the International Tribunal over competent domestic courts," an issue touching on state sovereignty (see para. 55). The Appeals Chamber's holding in *Tadić* had reversed that of the Trial Chamber, which had held that the accused could *not* raise the issue of unjustified primacy and alleged violations of State sovereignty, only States being competent to voice such complaints (*Tadić Jurisdiction Decision*, para. 41).

Authority of UNTAES

8.4.108 The arrest warrant against Dokmanović was executed by UNTAES, which the Trial Chamber found, in the above-mentioned Decision, had "complete executive authority" over Eastern Slavonia (*Decision on the Motion for Release by the Accused Slavko Dokmanović*, 22 October 1997, para. 45) by virtue of its Security Council mandate in Resolution 1037 of 15 January 1996. The Trial Chamber thus held that UNTAES was duly authorised under Rule 59 *bis* to execute the arrest warrant.

Transmission of Arrest Warrants to Prosecutor

8.4.109 See *Order under Rule 59* bis *for transmission of an arrest warrant* issued by Judge Rodrigues in *Zigić* on 15 April 1998, which ordered the transmission of an arrest warrant to the Prosecutor in the light of the following circumstances:

> (1) that the accused is presently in custody on other matters in Banja Luka, Republika Srpska, Bosnia and Herzegovina; (2) that he is willing to surrender himself to the Tribunal for trial; (3) that the authorities of Republika Srpska are prepared to release him from custody for the purposes of allowing him to surrender to members of the Prosecutor's staff; and (4) that members of the Prosecutor's staff stand ready in Banja Luka to take the accused into their custody, having made arrangements to allow the prompt transfer of the accused to the seat of the Tribunal in The Hague.

Dismissal of Indictment as a Result of Illegal Conduct During Course of Arrest

8.4.110 In *Nikolić, Decision on Defence Motion Challenging the Exercise of Jurisdiction by the Tribunal*, 9 October 2002, the Trial Chamber considered the question of whether illegal conduct during the course of arrest should result in the dismissal of the Indictment. It was alleged that Nikolić was kidnapped in Serbia by a number of unknown persons and delivered into the hands of SFOR officers stationed in Bosnia and Herzegovina. On 20 April 2000, he was arrested and detained by SFOR. On 21 April 2000 he was transferred to the Tribunal. Certain individuals were subsequently tried and sentenced in the Federal Republic of Yugoslavia (Serbia and Montenegro) for the acts relating to the apprehension of Nikolić.

8.4.111 The first issue before the Trial Chamber was whether the actions of those who apprehended Nikolić in Serbia could be attributed to SFOR. The Chamber held that there was no evidence that SFOR were in anyway involved in the actual apprehension of the accused in the FRY or in the transfer of the accused into the territory of Bosnia and Herzegovnia. Nor was it accepted that SFOR instructed, directed or controlled the apprehension and transfer. The Chamber held that once presented to them, SFOR acted in accordance with their mandate and pursuant to Article 29 and Rule 59 *bis* in informing the OTP and handing Nikolić over to its representatives. The Chamber held that there was no collusion or official involvement by SFOR in the alleged illegal acts and that SFOR had merely implemented its obligations under the Statute and Rules of the Tribunal. (paras 56–67). In light of their conclusion the Trial Chamber did not find it necessary to consider the relationship between SFOR and the OTP.

Mala Captus—Bene Detentus

8.4.112 The Trial Chamber in *Nikolić, Decision on Defence Motion Challenging the Exercise of Jurisdiction by the Tribunal*, 9 October 2002, conducted an extensive review of domestic and international jurisprudence relating to the principle of *mala capus—bene detentus* (paras 70–93). The Chamber held that, on the facts of the case, no violation of the territory of FRY had occurred by either SFOR or the OTP. It was therefore unnecessary for the Chamber to consider what the remedy should be in cases where sovereignty had been violated in the course of effecting an arrest. However the Chamber did note as *obiter dictum* that if a violation of State sovereignty had taken place, the accused should first have been returned to the FRY, whereupon the FRY would have been immediately under an obligation to return him pursuant to Article 29 of the ICTY Statute.

Remedy for Violation of Human Rights During Arrest

8.4.113 In *Nikolić, Decision on Defence Motion Challenging the Exercise of Jurisdiction by the Tribunal*, 9 October 2002, the defence asserted that the arrest and transfer of Nikolić amounted to a violation of internationally recognised human rights and a violation of the fundamental principle of due process of law. The defence did not assert that Nikolić could not receive a fair trial but instead argued that proceeding with the trial, in light of how he was brought within the jurisdiction of the Tribunal, would undermine the intergrity of the judicial process. The Trial Chamber rejected the motion, holding that:

> 114. . . . in a situation where an accused is very seriously mistreated, maybe even subjected to inhuman, cruel or degrading treatment, or torture, before being handed over to the Tribunal, this may constitute a legal impediment to the exercise of jurisdiction over such an accused. This would certainly be the case where persons acting for SFOR or the Prosecution were involved in such very serious mistreatment. But even without such involvement this Chamber finds it extremely difficult to justify the exercise of jurisdiction over a person if that person was brought into the jurisdiction of the Tribunal after having been seriously mistreated. This, the Chamber observes, is in keeping with the approach of the Appeals Chamber in the *Barayagwiza* case, according to which in cases of egregious violations of the rights of the Accused, it is "irrelevant which entity or entities were responsible for the alleged violations of the Appellant's rights." The Prosecution supports such an approach. Whether such a decision should be taken also depends entirely on the facts of the case and cannot be decided in the abstract. Accordingly, the level of violence used against the Accused must be assessed. Here, the Chamber observes that the assumed facts, although they do raise some concerns, do not at all show that the treatment of the Accused by the unknown individuals, [. . .] was of [such] egregious nature.

Cross References: Rules 54, 55 and 61(D) on the subject of arrest warrants.

Articles:

Figà-Talamanca, Niccoló, "The Role of NATO in the Peace Agreement for Bosnia and Herzegovina," 7 (2) *European Journal of International Law* 164 (1996); Gaeta, Paola, "Is NATO Authorised or Obliged to Arrest Persons Indicted by the International Criminal Tribunal for the Former Yugoslavia?" 9 *European Journal of International Law* 174–181 (1998); Susan Lamb, "The Powers of Arrest of the International Criminal Tribunal for the former Yugoslavia," *British Yearbook of International Law*, 1999.

8.4.114

ICTY Rule 60 Advertisement of Indictment	ICTR Rule 60 Publication of Indictment
At the request of the Prosecutor, a form of advertisement shall be transmitted by the Registrar to the national authorities of any State or States, for publication in newspapers or for broadcast via radio and television, notifying publicly the existence of an indictment and calling upon the accused to surrender to the Tribunal and inviting any person with information as to the whereabouts of the accused to communicate that information to the Tribunal.	At the request of the Prosecutor, a form of advertisement shall be transmitted by the Registrar to the national authorities of any State or States, for publication in newspapers or for broadcast via radio, transmission via internet or television, notifying publicly the existence of an indictment and calling upon the accused to surrender to the Tribunal and inviting any person with information as to the whereabouts of the accused to communicate that information to the Tribunal.

History of ICTY Rule 60

8.4.115 Rule 60 was amended at the thirteenth plenary session on 25 July 1997, adding the words, "and, where requested by the Prosecutor, for broadcast via radio and television." This Rule was further amended at the fourteenth plenary session on 12 November 1997.

History of ICTR Rule 60

8.4.116 ICTR Rule 60 was amended at the Fifth Plenary Session on 8 June 1998.

General

8.4.117 Recourse to Rule 60 is required to set Rule 61 proceedings in motion (see Rule 61(A)(ii)). Consequently, in each of the Rule 61 hearings held to date, the confirming Judge has first confirmed that there has been compliance with Rule 60.

Cross Reference:
ICTY/ICTR Rule 61.

Proof of Publication Not Necessary

8.4.118 The only requirement of Rule 60 is the transmission of the form of the advertisement by the Registrar to the competent authorities and not the need to prove that it was actually published (*Martić Rule 61 Decision*, p. 2).

8.4.119

ICTY Rule 61 Procedure in Case of Failure to Execute a Warrant	ICTR Rule 61 Procedure in Case of Failure to Execute a Warrant
(A) If, within a reasonable time, a warrant of arrest has not been executed, and personal service of the indictment has consequently not been effected, the Judge who confirmed the indictment shall invite the Prosecutor to report on the measures taken. When the Judge is satisfied that: (i) the Registrar and the Prosecutor have taken all reasonable steps to secure the arrest of the accused, including recourse to the appropriate authorities of the State in whose territory or under whose jurisdiction and control the person to be served resides or was last known to them to be; and (ii) if the whereabouts of the accused are unknown, the Prosecutor and the Registrar have taken all reasonable steps to ascertain those whereabouts, including by seeking publication of advertisements pursuant to Rule 60, the Judge shall order that the indictment be submitted by the Prosecutor to his Trial Chamber. (B) Upon obtaining such an order the Prosecutor shall submit the indictment to the Trial Chamber in open court, together with all the evidence that was before the Judge who initially confirmed the indictment. The Prosecutor may also call before the Trial Chamber and examine any witness whose statement has been submitted to the confirming Judge. In addition, the Trial Chamber may request the Prosecutor to call any other witness whose statement has been submitted to the confirming Judge. (C) If the Trial Chamber is satisfied on that evidence, together with such additional evidence as the Prosecutor may tender, that there are reasonable grounds for believing that the accused has committed all or any of the crimes charged in the indictment, it shall so determine. The Trial Chamber shall have the relevant parts of the indictment read out	(A) If, within a reasonable time, a warrant of arrest has not been executed, and personal service of the indictment has consequently not been effected, the Judge who confirmed the indictment shall invite the Prosecutor to report on the measures taken. When the Judge is satisfied that: (i) the Registrar and the Prosecutor have taken all reasonable steps to secure the arrest of the accused, including recourse to the appropriate authorities of the State in whose territory or under whose jurisdiction and control the person to be served resides or was last known to be; and (ii) if the whereabouts of the accused are unknown, the Registrar and the Prosecutor have taken all reasonable steps to ascertain those whereabouts, including by seeking publication of an advertisement pursuant to Rule 60, the Judge shall order that the indictment be submitted by the Prosecutor to his Trial Chamber. (B) Upon obtaining such an order the Prosecutor shall submit the indictment to the Trial Chamber in open court, together with all the evidence that was before the Judge who initially confirmed the indictment and any other evidence submitted to him after confirmation of the indictment. The Prosecutor may also call before the Trial Chamber and examine any witness whose statement has been submitted to the confirming Judge. (C) If the Trial Chamber is satisfied on that evidence, together with such additional evidence as the Prosecutor may tender, that there are reasonable grounds for believing that the accused has committed all or any of the crimes charged in the indictment, it shall so determine. The Trial Chamber shall have the relevant parts of the indictment read out by the Prosecutor together with an account of the efforts to effect service referred to in Sub-rule (A) above.

by the Prosecutor together with an account of the efforts to effect service referred to in Sub-rule (A) above. (D) The Trial Chamber shall also issue an international arrest warrant in respect of the accused which shall be transmitted to all States. Upon request by the Prosecutor or *proprio motu*, after having heard the Prosecutor, the Trial Chamber may order a State or States to adopt provisional measures to freeze the assets of the accused, without prejudice to the rights of third parties. (E) If the Prosecutor satisfies the Trial Chamber that the failure to effect personal service was due in whole or in part to a failure or refusal of a State to cooperate with the Tribunal in accordance with Article 29 of the Statute, the Trial Chamber shall so certify. After consulting the Presiding Judges of the Chambers, the President shall notify the Security Council thereof in such manner as the President thinks fit.	(D) The Trial Chamber shall also issue an international arrest warrant in respect of the accused which shall be transmitted to all States. Upon request by the Prosecutor or *proprio motu*, after having heard the Prosecutor, the Trial Chamber may order a State or States to adopt provisional measures to freeze the assets of the accused, without prejudice to the rights of third parties. (E) If, during the hearing, the Prosecutor satisfies the Trial Chamber that the failure to effect personal service was due in whole or in part to a failure or refusal of a State to co-operate with the Tribunal in accordance with Article 28 of the Statute, the Trial Chamber shall so certify. After consulting the Presiding Judges of the Chambers, the President shall notify the Security Council thereof in such manner as he thinks fit.

History of ICTY Rule 61

8.4.120 Para. (B) was amended at the fifth plenary session in January 1995 "to improve the working of the Tribunal" (second Annual Report, para. 24: "[the amendment] expressly allows the Prosecutor in the course of proceedings under Rule 61 to 'call before the Trial Chamber and examine any witness whose statement has been submitted to the confirming Judge'").

8.4.121 Para. (A) was amended at the sixth plenary session, held from 1–3 May 1995 to clarify how the work of the Tribunal would be divided between the two Trial Chambers. Formerly para. (A) called upon "a Judge of a Trial Chamber" to order that the indictment be submitted "to the Trial Chamber" once he or she was satisfied that certain steps relating to attempts to effect personal service or otherwise inform the accused of the existence of the indictment were taken. Based on the revised wording of para. (A) it is clear that the Judge who confirmed the indictment under Rule 47 must make the para. (A) determination and that it must be his or her Trial Chamber that hears the proceeding under Rule 61.

8.4.122 Para. (A) was again amended at the ninth plenary session in 17–18 January 1996 so as to allow the Judge who confirmed an indictment to invite the Prosecutor to report on the measures taken by him to serve the indictment on the accused. This report may lead to an order by the Judge that the indictment be submitted to the Judge's Trial Chamber for Rule 61 proceedings. Thus, the Rule now provides that it is the Judge, rather than the Prosecutor, who is responsible for initiating the Rule 61 procedure. This amendment was part of the pattern of amendments designed to shift power over the proceedings from the Prosecutor to the Judges, thereby, in theory, making the proceedings "more inquisitorial" or, perhaps, more balanced as between the adversarial and inquisitorial approaches. See 7.41 *et seq.*

8.4.123 At the same plenary, para. (E) was amended to provide that the President would notify the Security Council of a State's non-cooperation with the Tribunal "after consulting the Presiding Judges of the Chambers" and "in such manner as he thinks fit." These two amendments were intended to ensure uniformity of approach and flexibility, respectively, in the manner of notifying the Security Council.

8.4.124 Para. (D) was amended at the tenth plenary session, held on 22–23 April 1996, at the proposal of the Judicial Department of the Registry, to add the second sentence of the sub-Rule. To date, no such order for a State "to adopt provisional measures to freeze the assets of the accused" has been issued.

8.4.125 Para. (B) was amended at the thirteenth plenary session on 25 July 1997, adding the words, "In addition, the Trial Chamber may request the Prosecutor to call any other witness whose statement has been submitted to the confirming Judge." Para.(A) was again amended, in minor ways, at the fourteenth plenary session on 12 November 1997.

History of ICTR Rule 61

8.4.126 This Rule was amended in various ways at the Fifth Plenary Session on 8 June 1998, notably by inserting a reference to "the Registrar" in para. (A)(i) and (ii).

Differences Between ICTY and ICTR on Rule 61 Hearings

8.4.127 Interestingly, while there have been five Rule 61 proceedings at the ICTY, none have been held at the ICTR. This is a reflection of the different circumstances under which the two international tribunals operate. The ICTY experienced a long period after being established in which it had few accused in custody. Rule 61 proceedings were, therefore, important to fulfil its pedagogical role and to highlight the injustice of accused persons remaining at liberty when they had been accused of appalling crimes (see, in particular, the ICTY Rule 61 proceedings against Radovan Karadžić and Ratko Mladić in relation to Srebrenica). At the ICTR, by contrast, it was not long after it became operational that it received a large number of indictees in custody, whom it was a priority to try rather than to conduct Rule 61 proceedings. This, in turn, was a reflection of the fact that the Rwandan genocide ended with a military victory by the Tutsi-led Rwandan Patriotic Front, representing the victims of that genocide. "Ethnic cleansing" and war in Bosnia and Herzegovina, by contrast, were ended not by a military victory by the victims of that conflict but by a political compromise— the Dayton Peace Agreement. This Agreement left indicted persons at large and often, *de facto*, in positions of power (again, see Radovan Karadžić and Ratko Mladić, each twice accused of genocide of Bosniaks and Bosnian Croats, who remain at liberty). Moreover the Dayton Peace Agreement awarded territories captured by "ethnic cleansing" and genocide to the victors. Srebrenica, for example, was apportioned to the Bosnian Serb entity—Republika Srpska—despite the fact that the ICTY considered, in the *Karadžić and Mladić Rule 61 Decision* and in the *Krstić Trial Judgement*, that genocide and crimes against humanity had been committed in taking the town. Hence Rule 61 hearings were initially held at the ICTY, as sort of trials *in absentia*, to redress the imbalance created by so many indictees remaining at large.

Type of Proceedings

8.4.128 It is clear from para. (B) that it is not compulsory for witnesses to be called for a Rule 61 proceeding. Thus there are two main possibilities for Rule 61 proceedings: Rule 61 with live witnesses or Rule 61 on witness statements alone (i.e. "all the evidence that was before the Judge who initially confirmed the indictment," which would consist of witness statements, not live testimony). The five Rule 61 hearings held to date—in *Nikolić, Martić, Vukovar, Rajić,* and *Karadžić and Mladić*—have all been with live witnesses, partly due to the pedagogical role envisaged for these proceedings which is enhanced by having witnesses coming to the Tribunal to testify.

8.4.129 In this respect, Rule 61 proceedings are analogous to committal proceedings in the United Kingdom, which may be either "full," i.e. with witnesses, or "paper." See below, "Rule 61 akin to committal proceedings."

Rule 61 Hearing Not a Trial

8.4.130 A number of decisions of the Tribunal have insisted on the difference in character between Rule 61 proceedings and trial proceedings. See the *Rajić Rule 61 Decision*: "A Rule 61 proceeding is not a trial *in absentia*. There is no finding of guilt in this proceeding." See also the *Nikolić Rule 61 Decision*: "The Rule 61 procedure . . . cannot be considered a trial *in absentia*; it does not culminate in a verdict nor does it deprive the accused of the right to contest in person the charges brought against him before the Tribunal."

8.4.131 In his separate opinion to the *Rajić Rule 61 Decision*, Judge Sidhwa explained:

> Rule 61 is basically an apology for this Tribunal's helplessness in not being able to effectively carry out its duties, because of the attitude of certain States that do not want to arrest or surrender accused persons, or even to recognise or cooperate with the Tribunal. In such circumstances, it is the International Tribunal's painful and regrettable duty to adopt the next effective procedure to inform the world, through open public hearings, of the terrible crimes with which the accused is charged and the evidence against the accused that would support his conviction at trial. (para. 7, separate opinion).

Rule 61 Akin to Committal Proceedings

8.4.132 Judge Sidhwa added that, "the procedure relating to the oral examination of witnesses in Rule 61 proceedings is somewhat akin to that relating to committal proceedings prevailing in certain national jurisdictions" (para. 9, separate opinion). In England and Wales, committal proceedings are those by which a case is transferred to another court for trial, usually from the Magistrates to the Crown Court, but also to a foreign court in the case of extradition proceedings. Depending on the type of case, there may or may not be examination of whether the evidence against the accused establishes a *prima facie* case such that the accused should stand trial or be transferred for trial to a foreign jurisdiction. Judge Sidhwa evidently had in mind "old-style" committal proceedings in which the evidence is tested.

Representation of Accused

8.4.133 The Tribunal has not permitted counsel for the accused to be present during Rule 61 proceedings, although counsel may sit in the public gallery with "observer status." In the *Rajić* Rule 61 proceedings, counsel for the accused was informed in a Notice issued by the Registry that, "Rule 61 proceedings are *ex parte*. You may observe the hearing from the public gallery." In the *Karadžić and Mladić* case (IT-95-5-R61/IT-95-18-R61), upon receiving a request from counsel for Karadžić to be present during the Rule 61 proceedings, the Trial Chamber refused the request on the grounds that ". . . Rule 61 proceedings cannot be considered a trial," but it ordered the indictment to be read in the presence of counsel in open court (*Decision Partially Rejecting the Request Submitted By Mr Igor Pantelić, Counsel for Radovan Karadžić*, 27 June 1996). A similar decision was issued on 5 July 1996 by the same Chamber in the same case, but for different counsel (*Decision Rejecting the Request Submitted By Mr Medvene and Mr Hanley III, Defence Counsels for Radovan Karadžić*).

8.4.124 Counsel for the accused also may not file preliminary motions at the Rule 61 stage. In another Decision rendered in the *Karadžić and Mladić* case (IT-95-5-R61/IT-95-18-R61, *Decision Rejecting the Application presented by Messrs Medvene and Hanley III Seeking Leave to File Briefs Challenging the Fairness of the Statute and the Rules of Procedure and Evidence*, 24 July 1996) the Trial Chamber held that:

> pursuant to Rule 61, the . . . application does not fall within the jurisdiction of the Trial Chamber (and) could be filed by the accused only after his initial appearance before the Trial Chamber entitled to try him.

Amicus Curiae

8.4.135 *Amicus curiae* have been admitted, pursuant to Rule 74, in Rule 61 proceedings, for example in the *Karadžić and Mladić* case (IT-95-5-R61/ IT-95-18-R61), Mrs. Elizabeth Rehn, Special Rapporteur for the United Nations Commission on Human Rights, and Mrs. Christine Cleiren, member of the Commission of Experts established pursuant to Security Council Resolution 780 (1992), were invited to testify during the hearings.

8.4.136 Other applications have, however, been refused. In the same *Karadžić and Mladić* Rule 61 proceedings (IT-95-5-R61/IT-95-18-R61), the Trial Chamber rejected a request by the non-governmental organisation, Human Rights Watch, to submit a brief as *amicus curiae* (*Order on a Request to Submit an Amicus Curiae Brief During the Proceedings Pursuant to Rule 61 of the Rules of Procedure and Evidence*, 21 June 1996) on the grounds that:

it does not appear necessary that a brief presenting the proceedings organised by virtue of this text, whose principles and merits cannot be legally challenged, should be submitted. (1/333).

8.4.137 The Republic of Croatia filed a request on 30 April 1996 to appear as *amicus curiae* in all matters involving its responsibility, rights and legal interests. In particular, Croatia sought leave to be heard as *amicus curiae* in the Rule 61 proceedings against Ivica Rajić with respect to the nature of the conflict in the former Yugoslavia. On 24 May 1996, the Trial Chamber, before which the proceeding was pending, rejected Croatia's request, without prejudice to its ability to renew it at the time of trial (third Annual Report, para. 65).

Cross References:
See Commentary to Rule 10 under the heading, "Amicus Curiae." The use of *amicus curiae* in Rule 10 deferral proceedings may be contrasted with that in Rule 61. In the former, the State which is being requested to defer its proceedings in favour of the Tribunal typically appears as *amicus curiae*, although its status at such hearings is virtually that of a Party. In Rule 61 proceedings, on the other hand, States have been refused leave to appear as *amicus curiae* (see the IT-95-12-R61 proceedings, mentioned above). In such proceedings, those appearing as *amicus curiae* have more the character of being expert witnesses (see, for example, the *Karadžić and Mladić* proceedings, mentioned above). See also Rule 74 (*"Amicus Curiae"*).

Protection of Victims and Witnesses

8.4.138 The Chamber has granted protective measures for a number of victims and witnesses in Rule 61 proceedings. In the *Nikolić* Rule 61 proceedings, held 9–13 October 1995, protective measures were mostly limited to non-disclosure of addresses but one witness was granted confidentiality from the public. In this case, testimony was given in the courtroom but with protective screening shielding the witness from view from the public gallery and with the televised image subject to voice and image distortion.

"Reasonable Time" Dependent on Circumstances

8.4.139 Para. (A) provides that Rule 61 hearings shall take place if execution of the arrest warrants has not taken place "within a reasonable time." What is a "reasonable time" depends on the circumstances of the case. "The concept of reasonable time must be evaluated in respect of the circumstances specific to each case" (*Martić*, Tr. Ch., *Order for Review in Open Court of the Indictment by Trial Chamber I*, 13 February 1996, p. 1). In *Martić*, the Chamber considered that, since the arrest warrants had been issued seven months beforehand, a "reasonable time has long since elapsed" (*ibid.*). That "reasonable time" depends on the circumstances has been reaffirmed in a number of subsequent cases (see e.g. *Order to submit a Report on the Measures taken to effect Personal Service of the Indictment, Karadžić and Mladić*, 13 May 1997).

Additional Evidence Tendered by Prosecutor

8.4.140 "Such additional evidence as the Prosecutor may tender" includes "the testimony of witnesses whose statements were not before the confirming Judge" (*Rajić Rule 61 Decision*, para. 4).

8.4.141 In the *Rajić Rule 61 Decision*, however, the Chamber concurred with Judge Sidhwa, in his Separate Opinion to the Rule 61 Decision, that a person who is "a witness's proxy or substitute or a person who has recorded his statement, is not covered by Rule 61(B)" (para. 19, separate opinion). The Chamber agreed that such a witness's testimony—typically that of an investigator from the Office of the Prosecutor testifying as to the witnesses to whom he spoke and the content of their evidence—"is relevant to the decision of the Trial Chamber only to the extent that it evidences the taking of certain statements" (para. 5). See, on the subject of hearsay, 8.5.642 *et seq.*

Cross Reference:
Rule 89, on the admissibility and exclusionary principles of the Rules of Evidence.

International Arrest Warrants Sent to All States and to IFOR

8.4.142 Under Rule 61(D), international arrest warrants are sent to every Member State of the United Nations and, since the Dayton Agreement, to the International Implementation Force ("IFOR") established under that Agreement. See the *Vukovar Rule 61 Decision* of 3 April 1996, in which the Trial Chamber ordered "that the warrant shall be transmitted to all states and, if necessary, to the Implementation Force (IFOR)." Subsequently, on 18 April 1996, the Registrar transmitted the international arrest warrants to the Legal Advisor at Supreme Headquarters of the Allied Powers in Europe. This practice was followed by the Trial Chambers in the *Karadžić and Mladić, Martić* and *Rajić* Rule 61 proceedings.

8.4.143 The purpose of the international arrest warrant is to make the accused an "international fugitive." See the *Nikolić Rule 61 Decision:*

> In effect, all States in the international community will be bound, if the warrant is issued, to cooperate in searching for and arresting the accused, who would in consequence become an international fugitive. (para. 2)

See ICTR Rule 55 *bis*.

Provisional Measures to Freeze Assets

8.4.144 As noted above, Rule 61(D) has not yet been applied to order a State or States to adopt *provisional* measures to freeze the assets of the accused. See, however, orders made upon the confirmation of an indictment against Slobodan Milošević (4.4.11). Reference should also be made to Rules 98 *ter* (B), 105 (restitution) and 106 (compensation) in respect of *final* orders that the Tribunal has the power to make.

Notification to Security Council

8.4.145 In *Nikolić*, the Trial Chamber certified that the failure to effect service was due wholly to the failure or refusal of the Bosnian Serb administration in Pale to cooperate with the Tribunal and invited the President of the Tribunal to notify the Security Council accordingly. This was done on 30 October 1995 (S/1995/910).

8.4.146 In the *Vukovar* case (IT-95-13-R61), the Trial Chamber held that the failure to execute the warrants of arrest could be ascribed to the refusal of the Federal Republic of Yugoslavia (Serbia and Montenegro) to cooperate with the Tribunal and so certified for the purposes of notifying the Security Council. The President subsequently notified the Security Council on 24 April 1996.

8.4.147 In the *Rajić* case (IT-95-12-R61), the Trial Chamber held that the failure to execute the warrants of arrest could be ascribed to the refusal of the Federation of Bosnia and Herzegovina and the Republic of Croatia to cooperate with the Tribunal and so certified on 13 September 1996 for the purposes of notifying the Security Council. The President notified the Security Council on 16 September 1996 (S/1996/763).

8.4.148 The two indictments against Radovan Karadžić and Ratko Mladić were joined for the purposes of the Rule 61 hearing in the *Karadžić and Mladić* case (IT-95-5-R61/IT-95-18-R61). The indictments were confirmed in a reasoned Decision dated 11 July 1996. International warrants were duly issued for the arrest of Radovan Karadžić and Ratko Mladić. The Trial Chamber certified that the failure to execute the initial arrest warrants was due to the refusal of the Federal Republic of Yugoslavia (Serbia and Montenegro) and Republika Srpska to cooperate with the Tribunal. The President of the Tribunal sent a letter to this effect to the Security Council on 11 July 1996.

Articles:

Maison, Rafaëlle, "La décision de la Chambre de première instance No. 1 du Tribunal pénal international pour l'ex-Yougoslavie dans l'affaire Nikolić," 7 (2) *European Journal of International Law* 284 (1996).

Swaak-Goldman, Olivia, "International Decisions: The Prosecutor v. Rajić," 91 *American Journal of International Law* 523 (1997).

SECTION 5: COMMENCEMENT AND CONDUCT OF TRIAL PROCEEDINGS

8.5.1

ICTY Article 20 Commencement and Conduct of Trial Proceedings	ICTR Article 19 Commencement and Conduct of Trial Proceedings
1. The Trial Chambers shall ensure that a trial is fair and expeditious and that proceedings are conducted in accordance with the rules of procedure and evidence, with full respect for the rights of the accused and due regard for the protection of victims and witnesses. 2. A person against whom an indictment has been confirmed shall, pursuant to an order or an arrest warrant of the International Tribunal, be taken into custody, immediately informed of the charges against him and transferred to the International Tribunal. 3. The Trial Chamber shall read the indictment, satisfy itself that the rights of the accused are respected, confirm that the accused understands the indictment, and instruct the accused to enter a plea. The Trial Chamber shall then set the date for trial. 4. The hearings shall be public unless the Trial Chamber decides to close the proceedings in accordance with its rules of procedure and evidence.	1. The Trial Chambers shall ensure that a trial is fair and expeditious and that proceedings are conducted in accordance with the rules of procedure and evidence, with full respect for the rights of the accused and due regard for the protection of victims and witnesses. 2. A person against whom an indictment has been confirmed shall, pursuant to an order or an arrest warrant of the International Tribunal for Rwanda, be taken into custody, immediately informed of the charges against him and transferred to the International Tribunal for Rwanda. 3. The Trial Chamber shall read the indictment, satisfy itself that the rights of the accused are respected, confirm that the accused understands the indictment, and instruct the accused to enter a plea. The Trial Chamber shall then set the date for trial. 4. The hearings shall be public unless the Trial Chamber decides to close the proceedings in accordance with its rules of procedure and evidence.

General

8.5.2 ICTY Article 20 and ICTR Article 19 first set out the basic requirements on the part of the Trial Chambers to ensure that the trials are fair and conducted in accordance with the law and with respect for the rights of the accused. The Chambers are also mandated to have regard to the necessary protection of victims and witnesses. The articles then lay down the essentials of the pre-trial procedure: the accused being taken into custody, informed of the charges against him, instructed to enter a plea and then (in the event of a not guilty plea—this is spelt out in the rules but not in these articles) proceeding to trial.

Fair Trial, Truth-Finding and Effective Cross-Examination

8.5.3 The requirement of a fair trial implies, among other things, that both Parties must be able to conduct effective cross-examination. See *Decision on the Defence Motion for Protective Measures for Witnesses D/H and D/I* rendered by the Trial Chamber in *Blaškić* on 25 September 1998:

> CONSIDERING that the Trial Chamber must ensure that the trial is fair and expeditious,
>
> CONSIDERING that, in the view of establishing the truth, this principle requires that there be no excessive infringment on [sic] the rights of the Prosecution, *inter alia*, the right to conduct an effective cross-examination of the Defence witnesses. . . .

8.5.4 Of course the same applies, if not with considerably more force, to cross-examination of prosecution witnesses by the defence, both in terms of ensuring a fair trial and in terms of the "truth establishment" function, alluded to above.

8.5.5 See also, in terms of allegations of a violation of the right to a fair trial, the Appeals Chamber's *Decision on Motion to Preserve and Provide Evidence* in *Delalić et al.* of 22 April 1999. The Chamber admitted that the defence allegation that the Presiding Judge at trial had been asleep throughout substantial portions of the trial would, if proved, be a valid ground of appeal on the merits. In the event, the complaint did not succeed on the merits. See also the *Separate Opinion of Judge David Hunt on Motion by Esad Landžo to preserve and provide evidence* of 22 April 1999 in the same case.

Fair Trial and Appointment of *Amicus Curiae*

8.5.6 In *Milošević*, the Trial Chamber noted the requirement of Article 20 that a trial be fair and conducted with full respect for the rights of the accused in deciding to appoint *amicus curiae* where the accused stipulated that he had no intention of engaging a lawyer to represent him. See *Order Inviting Designation of Amicus Curiae*, 23 November 2001.

Custody

8.5.7 The ICTY and ICTR Statutes are silent as to the regime for detaining persons awaiting trial or appeal before the ICTs. However, the following instruments have been adopted by the ICTs, establishing the regime of detention of indictees who have been taken into custody (see the ICTY's *Basic Documents*, pp. 297–418):

- Rules of Detention (IT/38/Rev. 5);
- Regulations for the Establishment of a Complaints Procedure for Detainees (IT/96);
- Regulations for the Establishment of a Disciplinary Procedure for Detainees (IT/97);
- Regulations to Govern the Supervision of Visits to and Communications with Detainees (IT/98);

- House Rules for Detainees (IT/99);
- Letter dated 28 April 1995 appointing the International Committee of the Red Cross as Inspecting Authority for the Detention Unit; and,
- Agreement on Security and Order, signed 14 July 1994, between the Tribunal and the Ministry of Justice of the Kingdom of the Netherlands.

On the issue of release on bail, or provisional release, see Rule 65 ("*Provisional Release*") at 8.5.114 *et seq.*

Death in Custody: Inquest

8.5.8 An inquest will naturally follow any death of a person in the Tribunals' custody. Following the death, in the night of 29 June 1998, of the accused, Slavko Dokmanović, the Registry asked the Dutch authorities to conduct an inquest in accordance with the legal requirements of the Host State, as provided for by Rule 32(B) of the Rules governing the detention of persons awaiting trial or appeal before the Tribunal or otherwise detained on the authority of the Tribunal. Acting under Rule 32(C), the ICTY President, Judge McDonald, ordered an inquiry into the circumstances surrounding the death of the accused (see ICTY Press Release of 29 June 1998, CC/PIU/327-E).

Persons in ICTY Custody

8.5.9 For the latest information as to the persons currently in custody at the ICTY Detention Unit, see the Fact Sheet on ICTY Proceedings. (*http://www.un.org/icty/glance/procfact-e.htm*).

Persons in ICTR Custody

8.5.10 For the latest information as to the persons currently in custody at the ICTR Detention Unit, see See "ICTR Detainees" on the ICTR website (*http://www.ictr.org/*). Interestingly, the ICTR website classifes the detainees into the following categories: Political leaders, Military Leaders, Media Leaders, Administrators and "others" (this latter category including the Director of a Tea Factory, a Militia Leader and a Priest).

The Plea

8.5.11 Reference should be made to the *Erdemović Sentencing Judgement*, in which the Trial Chamber enquired into the validity of the plea to a charge of crimes against humanity. This matter went to the Appeals Chamber (see *Erdemović Appeals Judgement*), which found the plea to have been uninformed. The Appeals Chamber sent the case to a new Trial Chamber to take a new plea (see the *Erdemović Sentencing Judgement II*). See the commentary to Rule 62, 8.5.244.

Public Hearings

8.5.12 The principle before the ICTs is that the hearings are public. In the *Tadić Protective Measures Decision* of 10 August 1995, however, the majority of the Trial Chamber held that the benefits of public hearings were not unqualified, in particular, in relation to the protection of victims and witnesses:

> 32. The benefits of a public hearing are well known. The principal advantage of press and public access is that it helps to ensure that a trial is fair.... In addition, the International Tribunal has an educational function and the publication of its activities helps to achieve this goal. As such, the Judges of this Trial Chamber are, in general, in favour of an open and public trial.
>
> 33. Nevertheless, this preference for public hearings must be balanced with other mandated interests, such as the duty to protect victims and witnesses.... As such, in certain circumstances, the right to a public hearing may be qualified to take into account these other interests.

Cross Reference: See Part Six ("Proceedings before Trial Chambers") of the Rules of Procedure and Evidence.

* * * * *

RIGHTS OF THE ACCUSED

8.5.13

ICTY Article 21 Rights of the Accused	ICTR Article 20 Rights of the Accused
1. All persons shall be equal before the International Tribunal. 2. In the determination of charges against him, the accused shall be entitled to a fair and public hearing, subject to article 22 of the Statute. 3. The accused shall be presumed innocent until proved guilty according to the provisions of the present Statute. 4. In the determination of any charge against the accused pursuant to the present Statute, the accused shall be entitled to the following minimum guarantees, in full equality: (a) to be informed promptly and in detail in a language which he understands of the nature and cause of the charge against him; (b) to have adequate time and facilities for the preparation of his defence and to communicate with counsel of his own choosing;	1. All persons shall be equal before the International Tribunal for Rwanda. 2. In the determination of charges against him or her, the accused shall be entitled to a fair and public hearing, subject to article 21 of the Statute. 3. The accused shall be presumed innocent until proved guilty according to the provisions of the present Statute. 4. In the determination of any charge against the accused pursuant to the present Statute, the accused shall be entitled to the following minimum guarantees, in full equality: (a) to be informed promptly and in detail in a language which he or she understands of the nature and cause of the charge against him or her; (b) to have adequate time and facilities for the preparation of his or her defence and to communicate with counsel of his or her own choosing;

(c) to be tried without undue delay; (d) to be tried in his presence, and to defend himself in person or through legal assistance of his own choosing; to be informed, if he does not have legal assistance, of this right; and to have legal assistance assigned to him, in any case where the interests of justice so require, and without payment by him in any such case if he does not have sufficient means to pay for it; (e) to examine, or have examined, the witnesses against him and to obtain the attendance and examination of witnesses on his behalf under the same conditions as witnesses against him; (f) to have the free assistance of an interpreter if he cannot understand or speak the language used in the International Tribunal; (g) not to be compelled to testify against himself or to confess guilt.	(c) to be tried without undue delay; (d) to be tried in his or her presence, and to defend himself or herself in person or through legal assistance of his or her own choosing; to be informed, if he or she does not have legal assistance, of this right; and to have legal assistance assigned to him or her, in any case where the interests of justice so require, and without payment by him or her in any such case if he or she does not have sufficient means to pay for it; (e) to examine, or have examined, the witnesses against him or her and to obtain the attendance and examination of witnesses on his or her behalf under the same conditions as witnesses against him or her; (f) to have the free assistance of an interpreter if he or she cannot understand or speak the language used in the International Tribunal for Rwanda; (g) not to be compelled to testify against himself or herself or to confess guilt.

8.5.14   ICTR Article 20, but not ICTY Article 21, has been amended to appear in a, slightly cumbersome, gender-neutral manner ("he or she," "his or her," "himself or herself").

ICTY Article 21/ ICTR Article 20 Based on ICCPR Article 14

8.5.15   The fundamental rights of an accused in a criminal trial have attained near-universal status through the adoption of international human rights instruments (ICCPR, ECHR, IACHR, etc.) in the past half century. The "fair trial guarantees in Article 14 of the International Covenant on Civil and Political Rights ("ICCPR") have been adopted almost verbatim in Article 21 of the Statute" (*Tadić Jurisdiction Appeals Decision*, para. 46).

8.5.16   In the *Vujin Appeal Judgement On Allegations of Contempt Against Prior Counsel* of 27 February 2001, the Appeals Chamber relied upon Article 14 of the ICCPR in deciding that a right of appeal exists from a contempt conviction by the Appeals Chamber pursuant to Rule 77, despite the absence of a provision to that effect in Rule 77 itself. The Appeals Chamber stated that the Tribunal's Rules:

> must be interpreted in conformity with the International Tribunal's Statute, which, as the United Nations Secretary-General states in his report of 3 May 1993 (S/25704) must respect the "internationally recognized standards regarding the rights of the accused" including Article 14 of the International Covenant on Civil and Political Rights.

8.5.17 The Appeals Chamber stated that Article 14(5) of the ICCPR guarantees everyone convicted of a crime the right to have his conviction and sentence reviewed by a higher tribunal and that Article 14 of the ICCPR represents an "imperative norm of international law to which the Tribunal must adhere." Despite no provision for an appeal from a conviction by the Appeals Chamber in the Rules, the Appeals Chamber held:

> that it is the duty of the International Tribunal to guarantee and protect the rights of those who appear accused before it.

8.5.18 The Chamber accordingly decided to consider Vujin's complaints. It would appear from this Judgement that in certain circumstances, human rights considerations could override the clear language and meaning of the Tribunal's Rules (note, however, Judge Wald's strong dissent on this point—see commentary to ICTY Rule 77, at 4.2.590 *et seq.*).

8.5.19 The persuasiveness of decisions of the European Court of Human Rights, and the caution with which the Tribunal should consider the European Court's decisions was considered in the *Foča Trial Judgement* (paras. 465–497, discussing the definition of torture).

Equality Before the Tribunals

8.5.20 There has not been a lot of jurisprudence at the ICTs regarding the meaning of accused being "equal before" the tribunals. Conversely, there *has* been much discussion of the principle of "equality of arms" *between the parties* (see below, 8.5.70 and 8.5.73 *et seq.*).

8.5.21 The following *dicta*, however, touch on the issue of equality:

- Time-limits run only from when the party receives a notice in the language which he understands; the right to equal treatment does not, however, entitle both parties to receive something only one of them needs (*Talić*, Judge Hunt, Pre-Trial Judge, *Decision on Motion to Translate Procedural Documents into French*, 16 December 1999).
- In dealing with applications by the prosecution for protective measures for victims and witnesses under Rule 69(A), the rights of the accused come first and those of the victims and witnesses second (*Brdanin and Talić Decision on Motion by Prosecution for Protective Measures*, 3 July 2000, para. 30).

Public Hearing

8.5.22 Para. (2) of ICTY Article 21/ICTR Article 20 guarantees a public hearing, although this is subject to ICTY Article 22/ICTR Article 21, which deal with the protection of victims and witnesses. It is submitted that the correct understanding of this provision is that victims and witnesses may be protected *from publicity*, if need be. It is not the fairness of the proceedings, also referred to in para. (2), that is made subject to the need to protect victims and witnesses.

8.5.23 In the *Tadić Protective Measures Decision* of 10 August 1995, the Trial Chamber majority, held that the Chamber had to interpret the Statute and the Rules within the context of its own unique framework, and noted in that context that:

36. ... [T]he Statute of the International Tribunal, which is the legal framework for the application of the Rules, *does* provide that the protection of victims and witnesses is an acceptable reason to limit the accused's right to a public trial.

8.5.24 Judge Stephen appended a Separate Opinion to the Decision, in which he held that while the protection of victims and witnesses provided justification for limiting the *public* nature of a hearing, it did not justify measures which affected, not its public nature, but its *fairness:*

> That phrase "subject to Article 22" itself repays analysis. What it is in Article 21(2) that is to be subject to Article 22 can scarcely be the combined concept which precedes that phrase, the concept of "a fair and public hearing." It must rather be only one component of that concept, the public quality of the hearing and not its fairness, that is made subject to Article 22, and this for two reasons: first, because, while Article 22 specifically contemplates non-public hearings, it certainly does not contemplate unfair hearings; secondly, because Article 20(1) itself, unqualifiedly and quite separately from Article 21, requires a Trial Chamber to ensure that a trial is "fair." If this understanding of the phrase "subject to Article 22" be correct and it is primarily the public quality, not the fairness, of a hearing that may have to give way to the need to protect victims and witnesses, that in turn suggests that the kind of protection being thought of in Article 22 is essentially those measures that will affect the public nature of the trial, rather than its fairness. (p. 5027)

Presumption of Innocence

8.5.25 The presumption of innocence is enshrined in ICTY Article 21(3) and ICTR Article 20(3). While the presumption of innocence is practically a universal feature of criminal law, the precise meaning and implications of the phrase may vary from system to system. The presumption of innocence usually means, at a minimum, that the burden of proof is on the prosecution; the prosecution brings the case and the onus is, therefore, on the prosecution to prove that the accused is guilty and not on the accused to prove that he is innocent. The presumption of innocence may also carry with it the notion that the prosecution must prove the accused's guilt "beyond a reasonable doubt"; thus the presumption of innocence may relate not only to the burden of proof but also to the standard of proof. Lastly, the presumption of innocence may carry with it certain ancillary rules and presumptions, e.g., a right to bail (provisional release).

8.5.26 The ICTY and ICTR have affirmed the presumption of innocence on numerous occasions (see, e.g., *Delalić et al., Decision on the Prosecution's Alternative Request to Reopen the Prosecution's Case*, 19 August 1998, para. 20; *Ntuyahaga*, 18 March 1999), while ascribing different meanings to the phrase.

Burdens of Proof

8.5.27 The ICTY has accepted that the presumption of innocence entails that the burden of proving the accused's guilt is on the Prosecution (see the discussion in the *Delalić et al. Trial Judgement*, paras. 600–603 as to precisely what this *means*). However if the defence raise a material allegation, it may be for the defence to prove that allegation on a "balance of probabilities":

603. Whereas the Prosecution is bound to prove the allegations against the accused beyond a reasonable doubt, the accused is required to prove any issues which he might raise on the balance of probabilities.

8.5.28 In practice, this would mean that the Defence must show that it is more likely than not that their allegation is true, i.e., that it is 51% likely, to discharge the burden of proof. See the section on "Defences," at 6.3.1 *et seq.*, in particular in relation to the question of burdens of proof.

Independent and Impartial Tribunal

8.5.29 As stated above, ICTY Article 21 and ICTR Article 20 are based directly on Article 14 of the ICCPR and indirectly on Article 6 of the European Convention on Human Rights (ECHR). Yet both those articles refer to "a fair and public hearing *by a competent, independent and impartial tribunal established by law*" (Art. 14(1) ICCPR, emphasis added) and "a fair and public hearing within a reasonable time *by an independent and impartial tribunal established by law*" (Art. 6(1) ECHR).The italicised words do not appear in ICTY Article 21 and ICTR Article 20. The words, "established by law" were no doubt omitted because the UNSC considered that the ICTY and ICTR *were* established by law, or in any event it did not consider it appropriate for the tribunals to hear argument on the matter. The same applies to the requirements that the tribunals be independent and impartial. The requirement that *the Judges* be *impartial* is set out in various places in the ICTY and ICTR Statutes and Rules, in particular in ICTY Article 13 and ICTR Article 12(1). The requirement that the Judges be *independent* is, however, mentioned nowhere in the ICTY and ICTR Statutes, although, interestingly, the requirement that the Prosecutor act independently *is* mentioned (ICTY Article 16(2) and ICTR Article 15(2)).

8.5.30 The defence in *Kanyabashi* raised the objection that the Tribunal was neither impartial nor independent, which was rejected by the Trial Chamber in its *Kanyabashi Jurisdiction Decision* of 18 June 1997:

> 37. The Defense Motion asserted that the Tribunal was set up by the Security Council, a political body and as such the Tribunal is just another appendage of an international organ of policing and coercion, devoid of independence.
>
> 38. The Prosecutor, in response, challenged the claim in the Defense Motion that the Tribunal cannot act both as a subsidiary organ of the Security Council and as an independent Judicial body. He stated that although the ICTY and the ICTR share certain aspects of personnel, materials and means of operation, the Tribunal for Rwanda is a separate Tribunal with its own Statute, its own sphere of jurisdiction and its own rules of operation and as such it has legal independence.
>
> 39. This Trial Chamber is of the view that criminal courts worldwide are the creation of legislatures which are eminently political bodies. This was an observation also made by the Trial Chamber in the Tadić-case. To support this view, the Trial Chamber in that case relied on *Effect of Awards of Compensation made by the United Nations Administrative Tribunal* (1954) I.C.J. 47, 53; Advisory Opinion of 13 July, which specifically held that a political organ of the United Nations, in that case the General Assembly, could and had created "an inde-

pendent and truly judicial body." Likewise, the Security Council could create such a body using its wide discretion under Chapter VII.

40. This independence is, for example, demonstrated by the fact that the Tribunal is not bound by national rules of evidence as stated under rule 89 A of the Rules of Procedure and Evidence. The Tribunal is free to apply those Rules of Evidence which best favour a fair determination of the matter before it as stipulated in rule 89(B) of the Rules.

41. Further, the judges of the Tribunal exercise their *judicial* duties independently and freely and are under oath to act honourably, faithfully, impartially and conscientiously as stipulated in rule 14 of the Rules. Judges do not account to the Security Council for their judicial functions.

42. In this Trial Chamber's view, the personal independence of the judges of the Tribunal and the integrity of the Tribunal are underscored by Article 12 (1) of the Statute of the Tribunal which states that persons of high moral character, integrity, impartiality who possess adequate qualifications to become judges in their respective countries and having widespread experience in criminal law, international law including international humanitarian law and human rights law, shall be elected.

43. This Trial Chamber also subscribes to a view which was expressed by the Appeals Chamber in the Tadić case that when determining whether a tribunal has been 'established by law,' consideration should be made to the setting up of an organ in keeping with the proper international standards providing all the guarantees of fairness and justice.

44. Under the Statute and the Rules of Procedure and Evidence, the Tribunal will ensure that the accused receives a fair trial. This principle of fair trial is further entrenched in Article 20 which embodies the major principles for the provision of a fair trial, *inter alia*, the principles of public hearing and subject to cross-examination. The rights of the accused are also set out such as the right to counsel, presumption of innocence until the contrary is proved beyond a reasonable doubt, privilege against self-incrimination and the right to adequate time for the preparation of his/her case. These guarantees are further included in rules 62, 63 and 78 of the Rules. The rights of the accused enumerated above are based upon Article 14 of the International Covenant on Civil and Political Rights and are similar to those found in Article 6 of the European Convention on Human Rights.

45. Defence Counsel argued that the obligation imposed on the Tribunal to report to the Security Council derogates its independence as a judicial organ. . . . In Article 34 of the Statute, the Tribunal is duty bound to do this annually. This requirement is not only a link between it and the Security Council but it is also a channel of communication to the International community, which has an interest in the issues being addressed and the right to be informed of the activities of the Tribunal. In the Chamber's view, the Tribunal's obligation to report progress to the Security Council is purely administrative and not a judicial act and therefore does not in any way impinge upon the impartiality and independence of its judicial decision.

46. The Defence Counsel further contended that African jurisprudence and Human Rights Covenants were overlooked in the setting up the Tribunal. This contention cannot be correct because the important instruments on human rights in Africa, including the Charter of the Organization of African Unity (O.A.U.) and the African Charter On Human Rights ("the African Charter") were indirectly included in the law applicable to the Tribunal. Articles 3 and 7 of the

African Charter on Human and People's Rights, for example, contain rights which are similar to those guaranteed in the Statute.

47. The Defence Counsel argued that the impartiality of the Tribunal has not been demonstrated for the reason that there has been selective prosecution only of persons belonging to the Hutu ethnic group.

48. In his response, the Prosecutor dismissed these allegations and stated that indictments have been issued against leading perpetrators of the genocide and that subject to the availability of evidence, he intended to prosecute Hutu and Tutsi "extremists." The use of the word "extremist" is inaccurate and unfortunate, in view of Article 1 of the Statute.

49. The Trial Chamber simply reiterates that, pursuant to Article 1 of the Statute, all persons who are suspected of having committed crimes falling within the jurisdiction of the Tribunal are liable to prosecution.

50. The Trial Chamber is not persuaded by the arguments advanced by the Defence Counsel that the Tribunal is not impartial and independent and accordingly rejects this contention.

8.5.31 For further discussion of the concepts of independence and impartiality in the context of the ICC, see John R.W.D. Jones, "Composition of the Court," esp. Part III ("*Judges*"), in Cassese, Gaeta, Jones (eds.) *The Rome Statute of the International Criminal Court: A Commentary* (OUP, 2002).

Prompt, Detailed Information as to Nature and Cause of Charge

8.5.32 There has been much discussion at the ICTY and ICTR as to whether this requirement applies to *the indictment* or to the *charges* which must be read to the accused upon his arrest.

8.5.33 In fact, there are two separate "information" stages at which different rights of the accused come into play. When the accused is arrested, he has the right to know the reasons for his arrest. Typically, the accused is *charged* at this stage, i.e., informed summarily of the charges against him, which may not at that stage be contained in an indictment. When the accused is preparing for trial, he has the right to know the case he has to meet. This will be set out in the indictment, as well as in the Prosecutor's Pre-Trial Brief.

8.5.34 At the ICTY and ICTR, these two stages are often merged, since the indictment has usually been confirmed before the accused is arrested (unless he is provisionally arrested pursuant to Rule 40(i) and/or transferred to the Tribunal pursuant to Rule 40 *bis*), so that the indictment can be read to him upon his arrest. That does not, however, reduce the need to distinguish between the distinct functions and rights enjoyed at the two stages because this is the filter through which the accused's complaints must be viewed. In other words, it remains relevant to ask: is the accused's complaint that upon his arrest, he was inadequately informed of the reasons for his arrest, or is it that he is unable to prepare for trial because he is insufficiently informed of the charges he has to face? The tests to be applied by the Chamber in evaluating the accused's complaints will depend on the answer to that question.

8.5.35 So far, the approach taken by the tribunals has been to take ICTY Article 21/ICTR Article 20 in conjunction with ICTY Article 18/ICTR Article 17 to mean that "there is a minimum level of information that must be provided by the indictment; there is a floor below which the level of information must not fall if the indictment is to be valid as to form" (*Kvočka, Decision on Defence Preliminary Motions on the Form of the Indictment*, 12 April 1999, para. 14). See further the Commentary to ICTY/ICTR Rule 47 at 8.1.17 *et seq*.

8.5.36 In the *Decision* rendered by the ICTR Appeals Chamber in *Barayagwiza* on 3 November 1999, the Chamber held that the Statute and Rules recognise that a detainee must be given the opportunity to have recourse to a court to challenge the lawfulness of his detention. This is, in essence, what constitutes the writ of *habeas corpus*. It is also a right set out in ECHR Article 5 (4).

8.5.37 The *Barayagwiza Decision* was invoked by Radoslav Brdjanin in a petition dated 30 November 1999, requesting that the accused be promptly brought before a Trial Chamber and that the Prosecutor be ordered to present to the Trial Chamber the evidence in its possession supporting a *prima facie* case against the accused. The Trial Chamber rejected this petition in its *Decision on Petition for a Writ of Habeas Corpus on Behalf of Radoslav Brdjanin* dated 8 December 1999, ruling that the Chamber does not have the power to issue a writ of *habeas corpus* and that, in any event, the accused's detention was lawful.

8.5.38 See also *Decision on Motion for Release* rendered by the Trial Chamber in *Talić* on 10 December 1999 (an application by the Prosecution to amend the Indictment does not mean that the accused has been deprived of the right to be promptly informed of the charges against him).

Languages

8.5.39 It has been held (*Delalić*, Tr. Ch., *Decision on Defence Application for Forwarding the Documents in the Language of the Accused (Delalić)*, 25 September 1996) that the rights of the accused set out in para. 4(a) of ICTY Article 21/ICTR Article 20 entitle the accused to receive all items of evidence, including the material submitted in support of the indictment, in a language he understands. He also has the right to receive all Orders and Decisions issued by the Tribunal, which must be filed in both working languages of the Tribunal (i.e. French and English), in a language he understands.

8.5.40 Counsel for the accused may use the language of the accused during all proceedings before the Trial Chamber.

8.5.41 As regards discovery of documents, the Chamber ruled that if the item was originally obtained in the language of the accused (usually BCS—Bosnian/Croatian/Serbian), then discovery is made in that language. For documents not originally in the language of the accused (e.g. Danish), discovery is made in one of the working languages, with any translation desired being the responsibility of the party requesting it.

8.5.42 Otherwise, all of the following have to be filed in one of the working languages of the Tribunal: all motions, written arguments and other documents; all correspondence to or from an organ of the Tribunal, including the Office of the Prosecutor; transcripts of proceedings before the International Tribunal shall be made available in one or both of the working languages.

8.5.43 It follows from the above that the accused is *not* entitled to receive the transcripts in a language he understands, which is understandable given that it is not required by Article 21, that the transcripts are simply an *aide-memoire* which, in most criminal courts, does not exist, with the parties making their own notes, and finally given the limited resources of the Tribunal and the vast expense that would be involved in translating hundreds of pages of daily transcripts into the language of the accused.

8.5.44 A common difficulty arises where the accused is a B/C/S speaker and his counsel, or one of them, is not. Inevitably this means that the accused will have acess in his language to certain documents (e.g., documents originally discovered in B/C/S), which the Counsel will not have access to in French and English, and vice-versa (e.g., transcripts are available in French and English but not in B/C/S). In *Brdjanin and Talić*, for example, counsel complained that, in the midst of the trial, they were receiving exhibits in B/C/S which they were unable to comprehend.

8.5.45 See also *Naletilić and Martinović, Decision on Defence's Motion Concerning Translation of all Documents*, 18 October 2001, in which the Trial Chamber held that:

> the guarantees provided in Article 21(4) of the Statute do not extend to all documents, but only to evidence, which forms the basis of the determination by the Chamber of the charges against the accused; and that this right is ensured, *inter alia*, by the fact that all evidence admitted at trial is provided in a language the accused understands.

Cross Reference: Rule 3 ("Languages").

Adequate Time and Facilities

8.5.46 It is a fundamental right of an accused "to have adequate time and facilities for the preparation of his case." The phrase, "adequate time," is a flexible one, the meaning of which depends on the circumstances of each case. "It is impossible to set a standard of what constitutes adequate time to prepare a defence because this is something which can be affected by a number of factors including the complexity of the case, and the competing forces and claims at play, such as consideration of the interests of other accused persons." (*Delalić et al.*, Tr. Ch., *Decision on the Applications for Adjournment of the Trial Date*, 3 February 1997).

Expeditious Trial

Right To Be Tried Without Undue Delay

8.5.47 "Justice delayed is justice denied" (*Bagosora, Separate Opinion of Judge Yakov Ostrovsky on the Prosecution's Motion for Adjournment*, 17 March 1998, para. 9). In that case, Judge Ostrovsky considered that it was unacceptable that Bagosora's trial had not started despite his having been in custody for two years. He placed the blame for the delay on the Prosecutor and considered the situation to be a breach of the accused's right to a trial without undue delay in ICTR Article 20.

8.5.48 In the event, the Bagosora trial was not to start for another four years. This has been described as "*la plus longue détention provisoire des annales de la justice internationale. Pour un 'suspect numéro 1' qui, depuis qu'il est derrière les barreaux,* *n'a jamais fait obstruction à son procès*" ("Le mépris," *Diplomatie Judiciaire*, No. 84, April 2002, p. 8)

Expeditious Trial Not To Be Compromised by Motions to Amend Indictment

8.5.49 "The Prosecutor's right to submit a request for leave to amend the indictment pursuant to Rule 50 of the Rules must not be exercised to the prejudice of the accused's right to be tried without undue delay as stated in Article 21(4)(c) of the Statute" (*Kordić and Čerkez*, Tr. Ch., *Decision on the Prosecutor's Motion to hold pre-trial motions in abeyance*, 28 January 1998).

Use of Pre-Trial Briefs and Stipulations

8.5.50 After the first trial (*Tadić*), the Trial Chambers have sought to expedite trials by defining the issues in dispute before trial by means of pre-trial briefs and by requesting parties to stipulate, or formally admit, any non-disputed facts. See Rule 54, "Stipulations/formal admissions," 8.4.67 *et seq.*

8.5.51 To the same end of ensuring trial without undue delay, the Trial Chamber, ruling in *Dokmanović* on 28 November 1997, ordered that witness statements be presented to the Chamber before trial, not as evidence, but to enable the Chamber to familiarise itself with the case. Both Parties were ordered to file their Pre-trial Briefs and Opening Statements, and the defence was further ordered to file any alibi notice and a document "setting out those points, if any, in the . . . Indictment which are admitted, those which are denied and the grounds for so doing, and setting out in general terms the defence to the Indictment," as well as any Motions, by certain specified dates.

8.5.52 The same approach was taken by the Trial Chamber in *Aleksovski*. See *Scheduling Order* of 3 December 1997.

8.5.53 Rule 65 *ter* (F) now formally sets out these requirements, stipulating that, within a fixed time-period after receiving the Prosecutor's pre-trial brief and other materials, the defence must file "a pre-trial brief addressing the factual and legal issues, and including a written statement setting out: (i) in general terms, the nature of the accused's defence, (ii) the matters with which the accused takes issue in the Prosecutor's pre-trial brief; and (iii) in the case of each such matter, the reaon why the accused takes issue with it."

Use of Pre-Trial Judge

8.5.54 See *Order appointing a Pre-Trial Judge* issued by the Trial Chamber in *Kunarac* on 18 June 1998:

> CONSIDERING the provisions of Article 21(4)(C) of the Statute of the International Tribunal, which guarantees the accused's right "to be tried without undue delay" and Article 20(1) of the Statute of the International Tribunal, which enshrines the right to "a fair and expeditious [trial]";
>
> CONSIDERING that it is in the interests of justice and of a more expeditious and effectively managed trial to appoint a pre-trial Judge to be responsible for pre-trial matters on behalf of the Trial Chamber ("pre-trial Judge");

...

DESIGNATES Judge Florence Ndepele Mwachande Mumba to be the pre-trial Judge in this case, such appointment to take effect forthwith.

8.5.55 The institution of a pre-trial Judge has now been formalised in ICTY Rule 65 *ter* ("Pre-Trial Judge").

8.5.56 At the ICC, the institution of the Pre-Trial Chamber has important functions in the pre-trial phase. See, in particular, Article 57 of the Rome Statute of the ICC. Unlike the ICTY and ICTR, the Rome Statute provides that the Pre-Trial Chamber may, *inter alia*, take measures such "as may be necessary to assist the person in the preparation of his or her defence." (ICC Article 57 (3) (b))

No Oral Argument Unless Requested by Counsel

8.5.57 In general, the Tribunal has a preference for motions being made in writing and disposed of in writing, without an oral hearing. This has been justified by "the need to ensure a fair and expeditious trial" (*Radić et al.*, Tr. Ch., *Order for the filing of Motions*, 13 January 1999).

8.5.58 Even if counsel requests oral argument, it will not necessarily be granted. See *Decision on the Defence Preliminary Motion on the Form of the Indictment* of 24 February 1999 in *Krnojelac:*

> 65. The general practice of the International Tribunal is not to hear oral argument on [preliminary] motions prior to the trial unless good reason is shown for its need in a particular case. That general practice is soundly based upon the peculiar circumstances in which the International Tribunal operates, in that counsel appearing for accused persons before it invariably have to travel long distances from where they ordinarily practise in order to appear for such oral argument; counsel appearing for the prosecution are often appearing in other trials currently being heard; and the judges comprising the Trial Chamber in question are usually engaged in other trials at the time when the motion has to be determined.

8.5.59 Thus, in order to be granted a hearing, Counsel typically have to identify particular issues whish they wish to put orally and explain why they cannot be put in writing (para. 66, *ibid.*). In principle, this is a very hard challenge to meet; virtually any argument may be made in writing if it can be made orally. Nevertheless, it is submitted, certain issues should be debated orally, particularly where the complexity of the issues means that a dialectical approach and questioning from the bench is a more suitable way of determining the issues than resolving them on the papers alone.

Length of Trials

8.5.60 The Trial Chamber may limit the amount of time each party has to present evidence in the interests of an expeditious trial and the efficient administration of justice. See *Decision on the Length of the Proceedings and the time allocated to the Parties to present their evidence*, 17 December 1997, in which the Trial Chamber allocated a specific number of hearing days to each party to present their evidence. The Chamber

Accused May Not Waive Right to Expeditious Trial

8.5.61 In *Kvočka and Others, Decision on Interlocutory Appeal by the Accused Zoran Zigić Against the Decision of Trial Chamber I dated 5 December 2000*, 25 May 2001, the Appeals Chamber held that the Tribunal "has the primary obligation to ensure that the accused has a fair and expeditious trial." It added that "the right to an expeditious trial is an inseparable and constituent element of the right to a fair trial" and could therefore not be waived by the accused. The question arose in the context of the accused's request to adjourn the proceedings pending a ruling by the ICJ in the *Bosnia and Herzegovina v. FRY* case.

Assignment of Defence Counsel

8.5.62 When it comes to assiging defence counsel, the accused has the right to be consulted regarding his wishes and the Registrar may only refuse those wishes on "reasonable and valid grounds." This rule is applicable both to assignment of counsel and to appointment of co-counsel.

8.5.63 In *Gerard Ntakirutimana*, the accused requested the Trial Chamber to replace the defence counsel assigned to him. In numerous letters and in a *Motion to Trial Chambers to be assigned new Counsel*, filed on his behalf by Mr. Ramsey Clark on 25 April 1997, the accused requested that the counsel assigned to him by the Registrar on 17 March 1997, Mr. N.K. Loomu-Ojare of the Tanzania Bar Association, be replaced with a particular counsel of the accused's choice, namely Mr. Ramsey Clark of the United States. The accused based his objection to the assigned counsel solely on the ground that Mr. Loomu-Ojare was a Tanzanian national and that Tanzania maintained special ties with the present government of Rwanda.

8.5.64 The Trial Chamber, in its *Decision* of 11 June 1997, by two votes to one, refused to accede to the accused's request. The majority (Judges Kama and Aspegren) pointed out that the accused had already replaced his counsel once and declared that:

> Article 20(4) of the Statute cannot be interpreted as giving the indigent accused the absolute right to be assigned the legal representation of his or her choice.

8.5.65 They added:

> nonetheless . . . mindful to ensure that the indigent accused receives the most efficient defence possible in the context of a fair trial, and convinced of the importance to adopt a progressive practice in this area, an indigent accused should be offered the possibility of designating the counsel of his or her choice from the list drawn up by the Registrar for this purpose, the Registrar having to take into consideration the wishes of the accused, unless the Registrar has reasonable and valid grounds not to grant the request of the accused.

8.5.66 Thus it can be inferred from the above that the majority considered that the Registrar did have "reasonable and valid grounds" for refusing the accused's request in that particular case.

8.5.67 In an oral Decision rendered on 13 March 1998 in *Nyiramasuhuko*, on a defence motion requesting the appointment of a specifically named co-counsel, the Chamber held that the same test applies, *mutatis mutandis*, to appointment of co-counsel, i.e. the Registrar should take into account the wishes of the accused for a particular co-counsel and only refuse to accede to those wishes in the presence of "reasonable and valid grounds" for so doing.

8.5.68 In a Separate and Dissenting Opinion to the above *Ntakirutimana* Decision of 11 June 1997, the dissenting Judge—Judge Ostrovsky—agreed that Article 20(4)(d) gave the accused the right to be consulted concerning his choice of assigned counsel, but Judge Ostrovsky differed from the majority in holding that, in the circumstances of the case, this required that the request of the accused to replace his counsel be granted:

> 6. In conformity with Article 20(4)(d) of the Statute, Rule 45 of the Rules of Procedure and Evidence (the "Rules") and Article 13 of the Directive on Assignment of Defence Counsel (the "Directive"), the Registrar assigns a defence counsel to the indigent accused. But the accused has the right to choose his or her defence counsel from the list drawn up by the Registrar in accordance with Rules 44 and 45 of the Rules.
>
> The Registrar may refuse to assign a counsel to the accused of his or her choice if there are reasonable grounds for doing so. But in the light of Article 20(4)(d) of the Statute, the Registrar cannot impose his or her decision about the assignment of a defence counsel on the accused without taking into account his or her opinion.
>
> . . .
>
> 9. Therefore, I am of view that there is a sufficient legal basis to accept the request of the accused and replace his defence counsel in the interests of justice.

8.5.69 On this same point, see the Trial Chamber's *Decision on Request by Accused Mucić for Assignment of new Counsel*, 24 June 1996:

> 2. The Statute does not specifically state that the right to assigned counsel is also a right to assigned counsel of the accused's own choosing. . . . However, the practice of the Registry of the International Tribunal has been to permit the accused to select any available counsel from this list and to add counsel to the list if selected by an accused, provided that such counsel meets the necessary criteria. The Trial Chamber supports this practice, within practical limits.

See also the *Akayesu Appeals Judgement*, paras. 50–64. See also 2.6.15 *et seq.* on Rule 45 "Assignment of Counsel."

Equality of Arms Does Not Mean Equality of *Means and Resources*

8.5.70 In a motion filed in *Kayishema/Ruzindana*, the defence requested an order for the Prosecution "to divulge and limit its number of lawyers, consultants, assistants and investigators working on the case relating to Clement Kayishema," and to declare "the time spent and resources available to the Prosecution, since the opening of the Kayishema file." The defence made its request on the basis that the principle of equality of arms required the resources of Prosecution and Defence to be approximately equal. The Trial Chamber rejected this argument in its Decision rendered on 5 May 1997:

> the Tribunal finds that the rights of the accused and equality between the parties should not be confused with the equality of means and resources;
>
> ... the Tribunal determines that the rights of the accused as laid down in Article 20 and in particular (2) and (4) (b) of the Statute shall in no way be interpreted to mean that the Defence is entitled to [the] same means and resources as [are] available to the Prosecution;
>
> ... [the] Tribunal concludes that the Defence Counsel has not proved to its satisfaction any violation of the rights of the accused as laid down in Article 20(2) and (4)(b).

8.5.71 The Trial Chamber added that the Directive on the Assignment of Defence Counsel—the "legal aid" text for the Tribunal—comprehensively set out the resources available to the defence (Article 17(A) of the Directive provides that, ". . . the costs and expenses of legal representation of the suspect or accused necessarily or reasonably incurred shall be met by the Tribunal . . ."), and that the accused "has not shown anything on record to indicate that it has not been availed the remedies envisaged in . . . Article 17 of the Directive."

Proceeding in Absence of Counsel

8.5.72 If the accused is willing, pre-trial hearings may proceed in the absence of the accused's counsel, when the co-accused's counsel is present and willing to represent both accused for that session. See *Decision on the Motion filed by the Prosecutor on the Availability of the Defence Counsel* rendered by the Trial Chamber in *Kayishema* on 28 November 1997 (Decision delivered orally on 14 March 1997).

"Under the Same Conditions"—Equality of Arms

8.5.73 In the *Separate Opinion of Judge Vohrah on Prosecution Motion for Production of Defence Witness Statements*, in *Tadić* on 27 November 1996, Judge Vohrah said that the principle of equality of arms was intended principally to favour *the accused* (page 7):

> The principle is intended in an ordinary trial to ensure that the Defence has means to prepare and present its case equal to those available to the Prosecution which has all the advantages of the State on its side. . . . the European Commission of Human Rights equates the principle of equality of arms with the right of the accused to have procedural equality with the Prosecution. (p. 4)
>
> It seems to me from the above authorities that the application of the equality of arms principle especially in criminal proceedings should be inclined in favour of the Defence acquiring parity with the Prosecution in the presentation of the Defence case before the Court to preclude any injustice against the accused.

8.5.74 In a separate and dissenting opinion to this Decision, Judge McDonald considered, however, that in the context of the ICTY, the Prosecutor could not be presumed to enjoy inherent advantages vis-à-vis the defence, which the principle of equality of arms would then serve to correct. Judge McDonald questioned the validity of comparing "the resources and powers of the Prosecution of the International Tribunal with that of many national entities" (para. 32), since the Prosecutor of the Tribunal had perforce to rely on State cooperation for its investigations and prosecutions, which was often not forthcoming.

8.5.75 In a Decision in *Delalić et al* on 4 February 1998, the Trial Chamber disagreed with the view expressed in Judge Vohrah's *Separate Opinion* above. After citing the paras. reproduced above, the Chamber stated:

> 49. There is no doubt that procedural equality means what it says, equality between the Prosecution and the Defence. To suggest, as has been done in the above quotation, an inclination in favour of the Defence is tantamount to a procedural inequality in favour of the Defence and against the Prosecution, and will result in inequality of arms. This will be inconsistent with the minimum guarantee provided for in Article 21 para. 4(e) of the Statute. In the circumstances of the International Tribunal, the Prosecutor and the Defence rely on State cooperation for their investigation, so, *prima facie*, the basis for the inequality argument does not arise.

8.5.76 The Chamber used this rationale to order the Defence to provide to the Prosecution a list of the witnesses it intended to call at trial, since the Prosecution had done likewise (Tr. Ch., *Delalić et al, Decision on the Prosecutor's Motion for an Order requiring Advance Disclosure of Witnesses by the Defence*, 4 February 1998).

8.5.77 This was also followed by the Appeals Chamber in a Decision rendered in *Aleksovski* on 16 February 1999, in which it found that the principle of equality of arms should be interpreted in favour of both parties and not only in favour of the accused.

8.5.78 Again, this was followed in the *Tadić Appeals Judgement*. The accused's first ground of appeal was that:

> The Appellant's right to a fair trial was prejudiced as there was no 'equality of arms' between the Prosecution and the Defence due to the prevailing circumstances in which the trial was conducted. (para. 20)

8.5.79 Specifically, the Defence alleged that lack of cooperation and obstruction by Republika Srpska, and particularly the local Serb authorities in Prijedor, prevented the proper presentation of the defence case at trial.

8.5.80 The Appeals Chamber rejected this ground of appeal, accepting the Prosecution submission that equality meant procedural equality, not substantive equality, largely on the basis of the case-law of the European Court of Human Rights ("ECHR"):

> 49. There is nothing in the ECHR case law that suggests that the principle is applicable to conditions, outside the control of a court, that prevented a party from securing the attendance of certain witnesses. All the cases considered applications that the judicial body had the power to grant.

8.5.81 This is perhaps not surprising, however, since the ECHR hears cases from relatively stable, western democracies where police forces are able to provide law and order and thus to secure the appearance of witnesses before domestic courts. This was evidently not the situation in Prijedor, where the police chief, Simo Drljača, was himself indicted for genocide by the ICTY (and shot by SFOR troops trying to arrest him on 10 July 1997, two months after the *Tadić* Trial Judgement was rendered), and where the attendance of witnesses could not and would not be secured by the local police forces.

8.5.82 The reference to ECHR cases may also be inappropriate in that many of the cases referred to in the Appeals Chamber's Judgement (for example at para. 48) concerned civil, rather than criminal, matters. The emphasis on civil cases can too easily lead to the conclusion that the prosecutor and defence are equal parties in the proceedings, both the intended beneficiaries of the equality of arms principle. Thus, it is submitted that Judge Vohrah's view as expressed in his *Separate Opinion on Prosecution Motion for Production of Defence Witness Statements* of 27 November 1996 in *Tadić*, that the equality of arms principle is mainly intended, in criminal cases, to accrue to the benefit of the accused, is the correct approach.

Right of Confrontation and Exceptions

8.5.83 Article 21(4)(e) has been interpreted as an affirmation of the accused's right to confront the witnesses against him, a right recognised in many jurisdictions. Notably, the "Confrontation Clause" of the Sixth Amendment to the United States Constitution provides that, "In all criminal prosecutions, the accused shall enjoy the right . . . to be confronted with the witnesses against him; to have compulsory process for obtaining witnesses in his favour. . . ." Thus the Trial Chamber stated in its *Decision on the Motion to Allow Witnesses K, L And M to Give Their Testimony by Means of Video-Link Conference* of 28 May 1997:

> 15. It is important to re-emphasise the general rule requiring the physical presence of the witness. This is intended to ensure confrontation between the witness and the accused and to enable the Judges to observe the demeanour of the witness when giving evidence.

8.5.84 In this same Decision, however, the Trial Chamber recognised exceptions to the general rule requiring the physical presence of the accused—". . . there are exceptions to the general rule where the right of the accused under Article 21(4)(e) is not prejudicially affected" (para. 14)—including video-conferences:

> It is, however, well known that video-conferences not only allow the Chambers to hear the testimony of a witness who is unable or unwilling to present their evidence before the Trial Chamber at The Hague, but also allows the Judges to observe the demeanour of the witness whilst giving evidence. Furthermore, and importantly, counsel for the accused can cross-examine the witness and the Judges can put questions to clarify evidence given during testimony. Video-conferencing is, in actual fact, merely an extension of the Trial Chamber to the location of the witness. The accused is therefore neither denied his right to confront the witness, nor does he lose materially from the fact of the physical absence of the witness. It cannot, therefore, be said with any justification that testimony given by video-link conferencing is a violation of the right of the accused to confront the witness. Article 21(4)(e) is in no sense violated.

8.5.85 Note that Rule 90(A) was amended on 25 July 1997 at the thirteenth plenary session to make explicit reference to "video-conference link."

Cross Reference: Rules 71(D) and 90(A).

Trial Chamber Can Order Party to Close Its Case

8.5.86 Parties do not have an indefinite time in which to call witnesses. The Trial Chamber has, therefore, held that it may order a Party to close its case without infringing their rights.

8.5.87 See *Decision on the Alternative Request for renewed consideration of Delalic's Motion for an Adjournment until 22 June or Request for issue of subpoenas to individuals and requests for assistance to the Government of Bosnia and Herzegovina* rendered in *Delalić et al.* on 22 June 1998:

> 45. The Trial Chamber is of the opinion that where an accused person in a multiple accused trial is either unable or unwilling to call his witnesses to testify on his behalf on the particular dates directed by the Trial Chamber, and unreasonably and unilaterally chooses his own dates in such a manner as to prejudicially affect the course of the proceedings and cause delay in respect of the defence of other accused persons, the Trial Chamber is, in the interests of [an] expeditious and fair trial, empowered to order the accused to close his case. Otherwise, an accused person in a multiple accused trial, or indeed even in a trial of a single accused, may by devious reasons relying on Article 21(4)(e) prolong the trial unnecessarily.
>
> 46. All the accused persons involved in a multiple accused trial are entitled to the same protection of the provisions of Articles 20(1) and 21(4)(e) of the Statute and Rule 85 of the Rules. The Trial Chamber, vested with the duty in accordance with Article 20(1) to ensure [an] expeditious and fair trial, should not, in the face of such equal competing rights, allow the exercise of the right of one of the accused persons to operate to the prejudice of the others.

To Examine, or Have Examined, Witnesses Against Him

8.5.88 The above phrase was considered in hearings in *Akayesu*, on 14 January 1997, when the accused was given the right—pending a decision on his request for a change in assigned counsel—to cross-examine prosecution witnesses, while his defence counsel was also exercising the right of cross-examination.

8.5.89 The Prosecution objected to this way of proceeding:

> MR. PROSPER: . . . we would like to enter an objection on record. The Prosecution would object to the defence counsel engaging in cross-examination. In fact we object to the principle of double cross-examination. We feel that it is fundamentally unfair and not in accordance with the statute. It also appears that it is an "either or" proposition, meaning that the accused would cross-examine or his legal counsel would cross-examine and not both. When I look at Article 20, section 4, subsection "d," it says the accused certainly has the right to defend himself or herself in person or through legal assistance. And then when we look at subsection "e," the accused has a right to examine or have examined a witness against him or her. Therefore it would appear to us that it is again an "either

or" proposition and they get one bite at the apple and one opportunity to cross-examine . . . (transcripts of hearing, 14/1/97, p. 53)

8.5.90 The Trial Chamber, however, overruled this objection:

MR. PRESIDENT: Mr. Prosecutor, I would like to remind you the decision we took yesterday, which said there is no incompatibility between subparas d and e of Article 20. That is our opinion.(p. 54, 14/1/97)

Requests for Interpretation

8.5.91 In *Delalić et al.*, a Bosnian Croat accused requested interpretation of the trial proceedings into the Croatian language. The trial proceedings were then being translated into the Serbo-Croatian language. The Trial Chamber rejected the Motion, holding, on the basis of expert linguistic opinion, that "the varieties of Serbo-Croatian are mutually intelligible to all citizens of the former Yugoslavia" (*Order on Zdravko Mucić's Oral Request for Croatian Interpretation*, 23 June 1997). The Chamber referred to an earlier Decision of the Tribunal in this regard which had found that "the differences between Serbian and Croatian are small and that there was no valid reason to justify the refusal of Serbo-Croatian interpretation." The Chamber also noted that the accused had never complained in the past about an inability to understand and to follow the proceedings.

Cross Reference: Rule 3.

Privilege Against Self-Incrimination

8.5.92 In two oral decisions rendered by the Trial Chamber in *Akayesu*, on 17 and 26 February 1998, the Chamber held that to grant a defence motion requesting that several named accused persons be called to testify in the trial of *Akayesu* might violate those accused's privilege against self-incrimination. See, e.g. the oral decision of 17 February 1998:

le Tribunal, après en avoir délibéré, est d'avis que la comparution de ces accusés en tant que témoins au présent procès, est de nature à porter éventuellement atteinte à leur droit de ne pas être forcés à témoigner contre eux-mêmes ou de s'avouer coupables. Pour cette raison, le Tribunal a décidé de rejeter la requête de la Défense.

8.5.93 Para. (4)(g), *inter alia*, protects an accused from providing a handwriting sample that might prove his authorship of a letter having a tendency to incriminate him. See *Decision on the Prosecutor's Oral Request for the Admission of Exhibit 155 into evidence and for an Order to compel the accused, Zvdrako Mucić, to provide a handwriting sample* rendered by the Trial Chamber in *Delalić et al* on 19 January 1998:

47. . . . We hold that where the material factor absent in the incriminating elements is the handwriting sample of the accused, the Trial Chamber cannot compel the accused to supply the missing element. To do so will be to infringe the

provisions of Article 21 sub-para. 4(g) which protects the accused from self-incrimination. It is different where the accused voluntarily complies on demand without coercion.

59. ... It is the sacred and solemn duty of every judicial institution to respect and give benevolent construction to the provisions guaranteeing such rights instead of giving such a construction as to whittle down their effects.

60. ... Mucić cannot be ordered to provide a handwriting sample. This would involve him testifying against himself.

8.5.94 Equally the privilege against self-incrimination bars the drawing of adverse inferences from an accused's silence on any matter. The Chamber stated in the same Decision that an accused's silence is:

50. ... a legitimate exercise of his right implicit in Article 21 sub-para. 4(g) and express in Rule 63. The precise meaning of the right to silence is that an accused person can stay mute without reacting to the allegation. This is generally a legitimate reaction to the preceding warning of the right to silence. It is also in response and reaction to the exercise of the right to protection from self-incrimination.

8.5.95 Thus the Trial Chamber refused to draw any adverse inferences from the accused's silence; moreover, since it did not order him to produce a handwriting sample, the question of drawing adverse inferences from his refusal to provide a sample did not arise (para. 61).

8.5.96 An anomalous decision in this respect is the *Order for the Production of Documents used to prepare for testimony* rendered by the Trial Chamber in *Blaškić* on 22 April 1999, in which the accused was ordered to produce the notes which he used in testifying. The Chamber did not seem to consider that such an order could, if used against the accused, result in the accused being compelled to testify against himself.

Non-Enumerated Rights

Legitimate Expectation

8.5.97 The notion of Legitimate Expectation is well-known in public law. For an example of its application at the ICTY, see *Decision relating to the Trial Chamber's ruling on the basis of written submissions prior to hearing oral arguments as scheduled* rendered by the Appeals Chamber on 28 July 1999 in *Simić et al* (where the Trial Chamber had created the expectation that oral arguments would be heard, it violated the defence's legitimate expectation of an oral hearing when it rendered its Decision without a hearing, on the basis of written submissions alone).

8.5.98

| ICTY
Rule 63
Questioning of Accused | ICTR
Rule 63
Questioning of the Accused |
|---|---|
| (A) Questioning by the Prosecutor of an accused, including after the initial appearance, shall not proceed without the presence of counsel unless the accused has voluntarily and expressly agreed to proceed without counsel present. If the accused subsequently expresses a desire to have counsel, questioning shall thereupon cease, and shall only resume when the accused's counsel is present. (B) The questioning, including any waiver of the right to counsel, shall be audio-recorded or video-recorded in accordance with the procedure provided for in Rule 43. The Prosecutor shall at the beginning of the questioning caution the accused in accordance with Rule 42(A)(iii). | (A) Questioning by the Prosecutor of an accused, including after the initial appearance, shall not proceed without the presence of counsel unless the accused has voluntarily and expressly agreed to proceed without counsel present. If the accused subsequently expresses a desire to have counsel, questioning shall thereupon cease, and shall only resume when the accused's counsel is present. (B) The questioning, including any waiver of the right to counsel, shall be audio-recorded or video-recorded in accordance with the procedure provided for in Rule 43. The Prosecutor shall at the beginning of the questioning caution the accused in accordance with Rule 42 (A)(iii). |

History of ICTY Rule 63

8.5.99 ICTY Rule 63 was amended at the ICTY twelfth plenary session, held 2–3 December 1996, in order to achieve consistency with Rule 42, which concerns the questioning of suspects.

History of ICTR Rule 63

8.5.100 Para. (B) was added to this Rule at the ICTR fifth plenary session on 8 June 1998. This rule was amended at the eighth plenary session on 26 June 2000.

Right to Silence

8.5.101 Rule 63 was referred to in the context of the right to silence in the *Decision on the Prosecutor's Oral Requets for the Admission of Exhibit 155 into evidence and for an Order to compel the accused, Zvdrako Mucić, to provide a handwriting sample*, rendered by the Trial Chamber on 19 January 1998. The Chamber stated that the accused's silence is:

> 50. . . . a legitimate exercise of his right implicit in Article 21 sub-para. 4(g) and express in Rule 63. The precise meaning of the right to silence is that an accused person can stay mute without reacting to the allegation. This is generally a legitimate reaction to the preceding warning of the right to silence. It is also in response and reaction to the exercise of the right to protection from self-incrimination.

Questioning by the Prosecutor in the Absence of Counsel

8.5.102 See *Order on Representation by Counsel, Kvočka and Radić,* of 15 April 1998, in which Judge Rodrigues, noting that "the Prosecutor allegedly attempted to question the accused even though neither of them had counsel," ordered that "the questioning of either of the accused by the Prosecutor may not proceed before he [the accused] has received the permanent assistance of counsel."

8.5.103 Rule 63(A) has similarities to the Sixth Amendment to the Constitution of the United States, as interpreted by *Massiah v. U.S.*, Supreme Court of the United States, 377 U.S. 201, the rationale of which has been explained by Judge Higginbotham in *U.S. v. Johnson*, 954 F. 2d 1015 (5th Cir. 1992) (referred to by Saltzburg in *American Criminal Procedure* at p. 601):

> [The Sixth Amendment] recognizes that once the government has brought formal charges against an individual the adversary relationship between the parties is cemented. Once an accused has chosen to retain an attorney to act as his representative in the adversary process, the government may not try to circumvent the protection afforded by the presence of counsel during questioning. The vice is not deprivation of privacy, but interference with the parity required by the Sixth Amendment.

8.5.104 Professor Saltzburg comments on this right, "[it] is basically a constitutionalized version of a rule of professional ethics: that an adverse party may only be contacted through their lawyer."

8.5.105 For a national law comparison, see the *Massiah* line of cases decided by the United States Supreme Court under the 6th Amendment to the U.S. Constitution, according to which, once a person has been *indicted*, he may not be approached by the Prosecution for questioning except through his counsel.

Timing at Which to Challenge Compliance with Rule 63

8.5.106 In *Nyiramasuhuko and Ntahobali, Decision on the Defence Motion to Suppress Custodial Statements by the Accused*, 8 June 2001, the Trial Chamber held that the appropriate time for the Defence to challenge the Prosecutor's compliance with Rule 63 in the manner in which the accused was questioned would be if and when the Prosecutor seeks to use the accused's statements as evidence. At that stage it would be for the Defence to object to the admissibility of the statements. It would then be for the Chamber to decide whether a *voire dire* should take place.

History of ICTY Rule 64

8.5.107 ICTY Rule 64 was amended at the thirteenth plenary session on 25 July 1997, adding the words, "In exceptional circumstances, the accused may be held in facilities outside of the host country."

8.5.108

ICTY Rule 64 Detention on Remand	ICTR Rule 64 Detention on Remand
Upon his transfer to the seat of the Tribunal, the accused shall be detained in facilities provided by the host country, or by another country. In exceptional circumstances, the accused may be held in facilities outside of the host country. The President may, on the application of a party, request modification of the conditions of detention of an accused.	Upon his transfer to the seat of the Tribunal, the accused shall be detained in facilities provided by the host country or by another country. The President may, on the application of a party, request modification of the conditions of detention of an accused.

Modification of Conditions of Detention

8.5.109 For an example of modification of the conditions of detention, reference should be made to *Blaškić*. On 3 and 17 April 1996, the President of the Tribunal issued orders, pursuant to Rule 64, to modify the conditions of Blaškić's detention (*Decision of the President on the Defence Motion Filed Pursuant to Rule 64*). The Decision of 3 April 1996, which dealt at length with the international obligations of Croatia, as well as with the scope of Rules 64 and 65 and the meaning of "house arrest," permitted Blaškić, subject to the following conditions, to serve his pre-trial detention in a place other than the United Nations Detention Unit in The Hague:

> (1) that the residence of Blaškić be in the confines of a place designated by the Netherlands authorities in consultation with the Registrar;
>
> (2) that he be permitted to leave this place of residence only to meet his Counsel, the diplomatic and consular representatives of the Republic of Croatia accredited in the Netherlands, his family and friends, such meetings to take place in the Detention Unit;
>
> (3) that contacts with the media be prohibited;
>
> (4) that orders or requests of the Tribunal be promptly responded to;

8.5.110 Telephone calls were to be regulated by the Rules of Detention, and Blaškić would not be permitted to communicate his location to anyone.

8.5.111 On 17 April 1996, the President ordered further modifications to the condition of Blaškić's detention, which would permit the detainee to meet his wife, children and counsel in any place deemed appropriate by the Registrar and once a month he would be entitled to spend the night with his wife and children. Furthermore, Blaškić would be permitted to have a television, radio and to make outgoing telephone calls from his place of detention, subject to the provisions of the Rules of Detention. All costs relating to the special conditions of detention were to be borne by Blaškić.

8.5.112 Owing to practical difficulties, a new order was issued by the President on 9 May 1996 that Blaškić be held at the Detention Unit until arrangements could be made for him to be held in another appropriate place. In a later Decision on this matter, rendered on 9 January 1997, the President partly granted Blaškić's request for further modification of his conditions of detention. This arrangement had to be abrogated on 16 July 1997 (see Fourth Annual Report, para. 159).

Test to Be Applied

8.5.113 In reaching the above-mentioned Decision of 9 January 1997, the President weighed two main factors, namely:

> the right of all detainees to be treated in a humane manner in accordance with the fundamental principles of respect for their inherent dignity and of the presumption of innocence
>
> and, on the other hand, "the imperatives of security and order."

8.5.114

ICTY Rule 65 Provisional Release	ICTR Rule 65 Provisional Release
(A) Once detained, an accused may not be released except upon an order of a Chamber. (B) Release may be ordered by a Trial Chamber only after giving the host country and the State to which the accused seeks to be released the opportunity to be heard and only if it is satisfied that the accused will appear for trial and, if released, will not pose a danger to any victim, witness or other person. (C) The Trial Chamber may impose such conditions upon the release of the accused as it may determine appropriate, including the execution of a bail bond and the observance of such conditions as are necessary to ensure the presence of the accused for trial and the protection of others. (D) Any decision rendered under this Rule by a Trial Chamber shall be subject to appeal in cases where leave is granted by a bench of three Judges of the Appeals Chamber, upon good cause being shown. Subject to para. (F) below, applications for leave to appeal shall be filed within seven days of filing of the impugned decision. Where such decision is rendered orally, the application shall be filed within seven days of the oral decision, unless	(A) Once detained, an accused may not be released except upon an order of a Trial Chamber. (B) Provisional release may be ordered by a Trial Chamber only in exceptional circumstances, after hearing the host country and only if it is satisfied that the accused will appear for trial and, if released, will not pose a danger to any victim, witness or other person. (C) The Trial Chamber may impose such conditions upon the provisional release of the accused as it may determine appropriate, including the execution of a bail bond and the observance of such conditions as are necessary to ensure the presence of the accused at trial and the protection of others. (D) Any decision rendered under this Rule shall be subject to appeal in cases where leave is granted by a bench of three Judges of the Appeals Chamber, upon good cause being shown. Subject to paragraph (F) below, applications for leave to appeal shall be filed within seven days of filing of the impugned decision. Where such decision is rendered orally, the application shall be filed within seven days of the oral decision unless:

(i) the party challenging the decision was not present or represented when the decision was pronounced, in which case the time-limit shall run from the date on which the challenging party is notified of the oral decision; or
(ii) the Trial Chamber has indicated that a written decision will follow, in which case, the time-limit shall run from filing of the written decision.

(E) The Prosecutor may apply for a stay of a decision by the Trial Chamber to release an accused on the basis that the Prosecutor intends to appeal the decision, and shall make such an application at the time of filing his or her response to the initial application for provisional release by the accused.

(F) Where the Trial Chamber grants a stay of its decision to release an accused, the Prosecutor shall file his or her appeal not later than one day from the rendering of that decision.

(G) Where the Trial Chamber orders a stay of its decision to release the accused pending an appeal by the Prosecutor, the accused shall not be released until either:
(i) the time-limit for the filing of an application for leave to appeal by the Prosecutor has expired, and no such application is filed;
(ii) a bench of three Judges of the Appeals Chamber rejects the application for leave to appeal;
(iii) the Appeals Chamber dismisses the appeal; or
(iv) a bench of three Judges of the Appeals Chamber or the Appeals Chamber otherwise orders.

(H) If necessary, the Trial Chamber may issue a warrant of arrest to secure the presence of an accused who has been released or is for any other reason at liberty. The provisions of Section 2 of Part Five shall apply *mutatis mutandis*.

(I) Without prejudice to the provisions of Rule 107, the Appeals Chamber may grant provisional release to convicted persons pending an appeal or for a fixed period if it is satisfied that:

(i) the party challenging the decision was not present or represented when the decision was pronounced, in which case the time-limit shall run from the date on which the challenging party is notified of the oral decision; or
(ii) the Trial Chamber has indicated that a written decision will follow, in which case, the time-limit shall run from filing of the written decision.

(E) The Prosecutor may apply for a stay of a decision by the Trial Chamber to release an accused on the basis that the Prosecutor intends to appeal the decision, and shall make such an application at the time of filing his or her response to the initial application for provisional release by the accused.

(F) Where the Trial Chamber grants a stay of its decision to release an accused, the Prosecutor shall file his or her appeal not later than one day from the rendering of that decision.

(G) Where the Trial Chamber orders a stay of its decision to release the accused pending an appeal by the Prosecutor, the accused shall not be released until either:
(i) the time-limit for the filing of an application for leave to appeal by the Prosecutor has expired, and no such application is filed;
(ii) a bench of three Judges of the Appeals Chamber rejects the application for leave to appeal;
(iii) the Appeals Chamber dismisses the appeal; or
(iv) a bench of three Judges of the Appeals Chamber or the Appeals Chamber otherwise orders.

(H) If necessary, the Trial Chamber may issue a warrant of arrest to secure the presence of an accused who has been provisionally released or is for any other reason at large. The provisions of Section 2 of Part Five shall apply *mutatis mutandis*.

(I) Without prejudice to the provisions of Rule 107, the Appeals Chamber may grant provisional release to convicted persons pending an appeal or for a fixed period if it is satisfied that:

(i) the appellant, if released, will either appear at the hearing of the appeal or will surrender into detention at the conclusion of the fixed period, as the case may be; (ii) the appellant, if released, will not pose a danger to any victim, witness or other person, and (iii) special circumstances exist warranting such release. The provisions of paras. (C) and (H) shall apply *mutatis mutandis*.	(i) the appellant, if released, will either appear at the hearing of the appeal or will surrender into detention at the conclusion of the fixed period, as the case may be; (ii) the appellant, if released, will not pose a danger to any victim, witness or other person, and (iii) special circumstances exist warranting such release. The provisions of paragraphs (C) and (H) shall apply *mutatis mutandis*.

History of ICTY Rule 65

8.5.115 Para. (B) was amended at the fifth plenary session in January 1995 to add the reference to the host country in order to give the Dutch Government a role in the provisional release of an accused. Para. (D) was added at the thirteenth plenary session on 25 July 1997 to allow the possibility of appeal where the Trial Chamber has denied provisional release. Paras. (D) and (E) were again amended at the fourteenth plenary session on 12 November 1997.

8.5.116 Sections (i) and (ii) were added to para. (D) at the eighteenth plenary session on 9–10 July 1998. Identical amendments were added to Rules 72, 73 and 77. These amendments are designed to deal with the situation where a party seeks leave to appeal from an *oral* decision.

8.5.117 Paras (E), (F) and (G) were added at the twenty-first plenary session on 30 November 1999, with the previous para. (E) becoming para. (H). The reference to "exceptional circumstances" was also deleted from para. (B). Para. (I) was added on 2 August 2000, after the twenty-second plenary session. The rule was again amended in minor ways on 19 January 2001, after the twenty-third plenary session.

8.5.118 At the twenty-fifth plenary session, held on 12–13 December, 2001, para. (B) was amended to provide "the State to which the accused seeks to be released," in addition to the host country, the opportunity of being heard.

History of ICTR Rule 65

8.5.119 Para. (D) was added at the ICTR fifth plenary session on 8 June 1998, after a similar amendment allowing appeal from a decision to refuse bail adopted at the ICTY at its thirteenth plenary session on 25 July 1997. The Rule was further amended after the twelfth plenary session on 5–6 July 2002.

Granting of Provisional Release

8.5.120 Provisional release has been granted—always subject to a number of stringent conditions—in the case of eight accused, Đorđe Đukić, Milan Simić, Drago Josipović, Miroslav Tadić, Simo Zarić, Enver Hadžihadsanović, Mehmed Alagić and

Amir Kubura. Đukić and Simić were both granted provisional release for health reasons; Josipović to attend a funeral (see *Decision on the Motion of Defence Counsel for Drago Josipović (Request for permission to attend funeral)* as well as the *Registry Certificate*, both of 6 May 1999). Đukić died before his case came to trial. Milan Simić was provisionally released on 26 March 1998, on the condition that he surrender himself to the ICTY two weeks before the beginning of his trial. His provisional release was again ordered in a *Decision* dated 29 May 2000. As regards Miroslav Tadić and Simo Zarić, see the Trial Chamber's *Decision on Miroslav Tadić's Application for Provisional Release* and *Decision on Simo Zarić's Application for Provisional Release* both of 4 April 2000. One of the reasons for granting provisional release to these accused was pre-trial delay.

8.5.121 The three accused in *Hadžihasanović et al*—Enver Hadžihasanović, Mehmed Alagić and Amir Kubura—were all granted provisional release by the Trial Chamber in an oral decision rendered on 13 December 2001, which was confirmed in a written decision dated 19 December 2001. The Trial Chamber drew largely on human rights principles in reaching its decision, as well as the principle of proportionality in international law:

> 8. Moreover, when interpreting Rule 65, the general principle of proportionality must be taken into account. A measure in public international law is proportional only when (1) suitable, (2) necessary and when (3) its degree and scope remain in a reasonable relationship to the envisaged target. Procedural measures should never be capricious or excessive. If it is sufficient to use a more lenient measure, it must be applied.
>
> 9. In its application of these criteria, the Trial Chamber finds it no longer necessary to execute the order for detention on remand pending trial. The Trial Chamber is satisfied that the 17 guarantees offered by the accused and the 8 guarantees offered by the Government of Bosnia and Herzegovina reasonably safeguard the proper conduct of the procedure. It is aware, however, that there will never be a total guarantee that an accused will appear for trial and, if released, will not pose a danger to sources of evidence.

Timing of Application for Provisional Release

8.5.122 An application for Provisional Release can be made before or during the trial See the Decision of the Trial Chamber, 23 January 1998, in *Aleksovski*, which declared the defence motion for provisional release admissible (although it was denied on its merits), over the Prosecution's objection that the motion was inadmissible because the trial had started.

> the justification for provisional release must be seen as emanating from or as the corollary of the principle of the presumption of innocence. Thus, provisional release must accord with the presumption of innocence, and this principle applies until such time as the final decision [verdict] has been taken.
>
> In any case, in respect of questions of individual freedom, the Trial Chamber considers that an accused must be able to turn to it at any time.
>
> The request for provisional release may therefore be presented throughout the duration of the [detention on remand] and until such time as the final decision

has been taken. It may be granted as soon as the criteria and conditions provided in Sub-rule 65(B) have been satisfied.

State of Health a Factor To Be Considered in Granting Provisional Release

8.5.123 Provisional Release may be ordered when the accused's state of health is incompatible with any form of detention. See the *Ðukić Decision rejecting the Application to withdraw the Indictment and Order for Provisional Release* of 24 April 1996 by the Trial Chamber, and the *Decision on Provisional Release of the Accused* of 26 March 1998 and the *Decision sur la demande de l'accuse Milan Simić de quitter son lieu de residence pour des raisons medicales* of 17 April 1998, both rendered in *Simić* by the Trial Chamber.

8.5.124 In the case of Milan Simić, the fact that he had surrendered voluntarily to the Tribunal, that he was hemiplegic and suffering from serious medical problems requiring intensive daily care, that the Prosecutor was not opposed to provisional release and that Republika Srpska had posted a bail bond of US $25,000 were also deemed relevant. Simić was granted provisional release on condition that he:

> i. Return to The Hague and be present for any proceedings the Trial Chamber requires him to attend in person and to surrender himself immediately to the United Nations Detention Unit in The Hague;
>
> ii. Surrender his passport to the International Police Task Force (IPTF) in Orašje or to the Office of the Prosecutor in Sarajevo;
>
> iii. Remain within the confines of the municipality of Bosanski Šamac;
>
> iv. Provide the Registrar of the Tribunal with prior notice of any address change;
>
> v. Meet once a day with the local Bosanski Šamac police who will maintain a log and periodically file a written report confirming his presence each day;
>
> vi. Agree to have the IPTF check on a bi-monthly basis with the local police about his presence and be allowed to make occasional, unannounced visits to him;
>
> vii. Not have contact in any manner whatsoever with any of the co-accused;
>
> viii. Not have any contact whatsoever with any persons who may testify at his trial;
>
> ix. Assume responsibility for all expenses regarding transport from The Hague to Bosanski Šamac and back.

8.5.125 The Chamber further stated that "the parties must inform the Trial Chamber of any difficulty in respect of the execution of the above-listed obligations" and that "in case of violation of one of those obligations, the accused may again be placed in custody immediately."

8.5.126 See further the *Decisions on the Application of the Accused Milan Simić to leave his place of residence for medical reasons* rendered on 17 April 1998, 8 May 1998 and 29 July 1998. The accused was ordered to attend a hearing in The Hague in the *Order on Judicial Supervision of Milan Simić* issued on 2 September 1998 and ordered to surrender at least two weeks before the start of trial in an *Order requiring attendance of accused* of 10 May 1999.

Jurisdiction of Appeals Chamber to Order Provisional Release

8.5.127 In its Orders of 19 February 1999 and 31 May 1999 in *Delalić et al*, the majority of the Appeals Chamber (Judge Bennouna dissenting) held that, taking Rule 65 in conjunction with Rule 107, it had jurisdiction to rule on an application for provisional release.

Four Conditions for Provisional Release

8.5.128 In its *Decision on Motion for Provisional Release filed by the Accused Zejnil Delalić*, 25 September 1996, the Trial Chamber confirmed that four criteria must be met in order for provisional release to be granted:

> Sub-rule 65(B) establishes the criteria which must be satisfied before a Trial Chamber can authorise the release of an accused pending trial. These criteria are fourfold, three of which are substantive and one procedural. They are conjunctive in nature, and the burden of proof rests on the Defence. Thus, the Defence must establish that there are exceptional circumstances, that the accused will appear for trial, and that if released the accused will not pose a danger to any victim, witness or other person. Additionally, the host country must be heard. If any of these requirements are not met, the Trial Chamber is not authorised to grant provisional release and the accused must remain detained. (para. 1)

8.5.129 It has since been held that there is no burden of proof on the defence in this matter (see the *Decision in Hadžihasanović et al.*, 19 December 2001).

Exceptional Circumstances

8.5.130 The requirement that "exceptional circumstances" be shown in order for provisional release to be granted was deleted from ICTY Rule 65 at the ICTY twenty-first plenary session on 30 November 1999. The following considerations continue to apply, however, in respect of ICTR Rule 65. It should be noted, however, that some Chambers have held that the deletion of the term "exceptional circumstances" from ICTY Rule 65(B) did not make detention the exception and release the rule. Despite amendment, the focus is still on the particular circumstances of each case. See *Jokić and Others, Orders on Motions for Provisional Release*, 20 February 2002.

8.5.131 Defence submissions to the effect that the ICTR should also cease to apply the "exceptional circumstances" condition have not succeeded. See *Kanyabashi*, Tr. Ch., *Decision on the Defence Motion for the Provisional Release of the Accused*, 21 February 2001, in which the Defence requested the application of Rule 65(B) without the requirement of "exceptional circumstances" in accordance with the ICTY formulation of Rule 65(B). The Defence argued that the ICTR should apply the ICTY Rule instead of the ICTR provision in matters governing detention at the ICTR. The Trial Chamber rejected this argument on the ground that (i) pursuant to Article 1 of the ICTR Statute, the ICTR was established as a "separate and sovereign body, with a competence *ratione materiae* and *ratione temporis* distinct from that of the ICTY" and (ii) pursuant to Article 14 of the ICTR Statute, the ICTR judges are instructed to adopt the

ICTY Rules "with such changes as they deem necessary." Accordingly, the changes to Rule 65 by the ICTY on 30 November 1999 could only be incorporated into the ICTR Rules if the ICTR Judges decided to do so.

Presumption of Detention

8.5.132 The requirement that "exceptional circumstances" be shown in order for provisional release to be ordered means that detention is the rule and provisional release the exception. As stated, this consideration now only applies at the ICTR, not at the ICTY. Before amendment of ICTY Rule 65, however, the point was emphasised by the Trial Chamber in *Blaškić*, in its *Decision Rejecting a Request for Provisional Release*, rendered on 25 April 1996:

> the Prosecutor emphasised that . . . Rule 65 of the rules sets forth a presumption of opposition to provisional release; that pursuant to this rule, the Trial Chamber may order provisional release only in exceptional circumstances and that the existence of such circumstances has not been demonstrated by the Defence;
>
> Considering that the Rules have incorporated the principle of preventive detention [Detention on Remand] of accused persons because of the extreme gravity of the crimes for which they are being prosecuted by the International Tribunal, and, for this reason, subordinate any measure for provisional release to the existence of 'exceptional circumstances';
>
> . . .
>
> the Trial Chamber considers that it may order provisional release only in very rare cases in which the condition of the accused, notably the accused's state of health, is not compatible with any form of detention. . . ." (page 4)

8.5.133 See also *Decision on Motion for Provisional Release filed by the Accused Esad Landžo*, rendered in *Delalić et al* by the Trial Chamber on 16 January 1997:

> by international standards, pre-trial detention is the exception to the norm. The presumption is against detention and in favour of freedom. However, in certain circumstances, the gravity of the offence may justify pre-trial detention and the onus of showing exceptional circumstance to qualify for release before the trial is shifted to the accused. . . . Such an exception to the general rule is particularly apposite in cases before the International Tribunal, where accused persons are charged with very grave crimes, and in view of the unique circumstances under which the International Tribunal operates. The International Tribunal has no police force of its own, relying on national enforcement mechanisms to carry out its judicial orders. (para. 26)

8.5.134 The need to show "exceptional circumstances" was also emphasised in the *Decision on Defence Motion for Provisional Release* rendered in *Kupreškić* with respect to the accused Vlatko Kupreškić on 15 May 1998. "Exceptional circumstances" were not found to exist in that case.

8.5.135 In the Appeals Chamber *Order* in *Delić* of 31 May 1999, however, the Chamber granted that, "the funeral of a close relative may constitute an exceptional circumstance within the meaning of this provision," while refusing the application *in casu* for other reasons (risk of flight and danger posed to victims and witnesses).

8.5.136 The words "exceptional circumstances" have now been deleted from ICTY Rule 65 (B), so this Rule no longer requires an accused to demonstrate exceptional circumstances before release may be ordered. This amendment does not, however, affect the remaining requirements of this Rule nor does it have the effect of establishing release as the norm and detention as the exception (Tr. Ch., *Decision on Motions for Provisional Release of Miroslav Kvočka*, 2 February 2000, page 4).

8.5.137 See *Decision Granting Provisional Release to Enver Hadžihasanović and others*, 19 December 2001, in which the Trial Chamber stressed that mandatory detention on remand is incompatible with article 5(3) of the ECHR(Decision, para. 7). Article 5(3) of the ECHR provides that, "*Everyone arrested or detained in accordance with the provisions of paragraph 1.c. of this article shall be brought promptl before a judge or other officer authorised by law to exercise judicial power and shall be entitled to trial within a reasonable time or to release pending trial. Release may be conditioned by guarantees to appear for trial.*"

8.5.138 The ICTR still requires a demonstration of "exceptional circumstances" before it will order provisional release under ICTR Rule 65. For example, Kayishema's application for provisional release was refused by the Trial Chamber on the grounds of failure to demonstrate "exceptional circumstances" in its *Decision on the Preliminary Motion filed by the Defence* dated 6 November 1996.

Factors in Deciding Exceptional Circumstances

8.5.139 There are a number of factors for the Chamber to consider in deciding whether "exceptional circumstances" exist, for example "reasonable suspicion" that the accused committed the crime charged (this derives from Article 5(1)(c) of the ECHR), the accused's alleged rôle and length of the accused's detention.

8.5.140 In its *Decision on Motion for Provisional Release filed by the Accused Zejnil Delalić* of 25 September 1996, the Trial Chamber considered three factors in relation to the question of whether the accused had demonstrated "exceptional circumstances" justifying his provisional release:

> In determining whether an accused has established exceptional circumstances the Trial Chamber looks to determine whether there is reasonable suspicion that he committed the crime or crimes as charged, his alleged rôle in the said crime or crimes, and the length of the accused's detention. (para. 21)

8.5.141 On the question of "reasonable suspicion," the Chambers stated that it shall examine any new elements that the Defence may bring to its attention: ". . . To remain lawful the detention of the accused must be reviewed so that the Trial Chamber can assure itself that the reasons justifying detention remain" and ". . . the Trial Chamber rejects the Prosecutor's proposition that additional evidence is not admissible as it goes to the merits of the case" (para. 24).

8.5.142 On the question of the length of detention, the Chamber considered the standards enunciated by the European Commission on Human Rights:

> The European Commission of Human Rights has enumerated seven factors which should be used in examining cases brought under ECHR (the European Convention for the Protection of Human Rights and Fundamental Freedoms]. These factors are: (1) the actual length of detention; (2) the length of detention in relation to the nature of the offence . . . ; (3) the material, moral or other effects of detention . . . ; (4) the conduct of the accused relating to his role in delaying the proceedings . . . ; (5) the difficulties in the investigation of the case . . . ; (6) the manner in which the investigation was conducted; and (7) the conduct of the judicial authorities. (para. 26)

8.5.143 These standards were endorsed and applied in the *Order denying a Motion for Provisional Release*, rendered by the Trial Chamber in *Blaškić* on 20 December 1996:

> CONSIDERING that in the case in point the detention of the accused to date is less than nine months, having begun on 1 April 1996, whereas the crimes of which he is accused are extremely serious; and that, in respect of Article 5.3 of the European Convention, the Commission of Human Rights (hereinafter "the Commission"), as well as the European Court, could consider reasonable, in the cases in which the criteria it has identified were satisfied, time periods of 19 months to 5 years. . . . therefore, that the [detention on remand] does not exceed the reasonable time period pursuant to international principles and particularly those of the European Convention as interpreted by the Commission and the European Court. (pp. 6–7)

Length of Detention

8.5.144 The length of the accused's detention may be an exceptional circumstance. In *Kanyabashi, Decision on the Defence Motion for the Provisional Release of the Accused*, 21 February 2001, the Trial Chamber held that:

> The length of an accused's detention is a factor to be considered in determining whether the accused has shown exceptional circumstances sufficient to justify provisional release.

8.5.145 The Trial Chamber, however, clarified this stating that it remains consistent with international standards that the right to be tried without undue delay be assessed on a case by case basis. They cited the case of *Zimmerman and Steiner*, 13 July 1983, Series A, No. 66 at para. 24, in which the European Court of Human Rights held that:

> the reasonableness of the length of proceedings . . . must be assessed in each case according to the particular circumstances. The court has to have regard, *inter alia*, to the complexity of the factual or legal issues raised by the case, to the conduct of the applicants and the competent authorities and to what was at stake for the former, in addition to complying with the 'reasonable time' requirement.

8.5.146 In the *Kanyabashi Decision* of 21 February 2001, the Trial Chamber held that the length of proceedings and accordingly the accused's detention remained within the acceptable time limits.

Ill-Health of the Accused

8.5.147 As highlighted in *Blaškić*, mentioned above, (*Decision Rejecting a Request for Provisional Release*, Trial Chamber, 25 April 1996), the accused's state of health may be considered an exceptional circumstance justifying provisional release. In *Đukić, Decision Rejecting the Application to withdraw the Indictment and Order for Provisional Release*, rendered on 24 April 1996 by the Trial Chamber, the accused was granted provisional release on this ground, subject to the following conditions:

> (1) the accused or his counsel must inform the Registry before his release of his address and of any subsequent change to his address;
>
> (2) the accused or his counsel must send periodic reports of the accused's medical condition through the same channels;
>
> (3) the accused must respond to any summons from the Tribunal if his medical condition so permitted; and
>
> (4) the Government of the country to which Đukić intended to go would not obstruct the execution of requests from the Tribunal in respect of the accused.

8.5.148 In the event, the accused died while on provisional release and his case was discontinued.

8.5.149 A motion under Rule 65 of the ICTR's Rules of Procedure and Evidence for the provisional release of the accused on the grounds of his ill-health was refused by the Trial Chamber in *Rutaganda*, 25 September 1996, since the accused was already receiving appropriate medical attention at a civilian hospital.

8.5.150 Where the Trial Chamber is not satisfied of the existence of 'exceptional circumstances,' no provisional release shall be ordered and the Trial Chamber will not be required to consider any of the other three criteria. See *Kanyabashi, Decision on the Defence Motion for the Provisional Release of the Accused*, 21 February 2001, citing *inter alia*: *Blaškić, Decision portent rejet d'une demande de mise en liberte provisoire*, 25 April 1996; *Delalić et al, Decision on Motion for Provisional Release Filed by the Accused Zejnil Delalić*, 25 September 1996; *Drljaća and Kovacević, Decision on Defence Motion for Provisional Release*, 28 January 1998; *Simić, Decision Relative a la Requete depose par Simo Zaric aux fins mise en liberte provisoire*, 15 April 1999; *Rutaganda, Decision on the Request submitted by the Defence,* 25 September 1996 and *Decision on the Request filed by the Defence for Provisional Release of Georges Rutuganda*, 7 February 1997.

Accused Will Appear for Trial

8.5.151 Another criterion is that the Chamber must be satisfied that, if released, the accused will appear for trial. In the *Order denying a Motion for Provisional Release*, rendered by the Trial Chamber in *Blaškić* on 20 December 1996, the Chamber held that even the offer to post a very high bail bond—1 million Deutschmarks—was not sufficient to satisfy the Chamber that the accused would appear at his trial "because of the gravity of the criminal acts of which he stands accused; of the severity of penalties to which he is liable, and last of his sole offer to reside in his country in Zagreb." (p. 5)

8.5.152 See also *Decision on Defence Motion for Provisional Release* in *Kovačević* rendered by the Trial Chamber on 20 January 1998, which rejected the accused's motion on the grounds that none of the four-fold conditions were satisfied, and, in particular, as regards condition (2)—that the accused will appear for trial—because the authority which offered to accept the accused, Republika Srpska, had not arrested nor delivered a single accused to the Tribunal:

> 27. We find, having given due consideration to both letters submitted by the Defence, that we are not sufficiently satisfied that the accused will appear for trial. It is a matter of public record that the Republika Srpska has not arrested any one of the forty-eight persons publicly indicted by the International Tribunal and believed to be resident in that country. We are also alive to the difficulty of implementing any such guarantee or other conditions of release such as daily reporting to police authorities or house arrest.

8.5.153 In *Jokić and others*, *Decision on Motions for Provisional Release*, 20 February 2002, the Chamber held that the prior voluntary surrender of an accused was significant in the assessment of the risk that an accused may not appear for trial. It is submitted that it is correct to give some "credit" for a voluntary surrender, not least in order to encourage accused persons to surrender themselves to the Tribunal.

Accused Will Not Pose a Danger to Victims, Witnesses or Others

8.5.154 On conditions (2) and (3), see the *Decision on Motion for Provisional Release filed by the Accused Hazim Delić*, rendered on 24 October 1996 in *Delalić et al* by the Trial Chamber and the *Decision on Motion for Provisional Release filed by the Accused Esad Landžo*, rendered on 16 January 1997 in *Delalić et al* by the Trial Chamber.

8.5.155 In *Jokić and others*, 20 February 2002, it was held that the completion of the Prosecution's investigation may reduce the risk of potential destruction of documentary evidence. This reasoning may also apply in relation to the potential threat posed to witnesses.

Host Country Must Be Heard

Position of the Host Country with Regard to Provisional Release

8.5.156 Pursuant to Rule 65(B), provisional release may only be ordered, *inter alia*, "after hearing the host country." The ICTY's host country, i.e., the Netherlands, set out its position on matters of provisional release in a letter to the Registrar dated 18 July 1996 (see IT-95-14-T, p. 3036), in which it stated:

> 1. The Netherlands Government first submits that it is for the Tribunal to determine whether a request for provisional release should be honoured and, if so, under what conditions. The Netherlands Government therefore limits itself to the practical consequences relating to such a provisional release.
>
> 2. An accused person is under the jurisdiction of the Tribunal for as long as he is imprisoned in the Scheveningen detention centre. If released, however, that person will come under the jurisdiction of the Netherlands. If such a per-

son does not have a permit to stay in the Netherlands or has not applied for asylum—one of which will normally be the case—the Netherlands Government is obliged, on the basis of the Aliens Act and pursuant to its obligations under the Schengen agreement, to expel the person concerned from Dutch territory, back to the country from which he came.

3. Only if that person himself applies to the Netherlands authorities for a permit to stay, a permit may be issued—if that is not contrary to specific Dutch interests—for the sole purpose of staying in the Netherlands as long as his presence is required for the proceedings before the Tribunal. The power to take such a decision lies solely with the Minister of Justice of the Netherlands.

4. During such a stay, the Netherlands Government accepts no responsibility with respect to practical matters, such as housing or the protection (including possible surveillance measures) of the person concerned, or any conditions for provisional release which may be imposed by the Tribunal.

8.5.157 In light of this statement of the host country's position, the ICTY Chambers have not considered it necessary to consult the host country on each occasion on which there has been an application for provisional release (see the *Decision on Motion for Provisional Release filed by the Accused Esad Landžo*, rendered in *Delalić et al* by the Trial Chamber on 16 January 1997: "Consequently, it is unnecessary to seek the opinion of the host country unless the Trial Chamber is minded to grant the motion" (para. 2).

8.5.158 Note that Rule 65(B) was amended at the ICTY's twenty-fifth plenary session, held on 12–13 December 2001, to provide that, as well as the host country, "the State to which the accused seeks to be released," must also be afforded the opportunity to be heard. This is only logical, although one wonders why, if the accused seeks to be released to a country other than the host country, the host country needs to be heard on the matter at all. The answer may be that, if released to a third state, the accused must nonetheless pass in transit to and from the host country.

Appeal of Refusal to Grant Provisional Release

8.5.159 Since the introduction of Rule 65(D) at the thirteenth plenary session on 25 July 1997, provisional release *is* explicitly subject to appeal. The accused Dokmanović appealed the denial of his Motion for Provisional Release by a Trial Chamber on 22 October 1997; this appeal was denied by a Bench of the Appeals Chamber on 11 November 1997 (see Rule 59 *bis* commentary).

8.5.160 "Good cause" in para. (D) requires that the party satisfy the Bench of the Appeals Chamber "that the Trial Chamber may have erred in rendering the impugned Decision" (Bench of the App. Ch., *Decision on Application for Leave To Appeal, Simić et al*, 19 April 2000, page 3). The Bench was not satisfied of a possible error in this case and, therefore, refused to grant leave to appeal to the Prosecutor (the moving party).

Other Decisions on Rule 65

8.5.161 Decision of the Trial Chamber in *Kupreškić et al.* of 15 December 1997, denying motions for provisional release filed by six accused. Replying to the defence arguments, the Chamber noted that, "there are no exceptional circumstances involved in being a 'family' person, that the voluntary surrender of the accused and their 'subordinate' position (as opposed to persons in command of a situation) does not guarantee that they will appear for trial," and, finally, "that the fact that the accused are now in possession of statements of certain witnesses creates an enhanced risk of interference with the course of justice."

8.5.162 Decision of the Trial Chamber in *Aleksovski* of 23 January 1998, denying the defence motion for provisional release.

8.5.163 Decision of the Trial Chamber in *Kovačević* of 20 January 1998, denying the defence motion for provisional release.

8.5.164 *Decision Rejecting a Motion for Provisional Release* of 20 October 1998 in *Kvočka* (factual allegations regarding the accused's guilt or innocence and the national law governing provisional release in the State of which the accused is a citizen are both irrelevant to an application for provisional release).

8.5.165 Decision of the Trial Chamber in *Mucić* of 16 November 1998; and *Order of the Appeals Chamber on the Motion of the Appellant for a Provisional and Temporary Release* of 19 February 1999.

8.5.166 Decision of the Trial Chamber in *Hadžihasanović, Alagić, and Kubura,* 19 December 2001, in which all three accused were granted provisional release.

8.5.167 *Order of the Appeals Chamber on the Request by Hazim Delić for Provisional Release* rendered by a majority of the Appeals Chamber (Judge Bennouna dissenting on the grounds that there was no jurisdiction to entertain the request and declining to pronounce on the merits) on 31 May 1999; and *Order of the Appeals Chamber on Hazim Delić's Emergency Motion to Reconsider Denial of Request for Provisional Release* rendered by the Appeals Chamber on 1 June 1999.

8.5.168 In *Krajisnik,* ICTY, *Decision on Interlocutory Appeal by Momčilo Krajisnik,* 14 February 2002, the Appeals Chamber held that Krajisnik had no right pursuant to Article 21(4) of the ICTY Statute to be present at the hearing of an application for provisional release by his co-accused, Biljana Plavsić. Plavsić was subsequently granted provisional release.

Emergency Application for Provisional Release Can Be Considered by Duty Judge

8.5.169 In *Jokić and Ademi, Decisions on the Defence Motions for Provisional Release,* 21 December 2001, Judge Orie held that pursuant to Rule 28, a Duty Judge could consider an application for provisional release if the matter were urgent. However, he also held that, as a general rule, the Trial Chamber and not a duty judge should examine a motion for provisional release. Only where special circumstances exist, justifying an immediate consideration of the issues, such as a medical or family emergency, will the application warrant examination by the duty judge.

Cross Reference: See also commentary to Rule 72(B)(ii), below.

* * * * *

PROTECTION OF VICTIMS AND WITNESSES

8.5.170

ICTY Article 22 Protection of Victims and Witnesses	ICTR Article 21 Protection of Victims and Witnesses
The International Tribunal shall provide in its rules of procedure and evidence for the protection of victims and witnesses. Such protection measures shall include, but shall not be limited to, the conduct of *in camera* proceedings and the protection of the victim's identity.	The International Tribunal for Rwanda shall provide in its rules of procedure and evidence for the protection of victims and witnesses. Such protection measures shall include, but shall not be limited to, the conduct of *in camera* proceedings and the protection of the victim's identity.

General

8.5.171 A major innovation at the ICTY and ICTR was the emphasis placed from the start on the protection of victims and witnesses. Measures adopted to this end fall into two broad categories: first, institutionally, the establishment of a specialist Victims and Witnesses Unit (now the Victums and Witnesses Section), and second, normatively, the adoption of measures to protect the witness from the public and, in some cases, from the accused.

8.5.172 Information regarding the Victims and Witnesses Section may be found in the tribunals' annual reports. See also, John R.W.D. Jones, "Protection of Victims and Witnesses," Ch. 31.4, in Antonio Cassese, Paola Gaeta and John R.W.D. Jones (eds.), *The Rome Statute of the International Criminal Court: A Commentary* (Oxford Univesity Press, 2002).

8.5.173 For protective measures adopted in trials before the ICTY and ICTR, see the next section.

8.5.174

ICTY Rule 69 Protection of Victims and Witnesses	ICTR Rule 69 Protection of Victims and Witnesses
(A) In exceptional circumstances, the Prosecutor may apply to a Judge or Trial Chamber to order the non-disclosure of the identity of a victim or witness who may be in danger or at risk until such person is brought under the protection of the Tribunal. (B) In the determination of protective measures for victims and witnesses, the Judge or Trial Chamber may consult the Victims and Witnesses Section.	(A) In exceptional circumstances, the Prosecutor may apply to a Trial Chamber to order the non-disclosure of the identity of a victim or witness who may be in danger or at risk, until the Chamber decides otherwise. (B) In the determination of protective measures for victims and witnesses, the Trial Chamber may consult the Victims and Witnesses Support Unit.

(C) Subject to Rule 75, the identity of the victim or witness shall be disclosed in sufficient time prior to the trial to allow adequate time for preparation of the defence.	(C) Subject to Rule 75, the identity of the victim or witness shall be disclosed in sufficient time prior to the trial to allow adequate time for preparation of the prosecution and the defence.

History of ICTY Rule 69

8.5.175 ICTY Rule 69(B), like Rule 75, was amended at the ICTY seventh plenary session, held on 2–16 June 1995, in order to provide a rôle for the Victims and Witnesses Section in suggesting protective measures for victims and witnesses. The rule was amended at the twentieth plenary session to refer to the Victims and Witnesses Section rather than the Victims and Witnesses Unit, as it had previously been known.

8.5.176 The words, "Judge or," were added to paras. (A) and (B) at the ICTY's twenty-fifth plenary session, held on 12–13 December, 2001.

History of ICTR Rule 69

8.5.177 This Rule was amended at the ICTR fifth plenary session on 8 June 1998. The words, "until the Chamber decides otherwise," were added to para. (A) in substitution for the words, "until such person is brought under the protection of the Tribunal." The words, "the prosecution," were also added to para. (C), indicating thereby that the defence is also under an obligation, subject to Rule 75, to disclose the identity of its witnesses to the other party in sufficient time to allow that party adequately to prepare for trial. At the ICTY, defence disclosure of witness identities is regulated by Rule 65 *ter* (G)(i), which provides for disclosure by the defence of a list of defence witnesses "after the close of the Prosecutor's case and before the commencement of the defence case."

General

8.5.178 The following general comments regarding the protection of victims and witnesses were made by a majority of the Trial Chamber in *Tadić*, in its *Decision on the Prosecutor's Motion Requesting Protective Measures for Victims and Witnesses*, rendered on 10 August 1995:

> 24. In drafting the Rules . . . the Judges of the International Tribunal endeavoured to incorporate rules that addressed issues of particular concern, such as the protection of victims and witnesses, thus discharging the mandate of Article 22 of the Statute. (Annual Report, *supra*, paragraph 75.) Provisions are made for the submission of evidence by way of deposition, i.e., testimony given by a witness who is unable or unwilling to testify in open court (Rule 71). Another protection is that arrangements may be made for the identity of witnesses who may be at risk not to be disclosed to the accused until such time as the witness is brought under the protection of the International Tribunal (Rule 69). Additionally, appropriate measures for the privacy and protection of victims and witnesses may be ordered including, but not limited to, protection from public identification by a variety of methods (Rule 75). Also relevant is the establishment of a Victims and Witnesses Unit within the Registry to provide counselling and recommend protective measures (Rule 34).

Additionally, the Judges recognized that many victims of the conflict in the former Yugoslavia are women and have therefore placed special emphasis on crimes against women in the Rules. (Annual Report, *supra*, paragraph 82.) The Rules make special provisions as to the standard of evidence and matters of credibility of the witness which may be raised by the defence in cases of sexual assault (Rule 96). In particular, no corroboration of a victim's testimony is required and the victim's previous sexual conduct is inadmissible. Additionally, if the defence of consent is raised, the Trial Chamber may consider factors that vitiate consent, including physical violence and moral and psychological constraints.

Witness with a Criminal Record

8.5.179 The Chamber has held that where a witness has a criminal record, that does not disqualify the witness from being granted protective measures, but that it does exclude anonymity as one of those protective measures. In its *Decision on the Prosecutor's Motion Requesting Protective Measures for Witness L*, rendered in *Tadić* on 14 November 1995, the Trial Chamber pointed out that, in its view, "a person does not cease to qualify for the protective measures available to a witness under the Rules just because he has a criminal record." Nevertheless, it went on to say:

> 13. The Prosecutor has very correctly conceded that witness L's conviction in Bosnia-Herzegovina and his participation in crimes allegedly with the accused can be regarded as constituting an extensive criminal background which, because it fails to meet the third criterion [as set out in the *Protective Measures Decision* of 10 August 1995 laying down five criteria to be met before anonymity may be granted to a potential witness. The third criterion reads: "there must be no prima facie evidence that the witness is untrustworthy"], disqualifies witness L from seeking non-disclosure of his identify.

8.5.180 This should not, it is submitted, be interpreted as a *per se* rule that persons with criminal convictions may never qualify for protective measures; the matter natually has to be viewed on a case-by-case basis.

Cross Reference: Rule 67(A) ("reasonably practicable") and Rule 69(C).

Meaning of the "Identity" of the Victim or Witness

8.5.181 In its *Decision on the Defence Motion to compel the Discovery of Identity and Location of Witnesses*, rendered in *Delalić et al* on 18 March 1997, the Trial Chamber, denying the defence motion, held that the "identity" of a witness under Rule 69(C) must be taken to mean the witness's "name, sex, date of birth, place of origin, names of parents and place of residence at the time relevant to the charges to which the witness will testify." It did not, however, include the current address of the witness. Accordingly the Prosecution was ordered immediately to provide the said details of each witness it intended to call at trial. See also *Nyiramasuhuko et al, Decision on the Prosecutor's Motion for, inter alia, Modification of the Decision of 25 September 2001*, para. 22.

Cross Reference: Rule 67(A)(i).

Relationship of Rule 69 to Rule 75

8.5.182 In the Trial Chamber's *Decision on the Application of the Prosecutor dated 17 October 1996 requesting protective measures for victims and witnesses, Blaškić,* 5 November 1996, the Chamber stated, with regard to the relationship between these two Rules:

> 22. ... let us recall that the relief sought by the Prosecutor requires the presence of "exceptional circumstances" (Sub-rule 69(A)) and that, in any case, "the identity of the victim or witness shall be disclosed in sufficient time prior to the trial to allow adequate time for preparation of the defence" (Sub-rule 69(C)).
>
> 23. It is true that the last provision is stipulated "subject to Rule 75." (Sub-rule 69(C)). This reservation, however, serves only to raise once again the question which has already been asked [i.e. whether witness anonymity can be granted], since it subjects the protective measures to the "condition" that they be consistent with "the rights of the accused" (Sub-rule 75(A)). It is therefore completely logical that Sub-rule 75(B)(i) permits "measures to prevent disclosure to the public or the media" but stops short of including the accused.
>
> 24. The philosophy which imbues the Statute and the Rules of the Tribunal appears clear: the victims and witnesses merit protection, even from the accused, during the preliminary proceedings and continuing until a reasonable time before the start of the trial itself; from that time forth, however, the right of the accused to an equitable trial must take precedence and require that the veil of anonymity be lifted in his favour, even if the veil must continue to obstruct the view of the public and the media.

8.5.183 Thus the position would appear to be that Rule 69 allows, in exceptional circumstances, the identity of a witness to be kept from the defence *in the pre-trial phase*, but that once the trial begins, Rule 75 governs, and that this Rule, and Rule 69(C), require the witness's identity to be disclosed to the defence for the trial proper, although the witness may continue to be protected from the public, for example by means of a pseudonym, and/or face or voice distortion. This ruling would therefore seem to exclude witness anonymity (i.e. where the defence does not know the identity of the witness) at trial, contrary to the majority ruling in the *Tadić Protective Measures Decision* of 10 August 1995. However, the *Blaškić* Trial Chamber did not draw this conclusion, and indeed endorsed the criteria adopted by the *Tadić* majority for witness anonymity (see next heading, "Five conditions for witness anonymity").

8.5.184 On a similar point, namely the relation between Articles 21(2) and 22 of the Statute, see the Separate Opinion of Judge Stephen dissenting from the *Decision on the Prosecutor's Motion Requesting Protective Measures for Victims and Witnesses*, rendered by a majority of the Trial Chamber on 10 August 1995:

> That phrase "subject to Article 22" itself repays analysis. What it is in Article 21(2) that is to be subject to Article 22 can scarcely be the combined concept which precedes that phrase, the concept of "a fair and public hearing." It must rather be only one component of that concept, the public quality of the hearing and not its fairness, that is made subject to Article 22, and this for two reasons: first, because, while Article 22 specifically contemplates non-public

hearings, it certainly does not contemplate unfair hearings; secondly, because Article 20(1) itself, unqualifiedly and quite separately from Article 21, requires a Trial Chamber to ensure that a trial is "fair." If this understanding of the phrase "subject to Article 22" be correct and it is primarily the public quality, not the fairness, of a hearing that may have to give way to the need to protect victims and witnesses, that in turn suggests that the kind of protection being thought of in Article 22 is essentially those measures that will affect the public nature of the trial, rather than its fairness. (p. 5027)

8.5.185 Judge Stephen's analysis, it is submitted, is entirely correct. The prevailing position at the ICTs at present is that witness anonymity at trial is not permissible.

Witness Anonymity

8.5.186 In the terminology of the ICTs, witness anonymity refers to keeping the witness's identity from the accused. Confidentiality, or witness confidentiality, refers to keeping the witness's identity secret from the public and media, usually by means of employing a pseudonym, e.g., witness A, while the accused is aware of the witness's identity. While confidentiality is quite common in the tribunals' proceedings, anonymity is rare, if not entirely unheard of, at least at the ICTY.

Five Conditions for Witness Anonymity

8.5.187 Notwithstanding the position set out in 8.5.183 above—that witness anonymity is impermissible—it has to be acknowledged that in its early days, indeed in the first trial, the Tribunal did permit anonymity and laid down conditions for when it would be granted. This turned out to be a rather unfortunate experiment.

8.5.188 In its *Decision on the Application of the Prosecutor dated 17 October 1996 requesting protective measures for victims and witnesses*, rendered in *Blaškić* on 5 November 1996, the Trial Chamber, following the *Decision on the Prosecutor's Motion requesting protective measures for victims and witnesses* rendered by a majority of the Trial Chamber in *Tadić* on 10 August 1995, stipulated that for witness anonymity to be granted, the following five conditions would have to be met.

> First and foremost, there must be real fear for the safety of the witness or her or his family.
>
> Secondly, the testimony of the particular witness must be important to the Prosecutor's case.
>
> Thirdly, the Trial Chamber must be satisfied that there is no prima facie evidence that the witness is untrustworthy.
>
> Fourthly, the ineffectiveness or non-existence of a witness protection programme is another point that . . . has considerable bearing on any decision to grant anonymity . . .
>
> Finally, any measures taken should be strictly necessary. If a less restrictive measure can secure the required protection, that measure should be applied. (para. 41)

Three Further Criteria

8.5.189 In *Milošević, Decision on Prosecution Motion for Provisional Protective Measures Pursuant to Rule 69*, 19 February 2002, the Trial Chamber referred to three criteria which need to be considered in respect of applications made under Rule 69(A) for specific protective measures for witnesses. They are:

> (a) the likelihood that Prosecution witnesses will be identified with or intimidated once their identity is made known to the accused and his legal counsel, but not the public;
>
> (b) the extent to which the power to make protective orders can be used not only to protect individual victims and witnesses in the particular trial, and measures which simply make it easier for the Prosecution to bring cases against other persons in the future; and
>
> (c) the length of time before the trial at which the identity of the victims and witnesses must be disclosed to the accused.(The Prosecution accepted in [another] case that, although the shorter the time between the disclosure and testifying the less the opportunity will be for interference with that witness, the time allowed for preparation must be time *before trial commences* rather than before the witness gives evidence. What time frame is reasonable will depend on the category of the witness.)

8.5.190 In this decision in *Milošević*, the Trial Chamber noted with regret that the granting of such protective measures, which had started out as an exceptional practice, had become almost the norm in proceedings before the Tribunal. The Chamber further noted that the practice had followed *individual* applications for protective measures rather than *blanket* orders keeping the identity of witnesses from the accused. The Trial Chamber stated that while it is extremely important to provide adequately for the protection of victims and witnesses, the requirement that the accused be given a fair trial dictates that Trial Chambers only grant protective measures where it is properly shown in the circumstances of each such witness that the protective measures meet the standards set out in the Statute, Rules and expanded in the jurisprudence (para. 28).

Guidelines for Witness Anonymity

8.5.191 In the *Decision on the Prosecutor's Motion Requesting Protective Measures for Victims and Witnesses*, rendered by a majority in *Tadić* on 10 August 1995, with Judge Stephen dissenting, the Trial Chamber issued the following guidelines concerning witness anonymity:

> 71. Firstly, the Judges must be able to observe the demeanour of the witness, in order to assess the reliability of the testimony. . . . Secondly, the Judges must be aware of the identity of the witness, in order to test the reliability of the witness. . . . Thirdly, the defence must be allowed ample opportunity to question the witness on issues unrelated to his or her identity or current whereabouts, such as how the witness was able to obtain the incriminating information but still excluding information that would make the true name traceable. Finally, the identity of the witness must be released when there are no longer reasons to fear for the security of the witness.

...

73. ... As long as the Trial Chamber adheres to these guidelines, the Trial Chamber should order appropriate measures for anonymity of vulnerable witnesses, bound as it is by its mandated obligation to offer protection to them in the process of conducting a fair trial.

...

77. Initially, the Trial Chamber must consider the factors that apply to all witnesses. First, with respect to the objective aspect of the criterion that there must be real fear for the safety of the witness, it is generally sufficient for a court to find that the ruthless character of an alleged crime justifies such fear of the accused and his accomplices. The alleged crimes are, without doubt, of a nature that warrants such a finding. Secondly, the Prosecutor has sufficiently demonstrated the importance of the witnesses to prove the counts of the indictment to which they intend to testify. Thirdly, no evidence has been produced to indicate that any of the witnesses is untrustworthy. Fourthly, the International Tribunal is in no position to protect the witnesses and or members of their family after they have testified. When applying these principles to the specific circumstances that can justify anonymity in an individual case, the evidence with regard to each of the five witnesses pseudonymed G, H, I, J and K must be examined separately.

Withdrawal of Anonymity

8.5.192 The anonymity of a witness may be withdrawn by order of a Trial Chamber if the witness makes his or her willingness to testify in open session known. In its *Decision on the Prosecutor's Motion to Withdraw Protective Measures for Witness K*, dated 12 November 1996, the Trial Chamber granted the request of the Prosecutor to withdraw the protective measures for witness K, put in place by its *Decision on the Prosecutor's Motion Requesting Protective Measures for Victims and Witnesses* of 10 August 1995, on the grounds that witness K had made her willingness to testify in open session known. The Chamber noted the obligation on the parties to limit their requests for protective measures to those strictly necessary and the practice of the Chamber of implementing protective measures decisions that avoided undue prejudice to the rights of the accused, and further that the motion was unopposed. On these grounds, it granted the motion.

8.5.193 Subsequently, the Trial Chamber withdrew protective measures for witness L in its Decision rendered on 5 December 1996 in *Tadić*. As a consequence of this Decision, the Trial Chamber ruled that "the audiovisual record together with the transcript of the testimony given by witness L may now be released in full." However, this release remained "subject to any redactions that may be required to give effect to protective measures (. . .) granted with respect of other witnesses and to protect ongoing investigations or other confidential material."

8.5.194 Also in *Tadić*, the Trial Chamber applied Rule 75, in conjunction with Rule 71(D), to allow witnesses to testify by video-link. See following section and commentary to Rule 71(D) above.

Measures Stopping Short of Anonymity

8.5.195 For a standard example of measures ordered by a Chamber for the protection of a witness falling short of granting full anonymity, see, for example, the *Order on the Motion by the Prosecution for Protective Measures for the Witness designated by the Pseudonym "O,"* issued by the Trial Chamber on 3 June 1997 in *Delalić et al.*

Protective Measures Must Be Objectively Grounded

8.5.196 Protective measures cannot be granted *solely* on the basis of fears expressed by witness. The determination of the need to order protective measures for witnesses cannot be made purely on the *subjective* basis of either fear expressed by a witness or their willingness to testify at trial if their security is guaranteed. The Chamber must be satisfied that an *objective* situation exists whereby the security of the said witness is or may be at stake, which accounts for such a fear. Only in such a case would protective measures be warranted. See *Tadić, Decision on the Prosecutor's Motion Requesting Protective Measures for Victims and Witnesses*, 10 August 1995, "for a witness to qualify for protection . . . , there must be a real fear for the safety of the witness or her or his family, and that there must always be an objective basis to underscore this fear. . .":

> The Trial Chamber concludes, however, that for a witness to qualify for protection of his identity from disclosure to the public and the media, this fear must be expressed explicitly by the witness and based on circumstances which can objectively be seen to cause fear. (para. 25)

8.5.197 See also *Brdjanin and Talić, Decision on Motion for Protective Measures*, 3 July 2000 at paragraph 26, "Any fears expressed by potential witnesses themselves that they may be in danger or at risk are not in themselves sufficient to establish any real likelihood that they may be in danger or at risk. Something more than that must be demonstrated. . . ." This also makes sense inasmuch as witnesses may not be aware of the measures that may be put in place to assure their safety when they express their fear of testifying.

8.5.198 See also *Rutaganda, Decision on Protective Measures for Defence Witnesses*, 13 July 1998 at para. 9; *Bagilishema, Decision on the Prosecutor's Motion for Witness Protection*, 17 September 1999; and *Nteziryano, Decision on the Defence Motion for Protective Measures for Witnesses*, 18 September 2001, para. 6.

Redaction of Witness Statements

8.5.199 "Redaction" of a document refers to the practice of striking out parts of the document, usually with a thick, felt pen, to render those parts illegible, usually for the purpose of not revealing sensitive or confidential material.

8.5.200 The ICTR has held that the Prosecution should not redact witness statements without an order from the Chamber. See the *Decision on the Motion filed by the Prosecutor on the Protection of Victims and for Witnesses* rendered by the Trial Chamber in *Ruzindana* on 31 January 1997:

> WHEREAS, pursuant to Rule 69(A) of the Rules, non-disclosure by the Prosecutor of the identity of a victim or witness can only be administered if she has first obtained a court order for such measures from the Trial Chamber, and in any case, only when exceptional circumstances are shown;
>
> WHEREAS, in this case, the Tribunal notes *ex officio* that the Prosecutor independently decided not to disclose the identity of victims and witnesses to the Defence, without first requesting an order from a Trial Chamber as required under Rule 69(A) of the Rules;
>
> WHEREAS the Prosecutor thereby wrongfully submitted to the Defence versions in which identifying information on victims and witnesses were redacted, even if, had the Prosecutor first obtained an order to that effect, she would have been legally entitled to do so . . .

8.5.201 This does not mean, however, that redaction can only take place after the Chamber has ordered protective measures for victims and witnesses under Rule 69. The Chamber can authorise temporary redaction, pending a protective measures order. See *Decision to withdraw assigned counsel and to allow the Prosecutor temporarily to redact identifying information of her witnesses*, rendered by the Trial Chamber in *Musema* on 18 November 1997:

> HAVING RECEIVED, during the initial appearance of the accused, the Prosecutor's oral request pursuant to Rule 69 of the Rules for permission to temporarily redact the names and identifying information of the Prosecutor's witnesses in the supporting material until such time as the Chamber has ordered measures for the protection of her witnesses;
>
> . . .
>
> 9. The Tribunal finds that there are good reasons to grant the Prosecutor's request to redact the identifying information relating to her witnesses.

Decisions on the Protection of Victims and Witnesses

8.5.202 The ICTR ordered protective measures for witnesses in a *Decision on the Preliminary Motion submitted by the Prosecutor for Protective Measures for Witnesses*, rendered by the Trial Chamber on 26 September 1996 in *Rutaganda*. The Chamber based itself, in part, on the ICTY's early case-law on this subject:

> TAKING INTO CONSIDERATION the jurisprudence of the International Criminal Tribunal for the Former Yugoslavia, notably its decisions of 10 August 1995 and 14 November 1995. . . .

8.5.203 The Chamber granted a range of measures stopping short of full anonymity. The identities of the witnesses in question were not to be divulged to the defence "until such time that the witnesses are brought under the protection of the Tribunal," the wording of Rule 69. Subject to that proviso, it was ordered that, "the Prosecutor shall disclose the names and unredacted statements of the witnesses to the defence in sufficient time to allow the defence to prepare for trial . . ."

8.5.204 This Decision was followed in *Akayesu*, where the same Chamber, ruling on a Prosecution motion for the protection of witnesses, on 27 September 1996, ordered precisely the same range of measures as were ordered in *Rutaganda*.

See also: Decision on the Motion filed by the Prosecutor on the Protection of Victims and for Witnesses, Trial Chamber, *Kayishema*, 6 November 1996; *Decision on the Motion filed by the Prosecutor on the Protection of Victims and for Witnesses*, Trial Chamber, *Ruzindana*, 31 January 1997; *Decision on the Motion filed by the Prosecutor on the Protection of Victims and for Witnesses*, Trial Chamber, *Ruzindana*, 4 March 1997; *Decision on the Prosecutor's Motion for the Protection of Victims and Witnesses*, Trial Chamber, *Kanyabashi*, 6 March 1997; *Decision on the Motion filed by the Prosecutor for the Protection of Victims and for Witnesses*, Trial Chamber, *Ndajambaje*, 11 March 1997; *Decision on the Prosecutor's Motion for the Protection of Victims and Witnesses*, Trial Chamber, *Nsengiyumva*, 26 June 1997; *Decision on the Prosecutor's Motion for the Protection of Victims and Witnesses*, Trial Chamber, *Ntagerura*, 27 June 1997; *Decision on the Motion for the Protection of Defence Witnesses*, Trial Chamber, *Kayishema and Ruzindana*, 6 October 1997; *Decision on Protective Measures for Defence Witnesses and their Families and Relatives*, Trial Chamber, *Nsengiyumva*, 5 November 1997; *Nahimana, Decision on the Defence Motion Relating to Violations of the Witness Protection Order by the Prosecutor*, 5 July 2001 (Relationship of Rule 69 to Rule 67 on alibi witnesses).

Cross Reference: Rule 75.

8.5.205

ICTY Rule 75 Measures for the Protection of Victims and Witnesses	ICTR Rule 75 Measures for the Protection of Victims and Witnesses

(A) A Judge or a Chamber may, *proprio motu* or at the request of either party, or of the victim or witness concerned, or of the Victims and Witnesses Section, order appropriate measures for the privacy and protection of victims and witnesses, provided that the measures are consistent with the rights of the accused.
(B) A Chamber may hold an *in camera* proceeding to determine whether to order:
(i) measures to prevent disclosure to the public or the media of the identity or whereabouts of a victim or a witness, or of persons related to or associated with him by such means as:
  (a) expunging names and identifying information from the Tribunal's public records;
  (b) non-disclosure to the public of any records identifying the victim;
	(A) A Judge or a Chamber may, *proprio motu* or at the request of either party, or of the victim or witness concerned, or of the Victims and Witnesses Support Unit, order appropriate measures to safeguard the privacy and security of victims and witnesses, provided that the measures are consistent with the rights of the accused.
	(B) A Chamber may hold an *in camera* proceeding to determine whether to order notably:
	(i) measures to prevent disclosure to the public or the media of the identity or whereabouts of a victim or a witness, or of persons related to or associated with him by such means as:
	  (a) expunging names and identifying information from the Tribunal's public records;
	  (b) non-disclosure to the public of any records identifying the victim;

(c) giving of testimony through image- or voice-altering devices or closed circuit television; and
(d) assignment of a pseudonym;
(ii) closed sessions, in accordance with Rule 79;
(iii) appropriate measures to facilitate the testimony of vulnerable victims and witnesses, such as one-way closed circuit television.

(C) The Victims and Witnesses Section shall ensure that the witness has been informed before giving evidence that his or her testimony and his or her identity may be disclosed at a later date in another case, pursuant to Rule 75(F).

(D) A Chamber shall, whenever necessary, control the manner of questioning to avoid any harassment or intimidation.

(E) When making an order under paragraph (A) above, a Judge or Chamber shall wherever appropriate state in the order whether the transcript of those proceedings relating to the evidence of the witness to whom the measures relate shall be made available for use in other proceedings before the Tribunal.

(F) Once protective measures have been ordered in respect of a victim or witness in any proceedings before the Tribunal (the "first proceedings"), such protective measures:—
(i) Shall continue to have effect *mutatis mutandis* in any other proceedings before the Tribunal (the "second proceedings") unless and until they are rescinded, varied or augmented in accordance with the procedure set out in this Rule; but
(ii) shall not prevent the Prosecutor from discharging any disclosure obligation under the Rules in the second proceedings, provided that the Prosecutor notifies the Defence to whom the disclosure is being made of the nature of the protective measures ordered in the first proceedings.

(G) A party to the second proceedings seeking to rescind, vary or augment protective measures ordered in the first proceedings must apply:
(i) to any Chamber, however constituted, remaining seized of the first proceedings;

(c) giving of testimony through image- or voice-altering devices or closed circuit television; and
(d) assignment of a pseudonym;
(ii) closed sessions, in accordance with Rule 79;
(iii) appropriate measures to facilitate the testimony of vulnerable victims and witnesses, such as one-way closed circuit television.

(C) A Chamber shall control the manner of questioning to avoid any harassment or intimidation.

or
(ii) if no Chamber remains seized of the first proceedings, to the Chamber seized of the second proceedings.
(H) Before determining an application under paragraph (G) (ii) above, the Chamber seized of the second proceedings shall obtain all relevant information from the first proceedings, and shall consult with any Judge who ordered the protective measures in the first proceedings, if that Judge remains a Judge of the Tribunal.
(I) An application to a Chamber to rescind, vary or augment protective measures in respect of a victim or witness may be dealt with either by the Chamber or by a Judge of that Chamber, and any reference in this Rule to "a Chamber" shall include a reference to "a Judge of that Chamber."

History of ICTY Rule 75

8.5.206 The title of Rule 75 was amended at the fifth plenary session in January 1995 for the purpose of "clarifying the rules" (ICTY second Annual Report, para. 21, fn. 6). The previous heading, "Protection of Victims and Witnesses," had been identical to that of Rule 69, and the amendment was intended to avoid any possible confusion. The rule was amended at the fifth plenary session, replacing the phrase "*ex parte (non-contradictoire)*" with "*in camera*," to make clear that only the public are excluded from such proceedings and that the accused is entitled to be present. Rule 75 was again amended at the seventh plenary session, held on 2–16 June 1995. The amendment to Rule 75, like that to Rule 69(B), amended at the same plenary and for the same reason, enabled the Victims and Witnesses Section, in addition to a witness or the parties concerned, to request a Judge or Trial Chamber to order appropriate measures for the privacy and protection of witnesses. At the twentieth plenary session, 30 June 1999–2 July 1999, the reference in Rule 75(A) to the "Victims and Witnesses Unit" was changed to the "Victims and Witnesses Section," in line with the Unit's name-change. Para. (D) was added at the twenty-first plenary session on 30 November 1999. The last clause of para. (D) (". . . after consulting . . .") was added on 19 January 2001, after the twenty-third plenary session. Para. (D) was amended at the ICTY's twenty-fifth plenary session, held on 12–13 December, 2001, stylistically and to add the final sub-paragraph "During appellate proceedings . . . order made by the Trial Chamber."

8.5.207 The rule was further extensively amended at the twenty-sixth plenary session held on 11 and 12 July 2002, adding and/or modifying paras. (D), (E), (F), (G) and (H). A new para. (C) was added on 12 December 2002, with the other paras. being renumbered accordingly.

History of ICTR Rule 75

8.5.208 This Rule was amended in minor ways at the ICTR fifth plenary session on 8 June 1998.

Measures Taken

8.5.209 A range of measures has been taken to protect witnesses appearing before the ICTs. In principle, trial proceedings are open to the public and are televised. However, several witnesses have asked, and the court has granted, that their visual image and voice be distorted so that they cannot be recognised by the general public. A remote witness room is available from which witnesses can give testimony by way of closed circuit television. This enables them to testify without having to see the accused while technical arrangements have been made enabling those in court (or the judges alone) to see the witness while giving testimony. The Trial Chamber ordered certain of these protective measures in the first trial, *Tadić*.

Precarious Security Situation in Rwanda

8.5.210 Both Prosecution and defence have invoked the almost omnipresent danger to victims and witnesses in Rwanda to request blanket orders for the protection of all witnesses as opposed to specifically named witnesses. See *Decision on the Prosecutor's Motion for the Protection of Victims and Witnesses* rendered by the Trial Chamber in *Bagosora* on 31 October 1997. The Prosecutor requested blanket protection for two categories of witnesses:

> Category A: Any person residing in Rwanda who may be called as a prosecution witness during the trial of the accused unless he waives the application of the protective measures available, after having been notified about them.
>
> Category B: Any person residing outside Rwanda who may be called as a prosecution witness during the trial of the accused, who express fear for his or her safety and indicates to the office of the prosecutor his or her desire to have the protective measures extended to him or her.

8.5.212 In support of the Motion, the Prosecutor submitted affidavits to the effect that, ". . . the security situation in Rwanda is volatile and that, by January through December 1996, 227 genocide survivors and their associates were killed and 56 were injured and that Gisenyi prefecture, the birth place of the accused is also insecure."

8.5.213 The Chamber granted the request for non-disclosure to the public and media of the identities of the witnesses in question, providing however that the Prosecutor "furnish[ed] particulars of the victims and witnesses in category A and B . . . to the victims and witnesses support unit (VWU) thereby enabling the unit to initiate appropriate steps to implement the protective measures." The identities of the witnesses would temporarily not be revealed to the defence "until such time as they are under the protection of the Tribunal," but would have to be disclosed "in sufficient time prior to the trial to allow the defence to rebut any evidence that prosecution witnesses may raise."

Testifying Away from the Seat of the ICTR as a Safety Measure

8.5.214 In *Nahimana et al, Decision on the Prosecutor's Application to Add Witness X to its List of Witnesses and for Protective Measures*, 14 September 2001, the Prosecution argued that it was not possible to provide for the necessary security measures in Arusha and requested that their witness be allowed to testify in The Hague. The Trial Chamber held that under the Tribunal's Rules a change of venue is permitted (para. 33). However, on balance they considered that it would be possible to adopt sufficient measures to ensure that the witness could testify in Arusha.

Preventing Disclosure of Witness Statements to the Public and Media

8.5.215 Following the disclosure to the media of a prosecution witness statement in *Blaškić*, the Trial Chamber rendered a Decision, dated 6 June 1997, in which it ordered a set of measures designed to prevent the recurrence of such an episode:

> ORDERS that . . . the accused, his counsels and their representatives not disclose to the public or to the media the name of the witnesses residing in the territory of the former Yugoslavia or any information which would permit them to be identified, unless absolutely necessary for the preparation of the defence;
>
> ORDERS the Prosecutor and the Defence to maintain a log indicating the name, address and position of each person who has received a copy of a witness statement as well as the date it occurred and to submit the log to the Trial Chamber whenever it so requests;
>
> ORDERS the Prosecutor and the Defence to instruct those persons who have received a copy of the statements not to reproduce them—under pain of sanction for contempt of the Tribunal—and to return the said documents as soon as they are no longer required;
>
> ORDERS the Prosecutor and the Defence to verify that those individuals who have received a copy of the statements comply strictly with their obligation not to reproduce them and to return them as soon as they are no longer required.

Meaning of "Public" for Purposes of "Non-Disclosure to the Public"

8.5.216 See *Decision on Prosecution Motion to Protect Victims and Witnesses* rendered in *Kunarac* on 29 April 1998. The Trial Chamber stated:

> For the purposes of this Decision, the term "public" does not include those entities or persons who are assisting the accused, his counsel or the Prosecutor in the preparation of their cases.

Exception to Ban on Disclosure to Third Parties

8.5.217 Usually a Trial Chamber would not order a *complete* ban on disclosure to third parties, but would rather order no disclosure to third parties "unless absolutely necessary" for trial preparation. See, for example, the *Decision on the Defence Motion for Protective Measures for Defence Witnesses* dated 30 September 1998. Thus in that

Decision, the Chamber ordered the Prosecutor "not to disclose to any third party outside the Tribunal before their testimony the identity of the Defence witnesses residing in the territory of the former Yugoslavia, unless absolutely necessary for cross-examination by the Prosecutor."

Protective Orders for Victims of Sexual Offences

8.5.218 The ICTs have often recognised that special protective measures need to be adopted for victims of sexual offences. See, for example, *Order on Prosecutor's Motion requesting Protective Measures for Witnesses at Trial* issued in *Kunarac* by the Trial Chamber on 5 October 1998.

Ex Parte Hearings

8.5.219 *Ex parte* hearings have been requested for witness protection purposes, but so far such requests have been refused on the grounds of fairness. In *Blaškić*, in a Decision dated 2 October 1996 (*Decision of Trial Chamber I on the Applications of the Prosecutor dated 24 June and 30 August 1996 in respect of the protection of witnesses*), the Trial Chamber denied the Prosecutor's motion for an *ex parte* hearing based on Rule 75, considering that in the circumstances such a hearing was not consistent with the rights of the accused as provided by Rule 75 (A). The Chamber rejected the Prosecutor's submission that, "[t]here is an accused's right to be present at the trial, but there is no accused's right to be present at every aspect of that trial," holding that:

> The right of the accused to be present at his trial obviously includes every one of its stages, commences from the time the indictment is served, and must be respected both during the preliminary proceedings and the trial itself before the appropriate court. (p. 4).

Tadić Victims and Witnesses Decision of 10 August 1995

8.5.220 As this was the first protective measures adopted by either the ICTY or ICTR, it merits in-depth review.

8.5.221 In a majority decision rendered in *Tadić* on 10 August 1995 (*Decision on the Prosecutor's Motion requesting protective measures for victims and witnesses*), the Trial Chamber majority granted the Prosecutor's request for protection from public disclosure of the names and details of six witnesses and it ordered that their evidence be given in closed session, although edited recordings and transcripts of these sessions would be made available after review by the Victims and Witnesses Unit. The Chamber also authorised the use of screening or other appropriate methods for alleged victims of sexual assault to prevent them being retraumatised by seeing the accused. On the subject of witness anonymity, having reviewed the applicable principles of law and the circumstances of each case, the majority of the Chamber granted the Prosecutor's request in respect of three witnesses who would be allowed to testify without divulging their identity to the accused, subject to a number of safeguards, for example that the Judges should know the witness's identity and be permitted to observe their demeanour throughout the proceedings. The Chamber also ordered that the protected witnesses in this case should not be photographed, recorded or sketched while in the precincts of the Tribunal. A further motion for protective measures for an additional witness was subsequently submitted by the Prosecutor, which was granted by the Trial Chamber on 14 November 1995, in its *Decision on the Prosecutor's motion requesting protective measures for witness L.*

8.5.222 Judge Stephen delivered a separate opinion to the above-mentioned *Decision on the Prosecutor's Motion requesting protective measures for victims and witnesses* of 10 August 1995, denying, in principle, any anonymity of witnesses as far as the accused and his counsel were concerned. This was quoted with approval by the *Blaškić* Trial Chamber in its *Decision on the Application of the Prosecutor dated 17 October 1996 requesting protective measures for victims and witnesses* on 5 November 1996:

> 24. The philosophy which imbues the Statute and the Rules of the Tribunal appears clear: the victims and witnesses merit protection, even from the accused, during the preliminary proceedings and continuing until a reasonable time before the start of the trial itself; from that time forth, however, the right of the accused to an equitable trial must take precedence and require that the veil of anonymity be lifted in his favour, even if the veil must continue to obstruct the view of the public and the media.
>
> . . .
>
> 34. On this question, this Trial Chamber agrees with the conclusion of Judge Stephen in the case *The Prosecutor v. Tadić.*

On Witness Anonymity, see 8.5.186 *et seq.*, above.

Protective Measures Must Be *Exceptional*

8.5.223 Protective measures should not be ordered as a matter of routine. This would undermine the role of the Tribunal to do justice in an open and public manner. Thus the presence or otherwise of exceptional circumstances justifying protective measures must be reviewed case-by-case. See *Decision on Prosecutor's Motion requesting Protective Measures for Witnesses "A" and "D" at trial* rendered by the Trial Chamber in *Furundžija* on 11 June 1998:

> 7. The Trial Chamber finds that the case before it is exceptional for several reasons. The first of these is the situation in the former Yugoslavia, which remains volatile because of on-going ethnic tension and hatred. Witnesses therefore have more to fear for their own safety and that of their family than in countries where peace and stability prevail. Cases before the International Tribunal are therefore not comparable to cases before national jurisdictions in this respect.
>
> 8. This does not mean that every similar case merits the granting of protective measures; such measures should *only* be granted in exceptional circumstances. Each case must be determined on its own merits. The Trial Chamber holds such exceptional circumstances exist in this case. The allegations in this case concern, *inter alia*, a serious case of rape, and the protective measures requested are, therefore, warranted.

Witness Protection and State Cooperation Pursuant to Article 28

8.5.224 In *Semanza, Decision on the Defence Motion for Protection of Witnesses*, 24 May 2001, the Defence requested that the Trial Chamber order the Registry to take all measures to protect the legal status of witnesses in countries of their residence. The Trial Chamber, set out the general position as expressed in *Bagambiki*, that "the Chamber ought not to interfere with the sovereign prerogative of States to control the sojourn of aliens in their territories. . . ." *Bagambiki and Imanishimwe Decision on Motion by Emmanuel Bagambiki's Defence Seeking Orders for Protective Measures for its Witnesses*, 7 September 2000. The Chamber held that subject to this, and noting Article 28 of the Statute which provides for State cooperation with the Tribunal, the Chamber would direct the Registry to 'seek cooperation of States in facilitating the testimonies of Defence Witnesses.' (para. 12)

Refusal of Measures to Protect Against Self-Incrimination by a Witness

8.5.225 In *Nteziryano, Decision on the Defence Motion for Protective Measures for Witnesses*, 18 September 2001, the Defence sought a protective measure to ensure that a witness could refuse to make a statement which might incriminate him. The request was refused by the Chamber on the ground that the protections already provided by the Rules, particularly Rule 90(E), afford sufficient protection in such circumstances (para. 26).

Refusal to Limit Accused's Possession of Protected Material

8.5.226 See *Nsabimana and Nteziryayo, Decision on Prosecutor's Motion for protective measures for victims and witnesses*, 21 May 1999, where the Prosecution requested a prohibition on the accused individually from personally having possession of any material including, but not limited to, any copies of a statement of a witness even if the statement were in redacted form, unless the accused was, at the time of possession, in the presence of his assigned counsel. The Prosecution further requested that the Registry and UN Detention Facility ensure compliance with the prohibition. The Trial Chamber refused to make such an order stating that the request is "overly broad and may impinge (upon) Article 20(4)(b) of the Statute." See also *Nyiramasuhuko and Ntahobali, Decision on the Prosecutor's Motion for Protective Measures for Victims and Witnesses*, 27 March 2001, para. 24 and *Muvunyi et al, Decision on the Prosecutor's Motion for Orders for Protective Measures for Victims and Witnesses to Crimes Alleged in the Indictment*, 25 April 2001, para. 27.

Measures to Prevent Intimidation and Harassment of Witnesses

8.5.227 See *Decision on the Prosecution Motion to Delay Disclosure of Witness Statements*, Trial Chamber, 20 May 1998; and *Scheduling Order, Tadić*, 24 September 1998.

Prohibition on Making Independent Determination of the Identity of Any Protected Witness

8.5.228 See *Nsabimana and Nteziryayo, Decision on the Prosecutor's Motion for Protective Measures for Victims and Witnesses*, 17 June 1999, where the Trial Chamber granted a request prohibiting members of the defence from making an independent determination of the identity of any protected witness or from encouraging or abetting anyone else to try to determine the identity of protected persons. The Chamber held that "granting the Prosecution's request does not lower any ethical duty owed by both Parties." See also *Nyiramasuhuko and Ntahobali, Decision on Arsene Shalom Ntahobali's Motion for Protective Measures for Defence Witnesses*, 3 April 2001, para. 17, and *Decision on Pauline Nyiramasuhuko's motion for Protective Measures for Defence Witnesses and their Family Members*, 20 March 2001, where a similar measure was granted at the defence request.

8.5.229 Of course, in certain instances the defence may be able to ascertain, or at least form an educated guess, as to the identity of an anonymous witness. In such a case, there does not seem to be anything objectionable—on the contrary it is counsel's duty—to use that information to effect in cross-examination, provided that the purpose is not simply to elicit the witness's identity but rather to undermine the witness's credibility and/or otherwise elicit testimony favourable to the examining party.

Protective Measures for Family Members

8.5.230 See *Rutaganda, Decision on Protective Measures for Defence Witnesses*, 13 July 1998, in which protective measures were extended to the spouse and children of the witnesses. In *Nyiramasuhuko and Ntahobali, Decision on Pauline Nyiramasuhuko's motion for Protective Measures for Defence Witnesses and their Family Members*, 20 March 2001, para. 19, the Chamber held that there was a "sufficient showing of the real fear for the safety of the potential witnesses' father, mother, spouse(s) and children," and accordingly granted protective measures pursuant to Rule 75.

Review of Protective Measures

8.5.231 Review of protective measures can be requested at all times on the basis of new information. See *Nyiramasuhuko et al, Decision on the Prosecutor's Motion for, inter alia, Modification of the Decision of 25 September 2001*, paragraph 11, where the Trial Chamber stated

> a review of Decision on protective measures for witnesses, or, as in this case, of one having an impact on the protection of one party's witnesses can at all times be requested on the basis of new information, notably in regard of a change in the circumstances surrounding the initial Decision.

8.5.232 See also *Kamuhanda, Decision of Jean de Dieu Kamuhanda's Motion for Protective Measures for Defence Witnesses*, 22 March 2001, para. 24. The Trial Chamber stated that "the Defence is obviously at liberty pursuant to Rule 75 of the Rules, to request a Judge or Trial Chamber, at any time, to amend the protective measures sought or to seek additional measures for its witnesses."

Other Decisions and Orders Under Rule 75

8.5.233 See also *Decision on Prosecutor's Motion for the Protection of Victims and Witnesses*, Trial Chamber, *Kuprešić et al*, 22 January 1998; *Order to Protect Victims and Witnesses*, Trial Chamber, *Kordić and Čerkez*, 27 January 1998; *Decision on Prosecutor's Motion for Protective Measures*, Trial Chamber, *Dokmanović*, 6 February 1998; *Order to Protect Victims and Witnesses*, Trial Chamber (Judges Jorda and Rodrigues), *Milan Simić and Miroslav Tadić*, 17 February 1998; *Decision on the Prosecutor's Motion for Protective Measures*, Trial Chamber, *Blaškić*, 16 July 1998; *Order (Release of Transcript)*, Trial Chamber, *Kuprešić et al*, 10 May 1999.

8.5.234 For defence witnesses: *Order on the Motions for Protective Measures for the Witnesses designated by the Pseudonyms: DA.2, DB.2, DC.2, DD.2, DE.2, DF.2, DG.2 and DI.2., Delalić et al*, Trial Chamber, 11 June 1998; *Kajelijeli, Decision on Juvenal Kajelijeli's Motion for Protective Measures for Defence Witnesses*, 3 April 2001.

* * * * *

TIME LIMITS

8.5.235

ICTY Rule 126 General Provision
(A) Where the time prescribed by or under these Rules for the doing of any act is to run as from the occurrence of an event, that time shall begin to run as from the date of the event. (B) Should the last day of a time prescribed by a Rule or directed by a Chamber fall upon a day when the Registry of the Tribunal does not accept documents for filing it shall be considered as falling on the first day thereafter when the Registry does accept documents for filing.

History of ICTY Rule 126

8.5.236 This rule was amended at the twenty-fifth plenary session on 12–13 December, 2001, with time now running from the date of the event rather than from the date on which notification of the event would ordinarily have been transmitted. Para. (B) was added at the twenty-sixth plenary session held on 11 and 12 July 2002.

8.5.237

ICTY Rule 126 *bis* Time for Filing Responses to Motions
Unless otherwise ordered by a Chamber either generally or in the particular case, a response, if any, to a motion filed by a party shall be filed within fourteen days of the filing of the motion. A reply to the response, if any, shall be filed within seven days of the filing of the response, with the leave of the relevant Chamber.

History of ICTY Rule 126 bis

8.5.238 This rule was added at the twenty-fifth plenary session on 12–13 December 2001.

8.5.239

ICTY
Rule 127
Variation of Time-Limits

(A) Save as provided by paragraph (C), a Trial Chamber may, on good cause being shown by motion,
(i) enlarge or reduce any time prescribed by or under these Rules;
(ii) recognize as validly done any act done after the expiration of a time so prescribed,
on such terms, if any, as is thought just and whether or not that time has already expired.
(B) In relation to any step falling to be taken in connection with an appeal or application for leave to appeal, the Appeals Chamber or a bench of three Judges of that Chamber may exercise the like power as is conferred by paragraph (A) and in like manner and subject to the same conditions as are therein set out.
(C) This Rule shall not apply to the times prescribed in Rules 40 bis and 90 bis.

History of ICTY Rule 127

8.5.240 Part Ten—and consequently Rules 126 and 127—were adopted by the ICTY at the fourteenth plenary session on 12 November 1997. The ICTR has not adopted this Part. Rule 127 was amended in minor ways on 19 January 2001, after the twenty-third plenary session.

Orders Made Under Rule 127

8.5.241 See *Orders granting requests for Extension of Time* issued by the Appeals Chamber in *Tadić* on 13 May 1998 and 10 June 1998; *Order granting request for extension of time* of 2 July 1999 in *Kvočka et al; Order for Extension of Time* of 6 July 1999 in *Kovačević; Scheduling Order* in *Aleksovski* of 30 July 1999.

8.5.242

ICTR
Rule 7 ter
Time Limits

1. Unless otherwise ordered by the Chambers or otherwise provided by the Rules, where the time prescribed by or under the Rules for the doing of any act shall run as from the occurrence of an event, that time shall run from the date on which notice of the occurrence of the event has been received in the normal course of transmission by counsel for the accused or the Prosecutor as the case may be.
2. Where a time limit is expressed in days, only ordinary calendar days shall be counted. Weekdays, Saturdays, Sundays and public holidays shall be counted as days. However, should the time limit expire on a Saturday, Sunday or public holiday, the time limit shall automatically be extended to the subsequent working day.

History of ICTR Rule 7 *ter*

8.5.243 This rule was added at the tenth plenary session on 30–31 May, 2001.

* * * * *

PRELIMINARY PROCEEDINGS
8.5.244

ICTY Rule 62 Initial Appearance of Accused	ICTR Rule 62 Initial Appearance of Accused

Upon the transfer of an accused to the seat of the Tribunal, the President shall forthwith assign the case to a Trial Chamber. The accused shall be brought before that Trial Chamber or a Judge thereof without delay, and shall be formally charged. The Trial Chamber or the Judge shall:
(i) satisfy itself, himself or herself that the right of the accused to counsel is respected;
(ii) read or have the indictment read to the accused in a language the accused speaks and understands, and satisfy itself, himself or herself that the accused understands the indictment;
(iii) inform the accused that, within thirty days of the initial appearance, he or she will be called upon to enter a plea of guilty or not guilty on each count, but that, should the accused so request, he or she may immediately enter a plea of guilty or not guilty on one or more count;
(iv) if the accused fails to enter a plea at the initial or any further appearance, enter a plea of not guilty on the accused's behalf;
(v) in case of a plea of not guilty, instruct the Registrar to set a date for trial;
(vi) in case of a plea of guilty:
  (a) if before the Trial Chamber, act in accordance with Rule 62 *bis*, or
  (b) if before a Judge, refer the plea to the Trial Chamber so that it may act in accordance with Rule 62 *bis*;
(vii) instruct the Registrar to set such other dates as appropriate.
	(A) Upon his transfer to the Tribunal, the accused shall be brought before a Trial Chamber or a Judge thereof without delay, and shall be formally charged. The Trial Chamber or the Judge shall:
	(i) satisfy itself or himself that the right of the accused to counsel is respected;
	(ii) read or have the indictment read to the accused in a language he speaks and understands, and satisfy itself or himself that the accused understands the indictment;
	(iii) call upon the accused to enter a plea of guilty or not guilty on each count; should the accused fail to do so, enter a plea of not guilty on his behalf;
	(iv) in case of a plea of not guilty, instruct the Registrar to set a date for trial;
	(v) in case of a plea of guilty:
	  (a) if before a Judge, shall refer the plea to the Trial Chamber so that it may act in accordance with Rule 62 (B); or
	  (b) if before the Trial Chamber, act in accordance with Rule 62 (B);
	(B) If an accused pleads guilty in accordance with Rule 62(A)(v), or requests to change bhis plea to guilty, the Trial Chamber shall satisfy itself that the guilty plea:
	(i) is made freely and voluntarily;
	(ii) is an informed plea;
	(iii) is unequivocal; and
	(iv) is based on sufficient facts for the crime and the accused's participation in it, either on the basis of independent indicia or of lack of any material disagreement between the parties about the facts of the case.
	Thereafter the Trial Chamber may enter a finding of guilt and instruct the Registrar to set a date for the sentencing hearing.

History of ICTY Rule 62

8.5.245 Para. (iv) was amended, and paras. (v) and (vi) added, at the fifth plenary session in January 1995 for the purposes of "completeness" (second Annual Report, para. 21, fn. 6). Previously, para. (iv) simply read, "instruct the Registrar to set a date for trial." Para. (vi) fills a lacuna in the Rules as to the effects of a guilty plea, and para. (vii) provides a 'catch-all' for all the other various matters which have to be dealt with after the accused's initial appearance, notably status conferences. Para. (iii) was amended at the seventh plenary session held on 12–16 June 1995, to make clear that the defendant must plead *to each count* of the indictment, and not to the indictment as a whole, unless so agreed. The Rule was again amended in various ways at the fourteenth plenary session on 12 November 1997. A new para. (iii) was added at the nineteenth plenary session, on 17 December 1998, with the other paras. being renumbered accordingly. The purpose of the amendment appears to have been to ensure that the accused would have time to consider his plea and to consult with his counsel on the matter, rather than entering a plea immediately upon his first appearance before the Tribunal.

8.5.246 Rule 62 was amended at the twenty-first plenary session on 30 November 1999 to allow an initial appearance to be held before a single Judge, rather than the whole Trial Chamber. In the event of a guilty plea, the single Judge would not, however, be permitted to proceed in accordance with Rule 62 *bis* but would have to refer the matter to the full Trial Chamber to do so.

History of ICTR Rule 62

8.5.247 Para. (A) (v) of this Rule was amended at the Fifth Plenary Session on 8 June 1998 to incorporate the conditions for accepting a guilty plea which appear in ICTY Rule 62 *bis*. Rule 62 *bis* had been added at the ICTY in light of an uninformed plea which had been entered by the accused in the *Erdemović* case, and which he was subsequently allowed to change (see 8.5.263).

ICTY Initial Appearances

8.5.248 For information concerning ICTY detainees and the dates of their initial appearances, see www.un.org/icty/glance/index.htm.

8.5.249 Under an amendment to Rule 15(E) adopted on 5 July 1996, initial appearances are "routine matters" which may be conducted by a Chamber "in the absence of one or more of its members."

Prosecutor Has No Role in Assignment of a Case to a Trial Chamber

8.5.250 See the *Order of the President on Applications to assign a case to a Trial Chamber* of 21 April 1998, in *Meakić and others* and *Sikirica and others:*

> NOTING an "Application for Assignment of Case to Trial Chamber II *bis*" . . . filed by the Office of the Prosecutor ("Prosecution") on 9 April 1998 and the

"Application for Assignment of Case to Trial Chamber II" . . . filed by the Prosecution on 16 April 1998 (together the "Applications");

CONSIDERING that the Applications request that the Trial Chamber currently assigned to hear the case of *Prosecutor v. Milan Kovačević* (IT-97-24-PT) also be assigned to hear the present cases and further indicate the intention of the Prosecution to request the concurrent presentation of evidence against the accused Miroslav Kvočka, Mladen Radić, Zoran Zigić and Milan Kovačević;

FURTHER CONSIDERING the Applications to be a misuse of Article 14 of the Statute of the International Tribunal and Rule 62 of the Rules of Procedure and Evidence as neither of these provisions contemplate a role for the Prosecution in the assignment of cases to Trial Chambers and the request affects the rights of all of the aforementioned accused without affording them the opportunity to be heard;

. . .

HEREBY dismiss the Application AND

ORDER that these issues be discussed by the Prosecution and the Defence for Miroslav Kvočka, Mladen Radić, Zoran Zigić and Milan Kovačević before Trial Chamber II as part of the pre-trial proceedings in the case of *Prosecutor v. Milan Kovačević*.

Conditions for Accepting a Guilty Plea

8.5.251 To be accepted, a guilty plea must be made voluntarily and in full cognisance of the nature of the charge and its consequences.

8.5.254 The conditions for accepting a guilty plea are now explicitly addressed by Rule 62 *bis*. This Rule was introduced in light of the problems encountered in accepting the accused's guilty plea in *Erdemović*.

8.5.255 In its *Sentencing Judgement* rendered on 29 November 1996 in *Erdemović*, the Trial Chamber enquired into the validity of the guilty plea which had been entered by the accused to a count of crimes against humanity:

10. . . . Dražen Erdemović pleaded guilty, pursuant to the provisions of Article 20(3) of the Statute and Rule 62 of the Rules, to the count of a crime against humanity and stated his consent to the version of the events as set forth briefly by the Prosecutor. He added the following, however:

Your Honour, I had to do this. If I had refused, I would have been killed together with the victims. When I refused, they told me: 'If you're sorry for them, stand up, line up with them and we will kill you too.' I am not sorry for myself but for my family, my wife and son who then had nine months, and I could not refuse because then they would have killed me.

The Trial Chamber . . . considers that, at this point in the proceedings and before reviewing the merits of the case, it should examine the validity of the guilty plea. That validity must be assessed in formal as well as substantive terms.

1. *Formal validity*

11. The Trial Chamber wished to ensure that, starting from the initial appearance, the plea was made voluntarily and in full cognisance of the nature of the charge and its consequences. . . .

8.5.256 The Chamber then reviewed the grounds for believing that such was the case and concluded that the accused understood "the significance of his declarations when he pleaded guilty on 31 May 1996." The Chamber then went on to consider the question of the plea's substantive validity:

> 2. *Substantive validity*
>
> 13. ... the choice of pleading guilty relates not only to the fact that the accused was conscious of having committed a crime and admitted it, but also to his right, as formally acknowledged in the procedures of the International Tribunal and as established in common law legal systems, to adopt his own defence strategy. The plea is one of the elements which constitute such a defence strategy.
>
> ...
>
> While the Defence has full discretion over the strategy it decides to adopt in response to the Prosecution, the Trial Chamber must nonetheless ensure that the rights of the accused are actually respected and, more specifically, the accused's right to counsel. In the case in point, this was done in accordance with the provisions of Rule 62 of the Rules.

8.5.257 This reference to defence strategy in common law systems may be to the practice of an accused pleading guilty to a crime in the hope of receiving a lighter sentence thereby ("credit for a guilty plea"). Controversially, the accused may even be allowed to plead guilty for tactical reasons, while still maintaining his innocence: see for example, the "Alford plea" in the United States. Under *North Carolina v. Alford*, 400 U.S. 25 (1970), and the Model Code of Pre-Arraignment Procedure §350.4(4), a court may accept an accused's guilty plea even though the accused does not admit his guilt, if the court finds that it is reasonable for someone in the accused's position to plead guilty, for example if the evidence against the accused is overwhelming, so that he would almost certainly be convicted—and receive a heavier penalty—if he pleaded not guilty and were tried.

Equivocal Plea

8.5.258 While considering substantive validity in *Erdemović*, the Chamber considered the possibility that the accused's plea was equivocal. It ended, however, by accepting the plea:

> 14. Nevertheless, the very contents of a declaration which is ambiguous or equivocal might affect the plea's validity. In order to explain his conduct, the accused argued both an obligation to obey the orders of his military superior and physical and moral duress stemming from his fear for his own life and that of his wife and child. In and of themselves, these factors may mitigate the penalty. Depending on the probative value and force which may be given to them, they may also be regarded as a defence for the criminal conduct which might go so far as to eliminate the *mens rea* of the offence and therefore the offence itself. In consequence, the plea would be invalidated. The Trial Chamber considers that it must examine the possible defence for the elements invoked.

8.5.259 In this regard, the Chamber examined the Tribunal's Statute, the Secretary-General's Report thereon and post-World War Two jurisprudence and concluded that duress, but not superior orders, could constitute a complete defence:

> 16. In respect of the physical and moral duress accompanied by the order from a military superior (sometimes referred to as "extreme necessity"), which has been argued in this case, the Statute provides no guidance. At most, the Secretary-General refers to duress in paragraph 57 of his report and seems moreover to regard it as a mitigating circumstance.
>
> 17. A review by the United Nations War Crimes Commission of the post-World War Two international military case-law, as reproduced in the 1996 report of the International Law Commission (Supplement No. 10 (A/51/10) p. 93), shows that the post-World War Two military tribunals of nine nations considered the issue of duress as constituting a complete defence. . . .
>
> . . .
>
> 19. . . . while the complete defence based on moral duress and/or a state of necessity stemming from superior orders is not ruled out absolutely, its conditions of application are particularly strict. They must be sought not only in the very existence of a superior order—which must first be proven—but also and especially in the circumstances characterising how the order was given and how it was received.

8.5.260 Nevertheless, in the circumstances, the Chamber held that the plea of duress raised by the accused was not such as to invalidate the plea, but would be taken into account in mitigation at the sentencing stage:

> 20. . . . the Trial Chamber is of the view that proof of the specific circumstances which would fully exonerate the accused of his responsibility has not been provided. Thus, the defence of duress accompanying the superior order will, as the Secretary-General seems to suggest in his report, be taken into account at the same time as other factors in the consideration of mitigating circumstances.
>
> In conclusion, the Trial Chamber, for all the reasons of fact and law surrounding Dražen Erdemović's guilty plea, considers it valid.

8.5.261 This approach was mistaken. Once the Chamber was satisfied that the accused, while pleading guilty, was raising what might amount to a complete defence, then it was obliged to treat the plea as equivocal and thus enter a not guilty plea on the accused's behalf and proceed to trial. Reference to "proof" at the plea stage was misconceived. Proof is a matter of evidence and evidence is not adduced at the plea stage.

8.5.262 Thus the trial proceedings against Erdemović were flawed from the start and had to be reviewed by the Appeals Chamber (which found, by a three to two majority that duress could not be a defence to the killing of innocents and therefore that the plea was not equivocal, although it was uninformed—see next para.) and ultimately had to be remitted to a new Trial Chamber.

Cross Reference: Rule 62 *bis* ("Guilty Pleas").

Article:

Yee, Sienho, "The *Erdemović* Sentencing Judgement: A questionable milestone for the International Criminal Tribunal for the former Yugoslavia," 26 (2) *Georgia Journal of International and Comparative Law*, 263 (1997).

The *Erdemović* Case on Appeal

8.5.263 In its Decision rendered on 7 October 1997, the Appeals Chamber held that the conditions to be met in order for a guilty plea to be acceptable were that it be voluntary, informed, non-equivocal and that it have a factual basis. These conditions were subsequently codified in a new Rule, Rule 62 *bis* (see 8.5.282).

8.5.2664 The majority held on the facts that Erdemović's plea had been involuntary and uninformed, but that it had not been equivocal, since—the majority held—duress was not a complete defence, and so the fact of raising duress while pleading guilty did not vitiate the guilty plea.

8.5.265 Judge Cassese and Judge Stephen both dissented from this view, holding that duress could in certain circumstances constitute a complete defence, hence the plea had been unequivocal, as well as involuntary and uninformed. Moreover, Judge Cassese, while agreeing to the conditions to be met for a guilty plea, dissented from the majority's methodology in deriving the said conditions, which he felt relied unduly on common law authorities.

8.5.266 Judge Li dissented from the view that the accused's plea was uninformed, holding that it was indeed informed, and unequivocal, and acceptable in all respects.

Cross Reference: See ICTY Article 7(4) for commentary on the *Erdemović* Judgement, 6.2.152 *et seq.* and 6.3.38 *et seq.*

Failure to Enter a Plea

8.5.267 If the accused fails to enter a plea to any count, a not guilty plea is entered on his behalf. This was applied in *Kanyabashi* in the *Decision following the Initial Appearance* of the Trial Chamber of 29 November 1996:

> GIVEN THAT, during today's initial appearance, the accused declined to plead to the five counts of the indictment claiming that he was insufficiently represented by defence counsel, for which reason the Chamber registered a plea of being not-guilty to all counts on his behalf

8.5.268 This rule was also applied when Edouard Karemera refused to plead without a defence counsel at his initial appearance on 8 April 1999. The Trial Chamber entered a plea of "not guilty" on his behalf.

8.5.269 Stevan Todorović, at his initial appearance on 30 September 1998, declared himself unfit to plead for medical reasons and the Trial Chamber accordingly entered a provisional not guilty plea on the defendant's behalf.

8.5.270 The conditions explicitly included in Rule 62(v) had already been applied *de facto* when Jean Kambanda pleaded guilty at his initial appearance on 1 May 1998 (see 8.5.278).

Guilty Pleas

ICTY

8.5.271 The following guilty pleas have been received to date at the ICTY.

Erdemović

8.5.272 Drazen Erdemović pleaded guilty to one count of crimes against humanity. After this guilty plea was vacated by the Appeals Chamber, on re-plea, he pleaded guilty to one count of war crimes in respect of the same acts. He was sentenced to 5 years' imprisonment.

Kunarac

8.5.273 Dragoljub Kunarac pleaded guilty to rape as a crime against humanity on 9 March 1998. Pursuant to Rule 62 *bis*, the Trial Chamber undertook to satisfy itself that the guilty plea was not equivocal, involuntary or lacking a factual basis. Applying these criteria, the Chamber found the guilty plea unacceptable and rejected it, entering instead a plea of not guilty on the accused's behalf. Thus a trial proceeded on all counts of the indictment.

Jelisić

8.5.274 Goran Jelisić pleaded guilty to 14 murders, and four acts of torture and plunder as crimes against humanity which he committed in Brčko in the spring of 1992, but he denied genocide in relation to those events. See the document entitled *Factual Basis for the Charges to which Goran Jelisić intends to plead guilty* of 29 September 1998, which contains two annexes, one of which is confidential.

8.5.275 A trial proceeded on the genocide counts only, guilty pleas having been entered by Jelisić to the other counts. A proposal to sentence Jelisić for the charges to which he had pleaded guilty before completing the genocide trial was rejected (*Order in respect of the organisation of the work of the Trial Chamber*, 23 March 1999), and a single sentence of forty years' imprisonment for crimes against humanity and war crimes was imposed at the conclusion of that trial, after Jelisić was acquitted of genocide.

8.5.276 In the *Jelisić Trial Judgement*, the Trial Chamber stated that a guilty plea was not sufficient in itself to ground a conviction. The Chamber must also establish that the guilty plea is supported by the facts (para. 25). It found that the plea in that case *was* supported by the facts.

ICTR

8.5.277 The following guilty pleas received have been to date at the ICTR.

Kambanda

8.5.278 On 1 May 1998, at his initial appearance, Jean Kambanda, who was the former Prime Minister of the Interim Government of the Republic of Rwanda during the genocide and the highest-ranking person indicted by the ICTR, pleaded guilty to Genocide, Conspiracy to commit Genocide, Direct and Public Incitement to commit Genocide, Complicity in Genocide and Crimes against Humanity (murder and extermination). This was the first guilty plea to crimes of genocide ever recorded. At the ICTY, one accused—*Erdemović*—pleaded guilty to crimes against humanity but he was later permitted to withdraw that plea and to enter a plea of guilty to war crimes instead.

8.5.279 The procedure followed by the Trial Chamber in *Kambanda* was *de facto* based on ICTY Rule 62 *bis*—which had been adopted in light of the guilty pleas entered by the accused in *Erdemović* (see ICTY Rule 62 *bis*). In other words, the Chamber took pains to ensure that the accused understood the nature of the charges against him, that his plea was informed, voluntary and unequivocal, and that it had a factual basis. The factual basis for the plea was largely contained in a "Plea Bargain" agreement signed between the Prosecutor and the accused, which was submitted to the Chamber before the guilty plea was entered.

Serushago

8.5.280 Omar Serushago, a former militia leader of the *Interahamwe* in Gisenyi, at his initial appearance on 14 December 1998 pleaded guilty to four counts of genocide and crimes against humanity, and not guilty to a fifth count of crimes against humanity (rape) (see ICTR Press Release, ICTR/INFO-9-2-155). The fifth count was then withdrawn by the Prosecutor with the leave of the Trial Chamber. See *Decision relating to a plea of guilty* and *Sentence* of 5 February 1999.

Other Rule 62 Decisions

8.5.281 See, e.g., *Decision following the Initial Appearance*, Trial Chamber *Ndajambaje*, 29 November 1996; *Decision following the Initial Appearance*, Trial Chamber, *Gerard Ntakirutimana,* 2 December 1996.

8.5.282

ICTY
Rule 62 *bis*
Guilty Pleas

If an accused pleads guilty in accordance with Rule 62 (vi), or requests to change his or her plea to guilty and the Trial Chamber is satisfied that:
(i) the guilty plea has been made voluntarily;
(ii) the guilty plea is informed;
(iii) the guilty plea is not equivocal; and
(iv) there is a sufficient factual basis for the crime and the accused's participation in it, either on the basis of independent indicia or of lack of any material disagreement between the parties about the facts of the case,
the Trial Chamber may enter a finding of guilt and instruct the Registrar to set a date for the sentencing hearing.

History of ICTY Rule 62 *bis*

8.5.283 This Rule was adopted at the ICTY fourteenth plenary session on 12 November 1997. It has not been adopted by the ICTR. The amendment was adopted in light of the guilty plea entered by the accused in *Erdemović*, which was found by the majority of the Appeals Chamber to have been uninformed and hence *involuntary*, and, by a minority of the Appeals Chamber (Judges Cassese and Stephen), to have been *equivocal* too. See ICTY Article 7(4), 6.2.152 *et seq.*, "Defences . . . Duress," 6.3.38 *et seq.*, and Rule 62 commentary, 8.5.244 *et seq.*

8.5.284 The word "guilty" in the last line of this Rule was changed to "guilt" at the eighteenth plenary session on 9–10 July 1998. "Pre-sentencing hearing" was also changed to "sentencing hearing" in light of amendments to Rule 100 at the same plenary.

8.5.285 A new para. (ii) was added at the nineteenth plenary session, on 17 December 1998, namely the condition that "the guilty plea is informed," with the other paras. being re-numbered accordingly.

Plea Bargains

8.5.286 When *Erdemović* was remitted to a new Trial Chamber, following the Appeals Chamber's finding that his initial plea had been uninformed, the accused changed his guilty plea from that of guilty to crimes against humanity to guilty of war crimes. In its *Sentencing Judgement* of 5 March 1998, the Chamber referred to a "plea bargain":

> VI. PLEA BARGAIN AGREEMENT
>
> 18. On 8 January 1998, both sides filed with the Registry a "Joint Motion for Consideration of Plea Agreement between Drazen Erdemovic and the Office of the Prosecutor." Attached thereto was a plea agreement between the parties, the purpose of which was expressed to be to clarify the understanding of the parties as to the nature and consequences of the accused's plea of guilty, and to assist the parties and the Trial Chamber in ensuring that the plea entered into by the accused was valid, according to the rules of the International Tribunal. The essential elements of the plea agreement were that:
>
>> (a) The accused would plead guilty to count 2, a violation of the laws or customs of war, in full understanding of the distinction between that charge and the alternative charge of a crime against humanity, and the consequences of his plea.
>>
>> (b) The accused's plea was based on his guilt and his acknowledgement of full responsibility for the actions with which he is charged.
>>
>> (c) The parties agreed on the factual basis of the allegations against the accused, and in particular the fact that there was duress.
>>
>> (d) The parties, in full appreciation of the sole competence of the Trial Chamber to determine the sentence, recommended that seven years' imprisonment would be an appropriate sentence in this case, considering the mitigating circumstances.
>>
>> (e) In view of the accused's agreement to enter a plea of guilty to count 2, the Prosecutor agreed not to proceed with the alternative count of a crime against humanity.

19. Plea bargain agreements are common in certain jurisdictions of the world. There is no provision for such agreements in the Statute and Rules of Procedure and Evidence of the International Tribunal. This is the first time that such a document has been presented to the International Tribunal. The plea agreement in this case is simply an agreement between the parties, reached on their own initiative without the contribution or encouragement of the Trial Chamber. Upon being questioned by the Presiding Judge of the Trial Chamber, the accused confirmed his agreement to and understanding of the matters contained therein. The parties themselves acknowledge that the plea agreement has no binding effect on this Chamber, although submissions recommending it were made by both the Prosecutor and Defence Counsel at the hearing on 14 January 1998, in addition to the recommendations in the joint motion. Whilst in no way bound by this agreement, the Trial Chamber has taken it into careful consideration in determining the sentence to be imposed upon the accused.

8.5.287 It is difficult, however, to see the ingredients of a traditional "plea-bargain" agreement in this case since the accused had already pleaded guilty to crimes against humanity and been sentenced by the Trial Chamber. The Appeals Chamber had remitted the matter to this Trial Chamber because the plea had not been informed, and accordingly the accused had been allowed to change his plea to the lesser charge of war crimes. The accused could not, however, realistically have changed his plea to one of not guilty as he had always admitted his guilt and the majority of the Appeals Chamber had rejected the one possible defence—duress—he had raised on the facts. Hence it is hard to understand what this new plea would have been in *exchange* for, or what the "bargain" was, since Erdemović had always admitted his responsibility for the crimes charged. The reference to "plea bargain" seems to be an inappropriate importation of terminology from the American criminal justice system.

8.5.288 One may even question the appropriateness of the institution of allowing guilty pleas in a court such as the ICTY. The ICTY adjudicates international crimes, the elements of which are predicated on matters which an individual accused may not be in a position to admit or deny (such as whether an ethnic group was the target of attacks (for genocide), whether the conflict in question was an international armed conflict (for grave breaches of the Geneva Conventions) or whether a civilian population was subjected to a widespread or systematic attack (for crimes against humanity)). Thus an argument could be made for holding a trial in all cases, with any confession or admissions by the accused being but one element of the evidence in the case, rather than constituting a formal plea and waiver of the right to trial by the accused.

8.5.289 Notwithstanding this, "plea agreements" have also been employed at the ICTY in *Jelisić* and *Plavsić* and at the ICTR in *Kambanda* and *Serushago*.

8.5.290 Jelisić pleaded guilty on the basis of a plea agreement to 31 of 32 counts in a second amended indictment, confirmed on 19 October 1998, during his further initial appearance on 29 October 1998. The 31 counts comprise 15 counts of crimes against humanity and 16 counts of violations of the law or customs of war relating to 12 killings, four beatings and one count of plunder of private property in the Brčko area in 1992. Jelisić pleaded not guilty to the one count of genocide, on which a trial proceeded, with sentencing to take place after the genocide trial. In the event, Jelisić was acquitted of the genocide count at the close of the prosecution case; a finding disapproved of by the Appeals Chamber (see 8.6.9.)

8.5.291 At the twenty-fifth plenary session, held on 12–13 December, 2001, a rule specifically dealing with plea agreements was introduced. See Rule 62 *ter* below.

8.5.292

ICTY Rule 62 *ter* Plea Agreement Procedure
(A) The Prosecutor and the Defence may agree that, upon the accused entering a plea of guilty to the indictment or to one or more counts of the indictment, the Prosecutor shall do one or more of the following before the Trial Chamber: (i) apply to amend the indictment accordingly; (ii) submit that a specific sentence or sentencing range is appropriate; (iii) not oppose a request by the accused for a particular sentence or sentencing range. (B) The Trial Chamber shall not be bound by any agreement specified in paragraph (A). (C) If a plea agreement has been reached by the parties, the Trial Chamber shall require the disclosure of the agreement in open session or, on a showing of good cause, in closed session, at the time the accused pleads guilty in accordance with Rule 62(vi), or requests to change his or her plea to guilty.

History of ICTY Rule 62 *ter*

8.5.293 This rule was introduced at the ICTY's twenty-fifth plenary session, held on 12–13 December, 2001, codifying an existing practice (see Rule 62 *bis*, above).

8.5.294 The rule should, perhaps, also specify that the Prosecutor *is* bound by any agreement specified in para. (A), even if the Chamber is not. Otherwise, the Prosecutor could secure a guilty plea by agreeing with the defence to undertake any of (i), (ii) and (iii) in para. (A), and then, having secured the plea, renege on the agreement. In those circumstances, the rule should at least allow the accused to withdraw his plea.

8.5.295

ICTY Rule 65 *bis* Status Conferences	ICTR Rule 65 *bis* Status Conferences
(A) A Trial Chamber or a Trial Chamber Judge shall convene a status conference within one hundred and twenty days of the initial appearance of the accused and thereafter within one hundred and twenty days after the last status conference (i) to organise exchanges between the parties so as to ensure expeditious preparation for trial;	(A) A status conference may be convened by a Trial Chamber or a Judge thereof. Its purpose is to organise exchanges between the parties so as to ensure expeditious trial proceedings. (B) The Appeals Chamber or an Appeals Chamber Judge may convene a status conference.

(ii) to review the status of his or her case and to allow the accused the opportunity to raise issues in relation thereto, including the mental and physical condition of the accused.
(B) The Appeals Chamber or an Appeals Chamber Judge shall convene a status conference, within one hundred and twenty days of the filing of a notice of appeal and thereafter within one hundred and twenty days after the last status conference, to allow any person in custody pending appeal the opportunity to raise issues in relation thereto, including the mental and physical condition of that person.
(C) With the written consent of the accused, given after receiving advice from his counsel, a status conference under this Rule may be conducted
(i) in his presence, but with his counsel participating either via tele-conference or video-conference; or
(ii) in Chambers in his absence, but with his participation via tele-conference if he so wishes and/or the participation of his counsel via tele-conference or video-conference.

History of ICTY Rule 65 *bis*

8.5.296 Status conferences had been held at the ICTY since the first trial, but a rule confirming this practice was only adopted at the thirteenth plenary session on 25 July 1997. This rule was substantially amended at the nineteenth plenary session, on 17 December 1998. Para. (B) was added at the twenty-first plenary session on 30 November 1999. The old Rule became para. (A) and was amended in minor ways. Para. (C) was added on 12 December 2002, allowing tele- and video-conferencing for status conferences.

History of ICTR Rule 65 *bis*

8.5.297 This new Rule was adopted at the ICTR fifth plenary session on 8 June 1998, following the adoption of a similar rule by the ICTY at its thirteenth plenary session on 25 July 1997.

8.5.298

ICTY Rule 65 *ter*
Pre-Trial Judge

(A) The Presiding Judge of the Trial Chamber shall, no later than seven days after the initial appearance of the accused, designate from among its permanent members a Judge responsible for the pre-trial proceedings (hereinafter "pre-trial Judge").

(B) The pre-trial Judge shall, under the authority and supervision of the Trial Chamber seised of the case, coordinate communication between the parties during the pre-trial phase. The pre-trial Judge shall ensure that the proceedings are not unduly delayed and shall take any measure necessary to prepare the case for a fair and expeditious trial.

(C) The pre-trial Judge shall be entrusted with all of the pre-trial functions set forth in Rule 66, Rule 73 *bis* and Rule 73 *ter*, and with all or part of the functions set forth in Rule 73.

(D) (i) The pre-trial Judge may be assisted in the performance of his or her duties by one of the Senior Legal Officers assigned to Chambers.

(ii) The pre-trial Judge shall establish a work plan indicating, in general terms, the obligations that the parties are required to meet pursuant to this Rule and the dates by which these obligations must be fulfilled.

(iii) Acting under the supervision of the pre-trial Judge, the Senior Legal Officer shall oversee the implementation of the work plan and shall keep the pre-trial Judge informed of the progress of the discussions between and with the parties and, in particular, of any potential difficulty. He or she shall present the pre-trial Judge with reports as appropriate and shall communicate to the parties, without delay, any observations and decisions made by the pre-trial Judge.

(iv) the pre-trial Judge shall order the parties to meet to discuss issues related to the preparation of the case, in particular, so that the Prosecutor can meet his or her obligations pursuant to paragraphs (E)(i) to (iii) of this Rule and for the defence to meet its obligations pursuant to paragraph (G) of this Rule and of Rule 73 *ter*.

(v) Such meetings are held *inter partes* or, at his or he request, with the Senior Legal Officer and one or more of the parties. The Senior Legal Officer ensures that the obligations set out in paragraphs (E)(i) to (iii) of this Rule and, at the appropriate time, that the obligations in paragraph (G) and Rule 73 *ter*, are satisfied in accordance with the work plan set by the pre-trial Judge.

(vi) The presence of the accused is not necessary for meetings convened by the Senior Legal Officer.

(vii) The Senior Legal Officer may be assisted by a representative of the Registry in the performance of his or her duties pursuant to this Rule and may require a transcript to be made.

(E) Once disclosure pursuant to Rules 66 and 68 is completed and any existing preliminary motions filed within the time-limit provided by Rule 72 are disposed of, the pre-trial Judge shall order the Prosecutor, upon the report of the Senior Legal Officer, and within a time-limit set by the pre-trial Judge and not less than six weeks before the Pre-Trial Conference required by Rule 73 *bis*, to file the following:

(i) the final version of the Prosecutor's pre-trial brief including, for each count, a summary of the evidence which the Prosecutor intends to bring regarding the commission of the alleged crime and the form of responsibility incurred by the accused; this brief shall include any admissions by the parties and a statement of matters which are not in dispute; as well as a statement of contested matters of fact and law;

(ii) a list of witnesses the Prosecutor intends to call with:
   (a) the name or pseudonym of each witness;
   (b) a summary of the facts on which each witness will testify;
   (c) the points in the indictment as to which each witness will testify, including specific references to counts and relevant paragraphs in the indictment;

    (d) the total number of witnesses and the number of witnesses who will testify against each accused and on each count;
    (e) an indication of whether the witness will testify in person or pursuant to Rule 92 *bis* by way of written statement or use of a transcript of testimony from other proceedings before the Tribunal; and
    (f) the estimated length of time required for each witness and the total time estimated for presentation of the Prosecutor's case.
  (iii) the list of exhibits the Prosecutor intends to offer stating where possible whether the defence has any objection as to authenticity. The Prosecutor shall serve on the defence copies of the exhibits so listed.
(F) After the submission by the Prosecutor of the items mentioned in paragraph (E), the pre-trial Judge shall order the defence, within a time-limit set by the pre-trial Judge, and not later than three weeks before the Pre-Trial Conference, to file a pre-trial brief addressing the factual and legal issues, and including a written statement setting out:
(i) in general terms, the nature of the accused's defence;
(ii) the matters with which the accused takes issue in the Prosecutor's pre-trial brief; and
(iii) in the case of each such matter, the reason why the accused takes issue with it.
(G) After the close of the Prosecutor's case and before the commencement of the defence case, the pre-trial Judge shall order the defence to file the following:
(i) a list of witnesses the defence intends to call with:
    (a) the name or pseudonym of each witness;
    (b) a summary of the facts on which each witness will testify;
    (c) the points in the indictment as to which each witness will testify;
    (d) the total number of witnesses and the number of witnesses who will testify for each accused and on each count;
    (e) an indication of whether the witness will testify in person or pursuant to Rule 92 *bis* by way of written statement or use of a transcript of testimony from other proceedings before the Tribunal; and
    (f) the estimated length of time required for each witness and the total time estimated for presentation of the defence case; and
(ii) a list of exhibits the defence intends to offer in its case, stating where possible whether the Prosecutor has any objection as to authenticity. The defence shall serve on the Prosecutor copies of the exhibits so listed.
(H) The pre-trial Judge shall record the points of agreement and disagreement on matters of law and fact. In this connection, he or she may order the parties to file written submissions with either the pre-trial Judge or the Trial Chamber.
(I) In order to perform his or her functions, the pre-trial Judge may *proprio motu*, where appropriate, hear the parties without the accused being present. The pre-trial Judge may hear the parties in his or her private room, in which case minutes of the meeting shall be taken by a representative of the Registry.
(J) The pre-trial Judge shall keep the Trial Chamber regularly informed, particularly where issues are in dispute and may refer such disputes to the Trial Chamber.
(K) The pre-trial Judge may set a time for the making of pre-trial motions and, if required, any hearing thereon. A motion made before trial shall be determined before trial unless the Judge, for good cause, orders that it be deferred for determination at trial. Failure by a party to raise objections or to make requests which can be made prior to trial at the time set by the Judge shall constitute waiver thereof, but the Judge for cause may grant relief from the waiver.
(L) (i) After the filings by the Prosecutor pursuant to paragraph (E), the pre-trial Judge shall submit to the Trial Chamber a complete file consisting of all the filings of the parties, transcripts of status conferences and minutes of meetings held in the performance of his or her functions pursuant to this Rule.

> (ii) The pre-trial Judge shall submit a second file to the Trial Chamber after the defence filings pursuant to paragraph (G).
> (M) The Trial Chamber may *proprio motu* exercise any of the functions of the pre-trial Judge.
> (N) Upon a report of the pre-trial Judge, the Trial Chamber shall decide, should the case arise, on sanctions to be imposed on a party which fails to perform its obligations pursuant to the present Rule. Such sanctions may include the exclusion of testimonial or documentary evidence.

History of ICTY Rule 65 *ter*

8.5.299 This new Rule was added at the eighteenth plenary session on 9–10 July 1998. It was amended at the twenty-first plenary session on 30 November 1999. Paras. (E), (F), (G) and (L) were added, with the other paras. also being amended in various ways. The Rule was again substantially amended on 12 April 2001. In particular, new paras. (D), (K) and (N) were added. The Rule was again amended on 19 July, 2001, after the twenty-fourth plenary session.

8.5.300 Rule 65 *ter* was amended at the twenty-fifth plenary session, held on 12–13 December, 2001, to provide that when the Prosecutor and Defence file their list of exhibits on the other party, they must also serve *copies* of the exhibits so listed on the other party. Paras. (E)(iii) and (G)(ii) were amended accordingly.

Juge d'Instruction

8.5.301 The notion of a "pre-trial judge" is partly borrowed from civil law systems, e.g. *le juge d'instruction* in French law. See also the institution of the "Pre-Trial Chamber" in the Rome Statute for an International Criminal Court, Article 57 ("Functions and powers of the Pre-Trial Chamber") *et seq*.

Defence Pre-Trial Brief

8.5.302 Rule 65 *ter* (F) requires the defence to file a pre-trial brief in response to the prosecution's pre-tiral brief before trial. In *Brdjanin and Talić*, ICTY, *Decision on Prosecution Response to Defendant Brdjanin's Pre-Trial Brief*, 14 January 2002, the Pre-Trial Judge stated that the defence pre-trial brief is primarily intended to be a response to the Prosecution's pre-trial brief. It should therefore set some boundaries for the trial prior to its commencement and it is intended to be a tool for identifying areas of possible agreement between the parties so that the trial may be conducted as efficiently as possible.

8.5.303 In *Brdjanin*, the accused filed a three page pre-trial brief. The Pre-Trial Judge ordered the defence to file a statement setting out the defence's views on the legal issues in the case and specifying with which aspects of the Prosecution's pre-tral brief the defence disagreed and why.

8.5.304 See *Practice Direction on the Length of Briefs and Motions*, last revised 5 March 2002. Available at: *www.un.org/icty/legaldoc/index.htm*

* * * * *

PRODUCTION OF EVIDENCE

8.5.305

ICTY Rule 66 Disclosure by the Prosecutor	ICTR Rule 66 Disclosure of Materials by the Prosecutor
(A) Subject to the provisions of Rules 53 and 69, the Prosecutor shall make available to the defence in a language which the accused understands: (i) within thirty days of the initial appearance of the accused, copies of the supporting material which accompanied the indictment when confirmation was sought as well as all prior statements obtained by the Prosecutor from the accused, and (ii) within the time-limit prescribed by the Trial Chamber or by the pre-trial Judge appointed pursuant to Rule 65 *ter*, copies of the statements of all witnesses whom the Prosecutor intends to call to testify at trial, and copies of written statements taken in accordance with Rule 92 *bis*, copies of the statements of additional prosecution witnesses shall be made available to the defence as soon as a decision is made to call those witnesses. (B) The Prosecutor shall, on request, permit the defence to inspect any books, documents, photographs and tangible objects in the Prosecutor's custody or control, which are material to the preparation of the defence, or are intended for use by the Prosecutor as evidence at trial or were obtained from or belonged to the accused. (C) Where information is in the possession of the Prosecutor, the disclosure of which may prejudice further or ongoing investigations, or for any other reasons may be contrary to the public interest or affect the security interests of any State, the Prosecutor may apply to the Trial Chamber sitting *in camera* to be relieved from an obligation under the Rules to disclose that information. When making such application the Prosecutor shall provide the Trial Chamber (but only the Trial Chamber) with the information that is sought to be kept confidential.	Subject to the provisions of Rules 53 and 69: (A) The Prosecutor shall disclose to the defence (i) within 30 days of the initial appearance of the accused, copies of the supporting material which accompanied the indictment when confirmation was sought as well as all prior statements obtained by the Prosecutor from the accused, and (ii) no later than 60 days before the date set for trial, copies of the statements of all witnesses whom the Prosecutor intends to call to testify at trial. Upon good cause being shown, a Trial Chamber may order that copies of the statements of additional prosecution witnesses be made available to the defence within a prescribed time. (B) At the request of the defence, the Prosecutor shall, subject to Sub-rule (C), permit the defence to inspect any books, documents, photographs and tangible objects in his custody or control, which are material to the preparation of the defence, or are intended for use by the Prosecutor as evidence at trial or were obtained from or belonged to the accused. (C) Where information or materials are in the possession of the Prosecutor, the disclosure of which may prejudice further or ongoing investigations, or for any other reasons may be contrary to the public interest or affect the security interests of any State, the Prosecutor may apply to the Trial Chamber sitting *in camera* to be relieved from the obligation to disclose pursuant to Sub-rules (A) and (B). When making such an application the Prosecutor shall provide the Trial Chamber, and only the Trial Chamber, with the information or materials that are sought to be kept confidential.

History of ICTY Rule 66

8.5.306 Rule 66(A) was amended, at the suggestion of the International Law Committee of the Association of the Bar of the City of New York, at the fifth plenary session, "to broaden the rights of suspects and accused persons" (second Annual Report, para. 25: "Originally, (the rule) provided only that the Prosecutor must make available to the defence copies of supporting material 'which accompanied the indictment when confirmation was sought.' This obligation has now been extended to 'all prior statements obtained by the Prosecutor from the accused or from prosecution witnesses.'")

8.5.307 Para. (C) was added at the fifth plenary session in January 1995 "to take account of practical problems that have arisen or may arise in the implementation of the Statute or the Rules" (second Annual Report, para. 22: "It (the amendment) provides that the Prosecutor may apply for non-disclosure of information where its disclosure could prejudice investigations, affect the security interests of a State, or might otherwise be contrary to the public interest. This amendment, which was suggested by the Prosecutor, will facilitate the acquisition of information from governments and other sensitive sources"). As a consequential amendment, the words, "subject to Sub-rule (C)" were added to Rule 66(B) at the same plenary session.

8.5.308 Para. (A) was further amended at the twelfth plenary session, held 2–3 December 1996. The rule was substantially amended at the fourteenth plenary session on 12 November 1997 (see Revision 11 or ICTR Rule 66 for comparison).

8.5.309 The words, "in a language which the accused understands," were added to para. (A) at the eighteenth plenary session on 9–10 July 1998. The words, "within the time-limit prescribed by the Trial Chamber or by the pre-trial Judge appointed pursuant to Rule 65 *ter*," were added to para. (A)(ii) at the same plenary session in substitution for the words, "no later than sixty days before the date set for trial."

8.5.310 At the twenty-first plenary session, Rule 66 was amended in several ways, including by removing the words in para. (B), "subject to Sub-rule (C)." The para. remains in substance subject to para. (C), however, given that the Prosecutor may be relieved of, *inter alia*, an obligation under para. (B) to disclose information by invoking para. (C). Indeed, Rule 66 now provides the Prosecutor with an even broader possibility of not disclosing information since para. (C), as amended, extends beyond an obligation under para. (B) to cover, now, *any* obligation of disclosure under the Rules. The Prosecutor could now, therefore, invoke para. (C) to request non-disclosure of, for example, materials referred to in para. (A), i.e. copies of supporting material, affidavits and other statements. Such non-disclosure could, however, seriously prejudice the defence and vitiate the accused's right to know the case against him. It is to be hoped that para. (C) will not be applied to cover those materials.

8.5.311 Para. (A)(ii) was amended on 19 January 2001, after the twenty-third plenary session, to refer to all "written statements taken in accordance with Rule 92 *bis*."

History of ICTR Rule 66

8.5.312 Para. (A) was amended at the Fourth Plenary Session, held in Arusha on 1–5 June 1997, to introduce certain time-limits within which the Prosecutor must disclose to the Defence the supporting material which accompanied the indictment and witness statements, and also to align the provisions on matters not subject to disclosure with the like provisions in the Rules of Procedure and Evidence of the ICTY. The rule was further amended at the Fifth Plenary Session on 8 June 1998.

Orders Issued by the Accused Are Not "Prior Statements Obtained by the Prosecutor from the Accused" Within the Meaning of Rule 66(A)(i)

8.5.313 See *Decision on the Defence Motion for Sanctions for the Prosecutor's failure to comply with Sub-Rule 66(A) of the Rules and the Decision of 27 January 1997 compelling the production of all statements of the accused*, rendered on 15 July 1998 in *Blaškić*, in which the Trial Chamber refused to give a broad interpretation to the words, "prior statements," which would embrace orders issued by the accused, a military commander. Rather, the words "must be understood to refer to all statements made by the accused during questioning in any type of judicial proceeding which may be in the possession of the Prosecutor, but only such statements."

Accused's Access to His Prior Statements and Those of Prosecution Witnesses Applies Irrespective of How They Were Obtained by the Prosecution

8.5.314 In *Delalić et al*, the Trial Chamber held in its *Decision on motion by the accused Zejnil Delalić for the disclosure of evidence*, dated 26 September 1996, that the reference in Rule 66(A) to disclosure of "prior statements obtained by the Prosecutor from the accused":

> requires the Prosecution to disclose all statements of the accused that it has in its possession. This is a continuing obligation. (para.4)

8.5.315 This was followed in a *Decision on the Production of Discovery Materials*, rendered by the Trial Chamber in *Blaškić* on 27 January 1997. In that Decision, the Chamber, ruling on a defence motion for discovery from the Prosecutor, pronounced upon the application of Rules 66, 67, 68 and 70. Referring to the interpretation of Rule 66(A) just quoted, the Chamber stated:

> A literal reading of the Rules does not permit a different interpretation because such would restrict the rights of the accused as expressly indicated in Article 21 of the Statute.
>
> 35. The reference to the legal standards in effect in developed legal systems—such as those of the United States or France—leads to the same conclusion, namely, that the accused must have access to his own statements no matter how the Prosecution has obtained them.
>
> In this respect, it should be noted that [Rule] 16 (a) (1) (A) of the [Federal Rules of Criminal Procedure] whose wording is very similar to that of Rule 66, states:
>
>> Upon request of a defendant the government [shall] disclose to the defendant and make available for inspection, copying, or photographing: any relevant written or recorded statements made by the defendant, or copies thereof, within the possession, custody, or control of the government, the existence of which is known, or by the exercise of due diligence may become known, to the attorney for the government.

Although in French criminal proceedings the issue does not arise in the same terms because an investigation (*instruction*) is conducted by a specialised judge seeking exculpatory or inculpatory material, the principle posited by the French Code of Criminal Procedure still remains full disclosure of all information at all times (See *inter alia* Article 114, paragraph 3 of that Code).

36. The case-law of both those countries has not restricted the scope of the provisions which are highly protective of the rights of the accused.

37. The principles identified in support of the interpretation of Sub-rule 66(A) lead the Trial Chamber to the decision that all the previous statements of the accused which appear in the Prosecutor's file, whether collected by the Prosecution or originating from any other source, must be disclosed to the Defence immediately.

The same interpretation of Sub-rule 66(A) leads the Trial Chamber to draw no distinction between the form or forms which these statements may have. Moreover, nothing in the text permits the introduction of the distinctions suggested by the Prosecution between "the official statements taken under oath or signed and recognised by the accused" and the others.

38. Furthermore, the Trial Chamber considers that the same criteria as those identified in respect of the accused's previous statements must apply *mutatis mutandis* to the previous statements of the witnesses also indicated in Sub-rule 66(A).

8.5.316 The Chamber, however, made this ruling subject to two conditions, based on Rules 66(C) and 70(A):

— the first derives from Sub-rule 66(C) which permits the Prosecutor to apply to the Trial Chamber for relief from the obligation to disclose evidence which may prejudice further or ongoing investigations or be contrary to the public interest or affect the security interests of any State;

— the second is based on Sub-rule 70(A) which provides an exception from the disclosure obligation for reports, memoranda, or other internal documents prepared by a party, its assistants or representatives in connection with the investigation or preparation of the case. (paragraph 39)

8.5.317 Note, however, that Rule 66(A) is not *expressly* subject to Rule 66(C). Thus, on a literal reading of Rule 66, the Prosecutor cannot apply for relief from the obligation to disclose, under Rule 66(A), supporting material, and statements by the accused and prosecution witnesses, by claiming prejudice to ongoing investigations or that it would be against the public interest or would affect the security interests of a State. ICTR Rule 66(B), like ICTY Rule 66(B) before it was amended, is expressly "subject to sub-Rule (C)." This supports the *a contrario* argument that para. (A) is *not* "subject to sub-Rule (C)" otherwise it would have so stated.

Hearsay Declarant Is Not a Witness Whose Prior Statements Must Be Disclosed to the Defence, Although Prior Statements Must Be Disclosed if Exculpatory Pursuant to Rule 68

8.5.318 See *Decision on the Defence Motion to Compel the Disclosure of Rule 66 and 68 material relating to statements made by a Person known as "X,"* rendered by the Trial Chamber in *Blaškić* on 15 July 1998.

Accused Entitled to Witness Statements in Language He Understands

8.5.319 The Trial Chamber in *Milošević* held that the accused is entitled to receive all witness statements pursuant to Rule 66(A)(ii) in a language he understands so as to comply with Article 21(4) of the ICTY Statute. See *Milošević, Decision on Prosecution Motion for Permission to Disclose Witness Statements in English*, 19 September 2001.

Relationship Between Rule 66(A)(ii) and Rule 73 *bis* (E) on Variation of Witnesses to Be Called by Prosecution at Trial

8.5.320 In *Nahimana et al, Decision on the Prosecutor's Oral Motion for Leave to Amend the List of Selected Witnesses*, 26 June 2001, the Prosecution made an application, after commencement of trial, to vary its list of witnesses pursuant to Rule *73 bis*. It was argued by the Defence that the relevant test as to whether to allow variation was not the "interests of justice" test as set out in Rule 73 *bis* (F), but the showing of "good cause" in accordance with Rule 66(A)(ii) (this formula appears in ICTR Rule 66(A)(ii) but not in ICTY Rule 66(A)(ii)).

8.5.321 The Trial Chamber in *Nahimana* referred to a *Decision* of 2 December 1999 in *Bagilishema*, in which it was held that the purpose of Rule 66 was to give the Defence sufficient notice and adequate time to prepare for trial, and at the same time, to ensure that the relevant Prosecution evidence is not excluded merely on procedural grounds. The principle of "good cause" was accordingly applied at the trial stage. The Trial Chamber also referred to the 27 January 1997 *Decision* in *Blaškić*, in which the need for the Defence to have a clear and cohesive view of the Prosecution's strategy and to be able to make appropriate preparations was stressed.

8.5.322 In *Nahimana,* the Trial Chamber concluded that:

> In assessing the "interests of justice" and "good cause" Chambers have taken into account such considerations as the materiality of the testimony, the complexity of the case, prejudice to the Defence, including elements of surprise, on-going investigations, replacements and corroboration of evidence. The Prosecutor's duty under the Statute to present the best available evidence to prove its case has to be balanced against the right of the Accused to have adequate time and facilities to prepare his Defence and his right to be tried without undue delay. (paragraph 20)

See also *Nahimana, Decision on the Prosecutor's Application to Add Witness X to its List of Witnesses and for Protective Measures*, 14 September 2001.

Disclosure Must Be "Timely"

8.5.323 In *Nyiramasuhuko, Decision on Defence Motions*, 13 November 2001, the Trial Chamber held that in essence, Rule 66(A)(ii) is intended to assist the Defence in its understanding of the case, in accordance with the accused's rights under ICTR Articles 20 and 21 of the Statute. Accordingly, disclosure should be provided to the Defence in advance of trial so as to allow sufficient time for case preparation and investigation. The Chamber weighed the statutory rights of the Accused to prepare their defence in sufficient time prior to trial with the various orders for protective measures. The Chamber found the Prosecution's explanation for lack of disclosure unacceptable and accordingly ordered full disclosure of the Prosecution witness statements (para. 17).

8.5.324 See also *Nsabimana and Nteziryayo, Decision on the Defence Motions for Disclosure of Copies of the Prosecutor's Exhibits*, 18 September 2001, para. 22. The Trial Chamber stated that the Prosecution must disclose to the Accused "at the earliest available opportunity, and at least prior to the date of testimony by the witness" a copy of any items they intended to use during the testimony of its witnesses.

Prosecution Under Obligation to Obtain Previous Statements of Prosecution Witnesses Taken by Other Authorities

8.5.325 Rule 66(A)(ii) does not distinguish between statements taken by the Prosecution or national authorities. See *Nyiramasuhuko, Decision on the Defence Motion for Disclosure of the Declarations*, 18 September 2001, para. 6. See also *Delalić et al, Decision on the Motion by Accused Zejnil Delalic for Disclosure of Evidence*, 26 September 1996.

8.5.326 In *Kajelijeli, Decision on Juvenal Kajelijeli's Motion Requesting the Recalling of Prosecution Witness GAO*, 2 November 2001, paras. 17–22, the Trial Chamber decided that pursuant to Rule 66(A)(ii) the Prosecution were under a duty to have had possession of statements made by detained Prosecution witnesses during previous investigations and judicial proceedings. See also *Ndayambaje, Decision on the Defence Motions Seeking Documents Relating to Detained Witnesses*, 15 November 2001, para. 19.

Defence Not Entitled to Interview Prosecution Witnesses Prior to Trial or to Request a "Bill of Particulars"

8.5.327 In *Kajelejeli, Decision on Defence Motion Seeking to Interview Prosecutor's Witnesses or Alternatively to be Provided with a Bill of Particulars*, 12 March 2001, the Trial Chamber held that the neither the Rules or the Statute provided for the Defence to interview prosecution witnesses prior to testimony at trial. Furthermore, neither the Rules or Statute provided for a "Bill of Particulars." The Chamber was of the view that the matters that the Defence sought clarification of were matters that could be resolved by the Defence during cross-examination of the witnesses at trial (para. 10). Nonetheless, in other cases, e.g., *Hadžihasanović et al.*, the Defence have sought and been granted permission to interview prosecution witnesses prior to trial. There seems to be nothing objectionable in this practice, indeed, it facilitates discovery of the truth and accurate presentation of the issues in dispute at trial.

Requirement that Defence Show Materiality of Evidence Requested

8.5.328 In *Delalić et al.*, in the Trial Chamber's *Decision on motion by the accused Zejnil Delalić for the disclosure of evidence*, dated 26 September 1996, the Chamber ruled that the Defence in its motion ". . . must make a *prima facie* showing of materiality and that the requested evidence is in the custody or control of the Prosecutor" (para.9). The Chamber held that:

In this case, the Defence has noted its desire to have access to *all* documents and other objects within the Prosecution's custody and control having to do with the accused or Čelebići camp on the basis that they are all material to its preparation.... Given the absence of a specific identification of material evidence that the Defence alleges the Prosecution withheld, it is inappropriate for the Trial Chamber to intervene at this time. (paragraph 10)

8.5.329 In the Decision, the Chamber also referred to the U.S. Federal Rules of Criminal Procedure, noting that Rule 16(a)(1)(C) of the U.S. Federal Rules of Criminal Procedure had similar wording to Rule 66(B).

8.5.330 This test—of a *prima facie* showing of materiality—was also applied by the President of the Tribunal, Judge Cassese, in relation to the Prosecutor's request for production of material confiscated in the Detention Unit by the Registrar (*Decision of the President on the Prosecutor's Motion for the Production of Notes exchanged between Zejnil Delalić and Zdravko Mucić*, 11 November 1996) (see commentary to Rule 39, above). See also *Nsabimana and Nteziryayo, Decision on the Defence Motions for Disclosure of Copies of the Prosecutor's Exhibit*, 18 September 2001, para. 18.

8.5.331 Rule 66(B) imposes on the Prosecutor the responsibility of making the initial determination of materiality of evidence within its possession and if disputed, requires the Defence to specifically identify evidence material to the preparation of the Defence that is being withheld by the Prosecutor. (See *Delalić et al, Decision on Disclosure*, 6 September 1996, para. 11). When resorting to the Chamber, the Defence is required to show that their request is justified under Rule 66(B) and specifically satisfy the Chamber that the requested documents are material to the preparation of the Defence. See *Bagambiki, Decision on Bagambiki's Motion for Disclosure of the Guilty Pleas of Detained Witnesses and Statements by Jean Kambanda*, 1 December 2000. See also *Kajelejeli, Decision on Defence Motion Seeking to Interview Prosecutor's Witnesses or Alternatively to be Provided with a Bill of Particulars*, 12 March 2001, (para. 12) in which the Trial Chamber held that the "tape recordings, and/or transcripts of the tape recordings" of the taking of Prosecution witness statements could be pursued by the Defence pursuant to Rule 66(B). See also *Akayesu, Appeals Chamber Decision*, 1 June 2001, (para. 155) in which the Appeals Chamber agreed with the Trial Chamber that, on their face, the Rules do not provide for disclosure of tape recordings of interviews conducted with witnesses. The Appeals Chamber stated that it was unclear whether the Prosecution even had possession of the tape recordings, but that even if they did, it was under no obligation to disclose them (para. 159). The Appeals Chamber held that ultimately each case had to be determined on a case by case basis. The Chamber stated:

as a matter of principle an accused is not limited in any way, in the applications that he or she may bring before a Trial Chamber. Although it has not been a practice at the Tribunal to proffer "extrinsic evidence" of a prior statement, this does not imply that any application to do so would be automatically denied. On the contrary, as in all cases, a Trial Chamber would have to make a decision based on the facts before it (para. 167).

8.5.332 Note that a showing of materiality by the Defence is not required pursuant to Rule 66(B) for the disclosure of evidence that is (i) intended for use as evidence by the Prosecutor at trial, or (ii) that was obtained from or belonged to the Accused. See

Delalić et al, Decision on Disclosure, 6 September 1996, para. 5. Thus, the "materiality" test only applies to the first part of Rule 66(B).

Cross Reference: See 8.5.363 on reciprocal defence obligations pursuant to Rule 67(C).

Obligation to Disclose Arises only after the Initial Appearance of the Accused

8.5.333 In its *Decision Partially Rejecting the Request Submitted by Mr. Igor Pantelić, Counsel for Radovan Karadžić*, of 27 June 1996, the Trial Chamber noted that a Rule 61 hearing does not constitute a trial and therefore any documentation which the Prosecutor would have to provide according to Rule 66 could only be made available after the initial appearance of the accused in person:

> access to the relevant documents and case files . . . could only be granted as part of a trial following an initial appearance of the accused in person, pursuant to Rule 66. . . . [D1348/2bis]

See also a similar decision rendered in the same case on 5 July 1995 with respect to further lawyers representing Radovan Karadžić.

Sanctioning the Prosecution for Failure to Comply with Its Disclosure Obligations

8.5.334 If the Prosecution fails to fulfil its disclosure obligations under the Rules, it is only logical that there should be some form of sanction. So far that has been confined to adverse judicial comment. See, however, Rule 5 ("Non-compliance with Rules").

8.5.335 See *Scheduling Order* issued in *Furundžija* on 29 April 1998:

> NOTING FURTHER WITH GRAVE CONCERN AND DEPLORING THAT the Prosecution has failed to comply with its obligation under Rule 66(A)(ii) of the Rules of Procedure and Evidence to disclose to the Defence "no later than sixty days before the date set for trial, copies of the statements of all witnesses whom the Prosecutor intends to call to testify at trial."

8.5.336 See also the *Decision on Motion of Defendant Anto Furundžija to preclude testimony of certain Prosecution witnesses* rendered by the Trial Chamber in *Furundžija* on 29 April 1998 in which the Chamber expressed its "grave concern at the unjustifiable failure of the Prosecution to comply with its disclosure obligations" under Rule 66.

Other Decisions on Rule 66

8.5.337 *Decision on the Prosecution and Defence Motions dated 25 January 1999 and 25 March 1999 respectively, Blaškić*, 22 April 1999.

Redaction of Witness Statements May Only be Done Pursuant to an Order by the Chamber

8.5.338 The Prosecutor must not redact, i.e., edit, the supporting material and witness statements before disclosing them to the defence under Rule 66(A), unless she first obtains a relevant Order from the Trial Chamber. See *Decision on the Preliminary Motion filed by the Defence* rendered in *Kayishema* by the Trial Chamber on 6 November 1996:

> the Tribunal reminds the Prosecutor that, subject to an order of non-disclosure from the Tribunal, she is obliged to disclose to the Defence all materials provided under Rule 66(A) of the Rules which are presently in her possession. (p. 4)

8.5.339 If the supporting material were already redacted, e.g. by removing the names of witnesses, when it was before the confirming Judge, however, such an Order from the Trial Chamber would not appear to be necessary, since Rule 66(A)(i) only requires disclosure to the defence of "the supporting material which accompanied the indictment when confirmation was sought." On this subject, see also 8.2.11 *et seq.* and 8.2.17 *et seq.*, above.

Disclosure Pursuant to Rule 66(A) Not To Be Withheld Due to Pendency of a Motion for Protective Measures

8.5.340 Reference should be made to the *Decision on the Motion by the Defence Counsel for Disclosure* of the Trial Chamber on 27 November 1997:

> THE TRIAL CHAMBER FINDS:—
>
> (i) That the non-disclosure of the witnesses' statements by the Prosecution to the Defence Counsel is violative of rule 66(A)(i) of the Rules. The mere fact of filing a motion by the Prosecution for protective measures for its witnesses does not in any way relieve it of the obligations for disclosure to the defence under rules 66(A)(i) of the Rules. The Prosecution should note that the pendency of a motion under rule 53 of the Rules for protective measures does not exonerate the Prosecution of its other obligations imposed by the Rules;
>
> (ii) That if the Prosecution apprehends any potential risk to any of its witnesses in fulfilling her obligations of disclosure under rule 66(A) of the Rules, she should promptly approach the Trial Chamber for an appropriate order;
>
> (iii) That partial disclosure by the Prosecution to the defence 60 days before the scheduled date 24 October 1997 is in violation of rule 66(A)(ii) of the Rules

8.5.341 Nonetheless, the Chamber did not consider that the defence had been unduly prejudiced by the failure to disclose as the trial date had been postponed "and the defence will consequently have sufficient time to prepare for the trial."

8.5.342 Thus, the Trial Chamber directed in its Decision:

> (1) ... the Prosecution to fulfill its obligations under rules 66(A)(ii), by disclosing the witnesses' statements to the Defence Counsel within two weeks

from the signing of this decision, if need be, in redacted form;

(2) ... the Prosecution to disclose any other evidence to the Defence Counsel promptly, if it obtains the custody or control over any evidence, which it intends to use against the accused;

(3) ... the Prosecution to comply with the requirements of complete disclosure of evidence in accordance with rules 66 to 70 without undue delay. ...

Dilatory Disclosure by the Prosecutor

8.5.343 See *Separate Opinion of Judge Yakov Ostrovsky on the Prosecution's Motion for Adjournment* in *Bagosora* of 17 March 1998:

> 3. The first reason offered by the Office of the Prosecutor ("OTP") in favour of an adjournment, was not addressed in the Chamber's decision. The Prosecutor, in her written request, states that the disclosure process is not yet complete and "it has been impossible for the Prosecutor to make the disclosure required by rules 66 and 67 of the Rules of Procedure and Evidence ... in compliance with a 12 March 1998 set trial date."
>
> On 27 November 1997, the Trial Chamber issued a decision that the Prosecutor provide disclosure to the Defence within two weeks of the signing of the decision. More than three months later the Prosecutor claims that the disclosure process remains incomplete. This shows a blatant lack of respect for the decision of the Trial Chamber.

8.5.344

ICTY Rule 67 Reciprocal Disclosure	ICTR Rule 67 Reciprocal Disclosure of Evidence

(A) As early as reasonably practicable and in any event prior to the commencement of the trial:
(i) the Prosecutor shall notify the defence of the names of the witnesses that he intends to call in proof of the guilt of the accused and in rebuttal of any defence plea of which the Prosecutor has received notice in accordance with Sub-rule (ii) below;
(ii) the defence shall notify the Prosecutor of its intent to offer:
  (a) the defence of alibi; in which case the notification shall specify the place or places at which the accused claims to have been present at the time of the alleged crime and the names and addresses of witnesses and any other evidence upon which the accused intends to rely to establish the alibi;
	Subject to the provisions of Rules 53 and 69
	(A) As early as reasonably practicable and in any event prior to the commencement of the trial:
	(i) the Prosecutor shall notify the defence of the names of the witnesses that he intends to call to establish the guilt of the accused and in rebuttal of any defence plea of which the Prosecutor has received notice in accordance with Sub-rule (ii) below;
	(ii) the defence shall notify the Prosecutor of its intent to enter:
	  (a) the defence of alibi; in which case the notification shall specify the place or places at which the accused claims to have been present at the time of the alleged crime and the names and addresses of witnesses and any other evidence upon which the accused intends to rely to establish the alibi;

(b) any special defence, including that of diminished or lack of mental responsibility; in which case the notification shall specify the names and addresses of witnesses and any other evidence upon which the accused intends to rely to establish the special defence. (B) Failure of the defence to provide notice under this Rule shall not limit the right of the accused to testify on the above defences. (C) If the defence makes a request pursuant to Rule 66(B), the Prosecutor shall be entitled to inspect any books, documents, photographs and tangible objects, which are within the custody or control of the defence and which it intends to use as evidence at the trial. (D) If either party discovers additional evidence or material which should have been disclosed earlier pursuant to the Rules, that party shall immediately disclose that evidence or material to the other party and the Trial Chamber.	(b) any special defence, including that of diminished or lack of mental responsibility; in which case the notification shall specify the names and addresses of witnesses and any other evidence upon which the accused intends to rely to establish the special defence. (B) Failure of the defence to provide notice under this Rule shall not limit the right of the accused to rely on the above defences. (C) If the defence makes a request pursuant to Sub-rule 66(B), the Prosecutor shall in turn be entitled to inspect any books, documents, photographs and tangible objects, which are within the custody or control of the defence and which it intends to use as evidence at the trial. (D) If either party discovers additional evidence or information or materials which should have been produced earlier pursuant to the Rules, that party shall promptly notify the other party and the Trial Chamber of the existence of the additional evidence or information materials.

History of ICTY Rule 67

8.5.345 Para. (C) was amended at the twenty-fifth plenary session, held on 12–13 December 2001 to refer specifically to "disclosure" of material or evidence discovered at a later stage, rather than "prompt notification," to the other party and the Trial Chamber.

History of ICTR Rule 67

8.5.346 This Rule was amended at the ICTR fifth plenary session on 8 June 1998.

Names of Prosecution Witnesses Must Be Given in a Comprehensive Document

8.5.347 In a *Decision on the Production of Discovery Materials*, rendered by the Trial Chamber in *Blaškić* on 27 January 1997, the Chamber said that while a "list of prosecution witnesses" was not strictly required under Rule 67(A), the names should be clearly and comprehensively set out:

> 21. The Defence recognises that, to date, the identity of over one hundred prosecution witnesses has been transmitted to it but that it has not actually received a list in support of the initial indictment and thus of the amended indictment of 22 November 1996.

The Prosecution intends to disclose to the accused as soon as possible a list of the witnesses it plans to call.

22. The Trial Chamber would note that the dispute concerns both the notion of a list and the moment when such a list must be disclosed.

The Trial Chamber notes that Sub-rule 67(A) does not refer to an official list. However, by stipulating that the Prosecution has the obligation to inform the Defence of the names of the prosecution witnesses "as early as reasonably practicable and in any event prior to the commencement of the trial," the Rules support the idea that all the names of the prosecution witnesses must be disclosed at the same time in a comprehensive document which thus permits the Defence to have a clear and cohesive view of the Prosecution's strategy and to make the appropriate preparations.

Unlike Prosecution, Defence Is Not Obliged to Disclose Its Witnesses' Names Prior to Trial

8.5.348 It is clear from the plain terms of Rule 67(A)(i), that the *Defence* is not obliged to disclose the names of its witnesses to the Prosecution *prior to trial*. This was confirmed in the *Decision on the Applications filed by the Defence for the Accused Zejnil Delalić and Esad Landžo on 14 February 1997 and 18 February 1997 respectively*, rendered on 21 February 1997 in *Delalić et al.* by the Trial Chamber:

> 2. . . . The Defence argues that, according to the Rules of Procedure and Evidence ("the Rules"), it is under no obligation to notify the Prosecution of the names of its witnesses, whilst, by virtue of Sub-rule 67(A)(i), the Prosecution must notify the accused of the names of the witnesses it intends to call at trial. The Chamber is therefore requested to amend the Scheduling Order such that only the Prosecution is obliged to provide a witness list to the Defence.
>
> . . .
>
> 10. The Trial Chamber accepts the submission of the Defence that under the Rules there is no general reciprocal obligation on the Defence to give notice to the Prosecution of the witnesses it intends to call at trial. Sub-rule 67(A)(ii), however, imposes such an obligation upon the Defence when it intends to offer a defence of alibi or any other special defence, including that of diminished or lack of mental responsibility.
>
> 11. The Defence for the accused Zejnil Delalić has not given notice of its intent to offer any of the defences contemplated by Sub-rule 67(A)(ii). The Trial Chamber, therefore, accepts its submission that, at the present time, it is not obliged to provide a witness list to the Prosecution.

8.5.349 At trial, however, the Trial Chamber did decide to order the Defence to "provide the Prosecution with the names of the witnesses it intends to call at trial, in writing at least seven working days prior to the testimony of each witness." See *Decision on the Prosecutor's Motion for an Order requiring Advance Disclosure of Witnesses by the Defence, Delalić et al.*, 4 February 1998. The Chamber distinguished its earlier Decision, of 21 February 1997, by stating that the earlier Decision dealt with the defence's *pre-trial* privilege of not disclosing its witness list, but that, once the matter was at trial, Rule 54 could justify the Chamber ordering the defence to disclose its witness list if such was "necessary for the conduct of the trial" within the terms of that Rule.

8.5.350 See also *Separate Opinion of Judge Stephen on Prosecution Motion for Production of Defence Witness Statements*, dated 27 November 1996 in *Tadić:* "The Rules deal at some length with 'Production of Evidence' in Rules 66 to 70. . . . They impose very different obligations of disclosure on each of the two parties" (page 2).

8.5.351 See also *Decision of Trial Chamber I on the Prosecutor's Motion for Clarification of Order requiring advance disclosure of witnesses and for Order requiring reciprocal advance disclosure by the defence*, rendered by the Trial Chamber in *Blaškić* on 29 January 1998, in which the Chamber took the view that the defence was *not* obliged to disclose the names of the witnesses it intended to call, at least not while the Prosecution was still presenting its case.

8.5.352 It is important to emphasise, as Judge Stephen did, that the disclosure obligations on the Prosecution are very different from those on the defence. This is justified by the fact that it is the Prosecution which brings the case and which must prove the case; hence it has burdens and obligations not incumbent on the defence. Nonetheless, the Prosecution, and occasionally the Chambers, have sometimes sought to invoke the principle of equality of arms to impose equal, or comparable, disclosure obligations on the defence as are on the Prosecution. It is submitted that such attempts are misconceived; the principle of equality of arms in human rights law has always existed in order to help the defence achieve procedural equality with the prosecution. It was not intended to be used as a "sword" by the prosecution to impose obligations on the defence. See 8.5.73 *et seq.* on "equality of arms."

Cross Reference: Rule 65 *ter* (G) (i) and 69 (C).

Alibi Notice

8.5.353 Pursuant to Rule 67(A)(ii)(a), the defence is obliged to notify the Prosecutor of its intent to offer the defence of alibi. If it does so, the defence also has to "specify the place or places at which the accused claims to have been present at the time of the alleged crime and the names and addresses of witnesses and any other evidence upon which the accused intends to rely to establish the alibi."

8.5.354 In *Tadić*, the defence gave an alibi notice to the Prosecutor on 10 April 1996, and subsequently an amended notification on 3 May 1996 (See IT-94-1-T, *Amended notification ex Rule 67(A)(ii)(a)*, 3/5/96, pp. 8185–8191). See the *Opinion and Judgement* rendered in the *Tadić* case on 7 May 1997, paras. 478–528 of which discuss the accused's defence of alibi.

8.5.355 An alibi notice was also given in *Delalić et al* by the accused Esad Landžo. See *Motion Requesting Subsequent Submission of a Notice to the Prosecutor Offering the Defence of Alibi* filed on 14 January 1997, which was granted by Trial Chamber II in its *Order Disposing of Motions filed by the Defence* dated 27 January 1997. In its Order, the Chamber intimated that Rule 67(A)(ii) only required the Defence to serve such notice *on the Prosecutor:* ". . . the Motion . . . is granted, such Notice having already been served on the Prosecution" (para. 3).

Consequences of Failure to Serve Alibi Notice at the Proper Time

8.5.356 See the *Decision* of the Trial Chamber on 11 January 1999 in *Kupreškić* which held that if the accused failed to serve a proper alibi notice, he could, pursuant to Rule 67(B), still raise the defence, but the evidence of other witnesses corroborating the defence was liable to be excluded by the Trial Chamber.

8.5.357 In *Kayishema and Ruzindana*, both accused failed to respect the notice requirements for raising the defence of alibi under this rule. The sanction applied by the Trial Chamber was to weigh that fact in the balance when assessing the credibility of the defence (*Kayishema and Ruzindana Trial Judgement*, para. 237).

Notice of Special Defence

8.5.358 A notice of intent to offer a defence of diminished or lack of mental responsibility was filed by the accused Esad Landžo in *Delalić et al.* See *Notice of the Defence to the Prosecutor Pursuant to Rule 67(A)(ii)(b) of the Rules of Procedure and Evidence*, 15 November 1996. See also *Pre-Trial Brief of Esad Landžo and Response to Prosecutor's Pre-Trial Brief*, filed on 3 March 1997. The accused Hazim Delić also filed such a notice in the same case (see *Hazim Delić's Notice Pursuant to Rule 67(A)(b)(ii)*, filed on 3 March 1997).

Diminished Responsibility Versus Unfitness to Stand Trial

8.5.359 Diminished or lack of mental responsibility is to be distinguished from the notion of fitness to stand trial. See *Order on the Prosecution's Request for a Formal Finding of the Trial Chamber that the Accused Landžo is fit to stand trial*, issued on 23 June 1997 by the Trial Chamber in which, in response to a Motion by the Prosecutor, the Chamber found, on the basis of reports of mental health experts, the submissions of defence counsel and the behaviour of the accused—who had filed notice of his intent to offer the defence of diminished responsibility at trial—that the accused was fit to stand trial. The issue of diminished responsibility, by contrast, could only be determined at the end of the trial in the final Judgement rendered by the Chamber. See 6.3.1 on defences, in particular, diminished responsibility and insanity.

Disclosure of Addresses of Witnesses to Special Defence

8.5.360 Pursuant to Rule 67(A)(ii), the address of witnesses of a special defence must be disclosed to the Prosecution. The defence could, however, apply for protective measures. It was so held in a *Decision* rendered in *Delalić et al.* on 13 June 1997. The Trial Chamber affirmed that the defence was obliged to disclose to the Prosecution the addresses of witnesses to special defences such as alibi and diminished responsibility:

> 11. The provisions of Sub-rule 67(A)(ii) impose a clear and unambiguous obligation on the Defence to disclose the names and addresses of all witnesses which they intend to call to testify in relation to the defence of alibi and any

special defence, such as diminished or lack of mental responsibility. Where the language of a Rule is unequivocal, it is not open to either of the parties to challenge their duties thereunder.

8.5.361 The Chamber added, however, that it remained open to the defence to apply for protective measures under Rule 69 or Rule 75 for particular witnesses who may be at risk.

Decisions

8.5.362 See *Order on the Defence Motion for Discovery* rendered by the Trial Chamber in *Galić* on 11 May 2000, which interpreted a defence motion for discovery as a request pursuant to Rule 66(B) of the Rules, thereby calling Rule 67(C) into operation.

Para. (C) Only Requires Defence to Make Reciprocal Disclosure of Evidence That It "Intends" to Use at Trial

8.5.363 The requirement of Rule 67(C) for the Defence to disclose certain documents in its possession to the Prosecution forces the defence to reveal its strategy before the Prosecution has presented its case. To mitigate this potential violation of the rights of the accused, where the Defence makes a request pursuant to Rule 66(B) and the Prosecutor makes a reciprocal request pursuant to Rule 67(C), the Defence may decline the request on the grounds that it has not yet formed an intent to use the material in its possession as evidence at trial. Clearly, during the course of trial proceedings Defence strategy may change. The final decision on whether to use a particular document at trial may not be made until a matter of minutes before it is used. Accordingly, it would not be disingenuous of the Defence to argue that it does not "intend" to use any of the material in its possession until it actually does so. As a result the Defence would be under no obligation to disclose the material in question to the Prosecution.

Circumvention by Reliance Not on Rule 66(B) but on Rule 68 ("Disclosure of Exculpatory Evidence")

8.5.364 See the *Decision on the Production of Discovery Materials*, rendered by the Trial Chamber in *Blaškić* on 27 January 1997, on this point. The Chamber observed that:

> the Defence has clearly stated that its request does not fall within the ambit of this rule and thus evades its discovery obligation to the Prosecutor which would derive through the application of Sub-rule 67(C).

8.5.365 Given that fact, the Chamber considered that the Defence right to discovery was not an unqualified one:

> Thus, if the Trial Chamber notes that the Defence does not wish to honour the need for balanced reciprocal disclosure provided for in Sub-rules 66(B) and 67(C), it must then be particularly vigilant as to limiting the nature and extent of the request for exculpatory evidence from the Prosecutor's file because the accused has made such a scrutinising request compelling her to produce evidence.

8.5.366 The Chamber went on to consider the appropriate test to be applied in these circumstances (see following section).

8.5.367 It should be noted, however, that the reference to "the need for balanced reciprocal disclosure" is curious and arguably misconceived. As noted above at 8.5.352, the disclosure obligations on the prosecution are very different from those on the defence. Accordingly, they are not "balanced" at all. Nor is there any "need" for "balanced reciprocal disclosure." If the Prosecution believes it has a case against the defence—which it asserts when it submits an indictment for confirmation—it must have in its possession all the evidence it considers that it requires to secure a conviction. Thus it does not "need" anything from the defence. If the defence are able to prove the accused's innocence through the introduction of documents and other evidence at trial, then that is all the better. If when those documents are introduced, the Prosecution wishes to challenge them, they may do so in cross-examination, after an adjournment if necessary.

Defence Must Present a *Prima Facie* Case that Would Make Probable the Exculpatory Nature of the Materials Sought

8.5.368 In the above-mentioned *Blaškić Decision on the Production of Discovery Materials*, 27 January 1997, the Trial Chamber asked:

> Does the Defence which does not base its Motion on Sub-rule 66(B)—which would entail the obligation of mutual disclosure as required by Sub-rule 67(C)—have a general and unilateral right to inspect the Prosecutor's file by demanding and obtaining extensive and unrestricted disclosure? [pursuant to Rule 68]

8.5.369 The Chamber answered this question in the negative, drawing an analogy with Rule 66(B) as interpreted by the Trial Chamber in *Delalić et al* (Tr. Ch. *Decision on motion by the accused Zejnil Delalić for the disclosure of evidence*, 26 September 1996—see commentary to Rule 66(B) above), and it thus concluded that:

> after having previously shown that they were in the possession of the Prosecutor, the Defence must present a *prima facie* case which would make probable the exculpatory nature of the materials sought (para. 49).

8.5.370

ICTY Rule 68 Disclosure of Exculpatory Evidence	ICTR Rule 68 Disclosure of Exculpatory Evidence
The Prosecutor shall, as soon as practicable, disclose to the defence the existence of evidence known to the Prosecutor which in any way tends to suggest the innocence or mitigate the guilt of the accused or may affect the credibility of prosecution evidence.	The Prosecutor shall, as soon as practicable, disclose to the defence the existence of evidence known to the Prosecutor which in any way tends to suggest the innocence or mitigate the guilt of the accused or may affect the credibility of prosecution evidence.

History of ICTY Rule 68

8.5.371 Rule 68 was amended at the suggestion of the International Law Committee of the Association of the Bar of the City of New York, at the fifth plenary session in January 1995, "to broaden the rights of suspects and accused persons" by adding the last eight words (second Annual Report, paragraph 26: "Rule 68 was amended so that the Prosecutor's obligation to disclose to the defence exculpatory evidence which tended 'to suggest the innocence or mitigate the guilt of the accused,' now extends to any evidence which 'may affect the credibility of prosecution evidence'). The word, "evidence" was substituted for material on 19 July, 2001, after the twenty-fourth plenary session.

Definition of "Exculpatory Material"

8.5.372 In the *Decision on the Request of the Accused Pursuant to Rule 68 for Exculpatory Information* rendered on 24 June 1997 in *Delalić et al*, the Chamber defined exculpatory evidence under Rule 68 as "material which is known to the Prosecutor and which is favourable to the accused in the sense that it tends to suggest the innocence or mitigate the guilt of the accused or may affect the credibility of prosecution evidence" (para. 12, *Ibid*).

Lack of Evidence Is Not "Exculpatory Evidence"

8.5.373 The Prosecutor is obliged, under Rule 68, to provide exculpatory evidence to the defence. Lack of evidence is not, however, considered "exculpatory evidence" within the meaning of Rule 68. The defence cannot therefore call upon the Prosecution, as part of the latter's *disclosure obligations*, to admit that it does not have evidence on certain points, e.g. with respect to certain elements that the Prosecution has to prove at trial. Lack of evidence in this sense falls to be determined at trial.

8.5.374 In *Blaškić*, the defence, on a preliminary motion, requested the Prosecutor "to acknowledge that she lacks evidence in respect of certain points of the indictment. Such a lack of inculpatory evidence constitutes exculpatory evidence" within the meaning of Rule 68 (see *Decision on the Production of Discovery Materials*, Trial Chamber, 27 January 1997, para. 8). In its Decision, the Chamber rejected the defence argument, concurring with the Prosecutor that:

> the time and place to raise the possible question of the lack of evidence can only be at the trial on the merits. Possible evaluation of the exculpatory nature of this lack of evidence can take place at that time only. The Defence motion on this point therefore is, as such, denied (para. 25).

8.5.375 It may be, however, that with the introduction of pre-trial briefs (see Rule 65 *ter*, added to the Rules at the eighteenth plenary session on 9–10 July 1998, after the *Blaškić* Decision referred to in the last para.), there would be scope for the Defence to force an admission from the Prosecution that it did not have evidence regarding certain allegations at the stage of filing pre-trial briefs. Furthermore, it would appear to be in the interests of a fair and expeditious trial for such a matter to be brought to the Trial Chamber's attention at the earliest available opportunity.

Exculpatory Evidence in Case-Files of Other Accused

8.5.376 In the Trial Chamber's *Decision on the Production of Discovery Materials, Blaškić*, 27 January 1997, the Chamber considered that the Prosecutor's obligation under Rule 68 to disclose exculpatory evidence could in principle extend to such evidence contained in case-files of *other* accused (see paras. 26–30 of the Decision), although the Defence Motion to *inspect* the case-files of other accused was refused in that case on confidentiality and other grounds. See 8.5.534 on parties seeking access to confidential materials filed in other cases.

Duty on the Prosecutor

8.5.377 In the Trial Chamber's *Decision on the Production of Discovery Materials, Blaškić*, 27 January 1997, the Chamber pronounced upon the Prosecutor's duty in relation to Defence requests by motion for the disclosure of exculpatory evidence:

> in respect of all the materials mentioned by the Defence, the Prosecutor must state:
> — whether the materials are in fact in her possession;
> — whether the materials contain exculpatory evidence;
> — whether she believes that although she does possess exculpatory materials, Sub-rule 66(C) or any other relevant provision require that their confidentiality be protected.
>
> The Trial Chamber does not consider it sufficient that the Prosecutor declares that she "recognises her obligations under the Rule and has complied with them" (para. 47).

8.5.378 Once the Defence has established that certain material is in the possession of the Prosecutor, it must establish "a *prima facie* case which would make probable the exculpatory nature of the materials sought" (para. 49).

8.5.379 In the *Decision on Motion by Prosecution to modify Order for Compliance with Rule 68* in *Krnojelac* dated 1 November 1999, Judge Hunt, as Pre-Trial Judge of the Trial Chamber, held that, in order to ensure the Prosecution's compliance with its obligation to disclose exculpatory material to the accused in accordance with Rule 68, it may be appropriate to require a signed report from a representative of the Prosecution team certifying from his or her personal knowledge that a full search for the existence of Rule 68 material has been conducted of all the materials in the possession of the Prosecution or otherwise within its knowledge.

Exculpatory Evidence Must Be in Possession of Prosecutor

8.5.380 In *Bagilishema, Decision on the Request of the Defense for an Order For Disclosure by the Prosecutor of the Admissions of Guilt of Witnesses Y, Z, and AA*, 8

June 2000, the Trial Chamber held that Rule 68 has two main elements, (i) the evidence must be *known* to the Prosecutor, and (ii) it must be in some way exculpatory. The Trial Chamber equated "known" to being in the custody and control or possession of the material as these are the words used in Rule 66(B) and 67(C). The Chamber stated:

> the obligation on the Prosecutor to disclose possible exculpatory evidence would be effective only when the Prosecutor is in actual custody, possession, or has control of said evidence.

8.5.381 It is unclear from this whether custody, etc., is a necessary or a sufficient condition for the material being known to the Prosecutor, i.e., if the Prosecutor has custody of the material, is it thus "constructively known" to the Prosecutor? Or could the Prosecutor have custody of material yet claim not to know of it?

8.5.382 In *Kajelijeli, Decision on Kajelijeli's Urgent Motion and Certification*, 5 July 2001, the Trial Chamber held that the Defence had not convinced the Chamber that the items in question existed, let alone that they were in the possession of the Prosecutor (para. 14).

8.5.383 However, statements that Prosecution witnesses may have made in previous proceedings must be obtained and disclosed by the Prosecution. See *Kajelijeli, Decision on Juvenal Kajelijeli's Motion Requesting the Recalling of Prosecution Witness GAO*, 2 November 2001. The Trial Chamber was of the opinion that as the witnesses in question were to be called by the Prosecution in its case against the Accused, it was incumbent on them to have had, in their possession, the said statements, particularly as the said statements might have been used in weighing the credibility of the said witnesses. The Chamber held that in the interests of justice, the Prosecution bore the responsibility of obtaining the said statements from the Rwandan Authorities and providing them to the Defence pursuant to Rule 66(A)(ii) (see paras. 17–22 of the *Decision*).

Test To Be Applied for Discovery under Rule 68

8.5.384 The test applied under Rule 68 is that the Defence must present a *prima facie* case which would make probable the exculpatory nature of the materials sought.

8.5.385 In the Trial Chamber's *Decision on the Production of Discovery Materials, Blaškić*, 27 January 1997, the Chamber considered the test to be applied for discovery under Rule 68. The Chamber reasoned by analogy with Rule 66(B) as interpreted by the Trial Chamber in *Delalić et al.* (*Decision on motion by the accused Zejnil Delalić for the disclosure of evidence*, Trial Chamber, 26 September 1996—see commentary to Rule 66(B) above at 8.5.328 *et seq.*), that:

> after having previously shown that they were in the possession of the Prosecutor, the Defence must present a *prima facie* case which would make probable the exculpatory nature of the materials sought (para. 49).

8.5.386 This test was followed in the *Decision on the Request of the Accused Pursuant to Rule 68 for Exculpatory Information* rendered on 24 June 1997 in *Delalić et al.* by the Trial Chamber. Delić sought disclosure of material in the Prosecutor's possession which showed that Bosnian Serb forces violated the laws and customs of war, for the purposes of demonstrating that Bosnian Serb Prisoners of War failed to meet the requirement under Article 4(A)(2)(d) of the Geneva Prisoners of War Convention of 1949 of "conducting their operations in accordance with the laws and customs of war," and were thus not entitled to the "protected person" status which the Prosecution alleged, in the indictment, that they enjoyed. The Motion was denied by the Chamber, which, following the test laid down in *Blaškić* (above), concluded "that the Defence has failed to indicate the specific material it regards as exculpatory and which should be disclosed pursuant to Rule 68. Moreover, the Defence has failed to show *prima facie* that the information it seeks to be disclosed is in fact exculpatory" (para. 18).

8.5.387 This defence argument, that the victims in the indictment were not protected under the Prisoners of War (IIIrd) Geneva Convention because the forces to which they belonged did not conduct their operations in accordance with the laws of war, is an interesting one, but in the event it was not considered in the final Judgement since the victims were considered to be protected under the Civilian (IVth) Geneva Convention rather than under the Prisoners of War Convention.

Exculpatory Evidence Not Limited to Admissible Evidence

8.5.388 In *Kordić, Decision on Motions to Extend Time for Filing Appellant's Briefs*, 11 May 2001, Judge Hunt, the Pre-Appeal Judge, held that the reference to "evidence" in Rule 68 is not restricted to material in a form that would be admissible in evidence, but includes all information in any form which falls within the quoted description. This makes sense given that, even if the defence cannot directly admit such evidence in at trial, it may lead to further defence investigations which *will* produce admissible evidence. This is, in a sense, the opposite of the "fruits of the poisoned tree" scenario.

Obligation Pursuant to Rule 68 Continues after Trial

8.5.389 In both *Blaškić, Decision on the Appellant's Motions for the Production of Material, Suspension or Extension of the Briefing Schedule, and Additional Filings*, 26 September 2000, and *Kordić, Decision on Motions to Extend Time for Filing Appellant's Briefs*, 11 May 2001, it was held that the Prosecution's obligation to disclose exculpatory evidence continues after the Trial Judgement. This is only reasonable, as such material may be relevant to the appeal. Moreover, it is submitted that even if, years after a conviction, the Prosecution finds exculpatory evidence, it should be provided to the convicted person's legal representatives, as the latter may wish to consider recourse to review proceedings.

Subjective Element to What Is Exculpatory; Presumption of Good Faith on the Part of the Prosecutor

8.5.390 See the *Decision* rendered in *Blaškić* on 29 April 1998 on this point.

Cross Reference: Rule 66(B).

Sanctions for Prosecutor's Failure to Comply with Rule 68

8.5.391 The Trial Chamber said in *Blaškić* that it does not take a "sanctions approach" to non-compliance by the Prosecutor with Rule 68, but rather it examines in each case whether or not the Defence has been prejudiced by that non-compliance and then acts accordingly. See the *Decision on the Defence Motion for Sanctions for the Prosecutor's Continuing Violation of Rule 68* dated 28 September 1998.

Re-Opening of Trial Due to Failure to Comply with Rule 68

8.5.392 The Trial Chamber in *Furundžija* found "serious misconduct on the part of the Prosecution" in failing to disclose to the defence evidence to the effect that a prosecution witness, who was an alleged rape victim, had received psychological treatment following the rape. The defence alleged that this evidence could "affect the credibility of prosecution evidence," and hence should have been disclosed pursuant to Rule 68. The defence argued that the failure to disclose should be remedied by striking the witness's evidence or by ordering a new trial.

8.5.393 The Trial Chamber, in a *Decision* dated 16 July 1998 agreed that the Prosecution should have disclosed the evidence in question as it clearly affected the credibility of prosecution evidence (paras. 18 and 19 of the *Decision*), and stated that if the Prosecution had wished to withhold disclosure for public policy reasons, it should have followed the procedure laid down in Rule 66(C), which reads:

> (C) Where information is in the possession of the Prosecutor, the disclosure of which may prejudice further or ongoing investigations, or for any other reasons may be contrary to the public interest or affect the security interests of any State, the Prosecutor may apply to the Trial Chamber sitting *in camera* to be relieved from the obligation to disclose pursuant to Sub-rule (B). When making such application the Prosecutor shall provide the Trial Chamber (but only the Trial Chamber) with the information that is sought to be kept confidential.

8.5.394 However, the Chamber denied the relief sought by the Defence, and instead re-opened the trial to deal with this specific issue, to which end hearings were held in the week of 9 November 1998. See also the *Scheduling Order* of 17 July 1998.

8.5.395 The Defence sought to appeal the 16 July 1998 Order, but the application was refused by a Bench of the Appeals Chamber in a Decision dated 24 August 1998.

8.5.396 An application to submit an *amicus* brief was submitted on 5 November 1998 in relation to these proceedings by a coalition of women's groups. The *amicus* submission argued that it is a "rape myth" that female victims of sexual violence are uniquely prone to hysteria and emotional upheavals which impair their credibility (see, in particular, paras. 16, 19 and 20 of the application); moreover, that it violates women's rights to equality to be subject to discriminatory laws of evidence requiring higher proof for sexual offences against women than for other offences, and finally that it violated the privacy rights of the witness in question to conduct a hearing into the details of her psychological treatment. It is submitted that these arguments have a good deal of force. Moreover, it would be ironic if a rapist were to escape conviction by virtue of the trauma inevitably induced in the victim by the rape itself.

8.5.397

ICTY only Rule 68 *bis* Failure to Comply with Disclosure Obligations
The pre-trial Judge or the Trial Chamber may decide *proprio motu*, or at the request of either party, on sanctions to be imposed on a party which fails to perform its disclosure obligations pursuant to the Rules.

History of Rule 68 *bis*

8.5.398 This new rule was introduced at the ICTY's twenty-fifth plenary session, held on 12–13 December 2001. It makes explicit a power which in any event the Chambers had already assumed.

8.5.399

ICTY Rule 70 Matters Not Subject to Disclosure	ICTR Rule 70 Matters Not Subject to Disclosure
(A) Notwithstanding the provisions of Rules 66 and 67, reports, memoranda, or other internal documents prepared by a party, its assistants or representatives in connection with the investigation or preparation of the case, are not subject to disclosure or notification under those Rules. (B) If the Prosecutor is in possession of information which has been provided to him on a confidential basis and which has been used solely for the purpose of generating new evidence, that initial information and its origin shall not be disclosed by the Prosecutor without the consent of the person or entity providing the initial information and shall in any event not be given in evidence without prior disclosure to the accused. (C) If, after obtaining the consent of the person or entity providing information under this Rule, the Prosecutor elects to present as evidence any testimony, document or other material so provided, the Trial Chamber, notwithstanding Rule 98, may not order either party to produce additional evidence received from the person or entity providing the initial	(A) Notwithstanding the provisions of Rules 66 and 67, reports, memoranda, or other internal documents prepared by a party, its assistants or representatives in connection with the investigation or preparation of the case, are not subject to disclosure or notification under those Rules. (B) If the Prosecutor is in possession of information which has been provided to him on a confidential basis and which has been used solely for the purpose of generating new evidence, that initial information and its origin shall not be disclosed by the Prosecutor without the consent of the person or entity providing the initial information and shall in any event not be given in evidence without prior disclosure to the accused. (C) If, after obtaining the consent of the person or entity providing information under this Rule, the Prosecutor elects to present as evidence any testimony, document or other material so provided, the Trial Chamber, notwithstanding Rule 98, may not order either party to produce additional evidence received from the person or entity providing the initial

information, nor may the Trial Chamber for the purpose of obtaining such additional evidence itself summon that person or a representative of that entity as a witness or order their attendance. A Trial Chamber may not use its power to order the attendance of witnesses or to require production of documents in order to compel the production of such additional evidence. (D) If the Prosecutor calls a witness to introduce in evidence any information provided under this Rule, the Trial Chamber may not compel that witness to answer any question relating to the information or its origin, if the witness declines to answer on grounds of confidentiality. (E) The right of the accused to challenge the evidence presented by the Prosecution shall remain unaffected subject only to limitations contained in Sub-rules (C) and (D). (F) The Trial Chamber may order upon an application by the accused or defence counsel that, in the interests of justice, the provisions of this Rule shall apply *mutatis mutandis* to specific information in the possession of the accused. (G) Nothing in Sub-rule (C) or (D) above shall effect a Trial Chamber's power under Rule 89(D) to exclude evidence if its probative value is substantially outweighed by the need to ensure a fair trial.	information, nor may the Trial Chamber for the purpose of obtaining such additional evidence itself summon that person or a representative of that entity as a witness or order their attendance. (D) If the Prosecutor calls as a witness the person providing, or a representative of the entity providing, information under this Rule, the Trial Chamber may not compel the witness to answer any question the witness declines to answer on grounds of confidentiality. (E) The right of the accused to challenge the evidence presented by the Prosecution shall remain unaffected subject only to limitations contained in Sub-rules (C) and (D). (F) Nothing in Sub-rule (C) or (D) above shall effect a Trial Chamber's power under Rule 89(C) to exclude evidence if its probative value is substantially outweighed by the need to ensure a fair trial.

History of ICTY Rule 70

8.5.400 Rule 70(B) was added in October 1994, according to the amendment procedure laid down in Rule 6(B), by unanimous vote of the judges. The amendment was designed to meet a problem encountered by the Prosecutor in the field, namely that his investigations were being hampered by the fact that a number of bodies, in particular certain States and non-governmental organisations, had information which could help him to identify incidents worthy of further investigation, but which they were reluctant to release since it had been provided to them on a confidential basis. Hence the amendment was introduced to protect the source of such information.

8.5.401 The Rule was amended at the fifth plenary session "to improve the working of the Tribunal" (second Annual Report, para. 24). The words, "and shall in any event not be given in evidence without prior disclosure to the accused" were added to para. (B), to ensure disclosure to the accused prior to the presentation in court of any information covered by that para.

8.5.402 Paras. (C),(D), (E) and (F) were added at the eighth plenary session in October 1995, following a proposal by the Prosecutor, to allow the Prosecutor to use as evidence information provided to him on a confidential basis, while at the same time protecting the source by restricting the power of a Trial Chamber to order the source to produce additional evidence or to summon a representative of the source as a witness.

8.5.403 Paras. (C), (D) and (F) were further amended at the thirteenth plenary session on 25 July 1997 (see Revision 10 of the Rules or ICTR Rule 70 for comparison).

History of ICTR Rule 70

8.5.404 Paras. (C),(D), (E) and (F) were added at the Fourth Plenary Session, held 1–5 June 1997 in Arusha, to bring ICTR Rule 70 into line with ICTY Rule 70. Thus ICTR Rule 70 is now identical to ICTY Rule 70, except for para. (F) of ICTY Rule 70—applying the rule to the accused—which is absent from ICTR Rule 70.

Applicability of Rule 70 to the Accused

8.5.405 Although ICTY Rule 70(F) appears to make the rule applicable, *mutatis mutandis*, to the accused, it fails, in fact, to do so. The Prosecutor may set the rule in motion *proprio motu*, whereas the accused may do so only if a Trial Chamber grants its application, which would no doubt frequently be opposed by the Prosecutor. Moreover, para. (F) does not provide, as it should do, that any such application may be *ex parte* by the accused. If the application to protect a confidential source is made *inter partes*, however, the Prosecutor will learn of the source, thereby defeating the purpose of the application.

Applicability to Witness Statements

8.5.406 See the discussion by the Trial Chamber in two separate opinions (Judge Stephen and Judge Vohrah) and one separate and dissenting opinion (Judge McDonald) issued on 27 November 1996 on a *Prosecution Motion for Production of Defence Witness Statements*. The issue presented to the Chamber was "whether the Trial Chamber has the power to order the Defence to disclose to the Prosecution a witness's prior statement, taken by or on behalf of the Defence in anticipation of litigation, after the witness has testified" (para. 1, Opinion of Judge McDonald). The Chamber was unanimous in holding that the Rules did not specifically address this issue. Rule 70 does not specifically cover the issue since it refers to documents *prepared by a party, its assistants or representatives*, which does not strictly apply to a witness statement, being prepared primarily by the witness, albeit the defence team may have assisted in drawing it up and having it sworn. The majority (Judges Stephen and Vohrah) held in any event that such statements were protected by legal professional privilege and thus not subject to disclosure to the Prosecution.

Examples

8.5.407 See the commentary to Rule 66(A), above, and the *Decision on the Production of Discovery Materials*, rendered by the Trial Chamber in *Blaškić* on 27 January 1997. In that case, the Chamber held that:

the notes of the investigators ... as well as the internal reports at the Office of the Prosecutor from any expert witness ... must fall within the scope of Sub-rule 70(A) and not be the subject of any disclosure or exchange. (paragraph 40)

8.5.408 See also the *Order for the Production of Documents used to prepare for testimony* rendered in *Blaškić* on 22 April 1999, in which the Chamber held that materials used indirectly in the preparation of a defence did not constitute "internal documents" within the meaning of Rule 70(A) and accordingly their production to the opposite side could be ordered. See also *Ndayambaje, Decision on the Defence Motion for Disclosure*, 25 September 2001, in which the Trial Chamber held that questionnaires used by the Prosecution investigators and the specific questions asked to particular prosecution witnesses at the time of the collection of the witnesses statements constitute 'notes of investigators' falling under Rule 70(A). However, see also *Kajelijeli, Decision on Defence Motion Seeking to Interview Prosecutor's Witnesses or Alternatively to be Provided with a Bill of Particulars*, 12 March 2001, in which the Trial Chamber held that the "original tape recordings, and/or transcripts of tape recordings" of interviews of witnesses by the Prosecution could be sought by the Defence pursuant to Rule 66(B).

8.5.409 Rule 70 was applied to a witness in *Blaškić*. In its *Decision on the Prosecutor's Motion for Video Deposition and Protective Measures*, rendered on 11 November 1997, the Trial Chamber granted the Prosecutor's Motion, designed to bring a certain witness A to testify, subject to the following conditions:

— Witness A shall be heard at a closed session;

— classified documents the provision of which was sought by the Defence shall not be provided to it unless the Government concerned should decide to provide them on its own initiative;

— the scope of the Defence cross-examination shall be restricted to the scope of the direct examination, the Chamber reserving for itself the right to rule in any dispute in this respect;

— in accordance with Sub-rule 70(D), Witness A may decline to answer a question about the information involved or about its origin on grounds of its confidentiality;

— a representative of the Government concerned may be present in the courtroom at the time of Witness A's deposition.

8.5.410 The Government mentioned was that of which the witness was a national; it had imposed conditions for the witness to be heard before the Tribunal.

Cross Reference: Rules 90(E) and 97.

* * * * *

DEPOSITIONS

8.5.411

ICTY Rule 71 Depositions	ICTR Rule 71 Depositions
(A) Where it is in the interests of justice to do so, a Trial Chamber may order, *proprio motu* or at the request of a party, that a deposition be taken for use at trial, whether or not the person whose deposition is sought is able physically to appear before the Tribunal to give evidence. The Trial Chamber shall appoint a Presiding Officer for that purpose. (B) The motion for the taking of a deposition shall indicate the name and whereabouts of the person whose deposition is sought, the date and place at which the deposition is to be taken, a statement of the matters on which the person is to be examined, and of the circumstances justifying the taking of the deposition. (C) If the motion is granted, the party at whose request the deposition is to be taken shall give reasonable notice to the other party, who shall have the right to attend the taking of the deposition and cross-examine the person whose deposition is being taken. (D) Deposition evidence may be taken either at or away from the seat of the Tribunal, and it may also be given by means of a video-conference. (E) The Presiding Officer shall ensure that the deposition is taken in accordance with the Rules and that a record is made of the deposition, including cross-examination and objections raised by either party for decision by the Trial Chamber. He shall transmit the record to the Trial Chamber.	(A) At the request of either party, a Trial Chamber may, in exceptional circumstances and in the interests of justice, order that a deposition be taken for use at trial, and appoint, for that purpose, a Presiding Officer. (B) The motion for the taking of a deposition shall be in writing and shall indicate the name and whereabouts of the person whose deposition is sought, the date and place at which the deposition is to be taken, a statement of the matters on which the person is to be examined, and of the exceptional circumstances justifying the taking of the deposition. (C) If the motion is granted, the party at whose request the deposition is to be taken shall give reasonable notice to the other party, who shall have the right to attend the taking of the deposition and cross-examine the witness. (D) The deposition may also be given by means of a video-conference. (E) The Presiding Officer shall ensure that the deposition is taken in accordance with the Rules and that a record is made of the deposition, including cross-examination and objections raised by either party for decision by the Trial Chamber. He shall transmit the record to the Trial Chamber.

History of ICTY Rule 71

8.5.412 This rule was amended at the twenty-first plenary session on 30 November 1999 to remove the reference to "exceptional circumstances" and to provide that a Trial Chamber may order a deposition to be taken "whether or not the person whose deposition is sought is able physically to appear before the Tribunal to give evidence." The net effect of these changes should be to make depositions more common.

Use of Rule 71 in the Event of the Temporary Unavailability of a Judge

8.5.413 This seems to be considered permissible when all the parties consent (as in, for example, the *Kupreškić Decision on Prosecution and Defence Requests to Proceed by Deposition* of 11 February 1999), but not where one of the accused objects (see the Appeals Chamber's *Decision on Appeal by Dragan Papić against ruling to proceed by deposition* of 15 July 1999, invalidating the *Decision on Prosecution Request to Proceed by Deposition* rendered on 25 February 1999 by the Trial Chamber in *Kupreškić*).

8.5.414 Rule 71 was used in *Blaškić* to enable two of the Trial Chamber Judges to hear evidence in the temporary absence of the third Judge, in order to avoid delaying the trial. The Trial Chamber appointed the two Judges as Presiding Officers pursuant to Rule 71(A) to take the depositions of three Prosecution witnesses on 19 and 20 February 1998. The depositions of the witnesses were taken in a manner similar to that in which witness testimony is heard in the course of a trial, with examination-in-chief, cross-examination and re-examination, and the application of protective measures for the witnesses. The Judges, Prosecution and Defence were not robed for the deposition hearings. See *Blaškić Decision on the Prosecutor and Defence Motions to Proceed by Deposition*, Trial Chamber, 19 February 1998.

8.5.415 The same approach was taken in the *Kupreškić* trial on 11 February 1999, when one of the Judges was temporarily unavailable due to illness. The proceedings continued as the taking of depositions with the two remaining trial judges sitting as Presiding Officers, following a request made by the prosecution pursuant to Rule 71(A). See *Decision on Prosecution and Defence Requests to Proceed by Deposition* rendered on 11 February 1999.

8.5.416 This approach was again adopted in *Kordić and Čerkez* (see *Decision on Prosecution Request to Proceed by Deposition*, Trial Chamber, 13 April 1999).

8.5.417 The danger to be avoided is for it to become a matter of routine for only two judges to sit to hear evidence, with the third judge reading the transcripts. This danger has not, so far, materialised and the use of depositions in this way remains a rarity.

Video Conference

8.5.418 Rule 71(D) was applied by the Trial Chamber in *Tadić* to enable testimony to be given by video-link. In its *Decision on the Defence Motion to Summon and Protect Defence Witnesses, and on the Giving of Evidence by Video-Link*, dated 25 June 1996 (the "*Tadić Video-Link Decision*"), the Trial Chamber stated in relation to Video-Link Testimony:

> 18. . . . Rule 71 (D) is not intended to provide for the giving of testimony by video-link but is concerned with the admission of evidence taken by deposition for subsequent use at trial. However, because of the extraordinary circumstances attendant upon conducting a trial while a conflict is ongoing or recently ended, it is in the interest of justice for the Trial Chamber to be flexible and endeavour to provide the Parties with the opportunity to give evidence by video-link.

19. It cannot be stressed too strongly that the general rule is that a witness must physically be present at the seat of the International Tribunal. The Trial Chamber will, therefore, only allow video-link testimony if certain criteria are met, namely that the testimony of a witness is shown to be sufficiently important to make it unfair to proceed without it and that the witness is unable or unwilling to come to the International Tribunal.

8.5.419 "Acknowledg(ing) the need to provide for guidelines to be followed in order to ensure the orderly conduct of the proceedings when testimony is given by video-link," the Chamber then proceeded to lay down guidelines for testimony given by video-link (para. 22):

(1) the party making the application for video-link testimony should make arrangements for an appropriate location from which to conduct the proceedings. The venue must be conducive to the giving of truthful and open testimony. Furthermore, the safety and solemnity of the proceedings at the location must be guaranteed. The non-moving party and the Registry must be informed at every stage of the efforts of the moving party and they must be in agreement with the proposed location. Where no agreement is reached on an appropriate location, the Trial Chamber shall hear all parties, including the Registry, and make a final decision. The following locations should preferably be used: (i) an embassy or consulate, (ii) offices of the International Tribunal in Zagreb or Sarajevo, or, (iii) a court facility.

(2) the Trial Chamber will appoint a Presiding Officer to ensure that the testimony is given freely and voluntarily. The Presiding Officer will identify the witnesses and explain the nature of the proceedings and the obligation to speak the truth. He will inform the witnesses that they are liable to prosecution for perjury in case of false testimony, will administer the taking of the oath and will keep the Trial Chamber informed at all times of the conditions at the location.

(3) unless the Trial Chamber decides otherwise, the testimony shall be given in the physical presence only of the Presiding Officer and, if necessary, of a member of the Registry technical staff.

(4) the witnesses must by means of a monitor be able to see, at various times, the Judges, the accused and the questioner; similarly the Judges, the accused and the questioner must be able to observe the witness on their monitor.

(5) a statement made under solemn declaration by a witness shall be treated as having been made in the courtroom and the witness shall be liable to prosecution for perjury in exactly the same way as if he had given evidence at the seat of the International Tribunal.

8.5.420 In the same Decision, the Trial Chamber also granted safe conducts (temporary immunity from arrest) for a number of defence witnesses (see Rule 54, 8.4.47 et seq.).

8.5.421 This Decision was followed by the *Decision On The Motion To Allow Witnesses K, L And M To Give Their Testimony By Means Of Video-Link Conference*, rendered in *Delalić et al.* on 28 May 1997 by the Trial Chamber (see 8.5.424 et seq.).

8.5.422 See also the *Decision on the Prosecutor's Motion for Deposition Evidence* rendered in *Dokmanović* on 11 March 1998, in which the Chamber granted the Prosecutor's Motion to allow a witness to testify by video-conference. The Chamber insisted that the above-mentioned *Tadić* guidelines for the giving of evidence by video-link be followed. The same ruling was given in the *Decision on Defence Motions for Video Link Conference* in *Dokmanović* on 22 May 1998.

8.5.423 Note that ICTY Rule 71 *bis* now explicitly refers to the receipt of testimony via video-conference link if it is "in the interests of justice" for the Chamber to so order (see 8.5.428).

Video Conference and the Right of Confrontation

8.5.424 The *Tadić Video-Link Decision* was followed by the *Decision On The Motion To Allow Witnesses K, L And M To Give Their Testimony By Means Of Video-Link Conference* in *Delalić et al* on 28 May 1997, by the Trial Chamber. The Chamber applied the two criteria laid down in the *Tadić Video-Link Decision*, allowing video-conferencing only when it can be shown (1) that the testimony of the witness is sufficiently important to make it unfair to proceed without it and (2) that the witness is unable or unwilling to come to the Tribunal. The Chamber then added a third criterion—(3) that the accused will not thereby be prejudiced in the exercise of his right to confront the witness.

8.5.425 The Chamber also affirmed that testimony by video-conference may be less weighty than testimony given in the courtroom:

> 18. The Trial Chamber also notes that the Tadić Decision sets forth the view that the evidentiary value of testimony provided by video-link is not as weighty as testimony given in the courtroom (see paragraph 21). The distance of the witness from the solemnity of the courtroom proceedings and the fact that the witness is not able to see all those present in the courtroom at the same time, but only those on whom the video camera is focused, may detract from the reliance placed upon his or her evidence. The Trial Chamber agrees with this general principle, whilst also considering that it is a matter for the assessment of the Chamber when evaluating the evidence as a whole, to determine how credible each witness is.

8.5.426 The Trial Chamber also approved the guidelines for video-conference testimony laid down in the *Tadić Video-Link Decision* (see para. 22 of the *Tadić Decision*, quoted above) and stated that it "will ensure that these guidelines are scrupulously followed in the present case" (para. 21, *Delalić et al* Decision, 28 May 1997).

Cross Reference: ICTY Article 21(4)(e) and Rule 90(A).

8.5.427 For ICTR jurisprudence, see also the *Decision on the Extremely Urgent Request made by the Defence for the taking of a Teleconference Deposition* rendered on 6 March 1997 in *Rutaganda* by the Trial Chamber. The defence witnesses in question, in respect of whom video-conferencing had been requested by defence counsel, were dispersed from their refugee camp in Congo before the Chamber could consider the Motion; the Chamber therefore considered and granted an alternative request of the defence to the effect "(1) that every effort should be made to assist the Defence in locating the sixteen witnesses at issue . . . and isolating them from the main body of refugees; (2) that, to that end, the co-operation of States, the United Nations Organisation

... and any other organisation that could be of help in the matter, be solicited; (3) that the said witnesses be placed under the protection of the Tribunal as soon as possible after they are located and isolated from the main body of refugees."

8.5.428

ICTY Rule 71 *bis* Testimony by Video-Conference Link
At the request of either party, a Trial Chamber may, in the interests of justice, order that testimony be received via video-conference link.

History of ICTY Rule 71 *bis*

8.5.429 This rule was added at the twenty-first plenary session on 30 November 1999. See 8.5.418 *et seq.*, above, on video-conference link as a form of deposition.

* * * * *

MOTIONS

8.5.430

ICTY Rule 72 Preliminary Motions	ICTR Rule 72 Preliminary Motions
(A) Preliminary motions, being motions which (i) challenge jurisdiction; (ii) allege defects in the form of the indictment; (iii) seek the severance of counts joined in one indictment under Rule 49 or seek separate trials under Rule 82 (B), or (iv) raise objections based on the refusal of a request for assignment of counsel made under Rule 45 (C) shall be in writing and be brought not later than thirty days after disclosure by the Prosecutor to the defence of all material and statements referred to in Rule 66(A)(i) and shall be disposed of not later than sixty days after they were filed and before the commencement of the opening statements provided for in Rule 84. (B) Decisions on preliminary motions are without interlocutory appeal save (i) in the case of motions challenging jurisdiction;	(A) Preliminary motions by either party shall be brought within thirty days following disclosure by the Prosecutor to the Defence of all the material envisaged by Rule 66(A)(i). (B) Preliminary motions by the accused are: (i) Objections based on lack of jurisdiction; (ii) Objections based on defects in the form of the indictment; (iii) Applications for severance of crimes joined in one indictment under Rule 49, or for separate trials under Rule 82(B); (iv) Objections based on the denial of request for assignment of counsel. (C) The Trial Chamber shall dispose of preliminary motions *in limine litis*. (D) Decisions on preliminary motions are without interlocutory appeal, save in the case of dismissal of an objection based on lack of jurisdiction, where an appeal will lie as of right;

(ii) in other cases where certification has been granted by the Trial Chamber, which may grant such certification if the decision involves an issue that would significantly affect the fair and expeditious conduct of the proceedings or the outcome of the trial, and for which, in the opinion of the Trial Chamber, an immediate resolution by the Appeals Chamber may materially advance the proceedings.

(C) Appeals under paragraph (B)(i) shall be filed within fifteen days and requests for certification under paragraph (B)(ii) shall be filed within seven days of filing of the impugned decision. Where such decision is rendered orally, this time-limit shall run from the date of the oral decision, unless

(i) the party challenging the decision was not present or represented when the decision was pronounced, in which case the time-limit shall run from the date on which the challenging party is notified of the oral decision; or

(ii) the Trial Chamber has indicated that a written decision will follow, in which case, the time-limit shall run from filing of the written decision.

If certification is granted, a party shall appeal to the Appeals Chamber within seven days of the filing of the decision to certify.

(D) For the purposes of paragraphs (A)(i) and (B)(i), a motion challenging jurisdiction refers exclusively to a motion which challenges an indictment on the ground that it does not relate to:

(i) any of the persons indicated in Articles 1, 6, 7 and 9 of the Statute;
(ii) the territories indicated in Articles 1, 8 and 9 of the Statute;
(iii) the period indicated in Articles 1, 8 and 9 of the Statute;
(iv) any of the violations indicated in Articles 2, 3, 4, 5 and 7 of the Statute.

(E) An appeal brought under paragraph (B)(i) may not be proceeded with if a bench of three Judges of the Appeals Chamber, assigned by the President, decides that the appeal is not capable of satisfying the requirement of paragraph (D), in which case the appeal shall be dismissed.

(E) Notice of appeal envisaged by Sub-Rule (D) shall be filed within fifteen days from the impugned decision.

(F) Failure to comply with the time-limits prescribed in this Rule shall constitute a waiver of the rights. The Trial Chamber may, however, grant relief from the waiver upon showing good cause.

(G) Objections to the form of the indictment, including an amended indictment, shall be raised by a party in one motion only, unless otherwise allowed by a Trial Chamber.

(H) For purposes of Rule 72(B)(i) and (D) an objection based on lack of jurisdiction refers exclusively to a motion which challenges an indictment on the ground that it does not relate to:

(i) any of the persons indicated in Articles 1, 5, 6 and 8 of the Statute;
(ii) the territories indicated in Articles 1, 7 and 8 of the Statute;
(iii) the period indicated in Articles 1, 7, and 8 of the Statute, or
(iv) any of the violations indicated in Articles 2, 3, 4 and 6 of the Statute.

(I) An appeal brought under Rule 72 (D) my not be proceeded with if a bench of three Judges of the Appeals Chamber, assigned by the presiding Judge of the Appeals Chamber, decides that the appeal is not capable of satisfying the requirements of paragraph (H), in which case the appeal shall be dismissed.

History of ICTY Rule 72

8.5.431 This rule has been substantially amended since it was first adopted. This is perhaps not surprising since Motions are the principal mode of communication between the Parties and the Chamber and the means by which the Parties secure the desired orders or other action by the Chamber.

8.5.432 The old Rule 72 (before it was effectively "swapped" with Rule 73 and substantially amended at the fourteenth plenary session (see below)) was amended at the fifth plenary session in January 1995, adding the words, "and without interlocutory appeal, save in the case of dismissal of an objection based on lack of jurisdiction," to the then undivided para. (B). Para. (B) of the old rule was amended at the eleventh plenary session, as a result of an interlocutory appeal by the Prosecutor in Đukić, which was discontinued as a result of the death of the accused. It was not clear that the appeal was within the ambit of the interlocutory appeals allowed under the then Rule 72(B); hence a system was introduced for obtaining leave to appeal in such cases from a three-judge panel of the Appeals Chamber.

8.5.433 The old Rule 72(B)(ii) was amended at the thirteenth plenary session, on 25 July 1997, changing the time-period of seven days to fifteen days for filing interlocutory appeals (the time-period now appears in Rule 72(C), and has been changed back to seven days, subject to the exceptions in paragraphs (i) and (ii)).

8.5.434 The old Rule 72, with Rule 73, was comprehensively amended at the fourteenth plenary session on 12 November 1997. Before the fourteenth plenary, Rule 72 had read:

Rule 72
General Provisions

(A) After the initial appearance of the accused, either party may move before a Trial Chamber for appropriate relief or ruling. Such motions may be written or oral, at the discretion of the Trial Chamber.

(B) The Trial Chamber shall dispose of preliminary motions in limine litis and without interlocutory appeal, save

(i) in the case of dismissal of an objection based on lack of jurisdiction, where an appeal will lie as of right;

(ii) in other cases where leave is granted by a bench of three Judges of the Appeals Chamber, upon serious cause being shown, within fifteen days following the impugned decision.

8.5.435 The ICTY's fourteenth plenary amendments to Rules 72 and 73 largely follow the ICTR's amendments to these Rules, made at the ICTR's Fourth Plenary Session, held in Arusha, 2–6 June 1997 (see the History of ICTR Rules 72 and 73, below).

8.5.436 At the eighteenth plenary session on 9–10 July 1998, the period for bringing preliminary motions was changed from sixty days to thirty days. At the same plenary, the last sentence of Rule 72(C) and paragraphs (i) and (ii) were also added. Identical amendments were added to Rules 65, 73, and 77. These amendments are designed to deal with the situation where a party seeks leave to appeal from an *oral* decision. Rule 72(A) was further amended, removing the reference to the disposal of motions "*in limine litis*," at the twentieth plenary session held on 30 June–2 July 1999. The rule was amended at the twenty-first plenary session on 30 November 1999 to provide for a fifteen-day time limit for filing appeals as of right under Rule 72(B)(i). Paras. (D) and (E) were added on 19 January 2001, after the twenty-third plenary session.

8.5.437 At the extraordinary plenary session held on 23 April 2002, paras. (B) and (C) were amended to introduce a certification system for certain interlocutory appeals. The words "of the Appeals Chamber" were added to para. (E) on 12 December 2002.

History of ICTR Rule 72

8.5.438 ICTR Rules 72 and 73 were amended at the ICTR fourth plenary session, held in Arusha 1–5 June 1997. They were rearranged in order to clarify the substance of and time limits for both parties to submit preliminary and other motions.

8.5.439 Rule 72(B) was further amended at the fifth plenary session on 8 June 1998, altering the words "Preliminary motions by the accused *shall include*" to "Preliminary motions by the accused *are*," to indicate that the list of preliminary motions which follows is exhaustive rather than illustrative. The rule has since been amended in various ways to ensure inconsistency with ICTY Rule 72.

Motions Should Be Respectful

8.5.440 See the *Order* issued by the Trial Chamber in *Delalić et al.* on 18 May 1998:

> FURTHER CONSIDERING the Response to be unacceptable as a document filed with the International Tribunal, in the quality of its language, its attacks on the Office of the Prosecutor and its impugning of the proceedings of the International Tribunal itself;
>
> EXPRESSING CONCERN that there has been a pattern of filing documents of such disrespectful nature and that this should cease immediately.

Decisions on Motions Challenging Jurisdiction

8.5.441 Purely jurisdictional objections *must* be raised as a preliminary motion within the time-limit prescribed by Rule 72(A), while the Chamber will decide at trial whether to rule on mixed questions of fact and law. See *Decision on Defence Motion to Clarify* rendered by the Trial Chamber on 15 January 1999 in *Kordić*. See also the *Decision on the Defence Motion on Jurisdiction* rendered by the Trial Chamber on 18 June 1997 in *Kanyabashi*.

ICTY Challenges to Jurisdiction

8.5.442 In *Tadić*, the accused filed, on 23 June 1995, an objection based on lack of jurisdiction, challenging the legality of the establishment of the Tribunal by the Security Council, the primacy of the Tribunal and its competence *ratione materiae*.

8.5.443 The Trial Chamber denied the motion in its *Decision on the Defence Motion on Jurisdiction* of 10 August 1995. The Chamber held that the Tribunal lacked the competence to review the decision of the Security Council to establish the Tribunal, that the conferral of primacy did not violate principles of State sovereignty under international law and that in this case it was not necessary for its competence *ratione materiae* to decide whether or not the conflict in the former Yugoslavia was international in character. Accordingly, the Trial Chamber held that it was not competent to determine the first ground of challenge and dismissed the other two.

8.5.444 In relation to Rule 73(A)(i) (now Rule 72(A)(i)), the Chamber said:

> 5. ... this International Tribunal is not a constitutional court set up to scrutinise the actions of organs of the United Nations. It is, on the contrary, a criminal tribunal with clearly defined powers, involving a quite specific and limited criminal jurisdiction. If it is to confine itself to those specific limits, it will have no authority to investigate the legality of its creation by the Security Council.
>
> ...
>
> 9. [Rule 73(A)(i)] relates to challenges to jurisdiction and is no authority for engaging in investigation, not into jurisdiction, but into the legality of the action of the Security Council in establishing the International Tribunal.

8.5.445 See also Commentary to ICTY Article 2 above on the question of whether the internationality of the armed conflict is a jurisdictional prerequisite for the application of Article 2 (4.2.319 *et seq.*).

8.5.446 On 14 August 1995, Defence counsel filed notice of interlocutory appeal under Rule 72 against the Trial Chamber's *Decision on the Defence Motion on Jurisdiction*, pursuant to the expedited procedure of Rules 108 and 116 bis. See commentary to Rule 72(B), at 8.5.456 *et seq*.

ICTR Challenges to Jurisdiction

8.5.447 In *Karemera*, the Defence objected to the jurisdiction of the Tribunal over any accused on the bases of (i) the illegality of Security Council Resolution 955, and (2) the lack of independence of the Tribunal. The Trial Chamber held that objections based on the structural lack of jurisdiction of the Tribunal could not be entertained under Rule 72, as they did not relate to the indictment against the accused.

8.5.448 The Defence raised additional objections based on alleged lack of personal jurisdiction. These included allegations of (i) arbitrary detention, (ii) the denial of the right to choose counsel, and (iii) the absence of counsel during the accused's initial appearance. The Trial Chamber dismissed all of these objections. (See paras. 32–38 of the *Decision on the Defence Motion pursuant to Rule 72, Karemera*, 25 April 2001). Again, these are not properly issues of *personal* jurisdiction (which could be raised if, e.g. a corporation were indicted), but of complaints which could be raised on their merits.

Decisions on Objections Based on Defects in the Form of the Indictment

8.5.449 The following principles emerge from challenges that have been bought to the form of the indictment, pursuant to what is now ICTY Rule 72(A)(ii) and ICTR Rule 72(B)(ii).

- the indictment must describe with sufficient detail the acts, places and times of the crimes charged (Tr. Ch., *Delalić et al., Decision on the Motion by the Accused Zejnil Delalić based on Defects in the Form of the Indictment*, 2 October 1996);
- disagreements as to the facts are not sufficient to raise a claim that the indictment is defective. Factual questions are to be determined at trial. A challenge to the indictment is an inappropriate way of raising disagreements as to the facts (*ibid.*; this has been followed in a large number of decisions on challenges to jurisdiction and is firmly established in the Tribunal's jurisprudence);
- the indictment must separate the acts for which the accused is charged as a direct offender from those where he is accused as a superior (*ibid.*);
- the indictment must cite the applicable provisions of the Statute which support the alleged criminal responsibility of the acts mentioned in the indictment (*ibid.*);
- it is permissible for the indictment to charge an accused with two different crimes arising out of one act or omission (this is referred to as "cumulative charging"). Cumulative charging is only relevant to penalty considerations when the accused is found guilty of the charges and is therefore best dealt with at the sentencing stage (*ibid.*; see also *Krnojelac, Decision on the form of the indictment*, 24 February 1999, paras. 5–10) (8.3.1 *et seq.*);
- the principal function of the indictment is to notify the accused in a summary manner as to the nature of the crimes of which he is charged and to present the factual basis for the accusations (Tr. Ch., *Blaškić, Decision on the form of the indictment*, 4 April 1997);
- the indictment must contain certain information which permits the accused to prepare his defence (namely, the identity of the victim(s), the place(s) and approximate date(s) of the alleged crime(s) and the means used to perpetrate the crime(s) in order to avoid prejudicial surprise (*ibid.*);
- the question of knowing whether the allegations appearing in the indictment are vague will, in the final analysis, be settled at trial (*ibid.*). This view has not been held by Chambers in subsequent decisions, however, and vagueness of the indictment is generally a good challenge;
- there is a distinction between the accused's right to be informed in the indictment of the nature and cause of the charges against him, on the one hand, and on the other hand, his right to receive disclosure of evidence in order to be able adequately to prepare for his trial. The former is governed by ICTY Article 18(4) and Rule 47(B) of the Rules of Procedure and Evidence; the latter is governed by ICTY Article 21(4) and Rule 66 *et seq.* of the Rules (para. 11, *Blaškić, Decision on the form of the indictment*, 4 April 1997; see also *Krnojelac Decision on the form of the indictment*, 24 February 1999);

- there is a distinction between facts that must be pleaded in the indictment and evidence which must be disclosed to the accused (*Krnojelac Decision on the form of the indictment*, 24 February 1999, para. 12: "... There is thus a clear distinction drawn between the material facts on which the Prosecutor relies (which must be pleaded) and the evidence by which those material facts will be proved (which must be provided by way of pre-trial discovery)." (see also para. 14, *ibid.* and the discussion of the ICTR Decision in *Nyiramashuko* of 4 September 1998);
- there is equally a distinction between defects in the form of the indictment versus defects in the merits of the indictment (*Decision on the Preliminary Motion filed by the Defence based on Defects in the form of the Indictment*, Trial Chamber, *Nahimana*, 24 November 1997, para. 19);
- vague phrases such as "including, *but not limited to*," "attacks in, *among others*," "*about*," are unacceptable and will be ordered to be struck out (*ibid.*);
- the level of particularity required in an ICTY indictment is different from, and probably lower than, that of domestic jurisdictions, since "the massive scale of the crimes with which the International Tribunal has to deal makes it impracticable to require a high degree of specificity in such matters as the identity of the victims and the dates for the commission of the crimes" (*Kvočka Decision on the form of the indictment*, Trial Chamber, 12 April 1999, para. 17);
- The indictment "must be considered in its totality and it would be incorrect to make a conclusion as to any defect in it upon a selective reading of only certain paragraphs." (*Karemera, Decision on the Defence Motion*, Trial Chamber, 25 April 2001);
- The indictment must be sufficiently specific in terms of times and places. See the *Decision on the Preliminary Motion filed by the Defence based on Defects in the form of the Indictment*, rendered by the Trial Chamber in *Nahimana* on 24 November 1997, where the Chamber held that the Prosecutor had to be more specific in her temporal and geographic references:

    30. The Chamber acknowledges that, given the particular circumstances of the conflict in Rwanda and the alleged crimes, it could be difficult to determine the exact times and places of the acts with which the accused is charged. It is of the opinion, nonetheless, that the temporal and geographic references given by the Prosecutor are not sufficiently precise to enable the accused to unmistakably identify the acts or the sequence of acts for which he is criminally charged in the indictment. The Trial Chamber therefore suggests that the Prosecutor amend [...] the statement of facts in the indictment so as to include more specific indications of the time when and the place where the alleged crimes were committed by the accused.

8.5.450 This was affirmed by the Trial Chamber in the *Decision on the Preliminary Motion filed by the Defence based on defects in the form of the indictment* rendered in *Ntagerura* on 28 November 1997 (para. 23).

Distinguishing Between Forms of Individual Criminal Responsibility

8.5.451 In the *Decision on the Preliminary Motion filed by the Defence based on Defects in the form of the Indictment* rendered by the Trial Chamber in *Nahimana* on 24 November 1997, the Chamber held that the Prosecutor had to specify when the accused was charged with individual responsibility under ICTR Article 6(1) and when under ICTR Article 6(3):

> 33. ... The Chamber notes that the wording of the charges in question is not precise enough in that it does not provide the accused with information that would enable him to establish a link between his acts and the charges against him. The Chamber therefore suggests that the Prosecutor specif[y] which acts of the accused are covered by Article 6(1) and which fall under Article 6(3) of the Statute, or if there is a cumulation of charges.

Averring the Names of the Accused's Alleged Co-Conspirators

8.5.452 The Prosecutor has to provide the names of the accused's alleged co-conspirators in the indictment (*Nahimana*, Tr. Ch., *Decision on the Preliminary Motion filed by the Defence based on Defects in the form of the Indictment*, 24 November 1997). In that *Decision*, the Chamber held that:

> 34. The Chamber observes the same degree of vagueness in the expression "other persons" contained in count 1 [conspiracy to commit genocide]. The Chamber is, in fact, of the opinion that this expression must be clarified by mentioning the names or other identifying information concerning the persons with whom the accused allegedly conspired to commit genocide.

8.5.453 This was affirmed by the Trial Chamber in the *Decision on the Preliminary Motion filed by the Defence based on defects in the form of the indictment* rendered in *Ntagerura* on 28 November 1997:

> 19. ... this Trial Chamber is of the view that in order for the accused to fully understand the charge against him he needs to know who he is alleged to have conspired with and who are his alleged accomplices.

Decisions on Applications for Severance of Crimes Joined in One Indictment under Rule 49, or for Separate Trials under Sub-Rule 82(B)

8.5.454 This is dealt with under ICTY Rule 72(A)(iii) and ICTR Rule 72(B)(iii). In *Delalić et al.*, there were applications for separate trials by all four accused. The Trial Chamber denied the applications. See *Decision on Motions for Separate Trial filed by the Accused Zejnil Delalić and the accused Zdravko Mucić*, 25 September 1996. An application for severance was also lodged in *Dokmanović* on 7 July 1997, and in *Aleksovski* on 19 June 1997.

Objections Based on Denial of Request for Assignment of Counsel

8.5.455 To date, no preliminary motions have been filed under ICTY Rule 72 (A)(iv)/ICTR Rule 72 (B) (iv).

Interlocutory Appeal

8.5.456 No lesser weight is to be attached to decisions rendered by the Appeals Chamber on interlocutory appeals than to decisions rendered on final Appeal (App. Ch., *Judgement, Delalić et al*, 20 February 2001, para 122). The purpose of an appeal, whether on an interlocutory or on a final basis, is to determine the issues raised with finality.

Interlocutory Appeal on Jurisdiction in *Tadić*

8.5.457 In the appeal on jurisdiction in *Tadić*, the Defence appealed against the Decision of the Trial Chamber of 10 August 1995, on all three of the grounds which it had raised in its motion before the Trial Chamber, alleging that the ICTY was unlawfully established, that it enjoys unjustified primacy over competent domestic courts and that subject-matter jurisdiction under Articles 2, 3 and 5 of the Statute was lacking.

8.5.458 The *Tadić Jurisdiction Appeals Decision* was rendered by the Appeals Chamber on 2 October 1995, and has become a landmark decision and common reference point on a number of issues. The Appeals Chamber (1) held, by a majority of four to one, Judge Li dissenting, that the Tribunal was competent to entertain the motion; (2) unanimously dismissed the plea that the Tribunal was not lawfully established; (3) unanimously dismissed the challenge to primacy; and (4) held, Judge Sidhwa dissenting, that the Tribunal had subject-matter jurisdiction in respect of each of the three Articles of the Statute. Thus the Decision of the Trial Chamber was revised in respect of the competence of the Tribunal and confirmed in all other respects, although based on different reasoning in parts. Judges Li, Abi-Saab and Sidhwa appended separate opinions to the majority Decision and Judge Deschênes appended a Declaration concerning the working languages of the ICTY.

8.5.459 In its judgement, the Appeals Chamber considered at length the application of international humanitarian law to the situation in the former Yugoslavia insofar as was necessary for determination of issues of jurisdiction. The Appeals Chamber found that (para. 70):

> an armed conflict exists wherever there is a resort to armed force between States or protracted armed violence between governmental authorities and organised armed groups or between such groups within a State. International humanitarian law applies from the initiation of such armed conflicts and extends beyond the cessation of hostilities until a general conclusion of peace is reached; or, in the case of internal conflicts, a peaceful settlement is achieved. Until that moment, international humanitarian law continues to apply in the whole territory of the warring States or, in the case of internal conflicts, the whole territory under the control of a party, whether or not actual combat takes place there.

8.5.460 Applying these principles to the conflict in the former Yugoslavia, the Appeals Chamber found that an armed conflict existed at all relevant times.

8.5.461 Turning to the question of the characterisation of such conflicts as internal or international, the Appeals Chamber held that for the Tribunal to have jurisdiction under Article 2 of the Statute, the alleged offences must have been committed within the context of an *international* armed conflict. However, the Tribunal had jurisdiction under both Articles 3 and 5 in respect of any armed conflict, be it internal or international. The Appeals Chamber also considered and set out in detail in its Decision the conditions that must be fulfilled for a violation of international humanitarian law to be subject to the jurisdiction of the Tribunal under Article 3 of the Statute

Cross References: See also commentary to ICTY Articles 2–5 above.

Articles:

Alvarez, Jose E., "Nuremberg Revisited: The *Tadić* Case," 7(2) *European Journal of International Law*, (1996).

Greenwood, Christopher, "International Humanitarian Law and the *Tadić* Case," 7 (2) *European Journal of International Law*, 265 (1996).

Interlocutory Appeal Only Available to Parties

8.5.462 See *Decision on Application for Leave to Appeal*, rendered by a Bench of the Appeals Chamber (Judge Cassese, Li and Jan) on 3 June 1997 in the case of Dragan Opačić (IT-95-7-Misc. 1), in which the applicant—a detained witness—sought to appeal a decision of a Trial Chamber:

> 5. On even the most cursory examination of the application, however, it is clear that the applicant . . . lacks standing to invoke Rule 72 of the Rules of Procedure and Evidence. Rule 72 applies to preliminary motions filed by "either party." The term "party" is defined in Rule 2 of the Rules of Procedure and Evidence as "The Prosecutor or the accused." The detained witness, Dragan Opačić, who has not been indicted, being neither the Prosecutor nor the accused, is therefore not a party. Accordingly he has no standing to invoke Rule 72.
>
> 6. If this view of the matter appears overly legalistic, any other ruling would open up the Tribunal's appeals procedures to non-parties—witnesses, counsel, *amicus curiae*, even members of the public who might nurse a grievance against a Decision of the Trial Chamber. This could not be. The Tribunal has a limited appellate jurisdiction which categorically cannot be invoked by non-parties.

8.5.463 A new Rule was, however, introduced at the ICTY's thirteenth plenary session—Rule 108 *bis* ("State Request for Review")—which allows a State, a non-Party, to seek review of a Decision of the Trial Chamber, where its interests are "directly affected" by the Decision.

No Hearing Necessary

8.5.464 To date, the practice has been for applications for leave to appeal to be considered by the Bench of the Appeals Chamber, after receiving motions from the application and the respondent, *without* scheduling a hearing. The Appeals Chamber has denied that this offends the principle *audi alteram partes* ("hear the other side"). See the *Decision on the Prosecution Motion to set aside the Decision of the Appeals Chamber of 29 July 1997*, dated 12 August 1997, in particular para. 8 thereof. The same applies to applications to the Trial Chamber for certification under the amended ICTY Rule 72(B)(ii), which are made in writing.

Interpretation of ICTY Rule 72(B)(ii)

8.5.465 Until para. (B)(ii) was amended, at the extraordinary plenary session on 23 April 2002, to introduce a certification system for certain interlocutory appeals, the system for interlocutory appeal was one of seeking *leave* to appeal.

8.5.466 The system of seeking leave to appeal, or of seeking certification from the Trial Chamber that rendered the Decision, does not exist at the ICTR, where interlocutory appeal lies only from dismissal of a motion based on lack of jurisdiction, and there as of right.

8.5.467 For the case-law under the old ICTY Rule 72(B)(ii), where leave to appeal had to be sought from a bench of the Appeals Chamber, reference should be made to the second edition of this work.

8.5.468

ICTY Rule 73 Other Motions	ICTR Rule 73 Motions
(A) After a case is assigned to a Trial Chamber, either party may at any time move before the Chamber by way of motion, not being a preliminary motion, for appropriate ruling or relief. Such motions may be written or oral, at the discretion of the Trial Chamber. (B) Decisions on all motions are without interlocutory appeal save with certification by the Trial Chamber, which may grant such certification if the decision involves an issue that would significantly affect the fair and expeditious conduct of the proceedings or the outcome of the trial, and for which, in the opinion of the Trial Chamber, an immediate resolution by the Appeals Chamber may materially advance the proceedings (C) The Trial Chamber may certify that an interlocutory appeal during trial from a decision involving evidence or procedure is appropriate for the continuation of the trial, upon a request being made within seven days of the	(A) Subject to Rule 72, either party may move before a Trial Chamber for appropriate ruling or relief after the initial appearance of the accused. The Trial Chamber, or a Judge designated by the Chamber from among its members, may rule on such motions based solely on the briefs of the parties, unless it is decided to hear the motion in open Court. (B) Decisions rendered on such motions are without interlocutory appeal. (C) Where a date has been set for the hearing of a motion, including a preliminary motion, any additional motions to be heard on that date and any supporting material to the motions must be filed at least ten days before the hearing of the motion. Failure to observe this Rule will mean that the later motion will not be considered on the hearing date, nor will any adjournment of the original motion be granted on the basis of subsequent motions filed, save in exceptional circumstances.

issuing of the decision. If such certification is given, a party may appeal to the Appeals Chamber without leave, within seven days of the filing of the certification. If certification is given, a party shall appeal to the Appeals Chamber within seven days of the filing of the decision to certify.	(D) A responding party shall, thereafter, file any reply within five days from the date on which Counsel received the motion. (E) In addition to the sanctions envisaged by Rule 46, a Chamber may impose sanctions against Counsel if Counsel brings a motion, including a preliminary motion, that, in the opinion of the Chamber, is frivolous or is an abuse of process. Such sanctions may include non-payment, in whole or in part, of fees associated with the motion and/or costs thereof. (F) Notwithstanding the time limits in Rule 72(A), the time limit in the present Rule applies.

History of ICTY Rule 73

8.5.469 Like Rule 72, Rule 73 was comprehensively amended at the fourteenth plenary session on 12 November 1997. The old Rule 73 (before the fourteenth plenary) had read:

Rule 73
Preliminary Motions by Accused

(A) Preliminary motions by the accused shall include:
  (i) objections based on lack of jurisdiction;
  (ii) objections based on defects in the form of the indictment;
  (iii) applications for the exclusion of evidence obtained from the accused or having belonged to him;
  (iv) applications for severance of crimes joined in one indictment under Rule 49, or for separate trials under Sub-rule 82(B);
  (v) objections based on the denial of request for assignment of counsel.

(B) Any of the motions by the accused referred to in Sub-rule (A) shall be brought within sixty days after his initial appearance, and in any case before the hearing on the merits.

(C) Failure to apply within the time-limit prescribed shall constitute a waiver of the right. Upon a showing of good cause, the Trial Chamber may grant relief from the waiver.

8.5.470 The ICTY's fourteenth plenary amendments to Rules 72 and 73 largely follow the ICTR's amendments to these Rules, made at the ICTR fourth plenary session, held in Arusha, 2–6 June 1997 (see ICTR Rules 72 and 73, below). It can be seen that preliminary motions consisting of "applications for the exclusion of evidence obtained from the accused or having belonged to him" are no longer considered preliminary motions under the amended Rule 72(A).

8.5.471 At the eighteenth plenary session on 9–10 July 1998, para. (C) was amended. Identical amendments were added to Rules 65, 72 and 77. These amendments, which no longer appear in Rule 73 (C), concern a party seeking leave to appeal from an *oral* decision. Para. (C) was amended at the ICTY's twenty-fifth plenary session, held on 12–13 December, 2001, to add a seven-day time-limit for requesting interlocutory appeal from a decision involving evidence or procedure. At the extraordinary plenary session held on 23 April 2002, paras. (D) and (E) were deleted and paras. (B) and (C) were amended to introduce a certification system for interlocutory appeals for "other motions" (only interlocutory appeals on a challenge to jurisdiction brought by preliminary motion are appealable as of right). This system has not yet been tried and tested, so it remains to be seen how it will function. The fear is that Trial Chambers will be more reluctant to certify that their decisions should be subject to appeal than a bench of the Appeals Chamber would have been under the old system.

History of ICTR Rule 73

8.5.472   ICTR Rules 72 and 73 were substantially amended at the Fourth Plenary Session, held 1–5 June 1997 in Arusha. The ICTY subsequently followed suit, substantially amending the same two Rules at the thirteenth plenary session on 12 November 1997.

ICTY Motions Practice

8.5.473   Motions may be either written or oral. At the pre-trial stage, nearly all motions are written as there are no on-going proceedings at which motions may conveniently be made orally. The requirements concerning the length of written motions is set out in the *Practice Direction on the Length of Briefs and Motions* (IT/184, 19 January 2001). This *Practice Direction* was last revised on 5 March 2002 and is available at: www.un.org/icty/legaldoc/index.htm.

Written Motions

8.5.474   A moving party should include a draft order for relief with each motion submitted to the Trial Chamber, although this is not often done in practice. There is usually no oral argument on pre-trial motions unless specifically requested by counsel for either party and approved by the Trial Chamber taking into account the need to ensure a fair and expeditious trial (Tr. Ch., *Order regulating the filing of and response to Motions, Dosen and Kolundžija*, 12 November 1999). In fact, a request for a hearing in order to have oral argument on pre-trial motions is rarely granted, Chambers usually being of the view that there is sufficient opportunity for canvassing all the arguments in the written pleadings.

Oral Motions at Trial

8.5.475   The position is, however, different—indeed reversed—once the case is at trial, when all parties are at the seat of the Tribunal and appearing in court daily. Then the preference is for oral motions. Following a Bureau decision in the first half of 1999, motions should be made orally and ruled on orally. See the transcript of the *Kupreškić* trial of 3 May 1999:

JUDGE CASSESE: ... Motions. Now, in accordance with a decision by the Bureau ... we have decided that from now onwards, we should all endeavour to have motions made orally and ruled upon orally. Why? This is mainly to save money [and] time, because it has appeared that the translation of so many motions in all the various trials is time-consuming and it is also terribly expensive.

8.5.476 Thus the position would seem to be that where the court is sitting in a trial, oral motions should be submitted and oral decisions rendered, in order to save time and money. Conversely, when the court is not convened in trial proceedings, motions should be submitted in writing to obviate the need for a hearing and for counsel to travel to The Hague to make their arguments.

ICTR Motions Practice

8.5.477 At the ICTR, a Directive on Court Management was adopted at the ICTR fifth plenary session on 8 June 1998, which sets out the ICTR's Motions Practice in Article 37:

ARTICLE 37. MOTIONS PRACTICE

1. The Court Management Section will allocate two half-days every week (which at present are Monday and Friday afternoons) for the hearing of Motions. These days shall hereinafter be referred to as "motion days."

2. *Ordinary Motions Practice*. When the Party filing a Motion does not move for a prompt hearing or for an immediate decision or emergency relief, the following procedure shall be followed. The Court Management Section shall bring the motion and request for hearing to the attention of the Judge or Chamber assigned to the case, which will decide whether to grant a hearing, and if so, will instruct the Court Management Section to schedule such a hearing. The Judge or Chamber may postpone taking such a decision until all the relevant pleadings, including a brief from the opposing party and reply from the moving party, if allowed, have been filed.

3. Any party may move for a prompt hearing if an immediate decision or emergency relief from the court is desired. The Party should indicate whether the Motion is "Urgent" or "Extremely Urgent," in accordance with Article 30 of the present Directive.

4. *Urgent Motions*. An urgent Motion shall be set down for hearing no later than the first motion day after it is filed, provided that there is sufficient time between the date of filing and the first motion day to allow the Parties to make the appropriate arrangements to attend the hearing.

5. *Extremely Urgent Motions*. In the case of motions which are marked "Extremely Urgent," the Court Management Section, upon receiving such a Motion, shall immediately bring it to the attention of the appropriate Judge or Chamber. In the event that the appropriate Judge or Chamber is not available, any other, available Judge or Chamber shall be seized of the Motion. Extremely Urgent Motions shall be set down for hearing no more than three days from the date of filing and in any event as soon as possible. If necessary, the Court Management Section, under the direction of a Judge or Chamber, shall arrange telephone conference facilities for the Parties to be heard without delay by the Judge or Chamber.

6. Parties shall be cautioned against the unwarranted use of the "Urgent" and "Extremely Urgent" designations.

7. Whenever a hearing is granted, the Court Management Section shall immediately issue a written notice to the Judges, Parties and Press and Public Affairs Unit of the date and time of the hearing and, in case of urgency, shall despatch such notice by facsimile and notify the Parties by telephone.

8. *Pending Motions.* A list of pending motions in each case shall be maintained by the Court Management Section. The Court Management Section shall bring pending motions to the attention of the Judges and relevant Parties—and, where the Motions are public, to the Press and Public Affairs Unit—in a timely manner, and, in any event, at least on a weekly basis.

8.5.478 While these provision appear sensible, it is not clear whether and to what extent they are implemented in practice.

Types of Motion

8.5.479 Motions are the means by which a Party seeks to obtain some form of relief or order from the Chamber. They cover, therefore, every subject that may arise in the course of an investigation and trial (as well as an appeal or review).

Motions to Reconsider

8.5.480 Motions to reconsider are not a part of the practice of the ICTY nor provided for in the Rules of Procedure and Evidence. See *Decision on Defence Motion to Reconsider* rendered in *Kovačević* on 30 June 1998, refusing the motion on the grounds that, "motions to reconsider do not form part of the procedures of the International Tribunal and are not provided for in the Rules of Procedure and Evidence of the International Tribunal." See also *Decision refusing Defence Motion to Clarify and Reconsider* rendered in the same case on 30 June 1998 and based on the same reasoning. These decisions were followed in the Trial Chamber's *Decision on Prosecutor's Motion for Reconsideration* in *Kordić and Čerkez* on 15 February 1999.

8.5.481 A similar approach was taken by the ICTR in *Akayesu*, when the Trial Chamber rejected the Prosecutor's *Motion to Reconsider and Rescind the Order of 28 January 1997 for the Disclosure of Witness Statements* of 4 February 1997. This practice was also followed in the *Decision on Prosecutor's Motion for Reconsideration* rendered by the Trial Chamber in *Kordić and Čerkez* on 15 February 1999.

Interlocutory Appeal under Rule 73

8.5.482 Rule 73, like Rule 72 ("Preliminary Motions"), provides for interlocutory appeal (i.e., appeal before the trial has concluded) on denial of motions. The system for several years was of seeking leave to appeal from a bench (three judges) of the Appeals Chamber. That system was replaced, on 23 April 2002, by amendments to Rules 72 and 73, with a certification system, whereby a party whose motion has been refused by the Chamber may be appealed where the Trial Chamber certifies "that an interlocutory appeal during trial from a decision involving evidence or procedure is appropriate for the continuation of the trial."

8.5.483 For decisions under the old, "leave to appeal" system, see the decisions referred to in the second edition of this work.

Denial of Payment

8.5.484 When judges consider that, given the circumstances of the case, a motion is frivolous, without merit, misconceived, unnecessary or unreasonable and that the filing of the motion constitutes an abuse of process, the Trial and Appeals Chambers, in the exercise of their inherent powers, may direct the Registrar to withhold payment to defence counsel in respect of costs associated with preparing that motion.

8.5.485 See *Niyitegeka, Decision on Two Defence Motions*, 27 February 2001, in which the Trial Chamber warned that future frivolous motions could result in non-payment of the associated fees. See also *Kupreškić and Others, Decision on Motions by Zoran Kupreškić, Mirjan Kupreškić and Vladimir Šantic for leave to appeal the Decision of the Appeals Chamber dated 29 May 2001*, 18 June 2001, in which the ICTY Appeals Chamber requested that the Registrar consider withholding the payment of any fees involved in the preparation of what it considered frivolous motions.

* * * * *

CONFERENCES

8.5.486

ICTY Rule 73 *bis* Pre-Trial Conference	ICTR Rule 73 *bis* Pre-Trial Conference
(A) Prior to the commencement of the trial, the Trial Chamber shall hold a Pre-Trial Conference. (B) In the light of the file submitted to the Trial Chamber by the pre-trial Judge pursuant to Rule 65 *ter* (L)(i), the Trial Chamber may call upon the Prosecutor to shorten the estimated length of the examination-in-chief for some witnesses. (C) In the light of the file submitted to the Trial Chamber by the pre-trial Judge pursuant to Rule 65 *ter* (L)(i), the Trial Chamber, after having heard the Prosecutor, shall set the number of witnesses the Prosecutor may call. (D) After commencement of the trial, the Prosecutor may, if he or she considers it to be in the interests of justice, file a motion to reinstate the list of witnesses or to vary the decision as to which witnesses are to be called.	(A) The Trial Chamber shall hold a Pre-Trial Conference prior to the commencement of the trial. (B) At the Pre-Trial Conference, the Trial Chamber or a Judge, designated from among its members, may order the Prosecutor, within a time-limit set by the Trial Chamber or the said Judge, and before the date set for trial, to file the following: (i) a pre-trial brief addressing the factual and legal issues; (ii) admissions by the parties and a statement of other matters not in dispute; (iii) a statement of contested matters of fact and law; (iv) a list of witnesses the Prosecutor intends to call with: (a) the name or pseudonym of each witness;

(E) After having heard the Prosecutor, the Trial Chamber shall determine the time available to the Prosecutor for presenting evidence. (G) During a trial, the Trial Chamber may grant the Prosecutor's request for additional time to present evidence if this is in the interests of justice.	(b) a summary of the facts on which each witness will testify; (c) the points in the indictment on which each witness will testify; and (d) the estimated length of time required for each witness; (v) A list of exhibits the Prosecutor intends to offer stating, where possible, whether or not the defence has any objection as to authenticity. The Trial Chamber or the Judge may order the Prosecutor to provide the Trial Chamber with copies of the written statements of each witness whom the Prosecutor intends to call to testify. (C) The Trial Chamber or the designated Judge may order the Prosecutor to shorten the examination-in-chief of some witnesses. (D) The Trial Chamber or the designated Judge may order the Prosecutor to reduce the number of witnesses, if it considers that an excessive number of witnesses are being called to prove the same facts. (E) After commencement of the trial, the Prosecutor, if he considers it to be in the interests of justice, may move the Trial Chamber for leave to reinstate the list of witnesses or to vary his decision as to which witnesses are to be called. (F) At the Pre-Trial Conference, the Trial Chamber or the designated Judge may order the defence to file a statement of admitted facts and law and a pre-trial brief addressing the factual and legal issues, not later than seven days prior to the date set for trial.

History of ICTY Rule 73 *bis*

8.5.487 This new Rule—as well as Rule 73 *ter*, and indeed the section, Section 6: Conferences—were added at the eighteenth plenary session on 9–10 July 1998. These new rules introduce measures designed to expedite trial proceedings. The rule was amended at the twenty-first plenary session on 30 November 1999 in light of the amendments made at the same plenary session to Rule 65 *ter*. These amendments effectively transferred a number of functions from the Trial Chamber acting at the Pre-Trial Conference to the Pre-Trial Judge.

History of ICTR Rule 73 *bis*

8.5.488 This new Rule was introduced at the Fifth Plenary Session on 8 June 1998. A similar rule, also Rule 73 *bis*, was adopted by the ICTY on 9–10 July 1998. The object of the new Rule, as is apparent from its content, is to expedite the trial proceedings by having the Parties agree to the issues in dispute and efficiently to focus the evidence on those issues. Both the ICTR and ICTY had been criticised for over-lengthy trials. The words, "The Trial Chamber or the Judge may order the Prosecutor to provide the Trial Chamber with copies of the written statements of each witness whom the Prosecutor intends to call to testify," were added to para. (B) at the eighth plenary session on 26 June, 2000. Para. (E) was amended in a minor way at the tenth plenary session on 30–31 May, 2001.

Pre-Trial Brief

8.5.489 ICTY Rule 73 *bis* no longer deals with pre-trial briefs; this has been moved to Rule 65 *ter* (E)(i). ICTR Rule 73 *bis* does, however, continue to regulate this part of the proceedings (since the ICTR does not have Rule 65 *ter* in its Rules). The point of the prosecution filing a pre-trial brief, and the defence setting out with which matters it takes issue in the brief, is to define the issues in dispute before trial in order to avoid evidence being unnecessarily called in respect of matters not in dispute. For an example of an Order issuing from a Pre-Trial Conference, see the *Scheduling Order* of 10 May 1999 in *Simić and others*. As an example of a pre-trial brief, see *Prosecutor's Pre-Trial Brief* filed in *Kvočka et al.* on 9 April 1999.

Reinstatement of Witnesses

8.5.490 This is dealt with in ICTY Rule 73 *bis* (D) and ICTR Rule 73 *bis* (E). For a decision on this sub-rule, see *Decision on the Prosecutor's Motions to add a few more witnesses according to Rule 73(E) dated 17 and 24 March 1998* rendered by the Trial Chamber in *Jelisić* on 27 April 1999 (granting the motion in respect of three witnesses, but rejecting it in respect of a fourth who was deemed otiose). See also the ICTR case of *Semanza, Decision on the Defence Motion for Orders Calling Prosecution Witness VZ etc.*, 6 September 2001, in which the Trial Chamber considered Rule 73 *bis*. The Trial Chamber held that the Prosecution were under no obligation to call witnesses not included in the list of witnesses they indicated they would call. The defence, would be entitled to call these witnesses if it so required. A witness included in the Prosecution's list whom the Prosecution no longer wished to call to testify had not been removed from the list in accordance with Rule 73 *bis* (E). The Trial Chamber held that the Prosecution were not obliged to call the witness but that, if they so required, the Defence could call the witness. The Trial Chamber declined to admit the statements of the witnesses concerned into evidence, holding that the statements would have very little probative value and not assist the Chamber's deliberations.

Varying the Witness List at Trial

8.5.491 Pursuant to ICTR Rule 73 *bis* (E), "after commencement of the trial, the Prosecutor, if he considers it to be in the interests of justice, may move the Trial Chamber for leave to reinstate the list of witnesses or to vary his decision as to which witnesses are to be called." According to the ICTR's jurisprudence, "good cause" must be shown by Prosecutor to vary the list of witnesses at trial. See *Nahimana et al, Decision on the Prosecutor's Motion for Leave to Amend the List of Selected Witnesses*, 26 June 2001, para. 19. See also *Nahimana et al, Decision on the Prosecutor's Application to Add Witness X to its list of Witnesses and for Protective Measures*, 14 September 2001.

8.5.492

ICTY Rule 73 *ter* Pre-Defence Conference	ICTR Rule 73 *ter* Pre-Defence Conference

(A) Prior to the commencement by the defence of its case the Trial Chamber may hold a Conference.
(B) In the light of the file submitted to the Trial Chamber by the pre-trial Judge pursuant to Rule 65 *ter* (L)(ii), the Trial Chamber may call upon the defence to shorten the estimated length of the examination-in-chief for some witnesses.
(C) In the light of the file submitted to the Trial Chamber by the pre-trial Judge pursuant to Rule 65 *ter* (L)(ii), the Trial Chamber, after having heard the defence, shall set the number of witnesses the defence may call.
(D) After commencement of the defence case, the defence may, if it considers it to be in the interests of justice, file a motion to reinstate the list of witnesses or to vary the decision as to which witnesses are to be called.
(E) After having heard the defence, the Trial Chamber shall determine the time available to the defence for presenting evidence.
(F) During a trial, the Trial Chamber may grant a defence request for additional time to present evidence if this is in the interests of justice.
	(A) The Trial Chamber may hold a Conference prior to the commencement by the defence of its case.
	(B) At that Conference, the Trial Chamber or a Judge, designated from among its members, may order that the defence, before the commencement of its case but after the close of the case for the prosecution, file the following:
	(i) admissions by the parties and a statement of other matters which are not in dispute;
	(ii) a statement of contested matters of fact and law;
	(iii) a list of witnesses the defence intends to call with:
	  (a) the name or pseudonym of each witness;
	  (b) a summary of the facts on which each witness will testify;
	  (c) the points in the indictment as to which each witness will testify; and
	  (d) the estimated length of time required for each witness;
	(iv) a list of exhibits the defence intends to offer in its case, stating where possible whether or not the Prosecutor has any objection as to authenticity.
	The Trial Chamber or the Judge may order the Defence to provide the Trial Chamber with copies of the written statements of each witness whom the Defence intends to call to testify.
	(C) The Trial Chamber or the designated Judge may order the defence to shorten the estimated length of the examination-in-chief for some witnesses.

	(D) The Trial Chamber or the designated Judge may order the defence to reduce the number of witnesses, if it considers that an excessive number of witnesses are being called to prove the same facts. (E) After commencement of the defence case, the defence, if it considers it to be in the interests of justice, may move the Trial Chamber for leave to reinstate the list of witnesses or to vary its decision as to which witnesses are to be called.

History of ICTY Rule 73 *ter*

8.5.493 This new Rule—as well as Rule 73 *bis* (of which it is the mirror image for the defence), and indeed the section, Section 6: Conferences—were added at the eighteenth plenary session on 9–10 July 1998. These new rules introduce measures designed to expedite trial proceedings. The rule was amended at the twenty-first plenary session on 30 November 1999 in light of the amendments made at the same plenary session to Rule 65 *ter*. These amendments effectively transferred a number of functions from the Trial Chamber acting at the Pre-Trial Conference to the Pre-Trial Judge.

History of ICTR Rule 73 *ter*

8.5.494 This new Rule was introduced at the Fifth Plenary Session on 8 June 1998. A similar rule, also Rule 73 *ter*, was adopted by the ICTY on 9–10 July 1998. The object of the new Rule, as is apparent from its content, is to expedite the trial proceedings by having the Parties agree to the issues in dispute and efficiently to focus the evidence on those issues. Both the ICTR and ICTY had been criticised for over-lengthy trials. The words, "The Trial Chamber or the Judge may order the Prosecutor to provide the Trial Chamber with copies of the written statements of each witness whom the Prosecutor intends to call to testify," were added to para. (B) at the eighth plenary session on 26 June, 2000. Para. (E) was amended in a minor way at the tenth plenary session on 30–31 May, 2001.

Defence Can Be Ordered to Provide Information Identifying Their Witnesses and Summaries of Their Witnesses' Testimony

8.5.495 Using this Rule, applied in conjunction with Rule 54, and in the absence of protective measures ordered by the Trial Chamber, the Trial Chamber has ordered the Defence to disclose to the Prosecution the *names and identifying information* of its witnesses, as well as summaries of the facts to which the witness will testify. The Trial Chamber cannot, however, order the Defence to disclose prior statements made by the defence witnesses. See *Decision on the Prosecutor's Motion for Seven (7) days advance disclosure of defence witnesses and defence witness statements* rendered in *Blaškić* on 3 September 1998. See also *Scheduling Order* issued in the same case on 7 July 1998.

Order to Submit Detailed Witness Statements

8.5.496 Before ICTY Rule 73 *ter* was amended on 30 November 1999, it provided, like ICTR Rule 73 *ter*, that the defence could be ordered to produce summaries of statements of defence witnesses. In *Kupreškić*, the Prosecutor complained that the defence summaries were "extremely succinct and summary." The Trial Chamber, in its *Decision* of 11 January 1999, agreed with the Prosecution and ordered the defence to provide detailed statements of the statements indicated by the Prosecution, failing which the Prosecution would be granted the right to interview those witnesses before they testified. The Chamber based its decision on the principle of the equality of arms:

> CONSIDERING that the extremely succinct and summary nature of many Defence witness statements does violate the principle of equality of arms, since the Prosecution communicated much more detailed prosecution witness statements to the Defence and to the Trial Chamber before the presentation of its case, thereby enabling the Defence to prepare for cross-examination of prosecution witnesses;

8.5.497 This is somewhat doubtful inasmuch as Judges and Chambers of the ICTY have elsewhere held that the principle of equality of arms is designed to help the defence to achieve procedural parity with the prosecution, and is not meant to be invoked by the prosecution. See the *Separate Opinion of Judge Vohrah on Prosecution Motion for Production of Defence Witness Statements* dated 27 November 1996 in *Tadić*. See the commentary to ICTY Article 21(4)(e) above (8.5.13 *et seq.*).

8.5.498 In *Semanza, Decision on the Defence Motion for Extension of Time for Filing the List of Defence Witnesses*, 4 September 2001, the Trial Chamber held that pursuant to ICTR Rule 73 *ter* (B)(iii) the Defence needed only to consider and note which witnesses it *intended* to call during the trial and not their present whereabouts or availability to testify at trial.

* * * * *

PROCEEDINGS BEFORE TRIAL CHAMBERS

8.5.499

ICTY Rule 74 *Amicus Curiae*	ICTR Rule 74 *Amicus Curiae*
A Chamber may, if it considers it desirable for the proper determination of the case, invite or grant leave to a State, organization or person to appear before it and make submissions on any issue specified by the Chamber.	A Chamber may, if it considers it desirable for the proper determination of the case, invite or grant leave to a State, organization or person to appear before it and make submissions on any issue specified by the Chamber.

Guidelines for Submission of *Amicus* Briefs

8.5.500 Informal guidelines relating to *amicus curiae* practice were adopted by the ICTY Judges at the seventh plenary session held on 2–16 June 1995. The Registry adopted a document entitled "Information concerning the submission of amicus curiae briefs" (IT/122) on 27 March 1997.

History of *Amicus* Submissions

8.5.501 The Chambers have received several requests from a variety of sources, including States, non-governmental organisations and corporations for leave to appear as *amicus curiae*.

The UN Secretary-General as *Amicus*

8.5.502 A Chamber of the ICTR first granted an application to make submissions as *amicus curiae* to a representative of the Secretary-General, specifically Ms. Daphna Shraga from the Office of Legal Affairs in New York, in *Akayesu* on 20 February 1998. The submissions were for the purpose of addressing the scope of the waiver of immunity granted by the Secretary-General to General Romeo Dallaire in order for him to be able to testify under *subpoena* as a defence witness. General Dallaire was a former Force Commander of the United Nations Assistance Mission in Rwanda (UNAMIR). The United Nations Secretariat presented its *amicus curiae* submission at the hearing of 25 February 1998, and prior to General Dallaire's testimony, defining the scope of the waiver of immunity granted to General Dallaire. Ms. Shraga told the court that the waiver did not relate to the release of confidential documents of the United Nations which is subject to the authorisation of the Secretary-General. She further stated, on behalf of the United Nations Secretariat:

> The establishment of a peacekeeping operation, its mandate, nature, operational activities, and resources—both human and material—are the product of decision-making processes of the Security Council and of individual member states. While such decisions may be subject to different appreciations, the trial of an individual accused charged with genocide, crimes against humanity, and violations of Article 3 common to the Geneva Conventions, is not the appropriate context within which the performance of a peacekeeping operation, the propriety and adequacy of its mandate, its operational activities and the decision-making processes relating thereto, should be assessed.
>
> In waiving the immunity of General Dallaire, the Secretary-General has demonstrated his desire to cooperate with the Tribunal. The Secretary-General is convinced, however, that it is in the interest of all concerned that questions put to the witness are limited to matters of direct relevance to the charges made against the accused. It remains, of course, for the Tribunal to decide on the admissibility of any particular question.

8.5.503 In the course of the examination-in-chief of General Dallaire by counsel for the Defence, Judge Kama ruled that confidential reports sent by UNAMIR to the United Nations Secretariat Headquarters in New York were not relevant to the defence of the accused. The witness was therefore not required to answer questions on that aspect of his activities as force Commander of UNAMIR.

Governments as *Amicus*

8.5.504 Pursuant to Rule 74, the Government of the Federal Republic of Germany appeared in the *Tadić* deferral hearing (IT-94-1-D), the Government of the Republic of Bosnia and Herzegovina in the *Lašva River Valley* (IT-95-6-D) and *Bosnian Serb leadership* (IT-95-5-D) deferral hearings and the Federal Republic of Yugoslavia (Serbia and Montenegro) in the *Erdemović* deferral hearing (IT-96-22-D) (see Rules 9 and 10, 5.53 *et seq.* and 5.61 *et seq.*).

8.5.505 In *Tadić*, the Government of the United States of America was given leave to submit a brief on the preliminary motion by the accused objecting to the Tribunal's jurisdiction. The United States submitted its brief based "on its special interest and knowledge as a Permanent Member of the U.N. Security Council and its substantial involvement in the adoption of the Statute of the Tribunal" (Submission of the Government of the United States concerning certain arguments made by counsel for the accused in the case of *the Prosecutor of the Tribunal v. Dusan Tadić*, p. 1), and submitted, among other things, that objecting to the creation of the Tribunal because no such action had been taken before by the Security Council "would condemn the international community to refrain from actions necessary to maintain the peace because such actions had not been taken in the past (and) would effectively prevent the international community from developing and advancing the system of international law."

8.5.506 The Republic of Croatia filed a request on 30 April 1996 to appear as *amicus curiae* in all matters involving its responsibility, rights and legal interests. In particular, Croatia sought leave to be heard as *amicus curiae* in the Rule 61 proceedings against Ivica Rajić (IT-95-12-R61) with respect to the issue of the nature of the conflict in the former Yugoslavia. On 24 May 1996, the Trial Chamber before which the proceeding was pending rejected Croatia's request, without prejudice to its ability to renew it at the time of trial.

Blaškić Subpoena Hearings

8.5.507 In an *Order Submitting the Matter to Trial Chamber II and inviting Amicus Curiae*, issued on 14 March 1997 in *Blaškić*, Judge McDonald directed that a hearing on the issuance of a *subpoena duces tecum* (see Rule 54), scheduled for 16 April 1997, be held before the Trial Chamber, rather than before a single Judge, "considering the significance of the issues to be addressed." In the order, Judge McDonald invited requests for *amicus curiae* briefs on the following questions by 7 April 1997:

> the power of a Judge or Trial Chamber of the International Criminal Tribunal for the former Yugoslavia to issue a subpoena duces tecum to a sovereign State;
>
> the power of a Judge or Trial Chamber of the International Criminal Tribunal for the former Yugoslavia to make a request or issue a subpoena duces tecum to a high government official of a State;

the appropriate remedies to be taken if there is non-compliance [with] a subpoena duces tecum or request issued by a Judge or a Trial Chamber of the International Criminal Tribunal for the former Yugoslavia;

any other issue concerning this matter.

8.5.508 Several persons or organisations filed motions and were granted on 11 April 1997 leave to file *amicus* briefs or to appear as *amicus curiae*. Seven *amicus curiae* were additionally granted leave "to attend the hearing in order to respond to questions from the Judges of the Trial Chamber and to provide any further assistance the Trial Chamber may require."

8.5.509 An almost identical invitation was extended by the Appeals Chamber when this matter came under appeal/review. On this occasion, a number of States sent in *amicus* briefs.

Concerned Organisations

8.5.510 Shortly before the commencement of the *Tadić* trial, a request was filed by Courtroom Television Network. The Network sought leave to appear as *amicus curiae* to oppose a Defence motion to curtail press access to the trial in order to prevent the contamination of witness testimony. The Trial Chamber rejected this request, noting that the bulk of the Defence motion had been denied and that there was no need for a formal submission on behalf of Courtroom Television Network because its views had been fully set forth in its letter requesting leave to appear as *amicus curiae*.

8.5.511 In *Furundžija*, a coalition of women's organisations sought leave to submit an *amicus* brief on discrimination against women in the evidentiary standards applied to victims of sexual offences (see the *Application to file an Amicus Curiae Brief in the Case of the Prosecutor v. Anto Furundžija Case No. IT-95-17/1-T* dated 5 November 1998, discussed at 8.5.396, above). In *Brdjanin and Talić*, the Appeals Chamber permitted an *amicus curiae* brief on behalf of over 30 media organisations to be filed in the *Randal* journalistic privilege case. See 8.4.40.

Milošević and the Appointment of Amicus

8.5.512 In *Milošević*, in light of the fact that the accused indicated that he had no intention to engage a lawyer to represent him, the Trial Chamber order the appointment of three *amicus curiae* to appear at trial. The Trial Chamber stressed that the *amicus* were not representing the accused but to assist in the proper determination of the case. See *Order Inviting Designation of Amicus Curiae*, 23 November 2001, in which the Trial Chamber set out the parameters and issues upon which the *amicus* were invited to assist. On 10 October 2002, the Trial Chamber rendered an oral decision "*instructing the Registrar to revoke the appointment of Michail Wladimiroff as an amicus curiae*," following a complaint by the accused. In rendering the decision, Judge May, the presiding Judge, stated:

> The Chamber has considered this matter very carefully, and has concluded that the statements made by Mr. Wladimiroff, even with the explanations accepted, raise serious questions about the appropriateness of his continuing as amicus

curiae. The Chamber observes that not only did he comment on parts of the case in respect of which evidence has been given, but that he also made an assessment of parts in respect of which evidence had not yet been adduced, and that in both instances he appears to have formed a view of the case unfavourable to the accused. Of particular concern is the view expressed that the accused must be convicted of, at least, some of the charges. The statements taken as a whole, would, in the Chamber's view, give rise to a reasonable perception of bias on the part of the amicus curiae.

Implicit in the concept of an amicus curiae is the trust that the court reposes in "the friend" to act fairly in the performance of his duties. In the circumstances, the Chamber cannot be confident that the amicus curiae will discharge his duties (which include bringing to its attention any defences open to the accused) with the required impartiality.

Accordingly the Chamber has instructed the Registrar to revoke Mr. Wladimiroff's appointment as an amicus curiae. This is a decision that the Chamber has arrived at with regret, since Mr. Wladimiroff has, like the other amici, provided useful assistance to the court.

Relationship Between *Amicus* and *Partie Civile*

8.5.513 As is well known, the procedure of the ICTY and ICTR are based largely on the adversarial model of common law countries, rather than the inquisitorial models of continental, civil law systems. Accordingly, the institution of *Partie Civile*, where alleged victims of the accused's crimes come together in a class action as a Party which has standing before the court, does not exist at the ICTY and ICTR. While it also does not exist at the ICC, moves have been made towards *Partie Civile* in Article 68 of the Rome Statute which, among other things, enables victims to present their "views and concerns." Nonetheless, at the ICTR at least, there have been attempts to establish a *Partie Civile*.

Belgium

Bagosora and Nahimana

8.5.514 Thus, on 2 December 1997, the Government of the Kingdom of Belgium requested leave to appear in the *Bagosora* and *Nahimana* cases as *amicus curiae*, pursuant to Rule 74, to make submissions, *inter alia*, on:

> The right of the Belgians or their legal successors wronged by the massacres committed in 1994 in Rwanda to appear before the Tribunal as plaintiffs rather than as mere witnesses, on the basis notably of Article 23(3) of the Statute and Rules 105 and 106 of the Rules of Procedure and Evidence.

8.5.515 Belgium reiterated its request before the Trial Chamber on 10 February 1998. In a communication dated 26 January 1998, Belgium added the following information. Belgium desired to be permitted, as *amicus curiae*, to call witnesses to testify in the trial. Belgium also reaffirmed its desire that Belgium or those of its citizens harmed in the Rwandan massacres of 1994 appear before the Tribunal 'as plaintiffs and not mere witnesses.'

8.5.516 In a Memorial dated 10 February 1998 and filed on 6 March 1998 (but withdrawn on 10 March 1998), the Prosecutor opposed Belgium's request to be allowed to call witnesses, on the grounds of lack of standing, although it did not object to Belgium being granted leave to make submissions on any issue specified by the Trial Chamber, pursuant to Rule 74. The Prosecutor further stated:

> 14. A systematic appreciation of the Statute and Rules of the Tribunal, as well as general principles of law, will reveal that there are sufficient provisions, usage and principles by which the Prosecutor would accommodate such concerns as may motivate Belgium to seek to intervene in this case and call evidence.

8.5.517 The Prosecutor then went on to enumerate some of these principles:

> (a) as a representative of the aggregation of all member states of the United Nations—including Belgium—the Prosecutor must be presumed to take into account the interests of Belgium in seeing justice done, within the terms of the Statute;
>
> (b) as a representative of the aggregation of victims—including the Belgians who lost their lives during the conflict and their survivors—the Prosecutor must be presumed to take their collective plight into account, within the terms of the Statute;
>
> (c) the Prosecutor's duty to investigate and prosecute under the Statute envisages that she may receive information from governments—including the Government of Belgium; and
>
> (d) the Prosecutor must be presumed to discharge her responsibilities well and in good faith, for international law has recognised the legal principle in the maxim *omnia praesumuntur rite essa acta*.

8.5.518 See also *Ntagerura et al*, Decision of 24 May 2001 and *Decision on the Coalition for Women's Human Rights in Conflict Situations Motion for Reconsideration of the Decision on Application to File an Amicus Curiae Brief*, 24 September 2001, in which the filing of an *amicus* brief was refused.

8.5.519 On victims' rights, see also ICTY Article 24(3)/ICTR Article 23 (3), and Rules 105 and 106.

Semanza

8.5.520 On 15 August 2000, the Kingdom of Belgium filed a request to appear as *amicus curiae* in the case of *Laurent Semanza*. The Belgian Government submitted it had been particularly affected by the events that occurred in Rwanda in 1994. It indicated its intention to make submissions on the scope of Common Article 3 to the Geneva Conventions and Additional Protocol II. Belgium was of the opinion that the two texts had been too restrictively applied by the ICTR. It argued that the relevant test for the admissibility of its request for leave to appear as *amicus* is the "proper determination of the case." The Prosecution did not oppose the application but the defence argued that it was either *res judicata* or premature.

8.5.521 The Trial Chamber, on 9 February 2001, granted the request of Belgium to appear as *amicus* on the scope of Common Article 3 to the Geneva Conventions and

Additional Protocol II. The Trial Chamber stated that it might be useful to "gather additional legal views on the scope of the applicability of Article 3 common of the four Geneva Conventions and Additional Protocol II." However, the Chamber added that the Belgian Government's submission would only be maintainable with respect to the legal principles involved, and not to the particular circumstances of the case or any other ICTR case. The Chamber held that the matter was not *res judicata* and stated that the appropriate time for Belgium to make submissions would be after the presentation of the evidence by the parties and before the presentation of their closing arguments.

Cross References: See the sections on *amicus curiae* under Rules 10 and 61.

8.5.522

ICTY Rule 74 *bis* Medical Examination of the Accused	ICTR Rule 74 *bis* Medical Examination of the Accused
A Trial Chamber may, *proprio motu* or at the request of a party, order a medical, psychiatric or psychological examination of the accused. In such case, the Registrar shall entrust this task to one or several experts whose names appear on a list previously drawn up by the Registry and approved by the Bureau.	A Trial Chamber may, *proprio motu* or at the request of a party, order a medical, including a psychiatric examination or a psychological examination of the accused. In such case, the Registrar shall entrust this task to one or several experts whose names appear on a list previously drawn up by the Registry and approved by the Bureau.

History of ICTY Rule 74 *bis*

8.5.523 This new Rule was added at the eighteenth plenary session on 9–10 July 1998. The procedure of ordering medical examinations was nonetheless already in place before the Rule's introduction.

History of ICTR Rule 74 *bis*

8.5.524 This new Rule was introduced at the Fifth Plenary Session on 8 June 1998.

8.5.525

ICTY Rule 76 Solemn Declaration by Interpreters and Translators	ICTR Rule 76 Solemn Declaration by Interpreters and Translators
Before performing any duties, an interpreter or a translator shall solemnly declare to do so faithfully, independently, impartially and with full respect for the duty of confidentiality.	Before performing any duties, an interpreter or a translator shall solemnly declare to do so faithfully, independently, impartially and with full respect for the duty of confidentiality.

8.5.526 Pursuant to this Rule, the ICTY Registrar promulgated, on 5 March 1999, a *Code Of Ethics For Interpreters And Translators Employed By The International Criminal Tribunal For The Former Yugoslavia* (IT/144).

8.5.527

ICTY Rule 78 Open Sessions	ICTR Rule 78 Open Sessions
All proceedings before a Trial Chamber, other than deliberations of the Chamber, shall be held in public, unless otherwise provided.	All proceedings before a Trial Chamber, other than deliberations of the Chamber, shall be held in public, unless otherwise provided.

8.5.528 Open sessions should be the rule and closed sessions the exception. See in *Tadić*, the *Decision on the Prosecutor's Motion Requesting Protective Measures for witness 'R,'* 31 July 1996, in which the Trial Chamber stated, *inter alia*, with respect to Rule 78:

> The preference of the Trial Chamber is to have open sessions whenever possible so as not to restrict unduly the accused's right to a public hearing and the public's right to information and to ensure that closed sessions are utilized only when other measures will not provide the degree of protection required. (paragraph 7)

Cross Reference: Rule 79.

8.5.529

ICTY Rule 79 Closed Sessions	ICTR Rule 79 Closed Sessions
(A) The Trial Chamber may order that the press and the public be excluded from all or part of the proceedings for reasons of: (i) public order or morality; (ii) safety, security or non-disclosure of the identity of a victim or witness as provided in Rule 75; or (iii) the protection of the interests of justice. (B) The Trial Chamber shall make public the reasons for its order.	(A) The Trial Chamber may order that the press and the public be excluded from all or part of the proceedings for reasons of: (i) public order or morality; (ii) safety, security or non-disclosure of the identity of a victim or witness as provided in Rule 75; or (iii) the protection of the interests of justice. (B) The Trial Chamber shall make public the reasons for its order.

General Principle

8.5.530 Open sessions should be the rule and closed sessions the exception: ". . . it is of great importance that proceedings before this Tribunal should be public as far as possible. Non-public proceedings should be the exception and will be allowed only in accordance with the Statute and the Rules that do provide for certain limited instances where proceedings may be non-public. Over and above the reasons that public proceedings facilitate public knowledge and understanding and may have a general deterrent effect, the public should have the opportunity to assess the fairness of the proceedings. Justice should not only be done, it should also be seen to be done." (Tr. Ch., *Order on Defence Motion Pursuant to Rule 79, Foča*, 22 March 2000, para. 5).

National Security

8.5.531 See *Order for Closed Session* of 8 January 1999 in *Kordić and others* (national security matters may be disclosed in closed session).

Protection of Victims and Witnesses

8.5.532 Rule 79 was considered in *Tadić*. In its *Decision on the Prosecutor's Motion Requesting Protective Measures for witness 'R,'* rendered on 31 July 1996, the Trial Chamber stated, *inter alia*, with respect to Rule 79(A)(ii):

> In balancing the interests of the accused, the public and witness R, this Trial Chamber considers that the public's right to information and the accused's right to a public hearing must yield in the present circumstances to confidentiality in light of the affirmative obligation under the Statute and the Rules to afford protection to victims and witnesses. This Trial Chamber must take into account witness R's fear of the serious consequences to members of his family if information about his identity is made known to the public or the media (para. 6).

Transcripts of Closed Sessions

8.5.533 Even when the Chamber sits in closed session, a transcript continues to be made of the proceedings. These transcripts are not, however, public, unlike transcripts of open sessions. Accordingly, the question has sometimes arisen of the circumstances under which counsel in a related case can obtain access to closed session transcripts of hearings. This has particularly been the case in the Lašva River Valley cases, as there are a large number of such trials, all of which relate in one way or another to the others.

Lašva River Valley Cases: Access to Non-Public Materials

8.5.534 See a series of Orders and Motions in *Lašva River Valley cases* (i.e., *Blaškić, Kordić, Kupreškić et al, Aleksovski* and *Furundžija*), where defence counsel in one case applied for access to non-public materials in another case:

- *Decision on the Motion of the Accused for Access to Non-public Materials in the Lašva Valley and Related Cases*, rendered on 12 November 1998 by the Trial Chamber in *Kordić and Čerkez*.

- *Decision on the Prosecutor's Request to release testimony pursuant to Rule 66 of the Rules of procedure and Evidence given in closed session under Rule 79 of the Rules*, rendered by the Trial Chamber in *Kupreškić* on 29 July 1998, granting the Prosecutor's request to release closed hearing transcripts of witnesses testifying in the *Blaškić* trial to defence counsel in *Kupreškić*. The Prosecutor's request was based on Rule 66(A)(ii) and the requirement that the Prosecutor disclose to the defence "copies of the statements of all witnesses whom the Prosecutor intends to call to testify at trial." Several witnesses who had testified in *Blaškić* were to be called to testify in *Kupreškić*; their testimony in *Blaškić* was, in the opinion of the Chamber, a statement within the meaning of sub-Rule 66(A)(ii) and therefore had to be disclosed to defence counsel.
- Orders and Notices issued on this matter in *Kupreškić et al* and *Furundžija* on 10 December 1998.
- *Opinion further to the Decision of the Trial Chamber seized of the case the Prosecutor v. Dario Kordić and Mario Čerkez dated 12 November 1998* rendered by the *Blaškić* Trial Chamber on 16 December 1998.
- Opinion rendered by the Trial Chamber in *Aleksovski* on 9 February 1999. In that Opinion, the Chamber granted the Prosecution permission to disclose closed session transcripts from the *Aleksovski* case to the defendants in *Kordić*, but with measures to ensure the continuing protection of witnesses, for example the adoption of new pseudonyms, the maintenance of a log showing the names of the members of the defence team who were privy to the non-public information, etc. This Opinion deals with one of two situations. The first is where the Prosecution intends to call the witness in question and is therefore obliged under Rule 66 to disclose the witness's prior statements to the defence. The second is where the Prosecution considers the witness's testimony as exculpatory and therefore as disclosable under Rule 68. The Opinion does not, however, address the situation where (1) the Prosecution does not intend to call the witness (and is, therefore, not obliged to disclose the witness's prior statements under Rule 66); and (2) the Prosecution does not regard the witness's testimony as exculpatory (and is, therefore, not obliged to disclose the witness's statements under Rule 68), but (3) the defence is nonetheless interested in what the witness had said and in consulting the testimony with a view to calling the witness as a witness for the defence. In this scenario, the Chamber's Opinion could not be invoked to grant the defence disclosure of the witness statements.
- *Request Concerning The Release Of Transcripts Of Closed Session Testimony Of Witnesses* rendered in *Kupreškić* on 10 February 1999. The *Kupreškić* Trial Chamber requested the Registrar to disclose to the *Kordić* Trial Chamber the closed session transcripts of

Kupreškić witnesses who had been consulted and who had expressly consented to such release.
- *Further Order on Motion for Access to Non-Public Materials in the Lašva Valley and Related Cases*, Trial Chamber, *Kordić and Čerkez*, 16 February 1999. In this Order, the Chamber granted access to non-public materials produced in other ICTY cases provided that (1) (as concerns materials from the *Kupreškić* and *Furundžija* cases) protected witnesses consented to such access; and (2) (as concerns materials from the *Blaškić* and *Aleksovski* cases) the materials in question related to witnesses who had not objected to such access *and* who are either to be called to testify (in conformity with Rule 66(A)(ii)) or whose testimony constitutes exculpatory evidence (in conformity with Rule 68). The two alternative conditions reflect the two different approaches taken by the *Kupreškić* and *Furundžija* Trial Chamber, on the one hand, and the *Blaškić* and *Aleksovski* Trial Chamber, on the other, to requests for the disclosure of non-public materials from those trials to the defence in *Kordić* and *Čerkez*. The advantage of the approach of the *Kupreškić* and *Furundžija* Trial Chamber is that the defence would have access to *all* materials, where protected witnesses did not object, and the defence would thus be able to decide for itself whether to use that evidence or not. The approach of the *Blaškić* and *Aleksovski* Trial Chamber, on the other hand, simply reiterates the obligations of the Rules and leaves the defence in the hands of the Prosecutor depending on which witnesses the Prosecutor chooses to call and which evidence the Prosecutor deems exculpatory.
- *Decision on the Prosecution and Defence Motions dated 25 January 1999 and 25 March 1999 respectively, Blaškić*, 22 April 1999.

Other Decisions Under Rule 79

Order for Protection of Witnesses, Trial Chamber, *Dokmanović*, 16 March 1998; *Order for Closed Session*, Trial Chamber, *Dokmanović*, 17 March 1998; *Order for Protective Measures in the Matter of Allegations against Prior Counsel*, Appeals Chamber, 26 April 1999.

Cross Reference: Rule 78.

8.5.535

ICTY Rule 80 Control of Proceedings	ICTR Rule 80 Control of Proceedings
(A) The Trial Chamber may exclude a person from the courtroom in order to protect the right of the accused to a fair and public trial, or to maintain the dignity and decorum of the proceedings. (B) The Trial Chamber may order the removal of an accused from the courtroom and continue the proceedings in the absence of the accused if the accused has persisted in disruptive conduct following a warning that such conduct may warrant the removal of the accused from the courtroom.	(A) The Trial Chamber may exclude a person from the courtroom in order to protect the right of the accused to a fair and public trial, or to maintain the dignity and decorum of the proceedings. (B) The Trial Chamber may order the removal of an accused from the courtroom and continue the proceedings in his absence if he has persisted in disruptive conduct following a warning that he may be removed.

8.5.536 This rule has not, so far, been applied by the ICTY or ICTR.

8.5.537

ICTY Rule 81 Records of Proceedings and Evidence	ICTR Rule 81 Records of Proceedings and Evidence
(A) The Registrar shall cause to be made and preserve a full and accurate record of all proceedings, including audio recordings, transcripts and, when deemed necessary by the Trial Chamber, video recordings. (B) The Trial Chamber, after giving due consideration to any matters relating to witness protection, may order the disclosure of all or part of the record of closed proceedings when the reasons for ordering its non-disclosure no longer exist. (C) The Registrar shall retain and preserve all physical evidence offered during the proceedings subject to any Practice Direction or any Order which a Chamber may at any time make with respect to the control or disposition of physical evidence offered during proceedings before that Chamber. (D) Photography, video-recording or audio-recording of the trial, otherwise than by the Registrar, may be authorised at the discretion of the Trial Chamber.	(A) The Registrar shall cause to be made and preserve a full and accurate record of all proceedings, including audio recordings, transcripts and, when deemed necessary by the Trial Chamber, video recordings. (B) The Trial Chamber may order the disclosure of all or part of the record of closed proceedings when the reasons for ordering its non-disclosure no longer exist. (C) The Registrar shall retain and preserve all physical evidence offered during the proceedings. (D) Photography, video-recording or audio-recording of the trial, otherwise than by the Registry, may be authorised at the discretion of the Trial Chamber.

History of ICTY Rule 81

8.5.538 Para. (C) was amended at the thirteenth plenary session on 25 July 1997, adding the words "subject to" and the following. "Registry" was changed to "Registrar" in para. (D), at the fourteenth plenary session on 12 November 1997. The words, "after giving due consideration to any matters relating to witness protection," were added to para. (B) on 19 January 2001, after the twenty-third plenary session.

Orders and Decisions under Rule 81

8.5.539 The Trial and Appeals Chambers routinely issue orders under para. (D) to authorise the release of video- and audio-recordings of trial proceedings. As an example, see the *Order for release of audio-visual record* issued by the Trial Chamber in *Tadić* on 11 May 1995.

8.5.540 This rule was discussed in the *Decision on Motion to Preserve and Provide Evidence* rendered by the Appeals Chamber in an interlocutory motion in *Delalić et al.* on 22 April 1999. The accused applied for the preservation of the video-recordings of the trial because it claimed that they showed that the Presiding Judge was asleep for much of the trial—a ground for appeal from the accused's conviction. The Chamber rejected the motion, *inter qlia* because the Registrar was in any event under an obligation pursuant to Rule 81(A) to make and preserve a video-recording of the proceedings. See also the *Separate Opinion of Judge David Hunt on Motion by Esad Landžo to preserve and provide evidence* of 22 April 1999.

Authorisation of Photography

8.5.541 As an example of an Order under Rule 81(D), see *Order to Authorize Photographing* issued by the Trial Chamber in *Akayesu* on 9 January 1995.

Cross Reference: Rule 48 ("Joinder of Accused")

8.5.542

ICTY Rule 82 Joint and Separate Trials	ICTR Rule 82 Joint and Separate Trials
(A) In joint trials, each accused shall be accorded the same rights as if such accused were being tried separately. (B) The Trial Chamber may order that persons accused jointly under Rule 48 be tried separately if it considers it necessary in order to avoid a conflict of interests that might cause serious prejudice to an accused, or to protect the interests of justice.	(A) In joint trials, each accused shall be accorded the same rights as if he were being tried separately. (B) The Trial Chamber may order that persons accused jointly under Rule 48 be tried separately if it considers it necessary in order to avoid a conflict of interests that might cause serious prejudice to an accused, or to protect the interests of justice.

Conflict of Interest Necessitating Separate Trials

8.5.543 Pursuant to para. (B), "the Trial Chamber may order that persons accused jointly under Rule 48 be tried separately if it considers it necessary in order to avoid a conflict of interests that might cause serious prejudice to an accused. . . ." On this subject, see, e.g., *Decision on Defence Motions for Separate Trials* rendered in *Kupreškić et al* on 15 May 1998, in which the Trial Chamber declined to order separate trials. The Chamber found that the crimes alleged against the accused involved the attack on the Muslim population of Ahmići on 16 April 1993, and were thus part of the same transaction, so that the indictment met the requirements of Rule 48. The Chamber considered that the defence had failed to show how or why a conflict of interest would arise in the joint trial of the accused which would seriously prejudice the trial of the accused or otherwise threaten the interests of justice.

Relevance to Joint Trials of the Absence of a Jury

8.5.544 The fact that trials before the Tribunals are held before judges and not juries has significant implications for the question of whether or not to hold separate trials. See *Nyiramasuhuko and Ntahobali, Decision on the Motion for Separate Trials*, 8 June 2001, para. 16, quoting an oral decision from *Barayagwiza*, in which it was held that:

> A decision to grant or deny a motion for separate trial is left to the sound discretion of Judges of the Trial Chambers. It must be borne in mind that this is a trial by Judges and not by a Jury. The usual ground advanced by Defence seeking a separate trial is that evidence which may, in law, be admissible against one accused and not the others, will be heard by the Jury and may be relied upon by them in reaching a verdict. It is generally assumed that judges can rise above such risk of prejudice and apply their professional judicial minds to the assessment of evidence.

See also *Nsabimana, Decision on the Defence Motion Seeking Separate Trial for the Accused*, 8 September 2000.

Conflicting Defences

8.5.545 The fact that accused in a joint trial intend to present defences which are conflicting, or indeed mutually exclusive, does not consitute a "conflict of interest" within the meaning of Rule 82. See *Decision on Defence Motion to sever Defendants and Counts* rendered by the Trial Chamber in *Simić et al.* on 15 March 1999, rejecting the application for severance.

Concurrent Presentation of Evidence

8.5.546 The fact that the accused will have to sit through a quantity of evidence which is not relevant to him also does not amount to a conflict of interest, although it is no doubt highly inconvenient. See *Ndayambaje, Decision on the Defence Motion for Separate Trial*, 25 April 2001, para. 11 rejecting an application for separate trial on the ground that the "concurrent presentation of evidence of all the accused in this case could be unfair as most of the allegations in the indictment do not relate to [the accused]."

Intention to Call Co-Accused to Testify

8.5.547 A simple intimation that the accused intends to call his co-accused on his behalf is not enough for the Chamber to determine that there will be a conflict of interest sufficient to warrant a separate trial. See *Ndayambaje, Decision on the Defence Motion for Separate Trial*, 25 April 2001, para. 14. See also *Nyiramasuhuko and Ntahobali, Decision on the Motion for Separate Trials*, 8 June 2001, paras. 17–20.

8.5.548 This does, however, raise the problem that an accused enjoys the right under the Tribunals' statutes not to be compelled to testify against himself. If he is called to testify on behalf of a co-accused, this right may be compromised. See ICTY Article 21 (4) (g)/ICTR Article 20 (4) (g) and Rule 90 (E).

Command Responsibility

8.5.549 The fact that an accused seeking a separate trial is accused on the basis of command responsibility for the acts of his co-accused does not in itself make it necessary to order separate trials to avoid a conflict of interests (Tr. Ch., *Delalić et al., Decision on the Motions for Separate Trial filed by the accused Zejnil Delalić and the accused Zdravko Mucić*, 25 September 1996, para. 3: ". . . whatever degree of inconvenience this may involve is no such matter of conflict of interests with which Subrule 82(B) is concerned").

Drawbacks to Separate Trials

8.5.550 In the *Decision* referred to in the pervious paragraph, the Trial Chamber listed some of the disadvantages of separate trials:

> 6. . . . separate trials which have been sought would *in toto* be likely to involve much greater delay, at least for those unfortunate enough not to be the first to be tried. They would also mean considerable repetition of evidence.
>
> 7. . . . separate trials would involve much duplication of testimony and great hardship for already traumatised witnesses. . . .

Co-Accused Not in Custody

8.5.551 The fact that the accused's co-indictees are not in custody has justified the ordering of separate trials, essentially on the grounds of avoiding undue delay and assuring the accused's right to a speedy trial. In *Dokmanović* (IT-95-13a-PT), on 28 November 1997, a Trial Chamber granted a motion for separate trials on the grounds that "none of the co-accused of Slavko Dokmanović is in the custody of the Tribunal, nor appears to be in the process of being transferred to the custody of the Tribunal," and also considering Article 21(4)(c) of the ICTY's Statute "which guarantees that an accused has the right to be tried without undue delay." The Chamber reserved the right to reconsider its Decision "should the said co-accused come into the custody of the Tribunal before commencement of the trial of Slavko Dokmanović." In the event, this did not happen and Dokmanović was tried alone.

8.5.552 The position seems, therefore, to be the following: the fact that an accused's trial will be speedier if severance is granted is not in itself a reason for granting separate trials where the co-accused are also in custody and awaiting trial. In those circumstances, severance will not be granted (see the *Decision* in *Delalić et al.*, above, 8.5.549; see also *Ndayambaje, Decision on the Defence Motion for Separate Trial*, 25

April 2001, paras. 18–20, and *Nyiramasuhuko and Ntahobali, Decision on the Motion for Separate Trials*, 8 June 2001, paras. 23–26). However if the accused's co-accused have not yet been arrested and delivered to the Tribunal's custody, then it would be contrary to the interests of justice to detain the accused until his co-accused are arrested as it would then almost certainly violate his right to a speedy trial. In those circumstances, therefore, severance will be granted (see the *Decision* in *Dokmanović*, cited in the previous paragraph).

Deadline for Application for Severance

8.5.553 ICTY Rule 72(A)/ICTR Rule 72 (A) and (B) set a deadline for the filing of motions for "severance of counts joined in one indictment under Rule 49 or seek separate trials under Rule 82 (B)" ("not later than thirty days after disclosure by the Prosecutor to the defence of all material and statements referred to in Rule 66(A)(i)"). In fact, motions may be brought *after* the expiry of the time-limit, "whenever there is information that raises the issue of conflict of interests between the Accused and one or more of the accused charged in the same indictment or joined with him for trial." See *Nzirorera, Decision on the Defence Motion in opposition to joinder and Motion for severance and separate trial*, 12 July 2000; *Kajelijeli, Decision on the Defence Motion in opposition to Joinder and Motion for Severance and Separate trial*, 6 July 2000; *Nsabimana, Decision on the Defence Motion Seeking Separate Trial*, 8 September 2000; and *Ndayambaje, Decision on the Defence Motion for Separate Trial*, 25 April 2001.

8.5.554 See also *Nyiramasuhuko and Ntahobali, Decision on the Motion for Separate Trials*, 8 June 2001, in which the Trial Chamber held that:

> A motion pursuant to Rule 72 of the Rules cannot be left pending after having been decided by a Chamber. The Defence, though, is not prevented from bringing a Motion for severance of crimes joined in one indictment under Rule 49 of the Rules or for separate trials under Rule 82(B) of the Rules, during the course of trial whenever there is information that raises the issue of a conflict of interest. (para. 11)

8.5.555 In light of these rulings, it is submitted that Rule 72 should be amended, by deleting ICTY Rule 72(A)(iii)/ICTR Rule 72(B)(iii).

8.5.556

ICTY Rule 83 Instruments of Restraint	ICTR Rule 83 Instruments of Restraint
Instruments of restraint, such as handcuffs, shall be used only on the order of the Registrar as a precaution against escape during transfer or in order to prevent an accused from self-injury, injury to others or to prevent serious damage to property. Instruments of constraint shall be removed when the accused appears before a Chamber or a Judge.	Instruments of restraint, such as handcuffs, shall not be used except as a precaution against escape during transfer or for security reasons, and shall be removed when the accused appears before a Chamber.

History of ICTY Rule 83

8.5.557 This Rule was amended at the nineteenth plenary session, on 17 December 1998. It had previously read, "Instruments of restraint, such as handcuffs, shall not be used except as a precaution against escape during transfer or for security reasons, and shall be removed when the accused appears before a Chamber."

8.5.558 Counsel for Đukić objected to the handcuffing of his client because there was no danger that Đukić would try to escape (Transcript of hearing, IT-96-20-T, Monday 25th March 1996, p. 12). This issue became moot as Đukić was provisionally released shortly thereafter.

8.5.559

ICTY Rule 84 Opening Statements	ICTR Rule 84 Opening Statements
Before presentation of evidence by the Prosecutor, each party may make an opening statement. The defence may however elect to make its statement after the Prosecutor has concluded his presentation of evidence and before the presentation of evidence for the defence.	Before presentation of evidence by the Prosecutor, each party may make an opening statement. The defence may however elect to make its statement after the Prosecutor has concluded his presentation of evidence and before the presentation of evidence for the defence.

8.5.560 In *Tadić*, the defence elected to make an opening statement before the presentation of evidence by the Prosecutor (See Transcript of hearings, 7 May 1996).

8.5.561 In *Delalić et al.*, a multiple defendant trial, each defendant made an opening statement before the opening of the case *for that defendant*. Thus the order of presentation of evidence was prosecution opening speech, prosecution evidence, opening speech for Delalić, defence evidence for Delalić, opening speech for Mucić, defence evidence for Mucić, opening speech for Delić, defence evidence for Delić, opening speech for Landžo, defence evidence for Landžo, closing speeches.

8.5.562 In *Furundžija*, the defence elected to make an opening statement before the presentation of evidence by the Prosecution (Transcript of hearings, 8 June 1998). In *Blaškić*, the defence chose to make its opening statement before the presentation of the defence case (see Transcripts of hearings, 24 June 1997 and 7–8 September 1998). In *Kupreškić*, the defence did not make an opening statement before the presentation of evidence by the Prosecutor.

8.5.563

ICTY Rule 84 *bis* Statement of the Accused
(A) After the opening statements of the parties or, if the defence elects to defer its opening statement pursuant to Rule 84, after the opening statement of the Prosecutor, if any, the accused may, if he or she so wishes, and the Trial Chamber so decides, make a statement under the control of the Trial Chamber. The accused shall not be compelled to make a solemn declaration and shall not be examined about the content of the statement. (B) The Trial Chamber shall decide on the probative value, if any, of the statement.

History of ICTY Rule 84 *bis*

8.5.564 This new rule was introduced at the twentieth plenary session on 30 June–2 July 1999. Even before its adoption, however, an accused in *Kupreškić*, was, exceptionally, permitted to make a statement during the Prosecution case without first being sworn. Thus Rule 84 *bis* is, to a certain extent, the codification of an existing practice.

8.5.565 Slobodan Milosević invoked this rule after the Prosecution's opening of its case against him, giving a statement over a three-day period (see transcripts of the hearing, 14, 15 and 18 February 2002).

8.5.566 This procedure is to be contrasted with that under Rule 85, where the accused gives evidence but is sworn before so doing (see 8.5.584).

8.5.567

ICTY Rule 85 Presentation of Evidence	ICTR Rule 85 Presentation of Evidence
(A) Each party is entitled to call witnesses and present evidence. Unless otherwise directed by the Trial Chamber in the interests of justice, evidence at the trial shall be presented in the following sequence: (i) evidence for the prosecution; (ii) evidence for the defence; (iii) prosecution evidence in rebuttal; (iv) defence evidence in rejoinder; (v) evidence ordered by the Trial Chamber pursuant to Rule 98; and (vi) any relevant information that may assist the Trial Chamber in determining an appropriate sentence if the accused is found guilty on one or more of the charges in the indictment.	(A) Each party is entitled to call witnesses and present evidence. Unless otherwise directed by the Trial Chamber in the interests of justice, evidence at the trial shall be presented in the following sequence: (i) evidence for the prosecution; (ii) evidence for the defence; (iii) prosecution evidence in rebuttal; (iv) defence evidence in rejoinder; (v) evidence ordered by the Trial Chamber pursuant to Rule 98; (vi) any relevant information that may assist the Trial Chamber in determining an appropriate sentence, if the accused is found guilty on one or more of the charges in the indictment.

(B) Examination-in-chief, cross-examination and re-examination shall be allowed in each case. It shall be for the party calling a witness to examine such witness in chief, but a Judge may at any stage put any question to the witness. (C) The accused may, if he so desires, appear as a witness in his own defence.	(B) Examination-in-chief, cross-examination and re-examination shall be allowed in each case. It shall be for the party calling a witness to examine him in chief, but a Judge may at any stage put any question to the witness. (C) The accused may, if he so desires, appear as a witness in his own defence.

History of ICTY Rule 85

8.5.568 Rule 85(A)(vi) was added at the eighteenth plenary session on 9–10 July 1998.

History of ICTR Rule 85

8.5.569 Rule 85(A)(vi) was added at the ICTR fifth plenary session on 8 June 1998. An identical amendment was adopted by the ICTY on 9–10 July 1998.

Order of Presentation of Evidence

8.5.570 Where there are several accused, the presentation of evidence has been: examination-in-chief by the counsel for the accused calling the witness, cross-examination by other counsel, cross-examination by the Prosecutor and then re-examination by the counsel for the accused calling the witness. See *Decision on Order of Presentation of Evidence* of 21 January 1999 in *Kupreškić*.

Evidence Called at the Proper Time

8.5.571 Rule 85 expresses a well settled rule of practice that evidence should be called at the proper time. See *Decision on the Prosecution's Alternative Request to Reopen the Prosecution's Case* rendered in *Delalić et al* on 19 August 1998, para. 18. As a corollary to this general rule, there is the principle that matters probative of the Defendant's guilt should be adduced as part of the case of the prosecution. While the Prosecution in certain circumstances may be allowed to call further evidence at a later stage, this is exceptional and cannot be done merely in order to reinforce evidence already brought or to call evidence previously deemed unnecessary. See also para. 20 of this Decision.

8.5.572 Rebuttal evidence provides a limited exception to this general principle to rebut *new* issues raised in the defence case (see paras. 22 and 23, *ibid.*). Another limited exception is for fresh evidence adduced to re-open the case, which is only permitted on a "reasonable diligence" test (see paras. 26 and 27, *ibid.*).

Defence Motion to Dismiss Charges

8.5.573 Although there is no specific provision in Rule 85(A) for the submission of a motion to dismiss at the close of the Prosecution's case in chief, the Defence filed such a motion in *Tadić*, which was allowed by the Trial Chamber over the objection of the Prosecutor. The Motion itself did not, however, succeed.

8.5.574 The Trial Chamber, in its *Decision on Defence Motion to Dismiss Charges* of 13 September 1996, formulated the legal standard for evaluating such motions thus:

> The test to be applied in determining this motion is whether as a matter of law there is evidence, were it to be accepted by the Trial Chamber, as to each count charged in the indictment which could lawfully support a conviction of the accused.

8.5.575 See the *Jelisić Trial Judgement*, in which the Trial Chamber, *proprio motu* and without allowing the Prosecution to be heard on the matter, acquitted the accused of genocide at the close of the Prosecution case. The Trial Chamber was strongly criticised for this decision by the Appeals Chamber in the *Jelisić Appeals Judgement* (see 4.2.23 and 4.2.72).

Distinction between Motion to Dismiss and Judgement of Acquittal

8.5.576 These notions are not identical. In its *Order on the Motions to Dismiss the Indictment at the close of the Prosecutor's Case*, rendered in *Delalić et al* on 18 March 1998, the Chamber pointed out that the legal consequences differed as between a Motion to Dismiss and a Motion for Judgement of Acquittal:

> the two alternative requests differ in their content in that:
>
> (1) the submission of a motion for judgement of acquittal calls for a consideration, even at this stage of the proceedings, of the law and evidence adduced by the Prosecution. The accused persons, confident of the weakness of the Prosecution case, do not seek to offer any further evidence and are, therefore, closing their case. The Trial Chamber is, accordingly, entitled to consider the innocence or guilt of the accused in the light of the law and evidence presented to it by the Prosecution;
>
> (2) the alternative request for dismissal of the indictment is for the charges against the accused to be dismissed on the basis that the Prosecution has not, on the law and the evidence presented before the Trial Chamber, made out a case in relation to the charges at issue for the accused to defend themselves against;
>
> CONSIDERING that, whereas the implication of the two approaches is that a successful motion will in each case result in the termination of the case against the accused persons, the crucial and critical distinction is in respect of a failure of the motion:
>
> (1) in a motion for judgement of acquittal the Trial Chamber will determine the guilt or innocence of the accused persons, who have relied for their defence on the evidence led by the Prosecution;
>
> (2) conversely, an unsuccessful motion for request of dismissal of the indictment will afford the accused persons the opportunity to lead evidence and defend the case made out by the Prosecution.

8.5.577 The defence was requested to specify which motion they sought and the defence clarified that they requested *dismissal* of the counts of the indictment, i.e. (2) above, and thus the right to present the defence case should their motion be rejected. This motion for dismissal was rejected in the *Order* of 18 March 1998. Zejnil Delalić was, however, subsequently acquitted at the end of the defence case.

8.5.578 See *Prosecutor's Response to Defendants' Motion for Judgement of Acquittal, or in the alternative, Motion to Dismiss the Indictment at the close of the Prosecutor's case*, filed in *Delalić et al* on 6 March 1998.

Order of Presentation of Rebuttal Evidence

8.5.579 See *Scheduling Order* issued in *Delalić et al.* on 14 July 1998. See also a general *Scheduling Order* on the presentation of evidence under Rule 85 issued in *Delalić et al.* on 10 September 1998.

8.5.580 In the same case, Delalić proposed that the Prosecution should present its rebuttal evidence after Delalić had presented his defence case, followed by rejoinder evidence by Delalić, final arguments by Delalić and the OTP and then judgement by the Chamber as regards Delalić. The Chamber would then proceed to each of the other accused, presumably in the same fashion. The Chamber rejected this approach, stating that it would be analogous to conducting separate trials and it had already rejected applications for separate trials. See *Decision on the Motion by Defendant Delalić requesting procedures for final determination of the charges against him* rendered on 1 July 1998.

Re-Cross-Examination

8.5.581 Para. (B) of Rule 85 does not allow for a general right of re-cross-examination. In an oral Decision rendered in *Delalić et al* on 26 March 1997, the Trial Chamber pronounced on a defence motion to allow re-cross-examination of each witness. The Chamber denied the motion, holding that Rule 85(B) only contemplated examination-in-chief, cross-examination and re-examination. The Chamber added, however, that it might allow re-cross-examination when new matters arose in re-examination (See Draft Transcript of Hearing, 26 March 1997, pp. 1262–1265).

8.5.582 This Decision was confirmed in a written *Decision on the Motion on Presentation of Evidence by the Accused Esad Landžo* rendered by the Chamber on 1 May 1997. The Decision includes important *dicta* on principles of statutory interpretation, which the Chamber then applied to Rule 85. The Decision also affirmed that re-cross-examination, though not allowed *generally*, may be allowed in certain circumstances:

> 30. The Trial Chamber does not hold the view and has never stated, that a party can never be allowed to further cross-examine a witness after the re-examination of the witness . . . where during re-examination new material is introduced, the opposing party is entitled to further cross-examine the witness on such new material. Similarly, where questions put to a witness by the Trial Chamber after cross-examination raise entirely new matters, the opponent is entitled to further cross-examine the witness on such new matters.

8.5.583 As the Chamber pointed out, the reason for this is clear—"further cross-examination is to re-examination what cross-examination is to examination-in-chief." Therefore, not to permit re-cross-examination when new material is raised in re-examination "is tantamount to a denial of the right to cross-examination on such new material" (*Ibid*).

Accused Sworn before Giving Testimony

8.5.584 If an accused elects to appear as a witness in his own case, then he is first sworn to tell the truth. This is the approach taken in common law jurisdictions, but is alien to most civil law jurisdictions where the accused is allowed to speak on his own behalf without being sworn, enjoying, therefore, what is sometimes colloquially referred to as a "right to lie."

8.5.585 ICTY Rule 84 *bis* now permits the accused to "make a statement under the control of the Trial Chamber," without being compelled to make a solemn declaration and without being examined about the content of the statement. Under para. (B) of Rule 84 *bis*, "The Trial Chamber shall decide on the probative value, if any, of the statement." This is intended to approximate to the civil law approach to statements by the accused. It is, therefore, often cited as an example of the "hybrid" (i.e. mixed common law/civil law) nature of the Tribunal's proceedings.

8.5.586 For examples of each type of proceeding, see *Tadić*, where the accused appeared as a witness in his own defence under Rule 85(C). Before giving evidence, he took the oath prescribed for witnesses under Rule 90(B) (Transcript of Hearing, 25 October 1996). Rule 84 *bis* had not yet been adopted and was, therefore, not available to the accused.

8.5.587 In *Milošević*, on the other hand, Rule 84 *bis* had now been adopted by the Judges and the accused invoked it to make an unsworn statement over a three-day period (see transcripts of the hearing, 14, 15 and 18 February 2002). Many in the media mistook this lengthy statement for the actual presentation of evidence, whereas in fact it was for the Trial Chamber to decide what probative value, "*if any*," to accord the material.

8.5.588 Even before Rule 84 *bis* was adopted, an accused in *Kupreškić*, was, exceptionally, permitted to make a statement during the Prosecution case without first being sworn.

Accused Cannot Be Ordered to Appear as First Defence Witness

8.5.589 In *Delalić et al.*, the Prosecution requested an Order, *inter alia*, that:

> (1) should any of the accused choose to appear as a witness in their own defence, they are required to do so before calling the defence witnesses in their respective cases, subject to the discretion of the Trial Chamber on good cause being shown.

8.5.590 The Trial Chamber, quite rightly, rejected this request in an *Order* dated 3 April 1998, holding that the accused had the right to choose whether to appear as a witness in his own defence or not and that this right is not "restricted . . . to a particular stage of his defence"; in other words, the defence can exercise this right at any stage in the proceedings, including after other defence witnesses have testified. Accordingly, the Chamber rejected the Prosecution's request.

8.5.591 In its *Order,* the Chamber did, however, specify the order of examination for defence witnesses:

> HEREBY ORDERS that for each Defence witness the Defence complete their respective examination(s)-in-chief and respective cross-examination(s) before the Prosecution begins its cross-examination.

8.5.592 It should also be noted that although it is the accused's right as to whether and when to give evidence, it will be open to the Trial Chamber to draw an inference and afford less weight to the accused's evidence if he chooses to give evidence only after all of the other defence witness. See the Appeals Chamber's *Judgement on Allegations of Contempt against Prior Counsel, Milan Vujin, Tadić,* 31 January 2000.

Rules of Examination of Witnesses

Rule Against Comment

8.5.593 A party examining a witness should not interpose commentary on the witness's testimony. On this point, see *Akayesu*, hearings of 14 January 1997, and the following exchange between the Presiding Judge of the Trial Chamber, and the accused, who was then conducting cross-examination of the witness:

> MR. PRESIDENT: Madam, we asked you why calm reigned until April 18th, 1994 and you said that it was because Akayesu wanted there to be calm.
>
> THE WITNESS: Yes, I confirm that.
>
> MR. PRESIDENT: Is this a correct response?
>
> THE WITNESS: Yes, this is correct.
>
> THE ACCUSED: I think that this is more of a feeling on your part and this is not enough to prove that there was calm.
>
> MR. PRESIDENT: Let me remind the accused, again, that your commentary is superfluous. You have asked an important question, why was there calm? And she says thanks to you. That is sufficient as a response.
>
> THE ACCUSED: I understand, Mr. President.
>
> (pp. 12–13, Transcripts of hearings, 14/1/98))

8.5.594 See also, at page 9 of the same transcripts, the remark of the Presiding Judge, "I would also like to remind both the defence and the prosecution that questions put to a witness must be directly linked to the facts as they are described in the indictment and that they must not give general commentary."

Scope of Cross-Examination

8.5.595 In the common law tradition, there are two major rules regarding the permissible scope of cross-examination. The "American rule" is that "Cross-examination should be limited to the subject matter of the direct examination and matters affecting the credibility of the witness" (see Rule 611(b) of the Federal Rules of Evidence). The "English rule," by contrast, is that cross-examination is *not* limited to the subject matter of direct examination. See Adrian Keane, *The Modern Law of Evidence* (2nd edition, 1989), p. 118: "The questions of the cross-examiner are not restricted to matters proved in examination-in-chief but may relate to any fact in issue or relevant to a fact in issue," although of course the ordinary rules of admissibility and inadmissibility of evidence apply to cross-examination as well as to examination-in-chief.

8.5.596 At the ICTR, following the adoption of ICTR Rule 90(G) on 8 June 1998 (Rule 90(H) at the ICTY, adopted on 9–10 July 1998), it is clear that the "American rule" governs. ICTR Rule 90(G) now provides that "Cross-examination shall be limited to the subject-matter of the direct examination and matters affecting the credibility of the witness." However, "The Trial Chamber may, if it deems it advisable, permit enquiry into additional matters as if on direct examination." See Rule 90 (8.5.673 *et seq.*).

8.5.597 See also in *Akayesu*, comments of the Presiding Judge which suggested that the "American rule" governed:

> as regards the accused, the cross-examination of the witness must be done within the limits of the prosecutor's examination. In other words the accused is free to ask for clarification on any point on which the answer given was not clear. (pp. 8–9, Hearings of 14/1/98)

8.5.598 The Presiding Judge, however, immediately qualified this:

> He [the accused] may also ask other questions of the witness, given that these questions are only questions and that he does not provide commentary.(*Ibid.*)

Accused Has No Right to Polygraph Test

8.5.599 In *Naletilić and Martinović, Decision on the Request of the Accused to be Given the Opportunity to be Interrogated Under Applications of a Polygraph*, 27 November 2000, the Trial Chamber held that an accused does not have any right pursuant to the Statue or Rules to request a polygraph or lie-detector test. The determination of the credibility of any witness, including the accused should he decide to give evidence, is a matter that is ultimately for the Trial Chamber.

8.5.600 It is submitted that the Chamber must have considered that a lie detector test was intrinsically unreliable as a form of evidence; otherwise it is hard to understand why the Chamber would object to the admission of such evidence going to the veracity or otherwise of the accused's version of events.

8.5.601

ICTY Rule 86 Closing Arguments	ICTR Rule 86 Closing Arguments
(A) After the presentation of all the evidence, the Prosecutor may present a closing argument; whether or not the Prosecutor does so, the defence may make a closing argument. The Prosecutor may present a rebuttal argument to which the defence may present a rejoinder.	(A) After the presentation of all the evidence, the Prosecutor may present a closing argument. Whether or not the Prosecutor does so, the defence may make a closing argument. The Prosecutor may present a rebuttal argument to which the defence may present a rejoinder.

(B) Not later than five days prior to presenting a closing argument, a party shall file a final trial brief. (C) The parties shall also address matters of sentencing in closing arguments.	(B) A party shall file a final trial brief with the Trial Chamber not later than five days prior to the day set for the presentation of that party's closing argument,. (C) The parties shall also address matters of sentencing in closing arguments.

History of ICTY Rule 86

8.5.602 Rule 86(A) was amended at the eighteenth plenary session on 9–10 July 1998 to make clear that the defence could present a closing argument whether or not the Prosecutor did so. Paras. (B) and (C), concerning filing of trial briefs and sentencing respectively, were added at the same plenary session.

8.5.603 Rule 86 was amended in a minor way on 19 January 2001, after the twenty-third plenary session.

History of ICTR Rule 86

8.5.604 This Rule was amended at the ICTR fifth plenary session on 8 June 1998, adding paras. (B) and (C) and modifying para. (A). Similar amendments were adopted at the ICTY on 9–10 July 1998.

Unfairness to the Accused of Having to Address Sentencing Matters at the Sentencing Stage

8.5.605 Rule 86(C) obliges "the parties [to] also address matters of sentencing in closing arguments." While this requirement, being imposed on both parties—Prosecution and Defence equally—may seem fair, at least on that ground, in fact it is deeply unfair to the defence. The Prosecution has no difficulty addressing matters of sentencing in closing because the Prosecution case is that the accused committed the crimes as alleged in the indictment, and there is no difficulty in attaching a sentencing tariff to the Prosecution theory of the case, as well as addressing any aggravating or mitigating matters raised during the course of the defence case. For the defence, on the other hand, their case is that *the accused did not commit the crime at all*. If the defence case is correct, the accused should not be convicted and so there will be no sentencing, and no punishment, at all. To order the defence to address matters of sentencing in their closing speeches is, therefore, to force them into contradicting, and thus undermining, their own case that the accused is not guilty.

8.5.606 Moreover, it is virtually impossible for the defence to address sentencing when they do not know what factual findings the Chamber will make. For example, in a case in which an accused is charged in the alternative for direct perpetration (under Article 7(1) of the ICTY Statute) and command responsibility (under Article 7(3) of the Statute) with respect to a beating, the defence will be forced to present mitigating features in relation to the beating (e.g. that it was not particularly savage), when the

Chamber might eventually decide that the accused is guilty by virtue of command responsibility and not direct perpetration, in which case, the relevant sentencing factors will be what the accused knew about the beating and failed to do about it, not how savage the beating itself was.

Examples

8.5.607 In *Tadić*, the Prosecutor made a closing argument (see Transcript of hearings, 25 and 26 November 1996), to which the defence replied (see Transcript of hearings, 26, 27, 28 November 1996); the Prosecutor then made a rebuttal argument to which the defence rejoined (see Transcript of hearings, 28 November 1996).

8.5.608

ICTY Rule 87 Deliberations	ICTR Rule 87 Deliberations
(A) When both parties have completed their presentation of the case, the Presiding Judge shall declare the hearing closed, and the Trial Chamber shall deliberate in private. A finding of guilt may be reached only when a majority of the Trial Chamber is satisfied that guilt has been proved beyond reasonable doubt. (B) The Trial Chamber shall vote separately on each charge contained in the indictment. If two or more accused are tried together under Rule 48, separate findings shall be made as to each accused. (C) If the Trial Chamber finds the accused guilty on one or more of the charges contained in the indictment, it shall impose a sentence in respect of each finding of guilt and indicate whether such sentences shall be served consecutively or concurrently, unless it decides to exercise its power to impose a single sentence reflecting the totality of the criminal conduct of the accused.	(A) After presentation of closing arguments, the Presiding Judge shall declare the hearing closed, and the Trial Chamber shall deliberate in private. A finding of guilty may be reached only when a majority of the Trial Chamber is satisfied that guilt has been proved beyond reasonable doubt. (B) The Trial Chamber shall vote separately on each charge contained in the indictment. If two or more accused are tried together under Rule 48, separate findings shall be made as to each accused. (C) If the Trial Chamber finds the accused guilty on one or more of the counts contained in the indictment, it shall also determine the penalty to be imposed in respect of each of the counts.

History of ICTY Rule 87

8.5.609 Para. (C) was added at the eighteenth plenary session on 9–10 July 1998 to merge the judgement and sentencing stages (although the paragraph, as amended, no longer deals with the matter; see instead Rule 86(C) in this regard)

8.5.610 Para. (C) was substantially amended on 19 January 2001, after the twenty-third plenary session, to explicitly provide for the two sentencing approaches that had been adopted by Chambers: individual sentences for each finding of guilt indicating whether the sentences shall be served consecutively or concurrently (the approach taken, e.g., in *Tadić*) or a global sentence (the approach taken, e.g., in *Blaškić*).

History of ICTR Rule 87

8.5.611 This Rule was amended at the ICTR fifth plenary session on 8 June 1998. Para. (A) was modified and para. (C) added.

Proof of Guilt Beyond a Reasonable Doubt

8.5.612 The standard of proof beyond a reasonable doubt is, at least in common law jurisdictions, a universal standard of guilt in a criminal trial. It is widely considered to equate to the civil law standard expressed by the phrase, "*intime conviction*" (the intimate conviction which the judge must feel before pronouncing the accused guilty). For the meaning of "proof beyond a reasonable doubt," see, *inter alia*, the *Jelisić Trial Judgement*, para. 108; *Kunarac, Decision on Motion for Acquittal* para. 3; *Kvočka, Decision on Defence Motions for Acquittal*, para. 12; *Delalić et al. Appeals Judgement* para. 434; and *Jelisić Appeals Judgement* paras. 34–37.

8.5.613 In this regard, it is very important to point out that the standard of proof beyond a reasonable doubt is *not* a "probabilistic standard." An accused should not be convicted where it is merely "more probable than not" that the committed the crime, nor even where it is "extremely probable" that he committed the crime. The test is whether there is a reasonable doubt, that is a doubt to which a reason which is not fanciful can be assigned; in which case the accused deserves to be acquitted.

8.5.614 See the exposition of the standard of proof in the English case of *Miller v. Minister of Pensions* [1947] 2 All E.R. 372 per Denning J.:

> the degree of cogency as is required in a criminal case before an accused person is found guilty . . . is well settled. . . . Proof beyond reasonable doubt does not mean proof beyond the shadow of a doubt. The law would fail to protect the community if it admitted fanciful possibilities to deflect the course of justice. If the evidence is so strong against a man as to leave only a remote possibility in his favour which can be dismissed with the sentence "of course it is possible, but not in the least probable," the case is proved beyond reasonable doubt, but nothing short of that will suffice.

See also *Worthington v. DPP* [1935] A.C. 462 H.L.

8.5.615 The standard of proof beyond a reasonable doubt is the standard set for the International Criminal Court. See Article 66 ("Presumption of Innocence"), para. 3: "In order to convict an accused, the Court must be convinced of the guilt of the accused beyond reasonable doubt." That this is the standard adopted for the ICC would seem to indicate that the standard of proof beyond a reasonable doubt has become the customary standard of proof in international criminal trials.

Elements to Be Proved at Trial

8.5.616 It is not necessary for the Prosecution to prove the date or time of offences unless they are elements of the offence. See the *Tadić Opinion and Judgement*, para. 534:

> Whereas the Prosecution is bound to prove each of the elements of the offence charged, to specify and prove the exact date of an offence is not required when the date or time is not also an element of the offence. While it is usual to allege and prove the date on which the offence charged is asserted to have been committed, the date is not material unless it is an essential part of the offence. . . . However, in none of the offences here alleged was the date or time of the essence. For the foregoing reasons the events charged and the evidence adduced by the Prosecution was sufficiently precise and lack of specificity did not result in any denial of the accused's right to a fair trial.

Corroboration

8.5.617 See Rule 89(B) below.

Reliability of Witnesses

8.5.618 The reliability of witnesses, including that of victims of the conflicts in the former Yugoslavia and Rwanda, is assessed on a case-by-case basis. See the *Tadić Opinion and Judgement*, para. 541:

> The reliability of witnesses, including any motive they may have to give false testimony, is an estimation that must be made in the case of each individual witness. It is neither appropriate, nor correct, to conclude that a witness is deemed to be inherently unreliable solely because he was the victim of a crime committed by a person of the same (sic) creed, ethnic group, armed force or any other characteristic of the accused. . . . Such a conclusion can only be made . . . in the light of the circumstances of each individual witness, his individual testimony, and such concerns as the Defence may substantiate either in cross-examination or through its own evidence-in-chief.

Pre-Trial Media Coverage and the Infection of Testimonial Evidence

8.5.619 "In all trials, the potential impact of pre-trial media coverage is a factor that must be taken into account in considering the reliability of witnesses" (Tr. Ch., *Tadić Opinion and Judgement*, para. 544).

"Dock Identification"

8.5.620 "Dock i.d.," that is, the in-court identification of the accused by the witness, is of little evidentiary weight. In the *Tadić Opinion and Judgement*, the Chamber stated that it "places little weight upon mere dock identification" (para. 546). As the Chamber added, "the circumstances attendant upon such identification, with the accused seated between two guards in the courtroom, require the Trial Chamber to assess the credibility of each witness independently of that identification" (*Id.*).

8.5.621 The Chamber went on to discuss the probative value of a "photospread procedure," using "foils," which had been used as identification evidence (paras. 547–552). Despite some defects in the procedure that had been adopted, the Chamber accepted the identification evidence of the witnesses who had identified the accused from a photospread.

Hearsay

8.5.622 See Commentary to Rule 89(C) (8.5.626 *et seq.*).

Meaning of Separate Findings

8.5.623 Para. (B) of Rule 87 does not require separate decisions on motions by different accused. This point was raised in an application for leave to appeal filed under Rule 72(B)(ii) on 4 October 1996 by Zejnil Delalić in *Delalić et al* (IT-96-21-AR72.1). The accused sought leave to appeal the *Decision on Motions for Separate Trial filed by the Accused Zejnil Delalić and the Accused Zdravko Mucić*, rendered by the Trial Chamber on 25 September 1996. The accused argued that Rule 87(B) had been violated:

> 4. . . . the Applicant alleges non-compliance with the Tribunal's Rules of Procedure and Evidence by virtue of the fact that the Trial Chamber issued a joint decision on 25 September 1996 for him and his co-accused Mucić. The Applicant argues that his separate motion consisted of individualised facts and legal arguments which have "nothing [in] common with the arguments of the other accused persons." The Applicant argues that Rule 87(B) of the Rules of Procedure and Evidence which governs final deliberations should be followed in the preliminary phase *mutatis mutandis*.

8.5.624 In its Decision on the accused's application (*Decision On Application For Leave To Appeal* (*Separate Trials*, 14 October 1996), the Bench of the Appeals Chamber held that this argument did not raise a "serious cause," within the meaning of Rule 72(B)(ii), which would justify the granting of leave to appeal.

ICTY Rule 87(C)

8.5.625 The new Rule 87(C) was applied for the first time in the *Foča Trial Judgement*. The Trial Chamber took the approach of imposing a "single sentence reflecting the totality of the respective criminal conduct of each accused" (para. 855).

* * * * *

RULES OF EVIDENCE

8.5.626

ICTY Rule 89 General Provisions	ICTR Rule 89 General Provisions
(A) A Chamber shall apply the rules of evidence set forth in this Section, and shall not be bound by national rules of evidence. (B) In cases not otherwise provided for in this Section, a Chamber shall apply rules of evidence which will best favour a fair determination of the matter before it and are consonant with the spirit of the Statute and the general principles of law. (C) A Chamber may admit any relevant evidence which it deems to have probative value. (D) A Chamber may exclude evidence if its probative value is substantially outweighed by the need to ensure a fair trial. (E) A Chamber may request verification of the authenticity of evidence obtained out of court. (F) A Chamber may receive the evidence of a witness orally or, where the interests of justice allow, in written form.	(A) The rules of evidence set forth in this Section shall govern the proceedings before the Chambers. The Chambers shall not be bound by national rules of evidence. (B) In cases not otherwise provided for in this Section, a Chamber shall apply rules of evidence which will best favour a fair determination of the matter before it and are consonant with the spirit of the Statute and the general principles of law. (C) A Chamber may admit any relevant evidence which it deems to have probative value. (D) A Chamber may request verification of the authenticity of evidence obtained out of court.

History of ICTY Rule 89

8.5.627 Para. (F) was added, and para. (A) amended in terms of style, on 19 January 2001, after the twenty-third plenary session.

Comparison Between ICTY Rule 89 and ICTR Rule 89

8.5.628 ICTR Rule 89 is identical to ICTY Rule 89, except that ICTR Rule 89 curiously does not contain what is ICTY Rule 89(D), namely "A Chamber may exclude evidence if its probative value is substantially outweighed by the need to ensure a fair trial." Therefore, Rule 89(D) of the ICTR's Rules of Procedure and Evidence is instead Rule 89(E) of the ICTY's Rules of Procedure and Evidence.

8.5.629 Para. (F) having been added to ICTY Rule 89, that is also now a difference between the ICTY and ICTR Rules.

8.5.630 In the Final Document of the Arusha School on International Criminal Law and Human Rights, issued on 6 March 1998, the School proposed the addition of Rule 89(D) of the ICTY's Rules of Evidence to ICTR Rule 89, to guarantee the right of the accused to exclude from his trial prejudicial evidence of low probative value.

"Chambers Shall Not Be Bound by National Rules of Evidence"

8.5.631 The Judges of the Tribunal have, on a number of occasions, drawn attention to the concept that the Tribunal is not bound by national rules of evidence. See, e.g. the *Separate and Dissenting Opinion of Judge McDonald on Prosecution Motion for Production of Defence Witness Statements* in *Tadić*, on 27 November 1996, para. 34:

> The International Tribunal has ten rules of evidence which are designed only to provide the framework for the conduct of the proceedings. Certainly our Rules could not anticipate every trial procedure that litigants from a variety of countries may expect to utilise and the International Tribunal did not establish hyper-technical detailed rules typical of a jury system to cover every such possibility. In civil law systems technical rules are not available, and all evidence that aids in the search for truth is allowed. Our Rules provide the Judges with the power to review all relevant evidence, and when necessary, to make further rulings to aid in the adjudication before the Trial Chamber. Because of the absence of specific rules, the Trial Chamber has made rulings which it considered would best facilitate the process.

8.5.632 On Rule 89(A) in relation to hearsay, discussed further below, the Trial Chamber, in its *Blaškić* Hearsay Decision of 21 January 1998, stated, at para. 5:

> neither the rules issuing from the common law tradition in respect of the admissibility of hearsay evidence nor the general principle prevailing in the civil law systems, according to which, barring exceptions, all relevant evidence is admissible, including hearsay evidence, because it is the judge who finally takes a decision on the weight to ascribe to it, are directly applicable before this Tribunal. The International Tribunal is, in fact, a *sui generis* institution with its own rules of procedure which do not merely constitute a transposition of national legal systems. The same holds for the conduct of the trial which, contrary to the Defence arguments, is not similar to an adversarial trial, but is moving towards a more hybrid system.

Guidance as to What Constitute "General Principles of Law"

8.5.633 See *Separate Opinion of Judge Stephen on Prosecution Motion for Production of Defence Witness Statements*, dated 27 November 1996 in *Tadić:* ". . . where a substantial number of well-recognised legal systems adopt a particular solution to a problem it is appropriate to regard that solution as involving some quite general principle of law such as is referred to in Sub-rule 89(B)" (p. 6).

Proof of Death

8.5.634 In order for the Prosecutor to prove the death of a person, e.g. on a charge of killing, he is not required to produce the body. This is something which would clearly be impossible in the majority of cases in the former Yugoslavia and Rwanda, where the bodies were long ago disposed of in mass graves or elsewhere. There must, however, be some evidence of link between the injuries sustained by the victim and their subsequent death. This was the holding of the Trial Chamber in the *Tadić Opinion and Judgement*. The Chamber was faced with the question as to the standard and nature of proof required for conviction on a count the underlying crime for which is the killing of a human being. The Chamber stated, at para. 240:

> The Trial Chamber is cognisant of the fact that during the conflict there were widespread beatings and killings and indifferent, careless and even callous treatment of the dead. Dead prisoners were buried in makeshift graves and heaps of bodies were not infrequently to be seen in the grounds of the camps. Since these were not times of normalcy, it is inappropriate to apply rules of some national systems that require the production of a body as proof to death. However, there must be evidence to link injuries received to a resulting death. This the Prosecution has failed to do. Although the Defence has not raised this particular inadequacy of proof, it is incumbent upon the Trial Chamber to do so. When there is more than one conclusion reasonably open on the evidence, it is not for this Trial Chamber to draw the conclusion least favourable to the accused, which is what the Trial Chamber would be required to do in finding that any of the four prisoners died as a result of their injuries or, indeed, that they are in fact dead.

8.5.635 On the basis of this reasoning, the Chamber found that the Prosecution had failed to establish beyond reasonable doubt that any of the four persons in question had died as a result of the injuries they had received, and the accused was therefore acquitted on charges of having killed them.

Corroboration

8.5.636 The Tribunals do not have a general requirement of corroboration, i.e. that an item of evidence can only be considered proved if more than one source has testified to or substantiated it. The *unus testis, nullus testis* principle, according to which one person testifying on a matter is equivalent to nobody testifying, does not apply at the Tribunals. This was confirmed in the *Tadić Opinion and Judgement*, where the Chamber stated that there was no general requirement for corroboration at the Tribunal:

> 256. The final challenge made by the Defence in regards to the *unus testis, nullus testis* rule is a question of law. This principle still prevails in the civil law system, according to the Defence, and should be respected by the International Tribunal; therefore, because only one witness testified in support of paragraph 10, the accused cannot be found guilty. This principle is discussed elsewhere in this Opinion and Judgement but suffice it to say that the Trial Chamber does not accept this submission, which in effect asserts that corroboration is a prerequisite for acceptance of testimony.

8.5.637 The Chamber's reasoning is found at paras. 535 to 539 of the *Tadić Opinion and Judgement*, which concludes, " . . . there is no ground for concluding that this requirement of corroboration is any part of customary international law and should be required by this international tribunal" (para. 539).

8.5.638 This was followed in the *Delalić et al. Trial Judgement* of 16 November 1998, which likewise held, at para. 594, that there was no legal requirement of corroboration at the Tribunal.

Rules of Evidence/Comment

8.5.639 A rule in common law systems known as "comment" prohibits the asking of one witness to comment on the evidence of another witness, for example, to comment on whether another witness is telling the truth and, if not, why not. The basis for the rule is that the witness can only comment upon what he or she saw or heard, and can only speculate as to why another witness saw or heard the same event differently; speculation which is not particularly useful in ascertaining the truth.

8.5.640 To some extent this prohibition on comment has been incorporated at the ICTY. See the *Kupreškić* trial, 25 August 1998, page 54 of the daily transcript:

> JUDGE CASSESE: You can't ask him [the witness] to comment on the statement of another witness. It is not for the witness. You can only ask him about his own recollection, what he saw, what he remembers about a particular event. . . .

Weight To Be Given to Witness Testimony

8.5.641 In the *Delalić et al. Trial Judgement*, the Trial Chamber pointed out that inconsistencies in a witness's testimony may be due to the passage of time, and would go to the weight to be accorded such testimony rather than a basis for discarding the testimony altogether (para. 597).

Hearsay

Definition of Hearsay

8.5.642 "Hearsay" is commonly defined as an out-of-court statement tendered in court to prove the truth of its contents. See also the definition provided by the Appeals Chamber in the *Aleksovski Decision on Prosecutor's Appeal on Admissibility of Evidence*, 16 February 1999:

> (the) statement of a person made otherwise than in the proceedings in which it is being tendered, but nevertheless being tendered in those proceedings in order to establish the truth of what the person says.

Hearsay Not *Per Se* Excluded; Test Is Reliability of the Evidence

8.5.643 Hearsay statements are not excluded under the Rules of the ICTY or ICTR. However, before admitting hearsay evidence, the Trial Chamber must assess its "indicia of reliability." In *Kordić* and *Čerkez, Appeals Chamber Decision on Appeal Regarding Statement of a Deceased Witness*, 21 July 2000, the Appeals Chamber held that, even though Rule 89(C) grants the Trial Chamber a broad discretion to admit evidence, the Trial Chamber should consider reliability, as well as weight before admitting hearsay evidence (para. 24). In *Kordić*, the Trial Chamber had admitted the unsworn statement of a witness who had since died. The Appeals Chamber stated that the statement ought not to have been admitted as it was so lacking in reliability that it should have been excluded as without probative value under Rule 89(C). The Appeals Chamber directed Trial Chambers to consider various "indicia of reliability" before admitting hearsay evidence. Such indicia include whether the statement was:

(1) given under oath;
(2) subject to cross-examination;
(3) first-hand or removed;
(4) made contemporaneously to the events;
(5) made through many levels of translation;
(6) given under formal circumstances, such as before a judge (para. 28).

8.5.644 For the ICTR, see para. 136 of the *Akayesu Trial Judgement:* "The Chamber can freely assess the probative value of all relevant evidence. The Chamber had thus determined that in accordance with Rule 89, any relevant evidence having probative value may be admitted into evidence, provided that it is being in accordance with the requisites of a fair trial. The Chamber finds that hearsay evidence is not inadmissible per se and has considered such evidence, with caution, in accordance with Rule 89."

8.5.645 For the ICTY, see the *Decision on the Defence Motion on Hearsay, Tadić,* 5 August 1996, the Trial Chamber majority (Judges McDonald and Vohrah), para. 7:

> Under our Rules, specifically Sub-rule 89(C), out-of-court [hearsay] statements that are relevant and found to have probative value are admissible.

8.5.646 The Chamber went on to say, at para. 15:

> even without a specific Rule precluding the admission of hearsay, the Trial Chamber may exclude evidence that lacks probative value because it is unreliable. Thus, the focus in determining whether evidence is probative within the meaning of Sub-rule 89(C) should be at a minimum that the evidence is reliable (Footnote 1 reads: "Rule 95, while concerned with the methods by which evidence is obtained, also allows for its exclusion if it is unreliable.")
>
> 16. In evaluating the probative value of hearsay evidence, the Trial Chamber is compelled to pay special attention to indicia of its reliability. In reaching this determination, the Trial Chamber may consider whether the statement is voluntary, truthful, and trustworthy, as appropriate.
>
> . . .
>
> 19. In deciding whether or not hearsay evidence that has been objected to will be excluded, the Trial Chamber will determine whether the proferred evidence is relevant and has probative value, focusing on its reliability. In so doing, the Trial Chamber will hear both the circumstances under which the evidence arose as well as the content of the statement. The Trial Chamber may be guided by, but not bound to, hearsay exceptions generally recognized by some national legal systems, as well as the truthfulness, voluntariness, and trustworthiness of the evidence, as appropriate. In bench trial before the International Tribunal, this is the most efficient and fair method to determine the admissibility of out-of-court statements.

8.5.647 With respect to Rule 89 (D), the Chamber stated:

18. ... Sub-rule 89(D) provides further protection against prejudice to the Defence, for if evidence has been admitted as relevant and having probative value, it may later be excluded. Pursuant to this Sub-rule, the trial Judges have the opportunity to consider the evidence, place it in the context of the Trial, and then exclude it if it is substantially outweighed by the need to ensure a fair trial.

8.5.648 Judge Stephen, in a separate opinion, said with respect to Rule 89 (D):

It is to be noted that Sub-rule (D), while it may be applicable to some instances of hearsay evidence, is by no means confined to such evidence. It will obviously also have a role to play where, for example, highly prejudicial first-hand testimony is for any of a multitude of reasons, to be accorded very little weight because of low probative value and should therefore be excluded from evidence. (page 4).

8.5.649 See also the *Tadić Opinion and Judgement*, para. 555:

The use of hearsay evidence was debated at length before this Trial Chamber in an interlocutory motion in this case and was ruled upon in the Decision on the Defence Motion on Hearsay. Since that Decision may be consulted directly, all that need be said of it here is that it concluded that the mere fact that particular testimony was in the nature of hearsay did not operate to exclude it from the category of admissible evidence.

8.5.650 On hearsay, see also the Decision rendered on 21 January 1998 by the Trial Chamber in *Blaškić* on a defence motion objecting to the admission of hearsay evidence with no previous enquiry as to its reliability (see above under Rule 89(A)).

8.5.651 See also on Rule 89(C) and hearsay, the *Decision on Prosecutor's Appeal on Admissibility of Evidence* rendered by the Appeals Chamber (Robinson dissenting) in *Aleksovski* on 16 February 1999. This Decision, which allowed the admission of transcript evidence adduced in the *Blaškić* case into the *Aleksovski* case, upheld the Decisions rendered in *Tadić* (above) and *Blaškić* (below) holding that hearsay evidence is generally admissible before the Tribunal's proceedings. The decision also held that it was not strictly necessary for the party tendering the hearsay evidence to provide an adequate explanation of why the witness was unavailable to testify. The Appeals Chamber upheld the Trial Chamber's finding that the Prosecution's cross-examination of the witness in question in the *Blaškić* trial satisfied its right to cross-examine the witness in the *Aleksovski* trial. The two cases had very similar legal and factual themes and the Prosecution had not demonstrated any areas of cross-examination pertinent to the *Aleksovski* case which did not also arise in the *Blaškić* case.

8.5.652 In a *Dissenting Opinion* to the above *Decision*, Judge Robinson considered that the Rules did not allow transcripts to be admitted into evidence. In his view, Rule 90(A) established the principle that all evidence must be directly heard by the Chamber, subject to two exceptions: depositions and video-conference, neither of which applied in the case of transcripts. Nor did any of the other provisions for the taking of evidence that were exhaustively set out in the Rules provide for transcript evidence.

Non-Admission of Hearsay Evidence

8.5.653 A Trial Chamber has, however, ruled as hearsay and inadmissible for lack of probative value a summary of a document and witness statements that had not been tested by cross-examination. See *Decision on the Prosecution Application to admit the Tulica Report and Dossier into Evidence* rendered by the Trial Chamber on 29 July 1999 in *Kordić and Čerkez*. The Chamber did rule as admissible transcripts of the testimony of a witness who was cross-examined in another trial in which the defence allegedly had a common interest, while allowing the defence to apply to cross-examine the witness the transcript of whose testimony was admitted into evidence.

Admission of Hearsay Does Not Indicate Finding as to Its Probative Value

8.5.654 In the *Akayesu Appeal Judgement*, para. 292, the Appeals Chamber held that the admission of hearsay evidence does not automatically carry any particular finding as to its assessement. The fact that a Trial Chamber admits hearsay does not imply that it accepts it as reliable and probative. The probative value of hearsay evidence is something to be considered by the Trial Chamber at the end of the trial when weighing and evaluating the evidence as a whole, in light of the context and nature of the evidence itself, including the credibility and reliability of the relevant witness.

Hearsay and the Statement of a Deceased Witness

8.5.655 See *Defense Motion to admit into evidence the witness statement of deceased witness Midhat Haskić*, submitted in *Blaškić* on 18 December 1997. The Trial Chamber granted the Motion in its Decision of 29 April 1998. The Chamber added that it would determine in due course "the probative value such evidence would merit."

Relevant Evidence

8.5.656 By a Decision rendered on 19 January 1998, the Trial Chamber admitted into evidence a letter written to a Prosecution witness, which was allegedly written by the accused Mucić (*Decision on the Prosecutor's Oral Requests for the Admission of Exhibit 155 into Evidence and for an Order to Compel the Accused, Zdravko Mucić, to provide a handwriting sample*). The letter was authenticated by reference to the fact that it was signed "Pavo," the nickname by which Mucić was known, and that it mentioned several pieces of information which were of a non-public nature and which were peculiarly in the knowledge of Mucić and the addressee. The Prosecution further submitted that, in the event that the Trial Chamber did not find these elements sufficient to justify the inference that Mucić had indeed written the letter, the Chamber should then direct the accused to provide a hand-writing sample. The Chamber decided, in a ruling from the bench on 6 November 1997, to admit the letter into evidence but it denied the Prosecutor's request to order the accused to provide a hand-writing sample on the grounds that this would violate his privilege against self-incrimination under Article 21(4)(g) of the Statute.

732 • International Criminal Practice

8.5.657 In its Decision, the Chamber rejected the defence argument that the letter could only be admitted into evidence under Rule 89(C) if it had first been found to be *reliable*. Although the *Tadić Hearsay Decision* of 5 August 1996 emphasised the importance of the proferred evidence's reliability, the Trial Chamber ruling in the Mucić case refused to read into Rule 89(C) a separate requirement of reliability as a condition for admissibility of a given item into evidence:

> 32. . . . reliability is the invisible golden thread which runs through all the components of admissibility. Yet, it is a cardinal rule of construction of legislation, that where the words of a provision are clear and unambiguous, the task of interpretation does not arise. So it is with Sub-rule 89(C). Thus, it is neither necessary nor desirable to add to the provisions of Sub-rule 89 (C) a condition of admissibility which is not expressly prescribed by that provision.

8.5.658 In other words, while evidence may be excluded because it is unreliable, it is not required that evidence be shown to be reliable before it is admitted. The evidence need only be shown to be *relevant*, in order for it to be admissible.

8.5.659 This was affirmed by the same Chamber ruling in the same case in its *Decision on the Motion of the Prosecution for the Admissibility of Evidence* of 19 January 1998, para. 19.

8.5.660 Although admitting the letter into evidence, in its Decision of 19 January 1998, the Chamber did not find it established on the facts that Mucić did indeed write the letter:

> The contents of the letter that relate to him, such as his current address, are not facts peculiarly known only to Mucić and Witness P, but are matters of public knowledge. The Trial Chamber is, therefore, not convinced that these factors inexorably link Mucić to the letter. All that can be stated with any certainty at this stage is, thus, that sufficient indicia of reliability have been established of the letter as a document received by Witness P from an unknown third person.

8.5.661 The Chamber also rejected a Prosecution Motion to call an expert witness to testify with regard to the handwriting on the letter (*Order on the Motion to seek leave to call additional expert witness concerning handwriting*, 20 January 1998).

Character Evidence

8.5.662 It is generally inadmissible to adduce evidence of the accused's character in order to show his propensity to act in conformity therewith. See *Decision on evidence of the good character of the accused and the defence of* tu quoque rendered by the Trial Chamber in *Kupreškić* on 17 February 1999:

> (i) generally speaking, evidence of the accused's character prior to the events for which he is indicted before the International Tribunal is not a relevant issue inasmuch as (a) by their nature as crimes committed in the context of widespread violence and during a national or international emergency, war crimes and crimes against humanity may be committed by persons with no prior convictions or his-

tory of violence, and that consequently evidence of prior good, or bad, conduct on the part of the accused before the conflict began is rarely of any probative value before the International Tribunal, and (b) as a general principle of criminal law, evidence as to the character of an accused is generally inadmissible to show the accused's propensity to act in conformity therewith.

8.5.663 This principle has not, however, always been respected. In *Hadžihasanović et al.*, for example, the Prosecution has referred in the Amended Indictment to a criminal matter against one of the accused which is entirely extraneous to the war crimes charges. It seems the reference is included as allegedly going to character.

Direct Versus Indirect Evidence

8.5.664 While indirect evidence is admissible, it is obviously preferable, where direct evidence is available, for that to be adduced instead. In his separate opinion in the *Rajić Rule 61 Decision*, Judge Sidhwa said that while Rule 89(C) allowed "both direct and indirect testimony (to) be received" (para. 23, separate opinion), he doubted "that this Chamber can permit indirect evidence to be recorded in preliminary proceedings if direct evidence is available and can be produced." He was referring there to evidence given by an investigator as to what other witnesses had told him. Judge Sidhwa's view was that the witnesses themselves should be produced to give that evidence.

"Consciousness of Guilt" Not of Probative Value

8.5.665 In *Delalić et al.*, the Prosecution sought to lead evidence of statements allegedly made by two of the accused to each other in the courtroom "as evidence of consciousness of guilt of these accused." In an *Order* rendered by the Trial Chamber on 26 November 1997, the Chamber denied the Prosecution Motions, considering that, "the principle of consciousness of guilt is not a legal principle upon which the Motions may be based in the circumstances."

Evidence of Acts Not Charged in the Indictment

8.5.666 Evidence of acts not charged in the indictment must be disregarded. See the *Furundžija Decision* rendered by the Trial Chamber on 12 June 1998 in which it held that, "the Trial Chamber will only consider as relevant Witness A's testimony in so far as it relates to Paragraphs 25 and 26 as pleaded in the indictment against the accused."

8.5.667 See also the *Kupreškić Appeals Judgement*, in which the Trial Chamber was criticised for taking into consideration evidence of a killing in which some of the accused were alleged to have participated which had not been charged in the indictment.

Probative Value Outweighed by Prejudicial Effect

8.5.668 In *Kordić, Decision on Prosecutor's Submissions Concerning "Zagreb Exhibits" and Presidential Transcripts*, 1 December 2000, the Trial Chamber held that it would be contrary to ICTY Rule 89(D) to admit evidence and exhibits at that stage of the proceedings, as the defence would not have had an opportunity to cross-examine any witness about the reports. Moreover, some of the reports were based on anonymous sources (para. 40).

Authentication

8.5.669 In the *Blaškić* case, the Trial Chamber took the following approach to the authentication of documents (*Decision on the Defence Motion for Reconsideration of the Ruling to Exclude from Evidence authentic and exculpatory documentary evidence*, 30 January 1998):

(1) All documents produced by a party and identified or recognised by a witness are admitted into evidence;

(2) A document produced by a party and *not* identified by the witness is not admitted into evidence

(3) The weight to be attached to a document admitted into evidence will depend on the elements adduced to authenticate it, if a challenge to the document's authenticity is raised.

(4) The Prosecutor must transmit to the defence "any material relevant to the authenticity of any document forming part of exculpatory evidence which the Prosecution is required by Rule 68 of the Rules to transmit to the Defence."

No Corroboration Requirement

8.5.670 There is no *unus testis, nullus testis* rule, i.e. no corroboration requirement, at the ICTR. See paras. 132–135 of the *Akayesu Trial Judgement*, in particular para. 135, "the Chamber can rule on the basis of a single testimony provided such testimony is, in its opinion, relevant and credible." This conforms with the ruling in the *Tadić Opinion and Judgement*, paras. 256 and 535–539, which concluded, ". . . there is no ground for concluding that this requirement of corroboration is any part of customary international law and should be required by this international tribunal" (para. 539).

Submission of Documents to Chamber

8.5.671 ICTR Rule 89 was relied upon, in conjunction with Rule 98, by the Trial Chamber in *Akayesu* to order the Prosecutor to submit to the Chamber "all written witness statements already made available by her to the Defence Counsel in this case." (*Decision by the Tribunal on its Request to the Prosecutor to submit the written witness statements*, 28 January 1997). The Chamber did not give the reasons for the Decision, except to refer to "the exceptional nature of the offences" and "the particular character of the Tribunal." The Chamber entered a caveat, namely that "disclosure of all the written statements does not necessarily entail admissibility of the said statements as evidence." At the same time, however, it ordered "that all such statements *to which reference has been made by either the Prosecutor or the Defence* shall be admitted as evidence and form part of the record" (emphasis added). The Prosecutor filed a *Motion to Reconsider and Rescind the Order of 28 January 1997 for the Disclosure of Witness Statements* on 4 February 1997, which was rejected.

Other ICTY and ICTR Decisions on Rule 89

8.5.672 Tr. Ch., *Decision on the tendering of Prosecution Exhibits 104–108, Delalić et al*, 9 February 1998; Tr. Ch., *Decision on the Prosecution's Motion for Exclusion of Evidence and Limitation of Testimony, Kunarac et al*, 3 July 2000.

Cross Reference: Rule 98.

8.5.673

ICTY Rule 90 Testimony of Witnesses	ICTR Rule 90 Testimony of Witnesses
(A) Every witness shall, before giving evidence, make the following solemn declaration: "I solemnly declare that I will speak the truth, the whole truth and nothing but the truth." (B) A child who, in the opinion of the Chamber, does not understand the nature of a solemn declaration, may be permitted to testify without that formality, if the Chamber is of the opinion that he is sufficiently mature to be able to report the facts of which he had knowledge and that he understands the duty to tell the truth. A judgement, however, cannot be based on such testimony alone. (C) A witness, other than an expert, who has not yet testified shall not be present when the testimony of another witness is given. However, a witness who has heard the testimony of another witness shall not for that reason alone be disqualified from testifying. (D) Notwithstanding paragraph (C), upon Order of the Chamber, an investigator in charge of a party's investigation shall not be precluded from being called as a witness on the ground that he or she has been present in the courtroom during the proceedings. (E) A witness may object to making any statement which might tend to incriminate the witness. The Chamber may, however, compel the witness to answer the question. Testimony compelled in this way shall not be used as evidence in a subsequent prosecution against the witness for any offence other than false testimony. (F) The Trial Chamber shall exercise control over the mode and order of interrogating witnesses and presenting evidence so as to (i) make the interrogation and presentation effective for the ascertainment of the truth; and (ii) avoid needless consumption of time. (G) The Trial Chamber may refuse to hear a witness whose name does not appear on the list of witnesses compiled pursuant to Rules 73 *bis* (C) and 73 *ter* (C).	(A) Witnesses shall, in principle, be heard directly by the Chambers unless a Chamber has ordered that the witness be heard by means of a deposition as provided for in Rule 71. (B) Every witness shall, before giving evidence, make the following solemn declaration: "I solemnly declare that I will speak the truth, the whole truth and nothing but the truth." (C) A child who, in the opinion of the Chamber, does not understand the nature of a solemn declaration, may be permitted to testify without that formality, if the Chamber is of the opinion that the child is sufficiently mature to be able to report the facts of which the child had knowledge and understands the duty to tell the truth. A judgement, however, cannot be based on such testimony alone. (D) A witness, other than an expert, who has not yet testified shall not be present when the testimony of another witness is given. However, a witness who has heard the testimony of another witness shall not for that reason alone be disqualified from testifying. (E) A witness may refuse to make any statement which might tend to incriminate him. The Chamber may, however, compel the witness to answer the question. Testimony compelled in this way shall not be used as evidence in a subsequent prosecution against the witness for any offence other than perjury. (F) The Trial Chamber shall exercise control over the mode and order of interrogating witnesses and presenting evidence so as to (i) make the interrogation and presentation effective for the ascertainment of the truth; and (ii) avoid needless consumption of time. (G) Cross-examination shall be limited to points raised in the examination-in-chief or matters affecting the credibility of the witness. The Trial Chamber may, if it deems it advisable, permit enquiry into additional matters, as if on direct examination.

(H)
(i) Cross-examination shall be limited to the subject-matter of the evidence-in-chief and matters affecting the credibility of the witness and, where the witness is able to give evidence relevant to the case for the cross-examining party, to the subject-matter of that case.
(ii) In the cross-examination of a witness who is able to give evidence relevant to the case for the cross-examining party, counsel shall put to that witness the nature of the case of the party for whom that counsel appears which is in contradiction of the evidence given by the witness.
(iii) The Trial Chamber may, in the exercise of its discretion, permit enquiry into additional matters.

History of ICTY Rule 90

8.5.674 Rule 90 was amended at the fifth plenary session in January 1995. Para. (A) (now deleted) was amended, substituting the words, "unless a Chamber has ordered" for "in cases, however, where it is not possible to secure the presence of a witness, a Chamber may order." A new para. (C) (now para. (B)) was added, with the former (C) becoming (D), provision being made in the new para. for a child who is not able to understand the nature of a solemn declaration. Para. (E) was also amended at the fifth plenary session "to improve the working of the Tribunal" (second Annual Report, para. 24) (witness's privilege against self-incrimination). Rule 90 was again amended at the thirteenth plenary session on 25 July 1997. The exception for video-conferences was added to para. (A) (para. now deleted) and a new para. (E) was added, with old para. (E) becoming (F). Paras. (G) and (H) were added at the eighteenth plenary session on 9–10 July 1998. Like other amendments adopted at the same plenary, these amendments were intended to expedite trial proceedings. The rule was amended at the twenty-first plenary session on 30 November 1999, mainly to allow a cross-examining party to ask a witness questions "relevant to the case for the cross-examining party," where before that party was limited to the subject-matter of examination-in-chief (direct examination) and matters affecting the witness's credibility. Para. (H)(ii) now also provides that the cross-examining party has to "put" its case to the witness, but the form and sequence for putting the case is not specified in the rule.

8.5.675 Para. (A) was deleted, with the other paras. being renumbered accordingly, on 19 January 2001, after the twenty-third plenary session. This would seem to indicate that the ICTY has abandoned the preference for live, oral testimony. This would fit in with the other amendments, and general shift in the ICTY's practice, designed to allow more and more evidence to be admitted in written form (e.g., affidavits, transcript and exhibit evidence from other trials, etc.). At the same plenary session, the reference to "perjury" in para. (E) was changed to "false testimony," to be consistent with the wording used in Rule 91.

History of ICTR Rule 90

8.5.676 This Rule was amended at the ICTR fifth plenary session on 8 June 1998, notably by adding para. (G) on the scope of cross-examination.

The "Best Evidence Rule" at the ICTs

8.5.677 In his separate opinion to the *Rajić Rule 61 Decision*, Judge Sidhwa said that in a Rule 61 decision, "no laxity can be shown in the application of Rule 90(A)" (which then read as ICTR Rule 90(A) now does). In that context he considered that "a scribe who takes down the statement of an eye-witness on behalf of the Prosecution, by authority given to him, is not a witness to the occurrence" and therefore "cannot be permitted to give evidence as to what the eye-witnesses of the case told him because his evidence would be against the best evidence rule" (para. 28, separate opinion).

8.5.678 This is not, however, strictly speaking, what the "best evidence" rule provides. In the Unites States, where it is also referred to as the "original documents rule," the "best evidence rule" stipulates that, to prove the contents of a writing, the original document must be produced rather than a copy or other evidence of its contents such as an oral report (see Federal Rules of Evidence, Rule 1004). In England, the rule is so rarely applied "as to be virtually extinct" (Keane, *the Modern Law of Evidence*, 2nd ed., p. 18)

Video-Link Testimony

8.5.679 Before Rule 90(A) was deleted at the twenty-third plenary session on 19 January 2001, it provided that while evidence may be heard by video-link conference, the preference was, wherever possible, for oral testimony in court. As noted above, this para. has now been removed, and presumably, with it, the preference for oral testimony in court. On the old preference for live testimony, see *Decisions on Defence Motions for Video-link conference* rendered in *Dokmanović* on 18 May 1998 and 29 April 1998; *Order relat[ing] to the testimony of General Milivoj Petković* of 18 June 1999 in *Blaškić*.

Improper for Witness to Send *Ex Parte* Communications to Judge about Merits of Issues before the Tribunal

8.5.680 In the *Akayesu Appeal Judgement,* (para. 343), the Appeals Chamber held that it is improper for a person who is not a party to the proceedings—in that case, a witness—to send *ex parte* communications to a judge concerning the merits of issues in dispute in a matter pending before the judge. However, the Appeals Chamber held that even if and when this occurs, the judges of the Tribunal are professional judges and it must be assumed that they will consider each case before them on the basis of the evidence presented and admitted in that case and that they will disregard evidence not presented before them. Furthermore, it is to be presumed that they will only enter a conviction of guilt if, soley on the evidence before them, they are satisfied beyond a reasonable doubt of the guilt of the Accused.

Communications with a Witness after He Has Been Sworn

8.5.681 A Party calling a witness cannot communicate with that witness after the witness has taken the solemn declaration. The Trial Chamber so held in *Kupreškić*, in its *Decision on Communication between the Parties and their witnesses* of 21 September 1998. It ordered that, "the Prosecution and Defence henceforth must not communicate with a witness, once he or she has made the Solemn Declaration provided for in Rule 90(B) and commenced testifying except with the leave of the Chamber." In the event that a witness wished to communicate with the Party calling the witness after the witness had begun testifying, the witness would have to contact the Victims and Witnesses Section who would then report the matter to the relevant party.

8.5.682 The issue arose due to defence objections that evidence had been adduced in court as a result of out-of-court communications between the Prosecutor and its witnesses during the court recesses. The Chamber found no impropriety in these exchanges, but did consider that a genuine issue had been raised.

8.5.683 The Chamber based its reasoning in part on the notion that "a witness . . . once he or she has taken the Solemn Declaration . . . is a witness of truth before the Tribunal and, inasmuch as he or she is required to contribute to the establishment of the truth, not strictly a witness for either party."

8.5.684 This ruling was followed in *Jelisić* in the *Decision on Communication between Parties and Witnesses* rendered by the Trial Chamber on 11 December 1998.

8.5.685 Parties should also ordinarily not communicate with the witnesses of the other party, at least not unless they have obtained the permission of the adverse party. See *Order for Clarification of Possible Communications with Prosecution Witnesses*, rendered by the Trial Chamber in *Kupreškić et al.* on 11 August 1998. The position depends, however, on the orders that have been issued in each case and thus may vary from case to case. Where a party has sought a ruling that the other Party may not communicate with "its" witnesses without its prior authority, and the Chamber has refused to make such an Order, then it is clear that the other Party may communicate with the other Party's prospective witnesses, even without informing the adverse Party. See the Trial Chamber's *Order on Protective Measures, Hadžihasanović et al.*, 1 February 2002.

Prevention of Contamination of Witness Testimony

8.5.686 Para. (C) of ICTY Rule 70 (which was then (D)) was considered by the Trial Chamber in *Tadić*. In its *Decision on Defence Motion to Prevent the Contamination of Testimony*, rendered on 3 May 1996, the Chamber stated that:

> Counsel for both parties and the Victims and Witnesses Unit shall use their best efforts to ensure that the provisions of Rule 90(D) of the Rules are complied with in full. In particular, counsel for both parties shall provide all potential witnesses with a copy of Rule 90(D) notice and shall discuss its implementation with all witnesses both before the commencement of the trial and during their presence in the Hague to give evidence. (paragraph 2)

8.5.687 Appended to the Decision of 3 May 1996, was the "Notice to Witnesses," which instructs witnesses as to their responsibilities under Rule 90 (D):

> In addition to the basic instruction to witnesses not to be present in the courtroom when another witness is testifying, the Trial Chamber HEREBY DIRECTS you not to discuss testimony with other potential witnesses both prior to and during the trial.
>
> In practical terms this means that, from the time you are first advised that one of the parties wishes to list you as a potential witness for trial, you should not discuss any matters relating to the trial with persons other than members of the Office of the Prosecutor, counsel for the defence or their designated representatives, or officials of the International Tribunal.
>
> Witnesses must not watch or read media coverage or the proceedings prior to giving evidence . . . (p. 8182)

8.5.688 The purpose of this Rule is to prevent witnesses from hearing other testimony on the same subject as that on which they will be testifying and thus basing themselves, at least in part and possibly unconsciously, on what they have heard in the courtroom rather than on their own recollection. The same applies to witnesses discussing the subject of their testimony with other witnesses; it is undesirable in that the witnesses may then remember what they discussed with other witnesses about the event rather than their own direct recollections of it. Their recollection thus becomes "contaminated" by the contact with other witnesses.

Investigators Are Not "Expert Witnesses"

8.5.689 The ICTY has held that investigators are not "expert witnesses" for the purposes of Rule 90(C), and are not therefore entitled to be present when another witness is testifying. Notwithstanding this, para. (D) now provides that, "upon Order of the Chamber, an investigator in charge of a party's investigation shall not be precluded from being called as a witness on the ground that he or she has been present in the courtroom during the proceedings." Thus investigators appear to enjoy an intermediate status between "ordinary" witnesses and expert witnesses.

8.5.690 In its *Decision on the Motion by the Prosecution to allow the Investigators to follow the Trial during the testimonies of witnesses*, rendered in *Delalić et al* on 20 March 1997, the Trial Chamber held that Prosecution and Defence investigators did not qualify as "expert witnesses" under Rule 90(D) and accordingly "should not be present in the public gallery of the courtroom and should not, otherwise, follow the proceedings when other witnesses are testifying." On the subject of expert witnesses, the Chamber said:

> 10. An expert witness is one specially skilled in the field of knowledge about which he is required to testify. The question of whether a person is an expert is one of law for the determination of the Trial Chamber.
>
> . . .
>
> 11. . . . an investigator *simpliciter*, whose testimony is not founded on a special skill, knowledge, or expertise, will not be accorded the privileges of an expert witness.

8.5.691 See *Order permitting Investigator to follow Proceedings* issued in *Kovačević* on 12 May 1998 and *Order permitting investigators to follow proceedings* issued in *Kordić* on 19 April 1999.

Publications of Expert Witnesses Are Public Property and Do Not Have To Be Disclosed

8.5.692 It was so held in the *Decision on Defence Request to Cross-Examine the Prosecutor's Expert Witness* rendered in *Kovačević* on 3 July 1998, granting the request in part and rejecting it in part. The Chamber held, *inter alia*, that "the publications of expert witnesses are to be considered as public property and need not be disclosed" and that a report prepared by the expert witness "is analogous to the report of a historian reviewing and commenting upon supporting materials."

Expert Witnesses

8.5.693 For a number of purposes, expert witnesses are distinguished from lay witnesses. Under Rule 90(C), "a witness, other than an expert, who has not yet testified shall not be present when the testimony of another witness is given." The report of an expert witness must also be disclosed in advance to the other Party; see Rule 94 *bis*.

8.5.694 In *Akayesu*, the former Commander of the United Nations Assistance Mission in Rwanda (UNAMIR), General Romeo Dallaire, testified, explaining the role and operations of UNAMIR in late 1993 and early 1994. Before he began testifying, on 25 February 1998, the Presiding Judge of the Trial Chamber clarified that General Dallaire was not a witness for the Defence, but an *expert* witness *requested* by the Defence. The reference to "request" derives from the civil law notion that expert witnesses are called by the Court, not by the Parties.

Expert Witness Must Be Impartial and an Acknowledged Expert

8.5.695 In an oral decision rendered in *Akayesu* by the Trial Chamber on 9 March 1998, the Chamber rejected a defence motion to call, as an expert witness, an individual—Ferdinand Nahimana—who had been indicted by the Tribunal and was in custody. The Chamber rejected the motion on two grounds. First, to qualify as an expert witness, the witness must be a recognised expert in his field and impartial; since the proposed expert witness was indicted by the Tribunal, he could not be regarded as being impartial with respect to its proceedings. Second, that calling an accused to testify as an expert witness in another trial might violate his privilege against self-incrimination, as enshrined in Article 20(4)(g) of the Statute of the ICTR.

Sequestration of Witnesses

8.5.696 "Sequestration" refers to the practice, normally applied to juries, of separating or isolating them from contact with the public during the course of a sensational trial, usually in order to avoid their deliberations being influenced by public opinion or to avoid their learning about trial matters dealt with in their absence, e.g. rulings on evidence. At the ICTY, it has been applied to witnesses. See *Order on Defence Motion requesting Sequestration of Witnesses* issued in *Furundžija* on 10 June 1998.

Immunised Testimony

8.5.697 Rule 90 (E) recognises the privilege against self-incrimination, enshrined notably in the Fifth Amendment to the United States Constitution. As under U.S.

Constitutional Law, the privilege cannot be invoked when the testimony is immunised from being used as evidence in a subsequent prosecution against the witness except in a prosecution for perjury (this latter exception is necessary to prevent the immunisation being used as a "licence to lie" in subsequent proceedings).

Credibility of Witnesses

8.5.698 ICTY Rule 90(H)(i) and ICTR Rule 90(G) provide for the cross-examination of witnesses on matters "affecting the credibility of a witness." This can be used to determine whether witnesses have colluded or exchanged information on their testimony. In *Nyiramasuhuko et al.*, 24 July 2001, the Trial Chamber, (referring to a previous Trial Chamber Decision in *Bagambiki and Ntagerura*, 23 August 2000) held that in a situation where a number of witnesses are transferred to the Detention Unit pursuant to Rule 90 *bis*, ICTR Rule 90(G) provides sufficient safeguards against collusion while the witnesses are in custody by allowing a right for cross-examination on matters affecting the credibility of witnesses. While ICTR Rule 90(G) may enable a cross-examining party to determine the extent of possible communication between witnesses, the Tribunal should nonetheless take all reasonable measures to ensure that such communication does not take place.

Cross-Examination: Leading Questions

8.5.699 At trial in *Akayesu*, the accused, representing himself, was told by the presiding judge not to ask leading questions. Akayesu raised this on appeal. In the *Akayesu Appeals Judgement* (para. 232), the Appeals Chamber, although not explicating criticising the Trial Chamber, appeared to imply that it was incorrect to prohibit the accused from asking leading questions during cross-examination. The Appeals Chamber held, however, that the appellant had not been able to demonstrate how the restriction on asking leading questions had caused him any prejudice (para. 325).

8.5.700

ICTY Rule 90 *bis* Transfer of a Detained Witness	ICTR Rule 90 *bis* Transfer of a Detained Witness
(A) Any detained person whose personal appearance as a witness has been requested by the Tribunal shall be transferred temporarily to the detention unit of the Tribunal, conditional on the person's return within the period decided by the Tribunal. (B) The transfer order shall be issued by a Judge or Trial Chamber only after prior verification that the following conditions have been met:	(A) Any detained person whose personal appearance as a witness has been requested by the Tribunal shall be transferred temporarily to the detention unit of the Tribunal, conditional on his return within the period decided by the Tribunal. (B) The transfer order shall be issued by a Judge or Trial Chamber only after prior verification that the following conditions have been met:

(i) the presence of the detained witness is not required for any criminal proceedings in progress in the territory of the requested State during the period the witness is required by the Tribunal; (ii) transfer of the witness does not extend the period of detention as foreseen by the requested State. (C) The Registrar shall transmit the order of transfer to the national authorities of the State on whose territory, or under whose jurisdiction or control, the witness is detained. Transfer shall be arranged by the national authorities concerned in liaison with the host country and the Registrar. (D) The Registrar shall ensure the proper conduct of the transfer, including the supervision of the witness in the detention unit of the Tribunal; the Registrar shall remain abreast of any changes which might occur regarding the conditions of detention provided for by the requested State and which may possibly affect the length of the detention of the witness in the detention unit and, as promptly as possible, shall inform the relevant Judge or Chamber. (E) On expiration of the period decided by the Tribunal for the temporary transfer, the detained witness shall be remanded to the authorities of the requested State, unless the State, within that period, has transmitted an order of release of the witness, which shall take effect immediately. (F) If, by the end of the period decided by the Tribunal, the presence of the detained witness continues to be necessary, a Judge or Chamber may extend the period on the same conditions as stated in Sub-rule (B).	(i) the presence of the detained witness is not required for any criminal proceedings in progress in the territory of the requested State during the period the witness is required by the Tribunal; (ii) transfer of the witness does not extend the period of his detention as foreseen by the requested State; (C) The Registry shall transmit the order of transfer to the national authorities of the State on whose territory, or under whose jurisdiction or control, the witness is detained. Transfer shall be arranged by the national authorities concerned in liaison with the host country and the Registrar. (D) The Registry shall ensure the proper conduct of the transfer, including the supervision of the witness in the detention unit of the Tribunal; it shall remain abreast of any changes which might occur regarding the conditions of detention provided for by the requested State and which may possibly affect the length of the detention of the witness in the detention unit and, as promptly as possible, shall inform the relevant Judge or Chamber. (E) On expiration of the period decided by the Tribunal for the temporary transfer, the detained witness shall be remanded to the authorities of the requested State, unless the State, within that period, has transmitted an order of release of the witness, which shall take effect immediately. (F) If, by the end of the period decided by the Tribunal, the presence of the detained witness continues to be necessary, a Judge or Chamber may extend the period on the same conditions as stated in Sub-rule (B).

History of ICTY Rule 90 *bis*

8.5.701 This new Rule was adopted at the initiative of the Judicial Department of the Registry at the eighth plenary session in October 1995. It was amended at the fourteenth plenary session on 12 November 1997.

General

8.5.702 Rule 90 *bis* allows the Tribunal to obtain the transfer of a person who is required by the Tribunal as a witness and who is detained in a State. This Rule has been relied upon in several instances since its adoption. On 12 February 1996, Judge Stephen issued orders for the transfer from Bosnia and Herzegovina of Đorđe Đukić and Aleksa Krsmanović, who had been detained by the authorities there, and for their detention at the Tribunal's facilities in The Hague. Krsmanović refused to act as a witness for the Tribunal and was returned to the competent authorities of Bosnia and Herzegovina.

8.5.703 Rule 90 *bis* was also the basis for an order issued by Judge Riad on 28 March 1996, which requested the Federal Republic of Yugoslavia (Serbia and Montenegro) to transfer two persons who were required by the Tribunal as witnesses against the accused Radovan Karadžić and Ratko Mladić. One witness, Radoslav Kremenović, was remanded back to the authorities of the Federal Republic of Yugoslavia (Serbia and Montenegro) on 25 May 1996 because his continued presence as a witness was no longer required. The other witness, Dražen Erdemović, was the subject of a deferral hearing on 28 May 1996, was indicted on 29 May 1996 and sentenced on 29 November 1996.

Precursor to Rule 90 *bis:* The *Opačić* Case

8.5.704 Before the introduction, in October 1995, of Rule 90 *bis*, Rule 54 was used to make an order to the same effect. Under an Order made pursuant to Rule 54, Dragan Opačić (IT-95-7-Misc.1) was brought to the Tribunal as a detained witness to testify in the *Tadić* trial. At trial, his credibility was thoroughly impeached by defence counsel. Thereafter the Prosecution, on 25 October 1996, informed the Trial Chamber that it no longer regarded him as a witness of truth and invited the Trial Chamber to ignore his testimony. Subsequently—and on parity with the procedure which would be adopted under Rule 90 *bis*—Opačić was returned to the State on whose territory, or under whose jurisdiction or control, he had been detained, namely Bosnia and Herzegovina. See *Order for the Return of a Detained Witness*, issued by the Trial Chamber on 27 May 1997. Opačić unsuccessfully appealed the Trial Chamber's Decision. See *Decision on Application for Leave to Appeal*, rendered by a Bench of the Appeals Chamber on 3 June 1997.

8.5.705 Once a detained witness is no longer needed at the Tribunal, he can be transferred back to the State whence he came without the need for a new order (*Order Stating that an Order By a Judge is not Necessary to End the Temporary Transfer of a Detained Witness*, Judge Odio-Benito, *Karadžić and Mladić*, 9 May 1996).

Detention by National Authorities Not Justiciable

8.5.706 When it concerns the temporary transfer to the Tribunal of a witness detained in some other country, it is not for the Tribunal to look into whether the witness is validly detained in that other country. The Tribunal is not competent to enquire into such matters (*Decision on the Motion on Behalf of General Đorđe Đukić, Đukić* (IT-96-19-Misc.1), 28 February 1996; see also subsequent decision on the same matter of 1 March 1996).

Extension of Time for Detention

8.5.707 Under Rule 90 *bis* (F), a Judge of the Tribunal may extend the period for which a person is detained at the Tribunal pursuant to Rule 90 *bis*, provided the detained witness could still be detained by the national authority which transferred the witness. However, such an application for extension has been refused when the presence of the detainee as a witness had already been determined to be no longer necessary and no new element for the application of Rule 90 *bis* had been shown. See the Decision of Judge Odio-Benito in *Krsmanović*.

8.5.708 This Rule was applied by the ICTR in *Akayesu* in an Order issued by Judge Kama on 29 October 1996 and in an Order issued by the Trial Chamber on 31 October 1997. The Order of 31 October 1997 (*Order for Temporary Transfer of Three Detained Witnesses Pursuant to Rule 90 bis*) concerned three witnesses for the defence—given pseudonyms and other protection under Rule 75—who were then detained in the Taba Communal Prison in the Prefecture of Gitarama in Rwanda. The Order provided for the witnesses to "be transferred temporarily to the Tribunal's detention facilities in Arusha for a period not exceeding two months from 30 October 1997, in order to testify in the trial against [sic] the accused," and requested "the Government of Rwanda to comply with this order and to arrange for the transfer in liaison with the Tanzanian Government and the Registrar."

Expiry of Time Limits

8.5.709 Where the time limits set out in Rule 90 *bis* expire, the Tribunal may exceptionally use Rule 54, as a general rule, to extend the detention.

8.5.710 In *Bagambiki, Imanishimwe*, and *Ntagerura*, the Trial Chamber held, on 10 September 2001, that as a matter of principle, parties should bring motions for the extension of detention pursuant to Rule 90 *bis* in a timely manner, well in advance of the expiry of any previous detention orders. However, they held that in the event of the expiry of previous detention orders, Rule 54 permits the Chamber to issue orders as may be necessary for the conduct of the trial where Rule 90 *bis* (F) is no longer available and "when it is in the interests of justice and judicial efficiency to do so."

Cross Reference: Rule 54.

Necessity for the Request Must Be Demonstrated

8.5.711 In *Bagambiki, Imanishimwe*, and *Ntagerura*, a defence motion dated 25 February 1998, which requested the transfer of five witnesses pursuant to Rule 90 *bis*, and protective measures for the said witnesses, was rejected when the defence failed to provide reasons why the witnesses in question were needed. See oral decision rendered from the bench by the Trial Chamber on 26 February 1998. Contrasting the motion which had been granted in its Decision of 31 October 1997 (above), where the defence had convinced the Chamber of the imperative necessity of hearing the three witnesses and had explained the exculpatory nature of the evidence they would tender, the Chamber considered that the defence had not shown what steps they had taken to make contact with the witnesses. Accordingly the Chamber considered that the Defence was not able to show that the witnesses' testimony would necessarily be useful in establishing the truth. This seems to be part of a general approach whereby the Chambers will not step in to help a party unless the party can first show that it has taken all the measures within its power to obtain the desired result.

Detained Witness Not Required for Criminal Proceedings in Progress in the State

8.5.712 Rule 90 *bis* (B)(i) provides that a transfer issue shall only be ordered, *inter alia*, if "the presence of the detained witness is not required for any criminal proceedings in progress in the territory of the requested State during the period the witness is required by the Tribunal." This is designed to ensure that the removal of the witness to the Tribunal does not interfere with domestic criminal proceedings. This was the ground for the Trial Chamber refusing a defence request for a transfer order of 13 witnesses in *Akayesu*. See the oral decision of the Trial Chamber of 9 March 1998. The need to transfer detained witnesses arises more frequently at the ICTR than at the ICTY, since a great deal of Hutus are detained in Rwandan prisons on suspicion of having participated in genocide; these are often persons the defence wish to call as witnesses.

Communication between Detained Witnesses

8.5.713 In a Decision in *Nyiramasuhuko et al.*, 24 July 2001, the Trial Chamber held that where a number of witnesses are transferred at the same time to the Detention Unit, the right to cross-examine on credibility, set out in Rule 90(G), provides sufficient protection against the possibility of communication between those witnesses. This ruling was apparently in response to a party's request that measures be taken to ensure that the witnesses did not communicate with each other. The Tribunal considered that such steps were beyond its power but that any communications between witnesses could be exposed in the course of cross-examination.

Cross Reference: Rule 90(G).

8.5.714

ICTY Rule 92 Confessions	ICTR Rule 92 Confessions
A confession by the accused given during questioning by the Prosecutor shall, provided the requirements of Rule 63 were strictly complied with, be presumed to have been free and voluntary unless the contrary is proved.	A confession by the accused given during questioning by the Prosecutor shall, provided the requirements of Rule 63 were strictly complied with, be presumed to have been free and voluntary unless the contrary is proved.

Appropriate Stage to Challenge Admissibility of Confessions

8.5.715 In *Nyiramasuhuko and Ntahobali, Decision on the Defence Motion to Suppress Custodial Statements by the Accused*, 8 June 2001, the Trial Chamber held that the appropriate time for the defence to challenge whether the requirements of Rule 63 had been complied with by the Prosecution would be if and when the Prosecution sought to use the confession statements as evidence. It would then be for the Trial Chamber to decide whether to hold a *voire dire* on the admissibility of the statements.

8.5.716

ICTY Rule 92 *bis* Proof of Facts Other Than by Oral Evidence	ICTR Rule 92 *bis* Proof of Facts Other Than by Oral Evidence

(A) A Trial Chamber may admit, in whole or in part, the evidence of a witness in the form of a written statement in lieu of oral testimony which goes to proof of a matter other than the acts and conduct of the accused as charged in the indictment.
(i) Factors in favour of admitting evidence in the form of a written statement include but are not limited to circumstances in which the evidence in question:
  (a) is of a cumulative nature, in that other witnesses will give or have given oral testimony of similar facts;
  (b) relates to relevant historical, political or military background;
  (c) consists of a general or statistical analysis of the ethnic composition of the population in the places to which the indictment relates;
  (d) concerns the impact of crimes upon victims;
  (e) relates to issues of the character of the accused; or
  (f) relates to factors to be taken into account in determining sentence.
(ii) Factors against admitting evidence in the form of a written statement include whether:
  (a) there is an overriding public interest in the evidence in question being presented orally;
	(A) A Trial Chamber may admit, in whole or in part, the evidence of a witness in the form of a written statement in lieu of oral testimony which goes to proof of a matter other than the acts and conduct of the accused as charged in the indictment.
	(i) Factors in favour of admitting evidence in the form of a written statement include, but are not limited to, circumstances in which the evidence in question:
	  (a) is of a cumulative nature, in that other witnesses will give or have given oral testimony of similar facts;
	  (b) relates to relevant historical, political or military background;
	  (c) consists of a general or statistical analysis of the ethnic composition of the population in the places to which the indictment relates;
	  (d) concerns the impact of crimes upon victims;
	  (e) relates to issues of the character of the accused; or
	  (f) relates to factors to be taken into account in determining sentence.
	(ii) Factors against admitting evidence in the form of a written statement include whether:
	  (a) there is an overriding public interest in the evidence in question being presented orally;

(b) a party objecting can demonstrate that its nature and source renders it unreliable, or that its prejudicial effect outweighs its probative value; or
(c) there are any other factors which make it appropriate for the witness to attend for cross-examination.

(B) A written statement under this Rule shall be admissible if it attaches a declaration by the person making the written statement that the contents of the statement are true and correct to the best of that person's knowledge and belief and
(i) the declaration is witnessed by:
    (a) a person authorised to witness such a declaration in accordance with the law and procedure of a State; or
    (b) a Presiding Officer appointed by the Registrar of the Tribunal for that purpose; and
(ii) the person witnessing the declaration verifies in writing:
    (a) that the person making the statement is the person identified in the said statement;
    (b) that the person making the statement stated that the contents of the written statement are, to the best of that person's knowledge and belief, true and correct;
    (c) that the person making the statement was informed that if the content of the written statement is not true then he or she may be subject to proceedings for giving false testimony; and
    (d) the date and place of the declaration.

The declaration shall be attached to the written statement presented to the Trial Chamber.

(C) A written statement not in the form prescribed by paragraph (B) may nevertheless be admissible if made by a person who has subsequently died, or by a person who can no longer with reasonable diligence be traced, or by a person who is by reason of bodily or mental condition unable to testify orally, if the Trial Chamber:
(i) is so satisfied on a balance of probabilities; and

(ii) finds from the circumstances in which the statement was made and recorded that there are satisfactory *indicia* of its reliability. (D) A Chamber may admit a transcript of evidence given by a witness in proceedings before the Tribunal which goes to proof of a matter other than the acts and conduct of the accused. (E) Subject to Rule 127 or any order to the contrary, a party seeking to adduce a written statement or transcript shall give fourteen days notice to the opposing party, who may within seven days object. The Trial Chamber shall decide, after hearing the parties, whether to admit the statement or transcript in whole or in part and whether to require the witness to appear for cross-examination.	(ii) finds from the circumstances in which the statement was made and recorded that there are satisfactory *indicia* of its reliability. (D) A Chamber may admit a transcript of evidence given by a witness in proceedings before the Tribunal which goes to proof of a matter other than the acts and conduct of the accused. (E) Subject to any order of the Trial Chamber to the contrary, a party seeking to adduce a written statement or transcript shall give fourteen days notice to the opposing party, who may within seven days object. The Trial Chamber shall decide, after hearing the parties, whether to admit the statement or transcript in whole or in part and whether to require the witness to appear for cross-examination.

History of ICTY Rule 92 *bis*

8.5.717   This new rule was introduced on 19 January 2001, after the twenty-third plenary session. It superseded, and went beyond, Rule 94 *ter* ("Affidavit Evidence") which was deleted at the same plenary session.

8.5.718   Rule 94 *ter*, which was introduced at the nineteenth plenary session on 17 December 1998 and amended at the twenty-first plenary session on 30 November 1999, had read:

> To prove a fact in dispute, a party may propose to call a witness and to submit in corroboration of his or her testimony on that fact affidavits or formal statements signed by other witnesses in accordance with the law and procedure of the State in which such affidavits or statements are signed. These affidavits or statements are admissible provided they are filed prior to the giving of testimony by the witness to be called and the other party does not object within seven days after completion of the testimony of the witness through whom the affidavits are tendered. If the party objects and the Trial Chamber so rules, or if the Trial Chamber so orders, the witnesses shall be called for cross-examination.

8.5.719   See the *Practice Direction on Procedure for the Implementation of Rule 92bis (B)* of the Rules of Procedure and Evidence available at: www.un.org/icty/legal-doc/ index.htm.

8.5.720

ICTY Rule 93 Evidence of Consistent Pattern of Conduct	ICTR Rule 93 Evidence of Consistent Pattern of Conduct
(A) Evidence of a consistent pattern of conduct relevant to serious violations of international humanitarian law under the Statute may be admissible in the interests of justice. (B) Acts tending to show such a pattern of conduct shall be disclosed by the Prosecutor to the defence pursuant to Rule 66.	(A) Evidence of a consistent pattern of conduct relevant to serious violations of international humanitarian law under the Statute may be admissible in the interests of justice. (B) Acts tending to show such a pattern of conduct shall be disclosed by the Prosecutor to the defence pursuant to Rule 66.

History of ICTY Rule 93

8.5.721 Rule 93 was amended, at the suggestion of the International Law Committee of the Association of the Bar of the City of New York, at the fifth plenary session in January 1995, "to broaden the rights of suspects and accused persons . . . adding a requirement that the Prosecutor disclose evidence of a consistent pattern of conduct to the defence."

8.5.722 See the explanation of this rule given by Judge Cassese in *Kupreškić* at the hearing of 15 February 1999, stating that Rule 93 was not to be used to prove the good character of the accused (in order to prove behaviour in conformity therewith):

> As for the model of behaviour, I think with all due respect, Rule 93, on pattern of conduct, is not relevant to that. . . . I took some part in the drafting of this Rule 93, and I can tell you . . . this rule was conceived of as relating to crimes against humanity. When you may have to prove the existence of a consistent practice or systematic practice. I don't see why and [to] what extent Rule 93 could relate to the issue of character.

8.5.723

ICTY Rule 94 Judicial Notice	ICTR Rule 94 Judicial Notice
(A) A Trial Chamber shall not require proof of facts of common knowledge but shall take judicial notice thereof. (B) At the request of a party or *proprio motu*, a Trial Chamber, after hearing the parties, may decide to take judicial notice of adjudicated facts or documentary evidence from other proceedings of the Tribunal relating to matters at issue in the current proceedings.	(A) A Trial Chamber shall not require proof of facts of common knowledge but shall take judicial notice thereof. (B) At the request of a party or *proprio motu*, a Trial Chamber, after hearing the parties, may decide to take judicial notice of adjudicated facts or documentary evidence from other proceedings of the Tribunal relating to matters at issue in the current proceedings.

750 • *International Criminal Practice*

History of ICTY Rule 94

8.5.724 Para. (B) was added at the ICTY eighteenth plenary session on 9–10 July 1998.

History of ICTR Rule 94

8.5.725 Para. (B) was added at the ICTR ninth plenary session on 3 November 2000.

General

8.5.726 Reference may be made to a lengthy submission on judicial notice in international law by the Prosecutor in the hearings before the Appeals Chamber on the interlocutory appeal on jurisdiction in the *Tadić* case (IT-94-1-AR72, Transcript of Hearing, 7 September 1995, pp 107–110), reproduced in the first edition of this book. See also *Order on Prosecution Request for Judicial Notice* issued in *Kovačević* on 12 May 1998.

Judicial Notice and *Res Judicata*

8.5.727 These two concepts are sometimes confused. In *Simić and others*, the Prosecutor requested the Chamber to take judicial notice of the fact that the conflict in Bosnia and Herzegovina was, at least prior to 19 May 1992, *international* in that it was a conflict between two States—the FRY and Bosnia and Herzegovina. The Prosecutor made this request partly on the basis of previous rulings of the Chambers, in particular, in *Tadić* and *Delalić et al* (see Article 2 of the ICTY Statute). Thus the submission was, in effect, one of *res judicata*. The Trial Chamber, in its *Decision on the Pre-Trial Motion by the Prosecution requesting the Trial Chamber to take judicial Notice of the nature of the conflict in Bosnia and Herzegovina* of 25 March 1999, rejected this approach. It held that there was no doctrine of binding precedent at the Tribunal and that "Rule 94 is intended to cover facts and not legal consequences inferred from them." The Chamber did nevertheless take judicial notice of the fact that "(1) Bosnia and Herzegovina proclaimed its independence from the Socialist Federal Republic of Yugoslavia on 6 March 1992; (2) The independence of Bosnia and Herzegovina as a State was recognised by the European Community on 6 April 1992 and by the United States on 7 April 1992."

Judicial Notice and Stipulations/Formal Admissions

8.5.728 These two notions also seem to have been at times conflated. In a *Decision on Judicial Notice* rendered in *Kvočka* on 8 June 2000, the Trial Chamber took "judicial notice," on the basis of admissions agreed by the parties, of the fact that "at the times and places alleged in the indictment, there existed an armed conflict; that this conflict included a widespread and systematic attack against notably the Muslim and Croat civilian population; and that there was a nexus between this armed conflict and the widespread and systematic attack on the civilian population and the existence of the Omarska, Keraterm and Trnpolje camps and the mistreatment of the prisoners therein." These facts are not "facts of common knowledge" and so would not come within Rule 94(A). Although the situation might come within Rule 94(B), it would seem more appropriate to deal with this as a matter of stipulations rather than of judicial notice.

Judicial Notice of Adjudicated Facts

8.5.729 In *Decision on the Prosecutor's Motion for Judicial Notice of Adjudicated Facts* in *Ntakirutimana*, on 22 November 2001, the Trial Chamber stated that it follows from Rule 94(B) that the facts proposed for notice must have been 'adjudicated' in other proceedings before the ICTR. The Chamber was of the view that the reference to previous findings of the ICTR does not include judgements based on guilty pleas, or admissions voluntarily made by an accused during the proceedings. Such instances which do not call for the same scrutiny of facts by a Chamber as in a trial situation where the Prosecutor has the usual burden of proof, are not proper sources of judicial notice. The Trial Chamber noted the Appeals Chamber decision in *Kupreškić* (8 May 2001) where the Appeals Chamber had observed that only facts in a judgement, from which there has been no appeal, or as to which any appellate proceedings have concluded, can truly be deemed 'adjudicated facts' within the meaning of Rule 94(B) (para. 26 of the *Ntakirutimana Decision*).

8.5.730 The Trial Chamber further stated that Rule 94(B) requires that the proposed adjudicated facts must 'relate' to matters at issue in the proceedings in issue. Accordingly, matters which have only an indirect or remote bearing on the case at hand should not be the subject of judicial notice as this would not serve the main purpose of such notice, namely to ensure judicial economy (para. 27, *ibid.*).

8.5.731 The Chamber noted that Rule 94(B) grants the Chamber a 'discretionary' power to take judicial notice. The Chamber stressed that it is for the Chamber to decide whether justice is best served by taking judicial notice in ensuring (i) judicial economy and (ii) consistency of case law. It further emphasised that these aims must be balanced with the fundamental right of the accused to a fair trial in accordance with Article 20 of the ICTR Statute (para. 28, *ibid.*; see also *Simić et al.*, Decision of 27 September 2000; and *Semanza*, Decision of 15 March 2001). In striking this balance the Chamber should avoid taking judicial notice of facts that are the subject of reasonable dispute. Such matters should not be settled by judicial notice but instead be determined on the merits after the parties have had the opportunity to submit evidence and arguments (para. 29, *ibid.*;— see also *Sikirica*; Decision of 27 September 2000).

8.5.732 The Trial Chamber indicated that it was not inclined to take judicial notice of legal characterisations or legal conclusions based on interpretation of facts.

8.5.733 In *Ntakirutimana*, the Trial Chamber declined to take judicial notice of the 'widespread or systematic' nature of the attacks, the total number of people killed in Rwanda during the conflict, or the existence of a genocidal plan.

Citing Authorities and Judicial Notice

8.5.734 Citing authorities in support of a position is not the same as seeking judicial notice. In *Kajelijeli, Decision on Juvenal Kajelijeli's Motion in Objection to the Pre-Trial Brief*, 11 April 2001, the Defence asserted that the Prosecution were attempting to have judicial notice taken of facts pursuant to Rule 94. The Prosecution had made reference to a previous ICTR Decision as being authority on the extent and nature of evidence that could be presented before the Tribunal to establish 'Conspiracy to commit genocide.' The Trial Chamber rejected the Defence complaint noting that the Prosecution were not seeking judicial notice of a fact but simply referring to the authority of a judicial precedent on a legal question.

8.5.735

ICTY Rule 94 *bis* Testimony of Expert Witnesses	ICTR Rule 94 *bis* Testimony of Expert Witnesses
(A) The full statement of any expert witness to be called by a party shall be disclosed within the time-limit prescribed by the Trial Chamber or by the Pre-Trial Judge.	(A) Notwithstanding the provisions of Rule 66(A)(ii), Rule 73 *bis* (B)(iv)(b) and Rule 73 *ter* (B)(iii)(b), the full statement of any expert witness called by a party shall be disclosed to the opposing party as early as possible and shall be filed with the Trial Chamber not less than twenty-one days prior to the date on which the expert is expected to testify.
(B) Within thirty days of disclosure of the statement of the expert witness, or such other time prescribed by the Trial Chamber or pre-trial Judge, the opposing party shall file a notice indicating whether: (i) it accepts the expert witness statement; (ii) it wishes to cross-examine the expert witness; and (iii) it challenges the qualifications of the witness as an expert or the relevance of all or parts of the report and, if so, which parts.	(B) Within fourteen days of filing of the statement of the expert witness, the opposing party shall file a notice indicating whether: (i) it accepts the expert witness statement; or (ii) it wishes to cross-examine the expert witness.
(C) If the opposing party accepts the statement of the expert witness, the statement may be admitted into evidence by the Trial Chamber without calling the witness to testify in person.	(C) If the opposing party accepts the statement of the expert witness, the statement may be admitted into evidence by the Trial Chamber without calling the witness to testify in person.

History of ICTY Rule 94 *bis*

8.5.736 This Rule was added at the eighteenth plenary session on 9–10 July 1998. Like other amendments adopted at the same plenary, its purpose is to expedite trial proceedings, in this case by arranging for early exchange of expert reports to facilitate definition of the issues in dispute and to identify the need or otherwise to call the expert witness to testify in person.

8.5.737 The reference in para. (A) to Rule 73 *bis* and *ter* was changed, on 2 August 2000 after the twenty-second plenary session, to refer to Rule 65 *ter*. The para. was again amended in a minor way on 19 January 2001, after the twenty-third plenary session.

8.5.738 The rule was amended at the twenty-fifth plenary session on 12–13 December, 2001, to provide for the disclosure of the statement of the expert witness within the time-limit prescribed by the Trial Chamber or pre-trial Judge, rather than "as early as possible and shall be filed with the Trial Chamber not less than twenty-one days prior to the date on which the expert is expected to testify," as the rule had earlier provided. The time-period in para. (B) was also changed to thirty days. Para. (B)(iii) was added on 12 December 2002.

History of ICTR Rule 94 *bis*

8.5.739 This new Rule was added at the Fifth Plenary Session on 8 June 1998. An identical rule was added to the ICTY Rules of Procedure and Evidence on 9–10 July 1998. The object of the Rule, like the new Rules 73 *bis* and 73 *ter*, is to expedite the trial proceedings.

8.5.740 In *Nyiramasuhuko, Decision on the Defence Motions for an Extension of the Time Limits for Filing the Notice in Respect of Expert Witness Statements*, 25 May 2001, the Trial Chamber stipulated that Rule 94 *bis* (B) is to be read in conjunction with Rule 94 *bis* (A), and that the provisions clearly state that the time-frames under Rule 94 *bis* (B) run from the filing of the expert witnesses statements with the Trial Chamber.

8.5.741

ICTY Rule 95 Exclusion of Certain Evidence	ICTR Rule 95 Exclusion of Evidence on the Grounds of the Means by Which It Was Obtained
No evidence shall be admissible if obtained by methods which cast substantial doubt on its reliability or if its admission is antithetical to, and would seriously damage, the integrity of the proceedings.	No evidence shall be admissible if obtained by methods which cast substantial doubt on its reliability or if its admission is antithetical to, and would seriously damage, the integrity of the proceedings.

History of ICTY Rule 95

8.5.742 Rule 95 was amended at the fifth plenary session in January 1995 "to broaden the rights of suspects and accused persons" (exclusion of evidence because of how it was obtained). The Rule originally read, "Evidence obtained directly or indirectly by means which constitute a serious violation of internationally protected human rights shall not be admissible." See the second Annual Report, paragraph 26, fn. 9: "The amendment to Rule 95, which was made on the basis of proposals from the Governments of the United Kingdom and the United States, puts parties on notice that although a Trial Chamber is not bound by national rules of evidence, it will refuse to admit evidence—no matter how probative—if it was obtained by improper methods." Commentators had noted that the previous version of the Rule gave rise to ambiguities. Although this amendment meant that the rule no longer referred to violations of internationally protected human rights, the title remained, "Evidence Obtained by

Means Contrary to Internationally Protected Human Rights," until it was amended to the present title at the fourteenth plenary session on 12 November 1997. The title of ICTR Rule 95 is different again: "Exclusion of Evidence on the Grounds of the Means by which it was obtained."

Decisions, Orders, and Opinions under Rule 95

8.5.743 In his separate opinion in the *Rajić Rule 61 Decision*, Judge Sidhwa said, in relation to a witness who testified, in a summary manner, as to the facts given by eye-witnesses to him about the attack on a village, the subject of the indictment, that his testimony "violates the principle of Rules 61(A) and 95 and places the principle laid down in Rule 89(D) open to grave abuse" (paragraph 30). He concluded that he would therefore "reject that part of his testimony which seeks to recount what eye-witnesses 'A' to 'G' said to him (the witness)" (paragraph 30, separate opinion). See, on hearsay, 8.5.642 *et seq.*

8.5.744 See *Decision Stating Reasons for Trial Chamber's Ruling of 1 June 1999 rejecting Defence Motion to Suppress Evidence* of 25 June 1999 in *Kordić and Čerkez*, holding, on a defence motion to suppress evidence, that the Prosecution had authority to take direct enforcement action in the form of armed search and seizure operations within the boundaries of a sovereign state (Bosnia and Herzegovina) without that state's express permission, and that SFOR acted properly in assisting the ICTY in this task.

8.5.745

ICTY Rule 96 Evidence in Cases of Sexual Assault	ICTR Rule 96 Evidence in Cases of Sexual Assault

In cases of sexual assault:
(i) no corroboration of the victim's testimony shall be required;
 	
(ii) consent shall not be allowed as a defence if the victim
   (a) has been subjected to or threatened with or has had reason to fear violence, duress, detention or psychological oppression, or
   (b) reasonably believed that if the victim did not submit, another might be so subjected, threatened or put in fear;
(iii) before evidence of the victim's consent is admitted, the accused shall satisfy the Trial Chamber in camera that the evidence is relevant and credible;
(iv) prior sexual conduct of the victim shall not be admitted in evidence.
	In cases of sexual assault:
	(i) notwithstanding Rule 90(C), no corroboration of the victim's testimony shall be required;
	(ii) consent shall not be allowed as a defence if the victim
	   (a) has been subjected to or threatened with or has had reason to fear violence, duress, detention or psychological oppression, or
	   (b) reasonably believed that if the victim did not submit, another might be so subjected, threatened or put in fear;
	(iii) before evidence of the victim's consent is admitted, the accused shall satisfy the Trial Chamber in camera that the evidence is relevant and credible;
	(iv) prior sexual conduct of the victim shall not be admitted in evidence.

History of ICTY Rule 96

8.5.746 Para. (ii) of Rule 96 was amended at the third plenary session in May 1994 to add the words ". . . if the victim (a) has been subjected to or threatened with or has had reason to fear violence, duress, detention or psychological oppression, or (b) reasonably believed that if the victim did not submit, another might be so subjected, threatened or put in fear." Para. (iii) was added at the fifth plenary "to protect the rights of victims and witnesses" (second Annual Report, para. 27).

8.5.747 A corrigendum to (ii)(b) was adopted on 6 February 1995, which changed the pronoun "she" to the gender-neutral noun, "the victim," in recognition of the fact that men are also the victims of sexual assault.

Protection of Alleged Victims of Sexual Assault

8.5.748 The protective intent of Rule 96 was discussed by the Trial Chamber in *Tadić*. In its *Decision on the Prosecutor's Motion Requesting Protective Measures for Victims and Witnesses* of 10 August 1995, a majority of the Trial Chamber noted that special consideration was taken in the Rules of Procedure and Evidence to protect victims of sexual assault. After laying out the provisions of Rule 96, the Chamber discussed the importance of balancing the right of the accused to a fair and public trial against the protection of victims of sexual assault. Further, it asserted that measures which protect privacy and guard against re-traumatisation under Rule 75 do not adversely affect the accused's right to a fair and public trial. The Chamber discussed a range of possible steps which, if taken, would best protect the witness and safeguard the rights of the accused:

> 49. In consideration of the unique concerns of victims of sexual assault, a special Rule for the admittance of evidence in cases of sexual assault was included in the Rules of the International Tribunal. Rule 96 provides that corroboration of the victim's testimony is not required and consent is not allowed as a defence if the victim has been subject to physical or psychological constraints. Finally, the victim's prior sexual conduct is inadmissible.

> 50. In determining where the balance lies between the right of the accused to a fair and public trial and the protection of victims and witnesses, consideration has been given to the special concerns of victims of sexual assault. These concerns have been factored into the balance on an individual basis for each witness for whom protection is sought. . . . These measures in no way affect the accused's right to a fair and public trial. The protective measures sought pursuant to Rule 75 will afford these witnesses privacy and guard against their retraumatization should they choose to testify at trial. Given the individual circumstances of these four witnesses, the Trial Chamber has determined that protective measures are warranted, and are allowed by the Statute and Rules.

"Consent Shall Not Be Allowed as a Defence"

8.5.749 The meaning of this phrase was considered in the *Foča Trial Judgement* (paras. 461–464). According to the Trial Chamber, "consent" is not a defence as such; rather absence of consent is an element of the crime of rape. The point being made by Rule 96 is rather that the presence of force, violence, etc. would negate any apparent consent to intercourse on the part of the victim.

No Waiver of Victim's Right Not To Have His/Her Prior Sexual Conduct Admitted in Evidence

8.5.750 According to para. (iv) of Rule 96, "prior sexual conduct of the victim shall not be admitted in evidence." A Trial Chamber has held that the victim cannot, impliarly or explicitly, waive this right to exclude evidence of his or her prior sexual conduct. See *Decision on the Prosecution's Motion for the Redaction of the Public Record*, Trial Chamber, 5 June 1997, *Delalić et al.*:

> 58. Sub-rule 96(iv) is an exclusionary rule which totally forbids the introduction of evidence concerning prior sexual conduct in sexual assault cases and there can be no waiver of its imperative application.

Expert Medical Evidence Not Required in Relation to Sexual Offences

8.5.751 See *Order on Defence Experts* rendered in *Foča* on 29 March 2000 by the Trial Chamber:

> 5. . . . Expert medical evidence is not required in relation to the evidence of witnesses in relation to crimes such as rape, torture, outrages upon personal dignity and enslavement, and the circumstances in which expert medical evidence would even be relevant are rare. An example where such evidence may be relevant would be where a witness claims that a particular scar resulted from a cigarette burn, but where the expert was able to say that that scar was the result of a surgical procedure.
>
> 6. However, it would not be appropriate to permit a medical examination unless there is shown to be a reasonable likelihood in the particular case that it will assist the accused. Each case will have to be considered separately. Similarly, whether evidence may be given by the medical experts will also have to be considered on a case by case basis. As such evidence is governed by Rule 94 *bis* ("Testimony of Expert Witnesses"), full statements of the evidence will have to be filed in advance, and a determination will be made upon the basis of what they contain. Such witnesses will be defence witnesses, and not, as suggested by Defence counsel, as assisting the Trial Chamber.
>
> 7. It should be clearly understood—as both parties have conceded—that it is for the Trial Chamber, and for the Trial Chamber alone, to assess the credibility of the witnesses. At the hearing, it was suggested that a psychoanalyst could give evidence to assist the Trial Chamber as to the credibility of a witness who has allegedly given four different statements in relation to certain events. The Trial Chamber is not persuaded from what has been said so far that such evidence would be admissible.

8.5.752

ICTY Rule 97 Lawyer-Client Privilege	ICTR Rule 97 Lawyer-Client Privilege
All communications between lawyer and client shall be regarded as privileged, and consequently not subject to disclosure at trial, unless: (i) the client consents to such disclosure; or (ii) the client has voluntarily disclosed the content of the communication to a third party, and that third party then gives evidence of that disclosure.	All communications between lawyer and client shall be regarded as privileged, and consequently not subject to disclosure at trial, unless: (i) the client consents to such disclosure; or (ii) the client has voluntarily disclosed the content of the communication to a third party, and that third party then gives evidence of that disclosure.

General

8.5.753 The concept of Lawyer-Client privilege was extensively discussed by the Trial Chamber in two separate opinions (Judge Stephen and Judge Vohrah) and in one separate and dissenting opinion (Judge McDonald) issued on 27 November 1996 on a Prosecution Motion for Production of Defence Witness Statements. The issue presented to the Chamber was "whether the Trial Chamber has the power to order the Defence to disclose to the Prosecution a witness's prior statement, taken by or on behalf of the Defence in anticipation of litigation, after the witness has testified" (paragraph 1, Opinion of Judge McDonald). The Chamber was unanimous in holding that the Rules did not specifically address this issue. The majority (Judges Stephen and Vohrah), however, held that such statements were protected by legal professional privilege and were thus not subject to disclosure to the Prosecution.

Cross Reference: See Rule 70(A) and Rule 90(E).

Transmission of Privileged Correspondence between Counsel and Accused by Investigators

8.5.754 In *Rutaganda*, in a Decision of 11 June 1997, the Trial Chamber held that defence investigators do not have the same privileges as defence counsel with regard to visits to detainees. The Chamber ruled that:

> only visits to the detainees by their Defence [Counsel] can be rendered without any restriction or supervision, subject to prior consultation with the Commanding Officer.

8.5.755 Furthermore, defence investigators may only visit detainees at the UN Detention Facility:

subject to the restrictions and measures of supervision normally applied to visits by the accused's family, friends and 'others' within the meaning of Rule 61 of the Rules of Detention.

8.5.756 However:

[an] investigator employed by a Defence Counsel can . . . meet with the accused without any such restrictions or measures of supervision imposed by the Commanding Officer if he is accompanied by the Defence Counsel in person.

8.5.757 In *Mugiraneza*, in a Decision of 19 September 2001, the Trial Chamber held that a detainee is not entitled to communicate fully and without restraint with any person other than his Defence Counsel. The Chamber held that for the purposes of privileged communication, the term 'Counsel' does not include employees or associates of counsel. Accordingly, correspondence brought by a member of the Defence Team other than Counsel to the accused must be clearly identified as emanating from counsel and secured in such a manner to prevent persons other than the intended recipient seeing the contents to be considered privileged. Conversely, Security Officers may inspect the content of any communication that is not clearly identified as falling under lawyer-client privilege, regardless of format, when it is brought to the Detention Unit by members of the Defence Team other than Counsel. See also *Naletilić and Martinović, Order of the President on the Complaint of Defence Counsel for the accused Naletilić*, 5 June 2001, in which the President held that the privilege of confidential communication only applies between Defence Counsel and client and not to meetings between an investigator and the accused; and *Brdjanin and Talić, Decision on Motion for Production of Documents—Džonlić Testimony of 11 March 2002*, 9 April 2002.

8.5.758

ICTY Rule 98 Power of Chambers to Order Production of Additional Evidence	ICTR Rule 98 Power of Chambers to Order Production of Additional Evidence
A Trial Chamber may order either party to produce additional evidence. It may *proprio motu* summon witnesses and order their attendance.	A Trial Chamber may *proprio motu* order either party to produce additional evidence. It may itself summon witnesses and order their attendance.

History of ICTR Rule 98

8.5.759 The words *"proprio motu"* were added to this Rule at the ICTR fifth plenary session on 8 June 1998.

Witness Summoned by the Chamber

8.5.760 A Trial Chamber summoned a witness *proprio motu* pursuant to Rule 98 in the *Kupreškić* trial in an order dated 30 September 1998. In the Summons, the Trial

Chamber summoned the witness using a pseudonym and requested the Victims and Witnesses Unit "to manage all the practical arrangements related to bringing the witness to the Tribunal to testify and returning the witness to the witness's residence . . . and leaves it to the discretion of the Unit as to how to inform the said witness that the witness is being called by the Chamber to testify, taking into account the witness's infirmity." The Chamber went on to state that it did not at that stage contemplate any penalty for non-compliance and simply urged the witness to comply with the summons in the interests of justice. The Chamber also stated in the Summons that the order of examination of the witness would be examination by the Judges, followed by examination by the Prosecution and then examination by defence counsel.

8.5.761 In a series of decisions rendered on 25 March, 13 May and 21 May 1999, the *Blaškić* Trial Chamber applied Rule 98 to order General Phillippe Morillon (former UNPROFOR Commander), Colonel Robert Stewart (former BRITBAT Commander), a former Chief of Staff of the Croatian Defence Counsel (HVO), Commanders of the Bosnian Army and the former Chief of the European Community Monitoring Mission (ECMM) to appear as witnesses in the trial. The Chamber's decisions specified that each witness will "testify freely about matters of which he had knowledge that occurred within the scope of his then mission and that relate to the acts with which the accused has been charged as they appear in the indictment." The witnesses "may rely on personal notes" but "not read a prepared statement." The witnesses would then answer the questions put to them by the Judges, by the Prosecution and by the Defence. The Chamber's Decisions were transmitted on 25 March 1999 to the Embassies of France, the United Kingdom, Croatia and Bosnia and Herzegovina in order for the authorities "to take all the necessary measures to ensure that the witness(es) appear." For those witnesses who had served as United Nations Commanders, it was necessary to obtain a waiver of their immunity from the United Nations Secretariat, in line with the approach taken in *Akayesu* at the ICTR when General Dallaire testified (*Decision on the Motion to Subpoena a Witness* in *Akayesu* rendered by Trial Chamber 1 on 19 November 1997; see commentary to ICTR Rule 54, below).

8.5.762 Rule 98 was relied upon, in conjunction with Rule 89, by the Trial Chamber in *Akayesu* to order the Prosecutor to submit "all written witness statements already made available by her to the Defence Counsel in this case." (*Decision by the Tribunal on its Request to the Prosecutor to submit the written witness statements*, 28 January 1997).

Cross Reference: See ICTR's Rule 89 and commentary thereto above.

SECTION 6: JUDGEMENT

8.6.1

ICTY Article 23 Judgement	ICTR Article 22 Judgement
1. The Trial Chambers shall pronounce judgements and impose sentences and penalties on persons convicted of serious violations of international humanitarian law. 2. The judgement shall be rendered by a majority of the judges of the Trial Chamber, and shall be delivered by the Trial Chamber in public. It shall be accompanied by a reasoned opinion in writing, to which separate or dissenting opinions may be appended.	1. The Trial Chambers shall pronounce judgements and impose sentences and penalties on persons convicted of serious violations of international humanitarian law. 2. The judgement shall be rendered by a majority of the judges of the Trial Chamber, and shall be delivered by the Trial Chamber in public. It shall be accompanied by a reasoned opinion in writing, to which separate or dissenting opinions may be appended.

Judgements Drafted by Legal Assistants

8.6.2 Patricia Wald, former Judge at the ICTY, recently acknowledged that initial drafts of ICTY judgements are often prepared by legal assistants:

> Because ICTY trials are long and fact-specific and because legal assistants are often assigned to the Chambers as a whole, with only one junior legal assistant assigned to any individual judge, the task of initially drafting the Chamber's judgements, to a very considerable degree, is not infrequently delegated to the pool of legal assistants who commonly are selected by the Presiding Judge or the senior legal officers. Reading some of the . . . judgements of the ICTY, one can guess that many of the judgements are the work of a committee rather than an individual judge or judges.

8.6.3 See *The International Criminal Tribunal for the Former Yugoslavia Comes of Age: Some Observations on Day to Day Dilemmas of an International Court*, Vol.5 *Journal of Law and Policy* 87 at page 93. Nonetheless, it is imperative that the Tribunal's judges oversee and exercise the closest scrutiny over the work of legal assistants in the drafting of Tribunal Judgements. Moreover, such drafting cannot in any sense involve *substantive* decision-making, since the Judges' role, as triers of fact, in assessing the credibility of witnesses and of the accused, and ultimately of deciding upon the guilt or innocence of the accused, is fundamentally an exercise of their own judgement and therefore cannot be delegated to anyone. Delegation of findings of fact from the trier of fact would be *ultra vires*.

ICTY Trial Judgements

8.6.4 For a list of ICTY Judgements rendered, see Annex 1 ("Concluded Cases/ICTY").

Cross Reference: ICTY Rule 98 *ter*.

ICTR Final Judgements

8.6.5 Article 22 of the Statute of the ICTR is identical to Article 23 of the Statute of the ICTY. For a list of ICTR Judgements rendered, see Annex 1 ("Concluded Cases/ ICTR").

8.6.6

ICTY Rule 98 *bis* Motion for Judgement of Acquittal	ICTR Rule 98 *bis* Motion for Judgement of Acquittal
(A) An accused may file a motion for the entry of judgement of acquittal on one or more offences charged in the indictment within seven days after the close of the Prosecutor's case and, in any event, prior to the presentation of evidence by the defence pursuant to Rule 85(A)(ii). (B) The Trial Chamber shall order the entry of judgement of acquittal on motion of an accused or *proprio motu* if it finds that the evidence is insufficient to sustain a conviction on that or those charges.	If, after the close of the case for the prosecution, the Trial Chamber finds that the evidence is insufficient to sustain a conviction on one or more counts charged in the indictment, the Trial Chamber, on motion of an accused or *proprio motu*, shall order the entry of judgement of acquittal in respect of those counts.

History of ICTY Rule 98 *bis*

8.6.7 This Rule was added at the eighteenth plenary session on 9–10 July 1998. It was divided into paras. (A) and (B), and modified in minor ways, at the twenty-first plenary session on 30 November 1999.

History of ICTR Rule 98 *bis*

8.6.8 This Rule was introduced at the Fifth Plenary Session on 8 June 1998. A near-identical Rule 98 *bis* was added to the ICTY Rules of Procedure and Evidence on 9–10 July 1998.

Standard To Be Applied under Rule 98 *bis*

8.6.9 The test to be applied under Rule 98 *bis* is whether there was evidence on which a reasonable Trial Chamber could base a conviction. The test is *not* whether there was evidence that satisfied the Trial Chamber beyond a reasonable doubt. The broad purpose of the Rule is to determine whether the Prosecutor has put a case sufficient to warrant the defence being called upon to answer it (Tr. Ch., *Decision on Defence Motions for Judgement of Acquittal, Kordić and Čerkez*, 6 April 2000, paras. 11 and

26). In *Jelisić*, Appeals Judgement, 5 July 2001, paragraph 37, the Appeals Chamber stated:

> The Appeals Chamber considers that the reference in Rule 98 *bis* to a situation in which the evidence is insufficient to sustain a conviction means a case in which, in the opinion on the Trial Chamber, the prosecution evidence, if believed, is insufficient for any reasonable trier of fact to find that guilt has been proved beyond reasonable doubt.

Rule 98 *bis* Can Be Applied to Individual Incidents

8.6.10 In *Kvočka, Decision on Defence Motions for Acquittal*, 15 December 2000, the Trial Chamber held that it may enter a judgement of acquittal not only with regard to an entire count of the indictment, but also with regard to a factual incident or event cited in the indictment in support of the offence if the Prosecutor's evidence on that particular incident does not rise to the level of the standard required by Rule 98 *bis* (B). In essence, that means that the Chamber may make exculpatory findings of fact during the course of the trial.

Decisions under Rule 98 *bis*

8.6.11 A Motion for Judgement of Acquittal failed in *Blaškić*. See *Decision of Trial Chamber I on the Defence Motion to Dismiss* rendered by Trial Chamber on 3 September 1998. Although the Defence sought to rely on Rule 54, the Chamber considered it under Rule 98 *bis* on the principle of law *speciala derogant generalibus* (the special provision displaces the general one), Rule 54 being a general rule and Rule 98 *bis* the specific rule for this type of motion. The Chamber rejected the motion on the basis that the Prosecutor had neither failed to provide proof of any of the counts of the indictment, nor failed to demonstrate a serious *prima facie* case in support of its claims.

8.6.12 See also the *Decision on Motion for Withdrawal of the Indictment against the Accused Vlatko Kupreškić* rendered on 18 December 1998 in which, *inter alia*, the Trial Chamber stated that it did not consider it appropriate to apply Rule 98 *bis* to order a judgement of acquittal on one or more charges contained in the indictment against Vlatko Kupreškić. See also the subsequent decision of the Chamber rendered on 8 January 1999, in which Vlatko Kupreškić was convicted, and the Appeals Chamber's Judgement of 23 October 2001, overturning the conviction.

8.6.13 See *Decision on Motion for Acquittal* (denying the motion) rendered by the Trial Chamber in *Foča* on 3 July 2000.

8.6.14 The motion succeeded in *Jelisić*. See the *Jelisić Trial Judgement* of 14 December 1999, which was strongly criticised, but not overturned, by the Appeals Chamber in the *Jelisić Appeals Judgement* of 5 July 2001. See 4.2.23 and 4.2.72.

8.6.15 Rule 98 *bis* was considered for the first time by the ICTR in *Semanza, Decision on the Defence Motion for a Judgement of Acquittal in Respect of Laurent Semanza After Quashing the Counts Contained in the Third Amended Indictment*, 27 September 2001. The Trial Chamber held that Rule 98 *bis* means that a judgement of acquittal shall be ordered at the close of the case for the Prosecution if the Chamber finds that the evidence, if believed, is insufficient for a reasonable trier of fact to find that guilt has been proved beyond reasonable doubt. In *Semanza*, the Trial Chamber held that the Defence failed to show that the evidence, if believed, was insufficient for a conviction. They confirmed that all that was required of the Prosecution was to establish a *prima facie* case (para. 15). The Defence in *Semanza* had mistakenly argued that the evidence presented by the Prosecution was not credible or reliable. The Trial Chamber also stated that the Defence had mistakenly attempted to quash certain counts in the Indictment pursuant to Rule 98 *bis*. The Trial Chamber also held that the fact that not all Prosecution witnesses had testified on all counts in the indictment as indicated in the witness list was not an issue that the Chamber could consider under Rule 98 *bis* and nor would this amount to a sufficient ground for acquittal. (paras. 16–20).

8.6.16

ICTY Rule 98 *ter* Judgement	ICTR Rule 88 Judgement
(A) The judgement shall be pronounced in public, on a date of which notice shall have been given to the parties and counsel and at which they shall be entitled to be present, subject to the provisions of Sub-rule 102(B). (B) If the Trial Chamber finds the accused guilty of a crime and concludes from the evidence that unlawful taking of property by the accused was associated with it, it shall make a specific finding to that effect in its judgement. The Trial Chamber may order restitution as provided in Rule 105. (C) The judgement shall be rendered by a majority of the Judges. It shall be accompanied or followed as soon as possible by a reasoned opinion in writing, to which separate or dissenting opinions may be appended. (D) A copy of the Judgement and of the Judges' opinions in a language which the accused understands shall as soon as possible be served on the accused if in custody. Copies thereof in that language and in the language in which they were delivered shall also as soon as possible be provided to counsel for the accused.	(A) The judgement shall be pronounced in public, on a date of which notice shall have been given to the parties and counsel and at which they shall be entitled to be present. (B) If the Trial Chamber finds the accused guilty of a crime and concludes from the evidence that unlawful taking of property by the accused was associated with it, it shall make a specific finding to that effect in its judgement. The Trial Chamber may order restitution as provided in Rule 105. (C) The judgement shall be rendered by a majority of the Judges. It shall be accompanied or followed as soon as possible by a reasoned opinion in writing, to which separate or dissenting opinions may be appended.

History of ICTY Rule 98 *ter*

8.6.17 This Rule used to be ICTY Rule 88. It was re-numbered as Rule 98 *ter* at the eighteenth plenary session on 9–10 July 1998. At the same plenary, the rule was amended by adding the words, "subject to the provisions of Sub-rule 102(B)" to para. (A).

8.6.18 As Rule 88, this rule was amended at the fifth plenary session in January 1995 for the purpose of "clarifying the rules" (second Annual Report, para. 21, fn.6). The words, "and at which they shall be entitled to be present," were added, and the previous wording "in the presence of the accused" deleted, in order to be clear that an accused who is, for example, in hospital at the time the judgement is pronounced, does not have to be physically present before the court when judgement is pronounced. The words, "The judgement shall be rendered by a majority of the Judges. It shall be accompanied or followed as soon as possible by a reasoned opinion in writing . . ." were added, to reflect the wording of Article 23(2) of the Statute. The words, "as soon as possible," were added to indicate that judgement, in the sense of a verdict, need not be contemporaneous with the handing down of a reasoned decision.

Sentencing Matters May Be Dealt with Before Judgement Handed Down

8.6.19 See *Scheduling Order* issued in *Dokmanović* on 8 June 1998. The rule now indeed is that sentencing matters *must* be addressed in the Parties' closing speeches. See Rule 86(C) and, for criticism of this rule, 8.5.605.

8.6.20

ICTY Rule 99 Status of the Acquitted Person	ICTR Rule 99 Status of the Acquitted Person
(A) Subject to Sub-rule (B), in the case of an acquittal or the upholding of a challenge to jurisdiction, the accused shall be released immediately. (B) If, at the time the judgement is pronounced, the Prosecutor advises the Trial Chamber in open court of the Prosecutor's intention to file notice of appeal pursuant to Rule 108, the Trial Chamber may, on application in that behalf by the Prosecutor and upon hearing the parties, in its discretion issue an order for the continued detention of the acquitted person, pending the determination of the appeal.	(A) In case of acquittal, the accused shall be released immediately. (B) If, at the time the judgement is pronounced, the Prosecutor advises the Trial Chamber in open court of his intention to file notice of appeal pursuant to Rule 108, the Trial Chamber may, at the request of the Prosecutor, issue a warrant for the arrest and further detention of the accused to take effect immediately.

History of ICTY Rule 99

8.6.21 The French text of Rule 99(B) was amended at the sixth plenary session, held on 1–3 May 1995, to rectify a discrepancy between the French and English versions. Rule 99(B) was further amended at the fourteenth plenary session on 12 November 1997 (see ICTR Rule 99 for comparison). The reference to Rule 108 in Rule 99(B) was changed at the eighteenth plenary session, on 9–10 July 1998, from the previous reference to Rule 88 *bis*.

History of ICTR Rule 99

8.6.22 The words, "and further detention," were added to para. (B) at the fifth plenary session on 8 June 1998.

Application of Rule

8.6.23 ICTY Rule 99 was applied for the first time in the *Delalić et al Trial Judgement*, to release the acquitted Zejnil Delalić from custody (para. 1291 of the *Judgement*).

PART 9

SENTENCING PROCEDURE, PENALTIES AND ENFORCEMENT OF SENTENCES

ICTY Article 24/ICTR Article 23: Penalties	9.1
ICTY Rule 101/ICTR Rule 101: Penalties	9.2
History of ICTY Rule 101	9.3
History of ICTR Rule 101	9.6
Purposes of Sentencing in the Jurisprudence of the ICTs	9.7
Retribution	9.9
Role	9.9
Content	9.12
Deterrence	9.14
Rehabilitation	9.20
Protection of Society	9.23
Remarks	9.24
The Provisions of the Statutes	9.25
ICTY Article 24(1)/ICTR Article 23(1)	9.25
ICTY Article 24(2)/ICTR Article 23(2)	9.32
Gravity of the Offence and Discretionary Framework	9.33
Recourse to the General Practice Regarding Prison Sentences in the Courts of the Former Yugoslavia and to the Organic Law of Rwanda	9.39
Need for Consistency in Sentencing	9.41
Remarks	9.54
Powers of Appeals Chamber to Substitute Its Own Sentence Without Remitting the Matter to the Trial Chamber	9.58
Revision	9.60
Other Indications	9.61
Factors To Be Taken into Account in Sentencing	9.63
Aggravating Circumstances	9.66
The Accused's Superior Position	9.66
Abuse of Authority	9.68
Direct Participation of a Superior	9.72
A Factor Cannot Be Aggravating When It Is an Ingredient of the Crime	9.73
Premeditation	9.74
Other Aggravating Circumstances of Conduct: Youth or Old Age of the Victims	9.75
Conduct During the Trial	9.76
Aggravating Factors for Specific Crimes	9.77
Rape	9.78
Other Crimes	9.81
Mitigating Circumstances	9.82
Substantial Cooperation with the Prosecution before or after Conviction	9.83

Guilty Plea 9.86
Remorse 9.91
Superior Orders 9.94
Personal Circumstances of the Accused 9.98
Diminished Mental Capacity 9.101
Absence of Active Participation 9.102
ICTY Rule 100/ICTR Rule 100: Sentencing Procedure on a Guilty Plea 9.105
History of ICTY Rule 100 .... 9.106
History of ICTR Rule 100 .... 9.107
Psychiatric and Psychological Reports 9.108
Witnesses 9.109
Penalties in the Rome Statute 9.111
Punishment: General Reflections 9.115
Minimum Term Recommendation 9.118
Life Imprisonment 9.119
Meaning of Imprisonment for "the Remainder of His Life" 9.121
Burden and Standard of Proof for Aggravating Factors 9.123
Multiple Sentences 9.126
Credit for Time in Custody "Pending Surrender" 9.128
ICTY Rule 102/ICTR Rule 102: Status of the Convicted Person 9.130
History of ICTY Rule 102 .... 9.131
History of ICTR Rule 102 .... 9.133
ICTY Article 27/ICTR Article 26: Enforcement of Sentences 9.134
Enforcement of ICTY Sentences 9.135
Enforcement of Sentences in Rwanda 9.138
Enforcement of ICTR Sentences Outside Rwanda 9.139
The Position of the Government of Rwanda in the Security Council 9.140
ICTY Rule 103/ICTR Rule 103: Place of Imprisonment 9.141
History of ICTY Rule 103 .... 9.142
Agreement with Italy 9.145
The *Erdemović* Case 9.146
ICTY Rule 104/ICTR Rule 104: Supervision of Imprisonment 9.148
The *Erdemović* Case 9.149
ICTY Rule 105/ICTR Rule 105: Restitution of Property 9.150
History of ICTY Rule 105 .... 9.151
ICTY Rule 106/ICTR Rule 106: Compensation to Victims 9.153
Compensation for Deprivation of Liberty, Consequent upon Wrongful Arrest,
   Prosecution or Conviction or Unlawful Violation of Rights 9.155
ICTY Article 28/ICTR Article 27: Pardon or Commutation of Sentences 9.156
ICTY Rule 123/ICTR Rule 124: Notification by States 9.158
ICTY Rule 124/ICTR Rule 125: Determination by the President 9.159
ICTY Rule 125/ICTR Rule 126: General Standards for Granting Pardon or Commutation 9.161
Sentencing Bibliography 9.162

9.1

ICTY Article 24 Penalties	ICTR Article 23 Penalties
1. The penalty imposed by the Trial Chamber shall be limited to imprisonment. In determining the terms of imprisonment, the Trial Chambers shall have recourse to the general practice regarding prison sentences in the courts of the former Yugoslavia. 2. In imposing the sentences, the Trial Chambers should take into account such factors as the gravity of the offence and the individual circumstances of the convicted person. 3. In addition to imprisonment, the Trial Chambers may order the return of any property and proceeds acquired by criminal conduct, including by means of duress, to their rightful owners.	1. The penalty imposed by the Trial Chamber shall be limited to imprisonment. In determining the terms of imprisonment, the Trial Chambers shall have recourse to the general practice regarding prison sentences in the courts of Rwanda. 2. In imposing the sentences, the Trial Chambers should take into account such factors as the gravity of the offence and the individual circumstances of the convicted person. 3. In addition to imprisonment, the Trial Chambers may order the return of any property and proceeds acquired by criminal conduct, including by means of duress, to their rightful owners.

9.2

ICTY Rule 101 Penalties	ICTR Rule 101 Penalties
(A) A convicted person may be sentenced to imprisonment for a term up to and including the remainder of his life. (B) In determining the sentence, the Trial Chamber shall take into account the factors mentioned in Article 24(2) of the Statute, as well as such factors as: (i) any aggravating circumstances; (ii) any mitigating circumstances including the substantial cooperation with the Prosecutor by the convicted person before or after conviction; (iii) the general practice regarding prison sentences in the courts of the former Yugoslavia; (iv) the extent to which any penalty imposed by a court of any State on the convicted person for the same act has already been served, as referred to in Article 10(3) of the Statute.	(A) A person convicted by the Tribunal may be sentenced to imprisonment for a fixed term or the remainder of his life. (B) In determining the sentence, the Trial Chamber shall take into account the factors mentioned in Article 23(2) of the Statute, as well as such factors as: (i) any aggravating circumstances; (ii) any mitigating circumstances including the substantial co-operation with the Prosecutor by the convicted person before or after conviction; (iii) the general practice regarding prison sentences in the courts of Rwanda; (iv) the extent to which any penalty imposed by a court of any State on the convicted person for the same act has already been served, as referred to in Article 9(3) of the Statute.

(C) Credit shall be given to the convicted person for the period, if any, during which the convicted person was detained in custody pending his surrender to the Tribunal or pending trial or appeal.	(C) The Trial Chamber shall indicate whether multiple sentences shall be served consecutively or concurrently. (D) Credit shall be given to the convicted person for the period, if any, during which the convicted person was detained in custody pending his surrender to the Tribunal or pending trial or appeal.

* * * * *

History of ICTY Rule 101

9.3 Rule 101 was amended, at the suggestion of the International Law Committee of the Association of the Bar of the City of New York, at the fifth plenary session in January 1995. Old para. (B)(iv) was moved to para. (E), and the words, "Credit shall be given to the convicted person for" were added at the beginning, and the words, "or appeal," at the end of the para., to make clear that the time spent awaiting appeal may also be taken into consideration when determining an appropriate sentence.

9.4 Para. (D) was moved to Rule 100(B) at the eighteenth plenary session on 9–10 July 1998, with para. (E) becoming para. (D).

9.5 Para. (C) was deleted on 19 January 2001, after the twenty-third plenary session. The question of multiple sentencing is now dealt with in Rule 87 (C). Para. (D) became para. (C).

History of ICTR Rule 101

9.6 This Rule was amended at the ICTR fifth plenary session on 8 June 1998. Para. (A) was modified and old para. (D) deleted, with old para. (E) becoming (D).

Purposes of Sentencing in the Jurisprudence of the ICTs

9.7 The Tribunals have referred to different functions to be accomplished by sentencing.

9.8 The functions most often specified by the jurisprudence are four-fold:

- Retribution
- Deterrence
- Rehabilitation
- Protection of Society

Retribution

Role

9.9 The ICTY and ICTR have emphasised on numerous occasions the primary role of retribution. The jurisprudence of the International Tribunals seems to support deterrence and retribution as the main, if not the only, sentencing factors for international crimes (*Todorović Trial Judgement*, para. 28; *Aleksovski Appeals Judgement*, para. 185; *Kupreškić Trial Judgement* para. 848; *Delalić et al. Appeals Judgement*, para. 806; *Kordić and Čerkez Trial Judgement*, para. 847; *Foča Trial Judgement*, para. 857; *Kayishema and Ruzindana Trial Judgement*, para. 2).

9.10 Retribution requires the Chamber to enquire into the conduct of the accused in order to determine the just punishment for his crime (*Foča Trial Judgement*, para. 840, paras. 841 and 857). In the *Aleksovski* case, the Appeals Chamber explicitly endorsed the statement of the Trial Chamber in the *Delalić* case, that the "most important consideration, which may be regarded as the litmus test for the appropriate sentence, is the gravity of the offence" (*Aleksovski Appeals Judgement*, para. 182). In *Kupreškić*, the Trial Chamber found that "The sentences to be imposed must reflect the inherent gravity of the criminal conduct of the accused. The determination of the gravity of the crime requires a consideration of the particular circumstances of the case, as well as the form and degree of the participation of the accused in the crime" (*Kupreškić Trial Judgement*, para. 852).

9.11 Furthermore,

> the principle of retribution, if it is to be applied at all in the context of sentencing, must be understood as reflecting a fair and balanced approach to the exaction of punishment for wrongdoing. This means that the penalty imposed must be proportionate to the wrongdoing; in other words, that the punishment be made to fit the crime. (*Todorović Trial Judgement*, para. 29).

Content

9.12 Retribution "is not to be understood as fulfilling a desire for revenge but as duly expressing the outrage of the international community at these crimes. This factor has been widely recognised by Trial Chambers of this International Tribunal as well as Trial Chambers of the International Criminal Tribunal for Rwanda. Accordingly, a sentence of the International Tribunal should make plain the condemnation of the international community of the behaviour in question and show that the international community was not ready to tolerate serious violations of international humanitarian law and human rights." (*Erdemović Sentencing Judgement*, para. 64; *Delalić et al. Trial Judgement*, para. 1234; *Furundžija Trial Judgement*, para. 288; *Kambanda Trial Judgement*, para. 28; *Akayesu Trial Judgement*, para. 19; *Serushago Sentencing Judgement*, para. 20; *Rutaganda Trial Judgement*, para. 456; *Musema Trial Judgement*, para. 986; *Aleksovski Trial Judgement*, para. 185; *Foča Trial Judgement*, para. 841; *Kordić and Čerkez Trial Judgement*, para. 847).

9.13 Retribution sets a limit for determining a proportionate sentence:

> The principle of retribution, if it is to be applied at all in the context of sentencing, must be understood as reflecting a fair and balanced approach to the exaction of punishment for wrongdoing. This means that the penalty imposed must

be proportionate to the wrongdoing; in other words, that the punishment be made to fit the crime. The Chamber is of the view that this principle is reflected in the account, which the Chamber is obliged by the Statute and the Rules to take, of the gravity of the crime" (*Todorović Trial Judgement*, para. 29.)

Deterrence

9.14 The ICTY and ICTR systematically draw a distinction between general and special deterrence.

9.15 *General deterrence* is one of the general sentencing factors. It refers to "the need to punish an individual for the crimes committed and the need to deter other individuals from committing similar crimes" (*Foča Trial Judgement*, para. 836 *et seq.*; *Kordić and Čerkez Trial Judgement*, para. 847; *Krstić Trial Judgement*, para. 693).

9.16 The need for general deterrence has been expressed by Resolution 827 of the Security Council, which established the ICTY with the stated purpose of bringing to justice persons responsible for serious violations of international humanitarian law in the former Yugoslavia, *thereby deterring future violations* and contributing to the re-establishment of peace and security in the region.

9.17 The ICTY Appeals Chamber has accepted that this factor must not be accorded undue prominence in the overall assessment of the sentences to be imposed on persons convicted by the International Tribunal (*Tadić Judgement in Sentencing Appeals*, para. 48; following the *Aleksovski Appeals Judgement*, para. 185;, *Kordić and Čerkez Trial Judgement*, 26 February 2001, para. 847; *Delalić et al. Appeals Judgement*, para. 801). The moral dilemma presented by general deterrence is that it involves punishing one person in order to deter *others*. It therefore seems to fall foul of the categorical imperative, articulated by Immanuel Kant, that persons are to be treated as ends in themselves and not as a means to an end, in this case as a means to prevent other persons from committing crimes.

9.18 *Special deterrence* serves the function of deterring *the defendant* from re-committing, as opposed to deterring *others* from committing the crime.

9.19 In one case, the Chamber disapproved of deterrence, both specific and general:

> 840. Whether the Appeals Chamber considers special or general deterrence or both to be a main general sentencing factor is . . . not entirely clear. Given that uncertainty, this Trial Chamber considers it appropriate to express its view that special deterrence, as a general sentencing factor, is generally of little significance before this jurisdiction. The main reason is that the likelihood of persons convicted here ever again being faced with an opportunity to commit war crimes, crimes against humanity, genocide or grave breaches is so remote as to render its consideration in this way unreasonable and unfair. As to general deterrence, in line with the view of the Appeals Chamber, it is not to be accorded undue prominence in the assessment of an overall sentence to be imposed. The reason is that a sentence should in principle be imposed on an offender for *his* culpable conduct—it may be unfair to impose a sentence on an offender greater than is appropriate to that conduct solely in the *belief* that it will deter others (*Foča Trial Judgement*, para. 840).

Rehabilitation

> The factor of rehabilitation considers the circumstances of reintegrating the guilty accused into society. (. . .) The age of the accused, his circumstances, his ability to be rehabilitated and availability of facilities in the confinement facility can, and should, be relevant considerations in this regard (*Delalić et al. Trial Judgement*, para. 1233).

9.20 Concerning rehabilitation as a sentencing purpose, see also *Erdemović Sentencing Judgement*, para. 66; *Furundžija Trial Judgement*, para. 291; *Serushago Trial Judgement*, para. 39.

9.21 It should be stressed that, before the ICTs, rehabilitation does not play a primary role among the functions of sentencing. Thus the ICTY Appeals Chamber has affirmed that:

> The cases which come before the Tribunal differ in many respects from those which ordinarily come before national jurisdictions, primarily because of the serious nature of the crimes being prosecuted, that is "serious violations of international humanitarian law." Although both national jurisdictions and certain international and regional human rights instruments provide that rehabilitation should be one of the primary concerns for a court in sentencing, this cannot play a *predominant* role in the decision-making process of a Trial Chamber of the Tribunal. On the contrary, the Appeals Chamber (and Trial Chambers of both the Tribunal and the ICTR) have consistently pointed out that two of the main purposes of sentencing for these crimes are deterrence and retribution. Accordingly, although rehabilitation (in accordance with international human rights standards) should be considered as a relevant factor, it is not one which should be given undue weight (*Delalić et al. Appeals Judgement*, para. 806).

9.22 The Trial Chamber ruling in the *Foča Trial Judgement* held that rehabilitation is not the object of sentencing (para. 844).

Protection of Society

9.23 In the *Foča Trial Judgement*, the Trial Chamber held that protection of society was not a highly relevant aim since the accused before the tribunals were unlikely to be repeat offenders:

> 843. With respect to the protection of society, or the incapacitation of the dangerous, as the Prosecutor refers to it, the Trial Chamber considers that in this jurisdiction it would rarely play a role as a general sentencing factor. Protection from society or incapacitation as a general sentencing factor basically means that a convicted person receives a lengthier term of imprisonment to "remove" him from society because the crime for which he has been convicted is thought to show him to be dangerous to society. A convicted person, under this approach, is preventively detained, so to speak. In many, if not most cases before the International Tribunal, the convicted persons would have no record of previous criminal conduct *relevant to those committed during the armed conflict*. In practically all cases before the International Tribunal, the convicted persons would be first time offenders *in relation to international crimes*. Unless it can be shown that a particular convicted person has the propensity to commit violations of international humanitarian law, or, possibly, crimes relevant to such violations, such

as "hate" crimes or discriminatory crimes, it may not be fair and reasonable to use protection of society, or preventive detention, as a general sentencing factor. Violations of international humanitarian law, by their very nature, can be committed only in certain contexts which may not arise again in the society where the convicted person, once released, may eventually settle.

Remarks

9.24 In conclusion, the principal factors in international punishment are deterrence and retribution (*Todorović Trial Judgement*, para. 28; *Aleksovski Appeals Judgement*, para. 185; *Delalić et al. Appeals Judgement*, para. 806). Nevertheless, the former seems to be accorded a primary position in the ICTY's reasoning (*Kordić and Čerkez Trial Judgement*, para. 847). Furthermore, deterrence does not justify an increase in penalties, since the gravity of the offences which the Tribunal tries are already sufficiently serious to warrant heavy penalties. Retribution can play a role of limitation in sentencing; it imposes a requirement that the sentence must not be disproportionately severe in comparison to the gravity of the conduct.

The Provisions of the Statutes

ICTY Article 24 (1)/ICTR Article 23 (1)

9.25 The only penalty provided for in the ICTs Statutes is imprisonment. The Tribunals have had to deal with the question whether the Statutes authorise life imprisonment. The Statutes (Article 24 (1) ICTY / Article 23 (1) ICTR) provide that, in determining an appropriate sentence, the Trial Chambers shall have recourse to the general practice regarding prison sentences in the national courts of the former Yugoslavia and Rwanda.

9.26 Recourse to national practice raises two questions: First, whether the ICTY and ICTR are bound by national sentencing tariffs for international crimes (this problem will be dealt with in relation to the criteria for determining the sentence), and second, whether the scale of sentences applicable in the former Yugoslavia and Rwanda is mandatory or if it is to be used only as a reference.

9.27 In the debates on Resolution 955, establishing the ICTR (8 November 1994, S/PV.3453), the representative of Rwanda, Ambassador Bakuramutsa, made clear his government's view that the absence of the death penalty from the ICTR's Statute could lead to injustice:

> The International Tribunal as designed in the resolution, establishes a disparity in sentences since it rules out capital punishment, which is nevertheless provided for in the Rwandese penal code. Since it is foreseeable that the Tribunal will be dealing with suspects who devised, planned and organised the genocide, these may escape capital punishment whereas those who simply carried out their plans would be subjected to the harshness of this sentence.

The representative added:

That situation is not conducive to national reconciliation in Rwanda.

9.28 Under Article 14 of the Rwandan law, a person in category 1 (the categories applied in Rwanda for different levels of offenders, category 1 being the most serious offenders) would mandatorily receive the death penalty. In *Kambanda*, the Trial Chamber noted that the accused, the former Prime Minister of the Rwandan government during the genocide, who admitted participating in the planning and incitement of genocide, would fall into category 1. Trial Chamber affirmed that "The Chamber notes that it is logical that in the determination of the sentence, it has recourse only to prison sentences applicable in Rwanda, to the exclusion of other sentences applicable in Rwanda, including the death sentence, since the Statute and the Rules provide that the Tribunal cannot impose this one type of sentence" (*Kambanda Trial Judgement*, para. 22).

9.29 Article 24 of the ICTY's Statute states that, "The penalty imposed by the Trial Chamber shall be limited to imprisonment":

> In this regard, the Chamber observes that the laws in effect in the former Yugoslavia at the time of the commission of the crimes for which the accused stands convicted, allow for a maximum sentence of 20 years' imprisonment, in lieu of the death penalty (*Todorović Trial Judgement*, para. 106).

9.30 Article 38 of the SFRY Criminal Code is a provision of general application, setting out the terms of imprisonment. The punishment of imprisonment may not be shorter than 15 days nor longer than 15 years. The court may impose a punishment of imprisonment for a term of 20 years for criminal acts eligible for the death penalty. Chapter Sixteen of the SFRY Criminal Code is entitled "Criminal Acts against Humanity and International Law." Article 142(1) ("War crimes against the civilian population") of the SFRY Criminal Code falls within the said Chapter, and it provides as follows: "Whoever in violation of rules of international law effective at the time of war, armed conflict or occupation, orders that civilian population be subject to killings, torture; inhuman treatment . . . , immense suffering or violation of bodily integrity or health . . . ; forcible prostitution or rape; application of measures of intimidation and terror, . . . other illegal arrests and detention . . . ; forcible labor . . . or who commits one of the foregoing acts, shall be punished by imprisonment for not less than five years or by the death penalty." (See *Todorović Trial Judgement*, para. 105; see also *Kordić and Čerkez Trial Judgement*, para. 849).

> The question whether the Trial Chamber's discretion to impose a sentence of greater than 20 years is thus curtailed has been conclusively resolved by the Appeals Chamber, which has interpreted the relevant provisions of the Statute and Rules to mean that, while a Trial Chamber must consider the practice of courts in the former Yugoslavia, its discretion in imposing sentence is not bound by such practice. (*Prosecutor v. Todorović*, Trial Judgement, para. 107; *Prosecutor v. Jelisić*, Appeal Judgement, para. 117; ICTY, *Prosecutor v. Kunarac*, Trial Judgement, para. 829; *Prosecutor v. Tadić*, Ch. II, Sentencing judgement, para. 12).

> The Trial Chamber correctly followed this precedent and in doing so carried out a detailed analysis of the relevant provisions in the SFRY Penal Code, while also hearing testimony from an expert witness for the defence. It recognised the importance of the principle as being one of the "solid pillars on which the principle of legality stands, (*Prosecutor v. Delalić and others*, Trial Judgement,

para. 402) and found that the view that a higher penalty than that available under the SFRY would violate the principle of legality and *nulla poena sine lege* was "erroneous and overly restrictive" (*Prosecutor v. Delalić and others*, Trial Judgement, para. 1210).

9.31 The Chamber concluded that:

> There is no jurisprudential or juridical basis for the assertion that the International Tribunal is bound by decisions of the courts of the former Yugoslavia (*Prosecutor v. Delalić and others*, Trial Judgement, para. 1212). The Appeals Chamber finds no error in this approach (*Prosecutor v. Delalić and others*, Appeal Judgement, para. 814).

ICTY Article 24 (2)/ICTR Article 23 (2)

9.32 ICTY Article 24 and ICTR Article 23: the Chamber shall take into account such features as (i) gravity of the offence, (ii) individual circumstances of the accused person. These articles provide the Chamber with guidance as to which elements should be taken into account in fixing a penalty: this list is not exhaustive, however, since they clearly state that the Chamber has to take into account *such* factors *as* the gravity of the infraction or the personal situation of the convicted person, along with the sentencing tariffs for detention as applied in the courts of the former Yugoslavia and Rwanda. To these factors, as it will be seen, the Rules of Procedure and Evidence add specified aggravating and mitigating circumstances, including the behaviour of the accused during trial. Nevertheless, no conventional rule states precisely the relative weight of each of these criteria, nor the Chambers' margin for discretion in determining sentences (see the sentencing section of the *Kayishema and Ruzindana Trial Judgement*; see also the *Rutaganda Trial Judgement*, para. 449). On the one hand, the penal provisions of the Statute do not lay down a maximum penalty for each offence, as is often the case with municipal law. On the other hand, the Chambers cannot *rely* yet on a jurisprudence sufficiently detailed to provide sentencing guidelines. (thus there is, on the one hand, a tendency to discretion and autonomy of the Chambers—in fact there is great discretion as for the quantum of the penalty and the enforcement regime—in determining sentence, on the other hand, there is the opposite tendency to establish criteria for rendering homogeneous and harmonizing the determination of sentence, in accordance with the principle *nulla poena sine lege*). The Chamber's discretion has been referred to in the *Delalić et al. Appeals Judgement*, para. 757:

> This is not to suggest that a Trial Chamber is bound to impose the same sentence in the one case as that imposed in another case simply because the circumstances between the two cases are similar.

Gravity of the Offence and Discretionary Framework

9.33 Rule 101 and the practice of the ICTs clarify that the most important consideration to be taken into account in determining a sentence is the gravity of the offence (*Todorović Trial Judgement*, para. 31; *Delalić et al. Trial Judgement*, para. 1225;

Kupreškić Trial Judgement, para. 852; *Aleksovski Appeals Judgement*, para. 182; *Krstić Trial Judgement*, para. 698; *Tadić Opinion and Judgement; Delalić et al. Trial Judgement*, para. 1225).

9.34 The Appeals Chamber confirmed this analysis in reviewing the sentences in *Delalić et al.*, specifying that the gravity of the offence must also be taken into account whatever be the modes of criminal participation (*Delalić et al. Appeals Judgement*, para. 741). According to the Appeals Chamber, taking into account the seriousness of the offence is one of the elements permitting the evolution of a uniform jurisprudence and to avoid excessive disparities in the sentences imposed (*Delalić et al. Appeals Judgement*, paras. 756 to 758; see also the *Musema Appeals Judgement*, para. 393).

9.35 A review of the principles applied to sentencing by the ICTs reveals, therefore, that the Judges enjoy a wide discretion (see the *Ruggiu Trial Judgement*, para. 52; *Serushago Trial Judgement*, para. 22; *Kambanda Trial Judgement*, para. 30; *Rutaganda Trial Judgement*, para. 7.2.7). However, this amount of discretion is not unlimited (see, e.g., *Delalić et al. Appeals Judgement*, paras. 717, 721 and 731; *Todorović Trial Judgement; Sikirica Trial Judgement*, para. 105; *Kvočka Trial Judgement*, para. 701). Moreover, this autonomy is also limited by the control exercised by the Appeals Chamber.

9.36 In the *Delalić Appeals Judgement*, the Appeal Chamber held that:

> Trial Chambers exercise a considerable amount of discretion (although it is not unlimited) in determining an appropriate sentencing. This is largely because of the over-riding obligation to individualise a penalty to fit the individual circumstances of the accused and the gravity of the crime. To achieve this goal, Trial Chambers are obliged to consider both aggravating and mitigating circumstances relating to an individual accused. The many circumstances taken into account by the Trial Chambers to date are evident if one considers the sentencing judgements which have been rendered. As a result, the sentences imposed have varied, from the imposition of the maximum sentence of imprisonment for the remainder of life, to imprisonment for varying fixed terms (the lowest after appeal being five years). Although certain of these cases are now under appeal, the underlying principle is that the sentence imposed largely depended on the individual facts of the case and the individual circumstances of the convicted person (para. 717).

9.37 The Appeals Chamber in the *Delalić et al. Appeals Judgement* (para. 720) also affirmed that "In the case of *Anto Furundzija*, the Prosecution submitted that "every sentence imposed by a Trial Chamber must be individualised as there are a great many factors to which the Trial Chamber may have regard in exercising its discretion in each case."" (*Furundžija Appeals Judgement*, para. 222; see also *Delalić et al. Appeals Judgement*, para. 717; *Sikirica Trial Judgement*, para. 231). The Appeals Chamber endorsed the finding in that case:

> The sentencing provisions in the Statute and the Rules provide Trial Chambers with the discretion to take into account the circumstances of each crime in assessing the sentence to be given. A previous decision on sentence may indeed provide guidance if it relates to the same offence and was committed in substantially similar circumstances; otherwise a Trial Chamber is limited only by the provisions of the Statute and the Rules (*Furundžija Appeals Judgement*, para. 250).

9.38 Finally, in determining sentence, due regard must be had "to the relevant provisions in the Statute and the Rules which govern sentencing, as well as the relevant jurisprudence of this Tribunal and the ICTR, and of course to the circumstances of each case (*Furundžija Appeals Judgement*, para. 237); *Kvočka Trial Judgement*, para. 761; *Tadić Judgement in Sentencing Appeals*, para. 69).

Recourse to the General Practice Regarding Prison Sentences in the Courts of the Former Yugoslavia and to the Organic Law of Rwanda

9.39 The ICTs, in determining sentences, are not bound by any national practice regarding prison sentences. A Trial Chamber must nonetheless have regard to the sentencing practice of the former Yugoslavia although, as has been noted, no provision requires a Trial Chamber to follow this practice. (*Tadić Sentencing Judgement II*, para. 11: "the Trial Chamber may use the sentencing practice in the courts of the former Yugoslavia for guindance, but this is not binding"; *Todorović Trial Judgement*, para. 107; *Kupreškić Trial Judgement*, para. 840; *Blaškić Trial Judgement*, para. 759; *Delalić et al. Trial Judgement; Delalić et al. Appeals Judgement*, paras. 813 and 816; *Erdemović Sentencing Judgement; Kordić and Čerkez Trial Judgement*, para. 849; *Akayesu Trial Judgement; Akayesu Appeals Judgement*, para. 420; *Kambanda Trial Judgement*).

9.40 The rule established by ICTs' practice is that:

> the Tribunal may be informed in an appropriate case by the sentencing practices of the courts of one or more of the constituent republics of the former Yugoslavia where it has reason to believe that such specific consideration would aid it in appreciating "the general practice . . . in the courts of the former Yugoslavia (*Jelisić Appeals Judgement*, para. 116; *Ruggiu Judgement and Sentence*, para. 31; *Rutaganda Trial Judgement*, para. 454).

Need for Consistency in Sentencing

9.41 It is self-evident that the ICTY and ICTR should be consistent in sentencing convicted persons.

9.42 See the *Jelisić Appeals Judgement*, para. 96:

> The Appeals Chamber agrees that a sentence should not be capricious or excessive, and that, in principle, it may be thought to be capricious or excessive if it is out of reasonable proportion with a line of sentences passed in similar circumstances for the same offences. Where there is such disparity, the Appeals Chamber may infer that there was disregard of the standard criteria by which sentence should be assessed, as prescribed by the Statute and set out in the Rules. But it is difficult and unhelpful to lay down a hard and fast rule on the point; there are a number of variable factors to be considered in each case.

9.43 Sentencing practice at the ICTs has not, however, been consistent. The sentences imposed for the various types of conduct coming before the Tribunal have more often reflected the personal views of the sentencing Judges than an attempt to establish and follow a coherent sentencing policy. For example, *Blaškić* was sentenced to

45 years' imprisonment, largely on the basis that a superior bore a heavy responsibility for crimes committed by his subordinates. Yet his superior, Dario Kordić received a sentence of 25 years imprisonment. It is submitted that these discrepancies cannot be justified and must be remedied, if not by the Appeals Chamber, then by the Security Council or some organ thereof, possibly upon the conclusion of the tribunals' work once all the sentences have been imposed.

9.44 The following illustrates the ICTs' anomalous approach to sentencing.

9.45 Dražen Erdemović was the first accused to be sentenced by the Tribunal. He pleaded guilty to a count of crimes against humanity for his role in the massacres which took place following the fall of Srebrenica to Bosnian Serb forces in July 1995. On 29 November 1996, Erdemović was sentenced by Trial Chamber I to 10 years' imprisonment (*Erdemović Sentencing Judgement*, p. 57). On appeal, the matter was remitted to a new Trial Chamber which accepted a change of plea from guilty of crimes against humanity to guilty of violations of the laws or customs of war, and reduced Erdemović's sentence to 5 years' imprisonment (*Erdemović Sentencing Judgement II*).

9.46 Zdravko Mucić was sentenced to 7 years' imprisonment solely on a "command responsibility" theory for several beatings and murders committed by his subordinates (and for unlawful confinement of civilians under Article 7(1)).

9.47 In the *Furundžija Trial Judgement*, Furundžija was convicted of one count of torture as co-perpetrator and one count of rape as aider and abettor and sentenced to 10 years' imprisonment and 8 years' imprisonment respectively, to run concurrently.

9.48 Zlatko Aleksovski, whose case was similar to Mucic's in that he was convicted of crimes as a camp commander under Article 7(3) of the Statute and not of any acts of violence himself, was sentenced to two years and six months' imprisonment. This was revised to 7 years' imprisonment by the Appeals Chamber.

9.49 As stated above, the 45 year term of imprisonment to which Tihomir Blaškić was sentenced seems wildly disproportionate to the crimes, largely of omission, of which he was convicted (the Judgement itself is not entirely clear as to the factual basis on which Blaškić was being sentenced), particularly when compared with the sentences inflicted upon Goran Jelisić (40 years), Dario Kordić (25 years) and Mario Čerkez (15 years).

9.50 The first accused to be sentenced after a trial following a not guilty plea was Duško Tadić. The Trial Chamber imposed a number of concurrent sentences, the maximum being 20 years for a count of Crime against Humanity (persecution) involving, *inter alia*, the unlawful killing of two Bosnian policemen (*Tadić Sentencing Judgement*). For each count, the Crime against Humanity count was punished with a lengthier prison sentence than the corresponding war crimes count, to reflect that Crimes against Humanity are, other things being equal, more serious than war crimes (see Article 5, "Gravity of crimes against humanity").

9.51 The Trial Chamber convicted Jelisić of the counts alleging violations of the laws or customs of war and crimes against humanity, to which he had pleaded guilty, but acquitted him on the count of genocide and imposed a single sentence of 40 years' imprisonment. The Appeal Chamber confirmed this sentence, while criticising the Trial Chamber for dismissing the Prosecution case on genocide *proprio motu* at the close of the Prosecution case without giving the Prosecution the opportunity to be heard.

9.52 The Trial Chamber found Radislav Krstić guilty of genocide; persecution for murders, cruel and inhumane treatment, terrorising the civilian population, forcible transfer and destruction of personal property of Bosnian Muslim civilians; and murder as a violation of the Laws and Customs of War. The Trial Chamber sentenced Krstić to 46 years' imprisonment, the highest sentence imposed by the ICTY to date.

9.53 At the ICTR, the Trial Chamber found Jean Paul Akayesu guilty of genocide; direct and public incitement to commit genocide and crimes against humanity and sentenced him to life imprisonment. The Appeals Chamber confirmed this sentence. Kambanda, and several other persons convicted by the ICTR, also received a life sentence for genocide.

Remarks

9.54 Overall, it emerges from the practice of the ICTs that when it comes to determining sentences, the tribunals wish to retain a great deal of discretion and not to be bound by a predictable pattern of penalties.

9.55 This is confirmed by the refusal to specify a list of guidelines for determining sentences (*Furundžija Appeals Judgement*, para. 238: "The chamber considers it inappropriate to establish a definitive list of sentencing guidelines for future reference"). This tendency is also evident in the scant attention paid to the sentencing practice of the courts of the former Yugoslavia and Rwanda, which would in any event only be indicative and not mandatory.

9.56 At the same time, the ICTs seem to be aware of the limits of such practice: one Trial Chamber declared itself to be firmly convinced that, to bring the Tribunal's mission to a successful issue, a hierarchy of sanctions needed to be taken into account (*Aleksovski Trial Judgement*, para. 243).

9.57 However the Appeals Chamber has also stated that while:

> two accused convicted of similar crimes in similar circumstances should not in practice receive very different sentences, often the differences are more significant than the similarities, and the mitigating and aggravating factors dictate different results (*Delalić et al. Appeals Judgement*, para. 719).

Powers of Appeals Chamber to Substitute Its Own Sentence Without Remitting the Matter to the Trial Chamber

Cross Reference: See the section on "Appeals" (10.1.1 *et seq.*).

9.58 The Appeals Chamber has stated that:

> At the present time, there does not exist such a range or pattern of sentences imposed by the Tribunal. The offences which the Tribunal tries are of such a nature that there is little assistance to be gained from sentencing patterns in relation to often fundamentally different offences in domestic jurisdictions, beyond that which the Tribunal gains from the courts of the former Yugoslavia in accordance with Article 24 of the Tribunal's Statute. At the present time, therefore, in order

to avoid any unjustified disparity, it is possible for the Tribunal to have regard only to those sentences which have been imposed by it in generally similar circumstances as to both the offences and the offenders. It nevertheless must do so with considerable caution. As the Appeals Chamber discusses further below comparisons with sentences imposed in other cases will be of little assistance unless the circumstances of the cases are substantially similar. However, in cases involving similar factual circumstances and similar convictions, particularly where the sentences imposed in those other cases have been the subject of consideration in the Appeals Chamber, there should be no substantial disparity in sentence unless justified by the circumstances of particular accused (*Delalić et al. Appeals Judgement*, para. 758).

9.59 In the exercise of its power of revision of the sentences imposed by the Trial Chambers, and thus of discretion, the Appeal Chambers may either revise the sentence or indicate the sentence it would have imposed itself.

Revision

9.60 It is clear from the *Aleksovski Appeals Judgement* that, in the case of a successful appeal against sentence, it is open to the Appeals Chamber to consider and substitute its own sentence without remitting the matter to the Trial Chamber. (See *Aleksovski Trial Judgement*, para. 244.) The Appeals Chamber imposed a "revised sentence" of seven years, which took into account the "element of *double jeopardy*" in the process, in that Aleksovski had been required to appear for sentence twice for the same conduct, "suffering the consequent anxiety and distress" after having been released. According to the Appeals Chamber, if it were not for these considerations, "the [revised] sentence would have been considerably longer" (*Aleksovski Appeals Judgement*, para. 190; see also *Delalić et al. Appeals Judgement*, para. 719 and Disposition para. 4). (See also *Tadić Judgement in Sentencing Appeals*, para. 22; *Musema Appeals Judgement*, para. 379; *Serushago Sentencing Judgement*, para. 32).

Other Indications

9.61 The Appeal Chamber, in *Delalić et al. Appeals Judgement*, seemed to outline another form of control of the Trial Chamber's discretion:

> Taking into account the various considerations relating to the gravity of Mucić's offences and the aggravating circumstances already referred to, as well as the mitigating circumstances referred to by the Trial Chamber and the "double jeopardy" element involved in subjecting Mucić to a revised sentence, the Appeals Chamber would have imposed on Mucić a heavier sentence of a total of around ten years imprisonment (Para. 853).

9.62 That is, the Appeals Chamber may indicate the penalty it would have imposed. This practice is of questionable utility, since it does not change the sentence in fact imposed, except perhaps as providing indications to Trial Chambers as to how they should sentence in *future cases*.

Factors To Be Taken into Account in Sentencing

9.63   The factors that may be taken into account in imposing a sentence are described in articles 23 and 24 of the ICTs Statutes, as well as in Rule 101 of the Rules.

> Read together, Article 24 and Rule 101 allow for factors other than those expressly mentioned to be considered when determining the proper sentences to be imposed (*Foča Trial Judgement*, para. 827).

9.64   Thus, the factors represent an open list: it is in the power of ICTs to specify different circumstances.

9.65   It is necessary to distinguish between aggravating and mitigating factors. (Rules ICTY and ICTR 101 B, i) and ii)).

Aggravating Circumstances

The Accused's Superior Position

> The Trial Chamber finds that the direct participation of a high level superior in a crime is an aggravating circumstance, although to what degree depends on the actual level of authority and the form of direct participation (*Krstić Trial Judgement*, para. 708).

9.66   A hierarchically superior position is a very important criterion (*Kupreškić Trial Judgement*, paras. 826, 852 and 862; *Sikirica Trial Judgement*, para. 172; *Kayishema and Ruzindana Trial Judgement*, para. 15; *Kayishema and Ruzindana Appeals Judgement*, para. 357; *Blaškić Trial Judgement*, paras. 788 and 791; *Kambanda Trial Judgement*, para. 44; *Delalić et al. Trial Judgement*, para. 1240). It is, however, doubtful that a superior position could be considered an aggravating feature where the accused is convicted by virtue of Article 7(3) of the Statute, since a superior position is an essential element of that form of liability. A prerequisite for liability can hardly be at the same time an aggravating feature.

9.67   Reference should be made to the following decisions on the accused's superior position: *Foča Trial Judgement*, para. 863; *Serushago Sentencing Judgement*, para. 29 (*de facto* leaders); *Rutaganda Trial Judgement*, para. 469 ("the fact that a person in a high position abused his authority and commited crimes is to be viewed as an aggravating factor"); *Akayesu Sentencing Judgement*, para. 36; *Tadić Judgement in Sentencing Appeals*, paras. 56 and 57; *Rutaganda Trial Judgement*, 6 December 1999, para. 469.

Abuse of Authority

9.68   See, e.g., the *Todorović Trial Judgement*, on abuse of position as an aggravating feature.

> 61. (. . .) as Chief of Police, [the accused] had a responsibility to protect and defend all citizens of the municipality of Bosanski Samac. Instead, in his position as chief of an institution that is responsible for upholding the law, Stevan Todorović actively and directly took part in offences which he should have been working to prevent or punish. As discussed above, on one occasion, Stevan

Todorović also ordered three men to beat Omer Nalic. His direct participation in the crimes, as well as his abuse of his position of authority and of people's trust in the institution, clearly constitute an aggravating factor.

62. The fact that Stevan Todorović might, initially, have been reluctant to take on the position as Chief of Police does not negate the significance of his abuse of such a superior position. However, the Trial Chamber also recognises that, while the position of Chief of Police is a relatively senior one, Stevan Todorović was not in the very highest levels of the overall hierarchy in the conflict in the former Yugoslavia, nor was he one of its architects.

9.69 The Appeals Chamber in the *Tadić* case recognised the "need for sentences to reflect the relative significance of the role of the [accused] in the broader context of the conflict in the former Yugoslavia." (*Tadić Judgement in Sentencing Appeals*, para. 55; see also *Delalić et al. Appeals Judgement*, para. 845 and 847). The Appeals Chamber, in *Delalić et al.*, stated that in certain circumstances the gravity of the crime may be so great that a severe penalty is justified even in cases where the accused is not senior in the overall command structure (*Delalić et al. Appeals Judgement*, para. 847; *Tadić Judgement in Sentencing Appeals*, para. 56; *Aleksovski Appeals Judgement*, para. 184; *Musema Appeals Judgement*, para. 383).

9.70 In conclusion, "the fact that an accused held a position of superior responsibility may seriously aggravate an offence, but there must be regard to the position of the accused in the command structure (see also *Kambanda Trial Judgement*, para. 44).

9.71 In the *Krstić Trial Judgement*, the Trial Chamber found, "that the fact that General Krstić occupied the highest level of VRS Corps commander is an aggravating factor because he utilised that position to participate directly in a genocide" (*Krstić Trial Judgement*, para. 721).

Direct Participation of a Superior

9.72 The ICTY has considered that "direct participation in the crimes, as well as his abuse of his position of authority and of people's trust in the institution, clearly constitute an aggravating factor" (*Todorović Trial Judgement*, para. 61).

A Factor Cannot Be Aggravating When It Is an Ingredient of the Crime

9.73 The Trial Chamber affirmed in *Todorović* that: "since a discriminatory intent is one of the basic elements of the crime of persecution, this aspect of Todorovic's criminal conduct is already encompassed in a consideration of the offence. Therefore, it should not be treated separately as an aggravating factor" (*Todorović Trial Judgement*, para. 57). It would be more correct to say that that element *cannot* be treated separately as an aggravating factor rather than that it merely "should not." For this same observation with respect to Article 7(3) liability, see 9.66.

Premeditation

9.74 "The Trial Chamber agrees with the Prosecutor on the relevance of premeditation as an aggravating factor in the abstract but, based on the sequence of General Krstić's delayed participation in the genocidal scheme initiated by General Mladić and others, finds it not applicable to the situation" (*Krstić Trial Judgement*, para. 711; see also *Serushago Sentencing Judgement*, para. 30; *Blaškić Trial Judgement*, para. 793). Premeditation as an aggravating circumstance does not fit very well with certain crimes, for instance the crime of genocide, which requires planning and thus necessarily presupposes premeditation. Again, an element of the crime cannot also be an aggravating feature.

Other Aggravating Circumstances of Conduct: Youth or Old Age of the Victims

9.75 "The youthful age of certain of the victims" was an aggravating factor in the *Foča Trial Judgement*, para. 864, where the victims had been subjected to rape and other forms of sexual abuse; and *Kordić and Čerkez Trial Judgement*, par 852. *Cruel intention:* "The Trial Chamber considers the particular cruelty shown in connection with these beatings, and their lengthy duration, to be an aggravating factor" (*Todorović Trial Judgement*, para. 65); *involvement of more than one victim* in his offences also constitutes aggravation (*Foča Trial Judgement*, paras. 866 and 885; *Krstić Trial Judgement*, para. 701: "Thus, the Trial Chamber must assess the seriousness of the crimes in the light of their individual circumstances and consequences. This presupposes taking into account quantitatively the number of victims and qualitatively the suffering inflicted on the victims"; *Kambanda Trial Judgement*, para. 42; *Kayishema and Ruzindana Trial Judgement*, para. 26; *Kordić and Čerkez Trial Judgement*, para. 852; *Kvočka Trial Judgement*, para. 701): referring to this element as being relevant to the gravity of the offence see *Erdemović Sentencing Judgement II*, para. 15; concerning the interpretation of the concept of gravity of the offence c.f. art.78 para. 1 ICC) the commission of some of the offences by more than one perpetrator at the same time is also considered as aggravating (concerning gang rape, see the *Foča Trial Judgement*, para. 866); the fact that the crime was committed against civilians will not generally be accepted as an aggravating circumstance, since it is an element of most offences tried by the ICTs that the victims are civilians, or at any rate, non-combatants (*Todorović Trial Judgement*, para. 57).

Conduct During the Trial

9.76 In the *Delalić et al. Appeals Judgement*, the Chamber found that the Trial Chamber had erred by apparently taken into account Mucić's exercise of his right to silence as an aggravating factor in sentencing him (paras. 780–785). The Trial Chamber was, however, entitled to take into account Mucić's demeanour during the trial, *inter alia* as evidence of lack of remorse, as well as the fact that he apparently threatened witnesses (paras. 786–789).

Aggravating Factors for Specific Crimes

9.77 See 9.66 *et seq.*, above, on general aggravating features.

Rape

9.78 The Trial Chamber ruling in the *Foča Trial Judgement* set out the following factors as being aggravating circumstances in the commission of rape (para. 835):

- the youth of the victims;
- rapes committed with ethnically based motives;
- rapes committed against detainees;
- rapes committed against physically weak persons who could not defend themselves;
- rapes entailing multiple victims; and
- rapes at gunpoint.

9.79 The Chamber held that the effect of the crimes on third parties was not a factor to be taken into account in aggravation, but the effects of the crimes on the victims always was:

> 852. The Trial Chamber is unable to accept that a so-called *in personam* evaluation of the gravity of the crime could or should also concern the effect of that crime on third persons, as submitted by the Prosecutor. Such effects are irrelevant to the culpability of the offender, and it would be unfair to consider such effects in determining the sentence to be imposed. Consideration of the consequences of a crime upon the victim who is *directly* injured by it is, however, always relevant to the sentencing of the offender. Where such consequences are part and parcel of the definition of the offence, though, care should be taken to avoid considering them separately in imposing sentence. For example, the fact that an offender took someone's life cannot be considered as a *separate* sentencing circumstance when imposing a sentence for a murder conviction—it is part and parcel of the crime charged.

9.80 To take the example of rape, the degree of traumatisation suffered by the victim is not *an element* of the offence that has to be proved. While traumatisation can always be expected in rape, the *degree* of traumatisation, it is submitted, should always be an aggravating factor, with the greater the traumatisation of the victim, the greater the aggravation. This would entail that where the victim was an especially psychologically vulnerable person, the aggravation would be greater. This is consistent with the principle of tort law that the wrong-doer must take his victim as he finds him or her and therefore cannot be heard to complain that the victim was more than usually vulnerable. If a child is raped in front of her mother or father, the effect of the rape on the parents should, it is submitted, be taken into account in aggravation.

Other Crimes

9.81 See paras. 13–18 of the *Kayishema and Ruzindana Trial Judgement*.

Mitigating Circumstances

9.82 Mitigating circumstances are also an open-ended category: "Trial Chamber has the discretion to consider any factors it considers to be of a mitigating nature" (*Krstić Trial Judgement*, para. 713; see also *Musema Appeals Judgement*, para. 395).

Substantial Cooperation with the Prosecution before or after Conviction

9.83 Co-operation with the Prosecutor is the only circumstance explicitly provided for within the terms of the Rules. "Rule 101(B)(ii) requires the Trial Chamber to consider "any mitigating circumstances including the substantial co-operation with the Prosecutor by the convicted person ". (. . .) What constitutes "substantial co-operation" is not defined in the Rules and is left to the discretion of the Trial Chamber. It was for the Trial Chamber to weigh the circumstances relating to any co-operation" (*Jelisić Appeals Judgement*, para. 124). "The Appeals Chamber notes that the determination of whether the co-operation should be considered as substantial and therefore whether it constitutes a mitigating factor is for the Trial Chamber to determine" (*ibid.*):

> The earnestness and degree of co-operation with the Prosecutor decides whether there is reason to reduce the sentence on this ground. Therefore, the evaluation of the accused's co-operation depends both on the quantity and quality of the information he provides. Moreover, the Trial Chamber singles out for mention the spontaneity and selflessness of the co-operation which must be lent without asking for something in return. Providing that the co-operation lent respects the aforesaid requirements, the Trial Chamber classes such co-operation as a "significant mitigating factor (*Blaškić Trial Judgement*, para. 774).

9.84 The Trial Chamber "agree(d) with the finding in the *Blaškić* case that the accused's earnestness and the degree of his co-operation with the Prosecution should determine whether there is reason to reduce the sentence on this ground. Indeed, an evaluation of the accused's co-operation depends on the extent and quality of the information he provides. However, it is this Chamber's view that the fact that an accused has gained or may gain something pursuant to an agreement with the Prosecution does not preclude the Trial Chamber from considering his substantial co-operation as a mitigating circumstance in sentencing." This was the approach adopted in the *Todorović Sentencing Judgement*, 31 July 2001, para. 86.

9.85 On this subject, see also: the *Blaškić Trial Judgement*, para. 774; *Erdemović Sentencing Judgement*, paras. 99–101 and *Erdemović Sentencing Judgement II*, para. 16 iv; *Kambanda Trial Judgement*, para. 47; *Musema Judgement*, para. 1007; *Ruggiu Judgement and Sentence*, para. 53: the plea of guilty accelerates the procedure and allows for an economy of resources; *Jelisić* Judgement, para. 127; *Delalić et al. Trial Judgement*, para. 1279; *Kayishema and Ruzindana Trial Judgement*, para. 20; *Serushago Sentencing Judgement*, paras. 31–33; *Ruggiu Judgement and Sentence*, para. 58.

Guilty Plea

9.86 Four persons have been sentenced by the ICTY on the basis of a guilty plea: Erdemović, Jelisić, Todorović and Plavsić (see *Erdemović Sentencing Judgement II; Jelisić Trial Judgement* and *Todorović Sentencing Judgement*). At the ICTR also, three persons have pleaded guilty: Kambanda, Serushago and Ruggiu (see *Kambanda Trial Judgement*, para. 60; *Serushago Sentencing Judgement*, para. 35; and *Ruggiu Judgement and Sentence*, para. 55. See also *Sikirica Trial Judgement*, para. 148.

9.87 See the discussion in the *Todorović Trial Judgement* at paras. 75–83. The Tribunal's case-law (*Erdemović Sentencing Judgement*, p. 16) establishes that, "an admission of guilt demonstrates honesty and it is important for the International Tribunal to encourage people to come forth, whether already indicted or as unknown perpetrators." A voluntary admission of guilt saved the International Tribunal the time and effort of a lengthy investigation and trial, which was to be commended. Less credit for a guilty plea was given, however, where it was not accompanied by remorse (*Jelisić Trial Judgement*, para. 122). The weight to be attached to a guilty plea in mitigation is at the discretion of the Trial Chamber and, on appeal, "it falls on the cross-appellant to convince the Appeals Chamber that the Trial Chamber erred in the exercise of its discretion resulting in a sentence outside the discretionary framework provided in the Statute and the Rules." Jelisic's appeal was dismissed (*Jelisić Appeals Judgement*, paras. 119–123).

9.88 The *Kambanda* case also confirmed the principle that a guilty plea carries with it a reduction in sentence (*Kambanda Appeals Judgement*, para. 120; see also *Serushago, Reasons for Judgement*, 6 April 2000, para. 24).

9.89 In the *Todorović Trial Judgement*, the Chamber noted that it was in no way bound by the Plea Agreement entered into between the Prosecution and the Defence (para. 79: "Although the Plea Agreement does indicate a range within which the parties have agreed Todorović's sentence should fall, the Trial Chamber reiterates that it is in no way bound by this agreement. It is the Chamber's responsibility to determine an appropriate sentence in this case").

9.90 Of course, the timing of a guilty plea is arelevant factor to take into consideration in determining how much credit to give the accused for the plea:

> 81. A guilty plea is always important for the purpose of establishing the truth in relation to a crime. Generally, however, a plea of guilt will only contribute to the above-described public advantage if it is pleaded before the commencement of the trial against the accused. Needless to say, if pleaded at a later stage of the proceedings, or even after the conclusion of the trial, a voluntary admission of guilt will not save the International Tribunal the time and effort of a lengthy investigation and trial (*Todorović Trial Judgement*, para. 75–82).

Remorse

9.91 "Remorse has been considered as a mitigating factor in a number of cases before this International Tribunal. In order to accept remorse as a mitigating circumstance in its determination of the sentence, the Trial Chamber must be satisfied that the expressed remorse is sincere" (*Todorović Trial Judgement*, para. 89; see also *Erdemović Sentencing Judgement*, p. 16; *Jelisić Trial Judgement*, para. 127 (Jelisić's expression of remorse not accepted); *Blaškić Trial Judgement*, para. 775 (Blaškic's remorse not accepted); *Krstić Trial Judgement*, para. 715; *Foča Trial Judgement*, para. 869; *Serushago Sentencing Judgement*, paras. 40–41; ICTR, *Ruggiu Judgement and Sentence*, paras. 69–72; *Kayishema and Ruzindana Trial Judgement*, para. 20; *Kambanda Trial Judgement*, para. 56; *Akayesu Trial Judgement*, para. 35; *Sikirica Judgement*, paras. 192 and 227).

9.92 In *Todorović*, the Trial Chamber found that the accused was genuinely remorseful and took that into account in mitigation:

91. The Trial Chamber observes that Stevan Todorović has expressed the desire to channel his remorse into positive action by contributing to reconciliation in Bosnia and Herzegovina. This is a commendable aspiration which, in the Trial Chamber's view, further demonstrates Stevan Todorovic's remorse.

92. The Trial Chamber finds that Stevan Todorovic's statement and demeanour during the Sentencing Hearing reflect his remorse. This conclusion is supported by the fact that he has pleaded guilty and has cooperated with the Prosecution. Accordingly, the Trial Chamber finds that Stevan Todorovic's remorse is genuine and treats it as a mitigating circumstance in determining sentence (ICTY, *Prosecutor v. Todorović*, Judgement, paras. 91–92).

9.93 In conclusion, it seems that substantial cooperation, guilty plea and remorse are three different mitigating circumstances. However, in certain situations, these three mitigating factors blend into one another; it is hard to imagine an accused who feels remorse for his crimes but who nonethless pleads not guilty. Moreover, in given situations, as in the *Jelisić* case, a guilty plea without remorse loses all of its mitigating effect. See also: *Erdemović Sentencing Judgement*, paras. 96–98; *Erdemović Sentencing Judgement II*, para. 16; *Akayesu Trial Judgement*, para. 35 (i); *Serushago Sentencing Judgement*, paras. 40–41; *Ruggiu Judgement and Sentence*, paras. 69–72; *Foča Trial Judgement*, para. 869; *Blaškić Trial Judgement*, para. 775; *Jelisić Trial Judgement*, para. 127.

Superior Orders

9.94 In *Erdemović*, the Trial Chamber refused to take duress/extreme necessity into account in mitigation, on the grounds that it had been insufficiently proved. Having identified the following questions, "Could the accused have avoided the situation in which he found himself? Was the accused confronted with an insurmountable order which he had no way to circumvent? Was the accused, or one of his immediate family members, placed in danger of immediate death or death shortly afterwards? Did the accused possess the moral freedom to oppose the orders he had received? Had he possessed that freedom, would he have attempted to oppose the orders?," the Chamber held that:

91. ... the Defence has produced no testimony, evaluation or any other elements to corroborate what the accused has said. For this reason, the Judges deem that they are unable to accept the plea of extreme necessity.

9.95 This approach was wrong for a host of reasons. First, the only evidence against the accused was his own confession and testimony; it is therefore paradoxical, not to say unfair, to accept the accused's testimony only on the incriminating matters and not on exculpatory matters. Second, the ICTY's Rules do not require corroboration *as a matter of law*, except under Rule 90(C), for matters to be proved at trial. Much less then should corroboration be required outside the context of a trial, in a sentencing procedure. Hence the Chamber *could have* accepted the accused's account without further corroboration. Third, even the Prosecution had accepted that the accused had acted under duress.

9.96 In the second *Erdemović Sentencing Judgement* of 5 March 1998—after the Trial Chamber's Judgement had been reversed by the Appeals Chamber, which found that the guilty plea had been uninformed—a different Trial Chamber *did* take duress into account as a mitigating factor:

> 17. Duress
>
> The Trial Chamber has applied the ruling of the Appeals Chamber that "duress does not afford a complete defence to a soldier charged with a crime against humanity and/or a war crime involving the killing of innocent human beings. It may be taken into account only by way of mitigation.
>
> It has been accepted by the parties and the Trial Chamber that there was duress in this case. The earlier testimony of the accused has been cited above. Mr. Ruez has testified of the circumstances of a very vicious and cruelly fought war, the brutal nature of the battle for Srebrenica, the attendant environment of soldiers killing pursuant to superior orders, the accused's vulnerable position as a Bosnian Croat in the BSA and his history of disagreements with his commander, Milorad Pelemis, and subsequent demotion. He feels that had the accused refused to shoot, "most certainly, he would get into very deep trouble . . .
>
> The accused displays a tendency to feel the helpless victim; there are several references in his testimonies to his having no choice in a variety of situations. He speaks of his having to become a soldier, that he had no choice in leaving the Republic of Croatia for Republika Srpska, that he had to join the BSA "to feed my family," that he "simply had to" go to the military barracks and leave behind his bedridden wife and sick child, that he had no choice in taking part in the Srebrenica operation, and that he "had to shoot those people" murdered in the Pilica collective farm massacre. On the other hand, he has provided testimony of incidents when he broke out of this chain of helplessness and took positive action; such as when he saved some Serbs in Tuzla, when he saved Witness X, when he refused to comply with the orders of Lieutenant Milorad Pelemis, when he tried to refuse to kill at the collective farm and when he refused to kill at the hall in Pilica. Thus, he was capable of taking positive action, once he had weighed up his options. The risks that he took appear to have been calculated and considered.
>
> The evidence reveals the extremity of the situation faced by the accused. The Trial Chamber finds that there was a real risk that the accused would have been killed had he disobeyed the order. He voiced his feelings, but realised that he had no choice in the matter: he had to kill or be killed.

9.97 In fact, in fairness to the accused, it is apparent from his testimony that his main concern was the lives of his wife and child, not his own life; he feared that their lives would be forfeit if he did not participate in the killings in Srebrenica.

Cross Reference: ICTY Article 7 ("Duress").

Personal Circumstances of the Accused

9.98 Trial Chambers also take into account the following personal circumstances as mitigation in certain cases: a good personal character with no previous criminal record (see *Erdemović Sentencing Judgement II*, para. 16(i); *Ruggiu Judgement and Sentence*, paras. 59–68; *Kordić and Čerkez Trial Judgement*, para. 848; *Krstić Trial Judgement*, para. 714), poor health (see *Rutaganda Trial Judgement*, para. 472; *Krstić Trial Judgement*, para. 714), "Good character," "keen sense for the soldiering profession," or "poor family background" in combination with youth and an "immature and fragile" personality are also elements that may constitute mitigating circumstances": *Erdemović Sentencing Judgement II*, para. 16(i); *Furundžija Trial Judgement*, para. 284; *Blaškić Trial Judgement*, para. 778; *Jelisić Appeals Judgement*, para. 128; *Rutaganda Trial Judgement*, para. 471; *Sikirica Judgement*, para. 192 "assistance he provided to some of the detainees")

9.99 "The categories of mitigating circumstance cannot be considered as closed. Such factors will vary with the circumstances of each case, as must be contemplated by the reference to "individual circumstances" in Article 24 of the Statute" (*Kordić and Čerkez Trial Judgement*, para. 848).

9.100 The Appeals Chamber has held that mitigating circumstances included "youth of the accused, immature and fragile personality and the harsh environment of the armed conflict as a whole" (*Delalić et al. Appeals Judgement*, para. 827).

Diminished Mental Capacity

9.101 Diminished mental capacity does not "constitute a full defence. However, it has been accepted that it may be a matter appropriately considered in mitigation of sentence" (*Delalić et al. Appeals Judgement*, para. 839; see also *Todorović Trial Judgement*, paras. 93–95). "(. . .) In considering specifically those mitigating factors to which the Trial Chamber wished to attach weight, it expressly found that the evidence of "numerous" mental health experts had been taken into account and contributed to the consideration of an appropriate sentence" (*Delalić et al. Appeals Judgement*, para. 841).

Absence of Active Participation

9.102 It is not clear if the absence of active participation can be considered as a mitigating circumstance. In *Krstić*, the Trial Chamber held that:

> indirect participation is one circumstance that may go to mitigating a sentence. An act of assistance to a crime is a form of participation in a crime often considered less serious than personal participation or commission as a principal and may, depending on the circumstances, warrant a lighter sentence than that imposed for direct commission (*Krstić Trial Judgement*, para. 714).

9.103 Conversely, the Appeals Chamber has found that:

> It must also be recognised, however, that absence of such active participation is not a mitigating circumstance. Failure to prevent or punish subordinate crimes is the relevant culpable conduct and lack of active participation in the crimes does not reduce that culpability (*Delalić et al. Appeals Judgement*, para. 737).

9.104 This discrepancy is, however, more apparent than real. As noted above, the elements of command responsibility consist of a failure to prevent or punish; hence an accused convicted by virtue of command responsibility cannot claim in mitigation that he *only* failed to prevent or punish the crimes and did not actively participate in them, because he has in any event only been convicted of failure to prevent or punish, and not of direct commission. That is the point being made in the *Delalić et al. Appeals Judgement*, above. At the same time, if the Chamber is trying to arrive at an appropriate penalty for a crime, say genocide, by considering the sentences already meted out, it should of course take into consideration that an accused has been convicted "only" of failure to prevent or punish and not of direct commission, as the penalty for the former should, in principle, be less than for direct commission. That seems to be the point being made in the *Krstić Trial Judgement*, above.

9.105

ICTY Rule 100 Sentencing Procedure on a Guilty Plea	ICTR Rule 100 Sentencing Procedure on a Guilty Plea
(A) If the Trial Chamber convicts the accused on a guilty plea, the Prosecutor and the defence may submit any relevant information that may assist the Trial Chamber in determining an appropriate sentence. (B) The sentence shall be pronounced in a judgement in public and in the presence of the convicted person, subject to Sub-rule 102 (B).	(A) If the Trial Chamber convicts the accused on a guilty plea, the Prosecutor and the defence may submit any relevant information that may assist the Trial Chamber in determining an appropriate sentence. (B) The sentence shall be pronounced in a judgement in public and in the presence of the convicted person, subject to Sub-Rule 102(B).

History of ICTY Rule 100

9.106 Rule 100 was amended at the eleventh plenary session, adding the words, "if the accused pleads guilty," to make clear that the Rule applied to a guilty plea as well as to a conviction after a trial. Para. (A) was amended at the eighteenth plenary session on 9–10 July 1998 to clarify that when the accused pleads guilty, he is *convicted on that plea*. Thus if an accused pleads guilty, or if he is found guilty after a not guilty plea and trial, he is nonetheless in both cases *convicted by the Tribunal*. Para. (B) was also added at the same plenary session.

History of ICTR Rule 100

9.107 This Rule was amended to apply only to sentencing *on a guilty plea*, as opposed to conviction after a trial on a not guilty plea, at the Fifth Plenary Session on 8 June 1998. Para. (B) was added to this Rule at the same time.

Psychiatric and Psychological Reports

9.108 Psychiatric and psychological reports may be part of the "relevant information" which may be submitted pursuant to this Rule. Such reports, prepared by a "commission of three experts," two designated by the Tribunal and the third selected from a list presented by the defence, were submitted in *Erdemović*. See paras. 3–8 of the *Sentencing Judgement* rendered by Trial Chamber I on 29 November 1996 in that case. See also the *Scheduling Order* issued in *Tadić* on 12 June 1997, which contemplates the presentation of psychiatric, psychological or other expert reports. See also *Todorović Trial Judgement*, paras. 93–95.

Witnesses

9.109 Character witnesses were called in *Erdemović* at the pre-sentencing hearing. Erdemović himself, who had pleaded guilty, also appeared as a witness on his own behalf at the pre-sentencing hearing.

9.110 See also the *Scheduling Orders* issued on 27 May 1997 and 12 June 1997 by Trial Chamber II concerning sentencing in *Tadić*. The Order contemplated both written and oral submissions with respect to sentencing the accused, who was found guilty on a number of counts of the indictment after trial. In the Order of 12 June 1997, the Chamber also pointed out that, "it will receive only reports, written statements and oral statements which provide relevant information that may assist the Trial Chamber in determining an appropriate sentence and that it will reject any material relating to the guilt or innocence of Duško Tadić." It is logical that, after conviction, the Chamber would refuse to entertain any material submitted to prove the convicted person's innocence; any such matters should be brought before the Appeals Chamber to overturn the conviction.

Penalties in the Rome Statute

9.111 The ICC Statute, as well as the ICT Statutes, does not provide a scale of sentences for each crime. The provisions on penalties are in Part 7 of the Rome Statute. Article 77 provides, as the main penalty, imprisonment for a specified number of years or life imprisonment. The death penalty is excluded; article 80 clarifies that "nothing in this part of the Statute affects the application by States of penalties prescribed by their national law," making plain that the Statute's system of penalties does not prevent States Parties from providing for different penalties, including the death penalty.

9.112 Para. 2 of Article 77 provides that the Court may order a fine or a forfeiture of proceeds, property and assets derived directly or indirectly from that crime, without prejudice to the rights of bona fide third parties. Furthermore, article 79, in providing for a Trust Fund, provides in para. 2 that "The Court may order money and other property collected through fines or forfeiture to be transferred, by order of the Court, to the Trust Fund."

9.113 Article 78 contains the criteria for determining the appropriate sentence, but they are imprecise and insufficient. The article reproduces the formulation of Article 24(2) of the ICTY Statute and Article 23(2) of the ICTR Statute with an important clarifying element: the criterion otherwise described as gravity of the offence is defined, in the ICTs, as gravity of the crime (see para. 1). The concept of offence, in fact, may refer to the crime as well as to the specific conduct, creating partial superimpositions with the evaluation of circumstances.

9.114 Article 81(2) of the Rome Statute permits appeal against judgement in case of disproportionality between the crime and the sentence and thus seems, indirectly, to require proportionality.

Punishment: General Reflections

9.115 Punishment must conform to the general principles of criminal law (see bibliography at 9.162).

9.116 The typology of penalty, with regard to the structure and, most of all, the functions, in the International Criminal Tribunals, partially diverges from the type of penalty which is common to national systems of criminal justice. Concerning the structure, the International Criminal Tribunals have a wider margin of discretion in sentencing than courts on the national level enjoy. Concerning the aims of penalties, the ICTs, in determining sentence, pay particular attention to its exemplary role and the need for credibility. To such an extent, that jurisprudence founds the limits to the structure of its discretion on the need for consistent tariffs, and, in its turn, the need for consistency finds its ground in the need for exemplarity and credibility.

9.117 In particular, the ICTY Appeals Chamber has held that:

> 756. Public confidence in the integrity of the administration of criminal justice (whether international or domestic) is a matter of abiding importance to the survival of the institutions which are responsible for that administration. One of the fundamental elements in any rational and fair system of criminal justice is consistency in punishment. This is an important reflection of the notion of equal justice. The experience of many domestic jurisdictions over the years has been that such public confidence may be eroded if these institutions give an appearance of injustice by permitting substantial inconsistencies in the punishment of different offenders, where the circumstances of the different offences and of the offenders being punished are sufficiently similar that the punishments imposed would, in justice, be expected to be also generally similar.
>
> 757. This is not to suggest that a Trial Chamber is bound to impose the same sentence in the one case as that imposed in another case simply because the circumstances between the two cases are similar. As the number of sentences imposed by the Tribunal increase, there will eventually appear a range or pattern of sentences imposed in relation to persons where their circumstances and the circumstances of their offences are generally similar. When such a range or pattern has appeared, a Trial Chamber would be obliged to *consider* that range or pattern of sentences, without being *bound* by it, in order only to ensure that the sentence it imposes does not produce an unjustified disparity which may erode public confidence in the integrity of the Tribunal's administration of criminal justice (*Delalić et al. Appeals Judgement*).

Article: Schabas, William A., "Sentencing by International Tribunals: A Human Rights Approach," 7(2) *Duke Journal of Comparative & International Law*.

Minimum Term Recommendation

9.118 In the *Tadić Sentencing Judgement*, the Trial Chamber made a recommendation that, "unless exceptional circumstances apply, Duško Tadić's sentence should not be commuted or otherwise reduced to a term of imprisonment less than ten years from the date of this Sentencing Judgement or of the final determination of any appeal, whichever is the latter (sic)" (para. 76). There does not appear to be anything wrong with this practice; on the contrary, it is important that the Trial Chamber indicates precisely how long it thinks an accused should serve in jail, given that convicted persons will serve their sentences in prisons around the world which will have widely different practices of early release, automatic remission of part of the sentence, time off for good behaviour, etc..

Life Imprisonment

9.119 A controversial point concerns whether the ICTY has jurisdiction to sentence an individual to life imprisonment, given that, under Article 24(1) of the Statute, the Tribunal should have recourse to sentencing practice in the former Yugoslavia and that in the former Yugoslavia, life imprisonment did not exist (the maximum penalty was 20 years' imprisonment, although the death penalty existed for certain offences). Hence some commentators have argued that the ICTY cannot sentence convicted persons to life imprisonment. The validity of this position depends on whether life imprisonment can be considered the functional equivalent of the death penalty in the former Yugoslavia, or whether life imprisonment was excluded in the former Yugoslavia because it was considered "a fate worse than death."

9.120 The ICTY has not yet sentenced any convicted persons to life imprisonment. There is discussion of this issue in the *Delalić et al Trial Judgement* (paras. 1208–1212), but the Chamber did not finally state whether the ICTY could lawfully sentence someone to a term of more than 20 years, e.g. for 30 years or for life, or not.

Meaning of Imprisonment for "the Remainder of His Life"

9.121 The situation does not arise at the ICTR, presumably because life imprisonment was permitted in Rwanda.

9.122 According to the ICTR, the expression, imprisonment for "the remainder of his life," is to be given its plain, literal meaning, as distinct from the expression, "life imprisonment" under the laws of most national jurisdictions (*Kayishema and Ruzindana Trial Judgement*, para. 31). This would imply that a Trial Chamber sentencing an accused to life imprisonment intends, in effect, that the accused should die in prison. This does seem an exceptionally harsh sentence in that it contemplates not a period of years but rather permanent and irrevocable deprivation of the accused's liberty, irrespective of the numbers of years spent in custody, the detainee's health or rehabilitation. It is submitted that this approach is too harsh, and indeed might fall foul of the prohibition in international human rights law on inflicting "inhuman or degrading treatment or suffering" (Article 3, European Convention on Human Rights).

Burden and Standard of Proof for Aggravating Factors

9.123 The Trial Chamber in *Foča* held that the burden of proof regarding aggravating factors is on the Prosecutor and the standard of proof is that of beyond a reasonable doubt (paras. 846–847 of the *Foča Trial Judgement*). This is a departure from the standard applied in most national jurisdictions. The Chamber also held that the defence only has to prove mitigating factors on a balance of probabilities (para. 847).

9.124 The Chamber also ruled that acts not charged in the indictment will not be taken into account as aggravating factors *even if* they are proved beyond a reasonable doubt (para. 850: ". . . the Trial Chamber would not allow such an uncharged crime being used as an aggravating circumstance. The reason is this: an offender can only be sentenced for conduct for which he has been convicted.")

9.125 This is not entirely convincing. Lack of remorse is commonly recognised as an aggravating factor yet it is not charged in the indictment against an accused. The Chamber side-stepped this problem by saying that lack of remorse is a factor negating mitigation, not an aggravating factor (para. 854). This distinction seems somewhat artificial.

Multiple Sentences

9.126 The first occasion upon which multiple sentences were pronounced upon an accused was in the *Tadić Sentencing Judgement* rendered on 14 July 1997 by the Trial Chamber. The Chamber indicated that all sentences were to be served concurrently (see para. 75).

9.127 Concurrent sentences were also imposed in the *Delalić et al Judgement* of 16 November 1998 (para. 1286), and the *Furundžija* Judgement of 10 December 1998.

Credit for Time in Custody "Pending Surrender"

9.128 This provision was applied in the *Tadić Sentencing Judgement* to give the accused credit from the time *that the Tribunal requested deferral of the national proceedings against the accused* pursuant to Rule 10 of the Rules of Procedure and Evidence:

> I. *Credit for time served*
>
> 77. In accordance with Rule 101(E), Duško Tadić is entitled to credit for time for which he "was detained in custody pending his surrender to the Tribunal or pending trial or appeal." Although he was arrested on 12 February 1994, his detention pending surrender to the International Tribunal did not commence until 8 November 1994 when Trial Chamber I issued a formal request to the Government of the Federal Republic of Germany to defer to the jurisdiction of the International Tribunal (*Prosecutor v Duško Tadić*, Decision of the Trial Chamber on the Application by the Prosecutor for a Formal Request for Deferral, Case No. IT-94-1-D, T. Ch. I, 8 November 1994). Consequently, Duško Tadić is entitled to credit, except in respect of the minimum term recommendation made by the Trial Chamber in paragraph 76 of this Sentencing Judgement, for two years, eight months and six days of time served in relation to the sentence imposed by the Trial Chamber as at the date of this Sentencing Judgement together with such additional time as he may serve pending the determination of any appeal.

9.129 Thus the Trial Chamber only gave Tadić credit from the time he was detained in custody pending his surrender to the Tribunal, i.e. 8 November 1994, not from the time he was first arrested, i.e. 12 February 1994. This was overturned on appeal (App. Ch., *Judgement in Sentencing Appeals, Tadić*, 26 January 2000), as was the date from which the minimum term ran. The Appeals Chamber stated that the minimum term (10 years) should start to run from the date of the *Sentencing Judgement*, i.e. 14 July 1997, rather than from the date of determination of any final appeal, otherwise the effect might be to deter an accused from pursuing an appeal. See also the *Delalić et al. Trial Judgement*, paras. 1287–1289; and the Disposition of the *Furundžija Trial Judgement*. See also the oral Judgement rendered in *Aleksovski* on 7 May 1999. Aleksovski was initially sentenced to two years and six months' imprisonment for war crimes under Article 3 of the Statute. Since Aleksovski had been imprisoned for two years, ten months and 29 days by the time the oral Judgement was rendered, the Trial Chamber applied Rule 101(D) to order his immediate release, notwithstanding any appeal. This was confirmed in an *Order for the Immediate Release of Zlatko Aleksovski* rendered by Trial Chamber I on 7 May 1999. On appeal, however, Aleksovski was sentenced to 7 years' imprisonment.

9.130

ICTY Rule 102 Status of the Convicted Person	ICTR Rule 102 Status of the Convicted Person
(A) The sentence shall begin to run from the day it is pronounced. However, as soon as notice of appeal is given, the enforcement of the judgement shall thereupon be stayed until the decision on the appeal has been delivered, the convicted person meanwhile remaining in detention, as provided in Rule 64. (B) If, by a previous decision of the Trial Chamber, the convicted person has been released, or is for any other reason at liberty, and is not present when the judgement is pronounced, the Trial Chamber shall issue a warrant for the convicted person's arrest. On arrest, the convicted person shall be notified of the conviction and sentence, and the procedure provided in Rule 103 shall be followed.	(A) Subject to the Trial Chamber's directions in terms of Rule 101, the sentence shall begin to run from the day it is pronounced under Rule 100(B). However, as soon as notice of appeal is given, the enforcement of the judgement shall thereupon be stayed until the decision on the appeal has been delivered, the convicted person meanwhile remaining in detention, as provided in Rule 64. (B) If, by a previous decision of the Trial Chamber, the convicted person has been provisionally released, or is for any other reason at liberty, and he is not present when the judgement is pronounced, the Trial Chamber shall issue a warrant for his arrest. On arrest, he shall be notified of the conviction and sentence, and the procedure provided in Rule 103 shall be followed.

History of ICTY Rule 102

9.131   The words, "under Sub-rule 101(D)," were deleted from para. (A) at the eighteenth plenary session on 9–10 July 1998.

9.132   See para. 78 of the *Tadić Sentencing Judgement* rendered on 14 July 1997 by Trial Chamber II: "Until [such time as the Appeal Chamber has considered and determined the appeal of the parties], in accordance with Rule 102, Duško Tadić is to remain in the custody of the International Tribunal."

History of ICTR Rule 102

9.133   The words, "Subject to the Trial Chamber's directions in terms of Rule 101," were added to sub-Rule (A) at the ICTR fifth plenary session on 8 June 1998.

9.134

ICTY Article 27 Enforcement of Sentences	ICTR Article 26 Enforcement of Sentences
Imprisonment shall be served in a State designated by the International Tribunal from a list of States which have indicated to the Security Council their willingness to accept convicted persons. Such imprisonment shall be in accordance with the applicable law of the State concerned, subject to the supervision of the International Tribunal.	Imprisonment shall be served in Rwanda or any of the States on a list of States which have indicated to the Security Council their willingness to accept convicted persons, as designated by the International Tribunal for Rwanda. Such imprisonment shall be in accordance with the applicable law of the State concerned, subject to the supervision of the International Tribunal for Rwanda.

Enforcement of ICTY Sentences

9.135   Relevant material relating to enforcement of sentences can be found in "Responses of States Relating to Enforcement of Sentences" in the ICTY's *Yearbook 1994*, pp. 153–155, "the Enforcement of Sentences Imposed by the Tribunal" in the *Yearbook 1995*, pp. 319–321, and *Yearbook 1996*, pp. 226–227. Further information regarding enforcement of sentences can also be found in the Tribunal's Second Annual Report dated 23 August 1995 (A/50/365), at paragraphs 135–139, the Third Annual Report dated 16 August 1996 (A/51/292), at paragraphs 186–191, and the Fifth Annual Report, paragraphs 250–254.

9.136   On 6 February 1997, the Italian Government signed an *Agreement with the United Nations on the Enforcement of Sentences imposed by the Tribunal in Italian prisons*. Italy was the first State to sign such an agreement. The Agreement does not apply automatically, however, but only if Italy agrees to a request from the Registrar that a particular convict be sent to Italy to serve his sentence.

9.137   On 7 May 1997, the Government of Finland signed a similar Agreement, which entered into force on 7 June 1997. Like the Agreement with Italy, the Agreement with Finland does not apply automatically but on a case-by-case basis, following consultations between the Parties concerning a specific convicted person. Article 3(1) of the Agreement provides that Finland shall be bound by the duration of sentences handed down by the Tribunal, being given no latitude to alter the length of sentences. Article 3(2) provides, in accordance with Article 27 of the ICTY Statute, that the conditions of detention shall be governed by national law, subject to the Tribunal's supervision.

Cross References: Rules 103 and 104 of the Rules of Procedure and Evidence. See *Practice Direction on the Procedure for the International Tribunal's Designation of the State in which a Convicted Person is to serve his/her Sentence of Imprisonment* dated 9 July 1998 and available at: www.un.org/icty/legaldoc/index.htm.

Enforcement of Sentences in Rwanda

9.138 Article 26 of the Statute of the ICTR is virtually identical to Article 27 of the Statute of the ICTY, except that it also provides for imprisonment to be served in the country of the conflict, Rwanda. Article 27 of the Statute of the ICTY, on the other hand, does not contemplate imprisonment in the former Yugoslavia; indeed, in the Secretary-General's report, it is written that "the Secretary-General is of the view that, given the nature of the crimes in question and the international character of the tribunal, the enforcement of sentences should take place *outside the territory of the former Yugoslavia*." (§121, emphasis added)

Enforcement of ICTR Sentences Outside Rwanda

9.139 Three States so far have signed agreements to accept Rwandan convicts in their prisons: Mali, Benin and Swaziland.

The Position of the Government of Rwanda in the Security Council

9.140 In the debates on Resolution 955, establishing the ICTR (8 November 1994, S/PV.3453), the representative of Rwanda, Ambassador Bakuramutsa, expressed the view that convicts should serve their sentences in Rwanda:

> my delegation finds it hard to accept that the draft statute of the International Tribunal proposes that those condemned be imprisoned outside Rwanda and that those countries be given the authority to reach decisions about the detainees. This

9.141

ICTY Rule 103 Place of Imprisonment	ICTR Rule 103 Place of Imprisonment
(A) Imprisonment shall be served in a State designated by the President of the Tribunal from a list of States which have indicated their willingness to accept convicted persons. (B) Transfer of the convicted person to that State shall be effected as soon as possible after the time-limit for appeal has elapsed.	(A) Imprisonment shall be served in Rwanda or any State designated by the Tribunal from a list of States which have indicated their willingness to accept convicted persons. Prior to a decision on the place of imprisonment, the Chamber shall notify the Government of Rwanda.

(C) Pending the finalisation of arrangements for his or her transfer to the State where his or her sentence will be served, the convicted person shall remain in the custody of the Tribunal.	(B) Transfer of the convicted person to that State shall be effected as soon as possible after the time-limit for appeal has elapsed.

> is for the International Tribunal or at least for the Rwandese people to decide.
>
> . . .
>
> there [a]re countries in the world that would be inclined to let the perpetrators of the genocide go free and there can be no doubt that it would be those very countries that would rush to have in their prisons those Rwandese that are condemned by the International Tribunal.

History of ICTY Rule 103

9.142 Para. (C) was added at the nineteenth plenary session, on 17 December 1998, and para. (A) was amended to change "the Tribunal" to "the President of the Tribunal."

9.143 ICTR Rule 103 differs from ICTY Rule 103 in that the former explicitly refers to, and seems principally to contemplate, imprisonment in Rwanda, while the position is reversed at the ICTY. See ICTY Article 27, "Imprisonment shall be served in a State designated by the International Tribunal from a list of States which have indicated to the Security Council their willingness to accept convicted persons. Such imprisonment shall be in accordance with the applicable law of the State concerned, subject to the supervision of the International Tribunal," and the Secretary-General's view that the sentences should in fact be served *outside* the territory of the former Yugoslavia (S/25704, paragraph 121). This view was shared by ICTY Trial Chamber I rendering its *Sentencing Judgement* in the *Erdemović* case on 29 November 1996:

> the Trial Chamber . . . believes that because of the situation prevailing in that region, it would not be possible to ensure the security of the convicted person or the full respect of a decision of the International Tribunal in that regard.

9.144 This difference reflects the very different political circumstances from which the two international tribunals emerged—the ICTR having been created after a military victory by the erstwhile victims of genocide, and being the beneficiary of that victory; while the ICTY was created in the midst of on-going "ethnic cleansing" (the atrocities at Srebrenica took place in July 1995, and those in Kosovo in March–April 1999, when the ICTY was up-and-running) and had to operate, after November 1995, in the context of the diplomatic *impasse* created by the Dayton Peace Agreement.

Cross Reference: Article 26 of the Statute and Rule 104. See *Practice Direction on the Procedure for the International Tribunal's Designation of the State in which a Convicted Person is to serve his/her Sentence of Imprisonment* dated 9 July 1998 and available at: www.un.org/icty/legaldoc/index.htm.

Agreement with Italy

9.145 On 6 February 1997, the Italian Government signed an Agreement with the United Nations on the Enforcement of Sentences imposed by the ICTY in Italian prisons; Italy was the first State to sign such an agreement. The Agreement did not apply automatically, however, but only if Italy agreed to a request from the Registrar that a particular convict would be sent to Italy to serve his sentence.

The *Erdemović* Case

9.146 In the first *Sentencing Judgement* of the Tribunal, rendered in *Erdemović* on 29 November 1996 by Trial Chamber I, the Chamber "consider(ed) the question of where imprisonment will take place and the arrangements which will be made for the enforcement of the sentence" (para. 67). The Chamber started by noting that, under the Statute and Rules, "imprisonment shall be served in a State designated by the International Tribunal" and "shall be in accordance with the laws of the State concerned and under the supervision of the International Tribunal" (para. 68). The decision as to where the sentence should be enforced "shall be decided by the Registrar upon consultation with the President of the International Tribunal and with the approval of the Presiding Judge of the Trial Chamber which delivered the sentence" (para. 69). The Chamber then went on to state that it would "take account of the place and conditions of enforcement of the sentence in an effort to ensure due process, the proper administration of justice and equal treatment for convicted persons" (para. 70). Due process, and *nulla poena sine lege* required that every accused be aware "not only of the possible consequences of conviction for an international crime and the penalty but also the conditions under which the penalty is to be executed" (*ibid.*). The Chamber went on to express its concern "about reducing the disparities which may result from the execution of sentences" (*ibid.*) and to "provide guidance for the execution of international judicial decisions and, in particular, the rights of the convicted person" (*ibid.*). The Chamber then set out the applicable principles regarding the primacy of the Tribunal (para. 71), the fundamental basis of which is that "a State which has indicated its willingness and has been designated will execute the sentence *on behalf of the International Tribunal* in application of international criminal law and not domestic law. Therefore, that State may not in any way, including by legislative amendment, alter the nature of the penalty so as to affect its truly international character" (para. 71).

9.147 In light of these considerations, the Chamber held that "there can be no significant disparities from one State to another as regards the enforcement of penalties pronounced by an international tribunal" (para. 72). Therefore "some degree of uniformity and cohesion in the enforcement of international criminal sentences" was required (*ibid.*):

> The Trial Chamber concludes that two essential elements derive from the international character of the prison sentences set by the International Tribunal: respect for the duration of the penalty and respect for international rules governing the conditions of imprisonment.
>
> 3. *Duration of the penalty*
>
> 73. ... no measure which a State might take could have the effect of terminat-

ing a penalty or subverting it by reducing its length.

As regards the measures affecting the enforcement of the sentences, such as the remission of sentence and provisional release in effect in a certain number of States, the Trial Chamber can only recommend that these be taken into account when the choice of the State is made. The Trial Chamber wishes that all the measures of this type be brought beforehand to the attention of the President of the

9.148

ICTY Rule 104 Supervision of Imprisonment	ICTR Rule 104 Supervision of Imprisonment
All sentences of imprisonment shall be supervised by the Tribunal or a body designated by it.	All sentences of imprisonment shall be supervised by the Tribunal or a body designated by it.

International Tribunal who, pursuant to Article 28 of the Statute, moreover, is entitled to review pardons or commutations of penalties before such measures are granted or enforced."

See also on Rule 101(D), the *Delalić et al. Trial Judgement*, para. 1290 and the Disposition of the *Furundžija Trial Judgement*.

Cross Reference: Article 27 of the Statute and Rule 104.

The *Erdemović* Case

9.149 Rule 104 was considered in the first *Sentencing Judgement* of the Tribunal, rendered in *Erdemović* on 29 November 1996 by Trial Chamber I:

4. *Treatment of prisoners*

74. The International Tribunal bases its right to supervise how persons it has convicted are treated on Article 27 of the Statute and Rule 104 of the Rules.

The Trial Chamber considers that the penalty imposed as well as the enforcement of such penalty must always conform to the minimum principles of humanity and dignity which constitute the inspiration for the international standards governing the protection of the rights of convicted persons, which have *inter alia* been enshrined in article 10 of the International Covenant on Civil and Political Rights, article 5, paragraph 2 of the American Convention on Human Rights and, as regards penalties more specifically, article 5 of the Universal Declaration of Human Rights and article 3 of the European Convention on Human Rights.

The Trial Chamber would also refer to the following instruments: Standard Minimum Rules for the Treatment of Prisoners; Basic Principles for the Treatment of Prisoners; Body of Principles for the Protection of All Persons under Any Form of Detention or Imprisonment; European Prison Rules and Rules governing the Detention of Persons Awaiting Trial or Appeal before the Tribunal or otherwise Detained on the Authority of the Tribunal.

The significance of these principles resides in the fact that a person who has been convicted of a criminal act is not automatically stripped of all his rights. The Basic Principles for the Treatment of Prisoners state that "except for those limitations that are demonstrably necessitated by the fact of incarceration, all prisoners shall retain the human rights and fundamental freedoms set out in the Universal Declaration of Human Rights" (paragraph 5).

Last, the Trial Chamber considers that the penalty imposed on persons declared guilty of serious violations of humanitarian law must not be aggravated by the conditions of its enforcement.

75. In addition, because persons found guilty will be obliged to serve their sentences in institutions which are often far from their places of origin, the Trial Chamber takes note of the inevitable isolation into which they will have been placed. Moreover, cultural and linguistic differences will distinguish them from the other detainees. The situation is all the more true in cases of convicted persons who have co-operated with the Prosecutor because it is not unreasonable to assume that they will also be excluded from the very group to which they should normally belong.

Cross Reference: Article 27 of the Statute and Rule 103.

9.150

ICTY Rule 105 Restitution of Property	ICTR Rule 105 Restitution of Property
(A) After a judgement of conviction containing a specific finding as provided in Sub-rule 88(B), the Trial Chamber shall, at the request of the Prosecutor, or may, at its own initiative, hold a special hearing to determine the matter of the restitution of the property or the proceeds thereof, and may in the meantime order such provisional measures for the preservation and protection of the property or proceeds as it considers appropriate. (B) The determination may extend to such property or its proceeds, even in the hands of third parties not otherwise connected with the crime of which the convicted person has been found guilty. (C) Such third parties shall be summoned before the Trial Chamber and be given an opportunity to justify their claim to the property or its proceeds. (D) Should the Trial Chamber be able to determine the rightful owner on the balance of probabilities, it shall order the restitution either of the property or the proceeds or make such other order as it may deem appropriate.	(A) After a judgement of conviction containing a specific finding as provided in Rule 88(B), the Trial Chamber shall, at the request of the Prosecutor, or may, at its own initiative, hold a special hearing to determine the matter of the restitution of the property or the proceeds thereof, and may in the meantime order such provisional measures for the preservation and protection of the property or proceeds as it considers appropriate. (B) The determination may extend to such property or its proceeds, even in the hands of third parties not otherwise connected with the crime of which the convicted person has been found guilty. (C) Such third parties shall be summoned before the Trial Chamber and be given an opportunity to justify their claim to the property or its proceeds. (D) Should the Trial Chamber be able to determine the rightful owner on the balance of probabilities, it shall order the restitution either of the property or the proceeds or make such other order as it may deem appropriate.

(E) Should the Trial Chamber not be able to determine ownership, it shall notify the competent national authorities and request them so to determine. (F) Upon notice from the national authorities that an affirmative determination has been made, the Trial Chamber shall order the restitution either of the property or the proceeds or make such other order as it may deem appropriate. (G) The Registrar shall transmit to the competent national authorities any summonses, orders and requests issued by a Trial Chamber pursuant to Sub-rules (C),(D),(E) and (F).	(E) Should the Trial Chamber not be able to determine ownership, it shall notify the competent national authorities and request them so to determine. (F) Upon notice from the national authorities that an affirmative determination has been made, the Trial Chamber shall order the restitution either of the property or the proceeds or make such other order as it may deem appropriate. (G) The Registrar shall transmit to the competent national authorities any summonses, orders and requests issued by a Trial Chamber pursuant to Sub-rules (C),(D),(E) and (F).

History of ICTY Rule 105

9.151 Rule 105 was amended at the fifth plenary session in January 1995 "to improve the working of the Tribunal" (second Annual Report, para. 24). The words, "or make such other order as it may deem appropriate," were added to paras. (D) and (F) to allow the Chamber, for example, to make an order for compensation or costs in favour of an innocent third party where an order for straight restitution would not do justice. The words, "and (F)," were added to para. (G) to ensure that the Rule is fully effective.

9.152 The Rule was again amended in a minor way at the twenty-first plenary session on 30 November 1999.

9.153

ICTY Rule 106 Compensation to Victims	ICTR Rule 106 Compensation to Victims
(A) The Registrar shall transmit to the competent authorities of the States concerned the judgement finding the accused guilty of a crime which has caused injury to a victim. (B) Pursuant to the relevant national legislation, a victim or persons claiming through him may bring an action in a national court or other competent body to obtain compensation. (C) For the purposes of a claim made under Sub-rule (B) the judgement of the Tribunal shall be final and binding as to the criminal responsibility of the convicted person for such injury.	(A) The Registrar shall transmit to the competent authorities of the States concerned the judgement finding the accused guilty of a crime which has caused injury to a victim. (B) Pursuant to the relevant national legislation, a victim or persons claiming through him may bring an action in a national court or other competent body to obtain compensation. (C) For the purposes of a claim made under Sub-rule (B) the judgement of the Tribunal shall be final and binding as to the criminal responsibility of the convicted person for such injury.

Compensation for Deprivation of Liberty, Consequent upon Wrongful Arrest, Prosecution or Conviction or Unlawful Violation of Rights

9.155 In a letter dated 26 September 2000, ICTR President Judge Pillay wrote to the United Nations Secretary-General to suggest that the Security Council consider widening the ICTR's jurisdiction so as to permit the tribunal to order compensation for wrongful arrest, prosecution or conviction. Judge Pillay cited three instances at the ICTR of deprivation of liberty that had caused concern. She added that compensation was provided for in international human rights instruments (e.g. Article 14(6) of the International Covenant on Civil and Political Rights and Article 85 of the Rome Statute for an International Criminal Court).

9.156

ICTY Article 28 Pardon or Commutation of Sentences	ICTR Article 27 Pardon or Commutation of Sentences
If, pursuant to the applicable law of the State in which the convicted person is imprisoned, he or she is eligible for pardon or commutation of sentence, the State concerned shall notify the International Tribunal accordingly. The President of the International Tribunal, in consultation with the judges, shall decide the matter on the basis of the interests of justice and the general principles of law.	If, pursuant to the applicable law of the State in which the convicted person is imprisoned, he or she is eligible for pardon or commutation of sentence, the State concerned shall notify the International Tribunal for Rwanda accordingly. There shall only be pardon or commutation of sentence if the President of the International Tribunal for Rwanda, in consultation with the judges, so decides on the basis of the interests of justice and the general principles of law.

9.157 See *Sikirica and others*, ICTY, *Order of the President on the Early Release of Dragan Kolundzija*, 5 December 2001, in which the President ordered the early release of Kolundzija despite the fact that Kolundzija was not serving his sentence in one of the States signatory to the agreement on the enforcement of sentences. The President held that in such a situation, there was nothing in the Statute or Rules to preclude the Tribunal from ruling on the basis of its inherent powers to order a convicted person's early release.

Cross Reference: See Rule 125.

Practice Direction: See the *Practice Direction on the Procedure for the Determination of Applications for Pardon, Commutation of Sentence and early release of Persons convicted by the International Tribunal* (IT/146) issued by the ICTY President pursuant to Rule 19(B) on 7 April 1999 1999 available at: www.un.org/icty/legaldoc/index.htm.

9.158

ICTY Rule 123 Notification by States	ICTR Rule 124 Notification by States
If, according to the law of the State in which a convicted person is imprisoned, he is eligible for pardon or commutation of sentence, the State shall, in accordance with Article 28 of the Statute, notify the Tribunal of such eligibility.	If, according to the law of the State in which a convicted person is imprisoned, he is eligible for pardon or commutation of sentence, the State shall, in accordance with Article 27 of the Statute, notify the Tribunal of such eligibility.

9.159

ICTY Rule 124 Determination by the President	ICTR Rule 125 Determination by the President
The President shall, upon such notice, determine, in consultation with the Judges, whether pardon or commutation is appropriate.	The President shall, upon such notice, determine, in consultation with the Judges and after notification to the Government of Rwanda, whether pardon or commutation is appropriate.

9.160 ICTR Rule 125 differs from ICTY Rule 124 in the addition of the words, "and after notification to the Government of Rwanda." No comparable wording exists in ICTY Rule 125. This reflects the different political circumstances of the two tribunals: the ICTR is able to work in conjunction with the Rwandan government and to a certain extent operate as an adjunct to the Rwandan national justice system while there is no Yugoslav Government that could fulfil a comparable role.

Practice Direction:

See the *Practice Direction on the Procedure for the Determination of Applications for Pardon, Commutation of Sentence and early release of Persons convicted by the International Tribunal* (IT/146) issued by the ICTY President pursuant to Rule 19(B) on 7 April 1999 available at: www.un.org/icty/legaldoc/index.htm.

9.161

ICTY Rule 125 General Standards for Granting Pardon or Commutation	ICTR Rule 126 General Standards for Granting Pardon or Commutation
In determining whether pardon or commutation is appropriate, the President shall take into account, inter alia, the gravity of the crime or crimes for which the prisoner was convicted, the treatment of similarly-situated prisoners, the prisoner's demonstration of rehabilitation, as well as any substantial cooperation of the prisoner with the Prosecutor.	In determining whether pardon or commutation is appropriate, the President shall take into account, *inter alia*, the gravity of the crime or crimes for which the prisoner was convicted, the treatment of similarly-situated prisoners, the prisoner's demonstration of rehabilitation, as well as any substantial cooperation of the prisoner with the Prosecutor.

Sentencing Bibliography

9.162 Concerning sentencing by the International Criminal Tribunals, *see* Nemitz, J. C., *Sentencing in the jurisprudence of the International Criminal Tribunals for the Former Yugoslavia and Rwanda*, in Fischer—Kress—Lüder (eds.), *International and national prosecution of crimes under international law: current developments*, Berlin, Verlag Spitz, 2001, 873; Nemitz, J. C. *Aggravating and Mitigating Circumstances in International Humanitarian Law: The Erdemović Case*, 10 Humanitäres V-I, 1997, 22; Danner A. M., *Constructing a hierarchy of crimes in international criminal law Sentencing*, Virginia Law Review, 87 May 2001, 415; Yee, S., *The Erdemović Sentencing judgement: a questionable milestone for the International Criminal Tribunal for the former Yugoslavia*, 26 Georgia Journal International and Comparative Law, 1997, 263; Schabas, W., *Sentencing by International Tribunals: A Human rights Approach*, 7 Duke Journal of Comparative and International Law, 1997, 461; Safferling, C. J. M., *Towards an international Criminal Procedure*, Oxford University Press, 395; Klip—Sluiter (eds.), *Annotated Leading Cases of International Criminal Tribunals*, vol. I, 287–679; vol. II, 399–835;vol. III 363–877, Intersentia, Antwerp, 2001, 707; Ambos—Steiner, *Vom Sinn des Strafens auf innerstaatlicher und Supranationaler Ebene*, 40 juristische Schulung, 2000; Ackerman—O' Sullivan, E., *Practice and procedure of the International Criminal Tribunal for the Former Yugoslavia*, Kluwer Law International, The Hague, 2000, 145; Schabas, W., *Perverse Effects of the* Nulla Poena *Principle: National practice and the Ad Hoc Tribunals*, European Journal of International Law, 2000, 521; Schabas, "*International Sentencing: From Leipzig (1923) to Arusha (1996)*," in Bassiouni, *International Criminal Law, Vol. III* (1999, 2nd rev. ed.), pp. 171–193; Peglau, J., *Die Vorschriften zu Strafen und Strafzumessung für den Internationalen Strafgerichtshof und ihre Bedeutung für das nationale Strafrecht*, Humanitäres Völkerrecht, vol. 4, 2001, 247–251; Beresford, S., *Unshackling the paper tiger—the sentencing practices of the ad hoc International Criminal Tribunals fort he Former Yugoslavia and Rwanda*, International Criminal Law Review, 2001, n. 1–2, 33–90.

9.163 Concerning sentencing by the International Criminal Court, *see* Kress, K., *Sanciones penales, Ejecucion penal y cooperacion en el Estatuto de la Corte Penal Internacional*, in Ambos—Guerrero (eds.), *El Estatuto de Roma de la Corte Penal Internacional*, 1999, 345; Fife, *Article 77*, in Triffterer (ed.), *Commentary on the Rome Statute of the International Criminal Court, Observers' Notes, Article by Article* (1999), pp. 985–998; Fife, *Article 80*, in Triffterer, *ibid.*, pp. 1089–1014; Fife, *Penalties*, in Lee (ed.), *The International Criminal Court, The Making of the Rome Statute* (1999), pp. 319–344; Jennings, Article 78, in Triffterer, *ibid.*, pp. 999–1003; Jennings, *Article 79*, in Triffterer, *ibid.*, pp. 1005–1007; King & La Rosa, *Penalties under the ICC Statute*, in Lattanzi & Schabas (eds.), *Essays on the Rome Statute of the ICC*, 2000, pp. 311–338; Schabas, *Life, Death and the Crime of Crimes: Supreme Penalties and the ICC Statute*, 2 *Punishment & Society*, 2000, 263; Schabas, W., *Penalties*, in Lattanzi (ed.), *The International Criminal Court, Comments on the Draft Statute*, 1998, pp. 273–299; Schabas, W., *Penalties*, in Cassese, Gaeta and Jones, *The Rome Statute for the International Criminal Court. A Commentary*, three volumes 2002.

9.164 Concerning the aims of sentencing and judicial discretion, *see* in *English* Ashworth A.—von Hirsch A. (eds.), *Principled sentencing*, Edinburgh, 1992; Ashworth A.—Wasik M. (eds.), *Fundamentals of sentencing theory: essays in honour of Andrew von Hirsch*, Oxford, 1998; Ashworth, A., *Sentencing and Criminal Justice*, London, 2000; Frase R.S., *Sentencing in Germany and in the United States*, Freiburg i.Br., 2001; Frase R.S.—Tonry, M., *Sentencing and sanction in Western countries*, Oxford, 2001; Garland D., *Punishment in modern society*, Oxford, 1990; Gross H.—Hirsch A., *Sentencing*, New York—Oxford, 1981; Andeneas, J., *Punishment and Deterrence*, Ann Arbor, 1974; F. Zimring—G. Hawkins, *Deterrence: The Legal Treath in Crime Control*, Chicago, 1973; in *German:* Bruns, H. J., *Strafzumessungsrecht. Gesamtdarstellung*, 2. edition, Köln-Berlin-Bonn-München, 1974; Jakobs, G., *Schuld und Prävention*, Tübingen, 1976; Zipf, H., *Die Strafzumessung. Eine Systematische Darstellung für Strafrechtspraxis und Ausbildung*, Karlsruhe, 1977; Roxin, C., *Strafzumessung im Lichte der Strafzwecke*, in Schulz-FG, Bern, 1977, 463 ss.; Roxin C., *Prävention und Strafzumessung*, in Bruns-Festschrift, 1978; Köhler, M., *Über den Zusammenhang von Strafrechtsbegründung und Strafzumessung (erörtert am Problem der Generalprävention)*, Heidelberg, 1983; Neumann U., *Folgenorientierte versus schuldorientierte Strafzumessung*, in Jung/Neumann, *Rechtsbegründung—Rechtsberündungen. Günter Ellscheid zum 65. Geburtstag*, Baden-Baden, 1999, 118 ss.; Hörnle T., *Tatproportionale Strafzumessung*, Berlin, 1999; in *French:* Foucault, M., *Surveiller et punir. Naissance de la prison*, Paris, 1975; Delmas Marty, M., *Les grands systemes de politique criminelle*, Paris, 1992; Poncela, P., *Droit de la peine*, Paris, 2001; Ottenhof, R. (ed.), *L'individualisation de peine*, Paris, 2001; Garapon, A.-Gros, F.—Pech, T., *Et ce sera justice. Punir en democratie*, Paris, 2001; Tulkens, F.,—Van De Kerchove, M., *Introduction au droit pénal*, Bruxelles, 2000; in *Spanish:* Demetrio Crespo, E., *prevencion generale t individualizacion judicial de la pena*, Salamanca, 1999; Gallego Diaz, M., *El sistema espanol*, Madrid, 1985; Ziffer, P. S., *Lineamientos de la determinacion de la pena*, Buenos Aires, 1996; in *Italian:* Bricola, F., *La discrezionalità nel diritto penale*, Milano, 1965, in Raccolta degli Scritti, Milano, 2000; Dolcini, E., *Potere discrezionale del giudice (diritto processuale penale)*, Enciclopedia del Diritto, 1985, 744; Dolcini, E., *La commisurazione della pena. La pena detentiva*, Padova, 1979; Eusebi, L., *La funzione della pena: il commiato da Kant a Hegel*, Milan, 1989; Eusebi,

L., *La pena "in crisi." Il recente dibattito sulla funzione della pena*, Brescia 1991; Mannozzi, G., *Razionalità e giustizia nella commisurazione della pena : il just desert model e la riforma del sentencing nordamericano*, Padova, 1996; Pavarini, M., *I nuovi confini della penalità : introduzione alla sociologia della pena*, Bologna, 1996.

9.165 Concerning the relations between trial, sentencing and the general principles of criminal law, *see* in *English:* Damaska, M., *The Faces of Justice and State Authority*, New Haven, 1986; Henham R., *Sentence discounts and the criminal process*, Aldershot, Ashgate, 2001; in *French:* Lollini, A., *Réflexions à partir de la Commission sudafricaine pour la verité et la reconciliation*, Phd Dissertation, Ecole des Hautes Etudes en Sciences Sociales, Paris, 2002; in *Italian:* Donini, M., *Teoria del reato. Una introduzione.* Padova, 1996; Palazzo, F., *Introduzione ai principi di diritto penale*, Torino, 1999; Paliero, C. E., *Il principio di effettività nel diritto penale*, Rivista Italiana di Diritto e Procedura Penale, 1990, 455; Satta, S., *Il mistero del processo*, Milano, 1984.

PART 10

APPEAL AND REVIEW PROCEEDINGS

SECTION 1: APPEAL PROCEEDINGS
ICTY Article 25/ICTR Article 24: Appellate Proceedings 10.1.1
Right of Appeal 10.1.2
Scope of Appeal 10.1.4
    Appeals Chamber Not to Disturb Factual Conclusions of the Trial Chamber 10.1.4
    Errors of Fact Must Amount to Miscarriage of Justice 10.1.6
    Accused Cannot Raise a Defense for the First Time on Appeal 10.1.8
    Appeal only Available to Parties 10.1.9
    Appeal of Matters Outside the Scope of ICTY's (Article 25) and ICTR's (Article 24)
        Mandate 10.1.12
Interlocutory Appeals 10.1.13
    Appellate Jurisdiction of the ICTR More Limited Than the ICTY 10.1.15
ICTY Rule 107/ICTR Rule 107: General Provision 10.1.17
ICTR Rule 107 *bis*: Practice Directions for the Appeals Chamber 10.1.19
ICTY Rule 108/ICTR Rule 108: Notice of Appeal 10.1.20
History of ICTY Rule 108 .... 10.1.21
History of ICTR Rule 108 .... 10.1.22
ICTR Rule 108 *bis*: Pre-Appeal Judge 10.1.23
ICTY Rule 108 *bis*: State Request for Review 10.1.25
History of ICTY Rule 108 *bis* 10.1.26
Application of ICTY Rule 108 *bis* 10.1.27
Suspension of the Execution of an Order Pending Appellate Review 10.1.29
Other Decisions under Rule 108 *bis* 10.1.30
ICTY Rule 109/ICTR Rule 109: Record on Appeal 10.1.32
History of ICTY Rule 109 .... 10.1.33
History of ICTR Rule 109 .... 10.1.34
Decisions and Orders Rendered under Rule 109 .... 10.1.35
ICTY Rule 110/ICTR Rule 110: Copies of Record 10.1.36
ICTY Rule 111/ICTR Rule 111: Appellant's Brief 10.1.37
History of ICTY Rule 111 .... 10.1.38
History of ICTR Rule 111 .... 10.1.39
Practice Direction on Procedure for Filing Written Submissions 10.1.40
Calculation of Time Periods and Translation of Decisions 10.1.41
Supplemental Briefs 10.1.42
ICTY Rule 112/ICTR Rule 112: Respondent's Brief 10.1.43
History of ICTY Rule 112 .... 10.1.44
History of ICTR Rule 112 .... 10.1.46

ICTY Rule 113/ICTR Rule 113: Brief in Reply 10.1.47
ICTY Rule 114/ICTR Rule 114: Date of Hearing 10.1.48
ICTY Rule 115/ICTR Rule 115: Additional Evidence 10.1.51
History of ICTY Rule 115... 10.1.52
Definition of Additional Evidence: Unavailable at Trial 10.1.53
"The Interests of Justice ".. 10.1.56
Counsel's Negligence at Trial in Failing to Call Evidence Does Not Make It
    Unavailable 10.1.58
Admission of Evidence to Avoid Miscarriage of Justice 10.1.59
Admission of New Material Should Be at Early Stage of Appeal 10.1.60
Assessment of Additional Evidence... 10.1.61
Reconsideration of Factual Findings Where Additional Evidence Has Been Admitted..... 10.1.62
No Right of Appeal from Appeals Chamber Decision Not to Admit Additional Evidence 10.1.65
ICTR Rule 116: Extension of Time-Limits 10.166
ICTY Rule 116 *bis*/ICTR Rule 117: Expedited Appeals Procedure 10.1.67
History of ICTY Rule 116 *bis*.. 10.1.68
History of ICTR Rule 117.. 10.1.74
Orders Made under Rule 116 *bis*.. 10.1.75
ICTR Rule 117 *bis*: Parties' Books 10.1.76
History of ICTR Rule 117 *bis*.. 10.1.77
ICTR Rule 117 *ter*: Filing of the Trial Records 10.1.78
History of ICTR Rule 117 *ter*.. 10.1.79
ICTY Rule 117/ICTR Rule 118: Judgement on Appeal 10.1.81
History of ICTY Rule 117.. 10.1.82
History of ICTR Rule 118 .... 10.1.83
ICTY Rule 118/ICTR Rule 119: Status of the Accused Following Appeal............. 10.1.86

SECTION 2: REVIEW PROCEEDINGS

ICTY Article 26/ICTR Article 25: Review Proceedings................................. 10.2.1
ICTY Rule 119/ICTR Rule 120: Request for Review..................................... 10.2.2
History of ICTY Rule 119.. 10.2.3
ICTY Rule 120/ICTR Rule 121: Preliminary Examination 10.2.4
History of ICTY Rule 120.. 10.2.5
History of ICTR Rule 121 .... 10.2.6
ICTY Rule 121/ICTR Rule 122: Appeals 10.2.7
ICTY Rule 122/ICTR Rule 123: Return of Case to Trial Chamber 10.2.8
Four Criteria for Review.. 10.2.9
Review Only after Final Judgement... 10.2.11
    Decision on a Preliminary Motion May Not Be Reviewed 10.2.14
New Fact.. 10.2.15
    Change in Rules Does Not Constitute "New Fact" for Purposes of Review......... 10.2.15
Request for Review to Body that Rendered Final Judgement 10.2.16

* * * * *

SECTION 1: APPEAL PROCEEDINGS

10.1.1

ICTY Article 25 Appellate Proceedings	ICTR Article 24 Appellate Proceedings
1. The Appeals Chamber shall hear appeals from persons convicted by the Trial Chambers or from the Prosecutor on the following grounds: (a) an error on a question of law invalidating the decision; or (b) an error of fact which has occasioned a miscarriage of justice. 2. The Appeals Chamber may affirm, reverse or revise the decisions taken by the Trial Chambers.	1. The Appeals Chamber shall hear appeals from persons convicted by the Trial Chambers or from the Prosecutor on the following grounds: (a) an error on a question of law invalidating the decision; or (b) an error of fact which has occasioned a miscarriage of justice. 2. The Appeals Chamber may affirm, reverse or revise the decisions taken by the Trial Chambers.

Right of Appeal

10.1.2 The right of appeal is now generally recognised as a fundamental human right in criminal proceedings, although the Statutes of the Nuremberg and Tokyo Tribunals had no provisions on appeal. The evolution is in large part due to the development of international human rights law in the last half century. Particularly influential has been the 1966 International Covenant on Civil and Political Rights (ICCPR). Article 14(5) of the ICCPR provides that, "Everyone convicted of a crime shall have the right to have his conviction and sentence reviewed by a higher tribunal according to law." See the *Tadić Jurisdiction Appeals Decision* which confirmed that ICTY Article 25 "stands in conformity with the International Covenant on Civil and Political Rights which insists upon a right of appeal."

10.1.3 See also the Appeals Chamber Judgement in *Tadić*, Appeal Judgement on Allegations of Contempt Against Prior Counsel, Milan Vujin, 27 February 2001 (see 4.2.628 above). The Appeals Chamber held that, despite no provision for appeal from a conviction by the Appeals Chamber for contempt pursuant to Rule 77, the Rules of the Tribunal must be interpreted in conformity with the Tribunal's Statute which requires respect of the "internationally recognized standards regarding the rights of the accused" including Article 14 of the ICCPR. Article 14(5) of the ICCPR guarantees that "everyone convicted of a crime shall have the right to have his conviction and sentence reviewed by a *higher* tribunal according to law" [Emphasis added]. In allowing Vujin to appeal the decision of the Appeals Chamber to a differently constituted Appeals Chamber, it is submitted that the Appeals Chamber overlooked the fact that Article 14(5) was still not complied with as the differently constituted Appeals Chamber cannot be said to have been a "higher Tribunal" than the first. See also Judge Wald's dissenting opinion on the right of appeal in which she quoted Judge Sidhwa's separate opinion in the *Tadić Jurisdiction Appeals Decision*, para. 6, in which he stated:

The courts have no inherent powers to create appellate provisions or acquire jurisdiction where none is granted. . . . It is thus clear that a tribunal or court cannot assume appellate powers under any concept of inherent jurisdiction or by expanding its jurisdiction through any amendment to its rule.

Scope of Appeal

Appeals Chamber Not to Disturb Factual Conclusions of the Trial Chamber

10.1.4 The Appeals Chamber must give a margin of deference to a finding of fact reached by a Trial Chamber (App. Ch., *Judgement, Tadić*, 15 July 1999, para. 64):

> 64. . . . It is only where the evidence relied on by the Trial Chamber could not reasonably have been accepted by any reasonable person that the Appeals Chamber can substitute its own finding for that of the Trial Chamber. It is important to note that two judges, both acting reasonably, can come to different conclusions on the basis of the same evidence.

10.1.5 The "unreasonableness" test was also affirmed in *Aleksovski:* "unless there is good reason to believe that the Trial Chamber has drawn unreasonable inferences from the evidence, it is not open to the Appeals Chamber to disturb the factual conclusions of the Trial Chamber" (*Aleksovski Appeals Judgement*, para. 74).

Errors of Fact Must Amount to Miscarriage of Justice

10.1.6 The Appeals Chamber in *Furundžija* stated that:

> it is not any and every error of fact which will cause the Appeals Chamber to overturn a decision of the Trial Chamber, but one which has led to a miscarriage of justice.

10.1.7 Accordingly, the onus is on the Appellant to demonstrate that an error was committed by the Trial Chamber which occasioned a miscarriage of justice. The ICTY Appeals Chamber has on several occasions applied this standard which can be summarised as follows:

> The test to be applied in relation to the issue as to whether the evidence is *factually* sufficient to sustain a conviction is whether the conclusion of guilt beyond reasonable doubt is one which no reasonable tribunal of fact *could* have reached. If an appellant is not able to establish that the Trial Chamber's conclusion of guilt beyond reasonable doubt was one which no reasonable tribunal of fact could have reached, it follows that there must have been evidence upon which such a tribunal could have been satisfied beyond reasonable doubt of that guilt. Under those circumstances, the latter test of legal sufficiency is therefore redundant, and the appeal must be dismissed. Similarly, if an appellant is able to establish that no reasonable tribunal of fact could have reached a conclusion of guilt upon the evidence before it, the appeal against conviction must be allowed and a Judgement of acquittal entered. In such a situation it is unnecessary for an appel-

late court to determine whether there was evidence (if accepted) upon which such a tribunal could have reached such a conclusion. *Čelebići* Appeal Judgement (paras. 434 and 435).

Accused Cannot Raise a Defence for the First Time on Appeal

10.1.8 The general rule is that an accused cannot raise a defence for the first time on appeal (*Aleksovski Appeals Judgement*, para. 51).

Appeal Only Available to Parties

10.1.9 As a general rule, appeal is only open to Parties, i.e., the Accused or the Prosecutor. There are, however, exceptions, e.g., States can request "review," which is essentially appeal, of a decision under Rule 108 *bis*.

10.1.10 See *Decision on Application for Leave to Appeal*, rendered by a Bench of the Appeals Chamber (Judge Cassese, Li and Jan) on 3 June 1997 in the case of Dragan Opačić (IT-95-7-Misc. 1), in which the applicant—a detained witness—sought to appeal a decision of a Trial Chamber:

> 2. . . . It is readily apparent . . . that the applicant does not have standing to appeal to the full Appeals Chamber, since, according to Article 25 of the Statute, "The Appeals Chamber shall hear appeals from persons convicted by the Trial Chambers or from the Prosecutor . . ."; the applicant has not been convicted by the Trial Chamber nor may he appeal on behalf of the Prosecutor.
>
> . . .
>
> 6. If this view of the matter appears overly legalistic, any other ruling would open up the Tribunal's appeals procedures to non-parties—witnesses, counsel, *amicus curiae*, even members of the public who might nurse a grievance against a Decision of the Trial Chamber. This could not be. The Tribunal has a limited appellate jurisdiction which categorically cannot be invoked by non-parties.

10.1.11 The position has since changed with the introduction on 24 July 1997, at the Tribunal's thirteenth plenary session, of Rule 108 *bis* which allows interlocutory appeal/review by *States*, i.e., non-parties. This Rule was immediately invoked by the Republic of Croatia to appeal/review the *Decision on the Objection of the Republic of Croatia to the Issuance of Subpoenae Duces Tecum* rendered by a Trial Chamber in *Blaškić* on 18 July 1997.

Appeal of Matters Outside the Scope of ICTY's (Article 25) and ICTR's (Article 24) Mandate

10.1.12 The Appeals Chamber has held that it has jurisdiction to determine issues which, though they have no bearing on the verdict reached by a Trial Chamber, are of general significance to the Tribunal's jurisprudence. However, the Appeals Chamber will not consider all isses of general significance. The issues raised must be of "interest to legal practice of the Tribunal and must have a nexus with the case at hand." See *Akayesu Appeals Judgement*, paras. 12–28.

Interlocutory Appeals

10.1.13 The Judges of the Tribunal have introduced an interlocutory appeal jurisdiction in the Rules of Procedure and Evidence. See Rules 72 and 73. See also Rule 65(D) (appeal from denial of provisional release), Rule 77(D) (appeal from being found in Contempt of Court) and Rule 108 *bis* (interlocutory appeal by *States*).

10.1.14 For interlocutory appeals other than regarding challenges to jurisdiction, the ICTY moved to a "certification" system in amendments made to Rules 72 and 73 at the extraordinary plenary session held on 23 April 2002.

Appellate Jurisdiction of the ICTR More Limited Than the ICTY

10.1.15 Although ICTY Article 25 and ICTR Article 24, regarding appellate proceedings, are identical, the ICTR's interlocutory appellate jurisdiction under the Rules of Procedure and Evidence is more circumscribed than that of the ICTY. This is simply due to the choice of the ICTR judges. Rule 72(B) of the ICTR's Rules of Procedure and Evidence provides only for interlocutory appeals from the dismissal of an objection based on lack of jurisdiction and does not provide for a system of applying for certification in other cases, unlike Rule 72(B)(ii) and Rule 73(B) of the ICTY's Rules of Procedure and Evidence. The ICTR also has not enacted Rule 108 *bis* of the ICTY's Rules, which provides for appeal/review of a decision by *a State*.

10.1.16 Accordingly, the Appeals Chamber of the ICTR has been reluctant to entertain interlocutory appeals not covered by Rule 72(B). See *Scheduling Order (Ex parte)* in *Bagosora and 28 others* (an unconfirmed indictment, case no. ICTR-98-37-I) dated 23 April 1998, in which the Appeals Chamber, seized of an appeal by the Prosecutor of Judge Khan's Decision of 31 March 1998 dismissing an indictment, which the Chamber was not sure that it was competent to entertain, ordered the Prosecutor to "submit a written brief addressing the question of whether an appeal lies from the Decision."

10.1.17

ICTY Rule 107 General Provision	ICTR Rule 107 General Provision
The rules of procedure and evidence that govern proceedings in the Trial Chambers shall apply *mutatis mutandis* to proceedings in the Appeals Chamber.	The rules of procedure and evidence that govern proceedings in the Trial Chambers shall apply *mutatis mutandis* to proceedings in the Appeals Chamber.

10.1.18 This is a logical rule. It would be inconsistent, not to mention highly confusing, if different rules of evidence were applied at the appellate and trial levels. Being self-evident, the rule has been little discussed, although it was referred to in *Tadić* in the context of judicial notice (Rule 94) (see transcript of hearing, 7 September 1995, p. 107).

10.1.19

| ICTR
Rule 107 bis
Practice Directions for the Appeals Chamber |
|---|
| The Presiding Judge of the Appeals Chamber may issue Practice Directions, in consultation with the President of the Tribunal, addressing detailed aspects of the conduct of proceedings before the Appeals Chamber. |

10.1.20

ICTY Rule 108 Notice of Appeal	ICTR Rule 108 Notice of Appeal
A party seeking to appeal a judgement or sentence shall, not more than thirty days from the date on which the judgement or the sentence was pronounced, file a notice of appeal, setting forth the grounds. The Appellant should also identify the order, decision or ruling challenged with specific reference to the date of its filing, and/or the transcript page, and indicate the substance of the alleged errors and the relief sought. The Appeals Chamber may, on good cause being shown by motion, authorise a variation of the grounds of appeal.	(A) Subject to Sub-rule (B), a party seeking to appeal a judgement or sentence shall, not more than thirty days from the reception of the full judgement and sentence in both English and French, file with the Registrar and serve upon the other parties a written notice of appeal, setting forth the grounds. (B) In an appeal from a decision dismissing an objection based on lack of jurisdiction or a decision rendered under Rule 77 or Rule 91, such delay shall be fixed at seven days from the date on which the full decision is received in either French or English, whichever comes first. The party wishing to file a notice of appeal may apply to the Appeals Chamber under Rule 116 to enlarge the time so prescribed. Where the ability of the accused to make full answer and defence depends on the availability of the decision in an official language other than that in which it was originally issued, that circumstance shall be taken into account as a good cause under Rule 116.

History of ICTY Rule 108

10.1.21 This Rule was adopted as Rule 88 *bis* at the fourteenth plenary session on 12 November 1997. At the eighteenth plenary session on 9–10 July 1998, the Rule was re-numbered as Rule 108, with the previous text of Rule 108 being entirely deleted. At the same plenary, the words "or sentence" were removed. The previous Rule 108 had been amended at the fifth and thirteenth plenary sessions, in January 1995 and 25 July 1997 respectively. The words, "or notified pursuant to Rule 102 (B)," were added at the twentieth plenary session on 30 June–2 July 1999. They were then removed at the twenty-first plenary session on 30 November 1999. The rule was again amended at the twenty-fifth plenary session on 12–13 December, 2001, to change the time-limit for filing of notice of appeal from fifteen to thirty days. The words "setting forth the grounds" in the first sentence, and the whole of the second sentence, of the rule were also added at this plenary session.

History of ICTR Rule 108

10.1.22 This rule was amended at the ICTR ninth plenary session on 3 November 2000.

10.1.23

ICTR
Rule 108 *bis*
Pre-Appeal Judge

(A) The Presiding Judge of the Appeals Chamber may designate from among its members a Judge responsible for the pre-hearing proceedings (the "Pre-Appeal Judge").
(B) The Pre-Appeal Judge shall ensure that the proceedings are not unduly delayed and shall take any measures related to procedural matters, including the issuing of decisions, orders and directions with a view to preparing the case for a fair and expeditious hearing.
(C) The Pre-Appeal Judge shall record the points of agreement and disagreement between the parties on matters of law and fact. In this connection, he or she may order the parties to file further written submissions with the Pre-Appeal Judge or the Appeals Chamber.
(D) In order to perform his or her functions, the Pre-Appeal Judge may proprio motu, where appropriate, hear the parties without the convicted or acquitted person being present. The Pre-Appeal Judge may hear the parties in his or her office, in which case minutes of the meeting shall be taken by a representative of the Registry.

10.1.24 This rule exists only in this form at the ICTR. It first appeared in the version of the ICTR RPE dated 6 July 2002. The ICTR's Rule 108 *bis* (see next heading) is on an entirely different subject.

10.1.25

ICTY
Rule 108 *bis*
State Request for Review

(A) A State directly affected by an interlocutory decision of a Trial Chamber may, within fifteen days from the date of the decision, file a request for review of the decision by the Appeals Chamber if that decision concerns issues of general importance relating to the powers of the Tribunal.
(B) The party upon whose motion the Trial Chamber issued the impugned decision shall be heard by the Appeals Chamber. The other party may be heard if the Appeals Chamber considers that the interests of justice so require.
(C) The Appeals Chamber may at any stage suspend the execution of the impugned decision.
(D) Rule 116 *bis* shall apply *mutatis mutandis*.

History of ICTY Rule 108 *bis*

10.1.26 This new Rule was adopted on 25 July 1997 at the ICTY thirteenth plenary session to enable appeal/review by States of certain decisions of the Trial Chambers. Para. (D) was amended at the fourteenth plenary session on 12 November 1997 to refer to Rule 116(B) instead of Rule 116 *bis*, in accordance with the amendments to those two Rules that took place at the same plenary. This amendment was reversed at the eighteenth plenary session on 9–10 July 1998. The rule was amended at the twentieth plenary session, changing "seek" to "file a request for," presumably for the sake of precision. The rule was again amended at the twenty-first plenary session on 30 November 1999, to oblige the Appeals Chamber to hear the party whose motion led to the impugned decision and to provide that the Appeals Chamber may "at any stage" suspend the execution of the impugned decision.

Application of ICTY Rule 108 *bis*

10.1.27 Upon its adoption, Rule 108 *bis* was immediately invoked by the Republic of Croatia to appeal/review a decision of a Trial Chamber which had been rendered before the new Rule was adopted, but within the fifteen day time-limit which it prescribed. The decision appealed/reviewed was the *Decision on the Objection of the Republic of Croatia to the Issuance of Subpoenae Duces Tecum* rendered on 18 July by a Trial Chamber consisting of Judges McDonald, Odio-Benito and Jan. On 29 July 1997, the Appeals Chamber declared the request for review admissible, finding that:

> 13. . . . the said Decision meets these two requirements. First, Croatia is clearly "directly affected" by a Decision which holds that both Croatia and high officials of Croatia may be ordered to produce documents, in particular military records, before the Tribunal. Second, whether the Tribunal indeed has the power to subpoena States and high officials of States is clearly an issue "of general importance relating to the powers of the Tribunal," indeed it relates to the Tribunal's very competence.

10.1.28 The appeal/review was decided in a *Judgement* rendered by the Appeals Chamber on 29 October 1997 (see Article 29(2) and Rule 54 on *subpoenae*).

Suspension of the Execution of an Order Pending Appellate Review

10.1.29 See *Order on Admissibility of State Request for Review of Order to the Republic of Croatia for the Production of Documents issued by Trial Chamber III on 4 February 1999 and Request for Suspension of Execution of Order* issued by the Appeals Chamber in *Kordić and Čerkez* on 26 March 1999.

Other Decisions under Rule 108 *bis*

10.1.30 See the Appeals Chamber's *Decision on the Notice of State Request for Review of Order on the Motion of the Prosecutor for the Issuance of a binding order on the Republic of Croatia for the Production of Documents and Request for Stay of Trial Chamber's Order of 30 January 1998*, 26 February 1998.

10.1.31 See also the Appeals Chamber's *Decision on the Request of the Republic of Croatia for Review of a Binding Order, Kordić and Čerkez*, 9 September 1999.

10.1.32

ICTY Rule 109 Record on Appeal	ICTR Rule 109 Record on Appeal
The record on appeal shall consist of the trial record, as certified by the Registrar.	(A) The record on appeal shall consist of the parts of the trial record, as certified by the Registrar, and designated by the parties. (B) The parties shall, within thirty days of the certification of the trial record by the Registrar, by agreement designate the parts of that record which, in their opinion, are necessary for the decision on the appeal. (C) Should the parties fail so to agree within that time, the Appellant and the Respondent shall each designate to the Registrar, within sixty days of the certification, the parts of the trial record which he considers necessary for the decision on the appeal. (D) A party shall designate only parts of the trial record to which the party intends actually to refer the Appeals Judges in the party's submissions. (E) With leave of the Appeals Chamber, a party may designate such additional parts of the trial record as the party intends further to cite in the party's submissions. (F) The Appeals Chamber shall remain free to call for the whole of the trial record. (G) A certified true copy of the record on appeal shall be promptly transmitted to the Appeals Unit of the Appeals Chamber of the International Criminal Tribunal for Rwanda, located in The Hague.

History of ICTY Rule 109

10.1.33 ICTY Rule 109, upon its adoption, was identical to ICTR Rule 109. It was amended to its current form on 19 January 2001, after the twenty-third plenary session.

History of ICTR Rule 109

10.1.34 Para. (G) ("A certified true copy of the record on appeal shall be promptly transmitted to the Appeals Unit of the Appeals Chamber of the International Criminal

Tribunal for Rwanda, located in The Hague") was added at the eighth plenary session on 26 June 2000. The rule was again amended at the ICTR ninth plenary session on 3 November 2000.

Decisions and Orders Rendered under Rule 109

10.1.35 As an example of certification by the Registrar of the trial record under Rule 109(A), see *Registrar's Certificate* filed in *Erdemović* on 13 January 1997.

10.1.36

ICTY Rule 110 Copies of Record	ICTR Rule 110 Copies of Record
The Registrar shall make a sufficient number of copies of the record on appeal for the use of the Judges of the Appeals Chamber and of the parties.	The Registrar shall make a sufficient number of copies of the record on appeal for the use of the Judges of the Appeals Chamber and of the parties.

10.1.37

ICTY Rule 111 Appellant's Brief	ICTR Rule 111 Appellant's Brief
An Appellant's brief of argument setting out all the arguments and authorities shall be filed within seventy-five days of filing of the notice of appeal pursuant to Rule 108.	An Appellant's brief setting out all the arguments and authorities shall be filed within seventy-five days of filing of the notice of appeal pursuant to Rule 108.

History of ICTY Rule 111

10.1.38 This Rule was amended at the fourteenth plenary session on 12 November 1997 (see ICTR Rule 111 for comparison). The reference to Rule 108 was added at the eighteenth plenary session on 9–10 July 1998 in substitution for the former reference to Rule 88 *bis*. Rules 111 and 112 were amended at the twenty-first plenary session on 30 November 1999 to remove the words, "served on the other party" and "with the Registrar." The time-limit was changed from ninety to seventy-five days, and the reference to "the grounds of appeal and authorities" was changed to "all the arguments and authorities," at the twenty-fifth plenary session on 12–13 December, 2001.

History of ICTR Rule 111

10.1.39 This Rule was amended at the ICTR fifth plenary session on 8 June 1998. Note that, in any event, the Directive on Court Management, adopted also at the Fifth

Plenary Session, requires ordinary motions by parties to contain a brief of argument and a book of authority:

ARTICLE 27. RECEIVING DOCUMENTS

1. . . .

2. *Format of Motions and other processes.* The Court Management Section shall ensure that Motions and other processes which are filed are in proper form. In particular, when counsel files a Motion before a Judge or Chamber, Counsel must in all cases provide the court with the following documents:

(i) a Notice of Motion—appropriately entitled, informing the reader of the type and nature of the process.

(ii) a Memorial or Brief of Argument;

(iii) a supporting affidavit or Declaration. Note that a party who wishes the Chamber to make any determination on a question of fact in dispute should not make unsworn assertions of fact orally before the Chamber, but should, in his or her Motion, state contentious facts under oath, in an affidavit, affirmation or other solemn declaration.

(iv) a Book of Authority, in a standard format;

(v) a draft Order, in a standard format;

(vi) a Backing Sheet (Back Cover), in a standard format.

Motions and other processes not conforming to these requirements may be returned to the filing Party without filing and with instructions as to how to remedy the deficient filing, in accordance with Article 31 of the present Directive. . . .

Practice Direction on Procedure for Filing Written Submissions

10.1.40 See *Practice Direction on Procedure for the Filing of Written Submissions in Appeal Proceedings before the International Tribunal.* ICTY—last revised 7 March 2002. See also *Practice Direction on Formal Requirements for Appeals from Judgement.* ICTY—7 March 2002. Both are available at: *www.un.org/icty/legaldoc/index.htm.*

Calculation of Time Periods and Translation of Decisions

10.1.41 In *Erdemović*, the President of the Appeals Chamber, Judge Cassese, granted the request of the appellant defence counsel that the time-period for filing his brief of argument be calculated from the time of his receipt of the translation of the Decision under appeal into the Serbo-Croatian language, which Counsel alone could use and which he had been authorised to use by the Trial Chamber (See *Notice of Appeal* filed by Jovan Babić, dated 18 December 1996, page 22). See also, however, *Kordić, Decision on Motions to Extend Time for Filing Appellant's Briefs*, 11 May 2001, in which Judge Hunt held that delay in receiving a copy of the Trial Chamber Judgement in a language that the accused understands should not delay the commencement of work on the Appellant's Brief if the Judgement is available in a language which *counsel* understands.

Supplemental Briefs

10.1.42 See *Order on the Appellant—Cross Appellee's second motion for an extension of time to file briefs* of 15 June 1999 (where a final judgement yet to be rendered in another case is relevant to an appeal, the remedy is not to delay filing the briefs until the judgement is rendered but to apply for leave to submit a supplemental brief after the judgement has been rendered).

Cross Reference: See ICTY Rule 3(F), which now addresses this point.

10.1.43

ICTY Rule 112 Respondent's Brief	ICTR Rule 112 Respondent's Brief
A Respondent's brief of argument and authorities shall be filed within forty days of the filing of the Appellant's brief.	A Respondent's brief of argument and authorities shall be filed within forty days of the filing of the Appellant's brief.

History of ICTY Rule 112

10.1.44 Rules 111 and 112 were amended at the twenty-first plenary session on 30 November 1999 to remove the words, "served on the other party" and "with the Registrar."

10.1.45 The time-limit was changed from thirty to forty days at the twenty-fifth plenary session on 12–13 December, 2001.

History of ICTR Rule 112

10.1.46 This Rule was amended at the ICTR fifth plenary session on 8 June 1998.

10.1.47

ICTY Rule 113 Brief in Reply	ICTR Rule 113 Brief in Reply
An Appellant may file a brief in reply within fifteen days after the filing of the Respondent's brief.	An Appellant may file a brief in reply within fifteen days after the filing of the Respondent's brief.

10.1.48

ICTY Rule 114 Date of Hearing	ICTR Rule 114 Date of Hearing
After the expiry of the time-limits for filing the briefs provided for in Rules 111, 112 and 113, the Appeals Chamber shall set the date for the hearing and the Registrar shall notify the parties.	After the expiry of the time-limits for filing the briefs provided for in Rules 111, 112 and 113, the Appeals Chamber shall set the date for the hearing and the Registrar shall notify the parties.

10.1.49 In *Erdemović* (IT-96-22-A), after the filing of the Appellant's brief and the Respondent's brief, the Appeals Chamber *proprio motu*, in a *Scheduling Order* issued on 5 May 1997, set a hearing on "three preliminary questions" which was held on 26 May 1997. In the Order, the parties were instructed to submit written briefs on the following preliminary questions:

> (1) In law, may duress afford a complete defence to a charge of crimes against humanity and/or war crimes such that, if the defence is proved at trial, the accused is entitled to an acquittal?
>
> (2) If the answer to (1) is in the affirmative, was the guilty plea entered by the accused at his initial appearance equivocal in that the accused, while pleading guilty, invoked duress?
>
> (3) Was the acceptance of a guilty plea valid in view of the mental condition of the accused at the time the plea was entered? If not, was this defect cured by statements made by the accused in subsequent proceedings?

10.1.50 See ICTY Article 7(4) for the *Judgement* on these issues.

10.1.51

ICTY Rule 115 Additional Evidence	ICTR Rule 115 Additional Evidence
(A) A party may apply by motion to present before the Appeals Chamber additional evidence which was not available to it at the trial. Such motion shall clearly identify with precision the specific finding of fact made by the Trial Chamber to which the additional evidence is directed, and must be served on the other party and filed with the Registrar not later than 75 days from the date of the judgement, unless good cause is shown for further	(A) A party may apply by motion to present before the Appeals Chamber additional evidence which was not available to it at the trial. Such motion must be served on the other party and filed with the Registrar not less than fifteen days before the date of the hearing.

delay. Rebuttal material may be presented by any party affected by the motion. (B) If the Appeals Chamber finds that the additional evidence was not available at trial and is relevant and credible, it will determine if it could have been a decisive factor in reaching the decision at trial. If it could have been such a factor, the Appeals Chamber will consider the additional evidence and any rebuttal material along with that already on the record to arrive at a final judgement in accordance with Rule 117. (C) The Appeals Chamber may decide the motion prior to the appeal, or at the time of the hearing on appeal. It may decide the motion with or without an oral hearing. (D) If several defendants are parties to the appeal, the additional evidence admitted on behalf of any one of them will be considered with respect to all of them, where relevant.	(B) The Appeals Chamber shall authorise the presentation of such evidence if it considers that the interests of justice so require.

History of ICTY Rule 115

10.1.52 This rule was amended at the twenty-sixth plenary session held on 11 and 12 July 2002. The words, "not less than fifteen days before the not later than 75 days from the date of the judgement, unless good cause is shown for further delay. Rebuttal material may be presented by any party affected by the motion" were added to para. (A), para. (B) was amended, and new paras. (C) and (D) were added. Para. (A) was again amended, pursuant to Rule 6 (B), with effect from 17 October 2002, adding the words, "shall clearly identify with precision the specific finding of fact made by the Trial Chamber to which the additional evidence is directed, and. . . ."

Definition of Additional Evidence: Unavailable at Trial

10.1.53 "Additional evidence" which may adduced on appeal is limited to such "evidence which was not available to it at the trial." This, in turn, has been held to mean that the evidence's unavailability must not have resulted from the lack of due diligence on the part of counsel who undertook the defence of the accused before the Trial Chamber (*Tadić*, App. Ch., *Decision on Appellant's Motion for the Extension of the Time-Limit and Admission of Additional Evidence*, 15 October 1998—see next heading).

10.1.54 Of course, if genuinely relevant and credible evidence would have an impact on the appeal and it *was* discoverable by exercise of due diligence by trial counsel, but trial counsel acted negligently, it would be highly unfair for the appellant accused to suffer—indeed to remain convicted and sentenced where his conviction might be quashed if the additional evidence were admitted—as a result of his counsel's negligence.

It is, therefore, submitted that the correct interpretation of this rule is that *unless it is alleged as a separate ground of appeal that trial counsel was negligent*, additional evidence which could have been discovered by due diligence on the part of counsel will not be admitted.

10.1.55 A motion to present additional evidence filed before the Appeals Chamber in the *Tadić* appeal was dismissed by the Chamber in its *Decision on Appellant's Motion for the Extension of the Time-Limit and Admission of Additional Evidence* of 15 October 1998. The Appeals Chamber held that additional evidence should not be admitted lightly at the appellate stage. Construing the standard established by Rule 115, it noted that additional evidence is not admissible in the absence of a reasonable explanation as to why the evidence was not available at trial. The Appeals Chamber held that the evidence's unavailability must not have resulted from the lack of due diligence on the part of counsel who undertook the defence of the accused before the Trial Chamber.

"The Interests of Justice"

10.1.56 The interests of justice require admission of additional evidence only if (a) the evidence was relevant to a material issue, (b) the evidence was credible, and (c) the evidence was such that the failure to present it would render the conviction unsafe (*Tadić*, App. Ch., *Decision on Appellant's Motion for the Extension of the Time-Limit and Admission of Additional Evidence*, 15 October 1998—see next heading). In that case, the Appeals Chamber was not satisfied that the interests of justice required that any of the material which was said not to have been available at trial be presented on appeal. See also the Appeals Chamber's *Tadić Judgement* dated 15 July 1999 (paras. 14–17).

10.1.57 Further decisions: *Scheduling Order* dated 2 February 1998, *Order granting request for extension of time* dated 19 February 1998.

Counsel's Negligence at Trial in Failing to Call Evidence Does Not Make It Unavailable

10.1.58 The prohibition on a party from adducing evidence that was available to it at trial means that the party must put forward its best case at trial and cannot hold back evidence in reserve until the appeal. Where a party applies to admit evidence pursuant to Rule 115, there is a requirement that due diligence was exercised at the trial stage. Counsel is under a duty to act with competence, skill and diligence when investigating, gathering and presenting evidence before the Tribunal on behalf of an accused. Counsel is not required to do everything conceivable in performing these tasks, but he is expected to act with *reasonable* diligence in the discharge of his duties. Unless gross negligence is shown to exist, due diligence will be presumed. Subject to this exception, counsel's decision not to call evidence at trial does not make it unavailable. It follows that if the party applying to admit additional evidence can demonstrate that counsel at trial were grossly negligent in the discharge of their duty, this can form an exception to the strict application of Rule 115(A). See *Kupreškić, Decision on the Motions of Appellants Vlatko Kupreškić, Drago Josipović, Zoran Kupreškić and Mirjan Kupreškić to Admit Additional Evidence*, 26 February 2001 (paras. 15 and 16).

Appeal and Review Proceedings • *825*

Admission of Evidence to Avoid Miscarriage of Justice

10.1.59 In *Jelisić, Decision on Request to Admit Additional Evidence*, 15 November 2000, the Appeals Chamber held that in situations where evidence had been available at trial (meaning that the requirements of Rule 115(A) could not be met), the Appeals Chamber still had an inherent power to admit additional evidence to ensure that no miscarriage of justice would result.

Admission of New Material Should Be at Early Stage of Appeal

10.1.60 The Appeals Chamber has held that the admission of new material "in the interests of justice" should be considered at a relatively early stage in the appeal, i.e. before all the briefs have been received and argument taken place. This means in practical terms that the Appeals Chamber must give its best judgement as to the importance of the new material in light of its familiarity with the trial record at that time. This means that even after a finding that the material has satisfied the requirements of Rule 115(B), the Chamber, on further consideration and in light of the briefs and arguments, may decide that it is not so important that it would have changed the result and requires the overturning of the verdict or alteration of sentence. See *Kupreškić, Decision on the Admission of Additional Evidence Following Hearing of 30 March 2001*, 30 May 2001 (public version of Decision), para. 8.

Assessment of Additional Evidence

10.1.61 Once additional material is admitted, the Appeals Chamber will consider it alongside the material already in the trial record to see if the Trial Chamber's judgement is sustainable in light of the newly enlarged record on appeal. In so doing, the usual deference will be given to a Trial Chamber's findings of fact insofar as they were based on the material before the court at that time. See *Kupreškić, Decision on the Admission of Additional Evidence Following Hearing of 30 March 2001*, 30 May 2001 (public version of Decision), para. 8.

Reconsideration of Factual Findings Where Additional Evidence Has Been Admitted

10.1.62 The *Kupreškić Appeals Judgement* was the first major case in which the assessment of additional evidence admitted pursuant Rule 115 came under review. The Appeals Chamber underscored that it may exercise its discretion as to whether to decide on admissibility of additional evidence under Rule 115 during the pre-appeal phase of the proceedings or, alternatively, at the same time as the appeal hearing. The Appeals Chamber examined some of the standards governing the application of Rule 115 and, in particular, the standard to be applied by the Appeals Chamber in finally determining whether, in light of the additional evidence admitted, a miscarriage of justice occurred.

10.1.63 The Appeals Chamber expressed the view that "the more appropriate standard for the admission of additional evidence under Rule 115 on appeal is whether that evidence '*could*' have had an inpact on the verdict, rather than whether it 'would probably' have done so." It stressed that this change from the earlier formulation in the *Tadić* Rule 115 Decision "as more a matter of timing than substance (para. 69)." The Appeals Chamber considered that the 'would probably' standard is still basically appropriate for the ultimate determination of whether a miscarriage of justice has occurred requiring a reversal. It considered that "regardless of the standard used, it is a difficult task to determine whether the interests of justice require the admission of new evidence." The Appeals Chamber pointed out that it therefore "expects a party seeking to admit evidence to specify clearly the impact the additional evidence could have" on the Decision rendered by the Trial Chamber. It warned that if a party "fails to do so, it runs the risk of the evidence being rejected without detailed consideration" (*ibid.*).

10.1.64 The Appeals Chamber interpreted Rule 117 as suggesting that "even if the decision to admit the evidence is made at the same time as the main appeal, a two step process is nonetheless envisioned in which the new evidence, once admitted, will then be assessed as to the effect upon the appeal as a whole." It held that the test to be applied by the Appeals Chamber in deciding whether or not to uphold a conviction where additional evidence has been admitted before the Chamber is: "has the appellant established that no reasonable tribunal of fact could have reached a conclusion of guilt based upon the evidence before the Trial Chamber together with the additional evidence admitted during the appellate proceedings" (para. 76).

No Right of Appeal from Appeals Chamber Decision Not to Admit Additional Evidence

10.1.65 In *Kupreškić and others, Decision on Motions by Zoran Kupreškić, Mirjan Kupreškić and Vladimir Šantic for leave to appeal the Decision of the Appeals Chamber dated 29 May 2001*, 18 June 2001, the Appeals Chamber held that there is no provision in either the Statute or the Rules which allows for appeals from Decisions of the Appeals Chamber pursuant to Rule 115. The Chamber found the motions to be "manifestly ill-founded, an abuse of the court process and frivolous." As a result the Appeals Chamber requested that the Registrar consider withholding counsel's fees involved in the preparation of the motions.

10.1.66

ICTR
Rule 116
Extension of Time-Limits

(A) The Appeals Chamber may grant a motion to extend a time limit upon a showing of good cause.
(B) Where the ability of the accused to make full answer and defence depends on the availability of a decision in an official language other than that in which it was originally issued, that circumstance shall be taken into account as a good cause under the present Rule.

10.1.67

ICTY Rule 116 *bis* Expedited Appeals Procedure	ICTR Rule 117 Expedited Appeals Procedure
(A) An appeal under Rule 72 or Rule 73 or appeal from a decision rendered under Rule 54 *bis*, Rule 65, Rule 77 or Rule 91 shall be heard expeditiously on the basis of the original record of the Trial Chamber. Appeals may be determined entirely on the basis of written briefs. (B) Rules 109 to 114 shall not apply to such appeals. (C) The Presiding Judge, after consulting the members of the Appeals Chamber, may decide not to apply Rule 117 (D).	(A) An appeal under Rule 65, Rule 72 (D), Rule 77 or Rule 91 shall be heard expeditiously on the basis of the original record of the Trial Chamber. Appeals may be determined entirely on the basis of written briefs. (B) Rules 109 to 114 shall not apply to such appeals. (C) The Presiding Judge, after consulting the members of the Appeals Chamber, may decide not to apply Rule 118 (D).

History of ICTY Rule 116 *bis*

10.1.68 This new rule was adopted—as Rule 116 *bis*—at the ICTY fifth plenary session (January 1995) "to improve the working of the Tribunal" (second Annual Report, para. 24), by providing an expedited appeals procedure for appeals from judgements dismissing an objection based on lack of jurisdiction and decisions rendered under Rule 77 or Rule 91.

10.1.69 Para. (D) was added to then Rule 116 *bis* at the thirteenth plenary session on 25 July 1997.

10.1.70 Para. (A) was modified, and the existing Rule 116 was deleted, at the fourteenth plenary session on 12 November 1992.

10.1.71 The rule was further amended in minor ways and to provide that "appeals may be determined entirely on the basis of written briefs" at the twenty-first plenary session on 30 November 1999. It was also amended in a minor way on 2 August 2000 after the twenty-second plenary session.

10.1.72 Para. (B) was deleted, with the other paras. being renumbered accordingly, on 19 January 2001, after the twenty-third plenary session.

10.1.73 The paragraph references to Rules 72, 73 and 54 were removed from para. (A) at the twenty-fifth plenary session on 12–13 December, 2001.

History of ICTR Rule 117

10.1.74 This rule was amended at the ICTR ninth plenary session on 3 November 2000.

Orders Made under Rule 116 *bis*

10.1.75 This Rule only applies to appeals and not to trial proceedings. In an Order rendered in *Delalić et al* on 27 August 1998, President McDonald refused Delić's request to stay the trial proceedings on the basis of Rule 116(B).

10.1.76

ICTR
Rule 117 *bis*
Parties' Books

(A) In every appeal before the Appeals Chamber, the Appellant and the Respondent shall each prepare and file an Appeal Book respectively to be entitled "APPELLANT'S APPEAL BOOK" and "RESPONDENT'S APPEAL BOOK,' in consecutively numbered pages or tabs arranged in the following order:
(i) a table of contents describing each document, including each exhibit, by its nature, date, and where applicable, number, with an indication of the page or tab where the document will be found in the Appeal Book, and
(ii) a legible copy of the pages of or excerpts from every document in the case to which the party actually refers in the party's briefs or intends to refer in the party's oral arguments.
(B) In every appeal before the Appeals Chamber, the Appellant and the Respondent shall each prepare and file a Book of Authorities respectively to be entitled "APPELLANT'S BOOK OF AUTHORITIES" and "RESPONDENT'S BOOK OF AUTHORITIES," in consecutively numbered pages or tabs arranged in the following order:
(i) a table of contents describing each document, with an indication of the page or tab where the document will be found in the Book of Authorities, and
(ii) a legible copy of the pages of or excerpts from every reference material, including case law, statutory and regulatory provisions, from international and national sources, to which the party actually refers in the party's briefs or intends to refer in the party's oral arguments.
(C) Unless otherwise ordered in any particular case by the Appeals Chamber *proprio motu* or upon a motion by a party, each party shall file eight copies of his or her Appeal Book, and eight copies of his or her Book of Authorities, at the Registry two weeks before the date set for hearing.
(D) Failure to file the books prescribed above shall not bar the Appeals Chamber from rendering a judgement, a decision or an order as it sees fit in the appeal.

History of ICTR Rule 117 *bis*

10.1.77 Para. (C) was amended at the ICTR ninth plenary session on 3 November 2000 to change the time-limits therein.

10.1.78

ICTR **Rule 117 *ter*** **Filing of the Trial Records**
The notice of Appeal under Rule 108 and, where necessary, the briefs earmarked under Rules 111, 112, 113, 115 and 117 shall be filed, by the parties, either with the Registry or with an officer of the Registry specifically designated by the Registrar at the Appeals Unit of the Appeals Chamber of the International Criminal Tribunal for Rwanda, located in The Hague. Two similar records shall be kept: one at the Registry of the Tribunal and the other in The Hague. Depending on the place of filing, each record shall consist of the original documents or certified true copies thereof.

History of ICTR Rule 117 *ter*

10.1.79   This rule was added at the eighth plenary session on 26 June 2000.

10.1.80   This rule was amended at the ICTR ninth plenary session on 3 November 2000 to change the words, "trial records" to "documents."

10.1.81

ICTY **Rule 117** **Judgement on Appeal**	**ICTR** **Rule 118** **Judgement on Appeal**
(A) The Appeals Chamber shall pronounce judgement on the basis of the record on appeal together with such additional evidence as has been presented to it. (B) The judgement shall be rendered by a majority of the Judges. It shall be accompanied or followed as soon as possible by a reasoned opinion in writing, to which separate or dissenting opinions may be appended. (C) In appropriate circumstances the Appeals Chamber may order that the accused be retried according to law. (D) The judgement shall be pronounced in public, on a date of which notice shall have been given to the parties and counsel and at which they shall be entitled to be present.	(A) The Appeals Chamber shall pronounce judgement on the basis of the record on appeal together with such additional evidence as has been presented to it. (B) The judgement shall be rendered by a majority of the Judges. It shall be accompanied or followed as soon as possible by a reasoned opinion in writing, to which separate or dissenting opinions may be appended. (C) In appropriate circumstances the Appeals Chamber may order that the accused be re tried before the Trial Chamber. (D) The judgement shall be pronounced in public, on a date of which notice shall have been given to the parties and counsel and at which they shall be entitled to be present. (E) The written judgement shall be filed and registered with the Registry or with an officer of the Registry specifically designated by the Registrar at the Appeals Unit of the Appeals Chamber of the International Criminal Tribunal for Rwanda, located in The Hague.

History of ICTY Rule 117

10.1.82 Rule 117 and its title were amended at the fifth plenary session in January 1995 for the purposes of "clarification, consistency and completeness" (second Annual Report, para. 21, fn. 6). The title was changed from merely "Judgement" to "Judgement on Appeal," to avoid confusion with Rule 88 (now Rule 98 ter), which is also entitled, "Judgement" and to reflect more accurately the French title, "Arrêt."

10.1.83 Paras. (B) and (D) were also amended at the fifth plenary session, in line with similar amendments adopted to paras. (C) and (A), respectively, of Rule 88.

10.1.84 Para. (C) was also added, at the suggestion of the Prosecutor, at the fifth plenary session, to specify a measure which the Appeals Chamber may take by virtue of Article 25(2) of the Statute.

History of ICTR Rule 118

10.1.85 Para. (E) was added at the eighth plenary session on 26 June 2000.

10.1.86

ICTY Rule 118 Status of the Accused Following Appeal	ICTR Rule 119 Status of the Accused Following Appeal
(A) A sentence pronounced by the Appeals Chamber shall be enforced immediately. (B) Where the accused is not present when the judgement is due to be delivered, either as having been acquitted on all charges or as a result of an order issued pursuant to Rule 65, or for any other reason, the Appeals Chamber may deliver its judgement in the absence of the accused and shall, unless it pronounces his acquittal, order his arrest or surrender to the Tribunal.	(A) A sentence pronounced by the Appeals Chamber shall be enforced immediately. (B) Where the accused is not present when the judgement is due to be delivered, either as having been acquitted on all charges or as a result of an order issued pursuant to Rule 65, or for any other reason, the Appeals Chamber may deliver its judgement in the absence of the accused and shall, unless it pronounces his acquittal, order his arrest or surrender to the Tribunal.

SECTION 2: REVIEW PROCEEDINGS

10.2.1

ICTY Article 26 Review Proceedings	ICTR Article 25 Review Proceedings
Where a new fact has been discovered which was not known at the time of the proceedings before the Trial Chambers or the Appeals Chamber and which could have been a decisive factor in reaching the decision, the convicted person or the Prosecutor may submit to the International Tribunal an application for review of the judgement.	Where a new fact has been discovered which was not known at the time of the proceedings before the Trial Chambers or the Appeals Chamber and which could have been a decisive factor in reaching the decision, the convicted person or the Prosecutor may submit to the International Tribunal for Rwanda an application for review of the judgement.

10.2.2

ICTY Rule 119 Request for Review	ICTR Rule 120 Request for Review
(A) Where a new fact has been discovered which was not known to the moving party at the time of the proceedings before a Trial Chamber or the Appeals Chamber, and could not have been discovered through the exercise of due diligence, the defence or, within one year after the final judgement has been pronounced, the Prosecutor, may make a motion to that Chamber for review of the judgement. If, at the time of the request for review, any of the Judges who constituted the original Chamber are no longer Judges of the Tribunal, the President shall appoint a Judge or Judges in their place. (B) Any brief in response to a request for review shall be filed within forty days of the filing of the request. (C) Any brief in reply shall be filed within fifteen days after the filing of the response.	Where a new fact has been discovered which was not known to the moving party at the time of the proceedings before a Trial Chamber or the Appeals Chamber, and could not have been discovered through the exercise of due diligence, the defence or, within one year after the final judgement has been pronounced, the Prosecutor, may make a motion to that Chamber for review of the judgement.

History of ICTY Rule 119

10.2.3 The last sentence of this rule was added on 19 July 2001, after the twenty-fourth plenary session. Paras. (B) and (C), setting time-limits for the filing of briefs, were added at the twenty-sixth plenary session held on 11 and 12 July 2002.

10.2.4

ICTY Rule 120 Preliminary Examination	ICTR Rule 121 Preliminary Examination
If a majority of Judges of the Chamber constituted pursuant to Rule 119 that pronounced the judgement agree that the new fact, if proved, could have been a decisive factor in reaching a decision, the Chamber shall review the judgement, and pronounce a further judgement after hearing the parties.	If the Chamber which ruled on the matter decides that the new fact, if it had been proven, could have been a decisive factor in reaching a decision, the Chamber shall review the judgement, and pronounce a further judgement after hearing the parties.

History of ICTY Rule 120

10.2.5 The words, "constituted pursuant to Rule 119," were added to this Rule on 19 July 2001, after the twenty-fourth plenary session.

History of ICTR Rule 121

10.2.6 In the 6 July 2001 version of the ICTR RPE, the expression "the Chamber" was substituted for "a majority of Judges of the Chamber . . . ," which would seem to imply that at the ICTR unanimity is required before proceeding to review, where hitherto a majority sufficed, and continues to suffice at the ICTY. It is somewhat disquieting that the ICTY and ICTR should have different criteria for review. Moreover, the matter remains unclear, since it is "a Chamber" that convicts an accused, even if it does so only with a majority, so that the term, "Chamber" may still mean "a majority of the Judges."

10.2.7

ICTY Rule 121 Appeals	ICTR Rule 122 Appeals
The judgement of a Trial Chamber on review may be appealed in accordance with the provisions of Part Seven.	The judgement of a Trial Chamber on review may be appealed in accordance with the provisions of Part Seven.

10.2.8

ICTY Rule 122 Return of Case to Trial Chamber	ICTR Rule 123 Return of Case to Trial Chamber
If the judgement to be reviewed is under appeal at the time the motion for review is filed, the Appeals Chamber may return the case to the Trial Chamber for disposition of the motion.	If the judgement to be reviewed is under appeal at the time the motion for review is filed, the Appeals Chamber may return the case to the Trial Chamber for disposition of the motion.

Four Criteria for Review

10.2.9 The four criteria that must be met for a Chamber to carry out a review are:

- There must be a new fact;
- This new fact must not have been known to the moving party at the time of the original proceedings;
- The lack of discovery of the new fact must not have been due to lack of due diligence on the part of the moving party;
- It must be shown that the new fact could have been a decisive factor in reaching the original decision.

(App. Ch., *Barayagwiza, Decision (Prosecutor's Request for Review or Reconsideration)*, 31 March 2000, para. 41)

10.2.10 For a Chamber to conduct a review of a judgement it must be satisfied that all of these four criteria are met. However, in order to prevent a miscarriage of justice, the Appeals Chamber has stated that it may grant a motion for review based solely on the existence of a new fact that could have been decisive in reaching the original decision. Thus, even where the second and third criteria are not met, a Chamber may still conduct a Review. See *Delić, Decision on Motion for Review*, 25 April 2002 and *Tadić, Decision on Motion for Review*, 30 July 2002.

Review Only After Final Judgement

10.2.11 Review proceedings were set in motion by the Prosecutor in *Barayagwiza* following a *Decision* of the Appeals Chamber of 3 November 1999 that ordered the release of Bayagwiza "with prejudice to the Prosecutor." There had not been a final judgement in the sense of a conviction or acquittal on the merits; the Chamber found that the judgement was nonetheless final since the Decision sought to be reviewed had brought an end to the proceedings. Thus the Appeals Chamber ruled, in its *Barayagwiza, Decision (Prosecutor's Request for Review or Reconsideration)* of 31 March 2000, as a matter of admissibility, that review proceedings could be invoked by the Prosecutor even where there had not been a conviction (paras. 47–48), but that "only a final judgement may be reviewed pursuant to Article 25 of the [ICTR] Statute and to Rule 120" (para. 49). A final judgement in this sense is "one which terminates the proceedings" (*ibid*), which in this case applied to the *Decision* of 3 November 1999 since it dismissed the indictment against the accused and terminated the proceedings. See also *Nyiramasuhuko, Decision (Request for Review)*, 16 June 2001, in which the Appeals Chamber rejected a request for review on the ground that only a final judgement or a decision on an interlocutory appeal which terminates proceedings may be reviewed pursuant to Article 25 of the Statute and Rule 120 of the Rules.

10.2.12 The Appeals Chamber found that the four criteria had been met (albeit with a watered down "due diligence" requirement) and reversed the Decision of 3 November 1999. The Chamber decided that, as remedy for the violations of his rights, he would receive financial compensation if found not guilty and if found guilty, would have his sentence reduced to take account of the violation of his rights.

10.2.13 See also *Ntagerura et al, Decision on the Coalition for Women's Human Rights in Conflict Situations Motion for Reconsideration of the Decision on the Application to File an Amicus Curiae Brief*, 24 September 2001, where it was reiterated that only where a "new and potentially decisive fact has been discovered" will an application for review be entertained.

Decision on a Preliminary Motion May Not Be Reviewed

10.2.14 See *Nsabimana, Decision on the Defence Motion for Review*, 9 May 2000, and *Nyiramasuhuko, Decision on Pauline Nyiramasuhuko's Motion Seeking Review*, 14 February 2001, in both Decisions it was held that ". . . a Decision on a Preliminary Motion . . . may not be reviewed."

New Fact

Change in Rules Does Not Constitute "New Fact" for Purposes of Review

10.2.15 In *Semanza, Decision on the Prosecutor's urgent motion for review*, 7 February 2001, the Trial Chamber held that new law, such as a change in the Rules (Rule 94(B), in this case), did not constitute a "new fact" within the meaning of the Tribunal's review provisions and accordingly could not be a basis for review.

Request for Review to Body that Rendered Final Judgement

10.2.16 In *Tadić, Decision on Motion for Review*, 30 July 2002, the Appeals Chamber held that the proper forum for the filing of a request for review is before the body which rendered the final judgement. In the absence of the Judges who composed the Trial Chamber or Appeals Chamber which originally rendered the final judgement, a request for review shall still be filed with either of these two bodies and not with the President.

PART 11

STATE COOPERATION

SECTION 1: GENERAL OBLIGATION TO COOPERATE

ICTY Article 29/ICTR Article 28: Cooperation and Judicial Assistance 11.1.1
Duty to Cooperate 11.1.2
Implementing Legislation 11.1.6
    "Executive" Implementing Legislation 11.1.9
"States Shall Comply" 11.1.11
Subpoenae 11.1.13
Orders Addressed to States for the Production of Documents 11.1.16
National Security Concerns 11.1.17
Reporting Non-Cooperation to the Security Council 11.1.20
The Dayton Peace Agreement 11.1.21
International Arrest Warrants 11.1.23
Service of Documents 11.1.25
ICTR Article 28 . . . . 11.1.26
International Organisations 11.1.28
ICTY Rule 56/ICTR Rule 56: Cooperation of States 11.1.31
ICTR Rule 58/ICTR Rule 58: National Extradition Provisions 11.1.32
Relationship to ICTY Article 29 . . . . 11.1.33
Municipal Law No Excuse 11.1.34
    Federal Republic of Yugoslavia (Serbia and Montenegro):
        Extradition Argument 11.1.36

SECTION 2: CONSEQUENCES OF NON-COOPERATION

ICTY Rule 7 *bis*/ICTR Rule 7 *bis*: Non-Compliance with Obligations 11.2.1
History of Rule 7 *bis* 11.2.2
ICTY Rule 11/ICTR Rule 11: Non-Compliance with a Request for Deferral 11.2.4
ICTY Rule 59: Failure to Execute a Warrant or Transfer Order 11.2.7
ICTR Rule 59: Failure to Execute a Warrant of Arrest or Transfer Order 11.2.7
Failure to Execute Arrest Warrants 11.2.8
Reporting Failure to the Security Council 11.2.9
De Facto States 11.2.10

* * * * *

11.1.1

ICTY Article 29 Cooperation and Judicial Assistance	ICTR Article 28 Cooperation and Judicial Assistance
1. States shall cooperate with the International Tribunal in the investigation and prosecution of persons accused of committing serious violations of international humanitarian law. 2. States shall comply without undue delay with any request for assistance or an order issued by a Trial Chamber, including, but not limited to: (a) the identification and location of persons; (b) the taking of testimony and the production of evidence; (c) the service of documents; (d) the arrest or detention of persons; (e) the surrender or the transfer of the accused to the International Tribunal.	1. States shall cooperate with the International Tribunal for Rwanda in the investigation and prosecution of persons accused of committing serious violations of international humanitarian law. 2. States shall comply without undue delay with any request for assistance or an order issued by a Trial Chamber, including, but not limited to: (a) the identification and location of persons; (b) the taking of testimony and the production of evidence; (c) the service of documents; (d) the arrest or detention of persons; (e) the surrender or the transfer of the accused to the International Tribunal for Rwanda.

SECTION 1: GENERAL OBLIGATION TO COOPERATE

Duty to Cooperate

11.1.2   The duty of every State to cooperate with the Tribunals derives from the United Nations Charter, to which practically every State in the world is a signatory. Pursuant to Article 24 of the United Nations Charter, "In order to ensure prompt and effective action by the United Nations, its Members confer on the Security Council primary responsibility for the maintenance of international peace and security, and agree that in carrying out its duties under this responsibility the Security Council acts on their behalf." Resolutions of the Security Council are, therefore, binding on all Member States. The Security Council resolutions establishing the Tribunals lay down the obligation to cooperate with the Tribunals; accordingly this is binding on all Member States.

11.1.3   As the Secretary-General put it in his Report on the ICTY's Statute (S/25704), when considering whether the ICTY should be established by treaty or Security Council resolution:

22. In the light of the disadvantages of the treaty approach in this particular case and of the need indicated in resolution 808 (1993) for an effective and expeditious implementation of the decision to establish an international tribunal, the Secretary-General believes that the International Tribunal should be established by a decision of the Security Council on the basis of Chapter VII of the Charter of the United Nations. Such a decision would constitute a measure to maintain international peace and security, following the requisite determination of the existence of a threat to the peace, breach of the peace or act of aggression.

23. This approach would have the advantage of being expeditious and of being immediately effective as all States would be under a binding obligation to take whatever action is required to carry out a decision taken as an enforcement measure under Chapter VII.

[...]

28. In this particular case, the Security Council would be establishing, as an enforcement measure under Chapter VII, a subsidiary organ within the terms of Article 29 of the Charter, but one of a judicial nature.

[...]

125. As pointed out in paragraph 23 above, the establishment of the International Tribunal on the basis of a Chapter VII decision creates a binding obligation on all States to take whatever steps are required to implement the decision. In practical terms, this means that all States would be under an obligation to cooperate with the International Tribunal and to assist it in all stages of the proceedings to ensure compliance with requests for assistance in the gathering of evidence, hearing of witnesses, suspects and experts, identification and location of persons and the service of documents.

[...]

126. In this connection, an order by a Trial Chamber for the surrender or transfer of persons to the custody of the International Tribunal shall be considered to be the application of an enforcement measure under Chapter VII of the Charter of the United Nations.

11.1.4 The most immediate need for cooperation arises in the case of arrests of indicted persons by States. Since the Tribunal does not have its own police force capable of making arrests (although see the arrest of Dokmanović, which was at least partly carried out by Tribunal officers), it relies on States and international organisations (like NATO, IFOR, UNTAES, etc.) to do so.

11.1.5 The strongly mandatory nature of the obligation to cooperate with the two *ad hoc* international tribunals, and to comply with their orders, contrasts with the weaker, requests-based cooperative system of the ICC. The difference is due to the fact that the Tribunals were established by the Security Council acting under Chapter VII of the United Nations Charter, while the ICC was established by treaty, and the fact that the former enjoy primacy over national courts while the latter is based on "complementarity" with national courts. This has led some to refer to the Tribunal model as a "vertical" system (based on a hierarchical superiority of the Tribunals over States) compared to the "horizontal" system of the ICC (ICC and States on an equal footing).

Implementing Legislation

11.1.6 Typically States have to enact new legislation enabling them to cooperate with the ICTY and ICTR, as these are new institutions and, for example, transfer of the accused to the tribunals will not be dealt with in the existing extradition arrangements of the State. The same is true of the ICC.

11.1.7 In his *Decision on the Defence Motion Filed Pursuant to Rule 64*, rendered in *Blaškić* on 3 April 1996, President Cassese discussed the obligation incumbent on States to cooperate with the Tribunal. Blaškić had requested that the conditions of his detention be modified in light of the fact that he had surrendered voluntarily to the Tribunal. Counsel for Blaškić argued that the latter had appeared before the Tribunal voluntarily because the Republic of Croatia had not executed the Tribunal's warrant for his arrest. The non-execution of the arrest warrant was due, in turn, to Croatia's failure to enact implementing legislation enabling it to cooperate with the Tribunal in accordance with UN Security Council Resolution 827 (1993). On this point, President Cassese stated:

> 7. ... I am duty bound to point out that the Republic of Croatia is undisputedly in breach of an international legal obligation incumbent upon it, as much as on any other State or even any de facto Government. There exists in international law, a universally recognised principle whereby a gap or deficiency in municipal law, or any lack of the necessary national legislation, does not relieve States and other international subjects from their international obligations; consequently, no international legal subject can plead provisions of national legislation, or lacunae in that legislation, to be absolved of its obligations; when they do so, they are in breach of those obligations. This proposition is supported by copious international case law....
>
> 8. ... It follows that, since 1993, all States have been under an unquestionable obligation to enact any implementing legislation necessary to permit them to execute warrants and requests of the Tribunal (unless of course, no amendment to international law is needed for them to do so ...)
>
> It should be emphasised that this is not a generic obligation, but a very specific one. More precisely, this is an "obligation of conduct" (obligation de conduite) or "obligation of means (obligation de moyens) namely, an obligation requiring States to perform a specifically determined action, like "obligations of results" (obligation de résultat) which require States to bring about a certain situation or result, leaving them free to do so by whatever means they choose....
>
> 9. It is apparent from the above that, by not enacting implementing legislation, since 1993 the Republic of Croatia has undisputedly violated its obligation to implement the Statute, stemming from the relevant Security Council resolutions as well as Article 29 of the Tribunal's Statute.

11.1.8 Thus if a State, due to its internal legal system, is able to cooperate without enacting any implementing legislation, then it is not in breach of its obligations. Conversely, a State which has enacted legislation but then fails properly to put it into effect would be in breach. It is the *result* which is important, not the means by which the result is achieved.

"Executive" Implementing Legislation

11.1.9 The previous point is emphasised by considering the case of the United Kingdom, where the procedure for co-operation with the Tribunal was implemented by an Order in Council (The United Nations (International Tribunal)(Former Yugoslavia) Order 1996). An Order in Council is essentially an *executive* decree. Accordingly, the scope and legality of that Order has been challenged. Colin Warbrick, for example, has argued that implementing legislation should have been enacted by Parliament, after proper debate (Warbrick, *International and Comparative Law Quarterly*, Vol. 45 (1996) 947; see also Hazel Fox, *International and Comparative Law Quarterly*, Vol. 46 (1997) 434). Whatever the merits of this domestic debate, it is clear that it is a matter of supreme indifference *as far as the tribunals are concerned* whether the UK's cooperation with the tribunals was effected by executive decree or legislative action, provided cooperation is forthcoming.

11.1.10 The only *caveat* to this concerns the manner in which accused persons are brought before the Tribunal. While the traditional *mala captus bene detentus* rule (also known as the Kerr-Frisbie doctrine because of the leading cases), upheld in *Eichmann*, prescribes that the court need not be concerned with how accused are brought before the jurisdiction, the Tribunal has made clear, so far in *obiter dicta* (*Dokmanović, Todorović*), that it *will* enquire into the manner of an accused's detention. It appears, however, that if the accused were brought into the jurisdiction in breach of purely domestic law, the Tribunal would not necessaruily be concerned; it would only be if the accused's human rights were violated in some fundamental way that the Tribunal might react. See Rule 59 *bis* and commentary thereto.

"States Shall Comply"

11.1.11 As stated above, States are bound to comply with the Tribunal's requests or orders. The question arises as to what the sanction is where States fail so to comply. In the Tribunal's early years, the sole remedy was to report the States' non-compliance to the Security Council. This was done on a number of occasions with respect to the non-cooperation of the Federal Republic of Yugoslavia (Serbia and Montenegro) and Republika Srpska in arresting accused persons, notably at the conclusion of Rule 61 proceedings and, indirectly, in the ICTY's Annual Reports. (see below, 11.2.9) In the *Blaškić* subpoeanae proceedings, the Trial Chamber suggested broader powers to sanction specifically named State officials where they failed to appear ; the Appeals Chamber retrenched, however, on this, ruling that the Tribunal could only issue binding orders to States, not *subpoenae*, and could not address them to specifically named State officials. It was for the State to designate the appropriate official to respond to the order. Moreover, the only sanction was to report the State to the Security Council. It was not within the Tribunal's power to order financial penalties.

11.1.12 The Appeals Chamber set down the following criteria for issuing an Order for documents to a State. The request must:

> 1) identify specific documents and not broad categories of documents;
> 2) set out the relevance of the documents to trial;
> 3) not be unduly onerous; and
> 4) give the State sufficient time for compliance.
>
> (App. Ch., *Blaškic, Judgement on the Request of the Republic of Croatia for*

Review of the Decision of Trial Chamber II of 18 July 1997, 29 October 1997—"*Blaškić Subpoenae Appeals Judgement*")

See the next section, and for more detail, Rule 54/*subpoenae* at 8.4.8 *et seq.*

Subpoenae

11.1.13 Reference should be made to the Trial Chamber's *Decision on the Objection of the Republic of Croatia to the Issuance of subpoenae duces tecum*, rendered on 18 July 1997. The Chamber's conclusion that the Tribunal has express powers to issue a subpoena duces tecum, and its conclusion that States and their officials are under an obligation to comply with such subpoenae, was based to a large extent on Article 29's provisions.

11.1.14 The Decision was appealed upon request by Croatia under Rule 108 bis, and the Appeals Chamber rendered its *Blaškić Subpoenae Appeals Judgement* on 29 October 1997, reversing the Trial Chamber on a number of issues, in particular holding that subpoenae could not be addressed to States nor to State officials.

11.1.15 See now ICTY Rule 54 *bis* ("Orders Directed to States for the Production of Documents"), which has superseded subpoenae addressed to States.

Orders Addressed to States for the Production of Documents

11.1.16 Following the *Blaškić Subpoenae Appeals Judgement*, the Chambers have chosen to issue Orders to States for the Production of Documents rather than *subpoenae* (although the difference may be only one of terminology). See, for example, the *Binding Order to the Republika Srpska for the Production of Documents* issued by Judge Jorda in *Krstić* on 12 March 1999. Judge Jorda applied the criteria for ordering a State to produce documents set out in the Appeals Chamber's *subpoenae* decision in *Blaškić*.

National Security Concerns

11.1.17 States are naturally permitted to raise national security concerns in answer to a Tribunal Order that documents be produced. The *Blaškić Subpoenae Appeals Judgement* held that States could raise such concerns, which could, if necessary, in order to ensure the greatest confidentiality, be reviewed by a single Judge (Judge Karibi-Whyte dissenting). However if the single Judge decided that the States' national security concerns were unfounded, the implication is that the State would still be ordered to comply, notwithstanding their national security concerns. If the State continued to refuse to comply, the matter would be reported to the Security Council, which would resolve the matter.

11.1.18 For the ICC's (more detailed) provisions in this regard, see Article 72 of the Rome Statute. See also Malanczuk, "*Chapter 31.5: Protection of National Security Interests*" in Cassese, Gaeta and Jones (eds), *The Rome Statute of the International Criminal Court: A Commentary* (OUP, 2002); Dixon/Duffy, "*Article 72: Protection of national security information*" in Triffterer (ed.), *Commentary on the Rome Statute of the International Criminal Court*.

11.1.19 For an Order pursuant to Article 29 for an *ex parte* hearing for a State representative to explain why a State's national security concerns allegedly precluded it from complying with a binding order for the production of documents, see *Second Additional Order for a Witness to Appear* rendered by Trial Chamber I on 12 March 1999 in *Blaškić*.

Reporting Non-Cooperation to the Security Council

11.1.20 Pursuant to Rule 61, the ICTY has reported the failure of States and entities to co-operate with the Tribunal by arresting the persons the subject of the Rule 61 proceedings in the folllowing cases: *Vukovar Rule 61 Decision* (paras. 38–41: non-cooperation of the Federal Republic of Yugoslavia (Serbia and Montenegro)); *Karadžić and Mladić Rule 61 Decision* (paras. 98–101: non-cooperation of the Federal Republic of Yugoslavia (Serbia and Montenegro) and Republika Srpska); *Rajić Rule 61 Decision* (paras. 62–70; non-cooperation of the Republic of Croatia and the Federation of Bosnia and Herzegovina).

The Dayton Peace Agreement

11.1.21 The obligation of the States and entities of the former Yugoslavia to co-operate with the Tribunal and to comply with its orders, which already flowed from the Security Council resolutions establishing the Tribunal, as set out above (1.6 and 11.1.2), was reaffirmed in the Dayton Peace Agreement, signed on 14 December 1995. The Dayton Agreement in several places specifically affirms the duty of the signatories to co-operate with the ICTY.

11.1.22 On the relevance of the Dayton Peace Agreement to the obligation of States and Entities of the former Yugoslavia to co-operate with the Tribunal, see Payam Akhavan, "*The Yugoslav Tribunal at a Crossroads: The Dayton Peace Agreement and Beyond*," 18(2) *Human Rights Quarterly* (1996) 275; and John R.W.D. Jones, "*The Implications of the Dayton Peace Agreement for the International Criminal Tribunal for the former Yugoslavia*," European Journal of International Law, Vol. 7 (1996), No. 2, pp. 226–244.

International Arrest Warrants

11.1.23 When an indictment is confirmed, an arrest warrant is ordinarily sent to "the national authorities of a State in whose territory or under whose jurisdiction the accused resides, or was last known to be" (Rule 55(D)). However, the Tribunal also has the power to issue *international* arrest warrants, which are transmitted to all States and which impose on all States the obligation to search for and arrest the persons mentioned in the warrant:

> 2. . . . In effect, all States in the international community will be bound, if the warrant is issued, to cooperate in searching for and arresting the accused, who would in consequence become an international fugitive. (Tr. Ch., *Nikolić Rule 61 Decision*)

11.1.24 International arrest warrants are usually issued after Rule 61 proceedings, pursuant to Rule 61(D). Equally, however, an international arrest warrant could be sought pursuant to Rule 54 if the issuance of the warrant could be shown to be "necessary for the purposes of an investigation or for the preparation or conduct of the trial." Given that an accused has to be indicted in order for a warrant to issue, the reference to an investigation is probably not apt, and the second limb of Rule 54 ("necessary . . . for the preparation or conduct of the trial") would more properly be invoked, if it could be demonstrated that specifically an *international* arrest warrant was necessary to secure the accused's arrest (e.g. if the accused's whereabouts were completely unknown).

Service of Documents

11.1.25 Article 29(2)(c) of the ICTY Statute makes plain that States are obliged to comply with requests for assistance or orders for the service of documents. An arrest warrant is an order for the service of documents *par excellence*, and it is, therefore, not surprising that non-cooperation under this heading has mostly been certified with respect to failure to serve arrest warrants. See the *Karadžić and Mladić Rule 61 Decision*, paras. 98 to 101 ("98. . . . Despite the presence of Radovan KARADŽIĆ and Ratko MLADIĆ on the territory under its control, Republika Srpska has neither served the two indictments on the accused nor executed the warrants for their arrest"). See also the *Rajić Rule 61 Decision*, paras. 64–66 (". . . Ivica Rajić has been present in Croatia and in the territory of the Federation of Bosnia and Herzegovina on several occasions" and that "to date, personal service of the indictment has not been effected"). In the Disposition to the Decision, the Trial Chamber noted (at page 32):

> that the failure to effect personal service of the indictment can be ascribed to the refusal to cooperate with the International Tribunal by the Republic of Croatia and by the Federation of Bosnia and Herzegovina and entrusts the responsibility of so informing the Security Council to the President of the International Tribunal, pursuant to Sub-rule 61(E).

ICTR Article 28

11.1.26 Naturally, the same considerations noted above, with respect to the ICTY, apply equally to the ICTR. In the case of the ICTR, however, the Security Council took the additional step, in its resolution 978 (1995) of 27 February 1995, of urging States to arrest and detain persons found within their territory against whom there was sufficient evidence of responsibility for acts of violence within the jurisdiction of the Tribunal, and to inform the Secretary-General and the Tribunal's Prosecutor of the identity of any such persons detained and of the nature and of the crimes believed to have been committed by them (see paragraph 3 of the ICTR's Second Annual Report). This may have been partly a result of the fact that at the ICTR, the accused were dispersed across several (mostly African) States, following the victory of the RPF. Indeed, accused persons have been transferred to the ICTR from a great variety of States (Belgium, Benin, Burkina Faso, Cameroon, Denmark, France, Kenya, Togo, Mali, Namibia, Switzerland, Tanzania, UK, US, Zambia)

11.1.27 This contrasts with the ICTY where the accused almost exclusively remained on the territory of the former Yugoslavia, in particular in the Federal Republic of Yugoslavia (Serbia and Monenegro), the Republic of Croatia, Republika Srpska and the Federation of Bosnia and Herzegovina. Outside of the States of the former Yugoslavia, arrests have been made in comparatively few countries (to date, only Austria and Germany).

International Organisations

11.1.28 There has been much debate as to whether international organisations are obliged to cooperate with the Tribunal, in particular with regard to the question whether the NATO-led forces in Bosnia and Herzegovina are obliged to arrest suspects. On this subject, see 8.4.113.

11.1.29 Whatever the nature of the obligations which may or may not be owed by international organisations to the Tribunals, it cannot be disputed that the Tribunal is entitled to *request* assistance from them. Indeed, the help of international organisations, notably the United Nations High Commissioner for Refugees (UNHCR) has been solicited in several decisions, notably those concerning the protection of potential witnesses before the Tribunal. See, e.g. the *Decision on the Motion for the Protection of Defence Witnesses* rendered by Trial Chamber 2 in *Kayishema and Ruzindana* on 6 October 1997:

> NOW THEREFORE THE TRIAL CHAMBER ORDERS:—
>
> ...
>
> that pursuant to Security Council Resolution 955 (1994) and Article 28 of the Statute, the Registrar should solicit the assistance and cooperation of the Governments of the Republics of Kenya, Tanzania, Rwanda as well as the UNHCR and should take all possible measures to ensure the availability of the witnesses to testify before the Tribunal.

11.1.31

ICTY Rule 56 Cooperation of States	ICTR Rule 56 Cooperation of States
The State to which a warrant of arrest or a transfer order for a witness is transmitted shall act promptly and with all due diligence to ensure proper and effective execution thereof, in accordance with Article 29 of the Statute.	The State to which a warrant of arrest or a transfer order for a witness is transmitted shall act promptly and with all due diligence to ensure proper and effective execution thereof, in accordance with Article 28 of the Statute.

11.1.32

ICTY Rule 58 National Extradition Provisions	ICTR Rule 58 National Extradition Provisions
The obligations laid down in Article 29 of the Statute shall prevail over any legal impediment to the surrender or transfer of the accused or of a witness to the Tribunal which may exist under the national law or extradition treaties of the State concerned.	The obligations laid down in Article 28 of the Statute shall prevail over any legal impediment to the surrender or transfer of the accused or of a witness to the Tribunal which may exist under the national law or extradition treaties of the State concerned.

11.1.30 See also *Decision on Protective Measures for Defence Witnesses and their Families and Relatives* rendered by Trial Chamber in *Nsengiyumva* (ICTR-96-12-I) on 5 November 1997; *Decision on the Defence Extremely Urgent Motion for Request for Cooperation pursuant to Article 28 of the Statute of the Tribunal and Request for Cooperation by States*, Trial Chamber, in *Semanza* (ICTR-97-20-T) on 3 September 2001 and a further Decision in *Semanza* on 10 October 2001.

Relationship to ICTY Article 29

11.1.33 ICTY Rule 58 must be read in conjunction with Security Council resolution 827 (1993) of 25 May 1993, which requires "all States" to "cooperate fully" with the Tribunal and its organs and stipulates that all States "shall take any measures necessary under their domestic law to implement the provisions" of the Tribunal's Statute and comply with "requests for assistance or orders issued by a Trial Chamber." This principle of cooperation between States and the Tribunal "in the investigation and prosecution of persons accused of committing serious violations of international humanitarian law" is enshrined in the ICTY Statute under Article 29 and restated in Rule 58.

Municipal Law No Excuse

11.1.34 Under international law, a State cannot raise its national law or constitution ("municipal law" is the term used in international law to describe the domestic or national law of a State) as an obstacle to fulfilling its international obligations. "No international subject can plead provisions of national legislation, or lacunae in that legislation, to be absolved of its obligations; when they do so, they are in breach of those obligations" (*Decision of the President on the Defence Motion Filed Pursuant to Rule 64*, 3 April 1996). See *Decision on the Motion for Release by the Accused Slavko Dokmanović*, 22 October 1997, paragraph 36, referring to this "universally recognised principle."

11.1.35 Rule 58 is one aspect of that general principle, applied to the specific case of extradition.

Federal Republic of Yugoslavia (Serbia and Montenegro): Extradition Argument

11.1.36 The Federal Republic of Yugoslavia (Serbia and Montenegro) has often used the argument that its Constitution forbids the extradition of its nationals as grounds for refusing to arrest accused persons on its territory and to transfer them to the Tribunal. See, e.g., *Decision on the Motion for Release by the Accused Slavko Dokmanović*, 22 October 1997, para. 36: "[FRY has] failed to pass implementing legislation that would permit it to fulfil its obligations under Article 29. It has taken the position that its constitution bars the extradition of its nationals to the Tribunal, and thus legislation which provides for the surrender of Yugoslav nationals would be unconstitutional." The position of the ICTY on this matter is set out in the the ICTY's Fourth Annual Report (para. 188):

> it needs no argument to point out that the invocation by the Federal Republic of Yugoslavia (Serbia and Montenegro) of its Constitution is no answer for its failure to meet its international obligations, including the treaty obligations it solemnly took before the world community at Dayton.

11.1.37 See also the letter from the former United Nations Secretary-General, Boutros Boutros-Ghali, to the Deputy Prime Minister and Federal Minister for Foreign Affairs of the Federal Republic of Yugoslavia (Serbia and Montenegro) dated 27 April 1994, in reply to a letter from the latter in which he declined all co-operation by the Federal Republic of Yugoslavia (Serbia and Montenegro) with the Tribunal. The Secretary-General's letter concludes:

> It is therefore the position of the Secretary-General that the International Tribunal was established in full compliance with the provisions of the United Nations Charter, and that the Federal Republic of Yugoslavia, like all other States members of the United Nations, is bound to give effect to Security Council resolutions adopted under Chapter VII of the Charter, and to comply to that end with any requests of the International Tribunal for assistance, including, in particular, a request for the transfer or surrender of an accused, regardless of his nationality. It is the hope of the Secretary-General and that of the Security Council that the Federal Republic of Yugoslavia will cooperate with the Tribunal in the spirit of Security Council resolution 827 (1993) and the Statute of the International Tribunal.

11.1.38 See also the letter from Mr. Hans Corell, Under-Secretary-General for Legal Affairs and the Legal Counsel, to the Minister of Foreign Affairs of Bosnia and Herzegovina, dated 21 January 1997, in response to a letter from Mrs. Biljana Plavsić, President of Republika Srpska, in which the latter stated that Republika Srpska would not cooperate in the arrest and delivery to The Hague of Radovan Karadžić and Ratko Mladić. Mr. Corell's letter concludes:

> In consideration of the foregoing, it is the position of the United Nations that unconditional cooperation with the International Tribunal is imperative, and that the Republika Srpska should surrender Dr. Karadžić and General Mladić, as well as all other accused within this Entity to the International Tribunal to stand trial.

SECTION 2: CONSEQUENCES OF NON-COOPERATION

11.2.1

ICTY Rule 7 *bis* Non-Compliance with Obligations	ICTR Rule 7 *bis* Non-Compliance with Obligations
(A) In addition to cases to which Rule 11, Rule 13, Rule 59 or Rule 61 applies, where a Trial Chamber or a Judge is satisfied that a State has failed to comply with an obligation under Article 29 of the Statute relating to any proceedings before that Chamber or Judge, the Chamber or Judge may request the President to report the matter to the Security Council. (B) If the Prosecutor satisfies the President that a State has failed to comply with an obligation under Article 29 of the Statute in respect of a request by the Prosecutor under Rule 8 or 40, the President shall notify the Security Council thereof.	(A) Except in cases to which Rule 11, 13, 59 or 61 applies, where a Trial Chamber or a Judge is satisfied that a State has failed to comply with an obligation under Article 28 of the Statute relating to any proceedings before that Chamber or Judge, the Chamber or Judge may request the President to report the matter to the Security Council. (B) If the Prosecutor satisfies the President that a State has failed to comply with an obligation under Article 28 of the Statute in respect of a request by the Prosecutor under Rule 8 or 40, the President shall notify the Security Council thereof.

History of Rule 7 *bis*

11.2.2 This new Rule was added to the ICTR Rules of Procedure and Evidence at the Fourth Plenary Session, held in Arusha 1–5 June 1997, in order to authorise the President of the ICTR to report to the Security Council cases where States have failed to comply with requests for assistance or orders issued by a Trial Chamber pursuant to Article 28 of the ICTR Statute (Article 28 of the ICTR's Statute is equivalent to Article 29 of the ICTY's Statute).

11.2.3 The ICTY followed the ICTR by adopting Rule 7 *bis* at the ICTY's thirteenth plenary session on 25 July 1997. In a Decision dated 29 October 1997, the ICTY Appeals Chamber stated that, ". . . the adoption of Rule 7 *bis* is clearly to be regarded as falling within the authority of the International Tribunal" (paragraph 34).

11.2.4

ICTY Rule 11 Non-Compliance with a Request for Deferral	ICTR Rule 11 Non-Compliance with a Request for Deferral
If, within sixty days after a request for deferral has been notified by the Registrar to the State under whose jurisdiction the investigations or criminal proceedings have been instituted, the State fails to file a response which satisfies the Trial Chamber that the State has taken or is taking adequate steps to comply with the order, the Trial Chamber may request the President to report the matter to the Security Council.	If, within sixty days after a request for deferral has been notified by the Registrar to the State under whose jurisdiction the investigations or criminal proceedings have been instituted, the State fails to file a response which satisfies the Trial Chamber that the State has taken or is taking adequate steps to comply with the order, the Trial Chamber may request the President to report the matter to the Security Council.

11.2.5 The ICTY has not yet applied this Rule; in three of the four deferral applications, the State has acceded to the request and in the other application, the accused was already in the custody of the Tribunal, and, moreover, the government acceded to the request after the Chamber had issued a request for deferral (see Commentary to Rule 10 at 5.61 *et seq.*).

11.2.6 The rationale for notification of the Security Council in this and other Rules derives from ICTY Article 29 and ICTR Article 28.

11.2.7

ICTY Rule 59 Failure to Execute a Warrant or Transfer Order	ICTR Rule 59 Failure to Execute a Warrant of Arrest or Transfer Order
(A) Where the State to which a warrant of arrest or transfer order has been transmitted has been unable to execute the warrant, it shall report forthwith its inability to the Registrar, and the reasons therefor. (B) If, within a reasonable time after the warrant of arrest or transfer order has been transmitted to the State, no report is made on action taken, this shall be deemed a failure to execute the warrant of arrest or transfer order and the Tribunal, through the President, may notify the Security Council accordingly.	(A) Where the State to which a warrant of arrest or transfer order has been transmitted has been unable to execute the warrant of arrest or transfer order, it shall report forthwith its inability to the Registrar, and the reasons therefor. (B) If, within a reasonable time after the warrant of arrest or transfer order has been transmitted to the State, no report is made on action taken, this shall be deemed a failure to execute the warrant of arrest or transfer order and the Tribunal, through the President, may notify the Security Council accordingly.

Failure to Execute Arrest Warrants

11.2.8 See, for example, the *Vukovar Rule 61 Decision*, para. 39: "To date, these warrants of arrest have not been executed by the FRY. That state has not informed the Registrar of the Tribunal of the reasons for which it failed to execute the warrants of arrest; therefore it has not honoured its obligation to cooperate as required in Rule 59 (A) of the Rules of the Tribunal."

Reporting Failure to the Security Council

11.2.9 This Rule provides, with Rule 61, for notification to the Security Council of a State's failure to execute arrest warrants. The means of notification is not specified; in practice, the President may either write a letter to the Security Council or address the Security Council in a private session. The Tribunal's Annual Report is also a vehicle for reporting to the Security Council (see second Annual Report (A/50/365; S/1995/728), para. 191: "Regrettably, some States have witheld any cooperation: reference should be made in particular to the Federal Republic of Yugoslavia (Serbia and Montenegro), as well as some de facto authorities such as the self-styled Republics of Krajina and Srpska"; and the third Annual Report (A/51/292; S/1996/665), *passim*, and, especially, Annex II—"Detailed Survey of Instances of Failure to Execute Arrest Warrants"—which has been reproduced and up-dated in subsequent annual reports).

De Facto States

11.2.10 In accordance with the definition of "State" in ICTY Rule 2, ICTY Chambers have applied this Rule to "self-proclaimed entit(ies) *de facto* exercising governmental functions, whether recognised as a State or not," namely the Bosnian Serb administration in Pale (which became the entity, "Republika Srpska," within Bosnia and Herzegovina, after the Dayton Accord), the "Croatian Community of Herceg-Bosna," the former Krajina Serb Republic and the Federation of Bosnia and Herzegovina (also an entity within Bosnia and Herzegovina after the Dayton Accord). Rule 2 was indeed amended on 12 December 2002, after the ICTY's twenty-seventh plenary session, to add a new para. (ii) which further defined a "State" as "an entity recognised by the constitution of Bosnia and Herzegovina and the Republika Srpska." See ICTY Rule 2.

ANNEXES

ANNEX 1

SUMMARY OF CONCLUDED TRIALS

Note that the Decisions and Orders of the ICTY are now published in the Tribunal's *Judicial Reports/Recueils judiciaires*, published for and on behalf of the United Nations by Kluwer Law International, The Hague.

Visit the ICTY website for full case details of each concluded and pending case: *www. un.org/icty*.

INTERNATIONAL CRIMINAL TRIBUNAL FOR THE FORMER YUGOSLAVIA

For the purposes of this section, trials are concluded once a verdict has been announced, notwithstanding that the verdict may be under appeal.

Note the meaning of the symbols in the Case Number, e.g. IT-95-14-AR108.

- IT = International Tribunal
- 95 = year of indictment
- 14 = number of case
- A = Appeal (followed by Rule, if necessary, e.g. AR108 = Appeal of Rule 108)
- T = Trial
- PT = Pre-Trial
- I = Indictment
- R61 = Rule 61
- D = Deferral hearings (Rule 10)

The Erdemović Case (IT-96-22-T)

Dražen Erdemović, convicted and sentenced to five years' imprisonment.

Sentencing Judgement, Trial Chamber I, 29 November 1996.
Judgement, Appeals Chamber, 7 October 1997.
Sentencing Judgement, Trial Chamber, 5 March 1998.

The Tadić Case (IT-94-1-T)

Duško Tadić, convicted and sentenced to 20 years' imprisonment.

Decision on the Defence Motion on the Jurisdiction of the Tribunal, Trial Chamber II, 10 August 1995
Decision on the Defence Motion for Interlocutory Appeal on Jurisdiction, Appeals Chamber, 2 October 1995.
Opinion and Judgement, Trial Chamber II, 7 May 1997.
Judgement, Appeals Chamber, 15 July 1999.
Sentencing Judgement, Trial Chamber, 11 November 1999.
Judgement in Sentencing Appeals, 26 January 2000.

The Delalić, Mucić, Delić and Landžo Case (IT-96-21-T)

Zejnil Delalić, acquitted.
Zdravko Mucić, sentenced to 7 years' imprisonment.
Hazim Delić, sentenced to 20 years' imprisonment.
Esad Landžo, sentenced to 15 years' imprisonment.
Trial Chamber *Judgement*, 16 November 1998.
Appeals Chamber *Judgement*, 20 February 2001

The Furundžija Case (IT-95-17-T)

Anto Furundžija, convicted and sentenced to 10 years' imprisonment.
Judgement, 10 December 1998.
Appeals Judgement, 21 July 2000.

The Aleksovski Case (IT-95-14/1-T)

Zlatko Aleksovski, convicted and sentenced to 2 years and 6 months' imprisonment. Sentence revised to 7 years' imprisonment by the Appeals Chamber.
Oral Judgement, 7 May 1999
Written Judgement, 25 June 1999 (including *Joint Opinion of the majority, Judge Vohrah and Judge Nieto-Navia* and *Dissenting Opinion of Judge Rodrigues*, both on the applicability of Article 2 of the Statute)
Appeals Judgement, 24 March 2000.

The Jelisić Case (IT-95-10-I)

Goran Jelisić, convicted and sentenced to 40 years' imprisonment.
Judgement, 14 December 1999
Appeals Judgement, 5 July 2001

The Kupreškić et al. Case (IT-95-16-T)

Zoran Kupreškić, convicted and sentenced to 10 years' imprisonment. Conviction quashed on appeal.
Mirjan Kupreškić, convicted and sentenced to 8 years' imprisonment. Conviction quashed on appeal.
Vlatko Kupreškić, convicted and sentenced to 6 years' imprisonment. Conviction quashed on appeal.
Drago Josipović, convicted and sentenced to 15 years' imprisonment.
Dragan Papić, acquitted.
Vladimir Šantić, convicted and sentenced to 25 years' imprisonment.
Judgement, 14 January 2000
Appeals Judgement, 23 October 2001

The Blaškić Case (IT-95-14-T)

Tihomir Blaškić convicted and sentenced to 45 years' imprisonment.
Trial Judgement, 3 March 2000.

The Kunarac, Kovac and Vuković Case (IT-96-23-I)

Dragoljub Kunarac, convicted and sentenced to 28 years' imprisonment.
Radomir Kovac, convicted and sentenced to 20 years' imprisonment.
Zoran Vuković, convicted and sentenced to 12 years' imprisonment.

Trial Judgement, 22 February 2001.
Appeal Judgement, 12 June 2002.

The Kordić and Čerkez Case (IT-95-14/2-T)

Dario Kordić, convicted and sentenced to 25 years' imprisonment.
Mario Čerkez, convicted and sentenced to 15 years' imprisonment.

Trial Judgement, 26 February 2001.

The Krstić Case (IT-98-33-T)

Radoslav Krstić, convicted and sentenced to 46 years' imprisonment.

Trial Judgement, 2 August 2001.

The Todorović Case (IT-95-9-I)

Stevan Todorović, pleaded guilty and sentenced to 10 years' imprisonment.

Sentencing Judgement, 31 July 2001.

The Simić Case (IT-95-9/2)

Milan Simić, pleaded guilty and sentenced to 5 years' imprisonment.

Sentencing Judgement, 17 October 2002-10-25

Kvočka et al. Case (IT-98-30/1)

Miroslav Kvočka, convicted and sentenced to 7 years' imprisonment.
Dragoljub Prcac, convicted and sentenced to 5 years' imprisonment.
Mlado Radic, convicted and sentenced to 20 years' imprisonment.
Zoran Zigic, convicted and sentenced to 25 years' imprisonment.
Milojica Kos, convicted and sentenced to 6 years' imprisonment.

Trial Judgement, 2 November 2001

Kronjelac Case (IT-97-25)

Milorad Krnojelac, convicted and sentenced to 7 1/2 years' imprisonment.

Trial Judgement, 15 March 2002-10-25

Sikirica and Others Case (IT-95-8)

Duško Sikirica, pleaded guilty and sentenced to 15 years' imprisonment.
Damir Dosen, pleaded guilty and sentenced to 5 years' imprisonment.
Dragan Kolundzija, pleaded guilty and sentenced to 3 years' imprisonment.

Sentencing Judgement, 13 November 2001

INTERNATIONAL CRIMINAL TRIBUNAL FOR RWANDA

Visit the ICTY website for full case details of each concluded and pending case: *www.un.org/icty*.

The Akayesu Trial (ICTR-96-4-T)

Jean-Paul Akayesu, convicted and sentenced to life imprisonment.

Judgement, 2 September 1998.
Sentencing Judgement, 2 October 1998.
Appeals Judgement, 1 June 2001

The Kambanda Case (ICTR-97-23-I)

Jean Kambanda, pleaded guilty and was sentenced to life imprisonment.

Trial Judgement and Sentence, 4 September 1998.
Appeals Judgement, 19 October 2000.

The Serushago Case (ICTR-98-39-T)

Omar Serushago, pleaded guilty and was sentenced to fifteen years' imprisonment.

Decision relating to a Plea of Guilty, 14 December 1998
Sentence, 5 February 1999
Judgement (orally rendered by the Appeals Chamber), 14 February 2000
Reasons for Judgement (Appeals Chamber), 6 April 2000.

The Kayishema (ICTR-95-1-I) and Ruzindana (ICTR-95-1-T and ICTR-96-10-T) Case

Clément Kayishema, convicted and sentenced to life imprisonment.
Obed Ruzindana, convicted and sentenced to twenty-five years' imprisonment.

Trial Judgement, 21 May 1999.
Appeal Judgement, 1 June 2001

The Rutaganda Case (ICTR-96-3-T)

Georges Anderson Nderubumwe Rutaganda, convicted and sentenced to life imprisonment.

Trial Judgement, 6 December 1999.

The Musema Case (ICTR-96-13-I)

Alfred Musema, convicted and sentenced to life imprisonment.

Judgement and Sentence, 27 January 2000.
Appeals Judgement, 16 November 2001

The Ruggiu Case (ICTR-97-32-T)

Georges Ruggiu, sentenced to 12 years' imprisonment.

Judgement and Sentence, 1 June, 2000

The Bagilishema Case (ICTR-85-1)

Ignace Bagilishema, acquitted of all counts, Prosecution appeal dismissed

Trial Judgement 7 June 2001
Appeal Judgement 3 July 2002

See also information on ICTR cases provided by the websites of the independent press agency Hirondelle Foundation (*www.hirondelle.org*) and Ubutabera (*www.inter-media.org*)

THE SPECIAL PANEL FOR SERIOUS CRIMES IN EAST TIMOR

Introduction

1. For a historical background and introduction to this panel, see above, 1.142.
2. The Special Panel for the trial of Serious Crimes started with the hearing of some cases at the beginning of January 2001. It is working as a domestic tribunal with the standards, requirements and expectations of an international tribunal, since it is exercising jurisdiction for crimes against international law.
3. During the period, 1 January 2001–1 October 2002, the Special Panel rendered twenty-four judgements.
4. These judgements were rendered in the cases of *The Public Prosecutor* (here after "The Prosecutor") *v. Joao Fernandez, The Prosecutor v. Julio Fernandez, The Prosecutor v. Carlos Soares Carmona, The Prosecutor v. Joseph Leki, The Prosecutor v. Romerio Tilman, The Prosecutor v. Benjamin Sarmento, The Prosecutor v. Augustino da Costa, The Prosecutor v. Mateus Tilman, The Prosecutor v. Joni Marques and 9 others, The Prosecutor v. Manuel Gonzales Leto Bere, The Prosecutor v. Leonardus Kasa, The Prosecutor v. Carlos Suares, The Prosecutor v. Fransisco Pedro alias Geger, The Prosecutor v. Augusto Asameta Tavares, The Prosecutor v. Jose Valente, The Prosecutor v. Fransisco do Santos Laku alias Fransisco Lalu, The Prosecutor v. Cipriano da Costa, The Prosecutor v. Sergio da Costa, The Prosecutor v. Anigio Oliveira, The prosecutor v. Marcurious Jose De Deus* and *The Prosecutor v. Augusto do Santos*.
5. During this period, the Special Panel held 35 preliminary hearings, 32 trial hearings and 67 hearings to rule on pre-trial detention.

Judgements Rendered by the Special Panel

6. **The Prosecutor v. Joao Fernandez** (case n° 01/pid.c.g./2000). On 25 January 2001, the Special Panel rendered its Judgement in the above case. Joao Fernandez, also known as Joao Atabe, member of Dadarus Merah Militia, was convicted of murder, as stipulated in Section 8 of UNTAET Regulation N° 2000/15 and Article 340 of the Penal Code of Indonesia and sentenced to an imprisonment of 12 years. He has since filed an appeal against the judgement. The Court of Appeal confirmed the decision of the first instance with respect to the conviction and the sentence, except for the part relating to the payment of expenses.
7. **The Prosecutor v. Julio Fernandez** (case n°02/pid.c.g./2000). On 1 March 2001, the Special Panel rendered its Judgement in the above case. Julio Fernandez, a Falintil member, was convicted of murder, as stipulated in Section 8 of UNTAET Regulation N° 2000/15 and Article 340 of the Penal Code of Indonesia and sentenced to an imprisonment of 7 years. He has since filed an appeal against the judgement and the appeal Court has already decided the case. The appellant was convicted of homicide, as stipulated in article 338 of Indonesian Penal Code, and sentenced to 5 years of imprisonment.
8. **The Prosecutor v. Carlos Soares Carmona** (case n° 03/pid.c.g./2000). On 8 March 2001, the Special Panel rendered its Judgement in the above case. Carlos Soares Carmona, was convicted of murder, as stipulated in Section 8 of UNTAET Regulation N° 2000/15 and Article 340 of the Penal Code of Indonesia and sentenced to an imprisonment of 11 years. The Court of Appeal modified the decision of the Special panel. The appellant was

convicted of homicide, as stipulated in article 338 of Indonesian Penal Code, and sentenced to 8 years of imprisonment.
9. **The Prosecutor v. Joseph Leki** (case n° 05/pid.c.g./2000). On 8 June 2001, the Special Panel rendered its Judgement in the above case. Joseph Leki, was convicted of murder, as stipulated in Section 8 of UNTAET Regulation N° 2000/15 and Article 340 of the Penal Code of Indonesia and sentenced to imprisonment for 13 years.
10. **The Prosecutor v. Romerio Tilman** (case n° 04/pid.c.g./2000). On 5 July 2001, the Special Panel rendered its decision to admit the withdrawal of the indictment in the above case. The indictment was withdrawn after the submission of the case no 18/2002.
11. **The Prosecutor v. Benjamin Sarmento** (case n° 06/pid.c.g./2000). On 22 May 2001, the Special Panel gave leave to The Prosecutor to withdraw the indictment after the submission of the case n° 18/2002 in which the accused is indicted for the same facts.
12. **The Prosecutor v. Augustino da Costa** (case n° 07/pid.c.g./2000). On 11 October 2001, the Special Panel rendered its Judgement in the above case. Augustino da Costa was convicted of murder, as stipulated in Section 8 of UNTAET Regulation N° 2000/15 and Article 340 of the Penal Code of Indonesia and sentenced to imprisonment for 15 years.
13. **The Prosecutor v. Mateus Tilman** (case n° 08/pid.c.g./2000). On 24 August 2001, the Special Panel rendered its Judgement in the above case. Mateus Tilman, was convicted of attempted murder, as stipulated in Section 8 of UNTAET Regulation N° 2000/15 and Articles 53 and 340 of the Penal Code of Indonesia and sentenced to imprisonment for 4 years.
14. **The Prosecutor v. Joni Marques, Manuel da Costa, Joao da Costa alias Lemourai, Paulo da Costa, Amelio da Costa, Hilario da Silva, Gonsalo do Santos, Alarico Fernandes, Mautersa Monis and Gilberto Fernandes** (case n° 09/pid.c.g./2000). On 11 December 2001, the Special Panel rendered its Judgement in the above case. The accused were convicted of murder and torture as crimes against humanity, and or deportation or forcible transfer of civilian population and persecution as crimes against humanity, as stipulated in Section 5.1(a), (f), (d) and (h) of UNTAET Regulation N° 2000/15. They were sentenced to various lengthy terms of imprisonment, Joni Marques (33 years and 4 months), Manuel da Costa (19 years), Joao da Costa alias Lemourai (33 years and 4 months), Paulo da Costa (33 years and 4 months), Amelio da Costa (18 years), Hilario da Silva (17 years), Gonsalo do Santos (23 years), Alarico Fernandes (4 years), Mautersa Monis (4 years), and Gilberto Fernandes (5 years).
15. **The Prosecutor v. Manuel Gonzales Leto Bere** (case n°10/pid.c.g./2000). On 15 May 2001, the Special Panel rendered its Judgement in the above case. Manuel Gonzales Leto Bere was convicted of murder, as stipulated in Section 8 of UNTAET Regulation N° 2000/15 and Article 340 of the Penal Code of Indonesia and sentenced to imprisonment for 14 years.
16. **The Prosecutor v. Leornardus Kasa** (case n° 02/pid.c.g./2000). On 9 May 2001, the Special Panel rendered its decision of lack of jurisdiction in the above case.
17. **The Prosecutor v. Carlos Suares** (case n° 12/pid.c.g./2000). On 31 May 2001, the Special Panel rendered its Judgement in the above case. Carlos Suares, was convicted of murder, as stipulated in Section 8 of UNTAET Regulation N° 2000/15 and Article 340 of the Penal Code of Indonesia and sentenced to imprisonment for 15 years and 6 months.
18. **The Prosecutor v. Francisco Pedro alias Geger** (case n°01/pid.c.g./2001). On 23 May 2001, the Special Panel rendered its Judgement in the above case. The indictment was dismissed.
19. **The Prosecutor v. Augusto Asameta Tavares** (case n°02/pid.c.g./2002). On 28 September 2001, the Special Panel rendered its Judgement in the above case. Augusto Asameta Tavares, was convicted of murder, as stipulated in Section 8 of UNTAET Regulation N° 2000/15 and Article 340 of the Penal Code of Indonesia and sentenced to imprisonment for 16 years.
20. **The Prosecutor v. Jose Valente** (case n° 03/pid.c.g./2001). On 19 June 2001, the Special Panel rendered its Judgement in the above case. Jose Valente, was convicted of murder, as stipulated in Section 8 of UNTAET Regulation N° 2000/15 and Article 340 of the Penal

Code of Indonesia and sentenced to imprisonment for 12 years.
21. **The Prosecutor v. Fransisco do Santos Laku alias Fransisco Lalu** (case n° 08/pid.c.g./2001). On 27 July 2001, the Special Panel rendered its Judgement in the above case. Fransisco do Santos Laku alias Fransisco Lalu, was convicted of murder, as stipulated in Section 8 of UNTAET Regulation N° 2000/15 and Article 340 of the Penal Code of Indonesia and sentenced to imprisonment for 8 years.
22. **The Prosecutor v. Cipriano Da Costa** (case n° 17/pid.c.g./2001). On 21 January 2002, the Special Panel rendered its decision to permit the withdrawal of the indictment in the above case.
23. **The Prosecutor v. Sergio da Costa** (case n° 12/pid.c.g./2001). On 25 March 2002, the Special Panel rendered its decision to permit the withdrawal of the indictment in the above case.
24. **The Prosecutor v. Anigio de Oliveira** (case n° 07/pid.c.g./2001). On 27 March 2002, the Special Panel rendered its Judgement in the above case. Anigio de Oliveira, was convicted of homicide, as stipulated in Article 338 of the Penal Code of Indonesia and sentenced to imprisonment for 4 years.
25. **The Prosecutor v. Marcurious Jose De Deus** (case n°013/pid.c.g./2001). On 18 April 2002, the Special Panel rendered its Judgement in the above case. Marcurious Jose De Deus was convicted of murder, as stipulated in Section 8 of UNTAET Regulation N° 2000/15 and Article 340 of the Penal Code of Indonesia and sentenced to imprisonment for 5 years.
26. **The Prosecutor v. Augusto do Santos** (case n° 06/pid.c.g./2001). On 30 April 2002, the Special Panel rendered its Judgement in the above case. Augusto do Santos was convicted of murder, as stipulated in Section 8 of UNTAET Regulation N° 2000/15 and Article 340 of the Penal Code of Indonesia and sentenced to imprisonment for 5 years.
27. **The Prosecutor v. Gaspard Leki** (case n° 05/2001)
28. **The Prosecutor v. Fransisco Soares** (case n° 14/2001)
29. **The Prosecutor v. Armando do Santos** (case n° 15/2001)
30. **The Prosecutor v. Antonio Lemos** (case n° 16/2001)
31. These last four cases are pending.
32. **The Prosecutor v. Joao Franca da Silva**, alias Jhoni Franca (cae no. 04a/2001). The Special Panel rendered its Judgement on 5 December 2002. The Judgement deals, inter alia, with the definition of torture as a crime against humanity (at para. 140). The Judgement is available at www.intcrimpractice.com. The accused was convicted of imprisonment and torture as crimes against humanity, and sentenced to 5 years' imprisonment.

ANNEX 2

ROME STATUTE FOR AN ICC

PREAMBLE

The States Parties to this Statute,

Conscious that all peoples are united by common bonds, their cultures pieced together in a shared heritage, and concerned that this delicate mosaic may be shattered at any time,

Mindful that during this century millions of children, women and men have been victims of unimaginable atrocities that deeply shock the conscience of humanity,

Recognizing that such grave crimes threaten the peace, security and well-being of the world,

Affirming that the most serious crimes of concern to the international community as a whole must not go unpunished and that their effective prosecution must be ensured by taking measures at the national level and by enhancing international cooperation,

Determined to put an end to impunity for the perpetrators of these crimes and thus to contribute to the prevention of such crimes,

Recalling that it is the duty of every State to exercise its criminal jurisdiction over those responsible for international crimes,

Reaffirming the Purposes and Principles of the Charter of the United Nations, and in particular that all States shall refrain from the threat or use of force against the territorial integrity or political independence of any State, or in any other manner inconsistent with the Purposes of the United Nations,

Emphasizing in this connection that nothing in this Statute shall be taken as authorizing any State Party to intervene in an armed conflict or in the internal affairs of any State,

Determined to these ends and for the sake of present and future generations, to establish an independent permanent International Criminal Court in relationship with the United Nations system, with jurisdiction over the most serious crimes of concern to the international community as a whole,

Emphasizing that the International Criminal Court established under this Statute shall be complementary to national criminal jurisdictions,

Resolved to guarantee lasting respect for and the enforcement of international justice,

Have agreed as follows

PART 1. ESTABLISHMENT OF THE COURT
Article 1
The Court

An International Criminal Court ("the Court") is hereby established. It shall be a permanent institution and shall have the power to exercise its jurisdiction over persons for the most serious crimes of international concern, as referred to in this Statute, and shall be complementary to national criminal jurisdictions. The jurisdiction and functioning of the Court shall be governed by the provisions of this Statute.

Article 2
Relationship of the Court with the United Nations

The Court shall be brought into relationship with the United Nations through an agreement to be approved by the Assembly of States Parties to this Statute and thereafter concluded by the President of the Court on its behalf.

Article 3
Seat of the Court

1. The seat of the Court shall be established at The Hague in the Netherlands ("the host State").
2. The Court shall enter into a headquarters agreement with the host State, to be approved by the Assembly of States Parties and thereafter concluded by the President of the Court on its behalf.
3. The Court may sit elsewhere, whenever it considers it desirable, as provided in this Statute.

Article 4
Legal status and powers of the Court

1. The Court shall have international legal personality. It shall also have such legal capacity as may be necessary for the exercise of its functions and the fulfilment of its purposes.
2. The Court may exercise its functions and powers, as provided in this Statute, on the territory of any State Party and, by special agreement, on the territory of any other State.

PART 2. JURISDICTION, ADMISSIBILITY AND APPLICABLE LAW

Article 5
Crimes within the jurisdiction of the Court

1. The jurisdiction of the Court shall be limited to the most serious crimes of concern to the international community as a whole. The Court has jurisdiction in accordance with this Statute with respect to the following crimes:
   (a) The crime of genocide;
   (b) Crimes against humanity;
   (c) War crimes;
   (d) The crime of aggression.
2. The Court shall exercise jurisdiction over the crime of aggression once a provision is adopted in accordance with articles 121 and 123 defining the crime and setting out the conditions under which the Court shall exercise jurisdiction with respect to this crime. Such a provision shall be consistent with the relevant provisions of the Charter of the United Nations.

Article 6
Genocide

For the purpose of this Statute, "genocide" means any of the following acts committed with intent to destroy, in whole or in part, a national, ethnical, racial or religious group, as such:
   (a) Killing members of the group;
   (b) Causing serious bodily or mental harm to members of the group;

(c) Deliberately inflicting on the group conditions of life calculated to bring about its physical destruction in whole or in part;
(d) Imposing measures intended to prevent births within the group;
(e) Forcibly transferring children of the group to another group.

Article 7
Crimes against humanity

1. For the purpose of this Statute, "crime against humanity" means any of the following acts when committed as part of a widespread or systematic attack directed against any civilian population, with knowledge of the attack:
   (a) Murder;
   (b) Extermination;
   (c) Enslavement;
   (d) Deportation or forcible transfer of population;
   (e) Imprisonment or other severe deprivation of physical liberty in violation of fundamental rules of international law;
   (f) Torture;
   (g) Rape, sexual slavery, enforced prostitution, forced pregnancy, enforced sterilization, or any other form of sexual violence of comparable gravity;
   (h) Persecution against any identifiable group or collectivity on political, racial, national, ethnic, cultural, religious, gender as defined in paragraph 3, or other grounds that are universally recognized as impermissible under international law, in connection with any act referred to in this paragraph or any crime within the jurisdiction of the Court;
   (i) Enforced disappearance of persons;
   (j) The crime of apartheid;
   (k) Other inhumane acts of a similar character intentionally causing great suffering, or serious injury to body or to mental or physical health.
2. For the purpose of paragraph 1:
   (a) "Attack directed against any civilian population" means a course of conduct involving the multiple commission of acts referred to in paragraph 1 against any civilian population, pursuant to or in furtherance of a State or organizational policy to commit such attack;
   (b) "Extermination" includes the intentional infliction of conditions of life, *inter alia* the deprivation of access to food and medicine, calculated to bring about the destruction of part of a population;
   (c) "Enslavement" means the exercise of any or all of the powers attaching to the right of ownership over a person and includes the exercise of such power in the course of trafficking in persons, in particular women and children;
   (d) "Deportation or forcible transfer of population" means forced displacement of the persons concerned by expulsion or other coercive acts from the area in which they are lawfully present, without grounds permitted under international law;
   (e) "Torture" means the intentional infliction of severe pain or suffering, whether physical or mental, upon a person in the custody or under the control of the accused; except that torture shall not include pain or suffering arising only from, inherent in or incidental to, lawful sanctions;
   (f) "Forced pregnancy" means the unlawful confinement of a woman forcibly made pregnant, with the intent of affecting the ethnic composition of any population or carrying out other grave violations of international law. This definition shall not in any way be interpreted as affecting national laws relating to pregnancy;
   (g) "Persecution" means the intentional and severe deprivation of fundamental rights contrary to international law by reason of the identity of the group or collectivity;

(h) "The crime of apartheid" means inhumane acts of a character similar to those referred to in paragraph 1, committed in the context of an institutionalized regime of systematic oppression and domination by one racial group over any other racial group or groups and committed with the intention of maintaining that regime;
(i) "Enforced disappearance of persons" means the arrest, detention or abduction of persons by, or with the authorization, support or acquiescence of, a State or a political organization, followed by a refusal to acknowledge that deprivation of freedom or to give information on the fate or whereabouts of those persons, with the intention of removing them from the protection of the law for a prolonged period of time.

3. For the purpose of this Statute, it is understood that the term "gender" refers to the two sexes, male and female, within the context of society. The term "gender" does not indicate any meaning different from the above.

Article 8
War crimes

1. The Court shall have jurisdiction in respect of war crimes in particular when committed as part of a plan or policy or as part of a large-scale commission of such crimes.
2. For the purpose of this Statute, "war crimes" means:
   (a) Grave breaches of the Geneva Conventions of 12 August 1949, namely, any of the following acts against persons or property protected under the provisions of the relevant Geneva Convention:
       (i) Wilful killing;
       (ii) Torture or inhuman treatment, including biological experiments;
       (iii) Wilfully causing great suffering, or serious injury to body or health;
       (iv) Extensive destruction and appropriation of property, not justified by military necessity and carried out unlawfully and wantonly;
       (v) Compelling a prisoner of war or other protected person to serve in the forces of a hostile Power;
       (vi) Wilfully depriving a prisoner of war or other protected person of the rights of fair and regular trial;
       (vii) Unlawful deportation or transfer or unlawful confinement;
       (viii) Taking of hostages.
   (b) Other serious violations of the laws and customs applicable in international armed conflict, within the established framework of international law, namely, any of the following acts:
       (i) Intentionally directing attacks against the civilian population as such or against individual civilians not taking direct part in hostilities;
       (ii) Intentionally directing attacks against civilian objects, that is, objects which are not military objectives;
       (iii) Intentionally directing attacks against personnel, installations, material, units or vehicles involved in a humanitarian assistance or peacekeeping mission in accordance with the Charter of the United Nations, as long as they are entitled to the protection given to civilians or civilian objects under the international law of armed conflict;
       (iv) Intentionally launching an attack in the knowledge that such attack will cause incidental loss of life or injury to civilians or damage to civilian objects or widespread, long-term and severe damage to the natural environment which would be clearly excessive in relation to the concrete and direct overall military advantage anticipated;
       (v) Attacking or bombarding, by whatever means, towns, villages, dwellings or buildings which are undefended and which are not military objectives;

(vi) Killing or wounding a combatant who, having laid down his arms or having no longer means of defence, has surrendered at discretion;
(vii) Making improper use of a flag of truce, of the flag or of the military insignia and uniform of the enemy or of the United Nations, as well as of the distinctive emblems of the Geneva Conventions, resulting in death or serious personal injury;
(viii) The transfer, directly or indirectly, by the Occupying Power of parts of its own civilian population into the territory it occupies, or the deportation or transfer of all or parts of the population of the occupied territory within or outside this territory;
(ix) Intentionally directing attacks against buildings dedicated to religion, education, art, science or charitable purposes, historic monuments, hospitals and places where the sick and wounded are collected, provided they are not military objectives;
(x) Subjecting persons who are in the power of an adverse party to physical mutilation or to medical or scientific experiments of any kind which are neither justified by the medical, dental or hospital treatment of the person concerned nor carried out in his or her interest, and which cause death to or seriously endanger the health of such person or persons;
(xi) Killing or wounding treacherously individuals belonging to the hostile nation or army;
(xii) Declaring that no quarter will be given;
(xiii) Destroying or seizing the enemy's property unless such destruction or seizure be imperatively demanded by the necessities of war;
(xiv) Declaring abolished, suspended or inadmissible in a court of law the rights and actions of the nationals of the hostile party;
(xv) Compelling the nationals of the hostile party to take part in the operations of war directed against their own country, even if they were in the belligerent's service before the commencement of the war;
(xvi) Pillaging a town or place, even when taken by assault;
(xvii) Employing poison or poisoned weapons;
(xviii) Employing asphyxiating, poisonous or other gases, and all analogous liquids, materials or devices;
(xix) Employing bullets which expand or flatten easily in the human body, such as bullets with a hard envelope which does not entirely cover the core or is pierced with incisions;
(xx) Employing weapons, projectiles and material and methods of warfare which are of a nature to cause superfluous injury or unnecessary suffering or which are inherently indiscriminate in violation of the international law of armed conflict, provided that such weapons, projectiles and material and methods of warfare are the subject of a comprehensive prohibition and are included in an annex to this Statute, by an amendment in accordance with the relevant provisions set forth in articles 121 and 123;
(xxi) Committing outrages upon personal dignity, in particular humiliating and degrading treatment;
(xxii) Committing rape, sexual slavery, enforced prostitution, forced pregnancy, as defined in article 7, paragraph 2 (f), enforced sterilization, or any other form of sexual violence also constituting a grave breach of the Geneva Conventions;
(xxiii) Utilizing the presence of a civilian or other protected person to render certain points, areas or military forces immune from military operations;
(xxiv) Intentionally directing attacks against buildings, material, medical units and transport, and personnel using the distinctive emblems of the Geneva Conventions in conformity with international law;

- (xxv) Intentionally using starvation of civilians as a method of warfare by depriving them of objects indispensable to their survival, including wilfully impeding relief supplies as provided for under the Geneva Conventions;
- (xxvi) Conscripting or enlisting children under the age of fifteen years into the national armed forces or using them to participate actively in hostilities.

(c) In the case of an armed conflict not of an international character, serious violations of article 3 common to the four Geneva Conventions of 12 August 1949, namely, any of the following acts committed against persons taking no active part in the hostilities, including members of armed forces who have laid down their arms and those placed *hors de combat* by sickness, wounds, detention or any other cause:
- (i) Violence to life and person, in particular murder of all kinds, mutilation, cruel treatment and torture;
- (ii) Committing outrages upon personal dignity, in particular humiliating and degrading treatment;
- (iii) Taking of hostages;
- (iv) The passing of sentences and the carrying out of executions without previous judgement pronounced by a regularly constituted court, affording all judicial guarantees which are generally recognized as indispensable.

(d) Paragraph 2 (c) applies to armed conflicts not of an international character and thus does not apply to situations of internal disturbances and tensions, such as riots, isolated and sporadic acts of violence or other acts of a similar nature.

(e) Other serious violations of the laws and customs applicable in armed conflicts not of an international character, within the established framework of international law, namely, any of the following acts:
- (i) Intentionally directing attacks against the civilian population as such or against individual civilians not taking direct part in hostilities;
- (ii) Intentionally directing attacks against buildings, material, medical units and transport, and personnel using the distinctive emblems of the Geneva Conventions in conformity with international law;
- (iii) Intentionally directing attacks against personnel, installations, material, units or vehicles involved in a humanitarian assistance or peacekeeping mission in accordance with the Charter of the United Nations, as long as they are entitled to the protection given to civilians or civilian objects under the international law of armed conflict;
- (iv) Intentionally directing attacks against buildings dedicated to religion, education, art, science or charitable purposes, historic monuments, hospitals and places where the sick and wounded are collected, provided they are not military objectives;
- (v) Pillaging a town or place, even when taken by assault;
- (vi) Committing rape, sexual slavery, enforced prostitution, forced pregnancy, as defined in article 7, paragraph 2 (f), enforced sterilization, and any other form of sexual violence also constituting a serious violation of article 3 common to the four Geneva Conventions;
- (vii) Conscripting or enlisting children under the age of fifteen years into armed forces or groups or using them to participate actively in hostilities;
- (viii) Ordering the displacement of the civilian population for reasons related to the conflict, unless the security of the civilians involved or imperative military reasons so demand;
- (ix) Killing or wounding treacherously a combatant adversary;
- (x) Declaring that no quarter will be given;
- (xi) Subjecting persons who are in the power of another party to the conflict to physical mutilation or to medical or scientific experiments of any kind which

    are neither justified by the medical, dental or hospital treatment of the person concerned nor carried out in his or her interest, and which cause death to or seriously endanger the health of such person or persons;
  (xii) Destroying or seizing the property of an adversary unless such destruction or seizure be imperatively demanded by the necessities of the conflict;
 (f) Paragraph 2 (e) applies to armed conflicts not of an international character and thus does not apply to situations of internal disturbances and tensions, such as riots, isolated and sporadic acts of violence or other acts of a similar nature. It applies to armed conflicts that take place in the territory of a State when there is protracted armed conflict between governmental authorities and organized armed groups or between such groups.

3. Nothing in paragraph 2 (c) and (e) shall affect the responsibility of a Government to maintain or re-establish law and order in the State or to defend the unity and territorial integrity of the State, by all legitimate means.

Article 9
Elements of Crimes

1. Elements of Crimes shall assist the Court in the interpretation and application of articles 6, 7 and 8. They shall be adopted by a two-thirds majority of the members of the Assembly of States Parties.
2. Amendments to the Elements of Crimes may be proposed by:
   (a) Any State Party;
   (b) The judges acting by an absolute majority;
   (c) The Prosecutor.

   Such amendments shall be adopted by a two-thirds majority of the members of the Assembly of States Parties.
3. The Elements of Crimes and amendments thereto shall be consistent with this Statute.

Article 10

Nothing in this Part shall be interpreted as limiting or prejudicing in any way existing or developing rules of international law for purposes other than this Statute.

Article 11
Jurisdiction ratione temporis

1. The Court has jurisdiction only with respect to crimes committed after the entry into force of this Statute.
2. If a State becomes a Party to this Statute after its entry into force, the Court may exercise its jurisdiction only with respect to crimes committed after the entry into force of this Statute for that State, unless that State has made a declaration under article 12, paragraph 3.

Article 12
Preconditions to the exercise of jurisdiction

1. A State which becomes a Party to this Statute thereby accepts the jurisdiction of the Court with respect to the crimes referred to in article 5.
2. In the case of article 13, paragraph (a) or (c), the Court may exercise its jurisdiction if one or more of the following States are Parties to this Statute or have accepted the jurisdiction of the Court in accordance with paragraph 3:
   (a) The State on the territory of which the conduct in question occurred or, if the crime was committed on board a vessel or aircraft, the State of registration of that vessel or aircraft;
   (b) The State of which the person accused of the crime is a national.

3. If the acceptance of a State which is not a Party to this Statute is required under paragraph 2, that State may, by declaration lodged with the Registrar, accept the exercise of jurisdiction by the Court with respect to the crime in question. The accepting State shall cooperate with the Court without any delay or exception in accordance with Part 9.

Article 13
Exercise of jurisdiction

The Court may exercise its jurisdiction with respect to a crime referred to in article 5 in accordance with the provisions of this Statute if:
    (a) A situation in which one or more of such crimes appears to have been committed is referred to the Prosecutor by a State Party in accordance with article 14;
    (b) A situation in which one or more of such crimes appears to have been committed is referred to the Prosecutor by the Security Council acting under Chapter VII of the Charter of the United Nations; or
    (c) The Prosecutor has initiated an investigation in respect of such a crime in accordance with article 15.

Article 14
Referral of a situation by a State Party

1. A State Party may refer to the Prosecutor a situation in which one or more crimes within the jurisdiction of the Court appear to have been committed requesting the Prosecutor to investigate the situation for the purpose of determining whether one or more specific persons should be charged with the commission of such crimes.
2. As far as possible, a referral shall specify the relevant circumstances and be accompanied by such supporting documentation as is available to the State referring the situation.

Article 15
Prosecutor

1. The Prosecutor may initiate investigations *proprio motu* on the basis of information on crimes within the jurisdiction of the Court.
2. The Prosecutor shall analyse the seriousness of the information received. For this purpose, he or she may seek additional information from States, organs of the United Nations, intergovernmental or non-governmental organizations, or other reliable sources that he or she deems appropriate, and may receive written or oral testimony at the seat of the Court.
3. If the Prosecutor concludes that there is a reasonable basis to proceed with an investigation, he or she shall submit to the Pre-Trial Chamber a request for authorization of an investigation, together with any supporting material collected. Victims may make representations to the Pre-Trial Chamber, in accordance with the Rules of Procedure and Evidence.
4. If the Pre-Trial Chamber, upon examination of the request and the supporting material, considers that there is a reasonable basis to proceed with an investigation, and that the case appears to fall within the jurisdiction of the Court, it shall authorize the commencement of the investigation, without prejudice to subsequent determinations by the Court with regard to the jurisdiction and admissibility of a case.
5. The refusal of the Pre-Trial Chamber to authorize the investigation shall not preclude the presentation of a subsequent request by the Prosecutor based on new facts or evidence regarding the same situation.
6. If, after the preliminary examination referred to in paragraphs 1 and 2, the Prosecutor concludes that the information provided does not constitute a reasonable basis for an investigation, he or she shall inform those who provided the information. This shall not preclude

the Prosecutor from considering further information submitted to him or her regarding the same situation in the light of new facts or evidence.

Article 16
Deferral of investigation or prosecution

No investigation or prosecution may be commenced or proceeded with under this Statute for a period of 12 months after the Security Council, in a resolution adopted under Chapter VII of the Charter of the United Nations, has requested the Court to that effect; that request may be renewed by the Council under the same conditions.

Article 17
Issues of admissibility

1. Having regard to paragraph 10 of the Preamble and article 1, the Court shall determine that a case is inadmissible where:
   (a) The case is being investigated or prosecuted by a State which has jurisdiction over it, unless the State is unwilling or unable genuinely to carry out the investigation or prosecution;
   (b) The case has been investigated by a State which has jurisdiction over it and the State has decided not to prosecute the person concerned, unless the decision resulted from the unwillingness or inability of the State genuinely to prosecute;
   (c) The person concerned has already been tried for conduct which is the subject of the complaint, and a trial by the Court is not permitted under article 20, paragraph 3;
   (d) The case is not of sufficient gravity to justify further action by the Court.
2. In order to determine unwillingness in a particular case, the Court shall consider, having regard to the principles of due process recognized by international law, whether one or more of the following exist, as applicable:
   (a) The proceedings were or are being undertaken or the national decision was made for the purpose of shielding the person concerned from criminal responsibility for crimes within the jurisdiction of the Court referred to in article 5;
   (b) There has been an unjustified delay in the proceedings which in the circumstances is inconsistent with an intent to bring the person concerned to justice;
   (c) The proceedings were not or are not being conducted independently or impartially, and they were or are being conducted in a manner which, in the circumstances, is inconsistent with an intent to bring the person concerned to justice.
3. In order to determine inability in a particular case, the Court shall consider whether, due to a total or substantial collapse or unavailability of its national judicial system, the State is unable to obtain the accused or the necessary evidence and testimony or otherwise unable to carry out its proceedings.

Article 18
Preliminary rulings regarding admissibility

1. When a situation has been referred to the Court pursuant to article 13 (a) and the Prosecutor has determined that there would be a reasonable basis to commence an investigation, or the Prosecutor initiates an investigation pursuant to articles 13 (c) and 15, the Prosecutor shall notify all States Parties and those States which, taking into account the information available, would normally exercise jurisdiction over the crimes concerned. The Prosecutor may notify such States on a confidential basis and, where the Prosecutor believes it necessary to protect persons, prevent destruction of evidence or prevent the absconding of persons, may limit the scope of the information provided to States.

2. Within one month of receipt of that notification, a State may inform the Court that it is investigating or has investigated its nationals or others within its jurisdiction with respect to criminal acts which may constitute crimes referred to in article 5 and which relate to the information provided in the notification to States. At the request of that State, the Prosecutor shall defer to the State's investigation of those persons unless the Pre-Trial Chamber, on the application of the Prosecutor, decides to authorize the investigation.
3. The Prosecutor's deferral to a State's investigation shall be open to review by the Prosecutor six months after the date of deferral or at any time when there has been a significant change of circumstances based on the State's unwillingness or inability genuinely to carry out the investigation.
4. The State concerned or the Prosecutor may appeal to the Appeals Chamber against a ruling of the Pre-Trial Chamber, in accordance with article 82. The appeal may be heard on an expedited basis.
5. When the Prosecutor has deferred an investigation in accordance with paragraph 2, the Prosecutor may request that the State concerned periodically inform the Prosecutor of the progress of its investigations and any subsequent prosecutions. States Parties shall respond to such requests without undue delay.
6. Pending a ruling by the Pre-Trial Chamber, or at any time when the Prosecutor has deferred an investigation under this article, the Prosecutor may, on an exceptional basis, seek authority from the Pre-Trial Chamber to pursue necessary investigative steps for the purpose of preserving evidence where there is a unique opportunity to obtain important evidence or there is a significant risk that such evidence may not be subsequently available.
7. A State which has challenged a ruling of the Pre-Trial Chamber under this article may challenge the admissibility of a case under article 19 on the grounds of additional significant facts or significant change of circumstances.

Article 19
Challenges to the jurisdiction of the Court or the admissibility of a case

1. The Court shall satisfy itself that it has jurisdiction in any case brought before it. The Court may, on its own motion, determine the admissibility of a case in accordance with article 17.
2. Challenges to the admissibility of a case on the grounds referred to in article 17 or challenges to the jurisdiction of the Court may be made by:
    (a) An accused or a person for whom a warrant of arrest or a summons to appear has been issued under article 58;
    (b) A State which has jurisdiction over a case, on the ground that it is investigating or prosecuting the case or has investigated or prosecuted; or
    (c) A State from which acceptance of jurisdiction is required under article 12.
3. The Prosecutor may seek a ruling from the Court regarding a question of jurisdiction or admissibility. In proceedings with respect to jurisdiction or admissibility, those who have referred the situation under article 13, as well as victims, may also submit observations to the Court.
4. The admissibility of a case or the jurisdiction of the Court may be challenged only once by any person or State referred to in paragraph 2. The challenge shall take place prior to or at the commencement of the trial. In exceptional circumstances, the Court may grant leave for a challenge to be brought more than once or at a time later than the commencement of the trial. Challenges to the admissibility of a case, at the commencement of a trial, or subsequently with the leave of the Court, may be based only on article 17, paragraph 1 (c).
5. A State referred to in paragraph 2 (b) and (c) shall make a challenge at the earliest opportunity.
6. Prior to the confirmation of the charges, challenges to the admissibility of a case or challenges to the jurisdiction of the Court shall be referred to the Pre-Trial Chamber. After con-

firmation of the charges, they shall be referred to the Trial Chamber. Decisions with respect to jurisdiction or admissibility may be appealed to the Appeals Chamber in accordance with article 82.
7. If a challenge is made by a State referred to in paragraph 2 (b) or (c), the Prosecutor shall suspend the investigation until such time as the Court makes a determination in accordance with article 17.
8. Pending a ruling by the Court, the Prosecutor may seek authority from the Court:
   (a) To pursue necessary investigative steps of the kind referred to in article 18, paragraph 6;
   (b) To take a statement or testimony from a witness or complete the collection and examination of evidence which had begun prior to the making of the challenge; and
   (c) In cooperation with the relevant States, to prevent the absconding of persons in respect of whom the Prosecutor has already requested a warrant of arrest under article 58.
9. The making of a challenge shall not affect the validity of any act performed by the Prosecutor or any order or warrant issued by the Court prior to the making of the challenge.
10. If the Court has decided that a case is inadmissible under article 17, the Prosecutor may submit a request for a review of the decision when he or she is fully satisfied that new facts have arisen which negate the basis on which the case had previously been found inadmissible under article 17.
11. If the Prosecutor, having regard to the matters referred to in article 17, defers an investigation, the Prosecutor may request that the relevant State make available to the Prosecutor information on the proceedings. That information shall, at the request of the State concerned, be confidential. If the Prosecutor thereafter decides to proceed with an investigation, he or she shall notify the State to which deferral of the proceedings has taken place.

Article 20
Ne bis in idem

1. Except as provided in this Statute, no person shall be tried before the Court with respect to conduct which formed the basis of crimes for which the person has been convicted or acquitted by the Court.
2. No person shall be tried by another court for a crime referred to in article 5 for which that person has already been convicted or acquitted by the Court.
3. No person who has been tried by another court for conduct also proscribed under article 6, 7 or 8 shall be tried by the Court with respect to the same conduct unless the proceedings in the other court:
   (a) Were for the purpose of shielding the person concerned from criminal responsibility for crimes within the jurisdiction of the Court; or
   (b) Otherwise were not conducted independently or impartially in accordance with the norms of due process recognized by international law and were conducted in a manner which, in the circumstances, was inconsistent with an intent to bring the person concerned to justice.

Article 21
Applicable law

1. The Court shall apply:
   (a) In the first place, this Statute, Elements of Crimes and its Rules of Procedure and Evidence;
   (b) In the second place, where appropriate, applicable treaties and the principles and rules of international law, including the established principles of the international law of armed conflict;

(c) Failing that, general principles of law derived by the Court from national laws of legal systems of the world including, as appropriate, the national laws of States that would normally exercise jurisdiction over the crime, provided that those principles are not inconsistent with this Statute and with international law and internationally recognized norms and standards.
2. The Court may apply principles and rules of law as interpreted in its previous decisions.
3. The application and interpretation of law pursuant to this article must be consistent with internationally recognized human rights, and be without any adverse distinction founded on grounds such as gender as defined in article 7, paragraph 3, age, race, colour, language, religion or belief, political or other opinion, national, ethnic or social origin, wealth, birth or other status.

PART 3. GENERAL PRINCIPLES OF CRIMINAL LAW
Article 22
Nullum crimen sine lege

1. A person shall not be criminally responsible under this Statute unless the conduct in question constitutes, at the time it takes place, a crime within the jurisdiction of the Court.
2. The definition of a crime shall be strictly construed and shall not be extended by analogy. In case of ambiguity, the definition shall be interpreted in favour of the person being investigated, prosecuted or convicted.
3. This article shall not affect the characterization of any conduct as criminal under international law independently of this Statute.

Article 23
Nulla poena sine lege

A person convicted by the Court may be punished only in accordance with this Statute.

Article 24
Non-retroactivity ratione personae

1. No person shall be criminally responsible under this Statute for conduct prior to the entry into force of the Statute.
2. In the event of a change in the law applicable to a given case prior to a final judgement, the law more favourable to the person being investigated, prosecuted or convicted shall apply.

Article 25
Individual criminal responsibility

1. The Court shall have jurisdiction over natural persons pursuant to this Statute.
2. A person who commits a crime within the jurisdiction of the Court shall be individually responsible and liable for punishment in accordance with this Statute.
3. In accordance with this Statute, a person shall be criminally responsible and liable for punishment for a crime within the jurisdiction of the Court if that person:
   (a) Commits such a crime, whether as an individual, jointly with another or through another person, regardless of whether that other person is criminally responsible;
   (b) Orders, solicits or induces the commission of such a crime which in fact occurs or is attempted;
   (c) For the purpose of facilitating the commission of such a crime, aids, abets or otherwise assists in its commission or its attempted commission, including providing the means for its commission;

(d) In any other way contributes to the commission or attempted commission of such a crime by a group of persons acting with a common purpose. Such contribution shall be intentional and shall either:
    (i) Be made with the aim of furthering the criminal activity or criminal purpose of the group, where such activity or purpose involves the commission of a crime within the jurisdiction of the Court; or
    (ii) Be made in the knowledge of the intention of the group to commit the crime;
(e) In respect of the crime of genocide, directly and publicly incites others to commit genocide;
(f) Attempts to commit such a crime by taking action that commences its execution by means of a substantial step, but the crime does not occur because of circumstances independent of the person's intentions. However, a person who abandons the effort to commit the crime or otherwise prevents the completion of the crime shall not be liable for punishment under this Statute for the attempt to commit that crime if that person completely and voluntarily gave up the criminal purpose.

4. No provision in this Statute relating to individual criminal responsibility shall affect the responsibility of States under international law.

Article 26
Exclusion of jurisdiction over persons under eighteen

The Court shall have no jurisdiction over any person who was under the age of 18 at the time of the alleged commission of a crime.

Article 27
Irrelevance of official capacity

1. This Statute shall apply equally to all persons without any distinction based on official capacity. In particular, official capacity as a Head of State or Government, a member of a Government or parliament, an elected representative or a government official shall in no case exempt a person from criminal responsibility under this Statute, nor shall it, in and of itself, constitute a ground for reduction of sentence.
2. Immunities or special procedural rules which may attach to the official capacity of a person, whether under national or international law, shall not bar the Court from exercising its jurisdiction over such a person.

Article 28
Responsibility of commanders and other superiors

In addition to other grounds of criminal responsibility under this Statute for crimes within the jurisdiction of the Court:
(a) A military commander or person effectively acting as a military commander shall be criminally responsible for crimes within the jurisdiction of the Court committed by forces under his or her effective command and control, or effective authority and control as the case may be, as a result of his or her failure to exercise control properly over such forces, where:
    (i) That military commander or person either knew or, owing to the circumstances at the time, should have known that the forces were committing or about to commit such crimes; and
    (ii) That military commander or person failed to take all necessary and reasonable measures within his or her power to prevent or repress their commission or to submit the matter to the competent authorities for investigation and prosecution.

(b) With respect to superior and subordinate relationships not described in paragraph (a), a superior shall be criminally responsible for crimes within the jurisdiction of the Court committed by subordinates under his or her effective authority and control, as a result of his or her failure to exercise control properly over such subordinates, where:
  (i) The superior either knew, or consciously disregarded information which clearly indicated, that the subordinates were committing or about to commit such crimes;
  (ii) The crimes concerned activities that were within the effective responsibility and control of the superior; and
  (iii) The superior failed to take all necessary and reasonable measures within his or her power to prevent or repress their commission or to submit the matter to the competent authorities for investigation and prosecution.

Article 29
Non-applicability of statute of limitations

The crimes within the jurisdiction of the Court shall not be subject to any statute of limitations.

Article 30
Mental element

1. Unless otherwise provided, a person shall be criminally responsible and liable for punishment for a crime within the jurisdiction of the Court only if the material elements are committed with intent and knowledge.
2. For the purposes of this article, a person has intent where:
   (a) In relation to conduct, that person means to engage in the conduct;
   (b) In relation to a consequence, that person means to cause that consequence or is aware that it will occur in the ordinary course of events.
3. For the purposes of this article, "knowledge" means awareness that a circumstance exists or a consequence will occur in the ordinary course of events. "Know" and "knowingly" shall be construed accordingly.

Article 31
Grounds for excluding criminal responsibility

1. In addition to other grounds for excluding criminal responsibility provided for in this Statute, a person shall not be criminally responsible if, at the time of that person's conduct:
   (a) The person suffers from a mental disease or defect that destroys that person's capacity to appreciate the unlawfulness or nature of his or her conduct, or capacity to control his or her conduct to conform to the requirements of law;
   (b) The person is in a state of intoxication that destroys that person's capacity to appreciate the unlawfulness or nature of his or her conduct, or capacity to control his or her conduct to conform to the requirements of law, unless the person has become voluntarily intoxicated under such circumstances that the person knew, or disregarded the risk, that, as a result of the intoxication, he or she was likely to engage in conduct constituting a crime within the jurisdiction of the Court;
   (c) The person acts reasonably to defend himself or herself or another person or, in the case of war crimes, property which is essential for the survival of the person or another person or property which is essential for accomplishing a military mission, against an imminent and unlawful use of force in a manner proportionate to the degree of danger to the person or the other person or property protected. The fact that the person was

involved in a defensive operation conducted by forces shall not in itself constitute a ground for excluding criminal responsibility under this subparagraph;
  (d) The conduct which is alleged to constitute a crime within the jurisdiction of the Court has been caused by duress resulting from a threat of imminent death or of continuing or imminent serious bodily harm against that person or another person, and the person acts necessarily and reasonably to avoid this threat, provided that the person does not intend to cause a greater harm than the one sought to be avoided. Such a threat may either be:
    (i) Made by other persons; or
    (ii) Constituted by other circumstances beyond that person's control.
2. The Court shall determine the applicability of the grounds for excluding criminal responsibility provided for in this Statute to the case before it.
3. At trial, the Court may consider a ground for excluding criminal responsibility other than those referred to in paragraph 1 where such a ground is derived from applicable law as set forth in article 21. The procedures relating to the consideration of such a ground shall be provided for in the Rules of Procedure and Evidence.

Article 32
Mistake of fact or mistake of law

1. A mistake of fact shall be a ground for excluding criminal responsibility only if it negates the mental element required by the crime.
2. A mistake of law as to whether a particular type of conduct is a crime within the jurisdiction of the Court shall not be a ground for excluding criminal responsibility. A mistake of law may, however, be a ground for excluding criminal responsibility if it negates the mental element required by such a crime, or as provided for in article 33.

Article 33
Superior orders and prescription of law

1. The fact that a crime within the jurisdiction of the Court has been committed by a person pursuant to an order of a Government or of a superior, whether military or civilian, shall not relieve that person of criminal responsibility unless:
   (a) The person was under a legal obligation to obey orders of the Government or the superior in question;
   (b) The person did not know that the order was unlawful; and
   (c) The order was not manifestly unlawful.
2. For the purposes of this article, orders to commit genocide or crimes against humanity are manifestly unlawful.

PART 4. COMPOSITION AND ADMINISTRATION OF THE COURT
Article 34
Organs of the Court

The Court shall be composed of the following organs:
  (a) The Presidency;
  (b) An Appeals Division, a Trial Division and a Pre-Trial Division;
  (c) The Office of the Prosecutor;
  (d) The Registry.

Article 35
Service of judges

1. All judges shall be elected as full-time members of the Court and shall be available to serve on that basis from the commencement of their terms of office.
2. The judges composing the Presidency shall serve on a full-time basis as soon as they are elected.
3. The Presidency may, on the basis of the workload of the Court and in consultation with its members, decide from time to time to what extent the remaining judges shall be required to serve on a full-time basis. Any such arrangement shall be without prejudice to the provisions of article 40.
4. The financial arrangements for judges not required to serve on a full-time basis shall be made in accordance with article 49.

Article 36
Qualifications, nomination and election of judges

1. Subject to the provisions of paragraph 2, there shall be 18 judges of the Court.
2. (a) The Presidency, acting on behalf of the Court, may propose an increase in the number of judges specified in paragraph 1, indicating the reasons why this is considered necessary and appropriate. The Registrar shall promptly circulate any such proposal to all States Parties.
   (b) Any such proposal shall then be considered at a meeting of the Assembly of States Parties to be convened in accordance with article 112. The proposal shall be considered adopted if approved at the meeting by a vote of two thirds of the members of the Assembly of States Parties and shall enter into force at such time as decided by the Assembly of States Parties.
   (c) (i) Once a proposal for an increase in the number of judges has been adopted under subparagraph (b), the election of the additional judges shall take place at the next session of the Assembly of States Parties in accordance with paragraphs 3 to 8, and article 37, paragraph 2;
       (ii) Once a proposal for an increase in the number of judges has been adopted and brought into effect under subparagraphs (b) and (c) (i), it shall be open to the Presidency at any time thereafter, if the workload of the Court justifies it, to propose a reduction in the number of judges, provided that the number of judges shall not be reduced below that specified in paragraph 1. The proposal shall be dealt with in accordance with the procedure laid down in subparagraphs (a) and (b). In the event that the proposal is adopted, the number of judges shall be progressively decreased as the terms of office of serving judges expire, until the necessary number has been reached.
3. (a) The judges shall be chosen from among persons of high moral character, impartiality and integrity who possess the qualifications required in their respective States for appointment to the highest judicial offices.
   (b) Every candidate for election to the Court shall:
       (i) Have established competence in criminal law and procedure, and the necessary relevant experience, whether as judge, prosecutor, advocate or in other similar capacity, in criminal proceedings; or
       (ii) Have established competence in relevant areas of international law such as international humanitarian law and the law of human rights, and extensive experience in a professional legal capacity which is of relevance to the judicial work of the Court;

(c) Every candidate for election to the Court shall have an excellent knowledge of and be fluent in at least one of the working languages of the Court.

4. (a) Nominations of candidates for election to the Court may be made by any State Party to this Statute, and shall be made either:
   (i) By the procedure for the nomination of candidates for appointment to the highest judicial offices in the State in question; or
   (ii) By the procedure provided for the nomination of candidates for the International Court of Justice in the Statute of that Court.

Nominations shall be accompanied by a statement in the necessary detail specifying how the candidate fulfils the requirements of paragraph 3.

   (b) Each State Party may put forward one candidate for any given election who need not necessarily be a national of that State Party but shall in any case be a national of a State Party.
   (c) The Assembly of States Parties may decide to establish, if appropriate, an Advisory Committee on nominations. In that event, the Committee's composition and mandate shall be established by the Assembly of States Parties.

5. For the purposes of the election, there shall be two lists of candidates:

List A containing the names of candidates with the qualifications specified in paragraph 3 (b) (i); and

List B containing the names of candidates with the qualifications specified in paragraph 3 (b) (ii).

A candidate with sufficient qualifications for both lists may choose on which list to appear. At the first election to the Court, at least nine judges shall be elected from list A and at least five judges from list B. Subsequent elections shall be so organized as to maintain the equivalent proportion on the Court of judges qualified on the two lists.

6. (a) The judges shall be elected by secret ballot at a meeting of the Assembly of States Parties convened for that purpose under article 112. Subject to paragraph 7, the persons elected to the Court shall be the 18 candidates who obtain the highest number of votes and a two-thirds majority of the States Parties present and voting.
   (b) In the event that a sufficient number of judges is not elected on the first ballot, successive ballots shall be held in accordance with the procedures laid down in subparagraph (a) until the remaining places have been filled.

7. No two judges may be nationals of the same State. A person who, for the purposes of membership of the Court, could be regarded as a national of more than one State shall be deemed to be a national of the State in which that person ordinarily exercises civil and political rights.

8. (a) The States Parties shall, in the selection of judges, take into account the need, within the membership of the Court, for:
   (i) The representation of the principal legal systems of the world;
   (ii) Equitable geographical representation; and
   (iii) A fair representation of female and male judges.
   (b) States Parties shall also take into account the need to include judges with legal expertise on specific issues, including, but not limited to, violence against women or children.

9. (a) Subject to subparagraph (b), judges shall hold office for a term of nine years and, subject to subparagraph (c) and to article 37, paragraph 2, shall not be eligible for re-election.
   (b) At the first election, one third of the judges elected shall be selected by lot to serve for a term of three years; one third of the judges elected shall be selected by lot to serve for a term of six years; and the remainder shall serve for a term of nine years.
   (c) A judge who is selected to serve for a term of three years under subparagraph (b) shall be eligible for re-election for a full term.

10. Notwithstanding paragraph 9, a judge assigned to a Trial or Appeals Chamber in accordance with article 39 shall continue in office to complete any trial or appeal the hearing of which has already commenced before that Chamber.

Article 37
Judicial vacancies

1. In the event of a vacancy, an election shall be held in accordance with article 36 to fill the vacancy.
2. A judge elected to fill a vacancy shall serve for the remainder of the predecessor's term and, if that period is three years or less, shall be eligible for re-election for a full term under article 36.

Article 38
The Presidency

1. The President and the First and Second Vice-Presidents shall be elected by an absolute majority of the judges. They shall each serve for a term of three years or until the end of their respective terms of office as judges, whichever expires earlier. They shall be eligible for re-election once.
2. The First Vice-President shall act in place of the President in the event that the President is unavailable or disqualified. The Second Vice-President shall act in place of the President in the event that both the President and the First Vice-President are unavailable or disqualified.
3. The President, together with the First and Second Vice-Presidents, shall constitute the Presidency, which shall be responsible for:
   (a) The proper administration of the Court, with the exception of the Office of the Prosecutor; and
   (b) The other functions conferred upon it in accordance with this Statute.
4. In discharging its responsibility under paragraph 3 (a), the Presidency shall coordinate with and seek the concurrence of the Prosecutor on all matters of mutual concern.

Article 39
Chambers

1. As soon as possible after the election of the judges, the Court shall organize itself into the divisions specified in article 34, paragraph (b). The Appeals Division shall be composed of the President and four other judges, the Trial Division of not less than six judges and the Pre-Trial Division of not less than six judges. The assignment of judges to divisions shall be based on the nature of the functions to be performed by each division and the qualifications and experience of the judges elected to the Court, in such a way that each division shall contain an appropriate combination of expertise in criminal law and procedure and in international law. The Trial and Pre-Trial Divisions shall be composed predominantly of judges with criminal trial experience.
2. (a) The judicial functions of the Court shall be carried out in each division by Chambers.
   (b) (i) The Appeals Chamber shall be composed of all the judges of the Appeals Division;
       (ii) The functions of the Trial Chamber shall be carried out by three judges of the Trial Division;
       (iii) The functions of the Pre-Trial Chamber shall be carried out either by three judges of the Pre-Trial Division or by a single judge of that division in accordance with this Statute and the Rules of Procedure and Evidence;
   (c) Nothing in this paragraph shall preclude the simultaneous constitution of more than one Trial Chamber or Pre-Trial Chamber when the efficient management of the Court's workload so requires.
3. (a) Judges assigned to the Trial and Pre-Trial Divisions shall serve in those divisions for a period of three years, and thereafter until the completion of any case the hearing of which has already commenced in the division concerned.

(b) Judges assigned to the Appeals Division shall serve in that division for their entire term of office.
4. Judges assigned to the Appeals Division shall serve only in that division. Nothing in this article shall, however, preclude the temporary attachment of judges from the Trial Division to the Pre-Trial Division or vice versa, if the Presidency considers that the efficient management of the Court's workload so requires, provided that under no circumstances shall a judge who has participated in the pre-trial phase of a case be eligible to sit on the Trial Chamber hearing that case.

Article 40
Independence of the judges

1. The judges shall be independent in the performance of their functions.
2. Judges shall not engage in any activity which is likely to interfere with their judicial functions or to affect confidence in their independence.
3. Judges required to serve on a full-time basis at the seat of the Court shall not engage in any other occupation of a professional nature.
4. Any question regarding the application of paragraphs 2 and 3 shall be decided by an absolute majority of the judges. Where any such question concerns an individual judge, that judge shall not take part in the decision.

Article 41
Excusing and disqualification of judges

1. The Presidency may, at the request of a judge, excuse that judge from the exercise of a function under this Statute, in accordance with the Rules of Procedure and Evidence.
2. (a) A judge shall not participate in any case in which his or her impartiality might reasonably be doubted on any ground. A judge shall be disqualified from a case in accordance with this paragraph if, *inter alia*, that judge has previously been involved in any capacity in that case before the Court or in a related criminal case at the national level involving the person being investigated or prosecuted. A judge shall also be disqualified on such other grounds as may be provided for in the Rules of Procedure and Evidence.
   (b) The Prosecutor or the person being investigated or prosecuted may request the disqualification of a judge under this paragraph.
   (c) Any question as to the disqualification of a judge shall be decided by an absolute majority of the judges. The challenged judge shall be entitled to present his or her comments on the matter, but shall not take part in the decision.

Article 42
The Office of the Prosecutor

1. The Office of the Prosecutor shall act independently as a separate organ of the Court. It shall be responsible for receiving referrals and any substantiated information on crimes within the jurisdiction of the Court, for examining them and for conducting investigations and prosecutions before the Court. A member of the Office shall not seek or act on instructions from any external source.
2. The Office shall be headed by the Prosecutor. The Prosecutor shall have full authority over the management and administration of the Office, including the staff, facilities and other resources thereof. The Prosecutor shall be assisted by one or more Deputy Prosecutors, who shall be entitled to carry out any of the acts required of the Prosecutor under this Statute. The Prosecutor and the Deputy Prosecutors shall be of different nationalities. They shall serve on a full-time basis.

3. The Prosecutor and the Deputy Prosecutors shall be persons of high moral character, be highly competent in and have extensive practical experience in the prosecution or trial of criminal cases. They shall have an excellent knowledge of and be fluent in at least one of the working languages of the Court.
4. The Prosecutor shall be elected by secret ballot by an absolute majority of the members of the Assembly of States Parties. The Deputy Prosecutors shall be elected in the same way from a list of candidates provided by the Prosecutor. The Prosecutor shall nominate three candidates for each position of Deputy Prosecutor to be filled. Unless a shorter term is decided upon at the time of their election, the Prosecutor and the Deputy Prosecutors shall hold office for a term of nine years and shall not be eligible for re-election.
5. Neither the Prosecutor nor a Deputy Prosecutor shall engage in any activity which is likely to interfere with his or her prosecutorial functions or to affect confidence in his or her independence. They shall not engage in any other occupation of a professional nature.
6. The Presidency may excuse the Prosecutor or a Deputy Prosecutor, at his or her request, from acting in a particular case.
7. Neither the Prosecutor nor a Deputy Prosecutor shall participate in any matter in which their impartiality might reasonably be doubted on any ground. They shall be disqualified from a case in accordance with this paragraph if, *inter alia*, they have previously been involved in any capacity in that case before the Court or in a related criminal case at the national level involving the person being investigated or prosecuted.
8. Any question as to the disqualification of the Prosecutor or a Deputy Prosecutor shall be decided by the Appeals Chamber.
    (a) The person being investigated or prosecuted may at any time request the disqualification of the Prosecutor or a Deputy Prosecutor on the grounds set out in this article;
    (b) The Prosecutor or the Deputy Prosecutor, as appropriate, shall be entitled to present his or her comments on the matter;
9. The Prosecutor shall appoint advisers with legal expertise on specific issues, including, but not limited to, sexual and gender violence and violence against children.

Article 43
The Registry

1. The Registry shall be responsible for the non-judicial aspects of the administration and servicing of the Court, without prejudice to the functions and powers of the Prosecutor in accordance with article 42.
2. The Registry shall be headed by the Registrar, who shall be the principal administrative officer of the Court. The Registrar shall exercise his or her functions under the authority of the President of the Court.
3. The Registrar and the Deputy Registrar shall be persons of high moral character, be highly competent and have an excellent knowledge of and be fluent in at least one of the working languages of the Court.
4. The judges shall elect the Registrar by an absolute majority by secret ballot, taking into account any recommendation by the Assembly of States Parties. If the need arises and upon the recommendation of the Registrar, the judges shall elect, in the same manner, a Deputy Registrar.
5. The Registrar shall hold office for a term of five years, shall be eligible for re-election once and shall serve on a full-time basis. The Deputy Registrar shall hold office for a term of five years or such shorter term as may be decided upon by an absolute majority of the judges, and may be elected on the basis that the Deputy Registrar shall be called upon to serve as required.
6. The Registrar shall set up a Victims and Witnesses Unit within the Registry. This Unit shall provide, in consultation with the Office of the Prosecutor, protective measures and security arrangements, counselling and other appropriate assistance for witnesses, victims who

appear before the Court, and others who are at risk on account of testimony given by such witnesses. The Unit shall include staff with expertise in trauma, including trauma related to crimes of sexual violence.

Article 44
Staff

1. The Prosecutor and the Registrar shall appoint such qualified staff as may be required to their respective offices. In the case of the Prosecutor, this shall include the appointment of investigators.
2. In the employment of staff, the Prosecutor and the Registrar shall ensure the highest standards of efficiency, competency and integrity, and shall have regard, *mutatis mutandis*, to the criteria set forth in article 36, paragraph 8.
3. The Registrar, with the agreement of the Presidency and the Prosecutor, shall propose Staff Regulations which include the terms and conditions upon which the staff of the Court shall be appointed, remunerated and dismissed. The Staff Regulations shall be approved by the Assembly of States Parties.
4. The Court may, in exceptional circumstances, employ the expertise of gratis personnel offered by States Parties, intergovernmental organizations or non-governmental organizations to assist with the work of any of the organs of the Court. The Prosecutor may accept any such offer on behalf of the Office of the Prosecutor. Such gratis personnel shall be employed in accordance with guidelines to be established by the Assembly of States Parties.

Article 45
Solemn undertaking

Before taking up their respective duties under this Statute, the judges, the Prosecutor, the Deputy Prosecutors, the Registrar and the Deputy Registrar shall each make a solemn undertaking in open court to exercise his or her respective functions impartially and conscientiously.

Article 46
Removal from office

1. A judge, the Prosecutor, a Deputy Prosecutor, the Registrar or the Deputy Registrar shall be removed from office if a decision to this effect is made in accordance with paragraph 2, in cases where that person:
   (a) Is found to have committed serious misconduct or a serious breach of his or her duties under this Statute, as provided for in the Rules of Procedure and Evidence; or
   (b) Is unable to exercise the functions required by this Statute.
2. A decision as to the removal from office of a judge, the Prosecutor or a Deputy Prosecutor under paragraph 1 shall be made by the Assembly of States Parties, by secret ballot:
   (a) In the case of a judge, by a two-thirds majority of the States Parties upon a recommendation adopted by a two-thirds majority of the other judges;
   (b) In the case of the Prosecutor, by an absolute majority of the States Parties;
   (c) In the case of a Deputy Prosecutor, by an absolute majority of the States Parties upon the recommendation of the Prosecutor.
3. A decision as to the removal from office of the Registrar or Deputy Registrar shall be made by an absolute majority of the judges.
4. A judge, Prosecutor, Deputy Prosecutor, Registrar or Deputy Registrar whose conduct or ability to exercise the functions of the office as required by this Statute is challenged under this article shall have full opportunity to present and receive evidence and to make submissions in accordance with the Rules of Procedure and Evidence. The person in question shall not otherwise participate in the consideration of the matter.

Article 47
Disciplinary measures

A judge, Prosecutor, Deputy Prosecutor, Registrar or Deputy Registrar who has committed misconduct of a less serious nature than that set out in article 46, paragraph 1, shall be subject to disciplinary measures, in accordance with the Rules of Procedure and Evidence.

Article 48
Privileges and immunities

1. The Court shall enjoy in the territory of each State Party such privileges and immunities as are necessary for the fulfilment of its purposes.
2. The judges, the Prosecutor, the Deputy Prosecutors and the Registrar shall, when engaged on or with respect to the business of the Court, enjoy the same privileges and immunities as are accorded to heads of diplomatic missions and shall, after the expiry of their terms of office, continue to be accorded immunity from legal process of every kind in respect of words spoken or written and acts performed by them in their official capacity.
3. The Deputy Registrar, the staff of the Office of the Prosecutor and the staff of the Registry shall enjoy the privileges and immunities and facilities necessary for the performance of their functions, in accordance with the agreement on the privileges and immunities of the Court.
4. Counsel, experts, witnesses or any other person required to be present at the seat of the Court shall be accorded such treatment as is necessary for the proper functioning of the Court, in accordance with the agreement on the privileges and immunities of the Court.
5. The privileges and immunities of:
   (a) A judge or the Prosecutor may be waived by an absolute majority of the judges;
   (b) The Registrar may be waived by the Presidency;
   (c) The Deputy Prosecutors and staff of the Office of the Prosecutor may be waived by the Prosecutor;
   (d) The Deputy Registrar and staff of the Registry may be waived by the Registrar.

Article 49
Salaries, allowances and expenses

The judges, the Prosecutor, the Deputy Prosecutors, the Registrar and the Deputy Registrar shall receive such salaries, allowances and expenses as may be decided upon by the Assembly of States Parties. These salaries and allowances shall not be reduced during their terms of office.

Article 50
Official and working languages

1. The official languages of the Court shall be Arabic, Chinese, English, French, Russian and Spanish. The judgements of the Court, as well as other decisions resolving fundamental issues before the Court, shall be published in the official languages. The Presidency shall, in accordance with the criteria established by the Rules of Procedure and Evidence, determine which decisions may be considered as resolving fundamental issues for the purposes of this paragraph.
2. The working languages of the Court shall be English and French. The Rules of Procedure and Evidence shall determine the cases in which other official languages may be used as working languages.
3. At the request of any party to a proceeding or a State allowed to intervene in a proceeding, the Court shall authorize a language other than English or French to be used by such a party or State, provided that the Court considers such authorization to be adequately justified.

Article 51
Rules of Procedure and Evidence

1. The Rules of Procedure and Evidence shall enter into force upon adoption by a two-thirds majority of the members of the Assembly of States Parties.
2. Amendments to the Rules of Procedure and Evidence may be proposed by:
   (a) Any State Party;
   (b) The judges acting by an absolute majority; or
   (c) The Prosecutor.

   Such amendments shall enter into force upon adoption by a two-thirds majority of the members of the Assembly of States Parties.
3. After the adoption of the Rules of Procedure and Evidence, in urgent cases where the Rules do not provide for a specific situation before the Court, the judges may, by a two-thirds majority, draw up provisional Rules to be applied until adopted, amended or rejected at the next ordinary or special session of the Assembly of States Parties.
4. The Rules of Procedure and Evidence, amendments thereto and any provisional Rule shall be consistent with this Statute. Amendments to the Rules of Procedure and Evidence as well as provisional Rules shall not be applied retroactively to the detriment of the person who is being investigated or prosecuted or who has been convicted.
5. In the event of conflict between the Statute and the Rules of Procedure and Evidence, the Statute shall prevail.

Article 52
Regulations of the Court

1. The judges shall, in accordance with this Statute and the Rules of Procedure and Evidence, adopt, by an absolute majority, the Regulations of the Court necessary for its routine functioning.
2. The Prosecutor and the Registrar shall be consulted in the elaboration of the Regulations and any amendments thereto.
3. The Regulations and any amendments thereto shall take effect upon adoption unless otherwise decided by the judges. Immediately upon adoption, they shall be circulated to States Parties for comments. If within six months there are no objections from a majority of States Parties, they shall remain in force.

PART 5. INVESTIGATION AND PROSECUTION
Article 53
Initiation of an investigation

1. The Prosecutor shall, having evaluated the information made available to him or her, initiate an investigation unless he or she determines that there is no reasonable basis to proceed under this Statute. In deciding whether to initiate an investigation, the Prosecutor shall consider whether:
   (a) The information available to the Prosecutor provides a reasonable basis to believe that a crime within the jurisdiction of the Court has been or is being committed;
   (b) The case is or would be admissible under article 17; and
   (c) Taking into account the gravity of the crime and the interests of victims, there are nonetheless substantial reasons to believe that an investigation would not serve the interests of justice.

   If the Prosecutor determines that there is no reasonable basis to proceed and his or her determination is based solely on subparagraph (c) above, he or she shall inform the Pre-Trial Chamber.
2. If, upon investigation, the Prosecutor concludes that there is not a sufficient basis for a prosecution because:

(a) There is not a sufficient legal or factual basis to seek a warrant or summons under article 58;
(b) The case is inadmissible under article 17; or
(c) A prosecution is not in the interests of justice, taking into account all the circumstances, including the gravity of the crime, the interests of victims and the age or infirmity of the alleged perpetrator, and his or her role in the alleged crime;

the Prosecutor shall inform the Pre-Trial Chamber and the State making a referral under article 14 or the Security Council in a case under article 13, paragraph (b), of his or her conclusion and the reasons for the conclusion.

3. (a) At the request of the State making a referral under article 14 or the Security Council under article 13, paragraph (b), the Pre-Trial Chamber may review a decision of the Prosecutor under paragraph 1 or 2 not to proceed and may request the Prosecutor to reconsider that decision.
   (b) In addition, the Pre-Trial Chamber may, on its own initiative, review a decision of the Prosecutor not to proceed if it is based solely on paragraph 1 (c) or 2 (c). In such a case, the decision of the Prosecutor shall be effective only if confirmed by the Pre-Trial Chamber.
4. The Prosecutor may, at any time, reconsider a decision whether to initiate an investigation or prosecution based on new facts or information.

Article 54
Duties and powers of the Prosecutor with respect to investigations

1. The Prosecutor shall:
   (a) In order to establish the truth, extend the investigation to cover all facts and evidence relevant to an assessment of whether there is criminal responsibility under this Statute, and, in doing so, investigate incriminating and exonerating circumstances equally;
   (b) Take appropriate measures to ensure the effective investigation and prosecution of crimes within the jurisdiction of the Court, and in doing so, respect the interests and personal circumstances of victims and witnesses, including age, gender as defined in article 7, paragraph 3, and health, and take into account the nature of the crime, in particular where it involves sexual violence, gender violence or violence against children; and
   (c) Fully respect the rights of persons arising under this Statute.
2. The Prosecutor may conduct investigations on the territory of a State:
   (a) In accordance with the provisions of Part 9; or
   (b) As authorized by the Pre-Trial Chamber under article 57, paragraph 3 (d).
3. The Prosecutor may:
   (a) Collect and examine evidence;
   (b) Request the presence of and question persons being investigated, victims and witnesses;
   (c) Seek the cooperation of any State or intergovernmental organization or arrangement in accordance with its respective competence and/or mandate;
   (d) Enter into such arrangements or agreements, not inconsistent with this Statute, as may be necessary to facilitate the cooperation of a State, intergovernmental organization or person;
   (e) Agree not to disclose, at any stage of the proceedings, documents or information that the Prosecutor obtains on the condition of confidentiality and solely for the purpose of generating new evidence, unless the provider of the information consents; and
   (f) Take necessary measures, or request that necessary measures be taken, to ensure the confidentiality of information, the protection of any person or the preservation of evidence.

Article 55
Rights of persons during an investigation

1. In respect of an investigation under this Statute, a person:
   (a) Shall not be compelled to incriminate himself or herself or to confess guilt;
   (b) Shall not be subjected to any form of coercion, duress or threat, to torture or to any other form of cruel, inhuman or degrading treatment or punishment;
   (c) Shall, if questioned in a language other than a language the person fully understands and speaks, have, free of any cost, the assistance of a competent interpreter and such translations as are necessary to meet the requirements of fairness; and
   (d) Shall not be subjected to arbitrary arrest or detention, and shall not be deprived of his or her liberty except on such grounds and in accordance with such procedures as are established in this Statute.
2. Where there are grounds to believe that a person has committed a crime within the jurisdiction of the Court and that person is about to be questioned either by the Prosecutor, or by national authorities pursuant to a request made under Part 9, that person shall also have the following rights of which he or she shall be informed prior to being questioned:
   (a) To be informed, prior to being questioned, that there are grounds to believe that he or she has committed a crime within the jurisdiction of the Court;
   (b) To remain silent, without such silence being a consideration in the determination of guilt or innocence;
   (c) To have legal assistance of the person's choosing, or, if the person does not have legal assistance, to have legal assistance assigned to him or her, in any case where the interests of justice so require, and without payment by the person in any such case if the person does not have sufficient means to pay for it; and
   (d) To be questioned in the presence of counsel unless the person has voluntarily waived his or her right to counsel.

Article 56
Role of the Pre-Trial Chamber in relation to a unique investigative opportunity

1. (a) Where the Prosecutor considers an investigation to present a unique opportunity to take testimony or a statement from a witness or to examine, collect or test evidence, which may not be available subsequently for the purposes of a trial, the Prosecutor shall so inform the Pre-Trial Chamber.
   (b) In that case, the Pre-Trial Chamber may, upon request of the Prosecutor, take such measures as may be necessary to ensure the efficiency and integrity of the proceedings and, in particular, to protect the rights of the defence.
   (c) Unless the Pre-Trial Chamber orders otherwise, the Prosecutor shall provide the relevant information to the person who has been arrested or appeared in response to a summons in connection with the investigation referred to in subparagraph (a), in order that he or she may be heard on the matter.
2. The measures referred to in paragraph 1 (b) may include:
   (a) Making recommendations or orders regarding procedures to be followed;
   (b) Directing that a record be made of the proceedings;
   (c) Appointing an expert to assist;
   (d) Authorizing counsel for a person who has been arrested, or appeared before the Court in response to a summons, to participate, or where there has not yet been such an arrest or appearance or counsel has not been designated, appointing another counsel to attend and represent the interests of the defence;

(e) Naming one of its members or, if necessary, another available judge of the Pre-Trial or Trial Division to observe and make recommendations or orders regarding the collection and preservation of evidence and the questioning of persons;
(f) Taking such other action as may be necessary to collect or preserve evidence.
3. (a) Where the Prosecutor has not sought measures pursuant to this article but the Pre-Trial Chamber considers that such measures are required to preserve evidence that it deems would be essential for the defence at trial, it shall consult with the Prosecutor as to whether there is good reason for the Prosecutor's failure to request the measures. If upon consultation, the Pre-Trial Chamber concludes that the Prosecutor's failure to request such measures is unjustified, the Pre-Trial Chamber may take such measures on its own initiative.
(b) A decision of the Pre-Trial Chamber to act on its own initiative under this paragraph may be appealed by the Prosecutor. The appeal shall be heard on an expedited basis.
4. The admissibility of evidence preserved or collected for trial pursuant to this article, or the record thereof, shall be governed at trial by article 69, and given such weight as determined by the Trial Chamber.

Article 57
Functions and powers of the Pre-Trial Chamber

1. Unless otherwise provided in this Statute, the Pre-Trial Chamber shall exercise its functions in accordance with the provisions of this article.
2. (a) Orders or rulings of the Pre-Trial Chamber issued under articles 15, 18, 19, 54, paragraph 2, 61, paragraph 7, and 72 must be concurred in by a majority of its judges.
(b) In all other cases, a single judge of the Pre-Trial Chamber may exercise the functions provided for in this Statute, unless otherwise provided for in the Rules of Procedure and Evidence or by a majority of the Pre-Trial Chamber.
3. In addition to its other functions under this Statute, the Pre-Trial Chamber may:
(a) At the request of the Prosecutor, issue such orders and warrants as may be required for the purposes of an investigation;
(b) Upon the request of a person who has been arrested or has appeared pursuant to a summons under article 58, issue such orders, including measures such as those described in article 56, or seek such cooperation pursuant to Part 9 as may be necessary to assist the person in the preparation of his or her defence;
(c) Where necessary, provide for the protection and privacy of victims and witnesses, the preservation of evidence, the protection of persons who have been arrested or appeared in response to a summons, and the protection of national security information;
(d) Authorize the Prosecutor to take specific investigative steps within the territory of a State Party without having secured the cooperation of that State under Part 9 if, whenever possible having regard to the views of the State concerned, the Pre-Trial Chamber has determined in that case that the State is clearly unable to execute a request for cooperation due to the unavailability of any authority or any component of its judicial system competent to execute the request for cooperation under Part 9.
(e) Where a warrant of arrest or a summons has been issued under article 58, and having due regard to the strength of the evidence and the rights of the parties concerned, as provided for in this Statute and the Rules of Procedure and Evidence, seek the cooperation of States pursuant to article 93, paragraph 1 (k), to take protective measures for the purpose of forfeiture, in particular for the ultimate benefit of victims.

Article 58
Issuance by the Pre-Trial Chamber of a warrant of arrest or a summons to appear

1. At any time after the initiation of an investigation, the Pre-Trial Chamber shall, on the application of the Prosecutor, issue a warrant of arrest of a person if, having examined the application and the evidence or other information submitted by the Prosecutor, it is satisfied that:
   (a) There are reasonable grounds to believe that the person has committed a crime within the jurisdiction of the Court; and
   (b) The arrest of the person appears necessary:
      (i) To ensure the person's appearance at trial,
      (ii) To ensure that the person does not obstruct or endanger the investigation or the court proceedings, or
      (iii) Where applicable, to prevent the person from continuing with the commission of that crime or a related crime which is within the jurisdiction of the Court and which arises out of the same circumstances.
2. The application of the Prosecutor shall contain:
   (a) The name of the person and any other relevant identifying information;
   (b) A specific reference to the crimes within the jurisdiction of the Court which the person is alleged to have committed;
   (c) A concise statement of the facts which are alleged to constitute those crimes;
   (d) A summary of the evidence and any other information which establish reasonable grounds to believe that the person committed those crimes; and
   (e) The reason why the Prosecutor believes that the arrest of the person is necessary.
3. The warrant of arrest shall contain:
   (a) The name of the person and any other relevant identifying information;
   (b) A specific reference to the crimes within the jurisdiction of the Court for which the person's arrest is sought; and
   (c) A concise statement of the facts which are alleged to constitute those crimes.
4. The warrant of arrest shall remain in effect until otherwise ordered by the Court.
5. On the basis of the warrant of arrest, the Court may request the provisional arrest or the arrest and surrender of the person under Part 9.
6. The Prosecutor may request the Pre-Trial Chamber to amend the warrant of arrest by modifying or adding to the crimes specified therein. The Pre-Trial Chamber shall so amend the warrant if it is satisfied that there are reasonable grounds to believe that the person committed the modified or additional crimes.
7. As an alternative to seeking a warrant of arrest, the Prosecutor may submit an application requesting that the Pre-Trial Chamber issue a summons for the person to appear. If the Pre-Trial Chamber is satisfied that there are reasonable grounds to believe that the person committed the crime alleged and that a summons is sufficient to ensure the person's appearance, it shall issue the summons, with or without conditions restricting liberty (other than detention) if provided for by national law, for the person to appear. The summons shall contain:
   (a) The name of the person and any other relevant identifying information;
   (b) The specified date on which the person is to appear;
   (c) A specific reference to the crimes within the jurisdiction of the Court which the person is alleged to have committed; and
   (d) A concise statement of the facts which are alleged to constitute the crime.

The summons shall be served on the person.

Article 59
Arrest proceedings in the custodial State

1. A State Party which has received a request for provisional arrest or for arrest and surrender shall immediately take steps to arrest the person in question in accordance with its laws and the provisions of Part 9.
2. A person arrested shall be brought promptly before the competent judicial authority in the custodial State which shall determine, in accordance with the law of that State, that:
   (a) The warrant applies to that person;
   (b) The person has been arrested in accordance with the proper process; and
   (c) The person's rights have been respected.
3. The person arrested shall have the right to apply to the competent authority in the custodial State for interim release pending surrender.
4. In reaching a decision on any such application, the competent authority in the custodial State shall consider whether, given the gravity of the alleged crimes, there are urgent and exceptional circumstances to justify interim release and whether necessary safeguards exist to ensure that the custodial State can fulfil its duty to surrender the person to the Court. It shall not be open to the competent authority of the custodial State to consider whether the warrant of arrest was properly issued in accordance with article 58, paragraph 1 (a) and (b).
5. The Pre-Trial Chamber shall be notified of any request for interim release and shall make recommendations to the competent authority in the custodial State. The competent authority in the custodial State shall give full consideration to such recommendations, including any recommendations on measures to prevent the escape of the person, before rendering its decision.
6. If the person is granted interim release, the Pre-Trial Chamber may request periodic reports on the status of the interim release.
7. Once ordered to be surrendered by the custodial State, the person shall be delivered to the Court as soon as possible.

Article 60
Initial proceedings before the Court

1. Upon the surrender of the person to the Court, or the person's appearance before the Court voluntarily or pursuant to a summons, the Pre-Trial Chamber shall satisfy itself that the person has been informed of the crimes which he or she is alleged to have committed, and of his or her rights under this Statute, including the right to apply for interim release pending trial.
2. A person subject to a warrant of arrest may apply for interim release pending trial. If the Pre-Trial Chamber is satisfied that the conditions set forth in article 58, paragraph 1, are met, the person shall continue to be detained. If it is not so satisfied, the Pre-Trial Chamber shall release the person, with or without conditions.
3. The Pre-Trial Chamber shall periodically review its ruling on the release or detention of the person, and may do so at any time on the request of the Prosecutor or the person. Upon such review, it may modify its ruling as to detention, release or conditions of release, if it is satisfied that changed circumstances so require.
4. The Pre-Trial Chamber shall ensure that a person is not detained for an unreasonable period prior to trial due to inexcusable delay by the Prosecutor. If such delay occurs, the Court shall consider releasing the person, with or without conditions.
5. If necessary, the Pre-Trial Chamber may issue a warrant of arrest to secure the presence of a person who has been released.

Article 61
Confirmation of the charges before trial

1. Subject to the provisions of paragraph 2, within a reasonable time after the person's surrender or voluntary appearance before the Court, the Pre-Trial Chamber shall hold a hearing to confirm the charges on which the Prosecutor intends to seek trial. The hearing shall be held in the presence of the Prosecutor and the person charged, as well as his or her counsel.
2. The Pre-Trial Chamber may, upon request of the Prosecutor or on its own motion, hold a hearing in the absence of the person charged to confirm the charges on which the Prosecutor intends to seek trial when the person has:
   (a) Waived his or her right to be present; or
   (b) Fled or cannot be found and all reasonable steps have been taken to secure his or her appearance before the Court and to inform the person of the charges and that a hearing to confirm those charges will be held.

In that case, the person shall be represented by counsel where the Pre-Trial Chamber determines that it is in the interests of justice.

3. Within a reasonable time before the hearing, the person shall:
   (a) Be provided with a copy of the document containing the charges on which the Prosecutor intends to bring the person to trial; and
   (b) Be informed of the evidence on which the Prosecutor intends to rely at the hearing.

The Pre-Trial Chamber may issue orders regarding the disclosure of information for the purposes of the hearing.

4. Before the hearing, the Prosecutor may continue the investigation and may amend or withdraw any charges. The person shall be given reasonable notice before the hearing of any amendment to or withdrawal of charges. In case of a withdrawal of charges, the Prosecutor shall notify the Pre-Trial Chamber of the reasons for the withdrawal.
5. At the hearing, the Prosecutor shall support each charge with sufficient evidence to establish substantial grounds to believe that the person committed the crime charged. The Prosecutor may rely on documentary or summary evidence and need not call the witnesses expected to testify at the trial.
6. At the hearing, the person may:
   (a) Object to the charges;
   (b) Challenge the evidence presented by the Prosecutor; and
   (c) Present evidence.
7. The Pre-Trial Chamber shall, on the basis of the hearing, determine whether there is sufficient evidence to establish substantial grounds to believe that the person committed each of the crimes charged. Based on its determination, the Pre-Trial Chamber shall:
   (a) Confirm those charges in relation to which it has determined that there is sufficient evidence, and commit the person to a Trial Chamber for trial on the charges as confirmed;
   (b) Decline to confirm those charges in relation to which it has determined that there is insufficient evidence;
   (c) Adjourn the hearing and request the Prosecutor to consider:
      (i) Providing further evidence or conducting further investigation with respect to a particular charge; or
      (ii) Amending a charge because the evidence submitted appears to establish a different crime within the jurisdiction of the Court.
8. Where the Pre-Trial Chamber declines to confirm a charge, the Prosecutor shall not be precluded from subsequently requesting its confirmation if the request is supported by additional evidence.
9. After the charges are confirmed and before the trial has begun, the Prosecutor may, with the permission of the Pre-Trial Chamber and after notice to the accused, amend the charges. If the Prosecutor seeks to add additional charges or to substitute more serious charges, a

hearing under this article to confirm those charges must be held. After commencement of the trial, the Prosecutor may, with the permission of the Trial Chamber, withdraw the charges.
10. Any warrant previously issued shall cease to have effect with respect to any charges which have not been confirmed by the Pre-Trial Chamber or which have been withdrawn by the Prosecutor.
11. Once the charges have been confirmed in accordance with this article, the Presidency shall constitute a Trial Chamber which, subject to paragraph 9 and to article 64, paragraph 4, shall be responsible for the conduct of subsequent proceedings and may exercise any function of the Pre-Trial Chamber that is relevant and capable of application in those proceedings.

PART 6. THE TRIAL
Article 62
Place of trial

Unless otherwise decided, the place of the trial shall be the seat of the Court.

Article 63
Trial in the presence of the accused

1. The accused shall be present during the trial.
2. If the accused, being present before the Court, continues to disrupt the trial, the Trial Chamber may remove the accused and shall make provision for him or her to observe the trial and instruct counsel from outside the courtroom, through the use of communications technology, if required. Such measures shall be taken only in exceptional circumstances after other reasonable alternatives have proved inadequate, and only for such duration as is strictly required.

Article 64
Functions and powers of the Trial Chamber

1. The functions and powers of the Trial Chamber set out in this article shall be exercised in accordance with this Statute and the Rules of Procedure and Evidence.
2. The Trial Chamber shall ensure that a trial is fair and expeditious and is conducted with full respect for the rights of the accused and due regard for the protection of victims and witnesses.
3. Upon assignment of a case for trial in accordance with this Statute, the Trial Chamber assigned to deal with the case shall:
   (a) Confer with the parties and adopt such procedures as are necessary to facilitate the fair and expeditious conduct of the proceedings;
   (b) Determine the language or languages to be used at trial; and
   (c) Subject to any other relevant provisions of this Statute, provide for disclosure of documents or information not previously disclosed, sufficiently in advance of the commencement of the trial to enable adequate preparation for trial.
4. The Trial Chamber may, if necessary for its effective and fair functioning, refer preliminary issues to the Pre-Trial Chamber or, if necessary, to another available judge of the Pre-Trial Division.
5. Upon notice to the parties, the Trial Chamber may, as appropriate, direct that there be joinder or severance in respect of charges against more than one accused.
6. In performing its functions prior to trial or during the course of a trial, the Trial Chamber may, as necessary:

(a) Exercise any functions of the Pre-Trial Chamber referred to in article 61, paragraph 11;
(b) Require the attendance and testimony of witnesses and production of documents and other evidence by obtaining, if necessary, the assistance of States as provided in this Statute;
(c) Provide for the protection of confidential information;
(d) Order the production of evidence in addition to that already collected prior to the trial or presented during the trial by the parties;
(e) Provide for the protection of the accused, witnesses and victims; and
(f) Rule on any other relevant matters.

7. The trial shall be held in public. The Trial Chamber may, however, determine that special circumstances require that certain proceedings be in closed session for the purposes set forth in article 68, or to protect confidential or sensitive information to be given in evidence.
8. (a) At the commencement of the trial, the Trial Chamber shall have read to the accused the charges previously confirmed by the Pre-Trial Chamber. The Trial Chamber shall satisfy itself that the accused understands the nature of the charges. It shall afford him or her the opportunity to make an admission of guilt in accordance with article 65 or to plead not guilty.
   (b) At the trial, the presiding judge may give directions for the conduct of proceedings, including to ensure that they are conducted in a fair and impartial manner. Subject to any directions of the presiding judge, the parties may submit evidence in accordance with the provisions of this Statute.
9. The Trial Chamber shall have, *inter alia*, the power on application of a party or on its own motion to:
   (a) Rule on the admissibility or relevance of evidence; and
   (b) Take all necessary steps to maintain order in the course of a hearing.
10. The Trial Chamber shall ensure that a complete record of the trial, which accurately reflects the proceedings, is made and that it is maintained and preserved by the Registrar.

Article 65
Proceedings on an admission of guilt

1. Where the accused makes an admission of guilt pursuant to article 64, paragraph 8 (a), the Trial Chamber shall determine whether:
   (a) The accused understands the nature and consequences of the admission of guilt;
   (b) The admission is voluntarily made by the accused after sufficient consultation with defence counsel; and
   (c) The admission of guilt is supported by the facts of the case that are contained in:
       (i) The charges brought by the Prosecutor and admitted by the accused;
       (ii) Any materials presented by the Prosecutor which supplement the charges and which the accused accepts; and
       (iii) Any other evidence, such as the testimony of witnesses, presented by the Prosecutor or the accused.
2. Where the Trial Chamber is satisfied that the matters referred to in paragraph 1 are established, it shall consider the admission of guilt, together with any additional evidence presented, as establishing all the essential facts that are required to prove the crime to which the admission of guilt relates, and may convict the accused of that crime.
3. Where the Trial Chamber is not satisfied that the matters referred to in paragraph 1 are established, it shall consider the admission of guilt as not having been made, in which case it shall order that the trial be continued under the ordinary trial procedures provided by this Statute and may remit the case to another Trial Chamber.
4. Where the Trial Chamber is of the opinion that a more complete presentation of the facts of the case is required in the interests of justice, in particular the interests of the victims, the Trial Chamber may:

(a) Request the Prosecutor to present additional evidence, including the testimony of witnesses; or
(b) Order that the trial be continued under the ordinary trial procedures provided by this Statute, in which case it shall consider the admission of guilt as not having been made and may remit the case to another Trial Chamber.
5. Any discussions between the Prosecutor and the defence regarding modification of the charges, the admission of guilt or the penalty to be imposed shall not be binding on the Court.

Article 66
Presumption of innocence

1. Everyone shall be presumed innocent until proved guilty before the Court in accordance with the applicable law.
2. The onus is on the Prosecutor to prove the guilt of the accused.
3. In order to convict the accused, the Court must be convinced of the guilt of the accused beyond reasonable doubt.

Article 67
Rights of the accused

1. In the determination of any charge, the accused shall be entitled to a public hearing, having regard to the provisions of this Statute, to a fair hearing conducted impartially, and to the following minimum guarantees, in full equality:
   (a) To be informed promptly and in detail of the nature, cause and content of the charge, in a language which the accused fully understands and speaks;
   (b) To have adequate time and facilities for the preparation of the defence and to communicate freely with counsel of the accused's choosing in confidence;
   (c) To be tried without undue delay;
   (d) Subject to article 63, paragraph 2, to be present at the trial, to conduct the defence in person or through legal assistance of the accused's choosing, to be informed, if the accused does not have legal assistance, of this right and to have legal assistance assigned by the Court in any case where the interests of justice so require, and without payment if the accused lacks sufficient means to pay for it;
   (e) To examine, or have examined, the witnesses against him or her and to obtain the attendance and examination of witnesses on his or her behalf under the same conditions as witnesses against him or her. The accused shall also be entitled to raise defences and to present other evidence admissible under this Statute;
   (f) To have, free of any cost, the assistance of a competent interpreter and such translations as are necessary to meet the requirements of fairness, if any of the proceedings of or documents presented to the Court are not in a language which the accused fully understands and speaks;
   (g) Not to be compelled to testify or to confess guilt and to remain silent, without such silence being a consideration in the determination of guilt or innocence;
   (h) To make an unsworn oral or written statement in his or her defence; and
   (i) Not to have imposed on him or her any reversal of the burden of proof or any onus of rebuttal.
2. In addition to any other disclosure provided for in this Statute, the Prosecutor shall, as soon as practicable, disclose to the defence evidence in the Prosecutor's possession or control which he or she believes shows or tends to show the innocence of the accused, or to mitigate the guilt of the accused, or which may affect the credibility of prosecution evidence. In case of doubt as to the application of this paragraph, the Court shall decide.

Article 68
Protection of the victims and witnesses and their participation in the proceedings

1. The Court shall take appropriate measures to protect the safety, physical and psychological well-being, dignity and privacy of victims and witnesses. In so doing, the Court shall have regard to all relevant factors, including age, gender as defined in article 7, paragraph 3, and health, and the nature of the crime, in particular, but not limited to, where the crime involves sexual or gender violence or violence against children. The Prosecutor shall take such measures particularly during the investigation and prosecution of such crimes. These measures shall not be prejudicial to or inconsistent with the rights of the accused and a fair and impartial trial.
2. As an exception to the principle of public hearings provided for in article 67, the Chambers of the Court may, to protect victims and witnesses or an accused, conduct any part of the proceedings *in camera* or allow the presentation of evidence by electronic or other special means. In particular, such measures shall be implemented in the case of a victim of sexual violence or a child who is a victim or a witness, unless otherwise ordered by the Court, having regard to all the circumstances, particularly the views of the victim or witness.
3. Where the personal interests of the victims are affected, the Court shall permit their views and concerns to be presented and considered at stages of the proceedings determined to be appropriate by the Court and in a manner which is not prejudicial to or inconsistent with the rights of the accused and a fair and impartial trial. Such views and concerns may be presented by the legal representatives of the victims where the Court considers it appropriate, in accordance with the Rules of Procedure and Evidence.
4. The Victims and Witnesses Unit may advise the Prosecutor and the Court on appropriate protective measures, security arrangements, counselling and assistance as referred to in article 43, paragraph 6.
5. Where the disclosure of evidence or information pursuant to this Statute may lead to the grave endangerment of the security of a witness or his or her family, the Prosecutor may, for the purposes of any proceedings conducted prior to the commencement of the trial, withhold such evidence or information and instead submit a summary thereof. Such measures shall be exercised in a manner which is not prejudicial to or inconsistent with the rights of the accused and a fair and impartial trial.
6. A State may make an application for necessary measures to be taken in respect of the protection of its servants or agents and the protection of confidential or sensitive information.

Article 69
Evidence

1. Before testifying, each witness shall, in accordance with the Rules of Procedure and Evidence, give an undertaking as to the truthfulness of the evidence to be given by that witness.
2. The testimony of a witness at trial shall be given in person, except to the extent provided by the measures set forth in article 68 or in the Rules of Procedure and Evidence. The Court may also permit the giving of *viva voce* (oral) or recorded testimony of a witness by means of video or audio technology, as well as the introduction of documents or written transcripts, subject to this Statute and in accordance with the Rules of Procedure and Evidence. These measures shall not be prejudicial to or inconsistent with the rights of the accused.
3. The parties may submit evidence relevant to the case, in accordance with article 64. The Court shall have the authority to request the submission of all evidence that it considers necessary for the determination of the truth.
4. The Court may rule on the relevance or admissibility of any evidence, taking into account, *inter alia*, the probative value of the evidence and any prejudice that such evidence may

cause to a fair trial or to a fair evaluation of the testimony of a witness, in accordance with the Rules of Procedure and Evidence.
5. The Court shall respect and observe privileges on confidentiality as provided for in the Rules of Procedure and Evidence.
6. The Court shall not require proof of facts of common knowledge but may take judicial notice of them.
7. Evidence obtained by means of a violation of this Statute or internationally recognized human rights shall not be admissible if:
    (a) The violation casts substantial doubt on the reliability of the evidence; or
    (b) The admission of the evidence would be antithetical to and would seriously damage the integrity of the proceedings.
8. When deciding on the relevance or admissibility of evidence collected by a State, the Court shall not rule on the application of the State's national law.

Article 70
Offences against the administration of justice

1. The Court shall have jurisdiction over the following offences against its administration of justice when committed intentionally:
    (a) Giving false testimony when under an obligation pursuant to article 69, paragraph 1, to tell the truth;
    (b) Presenting evidence that the party knows is false or forged;
    (c) Corruptly influencing a witness, obstructing or interfering with the attendance or testimony of a witness, retaliating against a witness for giving testimony or destroying, tampering with or interfering with the collection of evidence;
    (d) Impeding, intimidating or corruptly influencing an official of the Court for the purpose of forcing or persuading the official not to perform, or to perform improperly, his or her duties;
    (e) Retaliating against an official of the Court on account of duties performed by that or another official;
    (f) Soliciting or accepting a bribe as an official of the Court in connection with his or her official duties.
2. The principles and procedures governing the Court's exercise of jurisdiction over offences under this article shall be those provided for in the Rules of Procedure and Evidence. The conditions for providing international cooperation to the Court with respect to its proceedings under this article shall be governed by the domestic laws of the requested State.
3. In the event of conviction, the Court may impose a term of imprisonment not exceeding five years, or a fine in accordance with the Rules of Procedure and Evidence, or both.
4. (a) Each State Party shall extend its criminal laws penalizing offences against the integrity of its own investigative or judicial process to offences against the administration of justice referred to in this article, committed on its territory, or by one of its nationals;
    (b) Upon request by the Court, whenever it deems it proper, the State Party shall submit the case to its competent authorities for the purpose of prosecution. Those authorities shall treat such cases with diligence and devote sufficient resources to enable them to be conducted effectively.

Article 71
Sanctions for misconduct before the Court

1. The Court may sanction persons present before it who commit misconduct, including disruption of its proceedings or deliberate refusal to comply with its directions, by administrative measures other than imprisonment, such as temporary or permanent removal from

the courtroom, a fine or other similar measures provided for in the Rules of Procedure and Evidence.
2. The procedures governing the imposition of the measures set forth in paragraph 1 shall be those provided for in the Rules of Procedure and Evidence.

Article 72
Protection of national security information

1. This article applies in any case where the disclosure of the information or documents of a State would, in the opinion of that State, prejudice its national security interests. Such cases include those falling within the scope of article 56, paragraphs 2 and 3, article 61, paragraph 3, article 64, paragraph 3, article 67, paragraph 2, article 68, paragraph 6, article 87, paragraph 6 and article 93, as well as cases arising at any other stage of the proceedings where such disclosure may be at issue.
2. This article shall also apply when a person who has been requested to give information or evidence has refused to do so or has referred the matter to the State on the ground that disclosure would prejudice the national security interests of a State and the State concerned confirms that it is of the opinion that disclosure would prejudice its national security interests.
3. Nothing in this article shall prejudice the requirements of confidentiality applicable under article 54, paragraph 3 (e) and (f), or the application of article 73.
4. If a State learns that information or documents of the State are being, or are likely to be, disclosed at any stage of the proceedings, and it is of the opinion that disclosure would prejudice its national security interests, that State shall have the right to intervene in order to obtain resolution of the issue in accordance with this article.
5. If, in the opinion of a State, disclosure of information would prejudice its national security interests, all reasonable steps will be taken by the State, acting in conjunction with the Prosecutor, the defence or the Pre-Trial Chamber or Trial Chamber, as the case may be, to seek to resolve the matter by cooperative means. Such steps may include:
   (a) Modification or clarification of the request;
   (b) A determination by the Court regarding the relevance of the information or evidence sought, or a determination as to whether the evidence, though relevant, could be or has been obtained from a source other than the requested State;
   (c) Obtaining the information or evidence from a different source or in a different form; or
   (d) Agreement on conditions under which the assistance could be provided including, among other things, providing summaries or redactions, limitations on disclosure, use of *in camera* or *ex parte* proceedings, or other protective measures permissible under the Statute and the Rules of Procedure and Evidence.
6. Once all reasonable steps have been taken to resolve the matter through cooperative means, and if the State considers that there are no means or conditions under which the information or documents could be provided or disclosed without prejudice to its national security interests, it shall so notify the Prosecutor or the Court of the specific reasons for its decision, unless a specific description of the reasons would itself necessarily result in such prejudice to the State's national security interests.
7. Thereafter, if the Court determines that the evidence is relevant and necessary for the establishment of the guilt or innocence of the accused, the Court may undertake the following actions:
   (a) Where disclosure of the information or document is sought pursuant to a request for cooperation under Part 9 or the circumstances described in paragraph 2, and the State has invoked the ground for refusal referred to in article 93, paragraph 4:
      (i) The Court may, before making any conclusion referred to in subparagraph 7 (a) (ii), request further consultations for the purpose of considering the State's representations, which may include, as appropriate, hearings *in camera* and *ex parte*;

(ii) If the Court concludes that, by invoking the ground for refusal under article 93, paragraph 4, in the circumstances of the case, the requested State is not acting in accordance with its obligations under this Statute, the Court may refer the matter in accordance with article 87, paragraph 7, specifying the reasons for its conclusion; and

(iii) The Court may make such inference in the trial of the accused as to the existence or non-existence of a fact, as may be appropriate in the circumstances; or

(b) In all other circumstances:
(i) Order disclosure; or
(ii) To the extent it does not order disclosure, make such inference in the trial of the accused as to the existence or non-existence of a fact, as may be appropriate in the circumstances.

Article 73
Third-party information or documents

If a State Party is requested by the Court to provide a document or information in its custody, possession or control, which was disclosed to it in confidence by a State, intergovernmental organization or international organization, it shall seek the consent of the originator to disclose that document or information. If the originator is a State Party, it shall either consent to disclosure of the information or document or undertake to resolve the issue of disclosure with the Court, subject to the provisions of article 72. If the originator is not a State Party and refuses to consent to disclosure, the requested State shall inform the Court that it is unable to provide the document or information because of a pre-existing obligation of confidentiality to the originator.

Article 74
Requirements for the decision

1. All the judges of the Trial Chamber shall be present at each stage of the trial and throughout their deliberations. The Presidency may, on a case-by-case basis, designate, as available, one or more alternate judges to be present at each stage of the trial and to replace a member of the Trial Chamber if that member is unable to continue attending.
2. The Trial Chamber's decision shall be based on its evaluation of the evidence and the entire proceedings. The decision shall not exceed the facts and circumstances described in the charges and any amendments to the charges. The Court may base its decision only on evidence submitted and discussed before it at the trial.
3. The judges shall attempt to achieve unanimity in their decision, failing which the decision shall be taken by a majority of the judges.
4. The deliberations of the Trial Chamber shall remain secret.
5. The decision shall be in writing and shall contain a full and reasoned statement of the Trial Chamber's findings on the evidence and conclusions. The Trial Chamber shall issue one decision. When there is no unanimity, the Trial Chamber's decision shall contain the views of the majority and the minority. The decision or a summary thereof shall be delivered in open court.

Article 75
Reparations to victims

1. The Court shall establish principles relating to reparations to, or in respect of, victims, including restitution, compensation and rehabilitation. On this basis, in its decision the Court may, either upon request or on its own motion in exceptional circumstances, determine the scope and extent of any damage, loss and injury to, or in respect of, victims and will state the principles on which it is acting.

2. The Court may make an order directly against a convicted person specifying appropriate reparations to, or in respect of, victims, including restitution, compensation and rehabilitation.

Where appropriate, the Court may order that the award for reparations be made through the Trust Fund provided for in article 79.

3. Before making an order under this article, the Court may invite and shall take account of representations from or on behalf of the convicted person, victims, other interested persons or interested States.
4. In exercising its power under this article, the Court may, after a person is convicted of a crime within the jurisdiction of the Court, determine whether, in order to give effect to an order which it may make under this article, it is necessary to seek measures under article 93, paragraph 1.
5. A State Party shall give effect to a decision under this article as if the provisions of article 109 were applicable to this article.
6. Nothing in this article shall be interpreted as prejudicing the rights of victims under national or international law.

Article 76
Sentencing

1. In the event of a conviction, the Trial Chamber shall consider the appropriate sentence to be imposed and shall take into account the evidence presented and submissions made during the trial that are relevant to the sentence.
2. Except where article 65 applies and before the completion of the trial, the Trial Chamber may on its own motion and shall, at the request of the Prosecutor or the accused, hold a further hearing to hear any additional evidence or submissions relevant to the sentence, in accordance with the Rules of Procedure and Evidence.
3. Where paragraph 2 applies, any representations under article 75 shall be heard during the further hearing referred to in paragraph 2 and, if necessary, during any additional hearing.
4. The sentence shall be pronounced in public and, wherever possible, in the presence of the accused.

PART 7. PENALTIES
Article 77
Applicable penalties

1. Subject to article 110, the Court may impose one of the following penalties on a person convicted of a crime referred to in article 5 of this Statute:
   (a) Imprisonment for a specified number of years, which may not exceed a maximum of 30 years; or
   (b) A term of life imprisonment when justified by the extreme gravity of the crime and the individual circumstances of the convicted person.
2. In addition to imprisonment, the Court may order:
   (a) A fine under the criteria provided for in the Rules of Procedure and Evidence;
   (b) A forfeiture of proceeds, property and assets derived directly or indirectly from that crime, without prejudice to the rights of bona fide third parties.

Article 78
Determination of the sentence

1. In determining the sentence, the Court shall, in accordance with the Rules of Procedure and Evidence, take into account such factors as the gravity of the crime and the individual circumstances of the convicted person.

2. In imposing a sentence of imprisonment, the Court shall deduct the time, if any, previously spent in detention in accordance with an order of the Court. The Court may deduct any time otherwise spent in detention in connection with conduct underlying the crime.
3. When a person has been convicted of more than one crime, the Court shall pronounce a sentence for each crime and a joint sentence specifying the total period of imprisonment. This period shall be no less than the highest individual sentence pronounced and shall not exceed 30 years imprisonment or a sentence of life imprisonment in conformity with article 77, paragraph 1 (b).

Article 79
Trust Fund

1. A Trust Fund shall be established by decision of the Assembly of States Parties for the benefit of victims of crimes within the jurisdiction of the Court, and of the families of such victims.
2. The Court may order money and other property collected through fines or forfeiture to be transferred, by order of the Court, to the Trust Fund.
3. The Trust Fund shall be managed according to criteria to be determined by the Assembly of States Parties.

Article 80
Non-prejudice to national application of penalties and national laws

Nothing in this Part affects the application by States of penalties prescribed by their national law, nor the law of States which do not provide for penalties prescribed in this Part.

PART 8. APPEAL AND REVISION
Article 81
Appeal against decision of acquittal or conviction or against sentence

1. A decision under article 74 may be appealed in accordance with the Rules of Procedure and Evidence as follows:
   (a) The Prosecutor may make an appeal on any of the following grounds:
      (i) Procedural error,
      (ii) Error of fact, or
      (iii) Error of law;
   (b) The convicted person, or the Prosecutor on that person's behalf, may make an appeal on any of the following grounds:
      (i) Procedural error,
      (ii) Error of fact,
      (iii) Error of law, or
      (iv) Any other ground that affects the fairness or reliability of the proceedings or decision.
2. (a) A sentence may be appealed, in accordance with the Rules of Procedure and Evidence, by the Prosecutor or the convicted person on the ground of disproportion between the crime and the sentence;
   (b) If on an appeal against sentence the Court considers that there are grounds on which the conviction might be set aside, wholly or in part, it may invite the Prosecutor and the convicted person to submit grounds under article 81, paragraph 1 (a) or (b), and may render a decision on conviction in accordance with article 83;
   (c) The same procedure applies when the Court, on an appeal against conviction only, considers that there are grounds to reduce the sentence under paragraph 2 (a).

3. (a) Unless the Trial Chamber orders otherwise, a convicted person shall remain in custody pending an appeal;
   (b) When a convicted person's time in custody exceeds the sentence of imprisonment imposed, that person shall be released, except that if the Prosecutor is also appealing, the release may be subject to the conditions under subparagraph (c) below;
   (c) In case of an acquittal, the accused shall be released immediately, subject to the following:
      (i) Under exceptional circumstances, and having regard, *inter alia*, to the concrete risk of flight, the seriousness of the offence charged and the probability of success on appeal, the Trial Chamber, at the request of the Prosecutor, may maintain the detention of the person pending appeal;
      (ii) A decision by the Trial Chamber under subparagraph (c) (i) may be appealed in accordance with the Rules of Procedure and Evidence.
4. Subject to the provisions of paragraph 3 (a) and (b), execution of the decision or sentence shall be suspended during the period allowed for appeal and for the duration of the appeal proceedings.

Article 82
Appeal against other decisions

1. Either party may appeal any of the following decisions in accordance with the Rules of Procedure and Evidence:
   (a) A decision with respect to jurisdiction or admissibility;
   (b) A decision granting or denying release of the person being investigated or prosecuted;
   (c) A decision of the Pre-Trial Chamber to act on its own initiative under article 56, paragraph 3;
   (d) A decision that involves an issue that would significantly affect the fair and expeditious conduct of the proceedings or the outcome of the trial, and for which, in the opinion of the Pre-Trial or Trial Chamber, an immediate resolution by the Appeals Chamber may materially advance the proceedings.
2. A decision of the Pre-Trial Chamber under article 57, paragraph 3 (d), may be appealed against by the State concerned or by the Prosecutor, with the leave of the Pre-Trial Chamber. The appeal shall be heard on an expedited basis.
3. An appeal shall not of itself have suspensive effect unless the Appeals Chamber so orders, upon request, in accordance with the Rules of Procedure and Evidence.
4. A legal representative of the victims, the convicted person or a bona fide owner of property adversely affected by an order under article 75 may appeal against the order for reparations, as provided in the Rules of Procedure and Evidence.

Article 83
Proceedings on appeal

1. For the purposes of proceedings under article 81 and this article, the Appeals Chamber shall have all the powers of the Trial Chamber.
2. If the Appeals Chamber finds that the proceedings appealed from were unfair in a way that affected the reliability of the decision or sentence, or that the decision or sentence appealed from was materially affected by error of fact or law or procedural error, it may:
   (a) Reverse or amend the decision or sentence; or
   (b) Order a new trial before a different Trial Chamber.

For these purposes, the Appeals Chamber may remand a factual issue to the original Trial Chamber for it to determine the issue and to report back accordingly, or may itself call evidence to determine the issue. When the decision or sentence has been appealed only by the person convicted, or the Prosecutor on that person's behalf, it cannot be amended to his or her detriment.

3. If in an appeal against sentence the Appeals Chamber finds that the sentence is disproportionate to the crime, it may vary the sentence in accordance with Part 7.
4. The judgement of the Appeals Chamber shall be taken by a majority of the judges and shall be delivered in open court. The judgement shall state the reasons on which it is based. When there is no unanimity, the judgement of the Appeals Chamber shall contain the views of the majority and the minority, but a judge may deliver a separate or dissenting opinion on a question of law.
5. The Appeals Chamber may deliver its judgement in the absence of the person acquitted or convicted.

Article 84
Revision of conviction or sentence

1. The convicted person or, after death, spouses, children, parents or one person alive at the time of the accused's death who has been given express written instructions from the accused to bring such a claim, or the Prosecutor on the person's behalf, may apply to the Appeals Chamber to revise the final judgement of conviction or sentence on the grounds that:
    (a) New evidence has been discovered that:
        (i) Was not available at the time of trial, and such unavailability was not wholly or partially attributable to the party making application; and
        (ii) Is sufficiently important that had it been proved at trial it would have been likely to have resulted in a different verdict;
    (b) It has been newly discovered that decisive evidence, taken into account at trial and upon which the conviction depends, was false, forged or falsified;
    (c) One or more of the judges who participated in conviction or confirmation of the charges has committed, in that case, an act of serious misconduct or serious breach of duty of sufficient gravity to justify the removal of that judge or those judges from office under article 46.
2. The Appeals Chamber shall reject the application if it considers it to be unfounded. If it determines that the application is meritorious, it may, as appropriate:
    (a) Reconvene the original Trial Chamber;
    (b) Constitute a new Trial Chamber; or
    (c) Retain jurisdiction over the matter,

with a view to, after hearing the parties in the manner set forth in the Rules of Procedure and Evidence, arriving at a determination on whether the judgement should be revised.

Article 85
Compensation to an arrested or convicted person

1. Anyone who has been the victim of unlawful arrest or detention shall have an enforceable right to compensation.
2. When a person has by a final decision been convicted of a criminal offence, and when subsequently his or her conviction has been reversed on the ground that a new or newly discovered fact shows conclusively that there has been a miscarriage of justice, the person who has suffered punishment as a result of such conviction shall be compensated according to law, unless it is proved that the non-disclosure of the unknown fact in time is wholly or partly attributable to him or her.
3. In exceptional circumstances, where the Court finds conclusive facts showing that there has been a grave and manifest miscarriage of justice, it may in its discretion award compensation, according to the criteria provided in the Rules of Procedure and Evidence, to a person who has been released from detention following a final decision of acquittal or a termination of the proceedings for that reason.

PART 9. INTERNATIONAL COOPERATION AND JUDICIAL ASSISTANCE
Article 86
General obligation to cooperate

States Parties shall, in accordance with the provisions of this Statute, cooperate fully with the Court in its investigation and prosecution of crimes within the jurisdiction of the Court.

Article 87
Requests for cooperation: general provisions

1. (a) The Court shall have the authority to make requests to States Parties for cooperation. The requests shall be transmitted through the diplomatic channel or any other appropriate channel as may be designated by each State Party upon ratification, acceptance, approval or accession.
   Subsequent changes to the designation shall be made by each State Party in accordance with the Rules of Procedure and Evidence.
   (b) When appropriate, without prejudice to the provisions of subparagraph (a), requests may also be transmitted through the International Criminal Police Organization or any appropriate regional organization.
2. Requests for cooperation and any documents supporting the request shall either be in or be accompanied by a translation into an official language of the requested State or one of the working languages of the Court, in accordance with the choice made by that State upon ratification, acceptance, approval or accession.
   Subsequent changes to this choice shall be made in accordance with the Rules of Procedure and Evidence.
3. The requested State shall keep confidential a request for cooperation and any documents supporting the request, except to the extent that the disclosure is necessary for execution of the request.
4. In relation to any request for assistance presented under this Part, the Court may take such measures, including measures related to the protection of information, as may be necessary to ensure the safety or physical or psychological well-being of any victims, potential witnesses and their families. The Court may request that any information that is made available under this Part shall be provided and handled in a manner that protects the safety and physical or psychological well-being of any victims, potential witnesses and their families.
5. (a) The Court may invite any State not party to this Statute to provide assistance under this Part on the basis of an ad hoc arrangement, an agreement with such State or any other appropriate basis.
   (b) Where a State not party to this Statute, which has entered into an ad hoc arrangement or an agreement with the Court, fails to cooperate with requests pursuant to any such arrangement or agreement, the Court may so inform the Assembly of States Parties or, where the Security Council referred the matter to the Court, the Security Council.
6. The Court may ask any intergovernmental organization to provide information or documents. The Court may also ask for other forms of cooperation and assistance which may be agreed upon with such an organization and which are in accordance with its competence or mandate.
7. Where a State Party fails to comply with a request to cooperate by the Court contrary to the provisions of this Statute, thereby preventing the Court from exercising its functions and powers under this Statute, the Court may make a finding to that effect and refer the matter to the Assembly of States Parties or, where the Security Council referred the matter to the Court, to the Security Council.

Article 88
Availability of procedures under national law

States Parties shall ensure that there are procedures available under their national law for all of the forms of cooperation which are specified under this Part.

Article 89
Surrender of persons to the Court

1. The Court may transmit a request for the arrest and surrender of a person, together with the material supporting the request outlined in article 91, to any State on the territory of which that person may be found and shall request the cooperation of that State in the arrest and surrender of such a person. States Parties shall, in accordance with the provisions of this Part and the procedure under their national law, comply with requests for arrest and surrender.
2. Where the person sought for surrender brings a challenge before a national court on the basis of the principle of *ne bis in idem* as provided in article 20, the requested State shall immediately consult with the Court to determine if there has been a relevant ruling on admissibility. If the case is admissible, the requested State shall proceed with the execution of the request. If an admissibility ruling is pending, the requested State may postpone the execution of the request for surrender of the person until the Court makes a determination on admissibility.
3. (a) A State Party shall authorize, in accordance with its national procedural law, transportation through its territory of a person being surrendered to the Court by another State, except where transit through that State would impede or delay the surrender.
   (b) A request by the Court for transit shall be transmitted in accordance with article 87. The request for transit shall contain:
   (i) A description of the person being transported;
   (ii) A brief statement of the facts of the case and their legal characterization; and
   (iii) The warrant for arrest and surrender;
   (c) A person being transported shall be detained in custody during the period of transit;
   (d) No authorization is required if the person is transported by air and no landing is scheduled on the territory of the transit State;
   (e) If an unscheduled landing occurs on the territory of the transit State, that State may require a request for transit from the Court as provided for in subparagraph (b). The transit State shall detain the person being transported until the request for transit is received and the transit is effected, provided that detention for purposes of this subparagraph may not be extended beyond 96 hours from the unscheduled landing unless the request is received within that time.
4. If the person sought is being proceeded against or is serving a sentence in the requested State for a crime different from that for which surrender to the Court is sought, the requested State, after making its decision to grant the request, shall consult with the Court.

Article 90
Competing requests

1. A State Party which receives a request from the Court for the surrender of a person under article 89 shall, if it also receives a request from any other State for the extradition of the same person for the same conduct which forms the basis of the crime for which the Court seeks the person's surrender, notify the Court and the requesting State of that fact.
2. Where the requesting State is a State Party, the requested State shall give priority to the request from the Court if:

(a) The Court has, pursuant to article 18 or 19, made a determination that the case in respect of which surrender is sought is admissible and that determination takes into account the investigation or prosecution conducted by the requesting State in respect of its request for extradition; or
(b) The Court makes the determination described in subparagraph (a) pursuant to the requested State's notification under paragraph 1.
3. Where a determination under paragraph 2 (a) has not been made, the requested State may, at its discretion, pending the determination of the Court under paragraph 2 (b), proceed to deal with the request for extradition from the requesting State but shall not extradite the person until the Court has determined that the case is inadmissible. The Court's determination shall be made on an expedited basis.
4. If the requesting State is a State not Party to this Statute the requested State, if it is not under an international obligation to extradite the person to the requesting State, shall give priority to the request for surrender from the Court, if the Court has determined that the case is admissible.
5. Where a case under paragraph 4 has not been determined to be admissible by the Court, the requested State may, at its discretion, proceed to deal with the request for extradition from the requesting State.
6. In cases where paragraph 4 applies except that the requested State is under an existing international obligation to extradite the person to the requesting State not Party to this Statute, the requested State shall determine whether to surrender the person to the Court or extradite the person to the requesting State. In making its decision, the requested State shall consider all the relevant factors, including but not limited to:
    (a) The respective dates of the requests;
    (b) The interests of the requesting State including, where relevant, whether the crime was committed in its territory and the nationality of the victims and of the person sought; and
    (c) The possibility of subsequent surrender between the Court and the requesting State.
7. Where a State Party which receives a request from the Court for the surrender of a person also receives a request from any State for the extradition of the same person for conduct other than that which constitutes the crime for which the Court seeks the person's surrender:
    (a) The requested State shall, if it is not under an existing international obligation to extradite the person to the requesting State, give priority to the request from the Court;
    (b) The requested State shall, if it is under an existing international obligation to extradite the person to the requesting State, determine whether to surrender the person to the Court or to extradite the person to the requesting State. In making its decision, the requested State shall consider all the relevant factors, including but not limited to those set out in paragraph 6, but shall give special consideration to the relative nature and gravity of the conduct in question.
8. Where pursuant to a notification under this article, the Court has determined a case to be inadmissible, and subsequently extradition to the requesting State is refused, the requested State shall notify the Court of this decision.

Article 91
Contents of request for arrest and surrender

1. A request for arrest and surrender shall be made in writing. In urgent cases, a request may be made by any medium capable of delivering a written record, provided that the request shall be confirmed through the channel provided for in article 87, paragraph 1 (a).
2. In the case of a request for the arrest and surrender of a person for whom a warrant of arrest has been issued by the Pre-Trial Chamber under article 58, the request shall contain or be supported by:

(a) Information describing the person sought, sufficient to identify the person, and information as to that person's probable location;
(b) A copy of the warrant of arrest; and
(c) Such documents, statements or information as may be necessary to meet the requirements for the surrender process in the requested State, except that those requirements should not be more burdensome than those applicable to requests for extradition pursuant to treaties or arrangements between the requested State and other States and should, if possible, be less burdensome, taking into account the distinct nature of the Court.

3. In the case of a request for the arrest and surrender of a person already convicted, the request shall contain or be supported by:
   (a) A copy of any warrant of arrest for that person;
   (b) A copy of the judgement of conviction;
   (c) Information to demonstrate that the person sought is the one referred to in the judgement of conviction; and
   (d) If the person sought has been sentenced, a copy of the sentence imposed and, in the case of a sentence for imprisonment, a statement of any time already served and the time remaining to be served.

4. Upon the request of the Court, a State Party shall consult with the Court, either generally or with respect to a specific matter, regarding any requirements under its national law that may apply under paragraph 2 (c). During the consultations, the State Party shall advise the Court of the specific requirements of its national law.

Article 92
Provisional arrest

1. In urgent cases, the Court may request the provisional arrest of the person sought, pending presentation of the request for surrender and the documents supporting the request as specified in article 91.

2. The request for provisional arrest shall be made by any medium capable of delivering a written record and shall contain:
   (a) Information describing the person sought, sufficient to identify the person, and information as to that person's probable location;
   (b) A concise statement of the crimes for which the person's arrest is sought and of the facts which are alleged to constitute those crimes, including, where possible, the date and location of the crime;
   (c) A statement of the existence of a warrant of arrest or a judgement of conviction against the person sought; and
   (d) A statement that a request for surrender of the person sought will follow.

3. A person who is provisionally arrested may be released from custody if the requested State has not received the request for surrender and the documents supporting the request as specified in article 91 within the time limits specified in the Rules of Procedure and Evidence. However, the person may consent to surrender before the expiration of this period if permitted by the law of the requested State. In such a case, the requested State shall proceed to surrender the person to the Court as soon as possible.

4. The fact that the person sought has been released from custody pursuant to paragraph 3 shall not prejudice the subsequent arrest and surrender of that person if the request for surrender and the documents supporting the request are delivered at a later date.

Article 93
Other forms of cooperation

1. States Parties shall, in accordance with the provisions of this Part and under procedures of national law, comply with requests by the Court to provide the following assistance in relation to investigations or prosecutions:

(a) The identification and whereabouts of persons or the location of items;
(b) The taking of evidence, including testimony under oath, and the production of evidence, including expert opinions and reports necessary to the Court;
(c) The questioning of any person being investigated or prosecuted;
(d) The service of documents, including judicial documents;
(e) Facilitating the voluntary appearance of persons as witnesses or experts before the Court;
(f) The temporary transfer of persons as provided in paragraph 7;
(g) The examination of places or sites, including the exhumation and examination of grave sites;
(h) The execution of searches and seizures;
(i) The provision of records and documents, including official records and documents;
(j) The protection of victims and witnesses and the preservation of evidence;
(k) The identification, tracing and freezing or seizure of proceeds, property and assets and instrumentalities of crimes for the purpose of eventual forfeiture, without prejudice to the rights of bona fide third parties; and
(l) Any other type of assistance which is not prohibited by the law of the requested State, with a view to facilitating the investigation and prosecution of crimes within the jurisdiction of the Court.

2. The Court shall have the authority to provide an assurance to a witness or an expert appearing before the Court that he or she will not be prosecuted, detained or subjected to any restriction of personal freedom by the Court in respect of any act or omission that preceded the departure of that person from the requested State.
3. Where execution of a particular measure of assistance detailed in a request presented under paragraph 1, is prohibited in the requested State on the basis of an existing fundamental legal principle of general application, the requested State shall promptly consult with the Court to try to resolve the matter. In the consultations, consideration should be given to whether the assistance can be rendered in another manner or subject to conditions. If after consultations the matter cannot be resolved, the Court shall modify the request as necessary.
4. In accordance with article 72, a State Party may deny a request for assistance, in whole or in part, only if the request concerns the production of any documents or disclosure of evidence which relates to its national security.
5. Before denying a request for assistance under paragraph 1 (l), the requested State shall consider whether the assistance can be provided subject to specified conditions, or whether the assistance can be provided at a later date or in an alternative manner, provided that if the Court or the Prosecutor accepts the assistance subject to conditions, the Court or the Prosecutor shall abide by them.
6. If a request for assistance is denied, the requested State Party shall promptly inform the Court or the Prosecutor of the reasons for such denial.
7. (a) The Court may request the temporary transfer of a person in custody for purposes of identification or for obtaining testimony or other assistance. The person may be transferred if the following conditions are fulfilled:
    (i) The person freely gives his or her informed consent to the transfer; and
    (ii) The requested State agrees to the transfer, subject to such conditions as that State and the Court may agree.
   (b) The person being transferred shall remain in custody. When the purposes of the transfer have been fulfilled, the Court shall return the person without delay to the requested State.
8. (a) The Court shall ensure the confidentiality of documents and information, except as required for the investigation and proceedings described in the request.
   (b) The requested State may, when necessary, transmit documents or information to the Prosecutor on a confidential basis. The Prosecutor may then use them solely for the purpose of generating new evidence.

(c) The requested State may, on its own motion or at the request of the Prosecutor, subsequently consent to the disclosure of such documents or information. They may then be used as evidence pursuant to the provisions of Parts 5 and 6 and in accordance with the Rules of Procedure and Evidence.

9. (a) (i) In the event that a State Party receives competing requests, other than for surrender or extradition, from the Court and from another State pursuant to an international obligation, the State Party shall endeavour, in consultation with the Court and the other State, to meet both requests, if necessary by postponing or attaching conditions to one or the other request.
  (ii) Failing that, competing requests shall be resolved in accordance with the principles established in article 90.
 (b) Where, however, the request from the Court concerns information, property or persons which are subject to the control of a third State or an international organization by virtue of an international agreement, the requested States shall so inform the Court and the Court shall direct its request to the third State or international organization.

10. (a) The Court may, upon request, cooperate with and provide assistance to a State Party conducting an investigation into or trial in respect of conduct which constitutes a crime within the jurisdiction of the Court or which constitutes a serious crime under the national law of the requesting State.
  (b) (i) The assistance provided under subparagraph (a) shall include, *inter alia:*
    a. The transmission of statements, documents or other types of evidence obtained in the course of an investigation or a trial conducted by the Court; and
    b. The questioning of any person detained by order of the Court;
   (ii) In the case of assistance under subparagraph (b) (i) a:
    a. If the documents or other types of evidence have been obtained with the assistance of a State, such transmission shall require the consent of that State;
    b. If the statements, documents or other types of evidence have been provided by a witness or expert, such transmission shall be subject to the provisions of article 68.
  (c) The Court may, under the conditions set out in this paragraph, grant a request for assistance under this paragraph from a State which is not a Party to this Statute.

Article 94
Postponement of execution of a request in respect of ongoing investigation or prosecution

1. If the immediate execution of a request would interfere with an ongoing investigation or prosecution of a case different from that to which the request relates, the requested State may postpone the execution of the request for a period of time agreed upon with the Court. However, the postponement shall be no longer than is necessary to complete the relevant investigation or prosecution in the requested State. Before making a decision to postpone, the requested State should consider whether the assistance may be immediately provided subject to certain conditions.
2. If a decision to postpone is taken pursuant to paragraph 1, the Prosecutor may, however, seek measures to preserve evidence, pursuant to article 93, paragraph 1 (j).

Article 95
Postponement of execution of a request in respect of an admissibility challenge

Where there is an admissibility challenge under consideration by the Court pursuant to article 18 or 19, the requested State may postpone the execution of a request under this Part pending a determination by the Court, unless the Court has specifically ordered that the Prosecutor may pursue the collection of such evidence pursuant to article 18 or 19.

Article 96
Contents of request for other forms of assistance under article 93

1. A request for other forms of assistance referred to in article 93 shall be made in writing. In urgent cases, a request may be made by any medium capable of delivering a written record, provided that the request shall be confirmed through the channel provided for in article 87, paragraph 1 (a).
2. The request shall, as applicable, contain or be supported by the following:
   (a) A concise statement of the purpose of the request and the assistance sought, including the legal basis and the grounds for the request;
   (b) As much detailed information as possible about the location or identification of any person or place that must be found or identified in order for the assistance sought to be provided;
   (c) A concise statement of the essential facts underlying the request;
   (d) The reasons for and details of any procedure or requirement to be followed;
   (e) Such information as may be required under the law of the requested State in order to execute the request; and
   (f) Any other information relevant in order for the assistance sought to be provided.
3. Upon the request of the Court, a State Party shall consult with the Court, either generally or with respect to a specific matter, regarding any requirements under its national law that may apply under paragraph 2 (e). During the consultations, the State Party shall advise the Court of the specific requirements of its national law.
4. The provisions of this article shall, where applicable, also apply in respect of a request for assistance made to the Court.

Article 97
Consultations

Where a State Party receives a request under this Part in relation to which it identifies problems which may impede or prevent the execution of the request, that State shall consult with the Court without delay in order to resolve the matter. Such problems may include, *inter alia:*
   (a) Insufficient information to execute the request;
   (b) In the case of a request for surrender, the fact that despite best efforts, the person sought cannot be located or that the investigation conducted has determined that the person in the requested State is clearly not the person named in the warrant; or
   (c) The fact that execution of the request in its current form would require the requested State to breach a pre-existing treaty obligation undertaken with respect to another State.

Article 98
Cooperation with respect to waiver of immunity and consent to surrender

1. The Court may not proceed with a request for surrender or assistance which would require the requested State to act inconsistently with its obligations under international law with respect to the State or diplomatic immunity of a person or property of a third State, unless the Court can first obtain the cooperation of that third State for the waiver of the immunity.
2. The Court may not proceed with a request for surrender which would require the requested State to act inconsistently with its obligations under international agreements pursuant to which the consent of a sending State is required to surrender a person of that State to the Court, unless the Court can first obtain the cooperation of the sending State for the giving of consent for the surrender.

Article 99
Execution of requests under articles 93 and 96

1. Requests for assistance shall be executed in accordance with the relevant procedure under the law of the requested State and, unless prohibited by such law, in the manner specified in the request, including following any procedure outlined therein or permitting persons specified in the request to be present at and assist in the execution process.
2. In the case of an urgent request, the documents or evidence produced in response shall, at the request of the Court, be sent urgently.
3. Replies from the requested State shall be transmitted in their original language and form.
4. Without prejudice to other articles in this Part, where it is necessary for the successful execution of a request which can be executed without any compulsory measures, including specifically the interview of or taking evidence from a person on a voluntary basis, including doing so without the presence of the authorities of the requested State Party if it is essential for the request to be executed, and the examination without modification of a public site or other public place, the Prosecutor may execute such request directly on the territory of a State as follows:
   (a) When the State Party requested is a State on the territory of which the crime is alleged to have been committed, and there has been a determination of admissibility pursuant to article 18 or 19, the Prosecutor may directly execute such request following all possible consultations with the requested State Party;
   (b) In other cases, the Prosecutor may execute such request following consultations with the requested State Party and subject to any reasonable conditions or concerns raised by that State Party. Where the requested State Party identifies problems with the execution of a request pursuant to this subparagraph it shall, without delay, consult with the Court to resolve the matter.
5. Provisions allowing a person heard or examined by the Court under article 72 to invoke restrictions designed to prevent disclosure of confidential information connected with national security shall also apply to the execution of requests for assistance under this article.

Article 100
Costs

1. The ordinary costs for execution of requests in the territory of the requested State shall be borne by that State, except for the following, which shall be borne by the Court:
   (a) Costs associated with the travel and security of witnesses and experts or the transfer under article 93 of persons in custody;
   (b) Costs of translation, interpretation and transcription;

(c) Travel and subsistence costs of the judges, the Prosecutor, the Deputy Prosecutors, the Registrar, the Deputy Registrar and staff of any organ of the Court;
  (d) Costs of any expert opinion or report requested by the Court;
  (e) Costs associated with the transport of a person being surrendered to the Court by a custodial State; and
  (f) Following consultations, any extraordinary costs that may result from the execution of a request.
2. The provisions of paragraph 1 shall, as appropriate, apply to requests from States Parties to the Court. In that case, the Court shall bear the ordinary costs of execution.

Article 101
Rule of speciality

1. A person surrendered to the Court under this Statute shall not be proceeded against, punished or detained for any conduct committed prior to surrender, other than the conduct or course of conduct which forms the basis of the crimes for which that person has been surrendered.
2. The Court may request a waiver of the requirements of paragraph 1 from the State which surrendered the person to the Court and, if necessary, the Court shall provide additional information in accordance with article 91. States Parties shall have the authority to provide a waiver to the Court and should endeavour to do so.

Article 102
Use of terms

For the purposes of this Statute:
  (a) "surrender" means the delivering up of a person by a State to the Court, pursuant to this Statute.
  (b) "extradition" means the delivering up of a person by one State to another as provided by treaty, convention or national legislation.

PART 10. ENFORCEMENT
Article 103
Role of States in enforcement of sentences of imprisonment

1. (a) A sentence of imprisonment shall be served in a State designated by the Court from a list of States which have indicated to the Court their willingness to accept sentenced persons.
   (b) At the time of declaring its willingness to accept sentenced persons, a State may attach conditions to its acceptance as agreed by the Court and in accordance with this Part.
   (c) A State designated in a particular case shall promptly inform the Court whether it accepts the Court's designation.
2. (a) The State of enforcement shall notify the Court of any circumstances, including the exercise of any conditions agreed under paragraph 1, which could materially affect the terms or extent of the imprisonment. The Court shall be given at least 45 days' notice of any such known or foreseeable circumstances. During this period, the State of enforcement shall take no action that might prejudice its obligations under article 110.
   (b) Where the Court cannot agree to the circumstances referred to in subparagraph (a), it shall notify the State of enforcement and proceed in accordance with article 104, paragraph 1.

3. In exercising its discretion to make a designation under paragraph 1, the Court shall take into account the following:
   (a) The principle that States Parties should share the responsibility for enforcing sentences of imprisonment, in accordance with principles of equitable distribution, as provided in the Rules of Procedure and Evidence;
   (b) The application of widely accepted international treaty standards governing the treatment of prisoners;
   (c) The views of the sentenced person;
   (d) The nationality of the sentenced person;
   (e) Such other factors regarding the circumstances of the crime or the person sentenced, or the effective enforcement of the sentence, as may be appropriate in designating the State of enforcement.
4. If no State is designated under paragraph 1, the sentence of imprisonment shall be served in a prison facility made available by the host State, in accordance with the conditions set out in the headquarters agreement referred to in article 3, paragraph 2. In such a case, the costs arising out of the enforcement of a sentence of imprisonment shall be borne by the Court.

Article 104
Change in designation of State of enforcement

1. The Court may, at any time, decide to transfer a sentenced person to a prison of another State.
2. A sentenced person may, at any time, apply to the Court to be transferred from the State of enforcement.

Article 105
Enforcement of the sentence

1. Subject to conditions which a State may have specified in accordance with article 103, paragraph 1 (b), the sentence of imprisonment shall be binding on the States Parties, which shall in no case modify it.
2. The Court alone shall have the right to decide any application for appeal and revision. The State of enforcement shall not impede the making of any such application by a sentenced person.

Article 106
Supervision of enforcement of sentences and conditions of imprisonment

1. The enforcement of a sentence of imprisonment shall be subject to the supervision of the Court and shall be consistent with widely accepted international treaty standards governing treatment of prisoners.
2. The conditions of imprisonment shall be governed by the law of the State of enforcement and shall be consistent with widely accepted international treaty standards governing treatment of prisoners; in no case shall such conditions be more or less favourable than those available to prisoners convicted of similar offences in the State of enforcement.
3. Communications between a sentenced person and the Court shall be unimpeded and confidential.

Article 107
Transfer of the person upon completion of sentence

1. Following completion of the sentence, a person who is not a national of the State of enforcement may, in accordance with the law of the State of enforcement, be transferred to a State which is obliged to receive him or her, or to another State which agrees to receive him or

her, taking into account any wishes of the person to be transferred to that State, unless the State of enforcement authorizes the person to remain in its territory.
2. If no State bears the costs arising out of transferring the person to another State pursuant to paragraph 1, such costs shall be borne by the Court.
3. Subject to the provisions of article 108, the State of enforcement may also, in accordance with its national law, extradite or otherwise surrender the person to a State which has requested the extradition or surrender of the person for purposes of trial or enforcement of a sentence.

Article 108
Limitation on the prosecution or punishment of other offences

1. A sentenced person in the custody of the State of enforcement shall not be subject to prosecution or punishment or to extradition to a third State for any conduct engaged in prior to that person's delivery to the State of enforcement, unless such prosecution, punishment or extradition has been approved by the Court at the request of the State of enforcement.
2. The Court shall decide the matter after having heard the views of the sentenced person.
3. Paragraph 1 shall cease to apply if the sentenced person remains voluntarily for more than 30 days in the territory of the State of enforcement after having served the full sentence imposed by the Court, or returns to the territory of that State after having left it.

Article 109
Enforcement of fines and forfeiture measures

1. States Parties shall give effect to fines or forfeitures ordered by the Court under Part 7, without prejudice to the rights of bona fide third parties, and in accordance with the procedure of their national law.
2. If a State Party is unable to give effect to an order for forfeiture, it shall take measures to recover the value of the proceeds, property or assets ordered by the Court to be forfeited, without prejudice to the rights of bona fide third parties.
3. Property, or the proceeds of the sale of real property or, where appropriate, the sale of other property, which is obtained by a State Party as a result of its enforcement of a judgement of the Court shall be transferred to the Court.

Article 110
Review by the Court concerning reduction of sentence

1. The State of enforcement shall not release the person before expiry of the sentence pronounced by the Court.
2. The Court alone shall have the right to decide any reduction of sentence, and shall rule on the matter after having heard the person.
3. When the person has served two thirds of the sentence, or 25 years in the case of life imprisonment, the Court shall review the sentence to determine whether it should be reduced. Such a review shall not be conducted before that time.
4. In its review under paragraph 3, the Court may reduce the sentence if it finds that one or more of the following factors are present:
   (a) The early and continuing willingness of the person to cooperate with the Court in its investigations and prosecutions;
   (b) The voluntary assistance of the person in enabling the enforcement of the judgements and orders of the Court in other cases, and in particular providing assistance in locating assets subject to orders of fine, forfeiture or reparation which may be used for the benefit of victims; or

(c) Other factors establishing a clear and significant change of circumstances sufficient to justify the reduction of sentence, as provided in the Rules of Procedure and Evidence.

5. If the Court determines in its initial review under paragraph 3 that it is not appropriate to reduce the sentence, it shall thereafter review the question of reduction of sentence at such intervals and applying such criteria as provided for in the Rules of Procedure and Evidence.

Article 111
Escape

If a convicted person escapes from custody and flees the State of enforcement, that State may, after consultation with the Court, request the person's surrender from the State in which the person is located pursuant to existing bilateral or multilateral arrangements, or may request that the Court seek the person's surrender, in accordance with Part 9. It may direct that the person be delivered to the State in which he or she was serving the sentence or to another State designated by the Court.

PART 11. ASSEMBLY OF STATES PARTIES
Article 112
Assembly of States Parties

1. An Assembly of States Parties to this Statute is hereby established. Each State Party shall have one representative in the Assembly who may be accompanied by alternates and advisers. Other States which have signed this Statute or the Final Act may be observers in the Assembly.
2. The Assembly shall:
   (a) Consider and adopt, as appropriate, recommendations of the Preparatory Commission;
   (b) Provide management oversight to the Presidency, the Prosecutor and the Registrar regarding the administration of the Court;
   (c) Consider the reports and activities of the Bureau established under paragraph 3 and take appropriate action in regard thereto;
   (d) Consider and decide the budget for the Court;
   (e) Decide whether to alter, in accordance with article 36, the number of judges;
   (f) Consider pursuant to article 87, paragraphs 5 and 7, any question relating to non-cooperation;
   (g) Perform any other function consistent with this Statute or the Rules of Procedure and Evidence.
3. (a) The Assembly shall have a Bureau consisting of a President, two Vice-Presidents and 18 members elected by the Assembly for three-year terms.
   (b) The Bureau shall have a representative character, taking into account, in particular, equitable geographical distribution and the adequate representation of the principal legal systems of the world.
   (c) The Bureau shall meet as often as necessary, but at least once a year. It shall assist the Assembly in the discharge of its responsibilities.
4. The Assembly may establish such subsidiary bodies as may be necessary, including an independent oversight mechanism for inspection, evaluation and investigation of the Court, in order to enhance its efficiency and economy.
5. The President of the Court, the Prosecutor and the Registrar or their representatives may participate, as appropriate, in meetings of the Assembly and of the Bureau.
6. The Assembly shall meet at the seat of the Court or at the Headquarters of the United Nations once a year and, when circumstances so require, hold special sessions. Except as otherwise specified in this Statute, special sessions shall be convened by the Bureau on its own initiative or at the request of one third of the States Parties.

7. Each State Party shall have one vote. Every effort shall be made to reach decisions by consensus in the Assembly and in the Bureau. If consensus cannot be reached, except as otherwise provided in the Statute:
   (a) Decisions on matters of substance must be approved by a two-thirds majority of those present and voting provided that an absolute majority of States Parties constitutes the quorum for voting;
   (b) Decisions on matters of procedure shall be taken by a simple majority of States Parties present and voting.
8. A State Party which is in arrears in the payment of its financial contributions towards the costs of the Court shall have no vote in the Assembly and in the Bureau if the amount of its arrears equals or exceeds the amount of the contributions due from it for the preceding two full years. The Assembly may, nevertheless, permit such a State Party to vote in the Assembly and in the Bureau if it is satisfied that the failure to pay is due to conditions beyond the control of the State Party.
9. The Assembly shall adopt its own rules of procedure.
10. The official and working languages of the Assembly shall be those of the General Assembly of the United Nations.

PART 12. FINANCING
Article 113
Financial Regulations

Except as otherwise specifically provided, all financial matters related to the Court and the meetings of the Assembly of States Parties, including its Bureau and subsidiary bodies, shall be governed by this Statute and the Financial Regulations and Rules adopted by the Assembly of States Parties.

Article 114
Payment of expenses

Expenses of the Court and the Assembly of States Parties, including its Bureau and subsidiary bodies, shall be paid from the funds of the Court.

Article 115
Funds of the Court and of the Assembly of States Parties

The expenses of the Court and the Assembly of States Parties, including its Bureau and subsidiary bodies, as provided for in the budget decided by the Assembly of States Parties, shall be provided by the following sources:
   (a) Assessed contributions made by States Parties;
   (b) Funds provided by the United Nations, subject to the approval of the General Assembly, in particular in relation to the expenses incurred due to referrals by the Security Council.

Article 116
Voluntary contributions

Without prejudice to article 115, the Court may receive and utilize, as additional funds, voluntary contributions from Governments, international organizations, individuals, corporations and other entities, in accordance with relevant criteria adopted by the Assembly of States Parties.

Article 117
Assessment of contributions

The contributions of States Parties shall be assessed in accordance with an agreed scale of assessment, based on the scale adopted by the United Nations for its regular budget and adjusted in accordance with the principles on which that scale is based.

Article 118
Annual audit

The records, books and accounts of the Court, including its annual financial statements, shall be audited annually by an independent auditor.

PART 13. FINAL CLAUSES

Article 119
Settlement of disputes

1. Any dispute concerning the judicial functions of the Court shall be settled by the decision of the Court.
2. Any other dispute between two or more States Parties relating to the interpretation or application of this Statute which is not settled through negotiations within three months of their commencement shall be referred to the Assembly of States Parties. The Assembly may itself seek to settle the dispute or may make recommendations on further means of settlement of the dispute, including referral to the International Court of Justice in conformity with the Statute of that Court.

Article 120
Reservations

No reservations may be made to this Statute.

Article 121
Amendments

1. After the expiry of seven years from the entry into force of this Statute, any State Party may propose amendments thereto. The text of any proposed amendment shall be submitted to the Secretary-General of the United Nations, who shall promptly circulate it to all States Parties.
2. No sooner than three months from the date of notification, the Assembly of States Parties, at its next meeting, shall, by a majority of those present and voting, decide whether to take up the proposal. The Assembly may deal with the proposal directly or convene a Review Conference if the issue involved so warrants.
3. The adoption of an amendment at a meeting of the Assembly of States Parties or at a Review Conference on which consensus cannot be reached shall require a two-thirds majority of States Parties.
4. Except as provided in paragraph 5, an amendment shall enter into force for all States Parties one year after instruments of ratification or acceptance have been deposited with the Secretary-General of the United Nations by seven-eighths of them.
5. Any amendment to articles 5, 6, 7 and 8 of this Statute shall enter into force for those States Parties which have accepted the amendment one year after the deposit of their instruments of ratification or acceptance. In respect of a State Party which has not accepted the amendment, the Court shall not exercise its jurisdiction regarding a crime covered by the amendment when committed by that State Party's nationals or on its territory.

6. If an amendment has been accepted by seven-eighths of States Parties in accordance with paragraph 4, any State Party which has not accepted the amendment may withdraw from this Statute with immediate effect, notwithstanding article 127, paragraph 1, but subject to article 127, paragraph 2, by giving notice no later than one year after the entry into force of such amendment.
7. The Secretary-General of the United Nations shall circulate to all States Parties any amendment adopted at a meeting of the Assembly of States Parties or at a Review Conference.

Article 122
Amendments to provisions of an institutional nature

1. Amendments to provisions of this Statute which are of an exclusively institutional nature, namely, article 35, article 36, paragraphs 8 and 9, article 37, article 38, article 39, paragraphs 1 (first two sentences), 2 and 4, article 42, paragraphs 4 to 9, article 43, paragraphs 2 and 3, and articles 44, 46, 47 and 49, may be proposed at any time, notwithstanding article 121, paragraph 1, by any State Party. The text of any proposed amendment shall be submitted to the Secretary-General of the United Nations or such other person designated by the Assembly of States Parties who shall promptly circulate it to all States Parties and to others participating in the Assembly.
2. Amendments under this article on which consensus cannot be reached shall be adopted by the Assembly of States Parties or by a Review Conference, by a two-thirds majority of States Parties. Such amendments shall enter into force for all States Parties six months after their adoption by the Assembly or, as the case may be, by the Conference.

Article 123
Review of the Statute

1. Seven years after the entry into force of this Statute the Secretary-General of the United Nations shall convene a Review Conference to consider any amendments to this Statute. Such review may include, but is not limited to, the list of crimes contained in article 5. The Conference shall be open to those participating in the Assembly of States Parties and on the same conditions.
2. At any time thereafter, at the request of a State Party and for the purposes set out in paragraph 1, the Secretary-General of the United Nations shall, upon approval by a majority of States Parties, convene a Review Conference.
3. The provisions of article 121, paragraphs 3 to 7, shall apply to the adoption and entry into force of any amendment to the Statute considered at a Review Conference.

Article 124
Transitional Provision

Notwithstanding article 12, paragraphs 1 and 2, a State, on becoming a party to this Statute, may declare that, for a period of seven years after the entry into force of this Statute for the State concerned, it does not accept the jurisdiction of the Court with respect to the category of crimes referred to in article 8 when a crime is alleged to have been committed by its nationals or on its territory. A declaration under this article may be withdrawn at any time. The provisions of this article shall be reviewed at the Review Conference convened in accordance with article 123, paragraph 1.

Article 125
Signature, ratification, acceptance, approval or accession

1. This Statute shall be open for signature by all States in Rome, at the headquarters of the Food and Agriculture Organization of the United Nations, on 17 July 1998. Thereafter, it shall remain open for signature in Rome at the Ministry of Foreign Affairs of Italy until 17 October 1998. After that date, the Statute shall remain open for signature in New York, at United Nations Headquarters, until 31 December 2000.
2. This Statute is subject to ratification, acceptance or approval by signatory States. Instruments of ratification, acceptance or approval shall be deposited with the Secretary-General of the United Nations.
3. This Statute shall be open to accession by all States. Instruments of accession shall be deposited with the Secretary-General of the United Nations.

Article 126
Entry into force

1. This Statute shall enter into force on the first day of the month after the 60th day following the date of the deposit of the 60th instrument of ratification, acceptance, approval or accession with the Secretary-General of the United Nations.
2. For each State ratifying, accepting, approving or acceding to this Statute after the deposit of the 60th instrument of ratification, acceptance, approval or accession, the Statute shall enter into force on the first day of the month after the 60th day following the deposit by such State of its instrument of ratification, acceptance, approval or accession.

Article 127
Withdrawal

1. A State Party may, by written notification addressed to the Secretary-General of the United Nations, withdraw from this Statute. The withdrawal shall take effect one year after the date of receipt of the notification, unless the notification specifies a later date.
2. A State shall not be discharged, by reason of its withdrawal, from the obligations arising from this Statute while it was a Party to the Statute, including any financial obligations which may have accrued. Its withdrawal shall not affect any cooperation with the Court in connection with criminal investigations and proceedings in relation to which the withdrawing State had a duty to cooperate and which were commenced prior to the date on which the withdrawal became effective, nor shall it prejudice in any way the continued consideration of any matter which was already under consideration by the Court prior to the date on which the withdrawal became effective.

Article 128
Authentic texts

The original of this Statute, of which the Arabic, Chinese, English, French, Russian and Spanish texts are equally authentic, shall be deposited with the Secretary-General of the United Nations, who shall send certified copies thereof to all States.

IN WITNESS WHEREOF, the undersigned, being duly authorized thereto by their respective Governments, have signed this Statute.

DONE at Rome, this 17th day of July 1998.

ANNEX 3

INTERNATIONAL CRIMINAL COURT RULES OF PROCEDURE AND EVIDENCE*

New York
13–31 March 2000
12–30 June 2000

Addendum

PART I
FINALIZED DRAFT TEXT OF THE RULES OF PROCEDURE AND EVIDENCE

Explanatory note

The Rules of Procedure and Evidence are an instrument for the application of the Rome Statute of the International Criminal Court, to which they are subordinate in all cases. In elaborating the Rules of Procedure and Evidence, care has been taken to avoid rephrasing and, to the extent possible, repeating the provisions of the Statute. Direct references to the Statute have been included in the Rules, where appropriate, in order to emphasize the relationship between the Rules and the Rome Statute, as provided for in article 51, in particular, paragraphs 4 and 5.

In all cases, the Rules of Procedure and Evidence should be read in conjunction with and subject to the provisions of the Statute.

The Rules of Procedure and Evidence of the International Criminal Court do not affect the procedural rules for any national court or legal system for the purpose of national proceedings.

In connection with rule 41, the Preparatory Commission considered whether the application of the rule would be facilitated by including a provision in the Regulations of the Court that at least one of the judges of the Chamber in which the case is heard knows the official language used as a working language in a given case. The Assembly of States Parties is invited to give further consideration to this issue.

Chapter 1
General provisions

Rule 1
Use of terms

In the present document:
— "article" refers to articles of the Rome Statute;
— "Chamber" refers to a Chamber of the Court;
— "Part" refers to the Parts of the Rome Statute;

---

* The ICC "Elements of Crimes" are included in the main text of this work at 4.2.585.

- "Presiding Judge" refers to the Presiding Judge of a Chamber;
- "the President" refers to the President of the Court;
- "the Regulations" refers to the Regulations of the Court;
- "the Rules" refers to the Rules of Procedure and Evidence.

Rule 2
Authentic texts

The Rules have been adopted in the official languages of the Court established by article 50, paragraph 1. All texts are equally authentic.

Rule 3
Amendments

1. Amendments to the rules that are proposed in accordance with article 51, paragraph 2, shall be forwarded to the President of the Bureau of the Assembly of States Parties.
2. The President of the Bureau of the Assembly of States Parties shall ensure that all proposed amendments are translated into the official languages of the Court and are transmitted to the States Parties.
3. The procedure described in sub-rules 1 and 2 shall also apply to the provisional rules referred to in article 51, paragraph 3.

Chapter 2
Composition and administration of the Court

Section I
General provisions relating to the composition and administration of the Court

Rule 4
Plenary sessions

1. The judges shall meet in plenary session not later than two months after their election. At that first session, after having made their solemn undertaking, in conformity with rule 5, the judges shall:
   (a) Elect the President and Vice-Presidents;
   (b) Assign judges to divisions.
2. The judges shall meet subsequently in plenary session at least once a year to exercise their functions under the Statute, the Rules and the Regulations and, if necessary, in special plenary sessions convened by the President on his or her own motion or at the request of one half of the judges.
3. The quorum for each plenary session shall be two-thirds of the judges.
4. Unless otherwise provided in the Statute or the Rules, the decisions of the plenary sessions shall be taken by the majority of the judges present. In the event of an equality of votes, the President, or the judge acting in the place of the President, shall have a casting vote.
5. The Regulations shall be adopted as soon as possible in plenary sessions.

Rule 5
Solemn undertaking under article 45

1. As provided in article 45, before exercising their functions under the Statute, the following solemn undertakings shall be made:
   (a) In the case of a judge:

"I solemnly undertake that I will perform my duties and exercise my powers as a judge of the International Criminal Court honourably, faithfully, impartially and conscientiously, and that I will respect the confidentiality of investigations and prosecutions and the secrecy of deliberations.";

(b) In the case of the Prosecutor, a Deputy Prosecutor, the Registrar and the Deputy Registrar of the Court:

"I solemnly undertake that I will perform my duties and exercise my powers as (title) of the International Criminal Court honourably, faithfully, impartially and conscientiously, and that I will respect the confidentiality of investigations and prosecutions."

2. The undertaking, signed by the person making it and witnessed by the President or a Vice-President of the Bureau of the Assembly of States Parties, shall be filed with the Registry and kept in the records of the Court.

Rule 6
Solemn undertaking by the staff of the Office of the Prosecutor, the Registry, interpreters and translators

1. Upon commencing employment, every staff member of the Office of the Prosecutor and the Registry shall make the following undertaking:

"I solemnly undertake that I will perform my duties and exercise my powers as (title) of the International Criminal Court honourably, faithfully, impartially and conscientiously, and that I will respect the confidentiality of investigations and prosecutions.";

The undertaking, signed by the person making it and witnessed, as appropriate, by the Prosecutor, the Deputy Prosecutor, the Registrar or the Deputy Registrar, shall be filed with the Registry and kept in the records of the Court.

2. Before performing any duties, an interpreter or a translator shall make the following undertaking:

"I solemnly declare that I will perform my duties faithfully, impartially and with full respect for the duty of confidentiality.";

The undertaking, signed by the person making it and witnessed by the President of the Court or his or her representative, shall be filed with the Registry and kept in the records of the Court.

Rule 7
Single judge under article 39, paragraph 2 (b) (iii)

1. Whenever the Pre-Trial Chamber designates a judge as a single judge in accordance with article 39, paragraph 2 (b) (iii), it shall do so on the basis of objective pre-established criteria.
2. The designated judge shall make the appropriate decisions on those questions on which decision by the full Chamber is not expressly provided for in the Statute or the Rules.
3. The Pre-Trial Chamber, on its own motion or, if appropriate, at the request of a party, may decide that the functions of the single judge be exercised by the full Chamber.

Rule 8
Code of Professional Conduct

1. The Presidency, on the basis of a proposal made by the Registrar, shall draw up a draft Code of Professional Conduct for counsel, after having consulted the Prosecutor. In the preparation of the proposal, the Registrar shall conduct the consultations in accordance with rule 20, sub-rule 3.
2. The draft Code shall then be transmitted to the Assembly of States Parties, for the purpose of adoption, according to article 112, paragraph 7.
3. The Code shall contain procedures for its amendment.

Section II
The Office of the Prosecutor

Rule 9
Operation of the Office of the Prosecutor

In discharging his or her responsibility for the management and administration of the Office of the Prosecutor, the Prosecutor shall put in place regulations to govern the operation of the Office. In preparing or amending these regulations, the Prosecutor shall consult with the Registrar on any matters that may affect the operation of the Registry.

Rule 10
Retention of information and evidence

The Prosecutor shall be responsible for the retention, storage and security of information and physical evidence obtained in the course of the investigations by his or her Office.

Rule 11
Delegation of the Prosecutor's functions

Except for the inherent powers of the Prosecutor set forth in the Statute, *inter alia*, those described in articles 15 and 53, the Prosecutor or a Deputy Prosecutor may authorize staff members of the Office of the Prosecutor, other than those referred to in article 44, paragraph 4, to represent him or her in the exercise of his or her functions.

Section III
The Registry

Subsection 1
General provisions relating to the Registry

Rule 12
Qualifications and election of the Registrar and the Deputy Registrar

1. As soon as it is elected, the Presidency shall establish a list of candidates who satisfy the criteria laid down in article 43, paragraph 3, and shall transmit the list to the Assembly of States Parties with a request for any recommendations.
2. Upon receipt of any recommendations from the Assembly of States Parties, the President shall, without delay, transmit the list together with the recommendations to the plenary session.
3. As provided for in article 43, paragraph 4, the Court, meeting in plenary session, shall, as soon as possible, elect the Registrar by an absolute majority, taking into account any recommendations by the Assembly of States Parties. In the event that no candidate obtains an absolute majority on the first ballot, successive ballots shall be held until one candidate obtains an absolute majority.
4. If the need for a Deputy Registrar arises, the Registrar may make a recommendation to the President to that effect. The President shall convene a plenary session to decide on the matter. If the Court, meeting in plenary session, decides by an absolute majority that a Deputy Registrar is to be elected, the Registrar shall submit a list of candidates to the Court.
5. The Deputy Registrar shall be elected by the Court, meeting in plenary session, in the same manner as the Registrar.

Rule 13
Functions of the Registrar

1. Without prejudice to the authority of the Office of the Prosecutor under the Statute to receive, obtain and provide information and to establish channels of communication for this purpose, the Registrar shall serve as the channel of communication of the Court.
2. The Registrar shall also be responsible for the internal security of the Court in consultation with the Presidency and the Prosecutor, as well as the host State.

Rule 14
Operation of the Registry

1. In discharging his or her responsibility for the organization and management of the Registry, the Registrar shall put in place regulations to govern the operation of the Registry. In preparing or amending these regulations, the Registrar shall consult with the Prosecutor on any matters which may affect the operation of the Office of the Prosecutor. The regulations shall be approved by the Presidency.
2. The regulations shall provide for defence counsel to have access to appropriate and reasonable administrative assistance from the Registry.

Rule 15
Records

1. The Registrar shall keep a database containing all the particulars of each case brought before the Court, subject to any order of a judge or Chamber providing for the non-disclosure of any document or information, and to the protection of sensitive personal data. Information on the database shall be available to the public in the working languages of the Court.
2. The Registrar shall also maintain the other records of the Court.

Subsection 2
Victims and Witnesses Unit

Rule 16
Responsibilities of the Registrar relating to victims and witnesses

1. In relation to victims, the Registrar shall be responsible for the performance of the following functions in accordance with the Statute and these Rules:
   (a) Providing notice or notification to victims or their legal representatives;
   (b) Assisting them in obtaining legal advice and organizing their legal representation, and providing their legal representatives with adequate support, assistance and information, including such facilities as may be necessary for the direct performance of their duty, for the purpose of protecting their rights during all stages of the proceedings in accordance with rules 89 to 91;
   (c) Assisting them in participating in the different phases of the proceedings in accordance with rules 89 to 91;
   (d) Taking gender-sensitive measures to facilitate the participation of victims of sexual violence at all stages of the proceedings.
2. In relation to victims, witnesses and others who are at risk on account of testimony given by such witnesses, the Registrar shall be responsible for the performance of the following functions in accordance with the Statute and these Rules:
   (a) Informing them of their rights under the Statute and the Rules, and of the existence, functions and availability of the Victims and Witnesses Unit;

(b) Ensuring that they are aware, in a timely manner, of the relevant decisions of the Court that may have an impact on their interests, subject to provisions on confidentiality.
3. For the fulfilment of his or her functions, the Registrar may keep a special register for victims who have expressed their intention to participate in relation to a specific case.
4. Agreements on relocation and provision of support services on the territory of a State of traumatized or threatened victims, witnesses and others who are at risk on account of testimony given by such witnesses may be negotiated with the States by the Registrar on behalf of the Court. Such agreements may remain confidential.

Rule 17
Functions of the Unit

1. The Victims and Witnesses Unit shall exercise its functions in accordance with article 43, paragraph 6.
2. The Victims and Witnesses Unit shall, *inter alia*, perform the following functions, in accordance with the Statute and the Rules, and in consultation with the Chamber, the Prosecutor and the defence, as appropriate:
    (a) With respect to all witnesses, victims who appear before the Court, and others who are at risk on account of testimony given by such witnesses, in accordance with their particular needs and circumstances:
        (i) Providing them with adequate protective and security measures and formulating long- and short-term plans for their protection;
        (ii) Recommending to the organs of the Court the adoption of protection measures and also advising relevant States of such measures;
        (iii) Assisting them in obtaining medical, psychological and other appropriate assistance;
        (iv) Making available to the Court and the parties training in issues of trauma, sexual violence, security and confidentiality;
        (v) Recommending, in consultation with the Office of the Prosecutor, the elaboration of a code of conduct, emphasizing the vital nature of security and confidentiality for investigators of the Court and of the defence and all intergovernmental and non-governmental organizations acting at the request of the Court, as appropriate;
        (vi) Cooperating with States, where necessary, in providing any of the measures stipulated in this rule;
    (b) With respect to witnesses:
        (i) Advising them where to obtain legal advice for the purpose of protecting their rights, in particular in relation to their testimony;
        (ii) Assisting them when they are called to testify before the Court;
        (iii) Taking gender-sensitive measures to facilitate the testimony of victims of sexual violence at all stages of the proceedings.
3. In performing its functions, the Unit shall give due regard to the particular needs of children, elderly persons and persons with disabilities. In order to facilitate the participation and protection of children as witnesses, the Unit may assign, as appropriate, and with the agreement of the parents or the legal guardian, a child-support person to assist a child through all stages of the proceedings.

Rule 18
Responsibilities of the Unit

For the efficient and effective performance of its work, the Victims and Witnesses Unit shall:
   (a) Ensure that the staff in the Unit maintain confidentiality at all times;
   (b) While recognizing the specific interests of the Office of the Prosecutor, the defence and the witnesses, respect the interests of the witness, including, where necessary, by maintaining an appropriate separation of the services provided to the prosecution and defence witnesses, and act impartially when cooperating with all parties and in accordance with the rulings and decisions of the Chambers;
   (c) Have administrative and technical assistance available for witnesses, victims who appear before the Court, and others who are at risk on account of testimony given by such witnesses, during all stages of the proceedings and thereafter, as reasonably appropriate;
   (d) Ensure training of its staff with respect to victims' and witnesses' security, integrity and dignity, including matters related to gender and cultural sensitivity;
   (e) Where appropriate, cooperate with intergovernmental and non-governmental organizations.

Rule 19
Expertise in the Unit

In addition to the staff mentioned in article 43, paragraph 6, and subject to article 44, the Victims and Witnesses Unit may include, as appropriate, persons with expertise, *inter alia*, in the following areas:
   (a) Witness protection and security;
   (b) Legal and administrative matters, including areas of humanitarian and criminal law;
   (c) Logistics administration;
   (d) Psychology in criminal proceedings;
   (e) Gender and cultural diversity;
   (f) Children, in particular traumatized children;
   (g) Elderly persons, in particular in connection with armed conflict and exile trauma;
   (h) Persons with disabilities;
   (i) Social work and counselling;
   (j) Health care;
   (k) Interpretation and translation.

Subsection 3
Counsel for the defence

Rule 20
Responsibilities of the Registrar relating to the rights of the defence

1. In accordance with article 43, paragraph 1, the Registrar shall organize the staff of the Registry in a manner that promotes the rights of the defence, consistent with the principle of fair trial as defined in the Statute. For that purpose, the Registrar shall, *inter alia:*
   (a) Facilitate the protection of confidentiality, as defined in article 67, paragraph 1 (b);
   (b) Provide support, assistance, and information to all defence counsel appearing before the Court and, as appropriate, support for professional investigators necessary for the efficient and effective conduct of the defence;
   (c) Assist arrested persons, persons to whom article 55, paragraph 2, applies and the accused in obtaining legal advice and the assistance of legal counsel;

(d) Advise the Prosecutor and the Chambers, as necessary, on relevant defence-related issues;
(e) Provide the defence with such facilities as may be necessary for the direct performance of the duty of the defence;
(f) Facilitate the dissemination of information and case law of the Court to defence counsel and, as appropriate, cooperate with national defence and bar associations or any independent representative body of counsel and legal associations referred to in sub-rule 3 to promote the specialization and training of lawyers in the law of the Statute and the Rules.

2. The Registrar shall carry out the functions stipulated in sub-rule 1, including the financial administration of the Registry, in such a manner as to ensure the professional independence of defence counsel.
3. For purposes such as the management of legal assistance in accordance with rule 21 and the development of a Code of Professional Conduct in accordance with rule 8, the Registrar shall consult, as appropriate, with any independent representative body of counsel or legal associations, including any such body the establishment of which may be facilitated by the Assembly of States Parties.

Rule 21
Assignment of legal assistance

1. Subject to article 55, paragraph 2 (c), and article 67, paragraph 1 (d), criteria and procedures for assignment of legal assistance shall be established in the Regulations, based on a proposal by the Registrar, following consultations with any independent representative body of counsel or legal associations, as referred to in rule 20, sub-rule 3.
2. The Registrar shall create and maintain a list of counsel who meet the criteria set forth in rule 22 and the Regulations. The person shall freely choose his or her counsel from this list or other counsel who meets the required criteria and is willing to be included in the list.
3. A person may seek from the Presidency a review of a decision to refuse a request for assignment of counsel. The decision of the Presidency shall be final. If a request is refused, a further request may be made by a person to the Registrar, upon showing a change in circumstances.
4. A person choosing to represent himself or herself shall so notify the Registrar in writing at the first opportunity.
5. Where a person claims to have insufficient means to pay for legal assistance and this is subsequently found not to be so, the Chamber dealing with the case at that time may make an order of contribution to recover the cost of providing counsel.

Rule 22
Appointment and qualifications of Counsel for the defence

1. A counsel for the defence shall have established competence in international or criminal law and procedure, as well as the necessary relevant experience, whether as judge, prosecutor, advocate or in other similar capacity, in criminal proceedings. A counsel for the defence shall have an excellent knowledge of and be fluent in at least one of the working languages of the Court. Counsel for the defence may be assisted by other persons, including professors of law, with relevant expertise.
2. Counsel for the defence engaged by a person exercising his or her right under the Statute to retain legal counsel of his or her choosing shall file a power of attorney with the Registrar at the earliest opportunity.
3. In the performance of their duties, Counsel for the defence shall be subject to the Statute, the Rules, the Regulations, the Code of Professional Conduct for Counsel adopted in accordance with rule 8 and any other document adopted by the Court that may be relevant to the performance of their duties.

Section IV
Situations that may affect the functioning of the Court

Subsection 1
Removal from office and disciplinary measures

Rule 23
General principle

A judge, the Prosecutor, a Deputy Prosecutor, the Registrar and a Deputy Registrar shall be removed from office or shall be subject to disciplinary measures in such cases and with such guarantees as are established in the Statute and the Rules.

Rule 24
Definition of serious misconduct and serious breach of duty

1. For the purposes of article 46, paragraph 1 (a), "serious misconduct" shall be constituted by conduct that:
   (a) If it occurs in the course of official duties, is incompatible with official functions, and causes or is likely to cause serious harm to the proper administration of justice before the Court or the proper internal functioning of the Court, such as:
      (i) Disclosing facts or information that he or she has acquired in the course of his or her duties or on a matter which is *sub judice*, where such disclosure is seriously prejudicial to the judicial proceedings or to any person;
      (ii) Concealing information or circumstances of a nature sufficiently serious to have precluded him or her from holding office;
      (iii) Abuse of judicial office in order to obtain unwarranted favourable treatment from any authorities, officials or professionals; or
   (b) If it occurs outside the course of official duties, is of a grave nature that causes or is likely to cause serious harm to the standing of the Court.
2. For the purposes of article 46, paragraph 1 (a), a "serious breach of duty" occurs where a person has been grossly negligent in the performance of his or her duties or has knowingly acted in contravention of those duties. This may include, *inter alia*, situations where the person:
   (a) Fails to comply with the duty to request to be excused, knowing that there are grounds for doing so;
   (b) Repeatedly causes unwarranted delay in the initiation, prosecution or trial of cases, or in the exercise of judicial powers.

Rule 25
Definition of misconduct of a less serious nature

1. For the purposes of article 47, "misconduct of a less serious nature" shall be constituted by conduct that:
   (a) If it occurs in the course of official duties, causes or is likely to cause harm to the proper administration of justice before the Court or the proper internal functioning of the Court, such as:
      (i) Interfering in the exercise of the functions of a person referred to in article 47;
      (ii) Repeatedly failing to comply with or ignoring requests made by the Presiding Judge or by the Presidency in the exercise of their lawful authority;
      (iii) Failing to enforce the disciplinary measures to which the Registrar or a Deputy Registrar and other officers of the Court are subject when a judge knows or should know of a serious breach of duty on their part; or

(b) If it occurs outside the course of official duties, causes or is likely to cause harm to the standing of the Court.

2. Nothing in this rule precludes the possibility of the conduct set out in sub-rule 1 (a) constituting "serious misconduct" or "serious breach of duty" for the purposes of article 46, paragraph 1 (a).

Rule 26
Receipt of complaints

1. For the purposes of article 46, paragraph 1, and article 47, any complaint concerning any conduct defined under rules 24 and 25 shall include the grounds on which it is based, the identity of the complainant and, if available, any relevant evidence. The complaint shall remain confidential.
2. All complaints shall be transmitted to the Presidency, which may also initiate proceedings on its own motion, and which shall, pursuant to the Regulations, set aside anonymous or manifestly unfounded complaints and transmit the other complaints to the competent organ. The Presidency shall be assisted in this task by one or more judges, appointed on the basis of automatic rotation, in accordance with the Regulations.

Rule 27
Common provisions on the rights of the defence

1. In any case in which removal from office under article 46 or disciplinary measures under article 47 is under consideration, the person concerned shall be so informed in a written statement.
2. The person concerned shall be afforded full opportunity to present and receive evidence, to make written submissions and to supply answers to any questions put to him or her.
3. The person may be represented by counsel during the process established under this rule.

Rule 28
Suspension from duty

Where an allegation against a person who is the subject of a complaint is of a sufficiently serious nature, the person may be suspended from duty pending the final decision of the competent organ.

Rule 29
Procedure in the event of a request for removal from office

1. In the case of a judge, the Registrar or a Deputy Registrar, the question of removal from office shall be put to a vote at a plenary session.
2. The Presidency shall advise the President of the Bureau of the Assembly of States Parties in writing of any recommendation adopted in the case of a judge, and any decision adopted in the case of the Registrar or a Deputy Registrar.
3. The Prosecutor shall advise the President of the Bureau of the Assembly of States Parties in writing of any recommendation he or she makes in the case of a Deputy Prosecutor.
4. Where the conduct is found not to amount to serious misconduct or a serious breach of duty, it may be decided in accordance with article 47 that the person concerned has engaged in misconduct of a less serious nature and a disciplinary measure imposed.

Rule 30
Procedure in the event of a request for disciplinary measures

1. In the case of a judge, the Registrar or a Deputy Registrar, any decision to impose a disciplinary measure shall be taken by the Presidency.
2. In the case of the Prosecutor, any decision to impose a disciplinary measure shall be taken by an absolute majority of the Bureau of the Assembly of States Parties.
3. In the case of a Deputy Prosecutor:
   (a) Any decision to give a reprimand shall be taken by the Prosecutor;
   (b) Any decision to impose a pecuniary sanction shall be taken by an absolute majority of the Bureau of the Assembly of States Parties upon the recommendation of the Prosecutor.
4. Reprimands shall be recorded in writing and shall be transmitted to the President of the Bureau of the Assembly of States Parties.

Rule 31
Removal from office

Once removal from office has been pronounced, it shall take effect immediately. The person concerned shall cease to form part of the Court, including for unfinished cases in which he or she was taking part.

Rule 32
Disciplinary measures

The disciplinary measures that may be imposed are:
   (a) A reprimand; or
   (b) A pecuniary sanction that may not exceed six months of the salary paid by the Court to the person concerned.

Subsection 2
Excusing, disqualification, death and resignation

Rule 33
Excusing of a judge, the Prosecutor or a Deputy Prosecutor

1. A judge, the Prosecutor or a Deputy Prosecutor seeking to be excused from his or her functions shall make a request in writing to the Presidency, setting out the grounds upon which he or she should be excused.
2. The Presidency shall treat the request as confidential and shall not make public the reasons for its decision without the consent of the person concerned.

Rule 34
Disqualification of a judge, the Prosecutor or a Deputy Prosecutor

1. In addition to the grounds set out in article 41, paragraph 2, and article 42, paragraph 7, the grounds for disqualification of a judge, the Prosecutor or a Deputy Prosecutor shall include, *inter alia*, the following:
   (a) Personal interest in the case, including a spousal, parental or other close family, personal or professional relationship, or a subordinate relationship, with any of the parties;
   (b) Involvement, in his or her private capacity, in any legal proceedings initiated prior to his or her involvement in the case, or initiated by him or her subsequently, in which the person being investigated or prosecuted was or is an opposing party;

(c) Performance of functions, prior to taking office, during which he or she could be expected to have formed an opinion on the case in question, on the parties or on their legal representatives that, objectively, could adversely affect the required impartiality of the person concerned;
(d) Expression of opinions, through the communications media, in writing or in public actions, that, objectively, could adversely affect the required impartiality of the person concerned.

2. Subject to the provisions set out in article 41, paragraph 2, and article 42, paragraph 8, a request for disqualification shall be made in writing as soon as there is knowledge of the grounds on which it is based. The request shall state the grounds and attach any relevant evidence, and shall be transmitted to the person concerned, who shall be entitled to present written submissions.
3. Any question relating to the disqualification of the Prosecutor or a Deputy Prosecutor shall be decided by a majority of the judges of the Appeals Chamber.

Rule 35
Duty of a judge, the Prosecutor or a Deputy Prosecutor to request to be excused

Where a judge, the Prosecutor or a Deputy Prosecutor has reason to believe that a ground for disqualification exists in relation to him or her, he or she shall make a request to be excused and shall not wait for a request for disqualification to be made in accordance with article 41, paragraph 2, or article 42, paragraph 7, and rule 34. The request shall be made and the Presidency shall deal with it in accordance with rule 33.

Rule 36
Death of a judge, the Prosecutor, a Deputy Prosecutor, the Registrar or a Deputy Registrar

The Presidency shall inform, in writing, the President of the Bureau of the Assembly of States Parties of the death of a judge, the Prosecutor, a Deputy Prosecutor, the Registrar or a Deputy Registrar.

Rule 37
Resignation of a judge, the Prosecutor, a Deputy Prosecutor, the Registrar or a Deputy Registrar

1. A judge, the Prosecutor, a Deputy Prosecutor, the Registrar or a Deputy Registrar shall communicate to the Presidency, in writing, his or her decision to resign. The Presidency shall inform, in writing, the President of the Bureau of the Assembly of States Parties.
2. A judge, the Prosecutor, a Deputy Prosecutor, the Registrar or a Deputy Registrar shall endeavour to give notice of the date on which his or her resignation will take effect at least six months in advance. Before the resignation of a judge takes effect, he or she shall make every effort to discharge his or her outstanding responsibilities.

Subsection 3
Replacements and alternate judges

Rule 38
Replacements

1. A judge may be replaced for objective and justified reasons, *inter alia:*
   (a) Resignation;
   (b) Accepted excuse;
   (c) Disqualification;

(d) Removal from office;
(e) Death.
2. Replacement shall take place in accordance with the pre-established procedure in the Statute, the Rules and the Regulations.

Rule 39
Alternate judges

Where an alternate judge has been assigned by the Presidency to a Trial Chamber pursuant to article 74, paragraph 1, he or she shall sit through all proceedings and deliberations of the case, but may not take any part therein and shall not exercise any of the functions of the members of the Trial Chamber hearing the case, unless and until he or she is required to replace a member of the Trial Chamber if that member is unable to continue attending. Alternate judges shall be designated in accordance with a procedure pre-established by the Court.

Section V
Publication, languages and translation

Rule 40
Publication of decisions in official languages of the Court

1. For the purposes of article 50, paragraph 1, the following decisions shall be considered as resolving fundamental issues:
   (a) All decisions of the Appeals Division;
   (b) All decisions of the Court on its jurisdiction or on the admissibility of a case pursuant to articles 17, 18, 19 and 20;
   (c) All decisions of a Trial Chamber on guilt or innocence, sentencing and reparations to victims pursuant to articles 74, 75 and 76;
   (d) All decisions of a Pre-Trial Chamber pursuant to article 57, paragraph 3 (d).
2. Decisions on confirmation of charges under article 61, paragraph 7, and on offences against the administration of justice under article 70, paragraph 3, shall be published in all the official languages of the Court when the Presidency determines that they resolve fundamental issues.
3. The Presidency may decide to publish other decisions in all the official languages when such decisions concern major issues relating to the interpretation or the implementation of the Statute or concern a major issue of general interest.

Rule 41
Working languages of the Court

1. For the purposes of article 50, paragraph 2, the Presidency shall authorize the use of an official language of the Court as a working language when:
   (a) That language is understood and spoken by the majority of those involved in a case before the Court and any of the participants in the proceedings so requests; or
   (b) The Prosecutor and the defence so request.
2. The Presidency may authorize the use of an official language of the Court as a working language if it considers that it would facilitate the efficiency of the proceedings.

Rule 42
Translation and interpretation services

The Court shall arrange for the translation and interpretation services necessary to ensure the implementation of its obligations under the Statute and the Rules.

Rule 43
Procedure applicable to the publication of documents of the Court

The Court shall ensure that all documents subject to publication in accordance with the Statute and the Rules respect the duty to protect the confidentiality of the proceedings and the security of victims and witnesses.

Chapter 3
Jurisdiction and admissibility

Section I
Declarations and referrals relating to articles 11, 12, 13 and 14

Rule 44
Declaration provided for in article 12, paragraph 3

1. The Registrar, at the request of the Prosecutor, may inquire of a State that is not a Party to the Statute or that has become a Party to the Statute after its entry into force, on a confidential basis, whether it intends to make the declaration provided for in article 12, paragraph 3.
2. When a State lodges, or declares to the Registrar its intent to lodge, a declaration with the Registrar pursuant to article 12, paragraph 3, or when the Registrar acts pursuant to sub-rule 1, the Registrar shall inform the State concerned that the declaration under article 12, paragraph 3, has as a consequence the acceptance of jurisdiction with respect to the crimes referred to in article 5 of relevance to the situation and the provisions of Part 9, and any rules thereunder concerning States Parties, shall apply.

Rule 45
Referral of a situation to the Prosecutor

A referral of a situation to the Prosecutor shall be in writing.

Section II
Initiation of investigations under article 15

Rule 46
Information provided to the Prosecutor under article 15, paragraphs 1 and 2

Where information is submitted under article 15, paragraph 1, or where oral or written testimony is received pursuant to article 15, paragraph 2, at the seat of the Court, the Prosecutor shall protect the confidentiality of such information and testimony or take any other necessary measures, pursuant to his or her duties under the Statute.

Rule 47
Testimony under article 15, paragraph 2

1. The provisions of rules 111 and 112 shall apply, *mutatis mutandis*, to testimony received by the Prosecutor pursuant to article 15, paragraph 2.
2. When the Prosecutor considers that there is a serious risk that it might not be possible for the testimony to be taken subsequently, he or she may request the Pre-Trial Chamber to take such measures as may be necessary to ensure the efficiency and integrity of the proceedings and, in particular, to appoint a counsel or a judge from the Pre-Trial Chamber to be present during the taking of the testimony in order to protect the rights of the defence. If

the testimony is subsequently presented in the proceedings, its admissibility shall be governed by article 69, paragraph 4, and given such weight as determined by the relevant Chamber.

Rule 48
Determination of reasonable basis to proceed with an investigation under article 15, paragraph 3

In determining whether there is a reasonable basis to proceed with an investigation under article 15, paragraph 3, the Prosecutor shall consider the factors set out in article 53, paragraph 1 (a) to (c).

Rule 49
Decision and notice under article 15, paragraph 6

1. Where a decision under article 15, paragraph 6, is taken, the Prosecutor shall promptly ensure that notice is provided, including reasons for his or her decision, in a manner that prevents any danger to the safety, well-being and privacy of those who provided information to him or her under article 15, paragraphs 1 and 2, or the integrity of investigations or proceedings.
2. The notice shall also advise of the possibility of submitting further information regarding the same situation in the light of new facts and evidence.

Rule 50
Procedure for authorization by the Pre-Trial Chamber of the commencement of the investigation

1. When the Prosecutor intends to seek authorization from the Pre-Trial Chamber to initiate an investigation pursuant to article 15, paragraph 3, the Prosecutor shall inform victims, known to him or her or to the Victims and Witnesses Unit, or their legal representatives, unless the Prosecutor decides that doing so would pose a danger to the integrity of the investigation or the life or well-being of victims and witnesses. The Prosecutor may also give notice by general means in order to reach groups of victims if he or she determines in the particular circumstances of the case that such notice could not pose a danger to the integrity and effective conduct of the investigation or to the security and well-being of victims and witnesses. In performing these functions, the Prosecutor may seek the assistance of the Victims and Witnesses Unit as appropriate.
2. A request for authorization by the Prosecutor shall be in writing.
3. Following information given in accordance with sub-rule 1, victims may make representations in writing to the Pre-Trial Chamber within such time limit as set forth in the Regulations.
4. The Pre-Trial Chamber, in deciding on the procedure to be followed, may request additional information from the Prosecutor and from any of the victims who have made representations, and, if it considers it appropriate, may hold a hearing.
5. The Pre-Trial Chamber shall issue its decision, including its reasons, as to whether to authorize the commencement of the investigation in accordance with article 15, paragraph 4, with respect to all or any part of the request by the Prosecutor. The Chamber shall give notice of the decision to victims who have made representations.
6. The above procedure shall also apply to a new request to the Pre-Trial Chamber pursuant to article 15, paragraph 5.

Section III
Challenges and preliminary rulings under articles 17, 18 and 19

Rule 51
Information provided under article 17

In considering the matters referred to in article 17, paragraph 2, and in the context of the circumstances of the case, the Court may consider, *inter alia*, information that the State referred to in article 17, paragraph 1, may choose to bring to the attention of the Court showing that its courts meet internationally recognized norms and standards for the independent and impartial prosecution of similar conduct, or that the State has confirmed in writing to the Prosecutor that the case is being investigated or prosecuted.

Rule 52
Notification provided for in article 18, paragraph 1

1. Subject to the limitations provided for in article 18, paragraph 1, the notification shall contain information about the acts that may constitute crimes referred to in article 5, relevant for the purposes of article 18, paragraph 2.
2. A State may request additional information from the Prosecutor to assist it in the application of article 18, paragraph 2. Such a request shall not affect the one-month time limit provided for in article 18, paragraph 2, and shall be responded to by the Prosecutor on an expedited basis.

Rule 53
Deferral provided for in article 18, paragraph 2

When a State requests a deferral pursuant to article 18, paragraph 2, that State shall make this request in writing and provide information concerning its investigation, taking into account article 18, paragraph 2. The Prosecutor may request additional information from that State.

Rule 54
Application by the Prosecutor under article 18, paragraph 2

1. An application submitted by the Prosecutor to the Pre-Trial Chamber in accordance with article 18, paragraph 2, shall be in writing and shall contain the basis for the application. The information provided by the State under rule 53 shall be communicated by the Prosecutor to the Pre-Trial Chamber.
2. The Prosecutor shall inform that State in writing when he or she makes an application to the Pre-Trial Chamber under article 18, paragraph 2, and shall include in the notice a summary of the basis of the application.

Rule 55
Proceedings concerning article 18, paragraph 2

1. The Pre-Trial Chamber shall decide on the procedure to be followed and may take appropriate measures for the proper conduct of the proceedings. It may hold a hearing.
2. The Pre-Trial Chamber shall examine the Prosecutor's application and any observations submitted by a State that requested a deferral in accordance with article 18, paragraph 2, and shall consider the factors in article 17 in deciding whether to authorize an investigation.
3. The decision and the basis for the decision of the Pre-Trial Chamber shall be communicated as soon as possible to the Prosecutor and to the State that requested a deferral of an investigation.

Rule 56
Application by the Prosecutor following review under article 18, paragraph 3

1. Following a review by the Prosecutor as set forth in article 18, paragraph 3, the Prosecutor may apply to the Pre-Trial Chamber for authorization in accordance with article 18, paragraph 2. The application to the Pre-Trial Chamber shall be in writing and shall contain the basis for the application.
2. Any further information provided by the State under article 18, paragraph 5, shall be communicated by the Prosecutor to the Pre-Trial Chamber.
3. The proceedings shall be conducted in accordance with rules 54, sub-rule 2, and 55.

Rule 57
Provisional measures under article 18, paragraph 6

An application to the Pre-Trial Chamber by the Prosecutor in the circumstances provided for in article 18, paragraph 6, shall be considered ex parte and in camera. The Pre-Trial Chamber shall rule on the application on an expedited basis.

Rule 58
Proceedings under article 19

1. A request or application made under article 19 shall be in writing and contain the basis for it.
2. When a Chamber receives a request or application raising a challenge or question concerning its jurisdiction or the admissibility of a case in accordance with article 19, paragraph 2 or 3, or is acting on its own motion as provided for in article 19, paragraph 1, it shall decide on the procedure to be followed and may take appropriate measures for the proper conduct of the proceedings. It may hold a hearing. It may join the challenge or question to a confirmation or a trial proceeding as long as this does not cause undue delay, and in this circumstance shall hear and decide on the challenge or question first.
3. The Court shall transmit a request or application received under sub-rule 2 to the Prosecutor and to the person referred to in article 19, paragraph 2, who has been surrendered to the Court or who has appeared voluntarily or pursuant to a summons, and shall allow them to submit written observations to the request or application within a period of time determined by the Chamber.
4. The Court shall rule on any challenge or question of jurisdiction first and then on any challenge or question of admissibility.

Rule 59
Participation in proceedings under article 19, paragraph 3

1. For the purpose of article 19, paragraph 3, the Registrar shall inform the following of any question or challenge of jurisdiction or admissibility which has arisen pursuant to article 19, paragraphs 1, 2 and 3:
   (a) Those who have referred a situation pursuant to article 13;
   (b) The victims who have already communicated with the Court in relation to that case or their legal representatives.
2. The Registrar shall provide those referred to in sub-rule 1, in a manner consistent with the duty of the Court regarding the confidentiality of information, the protection of any person and the preservation of evidence, with a summary of the grounds on which the jurisdiction of the Court or the admissibility of the case has been challenged.
3. Those receiving the information, as provided for in sub-rule 1, may make representation in writing to the competent Chamber within such time limit as it considers appropriate.

Rule 60
Competent organ to receive challenges

If a challenge to the jurisdiction of the Court or to the admissibility of a case is made after a confirmation of the charges but before the constitution or designation of the Trial Chamber, it shall be addressed to the Presidency, which shall refer it to the Trial Chamber as soon as the latter is constituted or designated in accordance with rule 130.

Rule 61
Provisional measures under article 19, paragraph 8

When the Prosecutor makes application to the competent Chamber in the circumstances provided for in article 19, paragraph 8, rule 57 shall apply.

Rule 62
Proceedings under article 19, paragraph 10

1. If the Prosecutor makes a request under article 19, paragraph 10, he or she shall make the request to the Chamber that made the latest ruling on admissibility. The provisions of rules 58, 59 and 61 shall be applicable.
2. The State or States whose challenge to admissibility under article 19, paragraph 2, provoked the decision of inadmissibility provided for in article 19, paragraph 10, shall be notified of the request of the Prosecutor and shall be given a time limit within which to make representations.

Chapter 4
Provisions relating to various stages of the proceedings

Section I
Evidence

Rule 63
General provisions relating to evidence

1. The rules of evidence set forth in this chapter, together with article 69, shall apply in proceedings before all Chambers.
2. A Chamber shall have the authority, in accordance with the discretion described in article 64, paragraph 9, to assess freely all evidence submitted in order to determine its relevance or admissibility in accordance with article 69.
3. A Chamber shall rule on an application of a party or on its own motion, made under article 64, subparagraph 9 (a), concerning admissibility when it is based on the grounds set out in article 69, paragraph 7.
4. Without prejudice to article 66, paragraph 3, a Chamber shall not impose a legal requirement that corroboration is required in order to prove any crime within the jurisdiction of the Court, in particular, crimes of sexual violence.
5. The Chambers shall not apply national laws governing evidence, other than in accordance with article 21.

Rule 64
Procedure relating to the relevance or admissibility of evidence

1. An issue relating to relevance or admissibility must be raised at the time when the evidence is submitted to a Chamber. Exceptionally, when those issues were not known at the time

when the evidence was submitted, it may be raised immediately after the issue has become known. The Chamber may request that the issue be raised in writing. The written motion shall be communicated by the Court to all those who participate in the proceedings, unless otherwise decided by the Court.
2. A Chamber shall give reasons for any rulings it makes on evidentiary matters. These reasons shall be placed in the record of the proceedings if they have not already been incorporated into the record during the course of the proceedings in accordance with article 64, paragraph 10, and rule 137, sub-rule 1.
3. Evidence ruled irrelevant or inadmissible shall not be considered by the Chamber.

Rule 65
Compellability of witnesses

1. A witness who appears before the Court is compellable by the Court to provide testimony, unless otherwise provided for in the Statute and the Rules, in particular rules 73, 74 and 75.
2. Rule 171 applies to a witness appearing before the Court who is compellable to provide testimony under sub-rule 1.

Rule 66
Solemn undertaking

1. Except as described in sub-rule 2, every witness shall, in accordance with article 69, paragraph 1, make the following solemn undertaking before testifying:
"I solemnly declare that I will speak the truth, the whole truth and nothing but the truth."
2. A person under the age of 18 or a person whose judgement has been impaired and who, in the opinion of the Chamber, does not understand the nature of a solemn undertaking may be allowed to testify without this solemn undertaking if the Chamber considers that the person is able to describe matters of which he or she has knowledge and that the person understands the meaning of the duty to speak the truth.
3. Before testifying, the witness shall be informed of the offence defined in article 70, paragraph 1 (a).

Rule 67
Live testimony by means of audio or video-link technology

1. In accordance with article 69, paragraph 2, a Chamber may allow a witness to give viva voce (oral) testimony before the Chamber by means of audio or video technology, provided that such technology permits the witness to be examined by the Prosecutor, the defence, and by the Chamber itself, at the time that the witness so testifies.
2. The examination of a witness under this rule shall be conducted in accordance with the relevant rules of this chapter.
3. The Chamber, with the assistance of the Registry, shall ensure that the venue chosen for the conduct of the audio or video-link testimony is conducive to the giving of truthful and open testimony and to the safety, physical and psychological well-being, dignity and privacy of the witness.

Rule 68
Prior recorded testimony

When the Pre-Trial Chamber has not taken measures under article 56, the Trial Chamber may, in accordance with article 69, paragraph 2, allow the introduction of previously recorded audio or video testimony of a witness, or the transcript or other documented evidence of such testimony, provided that:

(a) If the witness who gave the previously recorded testimony is not present before the Trial Chamber, both the Prosecutor and the defence had the opportunity to examine the witness during the recording; or
(b) If the witness who gave the previously recorded testimony is present before the Trial Chamber, he or she does not object to the submission of the previously recorded testimony and the Prosecutor, the defence and the Chamber have the opportunity to examine the witness during the proceedings.

Rule 69
Agreements as to evidence

The Prosecutor and the defence may agree that an alleged fact, which is contained in the charges, the contents of a document, the expected testimony of a witness or other evidence is not contested and, accordingly, a Chamber may consider such alleged fact as being proven, unless the Chamber is of the opinion that a more complete presentation of the alleged facts is required in the interests of justice, in particular the interests of the victims.

Rule 70
Principles of evidence in cases of sexual violence

In cases of sexual violence, the Court shall be guided by and, where appropriate, apply the following principles:
(a) Consent cannot be inferred by reason of any words or conduct of a victim where force, threat of force, coercion or taking advantage of a coercive environment undermined the victim's ability to give voluntary and genuine consent;
(b) Consent cannot be inferred by reason of any words or conduct of a victim where the victim is incapable of giving genuine consent;
(c) Consent cannot be inferred by reason of the silence of, or lack of resistance by, a victim to the alleged sexual violence;
(d) Credibility, character or predisposition to sexual availability of a victim or witness cannot be inferred by reason of the sexual nature of the prior or subsequent conduct of a victim or witness.

Rule 71
Evidence of other sexual conduct

In the light of the definition and nature of the crimes within the jurisdiction of the Court, and subject to article 69, paragraph 4, a Chamber shall not admit evidence of the prior or subsequent sexual conduct of a victim or witness.

Rule 72
In camera procedure to consider relevance or admissibility of evidence

1. Where there is an intention to introduce or elicit, including by means of the questioning of a victim or witness, evidence that the victim consented to an alleged crime of sexual violence, or evidence of the words, conduct, silence or lack of resistance of a victim or witness as referred to in principles (a) through (d) of rule 70, notification shall be provided to the Court which shall describe the substance of the evidence intended to be introduced or elicited and the relevance of the evidence to the issues in the case.
2. In deciding whether the evidence referred to in sub-rule 1 is relevant or admissible, a Chamber shall hear in camera the views of the Prosecutor, the defence, the witness and the victim or his or her legal representative, if any, and shall take into account whether that evi-

dence has a sufficient degree of probative value to an issue in the case and the prejudice that such evidence may cause, in accordance with article 69, paragraph 4. For this purpose, the Chamber shall have regard to article 21, paragraph 3, and articles 67 and 68, and shall be guided by principles (a) to (d) of rule 70, especially with respect to the proposed questioning of a victim.
3. Where the Chamber determines that the evidence referred to in sub-rule 2 is admissible in the proceedings, the Chamber shall state on the record the specific purpose for which the evidence is admissible. In evaluating the evidence during the proceedings, the Chamber shall apply principles (a) to (d) of rule 70.

Rule 73
Privileged communications and information

1. Without prejudice to article 67, paragraph 1 (b), communications made in the context of the professional relationship between a person and his or her legal counsel shall be regarded as privileged, and consequently not subject to disclosure, unless:
   (a) The person consents in writing to such disclosure; or
   (b) The person voluntarily disclosed the content of the communication to a third party, and that third party then gives evidence of that disclosure.
2. Having regard to rule 63, sub-rule 5, communications made in the context of a class of professional or other confidential relationships shall be regarded as privileged, and consequently not subject to disclosure, under the same terms as in sub-rules 1 (a) and 1 (b) if a Chamber decides in respect of that class that:
   (a) Communications occurring within that class of relationship are made in the course of a confidential relationship producing a reasonable expectation of privacy and non-disclosure;
   (b) Confidentiality is essential to the nature and type of relationship between the person and the confidant; and
   (c) Recognition of the privilege would further the objectives of the Statute and the Rules.
3. In making a decision under sub-rule 2, the Court shall give particular regard to recognizing as privileged those communications made in the context of the professional relationship between a person and his or her medical doctor, psychiatrist, psychologist or counsellor, in particular those related to or involving victims, or between a person and a member of a religious clergy; and in the latter case, the Court shall recognize as privileged those communications made in the context of a sacred confession where it is an integral part of the practice of that religion.
4. The Court shall regard as privileged, and consequently not subject to disclosure, including by way of testimony of any present or past official or employee of the International Committee of the Red Cross (ICRC), any information, documents or other evidence which it came into the possession of in the course, or as a consequence, of the performance by ICRC of its functions under the Statutes of the International Red Cross and Red Crescent Movement, unless:
   (a) After consultations undertaken pursuant to sub-rule 6, ICRC does not object in writing to such disclosure, or otherwise has waived this privilege; or
   (b) Such information, documents or other evidence is contained in public statements and documents of ICRC.
5. Nothing in sub-rule 4 shall affect the admissibility of the same evidence obtained from a source other than ICRC and its officials or employees when such evidence has also been acquired by this source independently of ICRC and its officials or employees.
6. If the Court determines that ICRC information, documents or other evidence are of great importance for a particular case, consultations shall be held between the Court and ICRC in order to seek to resolve the matter by cooperative means, bearing in mind the circum-

stances of the case, the relevance of the evidence sought, whether the evidence could be obtained from a source other than ICRC, the interests of justice and of victims, and the performance of the Court's and ICRC's functions.

Rule 74
Self-incrimination by a witness

1. Unless a witness has been notified pursuant to rule 190, the Chamber shall notify a witness of the provisions of this rule before his or her testimony.
2. Where the Court determines that an assurance with respect to self-incrimination should be provided to a particular witness, it shall provide the assurances under sub-rule 3, paragraph (c), before the witness attends, directly or pursuant to a request under article 93, paragraph (1) (e).
3. (a) A witness may object to making any statement that might tend to incriminate him or her.
   (b) Where the witness has attended after receiving an assurance under sub-rule 2, the Court may require the witness to answer the question or questions.
   (c) In the case of other witnesses, the Chamber may require the witness to answer the question or questions, after assuring the witness that the evidence provided in response to the questions:
      (i) Will be kept confidential and will not be disclosed to the public or any State; and
      (ii) Will not be used either directly or indirectly against that person in any subsequent prosecution by the Court, except under articles 70 and 71.
4. Before giving such an assurance, the Chamber shall seek the views of the Prosecutor, ex parte, to determine if the assurance should be given to this particular witness.
5. In determining whether to require the witness to answer, the Chamber shall consider:
   (a) The importance of the anticipated evidence;
   (b) Whether the witness would be providing unique evidence;
   (c) The nature of the possible incrimination, if known; and
   (d) The sufficiency of the protections for the witness, in the particular circumstances.
6. If the Chamber determines that it would not be appropriate to provide an assurance to this witness, it shall not require the witness to answer the question. If the Chamber determines not to require the witness to answer, it may still continue the questioning of the witness on other matters.
7. In order to give effect to the assurance, the Chamber shall:
   (a) Order that the evidence of the witness be given in camera;
   (b) Order that the identity of the witness and the content of the evidence given shall not be disclosed, in any manner, and provide that the breach of any such order will be subject to sanction under article 71;
   (c) Specifically advise the Prosecutor, the accused, the defence counsel, the legal representative of the victim and any Court staff present of the consequences of a breach of the order under subparagraph (b);
   (d) Order the sealing of any record of the proceedings; and
   (e) Use protective measures with respect to any decision of the Court to ensure that the identity of the witness and the content of the evidence given are not disclosed.
8. Where the Prosecutor is aware that the testimony of any witness may raise issues with respect to self-incrimination, he or she shall request an in camera hearing and advise the Chamber of this, in advance of the testimony of the witness. The Chamber may impose the measures outlined in sub-rule 7 for all or a part of the testimony of that witness.
9. The accused, the defence counsel or the witness may advise the Prosecutor or the Chamber that the testimony of a witness will raise issues of self-incrimination before the witness testifies and the Chamber may take the measures outlined in sub-rule 7.

10. If an issue of self-incrimination arises in the course of the proceedings, the Chamber shall suspend the taking of the testimony and provide the witness with an opportunity to obtain legal advice if he or she so requests for the purpose of the application of the rule.

Rule 75
Incrimination by family members

1. A witness appearing before the Court, who is a spouse, child or parent of an accused person, shall not be required by a Chamber to make any statement that might tend to incriminate that accused person. However, the witness may choose to make such a statement.
2. In evaluating the testimony of a witness, a Chamber may take into account that the witness, referred to in sub-rule 1, objected to reply to a question which was intended to contradict a previous statement made by the witness, or the witness was selective in choosing which questions to answer.

Section II
Disclosure

Rule 76
Pre-trial disclosure relating to prosecution witnesses

1. The Prosecutor shall provide the defence with the names of witnesses whom the Prosecutor intends to call to testify and copies of any prior statements made by those witnesses. This shall be done sufficiently in advance to enable the adequate preparation of the defence.
2. The Prosecutor shall subsequently advise the defence of the names of any additional prosecution witnesses and provide copies of their statements when the decision is made to call those witnesses.
3. The statements of prosecution witnesses shall be made available in original and in a language which the accused fully understands and speaks.
4. This rule is subject to the protection and privacy of victims and witnesses and the protection of confidential information as provided for in the Statute and rules 81 and 82.

Rule 77
Inspection of material in possession or control of the Prosecutor

The Prosecutor shall, subject to the restrictions on disclosure as provided for in the Statute and in rules 81 and 82, permit the defence to inspect any books, documents, photographs and other tangible objects in the possession or control of the Prosecutor, which are material to the preparation of the defence or are intended for use by the Prosecutor as evidence for the purposes of the confirmation hearing or at trial, as the case may be, or were obtained from or belonged to the person.

Rule 78
Inspection of material in possession or control of the defence

The defence shall permit the Prosecutor to inspect any books, documents, photographs and other tangible objects in the possession or control of the defence, which are intended for use by the defence as evidence for the purposes of the confirmation hearing or at trial.

Rule 79
Disclosure by the defence

1. The defence shall notify the Prosecutor of its intent to:

(a) Raise the existence of an alibi, in which case the notification shall specify the place or places at which the accused claims to have been present at the time of the alleged crime and the names of witnesses and any other evidence upon which the accused intends to rely to establish the alibi; or
(b) Raise a ground for excluding criminal responsibility provided for in article 31, paragraph 1, in which case the notification shall specify the names of witnesses and any other evidence upon which the accused intends to rely to establish the ground.
2. With due regard to time limits set forth in other rules, notification under sub-rule 1 shall be given sufficiently in advance to enable the Prosecutor to prepare adequately and to respond. The Chamber dealing with the matter may grant the Prosecutor an adjournment to address the issue raised by the defence.
3. Failure of the defence to provide notice under this rule shall not limit its right to raise matters dealt with in sub-rule 1 and to present evidence.
4. This rule does not prevent a Chamber from ordering disclosure of any other evidence.

Rule 80
Procedures for raising a ground for excluding criminal responsibility under article 31, paragraph 3

1. The defence shall give notice to both the Trial Chamber and the Prosecutor if it intends to raise a ground for excluding criminal responsibility under article 31, paragraph 3. This shall be done sufficiently in advance of the commencement of the trial to enable the Prosecutor to prepare adequately for trial.
2. Following notice given under sub-rule 1, the Trial Chamber shall hear both the Prosecutor and the defence before deciding whether the defence can raise a ground for excluding criminal responsibility.
3. If the defence is permitted to raise the ground, the Trial Chamber may grant the Prosecutor an adjournment to address that ground.

Rule 81
Restrictions on disclosure

1. Reports, memoranda or other internal documents prepared by a party, its assistants or representatives in connection with the investigation or preparation of the case are not subject to disclosure.
2. Where material or information is in the possession or control of the Prosecutor which must be disclosed in accordance with the Statute, but disclosure may prejudice further or ongoing investigations, the Prosecutor may apply to the Chamber dealing with the matter for a ruling as to whether the material or information must be disclosed to the defence. The matter shall be heard on an ex parte basis by the Chamber. However, the Prosecutor may not introduce such material or information into evidence during the confirmation hearing or the trial without adequate prior disclosure to the accused.
3. Where steps have been taken to ensure the confidentiality of information, in accordance with articles 54, 57, 64, 72 and 93, and, in accordance with article 68, to protect the safety of witnesses and victims and members of their families, such information shall not be disclosed, except in accordance with those articles. When the disclosure of such information may create a risk to the safety of the witness, the Court shall take measures to inform the witness in advance.
4. The Chamber dealing with the matter shall, on its own motion or at the request of the Prosecutor, the accused or any State, take the necessary steps to ensure the confidentiality of information, in accordance with articles 54, 72 and 93, and, in accordance with article 68, to protect the safety of witnesses and victims and members of their families, including by authorizing the non-disclosure of their identity prior to the commencement of the trial.

5. Where material or information is in the possession or control of the Prosecutor which is withheld under article 68, paragraph 5, such material and information may not be subsequently introduced into evidence during the confirmation hearing or the trial without adequate prior disclosure to the accused.
6. Where material or information is in the possession or control of the defence which is subject to disclosure, it may be withheld in circumstances similar to those which would allow the Prosecutor to rely on article 68, paragraph 5, and a summary thereof submitted instead. Such material and information may not be subsequently introduced into evidence during the confirmation hearing or the trial without adequate prior disclosure to the Prosecutor.

Rule 82
Restrictions on disclosure of material and information protected under article 54, paragraph 3 (e)

1. Where material or information is in the possession or control of the Prosecutor which is protected under article 54, paragraph 3 (e), the Prosecutor may not subsequently introduce such material or information into evidence without the prior consent of the provider of the material or information and adequate prior disclosure to the accused.
2. If the Prosecutor introduces material or information protected under article 54, paragraph 3 (e), into evidence, a Chamber may not order the production of additional evidence received from the provider of the initial material or information, nor may a Chamber for the purpose of obtaining such additional evidence itself summon the provider or a representative of the provider as a witness or order their attendance.
3. If the Prosecutor calls a witness to introduce in evidence any material or information which has been protected under article 54, paragraph 3 (e), a Chamber may not compel that witness to answer any question relating to the material or information or its origin, if the witness declines to answer on grounds of confidentiality.
4. The right of the accused to challenge evidence which has been protected under article 54, paragraph 3 (e), shall remain unaffected subject only to the limitations contained in sub-rules 2 and 3.
5. A Chamber dealing with the matter may order, upon application by the defence, that, in the interests of justice, material or information in the possession of the accused, which has been provided to the accused under the same conditions as set forth in article 54, paragraph 3 (e), and which is to be introduced into evidence, shall be subject *mutatis mutandis* to sub-rules 1, 2 and 3.

Rule 83
Ruling on exculpatory evidence under article 67, paragraph 2

The Prosecutor may request as soon as practicable a hearing on an ex parte basis before the Chamber dealing with the matter for the purpose of obtaining a ruling under article 67, paragraph 2.

Rule 84
Disclosure and additional evidence for trial

In order to enable the parties to prepare for trial and to facilitate the fair and expeditious conduct of the proceedings, the Trial Chamber shall, in accordance with article 64, paragraphs 3 (c) and 6 (d), and article 67, paragraph (2), and subject to article 68, paragraph 5, make any necessary orders for the disclosure of documents or information not previously disclosed and for the production of additional evidence. To avoid delay and to ensure that the trial commences on the set date, any such orders shall include strict time limits which shall be kept under review by the Trial Chamber.

Section III
Victims and witnesses

Subsection 1
Definition and general principle relating to victims

Rule 85
Definition of victims

For the purposes of the Statute and the Rules of Procedure and Evidence:
    (a) "Victims" means natural persons who have suffered harm as a result of the commission of any crime within the jurisdiction of the Court;
    (b) Victims may include organizations or institutions that have sustained direct harm to any of their property which is dedicated to religion, education, art or science or charitable purposes, and to their historic monuments, hospitals and other places and objects for humanitarian purposes.

Rule 86
General principle

A Chamber in making any direction or order, and other organs of the Court in performing their functions under the Statute or the Rules, shall take into account the needs of all victims and witnesses in accordance with article 68, in particular, children, elderly persons, persons with disabilities and victims of sexual or gender violence.

Subsection 2
Protection of victims and witnesses

Rule 87
Protective measures

1. Upon the motion of the Prosecutor or the defence or upon the request of a witness or a victim or his or her legal representative, if any, or on its own motion, and after having consulted with the Victims and Witnesses Unit, as appropriate, a Chamber may order measures to protect a victim, a witness or another person at risk on account of testimony given by a witness pursuant to article 68, paragraphs 1 and 2. The Chamber shall seek to obtain, whenever possible, the consent of the person in respect of whom the protective measure is sought prior to ordering the protective measure.
2. A motion or request under sub-rule 1 shall be governed by rule 134, provided that:
    (a) Such a motion or request shall not be submitted ex parte;
    (b) A request by a witness or by a victim or his or her legal representative, if any, shall be served on both the Prosecutor and the defence, each of whom shall have the opportunity to respond;
    (c) A motion or request affecting a particular witness or a particular victim shall be served on that witness or victim or his or her legal representative, if any, in addition to the other party, each of whom shall have the opportunity to respond;
    (d) When the Chamber proceeds on its own motion, notice and opportunity to respond shall be given to the Prosecutor and the defence, and to any witness or any victim or his or her legal representative, if any, who would be affected by such protective measure; and
    (e) A motion or request may be filed under seal, and, if so filed, shall remain sealed until otherwise ordered by a Chamber. Responses to motions or requests filed under seal shall also be filed under seal.

3. A Chamber may, on a motion or request under sub-rule 1, hold a hearing, which shall be conducted in camera, to determine whether to order measures to prevent the release to the public or press and information agencies, of the identity or the location of a victim, a witness or other person at risk on account of testimony given by a witness by ordering, *inter alia:*
   (a) That the name of the victim, witness or other person at risk on account of testimony given by a witness or any information which could lead to his or her identification, be expunged from the public records of the Chamber;
   (b) That the Prosecutor, the defence or any other participant in the proceedings be prohibited from disclosing such information to a third party;
   (c) That testimony be presented by electronic or other special means, including the use of technical means enabling the alteration of pictures or voice, the use of audio-visual technology, in particular videoconferencing and closed-circuit television, and the exclusive use of the sound media;
   (d) That a pseudonym be used for a victim, a witness or other person at risk on account of testimony given by a witness; or
   (e) That a Chamber conduct part of its proceedings in camera.

Rule 88
Special measures

1. Upon the motion of the Prosecutor or the defence, or upon the request of a witness or a victim or his or her legal representative, if any, or on its own motion, and after having consulted with the Victims and Witnesses Unit, as appropriate, a Chamber may, taking into account the views of the victim or witness, order special measures such as, but not limited to, measures to facilitate the testimony of a traumatized victim or witness, a child, an elderly person or a victim of sexual violence, pursuant to article 68, paragraphs 1 and 2. The Chamber shall seek to obtain, whenever possible, the consent of the person in respect of whom the special measure is sought prior to ordering that measure.
2. A Chamber may hold a hearing on a motion or a request under sub-rule 1, if necessary in camera or ex parte, to determine whether to order any such special measure, including but not limited to an order that a counsel, a legal representative, a psychologist or a family member be permitted to attend during the testimony of the victim or the witness.
3. For *inter partes* motions or requests filed under this rule, the provisions of rule 87, sub-rules 2 (b) to (d), shall apply *mutatis mutandis.*
4. A motion or request filed under this rule may be filed under seal, and if so filed shall remain sealed until otherwise ordered by a Chamber. Any responses to *inter partes* motions or requests filed under seal shall also be filed under seal.
5. Taking into consideration that violations of the privacy of a witness or victim may create risk to his or her security, a Chamber shall be vigilant in controlling the manner of questioning a witness or victim so as to avoid any harassment or intimidation, paying particular attention to attacks on victims of crimes of sexual violence.

Subsection 3
Participation of victims in the proceedings

Rule 89
Application for participation of victims in the proceedings

1. In order to present their views and concerns, victims shall make written application to the Registrar, who shall transmit the application to the relevant Chamber. Subject to the provisions of the Statute, in particular article 68, paragraph 1, the Registrar shall provide a copy of the application to the Prosecutor and the defence, who shall be entitled to reply within a time limit to be set by the Chamber. Subject to the provisions of sub-rule 2, the

Chamber shall then specify the proceedings and manner in which participation is considered appropriate, which may include making opening and closing statements.
2. The Chamber, on its own initiative or on the application of the Prosecutor or the defence, may reject the application if it considers that the person is not a victim or that the criteria set forth in article 68, paragraph 3, are not otherwise fulfilled. A victim whose application has been rejected may file a new application later in the proceedings.
3. An application referred to in this rule may also be made by a person acting with the consent of the victim, or a person acting on behalf of a victim, in the case of a victim who is a child or, when necessary, a victim who is disabled.
4. Where there are a number of applications, the Chamber may consider the applications in such a manner as to ensure the effectiveness of the proceedings and may issue one decision.

Rule 90
Legal representatives of victims

1. A victim shall be free to choose a legal representative.
2. Where there are a number of victims, the Chamber may, for the purposes of ensuring the effectiveness of the proceedings, request the victims or particular groups of victims, if necessary with the assistance of the Registry, to choose a common legal representative or representatives. In facilitating the coordination of victim representation, the Registry may provide assistance, *inter alia*, by referring the victims to a list of counsel, maintained by the Registry, or suggesting one or more common legal representatives.
3. If the victims are unable to choose a common legal representative or representatives within a time limit that the Chamber may decide, the Chamber may request the Registrar to choose one or more common legal representatives.
4. The Chamber and the Registry shall take all reasonable steps to ensure that in the selection of common legal representatives, the distinct interests of the victims, particularly as provided in article 68, paragraph 1, are represented and that any conflict of interest is avoided.
5. A victim or group of victims who lack the necessary means to pay for a common legal representative chosen by the Court may receive assistance from the Registry, including, as appropriate, financial assistance.
6. A legal representative of a victim or victims shall have the qualifications set forth in rule 22, sub-rule 1.

Rule 91
Participation of legal representatives in the proceedings

1. A Chamber may modify a previous ruling under rule 89.
2. A legal representative of a victim shall be entitled to attend and participate in the proceedings in accordance with the terms of the ruling of the Chamber and any modification thereof given under rules 89 and 90. This shall include participation in hearings unless, in the circumstances of the case, the Chamber concerned is of the view that the representative's intervention should be confined to written observations or submissions. The Prosecutor and the defence shall be allowed to reply to any oral or written observation by the legal representative for victims.
3. (a) When a legal representative attends and participates in accordance with this rule, and wishes to question a witness, including questioning under rules 67 and 68, an expert or the accused, the legal representative must make application to the Chamber. The Chamber may require the legal representative to provide a written note of the questions and in that case the questions shall be communicated to the Prosecutor and, if appropriate, the defence, who shall be allowed to make observations within a time limit set by the Chamber.

(b) The Chamber shall then issue a ruling on the request, taking into account the stage of the proceedings, the rights of the accused, the interests of witnesses, the need for a fair, impartial and expeditious trial and in order to give effect to article 68, paragraph 3. The ruling may include directions on the manner and order of the questions and the production of documents in accordance with the powers of the Chamber under article 64. The Chamber may, if it considers it appropriate, put the question to the witness, expert or accused on behalf of the victim's legal representative.

4. For a hearing limited to reparations under article 75, the restrictions on questioning by the legal representative set forth in sub-rule 2 shall not apply. In that case, the legal representative may, with the permission of the Chamber concerned, question witnesses, experts and the person concerned.

Rule 92
Notification to victims and their legal representatives

1. This rule on notification to victims and their legal representatives shall apply to all proceedings before the Court, except in proceedings provided for in Part 2.
2. In order to allow victims to apply for participation in the proceedings in accordance with rule 89, the Court shall notify victims concerning the decision of the Prosecutor not to initiate an investigation or not to prosecute pursuant to article 53. Such a notification shall be given to victims or their legal representatives who have already participated in the proceedings or, as far as possible, to those who have communicated with the Court in respect of the situation or case in question. The Chamber may order the measures outlined in sub-rule 8 if it considers it appropriate in the particular circumstances.
3. In order to allow victims to apply for participation in the proceedings in accordance with rule 89, the Court shall notify victims regarding its decision to hold a hearing to confirm charges pursuant to article 61. Such a notification shall be given to victims or their legal representatives who have already participated in the proceedings or, as far as possible, to those who have communicated with the Court in respect of the case in question.
4. When a notification for participation as provided for in sub-rules 2 and 3 has been given, any subsequent notification as referred to in sub-rules 5 and 6 shall only be provided to victims or their legal representatives who may participate in the proceedings in accordance with a ruling of the Chamber pursuant to rule 89 and any modification thereof.
5. In a manner consistent with the ruling made under rules 89 to 91, victims or their legal representatives participating in proceedings shall, in respect of those proceedings, be notified by the Registrar in a timely manner of:
   (a) Proceedings before the Court, including the date of hearings and any postponements thereof, and the date of delivery of the decision;
   (b) Requests, submissions, motions and other documents relating to such requests, submissions or motions.
6. Where victims or their legal representatives have participated in a certain stage of the proceedings, the Registrar shall notify them as soon as possible of the decisions of the Court in those proceedings.
7. Notifications as referred to in sub-rules 5 and 6 shall be in writing or, where written notification is not possible, in any other form as appropriate. The Registry shall keep a record of all notifications. Where necessary, the Registrar may seek the cooperation of States Parties in accordance with article 93, paragraph 1 (d) and (l).
8. For notification as referred to in sub-rule 3 and otherwise at the request of a Chamber, the Registrar shall take necessary measures to give adequate publicity to the proceedings. In doing so, the Registrar may seek, in accordance with Part 9, the cooperation of relevant States Parties, and seek the assistance of intergovernmental organizations.

Rule 93
Views of victims or their legal representatives

A Chamber may seek the views of victims or their legal representatives participating pursuant to rules 89 to 91 on any issue, *inter alia*, in relation to issues referred to in rules 107, 109, 125, 128, 136, 139 and 191. In addition, a Chamber may seek the views of other victims, as appropriate.

Subsection 4
Reparations to victims

Rule 94
Procedure upon request

1. A victim's request for reparations under article 75 shall be made in writing and filed with the Registrar. It shall contain the following particulars:
   (a) The identity and address of the claimant;
   (b) A description of the injury, loss or harm;
   (c) The location and date of the incident and, to the extent possible, the identity of the person or persons the victim believes to be responsible for the injury, loss or harm;
   (d) Where restitution of assets, property or other tangible items is sought, a description of them;
   (e) Claims for compensation;
   (f) Claims for rehabilitation and other forms of remedy;
   (g) To the extent possible, any relevant supporting documentation, including names and addresses of witnesses.
2. At commencement of the trial and subject to any protective measures, the Court shall ask the Registrar to provide notification of the request to the person or persons named in the request or identified in the charges and, to the extent possible, to any interested persons or any interested States. Those notified shall file with the Registry any representation made under article 75, paragraph 3.

Rule 95
Procedure on the motion of the Court

1. In cases where the Court intends to proceed on its own motion pursuant to article 75, paragraph 1, it shall ask the Registrar to provide notification of its intention to the person or persons against whom the Court is considering making a determination, and, to the extent possible, to victims, interested persons and interested States. Those notified shall file with the Registry any representation made under article 75, paragraph 3.
2. If, as a result of notification under sub-rule 1:
   (a) A victim makes a request for reparations, that request will be determined as if it had been brought under rule 94;
   (b) A victim requests that the Court does not make an order for reparations, the Court shall not proceed to make an individual order in respect of that victim.

Rule 96
Publication of reparation proceedings

1. Without prejudice to any other rules on notification of proceedings, the Registrar shall, insofar as practicable, notify the victims or their legal representatives and the person or persons concerned. The Registrar shall also, having regard to any information provided by the Prosecutor, take all the necessary measures to give adequate publicity of the reparation proceedings before the Court, to the extent possible, to other victims, interested persons and interested States.

2. In taking the measures described in sub-rule 1, the Court may seek, in accordance with Part 9, the cooperation of relevant States Parties, and seek the assistance of intergovernmental organizations in order to give publicity, as widely as possible and by all possible means, to the reparation proceedings before the Court.

Rule 97
Assessment of reparations

1. Taking into account the scope and extent of any damage, loss or injury, the Court may award reparations on an individualized basis or, where it deems it appropriate, on a collective basis or both.
2. At the request of victims or their legal representatives, or at the request of the convicted person, or on its own motion, the Court may appoint appropriate experts to assist it in determining the scope, extent of any damage, loss and injury to, or in respect of victims and to suggest various options concerning the appropriate types and modalities of reparations. The Court shall invite, as appropriate, victims or their legal representatives, the convicted person as well as interested persons and interested States to make observations on the reports of the experts.
3. In all cases, the Court shall respect the rights of victims and the convicted person.

Rule 98
Trust Fund

1. Individual awards for reparations shall be made directly against a convicted person.
2. The Court may order that an award for reparations against a convicted person be deposited with the Trust Fund where at the time of making the order it is impossible or impracticable to make individual awards directly to each victim. The award for reparations thus deposited in the Trust Fund shall be separated from other resources of the Trust Fund and shall be forwarded to each victim as soon as possible.
3. The Court may order that an award for reparations against a convicted person be made through the Trust Fund where the number of the victims and the scope, forms and modalities of reparations makes a collective award more appropriate.
4. Following consultations with interested States and the Trust Fund, the Court may order that an award for reparations be made through the Trust Fund to an intergovernmental, international or national organization approved by the Trust Fund.
5. Other resources of the Trust Fund may be used for the benefit of victims subject to the provisions of article 79.

Rule 99
Cooperation and protective measures for the purpose of forfeiture under articles 57, paragraph 3 (e), and 75, paragraph 4

1. The Pre-Trial Chamber, pursuant to article 57, paragraph 3 (e), or the Trial Chamber, pursuant to article 75, paragraph 4, may, on its own motion or on the application of the Prosecutor or at the request of the victims or their legal representatives who have made a request for reparations or who have given a written undertaking to do so, determine whether measures should be requested.
2. Notice is not required unless the Court determines, in the particular circumstances of the case, that notification could not jeopardize the effectiveness of the measures requested. In the latter case, the Registrar shall provide notification of the proceedings to the person against whom a request is made and so far as is possible to any interested persons or interested States.

3. If an order is made without prior notification, the relevant Chamber shall request the Registrar, as soon as is consistent with the effectiveness of the measures requested, to notify those against whom a request is made and, to the extent possible, to any interested persons or any interested States and invite them to make observations as to whether the order should be revoked or otherwise modified.
4. The Court may make orders as to the timing and conduct of any proceedings necessary to determine these issues.

Section IV
Miscellaneous provisions

Rule 100
Place of the proceedings

1. In a particular case, where the Court considers that it would be in the interests of justice, it may decide to sit in a State other than the host State.
2. An application or recommendation changing the place where the Court sits may be filed at any time after the initiation of an investigation, either by the Prosecutor, the defence or by a majority of the judges of the Court. Such an application or recommendation shall be addressed to the Presidency. It shall be made in writing and specify in which State the Court would sit. The Presidency shall satisfy itself of the views of the relevant Chamber.
3. The Presidency shall consult the State where the Court intends to sit. If that State agrees that the Court can sit in that State, then the decision to sit in a State other than the host State shall be taken by the judges, in plenary session, by a two-thirds majority.

Rule 101
Time limits

1. In making any order setting time limits regarding the conduct of any proceedings, the Court shall have regard to the need to facilitate fair and expeditious proceedings, bearing in mind in particular the rights of the defence and the victims.
2. Taking into account the rights of the accused, in particular under article 67, paragraph (1)(c), all those participating in the proceedings to whom any order is directed shall endeavour to act as expeditiously as possible, within the time limit ordered by the Court.

Rule 102
Communications other than in writing

Where a person is unable, due to a disability or illiteracy, to make a written request, application, observation or other communication to the Court, the person may make such request, application, observation or communication in audio, video or other electronic form.

Rule 103
Amicus curiae and other forms of submission

1. At any stage of the proceedings, a Chamber may, if it considers it desirable for the proper determination of the case, invite or grant leave to a State, organization or person to submit, in writing or orally, any observation on any issue that the Chamber deems appropriate.
2. The Prosecutor and the defence shall have the opportunity to respond to the observations submitted under sub-rule 1.
3. A written observation submitted under sub-rule 1 shall be filed with the Registrar, who shall provide copies to the Prosecutor and the defence. The Chamber shall determine what time limits shall apply to the filing of such observations.

Chapter 5
Investigation and prosecution

Section I
Decision of the Prosecutor regarding the initiation of an investigation under article 53, paragraphs 1 and 2

Rule 104
Evaluation of information by the Prosecutor

1. In acting pursuant to article 53, paragraph 1, the Prosecutor shall, in evaluating the information made available to him or her, analyse the seriousness of the information received.
2. For the purposes of sub-rule 1, the Prosecutor may seek additional information from States, organs of the United Nations, intergovernmental and non-governmental organizations, or other reliable sources that he or she deems appropriate, and may receive written or oral testimony at the seat of the Court. The procedure set out in rule 47 shall apply to the receiving of such testimony.

Rule 105
Notification of a decision by the Prosecutor not to initiate an investigation

1. When the Prosecutor decides not to initiate an investigation under article 53, paragraph 1, he or she shall promptly inform in writing the State or States that referred a situation under article 14, or the Security Council in respect of a situation covered by article 13, paragraph (b).
2. When the Prosecutor decides not to submit to the Pre-Trial Chamber a request for authorization of an investigation, rule 49 shall apply.
3. The notification referred to in sub-rule 1 shall contain the conclusion of the Prosecutor and, having regard to article 68, paragraph 1, the reasons for the conclusion.
4. In case the Prosecutor decides not to investigate solely on the basis of article 53, paragraph 1 (c), he or she shall inform in writing the Pre-Trial Chamber promptly after making that decision.
5. The notification shall contain the conclusion of the Prosecutor and the reasons for the conclusion.

Rule 106
Notification of a decision by the Prosecutor not to prosecute

1. When the Prosecutor decides that there is not a sufficient basis for prosecution under article 53, paragraph 2, he or she shall promptly inform in writing the Pre-Trial Chamber, together with the State or States that referred a situation under article 14, or the Security Council in respect of a situation covered by article 13, paragraph (b).
2. The notifications referred to in sub-rule 1 shall contain the conclusion of the Prosecutor and, having regard to article 68, paragraph 1, the reasons for the conclusion.

Section II
Procedure under article 53, paragraph 3

Rule 107
Request for review under article 53, paragraph 3 (a)

1. A request under article 53, paragraph 3, for a review of a decision by the Prosecutor not to initiate an investigation or not to prosecute shall be made in writing, and be supported with reasons, within 90 days following the notification given under rule 105 or 106.

2. The Pre-Trial Chamber may request the Prosecutor to transmit the information or documents in his or her possession, or summaries thereof, that the Chamber considers necessary for the conduct of the review.
3. The Pre-Trial Chamber shall take such measures as are necessary under articles 54, 72 and 93 to protect the information and documents referred to in sub-rule 2 and, under article 68, paragraph 5, to protect the safety of witnesses and victims and members of their families.
4. When a State or the Security Council makes a request referred to in sub-rule 1, the Pre-Trial Chamber may seek further observations from them.
5. Where an issue of jurisdiction or admissibility of the case is raised, rule 59 shall apply.

Rule 108
Decision of the Pre-Trial Chamber under article 53, paragraph 3 (a)

1. A decision of the Pre-Trial Chamber under article 53, paragraph 3 (a), must be concurred in by a majority of its judges and shall contain reasons. It shall be communicated to all those who participated in the review.
2. Where the Pre-Trial Chamber requests the Prosecutor to review, in whole or in part, his or her decision not to initiate an investigation or not to prosecute, the Prosecutor shall reconsider that decision as soon as possible.
3. Once the Prosecutor has taken a final decision, he or she shall notify the Pre-Trial Chamber in writing. This notification shall contain the conclusion of the Prosecutor and the reasons for the conclusion. It shall be communicated to all those who participated in the review.

Rule 109
Review by the Pre-Trial Chamber under article 53, paragraph 3 (b)

1. Within 180 days following a notification given under rule 105 or 106, the Pre-Trial Chamber may on its own initiative decide to review a decision of the Prosecutor taken solely under article 53, paragraph 1 (c) or 2 (c). The Pre-Trial Chamber shall inform the Prosecutor of its intention to review his or her decision and shall establish a time limit within which the Prosecutor may submit observations and other material.
2. In cases where a request has been submitted to the Pre-Trial Chamber by a State or by the Security Council, they shall also be informed and may submit observations in accordance with rule 107.

Rule 110
Decision by the Pre-Trial Chamber under article 53, paragraph 3 (b)

1. A decision by the Pre-Trial Chamber to confirm or not to confirm a decision taken by the Prosecutor solely under article 53, paragraph 1 (c) or 2 (c), must be concurred in by a majority of its judges and shall contain reasons. It shall be communicated to all those who participated in the review.
2. When the Pre-Trial Chamber does not confirm the decision by the Prosecutor referred to in sub-rule 1, he or she shall proceed with the investigation or prosecution.

Section III
Collection of evidence

Rule 111
Record of questioning in general

1. A record shall be made of formal statements made by any person who is questioned in connection with an investigation or with proceedings. The record shall be signed by the per-

son who records and conducts the questioning and by the person who is questioned and his or her counsel, if present, and, where applicable, the Prosecutor or the judge who is present. The record shall note the date, time and place of, and all persons present during the questioning. It shall also be noted when someone has not signed the record as well as the reasons therefor.
2. When the Prosecutor or national authorities question a person, due regard shall be given to article 55. When a person is informed of his or her rights under article 55, paragraph 2, the fact that this information has been provided shall be noted in the record.

Rule 112
Recording of questioning in particular cases

1. Whenever the Prosecutor questions a person to whom article 55, paragraph 2, applies, or for whom a warrant of arrest or a summons to appear has been issued under article 58, paragraph 7, the questioning shall be audio- or video-recorded, in accordance with the following procedure:
   (a) The person questioned shall be informed, in a language he or she fully understands and speaks, that the questioning is to be audio- or video-recorded, and that the person concerned may object if he or she so wishes. The fact that this information has been provided and the response given by the person concerned shall be noted in the record. The person may, before replying, speak in private with his or her counsel, if present. If the person questioned refuses to be audio- or video-recorded, the procedure in rule 111 shall be followed;
   (b) A waiver of the right to be questioned in the presence of counsel shall be recorded in writing and, if possible, be audio- or video-recorded;
   (c) In the event of an interruption in the course of questioning, the fact and the time of the interruption shall be recorded before the audio- or video-recording ends as well as the time of resumption of the questioning;
   (d) At the conclusion of the questioning, the person questioned shall be offered the opportunity to clarify anything he or she has said and to add anything he or she may wish. The time of conclusion of the questioning shall be noted;
   (e) The tape shall be transcribed as soon as practicable after the conclusion of the questioning and a copy of the transcript supplied to the person questioned together with a copy of the recorded tape or, if multiple recording apparatus was used, one of the original recorded tapes;
   (f) The original tape or one of the original tapes shall be sealed in the presence of the person questioned and his or her counsel, if present, under the signature of the Prosecutor and the person questioned and the counsel, if present.
2. The Prosecutor shall make every reasonable effort to record the questioning in accordance with sub-rule 1. As an exception, a person may be questioned without the questioning being audio- or video-recorded where the circumstances prevent such recording taking place. In this case, the reasons for not recording the questioning shall be stated in writing and the procedure in rule 111 shall be followed.
3. When, pursuant to sub-rule 1 (a) or 2, the questioning is not audio- or video-recorded, the person questioned shall be provided with a copy of his or her statement.
4. The Prosecutor may choose to follow the procedure in this rule when questioning other persons than those mentioned in sub-rule 1, in particular where the use of such procedures could assist in reducing any subsequent traumatization of a victim of sexual or gender violence, a child or a person with disabilities in providing their evidence. The Prosecutor may make an application to the relevant Chamber.
5. The Pre-Trial Chamber may, in pursuance of article 56, paragraph 2, order that the procedure in this rule be applied to the questioning of any person.

Rule 113
Collection of information regarding the state of health of the person concerned

1. The Pre-Trial Chamber may, on its own initiative or at the request of the Prosecutor, the person concerned or his or her counsel, order that a person having the rights in article 55, paragraph 2, be given a medical, psychological or psychiatric examination. In making its determination, the Pre-Trial Chamber shall consider the nature and purpose of the examination and whether the person consents to the examination.
2. The Pre-Trial Chamber shall appoint one or more experts from the list of experts approved by the Registrar, or an expert approved by the Pre-Trial Chamber at the request of a party.

Rule 114
Unique investigative opportunity under article 56

1. Upon being advised by the Prosecutor in accordance with article 56, paragraph 1 (a), the Pre-Trial Chamber shall hold consultations without delay with the Prosecutor and, subject to the provisions of article 56, paragraph 1 (c), with the person who has been arrested or who has appeared before the Court pursuant to summons and his or her counsel, in order to determine the measures to be taken and the modalities of their implementation, which may include measures to ensure that the right to communicate under article 67, paragraph 1 (b), is protected.
2. A decision of the Pre-Trial Chamber to take measures pursuant to article 56, paragraph 3, must be concurred in by a majority of its judges after consultations with the Prosecutor. During the consultations, the Prosecutor may advise the Pre-Trial Chamber that intended measures could jeopardize the proper conduct of the investigation.

Rule 115
Collection of evidence in the territory of a State Party under article 57, paragraph 3 (d)

1. Where the Prosecutor considers that article 57, paragraph 3 (d), applies, the Prosecutor may submit a written request to the Pre-Trial Chamber for authorization to take certain measures in the territory of the State Party in question. After a submission of such a request, the Pre-Trial Chamber shall, whenever possible, inform and invite views from the State Party concerned.
2. In arriving at its determination as to whether the request is well founded, the Pre-Trial Chamber shall take into account any views expressed by the State Party concerned. The Pre-Trial Chamber may, on its own initiative or at the request of the Prosecutor or the State Party concerned, decide to hold a hearing.
3. An authorization under article 57, paragraph 3 (d), shall be issued in the form of an order and shall state the reasons, based on the criteria set forth in that paragraph. The order may specify procedures to be followed in carrying out such collection of evidence.

Rule 116
Collection of evidence at the request of the defence under article 57, paragraph 3 (b)

1. The Pre-Trial Chamber shall issue an order or seek cooperation under article 57, paragraph 3 (b), where it is satisfied:
    (a) That such an order would facilitate the collection of evidence that may be material to the proper determination of the issues being adjudicated, or to the proper preparation of the person's defence; and
    (b) In a case of cooperation under Part 9, that sufficient information to comply with article 96, paragraph 2, has been provided.
2. Before taking a decision whether to issue an order or seek cooperation under article 57, paragraph 3 (b), the Pre-Trial Chamber may seek the views of the Prosecutor.

Section IV
Procedures in respect of restriction and deprivation of liberty

Rule 117
Detention in the custodial State

1. The Court shall take measures to ensure that it is informed of the arrest of a person in response to a request made by the Court under article 89 or 92. Once so informed, the Court shall ensure that the person receives a copy of the arrest warrant issued by the Pre-Trial Chamber under article 58 and any relevant provisions of the Statute. The documents shall be made available in a language that the person fully understands and speaks.
2. At any time after arrest, the person may make a request to the Pre-Trial Chamber for the appointment of counsel to assist with proceedings before the Court and the Pre-Trial Chamber shall take a decision on such request.
3. A challenge as to whether the warrant of arrest was properly issued in accordance with article 58, paragraph 1 (a) and (b), shall be made in writing to the Pre-Trial Chamber. The application shall set out the basis for the challenge. After having obtained the views of the Prosecutor, the Pre-Trial Chamber shall decide on the application without delay.
4. When the competent authority of the custodial State notifies the Pre-Trial Chamber that a request for release has been made by the person arrested, in accordance with article 59, paragraph 5, the Pre-Trial Chamber shall provide its recommendations within any time limit set by the custodial State.
5. When the Pre-Trial Chamber is informed that the person has been granted interim release by the competent authority of the custodial State, the Pre-Trial Chamber shall inform the custodial State how and when it would like to receive periodic reports on the status of the interim release.

Rule 118
Pre-trial detention at the seat of the Court

1. If the person surrendered to the Court makes an initial request for interim release pending trial, either upon first appearance in accordance with rule 121 or subsequently, the Pre-Trial Chamber shall decide upon the request without delay, after seeking the views of the Prosecutor.
2. The Pre-Trial Chamber shall review its ruling on the release or detention of a person in accordance with article 60, paragraph 3, at least every 120 days and may do so at any time on the request of the person or the Prosecutor.
3. After the first appearance, a request for interim release must be made in writing. The Prosecutor shall be given notice of such a request. The Pre-Trial Chamber shall decide after having received observations in writing of the Prosecutor and the detained person. The Pre-Trial Chamber may decide to hold a hearing, at the request of the Prosecutor or the detained person or on its own initiative. A hearing must be held at least once every year.

Rule 119
Conditional release

1. The Pre-Trial Chamber may set one or more conditions restricting liberty, including the following:
    (a) The person must not travel beyond territorial limits set by the Pre-Trial Chamber without the explicit agreement of the Chamber;
    (b) The person must not go to certain places or associate with certain persons as specified by the Pre-Trial Chamber;
    (c) The person must not contact directly or indirectly victims or witnesses;

    (d) The person must not engage in certain professional activities;
    (e) The person must reside at a particular address as specified by the Pre-Trial Chamber;
    (f) The person must respond when summoned by an authority or qualified person designated by the Pre-Trial Chamber;
    (g) The person must post bond or provide real or personal security or surety, for which the amount and the schedule and mode of payment shall be determined by the Pre-Trial Chamber;
    (h) The person must supply the Registrar with all identity documents, particularly his or her passport.
2. At the request of the person concerned or the Prosecutor or on its own initiative, the Pre-Trial Chamber may at any time decide to amend the conditions set pursuant to sub-rule 1.
3. Before imposing or amending any conditions restricting liberty, the Pre-Trial Chamber shall seek the views of the Prosecutor, the person concerned, any relevant State and victims that have communicated with the Court in that case and whom the Chamber considers could be at risk as a result of a release or conditions imposed.
4. If the Pre-Trial Chamber is convinced that the person concerned has failed to comply with one or more of the obligations imposed, it may, on such basis, at the request of the Prosecutor or on its own initiative, issue a warrant of arrest in respect of the person.
5. When the Pre-Trial Chamber issues a summons to appear pursuant to article 58, paragraph 7, and intends to set conditions restricting liberty, it shall ascertain the relevant provisions of the national law of the State receiving the summons. In a manner that is in keeping with the national law of the State receiving the summons, the Pre-Trial Chamber shall proceed in accordance with sub-rules 1, 2 and 3. If the Pre-Trial Chamber receives information that the person concerned has failed to comply with conditions imposed, it shall proceed in accordance with sub-rule 4.

Rule 120
Instruments of restraint

Personal instruments of restraint shall not be used except as a precaution against escape, for the protection of the person in the custody of the Court and others or for other security reasons, and shall be removed when the person appears before a Chamber.

Section V
Proceedings with regard to the confirmation of charges under article 61

Rule 121
Proceedings before the confirmation hearing

1. A person subject to a warrant of arrest or a summons to appear under article 58 shall appear before the Pre-Trial Chamber, in the presence of the Prosecutor, promptly upon arriving at the Court. Subject to the provisions of articles 60 and 61, the person shall enjoy the rights set forth in article 67. At this first appearance, the Pre-Trial Chamber shall set the date on which it intends to hold a hearing to confirm the charges. It shall ensure that this date, and any postponements under sub-rule 7, are made public.
2. In accordance with article 61, paragraph 3, the Pre-Trial Chamber shall take the necessary decisions regarding disclosure between the Prosecutor and the person in respect of whom a warrant of arrest or a summons to appear has been issued. During disclosure:
    (a) The person concerned may be assisted or represented by the counsel of his or her choice or by a counsel assigned to him or her;
    (b) The Pre-Trial Chamber shall hold status conferences to ensure that disclosure takes place under satisfactory conditions. For each case, a judge of the Pre-Trial Chamber

shall be appointed to organize such status conferences, on his or her own motion, or at the request of the Prosecutor or the person;
   (c) All evidence disclosed between the Prosecutor and the person for the purposes of the confirmation hearing shall be communicated to the Pre-Trial Chamber.
3. The Prosecutor shall provide to the Pre-Trial Chamber and the person, no later than 30 days before the date of the confirmation hearing, a detailed description of the charges together with a list of the evidence which he or she intends to present at the hearing.
4. Where the Prosecutor intends to amend the charges pursuant to article 61, paragraph 4, he or she shall notify the Pre-Trial Chamber and the person no later than 15 days before the date of the hearing of the amended charges together with a list of evidence that the Prosecutor intends to bring in support of those charges at the hearing.
5. Where the Prosecutor intends to present new evidence at the hearing, he or she shall provide the Pre-Trial Chamber and the person with a list of that evidence no later than 15 days before the date of the hearing.
6. If the person intends to present evidence under article 61, paragraph 6, he or she shall provide a list of that evidence to the Pre-Trial Chamber no later than 15 days before the date of the hearing. The Pre-Trial Chamber shall transmit the list to the Prosecutor without delay. The person shall provide a list of evidence that he or she intends to present in response to any amended charges or a new list of evidence provided by the Prosecutor.
7. The Prosecutor or the person may ask the Pre-Trial Chamber to postpone the date of the confirmation hearing. The Pre-Trial Chamber may also, on its own motion, decide to postpone the hearing.
8. The Pre-Trial Chamber shall not take into consideration charges and evidence presented after the time limit, or any extension thereof, has expired.
9. The Prosecutor and the person may lodge written submissions with the Pre-Trial Chamber, on points of fact and on law, including grounds for excluding criminal responsibility set forth in article 31, paragraph 1, no later than three days before the date of the hearing. A copy of these submissions shall be transmitted immediately to the Prosecutor or the person, as the case may be.
10. The Registry shall create and maintain a full and accurate record of all proceedings before the Pre-Trial Chamber, including all documents transmitted to the Chamber pursuant to this rule. Subject to any restrictions concerning confidentiality and the protection of national security information, the record may be consulted by the Prosecutor, the person and victims or their legal representatives participating in the proceedings pursuant to rules 89 to 91.

Rule 122
Proceedings at the confirmation hearing in the presence of the person charged

1. The Presiding Judge of the Pre-Trial Chamber shall ask the officer of the Registry assisting the Chamber to read out the charges as presented by the Prosecutor. The Presiding Judge shall determine how the hearing is to be conducted and, in particular, may establish the order and the conditions under which he or she intends the evidence contained in the record of the proceedings to be presented.
2. If a question or challenge concerning jurisdiction or admissibility arises, rule 58 applies.
3. Before hearing the matter on the merits, the Presiding Judge of the Pre-Trial Chamber shall ask the Prosecutor and the person whether they intend to raise objections or make observations concerning an issue related to the proper conduct of the proceedings prior to the confirmation hearing.
4. At no subsequent point may the objections and observations made under sub-rule 3 be raised or made again in the confirmation or trial proceedings.
5. If objections or observations referred to in sub-rule 3 are presented, the Presiding Judge of

the Pre-Trial Chamber shall invite those referred to in sub-rule 3 to present their arguments, in the order which he or she shall establish. The person shall have the right to reply.

6. If the objections raised or observations made are those referred to in sub-rule 3, the Pre-Trial Chamber shall decide whether to join the issue raised with the examination of the charges and the evidence, or to separate them, in which case it shall adjourn the confirmation hearing and render a decision on the issues raised.
7. During the hearing on the merits, the Prosecutor and the person shall present their arguments in accordance with article 61, paragraphs 5 and 6.
8. The Pre-Trial Chamber shall permit the Prosecutor and the person, in that order, to make final observations.
9. Subject to the provisions of article 61, article 69 shall apply *mutatis mutandis* at the confirmation hearing.

Rule 123
Measures to ensure the presence of the person concerned at the confirmation hearing

1. When a warrant of arrest or summons to appear in accordance with article 58, paragraph 7, has been issued for a person by the Pre-Trial Chamber and the person is arrested or served with the summons, the Pre-Trial Chamber shall ensure that the person is notified of the provisions of article 61, paragraph 2.
2. The Pre-Trial Chamber may hold consultations with the Prosecutor, at the request of the latter or on its own initiative, in order to determine whether there is cause to hold a hearing on confirmation of charges under the conditions set forth in article 61, paragraph 2 (b). When the person concerned has a counsel known to the Court, the consultations shall be held in the presence of the counsel unless the Pre-Trial Chamber decides otherwise.
3. The Pre-Trial Chamber shall ensure that a warrant of arrest for the person concerned has been issued and, if the warrant of arrest has not been executed within a reasonable period of time after the issuance of the warrant, that all reasonable measures have been taken to locate and arrest the person.

Rule 124
Waiver of the right to be present at the confirmation hearing

1. If the person concerned is available to the Court but wishes to waive the right to be present at the hearing on confirmation of charges, he or she shall submit a written request to the Pre-Trial Chamber, which may then hold consultations with the Prosecutor and the person concerned, assisted or represented by his or her counsel.
2. A confirmation hearing pursuant to article 61, paragraph 2 (a), shall only be held when the Pre-Trial Chamber is satisfied that the person concerned understands the right to be present at the hearing and the consequences of waiving this right.
3. The Pre-Trial Chamber may authorize and make provision for the person to observe the hearing from outside the courtroom through the use of communications technology, if required.
4. The waiving of the right to be present at the hearing does not prevent the Pre-Trial Chamber from receiving written observations on issues before the Chamber from the person concerned.

Rule 125
Decision to hold the confirmation hearing in the absence of the person concerned

1. After holding consultations under rules 123 and 124, the Pre-Trial Chamber shall decide whether there is cause to hold a hearing on confirmation of charges in the absence of the person concerned, and in that case, whether the person may be represented by counsel. The Pre-Trial Chamber shall, when appropriate, set a date for the hearing and make the date public.

2. The decision of the Pre-Trial Chamber shall be notified to the Prosecutor and, if possible, to the person concerned or his or her counsel.
3. If the Pre-Trial Chamber decides not to hold a hearing on confirmation of charges in the absence of the person concerned, and the person is not available to the Court, the confirmation of charges may not take place until the person is available to the Court. The Pre-Trial Chamber may review its decision at any time, at the request of the Prosecutor or on its own initiative.
4. If the Pre-Trial Chamber decides not to hold a hearing on confirmation of charges in the absence of the person concerned, and the person is available to the Court, it shall order the person to appear.

Rule 126
Confirmation hearing in the absence of the person concerned

1. The provisions of rules 121 and 122 shall apply *mutatis mutandis* to the preparation for and holding of a hearing on confirmation of charges in the absence of the person concerned.
2. If the Pre-Trial Chamber has determined that the person concerned shall be represented by counsel, the counsel shall have the opportunity to exercise the rights of that person.
3. When the person who has fled is subsequently arrested and the Court has confirmed the charges upon which the Prosecutor intends to pursue the trial, the person charged shall be committed to the Trial Chamber established under article 61, paragraph 11. The person charged may request in writing that the Trial Chamber refer issues to the Pre-Trial Chamber that are necessary for the Chamber's effective and fair functioning in accordance with article 64, paragraph 4.

Section VI
Closure of the pre-trial phase

Rule 127
Procedure in the event of different decisions on multiple charges

If the Pre-Trial Chamber is ready to confirm some of the charges but adjourns the hearing on other charges under article 61, paragraph 7 (c), it may decide that the committal of the person concerned to the Trial Chamber on the charges that it is ready to confirm shall be deferred pending the continuation of the hearing. The Pre-Trial Chamber may then establish a time limit within which the Prosecutor may proceed in accordance with article 61, paragraph 7 (c) (i) or (ii).

Rule 128
Amendment of the charges

1. If the Prosecutor seeks to amend charges already confirmed before the trial has begun, in accordance with article 61, the Prosecutor shall make a written request to the Pre-Trial Chamber, and that Chamber shall so notify the accused.
2. Before deciding whether to authorize the amendment, the Pre-Trial Chamber may request the accused and the Prosecutor to submit written observations on certain issues of fact or law.
3. If the Pre-Trial Chamber determines that the amendments proposed by the Prosecutor constitute additional or more serious charges, it shall proceed, as appropriate, in accordance with rules 121 and 122 or rules 123 to 126.

Rule 129
Notification of the decision on the confirmation of charges

The decision of the Pre-Trial Chamber on the confirmation of charges and the committal of the accused to the Trial Chamber shall be notified, if possible, to the Prosecutor, the person concerned and his or her counsel. Such decision and the record of the proceedings of the Pre-Trial Chamber shall be transmitted to the Presidency.

Rule 130
Constitution of the Trial Chamber

When the Presidency constitutes a Trial Chamber and refers the case to it, the Presidency shall transmit the decision of the Pre-Trial Chamber and the record of the proceedings to the Trial Chamber. The Presidency may also refer the case to a previously constituted Trial Chamber.

Chapter 6
Trial procedure

Rule 131
Record of the proceedings transmitted by the Pre-Trial Chamber

1. The Registrar shall maintain the record of the proceedings transmitted by the Pre-Trial Chamber, pursuant to rule 121, sub-rule 10.
2. Subject to any restrictions concerning confidentiality and the protection of national security information, the record may be consulted by the Prosecutor, the defence, the representatives of States when they participate in the proceedings, and the victims or their legal representatives participating in the proceedings pursuant to rules 89 to 91.

Rule 132
Status conferences

1. Promptly after it is constituted, the Trial Chamber shall hold a status conference in order to set the date of the trial. The Trial Chamber, on its own motion, or at the request of the Prosecutor or the defence, may postpone the date of the trial. The Trial Chamber shall notify the trial date to all those participating in the proceedings. The Trial Chamber shall ensure that this date and any postponements are made public.
2. In order to facilitate the fair and expeditious conduct of the proceedings, the Trial Chamber may confer with the parties by holding status conferences as necessary.

Rule 133
Motions challenging admissibility or jurisdiction

Challenges to the jurisdiction of the Court or the admissibility of the case at the commencement of the trial, or subsequently with the leave of the Court, shall be dealt with by the Presiding Judge and the Trial Chamber in accordance with rule 58.

Rule 134
Motions relating to the trial proceedings

1. Prior to the commencement of the trial, the Trial Chamber on its own motion, or at the request of the Prosecutor or the defence, may rule on any issue concerning the conduct of the proceedings. Any request from the Prosecutor or the defence shall be in writing and, unless the request is for an ex parte procedure, served on the other party. For all requests other than those submitted for an ex parte procedure, the other party shall have the opportunity to file a response.
2. At the commencement of the trial, the Trial Chamber shall ask the Prosecutor and the defence whether they have any objections or observations concerning the conduct of the proceedings which have arisen since the confirmation hearings. Such objections or observations

may not be raised or made again on a subsequent occasion in the trial proceedings, without leave of the Trial Chamber in this proceeding.

3. After the commencement of the trial, the Trial Chamber, on its own motion, or at the request of the Prosecutor or the defence, may rule on issues that arise during the course of the trial.

Rule 135
Medical examination of the accused

1. The Trial Chamber may, for the purpose of discharging its obligations under article 64, paragraph 8 (a), or for any other reasons, or at the request of a party, order a medical, psychiatric or psychological examination of the accused, under the conditions set forth in rule 113.
2. The Trial Chamber shall place its reasons for any such order on the record.
3. The Trial Chamber shall appoint one or more experts from the list of experts approved by the Registrar, or an expert approved by the Trial Chamber at the request of a party.
4. Where the Trial Chamber is satisfied that the accused is unfit to stand trial, it shall order that the trial be adjourned. The Trial Chamber may, on its own motion or at the request of the prosecution or the defence, review the case of the accused. In any event, the case shall be reviewed every 120 days unless there are reasons to do otherwise. If necessary, the Trial Chamber may order further examinations of the accused. When the Trial Chamber is satisfied that the accused has become fit to stand trial, it shall proceed in accordance with rule 132.

Rule 136
Joint and separate trials

1. Persons accused jointly shall be tried together unless the Trial Chamber, on its own motion or at the request of the Prosecutor or the defence, orders that separate trials are necessary, in order to avoid serious prejudice to the accused, to protect the interests of justice or because a person jointly accused has made an admission of guilt and can be proceeded against in accordance with article 65, paragraph 2.
2. In joint trials, each accused shall be accorded the same rights as if such accused were being tried separately.

Rule 137
Record of the trial proceedings

1. In accordance with article 64, paragraph 10, the Registrar shall take measures to make, and preserve, a full and accurate record of all proceedings, including transcripts, audio- and video-recordings and other means of capturing sound or image.
2. A Trial Chamber may order the disclosure of all or part of the record of closed proceedings when the reasons for ordering its non-disclosure no longer exist.
3. The Trial Chamber may authorize persons other than the Registrar to take photographs, audio- and video-recordings and other means of capturing the sound or image of the trial.

Rule 138
Custody of evidence

The Registrar shall retain and preserve, as necessary, all the evidence and other materials offered during the hearing, subject to any order of the Trial Chamber.

Rule 139
Decision on admission of guilt

1. After having proceeded in accordance with article 65, paragraph 1, the Trial Chamber, in order to decide whether to proceed in accordance with article 65, paragraph 4, may invite the views of the Prosecutor and the defence.

2. The Trial Chamber shall then make its decision on the admission of guilt and shall give reasons for this decision, which shall be placed on the record.

Rule 140
Directions for the conduct of the proceedings and testimony

1. If the Presiding Judge does not give directions under article 64, paragraph 8, the Prosecutor and the defence shall agree on the order and manner in which the evidence shall be submitted to the Trial Chamber. If no agreement can be reached, the Presiding Judge shall issue directions.
2. In all cases, subject to article 64, paragraphs 8 (b) and 9, article 69, paragraph 4, and rule 88, sub-rule 5, a witness may be questioned as follows:
   (a) A party that submits evidence in accordance with article 69, paragraph 3, by way of a witness, has the right to question that witness;
   (b) The prosecution and the defence have the right to question that witness about relevant matters related to the witness's testimony and its reliability, the credibility of the witness and other relevant matters;
   (c) The Trial Chamber has the right to question a witness before or after a witness is questioned by a participant referred to in sub-rules 2 (a) or (b);
   (d) The defence shall have the right to be the last to examine a witness.
3. Unless otherwise ordered by the Trial Chamber, a witness other than an expert, or an investigator if he or she has not yet testified, shall not be present when the testimony of another witness is given. However, a witness who has heard the testimony of another witness shall not for that reason alone be disqualified from testifying. When a witness testifies after hearing the testimony of others, this fact shall be noted in the record and considered by the Trial Chamber when evaluating the evidence.

Rule 141
Closure of evidence and closing statements

1. The Presiding Judge shall declare when the submission of evidence is closed.
2. The Presiding Judge shall invite the Prosecutor and the defence to make their closing statements. The defence shall always have the opportunity to speak last.

Rule 142
Deliberations

1. After the closing statements, the Trial Chamber shall retire to deliberate, in camera. The Trial Chamber shall inform all those who participated in the proceedings of the date on which the Trial Chamber will pronounce its decision. The pronouncement shall be made within a reasonable period of time after the Trial Chamber has retired to deliberate.
2. When there is more than one charge, the Trial Chamber shall decide separately on each charge. When there is more than one accused, the Trial Chamber shall decide separately on the charges against each accused.

Rule 143
Additional hearings on matters related to sentence or reparations

Pursuant to article 76, paragraphs 2 and 3, for the purpose of holding a further hearing on matters related to sentence and, if applicable, reparations, the Presiding Judge shall set the date of the further hearing. This hearing can be postponed, in exceptional circumstances, by the Trial Chamber, on its own motion or at the request of the Prosecutor, the defence or the legal representatives of the victims participating in the proceedings pursuant to rules 89 to 91 and, in respect of reparations hearings, those victims who have made a request under rule 94.

Rule 144
Delivery of the decisions of the Trial Chamber

1. Decisions of the Trial Chamber concerning admissibility of a case, the jurisdiction of the Court, criminal responsibility of the accused, sentence and reparations shall be pronounced in public and, wherever possible, in the presence of the accused, the Prosecutor, the victims or the legal representatives of the victims participating in the proceedings pursuant to rules 89 to 91, and the representatives of the States which have participated in the proceedings.
2. Copies of all the above-mentioned decisions shall be provided as soon as possible to:
   (a) All those who participated in the proceedings, in a working language of the Court;
   (b) The accused, in a language he or she fully understands or speaks, if necessary to meet the requirements of fairness under article 67, paragraph 1 (f).

Chapter 7
Penalties

Rule 145
Determination of sentence

1. In its determination of the sentence pursuant to article 78, paragraph 1, the Court shall:
   (a) Bear in mind that the totality of any sentence of imprisonment and fine, as the case may be, imposed under article 77 must reflect the culpability of the convicted person;
   (b) Balance all the relevant factors, including any mitigating and aggravating factors and consider the circumstances both of the convicted person and of the crime;
   (c) In addition to the factors mentioned in article 78, paragraph 1, give consideration, *inter alia*, to the extent of the damage caused, in particular the harm caused to the victims and their families, the nature of the unlawful behaviour and the means employed to execute the crime; the degree of participation of the convicted person; the degree of intent; the circumstances of manner, time and location; and the age, education, social and economic condition of the convicted person.
2. In addition to the factors mentioned above, the Court shall take into account, as appropriate:
   (a) Mitigating circumstances such as:
      (i) The circumstances falling short of constituting grounds for exclusion of criminal responsibility, such as substantially diminished mental capacity or duress;
      (ii) The convicted person's conduct after the act, including any efforts by the person to compensate the victims and any cooperation with the Court;
   (b) As aggravating circumstances:
      (i) Any relevant prior criminal convictions for crimes under the jurisdiction of the Court or of a similar nature;
      (ii) Abuse of power or official capacity;
      (iii) Commission of the crime where the victim is particularly defenceless;
      (iv) Commission of the crime with particular cruelty or where there were multiple victims;
      (v) Commission of the crime for any motive involving discrimination on any of the grounds referred to in article 21, paragraph 3;
      (vi) Other circumstances which, although not enumerated above, by virtue of their nature are similar to those mentioned.
3. Life imprisonment may be imposed when justified by the extreme gravity of the crime and the individual circumstances of the convicted person, as evidenced by the existence of one or more aggravating circumstances.

Rule 146
Imposition of fines under article 77

1. In determining whether to order a fine under article 77, paragraph 2 (a), and in fixing the amount of the fine, the Court shall determine whether imprisonment is a sufficient penalty. The Court shall give due consideration to the financial capacity of the convicted person, including any orders for forfeiture in accordance with article 77, paragraph 2 (b), and, as appropriate, any orders for reparation in accordance with article 75. The Court shall take into account, in addition to the factors referred to in rule 145, whether and to what degree the crime was motivated by personal financial gain.
2. A fine imposed under article 77, paragraph 2 (a), shall be set at an appropriate level. To this end, the Court shall, in addition to the factors referred to above, in particular take into consideration the damage and injuries caused as well as the proportionate gains derived from the crime by the perpetrator. Under no circumstances may the total amount exceed 75 per cent of the value of the convicted person's identifiable assets, liquid or realizable, and property, after deduction of an appropriate amount that would satisfy the financial needs of the convicted person and his or her dependants.
3. In imposing a fine, the Court shall allow the convicted person a reasonable period in which to pay the fine. The Court may provide for payment of a lump sum or by way of instalments during that period.
4. In imposing a fine, the Court may, as an option, calculate it according to a system of daily fines. In such cases, the minimum duration shall be 30 days and the maximum duration five years. The Court shall decide the total amount in accordance with sub-rules 1 and 2. It shall determine the amount of daily payment in the light of the individual circumstances of the convicted person, including the financial needs of his or her dependants.
5. If the convicted person does not pay the fine imposed in accordance with the conditions set above, appropriate measures may be taken by the Court pursuant to rules 217 to 222 and in accordance with article 109. Where, in cases of continued wilful non-payment, the Presidency, on its own motion or at the request of the Prosecutor, is satisfied that all available enforcement measures have been exhausted, it may as a last resort extend the term of imprisonment for a period not to exceed a quarter of such term or five years, whichever is less. In the determination of such period of extension, the Presidency shall take into account the amount of the fine, imposed and paid. Any such extension shall not apply in the case of life imprisonment. The extension may not lead to a total period of imprisonment in excess of 30 years.
6. In order to determine whether to order an extension and the period involved, the Presidency shall sit in camera for the purpose of obtaining the views of the sentenced person and the Prosecutor. The sentenced person shall have the right to be assisted by counsel.
7. In imposing a fine, the Court shall warn the convicted person that failure to pay the fine in accordance with the conditions set out above may result in an extension of the period of imprisonment as described in this rule.

Rule 147
Orders of forfeiture

1. In accordance with article 76, paragraphs 2 and 3, and rules 63, sub-rule 1, and 143, at any hearing to consider an order of forfeiture, Chamber shall hear evidence as to the identification and location of specific proceeds, property or assets which have been derived directly or indirectly from the crime.
2. If before or during the hearing, a Chamber becomes aware of any bona fide third party who appears to have an interest in relevant proceeds, property or assets, it shall give notice to that third party.

3. The Prosecutor, the convicted person and any bona fide third party with an interest in the relevant proceeds, property or assets may submit evidence relevant to the issue.
4. After considering any evidence submitted, a Chamber may issue an order of forfeiture in relation to specific proceeds, property or assets if it is satisfied that these have been derived directly or indirectly from the crime.

Rule 148
Orders to transfer fines or forfeitures to the Trust Fund

Before making an order pursuant to article 79, paragraph 2, a Chamber may request the representatives of the Fund to submit written or oral observations to it.

Chapter 8
Appeal and revision

Section I
General provisions

Rule 149
Rules governing proceedings in the Appeals Chamber

Parts 5 and 6 and rules governing proceedings and the submission of evidence in the Pre-Trial and Trial Chambers shall apply *mutatis mutandis* to proceedings in the Appeals Chamber.

Section II
Appeals against convictions, acquittals, sentences and reparation orders

Rule 150
Appeal

1. Subject to sub-rule 2, an appeal against a decision of conviction or acquittal under article 74, a sentence under article 76 or a reparation order under article 75 may be filed not later than 30 days from the date on which the party filing the appeal is notified of the decision, the sentence or the reparation order.
2. The Appeals Chamber may extend the time limit set out in sub-rule 1, for good cause, upon the application of the party seeking to file the appeal.
3. The appeal shall be filed with the Registrar.
4. If an appeal is not filed as set out in sub-rules 1 to 3, the decision, the sentence or the reparation order of the Trial Chamber shall become final.

Rule 151
Procedure for the appeal

1. Upon the filing of an appeal under rule 150, the Registrar shall transmit the trial record to the Appeals Chamber.
2. The Registrar shall notify all parties who participated in the proceedings before the Trial Chamber that an appeal has been filed.

Rule 152
Discontinuance of the appeal

1. Any party who has filed an appeal may discontinue the appeal at any time before judgement has been delivered. In such case, the party shall file with the Registrar a written notice

of discontinuance of appeal. The Registrar shall inform the other parties that such a notice has been filed.
2. If the Prosecutor has filed an appeal on behalf of a convicted person in accordance with article 81, paragraph 1 (b), before filing any notice of discontinuance, the Prosecutor shall inform the convicted person that he or she intends to discontinue the appeal in order to give him or her the opportunity to continue the appeal proceedings.

Rule 153
Judgement on appeals against reparation orders

1. The Appeals Chamber may confirm, reverse or amend a reparation order made under article 75.
2. The judgement of the Appeals Chamber shall be delivered in accordance with article 83, paragraphs 4 and 5.

Section III
Appeals against other decisions

Rule 154
Appeals that do not require the leave of the Court

1. An appeal may be filed under article 81, paragraph 3 (c) (ii), or article 82, paragraph 1 (a) or (b), not later than five days from the date upon which the party filing the appeal is notified of the decision.
2. An appeal may be filed under article 82, paragraph 1 (c), not later than two days from the date upon which the party filing the appeal is notified of the decision.
3. Rule 150, sub-rules 3 and 4, shall apply to appeals filed under sub-rules 1 and 2 of this rule.

Rule 155
Appeals that require leave of the Court

1. When a party wishes to appeal a decision under article 82, paragraph 1 (d), or article 82, paragraph 2, that party shall, within five days of being notified of that decision, make a written application to the Chamber that gave the decision, setting out the reasons for the request for leave to appeal.
2. The Chamber shall render a decision and shall notify all parties who participated in the proceedings that gave rise to the decision referred to in sub-rule 1.

Rule 156
Procedure for the appeal

1. As soon as an appeal has been filed under rule 154 or as soon as leave to appeal has been granted under rule 155, the Registrar shall transmit to the Appeals Chamber the record of the proceedings of the Chamber that made the decision that is the subject of the appeal.
2. The Registrar shall give notice of the appeal to all parties who participated in the proceedings before the Chamber that gave the decision that is the subject of the appeal, unless they have already been notified by the Chamber under rule 155, sub-rule 2.
3. The appeal proceedings shall be in writing unless the Appeals Chamber decides to convene a hearing.
4. The appeal shall be heard as expeditiously as possible.
5. When filing the appeal, the party appealing may request that the appeal have suspensive effect in accordance with article 82, paragraph 3.

Rule 157
Discontinuance of the appeal

Any party who has filed an appeal under rule 154 or who has obtained the leave of a Chamber to appeal a decision under rule 155 may discontinue the appeal at any time before judgement has been delivered. In such case, the party shall file with the Registrar a written notice of discontinuance of appeal. The Registrar shall inform the other parties that such a notice has been filed.

Rule 158
Judgement on the appeal

1. An Appeals Chamber which considers an appeal referred to in this section may confirm, reverse or amend the decision appealed.
2. The judgement of the Appeals Chamber shall be delivered in accordance with article 83, paragraph 4.

Section IV
Revision of conviction or sentence

Rule 159
Application for revision

1. An application for revision provided for in article 84, paragraph 1, shall be in writing and shall set out the grounds on which the revision is sought. It shall as far as possible be accompanied by supporting material.
2. The determination on whether the application is meritorious shall be taken by a majority of the judges of the Appeals Chamber and shall be supported by reasons in writing.
3. Notification of the decision shall be sent to the applicant and, as far as possible, to all the parties who participated in the proceedings related to the initial decision.

Rule 160
Transfer for the purpose of revision

1. For the conduct of the hearing provided for in rule 161, the relevant Chamber shall issue its order sufficiently in advance to enable the transfer of the sentenced person to the seat of the Court, as appropriate.
2. The determination of the Court shall be communicated without delay to the State of enforcement.
3. The provisions of rule 206, sub-rule 3, shall be applicable.

Rule 161
Determination on revision

1. On a date which it shall determine and shall communicate to the applicant and to all those having received notification under rule 159, sub-rule 3, the relevant Chamber shall hold a hearing to determine whether the conviction or sentence should be revised.
2. For the conduct of the hearing, the relevant Chamber shall exercise, *mutatis mutandis*, all the powers of the Trial Chamber pursuant to Part 6 and the rules governing proceedings and the submission of evidence in the Pre-Trial and Trial Chambers.
3. The determination on revision shall be governed by the applicable provisions of article 83, paragraph 4.

Chapter 9
Offences and misconduct against the Court

Section I
Offences against the administration of justice under article 70

Rule 162
Exercise of jurisdiction

1. Before deciding whether to exercise jurisdiction, the Court may consult with States Parties that may have jurisdiction over the offence.
2. In making a decision whether or not to exercise jurisdiction, the Court may consider, in particular:
   (a) The availability and effectiveness of prosecution in a State Party;
   (b) The seriousness of an offence;
   (c) The possible joinder of charges under article 70 with charges under articles 5 to 8;
   (d) The need to expedite proceedings;
   (e) Links with an ongoing investigation or a trial before the Court; and
   (f) Evidentiary considerations.
3. The Court shall give favourable consideration to a request from the host State for a waiver of the power of the Court to exercise jurisdiction in cases where the host State considers such a waiver to be of particular importance.
4. If the Court decides not to exercise its jurisdiction, it may request a State Party to exercise jurisdiction pursuant to article 70, paragraph 4.

Rule 163
Application of the Statute and the Rules

1. Unless otherwise provided in sub-rules 2 and 3, rule 162 and rules 164 to 169, the Statute and the Rules shall apply *mutatis mutandis* to the Court's investigation, prosecution and punishment of offences defined in article 70.
2. The provisions of Part 2, and any rules thereunder, shall not apply, with the exception of article 21.
3. The provisions of Part 10, and any rules thereunder, shall not apply, with the exception of articles 103, 107, 109 and 111.

Rule 164
Periods of limitation

1. If the Court exercises jurisdiction in accordance with rule 162, it shall apply the periods of limitation set forth in this rule.
2. Offences defined in article 70 shall be subject to a period of limitation of five years from the date on which the offence was committed, provided that during this period no investigation or prosecution has been initiated. The period of limitation shall be interrupted if an investigation or prosecution has been initiated during this period, either before the Court or by a State Party with jurisdiction over the case pursuant to article 70, paragraph 4 (a).
3. Enforcement of sanctions imposed with respect to offences defined in article 70 shall be subject to a period of limitation of 10 years from the date on which the sanction has become final. The period of limitation shall be interrupted with the detention of the convicted person or while the person concerned is outside the territory of the States Parties.

Rule 165
Investigation, prosecution and trial

1. The Prosecutor may initiate and conduct investigations with respect to the offences defined in article 70 on his or her own initiative, on the basis of information communicated by a Chamber or any reliable source.
2. Articles 53 and 59, and any rules thereunder, shall not apply.
3. For purposes of article 61, the Pre-Trial Chamber may make any of the determinations set forth in that article on the basis of written submissions, without a hearing, unless the interests of justice otherwise require.
4. A Trial Chamber may, as appropriate and taking into account the rights of the defence, direct that there be joinder of charges under article 70 with charges under articles 5 to 8.

Rule 166
Sanctions under article 70

1. If the Court imposes sanctions with respect to article 70, this rule shall apply.
2. Article 77, and any rules thereunder, shall not apply, with the exception of an order of forfeiture under article 77, paragraph 2 (b), which may be ordered in addition to imprisonment or a fine or both.
3. Each offence may be separately fined and those fines may be cumulative. Under no circumstances may the total amount exceed 50 per cent of the value of the convicted person's identifiable assets, liquid or realizable, and property, after deduction of an appropriate amount that would satisfy the financial needs of the convicted person and his or her dependants.
4. In imposing a fine the Court shall allow the convicted person a reasonable period in which to pay the fine. The Court may provide for payment of a lump sum or by way of instalments during that period.
5. If the convicted person does not pay a fine imposed in accordance with the conditions set forth in sub-rule 4, appropriate measures may be taken by the Court pursuant to rules 217 to 222 and in accordance with article 109. Where, in cases of continued wilful non-payment, the Court, on its own motion or at the request of the Prosecutor, is satisfied that all available enforcement measures have been exhausted, it may as a last resort impose a term of imprisonment in accordance with article 70, paragraph 3. In the determination of such term of imprisonment, the Court shall take into account the amount of fine paid.

Rule 167
International cooperation and judicial assistance

1. With regard to offences under article 70, the Court may request a State to provide any form of international cooperation or judicial assistance corresponding to those forms set forth in Part 9. In any such request, the Court shall indicate that the basis for the request is an investigation or prosecution of offences under article 70.
2. The conditions for providing international cooperation or judicial assistance to the Court with respect to offences under article 70 shall be those set forth in article 70, paragraph 2.

Rule 168
Ne bis in idem

In respect of offences under article 70, no person shall be tried before the Court with respect to conduct which formed the basis of an offence for which the person has already been convicted or acquitted by the Court or another court.

Rule 169
Immediate arrest

In the case of an alleged offence under article 70 committed in the presence of a Chamber, the Prosecutor may orally request that Chamber to order the immediate arrest of the person concerned.

Section II
Misconduct before the Court under article 71

Rule 170
Disruption of proceedings

Having regard to article 63, paragraph 2, the Presiding Judge of the Chamber dealing with the matter may, after giving a warning:
- (a) Order a person disrupting the proceedings of the Court to leave or be removed from the courtroom; or,
- (b) In case of repeated misconduct, order the interdiction of that person from attending the proceedings.

Rule 171
Refusal to comply with a direction by the Court

1. When the misconduct consists of deliberate refusal to comply with an oral or written direction by the Court, not covered by rule 170, and that direction is accompanied by a warning of sanctions in case of breach, the Presiding Judge of the Chamber dealing with the matter may order the interdiction of that person from the proceedings for a period not exceeding 30 days or, if the misconduct is of a more serious nature, impose a fine.
2. If the person committing misconduct as described in sub-rule 1 is an official of the Court, or a defence counsel, or a legal representative of victims, the Presiding Judge of the Chamber dealing with the matter may also order the interdiction of that person from exercising his or her functions before the Court for a period not exceeding 30 days.
3. If the Presiding Judge in cases under sub-rules 1 and 2 considers that a longer period of interdiction is appropriate, the Presiding Judge shall refer the matter to the Presidency, which may hold a hearing to determine whether to order a longer or permanent period of interdiction.
4. A fine imposed under sub-rule 1 shall not exceed 2,000 euros, or the equivalent amount in any currency, provided that in cases of continuing misconduct, a new fine may be imposed on each day that the misconduct continues, and such fines shall be cumulative.
5. The person concerned shall be given an opportunity to be heard before a sanction for misconduct, as described in this rule, is imposed.

Rule 172
Conduct covered by both articles 70 and 71

If conduct covered by article 71 also constitutes one of the offences defined in article 70, the Court shall proceed in accordance with article 70 and rules 162 to 169.

Chapter 10
Compensation to an arrested or convicted person

Rule 173
Request for compensation

1. Anyone seeking compensation on any of the grounds indicated in article 85 shall submit a request, in writing, to the Presidency, which shall designate a Chamber composed of three judges to consider the request. These judges shall not have participated in any earlier judgement of the Court regarding the person making the request.
2. The request for compensation shall be submitted not later than six months from the date the person making the request was notified of the decision of the Court concerning:
   (a) The unlawfulness of the arrest or detention under article 85, paragraph 1;
   (b) The reversal of the conviction under article 85, paragraph 2;
   (c) The existence of a grave and manifest miscarriage of justice under article 85, paragraph 3.
3. The request shall contain the grounds and the amount of compensation requested.
4. The person requesting compensation shall be entitled to legal assistance.

Rule 174
Procedure for seeking compensation

1. A request for compensation and any other written observation by the person filing the request shall be transmitted to the Prosecutor, who shall have an opportunity to respond in writing. Any observations by the Prosecutor shall be notified to the person filing the request.
2. The Chamber designated under rule 173, sub-rule 1, may either hold a hearing or determine the matter on the basis of the request and any written observations by the Prosecutor and the person filing the request. A hearing shall be held if the Prosecutor or the person seeking compensation so requests.
3. The decision shall be taken by the majority of the judges. The decision shall be notified to the Prosecutor and to the person filing the request.

Rule 175
Amount of compensation

In establishing the amount of any compensation in conformity with article 85, paragraph 3, the Chamber designated under rule 173, sub-rule 1, shall take into consideration the consequences of the grave and manifest miscarriage of justice on the personal, family, social and professional situation of the person filing the request.

Chapter 11
International cooperation and judicial assistance

Section I
Requests for cooperation under article 87

Rule 176
Organs of the Court responsible for the transmission and receipt of any communications relating to international cooperation and judicial assistance

1. Upon and subsequent to the establishment of the Court, the Registrar shall obtain from the Secretary-General of the United Nations any communication made by States pursuant to article 87, paragraphs 1 (a) and 2.

2. The Registrar shall transmit the requests for cooperation made by the Chambers and shall receive the responses, information and documents from requested States. The Office of the Prosecutor shall transmit the requests for cooperation made by the Prosecutor and shall receive the responses, information and documents from requested States.
3. The Registrar shall be the recipient of any communication from States concerning subsequent changes in the designation of the national channels charged with receiving requests for cooperation, as well as of any change in the language in which requests for cooperation should be made, and shall, upon request, make such information available to States Parties as may be appropriate.
4. The provisions of sub-rule 2 are applicable *mutatis mutandis* where the Court requests information, documents or other forms of cooperation and assistance from an intergovernmental organization.
5. The Registrar shall transmit any communications referred to in sub-rules 1 and 3 and rule 177, sub-rule 2, as appropriate, to the Presidency or the Office of the Prosecutor, or both.

Rule 177
Channels of communication

1. Communications concerning the national authority charged with receiving requests for cooperation made upon ratification, acceptance, approval or accession shall provide all relevant information about such authorities.
2. When an intergovernmental organization is asked to assist the Court under article 87, paragraph 6, the Registrar shall, when necessary, ascertain its designated channel of communication and obtain all relevant information relating thereto.

Rule 178
Language chosen by States Parties under article 87, paragraph 2

1. When a requested State Party has more than one official language, it may indicate upon ratification, acceptance, approval or accession that requests for cooperation and any supporting documents can be drafted in any one of its official languages.
2. When the requested State Party has not chosen a language for communication with the Court upon ratification, acceptance, accession or approval, the request for cooperation shall either be in or be accompanied by a translation into one of the working languages of the Court pursuant to article 87, paragraph 2.

Rule 179
Language of requests directed to States not party to the Statute

When a State not party to the Statute has agreed to provide assistance to the Court under article 87, paragraph 5, and has not made a choice of language for such requests, the requests for cooperation shall either be in or be accompanied by a translation into one of the working languages of the Court.

Rule 180
Changes in the channels of communication or the languages of requests for cooperation

1. Changes concerning the channel of communication or the language a State has chosen under article 87, paragraph 2, shall be communicated in writing to the Registrar at the earliest opportunity.
2. Such changes shall take effect in respect of requests for cooperation made by the Court at a time agreed between the Court and the State or, in the absence of such an agreement, 45 days after the Court has received the communication and, in all cases, without prejudice to current requests or requests in progress.

Section II
Surrender, transit and competing requests under articles 89 and 90

Rule 181
Challenge to admissibility of a case before a national court

When a situation described in article 89, paragraph 2, arises, and without prejudice to the provisions of article 19 and of rules 58 to 62 on procedures applicable to challenges to the jurisdiction of the Court or the admissibility of a case, the Chamber dealing with the case, if the admissibility ruling is still pending, shall take steps to obtain from the requested State all the relevant information about the *ne bis in idem* challenge brought by the person.

Rule 182
Request for transit under article 89, paragraph 3 (e)

1. In situations described in article 89, paragraph 3 (e), the Court may transmit the request for transit by any medium capable of delivering a written record.
2. When the time limit provided for in article 89, paragraph 3 (e), has expired and the person concerned has been released, such a release is without prejudice to a subsequent arrest of the person in accordance with the provisions of article 89 or article 92.

Rule 183
Possible temporary surrender

Following the consultations referred to in article 89, paragraph 4, the requested State may temporarily surrender the person sought in accordance with conditions determined between the requested State and the Court. In such case the person shall be kept in custody during his or her presence before the Court and shall be transferred to the requested State once his or her presence before the Court is no longer required, at the latest when the proceedings have been completed.

Rule 184
Arrangements for surrender

1. The requested State shall immediately inform the Registrar when the person sought by the Court is available for surrender.
2. The person shall be surrendered to the Court by the date and in the manner agreed upon between the authorities of the requested State and the Registrar.
3. If circumstances prevent the surrender of the person by the date agreed, the authorities of the requested State and the Registrar shall agree upon a new date and manner by which the person shall be surrendered.
4. The Registrar shall maintain contact with the authorities of the host State in relation to the arrangements for the surrender of the person to the Court.

Rule 185
Release of a person from the custody of the Court other than upon completion of sentence

1. Subject to sub-rule 2, where a person surrendered to the Court is released from the custody of the Court because the Court does not have jurisdiction, the case is inadmissible under article 17, paragraph 1 (b), (c) or (d), the charges have not been confirmed under article 61, the person has been acquitted at trial or on appeal, or for any other reason, the Court shall, as soon as possible, make such arrangements as it considers appropriate for the transfer of the person, taking into account the views of the person, to a State which is obliged to receive him or her, to another State which agrees to receive him or her, or to a State which

has requested his or her extradition with the consent of the original surrendering State. In this case, the host State shall facilitate the transfer in accordance with the agreement referred to in article 3, paragraph 2, and the related arrangements.

2. Where the Court has determined that the case is inadmissible under article 17, paragraph 1 (a), the Court shall make arrangements, as appropriate, for the transfer of the person to a State whose investigation or prosecution has formed the basis of the successful challenge to admissibility, unless the State that originally surrendered the person requests his or her return.

Rule 186
Competing requests in the context of a challenge to the admissibility of the case

In situations described in article 90, paragraph 8, the requested State shall provide the notification of its decision to the Prosecutor in order to enable him or her to act in accordance with article 19, paragraph 10.

Section III
Documents for arrest and surrender under articles 91 and 92

Rule 187
Translation of documents accompanying request for surrender

For the purposes of article 67, paragraph 1 (a), and in accordance with rule 117, sub-rule 1, the request under article 91 shall be accompanied, as appropriate, by a translation of the warrant of arrest or of the judgement of conviction and by a translation of the text of any relevant provisions of the Statute, in a language that the person fully understands and speaks.

Rule 188
Time limit for submission of documents after provisional arrest

For the purposes of article 92, paragraph 3, the time limit for receipt by the requested State of the request for surrender and the documents supporting the request shall be 60 days from the date of the provisional arrest.

Rule 189
Transmission of documents supporting the request

When a person has consented to surrender in accordance with the provisions of article 92, paragraph 3, and the requested State proceeds to surrender the person to the Court, the Court shall not be required to provide the documents described in article 91 unless the requested State indicates otherwise.

Section IV
Cooperation under article 93

Rule 190
Instruction on self-incrimination accompanying request for witness

When making a request under article 93, paragraph 1 (e), with respect to a witness, the Court shall annex an instruction, concerning rule 74 relating to self-incrimination, to be provided to the witness in question, in a language that the person fully understands and speaks.

Rule 191
Assurance provided by the Court under article 93, paragraph 2

The Chamber dealing with the case, on its own motion or at the request of the Prosecutor, defence or witness or expert concerned, may decide, after taking into account the views of the Prosecutor and the witness or expert concerned, to provide the assurance described in article 93, paragraph 2.

Rule 192
Transfer of a person in custody

1. Transfer of a person in custody to the Court in accordance with article 93, paragraph 7, shall be arranged by the national authorities concerned in liaison with the Registrar and the authorities of the host State.
2. The Registrar shall ensure the proper conduct of the transfer, including the supervision of the person while in the custody of the Court.
3. The person in custody before the Court shall have the right to raise matters concerning the conditions of his or her detention with the relevant Chamber.
4. In accordance with article 93, paragraph 7 (b), when the purposes of the transfer have been fulfilled, the Registrar shall arrange for the return of the person in custody to the requested State.

Rule 193
Temporary transfer of the person from the State of enforcement

1. The Chamber that is considering the case may order the temporary transfer from the State of enforcement to the seat of the Court of any person sentenced by the Court whose testimony or other assistance is necessary to the Court. The provisions of article 93, paragraph 7, shall not apply.
2. The Registrar shall ensure the proper conduct of the transfer, in liaison with the authorities of the State of enforcement and the authorities of the host State. When the purposes of the transfer have been fulfilled, the Court shall return the sentenced person to the State of enforcement.
3. The person shall be kept in custody during his or her presence before the Court. The entire period of detention spent at the seat of the Court shall be deducted from the sentence remaining to be served.

Rule 194
Cooperation requested from the Court

1. In accordance with article 93, paragraph 10, and consistent with article 96, mutatis mutandis, a State may transmit to the Court a request for cooperation or assistance to the Court, either in or accompanied by a translation into one of the working languages of the Court.
2. Requests described in sub-rule 1 are to be sent to the Registrar, which shall transmit them, as appropriate, either to the Prosecutor or to the Chamber concerned.
3. If protective measures within the meaning of article 68 have been adopted, the Prosecutor or Chamber, as appropriate, shall consider the views of the Chamber which ordered the measures as well as those of the relevant victim or witness, before deciding on the request.
4. If the request relates to documents or evidence as described in article 93, paragraph 10 (b) (ii), the Prosecutor or Chamber, as appropriate, shall obtain the written consent of the relevant State before proceeding with the request.
5. When the Court decides to grant the request for cooperation or assistance from a State, the request shall be executed, insofar as possible, following any procedure outlined therein by the requesting State and permitting persons specified in the request to be present.

Section V
Cooperation under article 98

Rule 195
Provision of information

1. When a requested State notifies the Court that a request for surrender or assistance raises a problem of execution in respect of article 98, the requested State shall provide any information relevant to assist the Court in the application of article 98. Any concerned third State or sending State may provide additional information to assist the Court.
2. The Court may not proceed with a request for the surrender of a person without the consent of a sending State if, under article 98, paragraph 2, such a request would be inconsistent with obligations under an international agreement pursuant to which the consent of a sending State is required prior to the surrender of a person of that State to the Court.

Section VI
Rule of speciality under article 101

Rule 196
Provision of views on article 101, paragraph 1

A person surrendered to the Court may provide views on a perceived violation of the provisions of article 101, paragraph 1.

Rule 197

Extension of the surrender

When the Court has requested a waiver of the requirements of article 101, paragraph 1, the requested State may ask the Court to obtain and provide the views of the person surrendered to the Court.

Chapter 12
Enforcement

Section I
Role of States in enforcement of sentences of imprisonment and change in designation of State of enforcement under articles 103 and 104

Rule 198
Communications between the Court and States

Unless the context otherwise requires, article 87 and rules 176 to 180 shall apply, as appropriate, to communications between the Court and a State on matters relating to enforcement of sentences.

Rule 199
Organ responsible under Part 10

Unless provided otherwise in the Rules, the functions of the Court under Part 10 shall be exercised by the Presidency.

Rule 200
List of States of enforcement

1. A list of States that have indicated their willingness to accept sentenced persons shall be established and maintained by the Registrar.
2. The Presidency shall not include a State on the list provided for in article 103, paragraph 1 (a), if it does not agree with the conditions that such a State attaches to its acceptance. The Presidency may request any additional information from that State prior to taking a decision.
3. A State that has attached conditions of acceptance may at any time withdraw such conditions. Any amendments or additions to such conditions shall be subject to confirmation by the Presidency.
4. A State may at any time inform the Registrar of its withdrawal from the list. Such withdrawal shall not affect the enforcement of the sentences in respect of persons that the State has already accepted.
5. The Court may enter bilateral arrangements with States with a view to establishing a framework for the acceptance of prisoners sentenced by the Court. Such arrangements shall be consistent with the Statute.

Rule 201
Principles of equitable distribution

Principles of equitable distribution for purposes of article 103, paragraph 3, shall include:
   (a) The principle of equitable geographical distribution;
   (b) The need to afford each State on the list an opportunity to receive sentenced persons;
   (c) The number of sentenced persons already received by that State and other States of enforcement;
   (d) Any other relevant factors.

Rule 202
Timing of delivery of the sentenced person to the State of enforcement

The delivery of a sentenced person from the Court to the designated State of enforcement shall not take place unless the decision on the conviction and the decision on the sentence have become final.

Rule 203
Views of the sentenced person

1. The Presidency shall give notice in writing to the sentenced person that it is addressing the designation of a State of enforcement. The sentenced person shall, within such time limit as the Presidency shall prescribe, submit in writing his or her views on the question to the Presidency.
2. The Presidency may allow the sentenced person to make oral presentations.
3. The Presidency shall allow the sentenced person:
   (a) To be assisted, as appropriate, by a competent interpreter and to benefit from any translation necessary for the presentation of his or her views;
   (b) To be granted adequate time and facilities necessary to prepare for the presentation of his or her views.

Rule 204
Information relating to designation

When the Presidency notifies the designated State of its decision, it shall also transmit the following information and documents:
   (a) The name, nationality, date and place of birth of the sentenced person;
   (b) A copy of the final judgement of conviction and of the sentence imposed;
   (c) The length and commencement date of the sentence and the time remaining to be served;
   (d) After having heard the views of the sentenced person, any necessary information concerning the state of his or her health, including any medical treatment that he or she is receiving.

Rule 205
Rejection of designation in a particular case

Where a State in a particular case rejects the designation by the Presidency, the Presidency may designate another State.

Rule 206
Delivery of the sentenced person to the State of enforcement

1. The Registrar shall inform the Prosecutor and the sentenced person of the State designated to enforce the sentence.
2. The sentenced person shall be delivered to the State of enforcement as soon as possible after the designated State of enforcement accepts.
3. The Registrar shall ensure the proper conduct of the delivery of the person in consultation with the authorities of the State of enforcement and the host State.

Rule 207
Transit

1. No authorization is required if the sentenced person is transported by air and no landing is scheduled on the territory of the transit State. If an unscheduled landing occurs on the territory of the transit State, that State shall, to the extent possible under the procedure of national law, detain the sentenced person in custody until a request for transit as provided in sub-rule 2 or a request under article 89, paragraph 1, or article 92 is received.
2. To the extent possible under the procedure of national law, a State Party shall authorize the transit of a sentenced person through its territory and the provisions of article 89, paragraph 3 (b) and (c), and articles 105 and 108 and any rules relating thereto shall, as appropriate, apply. A copy of the final judgement of conviction and of the sentence imposed shall be attached to such request for transit.

Rule 208
Costs

1. The ordinary costs for the enforcement of the sentence in the territory of the State of enforcement shall be borne by that State.
2. Other costs, including those for the transport of the sentenced person and those referred to in article 100, paragraph 1 (c), (d) and (e), shall be borne by the Court.

Rule 209
Change in designation of State of enforcement

1. The Presidency, acting on its own motion or at the request of the sentenced person or the Prosecutor, may at any time act in accordance with article 104, paragraph 1.
2. The request of the sentenced person or of the Prosecutor shall be made in writing and shall set out the grounds upon which the transfer is sought.

Rule 210
Procedure for change in the designation of a State of enforcement

1. Before deciding to change the designation of a State of enforcement, the Presidency may:
   (a) Request views from the State of enforcement;
   (b) Consider written or oral presentations of the sentenced person and the Prosecutor;
   (c) Consider written or oral expert opinion concerning, *inter alia*, the sentenced person;
   (d) Obtain any other relevant information from any reliable sources.
2. The provisions of rule 203, sub-rule 3, shall apply, as appropriate.
3. If the Presidency refuses to change the designation of the State of enforcement, it shall, as soon as possible, inform the sentenced person, the Prosecutor and the Registrar of its decision and of the reasons therefor. It shall also inform the State of enforcement.

Section II
Enforcement, supervision and transfer under articles 105, 106 and 107

Rule 211
Supervision of enforcement of sentences and conditions of imprisonment

1. In order to supervise the enforcement of sentences of imprisonment, the Presidency:
   (a) Shall, in consultation with the State of enforcement, ensure that in establishing appropriate arrangements for the exercise by any sentenced person of his or her right to communicate with the Court about the conditions of imprisonment, the provisions of article 106, paragraph 3, shall be respected;
   (b) May, when necessary, request any information, report or expert opinion from the State of enforcement or from any reliable sources;
   (c) May, where appropriate, delegate a judge of the Court or a member of the staff of the Court who will be responsible, after notifying the State of enforcement, for meeting the sentenced person and hearing his or her views, without the presence of national authorities;
   (d) May, where appropriate, give the State of enforcement an opportunity to comment on the views expressed by the sentenced person under sub-rule 1 (c).
2. When a sentenced person is eligible for a prison programme or benefit available under the domestic law of the State of enforcement which may entail some activity outside the prison facility, the State of enforcement shall communicate that fact to the Presidency, together with any relevant information or observation, to enable the Court to exercise its supervisory function.

Rule 212
Information on location of the person for enforcement of fines, forfeitures or reparation measures

For the purpose of enforcement of fines and forfeiture measures and of reparation measures ordered by the Court, the Presidency may, at any time or at least 30 days before the scheduled completion of the sentence served by the sentenced person, request the State of enforcement to transmit to it the relevant information concerning the intention of that State to authorize the person to remain in its territory or the location where it intends to transfer the person.

Rule 213
Procedure for article 107, paragraph 3

With respect to article 107, paragraph 3, the procedure set out in rules 214 and 215 shall apply, as appropriate.

Section III
Limitation on the prosecution or punishment of other offences under article 108

Rule 214
Request to prosecute or enforce a sentence for prior conduct

1. For the application of article 108, when the State of enforcement wishes to prosecute or enforce a sentence against the sentenced person for any conduct engaged in prior to that person's transfer, it shall notify its intention to the Presidency and transmit to it the following documents:
   (a) A statement of the facts of the case and their legal characterization;
   (b) A copy of any applicable legal provisions, including those concerning the statute of limitation and the applicable penalties;
   (c) A copy of any sentence, warrant of arrest or other document having the same force, or of any other legal writ which the State intends to enforce;
   (d) A protocol containing views of the sentenced person obtained after the person has been informed sufficiently about the proceedings.
2. In the event of a request for extradition made by another State, the State of enforcement shall transmit the entire request to the Presidency with a protocol containing the views of the sentenced person obtained after informing the person sufficiently about the extradition request.
3. The Presidency may in all cases request any document or additional information from the State of enforcement or the State requesting extradition.
4. If the person was surrendered to the Court by a State other than the State of enforcement or the State seeking extradition, the Presidency shall consult with the State that surrendered the person and take into account any views expressed by that State.
5. Any information or documents transmitted to the Presidency under sub-rules 1 to 4 shall be transmitted to the Prosecutor, who may comment.
6. The Presidency may decide to conduct a hearing.

Rule 215
Decision on request to prosecute or enforce a sentence

1. The Presidency shall make a determination as soon as possible. This determination shall be notified to all those who have participated in the proceedings.
2. If the request submitted under sub-rules 1 or 2 of rule 214 concerns the enforcement of a sentence, the sentenced person may serve that sentence in the State designated by the Court to enforce the sentence pronounced by it or be extradited to a third State only after having served the full sentence pronounced by the Court, subject to the provisions of article 110.
3. The Presidency may authorize the temporary extradition of the sentenced person to a third State for prosecution only if it has obtained assurances which it deems to be sufficient that the sentenced person will be kept in custody in the third State and transferred back to the State responsible for enforcement of the sentence pronounced by the Court, after the prosecution.

Rule 216
Information on enforcement

The Presidency shall request the State of enforcement to inform it of any important event concerning the sentenced person, and of any prosecution of that person for events subsequent to his or her transfer.

Section IV
Enforcement of fines, forfeiture measures and reparation orders

Rule 217
Cooperation and measures for enforcement of fines, forfeiture or reparation orders

For the enforcement of fines, forfeiture or reparation orders, the Presidency shall, as appropriate, seek cooperation and measures for enforcement in accordance with Part 9, as well as transmit copies of relevant orders to any State with which the sentenced person appears to have direct connection by reason of either nationality, domicile or habitual residence or by virtue of the location of the sentenced person's assets and property or with which the victim has such connection. The Presidency shall, as appropriate, inform the State of any third-party claims or of the fact that no claim was presented by a person who received notification of any proceedings conducted pursuant to article 75.

Rule 218
Orders for forfeiture and reparations

1. In order to enable States to give effect to an order for forfeiture, the order shall specify:
   (a) The identity of the person against whom the order has been issued;
   (b) The proceeds, property and assets that have been ordered by the Court to be forfeited; and
   (c) That if the State Party is unable to give effect to the order for forfeiture in relation to the specified proceeds, property or assets, it shall take measures to recover the value of the same.
2. In the request for cooperation and measures for enforcement, the Court shall also provide available information as to the location of the proceeds, property and assets that are covered by the order for forfeiture.
3. In order to enable States to give effect to an order for reparations, the order shall specify:
   (a) The identity of the person against whom the order has been issued;
   (b) In respect of reparations of a financial nature, the identity of the victims to whom individual reparations have been granted, and, where the award for reparations shall be deposited with the Trust Fund, the particulars of the Trust Fund for the deposit of the award; and
   (c) The scope and nature of the reparations ordered by the Court, including, where applicable, the property and assets for which restitution has been ordered.
4. Where the Court awards reparations on an individual basis, a copy of the reparation order shall be transmitted to the victim concerned.

Rule 219
Non-modification of orders for reparation

The Presidency shall, when transmitting copies of orders for reparations to States Parties under rule 217, inform them that, in giving effect to an order for reparations, the national authorities shall not modify the reparations specified by the Court, the scope or the extent of any damage, loss or injury determined by the Court or the principles stated in the order, and shall facilitate the enforcement of such order.

Rule 220
Non-modification of judgements in which fines were imposed

When transmitting copies of judgements in which fines were imposed to States Parties for the purpose of enforcement in accordance with article 109 and rule 217, the Presidency shall inform them that in enforcing the fines imposed, national authorities shall not modify them.

Rule 221
Decision on disposition or allocation of property or assets

1. The Presidency shall, after having consulted, as appropriate, with the Prosecutor, the sentenced person, the victims or their legal representatives, the national authorities of the State of enforcement or any relevant third party, or representatives of the Trust Fund provided for in article 79, decide on all matters related to the disposition or allocation of property or assets realized through enforcement of an order of the Court.
2. In all cases, when the Presidency decides on the disposition or allocation of property or assets belonging to the sentenced person, it shall give priority to the enforcement of measures concerning reparations to victims.

Rule 222
Assistance for service or any other measure

The Presidency shall assist the State in the enforcement of fines, forfeiture or reparation orders, as requested, with the service of any relevant notification on the sentenced person or any other relevant persons, or the carrying out of any other measures necessary for the enforcement of the order under the procedure of the national law of the enforcement State.

Section V
Review concerning reduction of sentence under article 110

Rule 223
Criteria for review concerning reduction of sentence

In reviewing the question of reduction of sentence pursuant to article 110, paragraphs 3 and 5, the three judges of the Appeals Chamber shall take into account the criteria listed in article 110, paragraph 4 (a) and (b), and the following criteria:
   (a) The conduct of the sentenced person while in detention, which shows a genuine dissociation from his or her crime;
   (b) The prospect of the resocialization and successful resettlement of the sentenced person;
   (c) Whether the early release of the sentenced person would give rise to significant social instability;
   (d) Any significant action taken by the sentenced person for the benefit of the victims as well as any impact on the victims and their families as a result of the early release;
   (e) Individual circumstances of the sentenced person, including a worsening state of physical or mental health or advanced age.

Rule 224
Procedure for review concerning reduction of sentence

1. For the application of article 110, paragraph 3, three judges of the Appeals Chamber appointed by that Chamber shall conduct a hearing, unless they decide otherwise in a particular case, for exceptional reasons. The hearing shall be conducted with the sentenced

person, who may be assisted by his or her counsel, with interpretation, as may be required. Those three judges shall invite the Prosecutor, the State of enforcement of any penalty under article 77 or any reparation order pursuant to article 75 and, to the extent possible, the victims or their legal representatives who participated in the proceedings, to participate in the hearing or to submit written observations. Under exceptional circumstances, this hearing may be conducted by way of a videoconference or in the State of enforcement by a judge delegated by the Appeals Chamber.

2. The same three judges shall communicate the decision and the reasons for it to all those who participated in the review proceedings as soon as possible.
3. For the application of article 110, paragraph 5, three judges of the Appeals Chamber appointed by that Chamber shall review the question of reduction of sentence every three years, unless it establishes a shorter interval in its decision taken pursuant to article 110, paragraph 3. In case of a significant change in circumstances, those three judges may permit the sentenced person to apply for a review within the three-year period or such shorter period as may have been set by the three judges.
4. For any review under article 110, paragraph 5, three judges of the Appeals Chamber appointed by that Chamber shall invite written representations from the sentenced person or his or her counsel, the Prosecutor, the State of enforcement of any penalty under article 77 and any reparation order pursuant to article 75 and, to the extent possible, the victims or their legal representatives who participated in the proceedings. The three judges may also decide to hold a hearing.
5. The decision and the reasons for it shall be communicated to all those who participated in the review proceedings as soon as possible.

Section VI
Escape

Rule 225
Measures under article 111 in the event of escape

1. If the sentenced person has escaped, the State of enforcement shall, as soon as possible, advise the Registrar by any medium capable of delivering a written record. The Presidency shall then proceed in accordance with Part 9.
2. However, if the State in which the sentenced person is located agrees to surrender him or her to the State of enforcement, pursuant to either international agreements or its national legislation, the State of enforcement shall so advise the Registrar in writing. The person shall be surrendered to the State of enforcement as soon as possible, if necessary in consultation with the Registrar, who shall provide all necessary assistance, including, if necessary, the presentation of requests for transit to the States concerned, in accordance with rule 207. The costs associated with the surrender of the sentenced person shall be borne by the Court if no State assumes responsibility for them.
3. If the sentenced person is surrendered to the Court pursuant to Part 9, the Court shall transfer him or her to the State of enforcement. Nevertheless, the Presidency may, acting on its own motion or at the request of the Prosecutor or of the initial State of enforcement and in accordance with article 103 and rules 203 to 206, designate another State, including the State to the territory of which the sentenced person has fled.
4. In all cases, the entire period of detention in the territory of the State in which the sentenced person was in custody after his or her escape and, where sub-rule 3 is applicable, the period of detention at the seat of the Court following the surrender of the sentenced person from the State in which he or she was located shall be deducted from the sentence remaining to be served.

ANNEX 4

ICTY DIRECTIVE ON THE ASSIGNMENT OF DEFENCE COUNSEL

(Directive No. 1/94)
(As amended 30 January 1995)
(AS AMENDED 25 JUNE 1996)
(as amended 1 August 1997)
(AS REVISED 17 NOVEMBER 1997)
(as amended 10 JULY 1998)
(AS AMENDED 19 JULY 1999)
(AS AMENDED 15 dECEMBER 2000)
(as amended 12 July 2002)
(IT/73/REV. 9)

I—PREAMBLE

The Registrar of the Tribunal,

Considering the Statute of the Tribunal as adopted by the Security Council under resolution 827 (1993) of 25 May 1993, as 00subsequently amended, and in particular Articles 18 and 21 thereof;

Considering the Rules of Procedure and Evidence as adopted by the Tribunal on 11 February 1994, as subsequently amended, and in particular Rules 42, 45 and 55 thereof;

Considering the host country agreement between the United Nations and the Kingdom of the Netherlands concerning the seat of the Tribunal signed at New York on 29 July 1994, and in particular Articles XIX and XX thereof;

Considering the Directive on the Assignment of Defence Counsel as adopted by the Tribunal on 28 July 1994, as subsequently amended, and as last amended on 15 December 2000;

ISSUES REVISION 9 OF THE DIRECTIVE ON THE ASSIGNMENT OF DEFENCE COUNSEL AS FOLLOWS:
II—GENERAL PROVISIONS

Article 1
Entry into force

This Directive establishes the conditions and arrangements for assignment of counsel and shall enter into force on the first day of August nineteen hundred and ninety four (1 August 1994).

Article 2
Definitions

Under this Directive, the following terms shall mean:

Accused: a person against whom one or more counts in an indictment have been confirmed in accordance with Rule 47 of the Rules of Procedure and Evidence;

Code of Conduct: the Code of Professional Conduct for Defence Counsel Appearing Before the International Tribunal as promulgated by the Registrar on 12 June 1997 as latest amended;

Counsel: a person eligible to be assigned pursuant to Rules 44, 45 and 45 *bis* of the Rules;

Directive: Directive No. 1/94 on the Assignment of Defence Counsel as latest amended;

President: the President of the Tribunal;

Prosecutor: the Prosecutor appointed pursuant to Article 16 of the Statute;

Registrar: the Registrar of the Tribunal;

Rules: the Rules of Procedure and Evidence adopted by the Tribunal on 11 February 1994, and as subsequently amended;

Stage of procedure: each of the stages of procedure laid down by the Rules in which the suspect or the accused may be involved (investigation, indictment, proceedings in the Trial Chamber, appeal, review).

Statute: the Statute of the Tribunal adopted by the Security Council under Resolution 827 (1993) of 25 May 1993, as subsequently amended;

Suspect: a person concerning whom the Prosecutor possesses reliable information which tends to show that the person may have committed a crime over which the Tribunal has jurisdiction;

Tribunal: the International Tribunal for the Prosecution of Persons Responsible for Serious Violations of International Humanitarian Law Committed in the Territory of the Former Yugoslavia since 1991

In this Directive, the masculine shall include the feminine and the singular the plural, and vice versa. All references in this Directive to suspects or accused shall also be understood to apply to any persons detained on the authority of the Tribunal.

Article 3
Authentic texts

The English and French texts of the Directive shall be equally authentic. In case of discrepancy, the version which is more consonant with the spirit of the Statute, Rules and the Directive shall prevail.

Article 4
Amendment of the Directive

A. Proposals for amendment of the Directive may be made by a Judge, the Registrar or the Advisory Panel. Amendments shall be promulgated by the Registrar in accordance with Rule 45 of the Rules.

B. Without prejudice to the rights of the accused in any pending case, an amendment of the Directive shall enter into force seven days after the day of issue of an official Tribunal document containing the amendment.

III—RIGHT TO HAVE COUNSEL ASSIGNED
Chapter 1: Basic principles

Article 5
Right to counsel

Without prejudice to the right of an accused to conduct his own defence:
i.   a suspect who is to be questioned by the Prosecutor during an investigation;
ii. an accused upon whom personal service of the indictment has been effected; and
iii. any person detained on the authority of the Tribunal, including any person detained in accordance with Rule 90 *bis*
iv. *shall have the right to be assisted by counsel.*

Article 6
Right to assigned counsel

A. Suspects or accused who lack the means to remunerate counsel shall be entitled to assignment of counsel paid for by the Tribunal.
B. A suspect or accused lacks the means to remunerate counsel if he does not dispose of means, which would allow him to remunerate counsel at the rates provided for by this Directive. For the purposes of Section III of this Directive, the remuneration of counsel also includes counsel's expenses.
C. For suspects or accused who dispose of means to partially remunerate counsel, the Tribunal shall pay that portion, which the suspect or accused does not have sufficient means to pay for.

Chapter 2: Procedure for assignment of counsel

Article 7
Request for assignment of counsel

A. Subject to the provisions of Article 17, a suspect or accused who wishes to be assigned counsel shall make a request to the Registrar of the Tribunal on the form provided by the Registry. A request shall be lodged with the Registry, or transmitted to it, by the suspect or accused himself or by a person authorised by him to do so on his behalf.
B. For the purposes of Article 8, a suspect or accused requesting the assignment of counsel is required to make a declaration of his means on the form provided by the Registry.
C. To ensure that the provisions of Article 8 are met, a suspect or accused must update his declaration of means at any time a change relevant to his declaration of means occurs.

Article 8
Determination of the means of suspects and accused

A. A suspect or accused who requests the assignment of counsel must produce evidence that he is unable to remunerate counsel.
B. In order to determine whether the suspect or accused is unable to remunerate counsel, there shall be taken into account means of all kinds of which he has direct or indirect enjoyment or freely disposes, including but not limited to direct income, bank accounts, real or personal property, pensions, and stocks, bonds, or other assets held, but excluding any family or social benefits to which he may be entitled. In assessing such means, account shall also be taken of the means of the spouse of a suspect or accused, as well as those of persons with whom he habitually resides.
C. Account may also be taken of the apparent lifestyle of a suspect or accused, and of his enjoyment of any property, movable or immovable, and whether or not he derives income from it.

Article 9
Certification of the declaration of means

A declaration must, so far as possible, be certified by an appropriate authority, either that of the place where the suspect or accused resides or is found or that of any other place considered appropriate in the circumstances which it shall be for the Registrar to assess.

Article 10
Information

A. For the purpose of establishing whether the suspect or accused satisfies the requisite conditions for assignment of counsel, the Registrar may inquire into his means, request the gathering of any information, hear the suspect or accused, consider any representation, or request the production of any documents likely to verify the request.
B. In executing this stipulation and even after counsel has been assigned, the Registrar shall be authorised to request any relevant information at any time from any person who appears to be able to supply relevant information.

Chapter 3: The decision

Article 11
Decision by the Registrar

A. After examining the declaration of means laid down in Article 7 (B) and (C) and relevant information obtained pursuant to Article 10, the Registrar shall determine how far the suspect or accused lacks means to remunerate counsel, and shall decide, providing reasons for his decision
   i. without prejudice to Article 18, to assign counsel and choose for this purpose a name from the list drawn up in accordance with Rule 45 (B) of the Rules and Article 14; or,
   ii. without prejudice to Article 18, that the suspect or accused disposes of means to partially remunerate counsel in which case the decision shall indicate which costs shall be borne by the Tribunal; or
   iii. not to grant the request for assignment of counsel.
B. To ensure that the right to counsel is not affected while the Registrar examines the declaration of means laid down in Article 7 (B) and (C) and the information obtained pursuant to Article 10 the Registrar may temporarily assign counsel to a suspect or an accused for a period not exceeding 120 days.
C. If a suspect or an accused, either
   i. requests an assignment of counsel but does not comply with the requirements set out above within a reasonable time; or
   ii. fails to obtain or to request assignment of counsel; or
   iii. fails to elect in writing that he intends to conduct his own defence;

the Registrar may nevertheless, in the interests of justice, assign him counsel from the list, and in accordance with Rule 45 (B) of the Rules, and without prejudice to Article 18.

Article 12
Notification of the decision

The Registrar shall notify the suspect or accused of his decision, and shall also notify the counsel so assigned and his professional or governing body of his decision.

Chapter 4: Remedy

Article 13
Remedy against the Registrar's decision

A. The suspect whose request for assignment of counsel has been denied may, within fifteen days of the date of notification to him, seek the President's review of the decision of the Registrar. The President may either confirm the Registrar's decision or decide that a counsel should be assigned.
B. The accused whose request for assignment of counsel has been denied, may, within two weeks of the date of notification to him, make a motion to the Chamber before which he is due to appear for immediate review of the Registrar's decision. The Chamber may
   i. confirm the Registrar's decision; or
   ii. rule that the suspect or accused has means to partially remunerate counsel, in which case it shall refer the matter again to the Registrar for determination of which parts shall be borne by the Tribunal; or
   iii. rule that a counsel should be assigned

IV—PREREQUISITES FOR ASSIGNMENT AS COUNSEL

Article 14
Qualifications and standing of counsel

A. Any person may be assigned as counsel if the Registrar is satisfied that he is admitted to the list of counsel envisaged in Rule 45 (B) of the Rules. A person is eligible for admission to the list if:
   i. he is admitted to the practice of law in a State, or is a university professor of law;
   ii. he has not been found guilty in relevant disciplinary proceedings against him where he is admitted to the practice of law or a university professor, and has not been found guilty in relevant criminal proceedings against him;
   iii. he speaks one of the two working languages of the Tribunal, except if the interests of justice do not require this;
   iv. he possesses reasonable experience in criminal and/or international law;
   v. he agrees to be assigned as counsel by the Tribunal to represent any indigent suspect or accused;
   vi. he is or is about to become a member of an association of counsel practising at the Tribunal.
B. The Registrar may remove the name of a counsel from the list upon:
   i. a decision by a Chamber to refuse audience to assigned counsel for misconduct under Rule 46 (A), in consultation with the Chamber; or
   ii. where counsel has been found to be in contempt pursuant to Rule 77 of the Rules, in consultation with the Chamber; or
   iii. where counsel has been found guilty of a disciplinary offense under the Code of Conduct, in accordance with the relevant provision of the Code, in consultation with the Chamber.

Counsel may seek recourse against the Registrar's decision before the President within two weeks of having been notified of that decision.

C. The Registrar must remove the name of counsel from the list referred to in Rule 45 (B) where counsel no-longer satisfies the requirements of Article 14 (A).
D. The Registrar may refuse a request for assignment of a counsel where a procedure pursuant to Rule 77 of the Rules, or, in accordance with Article 45 of the Code of Conduct, if a disciplinary procedure under Part Three of the Code of Professional Conduct has been initiated against that counsel. Counsel may seek recourse against the Registrar's decision before the President within two weeks of having been notified of that decision.

Article 15
Professional certification

In support of the pre-requisites provided for in Article 14 (A), the Registrar shall be supplied with a certificate of professional qualification issued by the competent professional or governing body and such other documentation the Registrar deems necessary.

V—SCOPE OF ASSIGNMENT

Article 16
Basic principles

A. A suspect or accused shall be entitled to have one counsel assigned to him and that counsel shall handle all stages of the procedure and all matters arising out of the conduct of the suspect's or accused's defence, including where two or more crimes are joined in one indictment.
B. Where persons accused of the same or different crimes are jointly charged or tried, each accused shall be entitled to request assignment of separate counsel.
C. In the interests of justice and at the request of the person assigned as counsel, the Registrar may, in accordance with Article 14 above, assign a second counsel to assist the lead counsel. The counsel first assigned shall be called the lead counsel.
D. Under the authority of lead counsel, who is responsible for the defence, co-counsel may deal with all stages of the procedure and all matters arising out of the representation of the accused or of the conduct of his defence. Lead counsel shall sign all documents submitted to the Tribunal unless he authorises co-counsel, in writing, to sign on his behalf.
E. No counsel shall be assigned to more than one suspect or accused at a time, unless an assignment to more than one suspect or accused would neither cause prejudice to the defence of either accused, nor a potential conflict of interest.

Article 17
Assignment of counsel away from the seat of the Tribunal

A. Away from the seat of the Tribunal, and in a case of urgency, a suspect who, during the investigation, requests assignment of counsel, may indicate the name of counsel if he knows one who may be assigned in accordance with the provisions of this Directive.
B. Where the suspect fails to indicate a name, the Prosecutor, or a person authorised by him or acting under his direction, may contact the local Bar Association and obtain the name of counsel who may be assigned in accordance with the provisions of this Directive.
C. In the situations envisaged in paragraphs (A) and (B), the procedure for assignment of counsel as set out in this Directive shall apply *mutatis mutandis* but shall be accelerated where necessary.

VI—SUSPENSION AND WITHDRAWAL OF ASSIGNMENT

Article 18
Ability of suspects or accused to remunerate counsel

A. Assignment of counsel or partial remuneration of counsel and/or payment of counsel's expenses may be withdrawn by the Registrar if:
  i. after his decision, the suspect or accused comes into means which, had they been available at the time the request in Article 7 was made, would have caused the Registrar not to grant the request;
  ii. information is obtained which establishes that the suspect or accused has sufficient means to allow him to pay for the cost of his defence.

B. The Registrar's decision shall be reasoned and notified to the suspect or accused and to the counsel assigned, and shall take effect from the date of receipt of the notification.
C. The provisions of Article 13 shall apply *mutatis mutandis* where a suspect or accused seeks a review of the Registrar's decision.

Article 19
Suspension and Withdrawal of counsel

A. In the interests of justice, the Registrar may:
   i. at the request of the accused, or his counsel, withdraw the assignment of counsel;
   ii. at the request of lead counsel withdraw the assignment of co-counsel.
B. The Registrar may suspend the assignment of counsel for a reasonable and limited time in consultation with the Chamber:
   i. if a disciplinary procedure under Part Three of the Code of Professional Conduct has been initiated against that counsel; or
   ii. if contempt proceedings have been initiated against that counsel.

The counsel may seek the President's review within two weeks from the notification of the decision to counsel.

C. The Registrar shall withdraw the assignment of counsel:
   i. upon the decision by a Chamber to refuse audience to assigned counsel for misconduct under Rule 46 (A);
   ii. where counsel no-longer satisfies the requirements of Article 14 (A); or
   iii. where counsel has been found to be in contempt pursuant to Rule 77 of the Rules.
D. In such cases the withdrawal or suspension shall be notified to the accused, to the counsel concerned and to his professional or governing body.
E. The Registrar shall immediately assign a new counsel to the suspect or accused.
F. Where a request for withdrawal, made pursuant to paragraph A, has been denied the person making the request may seek the President's review of the decision of the Registrar within two weeks from the notification of the decision to him.

Article 20
Replacement of counsel

A. Where the assignment of counsel is withdrawn by the Registrar or where the services of assigned counsel are discontinued, the counsel assigned may not withdraw from acting until either a replacement counsel has been provided by the Tribunal or by the suspect or accused, or the suspect or accused has declared his intention in writing to conduct his own defence.
B. In the interests of justice, the withdrawn counsel may continue to represent the suspect or the accused for a period of not exceeding 30 days after the date on which the replacement is assigned. During this period, the costs necessarily and reasonably incurred by both counsel shall be met by the Tribunal.

Article 21
Payment *pro rata temporis*

When, during engagement, an assigned counsel is replaced in the same capacity by another assigned counsel for whatever reason, the remuneration shall be paid to each of them *pro rata temporis*.

VII—COSTS OF REPRESENTATION

Article 22
Responsibility for remuneration and expenses

A. Where counsel has been assigned, the costs of legal representation of the suspect or accused necessarily and reasonably incurred shall be met by the Tribunal subject to the budgetary provisions, rules and regulations, and practice set by the United Nations. All costs are subject to prior authorization by the Registrar. If authorization was not obtained, the Registrar may refuse to meet costs. The Registrar establishes maximum allotments for each defence at the beginning of every stage of the procedure taking into account his estimate of the duration of the phase. In the event that a stage of the procedure is substantially longer or shorter than estimated, the Registrar may adapt the allotment. In the event of disagreement on the maximum allotment, the Registrar shall make a decision, after consulting the Chamber and, if necessary, the Advisory Panel.

B. Such costs to be met by the Tribunal shall include all remuneration due to counsel in accordance with Article 23. They shall also include expenses resulting from the assignment of legal and investigative assistance, expenses relating to the production of evidence for the defence, to the ascertainment of facts, expenses relating to temporary consultancy on specific questions, expert opinion paid at the rates established in Annex I, and accommodation and transportation of witnesses. They shall include travel expenses, travel taxes and similar duties. General office costs are included in the remuneration for counsel. This embraces in any case, but not exclusively costs for phone and mail or express mail, photocopies, books and journals, lease of office space, purchase of office equipment, office supplies and secretarial support.

C. The Registrar shall reimburse the sums claimed by assigned counsel for the remuneration and expenses as provided in paragraphs (A) and (B) above on receipt of a statement of expenses made out using the format provided by the Registry, which must be presented within 120 days from the last day of the month during which work was performed or an expense was incurred and be approved by the Registrar. Counsel may request monthly payment of equal parts of the maximum allotment established by the Registrar under paragraph (A) above. The statement shall in any case be submitted in an electronic version.

Article 23
Remuneration paid to assigned counsel

A. Without prejudice to Article 6 (C), the remuneration paid to assigned counsel for any one case and at any one stage of the procedure shall include:
   i. a fixed rate;
   ii. fees calculated on the basis of a fixed hourly rate applied at any stage of the procedure to the number of hours of work

The applicable rates shall be set by the Registrar and approved by the Judges.

B. Without prejudice to Article 6 (C), assigned counsel who receives remuneration from the Tribunal shall not accept remuneration for the assignment from any other source.

Article 24
Fixed rate

The fixed rate envisaged in Article 23 (A) (i) shall be equivalent to two thousand United States Dollars and cover the costs for the initial consultations with the suspect or accused, the initial appearance and plea before the Tribunal including its preparations as well as the indictment reading, refreshing of knowledge of rules and regulations and other general reading.

Article 25
Fees

The fixed hourly rate for fees envisaged in Article 23 (A) (ii) shall be assessed by the Registrar on the basis of the seniority and experience of counsel, according to Annex I. This rate includes general office costs.

Article 26
Travel expenses

A. Travel expenses shall be reimbursed for an assigned counsel who does not usually reside in the territory of the host country or in the country where the particular stage of the procedure is being conducted, on the basis of one economy class standard fixed-date round trip air ticket by the shortest route or within limits laid down by and subject to prior authorization of the Registrar, on presentation of a statement of travel expenses using the form provided by the Registry, accompanied by the original counterfoil of the ticket and the ticket stubs.
B. Travel expenses shall be reimbursed to assigned counsel residing in the territory of the host country but not in the town where he is serving, on the basis of either first class public transportation tickets or fixed rates as established by the United Nations Schedule of Rates of Reimbursement for Travel by Private Motor Vehicle applicable to different groups of Countries and Territories, per kilometre travelled on the outward and return journeys by the shortest route, on presentation of a statement of travel expenses using the form provided by the Registry.
C. Counsel shall submit all travel requests to the Registry at least one week before their scheduled travel, unless they can demonstrate that circumstances beyond their control prevent them from complying with this requirement. The Registry reserves the right to deduct cancellation fees, arising from changes in travel arrangement, from counsel's remuneration in cases where changes are not sufficiently related to his professional obligations as assigned counsel.

Article 27
Daily allowances

A. Counsel shall be entitled to a daily allowance calculated on the basis of fixed rates as established by the United Nations Schedule of Daily Subsistence Allowance Rates applied to the number of days of work. Counsel is not entitled to subsistence allowance while staying at his place of residence.
B. The rate for daily allowance shall be calculated on the basis of the current daily subsistence allowance rates applicable in the country where he is acting as an assigned counsel.
C. In accordance with the regulations in force at the United Nations, the applicable rate shall be lowered by twenty-five percent when counsel has spent more than 60 days in total from the date of his assignment in the country where he is acting as an assigned counsel.

Article 28
Family members and friends of suspects, accused and counsel

Members of the family or close friends of suspects, accused and counsel are not eligible for an assignment under the Directive as counsel, expert, legal assistant, investigator, translator or interpreter unless an assignment is in the interests of justice.

Article 29
Provisional payment

In exceptional circumstances and with the authorisation of the Registrar, a provisional payment of the daily allowance set out in Article 27 above or expenses of counsel may be made on presentation by counsel of a provisional statement using the forms provided by the Registry whether applicable covering the corresponding period or the expenses.

Article 30
Responsibility for payments

A. All sums payable to assigned counsel under the provisions of this Directive shall be paid by the Financial Officer of the Registry
B. The statement of remuneration and the statement of travel or other expenses, envisaged under Articles 23, 26, and 27, must receive the prior approval of the Registrar.

Article 31
Settlement of disputes

In the event of disagreement on questions relating to calculation and payment of remuneration or to reimbursement of expenses, the Registrar shall make a decision, after consulting the President and, if necessary, the Advisory Panel.

VIII—Advisory Panel

Article 32
Advisory panel

A. An Advisory Panel shall be set up consisting of two members chosen by the President by ballot from the list referred to in Article 14 and who have appeared before the Tribunal, two members proposed by the International Bar Association, two members proposed by the Union Internationale des Avocats, and the President of the Nederlandse Orde van Advokaten or his representative. Each member of the Advisory Panel must have a minimum of 10 years legal experience.
B. The President of the Advisory Panel will be the President of the Nederlandse Orde van Advokaten or his representative. The membership of the Advisory Panel shall come up for appointment every two years on the anniversary date of the entry into force of this Directive.
C. The Advisory Panel may be consulted as and when necessary by the Registrar or the President on matters relating to assignment of counsel.
D. The Advisory Panel may also of its own initiative refer to the Registrar, or to the Registrar and the President, any matter relating to the assignment of counsel.

ANNEX I:

Fixed gross hourly rate for Counsel in US $
(general office costs are included in this sum)
Lead Counsel / Counsel

20 years' professional experience or more 110 US$
15–19 years' professional experience 100 US$
10–14 years' professional experience 90 US$

0–9 years' professional experience 80 US$
Co-counsel
Fixed rate of 80 US$

>Fixed gross hourly rate for allotments to
>Legal Assistants and Investigators in Euros (€)
>(general office costs are included in this sum)

10 years' professional experience or more €25
5–9 years' professional experience €20
0–4 years' professional experience €15

ANNEX 5

STATUTE OF THE SPECIAL COURT FOR SIERRA LEONE

Having been established by an Agreement between the United Nations and the Government of Sierra Leone pursuant to Security Council resolution 1315 (2000) of 14 August 2000, the Special Court for Sierra Leone (hereinafter "the Special Court") shall function in accordance with the provisions of the present Statute.

Article 1: Competence of the Special Court

1. The Special Court shall, except as provided in subparagraph (2), have the power to prosecute persons who bear the greatest responsibility for serious violations of international humanitarian law and Sierra Leonean law committed in the territory of Sierra Leone since 30 November 1996, including those leaders who, in committing such crimes, have threatened the establishment of and implementation of the peace process in Sierra Leone.
2. Any transgressions by peacekeepers and related personnel present in Sierra Leone pursuant to the Status of Mission Agreement in force between the United Nations and the Government of Sierra Leone or agreements between Sierra Leone and other Governments or regional organizations, or, in the absence of such agreement, provided that the peacekeeping operations were undertaken with the consent of the Government of Sierra Leone, shall be within the primary jurisdiction of the sending State.
3. In the event the sending State is unwilling or unable genuinely to carry out an investigation or prosecution, the Court may, if authorized by the Security Council on the proposal of any State, exercise jurisdiction over such persons.

Article 2: Crimes against humanity

The Special Court shall have the power to prosecute persons who committed the following crimes as part of a widespread or systematic attack against any civilian population:
   a. Murder;
   b. Extermination;
   c. Enslavement;
   d. Deportation;
   e. Imprisonment;
   f. Torture;
   g. Rape, sexual slavery, enforced prostitution, forced pregnancy and any other form of sexual violence;
   h. Persecution on political, racial, ethnic or religious grounds;
   i. Other inhumane acts.

Article 3: Violations of Article 3 common to the Geneva Conventions and of Additional Protocol II

The Special Court shall have the power to prosecute persons who committed or ordered the commission of serious violations of article 3 common to the Geneva Conventions of 12 August 1949 for the Protection of War Victims, and of Additional Protocol II thereto of 8 June 1977. These violations shall include:

a. Violence to life, health and physical or mental well-being of persons, in particular murder as well as cruel treatment such as torture, mutilation or any form of corporal punishment;
b. Collective punishments;
c. Taking of hostages;
d. Acts of terrorism;
e. Outrages upon personal dignity, in particular humiliating and degrading treatment, rape, enforced prostitution and any form of indecent assault;
f. Pillage;
g. The passing of sentences and the carrying out of executions without previous judgement pronounced by a regularly constituted court, affording all the judicial guarantees which are recognized as indispensable by civilized peoples;
h. Threats to commit any of the foregoing acts.

Article 4: Other serious violations of international humanitarian law

The Special Court shall have the power to prosecute persons who committed the following serious violations of international humanitarian law:

a. Intentionally directing attacks against the civilian population as such or against individual civilians not taking direct part in hostilities;
b. Intentionally directing attacks against personnel, installations, material, units or vehicles involved in a humanitarian assistance or peacekeeping mission in accordance with the Charter of the United Nations, as long as they are entitled to the protection given to civilians or civilian objects under the international law of armed conflict;
c. Conscripting or enlisting children under the age of 15 years into armed forces or groups or using them to participate actively in hostilities.

Article 5: Crimes under Sierra Leonean law

The Special Court shall have the power to prosecute persons who have committed the following crimes under Sierra Leonean law:

a. Offences relating to the abuse of girls under the Prevention of Cruelty to Children Act, 1926 (Cap. 31):
   i. Abusing a girl under 13 years of age, contrary to section 6;
   ii. Abusing a girl between 13 and 14 years of age, contrary to section 7;
   iii. Abduction of a girl for immoral purposes, contrary to section 12.
b. Offences relating to the wanton destruction of property under the Malicious Damage Act, 1861:
   i. Setting fire to dwelling—houses, any person being therein, contrary to section 2;
   ii. Setting fire to public buildings, contrary to sections 5 and 6;
   iii. Setting fire to other buildings, contrary to section 6.

Article 6: Individual criminal responsibility

1. A person who planned, instigated, ordered, committed or otherwise aided and abetted in the planning, preparation or execution of a crime referred to in articles 2 to 4 of the present Statute shall be individually responsible for the crime.
2. The official position of any accused persons, whether as Head of State or Government or as a responsible government official, shall not relieve such person of criminal responsibility nor mitigate punishment.
3. The fact that any of the acts referred to in articles 2 to 4 of the present Statute was committed by a subordinate does not relieve his or her superior of criminal responsibility if he or she knew or had reason to know that the subordinate was about to commit such acts or had done so and the superior had failed to take the necessary and reasonable measures to prevent such acts or to punish the perpetrators thereof.
4. The fact that an accused person acted pursuant to an order of a Government or of a superior shall not relieve him or her of criminal responsibility, but may be considered in mitigation of punishment if the Special Court determines that justice so requires.
5. Individual criminal responsibility for the crimes referred to in article 5 shall be determined in accordance with the respective laws of Sierra Leone.

Article 7: Jurisdiction over persons of 15 years of age

1. The Special Court shall have no jurisdiction over any person who was under the age of 15 at the time of the alleged commission of the crime. Should any person who was at the time of the alleged commission of the crime between 15 and 18 years of age come before the Court, he or she shall be treated with dignity and a sense of worth, taking into account his or her young age and the desirability of promoting his or her rehabilitation, reintegration into and assumption of a constructive role in society, and in accordance with international human rights standards, in particular the rights of the child.
2. In the disposition of a case against a juvenile offender, the Special Court shall order any of the following: care guidance and supervision orders, community service orders, counselling, foster care, correctional, educational and vocational training programmes, approved schools and, as appropriate, any programmes of disarmament, demobilization and reintegration or programmes of child protection agencies.

Article 8: Concurrent jurisdiction

1. The Special Court and the national courts of Sierra Leone shall have concurrent jurisdiction.
2. The Special Court shall have primacy over the national courts of Sierra Leone. At any stage of the procedure, the Special Court may formally request a national court to defer to its competence in accordance with the present Statute and the Rules of Procedure and Evidence.

Article 9: Non bis in idem

1. No person shall be tried before a national court of Sierra Leone for acts for which he or she has already been tried by the Special Court.
2. A person who has been tried by a national court for the acts referred to in articles 2 to 4 of the present Statute may be subsequently tried by the Special Court if:
    a. The act for which he or she was tried was characterized as an ordinary crime; or
    b. The national court proceedings were not impartial or independent, were designed to shield the accused from international criminal responsibility or the case was not diligently prosecuted.

3. In considering the penalty to be imposed on a person convicted of a crime under the present Statute, the Special Court shall take into account the extent to which any penalty imposed by a national court on the same person for the same act has already been served.

Article 10: Amnesty

An amnesty granted to any person falling within the jurisdiction of the Special Court in respect of the crimes referred to in articles 2 to 4 of the present Statute shall not be a bar to prosecution.

Article 11: Organization of the Special Court

The Special Court shall consist of the following organs:

   a. The Chambers, comprising one or more Trial Chambers and an Appeals Chamber;
   b. The Prosecutor; and
   c. The Registry.

Article 12: Composition of the Chambers

1. The Chambers shall be composed of not less than eight (8) or more than eleven (11) independent judges, who shall serve as follows:
   a. Three judges shall serve in the Trial Chamber, of whom one shall be a judge appointed by the Government of Sierra Leone, and two judges appointed by the Secretary-General of the United Nations (hereinafter "the Secretary-General").
   b. Five judges shall serve in the Appeals Chamber, of whom two shall be judges appointed by the Government of Sierra Leone, and three judges appointed by the Secretary-General.
2. Each judge shall serve only in the Chamber to which he or she has been appointed.
3. The judges of the Appeals Chamber and the judges of the Trial Chamber, respectively, shall elect a presiding judge who shall conduct the proceedings in the Chamber to which he or she was elected. The presiding judge of the Appeals Chamber shall be the President of the Special Court.
4. If, at the request of the President of the Special Court, an alternate judge or judges have been appointed by the Government of Sierra Leone or the Secretary-General, the presiding judge of a Trial Chamber or the Appeals Chamber shall designate such an alternate judge to be present at each stage of the trial and to replace a judge if that judge is unable to continue sitting.

Article 13: Qualification and appointment of judges

1. The judges shall be persons of high moral character, impartiality and integrity who possess the qualifications required in their respective countries for appointment to the highest judicial offices. They shall be independent in the performance of their functions, and shall not accept or seek instructions from any Government or any other source.
2. In the overall composition of the Chambers, due account shall be taken of the experience of the judges in international law, including international humanitarian law and human rights law, criminal law and juvenile justice.
3. The judges shall be appointed for a three-year period and shall be eligible for reappointment.

Article 14: Rules of Procedure and Evidence

1. The Rules of Procedure and Evidence of the International Criminal Tribunal for Rwanda obtaining at the time of the establishment of the Special Court shall be applicable *mutatis mutandis* to the conduct of the legal proceedings before the Special Court.

2. The judges of the Special Court as a whole may amend the Rules of Procedure and Evidence or adopt additional rules where the applicable Rules do not, or do not adequately, provide for a specific situation. In so doing, they may be guided, as appropriate, by the Criminal Procedure Act, 1965, of Sierra Leone.

Article 15: The Prosecutor

1. The Prosecutor shall be responsible for the investigation and prosecution of persons who bear the greatest responsibility for serious violations of international humanitarian law and crimes under Sierra Leonean law committed in the territory of Sierra Leone since 30 November 1996. The Prosecutor shall act independently as a separate organ of the Special Court. He or she shall not seek or receive instructions from any Government or from any other source.
2. The Office of the Prosecutor shall have the power to question suspects, victims and witnesses, to collect evidence and to conduct on-site investigations. In carrying out these tasks, the Prosecutor shall, as appropriate, be assisted by the Sierra Leonean authorities concerned.
3. The Prosecutor shall be appointed by the Secretary-General for a three-year term and shall be eligible for re-appointment. He or she shall be of high moral character and possess the highest level of professional competence, and have extensive experience in the conduct of investigations and prosecutions of criminal cases.
4. The Prosecutor shall be assisted by a Sierra Leonean Deputy Prosecutor, and by such other Sierra Leonean and international staff as may be required to perform the functions assigned to him or her effectively and efficiently. Given the nature of the crimes committed and the particular sensitivities of girls, young women and children victims of rape, sexual assault, abduction and slavery of all kinds, due consideration should be given in the appointment of staff to the employment of prosecutors and investigators experienced in gender-related crimes and juvenile justice.
5. In the prosecution of juvenile offenders, the Prosecutor shall ensure that the child-rehabilitation programme is not placed at risk and that, where appropriate, resort should be had to alternative truth and reconciliation mechanisms, to the extent of their availability.

Article 16: The Registry

1. The Registry shall be responsible for the administration and servicing of the Special Court.
2. The Registry shall consist of a Registrar and such other staff as may be required.
3. The Registrar shall be appointed by the Secretary-General after consultation with the President of the Special Court and shall be a staff member of the United Nations. He or she shall serve for a three-year term and be eligible for re-appointment.
4. The Registrar shall set up a Victims and Witnesses Unit within the Registry. This Unit shall provide, in consultation with the Office of the Prosecutor, protective measures and security arrangements, counselling and other appropriate assistance for witnesses, victims who appear before the Court and others who are at risk on account of testimony given by such witnesses. The Unit personnel shall include experts in trauma, including trauma related to crimes of sexual violence and violence against children.

Article 17: Rights of the accused

1. All accused shall be equal before the Special Court.
2. The accused shall be entitled to a fair and public hearing, subject to measures ordered by the Special Court for the protection of victims and witnesses.
3. The accused shall be presumed innocent until proved guilty according to the provisions of the present Statute.

4. In the determination of any charge against the accused pursuant to the present Statute, he or she shall be entitled to the following minimum guarantees, in full equality:
   a. To be informed promptly and in detail in a language which he or she understands of the nature and cause of the charge against him or her;
   b. To have adequate time and facilities for the preparation of his or her defence and to communicate with counsel of his or her own choosing;
   c. To be tried without undue delay;
   d. To be tried in his or her presence, and to defend himself or herself in person or through legal assistance of his or her own choosing; to be informed, if he or she does not have legal assistance, of this right; and to have legal assistance assigned to him or her, in any case where the interests of justice so require, and without payment by him or her in any such case if he or she does not have sufficient means to pay for it;
   e. To examine, or have examined, the witnesses against him or her and to obtain the attendance and examination of witnesses on his or her behalf under the same conditions as witnesses against him or her;
   f. To have the free assistance of an interpreter if he or she cannot understand or speak the language used in the Special Court;
   g. Not to be compelled to testify against himself or herself or to confess guilt.

Article 18: Judgement

The judgement shall be rendered by a majority of the judges of the Trial Chamber or of the Appeals Chamber, and shall be delivered in public. It shall be accompanied by a reasoned opinion in writing, to which separate or dissenting opinions may be appended.

Article 19: Penalties

1. The Trial Chamber shall impose upon a convicted person, other than a juvenile offender, imprisonment for a specified number of years. In determining the terms of imprisonment, the Trial Chamber shall, as appropriate, have recourse to the practice regarding prison sentences in the International Criminal Tribunal for Rwanda and the national courts of Sierra Leone.
2. In imposing the sentences, the Trial Chamber should take into account such factors as the gravity of the offence and the individual circumstances of the convicted person.
3. In addition to imprisonment, the Trial Chamber may order the forfeiture of the property, proceeds and any assets acquired unlawfully or by criminal conduct, and their return to their rightful owner or to the State of Sierra Leone.

Article 20: Appellate proceedings

1. The Appeals Chamber shall hear appeals from persons convicted by the Trial Chamber or from the Prosecutor on the following grounds:
   a. A procedural error;
   b. An error on a question of law invalidating the decision;
   c. An error of fact which has occasioned a miscarriage of justice.
2. The Appeals Chamber may affirm, reverse or revise the decisions taken by the Trial Chamber.
3. The judges of the Appeals Chamber of the Special Court shall be guided by the decisions of the Appeals Chamber of the International Tribunals for the former Yugoslavia and for Rwanda. In the interpretation and application of the laws of Sierra Leone, they shall be guided by the decisions of the Supreme Court of Sierra Leone.

Article 21: Review proceedings

1. Where a new fact has been discovered which was not known at the time of the proceedings before the Trial Chamber or the Appeals Chamber and which could have been a decisive factor in reaching the decision, the convicted person or the Prosecutor may submit an application for review of the judgement.
2. An application for review shall be submitted to the Appeals Chamber. The Appeals Chamber may reject the application if it considers it to be unfounded. If it determines that the application is meritorious, it may, as appropriate:
   a. Reconvene the Trial Chamber;
   b. Retain jurisdiction over the matter.

Article 22: Enforcement of sentences

1. Imprisonment shall be served in Sierra Leone. If circumstances so require, imprisonment may also be served in any of the States which have concluded with the International Criminal Tribunal for Rwanda or the International Criminal Tribunal for the former Yugoslavia an agreement for the enforcement of sentences, and which have indicated to the Registrar of the Special Court their willingness to accept convicted persons. The Special Court may conclude similar agreements for the enforcement of sentences with other States.
2. Conditions of imprisonment, whether in Sierra Leone or in a third State, shall be governed by the law of the State of enforcement subject to the supervision of the Special Court. The State of enforcement shall be bound by the duration of the sentence, subject to article 23 of the present Statute.

Article 23: Pardon or commutation of sentences

If, pursuant to the applicable law of the State in which the convicted person is imprisoned, he or she is eligible for pardon or commutation of sentence, the State concerned shall notify the Special Court accordingly. There shall only be pardon or commutation of sentence if the President of the Special Court, in consultation with the judges, so decides on the basis of the interests of justice and the general principles of law.

Article 24: Working language

The working language of the Special Court shall be English.

Article 25: Annual Report

The President of the Special Court shall submit an annual report on the operation and activities of the Court to the Secretary-General and to the Government of Sierra Leone.

ANNEX 6

RULES OF PROCEDURE AND EVIDENCE OF THE SPECIAL COURT FOR SIERRA LEONE

(Revision 7, as corrected, 12 May 2003)

PART I—GENERAL PROVISIONS

Rule 1: Entry into Force

These Rules of Procedure and Evidence as first amended on 7 March 2003, are applicable pursuant to Article 14 of the Statute of the Special Court for Sierra Leone, and entered into force on 12 April 2002.

Rule 2: Definitions

(A) In the Rules, unless the context otherwise requires, the following terms shall mean:
- *Accused:* A person against whom one or more counts in an indictment have been approved in accordance with Rule 47;
- *Agreement:* The Agreement between the United Nations and the Government of Sierra Leone on the Establishment of a Special Court for Sierra Leone signed in Freetown on 16 January 2002;
- *Arrest:* The act of apprehending and taking a suspect or an accused into custody;
  Defence Office: The Office established by the Registrar for the purpose of ensuring the rights of suspects and accused in accordance with the Statute and the Rules of Procedure and Evidence;
- *The Deputy Prosecutor:* The Deputy Prosecutor appointed pursuant to Article 3 of the Agreement;
- *Detention Facility:* Detention Facilities of the Special Court shall include all such premises as designated by the Registrar with the approval of the Host State, for the purposes of detaining suspects and accused persons in accordance with these Rules and with the Rules of Detention;
- *Investigation:* All activities undertaken by the Prosecutor under the Statute and the Rules for the collection of information and evidence, whether before or after approval of an indictment;
- *Management Committee:* the Committee established pursuant to Article 7 of the Agreement;
- *Party:* The Prosecutor or the accused;
- *Principal Defender:* The Principal Defender as appointed by the Registrar;
- *President:* The President of the Special Court as referred to in Article 12 of the Statute;
- *Prosecutor:* The Prosecutor appointed pursuant to Article 3 of the Agreement;
- *Regulations:* The provisions framed by the Prosecutor pursuant to Rule 37 (A) for the purpose of directing the functions of the Office of the Prosecutor;

Rules: The Rules of Procedure and Evidence referred to in Rule 1;
- *Rules of Detention:* The Rules Governing the Detention of Persons Awaiting Trial or Appeal or otherwise detained by the Special Court;
- *Special Court:* The Special Court for Sierra Leone established by the Agreement between the United Nations and the Government of Sierra Leone of 16 January 2002 and consisting of the following organs: the Chambers, the Prosecutor and the Registry;
- *Statute:* The Statute of the Special Court annexed to the Agreement;
- *Suspect:* A person concerning whom the Prosecutor possesses reliable information which tends to show that he may have committed a crime over which the Special Court has jurisdiction in accordance with Article 1 of the Statute;
- *Transaction:* A number of acts or omissions whether occurring as one event or a number of events, at the same or different locations and being part of a common scheme, strategy or plan;
- *Victim:* A person against whom a crime over which the Special Court has jurisdiction has allegedly or has been found to have been committed.

(B) In the Rules, the masculine shall include the feminine and the singular the plural, and vice-versa.

Rule 3: Working Language

(A) The working language of the Special Court shall be English.
(B) The accused or suspect shall have the right to use his own language.
(C) Any person appearing before or giving evidence to the Special Court, who does not have sufficient knowledge of English, may ask for permission to use his own language.
(D) The Registrar shall make any necessary arrangements for interpretation and translation.

Rule 4: Sittings away from the Seat of the Special Court

A Chamber or a Judge may exercise their functions away from the Seat of the Special Court, if so authorized by the President. In so doing, audio or video-link technology, email or other available electronic instruments may be used if authorized by the President or Presiding Judge.

Rule 5: Non-compliance with the Rules

Where an objection on the ground of non-compliance with the Rules or Regulations is raised by a party at the earliest opportunity, the Trial Chamber may grant relief.

Rule 6: Amendment of the Rules

(A) Proposals for amendment of the Rules may be made by a Judge, the Prosecutor, the Registrar or the Defence Office, and by the Sierra Leone Bar Association or any other entity invited by the President to make proposals for amendments.
(B) Proposals for amendment may be adopted at a Plenary Meeting of the Special Court.
(C) An amendment of the Rules may be adopted otherwise than as stipulated in Sub-Rule (B) above, provided it is approved unanimously by any appropriate means either done in writing or confirmed in writing.
(D) An amendment shall, unless otherwise indicated, enter into force immediately. The Registrar shall publish the amendment by appropriate means.

Rule 7: Time limits

(A) Unless otherwise ordered by the Chambers or otherwise provided by the Rules, where the time prescribed by or under the Rules for the doing of any act shall run as from the occurrence of an event, that time shall run from the date on which notice of the occurrence of the event has been received in the normal course of transmission by counsel for the accused or the Prosecutor as the case may be.

(B) Where a time limit is expressed in days, only ordinary calendar days shall be counted. Weekdays, Saturdays, Sundays and public holidays shall be counted as days. However, should the time limit expire on a Saturday, Sunday or public holiday, the time limit shall automatically be extended to the subsequent working day.

(C) Unless otherwise ordered by a Chamber, any response to a motion shall be filed within seven days. Any reply to the response shall be filed within three days.

PART II—COOPERATION FROM STATES AND JUDICIAL ASSISTANCE

Rule 8: Requests and Orders

(A) The Government of Sierra Leone shall cooperate with all organs of the Special Court at all stages of the proceedings. Requests by any organ of the Special Court shall be complied with in accordance with Article 17 of the Agreement. An order issued by a Judge or Chamber shall have the same force or effect as if issued by a Judge, Magistrate or Justice of the Peace of a Sierra Leone court.

(B) Except in cases to which Rule 11, 13, 59 or 60 applies, where a Trial Chamber or a Judge is satisfied that the Government of Sierra Leone has failed to comply with a request made in relation to any proceedings before that Chamber or Judge, the Chamber or Judge may refer the matter to the President to take appropriate action.

(C) The Court may invite third States not party to the Agreement to provide assistance on the basis of an ad hoc arrangement, an agreement with such State or any other appropriate basis.

(D) Where a third State, which has entered into an ad hoc arrangement or an agreement with the Court, fails to cooperate with requests pursuant to any such arrangement or agreement, the President may take appropriate action.

(E) Where it appears to the Prosecutor that a crime within the jurisdiction of the Special Court is or has been the subject of investigations or criminal proceedings instituted in the courts of any State, he may request the State to forward to him all relevant information in that respect. The Government of Sierra Leone shall transmit to him such information forthwith in accordance with Article 17 of the Agreement.

Rule 9: Application for Deferral

Where it appears that crimes which are the subject of investigations or proceedings instituted in the courts of a State:
    (i) Are the subject of an investigation by the Prosecutor;
    (ii) Should be the subject of an investigation by the Prosecutor considering, amongst others:
        (a) The seriousness of the offences;
        (b) The status of the accused at the time of the alleged offences;
        (c) The general importance of the legal questions involved in the case; or
    (iii) Are the subject of an indictment in the Special Court, or
    (iv) Fall within Rule 72(B).
The Prosecutor may apply for an order or request for deferral under Rule 10.

Rule 10: Order for Deferral

(A) Where the Trial Chamber, seized of an application under Rule 9, determines that Sub-Rules (i), (ii) or (iii) of Rule 9 is satisfied, the Trial Chamber shall issue an order or request assistance to the effect that the court defer to the competence of the Special Court.

(B) An order or request for deferral shall include a request that the results of the investigation and a copy of the court's records and the judgement, if already delivered, be forwarded to the Registrar.

Rule 11: Non-compliance with an Order for Deferral

If, within 21 days after an order for deferral has been notified by the Registrar to the Government of Sierra Leone under whose jurisdiction the investigations or proceedings have been instituted, the Government of Sierra Leone fails to file a response which satisfies the Trial Chamber that it has taken or is taking adequate steps to comply with the order, the Trial Chamber may refer the matter to the President to take appropriate action.

Rule 12: Determinations of Courts of any State

Subject to Article 9 (2) of the Statute, determinations of courts of any State are not binding on the Special Court.

Rule 13: Double Jeopardy

When the President receives reliable information to show that criminal proceedings have been instituted against a person before a court of any State for acts for which that person has already been tried by the Special Court, he shall issue a reasoned order or request to such court seeking permanent discontinuance of its proceedings. If that court fails to do so, the President may take appropriate action.

PART III—ORGANIZATION OF THE SPECIAL COURT

Section 1: The Judges

Rule 14: Solemn Declaration

(A) Before taking up his duties each Judge shall make the following solemn declaration: "I solemnly declare that I will without fear or favour, affection or ill-will, serve as a Judge of the Special Court , honestly, faithfully, impartially and conscientiously."
(B) The text of the declaration, signed by the Judge and witnessed by the Secretary-General of the United Nations or his representative, and the President of Sierra Leone or his representative, shall be kept in the records of the Special Court.
(C) The members of the Special Court shall continue to discharge their duties until their places have been filled. Though replaced, they shall finish any cases which they may have begun.

Rule 15: Disqualification of Judges

(A) A Judge may not sit at a trial or appeal in any case in which he has a personal interest or concerning which he has or has had any personal association which might affect his impartiality. Where the Judge withdraws from the Trial Chamber, the President may assign the alternate judge, in accordance with Article 12(4) of the Statute, or another Trial Chamber Judge to sit in his place. Where a Judge withdraws from the Appeals Chamber, the Presiding Judge of that Chamber may assign another Judge to sit in his place.
(B) Any party may apply to the President for the disqualification of a Judge upon the above grounds. After the President has conferred with the Judge in question, and subject to Rule 23, he shall determine the matter. The President may assign another Judge to sit in place of the disqualified Judge, as necessary.
(C) Whenever the absence of a judge causes the membership of the Trial Chamber to fall below two judges, the President may assign another judge to sit in place of a missing judge.

(D) The Judge who approves an indictment or who is involved with any pre-trial or interlocutory matter against a suspect or accused, shall not for that reason be disqualified from sitting as a member of a Chamber for the trial or appeal of that suspect or accused.

Rule 16: Absence and Resignation

(A) If a Judge is unable to continue sitting in a part-heard case for a short duration and the remaining Judges are satisfied that it is in the interests of justice to do so, those remaining Judges may order that the hearing of the case continue in the absence of that Judge for a period of not more than five working days.
(B) If a Judge is, for any reason, unable to continue sitting in a part-heard case for a period which is or is likely to be longer than five days, the President may designate an alternate Judge as provided in Article 12(4) of the Statute.
   (i) If the case is in its advanced stages, and an alternate Judge was not available as provided in Article 12(4) of the Statute, and the remaining Judges are satisfied that it would not affect the verdict either way, the remaining Judges may continue in the absence of that Judge.
   (ii) Where a Trial or Appeal Chamber proceeds in the absence of one judge, in the event that the decision is split evenly a new trial or appeal may be ordered.
(C) A Judge who decides to resign shall give notice of his resignation in writing to the President, who shall transmit it to the Secretary-General of the United Nations and the Government of Sierra Leone.

Rule 17: Precedence

(A) All Judges are equal in the exercise of their judicial functions, regardless of dates of election, appointment, age or period of service.
(B) Judges elected or appointed on different dates shall take precedence according to the dates of their election or appointment; Judges elected or appointed on the same date shall take precedence according to age.
(C) In case of re-election, the total period of service as a Judge of the Special Court shall be taken into account.

Section 2: The Presidency

Rule 18: Election of the President

(A) The Presiding Judge of the Appeals Chamber shall be the President of the Special Court.
(B) The President shall be elected for a term of three years, or such shorter term as shall coincide with the duration of his term of office as a Judge. The President may be re-elected once.
(C) If the President ceases to be a member of the Special Court or resigns his office before the expiration of his term, the Judges of the Appeals Chamber shall elect from among their number a successor for the remainder of the term.
(D) The President shall be elected by a majority of the votes of the Judges appointed to the Appeals Chamber.

Rule 19: Functions of the President

(A) The President shall preside at all plenary meetings of the Special Court, co-ordinate the work of the Chambers and supervise the activities of the Registry as well as exercise all the other functions conferred on him by the Agreement, the Statute and the Rules.
(B) The President may after appropriate consultation issue Practice Directions, consistent with the Agreement, the Statute and the Rules, addressing detailed aspects of the conduct of proceedings before the Special Court.

Rule 20: The Vice-Presidency

The Vice-Presidency shall rotate in order of precedence amongst the other members of the Appeals Chamber commencing on 7 March 2003.

Rule 21: Functions of the Vice-President

The Vice-President shall exercise the functions of the President in case the latter is absent or is unable to act.

Rule 22: Replacements

If neither the President nor the Vice-President can carry out the functions of the Presidency, this shall be assumed by a senior Judge, determined in accordance with Rule 17.

Section 3: Internal Functioning of the Special Court

Rule 23: Consultations

The President, the Vice-President and the Presiding Judge of the Trial Chamber shall consult on major matters of concern relating to the functioning of the Tribunal where necessary and practicable.

Rule 24: Plenary Meetings of the Special Court

The Judges may meet in plenary to:
:(i) Adopt and amend the Rules;
(ii) Adopt the Annual Report provided for in Article 25 of the Statute;
(iii) Decide upon matters relating to the internal functioning of the Chambers and the Special Court;
(iv) Exercise any other functions provided for in the Agreement, the Statute or in the Rules.

Rule 25: Dates of Plenary Meetings

Plenary Meetings shall be convened by the President if so requested by at least five Judges, and may be convened whenever the exercise of his functions under the Agreement, the Statute or the Rules so requires.

Rule 26: Quorum and Vote

(A) The quorum for each Plenary Meeting of the Special Court shall be five Judges, including at least one judge from the Trial Chamber.
(B) Subject to Rule 6 (A) and (B) and Rule 18 (C), the decisions of the Plenary Meeting of the Special Court shall be taken by the majority of the Judges present. In the event of an equality of votes, the President or the Judge who acts in his place shall have a casting vote.

Section 4: The Chambers

Rule 27: Rotation of the Judges

(A) If a second Trial Chamber is created for the Special Court, Judges may rotate on a regular basis between the Trial Chambers. Rotation shall take into account the efficient disposal of cases.
(B) The Judges shall take their places in their assigned Chamber as soon as the President thinks it convenient, having regard to the disposal of pending cases.

(C) The President may at any time temporarily assign a member of one Trial Chamber to another Trial Chamber.

Rule 28: Designated Judges

(A) After consultation with the Judges concerned, the President or Presiding Judge of the Trial Chamber shall designate for a given period such Trial Judges as necessary to deal with pre-trial matters arising under:
- (i) Rule 40 (Provisional Measures) but excluding Rule 40(D)(i);
- (ii) Rule 40 *bis* (Transfer and Provisional Detention of Suspects);
- (iii) Rule 47 (Review of Indictment);
- (iv) Rule 50 (Amendment of Indictment), provided the circumstances described therein have been met;
- (v) Rule 51(A) (Withdrawal of Indictment), provided the circumstances described therein have been met; and
- (vi) Rule 53 (Non-Disclosure);
- (vii) Rule 54 (General Provision);
- (viii) Rule 61 (Initial Appearance of Accused and Plea);
- (ix) Rule 65 (Bail);
- (x) Rule 66 (Disclosure of Materials by the Prosecutor);
- (xi) Rule 74 *bis* (Medical Examination of the Accused);
- (xii) Rule 75(A) (Measures for the Protection of Victims or Witnesses);
- (xiii) Any other application of which a party has given notice and which appears to the President or presiding Judge of the Trial Chamber to be appropriately dealt with by a designated Judge.

(B) In the event that there is more than one Trial Chamber, the Presiding Judge of the Trial Chambers shall designate for given periods, in consultation with the Judges concerned, a Trial Judge to deal with pre-trial matters arising in a case not yet assigned to a Trial Chamber.

Rule 29: Deliberations

The deliberations of the Chambers shall take place in private and remain secret.

Section 5: The Registrar

Rule 30: Appointment of the Registrar

The Secretary-General of the United Nations, in consultation with the President of the Special Court, shall appoint a Registrar.

Rule 31: Appointment of the Deputy Registrar and Registry Staff

The Registrar shall appoint such other staff as may be required for the efficient functioning of the Registry, including a Deputy Registrar, if necessary.

Rule 32: Solemn Declaration

The Registrar shall make the following declaration before the President:

> "I solemnly declare that I will perform the duties incumbent upon me as Registrar of the Special Court in all loyalty, discretion and good conscience and that I will faithfully observe all the provisions of the Agreement, the Statute and the Rules of Procedure and Evidence of the Special Court."

Rule 33: Functions of the Registrar

(A) The Registrar shall assist the Chambers, the Plenary Meetings of the Special Court, the Judges and the Prosecutor, the Principal Defender and the Defence in the performance of their functions. Under the authority of the President, he shall be responsible for the administration and servicing of the Special Court and shall serve as its channel of communication.
(B) The Registrar, in the execution of his functions, may make oral or written representations to Chambers on any issue arising in the context of a specific case which affects or may affect the discharge of such functions, including that of implementing judicial decisions, with notice to the parties where necessary.
(C) The Registrar, mindful of the need to ensure respect for human rights and fundamental freedoms (particularly the presumption of innocence) shall in consultation with the President of the Special Court adopt and amend rules governing the detention of persons awaiting Trial or Appeal or otherwise detained by the Special Court and ensure conditions of detention.
(D) The Registrar may, in consultation with the President of the Special Court, issue Practice Directions addressing particular aspects of the practice and procedure in the Registry of the Special Court and in respect of other matters within the powers of the Registrar.

Rule 34: Victims and Witnesses Unit

(A) The Registrar shall set up a Victims and Witnesses Unit which, in accordance with the Statute, the Agreement and the Rules, and in consultation with the Office of the Prosecutor (for Prosecution witnesses) and the Defence Office or Defence Counsel (for Defence witnesses), shall, amongst other things, perform the following functions with respect to all witnesses, victims who appear before the Special Court, and others who are at risk on account of testimony given by such witnesses, in accordance with their particular needs and circumstances:
  (i) Recommend to the Court the adoption of protection and security measures for them;
  (ii) Provide them with adequate protective measures and security arrangements and develop long- and short-term plans for their protection and support;
  (iii) Ensure that they receive relevant support, counselling and other appropriate assistance, including medical assistance, physical and psychological rehabilitation, especially in cases of rape, sexual assault and crimes against children.
(B) The Unit personnel shall include experts in trauma, including trauma related to crimes of sexual violence and violence against children. Where appropriate the Unit shall cooperate with non-governmental and intergovernmental organizations.

Rule 35: Minutes

Except where a full record is made under Rule 81, the Registrar (or Registry staff designated by him) shall take minutes of the Plenary Meetings of the Special Court and of the sittings of the Chambers or a Judge, other than private deliberations.

Rule 36: Cause Book

The Registrar shall keep a Cause Book which shall list, subject to Rule 53, all the particulars of each case including the index of the contents of the case file.

Section 6: The Prosecutor

Rule 37: Functions of the Prosecutor

(A) The Prosecutor shall perform all the functions provided by the Statute in accordance with the Rules and with such Regulations, consistent with the Agreement and the Statute and the Rules, as may be framed by him.

(B) The Prosecutor's powers under Parts Four to Eight of the Rules may be exercised by staff members of the Office of the Prosecutor authorized by him, or by any person acting under his direction.

Rule 38: The Deputy Prosecutor

The Deputy Prosecutor shall exercise the functions of the Prosecutor in the event of his absence or inability to act or upon the Prosecutor's express instructions.

PART IV—INVESTIGATIONS, RIGHTS OF SUSPECTS AND ACCUSED

Section 1: Investigations

Rule 39: Conduct of Investigations

In the conduct of an investigation, the Prosecutor may:
  (i) Summon and question suspects, interview victims and witnesses and record their statements, collect evidence and conduct on-site investigations;
  (ii) Take all measures deemed necessary for the purpose of the investigation, including the taking of any special measures to provide for the safety, the support and the assistance of potential witnesses and sources;
  (iii) Seek, to that end, the assistance of any State authority concerned, as well as of any relevant international body including the International Criminal Police Organization (INTERPOL); and
  (iv) Request such orders as may be necessary from a Trial Chamber or a Judge.

Rule 40: Provisional Measures

(A) In case of urgency, the Prosecutor may request any State:
  (i) To arrest a suspect and place him in custody in accordance with the laws of that State;
  (ii) To seize all physical evidence;
  (iii) To take all necessary measures to prevent the escape of a suspect or an accused, injury to or intimidation of a victim or witness, or the destruction of evidence.
(B) The Prosecutor may apply to a Judge designated by the President in accordance with Rule 28 for an order to transfer the suspect to the seat of the Special Court or to such other place as the President may decide (with the advice of the Registrar) and to detain him provisionally. After consultation with the Prosecutor and the Registrar, the transfer shall be arranged between the authorities concerned, and the Registrar.
(C) In the cases referred to in Sub-Rule B, the suspect shall, from the moment of his transfer, enjoy all the rights provided for in Rule 42, and may apply for review to a Trial Chamber of the Special Court. The Chamber, after hearing the Prosecutor, shall rule upon the application.
(D) The suspect shall be released if:
  (i) the Chamber so rules; or
  (ii) the Prosecutor fails to submit an indictment within twenty days of the transfer; or
  (iii) the Prosecutor fails to obtain an order under rule 40 *bis* within twenty days of the transfer.

Rule 40 *bis*: Transfer and Provisional Detention of Suspects

(A) In the conduct of an investigation, the Prosecutor may transmit to the Registrar, for an order by a Judge designated pursuant to Rule 28, a request for the transfer and/or provisional detention of a suspect in the premises of the detention unit of the Special Court. This request shall indicate the grounds upon which the request is made and, unless the Prosecutor wishes only to question the suspect, shall include a provisional charge and a brief summary of the material upon which the Prosecutor relies.

(B) The Judge shall order the transfer and provisional detention of the suspect if the following conditions are met:
  (i) The Prosecutor has requested a State to arrest the suspect and to place him in custody, in accordance with Rule 40, or the suspect is otherwise detained by a State;
  (ii) Where there are provisional charges, and where there is reason to believe that the suspect may have committed a crime or crimes specified in those provisional charges over which the Special Court has jurisdiction; and
  (iii) The Judge considers provisional detention to be a necessary measure to prevent the escape of the suspect, physical or mental injury to or intimidation of a victim or witness or the destruction of evidence, or to be otherwise necessary for the conduct of the investigation.
(C) The provisional detention of the suspect may be ordered for a period not exceeding 30 days from the day after the transfer of the suspect to the detention unit of the Special Court.
(D) The order for the transfer and provisional detention of the suspect shall be signed by the Judge and bear the seal of the Special Court. The order shall set forth the basis of the request made by the Prosecutor under Sub-Rule (A), including the provisional charge, and shall state the Judge's grounds for making the order, having regard to Sub-Rule (B). The order, shall also specify the initial time limit for the provisional detention of the suspect and when served on the suspect be accompanied by a statement of his rights, as specified in this Rule and in Rules 42 and 43.
(E) As soon as possible, copies of the order and of the request by the Prosecutor shall be served upon the suspect and his counsel by the Registrar.
(F) At the Prosecutor's request indicating the grounds upon which it is made and if warranted by the needs of the investigation, the Judge who made the initial order, or another Judge designated under Rule 28, may decide, subsequent to an *inter partes* hearing and before the end of the period of detention, to extend the provisional detention for a period not exceeding 30 days.
(G) At the Prosecutor's request indicating the grounds upon which it is made and if warranted by special circumstances, the Judge who made the initial order, or another Judge designated under Rule 28, may decide, subsequent to an *inter partes* hearing and before the end of the period of detention, to extend the detention for a further period not exceeding 30 days.
(H) The total period of provisional detention shall in no case exceed 90 days after the day of transfer of the suspect to the Special Court, at the end of which, in the event the indictment has not been approved and an arrest warrant signed, the suspect shall be released or, if appropriate, be delivered to the authorities of the State to which the request was initially made.
(I) The provisions in Rules 55(B) to 59 shall apply to the execution of the order for the transfer and provisional detention of the suspect.
(J) After his transfer to the seat of the Special Court, the suspect, assisted by his counsel, shall be brought, without delay, before the Judge who made the initial order, or another Judge designated under Rule 28, who shall ensure that his rights are respected.
(K) During detention, the Prosecutor, the suspect or his counsel may submit to the Trial Chamber all applications relative to the propriety of provisional detention or to the suspect's release.
(L) Without prejudice to Sub-Rules (C) to (H), the Rules relating to the detention on remand of accused persons shall apply to the provisional detention of persons under this Rule.

Rule 41: Preservation of Information

(A) The Prosecutor shall be responsible for the preservation, storage and security of information and physical evidence obtained in the course of his investigations.
(B) The Prosecutor shall draw up an inventory of all materials seized from the accused, including documents, books, papers, and other objects, and shall serve a copy thereof on the accused. Materials that are of no evidentiary value shall be returned without delay to the accused.

Rule 42: Rights of Suspects during Investigation

(A) A suspect who is to be questioned by the Prosecutor shall have the following rights, of which he shall be informed by the Prosecutor prior to questioning, in a language he speaks and understands:
- (i) The right to legal assistance of his own choosing, including the right to have legal assistance provided by the Defence Office where the interests of justice so require and where the suspect does not have sufficient means to pay for it;
- (ii) The right to have the free assistance of an interpreter if he cannot understand or speak the language to be used for questioning; and
- (iii) The right to remain silent, and to be cautioned that any statement he makes shall be recorded and may be used in evidence.

(B) Questioning of a suspect shall not proceed without the presence of counsel unless the suspect has voluntarily waived his right to counsel. In case of waiver, if the suspect subsequently expresses a desire to have counsel, questioning shall thereupon cease, and shall only resume when the suspect has obtained or has been assigned counsel.

Rule 43: Recording Questioning of Suspects

Whenever the Prosecutor questions a suspect, the questioning shall be audio-recorded or video-recorded, in accordance with the following procedure:

- (ii) In the event of a break in the course of the questioning, the fact and the time of the break shall be recorded before audio-recording or video-recording ends and the time of resumption of the questioning shall also be recorded;
- (iii) At the conclusion of the questioning the suspect shall be offered the opportunity to clarify anything he has said, and to add anything he may wish, and the time of conclusion shall be recorded;
- (iv) The content of the recording shall then be transcribed as soon as practicable after the conclusion of questioning and a copy of the transcript supplied to the suspect, together with a copy of the recording or, if multiple recording apparatus was used, one of the original recorded tapes; and
- (v) After a copy has been made, if necessary, of the recorded tape for purposes of transcription, the original recorded tape or one of the original tapes shall be sealed in the presence of the suspect under the signature of the Prosecutor and the suspect.

Section 2: Defence Counsel

Rule 44: Appointment and Qualifications of Counsel

(A) Counsel engaged by a suspect or an accused shall file his power of attorney with the Registrar at the earliest opportunity. Subject to verification by the Registrar, a counsel shall be considered qualified to represent a suspect or accused, provided that he has been admitted to the practice of law in a State for a minimum of five years.

(B) In the performance of their duties counsel shall be subject to the relevant provisions of the Agreement, the Statute, the Rules, the Rules of Detention and any other rules or regulations adopted by the Special Court, the Host Country Agreement, the Code of Professional Conduct and the codes of practice and ethics governing their profession and, if applicable, the Directive on the Assignment of Defence Counsel.

Rule 45: Defence Office

The Registrar shall establish, maintain and develop a Defence Office, for the purpose of ensuring the rights of suspects and accused. The Defence Office shall be headed by the Special Court Principal Defender.

(A) The Defence Office shall, in accordance with the Statute and Rules, provide advice, assistance and representation to:
 (I) suspects being questioned by the Special Court or its agents under Rule 42, including non-custodial questioning;
 (ii) accused persons before the Special Court.
(B) The Defence Office shall fulfil its functions by providing, amongst other things,
 (i) initial legal advice and assistance by duty counsel who shall be situated within a reasonable proximity to the Detention Facility and the Seat of the Special Court and shall be available as far as practicable to attend the Detention Facility in the event of being summoned;
 (ii) legal aid as ordered by the Special Court in accordance with Rule 61, if the accused does not have sufficient means to pay for it, as the interests of justice may so require;
 (iii) adequate facilities for counsel in the preparation of the defence.
(C) The Principal Defender, may, in providing an effective defence, maintain a list of highly qualified criminal defence counsel whom he believes appropriate to act as duty counsel or to lead the defence or appeal of an accused. Such counsel (who may include members of the Defence Office) shall:
 (i) speak fluent English;
 (ii) be admitted to practice law in any State;
 (iii) have at least 7 years' relevant experience; and
 (iv) have indicated their willingness and full-time availability to be assigned by the Special Court to suspects or accused.
(D) Any request for replacement of an assigned counsel shall be made to the Principal Defender. Under exceptional circumstances, the request may be made to a Chamber upon good cause being shown and after having been satisfied that the request is not designed to delay the proceedings.
(E) Counsel will represent the accused and conduct the case to finality. Failure to do so, absent just cause approved by the Chamber, may result in forfeiture of fees in whole or in part. In such circumstances the Chamber may make an order accordingly. Counsel shall only be permitted to withdraw from the case to which he has been assigned in the most exceptional circumstances. In the event of such withdrawal the Principal Defender shall assign another Counsel who may be a member of the Defence Office, to the indigent accused.

Rule 45*bis*: Declaration of Means by the Accused

(A) Upon his transfer to the Special Court, and when he first appears before a Judge or a Trial Chamber, the suspect or accused shall be requested by the Registrar to:
 (i) make a declaration of his means, and if applicable
 (ii) make a request for legal assistance.
(B) If a suspect or an accused elects to conduct his own defence, he shall so notify the Registrar in writing at the first opportunity.

Rule 46: Misconduct of Counsel

(A) A Judge or Chamber may, after a warning, impose sanctions against or refuse audience to a counsel if, in its opinion, his conduct remains offensive or abusive, obstructs the proceedings, or is otherwise contrary to the interests of justice.

(B) The Chamber may determine that counsel is no longer eligible to represent a suspect or accused before the Special Court, pursuant to Rule 45. If declared ineligible, removed counsel shall transmit to replacement counsel all materials relevant to the representation.
(C) Counsel who bring motions, or conduct other activities, that in the opinion of the Chamber are either frivolous or constitute abuse of process may be sanctioned for those actions as the Chamber may direct. Sanctions may include fines upon counsel; non-payment, in whole or in part, of fees associated with the motion or its costs, or such other sanctions as the Chamber may direct.
(D) A Judge or a Chamber may also, with the approval of the President, communicate any misconduct of counsel to the professional body regulating the conduct of counsel in his State of admission.
(E) If a counsel assigned pursuant to Rule 45 is sanctioned by being refused audience, the Chamber shall instruct the Registrar to replace the counsel.
(F) This Rule is applicable to counsel for the prosecution as well as counsel appearing for the defence as for the intervenors.
(G) The Registrar may set up a Code of Professional Conduct enunciating the principles of professional ethics to be observed by counsel appearing before the Special Court, subject to adoption by the Plenary Meeting. Amendments to the Code shall be made in consultation with representatives of the Prosecutor and Defence counsel, and subject to adoption by the Plenary Meeting. If the Registrar has strong grounds for believing that Counsel has committed a serious violation of the Code of Professional Conduct so adopted, he may report the matter to the President for appropriate action under this rule.

PART V—PRE-TRIAL PROCEEDINGS

Section 1: Indictments

Rule 47: Review of Indictment

(A) An indictment submitted in accordance with the following procedure shall be approved by a Judge designated in accordance with Rule 28 for this purpose.
(B) The Prosecutor, if satisfied in the course of an investigation that a suspect has committed a crime or crimes within the jurisdiction of the Special Court, shall prepare and submit to the Registrar an indictment for approval by the aforementioned Judge.
(C) The indictment shall contain, and be sufficient if it contains, the name and particulars of the suspect, a statement of each specific offence of which the named suspect is charged and a short description of the particulars of the offence. It shall be accompanied by a Prosecutor's case summary briefly setting out the allegations he proposes to prove in making his case.
(D) The Registrar shall submit the indictment and accompanying material to the designated Judge for review.
(E) The designated Judge shall review the indictment and the accompanying material to determine whether the indictment should be approved. The Judge shall approve the indictment if he is satisfied that:
  (i) the indictment charges the suspect with a crime or crimes within the jurisdiction of the Special Court; and
  (ii) that the allegations in the Prosecution's case summary would, if proven, amount to the crime or crimes as specified and particularised in the indictment.
(F) The designated Judge may approve or dismiss each count.
(G) If at least one count is approved, the indictment shall go forward. If no count is approved, the indictment shall be returned to the Prosecutor.
(H) Upon approval of the indictment:

(i) The judge may, at the request of the Prosecutor, issue such orders and warrants for the arrest, detention, surrender or transfer of persons, and any other orders as may be required for the proceedings in accordance with these Rules.; and
(ii) The suspect shall have the status of an accused.
(I) The dismissal of a count in an indictment shall not preclude the Prosecutor from subsequently submitting an amended indictment including that count.

Rule 48: Joinder of Accused or Trials

(A) Persons accused of the same or different crimes committed in the course of the same transaction may be jointly charged and tried.
(B) Persons who are separately indicted, accused of the same or different crimes committed in the course of the same transaction, may be tried together, with leave granted by a Trial Chamber pursuant to Rule 73.

Rule 49: Joinder of Crimes

Two or more crimes may be joined in one indictment if the series of acts committed together form the same transaction, and the said crimes were committed by the same accused.

Rule 50: Amendment of Indictment

(A) The Prosecutor may amend an indictment, without prior leave, at any time before its approval, but thereafter, until the initial appearance of the accused pursuant to Rule 61, only with leave of the Judge who reviewed it but, in exceptional circumstances, by leave of a Judge assigned by the President. At or after such initial appearance, an amendment of an indictment may only be made by leave granted by a Trial Chamber pursuant to Rule 73. If leave to amend is granted, Rule 47 (G) and Rule 52 apply to the amended indictment.
(B) If the amended indictment includes new charges and the accused has already made his initial appearance in accordance with Rule 61, a further appearance shall be held as soon as practicable to enable the accused to enter a plea on the new charges.
(C) The accused shall have a further period of fourteen days from the date of the initial appearance on the new charges in which to file preliminary motions.

Rule 51: Withdrawal of Indictment

(A) The Prosecutor may withdraw an indictment at any time before the commencement of the trial of the accused. Following the commencement of trial, an indictment may only be withdrawn by leave granted by a Trial Chamber pursuant to Rule 73 but, in exceptional circumstances, by leave of a Judge assigned by the President.
(B) The withdrawal of the indictment shall be promptly notified to the suspect or the accused and to the counsel of the suspect or accused.

Rule 52: Service of Indictment

(A) Service of the indictment shall be effected personally on the accused at the time the accused is taken into the custody of the Special Court or as soon as possible thereafter.
(B) Personal service of an indictment on the accused is effected by giving the accused a copy of the indictment that has been certified in accordance with Rule 47.
(C) An indictment that has been permitted to proceed by the Judge shall be retained by the Registrar, who shall prepare certified copies bearing the seal of the Special Court. If the accused does not understand English and if the language understood is a written language known to the Registrar, a translation of the indictment in that language shall also be pre-

pared. In the case that the accused is illiterate or his language is an oral language, the Registrar will ensure that the indictment is read to the accused by an interpreter, and that he is served with a recording of the interpretation.
(D) Subject to Rule 53, upon approval by a designated Judge the indictment shall be made public.

Rule 53: Non-disclosure

(A) In exceptional circumstances, a Judge designated pursuant to Rule 28 may, in the interests of justice, order the non-disclosure to the public of any documents or information until further order.
(B) When approving an indictment the Judge may, on the application of the Prosecutor, order that there be no public disclosure of the indictment until it is served on the accused, or, in the case of joint accused, on all the accused.
(C) A Judge or Trial Chamber may, on the application of the Prosecutor, also order that there be no disclosure of an indictment, or part thereof, or of all or any part of any particular document or information, if satisfied that the making of such an order is required to give effect to a provision of the Rules, to protect confidential information obtained by the Prosecutor, or is otherwise in the interests of justice.

Section 2: Orders and Warrants

Rule 54: General Provision

At the request of either party or of its own motion, a Judge or a Trial Chamber may issue such orders, summonses, subpoenas, warrants and transfer orders as may be necessary for the purposes of an investigation or for the preparation or conduct of the trial.

Rule 55: Execution of Arrest Warrants

(A) An Arrest Warrant shall be signed by a Judge and shall bear the seal of the Special Court. It shall be accompanied by a copy of the indictment, and a statement of the rights of the accused.
(B) The Registrar shall transmit to the relevant authorities of Sierra Leone in whose territory or under whose jurisdiction or control the accused resides, or was last known to be, three sets of certified copies of:
  ii) The approved indictment;
  (iii) A statement of the rights of the accused; and if necessary a translation thereof in a language understood by the accused.
(C) The Registrar shall request the said authorities to:
  (i) Arrange for the arrest of the accused and his transfer to the Special Court;
  (ii) Serve a set of the aforementioned documents upon the accused;
  (iii) Cause the documents to be read to the accused in a language understood by him and to caution him as to his rights in that language; and
  (iv) Return one set of the documents together with proof of service, to the Special Court.
(D) When an arrest warrant issued by the Special Court is executed, a member of the Prosecutor's Office may be present at the time of arrest.

Rule 56: Arrest Warrants to Third States

(A) Upon the request of the Prosecutor, and if satisfied that to do so would facilitate the arrest of an accused who may move from State to State, or whose whereabouts are unknown, a Judge may address an arrest warrant to any third State, as well as any relevant international body including the International Criminal Police Organisation (INTERPOL).

(B) The Registrar shall transmit such a warrant to the national authorities of such States, or to the relevant international body, as may be indicated by the Prosecutor.

Rule 57: Procedure after Arrest

Upon the arrest of the accused, the State concerned shall detain him, and shall promptly notify the Registrar. The transfer of the accused to the seat of the Special Court, or to such other place as the President may decide, after consultation with the Registrar (who shall have consulted the Prosecutor) and the Vice-President if practicable, shall be arranged by the State authorities concerned, in liaison with the authorities of the host country and the Registrar.

Rule 58: Transfer to the Special Court from third States

The Special Court may invite third States to enter into agreements and or ad hoc arrangements which may facilitate arrest and transfer to the Special Court.

Rule 59: Failure to Execute an Arrest Warrant or Transfer Order

(A) Where the Sierra Leone authorities, to whom an arrest warrant or transfer order has been transmitted, are unable to execute the arrest warrant or transfer order, they shall report forthwith their inability to the Registrar, and the reasons therefore.
(B) If, within a reasonable time after the arrest warrant or transfer order has been transmitted to the Sierra Leone authorities, no report is made on action taken, this shall be deemed a failure to execute the arrest warrant or transfer order and the Special Court may request the President to take appropriate action.

Rule 60: Trial in the Absence of the Accused

(A) An accused may not be tried in his absence, unless:
 (i) the accused has made his initial appearance, has been afforded the right to appear at his own trial, but refuses so to do; or
 (ii) the accused, having made his initial appearance, is at large and refuses to appear in court.
(B) In either case the accused may be represented by counsel of his choice, or as directed by a Judge or Trial Chamber. The matter may be permitted to proceed if the Judge or Trial Chamber is satisfied that the accused has, expressly or impliedly, unequivocally waived his right to be present.

Rule 61: Initial Appearance of Accused and Plea

Upon his transfer to the Special Court, the accused shall be brought before a Trial Judge as soon as practicable, and shall be formally charged. The Judge shall:

 (i) Satisfy himself that the right of the accused to counsel is respected, and in so doing, shall question the accused with regard to his means and instruct the Registrar to provide legal aid to the accused as the interests of justice so require;
 (ii) Read or have the indictment read to the accused in a language he speaks and understands, and satisfy himself that the accused understands the indictment;
 (iii) Call upon the accused to enter a plea of guilty or not guilty on each count; should the accused fail to do so, enter a plea of not guilty on his behalf;
 (iv) In case of a plea of not guilty, instruct the Registrar to set a date for trial;
 (v) In case of a plea of guilty, shall refer the plea to the Trial Chamber so that it may act in accordance with Rule 62.

Rule 62: Procedure upon Guilty Plea

(A) If an accused pleads guilty in accordance with Rule 61, or requests to change his plea to guilty, the Trial Chamber shall satisfy itself that the guilty plea:
  (i) is made freely and voluntarily;
  (ii) is an informed plea;
  (iii) is unequivocal;
(B) Thereafter the Trial Chamber may enter a finding of guilt and instruct the Registrar to set a date for the sentencing hearing.

Rule 63: Questioning of the Accused

(A) Questioning by the Prosecutor of an accused, including after the initial appearance, shall not proceed without the presence of counsel unless the accused has voluntarily and expressly agreed to proceed without counsel present. If the accused subsequently expresses a desire to have counsel, questioning shall thereupon cease, and shall only resume when the accused's counsel is present.
(B) The questioning, including any waiver of the right to counsel, shall be audio-recorded or, (and if possible) video-recorded, in accordance with the procedure provided for in Rule 43. The Prosecutor shall at the beginning of the questioning caution the accused in accordance with Rule 42 (A)(iii).

Rule 64: Detention on Remand

Upon his transfer to the Special Court, the accused shall be detained in the facilities of the Special Court, or facilities otherwise made available pursuant to Article 22 of the Statute. The President may, on the application of a party or the Registrar, order special measures of detention of an accused.

Rule 65: Bail

(A) Once detained, an accused shall not be granted bail except upon an order of a Judge or Trial Chamber.
(B) Bail may be ordered by a Judge or a Trial Chamber after hearing the State to which the accused seeks to be released and only if it is satisfied that the accused will appear for trial and, if released, will not pose a danger to any victim, witness or other person.
(C) An accused may only make one application for bail to the Judge or Trial Chamber unless there has been a material change in circumstances.
(D) The Judge or Trial Chamber may impose such conditions upon the granting of bail to the accused as it may determine appropriate, including the execution of a bail bond and the observance of such conditions as are necessary to ensure the presence of the accused at trial and the protection of others.
(E) Any decision rendered under this Rule shall be subject to appeal in cases where leave is granted by a Single Judge of the Appeals Chamber designated under Rule 28, upon good cause being shown. Applications for leave to appeal shall be filed within seven days of the impugned decision.
(F) If necessary, the Trial Chamber may issue a arrest warrant to secure the presence of an accused who has been granted bail or is for any other reason at large. The provisions of Section 2 of Part V shall apply.
(G) The Prosecutor may appeal a decision to grant bail. In the event of such an appeal, the accused shall remain in custody until the appeal is heard, and determined.
(H) Appeals from bail decisions shall be heard by a bench of at least three Appeals Chamber Judges.

Rule 65 bis: Status Conferences

A status conference may be convened by a Trial Chamber or a Judge thereof as necessary. The status conference shall:

(ii) review the status of his case and to allow the accused the opportunity to raise issues in relation thereto.

Section 3: Production of Evidence

Rule 66: Disclosure of materials by the Prosecutor

(A) Subject to the provisions of Rules 53, 69 and 75, the Prosecutor shall:
 (i) Within 30 days of the initial appearance of an accused, disclose to the Defence copies of the statements of all witnesses whom the Prosecutor intends to call to testify and all evidence to be presented pursuant to Rule 92 *bis* at trial. Upon good cause being shown, a Judge of the Trial Chamber may order that copies of the statements of additional prosecution witnesses be made available to the defence within a prescribed time.
 (ii) At the request of the defence, subject to Sub-Rule (B), permit the defence to inspect any books, documents, photographs and tangible objects in his custody or control, which are material to the preparation of the defence, upon a showing by the defence of categories of, or specific, books, documents, photographs and tangible objects which the defence considers to be material to the preparation of a defence, or to inspect any books, documents, photographs and tangible objects in his custody or control which are intended for use by the Prosecutor as evidence at trial or were obtained from or belonged to the accused.
(B) Where information or materials are in the possession of the Prosecutor, the disclosure of which may prejudice further or ongoing investigations, or for any other reasons may be contrary to the public interest or affect the security interests of any State, the Prosecutor may apply to a Judge designated by the President sitting *ex parte* in private to be relieved from the obligation to disclose pursuant to Sub-Rule (A). When making such an application the Prosecutor shall provide, only to the designated Judge, the information or materials that are sought to be kept confidential.

Rule 67: Reciprocal Disclosure of Evidence

Subject to the provisions of Rules 53 and 69:

(A) As early as reasonably practicable and in any event prior to the commencement of the trial:
 (i) The Prosecutor shall notify the defence of the names of the witnesses that he intends to call to establish the guilt of the accused and in rebuttal of any defence plea of which the Prosecutor has received notice in accordance with Sub-Rule (ii) below, or any defence pleaded in the Defence Case Statement served under Sub-Rule (C);
 (ii) The defence shall notify the Prosecutor of its intent to enter:
  (a) The defence of alibi; in which case the notification shall specify the place or places at which the accused claims to have been present at the time of the alleged crime and the names and addresses of witnesses and any other evidence upon which the accused intends to rely to establish the alibi;
  (b) Any special defence, including that of diminished or lack of mental responsibility; in which case the notification shall specify the names and addresses of witnesses and any other evidence upon which the accused intends to rely to establish the special defence.

(B) Failure of the defence to provide such notice under this Rule shall not limit the right of the accused to rely on the above defences.
(C) To assist the Prosecutor with its disclosure obligations pursuant to Rule 68, the defence may prior to trial provide the Prosecutor with a Defence Case Statement. The Defence Case Statement shall:
   (i) set out in general terms the nature of the accused's defence;
   (ii) indicate the matters on which he takes issue with the prosecution; and
   (iii) set out, in the case of each such matter, the reason why he takes issue with the prosecution.
(D) If either party discovers additional evidence or information or materials which should have been produced earlier pursuant to the Rules, that party shall promptly notify the other party and the Trial Chamber of the existence of the additional evidence or information or materials.

Rule 68: Disclosure of Exculpatory Evidence

(A) The Prosecutor shall, within 14 days of receipt of the Defence Case Statement, disclose to the defence the existence of evidence known to the Prosecutor which may be relevant to issues raised in the Defence Case Statement.
(B) The Prosecutor shall, within 30 days of the initial appearance of the accused disclose to the defence the existence of evidence known to the Prosecutor which in any way tends to suggest the innocence or mitigate the guilt of the accused or may affect the credibility of prosecution evidence. The Prosecutor shall be under a continuing obligation to disclose any such exculpatory material.

Rule 69: Protection of Victims and Witnesses

(A) In exceptional circumstances, either of the parties may apply to a Judge of the Trial Chamber or the Trial Chamber to order the non-disclosure of the identity of a victim or witness who may be in danger or at risk, until the Judge or Chamber decides otherwise.
(B) In the determination of protective measures for victims and witnesses, the Judge or Trial Chamber may consult the Victims and Witnesses Unit.
(C) Subject to Rule 75, the identity of the victim or witness shall be disclosed in sufficient time before a witness is to be called to allow adequate time for preparation of the prosecution and the defence.

Rule 70: Matters not Subject to Disclosure

(A) Notwithstanding the provisions of Rules 66 and 67, reports, memoranda, or other internal documents prepared by a party, its assistants or representatives in connection with the investigation or preparation of the case, are not subject to disclosure or notification under the aforementioned provisions.
(B) If the Prosecutor is in possession of information which has been provided to him on a confidential basis and which has been used solely for the purpose of generating new evidence, that initial information and its origin shall not be disclosed by the Prosecutor without the consent of the person or entity providing the initial information and shall in any event not be given in evidence without prior disclosure to the accused.
(C) If, after obtaining the consent of the person or entity providing information under this Rule, the Prosecutor elects to present as evidence any testimony, document or other material so provided, the Trial Chamber may not order either party to produce additional evidence received from the person or entity providing the initial information, nor may the Trial Chamber for the purpose of obtaining such additional evidence itself summon that person or a representative of that entity as a witness or order their attendance. The consent shall be in writing.

(D) If the Prosecutor calls as a witness the person providing or a representative of the entity providing information under this Rule, the Trial Chamber may not compel the witness to answer any question the witness declines to answer on grounds of confidentiality.
(E) The right of the accused to challenge the evidence presented by the Prosecution shall remain unaffected subject only to limitations contained in Sub-Rules (C) and (D).
(F) Nothing in Sub-Rule (C) or (D) above shall affect a Trial Chamber's power under Rule 95 to exclude evidence if its admission would bring the administration of justice in the Special Court into serious disrepute.

Section 4: Depositions

Rule 71: Depositions

(A) At the request of either party, a Trial Chamber may, in exceptional circumstances and in the interests of justice, order that a deposition be taken for use at trial and appoint for that purpose, a Legal Officer.
(B) The motion for the taking of a deposition shall be in writing and shall indicate the name and whereabouts of the witness whose deposition is sought, the date and place at which the deposition is to be taken, a statement of the matters on which the person is to be examined, and of the interests of justice justifying the taking of the deposition.
(C) If the motion is granted, the party at whose request the deposition is to be taken shall give reasonable notice to the other party, who shall have the right to attend the taking of the deposition and cross-examine the witness.
(D) The deposition may also be given by means of a video-conference.
(E) The Legal Officer shall ensure that the deposition is taken in accordance with the Rules and that a record is made of the deposition, including cross-examination and objections raised by either party for decision by the Trial Chamber. He shall transmit the record to the Trial Chamber.

Section 5: Preliminary Motions

Rule 72: Preliminary Motions

(A) Preliminary motions by either party shall be brought within 21 days following disclosure by the Prosecutor to the Defence of all the material envisaged by Rule 66(A)(i).
(B) Preliminary motions by the accused are:
  (i) Objections based on lack of jurisdiction;
  (ii) Objections based on defects in the form of the indictment;
  (iii) Applications for severance of crimes joined in one indictment under Rule 49, or for separate trials under Rule 82 (B);
  (iv) Objections based on the denial of request for assignment of counsel; or
  (v) Objections based on abuse of process.
(C) The Trial Chamber shall, except as provided by (D) and (E) below, dispose of preliminary motions before the trial, and such decisions shall not be subject to interlocutory appeal.
(D) Preliminary or other motions made in the Trial Chamber prior to the Prosecutor's opening statement, if in the opinion of that Chamber, they raise:
  (i) a substantial issue relating to jurisdiction; or
  (ii) an issue that would significantly affect the fair and expeditious conduct of the proceedings or the outcome of a trial, and for which an immediate resolution by the Appeals Chamber may materially advance the proceedings, may be referred to the Appeals Chamber, where they will proceed to a determination as soon as practicable.

(E) The Trial Chamber shall certify the issue for appeal, which will proceed if, within seven days of such certification, any party files a notice of appeal. Such notice shall not operate as a stay of the Trial proceedings unless the Trial Chamber so orders.
(F) Failure to comply with the time limits prescribed in this Rule shall constitute a waiver of the rights. The Trial Chamber may, however, grant relief from the waiver upon showing good cause.
(G) Objections to the form of the indictment, including an amended indictment, shall be raised by a party in one motion only, unless otherwise allowed by a Trial Chamber.

PART VI—PROCEEDINGS BEFORE TRIAL CHAMBERS

Section 1: General Provisions

Rule 73: Motions

(A) Subject to Rule 72, either party may move before a Trial Chamber for appropriate ruling or relief after the initial appearance of the accused. The Trial Chamber, or a Judge designated by the Chamber from among its members, may rule on such motions having heard the parties in open Court. The Trial Chamber may request that the parties submit written submissions in support of a motion.
(B) Decisions rendered on such motions are without interlocutory appeal save where leave is granted by the Trial Chamber on the grounds that a decision would be in the interest of a fair and expeditious trial.

Rule 73 *bis*: Pre-Trial Conference

(A) The Trial Chamber may hold a Pre-Trial Conference prior to the commencement of the trial.
(B) At the Pre-Trial Conference the Trial Chamber or a Judge designated from among its members may order the Prosecutor, within a time limit set by the Trial Chamber or the said Judge, and before the date set for trial, to file:
   (i) A pre-trial brief addressing the factual and legal issues;
   (ii) Admissions by the parties and a statement of other matters not in dispute;
   (iii) A statement of contested matters of fact and law;
   (iv) A list of witnesses the Prosecutor intends to call with:
      (a) The name or pseudonym of each witness;
      (b) A summary of the facts on which each witness will testify;
      (c) The points in the indictment on which each witness will testify; and
      (d) The estimated length of time required for each witness;
   (v) A list of exhibits the Prosecutor intends to offer stating, where possible, whether or not the defence has any objection as to authenticity.
(C) The Trial Chamber or the designated Judge may order the Prosecutor to shorten the examination-in-chief of some witnesses.
(D) The Trial Chamber or the designated Judge may order the Prosecutor to reduce the number of witnesses, if it considers that an excessive number of witnesses are being called to prove the same facts.
(E) After commencement of Trial, the Prosecutor may, if he considers it to be in the interests of justice, move the Trial Chamber for leave to reinstate the list of witnesses or to vary his decision as to which witnesses are to be called.
(F) At the Pre-Trial Conference, the Trial Chamber or the designated Judge may order the defence to file a statement of admitted facts and law and a pre-trial brief addressing the factual and legal issues, not later than seven days prior to the date set for trial.

Rule 73 ter: Pre-Defence Conference

(A) The Trial Chamber may hold a Conference prior to the commencement by the defence of its case.
(B) At that Conference, the Trial Chamber or a Judge, designated from among its members, may order that the defence, before the commencement of its case but after the close of the case for the prosecution, file the following:
    (i) Admissions by the parties and a statement of other matters which are not in dispute;
    (ii) A statement of contested matters of fact and law;
    (iii) A list of witnesses the defence intends to call with:
        (a) The name or pseudonym of each witness;
        (b) A summary of the facts on which each witness will testify;
        (c) The points in the indictment as to which each witness will testify; and
        (d) The estimated length of time required for each witness;
    (iv) A list of exhibits the defence intends to offer in its case, stating where possible whether or not the Prosecutor has any objection as to authenticity.
(C) The Trial Chamber or the designated Judge may order the defence to shorten the estimated length of the examination-in-chief for some witnesses.
(D) The Trial Chamber or the designated Judge may order the defence to reduce the number of witnesses, if it considers that an excessive number of witnesses are being called to prove the same facts.
(E) After commencement of the defence case, the defence may, if it considers it to be in the interests of justice, move the Trial Chamber for leave to reinstate the list of witnesses or to vary its decision as to which witnesses are to be called.

Rule 74: Intervenors

A Chamber may, if it considers it desirable for the proper determination of the case, invite or grant leave to any State, organization or person to make submissions on any issue specified by the Chamber.

Rule 74 bis: Medical examination of the accused

A Judge or Trial Chamber may, on its own motion, or at the request of a party, order a medical, including psychiatric examination or a psychological examination of the accused.

Rule 75: Measures for the Protection of Victims and Witnesses

(A) A Judge or a Chamber may, on its own motion, or at the request of either party, or of the victim or witness concerned, or of the Victims and Witnesses Unit, order appropriate measures to safeguard the privacy and security of victims and witnesses, provided that the measures are consistent with the rights of the accused.
(B) A Chamber may hold proceeding in private to determine whether to order:
    (i) Measures to prevent disclosure to the public or the media of the identity or whereabouts of a victim or a witness, or of persons related to or associated with him by such means as:
        (a) Expunging names and identifying information from the Special Court's public records;
        (b) Non-disclosure to the public of any records identifying the victim or witness;
        (c) Giving of testimony through image- or voice- altering devices or closed circuit television, video link or other similar technologies; and
        (d) Assignment of a pseudonym;

(ii) Closed sessions, in accordance with Rule 79;
(iii) Appropriate measures to facilitate the testimony of vulnerable victims and witnesses, such as one-way closed circuit television.
(C) A Chamber shall control the manner of questioning to avoid any harassment or intimidation.
(D) The Victims and Witnesses Unit shall ensure that the witness has been informed before giving evidence that his or her testimony and his or her identity may be disclosed at a later date in another case, pursuant to Rule 75 (F).
(E) When making an order under Sub-Rule (A) above, a Judge or Chamber shall wherever appropriate state in the order whether the transcript of those proceedings relating to the evidence of the witness to whom the measures relate shall be made available for use in other proceedings before the Court.
(F) Once protective measures have been ordered in respect of a witness or victim in any proceedings before the Court (the "first proceedings"), such protective measures:
  (i) shall continue to have effect mutatis mutandis in any other proceedings before the Court (the "second proceedings") unless and until they are rescinded, varied or augmented in accordance with the procedure set out in this Rule; but;
  (ii) shall not prevent the Prosecutor from discharging any disclosure obligation under the Rules in the second proceedings, provided that the Prosecutor notifies the Defence to whom the disclosure is being made of the nature of the protective measures ordered in the first proceedings.
(G) A party to the second proceedings seeking to rescind, vary or augment protective measures ordered in the first proceedings must apply:
  (i) to any Chamber, however constituted, remaining seized of the first proceedings; or
  (ii) if no Chamber remains seized of the first proceedings, to the Chamber seized of the second proceedings.
(H) Before determining an application under Sub-Rule (F) (ii) above, the Chamber seized of the second proceedings shall obtain all relevant information from the first proceedings, and shall consult with any Judge who ordered the protective measures in the first proceedings, if that Judge remains a Judge of the Court.
(I) An application to a Chamber to rescind, vary or augment protective measures in respect of a victim or witness may be dealt with either by the Chamber or by a Judge of that Chamber, and any reference in this Rule to "a Chamber" shall include a reference to "a Judge of that Chamber".

Rule 76: Solemn Declaration by Interpreters and Translators

Before performing any duties, an interpreter or a translator shall solemnly declare to do so faithfully, independently, impartially and with full respect for the duty of confidentiality.

Rule 77: Contempt of the Special Court

(A) The Special Court, in the exercise of its inherent power, may punish for contempt any person who knowingly and willfully interferes with its administration of justice, including any person who:
  ii) discloses information relating to proceedings in knowing violation of an order of a Chamber;
  (iii) without just excuse fails to comply with an order to attend before or produce documents before a Chamber;
  (iv) threatens, intimidates, causes any injury or offers a bribe to, or otherwise interferes with, a witness who is giving, has given, or is about to give evidence in proceedings before a Chamber, or a potential witness;

(v) threatens, intimidates, offers a bribe to, or otherwise seeks to coerce any other person, with the intention of preventing that other person from complying with an obligation under an order of a Judge or Chamber; or
(vi) knowingly assists an accused person to evade the jurisdiction of the Special Court.

(B) Any incitement or attempt to commit any of the acts punishable under Sub-Rule (A) is punishable as contempt of the Special Court with the same penalties.

(C) When a Judge or Trial Chamber has reason to believe that a person may be in contempt of the Special Court, it may:
(i) deal with the matter summarily itself;
(ii) refer the matter to the appropriate authorities of Sierra Leone; or
(iii) direct the Registrar to appoint an experienced independent counsel to investigate the matter and report back to the Chamber as to whether there are sufficient grounds for instigating contempt proceedings. If the Chamber considers that there are sufficient grounds to proceed against a person for contempt, the Chamber may issue an order in lieu of an indictment and direct the amicus curiae to prosecute the matter.

(D) Proceedings under Sub-Rule (C)(iii) above may be assigned to be heard by a single judge of the Trial Chamber or a Trial Chamber.

(E) The rules of procedure and evidence in Parts Four to Eight shall apply, as appropriate, to proceedings under this Rule.

(F) Any person indicted for or charged with contempt shall, if that person satisfies the criteria for determination of indigence established by the Registrar, be entitled to legal assistance in accordance with Rule 45.

(G) The maximum penalty that may be imposed on a person found to be in contempt of the Special Court pursuant to Sub-Rule (C)(i) shall be a term of imprisonment not exceeding six months, or a fine not exceeding 2 million leones, or both; and the maximum penalty pursuant to Sub-Rule (C)(iii) shall be a term of imprisonment for seven years or a fine not exceeding 2 million leones, or both.

(H) Payment of a fine shall be made to the Registrar on a separate account.

(I) If a counsel is found guilty of contempt of the Special Court pursuant to this Rule, the Chamber making such finding may also determine that counsel is no longer eligible to appear before the Court or that such conduct amounts to misconduct of counsel pursuant to Rule 46, or both.

(J) Any decision rendered by a Single Judge or Trial Chamber under this Rule shall be subject to appeal. Notice of appeal shall be filed within seven days of the impugned decision.

(K) Appeals pursuant to this Rule shall be heard by three Judges of the Appeals Chamber. In accordance with Rule 117 such appeals may be determined entirely on the basis of written submissions.

(L) In the event of contempt occurring during proceedings before the Appeals Chamber or a Judge of the Appeals Chamber, the matter may be dealt with summarily from which there shall be no right of appeal or referred to a Trial Chamber for proceedings in accordance with Sub-Rules (C) to (I) above.

Rule 78: Open Sessions

All proceedings before a Trial Chamber, other than deliberations of the Chamber, shall be held in public, unless otherwise provided.

Rule 79: Closed Sessions

(A) The Trial Chamber may order that the press and the public be excluded from all or part of the proceedings if:

Rules of Procedure and Evidence of the Special Court for Sierra Leone • 1025

    (i) information prejudicial to national security or to the security of the Special Court may be disclosed; or
    (ii) it is necessary to protect the privacy of persons, as in cases of sexual offences or cases involving minors; or
    (iii) publicity would prejudice the interests of justice.
(B) The Trial Chamber shall make public the reasons for its order.
(C) In the event that it is necessary to exclude the public, the Trial Chamber should if appropriate permit representatives of the press and/or monitoring agencies to remain.

Rule 80: Control of Proceedings

(A) The Trial Chamber may exclude a person from the proceedings in order to protect the right of the accused to a fair and public trial, or to maintain the dignity and decorum of the proceedings.
(B) The Trial Chamber may order the removal of an accused from the proceedings and continue the proceedings in his absence if he has persisted in disruptive conduct following a warning that he may be removed. In the event of removal, where possible, provision should be made for the accused to follow the proceedings by video link.

Rule 81: Records of Proceedings and Preservation of Evidence

(A) The Registrar shall cause to be made and preserve a full and accurate record of all proceedings, including audio recordings, transcripts and, when deemed necessary by the Trial Chamber, video recordings.
(B) The Trial Chamber may order the disclosure of all or part of the record of closed proceedings when the reasons for ordering the non disclosure no longer exist.
(C) The Registrar shall retain and preserve all physical evidence offered during the proceedings.
(D) Photography, video-recording or audio-recording of the trial, otherwise than by the Registry, may be authorised at the discretion of the Trial Chamber.

Section 2: Case Presentation

Rule 82: Joint and Separate Trials

(A) In joint trials, each accused shall be accorded the same rights as if he were being tried separately.
(B) The Trial Chamber may order that persons accused jointly under Rule 48 be tried separately if it considers it necessary in order to avoid a conflict of interests that might cause serious prejudice to an accused, or to protect the interests of justice.

Rule 83: Instruments of Restraint

Instruments of restraint, such as handcuffs, shall not be used except as a precaution against escape during transfer or for security reasons, and shall be removed when the accused appears before a Chamber unless otherwise ordered by the Chamber.

Rule 84: Opening Statements

At the opening of his case, each party may make an opening statement confined to the evidence he intends to present in support of his case. The Court may limit the length of those statements in the interests of justice.

Rule 85: Presentation of Evidence

(A) Each party is entitled to call witnesses and present evidence. Unless otherwise directed by the Trial Chamber in the interests of justice, evidence at the trial shall be presented in the following sequence:
  (i) Evidence for the prosecution;
  (ii) Evidence for the defence;
  (iii) Prosecution evidence in rebuttal, with leave of the Trial Chamber;
  (iv) Evidence ordered by the Trial Chamber pursuant to Rule 98.
(B) Examination-in-chief, cross-examination and re-examination shall be allowed in each case. It shall be for the party calling a witness to examine him in chief, but a Judge may at any stage put any question to the witness.
(C) The accused may, if he so desires, appear as a witness in his own defence.
(D) Evidence may be given directly in court, or via such communications media (including video, closed-circuit television) as the Trial Chamber may order.

Rule 86: Closing Arguments

(A) After the presentation of all the evidence, the Prosecutor shall and the defence may present a closing argument.
(B) A party may file a final trial submissions with the Trial Chamber before the day set for the presentation of that party's closing argument.
(C) The parties shall inform the Court of the anticipated length of closing arguments; the Court may limit the length of those arguments in the interests of justice.

Rule 87: Deliberations

(A) After presentation of closing arguments, the Presiding Judge shall declare the hearing closed, and the Trial Chamber shall deliberate in private. A finding of guilty may be reached only when a majority of the Trial Chamber is satisfied that guilt has been proved beyond reasonable doubt.
(B) The Trial Chamber shall vote separately on each count contained in the indictment. If two or more accused are tried together under Rule 48, separate findings shall be made as to each accused.
(C) If the Trial Chamber finds the accused guilty on one or more of the counts contained in the indictment, it shall also determine the penalty to be imposed in respect of each of the counts.

Rule 88: Judgement

(A) The judgement shall be pronounced in public.
(B) If the Trial Chamber finds the accused guilty of a crime, the Trial Chamber may order the forfeiture of the property, proceeds and any assets acquired unlawfully or by criminal conduct as provided in Rule 104.
(C) The judgement shall be rendered by a majority of the Judges. It shall be accompanied by a reasoned opinion in writing. Separate or dissenting opinions may be appended.

Section 3: Rules of Evidence

Rule 89: General Provisions

(A) The rules of evidence set forth in this Section shall govern the proceedings before the Chambers. The Chambers shall not be bound by national rules of evidence.

(B) In cases not otherwise provided for in this Section, a Chamber shall apply rules of evidence which will best favour a fair determination of the matter before it and are consonant with the spirit of the Statute and the general principles of law.
(C) A Chamber may admit any relevant evidence.

Rule 90: Testimony of Witnesses

(A) Witnesses may give evidence directly, or as described in Rules 71 and 85(D).
(B) Every adult witness shall, before giving evidence, make one of the following solemn declarations:

> "I solemnly declare that I will speak the truth, the whole truth and nothing but the truth."

Or

> "I solemnly swear on the [insert holy book] that I will speak the truth, the whole truth and nothing but the truth."

(C) A child shall, be permitted to testify if the Chamber is of the opinion that he is sufficiently mature to be able to report the facts of which he had knowledge, that he understands the duty to tell the truth, and is not subject to undue influence. However, he shall not be compelled to testify by solemn declaration.
(D) A witness, other than an expert or an investigator, who has not yet testified may not be present without leave of the Chamber when the testimony of another witness is given. However, a witness who has heard the testimony of another witness shall not be disqualified from testifying.
(E) A witness may refuse to make any statement which might tend to incriminate him. The Chamber may, however, compel the witness to answer the question. Testimony compelled in this way shall not be used as evidence in a subsequent prosecution against the witness for any offence other than false testimony under solemn declaration.
(F) The Trial Chamber shall exercise control over the mode and order of interrogating witnesses and presenting evidence so as to:
  (i) Make the interrogation and presentation effective for the ascertainment of the truth; and
  (ii) Avoid the wasting of time.

Rule 91: False Testimony under Solemn Declaration

(A) A Chamber, on its own initiative or at the request of a party, may warn a witness of the duty to tell the truth and the consequences that may result from a failure to do so.
(B) If a Chamber has strong grounds for believing that a witness may have knowingly and wilfully given false testimony, the Chamber may follow the procedure, as applicable, in Rule 77.
(C) The maximum penalty for false testimony under solemn declaration shall be a fine of 2 million leones or a term of imprisonment of 2 years, or both. The payment of any fine imposed shall be made to the Registrar to be held in the separate account referred to in Rule 77(H).
(D) Sub-Rules (A) to (C) shall apply to a person who knowingly and wilfully makes a false statement in a written statement which the person knows, or has reason to know, may be used in evidence in proceedings before the Special Court.

Rule 92: Confessions

A confession by the accused given during questioning by the Prosecutor shall, provided the requirements of Rule 63 were complied with, be presumed to have been free and voluntary unless the contrary is proved.

Rule 92 bis: Alternative Proof of Facts

(A) A Trial Chamber may admit as evidence, in whole or in part, information in lieu of oral testimony.
(B) The information submitted may be received in evidence if, in the view of the Trial Chamber, it is relevant to the purpose for which it is submitted and if its reliability is susceptible of confirmation.
(C) A party wishing submit information as evidence shall give 10 days notice to the opposing party. Objections, if any, must be submitted within 5 days.

Rule 93: Evidence of Consistent Pattern of Conduct

(A) Evidence of a consistent pattern of conduct relevant to serious violations of international humanitarian law under the Statute may be admissible in the interests of justice.
(B) Acts tending to show such a pattern of conduct shall be disclosed by the Prosecutor to the defence pursuant to Rule 66.

Rule 94: Judicial Notice

(A) A Trial Chamber shall not require proof of facts of common knowledge but shall take judicial notice thereof.
(B) At the request of a party or of its own motion, a Trial Chamber, after hearing the parties, may decide to take judicial notice of adjudicated facts or documentary evidence from other proceedings of the Special Court relating to the matter at issue in the current proceedings.

Rule 94 bis: Testimony of Expert Witnesses

(A) Notwithstanding the provisions of Rule 66 (A), Rule 73 bis (B) (iv) (b) and Rule 73 ter (B) (iii) (b) of the present Rules, the full statement of any expert witness called by a party shall be disclosed to the opposing party as early as possible and shall be filed with the Trial Chamber not less than twenty-one days prior to the date on which the expert is expected to testify.
(B) Within fourteen days of filing of the statement of the expert witness, the opposing party shall file a notice to the Trial Chamber indicating whether:
  (i) It accepts the expert witness statement; or
  (ii) It wishes to cross-examine the expert witness.
(C) If the opposing party accepts the statement of the expert witness, the statement may be admitted into evidence by the Trial Chamber without calling the witness to testify in person.

Rule 95: Exclusion of Evidence

No evidence shall be admitted if its admission would bring the administration of justice into serious disrepute.

Rule 96: Rules of Evidence in Cases of Sexual Assault

In cases of sexual violence, the Court shall be guided by and, where appropriate, apply the following principles:
  ii) Consent cannot be inferred by reason of any words or conduct of a victim where the victim is incapable of giving genuine consent;
  (iii) Consent cannot be inferred by reason of the silence of, or lack of resistance by, a victim to the alleged sexual violence;
  (iv) Credibility, character or predisposition to sexual availability of a victim or witness cannot be inferred by reason of sexual nature of the prior or subsequent conduct of a victim or witness.

Rule 97: Lawyer-Client Privilege

All communications between lawyer and client shall be regarded as privileged, and consequently disclosure cannot be ordered, unless:
  (i) The client consents to such disclosure; or
  (ii) The client has voluntarily disclosed the content of the communication to a third party, and that third party then gives evidence of that disclosure.
  (iii) The client has alleged ineffective assistance of counsel, in which case the privilege is waived as to all communications relevant to the claim of ineffective assistance.

Rule 98: Motion for Judgement of Acquittal

If, after the close of the case for the prosecution, the evidence is such that no reasonable tribunal of fact could be satisfied beyond a reasonable doubt of the accused's guilt on one or more counts of the indictment, the Trial Chamber shall enter a judgment of acquittal on those counts.

Section 4: Sentencing Procedure

Rule 99: Status of the Acquitted Person

(A) In case of acquittal, subject to Sub-Rule (B) below, the Special Court shall order the release of the accused.
(B) If, at the time the judgement of acquittal is pronounced, the Prosecutor advises the Trial Chamber in open court of his intention to file notice of appeal pursuant to Rule 108, the Trial Chamber may, on application of the Prosecutor and upon hearing the parties, in its discretion, issue an order for the continued detention of the accused, pending the determination of the appeal

Rule 100: Sentencing Procedure

(A) If the Trial Chamber convicts the accused or the accused enters a guilty plea, the Prosecutor shall submit any relevant information that may assist the Trial Chamber in determining an appropriate sentence no more than 14 days after such conviction or guilty plea. The defendant shall thereafter, but no more that 21 days after the Prosecutor's filing submit any relevant information that may assist the Trial Chamber in determining an appropriate sentence.
(B) Where the accused has entered a guilty plea, the Trial Chamber shall hear submissions of the parties at a sentencing hearing. Where the accused has been convicted by a Trial Chamber, the Trial Chamber may hear submissions of the parties at a sentencing.
(C) The sentence may be pronounced in a judgement in public and in the presence of the convicted person, subject to Sub-Rule 102 (B).

Rule 101: Penalties

(A) A person convicted by the Special Court, other than a juvenile offender, may be sentenced to imprisonment for a specific number of years.
(B) In determining the sentence, the Trial Chamber shall take into account the factors mentioned in Article 19 (2) of the Statute, as well as such factors as:
ii) Any mitigating circumstances including the substantial cooperation with the Prosecutor by the convicted person before or after conviction;
(iii) The extent to which any penalty imposed by a court of any State on the convicted person for the same act has already been served, as referred to in Article 9 (3) of the Statute.
(D) The Trial Chamber shall indicate whether multiple sentences shall be served consecutively or concurrently.

(D) Credit shall be given to the convicted person for the period, if any, during which the convicted person was detained in custody pending his surrender to the Special Court or pending trial or appeal.

Rule 102: Status of the Convicted Person

(A) Subject to the Trial Chamber's directions in terms of Rule 101, the sentence shall begin to run from the day it is pronounced under Rule 100 (B). However, as soon as notice of appeal is given, the enforcement of the judgement shall thereupon be stayed until the decision on the appeal has been delivered, the convicted person meanwhile remaining in detention, as provided in Rule 64.
(B) If, by a previous decision of the Trial Chamber, the convicted person has been provisionally released, or is for any other reason at liberty, and he is not present when the judgement is pronounced, the Trial Chamber shall issue a warrant for his arrest. On arrest, he shall be notified of the conviction and sentence, and the procedure provided in Rule 103 shall be followed.

Rule 103: Place of Imprisonment

(A) Imprisonment shall be served in Sierra Leone, unless circumstances require otherwise. The Special Court may conclude agreements with other countries willing to accept and imprison convicted persons.
(B) Transfer of the convicted person to the place of imprisonment shall be effected as soon as possible after the time limit for appeal has lapsed.

Rule 104: Forfeiture of Property

(A) After a judgement of conviction containing a specific finding as provided in Rule 88 (B), the Trial Chamber, at the request of the Prosecutor or at its own initiative, may hold a special hearing to determine the matter of property forfeiture, including the proceeds thereof, and may in the meantime order such provisional measures for the preservation and protection of the property or proceeds as it considers appropriate.
(B) The determination may extend to such property or proceeds, even in the hands of third parties not otherwise connected with the crime, for which the convicted person has been found guilty. Such third parties shall be entitled to appear at the hearing.
(C) The Trial Chamber may order the forfeiture of any property, proceeds and any assets it finds has been acquired unlawfully or by criminal conduct, and order its return to the rightful owner, or its transfer to the State of Sierra Leone, as circumstances may require.

Rule 105: Compensation to Victims

(A) The Registrar shall transmit to the competent authorities of the States concerned the judgement finding the accused guilty of a crime which has caused injury to a victim.
(B) Pursuant to the relevant national legislation, a victim or persons claiming through him may bring an action in a national court or other competent body to obtain compensation.
(C) For the purposes of a claim made under Sub-Rule (B) the judgement of the Special Court shall be final and binding as to the criminal responsibility of the convicted person for such injury.

PART VII—APPELLATE PROCEEDINGS

Rule 106: General Provisions

The rules of procedure and evidence that govern proceedings in the Trial Chambers shall apply as appropriate to proceedings in the Appeals Chamber.

Rule 107: Practice Directions for the Appeals Chamber

The President may issue Practice Directions, in consultation with the Vice-President, addressing detailed aspects of the conduct of proceedings before the Appeals Chamber.

Rule 108: Notice of Appeal

(A) Subject to Sub-Rule (B), a party seeking to appeal a judgement or sentence shall, not more than 14 days from the reception of the full judgement and sentence in English, file with the Registrar and serve upon the other parties a written notice of appeal, setting forth the grounds.

(B) In an appeal from a decision dismissing an objection based on lack of jurisdiction or a decision rendered under Rule 77 or Rule 91, such delay shall be fixed at seven days from the date on which the full decision is received in English. The party wishing to file a notice of appeal may apply to the Appeals Chamber under Rule 116 to enlarge the time so prescribed.

Rule 109 : Pre-Hearing Judge

(A) The Presiding Judge of the Appeals Chamber may designate from among its members a Judge responsible for the pre-hearing proceedings (the "Pre-Hearing Judge").

(B) The Pre-Hearing Judge shall ensure that the proceedings are not unduly delayed and shall take any measures related to procedural matters, including the issuing of decisions, orders and directions with a view to preparing the case for a fair and expeditious hearing.

(C) The Pre-Hearing Judge shall record the points of agreement and disagreement between the parties on matters of law and fact. In this connection, he or she may order the parties to file further written submissions with the Pre-Hearing Judge or the Appeals Chamber.

(D) The Appeals Chamber may of its own initiative exercise any of the functions of the Pre-Hearing Judge.

Rule 110: Record on Appeal

The record on appeal shall consist of the parts of the trial record as designated by the Pre-Hearing Judge, certified by the Registrar.

Rule 111: Appellant's Submissions

An Appellant's submissions shall be served on the other party or parties and filed with the Registrar within twenty one days of the notice of appeal pursuant to Rule 108.

Rule 112: Respondent's Submissions

A Respondent's submissions shall be served on the other party or parties and filed with the Registrar within fourteen days of the filing of the Appellant's submissions .

Rule 113: Submissions in Reply

(A) An Appellant may file submissions in reply within five days after the filing of the Respondent's submissions.

(B) No further submissions may be filed except with leave of the Appeals Chamber.

Rule 114: Date of Hearing

After the expiration of the time-limits for filing the submissions provided for in Rules 111, 112 and 113, the Appeals Chamber shall set the date for the hearing in open court, unless it decides to rule on such appeals based solely on the submissions of the parties. The Registrar shall notify the parties accordingly.

Rule 115: Additional Evidence

(A) A party may apply by motion to present before the Appeals Chamber additional evidence which was not available to it at the trial. Such motion must be served on the other party and filed with the Registrar not less than fifteen days before the date of the hearing.
(B) The Appeals Chamber shall authorize the presentation of such evidence if it considers that the interests of justice so require.

Rule 116: Extension of Time Limits

The Appeals Chamber may grant a motion to extend a time limit upon a showing of good cause.

Rule 117: Expedited Appeals Procedure

(A) An appeal under Rule 72 (D), 77 or 91 shall be heard expeditiously and may be determined entirely on the basis of written submissions. The record on appeal shall be the record of the Trial Chamber in the particular phase of proceeding that resulted in the impugned decision.
(B) All delays and other procedural requirements shall be fixed by an order of the Presiding Judge.
(C) Rules 109 to 114 and 118 (D) shall not apply to such appeals.

Rule 118: Judgement on Appeal

(A) The Appeals Chamber shall pronounce judgement on the basis of the record on appeal and on any additional evidence as has been presented to it.
(B) The judgement shall be rendered by a majority of the Judges. It shall be accompanied or followed as soon as possible by a reasoned opinion in writing, to which separate or dissenting opinions may be appended.
(C) In appropriate circumstances the Appeals Chamber may order that the accused be retried before the Trial Chamber.
(D) If the Appeals Chamber reverses an acquittal of an accused by the Trial Chamber on any count, the Appeals Chamber shall proceed to sentence the accused in respect of that offence.
(E) The judgement shall be pronounced in public, on a date of which notice shall have been given to the parties and counsel and at which they shall be entitled to be present.
(F) The written judgement shall be filed and registered with the Registry.

Rule 119: Status of the Accused Following Judgement on Appeal

(A) A sentence pronounced by the Appeals Chamber shall be enforced immediately.
(B) Where the accused is not present when the Appeal judgement is due to be delivered, it may, unless it pronounces his acquittal, order his arrest or surrender to the Special Court.

PART VIII—REVIEW PROCEEDINGS

Rule 120: Request for Review

Where a new fact has been discovered which was not known at the time of the proceedings before the Trial Chamber or Appeals Chamber and which could have been a decisive factor in reaching the decision, the convicted person or the Prosecutor may submit an application for a review of the judgement.

Rule 121: Preliminary Examination

An application for review shall be submitted to the Appeals Chamber. The Appeals Chamber may reject the application if it considers it to be unfounded. If it determines that the application is meritorious, it may, as appropriate:
    (i) Reconvene the Trial Chamber;
    (ii) Retain jurisdiction over the matter.

Rule 122: Appeals

The judgement of a Trial Chamber on review may be appealed in accordance with the provisions of Part VII.

PART IX—PARDON AND COMMUTATION OF SENTENCE

Rule 123: Notification by States

If, pursuant to the applicable law of the State in which the convicted person is imprisoned, he is eligible for pardon or commutation of sentence, the State concerned shall, in accordance with Article 23 of the Statute, notify the Special Court.

Rule 124: Determination by the President

There shall only be pardon or commutation of sentence if the President of the Special Court, in consultation with the judges, so decides on the basis of the interests of justice and the general principles of law.

Done in Middle Temple, London
7 March 2003

Judge Robertson
President

Judge Jallow

Judge King
Vice-President

Judge Thompson

Judge Ayoola

Judge Itoe

Judge Winter

Judge Boutet

INDICES

BIBLIOGRAPHY

ADJOVI and DELLA MORTE, "La notion de procès équitable devant les Tribunaux Pénaux Internationaux," *in* Ruiz Fabri (ed.), *La notion de procès equitable en droit international* (Paris, forthcoming 2002).

AKHAVAN, P., "Punishing War Crimes in the Former Yugoslavia: A Critical Juncture for the New World Order," 15 *Human Rights Quarterly* 262 (1993).

———, "The Yugoslav Tribunal at a Crossroads: The Dayton Peace Agreement and Beyond," 18 *Human Rights Quarterly* 259 (1996).

ALDRICH, G.H., "Jurisdiction of the International Criminal Tribunal for the Former Yugoslavia," 90 *American Journal of International Law* 64 (1996).

ALVAREZ, J.E., "Nuremberg Revisited: The *Tadić* Case," 7 *European Journal of International Law* 245 (1996).

AMATI, E., "La repressione dei crimini di guerra tra diritto internazionale e diritto interno," *in* Illuminati, G., L. Stortoni, M. Virgilio (a cura di), *Crimini internazionali e giustizia. Dai Tribunali Internazionali alle Commissioni Verità e Riconciliazione*, 98 ss. (Torino, 2000).

AMBOS, K., *Der "Allgemeiner Teil" des Völkerstrafrechts. Ansätze einer Dogmatisierung* (Berlin, 2002).

———, "Straflosigkeit (impunity) von schweren Menschenrechtsverletzungen und die Rolle des Völkerstrafrechts," *in* Arnold, Jörg, Björn Burkhardt, Walter Gropp, Hans-Georg Koch (Hrsg.), *Grenzüberschreitungen. Beiträge zum 60. Geburtstag von Albin Eser*. 249–277 (Freiburg i. Br.: 1995).

———, "Establishing an International Criminal Court and an International Criminal Code: Observations from an International Criminal Law Viewpoint," *European Journal of International Law* 519–544 (1996).

———, "Verbrechenselemente sowie Verfahrens- und Beweisregeln des Internationalen Strafgerichtshofs," *Neue Juristische Wochenschrift* 405–410 (2001).

AMBOS, K., and S. WIRTH, "Genocide and War Crimes in the Former Yugoslavia before German Criminal Courts (1994–2000)," *in* Fischer, Horst, Claus Kreß and Sascha Rolf Lüder (dir.), *International and National Prosecution of Crimes under International Law* 769–797 (Berlin: 2001).

ANDUJAR, F.C., "Individuel Aansprakelijkheid Voor Misdrijven Begaan Tijdens Niet—Internationaal Gewapend Conflict: Het Statuut Van Den Haag," 44 *Ars Aequi Jurisdisch Studentenblad* 170 (1995).

ARBOUR and BERGSMO, "Conspicuous Absence of Jurisdictional Overreach," *in* H. von Hebel, J. Lammers and J. Schukking (eds.), *Reflections on the International Criminal Court—Essays in Honour of Adriaan Bos* 129–140 (The Hague: T.M.C. Asser Press, 1999).

ARSANJANI, M., "Reflections on the Jurisdiction and Trigger-Mechanism of the International Criminal Court," in *Reflections on the International Criminal Court Court—Essays in Honour of Adriaan Bos* 57–77 (The Hague: T.M.C. Asser Press, 1999).

ASCENSIO, H., E. DECAUX, and A. PELLET, *Droit International Pénal* (Paris: Pedone, 2000).

ASCENSIO, H. and A. PELLET, "L'activité du Tribunal pénal international pour l'ex-Yougoslavie (1993–1995)," 41 *Annuaire français de droit international* 101 (1995).

ASCENSIO, H. and R. MAISON, "L'activité des Tribunaux pénaux internationaux pour l'ex-Yougoslavie (1995–1997) et pour le Rwanda (1994–1997)," *Annuaire français de droit international* 368–402 (1997).

ASHWORTH, A., *Principles of Criminal Law*. Oxford 3. Aufl. 1999 (2d ed. 1995).

ASKIN, Kelly D., "Sexual Violence in Decisions and Indictments of the Yugoslav and Rwandan Tribunals: Current Status," 93 *American Journal of International Law* 97–123 (1999).

ASKIN, Kelly D., "The International War Crimes Trial of Anto Furund_ija: Major Progress Toward Ending the Cycle of Impunity for Rape Crimes," *Leiden Journal for International Law* 935–955 (1999).

BAARDA, T. and R.M. KAMPHORST, "Het Joegoslavie Tribunaal en de Hoge Raad: een Onwennige Relatie," 71 *Nederlands Juristenblad* 1163 (1996).

BALCHETTI, P., "Il potere del consiglio di sicurezza di istituire tribunali penali internazionali," *Rivista di Diritto Internazionale* 413 (1996).

BARKHUIS, N., "Het slachtoffer als getuige: Een Week bij de Nikolić orzitting voor het Joegoslavie Tribunaal," *Nemesis* 81 (Special Edition,1996).

BASSIOUNI, M. Cherif, *Crimes Against Humanity in International Criminal Law*. (The Hague: 1999).

———, "Enslavement," *International Criminal Law—Crimes* 663–704. (3 vols., M.C. Bassiouni ed., Transnational Publishers, 1998).

———, "The United Nations ad hoc Tribunal for the Former Yugoslavia," *1993 Proceedings of the American Society of International Law* 20.

———, "The United Nations Commission of Experts Established Pursuant to Security Council Resolution 780 (1992)," 88 *American Journal of International Law* 784 (1994).

———, "Former Yugoslavia, Investigating Violations of International Humanitarian Law and Establishing an International Criminal Tribunal," 25 *Security Dialogue* 409 (1994).

———, "Former Yugoslavia: Investigating Violations of International Humanitarian Law and Establishing an International Criminal Tribunal," 18 *Fordham International Law Journal* 1191 (1995).

———, *Crimes Against Humanity in International Criminal Law* (Kluwer Law International, 2d. rev. ed.).

———, and P. MANIKAS, *The Law of the International Criminal Tribunal for the Former Yugoslavia* (Transnational Publishers, Inc., 1996).

BEAMON, Martine M., "*Illinois v. Perkins:* Has Our Criminal Justice System Turned 'Accusatorial' to 'Inquisitorial'?," 59 *University of Pittsburgh Law Review* 669–687.

BEANE, D.A. and L. HEFFERNAN, "The International Tribunal for the Former Yugoslavia: A Progress Report: Part I," 14 *Irish Law Times* 226 (1996).

———, "The International Tribunal for the Former Yugoslavia: A Progress Report: Part II," 14 *Irish Law Times* 250 (1996).

BEM Achour R., and S. LAGHMANI (Sous la direction de), *Justice et Juridictions Internationales*, Rencontres Internationales de la FacultÈ des Sciences Juridiques Politiques et Sociales de Tunis. Ed. A Pedone, Paris, 2000.

BENVENUTI, P., "Complementarity of the International Criminal Court to National Criminal Jurisdictions," *in* F. Lattanzi and W.A. Schabas (eds.), 1 *Essays on the Rome Statute of the International Criminal Court* 21–51 (Il Sirente, Ripa Fagnano Alto (AQ), 1999).

BERGSMO, M., "The Establishment of the International Tribunal on War Crimes," 14 *Human Rights Law Journal* 371 (1993).

———, "International Criminal Tribunal for the Former Yugoslavia: Recent Developments," 15 *Human Rights Law Journal* 405 (1994).

BERNARDINI, A., "Il Tribunale penale internazionale per la (ex) Jugoslavia: considerazioni giuridiche," IV *I Diritti Dell'Uomo* 15 (1993).

BESON DE VEZAC, Marie-Pierre, "La Convention du 17 juillet 1998 instituant la Cour pénale internationale: coup d'épée dans l'eau ou avancée décisive?," 225 *Les Petites Affiches* (11 novembre 1999).

BLAKESLEY, C., "Comparing the *Ad Hoc* Tribunal for Crimes against Humanitarian Law in the Former Yugoslavia and the Project for an International Criminal Court Prepared by the International Law Commission," 67 *Revue Internationale de Droit Pénal* 139 (1996).

BOHLANDER, Michael, "International Criminal Tribunals and Their Power to Punish Contempt and False Testimony," 12 *Criminal Law Forum* 91–118 (2001).

———, "Possible Conflicts of Jurisdiction with Ad-hoc International Tribunal," *in* A. Cassese, P. Gaeta, J.R.W.D. Jones (eds.), *The Rome Statute of the International Criminal Court. A Commentary* (3 vols., Oxford University Press, 2002).

BONINO Emma, "Droits de l'Homme, actions humanitaire et justice internationale," 1 *Revue du marché unique* 5–8 (1er janvier 1997).

BOSLY, H.D., "Actualite du Tribunal International Penal," 55 *Annales de Droit de Louvain* 3 (1995).

BOYLE, D., "Quelle justice pour les Khmers rouges?,"40 *Revue trimestrielle des Droits de l'homme* 773–826 (1er octobre 1999).

BRINGA, T., *Being Muslim the Bosnian Way: Identity and Community in a Central Bosnian Village* (Princeton University Press, 1995).

BROOMHALL, B., "La Cour Pénale Internationale: Présentation générale et Coopération des Etats," 13(4) *Nouvelles études pénales* 48–81 (1999).

BROWN, Bartram S., "International Prosecutor, Independent Counsel," 144(77) *Chigaco Daily Law Bulletin* 6.

———, "Nationality and Internationality in International Humanitarian Law," 34(2) *Stanford Journal of International Law* 347–406 (1998).

———, "Primacy or Complementarity: Reconciling the Jurisdiction of National Courts and International Criminal Tribunals," 23 *Yale Journal of International Law* 383 (1998).

BULLIER, Antoine J., "Les Etats face à la justice pénale internationale, coopération ou contrainte?," 185 *Les Petites Affiches* 6–7 (16 septembre 1999).

BYRNES, A., "Torture and Other Offences Involving the Violation of the Physical or Mental Integrity of the Human Person," *in* G.K. McDonald and O. Swaak-Goldman (eds.), *Substantive and Procedural Aspect of International Law* 197–245 (Kluwer Law International, 2000).

CAIANIELLO, M.-Fronza, E., "Il principio di legalità nello Statuto della Corte penale internazionale," *Indice penale* 307 (2002).

CARELLA, G., "Il Tribunale penale internazionale per l'ex Jugoslavia," *in* Picone, P. (ed.), *Interventi delle nazione unite i diritto internazionale* (Cedam: Padua, 1995).

CASSESE, Antonio, "Il Tribunale internazionale per l'ex Jugoslavia: Al passo decisivo," 1 *Diritto Penale e Processo* 12 (1995).

———, "The Statute of the International Criminal Court: Some Preliminary Reflections," 10 *European Journal of International Law* 144–172 (1999).

———, P. Gaeta, and John R.W.D. Jones, (eds.), *The Rome Statute of the International Criminal Court: A Commentary* (3 vols., Oxford University Press, 2002).

———, and M. Delmas-Marty (dir.), *Crimes internationaux et juridictions internationales. Valeurs, politique et droit* (Paris: PUF, 2002).

———, *Juridictions nationales et crimes internationaux* (Paris: PUF, 2002). PUF, Paris, 2002.

CASTILLO, M., "La compétence du tribunal pour l'ex-Yougoslavie." 98 *Revue Generale de Droit International Public* 61 (1994).

CATENACCI, M., "Nullum crimen sine lege," *in* Lattanzi, Flavio (dir.), *The International Criminal Court. Comments on the Draft Statute* 159–170 (Naples: 1998).

CHAVRIN, R., "Premières observations sur la création du Tribunal Permanent international de la résolution 808 du Conseil de Sécurité des Nations Unies," IV *I Diritti Dell'Uomo* 26 (1993).

CHINKIN, C., "Rape and Sexual Abuse of Women in International Law," 5 *European Journal of International Law* 326 (1994).

CHRESTIA Philippe, "L'influence des Droits de l'Homme sur l'évolution du droit international contemporain," 40 *Revue Trimestrielle des Droits de l'Homme* 715–738 (1er octobre 1999).

CLEIREN, C.P.M., "Het Joegoslavië-tribunaal: een noodzakelijk surplus," 24 *Nederlands Tijdschrift voor Rechtsfilosofie en Rechtstheorie* 43 (1995).

COHEN, P. J., "Ending the War and Securing Peace in Former Yugoslavia," 6 *Pace International Law Review* 19 (1994).

COOLEN, G.L., "Is de militaire rechter wel bevoegd kennis te nemen van oorlogsmisdaden gepleegd in het voormalig Joegoslavië?," 88 *Militair Rechtelijk Tijdschrift* 65 (1995).

COOLEN, G.L., "Nogmaals: oorlogsmisdrijven gepleegd in het voormalig Joegoslavië," 88 *Militair Rechtelijk Tijdschrift* 104 (1995).

COONAN, T., "Prosecuting and Defending Violations of Genocide and Humanitarian Law: The International Tribunal for the Former Yugoslavia," *1994 Proceedings of the American Society of International Law* 239.

CROWE, C., "Command Responsibility in the Former Yugoslavia: The Chances for Successful Prosecution," 29 *University of Richmond Law Review* 191 (1995).

D'AMATO, Anthony, "Peace vs. Accountability in Bosnia," 88 *American Journal of International Law* 500 (1994).

DAVID, E., "Le tribunal international pénal pour l'ex-Yougoslavie," 6 *Revue Belge de Droit International* 565 (1993).

DAVIS, P.H., "The Politics of Prosecuting Rape as War Crime," *The International Lawyer* 1223–1248 (2000).

DEAK, L., "For the Former Yugoslavia," *1993 Proceedings of the American Society of International Law* 20.

DE GOUTTES, R., "A propos du tribunal international institué pour les crimes de guerre commis depuis 1991 dans l'ex-Yougoslavie: aperáu des différentes positions adoptées par les Etats lors des travaux préparatoires," *in Archives de Politique Criminelle* 35 (Paris: 1994).

DELLA MORTE, G., "La potestà giurisdizione della Corte Penale Internazionale: complementavità, condizione di procedibilità, soggetti legittimati a richiedere l'esercizio dell'azione penale e ne bis in idem," *in* G. Della Morte, A. Marchesi and S. Laurenti (eds.), *La Corte Penale Internazionale: problemi e prospettive (The International Criminal Court: Issues and Perspectives)* (Napoliz: Vivarium, 2002) (forthcoming).

DELMAS MARTY, M. (Dir.), "Du droit international au droit national: l'exemple du génocide," *in* VII *Criminalité économique et atteintes à la dignité de la personne*, Partie II, 171–330 (Paris: Ed. de la Maison des Sciences de Lí Homme, 2001).

———, The ICC and the Interaction of International and National Systems," *in* Cassese, A., P. Gaeta, and J.R.W.D. Jones (eds), *The Rome Statute of the International Criminal Court* (Oxford University Press, 2002).

———, *Pour un droit commun*, (Paris: 1994).

———, *Trois défis pour un droit mondial* (Paris: 1998).

———, "Criminalité économique et atteintes à la dignité de la personne," VII *Les processus d'internationalisation* (Paris: 2001).

———, Variations autour d'un droit commun. Travaux préparatoires, Société de législation comparée (Paris: 2001).

DERBY, D., "Torture" *in* M. Cherif Bassiouni (ed.), *International Criminal Law—Crimes* 705–749 (3 vols., Transnational Publishers, 1998).

DI MARINO, G., "Le tribunal pénal international crée par la résolution 808 du Conseil de sécurité de l'O.N.U.," 63 *Revue Internationale de Droit Pénal* 1485 (1993).

DIXON, Rosalind, "New Developments in the International Criminal Tribunal for the Former Yugoslavia: Prominent Leaders Indicted and Jurisdiction Established," 8 *Leiden Journal of International Law* 449 (1995).

———, "Rape as a Crime in International Humanitarian Law: Where to from Here?," 13(3) *European Journal of International Law* 697–719 (June 2002).

———, "The International Criminal Tribunal for the Former Yugoslavia: Working for Peace and Justice in the Balkans," 20 *South African Yearbook of International Law* 25 (1995).

DREW, Catriona, "The East Timor Story: International Law on Trial," 12(4) *European Journal of International Law* 651–684 (September 2001) (on the self-determination aspects of East Timor's struggle for independence).

DUGARD, J., "Possible Conflicts of Jurisdiction with Truth Commission," *in* A. Cassese, P. Gaeta, J.R.W.D. Jones (eds.), *The Rome Statute of the International Criminal Court. A Commentary* (3 vols., Oxford University Press, 2002).

DUNN, James, "Crimes Against Humanity in East Timor, January to October 1999: Their Nature and Causes," *available at* www.etan.org/news/2001a/dunn1.htm.

DUPUY, Pierre-Marie, "La genèse de la Cour Pénale Internationale," *L'Astrée* 7–12 (1er septembre 1999).

ECONOMIDES, S. and P. TAYLOR, "United Nations Experience in Cambodia, Former Yugoslavia, and Somalia," *The New Interventionism 1991–1994*. Ed. J. Mayall. (Cambridge University Press, 1996).

EDWARDS, C. and P. ROWE, "The International Criminal Tribunal for the Former Yugoslavia: The Decision of the Appeals Chamber on the Interlocutory Appeal on Jurisdiction in the Tadić Case," 45 *International and Comparative Law Quarterly* 691 (1996).

ELST, R. van, "Afscheid van Joegoslavië: over oorlogsmisdrijven tegen de menselijkheid begaan in voormalig Joegoslavië en de Nederlandse rechter," 69 *Nederlands Juristenblad* 1401 (1994).

ESER, Albin, "Defences in Strafverfahren wegen Kriegsverbrechen," *in* Schmoller, Kurt (Hrsg.), *Festschrift für Otto Triffterer zum 65* 755–775, Geburtstag. (New York:Wien 1996). 755–775.

———, "Funktionen, Methoden und Grenzen der Strafrechtsvergleichung," *in* Albrecht, Hans-Jörg, F. Dünkel, H.J. Kerner, J. Kürzinger, H. Schöch, K. Sessar, and B. Villmow, (Hrsg.), *Internationale Perspektiven in Kriminologie und Strafrecht. Festschrift für Günther Kaiser zum 70, Geburtstag* 1499–1529 (Berlin: Band 2., 1998).

———, "Verhaltensregeln und Behandlungsnormen. Bedenkliches zur Rolle des Normadressaten im Strafrecht," *in* Eser, Albin, Ulrike Schittenhelm and Heribert Schumann (Hrsg.), *Festschrift für Theodor Lenckner zum 70, Geburtstag* 25–54 (München 1998).

———, and J. Arnold (Hrsg.), "Strafrecht in Reaktion auf Systemunrecht. Vergleichende Einblicke" *in Transitionsprozesse. Band 2 Deutschland* (H. Kreicker, M. Ludwig, K. Rossig, A. Rost, S. Zimmermann, Freiburg i.Br.: 2000).

FALVEY, J.L., "United Nations Justice or Military Justice: Which Is the Oxymoron? An Analysis of the Rules of Procedure and Evidence of the International Tribunal for the Former Yugoslavia," 19 *Fordham International Law Journal* 475 (1995).

FENRICK, W., "Some International Law Problems Related to Prosecutions Before the International Criminal Tribunal for the Former Yugoslavia," 6 *Duke Journal of Comparative and International Law* 103 (1995).

FITZGERALD, K., "Problems of Prosecution and Adjudication of Rape and Other Sexual Assaults under International Law," *European Journal of International Law* 638–663 (1997).

FLETCHER, G., *Rethinking Criminal Law*. (Boston/Toronto 1978: Oxford, 2000).

———, *Basic Concepts of Criminal Law* (New York: Oxford, 1998).

FRONZA, E., "Genocide in the Rome Statute," *in* Lattanzi, Flavia and William A. Schabas (dir.), I *Essays on the Rome Statute of the International Criminal Court* 105–137 (Italy: Ripa Fagnano Alto, 1999).

FRULLI, Micaela, "The Special Court for Sierra Leone: Some Preliminary Comments," 11 *European Journal of International Law* 857–870 (2000).

———, "I crimini di diritto internazionale nell'interpretazione della giurisprudenza internazionale: il caso Akayesu," *in Illuminati*, G., L. Stortoni, and M. Virgilio (a cura di), *Crimini internazionali e giustizia. Dai Tribunali Internazionali alle Commissioni Verità e Riconciliazione* 96 (Torino, 2000).

———, and N. Guillou, "Droit pénal commun et méthodes comparées: réflexions à partir du crime de génocide," in Delmas-Marty, M., H. Muir Watt, and H. Ruiz Fabri (dir.), *Variations autour du droit commun, Société de législation comparée* 277–300 (Paris: 2002).

GAETA, P., "Is NATO Authorised or Obliged to Arrest Persons Indicted by the International Criminal Tribunal for the Former Yugoslavia?," 9 *European Journal of International Law* 174 (1998).

GALLANT, K.S., "Securing the Presence of Defendants in the International Tribunal for the Former Yugoslavia, International Experts Conference on International Criminal Justice: Historic and Contemporary Perspectives," I.S.I.S.C., Siracusa, Italy, December 4–8 1994.

GAUTRON, Jérôme and Pierre-Yves MONJAL, "La décision 98–408 du Conseil Constitutionnel relative au statut de la Cour pénale internationale: un soutien juridique aux réticences nationale," 4 *Revue de la recherche juridique, Droit prospectif* 1207–1235 (1er octobre 1999).

GENUGTEN, W.J.M. van, "Het Joegoslavië-tribunaal: pervertering van het internationale recht?," 24 *Nederlands Tijdschrift voor Rechtsfilosofie en Rechtstheorie* 49 (1995).

GENTILI, A. M., and A. LOLLINI, "L'esperienza delle Commissioni per la verità e la riconciliazione: il caso sudafricano in una prospettiva giuridico-politica," *dans* Illuminati, Stortoni, et Virgilio (dir.), *Crimini internazionali tra diritto e giustizia. Dai Tribunali internazionali alle Commissioni Verità e Riconciliazione* 163 (Turin, 2000).

GETTI, J.P., and K. LESCURE, "Historique du fonctionnement du Tribunal pénal international pour l'ex-Yougoslavie," 67 *Revue Internationale de Droit Pénal* 233 (1996).

GIESE, M., "Das Internationale Jugoslawien-Tribunal: Rechtsgrundlage, Ausgestaltung und erste Arbeitsergebnisse," 36 *WGO: Monatshefte fur Osteuropäisches Recht* 23 (1994).

GIL GIL, A., *Derecho Penal Internacional. Especial consideración del delito de genocidio* (Madrid 1999).

———, "Die Tatbestände der Verbrechen gegen die Menschlichkeit und des Völkermords im Römischen Statut des Internationalen Strafgerichtshofs," 112 *Zeitschrift für Gesamte Strafrechtswissenschaft* 382–397 (2000).

GOLDSTONE, Richard J., "The International Tribunal for the Former Yugoslavia: A Case Study of Security Council Action," 6 *Duke Journal of Comparative and International Law* (1995).

———, "International Jurisdiction and Prosecutorial Crimes," 47 *Cleveland State Law Review* 473–481.

GONZALEZ, J.S., "El Tribunal Internacional de Yugoslavia," 95/1–2 *Justicia* 207 (1995).

GRADITZKY, "Individual Criminal Responsibility for Violations of International Humanitarian Law Committed in Non-International Armed Conflicts," 322 *International Review of the Red Cross* 29–56 (1 March 1998).

GRAEFRATH, B., "Jugoslawientribunal—Präzedenzfall trotz fragwürdiger Rechtsgrundlage," 47 *Neue Justiz* 433 (1993).

GRANT, S., "Protection Mechanisms and the Yugoslav Crisis," 8.1 *Interights Bulletin* 3 (1994).

GRAVEN, J., "Les crimes contre l'Humanité. La Convention internationale sur le génocide," 76 *Recueil des cours de l'Académie de droit international de La Haye* (1950).

GREENWOOD, Christopher, "The International Tribunal for Former Yugoslavia," 69 *International Affairs* 641 (1993).

———, "International Humanitarian Law and the *Tadić* Case," 7 *European Journal of International Law* 265 (1996).

GROSS, O., "The Grave Breaches System and the Armed Conflict in the Former Yugoslavia," 16 *Michigan Journal of International Law* 783 (1995).

GUILLAUME, G., "Terrorisme et droit international," 215 *Recueil des cours de l'Académie de droit international de La Haye* (1998-III).

HADDAD, Judith, "Décision du Conseil constitutionnel du 22 janvier 1999: examen de la compatibilité du statut de la Cour pénale internationale avec la constitution française," 2 *Revue générale de droit international public* 464–470 (1er mars 1999).

HAJAM, M., "Creation et Competences du Tribunal Pénal International," 26 *Etudes Internationales* 503 (1995).

HALL, Christopher Keith, "The Third and Fourth Sessions of the Preparatory Comittee Establishment of an International Criminal Court," 92 *American Journal of International Law* 124–133.

HALL, K., "The Principle of Complementarity," *in The International Criminal Court, The Making of the Rome Statute, Issues, Negotiations, Results* 41–79 (The Hague/London/Boston: 1999).

HAMPSON, F.J., "Violation of Fundamental Rights in the Former Yugoslavia: The Case for a War Crimes Tribunal," David Davies Memorial Institute of International Studies, Occasional Paper No. 3 (1993).

HEALEY, S., "Prosecuting Rape Under the Statute of the War Crimes Tribunal for the Former Yugoslavia," 21 *Brooklyn Journal of International Law* 327 (1995).

HEBEL, H. von, "An International Tribunal for the Former Yugoslavia; An Act of Powerlessness or a New Challenge for the International Community?," 4 *Netherlands Quarterly of Human Rights* 437 (1994).

———, "Het straftribunaal voor voormalig Joegoslavië; Een korte toelichting," 6 *VN Forum* 1 (1993).

———, "Tribunaal voor Joegoslavië; een gerechtvaardigde doch riskante onderneming," 43 *Ars Aequi* 145 (1994).

———, and M. Kelt, "Some Comments on the Elements of Crimes for the Crimes of the ICC Statute," *in* 3 *Yearbook of International Humanitarian Law* 273–288 (H. Fischer, and A. McDonald, Edís 2000) (TMC Asser Press, 2002).

HEINTSCHEL V. HEINEGG, W., "Zur Zulassigkeit der Errichtung des Jugoslawien-Strafgerichtshofes durch Resolution 827 (1993)," 9 *Humanitäres Völkerrecht* 75 (1996).

HERDER, Stephen and TITTEMORE, Brian D., "Seven Candidates for the Prosecution: Accountability for the Crimes of the Khmer Rouge," *available at* www.wcl.american.edu/pub/humright/wcrimes/khmerrouge.pdf.

HIGGINS, R., "The New United Nations and Former Yugoslavia," 69 *International Affairs* 3 (1993).

——— (ed.), *Terrorism and International Law* (London:Routledge, 1997).

HOCHKAMMER, K.A., "The Yugoslavia War Crimes Tribunal: The Compatibility of Peace, Politics, and International Law," 28 *Vanderbuilt Journal of Transnational Law* 119 (1995).

HOGAN-DORAN, J., "Murder as a Crime Under International Law and the Statute of the International Criminal Tribunal for the Former Yugoslavia: Of Law, Legal Language, and a Comparative Approach to Legal Meaning," *Leiden Journal of International Law* 165–181 (1998).

HOLLWEG, C., "Le nouveau Tribunal international de l'O.N.U. et le conflit en ex-Yougoslavie: un défi pour le droit humanitaire dans le nouvel ordre mondial," 105 (5) *Revue du Droit Public et de la Science Politique en France et a l'Etranger 1357* 1357–1397 (octobre 1994).

———, "Vom Jugoslawientribunal der UNO zum allgemein Internationalen Strafgerichtshof?," 112 *Schwizerische Zeitschrift fur Strafrecht* 251 (1994).

HOLMES, J., "Complementarity: National Courts versus the ICC," *in* A. Cassese, P. Gaeta, J.R.W.D. Jones (eds.), *The Rome Statute of the International Criminal Court. A Commentary* (3 vols., Oxford University Press, 2002).

JESCHECK, H. H., *Die Verantwortlichkeit der Staatsorgane nach Völkerstrafrecht* (Bonn: 1952).

———, "Die internationale Genocidium-Konvention vom 9. Dezember 1948 und die Lehre vom Völkerstrafrecht," 66 *Zeitschrift für Gesamte Strafrechtswissenschaft* 193–217 (1954).

———, *Entwicklung, Aufgaben und Methoden der Strafrechtsvergleichung* (Tübingen, 1955).

———, "Gegenwärtiger Stand und Zukunftsaussichten der Entwurfsarbeiten auf dem Gebiet des Völkerstrafrechts," *in* Hilde Kaufmann, Erich Schwinge, and Hans Welzel (Hrsg.), *Erinnerungsgabe für Max Grünhut. Marburg* 47–60 (1965).

———, and Weigend, T., *Lehrbuch des Strafrechts* (Allgemeiner Teil. 5 Aufl. Berlin: 1996).

JONES, John R.W.D., "The Implications of the Dayton Peace Agreement for the International Criminal Tribunal for the Former Yugoslavia," 7 *European Journal of International Law* 226 (1996).

———, "Immunity and Double Criminality: General Augusto Pinochet before the House of Lords" *in International Law in the Post-Cold War World: Essays in Honour of Judge Li*, (Sienho Yee and Wang Tieya eds., Routledge, 2001).

JOYNER, C., "Enforcing Human Rights Standards in the Former Yugoslavia: The Case for an International War Crimes Tribunal," 22 *Denver Journal of International Law and Policy* 235 (1994).

———, "Strengthening Enforcement of Humanitarian Law: Reflections on the International Criminal Tribunal for the Former Yugoslavia," 6 *Duke Journal of Comparative and International Law* 79 (1995).

KIRSCH, P., and J. HOLMES, "The Rome Conference on an International Criminal Court: The Negotiating Process," 93 *American Journal of International Law* 2–12 (1999).

KLIPP, A., "Witnesses before the International Criminal Tribunal for the Former Yugoslavia," 67 *Revue Internationale de Droit Pénal* 267 (1996).

KOOIJMANS, P.H., "The Judging of War Criminals: Individual Responsibility and Jurisdiction," 8 *Leiden Journal of International Law* 443 (1995).

KRASS, C. D., "Bringing the Perpetrators of Rape in the Balkans to Justice: Time for an International Criminal Court," 22 *Denver Journal of International Law and Policy* 317 (1994).

KRESS, C., Strafen, *Strafvollstreckung und internationale Zusammenarbeit im Statut des Internationalen Strafgerichtshofes* 151–161 (HuV 1998).

———, *Die Kristallisation eines Allgemeinen Teils des Völkerstrafrechts: Die Allgemeinen Prinzipien des Strafrechts im Statut des Internationalen Strafgerichtshofs* 4–10 (HuV 1999).

———, *Die Kristallisation eines Allgemeinen Teils des Völkerstrafrechts: Die Allgemeinen Prinzipien des Strafrechts im Statut des Internationalen Strafgerichtshofs* 4–10 (HuV, 1999).

———, "Zur Methode der Rechtsfindung im Allgemeinen Teil des Völkerstrafrechts. Die Bewertung von Tötungen im Nötigungsnotstand durch die Rechtsmittelkammer des Internationalen Straftribunals für das ehemalige Jugoslawien im Fall Erdemovic," 111 *ZStW* 597–623 (1999).

———, *Vom Nutzen eines deutschen Völkerstrafgesetzbuchs* (Baden-Baden: 2000).

———, "Völkerstrafrecht in Deutschland," *NstZ* 617–626 (2000).

———, "War Crimes Committed in Non-International Armed Conflict and the Emerging System of International Criminal Justice," 30 *IYHR* 103–177 (2000).

——— and F. LATTANZI (dir.), I *The Rome Statute and Domestic Legal Orders* (Baden-Baden: Ripa Fagnano Alto (Italien), 2000).

KRIEG Jean-François, "L'autorité des juridictions internationales confrontée aux principes d'indépendance et d'impartialité du juge," 209 *Les Petites Affiches* 4–12 (19 octobre 2000).

KRITZ and FINCI, "A Truth Reconciliation Commission in Bosnia and Herzegovina: An Idea Whose Time Has Come," 3(1) *International Law FORUM du droit international* (2001).

KUPFERBERG, M. I., "Balkan War Crimes Trials: Forum Selection," XVII *Boston College International and Comparative Law Review* 375 (1994).

LABER, J. and NIZICH, I., "The War Crimes Tribunal for the Former Yugoslavia: Problems and Prospects," *The Fletcher Forum* 7 (Summer/Fall 1994).

LAKATOS, A.C., "Evaluating the Rules of Procedure & Evidence for the International Tribunal in the Former Yugoslavia: Balancing Witnesses' Needs Against Defendants' Rights," 46 *Hastings Law Journal* 909 (1995).

LAMB, S., "The Powers of Arrest of the International Criminal Tribunal for the Former Yugoslavia," *British Yearbook of International Law* (1999).

LATTANZI, F., "Alcune riflessioni su un Tribunale ad hoc per la ex Jugoslavia," IV *I Diritti Dell'Uomo* 32 (1993).

———, "La primazia del Tribunale penale internazionale per la ex-Iugoslavia sulle giurisdizioni interne," 79 *Rivista di Diritto Internazionale* 597 (1996).

———, "The Rome Statute and State Sovereignty, ICC Competence, Jurisdiction Links, Trigger Mechanism," *in Essays on the Rome Statute of the International Criminal Court* 51–67 (Il Sirente: Teramo, 2000).

———, "Compétence de la Cour pénale internationale et consentement des Etats," *in* 2 *RGDIP*, 426–444 (1999).

———, "Rapporti fra giurisdizioni penali internazionali e giurisdizioni penali interne," *in Crimini di guerra e competenza delle giurisdizioni nazionali* 47–75 (Milano).

——— and Schabas W. (eds.), I *Essays on the Rome Statute of the International Criminal Court* (Il Sirente: Teramo, 2000).

——— and Sciso, E. (eds.), *Di tribunali penali internazionale ad hoc a una corte permanente.* (Editoriale Scientisica. Napoli: 1996).

LEE, Roy S., *The International Criminal Court: The Making of the Rome Statute* (Kluwer: 1999).

LEIGH, M., "The Yugoslav Tribunal: Use of Unnamed Witnesses Against Accused," 90 *American Journal Of International Law* 235 (1996).

LEMKIN, R., "Genocide as Crime under International Law," 41 *American Journal of International Law* 145 et seq. (1947).

LEVIE, H.S., "Prosecuting War Crimes Before an International Tribunal," 28 *Akron Law Review* 429 (1995).

LINTON, Suzanna, "Cambodia, East Timor and Sierra Leone: Experiments in International Justice," 12 *Criminal Law Forum* 185 (2001).

———, "Rising from the Ashes: The Creation of a Viable Criminal Justice System in East Timor," 25 *Melbourne University Law Review* 122 (2001).

LOLLINI, A., "La construction d'une mémoire collective en Afrique du Sud. La Commission vérité et réconciliation: hypertrophie de la sentence ou hypertrophie de l'histoire?," *L'Astrée* 25 n. 8 (1999).

LOPEZ, L., "Uncivil Wars: The Challenge of Applying International Humanitarian Law to Internal Armed Conflicts," 79 *Minnesota Law Review* 1413 (1995).

LUCHAIRE François, "La Cour pénale internationale et la responsabilité du chef de l'Etat devant le Conseil constitutionnel," 2 *Revue du Droit public* 457–479 (1 avril 1999).

MAISON, R., "Les Premiers Cas d'Application des Dispositions Pénales des Convention de Genève par les Juridictions Internes," 6 *European Journal of International Law* 260 (1995).

———, "La décision de la Chambre de première instance No. 1 du Tribunal pénal international pour l'ex-Yougoslavie dans l'affaire Nikolić," 7 *European Journal of International Law* 284 (1996).

———, "Le crime de génocide dans les premiers jugements du tribunal pénal international pour Rwanda," *R.G.D.P.* 129–145 (1999).

MALCOLM, N., *Bosnia: A Short History* (New York University Press: 1998).

———, *Kosovo: A Short History* (Macmillan: 1998).

MANACORDA, S. *L'armonizzazione dei sistemi penali: una introduzione*, dans Centro nazionale di prevenzione e difesa sociale, *La giustizia penale italiana nella prospettiva internazionale* (Milano: 2000).

MARTIN, D.A., "Reluctance to Prosecute War Crimes: Of Causes and Cures," 34 *Virginia Journal of International Law* 255 (1994).

MARTIN, P.M., "La compétence de la compétence (à propos de l'arrêt Tadić, Tribunal pénal international, Chambre d'appel, 2 octobre 1995)," 1996 *Recueil Dalloz Sirey* 157 (1996).

MAYER Danièle, "La Cour pénale internationale: droit pénal et procédure applicables," 8 *L'Astrée* 13–18 (1 septembre 1999).

MCCOUBREY, H., "The Armed Conflict in Bosnia and Proposed War Crimes Trials," XI

International Relations 411 (1993).
MELTZER, B.D., "War Crimes: The Nuremberg Trial and the Tribunal for the Former Yugoslavia," 30 *Valparaiso University Law Review* 895 (1996).
MERLE, M., "La sanction des atteintes au droit humanitaire commises dans l'ex-Yougoslavie," 2 *Transnational Associations* 119 (1994).
MERON, T., "Rape as a Crime Under International Humanitarian Law," 87 *American Journal of International Law* 424 (1993).
———, "The Case for War Crimes Trials in Yugoslavia," 73 *Foreign Affairs* 122 (1993).
———, "War Crimes in Yugoslavia and the Development of International Law," 88 *American Journal of International Law* 78 (1994).
———, "International Criminalization of Internal Atrocities," 89 *American Journal of International Law* 554 (1995).
———, "The Continuing Role of Custom in the Formation of International Humanitarian Law," 90 *American Journal of International Law* 238 (1996).
———, "Classification of Armed Conflict in the Former Yugoslavia: Nicaragua's Fallout," 92(2) *American Journal of International Law* 236 (April 1998).
MORRIS, V. and SCHARF, M., "The Precedential Value of the International Tribunal," paper presented at: International Experts Conference on International Criminal Justice: Historic and Contemporary Perspectives," (Siracusa, Italy: I.S.I.S.C., 4–8 December 1994).
———, *An Insider's Guide to the International Criminal Tribunal for the Former Yugoslavia* (New York: Transnational Publishers, Inc., 1995).
———, *The International Criminal Tribunal for Rwanda* (New York: Transnational Publishers, Inc.: 1997).
NAGAN, W.P., "Strengthening Humanitarian Law: Sovereignty, International Criminal Law and the *ad hoc* Tribunal for the Former Yugoslavia," 6 *Duke Journal of Comparative and International Law* 127 (1995).
NASH, M. L., "Proposed Tribunal for Crimes Against International Humanitarian Law and Draft Charter of the International Tribunal for Violations of International Humanitarian Law in the Former Yugoslavia," 87 *American Journal of International Law* 435 (1993).
NIANG Mandiaye, "Les obligations du Procureur face à la défense devant le Tribunal pénal international pour le Rwanda," 2 *Revue de science criminelle et de droit pénal comparé* 277–289 (April–June 2001).
NIARCHOS, C., "Women, War, and Rape: Challenges Facing the International Tribunal for the Former Yugoslavia," 17 *Human Rights Quarterly* 649 (1995).
NIEMANN, G.R., "Aspects of Investigation and Prosecution," 89 *Militair Rechtelijk Tijdschrift* 99 (1996).
NIER, C. L., "The Yugoslavian Civil War: An Analysis of the Applicability of the Laws of War Governing Non-International Armed Conflicts in the Modern World," 10 *Dickinson Journal of International Law* 303 (1992).
NOUVEL, Y., "La preuve devant le tribunal pénal international pour l'ex-Yougoslavie," 4 *Revue générale de droit international public ("R.G.D.I.P")* 905–943 (1 octobre 1997).
———, "Précisions sur le pouvoir du tribunal pour l'ex-Yougoslavie d'ordonner la production des preuves et la comparution des témoins: l'arrêt de la chambre d'appel du 29 octobre 1997 dans l'affaire Blaskic," *R.G.D.I.P* 157–164 (1998).
NUNES, Keith D., "'You can Run but You Can't Hide': A Case for Criminal Trial Under International Auspices to Prosecute the Human Right to Personal Security," 6 *Pace International Law Review* 41 (1994).
NUSS Pierre, "La France et la Cour pénale internationale," 56 *La Gazette du Palais* 21–37 (25 février 2000).
O'BRIEN, J. C., "The International Tribunal for Violations of International Humanitarian Law in the Former Yugoslavia," 87 *American Journal of International Law* 640 (1993).
ORDÓÑEZ Solis, D., "Tribunal internacional sobre crímines internacionales en la Antigua

Yugoslavia Resolución 827(1993) del Consejo de Seguridad de las Naciones Unidas: Publicación y ejecución en el Derecho español," XLVI *Revista Española de Derecho Internacional* 433 (1994).

O'REILLY Gregory W., "England Limits the Right to Silence and Moves Towards an Inquisitorial System of Justice," 85 *Journal of Criminal Law and Criminology* 402–452.

PANIAGUA Redondo, R., "Un tribunal internacional para la extinta Yugoslavia," 35 *Naciones Unidas* (1993).

PARTSCH, K.J., "Der Sicherheitstrat als Gerichtsgründer—Zur Entschung des besonderen internationalen Strafgerichts für Jugoslawien," 42 *Vereinte Nationen* 11 (1994).

PATRY Didier, "Le contentieux du génocide rwandais ou l'impasse judiciaire," 84 *La Gazette du Palais* 3–7 (25 March 2001).

———, "Le transfert de Slobodan Milosevic à La Haye ou le tournant de la justice pénale internationale," 294 *La Gazette du Palais* 11–12 (21 octobre 2001).

PAUST, J.J., "Applicability of International Criminal Laws to Events in the Former Yugoslavia," 9 *American University Journal of International Law* 499 (1994).

PEGRAU Solé, A., "Reflexiones sobre el Tribunal internacional para la antigua Yugoslavia desde la perspectiva de la codificación y el desarrollo progresivo del Derecho internacional," XI *Anuario del Instituto Hispano-Luso-Americano de Derecho International* 211 (1994).

PELLET, A., "Le tribunal criminel international pour l'ex-Yougoslavie: poudre aux yeux ou avancée décisive?," 98 *Revue Générale de Droit International Public* 7 (1994).

PICONE, p., "Sul Fonamento Giuridico del Tribunale Penale per la ex-Iugoslavia," 51 *La Comunita Internazionale* 3 (1996).

PIPE, S.C. Kennedy, "Rape in War: Lessons of the Balkan Conflicts in the 1990s," *International Journal of Human Rights* 67–84 (2000).

PRUNIER, G., *The Rwanda Crisis: History of a Genocide* (Columbia University Press: 1997).

PULS, K.E., "Report on the International Tribunal to Adjudicate War Crimes Committed in the Former Yugoslavia," 12 *Boston University International Law Journal* 139 (1993).

QUEL LÓPEZ, F.J., "Los efectos de la creación del Tribunal Internacional Penal para la Antigua Yugoslavia en el orden interno español," XLVI *Revista Española de Derecho Internacional* 61 (1994).

QUINTANA, J., "Violations of International Humanitarian Law and Measures of repression: The International Tribunal for the Former Yugoslavia," 34 *International Review for the Red Cross* 223 (1994).

REES, M. & S. MAGUIRE, "Rape as a Crime Against Humanity," 6 *Tribunal* (Nov.–Dec. 1996) (a Publication of the Institute for War & Peace Reporting).

REINISCH, A., "Das Jugoslawien-Tribunal der Vereinten Nationen und die Verfahrensgarantien des II.VN-Menschenrechtspaktes. En Bietrag zur Frage der Bindung der Vereinten Nationen an nicht-ratifiziertes Vertragsrecht," 47 *Austrian Journal of Public International Law* 173 (1995).

REYDAMS, L., "Justice dans l'après-Apartheid. La Commission de vérité et de réconciliation sud-africaine," 9 *Yearbook of African Law* (1995).

ROWE, P., "War Crimes and the Former Yugoslavia: The Legal Difficulties," XXXII *Military Law and Law of War Review* 317 (1993).

ROGGEMANN, H., *Der Internationale strafgerichtshof der Vereinten Nationen von 1993 und der Krieg auf dem Balkan* (Berlin: 1994).

———, "Der Internationale strafgerichtshof der Vereinten Nationen von 1993 und die Balkankriegsverbrechen," 8 *Zeitschrift Für Rechtspolitik* 297 (1994).

RUBIN, Alfred P., "An International Criminal Tribunal for Former Yugoslavia?," 6 *Pace International Law Review* 7 (1994).

———, "The International Criminal Court: Possibilities for Abuse," 64 *Law and Contemporary Problems* 153–165.

RUDOLF BEATE, "Considérations constitutionnelles à propos de l'établissement d'une justice pénale internationale," 39 *Revue Française de Droit Constitutionnel* 451–482 (1 septembre 1999).

RUSSBACH, O., *ONU contre ONU, le Droit International Confisqué* (Paris 1994).

SAINT-JUST (De) Wallerand, "Le statut de la Cour pénale internationale est-il en "amélioration" par rapport à ceux du Tribunal pénal international pour l'ex-Yougoslavie et du Tribunal international pour le Rwanda ?," 320 *La Gazette du Palais* 2–3 (16 novembre 1999).

SANDOZ, Y., "Réflexions sur la mise en œuvre du droit international humanitaire et sur le rôle du C.I.C.R. en ex-Yougoslavie," 4 *Revue Suisse de Droit International et de Droit Européen* 461 (1993).

SASSOLI, M., "La première décision de la Chambre d'appel du Tribunal pénal international pour l'ex-Yougoslavie: Tadi} (Compétence)," 100 *Revue Générale de Droit International Public* 101 (1996).

SAUNDERS, B.L., "The World's Forgotten Lesson: The Punishment of War Criminals in the Former Yugoslavia," 8 *Temple International and Comparative Law Journal* 357 (1994).

SCHABAS, W.A., "Le Règlement de preuve et de procédure du tribunal international chargé de poursuivre les personnes présumées responsables de violations graves du droit international humanitaire commises sur le territoire de l'ex-Yougoslavie depuis 1991," (paper presented at: Colloque sur les développements récents en droit international humanitaire, Montréal, 7 April 1994).

———, *An Introduction to the International Criminal Court* 54–70 (Cambridge, 2001).

———, *Genocide in International Law: The Crime of Crimes* (Cambridge University Press: Cambridge, U.K.; New York, 2000).

———, "Justice, Democracy and Impunity in Post-Genocide Rwanda: Searching for Solutions to Impossible Problems," 7(3) *Criminal Law Forum*.

SCHARF, Michael P., "The Special Court for Sierra Leone," *ASIL Insight* (American Society of International Law: October 2000).

———, "International Decisions: *Prosecutor v. Tadić*," 91(4) *American Journal of International Law* (October 1997).

SCHOUWEY, J-D., *Criminels de Guerre: un État des Lieux du Droit Suisse* (Berne 1994).

SCHRAG, M., "The Yugoslavia Crimes Tribunal: A Prosecutor's View," 6 *Duke Journal of Comparative and International Law* 186 (1995).

SELLERS, P.V., "The Context of Sexual Violence: Sexual Violence as Violations of International Humanitarian Law," in G.K. McDonald and O. Swaak-Goldman (eds.), *Substantive and Procedural Aspects of International Law* 263–322 (Kluwer Law International, 2000).

SHRAGA, D. and ZACKLIN, R., "The International Criminal Tribunal for the Former Yugoslavia," 5 *European Journal of International Law* 360 (1994).

SIESBY, E., "An International Court of Civil Claims Arising from Criminal Acts Committed during the War in the Former Yugoslavia," (Paper, The Danish Helsinki Committee, 1994).

SILBER, L. and LITTLE, A, *Yugoslavia: Death of a Nation* (BBC: 1996).

SIMMA, B. and PAULUS, A., "The Responsibility of Individuals for Human Rights Abuses in Internal Conflicts: A Positivist View," 93 *American Journal of International Law* 302–316 (1999).

———, "Le rôle relatif des différentes sources du droit pénal (dont les principes généraux de droit)," in Ascensio, Decaux, Pellet (Hrsg.), *Droit international pénal* 55–69 (Paris: 2000).

SINHA, S.P., "Symposium: Should There Be an International Tribunal for Crimes Against Humanity? An Introductory Note," 6 *Pace International Law Review* 1 (1994).

SJÖCRONA, J.M., "Oorlogstribunaal in Den Haag," 68 *Nederlands Juristenblad* 1435 (1993).

———, "The International Criminal Tribunal for the Former Yugoslavia: Some Introductory Remarks From a Defence Point of View," 8 *Leiden Journal of International Law* 463 (1995).

SLUITER, G.K. and KLIP, A.H., "Uitwerking van vredesakkoord van Dayton staat op gespannen voet met principiîle uitgangspunten van het Statuut voor het Joegoslavie Tribunal," 71 *Nederlands Juristenblad* 353 (1996).

SOHN, L.B., "International War Crimes Tribunal," 28 *International Lawyer* 545 (1994).
STERNBERG, M.R., "A Comparison of the Yugoslavian and Rwandan War Crimes Tribunals: Universal Jurisdiction and the 'Elementary Dictates of Humanity'," 22 *Brooklyn Journal of International Law* 111 (1996).
STEWART, M., "Bosnia War Crimes Trials," 19(4) *London Review of Books* (11 December 1997).
———, "Atone and Move Forward," 19(4) *London Review of Books* (11 December 1997).
STRIER FRANKLIN, "What Can the American Adversary System Learn from an System of Justice?," 76 *Judicature* 109–111.
STROHMEYER, HANSJORG, "Collapse and Reconstruction of a Judicial System: The United Nations Missions in Kosovo and East Timor," 95 *American Journal of International Law* (2001).
SUNGA, L.S., *The Emerging System of International Criminal Law: Developments in Codification and Implementation* (Kluwer Law International, The Hague, Netherlands, 1997).
SUR SERGE, "Le droit international pénal, entre l'Etat et la société internationale," *Actualité et droit international* (octobre 2001) (www.ridi.org/adi).
SWART, A.H.J., "Een International Gerechtshof voor Joegoslavië: een stap vooruit of slag in de lucht?," 18 *N.J.C.M. Bulletin* 374 (1993).
SZASZ, P., "The Proposed War Crimes Tribunal for Ex-Yugoslavia," 25 *New York University Journal of International Law and Politics* 405 (1994).
TALLGREN, "Article 20—Ne bis in idem," in *Commentary on the Rome Statute of the International Criminal Court—Observers' Notes, Article by Article* 319–443 (Baden-Baden: Nomos Verlagsgesellschaft, 1999).
THURER, D., "Vom Nurnberger Tribunal zum Jugoslawien-Tribunal und weiter zu einem Weltstrafgerichtshof?," 4 *Revue Suisse de Droit International et de Droit EuropÈen* 491 (1993).
TOMPKINS, T., "Prosecuting Rape as a War Crime: Speaking the Unspeakable," 70 *Notre Dame Law Review* 845 (1995).
TOMUSCHAT, C., "A System of International Criminal Prosecution is Taking Shape," 50 *Review International Commission of Jurists* 56 (1993).
———, "Ein Internationaler Strafgerichtshof als Element einer Weltfriedensordnung," 3 *Europa Archiv* 61 (1994).
TRAUTWEIN, T., "Das Internationale Jugoslawien-Tribunal und das Völkerrecht," 88 *Zeitschrift f,r Rechtspolitik* 104 (1995).
TRIFFTERER, O., "Grundlagen, Moglichkeiten und Grenzen des Internatio-nalen Tribunals zur Verfolgung der Humanitatsverbrechen im ehemaligen Jugoslawien," 49 *Ostereichische Juristenzeitung* 825 (1994).
——— (ed.), *Commentary on the Rome Statute of the International Criminal Court. Observers' Notes, Article by Article* (Baden-Baden: Nomos, 1999).
———, "Kriminalpolitische und dogmatische überlegungen zum Entwurf gleichlautender "Elements of Crimes" für alle Tatbestände des Völkermords," in Bernd Schünemann, Wilfried Bottke, Hans Achenbach, Bernhard Haffke, Hans-Joachim Rudolphi (Hrsg.), *Festschrift für Claus Roxin* 1415-1415-1445 (M,nchen 2001).
TRUCHE PIERRE, "L'émergence d'une justice pénale internationale : les expériences en cours," 8 *L'Astrée* 3–6 (1 septembre 1999).
UNGARI, P., "Il tempo è venuto," IV *I Diritti Dell'Uomo* 39 (1993).
VAN DEN WYNGAERT, C. and ONGENA, "Ne bis in idem Principle, Including the Issue of Amnesty," in A. Cassese, P. Gaeta, J.R.W.D. Jones (eds.), *The Rome Statute of the International Criminal Court. A Commentary* (3 vols., Oxford University Press, 2002).
VANDERMEERSCH, D., "La loi du 22 mars 1996 relative à la reconnaissance du Tribunal international pour l'ex-Yougoslavie et du Tribunal international pour le Rwanda et à la coopération avec ces Tribunaux," 76 *Revue de Droit Pénal et de Criminologie* 855 (1996).
VASSALLI, G., "Diritti del'uomo e diritto internazionale penale," IV I *Diritti Dell'Uomo* 42 (1993).

―――, *La giustizia internazionale penale: studi* (Milano: 1995).
VERDIRAME, G., "The Genocide Definition in the Jurisprudence of the ad hoc Tribunals," 49 *International and Comparative Law Quarterly* 578–598 (July 2000).
VERHOEVEN, J., "La spécificité du crime du génocide," *in* A. Destexhe, *De Nuremberg à La Haye et Arusha* 39–47 (Bruxelles: 1997).
VERRIJN S., and HEIKELIEN M., "Viva Voce: Aantekeningen bij het Joegoslavie Tribunaal," *NEMESIS* 93 (Special Edition, 1996).
VEST, H., *Genozid durch organisatorische Machtapparate* (Berlin: 2001).
VIERUCCI, L., "The First Steps of the International Criminal Tribunal for the Former Yugoslavia," 6 *European Journal of International Law* 134 (1995).
―――, "Gli Emendamenti al Regolamento di Procedura del Tribunale Penale Internazionale per la Ex Jugoslavia," 79 *Rivista di Diritto Internazionale* 71 (1996).
VOETELINK, J.E.D., "Het Joegoslavie-Tribunaal en de Vredesovereenkomst van Dayton," 89 *Militair Rechtelijk Tijdschrift* 93 (1996).
WARBRICK, C., "International Criminal Law," 44 *International and Comparative Law Quarterly* 466 (1995).
WAUTERS, J.M., "Torture and Related Crimes—A Discussion of the Crimes Before the International Criminal Tribunal for the Former Yugoslavia," *Leiden Journal of International Law* 155–164 (1998).
WEBB, J., "Genocide Treaty—Ethnic Cleansing—Substantive and Procedural Hurdles in the Application of the Genocide Convention to Alleged Crimes in the Former Yugoslavia," 23 *Georgia Journal of International and Comparative Law* 377 (1993).
WECKEL, PHILIPPE., "L'institution d'un tribunal international pour la répression des crimes de droit humanitaire en Yougoslavie," 39 *Annuaire FranÁais de Droit International* 232–261 (1 janvier 1993).
―――, and HELALI EDDIN, "Tribunal pénal international pour l'ex-Yougoslavie, avis du Comité consultatif pour l'examen de la campagne militaire de l'OTAN contre la Yougoslavie, 12 juin 2000," 4 *Revue gÈnÈrale de droit international public* 1059–1065 (1 octobre 2000).
WEDGWOOD, R., "War Crimes in the Former Yugoslavia: Comments on the International War Crimes Tribunal," 34 *Virginia Journal of International Law* 267 (1994).
WERLE, G., "Menschenrechtsschutz durch Völkerstrafrecht," 109 *ZStW* 808–829 (1997).
―――, "Völkerstrafrecht und geltendes deutsches Strafrecht," *JZ* 755–760 (2000).
―――, "Konturen eines deutschen Völkerstrafrechts," *JZ* 885–895 (2001).
―――, "Rückwirkungsverbot und Staatskriminalität," *NJW* 3001–3008 (2001).
WIERUSZEWSKI, R., "International Response to the Human Rights Violations in the Territory of the Former Yugoslavia," 19 *Polish Yearbook of International Law* 203 (1991–92).
WILBERS, M.T.A., "Sexual Abuse in Times of Armed Conflict," 7 *Leiden Journal of International Law* 43 (1994).
WILT, H. VAN DER, "Een Internationaal Starftribunaal voor ex-Joegoslavië: de spanning tussen legaliteit en effectiviteit," 20 *Rech en Kritiek* 8 (1994).
―――, "De tenuitvoerlegging in Nederland van strfvonnissen, geweze door het VN-Tribunaal voor ex-Joegoslavië," 88 *Militair Rechtelijk Tijdschrift* 49 (1995).
―――, "De tenuitvoerlegging in Nederland van strafvonnissen, gewezen door het VN-Tribunaal voor Ex-Joegoslavië," 88 *Militair Rechtelijk Tijdschrift* 49 (1995).
WILLIAMS, "Article 17—Issues of Admissibility," *in Commentary on the Rome Statute of the International Criminal Court—Observers' Notes, Article by Article* 383–394 (Baden-Baden: Nomos Verlagsgesellschaft, 1999).
WIRTH, S., "Zum subjektiven Tatbestand des Völkermords—Zerstörungsabsicht und Vertreibungsverbrechen," *in* Bernd Rill (Hrsg.), *Gegen Völkermord und Vertreibung, Die überwindung des zwanzigsten Jahrhunderts. München (Hanns Seidel Stiftung)* 59–74 (2001).

WOLFE JEFFREY S., PROSZEK LISA B., "Interaction dynamics in federal administrative decision making : of the inquisitorial judge and the adversarial lawyer," 33 *Tulsa Law Journal* 293–347.

YARNOLD, B.M., "Doctrinal Basis for the International Criminalization Process," 8 *Temple International and Comparative Law Journal* 85 (1994).

YEE, S., "The *Erdemović* Sentencing Judgement: A Questionable Milestone for the International Criminal Tribunal for the Former Yugoslavia," 26(2) *Georgia Journal of International and Comparative Law* 263 (1997).

ZACKLIN, R., "Bosnia and Beyond," 34 *Virginia Journal of International Law* 277 (1994).

ZAPPALÀ, S., "Il Procuratore della Corte Penale Internazionale: luci e ombre," 1 *RDI* 39–85 (1999).

Collections and Symposia

Collected Courses of the Hague Academy of International Law. Martinus Nijhoff Publishers, Tome 280-1999, The Hague/Boston/London, 2000.

"Symposium: The International Tribunal for the former Yugoslavia Comes of Age," 7 *European Journal of International Law* 245 (1996).

ICTY and ICTR documents

ICTR Yearbooks
ICTR Annual Reports, 1995–2002
ICTR Manual for Practitioners
ICTY Yearbooks, 1994–1996
ICTY Annual Reports, 1994-2002
ICTY Basic Documents 1998
ICTY Manual for Practitioners

UN Reports

International Law Commission, *Draft Code of Crimes*, Report of the ILC on its 48th session, 1996, Chapter II, UNDoc. A/51/10, 6 May–26 July 1996. "*http://www.un.org/law/ilc/reports/1996/chap02.htm.*"

Preparatory Commission for the International Criminal Court, *Finalized draft text of the Elements of Crimes*, UN Doc. PCNICC/2000/1/Add.2, 2 November 2000.

Ruhashyankiko N., Special Rapporteur, Report on the Question of the Prevention and Punishment of the crime of genocide, UN Doc. E/CN.4/Sub.2/416, 4 July 1978.

Whitaker M., Special Rapporteur, Revised and Updated Report on the Question of the Prevention and Punishment of the crime of Genocide, 2 July 1985, UN Doc. E/CN.4/Sub.2/1985/6.

Websites on International Criminal Law

Actualité et Droit international, *www.ridi.org*
Diplomatie Judiciaire, *www.diplomatiejudiciaire.com*
Fondation Hirondelle, *www.hirondelle.org*
Justice Internationale, *www.toile.org*
International Criminal Court, *www.icc.int*
International Criminal Law, *www.fo.unibo.it/spolfo/CRIMLAW*
International Criminal Tribunal for the Former Yugoslavia, *www.un.org/icty*
International Criminal Tribunal for Rwanda, *www.ictr.org*
International legal studies websites, *www.qsilver.queensu.ca*
McGill Law Journal, *www.journal.law.mcgill*
Special Court for Sierra Leone, *www.specialcourt.org*
United Nations, *www.un.org*

ICTY and ICTR documents referred to in this publication may be obtained from:

Press and Public Information Office
International Criminal Tribunal for the Former Yugoslavia
Churchillplein 1, 2517 JW, The Hague, The Netherlands
www.un.org/icty

and

Registry
International Criminal Tribunal for Rwanda
P.O.Box 6016
Arusha International Conference Centre
Arusha, Tanzania
www.ictr.org

This book is periodically updated at *www.intcrimpractice.com*. E-mails may be sent with comments, information, suggestions, etc.

BIOGRAPHICAL NOTES

John Richard William Day Jones is a barrister specialising in international criminal law, extradition, asylum and prisoner's rights. He practices from Charter Chambers, 2 Dr. Johnson's Buildings, Temple, London. He acted as co-counsel for General Mehmed Alagic before the International Criminal Tribunal for the former Yugoslavia ("ICTY") and is currently representing Naser Oric before the ICTY. From April–July 2003, he will be acting Principal Defender of the Special Court for Sierra Leone in Freetown, Sierra Leone.

John Jones was educated at St. Edmund Hall, Oxford University, where he read Philosophy, Politics and Economics. He was called to the Bar of England and Wales in 1992 by Lincoln's Inn and became a Member of the Bar of the District of Columbia in 1999.

He went to The Hague in January 1995 in the first group of eight law clerks seconded by the International Commission of Jurists to work in the Registry and with the Judges of the ICTY. He was the law clerk to Judge Antonio Cassese, the first President of the ICTY, between 1996 and 1999. For most of 1998, he worked in Arusha as a legal officer with the Judges of the International Criminal Tribunal for Rwanda.

He has lectured widely, published numerous articles and spoken on the BBC World Service on international criminal law. He has also worked as a consultant on war crimes issues for, among others, the OSCE.

John Jones is co-editor of *The Rome Statute for an International Criminal Court: A Commentary* (eds. Cassese, Gaeta and Jones, Oxford University Press, 2002).

Steven Powles is a barrister specialising in international criminal law, extradition, crime and human rights. He practices at Doughty Street Chambers, London. He is currently acting as co-counsel in cases before the ICTY and Special Court for Sierra Leone.

He was educated at the London School of Economics, where he read law, and Cambridge University where he received an LL.M. in international law. He was called to the Bar of England and Wales in 1997.

He spent one year at the ICTY in 2000/2001 where he was a legal assistant to Judge Liu Daqun. He has also served as legal assistant to the delegation of Trinidad and Tobago at negotiations at the United Nations on the Rules of Procedure and Evidence for the permanent International Criminal Court. He also served as a consultant to the first Plenary of Judges of the Special Court for Sierra Leone in producing the first Rules of Procedure and Evidence for the Court. He has appeared in cases before the ICTY, including the landmark case of Washington Post reporter Jonathan Randal, establishing a qualified journalistic privilege for conflict zone reporters. He has undertaken various projects in the field and in 1999 spent two months in Kosovo with the International Crisis Group documenting violations of international humanitarian law.

Steven Powles has worked closely with a number of NGOs on international crime and human rights related matters including *No Peace Without Justice*, the *Redress Trust*, and *Human Rights Watch*. He has written on specialist areas in a number of publications including *The Times* and has spoken at various seminars including a NATO lawyers' conference. He is on the Executive of the Bar Human Rights Committee and an active member of the International Criminal Defence Attorneys Association.

INDEX

Abbaye-Ardenne case, 6.2.80
Abi Saab, Georges, 1.49, 4.2.331–4.2.333
Abnormality of mind
  See McNaghten's Case
  Absence, 8.5.102–8.5.105, 8.5.742
  Of Accused, continuation of proceedings in his absence, 4.2.643, 8.5.72, 9.102–9.104
  Of judge, 2.174–2.1.79
  Of jury, 8.5.544
  Of Prosecutor, 8.5.102–8.5.105
Abuse of authority, 9.68–9.69
Abuse of process, 8.1.21
Access of public to hearings, 8.5.22–8.5.24
Accessorial liability, 6.2.148
Accusatorial system, 7.41–7.42
Accused
  Absence of counsel, 8.5.72
  Adequate time and facilities, 8.5.46
  Appearance, initial, 8.5.248–8.5.249
  Arrest, procedure upon, 8.4.90–8.4.92
  Arrest, State obligation to assist with
  See State cooperation
  Assignment of defence counsel, 8.5.62–8.5.69
  Burden of proof, 6.3.4–6.3.8, 8.5.27–8.5.28
  Co-accused not in custody, 8.5.551–8.5.552
  Confession, 8.5.714–8.5.715
  Confrontation and exceptions, right of, 8.5.83–8.5.88
  Counsel, appointment of, 2.6.1–2.613, 8.5.6, 8.5.12
  Counsel, assignment of to indigent, 8.5.628, 5.69
  See also Counsel
  Definition, 7.50
  Equality of, 8.5.70, 8.5.73–8.5.82
  Examination of witnesses, 8.5.93–8.5.94
  Expeditious trial, 8.5.47–8.5.61
  Fundamental rights of, 8.5.15
  Independent and impartial tribunal, 8.5.29–8.5.31

  Joinder, 8.2.39–8.2.54
  Joinder, crimes, 8.2.58–8.2.68
  Independent and impartial tribunal, 8.5.29–8.5.31
  Interpretation, requests for, 8.5.91
  Language, right to use own, 8.5.39–8.5.45
  Legal aid, 8.5.71
  Length of trials, 8.5.60
  Luring of, 8.4.98–8.4.105
  Medical examination of, 8.5.522–8.5.524
  Nature and cause of charge, 8.5.32–8.5.38
  Non-enumerated rights, 8.5.97
  Oral argument, 8.5.57–8.5.59
  Pretrial judge, use of, 8.5.54–8.5.56
  Presence of, 6.2.57–6.2.61
  Presumption of innocence, 8.5.25–8.5.26
  Privileges and immunities of, 3.1–3.21
  Provisional release, 8.5.127
  Public hearing, 8.5.22–8.5.24
  Questioning, 8.5.98–8.5.107
  Release, provisional, 8.5.127
  Remand, 8.5.108–8.5.113
  Rights of, generally, 8.5.13–8.5.97
  Right to fair and public hearing, 4.2.421–4.2.422, 8.5.3–8.5.6
  Rights, protective measures to be consistent with
  See Protective measures
  Self-incrimination, 8.5.92–8.5.96
  Standing to raise violation of state sovereignty, 8.4.106–8.4.107
  Statements of, 8.5.563–8.5.566
  Status of the accused following appeal, 10.1.86
  Surrender, State obligation to assist with
  See State
  Testimony of, 8.5.584–8.5.588
  Time and facilities, 8.5.46
  Trial chamber can order party to close the case, 8.5.86–8.5.87
  Witnesses, examine, 8.5.88–8.5.90

Acquittal
　Acquitted person, status of, 8.6.20–8.6.23
　Motion for judgement of acquittal,
　　8.5.576–8.5.578, 8.6.6–8.6.15
　Non bis in idem
　　See *Non bis in idem*
Actus reus
　Complicity in genocide, 4.2.132–4.2.138,
　　4.2.148
　Mens rea and, 4.2.35–4.2.51
　Persecution and, 4.2.284–4.2.286
　War crimes, 4.2.402–4.2.429
Ad hoc International Tribunals
　See International Criminal Tribunal for
　　Rwanda (ICTR) and International
　　Criminal Tribunal for the Former
　　Yugoslavia (ICTY), 4.1.8 et seq;
　Additional Protocol I to the 1949 Geneva
　　Conventions (API), 6.2.87–6.2.94;
　Additional Protocol II to the 1949 Geneva
　　Conventions (APII), 6.2.87–6.2.94
Ad litem judge
　At ICTY, 1.9
　Definition, 7.50
　　ICTR, 1.9
　　Status of, 2.1.13
Ademi, 8.5.169
Administration of justice, offences against,
　　4.2.590–4.2.674
　ICC, 4.2.655
Admissibility, issues of, 5.103 et seq.
　See also Evidence
Admissions
　See Stipulations
　Adversarial system, 8.5.515
　See also accusatorial system
Advocates
　See Counsel
Affidavit evidence, 8.5.717
Age
　See Children
Aggravation, aggravating factors, 9.65 et seq.
　See also Sentencing
Aid and abet, aiding and abetting,
　　6.2.49–6.2.63
　Accused's presence at crime,
　　6.2.57–6.2.61
　Torture: co-perpetrator or aider and abet-
　　tor, 6.2.62–6.2.63
Akayesu, JeanPaul, 2.6.32–2.6.33, 2.6.62,
　　2.6.68, 3.11, 4.2.31–4.2.33, 4.2.37,
　　4.2.41–4.2.42, 4.2.44, 4.2.46,
　　4.2.48–4.2.49, 4.2.51, 4.2.53, 4.2.58,
　　4.2.84, 4.2.86, 4.2.88, 4.2.89, 4.2.93,
　　4.2.99, 4.2.105, 4.2.106, 4.2.116,
　　4.2.120 et seq1., 4.2.130 et seq,
　　4.2.140 et seq., 4.2.173, 4.2.178,
　　4.2.195, 4.2.207, 4.2.214, 4.2.237,
　　4.2.240, 4.2.246, 4.2.264 et seq.,
　　4.2.271, 4.2.296, 4.2.462, 5.2.502 et
　　seq., 4.2.510, 4.2.539, 4.2.541,
　　4.2.545, 4.2.548, 4.2.552, 4.2.559,
　　4.2.560, 4.2.563, 4.2.653, 4.2.655,
　　4.2.657, 6.2.35, 6.2.46–6.2.48, 6.2.50,
　　6.2.55, 6.2.58, 6.2.60, 6.2.102,
　　6.2.131, 6.2.146, 7.85, 8.2.85, 8.2.87,
　　8.3.3, 8.4.55– 8.4.57, 8.5.69, 8.5.88,
　　8.5.92, 8.5.331, 8.5.481, 8.5.593,
　　8.5.597, 8.5.644, 8.5.654, 8.5.670,
　　8.5.671, 8.5.680, 8.5.694, 8.5.695,
　　8.5.699, 8.5.712, 8.5.761, 8.5.762,
　　9.39, 9.53, 9.67, 9.91, 9.93, 10.1.12
Alagić, Mehmed, 2.6.38, 4.2.468, 6.1.25,
　　6.2.106, 8.5.120, 8.5.121, 8.5.166
Albright, Madeleine, 4.2.176
Aleksovski, Zlatko, 4.1.14, 4.2.335, 4.2.354,
　　4.2.380–4.2.391, 4.2.440, 4f.2.581,
　　4.2.583, 4.2.604, 4.2.608, 4.2.633,
　　6.2.31, 6.2.50, 6.2.59, 6.2.114,
　　6.2.122, 6.2.137, 6.3.7, 6.3.52, 6.3.53,
　　8.4.68, 8.5.52, 8.5.122, 8.5.162,
　　8.5.241, 8.5.454, 8.5.534, 8.5.642,
　　8.5.651, 9.9, 9.10, 9.12, 9.17, 9.24,
　　9.33, 9.48, 9.56, 9.60, 9.69, 9.129,
　　10.1.5, 10.1.8
　Aleksovski Appeals Judgement,
　　4.2.388–4.2.391, 4.1.11, 4.1.15
　Aleksovski Trial Judgement,
　　4.2.380–4.2.387
Alford
　See *North Carolina v. Alford*
Alibi, 6.3.9–6.3.16
　See also Defences
Alibi notice, matters not subject to ,
　　8.5.353–8.5.357
Alilović, Stipo, 8.2.92
Alvarez-Machain, 8.4.99
Amendment of the Rules of Procedure and
　　Evidence, 7.72–7.81
American Indians, 4.2.5
Amicus curiae, 5.82, 8.4.11,
　　8.4.135–8.4.137, 8.5.396, 8.5.50,
　　8.5.511, 8.5.512
　Appointment of, 8.5.6, 8.5.512

Government as amicus, 8.5.504–8.5.506
  Partie Civile and, 8.5.513
  Proceedings before trial chambers, 8.5.499–8.5.506
  UN Secretary-General as amicus, 8.5.502–8.5.503
Amicus curiae, 8.5.6, 8.5.12
Amicus curiae briefs, 4.2.334, 4.2.387, 4.2.639, 8.5.396
Annual Report, 3.19 et seq., 3.20–3.22
Anonymity\of a witness, 8.5.186–8.5.195
Apartheid, 4.2.237, 4.2.588
Appeal and review proceedings, 10.1.1–10.2.16
Appellant's appeal book, 10.1.76
  Respondent's appeal book, 10.1.76
Appeal proceedings, 10.1.1–10.1.86
  Additional evidence, 10.1.51–10.1.65
  Appellant's brief, 10.1.37–10.1.41
  Brief in reply, 10.1.47
  Copies of record, 10.1.36
  Counsel's negligence, 10.1.58
  Expedited appeals procedure, 10.1.67–10.1.75
  Hearing, date of, 10.1.48–10.1.50
  Interlocutory appeals, 10.1.13–10.1.16
  Judgement on appeal, 10.1.81–10.1.85
  Miscarriage of justice, 10.1.59
  Notice of appeal, 10.1.20–10.1.22
  Parties' books, 10.1.76–10.1.77
  Parties, available to, 10.1.9–10.1.11
  Practice directions for the Appeals Chamber, 10.1.19
  Pre-Appeal judge, 10.1.23–10.1.24
  Preliminary examination, 10.2.4–10.2.6
  Record on appeal, 10.1.32–10.1.34
  Request for review, 10.2.2–10.2.3
  Respondent's brief, 10.1.43–10.1.45
  Review proceedings, 10.2.1–10.2.16
  Right of appeal, 10.1.2–10.1.3
  Scope of appeal, 10.1.4–10.1.7
  State request for review, 10.1.25–10.1.28
  Status of the accused following appeal, 10.1.86
  Supplemental briefs, 10.1.42
  Time limits, extension of, 10.1.66
  Trial chambers and, 10.1.17–10.1.18
  Trial records, filing of, 10.1.78–10.180
Appeal(s)
  See Appeals Chamber, Appeals Proceedings, Appellate
Appeals Chamber
  Sentencing and, 9.58–9.59

Appeals proceedings
Appearance
  Initial, 8.5.248–8.5.249
Appellant, 10.1.37–10.1.42
Appellate proceedings, 10.1.1 et seq.
Appointment of Counsel, 2.6.1–2.6.13, 8.5.6, 8.5.12
Appointment of judges
  See Judges
Appropriation of property
  See Property
Arkan, 8.2.108, 8.2.109
Armed conflict
  Crimes against humanity and, 4.2.179–4.2.182, 4.2.185–4.2.189
  Existence of, 4.2.184–4.2.189
Armenian genocide, 4.2.163, 6.2.3
Arrest
  By UNTAES, 8.4.96
  Definition, 7.50 et seq.
  Habeas corpus
    See Habeas corpus
  Immediate arrest, 4.2.673
  Immunities, 3.13.2
  Meaning of, 8.4.82
  Procedure after, 8.4.90–8.4.92
  Provisional, 8.5.127
  Violation of human rights during, 8.4.113
  Wrongful, 9.154
Arrest warrant(s)
  Execution of, 8.4.75–8.4.86
  Failure to execute, 11.2.8, 11.2.9
  International, 8.4.5–8, 11.1.23–11.1.24
  Transmission of arrest warrants, 8.4.93–8.4.113
  Warrant of arrest to all states, 8.4.88–8.4.89
Aspegren, Lennart, 8.5.64
Assets, freezing of, 8.4.144–8.4.148
Assignment of Counsel, 2.6.6–2.6.10
Attack(s), 4.2.211
  On civilian population, 4.2.211–4.2.212
Attempt(s)
  See as subhead to other topics
  See also ICTY Article 7(1) and ICTR and SCSL Article 6(1))
Auschwitz Concentration Camp case, 6.2.54
Authentic texts
  See Documents
Authentication, 8.5.669

Babić, 2.6.22, 8.2.95
Bagambiki, Emmanuel, 8.2.57, 8.5.224, 8.5.331, 8.5.698, 8.5.710, 8.5.711
Bagilishema, Ignace (Ntaganda), 4.2.30, 4.2.33, 4.2.35, 4.2.41, 4.2.45, 4.2.85, 4.2.86, 4.2.113, 4.2.119, 4.2.133, 4.2.138, 4.2.657, 6.2.53, 6.2.55, 6.2.6, 8.5.198, 8.5.380
Bagosora, Théoneste, 8.1.16, 8.2.36, 8.2.38, 8.2.54, 8.5.14–8.5.19, 8.5.47, 8.5.48, 8.5.210, 8.5.343, 8.5.514, 10.1.16
Bail
  See Provisional Release
Barayagwiza, Jean-Bosco, 8.1.21, 8.5.36, 8.5.37, 10.2.9, 10.2.11
Beatings
  See crimes against humanity
Belgium, 5.11–5.12, 8.2.98, 8.5.514
Bennett v. Horseferry Road Magistrates Court, 8.4.102
Best evidence rule, 8.5677–8.5.678
Bias
  See Impartiality
Bill of particulars, 8.5.408
Binding Orders
  See Orders
Biological experiments, 4.2.413–4.2.414
Births
  Genocide to prevent, 4.2.586
Blanket orders, 8.5.190
Blaškić, 4.2.194, 4.2.199, 4.2.209, 4.2.222, 4.2.229, 4.2.230, 4.2.286, 4.2.288, 4.2.295, 4.2.313, 4.2.321, 4.2.335, 4.2.355, 4.2.356, 4.2.358, 4.2.392, 4.2.393, 4.2.400, 4.2.402, 4.2.404, 4.2.405, 4.2.407, 4.2.415, , 4.2.428, 4.2.429, 4.2.439, 4.2.462, 4.2.473, 4.2.481, 4.2.485, 4.2.486, 4.2.488, 4.2.490–4.2.492, 4.2.496, 4.2.541, 4.2.572, 4.2.578, 4.2.608, 4.2.638, 4.2.641, 4.2.644, 6.2.35, 6.2.48, 6.2.51, 6.2.104, 6.2.126, 6.2.133, 6.2.138, 6.2.142, 6.2.148, 7.77, 7.78, 8.2.26, 8.2.29, 8.2.76, 8.4.8, 8.4.13–8.4.15, 8.4.19, 8.4.21, 8.4.63, 8.5.3, 8.5.96, 8.5.109, 8.5.111, 8.5.112, 8.5.132, 8.5.143, 8.5.147, 8.5.150, 8.5.151, 8.5.182, 8.5.183, 8.5.188, 8.5.215, 8.5.219, 8.5.221, 8.5.233, 8.5.313, 8.5.315, 8.5.318, 8.5.321, 8.5.337, 8.5.347, 8.5.3518.5.364, 8.5.368, 8.5.374–8.5.377, 8.5.385, 8.5.386, 8.5.389–8.5.391, 8.5.407, 8.5.408, 8.5.414, 8.5.449, 8.5.495, 8.5.507, 8.5.534, 8.5.562, 8.5.610, 8.5.632, 8.5.650, 8.5.651, 8.5.669, 8.5.679, 8.6.11, 9.43, 9.49, 9.66, 9.74, 9.83– 9.85, 9.91, 9.93, 9.98, 10.1.11, 11.1.7, 11.1.11, 11.1.12, 11.1.14, 11.1.16, 11.1.17, 11.1.19
  Blaškić Trial Judgement, 4.2.355–4.2.356, 4.2.392–4.2.393
  Subpoena hearings, 8.5.507–8.5.509
"Blockburger" test, 8.3.4
  See Cumulative convictions
Bombardment
  Undefended towns, villages, dwellings, 4.2.480
Borman, 4.2.286
Bosnia and Herzegovina v. Fry case, 8.5.61
Bosnia-Herzegovina v. Yugoslavia, 1.52
Bosnian Serb leadership, 5.60, 5.71, 5.74, 5.82
Brdjanin, Radoslav, 4.2.22, 6.2.41, 6.2.45, 8.2.4, 8.2.33, 8.2.60, 8.4.40, 8.5.21, 8.5.37, 8.5.44, 8.5.197, 8.5.302, 8.5.303, 8.5.511, 8.5.757
Brief
  Appellant's brief, 10.1.37–10.1.42
Brief in reply, 10.1.47
  Respondent's brief, 10.1.43–10.1.46
Buildings
  See, in general, War crimes
Bullets, prohibited
Burden(s) of Proof, 8.5.27–8.5.28
  See also Accused
Bureau
  Definition, 7.50
  ICTR, 2.1.98–2.1.101
Butare Four case, 5.12

Calley, Lt., 6.2.84
Cambodia
  Proposed Extraordinary Chambers of the Courts of, 1.156–1.165
Capital punishment, 9.27–9.28
Cassese, Antonio, 6.3.42–6.3.45, 11.1.7
Čelebići camp case (ICTY case No. IT9621T)), a.k.a. *Delalić et al.*
  See Delalić, Zejnil
  See Mucić, Zdravko
  See Delić, Hazim
  See Landžo, Esad
Chambers

Index • 1061

Composition of, 2.1.1–2.1.54
Deliberations in secret, 2.1.26
Officers and members of, 2.1.38–2.1.54
Character evidence
  See Evidence
Charge, charging
  Cumulative, 8.3.1–8.3.20
  Nature and cause of charge, 8.5.32–8.5.38
Charter
  United Nations, 1.2
  See also Nuremberg, Tokyo, etc.
Chemical weapons
  War crime of employing weapons in Annex to the Statute, 4.2.589
Child, Children
  Forcibly transferring children, 4.2.586
  Prevention of Cruelty to Act, 1.99
  War crime of using, conscripting or enlisting, 4.2.589
Citizens and citizenship
  Nottebohm case, I.C.J. 4.2.116–4.2.117
Civilian(s) Attacking, as a war crime, 4.2.193–4.2.199, 4.2.589
  Attacking civilian objects, 1.99, 4.2.589
  Definition, 4.2.193
Clark, Ramsey, 8.5.63
Closed hearing
  See Hearing
Closed sessions, 8.5.530, 8.5.529–8.5.534
  Protection of victims and witnesses, 8.5.532
  Transcripts of, 8.5.533
Closing arguments, 8.5.601–8.5.607
  Sentencing stage and , 8.5.605–8.5.607
Coalition for an International Criminal Court
  See, in general, International Criminal Court
Code of conduct, 2.6–39–2.6.49
Command responsibility (ICTY Article 7(3), ICTR Article 6(3) and SCSL Article 6(3)), 6.2.69– 6.2.158
  Additional Protocol I of 1977, 6.2.87–6.2.94
  Causation not required, 6.2.143
  Charging command responsibility, 6.2.100–6.2.102
Command responsibility at the ICTs, 6.2.95–6.2.99
Commanders and other superiors
  Responsibility of, 6.2.149–6.2.155
  Customary nature of, 6.2.103–6.2.105
  Elements of, 6.2.112–6.2.148

Failure to take necessary and reasonable measures, 6.2.136–6.2.142
Had reason to know, 6.2.126–6.2.135
ICTY Art. 7/ICTR Art. 6
  Relationship between Para. (1) and (3), 6.2.144–6.2.148
Internal conflict, in, 6.2.106–6.2.111
Origins of, 6.2.70
Position of command as aiding and abetting, 6.2.145–6.2.147
PostWorld War II cases, 6.2.81–6.2.86
PreWorld War II cases, 6.2.71–6.2.74
Simultaneous liability for same conduct, 6.2.148
Superior orders, 6.2.152–6.2.155
  Mitigation of punishment and, 6.2.158
  Prescription of law, and, 6.2.156–6.2.158
Superior/subordinate relationship, 6.2.113–6.2.123
World War II cases, 6.2.75–6.2.80
Commission of Experts
  See Expert
Common and civil law
  Fusion of two, 4.1.8–4.1.21
Common Article 3 to the Geneva Convention, 4.2.461
Common criminal purpose, 6.2.38–6.2.45
  See also Joint criminal enterprise
Commutation of sentence, 9.160
Compensation
  Victims, 9.153–9.155
Competence of the Tribunals, 4.1–.4.19
  See also Jurisdiction
Complementarity with national courts, 5.94–5.97
  Lower-ranking accused and, 6.2.21–6.2.27
Complementarity, between the ICC and national courts, 5.94–5.97, 6.2.23, 8.2.95
Complicity, 4.2.130
Composition of the ICC
  See International Criminal Court
Concurrent jurisdiction
  See Jurisdiction
Conferences
  Pre-Defence, 8.5.492–8.5.498
  Pre-Trial, 8.5.486–8.5.491
Confession(s), 8.5.714–8.5.715
  See also Evidence
Confidential communication, 8.5.757

Confinement, unlawful, 4.2.589
Conflict of interest, 8.5.543, 8.5.545
Confrontation of witnesses, 8.5.83–8.5.85
Conscription
  See Children
Conspiracy
  To commit genocide, 4.2.147–4.2.156
Constituent crimes under Article 4, 4.2.522–4.2.531
Contempt of Tribunal (ICTY and ICTR Rule 77), 4.2.674 et seq.
  Appeal, 4.2.630
  Cautioning counsel, 4.2.631
  Convictions, 4.2.607–4.2.618
  Counsel, 2.6.46
  Counsel's absence from hearing, 4.2.643
  History of, 4.2.646–4.2.647
  Jurisdiction, 4.2.599–4.2.600
  Need to specify the charge, 4.2.601–4.2.606
  Order for cessation of, 4.2.644
  Payment of fines, 4.2.645
  Prerogative of the Chambers, 4.2.632
  Proprio Motu, 4.2.633
  Right to appeal conviction, 4.2.628–4.2.629
  Severance of joint trials, 4.2634–4.2.635
  Striking counsel of list to be assigned, 4.2.619–4.2.627
  Subpoena, failure to comply with, 4.2.638
  Trial in absentia, 4.2.639
Common criminal purpose doctrine, 6.2.32
Compelling to serve hostile force, 4.2.419–4.2.420
  Displacing, 4.2.589
  Fair and regular trial, 4.2.421–4.2.422
  Hostage taking, 4.2.428–4.2.429, 4.2.589
  Unlawful confinement of, 4.2.423–4.2.425, 4.2.574, 4.2.575
  Unlawful transfer or deportation of, 4.2.426–4.2.427, 4.2.589
Control of proceedings, 8.5.535–8.5.536
Convicted person
  Status of, 9.130–9.133
  Cooperation
  Duty to cooperate, 11.1.2–11.1.10
  State cooperation, 11.1.1–11.2.10
Coordination Council
  ICTR, 2.1.102–2.1.103
Corroboration
  See Evidence

Counsel
  Appointment, qualifications and duties of defence counsel, 2.6.1
  Assignment of counsel, 2.6.6–2.6.11, 2.6.15, 2.6.49
  Co-counsel, investigators, etc., 2.6.35–2.6.37
  Code of Conduct, 2.6.39–2.6.49
  Duty counsel (ICTR), 2.6.12–2.6.14
  Experience, 2.6.23–2.6.25
  List of counsel willing to be assigned to indigent suspects and accused
  Withdrawal, 2.6.26–2.6.34
Credibility
  See Accused
Crimes against Humanity (ICTY Article 5, ICTR Article 3 and SCSL Article 3), 4.2.161–4.2.301, 4.2.587–4.2.598
  Apartheid, 4.2.588
  Conditions of applicability, 4.2.183–4.2.232
  Constituent offenses of, 4.2.236–4.2.239
  Deportation, 4.2.253–4.2.256, 4.2.587
  Enforced disappearance of persons, 4.2.588
  Enslavement, 4.2.252, 4.2.587
  Extermination, 4.2.246–4.2.251, 4.2.587
  Gravity of, 4.2.169–4.2.172
  Historical background, 4.2.162–4.2.168
  ICC and, 4.2.587
  ICT Statutes and, 4.2.173–4.2.178
  Imprisonment, 4.2.257–4.2.263, 4.2.587
  Mens rea requirement, 4.2.225–4.2.227
  Murder, 4.2.240–4.2.245, 4.2.587
  Nexus with armed conflict, 4.2.179–4.2.182
  No need for formal or state policy, 4.2.220–4.2.24
  Other inhumane acts. 4.2.295–4.2.299, 4.2.588
  Persecutions on political, racial and religious grounds, 4.2.276–4.2.294, 4.2.588
  Pregnancy, forced, 4.2.588
  Prostitution, 4.2.588
  Rape, 4.2.266–4.2.272, 4.2.587, 4.2.588
  Rape as torture, 4.2.273–4.2.275
  Sexual slavery, 4.2.587, 4.2.588
  Sexual violence, 4.2.588
  Sterilization, 4.2.588
  Torture, 4.2.264–4.2.265, 4.2.587
Criminal law
  General principles of, 6.1.1–6.367
  See also specific topics

Strict interpretation, 6.1.14–6.1.17
Who makes the law? 6.1.10–6.1.11
Criminal record
   Witness with, 8.5.179–8.5.180
Criminal responsibility, scope of
   Grounds for excluding (ICC), 6.3.64
   Individual, 4.2.507
Cross-examination
   See Evidence, Witnesses
Cruel treatment (also Inhuman treatment), 4.2.488–4.2.489, 4.2.589
Cultural destruction, 4.2.40, 4.2.48, 4.2.98
Cultural genocide, 4.2.49
Cumulative charging, 8.3.18.3.20
Cumulative convictions
   Blockburger test
      See Blockburger test
Custody, 8.5.7–8.5.10
Customs of war
   See Laws or Customs of war, violations of

Dachau Concentration Camp case, 6.2.54
Damages
   See Compensation
   Dayton Peace Agreement, 4.2.316, 8.4.127, 11.1.21–11.1.22
   Death penalty
   See Capital punishment
Death, proof of, 8.5.634–8.5.635
Decisions
   of the Trial Chamber, 8.5.86–8.5.87
De facto
   De facto states, 11.2.10
   Superior/subordinate
      See Command Responsibility
De jure
   Superior/subordinate
      See Command Responsibility
Defects, in the indictment
   See, *in general,* Indictment)
Defence Counsel
   Appointment, qualifications and duties, 2.6.1–2.6.13
   Assignment of, 2.6.11, 2.6.15–2.6.49, 8.5.62–8.5.69
   Availability of, 2.6.53–2.6.54
   Misconduct of, 2.6.57–2.6.70
   Proceedings in absence of, 8.5.72, 8.5.102–8.5.105
Defence(s), to international crimes, 6.3.1–6.3.63
   Alibi, 6.3.9–6.3.16

Alibi notice, 8.5.353–8.5.357
Burden of proof, 6.3.4–6.3.8, 9.123
Conflicting, 8.5.545
Diminished responsibility and lack of mental capacity, 6.3.17–6.3.37, 9.101–9104
   Unfitness to stand trial and, 8.5.359
Duress, 6.3.38–6.3.53
ICC, 6.3.1, 6.3.67
Mistake of fact, 6.3.65
Mistake of law, 6.3.65
Notice of special defence, 8.5.358
Reprisals, 6.3.58–6.3.61
Self-defence, 6.3.62–6.3.63
Standard of proof, 9.123–9.125
Tu quoque, 6.3.54–6.3.57
Deferral of national court proceedings, 5.53 et seq., 11.2.4–11.2.6
Definitions, 7.50–7.55
Delalić et al, 4.2.139, 4.2.257, 4.2.315, 4.2.318,, 4.2.335, 4.2.348–4.2.354, 4.2.375–4.2.379, 4.2.404, 4.2.405, 4.2.407, 4.2.408, 4.2.410, 4.2.415, 4.2.424, 4.2.425, 4.2.444–4.2.446, 4.2.462, 4.2.463, 4.2.465, 4.2.485, 4.2.488, 4.2.540, 4.2.542, 4.2.546, 4.2.548, 4.2.555, 4.2.559, 4.2.560, 4.2.563, 4.2.568, 4.2.570, 4.2.571, 4.2.573–4.2.575, 4.2.577–4.2.579, 4.2.632, 4.2.640, 5.31, 5.68, 6.1.7, 6.1.8, 6.1.10, 6.1.14, 6.1.26, 6.2.15, 6.2.33, 6.2.36, 6.2.38, 6.2.58, 6.2.103, 6.2.105, 6.2.112–6.2.115, 6.2.118, 6.2.121, 6.2.124–6.2.128, 6.2.130, 6.2.136, 6.2.140, 6.2.143, 6.3.18, 6.3.27–6.3.29, 6.3.36, 6.3.9, 7.63, 8.1.4, 8.1.5, 8.1.34, 8.1.38, 8.2.12, 8.2.24, 8.2.44, 8.2.75, 8.3.4, 8.3.12, 8.4.3, 8.4.4, 8.4.29, 8.4.35, 8.4.39, 8.4.45, 8.4.46, 8.4.54, 8.4.66, 8.5.5, 8.5.26, 8.5.27, 8.5.39, 8.5.46, 8.5.75, 8.5.76, 8.5.87, 8.5.91, 8.5.93, 8.5.127, 8.5.128, 8.5.133, 8.5.140, 8.5.150, 8.5.154, 8.5.157, 8.5.181, 8.5.234, 8.5.314, 8.5.325, 8.5.328, 8.5.330, 8.5.331, 8.5.332, 8.5.348, 8.5.349, 8.5.355, 8.5.358, 8.5.360, 8.5.369, 8.5.372, 8.5.385, 8.5.386, 8.5.421, 8.5.426, 8.5.440, 8.5.449, 8.5.454, 8.5.456, 8.5.549, 9.9, 9.12, 9.21, 9.24, 9.30, 9.31, 9.32, 9.33, 9.34, 9.36, 9.37, 9.39, 9.58, 9.60, 9.66, 9.69,

Delalić et al (continued)
    9.76, 9.100, 9.101, 9.103, 9.104,
    9.117, 9.120, 9.127, 9.129, 9.148,
    8.5.549, 8.5.552, 8.5.561, 8.5.571,
    8.5.576, 8.5.577, 8.5.578, 8.5.579,
    8.5.580, 8.5.581, 8.5.589, 8.5.612,
    8.5.623, 8.5.638, 8.5.641, 8.5.665,
    8.5.672, 8.5.690, 8.5.727, 8.6.23,
    9.17, 9.21, 9.30, 9.31, 9.32, 9.33,
    9.34–9.37, 9.39, 9.57, 9.60, 9.66,
    9.69, 9.76, 9.85
  Delalić Appeals Judgement, 4.2.35–4,
    4.2.379
  Delalić Trial Judgement, 4.2.348–4.2.353,
    4.2.375–4.2.378l
Delay
  Undue, 8.5.47
Deliberations, 8.5.608–8.5.625
Delić, Hazim 8.29, 8.2.24, 8.3.12, 8.5.135,
  8.5.167, 10.210
Denmark, 5.13
Deportation, 4.2.589
Depositions, 8.5.411–8.5.429
Deprivation of physical liberty, 9.155
Deputy Prosecutor, 2.5.45
Deputy Registrar, 2.2.18–2.2.19
Deschenes, Jules, 3.18, 7.83
Destruction of property
  See Property
Detained persons, 2.6.50–2.6.52
Detained witness
  Transfer of, 8.5.700–8.5.713
Detention
  Detention Unit, 8.5.10, 8.5.757
  Length of, 8.5.144–8.5.146
  On remand, 8.5.108–8.5.113
  Pre-trial, 1.150
  Presumption of, 8.5.132–8.5.138
  Suspects, 8.1.12–8.1.18
Deterrence, sentencing and, 9.14–9.19
Devastation not justified by military
  necessity
  As a war crime, 4.2.476–4.2.479
Dignity, personal, 4.2.589
Diminished responsibility, 6.3.17–6.3.36
  See also Defences
Directive on the Assignment of Counsel,
  6.3.17–6.3.37
Disappearance of persons, enforced, 4.2.588
Disclosure, 8.5.340
  By Prosecution (ICTY and ICTR Rules 66
    to 68), 8.5.305–8.5.396

Dilatory disclosure by the prosecutor,
  8.5.343
Exculpatory Evidence
  See Exculpatory evidence
Matters not subject to, 8.5.399–8.5.410
Objection to, 8.5.333
Pendency of a motion for protective measures, 8.5.340–8.5.343
Public and media, 8.5.215
Reciprocal (ICTY and ICTR Rules 66(B)
  and 67), 8.5.344–8.5.396
Sanctions, 4.2.674, 8.5.334–8.5.336
Timely, 8.5.323–8.5.324
Discretion, 2.5.30–2.5.33
Discriminatory intent, 4.2.213–4.2.219
Disqualification of Judges, 2.1.56 et seq.
Djajić, 5.17
Dock identification, 8.5.620
Documents
  Authentification of, 7.82–7.84
  In the language of the accused, 7.63–7.67
  Order to state for production of documents, 8.4.71–8.4.74
  Registrar must serve documents on
    national states, 8.4.84–8.4.86
  Service of, 11.1.25
  Warrant of arrest to all states,
    8.4.88–8.4.89
Dokmanović, Slavko, 8.2.106, 8.3.19, 8.4.51,
  8.4.52, 8.4.53., 8.4.54, 8.4.66, 8.4.67,
  8.4.82, 8.4.83, 8.4.96, 8.4.97, 8.4.98,
  8.4.106, 8.4.108, 8.5.51, 8.5.159,
  8.5.233, 8.5.422, 8.5.454, 8.5.534,
  8.5.551, 8.5.679, 8.5.750, 11.1.4,
  11.1.10, 11.1.34, 11.136
Dolus specialis, 4.2.53
Domestic courts
  Withdrawal for trial in, 8.2.95–8.2.99
Došen, Damir, 8.2.21, 8.5.474
Double jeopardy, 9.60
Draft Statute of ICC
  See, in general, International Criminal
    Code
Drljača, Simo, 8.5.81, 8.5.150
Due diligence, 10.2.12
Due process, 1.41
  Sentencing or executing without, 4.2.589
Đukić, 2.2.14, 2.6.10, 5.69, 8.2.25, 8.2.91,
  8.4.60, 8.5.120, 8.5.123 8.5.557,
  8.5.702, 8.5.706
Dum Dum bullets
  See Bullets

Duplicity, 8.2.5–8.2.7
Duress
  as a defence, 6.3.38–63.53
  See also Defences
Duty counsel, 2.6.12–2.6.14
Džonlić, 8.5.757

East Timor
  Serious Crimes Panel of the Dili District Court, 1.142–1.155
Education
  Destruction or willful damage to property of, 4.2.481–4.2.483
Effective control
  See, in general, Command responsibility test of superior-subordinate relationship
  See, in general, Command responsibility
Eichmann, 4.2.43, 4.2.160, 8.4.99, 11.1.10
Einsatzgruppen Concentration Camp case, 6.2.54
Election
  Of Judges, 2.1.10–2.1.32, 2.1.36
  Of the Prosecutor
    See, in general, Prosecutor
Elements, of the offences/crimes, 4.2.535–4.2.589
Elements of crimes, 4.2.585
  ICTY and ICTR offences, 4.2.535–4.2.583
Emblems, improper use of, 4.2.589
Enforcement, of sentences
  See Sentencing
Enslavement, 4.2.587
Entry into force, 7.4.9
  Of the ICTY AND ICTR, 7.4
Equality
  Before the tribunals, 8.5.20–8.5.21
Equality of arms, the principle of, 8.5.20, 8.5.70–8.5.71
  Under the same conditions, 8.5.73–8.5.82
  See also Accused
Erdemović, 4.2.170, 4.2.172, 5.66, 5.71, 5.74, 5.82, 6.2.12, 6.2.158, 6.3.38, 6.3.41, 6.3.47–6.3.49, 8.5.11, 8.5.247.8.5.254, 8.5.255, 8.5.258, 8.5.262, 8.5.263, 8.5.266 , 8.5.272, 8.5.279, 8.5.283, 8.5.286, 8.5.703, 9.12, 9.20, 9.45, 9.75, 9.94, 9.96, 9.98, 9.108, 9.109, 9.143, 9.146–9,147, 9.149, 10.1.35, 10.1.41, 10.1.49

Establishment
  East Timor Serious Crime Panels, 1.142–1.145
"Ethnic cleansing," 1.6, 1.39, 8.4.127
  Crimes against humanity and, 4.2.233–4.2.234
  Relationship to genocide, 4.2.19
Ethics, code of, 8.5.526
Ethnic group, 4.2.119–4.2.121
European Court of Human Rights (ECHR), 8.5.15, 8.5.19, 8.5.80
  Equality of arms, 8.5.80–8.5.82
  Relationship between ICTY and, 1.57–1.61
European Union, 2.5.44\
Euthenasia, 4.2.219
Evidence
  See also Rules of Procedure and Evidence
  Accused as first defence witness, 8.5.589–8.5.592
  Accused sworn before giving testimony, 8.5.584–8.5.588
  Acts not charged in the indictment, 8.5.666–8.5667
  Additional evidenced, 10.1.51–10.1.55
  Power of chambers to order, 8.5.75–88.5.761
  Admissibility of
  Chamber not bound by national rules of evidence, 8.5.631–8.5.632
  Character, 8.5.662–8.5.663
  Concurrent presentation of, 8.5.546
  Comment, 8.5.639–8.5.640
  Confessions, 8.5.714–8.5.715
  Consciousness of guilty, 8.5.665
  Consistent pattern of conduct, 8.5.720–8.5.722
  Corroboration, 8.5.636–8.5.638, 8.5.670
  Defence motion to dismiss charges, 8.5.573–8.5.575
  Direct versus indirect, 8.5.664
  Exclusion of, 8.5.741–8.5.744
  Hearsay, 8.5.642–8.5.655
  Materiality of evidence, 8.5.328–8.5.332
  Motion to dismiss
    Judgement of acquittal and, 8.5.576–8.5.578
  Order of, 8.5.570
  Polygraph, 8.5.599–8.5.600
  Presentation of, 8.5.567–8.5.600
  Privilege
    See Accused

Evidence *(continued)*
  Probative value outweighed by prejudicial effect, 8.5.668
  Proper time, 8.5.571–8.5.572
  Recross-examination, 8.5.581–8.5.583
  Rebuttal, 8.5.579–8.5.580
  Records of, 8.5.537–8.5.541
  Relevant evidence, 8.5.656–8.5.661
  Rules of Evidence (ICTY and ICTR Rules 89 to 98 bis)
  Sexual offences, in relation to, 8.5.745–8.5.751
  Weight to be given to witness testimony, 8.5.641
    Submission of documents to chamber, 8.5.671
Ex parte communication
  Improper for witness to send, 8.5.680
  Examination of witnesses, also See Accused, Witnesses, Testimony
  Exceptional circumstances, 8.5.130–8.5.131
  Excessive incidental death, injury, or damage
    War crime of, 4.2.589
  Exculpatory evidence (ICTY and ICTR Rule 68), 8.5.364–8.5.369
    Admissible evidence and, 8.5.388
    Disclosure of, 8.5.370–8.5.396
    Duty of prosecutor, 8.5.377–8.5.379
    Exculpatory material, 8.5.372
    failure to comply, 8.5.392–8.5.397
    Lack of evidence and, 8.5.373–8.5.375
    Possession of prosecutor, 8.5.380–8.5.383
    Presumption of good faith, 8.5.390
    Prima facie case, 8.5.384
    Sanctions, 8.5.391
  Execute, executed, execution
    In the sense of carried out
      See ICTY Article 7(1) and ICTR and SCSL Article 6(1)
    In the sense of killed
      See killing
Ex parte hearing(s), 8.5.219
Expeditious trial, 8.5.47–8.5.61
  See also Accused
Expenses
  International tribunals, 3.123.15
Expert (witness)
  Testimony of, 8.5.693–8.5.695
  See also Witnesses

Extensive destruction, not justified by military necessity
  See Property
Extermination,, 4.2.587
  As a crime against humanity (ICTY Article 5(b) and ICTR Article 3(b))
  See also Killing
Extradition, 11.1.35, 11.1.36
  National extradition provisions, 11.1.32–11.1.38
Extraterritoriality
  See, in general, Jurisdiction

Facilities for Defence counsel
  See, in general, Defence counsel
Facts
  Adjudicated, 8.5.729–8.5.733
  Facts of common knowledge, 8.5.728
  Statement of, 8.2.8–8.2.10
Fair trial, 4.2.421, 8.2.9, 8.5.3–8.5.6
  Denial of, as a war crime, 4.2.589
  Guarantees, before international courts and tribunals (ICTY Article 21 and ICTR Article 20
  See also Independent and impartial tribunal
False testimony
  Contempt and false testimony before ICC, 4.2.661–4.2.664
  Contradiction and, 4.2.653–4.2.655
  Direction to investigate, 4.2.652
  Elements of, 4.2.657–4.2.660
  History of ICTR Rule 91, 4.2.651
  History of ICTY Rule 91, 4.2.649–4.2.650
  Onus to prove knowingly and wilfully, 4.2.656
  Under solemn declaration (ICTY and ICTR Rule 91), 4.2.648–4.2.664
Families of victims
  See, in general, Victims
Federal Republic of Yugoslavia (Serbia and Montenegro)(FRY), 8.4.97 et seq
  See, in general, Yugoslavia
Federal Rules of Criminal Procedure, 8.5.329
Federal Rules of Evidence, 7.42
Fee splitting, 2.6.71–2.6.72
Fifth Amendment, 8.5.697
Fine
  payment of, for contempt, 4.2.645
Fitness to stand trial, 8.5.359
Flag of truce, improper use of, as a war crime, 4.2.589

Foča case (ICTY case No. IT96231), 4.2.171, 4.2.188, 4.2.191, 4.2.201, 4.2.211, 4.2.252, 4.2.265, 4.2.269, 4.2.270, 4.2.271, 4.2.444, 4.2.449, 4.2.549, 4.2.565, 4.2.566, 4.2.583, 6.2.34, 6.2.50, 6.2.55, 6.2.60, 6.2.114, 6.3.14, 8.3.6, 8.5.19, 8.5.530, 8.5.625, 8.5.749, 8.5.751, 8.6.13, 9.9, 912, 9.15, 9.19, 9.22, 9.23, 9.63, 9.67, 9.75, , 9.85, 9.86, 9.87, 9.91, 9.93, 9.96, 9.98, 9.108, 9.143, 9.146, 9.1499.78, 9.91, 9.93, 9.123
  See Janković, Janjić, Kovać, Vuković, Zelenović, and *Stanković*
  See Rape
Forcible transfer of children, 4.2.586
Franca, Jhoni, 4.2.551
France, 5.14–5.15
Freezing assets
  See Assets, freezing of
Frivolous motion, 10.1.65
Fundamental rights
  See, in general, Accused and other topics
Furundžija, 4.2.171, 4.2.268, 4.2.269–4.2.271, 4.2.464, 4.2.547, 4.2.566, 4.2.561–4.2.566, 6.2.28, 6.2.33, 6.2.49, 6.2.54, 6.2.55, 6.2.58, 6.2.62, 6.2.145, 8.5.11, 8.5.223, 8.5.334, 8.5.335, 8.5.336, 8.5.392, 8.5.511, 9.12, 9.20, 9.37, 9.38, 9.55, 8.5.534, 8.5.562, 8.5.666, 8.5.696, 9.47, 9.98, 9.127, 9.129, 9.148, 10.1.6

Gagović, 4.2.643, 8.4.59
Galić, 8.5.362
Gases
  War crime of employing gases, liquids, etc., 4.2.589
Gender
  See Sexual offences
General principles of criminal law, 6.1.1–6.3.67
General principles of law, 8.5.633
General provisions, 8.5.626–8.5.672
Geneva Convention, 6.2.87
  See also Protected Persons, Protected Property
  Common Article 3 of the, 4.2.461, 4.2.497–4.2.531
  Grave breaches of, 4.2.303 et seq.
  Improper use of emblems, 4.2.589
"Geneva Law," 4.2.431, 4.2.442, 4.2.500

Genocide, 4.2.1–4.2.159, 4.2.586
  In general (ICTY Article 4 and ICTR Article 2), 4.2.1
  Attempt to commit genocide (ICTY Article 4(3)(d) and ICTR Article 2(3)(d)), 4.2.1 et seq.
  Complicity in genocide (ICTY Article 4(3)(e) and ICTR Article 2(3)(e)), 4.2.1 et seq., 4.2.130–4.2.139
  Conspiracy to commit genocide (ICTY Article 4(3)(b) and ICTR Article 2(3)(b)), 4.2.147–4.2.156
  Cultural, 4.2.39
  Definition, 4.2.2
  Direct and public incitement to commit genocide (ICTY Art 4(3)(c) and ICTR Art 2(3)(c)), 4.2.140
  Existence of genocidal plan, 4.2.87–4.2.94
  Former Yugoslavia, 4.2.16–4.2.24
  ICC and, 4.2.586
  Mens rea requirement for incident, 4.2.144
  Participation in a genocidal plan, 4.2.77–4.2..82
  Proof of specific intent, 4.2.83–4.2.86
  Relative scale of the crimes, 4.2.95–4.2.96
  Rwanda, 4.2.25–4.2.33
  Variable standard of proof, 4.2.75–4.2.76
Germany, 5.165.17
Goldsteon, Richard, 2.5.5, 8.4.40
Good cause, 8.5.160
Good character, 8.5.722, 9.98
Goodwin v. UK, 8.4.41
Govedarica, Zdravko, 8.2.95
Government
  Amicus, as, 8.5.504–8.5.506
Gravity of the crime, 9.33–9.38
"Greater Serbia" Project, 8.2.62
Gruban, 8.2.95
Guilty Plea, 8.5.282–8.5.291, 9.86–9.90
  See also Plea
  Burden and standard of proof for aggravating factors, 9.123–9.125
  Conditions for accepting, 8.5.251–8.5.257
  Credit for time in custody pending surrender, 9.128–9.129
  Equivocal plea, 8.5.258–8.5.262
  Life imprisonment, 9.119–9.120
  Minimum term recommendation, 9.118
  Penalties in the Rome Statute, 9.111–9.114
  Sentencing procedures on, 9.105–9.129
Guzzardi v. Italy, 8.4.82

Hadžihasanović, Enver, 2.6.37, 2.6.38, 4.2.322, 4.2.360, 4.2.468, 6.1.25, 6.2.94, 6.2.106, 8.5.120, 8.5.121, 8.5.127, 8.5.129, 8.5.166, 8.5.327, 8.5.663, 8.5.685
Habeas corpus, 8.1.21
Hague Conventions respecting the Laws and Customs of War on Land, 4.2.302
"Hague law," 4.2.302, 4.2.431, 4.2.442, 4.2.487, 4.2.500
  Article 3 not confined to, 4.2.446–4.2.447
Haskić, Midhat, 8.5.655
Headquarters Agreement, 3.43.5
Health
  Factor in provisional release, 8.5.123–8.5.126
  Ill-health of accused, 8.5.147–8.5.150
Hearings, 8.5.464
  See also as subhead to other topics
  Closed, 8.5.206
  Ex parte, 8.5.219
  Fair and public, 8.5.29
  In camera, 8.5.206
  Public, 8.5.22–8.5.24
Hearsay, 8.5.218
  See also Evidence
  Definition, 8.5.642
Hechingen deportation case, 6.2.54
Hideki Tojo, Trial of, 6.2.80
Higaniro, Alphonse, 5.79
High command case, 6.2.77
Hors de combat
  Killing or wounding a person in, 4.2.589
Hostage(s), hostage-taking, 4.2.490–4.2.494, 4.2.524
  Hostage case, 6.2.80
  War crime of, 4.2.589
Host Country, 8.5.156–8.5.158
Hostile forces
  war crime of compelling service in, 4.2.589
Hostilities
  Persons taking no part in, 4.2.469–4.2.470
Humanitarian Intervention, 1.34–1.35
  War crimes and, 4.2.589
Human rights, 1.31, 1.57, 8.4.136
  See Accused, rights of
  Commission on, 4.4.9

ICTR (the International Criminal Tribunal for the Prosecution of Persons Responsible for Genocide and Other Serious Violations of International Humanitarian Law Committed in the Territory of Rwanda and Rwandan Citizens Responsible for Genocide and other such violations committed in the territory of neighbouring States, between 1 January 1994 and 31 December 1994)
  Amendment of Statute, 1.14–1.17
  Appeals Chamber, 2.1.46–2.1.47
  Article 5 (personal jurisdiction), 4.3.1–4.3.14
  Article 13, 2.1.40–2.1.41
  Article 29, 3.2
  Changing structure of, 2.1.14–2.1.19
  Composition of the Chambers, 2.1.1 et seq.
  Concurrent jurisdiction, 5.21–5.34
  Election of judges, 2.1.28–2.1.35
  Elements of the offences, 4.2.535–4.2589
  Establishment of, 1.1, 1.11
  History of, 2.32.7
  Lawfulness of, 1.18–1.33
  President, 2.1.48
  Request for information, 5.51–5.52
  Rule 77, 4.2.590 et seq.
  Updated statute of, 1.1
ICTY (the International Tribunal for the Prosecution of Persons Responsible for Serious Violations of International Humanitarian Law Committed in the Territory of the Former Yugoslavia since 1991)
  Amendment of Statute, 1.71.10
  Appeals chamber, 2.1.46–2.1.47
  Article 6 (Personal jurisdiction), 4.3.1–4.3.14
  Article 14, 2.1.39
  Article 31, 3.4
  Changing structure of, 2.1.14–2.1.19
  Composition of the Chambers, 2.1 et seq.
  Concurrent jurisdiction, 5.21–5.34
  Election of judges, 2.1.21–2.1.26
  Elements of the offences, 4.2.535–4.2.589
  Establishment of, 1.1 et seq.
  Lawfulness of, 1.18–1.33
  Historical background, 1.2
  Jurisdiction
  Military tribunal, 1.40–1.41
  Organization of, 2.1
  Qualification and election of judges, 2.1.10–2.1.32
  Request for information, 5.51–5.52
  Rule 77, 4.2.590 et seq.
  Updated statute of, 1.1

Identification, of the Accused
  Dock, 8.5.620–8.5.622
IFOR (NATO led Implementation Force),
    8.4.80
  International arrest warrants sent to all
    states and, 8.4.142–8.4.143
Imanishimwe, 8.2.57, 8.5.710, 8.5.711
Immunity
  No state immunity, 6.2.64–6.2.68
  Personal (immunity *ratione personae*),
    4.2.510–4.2.513
  State immunity (immunity *ratione
    materiae*), 4.2.510–4.2.513
Impartiality, 2.1.20
Imprisonment
  Place of, 9.141–9.147
  Remainder of his life, 9.121–9.122
  Supervision of, 9.148–9.149
In camera hearings, 8.5.206
  See also Hearings
Incapacity
  See McNaghten's Case
Incitement, 4.2.140
  See also Instigation
  Direct and public, to commit genocide
    (ICTY Article 4(3)(c) and ICTR
    Article 2(3)(c)), 4.2.140–4.2.146
Independent and impartial tribunal,
    8.5.29–8.5.31
  See also Accused
Indictment, 8.2.1–8.2.112
  Advertisement of (ICTY and ICTR Rule
    60), 8.4114–8.4.118
  Amendment of (ICTY and ICTR Rule 50),
    8.2.69–8.2.87
  Concise statement of facts and crimes
    charged, 8.2.8–8.2.10, 8.2.23–8.2.25
  Cumulative charging, 8.3.1–8.3.20
  Defects in, 8.2.9, 8.2.84
  Dismissal of counts, 8.2.34
  Dismissal of illegal conduct during arrest,
    8.4.110–8.4.111
  Duplicity, 8.2.5–8.2.7
  Excessive vagueness, 8.2.26–8.2.29
  Investigation and preparation of,
    8.2.1–8.2.10
  Nondisclosure of (ICTY and ICTR Rule
    53), 8.2.102–8.2.109
  Orders and warrants, 8.4.1–8.4.145
  Public character of (ICTY and ICTR Rule
    52), 8.2.100–8.2.101
  Publication of, 8.4.113–8.4.118

  Referral of indictment to another court,
    5.84–5.91
  Requirements of, 8.2.4
  Review of, 8.2.11–8.2.12
  Same transaction, 8.2.44 et seq., 8.2.63,
    8.2.68
  Schedule to
  Sealed, 8.2.105–8.2.109
    under seal (ICTY and ICTR Rule 54)
  Service of (ICTY and ICTR Rule 53 bis),
    8.2.110–8.2.112
  Submission of indictment by the prosecu-
    tor (Rule 47), 8.2.17–8.2.38
  Superceding, 8.2.35
  Suspension of (ICTR Rule 11 bis)
  Withdrawal (ICTY and ICTR Rule 51),
    8.2.88–8.2.99
Indigency, 2.6.6
Individual Criminal Responsibility (ICTY
    Article 7 and ICTR Article 6),
    6.2.1–6.2.158
  Levels of, 6.2.9–6.2.20
  Lowerranking accused and complementar-
    ity with national courts, 6.2.21–6.2.25
  Need to determine form of liability,
    6.2.28–6.2.29
  Participation
    Forms of, 6.2.32–6.2.37
    Intent and, 6.2.30–6.2.31
Information, retention of/ preservation of,
    8.1.28–8.1.31
Inhuman treatment (also Cruel treatment),
    4.2.407–4.2.411, 4.2.570–4.2.572,
    4.2.589
  Detention under inhumane treatment,
    4.2.573
Inhumane acts, 4.2.407–4.2.411
Initial appearance, 8.5.248–8.5.249
Innocence, presumption of, 8.5.25–8.5.26
Insanity
  Diminished responsibility, 6.3.17–6.3.37
Instigation, instigating (ICTY Article 7(1)
    and ICTR and SCSL Article 6(1)),
    6.2.46–6.2.48
Instruments of restraint, use of,
    8.5.556–8.5.558
Inter pares hearings, 8.2.41
Interlocutory appeals, 8.5.456–8.5.464,
    10.1.13–10.1.16
  Available to parties, 8.5.462–8.5.463
  Hearing, 8.5.464
  On jurisdiction, 8.5.457–8.5.461

1070 • *International Criminal Practice*

Internal
  Application of Art. 3 to, 4.2.454–4.2.460, 4.2.464–4.2.468
International
  Arrest warrant, 8.4.58
  Criminal law
    See Criminal law
  Humanitarian law, 1.34–1.35
International Committee of the Red Cross (ICRC), 6.2.90, 6.2.91, 8.4.32
International cooperation and judicial assistance
  ICC Rule 167, 4.2.671
International Court of Justice (ICJ)
  Concurrent jurisdiction between ICTs and, 5.31–5.34
  Relationahips of the ICTs to, 1.42–1.56
International Covenant on Civil and Political Rights (ICCPR), 2.6.18, 8.2.81, 8.5.15, 8.5.16, 10.1.2
International Criminal Court (ICC)
  Admissibility, , 5.103–5.119
  Apartheid, 4.2.588
  Application of the Statute and the Rules, 4.2.667
  Article 1, 5.99–5.102
  Complementarity with national courts, 5.94–5.97
  Crimes against humanity (Article 7), 4.2.300–4.2.301, 4.2.587
  Election of judges, 2.1.36
  Elements of crime, 4.2.584–4.2.589
  Enforced disappearance of persons, 4.2.588
  Enforced prostitution, 4.2.588
  Enforced sterilization, 4.2.588
  Establishment of, 1.62
  Exercise of jurisdiction, 4.2.666
  Forced pregnancy, 4.2.588
  Genocide and, 4.2.158–4.2.160, 4.2.586
  Immediate arrest, 4.2.673
  Individual criminal responsibility, 4.3.12, 6.2.2–6.2.158, 6.3.64, 8.5.451
  Inhumane acts, 4.2.588
  International cooperation and judicial assistance, 4.2.671
  Investigation, prosecution, and trial, 4.2.669
  Jurisdiction ratione temporis, 4.4.19–4.4.22
  Ne bis in idem, 4.2.672, 4.2.672, 5.120–5.125
  Offences against the administration of justice, 4.2.655
  Organization of, 2.9
  Periods of limitation, 4.2.668
  Persecution and, 4.2.291–4.2.293, 4.2.588
  Personal jurisdiction, 4.3.11–4.3.19
  Persons under 18, 4.3.13
  Preamble, 5.98
  Rape, 4.2.588
  Sanctions for misconduct before the court, 4.2.674
  Sanctions under Article 70, 4.2.670
  Sexual slavery, 4.2.588
  Sexual violence, 4.2.588
  Superior orders and prescription of law, 6.3.66
  Territorial jurisdiction, 4.4.23–4.4.29
  Trial and appellate levels at, 2.1.9
  War crimes, Article 8, 4.2.532–4.2.534, 4.2.589
  See also specific crimes
International criminal tribunals
  Concurrent jurisdiction, 5.21–5.31
  Deferral
    Justification for deferral to the ICTs, 5.49–5.50
  Determination of courts of any state, 5.92–5.97
  Formal request for deferral, 5.61–5.83
  Historical background, 5.25.3
  In general, 5.45.7
  Indictment, 5.84–5.91
  National war crimes cases, 5.8–5.20
  Non bis in idem, 5.35–5.50
  Preamble to ICC, 5.98, 8.2.96
  Primacy of, 5.1–5.120
  Prosecutor's request for deferral5.535.60
  Request for information, 5.51–5.52
International Criminal Tribunal for Rwanda (ICTR)
  See ICTR
International criminal proceedings, 8.1.1–8.6.23
  See also Indictment, Investigations and other topics
International Criminal Tribunal for the former Yugoslavia (ICTY)
  See ICTY
International Implementation Force (IFOR), 8.4.80
International Military Tribunal (IMT)
  at Nuremberg

See Nuremberg Tribunal for the Far East
See Tokyo Tribunal
International organizations, 8.4.31, 11.1.28–11.1.29
International Tribunals
See also specific topics
Article 30, 3.2
Organisation of, 2.12.6.72
Status, privileges, and immunities of, 3.1–3.21
Interpretation
See also Language, Interpreters, Solemn Declaration, Interpreters, Translation
Requests for, 8.5.91
Interpreter(s)
Solemn declaration by, 8.5.525–8.5.526
Intervention
See Humanitarian Intervention
Investigations, Investigators, 4.2.669, 8.1.1–8.1.37
Conduct of, 8.1.1–8.1.7
Provisional measures, 8.1.8–8.1.11
Israel, 6.2.81, 6.2.85

Jan, Saad Saood, 8.4.12
Janjić, Janko, 8.2.95, 8.2.97
Janjić, Nikica, 6.2.21
Janković, Gojko
Javor, 5.14
Jelisić, Goran, 4.2.34, 4.2.56, 4.2.58, 4.2.59, 4.2.65, , 4.2.66, 4.2.69, 4.2.70, 4.2.72, 4.2.75, 4.2.77, 4.2.80, 4.2.86, 4.2.91, 4.2.99, 4.2.101, 4.2.112, 4.2.114, 4.2.123, 4.2.126, 4.2.160, 4.2.322, 6.3.51, 8.2.77, 8.5.274–8.5.276, 8.5.289, 8.5.290, 8.5.490, 8.5.575, 8.5.612, 8.5.684, 8.6.9, 8.6.14, 9.30, 9.40, 9.42, 9.49, 9.51, 9.83, 9.85, 9.86, 9.87, 9.91, 9.93, 9.98, 10.1.59
Joinder
Of accused (ICTY and ICTR Rule 48), 8.2.39–8.2.54
Of crimes (ICTY and ICTR Rule 49), 8.2.58–8.2.68
Of trials (ICTR Rule 48 bis), 8.2.42, 8.2.55–8.2.57
To protect victims and witnesses, 8.2.51–8.2.54
Joint criminal enterprise (See also common criminal purpose), 6.2.38–6.2.45
Joint and separate trials (Joinder), 8.5.542–8.5.555

Jokić, 8.5.153, 8.5.154, 8.5.169
Jokić and Ademi, 2.1.125
Jorda, Claude, 8.1.25
Jorgić, 4.2.20, 5.16
Josipović, Drago, 8.5.120, 10.1.58
Journalists, 8.4.40–8.4.44
See also Media
Judgement(s), 8.6.1–8.6.23
ICTR final judgments, 8.6.5
ICTY trial judgements, 8.6.4
Judgement on appeal, 10.1.81–10.1.85
Legal assistants, drafting by, 8.6.2–8.6.3
Motion for judgement of acquittal, 8.6.6–8.6.15
Rule 98 (ICTY), Rule 88 (ICTR), 8.6.16–8.6.19
Status of the acquitted person, 8.6.20–8.6.23
Judges
Absence of, 2.1.74–2.1.79
Disqualification of, 2.1.56 et seq.
Disqualification by Bureau, 2.1.63–2.1.73
Duty judge, 2.1.122–2.1.125
Election of ICC judges, 2.1.36–2.1.37
Election of ICTR judges, 2.1.28–2.1.31
Election of ICTY judges, 2.1.21–2.1.26
Impartiality of, 2.1.20, 2.1.45, 2.1.52, 8.5.29–8.5.30
Judge shopping, 2.1.44
Power of incrimination, 6.1.12–6.1.13
Qualification and election of, 2.1.10–2.1.12
Rotation of judges and deliberations, 2.1.111–2.1.127
Rule-making and, 7.44
Solemn declaration, 2.1.49–2.1.51
Judicial notice, 8.5.723–8.5.734
Adjudicated facts, 8.5.729–8.5.733
Citing authorities and, 8.5.734
Res judicata and, 8.5.727
Stipulations and, 8.5.728
Judicial orders, See Orders
Juge d'instruction, 8.5.301
Jurisdiction
Challenge to, 8.5.447–8.5.448
Concurrent jurisdiction, 5.21–5.34, 8.2.96
Challenge of grant of primacy to the ICTR, 5.30
ICT and ICJ, 5.31–5.34
Justification for trying crimes before ICTs, 5.28–5.29
Contempt
See Contempt

Jurisdiction *(continued)*
  Exercise of at ICC, 4.2.666
  Provisional release, 8.5.127
  Ratione materiae (subjectmatter jurisdiction), 4.7, 4.2.1, 4.7, 4.2.67
  Ratione personae (personal jurisdiction), 4.3.1–4.3.14, 4.18, 4.2.510–4.2.513, 4.3.1–4.3.14
  Ratione loci (territorial jurisdiction), 4.4.1–4.4.23, 4.19
  Ratione temporis (temporal jurisdiction), 4.4.1–4.4.23, 4.19
  Subject-matter jurisdiction, 4.2.1–4.2.674
Jurisprudence
  See Precedent
Jurović, 4.2.91
Jury
  Joint trials and absence of jury, 8.5.544
Justice
  Interests of justice, 10.1.56–10.1.57

Kabiligi and Ntabakuze, 4.41.18, 8.2.49
Kajelijeli, 4.4.18, 7.67, 8.5.234, 8.5.326, 8.5.327, 8.5.331, 8.5.382, 8.5.383, 8.5.408, 8.5.553, 8.5.734
Kama, Laity, 8.1.16, 8.4.57, 8.5.64
Kambanda, Jean, 4.2.26, 4.2.29, 4.2.33, 4.2.59, 4.2.139, 8.1.20, 8.5.270, 8.5.278, 8.5.279, 8.5.289, 8.5.331, 9.12, 9.28, 9.35, 9.39, 9.66, 9.70, 9.75, 9.86, 9.88, 9.91
Kamuhanda, 8.5.232
Kant, Immanuel, 9.17
Kanyabashi, Joseph, 4.2.602, 4.3.7, 5.30, 5.79, 5.116, 7.39, 7.71, 8.5.30, 8.5.131, 8.5.144, 8.5.146, 8.5.150, 8.5.204, 8.5.267, 8.5.441
Karadžić, Radovan, 4.268, 4.2.83, 4.2.86, 4.2.87, 4.2.89, 4.2.96, 4.2.97, 4.2.275, 4.2.335, 4.2.544, 5.66, 6.71, 5.82, 6.2.11, 6.2.19, 7.51, 8.1.6, 8.4.127, 8.4.128, 8.4.133, 8.4.134, 8.4.136, 8.4.139, 8.4.142, 8.4.148, 8.5.333, 8.5.703, 8.5.705, 11.1.20, 11.1.25, 11.1.38
Karemera, 7.85, 8.5.268, 8.5.447–8.5.449
Katava, Marinko , 8.2.93
Kayishema, Clement , 4.2.30, 4.2.32, 4.2.33, 4.2.37, 4.2.41, 4.2.45–4.2.49, 4.2.55, 4.2.58, 4.2.59, 4.2.67, 4.2.73, 4.2.81, 4.2.86, 4.2.90, 4.2.91, 4.2.95, 4.2.96, 4.2.105, 4.2.108, 4.2.119–4.2.122,
4.2.125, 4.2.160, 4.2.192, 4.2.196, 4.2.208, 4.2.221, 4.2.228, 4.2.236, 4.2.238, 4.2.239, 4.2.241, 4.2.247, 4.2.248, 4.2.297, 4.2.298, 4.2.506, 4.2.510, 4.2.513, 4.2.516–4.2.521, 4.2.541 6.1.17, 6.2.34, 6.2.60, 6.2.114, 6.2.132, 6.2.148, 7.2.151, 6.3.10, 6.3.12, 6.3.13, 7.71, 8.2.35, 8.2.42, 8.2.45, 8.2.49, 8.2.51, 8.3.9, 8.5.70, 8.5.72, 8.5.204, 8.5.338, 8.5.357, 9.9, 9.32, 9.66, 9.75, 9.80, 9.85, 9.91, 9.122, 11.1.29
Keraterm camp case (ICTY case No. IT958I), 8.4.61, 8.4.62
Kerr-Frisbie doctrine, 8.4.99, 11.1.10
Khan, Tafazzal, 8.2.88, 8.3.10
Khmer Rouge, 1.156 et seq., 4.2.117, 4.2.218
Kidnapping, 8.4.110
Killing, 4.2.35
  See also Execute, Extermination, murder
  Members of a national, ethnical, racial or religious group, as genocide (ICTY Article 4(2)(a) and ICTR Article 2(2)(a)), 4.2.41
  Murder
    See Murder
  Violation of Additional Protocol II and Common Article 3 (ICTR Article 4)
  Treacherously killing or wounding, 4.2.589
  War crime of wilful killing, 4.2.589
  Wilful, 4.2.589
    as a Grave Breach of the Geneva Conventions (ICTY Article 2), 4.2.538–4.2.541
Kiseljak (Bosnia and Herzegovina)
  See Rajić
Knesen, 5.18
Knezević, 2.6.38
Knowledge, 4.2.228–4.2.232
  Command responsibility and, 6.2.125
Kolundžija, Dragan, 8.2.21, 8.2.41, 8.5.474, 9.157
Kondić, Dragan, 4.2.197, 4.2.223, 4.2.278, 4.2.443, 4.2.479, 4.2.483, 4.2.485, 4.2.486, 6.2.21, 8.2.97
Konjić Hospital, 8.4.29
Kordić and Čerkez, 4.2.210, 4.2.223, 4.2.257, 4.2.258, 4.2.260, 4.2.277, 4.2.279, 4.2.289, 4.2.293, 4.2.299, 4.2.321, 4.2.335, 4.2.357, 4.2.359, 4.2.394–4.2.396, 4.2.405, 4.2.407,

4.2.416, 4.2.418, 4.2.424, 4.2.428,
4.2.447, 4.2.475, 4.2.495, 4.2.580,
6.2.35, 6.2.48, 6.2.50, 6.2.104,
6.2.142, 6.2.147, 6.2.148, 6.3.56,
6.3.62, 6.3.63,, 8.2.83, 8.3.8, 8.4.17,
8.5.49, 8.5. 233, 8.5.416, 8.5.480,
8.5.481, 8.5.534, 8.5.643, 8.5.653,
8.5.744, 8.6.9, 9.9, 9.12, 9.15, 9.17,
9.24, 9.30, 9.39, 9.49, 9.75, 9.98,
10.1.29, 10.1.31
Kordić and Čerkez Trial Judgement,
4.2.357, 4.2.394–4.2.397, 8.5.534
Kordice, 8.2.15, 8.4.63
Kos, Milojica , 6.2.48
Kosovo, 1.3 et seq., 8.2.68
  Prosecution of war and ethnic crimes, 1.116–1.141
Kostić, Predrag, 8.2.95
Kovac, Radomir, 8.2.20
Kovačević, Milan, 8.2.63, 8.2.78, 8.2.86,
  8.2.106, 8.4.27, 8.4.31, 8.4.64, 8.4.66,
  8.4.68, 8.5.150, 8.5.152, 8.5.163,
  8.5.241, 8.5.250, 8.5.480, 8.5.691,
  8.5.692, 8.5.726
Krajisnik, Momcito, 1.20, 2.1.122, 2.5.33,
  4.2.22, 8.5.168
Krauch, Iarl, U.S. v., 4.2.576
Krnojelac, 6.2.43, 6.2.100, 6.2.132, 8.284,
  8.5.58, 8.5.79, 8.5.449
Kremenović, 2.6.10
Krsmanović, Aleksa, 8.4.60, 8.5.702, 8.5.707
Krstić, Radislav, 4.2.38, 4.2.39, 4.2.54, 4.2.67,
  4.2.72, 4.2.79, 4.2.98–4.2.100, 4.2.102,
  4.2.109, 4.2.110, 4.2.115, 4.2.118,
  4.2.160, 4.2.232, 4.2.250, 4.2.254,
  4.2.255, 4.2.126, 4.2.295, 4.2.427,
  4.2.541, 6.2.34, 6.2.35, 6.2.41, 6.2.48,
  6.2.50, 8.2.106, 8.4.70, 9.15, 9.33,
  9.52, 9.65, 9.71, 9.74, 9.75, 9.82, 9.91,
  9.98, 9.102, 9.104, 11.1.16
Krupp von Bohlen und Halbach, 8.2.91
Kubura, Amir, 4.2.468, 6.125, 6.2.106,
  8.5.120, 8.5.121, 8.5.166
Kusijić, 4.2.20
Kunarac, Dragoljub, 2.6.46, 8.5.54, 8.5.216,
  8.5.218, 8.5.273, 8.5.612, 8.5.672
Kupreškić, 2.1.67, 2.5.28, 2.6.30, 2.6.49, 3.8,
  4.2.190, 4.2.194, 4.2.222, 4.2.223,
  4.2.444, 4.2.276, 4.2.277, 4.2.284,
  4.2.285, 4.2.287, 4.2.295, 4.2.299,
  4.2.322, 4.2.541, 4.2.631, 6.1.19,
  6.3.54, 6.3.55, 6.3.57, 6.3.59, 6.3.61,

8.2.4, 8.2.82, 8.3.3, 8.3.18, 8.4.7,
8.5.134, 8.5.161, 8.5.233, 8.5.356,
8.5.413, 8.5.415, 8.5.475, 8.5.485,
8.5.496, 8.5.534,8.5.543, 8.5.562,
8.5.564, 8.5.570, 8.5.588, 8.5.640,
8.5.662, 8.5.667, 8.5.681, 8.5.685,
8.5.722, 8.5.760, 8.6.12, 9.9, 9.10,
9.33, 9.39, 9.66, 10.1.58,
10.1.60–10.1.62, 10.1.65
Kvočka, Miroslav, 1.48, 4.2.442, 4.2.443,
  4.2.550, 4.8, 4.17, 5.33, 5.34, 6.2.48,
  8.2.4, 8.5.35, 8.5.61, 8.5.102, 8.5.136,
  8.5.164, 8.5.241, 8.5.250, 8.5.449,
  8.5.489, 8.5.612, 8.5.728, 8.6.10,
  9.35, 9.38, 9.75

Lajić, Goran, 6.2.21, 8.2.97, 8.4.61
Landžo, Esad, 2.5.31, 2.5.82, 2.6.28, 6.3.5,
  6.3.6, 6.3.19, 6.3.24, 6.3.25, 8.3.12,
  8.4.37, 8.4.65, 8.5.5, 8.5.133, 8.5.154,
  8.5.157, 8.5.348, 8.5.355, 8.5.358,
  8.5.359, 8.5.540, 8.5.561, 8.5.582
Language(s), 8.5.39–8.5.45
  See also Interpretation, Interpreters,
    Solemn Declaration, Translation
  Accused entitled to statements in language
    he understands, 8.5.319
  Defence counsel, 2.6.21–2.6.22
  Version most favourable to accused, 7.85
  Working languages, 3.17–3.18, 7.57–7.62
Lasva River Valley cases, 5.66, 5.73, 5.74,
  5.82, 8.5.504, 8.5.534
  See also Aleksovksi, Zlatko (ICTY Case
    No IT9514/1T), 8.5.534
  See Blaškić, Tihomir (ICTY Case No.
    IT9514T), 8.5.534
  See Furundžija, Anto (ICTY Case No.
    IT9517T), 8.5.534
  See Kordić, Dario and Čerkez, Mario
    (ICTY Case No. IT9514/2T), 8.5.534
  See Kupreškić et al. (ICTY Case No.
    IT9516T), 8.5.534
  See Marinić, Zoran (ICTY Case No.
    IT9515I), 8.5.534
Laws or customs of war, violations of (ICTY
    Article 3), 4.2.430–4.2.495
  Applicability to internal conflict,
    4.2.454–4.2.460
  Background, 4.2.431–4.2.435
  Common to both internal and
    international armed conflicts,
    4.2.464–4.2.468

Laws or customs of war, violations of (ICTY Article 3) *(continued)*
   Common to Geneva Convention, 4.2.461–4.2.462
   Conditions for application of Art. 3, 4.2.452–4.2.453
   Constituent offenses of Art. 3, 4.2.471–4.2.484
   ICTY Art. 3, 4.2.485–4.2.494
   Mens rea requirement, 4.2.439–4.2.441
   Persons taking no part in the hostilities, 4.2.469–4.2.470
   Residual nature of Art. 3, 4.2.448–4.2.451
   Security Council interpretation of Art. 3, 4.2.436–4.2.438
   Violations of Additional Protocol 1, 4.2.495–4.2.496
Lawyer-client privilege, 8.5.752–8.5.757
Lebanon, 6.2.85
Leandovery Castle, 6.2.2
Legal aid, 8.5.71
Legality, principle of, 6.1.4–6.1.8
Legislation
   ICTY and ICTR and, 4.5
Legitimate expectation, 8.5.97
Li, Haopei, 1.25, 4.2.334, 4.2.459, 6.3.41
Life imprisonment, 9.119–9.120
Life and person
   Violence to and customs of war, 4.2.486–4.2.487
Limitation periods, 4.2.668
Ljuboten, 5.77
Lome Peace Agreement, 1.64, 1.69
London Charter for the IMT at Nuremberg
   See Nuremberg Tribunal

Male captus, bene detentus rule, 8.4.112
Management Committee
   ICTY, 2.1.104–2.1.105
Martić, Milan, 6.2.11, 6.3.58, 8.1.6, 8.4.118, 8.4.128, 8.4.139
Martinović, Vinko, a.k.a. "[Tela]", 8.5.45, 8.5.599, 8.5.757
Massiah v. U.S., 8.5.103, 8.5.105
Materiality, 8.5.330
   Defense show materiality of evidence, 8.5.328–8.5.332
Mavrova Road Workers, 5.77
McDonald, Gabrielle Kirk, 1.40, 4.2.339, 4.2.352, 4.2.368, 4.2.369, 4.2.370, 6.3.41, 8.1.21, 8.2.15, 8.4.12, 8.5.8, 8.5.74, 8.5.507, 8.5.753

McNaghten's Case (1843) (definition of insanity), 6.3.36
   See also Fitness to stand trial
Meakić, 8.5.215, 8.5.250
Measures for the Protection of victims and witnesses, 8.5.205–8.5.234
Media, 8.2.215, 8.5.215
   See also Journalists
   Pretrial media coverage and, 8.5.619
Medical examination
   Of accused, 8.5.522–8.5.524
Medical evidence
   See Evidence
Medical or scientific experiments, war crime of, 4.2.589
Medina, Ernest, U.S. v. 6.2.83, 6.2.84
Melenki v. Chief Military Prosecutor, 6.2.81
Mens rea
   Actus rea and, 4.2.35–4.2.51
   Customs of war, 4.2.439–4.2.441
   Genocide and, 4.2.52–4.2.67, 4.2.149–4.2.151
   Knew or had reason to know, command responsibility and, 6.2.124
   Persecution and, 4.2.287–4.2.290
   War crimes, 4.2.402–4.2429
Mental element
   See Mens Rea
Meron, Theodor, 1.34, 4.1.23, 6.2.71
Military insignia, 4.2.589
Military operations
   War crime of compelling participation, 4.2.589
Military superiors
   See Command responsibility
Miller v. Minister of Pensions, 8.5.614
Milošević, Slobodan, 1.33, 1.58, 1.59, 2.5.34, 4.2.17, 4.2.22, 4.2.644, 4.4.10, 6.2.65, 7.62, 8.2.16, 8.2.62, 8.2.65, 8.2.67, 8.2.68, 8.4.144, 8.5.6, 8.5.189, 8.5.190, 8.5.319, 8.5.512, 8.5.565, 8.5.587
   Amicus and, 8.5.12
Milutinović, Milan, 4.4.10
Ministries case, 4.2.419
Minutes and records, 2.4.1–2.4.2
Miscarriage of justice, 10.1.6–10.1.7, 10.1.59
Misconduct of counsel, 2.6.57–2.6.70
Mistake of fact, 6.3.65
Mistake of law, 6.3.65
Mitigation, mitigating factors

See Sentencing
Mladić, Ratko, 4.2.17, 4.2.19–4.2.22, 4.2.68, 4.2.83, 4.2.86, 4.2.87, 4.2.89, 4.2.96, 4.2.97, 4.2.275, 4.2.335, 4.2.544, 5.66, 5.71, 5.82, 6.2.11, 6.2.19, Ratko, 7.51, 8.1.6, 8.4.127, 8.4.128, 8.4.133, 8.4.134, 8.4.135, 8.4.136, 8.4.139, 8.4.142, 8.4.148, 8.5.703, 8.5.705, 9.74, 11.1.20, 11.1.25, 11.1.38
Model Code of Pre-Arraignment Procedure, 8.5.257
Morillon, Philippe, 8.4.25, 8.4.26, 8.4.36
Motions
  Denial of payment, 8.5.484–8.5.485
  ICTR motions practice, 8.5.477–8.5.478
  ICTY motions practice, 8.5.473–8.5.476
  Interlocutory appeal, 8.5.482
  Oral motions at trial, 8.5.475–8.5.476
  Preliminary, 8.5.430–8.5.485
  Protective measures, 8.5.340–8.5.342
  Reconsider, 8.5.480–8.5.481
  Rule 73, 8.5.468–8.5.485
  Time for filing responses to, 8.5.237–8.5.238
  Types of motions, 8.5.479–8.5.481
  Written motions, 8.5.474
Motive
  Aggravating circumstance, 9.65 et seq.
  Irrelevance of, 4.2.190–4.2.192
Mrkšić, Mile, 8.4.66
Mucić, Zdravko, 2.2.16, 2.2.17, 2.6.26, 2.6.63, 4.2.424, 4.2.632, 5.68, 6.2.121, 7.1.4, 8.2.44, 8.4.3, 8.5.69, 8.5.93, 8.5.101, 8.5.165, 8.5.330, 8.5.454, 8.5.549, 8.5.561, 8.5.623, 8.5.656, 9.46, 9.48, 9.61, 9.76
Mugiraneza, 8.5.757
Multiple sentences, 9.126–9.127
Municipal law, 11.1.34–11.1.38
Munyakazi, 8.2.57
Munyeshyaka, 5.15
Murder
  As crime against humanity (ICTY Article 5(a) and ICTR Article 3(a)
  As a violation of the laws or customs of war (ICTY Article 3), 4.2.485
  As a violation of Article 3 common to the Geneva Conventions and of Additional Protocol II (ICTR Article 4(a)), 4.2.497–4.2.533
  ICC, 4.2.587
  War crime, 4.2.589

Musema, Alfred, 2.6.64, 4.2.30, 4.2.33, 4.2.130, 4.2.131, 4.2.133, 4.2.138, 4.2.148, 4.2.149, 4.2.152, 4.2.154, 4.2.156, 4.2.237, 4.2.269, 4.2.271, 5.80, 8.5.201, 9.12, 9.34, 9.60, 9.69, 9.82, 9.85
Mutilation, 4.2.589
  War crime, 4.2.589
Muvunyi, 8.5.226

Nahimana, Ferdinand, 4.2.153, 4.2.656, 4.2.659, 4.4.18, Nahimana, 8.1.16, 8.2.30, 8.2.32, 8.5.14–8.5.19, 8.5.204, 8.5.214, 8.5.320, 8.5.321, 8.5.322, 8.5.449, 8.5.451, 8.5.452, 8.5.514, 8.5.517
Naletilić, Mladen, a.k.a. "Tuta," 8.5.45, 8.5.599, 8.5.757
Naletelić v. Croatia, 1.60
National courts, 8.2.95
  ICTs not excluded from trying cases, 5.445.45
  Lower-ranking accused and, 6.2.21–6.2.27
National flags, use of, 4.2.589
National group, 4.2.115–4.2.118
National law, 4.1.4–4.1.7
National security, 8.4.21–8.4.27, 8.5.531, 11.1.17–11.1.19
National war crimes prosecutions, 5.85.20
NATO, 2.5.44
Nazis, 4.2.2, 4.2.206
  See also Nuremberg Tribunal
Ndajambaje, Elie, 5.79, 8.5.204, 8.5.281, 8.5.326, 8.5.408, 8.5.546, 8.5.547, 8.5.552, 8.5.553
Negligence
  Counsel's negligence at trial, 10.1.58
  Criminal negligence, 4.2.403
Netherlands, 5.18
New offences, 4.54.10
Necessity, See Duress
Neprosteno, 5.77
Netherlands, 5.18
Ngeze, 2.6.35, 8.1.27, 8.2.34
Nicaragua case, International Court of Justice (1986 ICJ Reports 14), 1.53, 4.2.341, 4.2.351, 4.2.352, 4.2.369, 4.2.370, 4.2.381
Nieto-Navia, Rafael, 4.2.380, 8.1.21, 8.11.23
Nikolić, Dragan, 4.2.18–4.2.19, 4.2.83, 4.2.202, 4.2.234, 4.2.263, 4.2.274, 4.2.318, 4.2.335, 4.2.362, 4.2.544,

Nikolić, Dragan *(continued)*
    7.51, 8.2.73, 8.4.110– 8.4.113,
    8.4.128, 8.4.130, 8.4.138, 8.4.145,
    11.1.23
Niyanteze, 5.19
Niyitigeka, Eliezer, 4.4.18, 7.71, 8.5.485
NLA Leadership case, 5.77
Non-public materials, 8.5.534
Nondisclosure, 8.2.102–8.2.109
Nobilo, Anto, 4.2.608–4.2.614, 4.2.633
Non bis in idem, Ne bis in idem, 4.2.672,
    5.35–5.43, 5.120–5.125
    Exceptions to, 5.46–5.48
Noncompliance with rules (ICTY and ICTR
    Rule 5), 7.68–7.71
Non-disclosure, 8.2.102–8.2.109
Non-governmental organizations (NGO),
    8.4.136
Non-retroactivity ratione personae, 6.1.3,
    6.1.21–6.1.27
North Carolina v. Alford, 8.5.257
Notices
    Notice of appeal, 10.1.20–10.1.22
Not Guilty Plea
    See, in general, Plea
Nottebohm, 4.2.116–4.2.117
Nsabimana, 8.1.27, 8.5.226, 8.5.228, 8.5.330,
    8.5.491, 8.5.544, 8.5.553, 10.2.14
Nsengiyumva, Anatole, 4.4.18, 8.1.16,
    8.1.27, 8.5.204, 11.1.30
Ntabakuze, 8.2.49
Ntagerura, André, 4.2.139, 8.1.16, 8.1.27,
    8.2.32, 8.2.57, 8.4.85, 8.5.18,8.5.204,
    8.5.450, 8.5.453, 8.5.698, 8.5.710,
    8.5.711, 10.2.13
Ntahobali, 2.6.14,2.6.27, 2.6.70, 8.5.106,
    8.5.226, 8.5.228, 8.5.230, 8.5.544,
    8.5.547, 8.5.552, 8.5.554, 8.5.715
Ntakirutimana, 2.6.24, 4.2.642, 7.80, 8.2.6,
    8.2.45, 8.2.50, 8.2.51, 8.2.57, 8.5.63,
    8.5.68, 8.5.281, 8.5.729, 8.5.733
Nteziryano, 8.5.198, 8.5.225, 8.5.226,
    8.5.228, 8.5.330
Ntuyahaga, 5.89–5.91, 8.2.98, 8.5.26
Nulla poena sine lege, 4.9, 6.1.2,
    6.1.18–6.1.20, 9.146
Nullum crimen sine lege, 4.2.39, 4.2.463,
    4.9, 8.2.9
Nuremberg Tribunal (International Military
    Tribunal at Nuremberg), 1.35, 4.2.165
    et seq., 4.2.286, 4.2.432–4.2.433, 5.2,
    8.2.91

Nyiramasuhuko, 2.6.14,2.6.27, 2.6.70,
    4.2.633, 8.5.67, 8.5.106, 8.5.181,
    8.5.226, 8.5.228, 8.5.230, 8.5.231,
    8.5.323, 8.5.325, 8.5.544, 8.5.547,
    8.5.552, 8.5.554, 8.5.698, 8.5.713,
    8.5.715, 8.5.740, 10.2.11, 10.2.14
Nzirorera, 2.2.14, 2.6.34, 8.5.553

Obrenevic, Dragon, 4.2.22
Odio-Benito, Elizabeth, 8.4.12
Offences against the Administration of
    Justice, 4.2,590–4.2674
    See ICC Article 70
Office of the Prosecutor (OTP),
    2.5.1–2.5.46
    See also Prosecutor
Ojdanić, Dragoljub, 4.4.10
Omarska camp case (ICTY Case No. IT9541)
Ombudsman, 1.137–1.140
Onsite visit, 3.83.10
Onus of proof
    See Burden of proof
Opacić, Dragan, 4.2.652,8.5.462,
    8.5.704–8.5.705, 10.110
Open sessions, 8.5.527–8.5.528, 8.5.530
Opening statements, 8.5.559–8.5.562
Oral argument, 8.5.57–8.5.59
Oral evidence
    See, in general, Evidence, Witnesses
Order, ordering, ordered
    See ICTY Article 7(1) and ICTR and SCSL
    Article 6(1)
    Detention of suspects, 8.4.60
    Fitness to stand trial, 8.4.65
    Production of documents, 8.4.71–8.4.74
    Remedy error in personam, 8.4.61–8.4.62
    Return of materials, 8.4.64
    Superior orders, 6.3.66
Orders and warrants (ICTR AND ICTY Rule
    54), 8.4.1–8.4.145
Organization for Security and Cooperation in
    Europe (OSCE), 8.4.31
Osawa, 8.2.91
Ostrovsky, Yakov, 8.1.20, 8.2.37, 8.2.54,
    8.5.47
OTP (Office of the Prosecutor), 2.59, 8.4.11
    See Prosecutor
Outrages upon personal dignity, 4.2.528,
    4.2.581–4.2.583

Pandurevic, Vinko, 4.2.22
Papić, Dragan, 2.1.7, 2.1.79, 8.5.413

Papon, Dragan, 4.2.229
Pardon or commutation of sentences, 9.156–9.160
  General standards for, 9.161–9.165
Partie civile, 8.5.513
Parties' books, 10.1.76–10.1.77
Party, definition of, 8.2.31
Paspalj, 8.2.95
Peacekeeping mission
  War crime of attacking personnel involved in, 4.2.589
Penalties, 9.1 et seq
  See also Sentencing
Per curiam, 4.1.11
Perpetrators
  Class of, 4.2.511–4.2.516
Persecution, 4.2.276–4.2.294, 4.2.588
  Definition, 4.2.276–4.2.281
  Murder as persecution, 4.2.282
Personal circumstances of accused, 9.98–9.100
Personality disorder
  See, Fitness to stand trial, *McNaghten's Case*
Photography, 8.5.541
Pillage
  See Plunder
Pinochet, General Augusto, the *Pinochet case*, 6.2.63, 6.2.65, 6.2.67
Pisarević, Borislav, 2.6.47
Plan, planning, planned (ICTY Article 7(1) and ICTR and SCSL Article 6(1))
Plavsić, Biljana, 4.2.22–4.2.24, 8.5.168, 8.5.289, 9.86
Plea
  Bargain(s), bargaining, 8.5.279, 8.5.286–8.5.291
  Equivocal, 8.5.258–8.5.262
  Failure to enter, 8.5.267–8.5.270
  Guilty plea, 9.86–9.90
  Informed, uninformed, 8.5.11
  Plea agreement procedure, 8.5.292–8.5.294
Plenary
  Meetings/sessions, 2.1.106 et seq., 7.81
  Quorum, 2.1.109–2.1.110
Plunder, 4.2.529–4.2.530, 4.2.533, 4.2.576–4.2.580, 4.2.589
Poison, poisoned weapons, 4.2.472
  war crime of employing, 4.2.589
Polygraph test, 8.5.599–8.5.600
Popović, Milutin, 8.2.95

Population
  Crimes against humanity and, 4.2.200–4.2.212, 4.2.587
Powers of Trial Chamber, 8.5.86–8.5.87
Practice Directions, 2.1.88–2.1.90
Prcać, Dragoljub, 6.2.48
Pre-appeal judge, 10.1.23
Precedence of Judges, 2.1.56, 2.182–2.1.83
Precedent, doctrine of (*stare decisis*), 4.1.9, 4.1.12, 4.1.13
Pre-defence conferences, 8.5.492–8.5.498
  Order to submit detailed witness statements, 8.5.496–8.5.498
  Witness obligations, 8.5.495
Predojević, 8.2.95
Pregnancy, forced, 4.2.588
  See Prostitution, Rape, Sexual offences
Preliminary examination, 10.2.4–10.2.6
Preliminary Motions, 8.5.430–8.5.467
  Assignment of counsel, 8.5.455
  Defect in indictment, 8.5.449–8.5.450
  Decisions on motions challenging jurisdiction, 8.5.441–8.5.448
  Severance of crimes, 8.5.454
Preliminary proceedings, 8.5.244–8.5.281
  Equivocal plea, 8.5.258–8.5.262
  Guilty plea, 8.5.251–8.5.257, 8.5.271–8.5.280
  Failure to enter, 8.5.267–8.5.270
  Initial appearances, 8.5.248–8.5.249
  Prosecutor, role of, 8.5.250
Premeditation, 4.2.37, 4.2.42, 9.74
Prepare, preparing, prepared (See ICTY Article 7(1) and ICTR and SCSL Article 6(1))
Prescription of law, 6.3.66
President
  of the ICTY, 2.1.84
  of the ICTR, 2.1.84
Press, access, 8.5.510
  See also Media
Presumption of Innocence, 8.5.25–8.5.26, 8.5.615
  See also Accused
Pre-trial brief, 8.5.489
  Citing authorities, 8.5.734
  For Defence, 8.5.302–8.5.304
  Use of, 8.5.54–8.5.56
Pretrial conference
  ICTY and ICTR Rule 73, 8.5.486–8.5.491
  Varying the witness list at trial, 8.5.491

Pretrial judge, 8.5.55, 8.5.298–8.5.304
  Defence pretrial brief, 8.5.302–8.5.304
Primacy, of the ICTs, 5.15.120
Prima facie case, 8.2.2, 8.2.13, 8.2.14,
  8.2.14–8.2.16, 8.5.368–8.5.369
Principles of interpretation, 4.1.22–4.1.23
Prior statements, 8.5.313–8.5.317
  Hearsay declarant and, 8.5.318
Prisoners of War, Prisoners of War
  Convention (Third Geneva
  Convention of 1949)
  Compelling to serve hostile power,
    4.2.419–4.2.420
  Fair and regular trial, 4.2.421–4.2.422
Privilege
  See also Disclosure, Evidence
  Lawyer/client , 8.5.752–8.5.757
Privileges and immunities, 3.13.21
Proceedings appellate
  Control of, 8.5.535–8.5.536
  records of, 8.5.537–8.5.540
Professional conduct
  Misconduct of counsel, 2.6.57–2.6.70
Proof of facts
  Other than by oral evidence,
    8.5.716–8.5.719
Property
  Extensive destruction of, 4.2.417–4.2.418,
    4.2.589
  Plunder of, 4.2.484
  Restitution, 9.150–9.152
  War crime of destroying or seizing the
    enemy's property, 4.2.589
Proprio motu, 8.5.759, 9.51
Prosecutor (OTP), 2.5.1–2.5.46, 2.59 et seq.
  Assignment of case, role in, 8.2.250
  Deputy Prosecutor, 2.5.45
  Definition, 7.50
  Dilatory disclosure by, 8.5.343
  Disclosure by, 8.3.305–8.3.344
  Discretion, 2.5.30–2.5.33
  Functions, 2.5.19–2.5.27
  ICC Prosecutor, 2.5.38–2.5.44
  Role of, 2.5.282.5.29
  Structure of OTP, 2.5.12–2.5.14
  Submission of indictment by,
    8.2.17–8.2.38
Prostitution, enforced, 4.2.588, 4.2.589
  See also Pregnancy, forced; Rape; Sexual
    offences
Protected objects, 4.2.589
Protected Persons

War crimes and, 4.2.361–4.2.397
Protected Property, 4.2.398–4.2.429
Protection of victims and witnesses, 8.4.138,
  8.5.170–8.5.204
  Ex parte hearings, 8.5.219
  Family members, 8.5.230
  Identity of the victim or witness, 8.5.181
  Intimidation and harassment of witnesses,
    8.5.227
  Measures for, 8.5.205–8.5.234
  Objectively grounded measures,
    8.5.196–8.5.198
  Preventing disclosure of witness state-
    ments to public or media, 8.5.215
  Protected material, 8.5.226
  Protective measures must be exceptional,
    8.5.223
  Public, meaning of, 8.5.216
  Redaction of witness statements,
    8.5.199–8.5.201, 8.5.338–8.5.339
  Relationship of Rule 69 to Rule 75,
    8.5.182–8.5.185
  Review of protective measures, 8.5.231
  Self-incrimination by a witness, 8.5.225
  Sexual offences
    Protective orders for victims of, 8.5.218
  State cooperation pursuant to Art. 28,
    8.5.224, 11.1.111.2.10
  Tadić victims and witnesses decision of 10
    Aug. 1995, 8.5.220–8.5.222
  Third parties
    Exception to ban on disclosure to,
      8.5.217
  Witness anonymity, 8.5.186–8.5.195
    Withdrawal of, 8.5.192–8.5.195
  Witnesses with a criminal record,
    8.5.1798.5.180
Protective measures, 8.5.205–8.5.234
  See also Protection of victims and
    witnesses
  Disclosure of identity/identities, 8.5.181
  Exceptional nature of, 8.5.223
  Family members, 8.5.230
  Public disclosure, 8.5.213
  Review of, 8.5.231
  Testifying away from seat, 8.5.214
Provisional measures, 8.1.8–8.1.11
Provisional release, 8.5.113–8.5.169
  Accused will appear for trial,
    8.5.151–8.5.153
  Appeal of refusal to grant,
    8.5.159–8.5.160

Emergency application, 8.5.169
Exceptional circumstances,
  8.5.130–8.5.131, 8.5.139–8.5.143
Generally, 8.5.115 et seq.
Granting of, 8.5.120–8.5.121
Host country, 8.5.156–8.5.158
Jurisdiction, 8.5.127
Length of detention, 8.5.144–8.5.146
Presumption of detention, 8.5.132–8.5.138
State of health, 8.5.123–8.5.126,
  8.5.147–8.5.150
Timing of application, 8.5.122
Victims and witnesses
  Not to pose danger to, 8.5.154–8.5.155
Psychiatric and psychological reports, 9.108
Public
  Meaning of for purposes of non-disclosure, 8.5.216
Public hearings, 8.5.12, 8.5.22–8.5.24
  See also Hearings
Punishment
  General reflections, 9.115–9.117
  Legality of punishment, 6.1.18–6.1.20
  See also Sentencing
  Collective punishments, 4.2.523

Quarter, denial of
  as a war crime, 4.2.589
Quater, 2.6.56
Questioning
  Of an accused, 8.5.98–8.5.107
  See also Accused
  Prosecutor in absence of counsel,
    8.5.102–8.5.105
Quorum, 7.827.85
  See also Plenary

Racial group, 4.2.122–4.2.126
Radić, 4.2.443, 6.2.48, 8.5.57, 8.5.102,
  8.5.250
Radio TV Libre des Mille Collines, 5.50,
  5.73, 5.80
Radovan, 8.4.127
Radović, Ranko, 4.2.631
Rajić, Ivica, 4.2.335, 4.2.364, 4.2.382,
  4.2.399, 4.2.474, 4.2.477, 6.2.120 ,
  8.2.14, 8.4.128, 8.4.130, 8.4.131,
  8.4.137, 8.4.140, 8.4.141, 8.4.147,
  8.5.506, 8.5.664, 8.5.677, 8.5.743,
  11.1.20, 11.1.25
Randal's case, 8.4.41
Rape, 4.2.266–4.2.275, 4.2.557–4.2.567

See also Pregnancy, forced; Prostitution;
  Sexual offences; Torture
Aggravating circumstances, 9.789.80
Crime against humanity, 4.2.588
Definition, 4.2.588
Under Common Article 3
Elements of the Offence
  As a war crime, 4.2.589
Rape myth, 8.5.396
Ratio decidendi, 4.1.12
Ratione materiae, 4.4
Reasonable doubt
  Proof of guilt beyond, 8.5.612–8.5.615
Reasonable time, 8.4.139
Record book, 2.4.5–2.4.6
Record on appeal, 10.1.32–10.1.35
  Copies of, 10.1.36
Recording of proceedings, 8.5.537–8.5.538
Recording of questioning (ICTY, ICTR and
  SCSL Rule 43)
Red Cross
  See International Committee of the Red
    Cross (ICRC)
Redaction, 8.5.199–8.5.201
Referral to national court proceedings (ICTY
  Rule 11 bis)
Registrar, 8.5.538
Registry, 2.2.1–2.2.19
  Deputy registrar, 2.2.18–2.2.19
  President's authority over, 2.2.15–2.2.17
Regulations of the court, 7.48
Rehabilitation, 9.20–9.22
Rehearing
  See, in general, Hearing
Religion
  Destruction or willful damage to property
    of, 4.2.481–4.2.483
Relocation, 2.3.10
Remand
  See also Accuse
  Detention on, 8.5.108–8.5.113
Replacements, 2.1.94–2.1.97
Reprisals, 6.3.58–6.3.61
  See also Defences
Republika Srpska, 8.4.127, 8.4.148,
  8.5.152
Request
  For deferral (ICTY and ICTR Rule 9),
    5.53–5.60, 5.61–5.70, 5.79–5.81
  For information (ICTY and ICTR Rule 8),
    5.51–5.52
Res judicata, 8.5.520, 8.5.727

Resignation
  of judges, 2.1.56, 2.1.80–2.1.81
Restitution of property, 9.150–9.152
Restraint
  Instruments of, 8.5.556–8.5.558
Retribution
  Content, 9.12–9.13
  Role of, 9.9–9.11
Review proceedings, 10.2.1–10.2.16
  Appeals, 10.2.7
  Criterial for review, 10.2.9–10.2.16
  Final judgment, 10.2.11–10.2.13
  New fact, 10.2.15
  Preliminary examination, 10.2.4–10.2.6
  Request for review, 10.2.2–10.2.3
  Return of case to trial Chamber, 10.2.8
Review of indictment, 8.2.11–8.2.12
Riad, Fouad, 8.4.96
Rights
  of accused
    See Accused
  of suspects during investigation,
    8.1.32–8.1.35
Rights of action
  Depriving nationals of the hostile power
    of, 4.2.589
Robinson, Patrick, 8.5.652
Rohde, 6.2.54
Rome Conference, 1.3
Rome Statute, 1.62, 1.63, 8.2.96, 8.5.56,
  9.111–9.114
Rotation of Judges, 2.1.111
Ruggiu, Georges, 4.2.33, 9.35, 9.40, 9.85,
  9.86, 9.91, 9.93, 9.98
Ruhashyankiko, 4.2.55, 4.2.57
Rulemakers, judges as, 7.44–7.45
Rulemaking, 7.43
Rules of interpretation, 4.1.8
Rules of Detention
  See, in general, Detention
Rules of Hearing
  Amicus curiae, 8.4.135–8.4.137
  Representation of accused, See Accused
Rules of Procedure and Evidence, 7.1–7.85
  See also Evidence
  Amendments, 7.72–7.81
  Plenary sessions, 7.5., 7.31
  Noncompliance with, 7.68–7.71
Rusatira, 8.2.94
Rutaganda, Georges, 4.1.15, 4.2.33, 4.2.41,
  4.2.44, 4.2.46, 4.2.48, 4.2.49, 4.2.64,
  4.2.73, 4.2.108, 4.2.237, 4.2.245,
  4.2.248, 4.2.541, 4.2.656, 6.3.15,
  8.5.149, 8.5150, 8.5.198, 8.5.202,
  8.5.204, 8.5.427, 8.5.754, 9.12, 9.32,
  9.35, 9.40, 9.67, 9.98
Ruzindana, Obed, 4.1.23, 4.2.30, 4.2.32,
  4.2.33, 4.2.37, 4.2.41, 4.2.45–4.2.49,
  4.2.56, 4.2.58, 4.2.59, 4.2.67, 4.2.73,
  4.2.81, 4.2.86, 4.2.90, 4.2.91, 4.2.95,
  4.2.96, 4.2.105, 4.2.108,
  4.2.119–4.2.122, 4.2.125, 4.2.160,
  4.2.192, 4.2.196, 4.2.208, 4.2.221,
  4.2.228, 4.2.236, 4.2.238, 4.2.239,
  4.2.241, 4.2.247, 4.2.248, 4.2.297,
  4.2.298, 4.2.506, 4.2.510, 4.2.513,
  4.2.516–4.2.521, 4.2.541, 6.1.17,
  6.2.60, 6.2.114, 6.2.132, 6.2.148,
  6.2.151, 6.3.10, 6.3.12, 6.3.13, 8.2.35,
  8.2.42, 8.2.43, 8.2.45, 8.3.9, 8.5.70,
  8.5.200, 8.5.204, 8.5.357, 9.9, 9.32,
  9.66, 9.75, 9.81, 9.85, 9.91, 9.122,
  11.1.29
Rwamakuba, 4.2.642
  See also ICTR
Rwanda
  Applicability of Additional Protocol II and
    Common Art.3 to events in,
    4.2.502–4.2.520
  Enforcement of sentences in, 9.138–9.140
  National war crime cases, 5.10
  Precarious security situation in,
    8.5.210–8.5.213
  UNAMIR, 8.4.55

S(h)abra and Shatila, 4.2.102, 6.2.85
Safe conducts, 8.4.47–8.4.66
Šainović, Nikola, 4.4.10
Sanctions
  ICC, 4.2.670
Šantić, Ivan, 2.6.49, 8.2.93, 8.5.485
Šantić, Vladimir or Vlado, 10.1.65
Šaponja, Dragomir, 6.2.21, 8.2.95, 8.2.97
Sarik case, 5.13
Savić, 8.2.95
Schmid, Max, 4.2.409
Schonfeld, 6.2.54
Sealed indictments (ICTY Rule 54
Security
  See National security
Security Council,, 1.2, 1.27 et seq.
  Notification to, 8.4.145–8.4.148
  Report failure to cooperate to, 11.2.9
Self-defence, 6.3.62

See also Defences
Self-incrimination,
  See also Accused
  Privilege against, 8.5.92 8.5.96
Semanza, 5.32, 8.5.520–8.5.521, 8.5.224, 8.5.498, 8.6.15, 10.2.15, 11.1.30
Sentencing
  Absence of active participation, 9.102–9.104
  Abuse of authority, 9.68–9.71
  Aggravating circumstances, 9.66–9.67, 9.73, 9.75, 9.77 et seq.
  Appeals chamber and, 9.58–9.62
  Bibliography, 9.162–9.165
    International Criminal Court, 9.163
    International criminal tribunals, 9.162
    Judicial discretion, 9.164
    Trial, sentencing and general principles of criminal law, 9.165
  Conduct during the trial, 9.76
  Enforcement of
    ICTY sentences, 9.135–9.137
    Rwanda, 9.138–9.140
  Imprisonment, 9.25
  Aggravation, aggravating factors, 9.65
  Consistency in, 9.41–9.53
  Diminished mental capacity, 9.101
  Factors to be taken into account, 9.63–9.104
  Gravity of the offence and discretionary framework, 9.33–9.38
  Guilty plea, 9.86–9.90
  Minimum term recommendation, 9.118
  Mitigation, mitigating factors, 9.82
  National practices, 9.39
  Premeditation, 9.74
  Provisions of the statutes, 9.25–9.40
  Purpose of, 9.79.9
  Personal circumstances of the accused, 9.98–9.100
  Rape, 9.78–9.80
  Remorse, 9.91–9.93
  Substantial cooperation with the prosecution, 9.83–9.85
  Superior orders, 9.94–9.97
  Witnesses, 9.109–9.110
  Youth or old age of the victims, 9.75
Separate findings
  Meaning of, 8.5.623–8.5.624
Serious violations
  Prosecutions for, 4.1.1–4.1.6

Serushago, Omar, 4.2.33, 8.5.280, 8.5.289, 9.12, 9.60, 9.67, 9.86, 9.88, 9.91, 9.93
Sessions
  Closed, 8.5.529–8.5.534
  Open, 8.5.527–8.5.528
Severance, 8.5.553–8.5.555
Sexual offences
  See also Pregnancy, forced; Prostitution; Rape
  Consent as a defence, 8.5.749
  Evidence in cases of, 8.5.745–8.5.751
  Expert medical evidence, 8.5.751
  Protective orders for victims of, 8.5.218
  Sexual assault, 4.1.7–4.1.9
  Sexual mutilation, 4.2.48
  Sexual slavery, 4.2.589
  Sexual violence, 4.2.588, 4.2.589
  Sexual slavery, 4.2.588
SFOR (NATO-led Stabilization Force), 8.4.110–8.4.111, 8.5.81
Shahabuddeen, Mohamed, 4.2.347, 5.32, 8.1.21, 8.1.22, 8.2.63, 8.2.64, 8.2.80, 8.2.81, 8.4.19, 8.4.20
Sharon, Ariel, 6.2.86
Shields, human
  See Human Shields
  War crime of using, 4.2.589
Sidhwa, Rustam, 8.4.131, 8.4.132, 8.5.664
Sierra Leone, 1.3
  See also Special Court for Sierra Leone
Sikirica, Dusko, 4.2.61, 4.2.67, 4.2.102, 4.2.160, 8.5.250, 8.5.731, 9.35, 9.66, 9.91, 9.98, 9.157
Silence, right to, 8.5.101
Šimić, Milan, 3.1, 4.2.604, 4.2.630, 4.2.634, 4.2.635, 8.4.32, 8.4.74, 8.5.120, 8.5.123, 8.5.124, 8.5.126, 8.5.150, 8.5.160, 8.5.233, 8.5.489, 8.5.545, 8.5.727, 8.5.731
Sixth Amendment, 8.5.83
Slavery, 4.2.162
Society, protection of, 9.23
Sokolović, 4.2.20
Solemn declaration, 2.1.49
  False testimony, 4.2.648
  Interpreters and translators, 8.5.525–8.5.526
Sources of law, 4.1.1–4.1.22
South West Africa case, 4.1.5
Special Court for Sierra Leone, 1.4, 1.64–1.115
Speciala derogant generalibus, 8.6.11

Srebrenica case (ICTY Case No. IT95181), 4.2.102
  See indictments of Radovan Karadic},
    Ratko Mladic, Erdemovic and
    Radislav Krstic
Srpska, Republika, 8.5.151
Stakic, Milomir, 4.2.22
Standard of proof, 8.2.13, 9.123–9.125
Stanisić, 5.66, 5.82, 6.2.17
Stare decisis, 4.1.9, 4.1.12
Starvation
  as a method of warfare, 4.2.589
State
  Definition, 7.51
  Serve documents on, 8.4.84
  Subpoenas to, 8.4.12–8.4.20
State cooperation, 11.1.1–11.2.10
  Consequences of noncooperation, 11.2.1–11.2.10
  ICTY and ICTR Rule 56, 11.1.31
  Production of documents, 11.1.16
  States shall comply, 11.1.11–11.1.12
State immunity
  No state immunity, 6.2.64–6.2.68
State request for review, 10.1.25–10.1.28
State security
  See national security
State sovereignty, 8.4.106–8.4.107
Status conference, 8.5.295–8.5.297
Stephen, Ninian, 6.3.42, 6.3.45, 8.5.222, 8.5.753
Sterilisation, enforced, 4.2.588, 4.2.589
  See also Pregnancy, forced
Stipulations (Admissions, formal), 8.4.67–8.4.70
  Judicial notice and, 8.5.728
Stojiljković, Vlajko, 4.4.10
Stupni Do case (ICTY Case No. IT9512R61)
  See Rajić, Ivica or Kiseljak (Bosnia and Herzegovina)
Subpoena (ICTY Rule 54), also See Orders
  Binding orders to states, 8.4.15–8.4.20
  Examples of, 8.4.5–8.4.46
  International organisations, 8.4.31–8.4.34
  ICTR subpoena, 8.4.55–8.4.57
  Journalists and war correspondents, 8.4.40–8.4.44
  Not issued in vain,.8.4.45
  Private individuals, 8.4.28–8.4.30
  Protection of national security and, 8.4.21–8.4.27
  State cooperation, 11.1.13–11.1.15

Subpoenae duces tecum, 8.4.8–8.4.11
Subpoenas to states, 8.4.12–8.4.14
Tribunal officials, 8.4.35–8.4.39
Vacating, 8.4.46
Suffering, causing unnecessary, 4.2.415, 4.2.416, 4.2.472
  Great suffering or serious injury to body or health, 4.2.568–4.2.569, 4.2.589
Summons (ICTY and ICTR Rule 54)
  See also Orders
  Examples, 8.4.5–8.4.46
Superior Order(s) (ICTY Article 7(4) and ICTR Article 6(4))
  See also Orders
  Sentencing, 9.94–9.97
Superior Responsibility
  See Command Responsibility
Surrender of accused (ICTY Rule 54)
Suspect(s)
  Transfer and provisional detention of, 8.1.12–8.1.27
  Recording questioning of, 8.1.36–8.1.38
  Rights of during investigation, 8.1.32–8.1.35
Switzerland, 5.19–5.20
Synagogue case, 6.2.54

Tadić, 4.2.169, 4.2.171–4.2.173, 4.2.180, 4.2.183, 4.2.185, 4.2.187, 4.2.190, 4.2.191, 4.2.193, 4.2.196, 4.2.200, 4.2.203, 4.2.204, 4.2.217, 4.2.218, 4.2.220, 4.2.225–4.2.227, 4.2.282, 4.2.283, 4.2.294, 4.2.295, 4.2.306, 4.2.308, 4.2.309, 4.2.311, 4.2.312,4.2.314, 4.2.318, 4.2.320, 4.2.323–4.2.347, 4.2.351, 4.2.356, 4.2.358, 4.2.365, 4.2.370, 4.2.372, 4.2.381, 4.2.385, 4.2.387, 4.2.390, 4.2.392, 4.2.405, 4.2.409, 4.2.429, 4.2.443, 4.2.448, 4.2.450, 4.2.452, 4.2.454, 4.2.456, 4.2.458, 4.2.460, 4.2.462, 4.2.469, 4.2.470, 4.2.491, 4.2.501, 4.2.507, 4.2.579, 4.2.468, 4.42, 5.28, 5.41, 5.42, 5.46, 5.47, 5.66, 5.71, 5.74, 5.116, 6.2.26, 6.2.30, 6.3.39, 6.2.42, 6.2.54, 6.2.56, 6.2.57, 6.2.120, 6.2.140, 7.83, 8.2.23, 8.3.11, 8.3.13, 8.3.15, 8.4.6, 8.4.47, 8.4.107, 8.5.12, 8.5.15, 8.5.23, 8.5.30, 8.5.50, 8.5.78, 8.5.81, 8.5.120, 8.5.178, 8.5.179, 8.5.188, 8.5.191, 8.5.194, 8.5.196, 8.5.197, 8.5.209, 8.5.221,

8.5.222, 8.5.227, 8.5.233, 8.5.241,
8.5.350, 8.5.354, 8.5.418, 8.5.424,
8.5.426, 8.5.442, 8.5.457, 8.5.458,
8.5.497, 8.5.504, 8.5.505, 8.5.510,
8.5.528, 8.5.532, 8.5.560, 8.5.573,
8.5.586, 8.5.592, 8.5.607, 8.5.616,
8.5.619, 8.5.620, 8.5.631, 8.5.636,
8.5.637, , 8.5.645, 8.5.649, 8.5.651,
8.5.657, 8.5.670, 8.5.686, 8.5.704,
8.5.727, 8.5.748, 8.5.757, 9.17, 9.30,
9.33, 9.39, 9.50, 9.60, 9.67, 9.60, 9.108,
9.110, 9.118, 9.126, 9.128, 9.129,
10.1.2, 10.1.3, 10.1.4, 10.1.53, 10.1.55,
10.1.56, 10.1.63, 10.2.10, 10.2.16
Appeals Chamber's Tadić Jurisdiction Appeals decision, 4.2.325–4.2.334
Developments after Tadić Jurisdiction Appeals decision, 4.2.335–4.2.336
Decision of 10 August 1995, 8.5.220–8.5.222
Interlocutory appeal on jurisdiction, 8.5.457–8.5.461
Jurisdiction decision of 10 August 1995, 4.2.323–42.324
Tadić Appeals Judgement of 15 July 1999, 4.2.340–4.2.347, 4.2.372–4.2.374
Tadić Opinion and Judgement of 7 May 1997, 4.2.337–4.2.339, 4.2.365–4.2.371
Tadić, Momir, 2.1.69, 4.2.22, 6.2.41, 6.2.45, 8.2.33, 8.2.60, 8.4.40, 8.5.21, 8.5.38, 8.5.44, 8.5.302, 8.5.511
Terrorism
  Acts of, 4.2.525–4.2.527
Terry v. Ohio, 8.4.82
  Testimony
    See Evidence, Witness
  Expert witnesses, 8.5.693–8.5.695, 8.5.735–8.5.740
Third parties
  Exception to ban on disclosure to, 8.5.217
Timarac, Nedjeljko, 6.2.21, 8.2.97
Time, Timelimits, 8.5.235–8.5.236, 8.5.242–8.5.243, 10.1.66
  Variation of, 8.5.239–8.5.241
Todorović, Stevan, 4.2.634, 4.2.635, 6.3.35, 6.3.51, 8.4.33, 8.4.100, 8.4.104, 8.5.269, 9.9, 9.11, 9.13, 9.24, 9.29, 9.30, 9.33, 9.35, 9.39, 9.68, 9.72, 9.73, 9.75, 9.84 9.86, 9.87, 9.89–9.92, 9.101, 9.108, 11.1.10

Tokyo trial, 8.2.91
Tokyo Tribunal (International Military Tribunal for the Far East), 8.2.91
Torture, including inhuman treatment, 4.2.412, 4.2.542–4.2.551, 4.2.588
  Rape as torture, 4.2.552–4.2.556
  War crime of, 4.2.589
Tradić, 8.2.4
Translation
  See also Interpretation, Interpreters, Language, Solemn Declaration
  Solemn declaration by, 8.5.525–8.5.526
Treaty of Neuilly-sur-Seine, 6.2.3
Treaty of Sevrfes, 6.2.3
Treaty of Versailles, 6.2.3
Trial Chamber
  Amicus curiae, 8.5.499–8.5.506
    Partie Civile and, 8.5.513
  Proceedings before, 8.5.499–8.5.521
  Requests to, 8.1.3–8.1.7
  Return of case to, 10.2.8–10.2.14
Trial proceedings
  Commencement and conduct of, 8.5.1–8.5.12
  Custody, 8.5.7–8.5.10
  Elements to be proved at, 8.5.616
  Fair trial and appointment of amicus curiae, 8.5.6
  Fair trial, truth-finding and crosse-xamination, 8.5.3–8.5.5
  Length of trials, 8.5.60
  Plea, 8.5.11
  Public hearings, 8.5.12
Trial records
  Filing of, 10.1.78–10.1.80
Trials of War Criminals, 6.2.80
Truce flags, improper use of, 4.2.589
Tu quoque, as a defence to war crimes of, 6.3.54–6.3.57
  See also Defences
"Tuta" (Naletilic, Mladen), 8.2.108
Tutsi, 4.2.30, 4.2.58, 4.2.107, 4.2.121–4.2.122

UN Assistance Mission in Rwanda (UNAMIR), 8.4.55
UN Commission on Human Rights, 8.4.135
UN High Commissioner for Refugees (UNHCR), 11.1.29
Undefended places, acts on, 4.2.589
Unfit to stand trial
  See McNaghten's Case

Uniform, improper use of, 4.2.589
United Nations
  Inviolibility of Archives of, 3.1
  Secretary General as amicus, 8.5.502–8.5.503
United States v. Johnson, 8.5.103
United State v. Keenan, 6.2.154
United States v. Mendenhall, 8.4.82
United States v. Walter Griffin, 6.2.154
Universal Declaration of Human Rights, 4.2.262
Unsworn statements, right of the accused to make
  See Accused
UNTAES (UN Transitional Administration for Eastern Slavonia), 8.4.96–8.4.97
  Authority of, 8.4.108

Velasguez-Rodriguez, 4.2.588
Versailles Treaty, 6.2.3
Vice-President
  ICTR, 2.1.91–2.1.93
  ICTY, 2.1.91–2.1.93
Victim(s)
  Class of, 4.2.510
  Compensation to, 9.153–9.155
  Definition, 7.50
  Identity of, 8.5.181
  Measures for the protection of, 8.5.205–8.5.234
  Protection of
    ICTY Art. 22/ICTR Art. 21, 8.5.170–8.5.173
    ICTY/ICTR Rules 69 and 75, 8.5.174, 8.5.205
  Victim's rights, 8.5.19
  Youth or old age of, 9.75
Victims and Witnesses Unit, 2.3.1–2.3.10
Video
  Conference, 8.5.418–8.5.427
  Deposition, 8.5.409
  Link, 4.1.9, 8.4.6, 8.4.47, 8.5.83– 8.5.85, 8.5.193, 8.5.296, 8.5.418 et seq., 8.5.428, 8.5.679
Vienna Convention on the Law of Treaties 1969, 6.2.47
Vietnam War, 4.2.168, 6.2.83
Violations of Common Article 3 and Additional Protocol II (*see* ICTR Article 4), 4.2.497–4.2.533
Violation of rights, 9.154

Violations of the laws or customs of war (See ICTY Article 3)
  See Law or Customs of War
Vohrah, Lal Chand, 1.40, 4.2.380, 6.3.41, 8.1.21, 8.2.41, 8.5.73 et seq, 8.5.753
Vujin, Milan, 4.2.615–4.2.618, 4.2.596, 4.2.599, 4.2.600, 4.2.615–4.2.619, 4.2.623–4.2.624, 6.1.12, 8.5.16, 8.5.592, 10.1.3
Vukovar case (ICTY Case No. IT9513R61), 4.2.193, 4.2.194, 4.2.206, 4.2.335, 4.2.363, 5.66, 5.67, 5.72, 8.4.96, 8.4.128, 8.4.142, 8.4.146, 11.1.20, 11.2.8

Wald, 4.2.629, 6.1.13, 8.1.21, 8.5.18
Wanton, wantonly
Wanton destruction of towns, etc., 4.2.473–42.475, 4.2.480
War crimes, 4.2.304–4.2.428,
  Actus reus and mens rea, 4.2.402–4.2.429
  Depriving a prisoner of war or a civilian of the rights of fair and regular trial
    See ICTY Article 2(f)
  Generally, 4.2.305–4.2.318
  ICC, Art. 8, 4.2.532–4.2.534, 4.2.589
  In international armed conflict, 4.2.319–4.2.397
  Internationality of conflict to be proved at trial, 4.2.358–4.2.360
  Protected persons, 4.2.361–4.2.397
  Protected property/occupation, 4.2.398
  Weapons, See Chemical weapons, Bullets
  Wilful, wilfully
    Causing of great suffering or serious injury to body or health
      See ICTY Article 2(c)
    Killing
      See ICTY Article 2(a), 4.2.538–4.2.540
Warrants
  Examples of, 8.4.58.4.8.4.46
  Failure to execute a warrant or transfer order, 11.2.7–11.2.10
  Orders and, 8.4.1–8.4.145
  Procedure in case of failure to execute (ICTY AND ICTR Rule 61), 8.4.119–8.4.148
    Akin to committal proceedings, 8.4.132
    Amicus curiae, 8.4.135–8.4.137
    Hearing not a trial, 8.4.130–8.4.131

Web sites, 2.1.42, 8.5.9, 8.5.10, 8.5.248, 8.5.304, 9.144
   Avalon Project of the Yale Law School, 1.34, 5.3
   Cambodia, 1.165
   International Courts and Tribunals in Amsterdam cases, 1.155
   Rome Statute of the ICC, 1.62
Weizsaecker et al, In re, 4.2.419
Wilful killing, 4.2.404–4.2.406, 4.2.538–4.2.541
Witness(es)
   Anonymity of, 8.5.186–8.5.195
     Withdrawal of, 8.5.192–8.5.195
   Communication with witness after swearing, 8.5.681–8.5685
   Confrontation of
   Credibility of, 8.5.698
   Criminal record of, 8.5.179–8.5.180
   Cross-examination of, 8.5.88–8.5.90
     Leading questions, 8.5.699
     Scope of, 8.5.595–8.5.598
   Defense not obliged to disclose witnesses' names, 8.5.348–8.5.352
   Detained witness
   Communication between, 8.5.713
   Transfer of, 8.5.700–8.5.713
   Disclosure by prosecutor, 8.5.305 et seq.
   Disclosure of addresses of witnesses to special defence, 8.5.360–8.5.362
   Disclosure of protected witness's statement, 4.2.642
   Examination of witnesses, 8.5.593–8.5.594
   Expert witness, 8.5.693–8.5.695
     Investigators and, 8.5.689–8.5.691
     Publications of, 8.5.692
     Testimony of, 8.5.735–8.5.740
   Identity of, 8.5.181
   Immunised testimony, 8.5.697
   Interfering with or intimidating, as contempt, 4.2.640–4.2.641
   Intimidation and harassment, 8.5.224–8.5.227
   Measures for protection of, 8.5.205–8.5.234
   Names of prosecution witnesses, 8.5.347
   Previous statements and prosecution, 8.5.325–8.5.326
   Protection of
     ICTY Art 22/ICTR Art. 21, 8.5.170–8.5.173
     ICTY/ICTR Rules 69 and 75, 8.5.174, 8.5.205
   Redaction of witness statements, 8.5.199, 8.5.201
   Reliability of, 8.5.618
   Relocation, 2.3.10
   Reinstatement of, 8.5.490
   Self-incrimination, 8.5.225
   Sequestration of, 8.5.696
   Summoned by chamber for additional evidence, 8.5.760
   Testimony of witnesses, 8.5.673–8.5.699
     Contamination of, 8.5.686–8.5.688
   Variation of to be called by prosecution, 8.5.320–8.5.322
Women's human rights, 10.2.13
Women's organizations, 8.5.511
Working languages
   See Languages
Worthington v. DPP, 8.5.614

Yamashita, In re, 6.2.75, 6.2.84
Young persons
   See Children
Yugoslavia
   Prosecutions in Former Yugoslavia, 5.9
   Territory of Former Yugoslavia, 4.4.3–4.4.15

Zarić, Simo, 8.2.40, 8.5.120, 8.5.150
Žigić, Zoran, 1.48, 8.4.109, 8.5.250
Zimmerman and Steiner, 8.5.145
Zogoc, Zoran, 5.33
Zyklin 13 case, 6.2.54